The Making of Modern Japan

The
MAKING
of
MODERN
JAPAN

Marius B. Jansen

THE BELKNAP PRESS OF
HARVARD UNIVERSITY PRESS
Cambridge, Massachusetts
London, England
2000

Book design by Marianne Perlak

Library of Congress Cataloging-in-Publication Data

Jansen, Marius B.
The making of modern Japan / Marius B. Jansen.
p.   cm.
Includes bibliographical references and index.
ISBN 0-674-00334-9 (alk. paper)
1. Japan—History—Tokugawa period, 1600–1868.
2. Japan—History—Meiji period, 1868–   I. Title.

DS871.J35 2000
952'.025—dc21   00-041352

CONTENTS

Illustrations follow pages 140, 364, and 588.

MAPS

PREFACE

My entry into the field of Japanese history was fortuitous. As an undergraduate at Princeton I had decided on a career in Reformation and Renaissance history, but World War II and the military duty I began in 1943 changed that. An army language program, followed by service in Okinawa and Japan, brought experiences and interests that proved compelling. The army program was directed by a pioneer in the study of Japan, Serge Elisséeff, who was himself a chapter in the West's encounter with Japan. Son of a wealthy Russian merchant, he had studied at Tokyo Imperial University in the last years of the Meiji period majoring in Japanese literature, the first non-Japanese to do so, and became a member of the student group that met with the great novelist Natsume Sōseki. Returning to Moscow, he narrowly survived the Bolshevik Revolution and made his way to Paris before coming to head the Harvard-Yenching Institute in 1935. He was a splendid teacher, with a personal anecdote to underscore the usage of almost any word or term.

I was astonished by a language so different from those I knew, and to acquire it was almost like learning to think a second time. There were gradations of status so clearly established that they seemed terraces of courtesy, and all transcribed in a nonalphabetic script. Long before the course was completed I had decided to return for more systematic study once the war was over.

Acquaintance with Japanese society confirmed me in that resolution. On Okinawa I found a gentle, warm, and forgiving people, stripped of everything except their dignity, dazed and surprised to find themselves alive after the carnage of a battle that had reduced their numbers by one-quarter. They seemed courteous, deferential, and quietly skeptical of all authority. In the Japan to which I was soon transferred shadowy figures moved along darkened streets in the rubble of the cities, far more fearful, and far less open, than the Okinawans had seemed.

There followed an assignment to join a small detachment in the magnificent mountains of Hakone, among villages to which Japanese authorities had sent the "friendly" European community for shelter when the cities were set ablaze by fire raids. The little unit to which I found myself attached had as its mission the investigation of the master spy Richard Sorge, whose story the Intelligence Section of General Headquarters wanted clarified as an object lesson in the dangers of Communist subversion. Sorge, a German of Russian birth, combined brilliance with extraordinary recklessness. As columnist for the *Frankfurter Zeitung* he had secured access to the military men who headed the Nazi embassy in Tokyo, mixed easily with Japanese social scientists, many of them Marxist, who staffed a research institute established by Prince Konoe, three times prime minister, and then transmitted to Moscow reel after reel of secret documents which indicated that Japan would strike south and not north against the Russians. Our office contained the relevant files from the German embassy, and former ambassador general Eugen Ott, who had lost his post when Sorge was unmasked, lived nearby; his successor, Heinrich Stahmer, lived upstairs in the hotel in which we had our office. So too the German embassy's military attaché, who described for us his astonishment, on walking his dog in Hibiya Park one December morning, at hearing that the Japanese navy had attacked Pearl Harbor and war had broken out with the United States. It would be difficult to imagine a better introduction to contemporary East Asian history.

That same good fortune continued during my years of graduate training in Chinese and Japanese studies at Harvard after the war. Some of our number, most of them with prewar experience of East Asia, were following plans they had had to defer because of military service during the war, but the great majority of us were wartime converts, eager to place what we had learned and experienced in a larger and longer historical context. Edwin Reischauer, newly returned as professor from service in Washington and little more than a decade senior to most of us, was the coach and leader of the team, and his vitality and energy balanced Professor Elisséeff's quiet astonishment at this sudden influx of enthusiastic students. There was an air of excitement and discovery about our work; the world we were studying seemed newly opened, and its paths were still uncharted.

My first research topic was chosen almost as accidentally as my entrance into Japanese studies. I needed a topic that could be researched in Japanese sources for John Fairbank's seminar in Chinese history, and out of that came a concern with Sino-Japanese cultural and political contacts that never left me and is reflected in the chapters that follow. *The Japanese and Sun Yat-sen* (Harvard University Press, 1954) traced friendships that developed between Chinese and Japanese in shared distress at the rise of Western imperialism in the last decades of the nineteenth century, and closer study of Japanese participants in those events opened windows on the aspirations of a generation of young Japanese whose identities had been shaken to the core by the tidal wave of foreign culture they encountered. Miyazaki Tōten and Chiba Takusaburō, two young men who figure in this narrative, exemplify that shock and cultural confusion.

For most of that generation a desperate drive to shelter what was central led to concentration on the construction of a modern state. Sun Yat-sen and other Chinese exiles in Japan sometimes styled themselves after the state builders of Meiji Japan, while the young Miyazaki and Chiba looked for ways to broaden the mandate their predecessors had worked out. To better understand this I turned next to the study of the thought and political world of pre-Meiji activists, and tried to locate my subject in the political and intellectual ferment whose echoes still moved Meiji-era Japanese like Miyazaki as well as their Chinese friends. For this a young enthusiast whose political growth was mirrored in letters to the family he had left behind, and whose early death at the hands of assassins, on the very eve of the Tokugawa fall, removed the possibility of distraction by a later career, proved a happy choice. *Sakamoto Ryōma and the Meiji Restoration* (Princeton University Press, 1961) also immersed me in problems of local history in late and post-feudal institutions in Tokugawa Japan, and these in turn traced their origin to the founding of the shogunate in 1600.

That sweep of Japanese history, from 1600 to the present, has been the subject of my teaching and research in the decades that have followed, and it is the field I have taken as my problem in this book. It would have been an easier task fifty years ago, when I began my career at the University of Washington. It is difficult today to imagine a field in which there were almost no books, few articles, and not very many ideas. The study of Japanese history has grown exponentially in this half century, and the flood of publications and variety of topics have forced students to specialize in ways that my generation could not. We were less learned, no doubt, but perhaps also more fortunate, for every topic lay ready to hand and needed to be examined. Concepts like feudalism, militarism, modernization, statism, civil society, and social history have changed the landscape, each leaving awareness of new problems and possibilities in its wake.

My generation of historians of Japan has also benefited immeasurably from the accessibility and cooperation of scholars in Japan. In my case, a year spent as executive associate at the International House of Japan in Tokyo during 1960–61 led to friendships that have deepened over the years. It has been quite different for our counterparts in Chinese history; however great the contributions of expatriate Chinese scholars and institutions on the edges of China itself, universities in the People's Republic were beyond reach, personally and intellectually, for the greater part of the last half century. In contrast the flow of visiting scholars from Japan, and their receptivity to colleagues, students, and publications on this side of the Pacific, created a universe of shared discovery that has been central to all our work. Visiting scholars became partners in projects by the 1950s; they were taking part in multinational and binational research conferences by the 1960s, joined committees to plan research programs in the 1970s, and took part in editorial boards and manuscript preparation for projects like the *Cambridge History of Japan* in the 1980s and 1990s. They translated and discussed our work and visited major institutions to expound their own ideas. In the last decades the support of the Japan Foundation and, most recently, the International Research Center for Japan Studies have made the study of Japanese society and culture even more of a binational effort.

The other major change has come with the emergence of a generation of specialists who encountered Japanese history and society as standard fare within established college and university curricula, and did not have to wait for international crises or governmental directives to draw them into the study of Japanese. Students educate one another, with the help, or sometimes in spite of, the efforts of their teachers. The greatest pleasure of my pursuit of Japanese history has been the companionship and stimulation of undergraduate and graduate participants in that effort at Princeton since 1959. Not a few will find their work cited in the notes and suggestions for further reading provided here, and it is to them that this book is dedicated.

ACKNOWLEDGMENTS

Every author owes thanks to those who helped, but my gratitude has grown as my eyesight has weakened. I am enormously indebted to Ronald P. Toby for the care with which he went through the manuscript. In addition it was he who worked with James A. Bier to produce the maps. Computers were meant for younger people; Ralph Meyer responded to numerous emergencies with house calls, and Eileen Moffett unearthed a font that I could almost read. Morgan Pitelka rejuvenated the manuscript and its author by clearing the manuscript of technical errors. Izumi Koide and Yasuko Makino, librarians at the International House of Japan and Princeton University's Gest Oriental Library, were unfailingly prompt with materials and answers. Martin Heijdra, Yoshiaki Shimizu, Masako Shinn, Robert Singer, and Yutaka Yabuta helped in various ways with illustrations. My colleagues Martin Collcutt, Sheldon Garon, and David Howell were always on hand when needed. At Harvard University Press Aïda D. Donald, Elizabeth Suttell, and especially my manuscript editor Elizabeth Gilbert have been models of forbearance. Jean, as always, has been more central to this enterprise than she can ever know. To all, my thanks for what is here and my apologies for what is not.

Princeton, N.J.
April 2000

NOTE ON NAMES
AND ROMANIZATION

In Japan, as in China and Korea, the family name precedes the given, and this order has been followed throughout the text. Japanese authors whose works appear in translation or who publish in English sometimes prefer to use the Western sequence with family names last, however, and where this is the case citations in the notes follow the original. There are other pitfalls. Japanese are sometimes better known by their pen names or, more inconvenient still, by alternate readings of the Chinese characters with which their first name is written. Where this is the case the text and the index indicate the alternate possibility in parentheses. Japanese romanization follows *Kenkyūsha's New Japanese-English Dictionary*, 4th ed. (1974), a modification of the system worked out by the pioneer missionary James Hepburn, a Princeton graduate of 1832. Macrons to indicate long vowels in names have been used except in reference to well-known terms and places like shogun and Tokyo. For readings of names and for dates, I have followed *Kadokawa Nihonshi jiten*, 2d ed. (Tokyo: Kadokawa, 1976). For Chinese I have retained the Wade-Giles system, except for familiar place names like Peking, but that too, in deference to current usage, becomes Beijing after 1949.

The Making of Modern Japan

1

In 1610 Ieyasu, the founder of the Tokugawa shogunate, gave
his adopted daughter a pair of eight-fold screens as part of her
dowry before sending her off to be the bride of Tsugaru Nobu-
hira. The screens depict the battle of Sekigahara, which took
place in the ninth month of 1600, and established the political
foundation for two and a half centuries of Tokugawa rule. They
are in the style of the court school of Tosa painters, richly detailed and splendidly colored, painted on thin sheets of hammered gold that set off the epic deeds that they record. The
narrative moves from right to left, as in a page of written Japanese, and begins with the arrival of the competing hosts the day
before the battle. The village of Sekigahara is set in a narrow
valley between the mountains of Mino Province. The rice harvest has been gathered; fall was a favorite time for the military
commanders of the day, as they could seize the peasants' produce after the harvest and avoid the work of transporting mountains of supplies. At the top the army of Ieyasu is shown joining
the battle line; the future shogun himself is splendidly mounted
and surrounded by his guard. Lower on those panels is the castle
of Ōgaki, which served as headquarters for the coalition of feudal chiefs, the daimyo, drawn up to oppose Ieyasu. Everywhere
throughout the sixteen panels there are formations of soldiers,
arranged below the tall cloth banners that announce their formation and lord. The men throng to the scenes of struggle, and
break in defeat and flight. The samurai, resplendent in their
armor, are on horseback; larger groups of foot soldiers armed
with lances and swords surround and follow them. By the time
the scene shifts to the sixteenth and final screen the army at the
lower part of the screen is in flight, and from the surrounding
hills men equipped with firearms are adding to the carnage by
picking them off. Soon the heads of those who have fallen will

be stacked in orderly piles to make possible a count of enemy dead. For the losing side modern estimates range from four thousand to twice that number; in any case an awesome harvest of the defeated host will be executed a few days later, and their gibbeted heads displayed in the nearby city.

The number of fighting men arrayed against each other was formidable. There were probably over 100,000 on each side, although the nature of the terrain meant that about half that many, perhaps 110,000, were actually committed to the battle. Sekigahara came as the climax to almost a century of intermittent warfare during which commanders had gained experience in moving large numbers of troops. The night before the battle not even a driving rain kept the hosts from assembling and taking up their positions, and on the morning hostilities broke out a dense fog brought units into contact before the word to attack had been given. Battle management was difficult because there were divisions sent by feudal lords from all parts of the country on both sides. From one such, the detachment of 3,000 men contributed by Date Masamune, daimyo of the northeastern domain of Sendai, one can get some idea of the proportions of weaponry in use. Date had 420 horsemen, 200 archers, 850 men carrying long spears, and 1,200 armed with matchlock firearms. Many also carried swords, the samurai two, one long and the other short, but the other weapons were the ones that counted more.

1. The Sengoku Background

Tokugawa rule was to be praised as the "great peace," and to understand how grateful writers in early modern Japan were for the more than two centuries without conflict—a period during which China was overrun by the Manchus, India by the Moguls, and Europe was engulfed in a series of wars that culminated in the rise and fall of the Napoleonic empire—it is necessary to explain what had gone before. Tokugawa rule was not Japan's first experience of unity and order. In the seventh and eighth centuries the introduction of institutions of central government modeled on those of China had also been followed by several centuries of peace broken only by border conflict to the north. The early government had purchased Chinese-style centralization for its heartland at the price of continued dominance for regional leaders at the periphery, however, and by the tenth century a movement of privatization had begun to replace the institutions of central rule. Grants of tax-free land to court favorites and to temples restricted the fiscal base of central government, and additional offices for the maintenance of order and land registration began to usurp the functions that had been set aside for the institutions of the imperial state. By the twelfth century power struggles between local grandees were affecting life in the capital. At the center the great Fujiwara clan, subdivided into several houses, reached into the court through marriage alliances and patronage, and so dominated life that emperors began to seek early abdication in order to be able to arrange their own lives and manage their own estates. The court itself was becoming more a private than a governmental institution, though its members continued to function as the most important of the lineages with which it was connected. Great Buddhist temples too served as centers of a network of subsidiaries with landed interests throughout the country. Ambitious men developed personal followings in the course of accumulating and managing private estates and managing the diminished part of the once universal public realm that remained. They began to arrange themselves in leagues that claimed and sometimes had lineage connections, and as their power grew the aristocrats at court tried also to utilize them for their needs.

In the twelfth century a series of wars among these aristocratic warriors—few in number, fiercely proud of their heritage, and splendidly accoutered and horsed—ended with victory for the Minamoto clan, which installed itself in headquarters at Kamakura on the Sagami Bay in eastern Japan. The office of shogun, theretofore a temporary commission used in pacification campaigns against the Ainu to the north, now became a permanent and hereditary title used to designate the head of warrior houses. Japan entered a period of warrior rule from which it did not emerge until the fall of the Tokugawa in 1868.

That period was nevertheless one of constant development and change. The first line of Minamoto shoguns—from whom the Tokugawa were to claim descent, albeit on dubious grounds—established a line of military authority that supplemented, and in time overshadowed, that of the imperial court. It forced from the court permission to appoint stewards to private estates throughout the land, and constables or military governors in the provinces to serve as officials of the new system of justice that was established. Although the Minamoto line itself soon ended, a line of regents, hereditary in the Hōjō family, carried on its functions. At the imperial capital the wishes of emperors, who frequently abdicated to exercise greater influence from monastic establishments, counted for much less. An attempt by a retired emperor to challenge Kamakura dominance was quickly snuffed out and led to more forceful measures by the Kamakura leaders. Shadow shoguns dealt with shadow emperors, and Kamakura institutions remained an overlay on those of the court. Gradually provincial and local interests came to count for more. The tenuous balance was brought to an end by the great invasions launched by the Mongol overlords of China in 1274 and 1281. Japan emerged from this crisis with its sovereignty intact, but its leaders had conquered no new lands with which they could reward their men. By 1333 a discontented emperor was able to rally enough discontented warriors to bring the Kamakura shogunate to its final crisis.

The second shogunal line, that of the Ashikaga, chose to establish its headquarters in the imperial capital of Kyoto. The title of shogun was now formally linked with the designation of leader of the military houses (*buke no tōryō*), but in fact he experienced increasing difficulty asserting his primacy over the provincial warrior administrators. The discontent the emperor had exploited to bring on the crisis of 1333 extended throughout that century. At a time when rival papacies at Avignon and Rome vied for authority in the West, competing military houses in Japan maintained rival imperial lines. Three-quarters of a century of warfare were brought to an end only by a compromise under which the two lines alternated in office. Meanwhile the power of the imperial house continued to diminish. Although the Ashikaga shogun's writ did not run far beyond the heartland of classical Japan, within it his pretensions grew until the shogun Ashikaga Yoshimitsu styled himself "King of Japan" when he engaged in foreign policy with the Ming emperors of China.

Yoshimitsu (1358–1408) was passionately eager to show himself a cultured aesthete capable of dealing with continental culture, and he was assiduous in collecting evidence of that cultivation in the form of paintings and ceramics. He had hundreds, perhaps thousands, of contemporaries who were no less eager, and much less restrained, in taking what they wanted. The fourteenth and fifteenth centuries were conspicuous for the appearance of piracy that preyed on the settled civilizations of Korea and China. The *wakō*, as the raiders were called, were based for the most part on islands off the coast of the Japanese island of Kyushu. The weakness of central power and public order, and the high degree of commercial and military vigor that Japan's warrior society began to generate, made Kyushu and its environs a perfect base from which Japanese buccaneers, Chinese expatriates, and Korean renegades could become a scourge for Japan's neighbors. After the Koreans made adjustments that permitted a limited amount of trade for them at authorized ports, the brigands turned to Ming China, which brooked no compromise. In periods of relative strength, like that under Yoshimitsu, the Ashikaga shogunate was able to restrain the pirates, but after his death in 1408 the tide ran stronger than before. Within Japan political order disintegrated almost totally after a shogunal succession dispute in 1467 split the warrior leaders and led to the War of the Ōnin era. With Ming prohibitions on all trade the inhabitants of China's coastal provinces were often willing to encourage "secret" trade that could easily degenerate into pirate raids, and in the mid-sixteenth century the situation reached crisis proportions. Flotillas of *wakō* ships carrying as many as several thousand armed men raided Chinese coastal areas for food supplies and anything else of value, in one case sweeping up to the very gates of Nanking. As in Elizabethan England, trade and piracy went hand in hand, but without the central authority and reward that London could contribute.

The Ōnin War began a long conflagration that effectively ended Ashikaga influence and rule. Japanese familiar with Chinese history referred to the era as "Sengoku," the Age of Warring States that had preceded the establishment of China's unitary empire. If the influence of the shogun was at a low ebb, so was that of the imperial court. In 1500 a new emperor, Go-Kashiwabara, had to wait twenty years for formal enthronement because funds were lacking. Not one of the Ashikaga shoguns of the sixteenth century served out his term without being driven from Kyoto at least once, and the only one to die in his capital was murdered there.[1] Real power was beginning to lie with regional commanders, who were consolidating their holdings and followers while their betters fought themselves to a standstill at the center.

After the Ming rulers banned Japanese ships from their shores, trade for Chinese goods continued through the network of trading stations that was being developed by Chinese merchants throughout Southeast Asia. It was into this network that European traders and pirates, first Portuguese and then Spanish, English, and Dutch, worked their way from their bases in Macao, Manila, Indonesia, and India in the sixteenth century. The wave of Chinese commerce carried them to Japan. The Chinese privateer Wang Chih had based himself there, and the conqueror of Taiwan and chief problem for Manchu rulers (as well as for Dutch competitors), Cheng Ch'eng-kung (whom the Europeans and Japanese would refer to as Koxinga), was born on Kyushu of a Japanese mother and a Chinese father.

In 1543 two or three Portuguese traders arrived on board a Chinese junk at the island of Tanegashima, south of Kyushu. The island was, in the words of one authority, a "prolific breeding ground of pirates";[2] today it is the site of Japan's principal rocket station. The Portuguese were carried to Japan "in the backwash of the *wakō* tide,"[3] but they inaugurated a century of Iberian contact that included missionaries from the Society of Jesus, which had been formed a few years earlier; its disciplined, courageous, and often brilliant members were to play a remarkable role in Japan for the next half century. One of the most notorious *wakō* captains acted as their first interpreter, and St. Francis Xavier himself arrived from Malacca on board a pirate ship in 1549. As will be noted below, the missionaries' courage and devotion were phenomenal; by the time Japan's rulers turned against Christianity, expelling its missionaries and persecuting their converts, thousands had embraced the new faith. Konishi Yukinaga, a Kyushu daimyo who was on the losing side at Sekigahara, refused his followers' entreaty to commit suicide and chose the

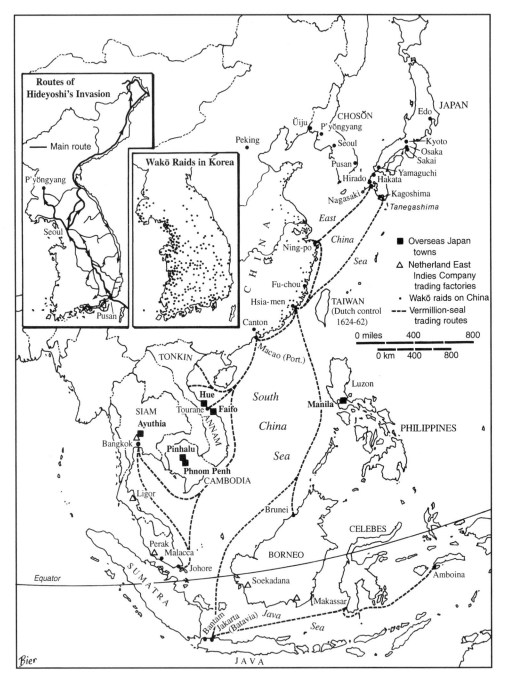

Routes of
Hideyoshi's Invasion

— Main route

P'yŏngyang

Seoul

Pusan

Wakō Raids in Korea

CHOSŎN

Ŭiju P'yŏngyang

Seoul

Pusan

Hirado Hakata

Nagasaki

Peking

Ning-po

East

China

Sea

Fu-chou

Hsia-men

Canton

Macao (Port.)

JAPAN

Edo

Kyoto
Osaka
Sakai

Yamaguchi

Kagoshima

Tanegashima

■ Overseas Japan
  towns

△ Netherland East
  Indies Company
  trading factories

• Wakō raids on China

--- Vermillion-seal
  trading routes

TAIWAN
(Dutch control
1624-62)

0 miles   400   800

0 km   400   800

TONKIN

Hue

Tourane Faifo

SIAM

Ayuthia

Bangkok

Pinhalu

Phnom Penh

CAMBODIA

Ligor

Perak

Malacca

Johore

South

China

Sea

Luzon

Manila

PHILIPPINES

Brunei

CELEBES

BORNEO

Soekadana

Makassar

Amboina

Equator

SUMATRA

Bantam

Jakarta
(Batavia)

Java

Sea

JAVA

Bier

1. Japanese raids, wars, and settlements in Asia in the fifteenth and sixteenth centuries. *Wakō* pirates, largely but not exclusively made up of Japanese, raided the Korean and Chinese coasts at the points indicated. In Southeast Asia Japanese trading ships led to the rise of "Japantowns" in Siam, Luzon, and other places. The left insert shows the route of Hideyoshi's daimyo in the invasions of Korea in 1592 and 1598.

humiliation of surrender and public execution rather than violate his Christian scruples against self-destruction.

Yet the most immediate product of the first contact with the West was the introduction of firearms. The harquebus impressed the Japanese immediately, and the "Tanegashima iron rod," as it became known from the place of its introduction, was speedily copied, improved, and produced in such numbers that, as the screen illustrations of the battle of Sekigahara show, it transformed warfare and became the instrument of the unification of Japan.

The *Teppō-ki* (The story of the gun) that was compiled for Hisatoki, lord of Tanegashima, gives this description of the islanders' effort to square the new weapon with inherited philosophical ideas by describing how a Buddhist monk told about the encounter.

In their hands [the strangers] carried something two or three feet long, straight on the outside with a passage inside, and made of a heavy substance. The inner passage runs through it although it is closed at the end. At its side there is an aperture which is the passageway for fire. Its shape defied comparison with anything I know. To use it, fill it with powder and small lead pellets. Set up a small white target on a bank. Grip the object in your hand, compose your body, and closing one eye, apply fire to the aperture. Then the pellet hits the target squarely. The explosion is like lightning and the report like thunder. Bystanders must cover their ears . . .

Lord Tokitaka saw it and thought it was the wonder of wonders. He did not know its name at first, or the details of its use. Then someone called it "iron-arms" although it was not known whether the Chinese called it so, or whether it was so called only on our island. Thus, one day, Tokitaka spoke to the two alien leaders through an interpreter: "Incapable though I am, I should like to learn about it." Thereupon, the chiefs answered, also through an interpreter: "If you wish to learn about it, we shall teach you its mysteries." Tokitaka then asked, "What is its secret?" The chiefs replied: "The secret is to put your mind aright and close one eye." Tokitaka said: "The ancient sages have often taught how to set one's mind aright, and I have learned something of it. If the mind is not set aright, there will be no logic for what we say or do. Thus, I understand what you say about setting our minds aright. However, will it not impair our vision for objects at a distance if we close one eye? Why should we close an eye?" To which the chiefs replied: "That is because concentration is important in everything. When one concentrates, a broad vision is not necessary. To close an eye is not to dim one's eyesight but rather to project one's concentration further. You should know this." Delighted, Lord Tokitaka said: "That corresponds to what Lao Tzu has said, 'Good sight means seeing what is very small'"...

It is more than sixty years since the introduction of this weapon into our country. There are some gray-haired men who still remember the event clearly. The fact is that Tokitaka procured two pieces of the weapon and studied them, and with one volley of the weapon startled sixty provinces [i.e., all Japan] of our country. Moreover, it was he who made the iron-workers learn the method of their manufacture and made it possible for that knowledge to spread over the entire length and breadth of the country.[4]

2. The New Sengoku Daimyo

The early decades of sixteenth-century Japan were remarkable for the variety of patterns of control, landholding, and taxation that prevailed. In some areas the *shōen*, estates granted to powerful families or temples by the Heian (Kyoto) court as its power waned in the eleventh and twelfth centuries, survived, but they had become steadily more free from outside interference. Proprietors delegated administration and order to local notables; *myōshu*, lineage members whose names became attached to their lands, dominated lesser farming families and kept order for representatives of shogunal power who held titles like "military steward" or "provincial constable." In areas more distant from the imperial capital local warrior families had substantially taken over from the representatives of the center, and "men of the land" *(kokujin)* became forces to be reckoned with. Still other local military men, who styled themselves samurai (from *saburau*, to serve) in evocation of the professional warriors at the capital, emerged as keepers of the peace in areas where government lands had never been transferred to the private estates. The warfare that followed the succession dispute of the Ōnin era in the fifteenth century naturally accentuated the variety and confusion, until parts of Japan became a welter of conflicting jurisdictions and procedures.

In the 1500s, however, parallel and uniform trends in major parts of the country began to bring pattern to this confusion. Quiet but significant increases in agricultural productivity were accompanied by greater commercial growth and monetization of transactions. The explosion of brigandage that swept the coasts of China and Korea was in part a reflection and in part a by-product of this economic growth. With it came institutional changes and improvements in the technology of rule. Add the changes in military technology that followed the introduction of firearms, the larger scale of control, and more effective methods of exploitation, and profound change came to most areas of central Japan. In explaining this, Japanese historians frequently refer to "Sengoku daimyo," who differ from "shugo [constable] daimyo" of late medieval times, to illustrate the contrast between the variety and confusion of conditions in the fourteenth century chaos and the emerging order of the sixteenth century.

The new daimyo were far more powerful within their realms than the shugo daimyo had been in theirs; the latter had been appointees and subject to constraints of shogunal power and aristocratic and temple proprietors who were quick to complain about their excesses at the court, but the Sengoku daimyo, their power established through military tactics and buttressed by greater resources, were able to make greater demands of their vassals and hold their own against complaints from outside their realm. Many of them, notably those able to survive into the period of warfare that culminated in the battle of Sekigahara, were eager, as some scholars put it, to portray themselves as absolute rulers of their realms. This notwithstanding, they were also eager to maximize their ties to the faltering Ashikaga shogunate and the imperial court in Kyoto, and maintained what Asao Naohiro calls a "Kyoto orientation"[5] with a lively awareness of the way the faltering central powers could affect and assist them in their tasks. The Ashikaga shogunate was, as Asao puts it, built into both the imperial-official and the lord-vassal system.

There were several ingredients involved in the rise of new local hegemons. First was surely the collapse of the landholding and tax exempt status that *shōen* proprietors had enjoyed for centuries. The need to work out new ways of controlling and exploiting the subject peasantry led to new systems of household registration and implementation of land and other resources. Where the earlier system had concentrated on a tax in kind on rice paddies, a new trend of reckoning obligations and assets in coin, which historians call the *kandaka* system, became widespread. Unlike the earlier system, this laid the basis for levies that could be charged against all arable land. As daimyo struggled to increase their resources they charged their vassals with new surveys that were more inclusive and systematic than those that had gone before. In an age of intermittent struggle the daimyo was concerned with the responsibilities of his vassals in warfare, and the result was a far more inclusive registration. Assessments made specific the military responsibilities that fief holders were expected to meet. Ōi Samanojō, for instance, a vassal of the Takeda daimyo in Kōfu, found his military assessment of 227 *kan* of copper coins obligated him to muster four mounted warriors and thirty-four foot soldiers whenever his daimyo gave the signal.[6] Earlier appointments from shogunal headquarters had had an almost official character, but now, really for the first time, enfeoffment began to carry clear contractual obligations to the feudal lord. Lords became severe and specific in the instructions and warnings they issued to their vassals, and as the powers of the overlord became more unconditional long-standard terms of "loyalty" and "filiality" took on new meanings of total subordination.

The lords were also hard-pressed to fill their own coffers, for only a part of their realm was under their own administration. The sure knowledge of productivity embodied in the cadastral surveys made possible heavier exactions on the countryside. Many daimyo established tariff stations, and new market towns and did their best to exploit commercial networks that led to vassals' or competitors' markets. Japan was plagued by inadequate and often inferior coinage, and daimyo issued regulations calling for the payment of taxes in high-grade coins only. Both vassals and peasants could register distress, the former sometimes through sale or alienation of their fiefs and the latter through petitions and protests. On the other hand, sustained daimyo control of regional valley systems gradually made large-scale riparian works possible; these extended and safeguarded acreage, all of which added to the daimyo's economic potential.

Japan was now moving toward a matured system of feudal rule. More and more the new local rulers set aside what remained of the old private estates whose revenue could be claimed by aristocrats or temples at the national center of Kyoto. Land under daimyo control was parceled out to vassals who were responsible for military support in the fighting that became endemic. With new patterns of administration taking hold and new technology of warfare made possible by the introduction of firearms, armies grew larger. Provincial overlords began to think of themselves as candidates for national governance. Phrases like *kōgi,* "public business," or *tenka,* "the realm," began to appear in codes of instructions that lords issued to their vassals.

Yet it must be remembered that these developments came slowly and that they did not replace, so much as they complicated, the earlier focus on the imperial court and shogunate. One complication was provided by a restless countryside in which local men of eminence resisted the new exactions required of them. Peasants who challenged samurai government did so under the shadow of an ideology that had imperial and religious overtones. They appealed to the more distant governance of earlier times in which the military class had not come to stand between them and the court, and frequently claimed for themselves the standing of imperial servants.[7] Consequently the warriors had to insist that their control over the countryside derived from the imperial court as well as from the authority of the shogun, however faltering, as he was supreme commander of all warriors *(buke no tōryō).* Since, however, the Ashikaga shoguns were so weak by the sixteenth century, regional lords found it more and more necessary to issue statements that had language like "reluctant as we are," the times made it necessary to "maintain order on our own," and issue codes of law for their provinces.[8] Most of the powerful daimyo of Sengoku times found it wise to make special trips to Kyoto themselves or to send emissaries to pay respects to the shogun, the emperor, and court nobles and present them with gifts. One can say they shared a "Kyoto orientation"; it was in part defensive, to strengthen their position with the peasants whose produce was their chief resource, in part competitive, to make sure their peers could not blindside them, and in part aggressive, in the hope of "graduating" to a role in governance at the Kyoto center.

3. The Unifiers: Oda Nobunaga

Out of this ferment emerged three men who managed, in four decades of almost constant warfare, to dominate their peers, eliminate the Ashikaga shoguns, and bend the imperial court to their will. In the years after the coming of the Europeans the conflict was so savage that Portuguese traders and missionaries wrote correctly of the constant treachery and violence that characterized competition among the contenders for power. After the Tokugawa victories at Sekigahara in 1600 and Osaka in 1615, however, writers praised the "Great Tokugawa Peace" that had settled on the land and wrote of loyalty as the center of warrior values with such earnestness that the carnage in men and pervasive distrust of the late 1500s seemed almost to have been forgotten.

Historians naturally focus on those who win the power struggles, and the revolution in institutional and economic change that Japan underwent is sometimes credited to the three successive hegemons who left their Japan very different. That is of course too simple. The changes that were going on could be seen in most parts of Japan, and virtually all of the emerging lords used comparable tactics and pursued similar goals. But because the other houses failed to prevail and endure it is convenient to treat the unifiers as system builders, innovators whose work brought Japan its greatest institutional change since the introduction of Chinese patterns of governance in the seventh and eighth centuries.

Nobunaga (1534–1582) was the son of a deputy military governor in Owari, on the Nagoya plain of central Japan. The province was strategically placed, within ready marching distance of the capital but sufficiently removed to make it possible to avoid the chaotic strife of the central provinces. His father's death in 1551 was the signal for a series of battles in which Nobunaga fought off the attempts of relatives to encroach on his authority. He had a younger brother killed and ousted other possible competitors. He quickly established his skill in exploitation of the new weapons of war that Europeans had brought to Japan; as early as 1549 he bought five hundred guns for his troops. His forces were quick to master the tactics required for the effective utilization of guns; it took time to prime a musket and light the fuse, and they had to be fired in sequence rather than simultaneously in order to prevent the enemy's charge during the process. Nobunaga arranged his men in ranks. He abandoned the medieval ritual of battle in which magnificently armed samurai had introduced themselves in the field of battle before charging. Henceforth such courtesy would be fatal.

In 1560 Nobunaga defeated a massive army sent against him by Imagawa Yoshimoto. One of the latter's vassals, Matsudaira Motoyasu (the future Tokugawa Ieyasu) now entered into a firm alliance with Nobunaga. In the course of decades of warfare Nobunaga moved swiftly from one border to another, throwing his enemies off balance and gradually enlarging his lands. As his victories grew other daimyo tried to ally against him. The turning point in his military career was the battle of Nagashino in 1575 in which his army of 40,000, 3,000 of them armed with muskets and fighting from well-prepared defensive positions, routed a force of mounted warriors who tried to attack him.

Nobunaga's struggles against Buddhist sectarians were particularly remorseless, and earned him the condemnation of historians including George Sansom, who summed him up as a "cruel and callous brute."[9] His was not, to be sure, an age of compassion, and his peers were not a great deal kinder. But if he was not more cruel, he was a great deal more thorough in his destruction of those who gave him trouble. He earned his reputation through his ruthless extirpation of those who opposed him and his complete disregard for conventional taboos about sacred places and communities. Honganji, the head temple of the Jōdo (Pure Land) Buddhist persuasion, was his most tenacious opponent, and its armed sectarians fought him tooth and nail for the entire decade of the 1570s. In several operations, notably one in Ise in 1574, his forces were credited with the wholesale slaughter of about 20,000 of the sectarians. More startling still was his remorseless assault of 1571 on the Buddhist center of Enryakuji on Hieizan, the mountain northeast of Kyoto sacred to the monks of Tendai. On several occasions the mountain, whose monks were armed with traditional weapons and totemic symbols with which they intimidated the capital, had given support to Nobunaga's enemies despite his warnings of future retribution. When his opportunity came Nobunaga surrounded the mountain with his troops and ordered them burn every building and kill every inhabitant, ignoring the pleas of those who argued that this mountain center, since its founding in the eighth century, had been the guardian of the imperial palace for eight hundred years. "Although it is said that ours is a degenerate age," they said, "such an act as the destruction of the center is an unprecedented, unheard-of act." To no avail; a contemporary account concludes that "the roar of the huge burning monastery, magnified by the cries of countless numbers of the old and the young, sounded and resounded to the ends of heaven and earth. The noise was at once deafening and pathetic."[10]

Nobunaga marched on Kyoto in 1568, ostensibly in response to requests from the Emperor Ōgimachi and Ashikaga Yoshiaki, who was confirmed as fifteenth (and last) Ashikaga shogun by the emperor shortly after Nobunaga gained control of the city. Once there, however, it was clear that Nobunaga had no intention of fitting into the pattern of subordination that this act of "loyalty" implied. The shogun quickly offered him appointments as vice-shogun or chief executive officer, and the emperor also attempted to have him accept such appointments. Grateful to his rescuer, the shogun addressed Nobunaga with terms of lavish praise, while the emperor, though more restrained, also praised Nobunaga's "unparalleled designs." The aims proved to live up to that description, but not in the way the authorities had hoped. Their new protector and guest instead took things into his own hands. Prior to this he had adopted as his seal the slogan *Tenka fubu,* "the realm [tenka] subject to the military," and his actions now showed his intent to live up to that goal. From 1570 on, documents he issued often coupled the phrase *tenka no tame,* "for the sake of the realm," with "Nobunaga no tame," "for the sake of Nobunaga." Clearly he was anticipating somewhat Louis XIV's "l'état, c'est moi"; he was the realm.

Nobunaga's first problem was to deal with the shogun. Harassed though Nobunaga was by continued resistance from Buddhist and secular leaders, he was intent on seeing to it that the shogun kept out of military affairs and left to him all communication with feudal lords. In articles he issued in 1569 he spelled out limitations on the shogun's contacts and administrative and legal authority, and ruled out direct petitions to the shogun. A year later he ordered that the shogun refer to him all correspondence and grants of proprietorships in the provinces. "Since the affairs of the realm [tenka] have in fact been put in Nobunaga's hands," one clause read, "Nobunaga may take measures against anyone whatsoever according to his own discretion and without the need to obtain the shogun's agreement." Nobunaga did not stop there, but went on to criticize the shogun's service to the imperial court as a way of publicly reprimanding him. The shogun was informed that people at large were beginning to have doubts about his probity and intentions. By 1573 the shogun had to choose between groveling subservience and resistance. He chose the latter, hoping that other warrior chieftains would come to his rescue, just as he had earlier petitioned for Nobunaga's help. In response Nobunaga had his army encircle Kyoto and begin a systematic burning of its outer periphery. This brought shogunal professions of contrition, only to be followed by his flight from the capital, defeat, "pardon," and exile. Yoshiaki, destined to be the last Ashikaga shogun, lived on until 1597, irrelevant to national politics and in virtual exile as nominal lord of a mean and insignificant realm.[11]

Nobunaga thus succeeded in his determination to break ties between the institution of the shogunate, with its built-in subordination to the imperial court, and leaders of the samurai estate. He himself would demand total subordination from the samurai. As he demanded of one retainer in 1575, "you must resolve to do everything as I say . . . you shall revere me and bear me no evil thought behind my back. Your feelings toward me must be such that you do not even point your feet in my direction. If you act that way, you will be blessed with good fortune forever, as befits a proper samurai."[12]

The imperial court was important to Nobunaga's concerns of legitimacy, but here too he was careful to avoid becoming entangled in its web of protocol and precedent while moving to establish his control over its functions. Immediately after the expulsion of the Ashikaga shogun from Kyoto, Nobunaga presented an urgent request for change of the era name, a function normally restricted to the shogun for ultimate disposition by the court. That accomplished, he accepted, over a period of four years, steady promotion in rank and appointment until he held the title of Grand Minister of State *(daijō daijin)*, after which he resigned those honors, pleading the urgency of military duties, and requested that they be transferred to his son. That request, however, was not met. In a series of steps Nobunaga infringed upon the few prerogatives the court still retained, among them adjudication of land disputes between major temples. Meanwhile he was also urging the abdication of the Emperor Ōgimachi in favor of his son and preparing an elaborate reception hall for the latter, once he was enthroned, at the splendid new castle he had constructed at Azuchi.

Emperor Ōgimachi's abdication came only after Nobunaga's death, and Nobunaga's ultimate plans for the exercise of power once unification was complete remain unclear. He may have planned to have himself appointed shogun. In any case, he would have seen to it that he personally remained the ultimate arbiter of power.

Nobunaga's construction of the Nijō Castle in Kyoto was witnessed by the Jesuit Luis Frois, whose description of the operation suggests the fear that

Nobunaga inspired. Frois referred to Nobunaga as "king" and his retainers as "princes," for he was not conscious of any other power structure.

> Nobunaga built a castle there, the like of which has never been seen before in Japan. First of all he gave orders for both temples to be razed and then commandeered the site, measuring four streets long and four wide. All the princes and nobles of Japan came to help in the building operations; usually there were from 15,000 to 25,000 men at work, all dressed in cloth breeches and short jackets made of skins. When he went around supervising the operations, he carried his sword in his hand or rested it on his shoulder, or else he carried a baton in his hand . . . As there was no stone available for the work, he ordered many stone idols to be pulled down, and the men tied ropes around the necks of these and dragged them to the site. All this struck terror and amazement in the hearts of the Miyako [Kyoto] citizens for they deeply venerated their idols. And so a noble and his retainers would carry away a certain number of stones from each monastery every day, and as all were eager to please Nobunaga and not depart one iota from his wishes, they smashed the stone altars, toppled over and broke up the *hotoke* [Buddha images] and carried away the pieces in carts. Other men went off to work in quarries, others carted away earth, others cut down timber in the hills; in fact the whole operation resembled the building of the Temple in Jerusalem or the labours of Dido in Carthage . . . He decreed that while the work was in progress none of the monasteries either inside or outside the city should toll its bells. He set up a bell in the castle to summon and dismiss the men, and as soon as it was rung all the chief nobles and their retainers would begin working . . . He always strode around girded about with a tiger skin on which to sit and wearing rough and coarse clothing; following his example everyone wore skins and no-one dared to appear before him in court dress while the building was still in progress . . . while on the site one day, he happened to see a soldier lifting up a woman's cloak slightly in order to get a glimpse of her face, and there and then the king struck off his head with his own hand . . . The most marvelous thing about the whole operation was the incredible speed with which the work was carried out. It looked as if four or five years would be needed to complete the masonry work, yet he had it finished within 70 days.[13]

At the time of his death in 1582 Nobunaga's task of military unification remained incomplete. He had, however, become master of the central plains and conquered approximately one-third of Japan. His plans next involved reduction of the Inland Sea provinces dominated by the house of Mōri. In

1582, as he was headquartered at the Kyoto Honnōji temple, he was surprised by the sudden attack of a vassal lord who had just been ordered to the front and instead directed his troops to attack Nobunaga. Nobunaga fought until the battle was clearly lost, and then retired to disembowel himself in the warrior rite of *seppuku* or, a less elegant expression, *hara-kiri*.

Concentration on Nobunaga's ruthless brutality risks neglect of the innovations that contributed to the unification of Japan. His reduction of the Buddhist military centers at Enryakuji and Osaka brought to an end religious monarchies that had prevailed since the middle ages. His forcible demolition of provincial forts and defense works in areas under his control foreshadowed measures that would be continued by later hegemons. Land surveys were carried out with rigor and grim sanctions against those who falsified returns. Several vassal lords were ordered from their lands and arbitrarily moved to new settings, foreshadowing the firmer central power that lay ahead. Tangled skeins of control and authority that linked metropolitan temples and aristocrats with provincial holdings were cut away. Local toll stations that operated to enrich petty rulers by levying taxes on goods in transit were abolished to speed and facilitate commerce. "Open" trade and guilds *(rakuza)* would take their place. Constant warfare required the assemblage of large bodies of men at the commanders' headquarters and began the separation of samurai from landholding. The commanders' headquarters became castle towns that centered on huge structures set on massive stone bases that commanded fields of fire and symbolized the new power structure that was coming into existence. None better represented these trends than Nobunaga's own structures, first at Gifu and then at Azuchi on the shores of Lake Biwa. They shone as marvels of construction and opulence to the European visitors whom Nobunaga permitted to see them.

"I wish I were a skilled architect or had the gift of describing places well," wrote the Jesuit Luis Frois about Gifu, "because I sincerely assure you that of all the palaces and houses I have seen in Portugal, India, and Japan, there has been nothing to compare with this as regards luxury, wealth, and cleanliness. You will be better able to realize this when I tell you that Nobunaga does not believe in an after-life or in anything he cannot see; as he is extremely wealthy, he will not allow himself to be outdone in anything by any other king but strives to surpass them all."

Azuchi, however, outdid this once more: ". . . as regards architecture, strength, wealth and grandeur [it] may well be compared with the greatest buildings of Europe. Its strong and well constructed surrounding walls of stone are over 60 spans in height and even higher in many places; inside

the walls there are many beautiful and exquisite houses, all of them decorated with gold and so neat and well fashioned that they seem to reach
the acme of human elegance. And in the middle there is a sort of tower
which they call *tenshu* and it indeed has a far more noble and splendid
appearance than our towers. It consists of seven floors, all of which, both
inside and out, have been fashioned to a wonderful architectural design;
for both inside and out, I mean, inside, the walls are decorated with designs
richly painted in gold and different colours, while the outside of each of
these stories is painted in various colours. Some are painted white with
their windows varnished black according to Japanese usage and they look
extremely beautiful, . . . the uppermost one is entirely gilded . . . In a word
the whole edifice is beautiful, excellent, and brilliant."[14]

Nor was Nobunaga unaware of or indifferent to traditional Japanese culture.
Offered a reward by the Emperor Ōgimachi after his entry into Kyoto, he
combined arrogance with connoisseurship by choosing a chip of a near-sacred
incense stick of Indian provenance from the imperial storehouse at Nara, the
Shosōin. He was a passionate devotee of the tea ceremony; at the time of his
death he had just finished entertaining an assemblage of court aristocrats to
display his precious tea ceremony utensils. His freedom from traditional taboos led the Jesuits, whom he occasionally befriended, to describe him as a
coolly rationalist, fearless person with a lively curiosity about them and their
cause. And since they were convinced of the corruptions of contemporary
Buddhism, this provided an additional avenue of contact.

4. Toyotomi Hideyoshi

Hideyoshi, who was born the son of one of Nobunaga's foot soldiers in 1537,
achieved such remarkable successes by the time of his death in 1598 that all
historians signal his achievements, though not all would agree with the early
twentieth century Scottish historian of Japan who praised him as "the greatest
man Japan has ever seen."[15] He found favor with Nobunaga at an early age,
emerged as a brilliant strategist in his service, was created a daimyo, and
quickly avenged Nobunaga's death by defeating Akechi Mitsuhide, the vassal
whose treachery brought Nobunaga down. Although Nobunaga's principal
subordinates and allies agreed on a grandson as his heir and established four
regents to serve as guardians, there was never much doubt that the struggle
would be between the two greatest, Hideyoshi and Tokugawa Ieyasu. After the
two matched their abilities in battles that proved inconclusive, Ieyasu accepted
Hideyoshi as his superior and became his most important subordinate.

Hideyoshi had all Nobunaga's ambition, but gained a reputation for magnanimity through his preference for co-opting allies instead of intimidating them, and using his opponents instead of exterminating them. He continued and completed the military unification of Japan. In 1583 he conquered a group of daimyo on the Japan Sea coast and installed his own men there. He continued Nobunaga's work of pacifying Buddhist sectarians in the province of Kii. Two years later he took control of the island of Shikoku, and in 1587 he conquered Kyushu by defeating the greatest of the island's daimyo, the Shimazu. There remained only the northeast, and this bastion fell with the successful siege of Odawara in 1590.

With this unparalleled series of successes his prospects and standing changed, as did his name. Beginning with the rustic name "Kinoshita" (under the tree) he moved on to something more appropriate with Hashiba, and then was granted Toyotomi (Bountiful Minister) by the court. With this came the same honors that Nobunaga had received, and more: he was appointed Imperial Regent *(kanpaku)* in 1585 and, a year later, Grand Minister of State *(daijō daijin)*. He now manufactured an illustrious genealogy that related him to the Fujiwara family of classical times. More successful than Nobunaga, he succeeded in having these honors transferred to his nephew and himself used the title Taikō, restricted to retired *kanpaku,* and that is the way he is usually known in Japan.

Hideyoshi regularized the practice of delegating rule over subject areas to his leading vassals, and extended that to defeated rivals who accepted him as overlord, a practice in which he was considerably more generous than Nobunaga. A modern historian goes so far as to use the term "federalism" to describe the polity that resulted.[16] Most Nobunaga followers, accustomed to obedience, accepted Hideyoshi's leadership; transfers and long years of fighting had usually left them without secure land bases from which they could have launched challenges. Hideyoshi thus retreated from the reign of terror associated with Nobunaga, began to adopt sons of rivals, and refrained from major purges. Toward the end of his career he seems to have become paranoid, moody, and dangerous. His longtime friend and tea master Sen no Rikyū was ordered to commit *seppuku* in a tragic end that continues to puzzle historians and dramatists. When, late in life, Hideyoshi found himself father of a son on whose succession he could focus his hopes, he turned against his designated heir and nephew Hidetsugu to execute him and display his head in savagery that included the public execution of his entire household; in the description of the Jesuit Luis Frois, "the bloudie and black daye came that [Hideyoshi's] commandment must be exequuted, there were drawen alonge in the streates in cartes to the open view of the world 31 Ladies and gentlewoemen, with the two sonnes and one daughter of [Hidetsugu] the eldest of which was not above five yeares olde, how greivous a spectacle this was unto the beholders eyes everie man maie imagyne . . . All their boddies by order from [Hideyoshi] were throwne into a pitte, made for the nonce, over the whiche he caused to be buylded a little Chappell with a Tombe in it with this inscription: The Tombe of the Traitors."[17]

With Japan united and no further provinces to conquer, Hideyoshi turned to thoughts of empire in Korea and China. Historians argue that one purpose of the campaign was to occupy the daimyo armies, since there was no further territory in Japan with which to reward them; others suggest that Hideyoshi desired to renew licensed trade with Ming China. The Taikō's behavior in his last years was increasingly irrational, however, and his megalomania grew steadily. Imperious letters went to Ryukyu (Okinawa), the Philippines, Taiwan, and Goa, the Portuguese base in India. Hideyoshi expected others to know of his conquests and come to pay him honor. His plan seems to have been to transfer the imperial court to Peking, thereby enlarging its rule. The responses, however, could have been anticipated; they ranged from refusal to silence. Accordingly, he set up headquarters in Nagoya (modern Karatsu) in northern Kyushu and summoned his vassals and allies to join the contest. He himself planned to go after the fall of Seoul to take personal command, but he was dissuaded from doing so by the Emperor Goyōzei and the daimyo Tokugawa Ieyasu and Maeda Toshiie, who also managed to stay in Japan.

Hideyoshi's confidence can be gauged by this letter sent to Taiwan after the fall of the Korean capital of Seoul. In tones reminiscent of central Asian empire builders, he claimed supernatural gifts for himself:

When my mother conceived me, she was given a miraculous omen with respect to the sun, and on the very night that I was born the room was suddenly aglow with sunlight, thus changing night to day. All persons present were astounded. Physiognomists gathered and debated upon this wonderful happening. They finally divined that the child whose birth was attended by these miracles was destined to become a man of unusual attainments. His benevolent virtues would shine brilliantly in every land within the four seas. His dignity and authority would extend in all directions. This prediction is fulfilled in me. Within less than ten years, I have conquered and overcome all people of the unruly classes, thus unifying and pacifying the whole of the Nation Within the Sea. Even distant nations in the outside world have learned to admire our benevolent rule and to express their urgent desire to become our dependencies. Envoys have sailed from their respective countries and have rivaled each other in speed, hoping to be the first in making obeisance to our throne.

However, Korea, a land that was long our tributary state, has failed to live up to her pledge of loyalty. At the very time that our troops started out to conquer the Great Ming, Korea rebelled. I therefore sent a punitive expedition under the command of prominent military leaders. Having lost all hope, the Korean king abandoned his national capital, setting fire to it and reducing it to ashes. Upon hearing of the national crisis in Korea, Great Ming sent several hundreds of thousands of troops with the hope of saving that kingdom. In spite of the fact that those Chinese armies engaged in a number of desperate battles with our troops, they always suffered defeat. Great Ming therefore sent an envoy to sue for peace . . .

The Philippines and Ryūkyū have sent tribute-bearing envoys to our country . . . Your country, however, has not yet sent any envoy to our military headquarters. This lack of loyalty will certainly bring the curse of Heaven upon you.[18]

In 1592 a host of more than 158,000 men crossed to Korea, with China as their ultimate destination. In less than a month they had taken Seoul; rival daimyo armies then raced north and soon had control of the main Korean cities and communication lines. The Japanese were veterans seasoned in the fighting involved in the unification of Japan, and their muskets gave them important advantages over the unprepared Koreans. Two months later, however, a Ming army crossed the Yalu and engaged the Japanese, who fell back to Seoul. There followed a long period of almost four years of stalemate during which Korean guerrillas harassed the Japanese. The commanders tried to extricate themselves through negotiations, and tried to deceive Hideyoshi about their details. Hideyoshi demanded that the Chinese court provide a consort for the Japanese emperor, reopen licensed trade with Japan, and that four provinces of Korea be ceded to Japan. The Chinese in turn assumed Japanese subservience as the prerequisite for trade, and grandly invested Hideyoshi as "king of Japan" with gifts of official garments and seals. When Hideyoshi found that his negotiators had presented him with a hollow victory he once again flew into a rage and ordered a second invasion of Korea.

This invasion began in early 1597 with the dispatch of another 140,000 Japanese troops to Korea, and it came to an end with Hideyoshi's death the following year. The Japanese goal was the implementation of the peace treaty Hideyoshi thought he had won, but their tactics became increasingly punitive and brutal. Now resistance from Korea and Chinese armies was strong, and Japanese maritime supply lines were cut by the famous iron-clad "turtle ships" of Korea. Gradually the struggle assumed degrees of bitterness and barbarity that culminated in the famous mound of ears, symbols of "body count," in Kyoto. Upon Hideyoshi's death leaders of the Japanese coalition hurriedly withdrew the armies from Korea while trying to conceal their commander's demise. The Korean adventure left the future Tokugawa regime a legacy of hatred and suspicion that boded ill for subsequent Korean-Japanese relations.

Although the attempt at continental conquest ended in failure, the Hideyoshi years marked a culminating stage in the transformation of Japanese institutions from late medieval to early modern. Hideyoshi's orders to his daimyo were enforced to varying degree and time depending on the place and its local problems, but they set a standard that remained the basis for the Tokugawa rule that followed. His grants of daimyo status for those who submitted to his rule set the example for what would become the Tokugawa daimyo system. He was able to arrogate to himself a monopoly of daimyo proprietary rights; Nobunaga's writ had never extended to all parts of Japan. For the daimyo, many of whom had had to put down sectarian and village resistance to their rule, subordination to the hegemon was also the price of domination within their realm; they consequently developed a symbiotic relationship with the center.

There could certainly be no doubt of the vassal's subordination to his lord. From late Ashikaga times samurai (and sometimes temples) had presented oaths of total loyalty to the local lord, swearing that they would accept the vengeance of Shinto and Buddhist gods if they were found unfaithful. Hideyoshi now tried to strengthen these bonds by linking them with loyalty to the imperial court. In 1588, on the occasion of a visit from the Emperor Goyōzei to his splendid new castle at Fushimi, he ordered all his vassals to be present and invited the assembled daimyo to subscribe to the following: "We shed tears of gratitude that His Majesty has honored us with his presence. If any evil person should interfere with the estates and lands of the Imperial House or with the fiefs of the Court Nobles, we will take firm action. Without equivocation we commit not only ourselves but our children and grandchildren as well. We will obey the command of the Regent [Hideyoshi] down to the smallest details. If any of the above provisions should be violated even in the slightest, then may punishments of . . . [names of Shinto and Buddhist deities] be visited on us."[19] Thus loyalty to the throne was related to obedience to Hideyoshi, and disloyalty associated with supernatural punishment from the gods.

In addition to finalizing the "daimyo system," Hideyoshi also structured the "samurai system." Edicts stipulated that samurai should not be harbored in the countryside. Instead of an earlier system in which warriors could be part farmer and part soldier, they now had to choose one role or the other. The warfare of Hideyoshi's decades required standing armies of full-time military men. By 1591 Hideyoshi could order that "if there should be living among you any men formerly in military service who have taken up the life of a peasant since the seventh month of last year . . . you are hereby authorized to take them under surveillance and expel them . . . No military retainer who has left his master without permission shall be given employment by another . . . Those who fail to report that they already have a master are to be arrested for violating the law and returned to their former master. Whenever this regulation is violated and the offender allowed to go free, the heads of three men shall be offered in compensation to the original master."[20] Warriors could not, in other words, find cover in the countryside. They had to stay with their lords. In consequence the farmer-warrior types of Sengoku years became members of standing armies, provisioned in barracks in the new castle towns that dotted the communication routes throughout the land. *Hei-nō bunri*, or separation of warriors and farmers, is the shorthand term Japanese historians use for this.

Along with this came orders for nationwide land surveys that were more systematic and thorough than any previously undertaken. The *Taikō Survey*, as it is known, specified plot-by-plot measurement of cultivated land with the use of a newly standardized chain measure, recorded the quality and productive capacity of each plot, and specified the individual responsible for its tax payment. Where earlier surveys had registered lands and areas by the tax they produced, this measure concerned itself with tax potential. Most earlier surveys had been submitted by local authorities, who frequently used the cadastral documents they had as base. Under Hideyoshi measuring teams under orders from the hegemon or his vassals were supposed to enter the village to measure its area, note its productivity on the basis of past records, and name the owner. Areas for which the complete survey has survived, as in Tosa, show the massive effort that went into the project.[21] On the other hand it must be remembered that full implementation of this all over Japan would have required a complex bureaucratic structure that was not yet in being. As late as the 1870s, when the modern Meiji government issued ownership certificates to landholders, it took the better part of a decade to complete the work. Recent studies in local history indicate that appraisals of the effectiveness of Hideyoshi's measures, based too often upon the edicts he issued, underestimate the amount of continuity and degree of local variation that survived his years.[22]

One should probably take the *Taikō Survey* as shorthand for changes that required the better part of a half century to mature. Hideyoshi's edicts serve as important benchmarks in that development.

Vital to this process was a change from tax assessment in coin to productivity figures expressed in *koku* of rice. Tax records, land survey appraisals, and samurai income now came to be expressed in terms converted into rice equivalents: the *koku,* approximately 5 bushels; *hyō,* bales; and *fuchi,* rations. This became fully standardized in the Tokugawa years of peace. At first glance this may seem a backward step away from monetization, but in actuality it represented a much more ambitious effort to quantify total production; it is difficult to exaggerate the importance of this development. Prices could fluctuate, but productivity, except in years of crop failure and famine, was a much more stable measure of the production of an agrarian-based society. This single measure of the gross product made it possible to arrange daimyo lands, retainer fiefs, and village income and represented a startling new, objective, and rational measure of power, influence, and status. We shall be dealing with it throughout the Tokugawa period. It also expressed a zero-sum view of competition. In a land fully surveyed and allocated and absent the possibilities offered by foreign conquest, one man's gain could only be made at cost to his fellows. The total rice productivity, or *kokudaka,* was now, in theory at least, known and accounted for. Only the appearance of a new hegemon could change those rules.

This would not have been binding, however, without disarming the countryside. In 1588 an edict of Hideyoshi announced that "the people of the various provinces are strictly forbidden to have in their possession any swords, short swords, bows, spears, firearms or other form of weapon." The edict was frank in its purpose: "The possession of unnecessary implements [of war] makes difficult the collection of taxes and dues and tends to foment uprising." Of course weapons did not disappear from the countryside overnight; nevertheless there is good documentary evidence to show that daimyo all over Japan took it seriously. So distant and great a daimyo as Shimazu of Satsuma, for one, recently the loser in his struggle against Hideyoshi, made it a point to comply; as Mary Elizabeth Berry notes, "given the fame of the long blades from that province . . . any failure on the part of the Shimazu to comply with the edict would be particularly conspicuous."[23] Of course it also coincided with daimyo self-interest, as it lessened the danger of peasant rebellions.

Together these edicts—land survey, sword hunt, separation of samurai and cultivators, marshaling of daimyo in presumed obedience to the throne—established new bases for legitimacy, new status regulations for military and nonmilitary, and new pacification of the countryside. They had been in process for some time, to be sure, and they were not completed in some districts during Hideyoshi's lifetime, but they are properly associated with his governance.

Hideyoshi never took the office of shogun. The last Ashikaga shogun, to be sure, died only one year before Hideyoshi. But Hideyoshi was more concerned with associating himself with the imperial court through his fabricated lineage of Fujiwara, his assumption of the traditional Fujiwara titles of *kanpaku* and *daijō daijin,* and his exploitation of the prestige of the court for his own purposes. Perhaps because his lineage and background were less illustrious than was the case with Nobunaga or Ieyasu, he deliberately associated himself with the imperial court in order to make use of its prestige. When he arranged the emperor's visit to his residence in 1588 he had thirty-one daimyo pledge to guarantee the lands of the court and nobility, thus binding court, daimyo, and himself into a polity (the *kōgi*) that expressed their common interests. Henceforth a challenge to any part of it could be disloyalty to the throne at the center. In addition to his concern with the emperor, Hideyoshi's efforts to master traditional arts like Nō dancing and his flamboyant advocacy of and participation in the tea ceremony showed additional utilization (and alteration) of the aristocratic aura. Designed to be a small gathering of intimate friends, the tea ceremony, Hideyoshi-style, became a public display of magnificence and opulence. In addition Hideyoshi, like Nobunaga, reached for the legitimacy that designation as a Shinto divinity *(kami)* might confer. His turn against the Iberian missionaries he first tolerated was also related to this. In 1587 he ordered them out of the country with the stern warning that Japan was the "land of the gods." In this way tradition was invoked to justify revolutionary changes, something that would be seen again at the end of the Tokugawa period.

5. Azuchi-Momoyama Culture

The years of unification were filled with violence, treachery, and cruelty. But they were also years of economic vigor and prosperity, and they included a virtual explosion of cultural activity. Most of the military hegemons who bestrode the land had little time or inclination for bookish learning, but others made impressive efforts to master and transmit traditional culture. Inhabitants of the growing urban centers that sprouted along strategic routes also had limited aptitude for works of literary merit, for literacy was not yet widespread. The highly cultured court nobility and priestly aristocrats lived in some sense at the mercy of the military despots but they, in turn, were hungry for the cultural legitimacy the aristocracy of court and temples could confer, and their eagerness for self-promotion made them unparalleled sponsors and patrons of visual arts of every sort. Their realization of the need for discipline in life and battle also brought them to the quiet arts of tea, ceramics, and brushwork. At the same time liberation from the constraints of traditional hierarchy made them relatively open to influences from abroad, and their unprecedented ability to commandeer the fruits of commerce, mining, and war made them unstinting patrons of art and architecture as well as martial arts.

The age was typified by the towering castles that stood as symbols of the builders' might. Massive stone parapets surrounded by a network of moats opened to reveal a bewildering labyrinth in which attackers would find themselves funneled toward barriers which, even if surmounted, led on to 90-degree turns along an upward course dominated on every side and sometimes from above by parapets from which a withering flanking fire could be directed at them. Within were quarters for the defenders, sometimes a standing guard of thousands, as well as residences for the daimyo and his principal retainers. The whole was crowned by an imposing five- to seven-story keep or *donjon* with narrow black apertures set in a brilliant white-plastered wall that concealed the massive beams of the structure. Above it all the heavy tiles of a complex pattern of eves and parapets crowned the structure with flamboyant tile representations of the daimyo's logo and representations of dolphin, crane, phoenix, or carp.

The whole was planned with an eye to the beauties of the site and proportion. The Jesuit father d'Almeida wrote of a keep in Nara that "there can scarcely be a more beautiful sight in the world than this fortress seen from outside, for it is a sheer joy to look on it . . . To enter in this town (for so I may call it) and to walk about its streets seems to be like entering Paradise . . . it does not appear to be the work of human hands . . . the walls are all decorated with paintings of ancient stories on a background of gold leaf. The pillars are sheathed with lead for about a span at the top and bottom respectively, and gilded and carven in such a way that everything looks as if it were covered with gold . . . As for the gardens . . . which I saw in the palace grounds, I cannot imagine anything more delightfully cool and fresh . . . I am sure that in the whole world it would be impossible to find anything more splendid and attractive than this fortress."[24]

These structures had dark interiors. To decorate the walls of public rooms artists utilized great amounts of thinly hammered gold and silver leaf. The age was one that began a century and more of the production of precious metal in Japan; until the mines began to be exhausted a century later Japan was a major producer and exporter of silver. Hammering, mounting, and painting on gold and silver leaf is not a gentleman's avocation, but requires the highest standards of craftsmanship. This challenge, and this sponsorship, coincided with the great age of painters of the Kanō school. Eitoku (1543–

1590), who did the screens at many of the Kyoto temples, worked as court decorator for castle reception rooms for Nobunaga and Hideyoshi and did the screens for Nobunaga's castle at Azuchi and Hideyoshi's great Jurakutei, part of which is preserved in the Nishi Honganji Temple in Kyoto. He was one of the great masters in the history of Japanese art, and influenced all his contemporaries and many students. He stands as the originator of the new and magnificent wall decorations appropriate to the scale and grandeur of the new palaces and castles of the period, combining in his style the decorative qualities of the Tosa school of artists with Chinese-inspired ink painting. With his lavish use of gold background, strong black ink, vivid color, and immense scale, his exuberant flair was perfectly suited to the age. Eitoku did not work alone, but served as master of a workshop of artists. Present-day visitors to the Nijō Castle can still sense the awe and power the artist and his patron expected guests to feel when they encountered the giant wall paintings of mighty pines that greeted them in the entrance hall. Interior, residential quarters had less need to overpower and brought more soothing depictions of peace with sages illustrating the virtues and pastimes of the Chinese classical tradition.

Nobunaga's Azuchi Castle, one he began to build in 1576, and Hideyoshi's keep at Momoyama thus gave their name to an era of cultural history remarkable for its exuberance and opulence. But everywhere in Japan, particularly along the major routes of communication, daimyo developed castles appropriate to their wealth and potential. The 1590s were a remarkable decade in which the foundations of the castle, and the castle town surrounding it with its standing army of samurai as consumers, began to transform urban life in Japan.

Hideyoshi's zest for display extended to the tea ceremony; the standard ideal was one of restraint and sobriety, but he did not hesitate to construct for himself a tea house covered with gold leaf. He also showed that side of his taste in his Grand Kitano Tea Ceremony in 1587, when he invited the entire population of Kyoto to admire his finest tea implements and personally served tea to some eight hundred people on the opening day. Participants were invited to show their treasures too, though one wonders how many took the risk. Admiration from the hegemon would surely have required that the object be presented to him by the owner. One explanation for Hideyoshi's order to Sen no Rikyū to commit suicide relates it to the tea master's possession of a particularly fine tea bowl that had inspired Hideyoshi's jealousy.

The culture of the age was dominated by the arts, of course; musket manufacturers and wealthy specialists like Sen no Rikyū could mix with military despots almost as equals. What they had to contribute was expertise in the tea ceremony that was at once most demanding and most austere. The aesthetics of the simple hut, the rustic walls and single scroll, simple flower, and quiet bowl spoke of the breeding and taste of the host. Nobunaga studied tea with Sakai masters and sometimes gave tea utensils to his vassals as reward for particularly outstanding and valorous service. He also exchanged congratulatory poems with leading poets of the era. Hideyoshi, whose correspondence shows him to have been anything but learned and eloquent, patronized the Nō theater and struggled to master the art of Nō dance. He treated the (no doubt long-suffering) emperor to displays of his accomplishments, and compelled leading vassals like Tokugawa Ieyasu and Maeda Toshiie to perform alongside him. Some daimyo patrons of culture were major cultural luminaries in their own right. Furuta Oribe, who disemboweled himself when he came under suspicion first from Hideyoshi and finally from Ieyasu, was a ceramicist of note, and Hosokawa Yūsai (1534–1610), scion of a distinguished daimyo family (and ancestor of a prime minister in the 1990s) who fought under Hideyoshi and Ieyasu, established a formidable reputation for his mastery of culture ranging from poetry and prose classics to tea, food, music, swords, and ancient military practices. His expertise in a secretly transmitted commentary of the *Kokin wakashū*, a medieval poetry anthology, was considered so unique a national asset that when his life was endangered because the western army had encircled his castle at the time of Sekigahara the appeal of a court prince and a special rescript from the Emperor Goyōzei secured the lifting of the siege.

The most highly prized ceramics of the period were the rough, irregular hand-shaped bowls whose integrity served as symbols of the ideals of tea. Japanese ceramics were enriched by the fortunes of war, for many of the daimyo who led the armies to Korea brought Korean potters, in some cases entire communities, back with them. In the Satsuma village of Naeshirogawa a community of Korean exiles maintained their ethnic identity and ceramic traditions into the nineteenth century, as did a group brought to Kumamoto by Katō Kiyomasa. The greatest advances came in Saga, where Korean potters brought by the Nabeshima daimyo discovered a vein of kaolin that became the basis for Japan's first porcelain. There Japanese and Korean potters worked under the protection of the domain to produce a ware of blue and white, originally modeled on that of Ming China, that was shipped to all parts of Japan. Other forms of art flourished as well. A tradition of rare and radiant beauty developed in exquisite techniques that set new standards of decorative skill. *Rimpa* artists specializing in calligraphy, painting, and decorative glazes transformed the artistic life and standards of early modern Japan.

The age was also open to the outside world to a remarkable degree. Japanese traders and adventurers were to be found in many areas of Southeast

Asia where they operated along the network of ports developed by Chinese traders. The materials they brought back, ranging from raw materials for munitions to fine Chinese silk thread that was prized for embroidery, were eagerly sought by the urban merchants who purveyed their wares to the military despots of the castle towns and their ladies. Permits for such trade were issued by Hideyoshi and, after him, the Tokugawa; great temples, wealthy merchants, and frequently military lords cooperated in sponsoring such voyages. The Iberian traders and missionaries who first came to southern Kyushu in the 1540s were followed by many more. The art and patterns they brought quickly resonated with themes in Japan, and a series of "Southern Barbarian" paintings depicted their ships, missionaries, and servants. Within decades the Kyushu daimyo Ōmura Sumitada, fearing for his rule as rivals closed in on him, offered the Westerners the port of Nagasaki as a base for their trade. Nagasaki became the site of the mission headquarters with an academy for the training of Japanese and a printing press for the diffusion of translations of literature ranging from Aesop's fables to Thomas à Kempis's *Imitation of Christ*. Members of the Society of Jesus, many of them members of the feudal order in Italy and the Iberian peninsula, chose to work among the Japanese feudality, confident that if they won the lords and their vassals the commoners would follow. To preach among ordinary Japanese, they reasoned, would stir suspicions of subversion. In this they proved correct; a number of powerful daimyo became converts. When missionaries of other orders—Dominicans, Augustinians—joined their efforts by preaching to commoners, the Christian community grew rapidly. By the end of the sixteenth century Catholic converts may have neared 2 percent of the population, a higher percentage than are Christian in Japan today. Unlike in China, where the Jesuits chose to become intellectuals and scholars in order to penetrate the class of literati, in Japan they could concentrate on their religious tasks, as the principal intellectual class, that of Buddhist clergy, was in any case closed to them. Their hostility to Buddhism of every kind ingratiated them to some extent to the military hegemons like Nobunaga and Hideyoshi who had waged relentless war against Buddhist sectarians. They invited the Westerners to see their castles, expressed interest in the world from which they had come, and respected the dedication and courage of their lives. In addition, as he discovered to his sorrow when he was betrayed by a vassal in 1582, Nobunaga, like other hegemons, could hardly afford to relax with his own men, and it may well be that the disinterested, learned, and cultivated Europeans who directed the Jesuit mission were some of the few with whom he could interact without looking over his shoulder. Whatever the case, the Jesuits found the Japanese leaders fascinating and honorable people, though they never professed to understand them fully. The missionaries worked hard and successfully at their studies of language; their discretion and tact made them welcome at the headquarters of the despots even, for a time, after Hideyoshi ruled against Christianity in 1587. The affectation of Western costume, in turn, became something of a fad at many daimyo headquarters. Many of the conversions may have been expressions of this, but the constancy of other daimyo converts leaves no doubt of missionary success. Mention has been made of Konishi Yukinaga, one of Hideyoshi's leading generals in the Korean campaign; unable to bring himself to commit suicide after the loss of the battle of Sekigahara, he chose capture, mockery and execution. The Christian movement will receive further attention in a later chapter.

6. The Spoils of Sekigahara: Tokugawa Ieyasu

The third of the unifiers was Tokugawa Ieyasu, who was able to seize the gains scored by his two predecessors. He lived long enough to complete his work, he had enough sons to relieve him of dependency on the loyalty of his vassals, and he established a shogunate that endured until 1868.

Ieyasu's personal history can stand as a textbook case of the insecurities and qualities that produced leadership in the Sengoku years. He was born in 1543, the son of a petty military chief in Mikawa (present-day Shizuoka). When he was four years old his father packed him off to a more powerful neighbor, Imagawa, as a hostage. On the way there, however, he was kidnapped by men of the Oda house, later to be led by Nobunaga, and held by them for two years. When, at the age of seven, he was released, earlier plans for sending him as hostage to the Imagawa were carried out, and he remained in that status until his eighteenth year. By that time he had taken his first wife and fathered a son. In 1560, when Nobunaga defeated the Imagawa in his first great victory, Ieyasu went with the winner and fought as a Nobunaga supporter until Nobunaga's death. This permitted him to take charge of his old family vassals and encroach on the lands of the Imagawa to his own advantage. He was now permitted by imperial consent to change his (Matsudaira) family name to the more ancient name of Tokugawa. The alliance with Nobunaga brought demands that he show his loyalty by putting his (Imagawa-related) wife to death and ordering his son to disembowel himself. Upon Nobunaga's death, however, he was able to seize the rest of the Takeda domains to his north. By 1583 he was master of five provinces. He had a highly respectable background, sufficiently so to have been worth keeping alive by his more powerful neighbors. He was schooled in adversity. His education in marriage politics would continue with Hideyoshi. When, after some indecisive military sparring the two decided to cooperate, Ieyasu offered another son to Hide-yoshi for adoption, and accepted Hideyoshi's sister, freshly divorced for the occasion, as his wife.

Ieyasu developed his administrative skills while Hideyoshi busied himself with the reduction of Shikoku and Kyushu. Then, in 1590, they embarked on the most important military cooperation of their careers, the successful siege of Odawara. This brought the northeast provinces of Japan into the coalition of daimyo who now supported Hideyoshi. Hideyoshi's reward for Ieyasu was to order him to pack up and move, lock, stock and barrel, into the lands newly conquered and give up his provinces in central Japan for reassignment. This move, which must have seemed a blow at first, was ultimately to Ieyasu's benefit. He was now in command of the largest consolidated plain, the Kantō, with amassed revenue of 2.5 million *koku*. It was foreign to Ieyasu and, more important, to his vassals; they had no local base of support, and they were completely dependent upon their lord. Ieyasu occupied himself with the de-velopment of the Kantō while Hideyoshi was mustering the daimyo of western Japan for his invasion of Korea. Ieyasu was not involved in that expensive folly, and diplomatically urged Hideyoshi not to leave the country himself.

Ieyasu's administrative developments in Kantō proved the perfect prepa-ration for his exercise of national power after the battle of Sekigahara. He placed his most trustworthy vassals in locations of strategic importance. He set up a machinery of local administration and taxation. As his headquarters he selected a small fortress town in the middle of his new realm instead of rebuilding Odawara, from which the Hōjō daimyo had dominated the area. The place he chose became Edo, modern Tokyo. There he set in progress a massive building plan that required fifteen and more years for its completion. Swamps had to be drained. The ramparts of the great Chiyoda Castle (the present imperial palace grounds) that rose in its center were made of giant rocks cut from the cliffs of the Izu Peninsula to the south. To transport them to the castle site a series of moats were cut through the coastal plain. Still other public works were necessary for the water supply of what became, within a century or so, the world's most populous city.

Hideyoshi, when he sensed his death at hand in 1598, appointed Ieyasu one of five great councillors who were to be charged with the welfare and safety of his young son Hideyori in Osaka. Ieyasu and the others swore to serve Hideyori as faithfully as they had served his father. Probably none of them intended to do so, but in any case Ieyasu, with his vast and integrated realm under control and an abundance of progeny from his wives with which to make alliances, was best placed and most ambitious. Soon he had placed a son, an adopted daughter, and two granddaughters with strategically placed families to strengthen his position. When challenged by another group of Hideyoshi vassals led by Ishida Mitsunari, Ieyasu set in motion the events that led to Sekigahara and victory.

Sekigahara was not, however, a line-up of pro- and anti-Hideyoshi daimyo. They all professed loyalty to his memory and heir. But Ieyasu was acknowledged leader of the eastern host, and no one else was as well placed to capitalize on the outcome of the battle. It was Ieyasu who had forced the issue and dominated the fight. Even so, the successful conclusion left him with much to do. Hideyori remained alive and well in Osaka as reminder of Ieyasu's pledge of loyalty, and many of the most important Hideyoshi daimyo were still in their realms. Hideyori was only eight years old, but his rank and office at court put him on a level with Ieyasu. Until the fall of Osaka in 1615, the power to guarantee status was still divided between Hideyori and Ieyasu.

In 1603 Ieyasu accepted appointment as shogun, but that did not resolve the problem of Hideyori at Osaka. Ieyasu felt it necessary to spend a year and nine months in Fushimi, near the capital, to keep his eye on both Kyoto and Osaka. In 1605 he passed the title of shogun on to his son Hidetada and returned farther east to Sunpu in Shizuoka, but he continued to supervise the construction of the new order; *ōgosho,* literally "the great palace," actually refers to its occupant, a retired eminence, but since Ieyasu's day it has entered into colloquial Japanese to indicate a behind-the-scenes mover and shaker of events. Daimyo were ordered to submit registers of their villages and maps of their territories. In 1606 the court was told that future recommendations of court rank and offices for military houses would come from Ieyasu. Work began on the institutions that would distinguish the Tokugawa system for the next two centuries.

Each of the unifiers thus built on the work of his predecessor. Nobunaga destroyed the old order and began the process of centralization; Hideyoshi regularized the daimyo system, but relied upon the prestige of the imperial court instead of working out a consistent hierarchy of vassals. Ieyasu, however, lived sixteen years after his greatest victory and concentrated on steps that would enable his line to endure. He was able to place his five sons in a ring of outer support and call on the practical experience of disorder and distrust he had accumulated to work out a system of checks without balance. The system that resulted stood until 1868.

2

There has always been a lively argument about the nature of the Japanese polity during the Tokugawa, or Edo, period. Eighteenth-century Japanese scholars were well versed in the nature of the Chinese state and fully aware that their own was very different. In China the polity had progressed from "feudal" to central under the empire. The Japanese reading of the Chinese characters used to telegraph these systems distinguished between *hōken*, or feudal, and *gunken*, centralized government based on districts and prefectures. By late Tokugawa times even elementary compendia of knowledge prepared for commoners could note that while China had started with *hōken* and moved on to *gunken* government, in Japan the sequence had been reversed. Chinese-style institutions introduced into Japan in the seventh century had produced a centralized government under the emperor, but warrior rule had led to feudalism thereafter.

Later, familiarity with Western historical writing in the nineteenth century was quickly followed by attempts to fit Japan's history into world history. This produced a large volume of writing, some of which argued the case for the Tokugawa shogun as having had the "power of kingship" on the order of feudal monarchs in the West. Those who agreed held that it made more sense to compare the place of the emperor, whose functions were ritual and who held no political power, with that of the pope in the West. This position too had precedents in Tokugawa days, when the Dutch representatives who traveled to Edo routinely referred to the shogun as the "emperor." The documents prepared for Perry's mission to Japan in 1853 also addressed the shogun as "emperor." In the early eighteenth century the shogunal adviser Arai Hakuseki had tried to institutionalize this by referring to the shogun as Japan's "king" *(kokuō)*, but Arai's efforts did not long survive his period in office.

The problem has its origins in the fact that Tokugawa Japan was pacified and bureaucratized but not really unified. The daimyo domains, with their administrative structures, armies, and fiscal systems, retained important elements of autonomy although they were dependent on shogunal favor. Edwin O. Reischauer's term "centralized feudalism" encapsulates this paradox and identifies the problem: Japan was neither fully centralized nor fully feudal. Since World War II historians in Japan have followed substantially the same path by analyzing the Tokugawa system as a *baku-han kokka,* or "bakufu-han state," to indicate the duality between central shogun (bakufu) and regional daimyo (han) polities. To cap these distinctions, in recent years the dissolution of communist authoritarianism elsewhere has brought interest in the possibility that nongovernmental space can grow within an apparently closed system, and this in turn has led to efforts to see whether the limitations on shogunal rule at the center suffice to make it possible to consider early modern Japan under the rubric of "civil society." Limitations on both center and periphery, it can be argued, created interstices in which preconditions for participatory and limited government might have anticipated, or speeded, the changes of modern times.

It is interesting to examine the Edo system with some of these questions in mind, but it is necessary to begin with the assertion that the system changed considerably over time. In the period's first century, when Ieyasu emerged victorious from cataclysmic battles at Sekigahara and Osaka, he and his successors stood out as the most powerful among their peers. But they did have peers, and their victories were victories of allied armies, however hegemonic the leader's position came to seem. Still, the early shoguns were able to discipline, reward, and punish with relative impunity. A century later, once major feudal barons had been in place for a generation or more, dominance of that sort was exercised less frequently, and daimyo tenure became relatively secure. Political institutions did not move in the direction of greater centralization, but economic integration did. The needs of peace, commerce, and communications created waves that washed over political boundaries with increasing frequency. As conflict receded, so too did the shogun's need or inclination to marshal and to discipline his vassals.

1. Taking Control

Tokugawa Ieyasu moved carefully and systematically to exploit his victory at Sekigahara. His goal was to structure a system that would be more enduring than those built by his predecessors. He was in a stronger position from the start. Nobunaga had been survived by three sons, Hideyoshi by one, but Ieyasu left five of his nine sons behind him. By the time he died in 1616 one, Hidetada, had already been shogun and three others had been settled as major daimyo in the cadet houses of Owari, Kii, and Mito, which were eligible to provide sons for adoption into the main line in the event a shogun failed to father an appropriate successor. Nevertheless Ieyasu's success required astute judgment, determination, and patience.

The first and obvious steps were disposition of the territories held by leaders of the western coalition that had opposed him at Sekigahara. Eighty-seven warrior houses were extinguished and three were reduced in size, as a total of 6,221,690 *koku* of assessed land changed hands. Hideyoshi's son Hideyori alone found his holdings reduced by 1.3 million *koku*. The immediate beneficiaries were the Tokugawa vassals who had served Ieyasu from the first. They had been in charge of territories on the Kantō (Edo, or Tokyo) plain since Hideyoshi had ordered Ieyasu to move there in 1590; several had held territories larger than those of many daimyo, but as subordinates to Ieyasu they had not had formal daimyo status. Now that rank and title were Ieyasu's to convey he made this good, and the vassals were relocated to strategic points throughout central Japan. Next, the need for additional rewards was combined with doubts about loyalty to affect tenure in lands already granted. Kobayakawa Hideaki, the turncoat whose defection from the western cause had sealed its fate at Sekigahara, was enfeoffed in the great Inland Sea domain of Okayama (Bizen), but when he died without an heir in 1602 the territory was reclaimed and his house came to an end. This was the first time a transfer of this order had not been related to fortunes of war, and it testified to the strength of the central power that was emerging.

The greatest problems came with the greatest lords. Shimazu, daimyo of Satsuma, had beat a hasty retreat to his domains in southern Kyushu after the disaster at Sekigahara. It would have required further warfare with a deeply entrenched leader to eliminate him altogether, and instead the arts of diplomacy came into play. Soon messengers were moving between Ieyasu's headquarters and the distant port of Kagoshima. Late in 1602 a meeting was arranged between Ieyasu and Shimazu Yoshihiro at Ieyasu's Fushimi headquarters. Significantly, Ieyasu was absent in Edo when Shimazu first made the trip, and chose to keep his guest waiting until he made a leisurely return to Fushimi. Now it became possible for Shimazu to explain that his participation at Sekigahara had been based on the mistaken belief that it had been mandated by his loyalty to Hideyoshi's son. Mollified, Ieyasu confirmed him in the rule of his ancestral territory, and Shimazu pledged his loyalty to the new Tokugawa hegemon. Prior to this the imperial court had offered to invest Ieyasu with the title of head of the shogunal house of Minamoto, only to have him decline, but in 1603, with Shimazu on board, Ieyasu accepted appointment as shogun, head of the Minamoto and of the military houses, second court rank, and Minister of the Right in the old administrative structure of honors. Two years later he transferred the office of shogun to his son Hidetada, who led a host of 100,000 men to Kyoto to accept the commission. The ceremonies for Ieyasu's appointment had followed so soon after Sekigahara that few of the major lords (as opposed to Tokugawa vassals) were present, but for Hidetada's investment the retinues of almost all the major barons, including Shimazu Iehisa of Satsuma, thronged the streets of Kyoto. Significantly, not one of them thought it politic to combine this with a visit to young Hideyori at Osaka.

Ieyasu, free of burdensome ritual, was now at liberty to plan the reduction of Osaka. Toyotomi Hideyori remained in charge of Japan's largest and strongest castle complex in a city swollen by adherents of defeated lords whose lands had been confiscated. It was a host increasingly desperate and fearful, but without an unlikely military upset it was not going to get the support of other daimyo, who saw the writing on the wall. The Shimazu capitulation had been followed by pledges from most others who counted. The year 1611 brought oaths of loyalty from all the major daimyo who had been Ieyasu's peers.

As a first step Ieyasu suggested a visit with Hideyori. The boy was now ten years old; he was being educated in the aristocratic arts of the capital, and advised by his mother. Though his holdings had been reduced to lands producing 650,000 *koku*, he remained a threat to Tokugawa legitimacy because Ieyasu and his peers were pledged to guard his interests. Hideyori and his mother resisted and vacillated in responding to Ieyasu's request for a meeting, uncertain whether his professions of concern and respect for the Toyotomi legacy were more than a carefully planned ruse. A meeting finally took place in 1611, in the relatively neutral ground of the Kyoto Nijō Castle and not at Ieyasu's Fushimi headquarters, but it did little to improve the relationship between the two.

Further moves focused on the imperial court, which could be expected to see Hideyori as a balance against Ieyasu and as a guarantee of its own influence. Hideyori had been appointed Minister of the Interior (*nai daijin*) at the same time Ieyasu had received his titles; the boy seemed able and was becoming popular at the court, and there was beginning to be talk about the possibility of appointing him to his father's old title of *kanpaku*, or regent. It became urgent to neutralize the court and keep it out of warrior politics. This would have been difficult for Hideyoshi, who had made such use of court titles, but Ieyasu's new standing as head of the military houses made it possible for him. In 1613 Ieyasu issued a set of instructions for the court nobility (the *kuge shohatto*) that was designed to restrict court involvement in warrior affairs, and particularly to prevent it from issuing promotions and titles. This was only part of a much more ambitious program to regulate matters at court by researching ancient documents for precedents that would settle once and for all disputes about priority and protocol at the innumerable ceremonial occasions that dominated the tedious routine of aristocratic life. Ieyasu paid close attention to this project as it unfolded, urged haste on those assigned to it, and attached great importance to it. Priority in such matters would bring pacification and eliminate rancor at court, and lessen the likelihood or need to seek assistance from contacts within the warrior class. It would also, of course, demonstrate his ascendancy over the court. There is also a good deal of evidence that Ieyasu had genuine respect for the court, and that he showed deference as well as determination in his dealings with it.

In 1613 the court nobles were ordered to be "diligent in their studies," arrange guard duty around the emperor's person, resist the temptation to wander through the streets day or night, avoid sports and games, and above all to avoid contact with the many unruly young dandies and roughnecks who thronged the streets of Kyoto. Moreover, it would be the shogun or his deputies, and not the court, that would examine reported infractions of these rules.

Meanwhile work continued on a longer code of procedure, the *Kinchū narabi ni kuge shohatto* (Regulations for the court and the nobility), that was issued immediately after the fall of Osaka in 1615.[1] The emperor's concerns were to be cultural, concentrated on proficiency in the arts of peace. It then listed the orders of priority to be observed at court, procedures to be followed in assigning era names *(nengō),* and went on to specify in elaborate detail the materials, dyes, and patterns appropriate for the several ranks involved in ceremonial duties at court. Further regulations applying to appointments for Buddhist primates at court-related temples *(monzeki)* completed the document.

Ieyasu extended this concern for the resolution of disputes to Buddhist temples by ordering distribution of major Ming dynasty Buddhist texts in the hope that prelates would abandon politics for doctrine.

Nevertheless the presence of Hideyori in Osaka was a reminder that the Tokugawa primacy was to some degree a usurpation. In 1614 Ieyasu decided that it was safe to launch an attack on the castle. He used a rather thin pretext about an imagined slight conveyed by use of the characters for his name in the inscription on a temple bell. Some 90,000 defenders, helped by the defensive arrangements of Japan's greatest castle, held off an attack by twice their number. Ieyasu now turned to crafty negotiation, and suggested a truce in which, as a show of good faith, part of the Osaka castle's defensive moats would be filled in. As those terms were being carried out, treachery on the part of the Tokugawa force, which obligingly provided the labor, tipped the balance. The Tokugawa labor squads, in an excess of zeal, filled in more of the moats than was called for by the agreement. After they were through and the attack was renewed in the summer of 1615, things went better. When defeat was certain young Hideyori and his mother committed suicide, the castle was put to flames, and the problem of loyalty to the memory of Hideyoshi was laid to rest.

2. Ranking the Daimyo

The task of rearranging the daimyo had been substantially achieved by 1615, but the fall of Osaka left the Tokugawa free to reassign the domains that had remained in Hideyori's care. It now became possible to finalize the divisions of the country.

In considering the shape of territorial disposition it is clear that the Tokugawa arrangement grew organically out of what had gone before. The Kamakura and Ashikaga shoguns had worked with and through the administrative and territorial patterns laid down by the imperial court, and they had structured their own house band and retainers into existing administrative units, after which they squelched attempts by aristocratic and temple networks of Kyoto to retain control of the assets within their realms. Of the unifiers, Nobunaga had been ruthless in removing clerical and administrative interference with his activities, while Hideyoshi had done his best to co-opt the prestige of the court through his assumption of court titles. Ieyasu's first moves, as shown in his instructions for the court nobility, were to keep them out of warrior politics, and in a short time he managed to hamstring the Kyoto establishment in such a way that it was probably less effective, in terms of real power, than it had been since the seventh century.

The vassal bands that the Sengoku unifiers developed were far more intimately a part of the clan structure than their predecessors had been. John Hall has observed that throughout history Japan has alternated between familial and bureaucratic structures;[2] and that with time each took on an overlay of the other. In Tokugawa Japan this reached a high point, as fictive family terms came to cloak most relationships of status dependency.

The house, or *ie*, was everywhere the enduring unit, and all obligations were subordinated to its preservation. This was not limited to the warrior class. In the seventeenth-century Japanese countryside large households staffed by subordinates with varying degrees of bondage were everywhere. The principal tenants or servants were classed as *fudai*, "hereditary"; below them a network of lesser orders with varying degrees of indentured bondage looked to their immediate superiors as representing a quasi-paternal presence. Those who lived alongside such a network were outsiders, perhaps of equal rank, but inhabitants of a different universe of relationships.[3] In contemporary Japan this lives on to some degree as the non-Asian "outsiders," *gaijin*, move in their own and distinctive orbit, forever "different."

Translated to the world of Edo feudality, this brought a distinction between the traditional Tokugawa house vassals, the *fudai* daimyo, and the *tozama* or "outside lords." Some had opposed the Tokugawa forces at Sekigahara while others had cooperated, but as heads of completely distinct systems of subordination and command they could never change their classification. What was true at the high level of daimyo was even more so at the level of ordinary samurai. Daimyo could interact, compete, and rank themselves in relationships to the shogunal hegemon, but their vassals lived within a world structured around the daimyo. The categories of *fudai* and *tozama* thus served to separate the Tokugawa house from its peers. Tokugawa house vassals could serve in the bakufu organization, while *tozama* were forever outside it.

To this must be added the fact that some daimyo houses retained and even treasured long-standing resentment of defeat. In Chōshū the Mōri suffered sharp reductions in territory after the defeat at Sekigahara (from 1,205,000 to 298,480 *koku*), and one can imagine the deep-laid hope for future revenge, particularly among the lower ranks whose members might have fared differently in different times. Albert Craig reports a Chōshū tradition in which, on the first day of the new year, domain elders and inspectors appeared before the daimyo to ask, "Has the time come to begin the subjugation of the bakufu?" and received the ritual response "It is still too early; the time has not yet come."[4]

A second aspect of the daimyo system as it crystallized during the Edo period was the precision of its ranking. A daimyo was defined as a feudal lord enfeoffed with an area assessed at the level of 10,000 *koku* or higher and directly invested by the shogun. This last was a crucial distinction; many vassals of daimyo were invested with subfiefs larger than that, but they remained rear-vassals *(baishin)* and moved in their daimyo's orbit and not the shogun's national galaxy. A distinctive aspect of each galaxy was the way in which assessed *koku* income *(kokudaka)*, status rank, and military power as expressed in army size or vassal band coincided. The *kokudaka* figure was based on domain surveys conducted at the beginning of the period. It was termed the "official" or "outer" *(omote)* yield of the domain; as time passed that might be less than the "real" or "inner" *(uchi)* productivity, but it remained the measure of status rank because to alter it by bringing it up to date would involve restructuring the daimyo's standing relative to that of his peers and hence involve rearranging the whole system. That standing determined everything from the location and size of the *yashiki,* the daimyo's Edo residence, and particularly its entrance gate,[5] to the entourage of samurai he could bring with him to the capital, the audience chamber or gallery where he would be seated in the shogun's castle, and where he would line up with his peers—in short, his quality as a feudal lord, as demonstrated by his conspicuous consumption. It was no less important to his retainers, since it provided the basis for their self-esteem too. It also mattered to the Edo townsmen and merchants who had access to the handbook of heraldry, the daimyo *bukan,* which listed the feudal lords, their principal vassals, their *kokudaka,* their heraldry and insignia, the size of their entourage, their mansions, and the schedules of their rites of homage to the shogun, for all this was highly relevant to the commercial dealings with the daimyo's samurai and provided, so to speak, their credit rating.

Officially, however, two other ratings for lords were used. One related to the size of the domain. If it incorporated an entire province the daimyo was a *kokushu,* or province holder; he could also be close to that, as a "quasi-" province holder. Similar conditions came to apply to whether the domain included a castle or not; postage-stamp sized principalities often did not. Consequently considerations of "province" and "castle," each made flexible by the possibility of the further gradations "quasi" or "having the status of," provided instant indicators of ceremonial importance. An additional index was that of rank in the ancient nine-step hierarchy the Japanese court had taken over from China in the seventh century. The Edo bakufu, however, had seen to it that the court would steer clear of the aristocratic distinctions that were so dear to warriors trying to better themselves; in 1606 it ordered that it alone could petition for court rank and title for warriors. In doing so it manipulated the lists greatly to the advantage of the Tokugawa house and its affiliates. Then, in 1611 and 1615, it went on to order the deletion of warriors from court rosters; warrior offices and ranks were to be distinct from those for the nobility. By 1680 and after the highest ranks were largely closed to any but Tokugawa houses.[6]

It now becomes possible to examine the division of lands according to categories of daimyo. One additional category of shogunal retainers, *hatamoto* (bannermen), were of sub-daimyo level but invested separately; they were to play an important role in staffing the bakufu bureaucracy. Shoguns made modifications as they promoted favorites and penalized others, but by the end

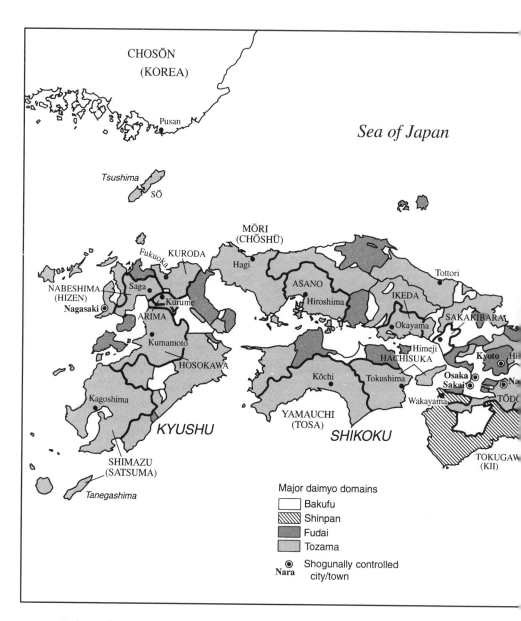

2. Daimyo domains, as reassigned by the early Tokugawa shoguns, in 1664. Tokugawa houses and *fudai* vassals held the productive Kantō and Kansai plains and strategic communication routes, while *tozama* domains, though often larger, were on the periphery. This pattern endured for two centuries.

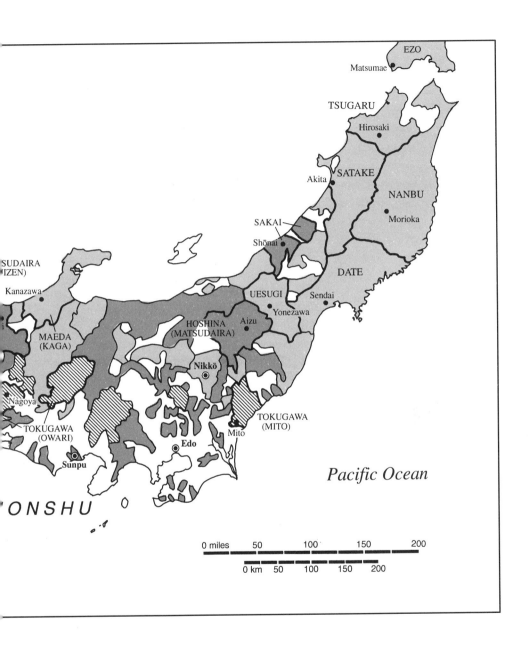

EZO

Matsumae

TSUGARU

Hirosaki

SATAKE

Akita

NANBU

Morioka

SAKAI

Shōnai

DATE

SUDAIRA
IZEN)

UESUGI

Sendai

Kanazawa

Yonezawa

MAEDA
(KAGA)

HOSHINA
(MATSUDAIRA)

Aizu

Nikkō

Nagoya

TOKUGAWA
(MITO)

TOKUGAWA
(OWARI)

Mito

Edo

Sunpu

Pacific Ocean

ONSHU

| 0 miles | 50 | 100 | 150 | 200 |

| 0 km | 50 | 100 | 150 | 200 |

of the formative decades of the Edo bakufu the following arrangements were in place:[7]

Imperial court lands	141,151 *koku*
Shogunal lands (*tenryō*)	4,213,171 *koku*
Shogunal sub-daimyo vassals	2,606,545 *koku*
Fudai and collaterals (*shimpan*)	9,325,300 *koku*
Tozama ("outside") lords	9,834,700 *koku*
Shrine and temple lands	316,230 *koku*

It will be seen that shogunal lands totaled 6,819,716 *koku*, approximately one-quarter of the national total. If to this one adds the almost ten million *koku* in *fudai* daimyo hands, the overwhelming predominance of the Edo bakufu is clear.

A geographic balance of power made this possible. Each of the most productive plains of the central island of Honshu was in Tokugawa hands, and the major *fudai* vassals and Tokugawa related collateral houses controlled the access routes to Edo. The Kantō plain itself was in the hands of Tokugawa sub-daimyo houses, most of them bannermen (*hatamoto*). The great *tozama* houses were to be found in the west and northeast, to some degree at the periphery of the land. Lands set aside for the imperial court, whose 137 noble families were also assigned a *koku* income, were around the old capital of Kyoto. Interestingly, the distinction between *fudai* and *tozama* was also used to some extent within the court families.

But this overview does little to indicate the crazy quilt pattern of holdings. The outside lords, who numbered about eighty-five, had large areas; their lines had been established by Sengoku times, some much earlier, and they agreed to Tokugawa leadership after Sekigahara. The greatest of them, the house of Maeda at modern Kanazawa, was rated at 1,022,700 *koku*, second only to the Tokugawa house itself. Of the sixteen largest daimyo holdings, all but five were *tozama*; of those five one was the greatest of the *fudai*, the house of Ii, and the other four were Tokugawa collateral houses. In all only sixteen daimyo ruled lands assessed at more than 300,000 *koku*. In contrast to this was the prevalence of petty, postage-stamp-sized domains among the *fudai*, who numbered about 145. Most of them were without even a castle town and were close to the definitional limit for daimyo of 10,000 *koku* assessed productivity. The coastal area of the Nagoya plain shows this in startling clarity. Its territory was a sandy spit of waterfront land. Although highly developed as resort country today, in Edo times its productivity was negligible. Even its high officials lived in relative poverty. Nevertheless Tawara, as the domain was called, was still fortunate compared with many of its inland neighbors whose lands were isolated spots surrounded by those of other daimyo. On the Kantō plain the holdings of the *hatamoto* were frequently so mangled that villages might be divided between two fief-holders. Hence, although *fudai* outnumbered the *tozama* by almost half, and *hatamoto* certainly outnumbered *fudai*, in no case did their individual *kokudaka* approach that of the major *tozama* daimyo. To complicate things further, the bakufu lands were widely scattered; the bakufu also frequently allocated, or requisitioned, lands for one or another infraction, and ordered neighboring daimyo to take on the burden of running them on its behalf. It is not without reason that Kären Wigen has coined the term "parcellized sovereignty" for the Tokugawa system.[8]

3. The Structure of the Tokugawa Bakufu

The Tokugawa house began its rule under the dominating presence of Ieyasu. Until his death in 1616, by which time Hidetada had already been shogun for a decade, the decisions that mattered were Ieyasu's. Hidetada, historians conclude, was his choice as successor not because of his brilliance but because he could be considered careful and cautious. These characteristics, indeed, almost cost him the succession, for he was late in arriving at Sekigahara with his army, having waited to besiege a castle that he could have bypassed. Ieyasu was reportedly so incensed that he refused to meet with him for some time thereafter. Once he was shogun, Hidetada showed less sensitivity to court and imperial wishes than his father had. He insisted on placing his daughter Kazuko as consort for the emperor. A daughter, who took the throne as Empress Meishō (r. 1629–1643), was born of this union, and became the first empress to reign in many centuries. At the birth of the child in 1626 Hidetada and his son, Iemitsu, who had already succeeded him as shogun, journeyed to Kyoto where they made lavish grants of gold to nobles and townsmen alike. Ieyasu had left the bakufu with six million *ryō*, the basic gold coin of the realm, in its coffers; but that surplus did not long survive him.

Iemitsu, the third shogun, was also the first to be born as putative successor, a fact that may account for his overbearing attitude toward the daimyo. Once he had freed himself from the restraints of his father's advisers he surrounded himself with personal friends he felt he could trust. He was a harsh and self-centered autocrat with the feudality, but he also tried to communicate with ordinary people by going on hawking trips alone. Informality of that sort would have been unthinkable by the time of Yoshimune, the eighth shogun, who was also fond of hawking. Under Iemitsu's rule bakufu institutions took on the form they would retain until the end. At the time of his death five of his senior aides accompanied him in ritual suicide *(junshi)*, a procedure that was later, in 1663, forbidden by the bakufu.

Once a shogun was invested by the court he was absolute ruler. During his minority there might be a regent, and after he reached maturity he issued orders through bureaucratic institutions that developed, but in theory there was nothing that could restrain him. The more important, then, that he be tutored in the merits of virtuous government in his youth. By Ieyasu's provisions shogunal successors were to be chosen from the three great cadet lines of Owari, Kii, and Mito if a shogun failed to produce an heir. Yoshimune, the eighth shogun, added three additional cadet lines from which successors might be chosen. In the nature of things, shoguns kept a wary eye on those houses from which competitors or successors might come, and heads of cadet and collateral houses seldom if ever found it possible to receive appointments of national significance. The shogunal councils were staffed by Tokugawa vassals; at the highest levels by *fudai* daimyo, and below that by bannermen. There were fifteen Tokugawa shoguns.

The Tokugawa Shoguns

1. Ieyasu (1542–1616), shogun 1603–1605
2. Hidetada (1579–1632), shogun 1605–1623
3. Iemitsu (1604–1651), shogun 1623–1651
4. Ietsuna (1641–1680), shogun 1651–1680
5. Tsunayoshi (1646–1709), shogun 1680–1709
6. Ienobu (1662–1712), shogun 1709–1712 (Kōfu cadet line)
7. Ietsugu (1709–1716), shogun 1713–1716
8. Yoshimune (1684–1751), shogun 1716–1745 (Kii cadet line)
9. Ieshige (1711–1761), shogun 1745–1760
10. Ieharu (1737–1786), shogun 1760–1786
11. Ienari (1773–1841), shogun 1787–1837 (Hitotsubashi cadet line)
12. Ieyoshi (1793–1853), shogun 1837–1853
13. Iesada (1824–1858), shogun 1853–1858
14. Iemochi (1846–1866), shogun 1858–1866 (Kii cadet line)
15. Yoshinobu (Keiki) (1837–1913), shogun 1866–1867 (Mito/Hitotsubashi cadet line)

Note: It will be seen from this chart that cadet lines provided successors five times. On several occasions, however, younger sons who had been adopted into related lines, and even grandsons of previous shoguns, were adopted into the main line. In Yoshimune's case, his status as a great-grandson (of Ieyasu) helped swing the balance in his favor.

In accordance with the primogeniture tradition that had become firm in Japan by Ashikaga times, the shogun was to be succeeded by his eldest son. At the very end of the Edo period the importance of blood over ability was emphasized by a Tokugawa vassal in discussing a succession choice: "The peace and order of the nation are due to the dignity and virtue of the great shogunal family, not just to the relative intelligence [of an individual shogun]. This is the custom of our empire, different from that of other countries [i.e., China]."[9] But youth and adolescence in the pampered interior of the Chiyoda Castle was not likely to produce effective leadership. Moreover, after a successful assassination attempt on the life of a high official in 1684, steps were taken to make the shogun and his top officials less approachable; guards saw to it that chamberlains, pages, and personal attendants were the only ones able to approach the leader.[10]

This began a period in which chamberlains became central. Thereafter, unless the shogun was a person of unusually strong personal determination and presence, jockeying for influence between heads of bakufu councils and personal advisers characterized Edo politics. It is notable that in almost every case in which the shogun really counted he proved to have come to the top through irregular, "outside" channels through adoption and not through birth, youth, and adolescence in the Great Interior (*Ōoku*) of the Edo Castle. To a remarkable degree this was true in daimyo houses as well; innovative and strong individuals were usually adopted into the main line. Not only that: the shoguns who made a difference frequently had mothers whose plebeian origins refreshed the Tokugawa blood line. Consider three.

Tsunayoshi, the fifth shogun, presided over the Genroku era (1688–1704), which stands as a turning point in Japanese culture, and enjoyed a twenty-nine-year rule as arbitrary despot.[11] A son of Iemitsu and great-grandson of Ieyasu, he was probably the most scholarly of all the shoguns. Tsunayoshi has nevertheless been ridiculed as the *inu kubō* or "dog shogun" for the misguided edicts he issued to protect animals in an effort to promote compassion.[12]

He was a major sponsor of Confucian studies, and during his rule the Edo court became a scholarly center of studies of Chinese and of Buddhism. He was also notorious for the easy favoritism he showed handsome young pages, many of whom he promoted to daimyo if they pleased him. Tsunayoshi's mother was the daughter of a Kyoto greengrocer; when her father died she went to serve in the household of a court aristocrat, after which she was sent as a lady-in-waiting to the women's quarters of the shogun's castle. There she came to Iemitsu's attention and bore him a son, the future shogun Tsunayoshi. Since he seemed unlikely to succeed to rule, Tsunayoshi was appointed daimyo of Tatebayashi, but he continued to live in Edo to be tutored in Confucian learning. One elder brother committed suicide, and when the other, the shogun Ietsuna, was on his deathbed, Tsunayoshi was brought in for a bedside adoption and succession to the rule. Thus in this case birth from a plebeian (but highly intelligent and famously beautiful) mother and an independent upbringing that was not geared for heading the bakufu produced a strong-willed and intelligent, albeit idiosyncratic, shogun.

Yoshimune, the eighth shogun, provides an even better case. By any measure he was a major shogun, perhaps the most important after Ieyasu, whose achievements he tried to emulate. He reacted against the luxury and corruption of the Genroku age by limiting himself and his staff to two meals per day. He tried to restore martial values in his samurai corps. Concerned about the outflow of precious metals in foreign trade, he inaugurated programs of agricultural experimentation by importing pharmacopoeia from China. An avid student of Chinese institutional history, he sponsored studies of Ming dynasty law, set about revising the calendar, and did his best to import military and technological knowledge from China and from Holland. He tried hard, and with some success, to free himself from the conventions that had developed to keep the shogun in the recesses of the palace during most of his waking day.

Yoshimune's lineage on his father's side was impeccable; he was a great-grandson of Ieyasu and the third son of the daimyo of the Kii cadet house. His mother, however, was of townsman extraction. She became a lady-in-waiting, no doubt because of her beauty, but she was so low in rank that she was not permitted to rear her son. Since there seemed little likelihood of promotion for the young Yoshimune, he was given a petty fief with a paltry rating of 2,000 *koku,* so insignificant that he had difficulty in meeting the ceremonial requirements of his court rank. Then, following the deaths of his two elder brothers, he emerged as daimyo of Kii (Wakayama), suddenly eligible for succession to the shogunate. Thus a fortuitous pattern of illness and premature death in Edo and within his own paternal family made it possible for him to be appointed shogunal regent; and from that post he was able to maneuver for support among the *rōjū* (senior councillors) for his elevation to shogun. He represents another instance in which commoner blood combined with unexpected mortality in high places to make it possible for a relative outsider to come to the rule.

Ienari, the longest lived of all the Tokugawa shoguns, has fared less well at the hands of historians, who characterize his era as the "Age of the [Harem] Great Interior" *(Ōoku jidai).* He came into office from the (Yoshimune-created) cadet family of Hitotsubashi, and was named heir to the childless Ieharu at the age of thirteen. Shogun from 1787 to 1837, he first sponsored and then repudiated the reform program of Matsudaira Sadanobu (a grandson of Yoshimune) and chose instead an easygoing style of court and marriage politics in which most of the traditional barriers of *tozama-fudai* distinctions were ignored. His formal consort was the daughter of the Satsuma daimyo. With the help of dozens of secondary consorts he sired over fifty children, many of whom were adopted into daimyo houses. As a result a startling number of daimyo in late Tokugawa decades were half-brothers by virtue of Ienari's parentage. Of the powerful and self-willed daimyo of Edo days, therefore, the three most remarkable—and the fourth (also from Mito via Hitotsubashi), who chose to surrender the office in 1867—were "outsiders" and relatively free from the aristocratic inhibitions of an upbringing in the Edo castle.

Below the shogun the Edo administration developed into a formidable bureaucracy that came to number some 17,000 men. This was still a small fraction of the Tokugawa and *fudai* retainer corps. Moreover, major posts tended to become traditional for, and monopolized within, certain vassal houses. The result was underemployment, alternation between several men assigned to the same office during employment, and no doubt boredom for the majority.

The accompanying chart showing principal figures in the Tokugawa bureaucracy only begins to suggest the number of offices and those who filled them.[13] The vast space of the Chiyoda Castle in Edo provided office space for these and many more. Because most offices were held by more than one individual, a city magistrate on duty in Osaka, for instance, would have a counterpart in Edo.

Principal Figures in the Tokugawa Bureaucracy

Tairō (great elder)
Rōjū (elders; senior councillors) (4–5) were in charge of:
    Chamberlains *(sobashū)*
    City magistrates (for Edo, Kyoto, Osaka, Nagasaki)
    Superintendents *(bugyō)* of finance, temples and shrines, public works
    Inspectors general *(ōmetsuke)*
    Kantō deputy
    Masters of court ceremony
Junior Council (Wakatoshiyori)
Supreme Court of Justice (Hyōjōsho)

Let us look more closely at the council of elders, the *rōjū*. Ieyasu and Hidetada retained as special advisers men who had served them in war and peace, but Iemitsu set about structuring an administration that would be loyal to him personally. In 1634 he ordered that the *rōjū* be responsible for all matters relating to the imperial court. Ieyasu had installed a trusted vassal at Kyoto in a post that became known as the *shōshidai*, and the court in turn named a court noble *(buke denso)* to deal with the bakufu.

Rōjū were the bakufu's most important officials. They were in charge of foreign policy, and they were also responsible for relations with all but the largest daimyo. To them fell responsibility for major construction projects, stipends for samurai who had given up or wished to surrender their land, matters relating to the shogunal household, schedules for attendance at the shogun's capital, the reconstruction of castles, the retirement and succession of daimyo, and the creation of new domains. When necessary *rōjū* were also to organize daimyo to suppress rebellions. In short, all matters of national significance were entrusted to them.

A Junior Council, the Wakatoshiyori, was responsible for matters within the shogunal retainer band. The council was briefly abolished between 1649 and 1662, but thereafter it dealt with matters of the sub-daimyo level.

Membership on the board of *rōjū* was restricted to *fudai* daimyo with incomes rated between 30,000 and 100,000 *koku*. They would normally have had previous experience as superintendents of shrines and temples, masters of shogunal ceremony, and Kyoto or castle deputies. Thus the post was restricted to the highest-ranking and most trusted of the *fudai* daimyo. Study of the membership of the board throughout the period, however, shows that it drew on a very limited number of families; the same family names appear over and over again. It is relevant to this that, as Thomas Smith has written, "merit appointment may have become a sore issue in the second half of the Tokugawa period partly because rank was a *more* severe bar to advancement than previously."[14]

The *rōjū* worked as a committee and reported their decisions to the shogun. They served on a monthly rotation system. Even when not on duty call, however, they were expected to be present at the castle each morning. The duty *rōjū* called on the shogun each morning to pay his respects. Under the *rōjū* a large staff of secretaries generated imposing volumes of paperwork that had to be reviewed. The office was honored with the grant of fourth (imperial) court rank. *Rōjū* received gifts from fellow daimyo and officials at the end of the year, from the Dutch when they came to Edo, and from all daimyo when they came to Edo on rotation duty. Lower officials were expected to sink to their knees when they encountered *rōjū*, and even the heads of the three great cadet houses bowed to them. Outside the castle they enjoyed precedence over daimyo processions. When a *rōjū* died there was no public singing, dancing, or music allowed for three days, and daimyo would send messages of condolence. Most of the central bureaucracy reported to *rōjū;* they were clearly the fulcrum of the Edo administration.

The bakufu retained within its territory each of the great cities of Edo, Osaka, and Kyoto as well as Nagasaki. The city magistrates for the great centers of Edo and of Osaka were also in important posts; they too operated on a monthly alternation system, with one on duty in the Edo home office and the other at his post. Kyoto, for the imperial court, and Nagasaki, for its foreign trade, were similarly governed.

Where technical knowledge was required rank became less important than competence. The superintendents of finance *(kanjō bugyō)* were bannermen with modest family stipends of 500–2,500 *koku,* which was augmented when in office with a salary of 3,000 *koku.* They were responsible for the shogun's granary lands, and the various bailiffs and intendants *(daikan)* who administered and taxed those lands reported to them. In all, close to five or six thousand officials were supervised by the eight superintendents *(bugyō),* who in turn reported to the *rōjū.*

An office much remarked upon by writers was the intelligence service of *metsuke,* literally "observer" or "inspector," that operated at all levels, from Ōmetsuke to "yokome" ("side glance"?) to keep the administration posted on performance and apprised of political or religious subversion. There was not a hierarchy of political intelligence centered in a single apparatus of distrust, but it may well be that few administrative systems have built counterintelligence so prominently and permanently into all branches of their governing structures. The injunctions against Christianity and some forms of Buddhism provided the bakufu with excuse for checks that gave it the ability to maintain vigilance against any kind of dissidence. At the same time the network of inspectors made it possible to check on the performance and quality of local administration.

4. The Domains *(han)*

Three-quarters of Japan was under the control of daimyo; their domains stretched from Kyushu in the southwest to the fringes of Hokkaido in the north. The number of domains, and of daimyo, changed throughout the period as a result of rewards and penalties; over 500 existed at least briefly, and at any point there were slightly more than 250. The Japanese term for domain, *han,* is a modern designation and dates from the nineteenth century, as does the term "feudalism" in the West; it was only after people thought it unusual or special that attention began to focus on the domain. In prewar Japan historians were preoccupied with the foundations of the imperial state, and little study of the domain was made before the end of World War II. After 1945 there came a flood of studies of domains and analysis of the "bakuhan state"; as three-quarters of the country were under daimyo rule, that meant that three-quarters of the country was not under direct shogunal rule. It is essential to look at that area.

Domains varied enormously in size and importance. The largest was that of the Maeda house, with its capital at the city of Kanazawa and a *koku* rating of over one million. But many more just passed the definitional line of 10,000 *koku*. Only sixteen domains had a *koku* rating of more than 300,000, and only a few dozen daimyo houses managed to stay in place throughout the two and a half centuries of Tokugawa rule.

Domains varied also in their social structure, depending on the proportion of their population that was samurai. Some had so many samurai that the castle town could not contain them, and in consequence allowed them to live in the countryside. Satsuma, whose swollen military establishment of Sengoku times was retained throughout the period, had samurai families everywhere, forming 20 or 30 percent of the total population, while the figure elsewhere was 2 or 3 percent, for an overall total of 5 to 6 percent including dependents. Consequently most of the great *tozama* domains were relatively more highly militarized and, with samurai scattered throughout the area, economically less developed than the Tokugawa heartland.

We have already noted that some of the great *tozama* domains like Chōshū fostered a hereditary resentment of Tokugawa dominance. In Satsuma, too, upper samurai donned their armor each year on the anniversary of the defeat at Sekigahara and headed for their temple to meditate on that event. Satsuma had special arrangements for the reception of bakufu inspectors that guaranteed that they would not learn much about the domain. Special villages would be readied for such visits by shooing the farmers away and populating the paddies with samurai pretending to be farmers, in order to maintain security.[15] On the other hand, many daimyo were grateful to the bakufu for having authorized their rule and treated bakufu inspectors with elaborate courtesy.

The factor of size probably provides the most important distinction among domains. The domain of Tawara, which became famous to modern readers through the career of the official-painter Watanabe Kazan (1793–1841), was about as small and poor as an area could be. It was rated at 12,000 *koku*.

A seven days' walk from Edo, it had only a scruffy castle. But because the daimyo had fought for Ieyasu from the first he was granted a location for his Edo estate that placed him among the great Tokugawa vassals. Unfortunately this was an extremely expensive honor for a domain consisting of 24 villages with a population of about 20,000. There were 598 military families, 296 of them foot soldiers; 212 were registered as temple staff, 27 for Shinto shrines, and 32 were listed as "criminals and beggars."

Consequently even someone near the top of the Tawara samurai structure like Watanabe, whose family tax base was rated at 130 *koku*, experienced grinding poverty. His family normally received less than half of its stipend. He provides a graphic description of that hardship:

> The condition of our poverty was such that I cannot do justice to it in words. Because of our reduced food supply one brother had to be sent out of our home to apprentice in a temple, and later to serve in the home of a *hatamoto*. I was 14 when I was told to lead this little brother to Itabashi [in Edo, where the family lived at the daimyo residence]. I remember that in a lightly falling snow this little boy of 8 or 9 was led off by a rough looking stranger. I recall as though it was yesterday how we both watched over our shoulders until we were out of each other's sight.[16]

If this was true for the Watanabe family, high in the Tawara establishment, it can be imagined what life was like for those less fortunately placed. A tiny principality like Tawara could not constitute much of a restraint on the authority of the central bakufu at Edo.

A substantial domain presented a very different picture. Tosa, on the island of Shikoku, was a fan-shaped, mountainous, and relatively inaccessible area. It was an integrated realm with natural frontiers; probably only Satsuma was a better-integrated geographic entity. The Tosa population in 1600 was about 200,000, although it grew to be almost double that by late Tokugawa times. In officially rated *koku* productivity the domain was nineteenth in Japan. It possessed great natural wealth in its splendid forests and forest products like paper, and its warm bay made fishing for bonito, a major ingredient of the diet, and whaling profitable.

Tosa had developed as a domain under a Sengoku daimyo named Chōsokabe. In the 1580s the family head led local warriors to unite the realm. For a brief moment he seemed likely to incorporate all of Shikoku under his rule, but Hideyoshi thwarted those plans by defeating him in 1585. Thereafter the Chōsokabe daimyo fought Hideyoshi's battles in Kyushu and Korea, and joined the western host at Sekigahara. That ended his rule in Tosa. Before then a cadastral survey that was inherited by his successor laid the basis for Tokugawa-era rule in Kochi. Codes of administrative procedure and law brought the island into broad conformity with developments elsewhere in Japan.[17]

After his victory at Sekigahara, Tokugawa Ieyasu granted the domain to Yamauchi Kazutoyo. It was a striking reward for a non-Tokugawa retainer who had played a useful, but last-minute and minor role at Sekigahara. Gratitude for this kindness affected Yamauchi politics into the closing days of the bakufu. Yamauchi was the younger brother of a local grandee in Owari, where one of the three Tokugawa cadet houses was established after Sekigahara. The Tosa squirarchy of Chōsokabe retainers, however, was mutinous at having to acknowledge the new daimyo, and farmers also feared increased exploitation under the new lord; they withheld their cooperation, and many fled across the border to the neighboring domain.

The new daimyo came in with only 158 mounted men, and he found it wise to petition for help in claiming his prize. Suppression of dissent by ruse and by violence soon put him in control. Two boatloads containing 273 heads were sent to Tokugawa headquarters to demonstrate Yamauchi efficiency, and another 73 dissidents were crucified on the beach.

The Yamauchi daimyo now concentrated his efforts on the exploitation of his realm. Major vassals were established as landed rulers, while the Yamauchi house retained for itself lands producing double those that had been Chōsokabe granary land. Similarly, Ieyasu had retained more for himself than Hideyoshi had. A fine new castle was built at Kōchi on the bay. Before long incentives for cooperation were designed to win the cooperation of local leaders, many of whom were former Chōsokabe adherents, by naming some 900 of them as "country samurai" (gōshi) in return for their work in agricultural reclamation. A large-scale riparian work project to increase productivity was undertaken by a domain official named Nonaka Kenzan. An intensive search for revenue was necessary because of the heavy financial obligations placed on the domain by Tokugawa building projects. With peace and no further need for service in war, daimyo obligations could be set and measured in large contributions for bakufu projects. New castles for the shoguns, temple restoration, and public works of all sorts required the delivery of massive amounts of lumber from Tosa. So heavy were those burdens that most of the Tosa foot soldiers (ashigaru) found themselves transformed into a labor corps, cutting and dragging giant timbers from the mountainous forests to rivers from which they could be floated to coastal points for shipment to Osaka and Edo.[18]

The polity of major daimyo domains like Tosa was that of the Edo bakufu writ small. Principal vassals were enfeoffed, their ranks infiltrated with adoptive sons from the main house, and set up as cadet houses. Kōchi had eleven "elders," *rōjū*, who rated between 1,500 and 10,000 *koku* in land assignments. Another eleven *chūrō*, "middle-rank elders," rated between 450 and 1,500 *koku*. The "mounted guard" of regular samurai *(umamawari)*, eight hundred strong, were assigned lands between 100 and 700 *koku* and furnished the bulk of officials for controlling and taxing the villages whose produce made this all possible. The *umamawari* were, in other words, like the Tokugawa bannermen. Upper samurai maintained residences in the castle town of Kōchi as well as on their lands, and in town their residences were neatly arranged in order of power and income.

Before long a complex administrative structure resembling that of the bakufu developed. The chief administrators were charged with relations with the bakufu and the supervision of magistrates who dealt with county governance, fishing villages, taxes, and temples and shrines. Inspectors toured the realm. Separate divisions of samurai administrators were charged with governing the domain, managing the affairs of the daimyo household and its granary land, and maintaining and supporting the residences in Edo. As with the bakufu *fudai*, leading families predominated in important posts. In the countryside, long-standing memory and preference for the pre-Yamauchi rule kept the Chōsokabe tradition alive; it would be fanned to life by the nineteenth-century crises in the form of antagonisms between castle-town samurai, the "insiders," and the country samurai *(gōshi)* and village headmen.

Domains were called upon for cooperation in connection with building projects, but they were not directly taxed by the bakufu. A domain lived on the income derived from its own lands. The bakufu set guidelines for military forces, but it had no control over domain armed forces. The bakufu could issue instructions about permissible currency within its borders, but the daimyo, although he was supposed to get bakufu approval, could issue paper money for use within his territories and could even mint copper cash. At the end of the Tokugawa period there were hundreds of forms of exchange in circulation, most of them limited to use within domain borders. In sum, several dozen of the domains were very nearly independent states, with their own armies, administrative and law codes, tax systems, and tax codes. Small wonder that residents of a large domain like Tosa or Satsuma thought of it as a country and could not conceive of a hierarchy of authority that extended beyond their lord. The "han" part of the "bakuhan state" thus represented a significant limitation on centralization and Japan's development as a nation state.

5. Center and Periphery: Bakufu-Han Relations

The real test of statehood for early modern Japan thus lay in the relations between the bakufu and the daimyo domains. Among the greatest of the latter were houses whose history of rule was much longer than that of the Tokugawa, and it is no accident that the nineteenth-century movement for imperial restoration found its leadership among such domains.

The early shoguns won their hegemony by victory in battle, and consequently they were able to confiscate and redistribute daimyo lands with relative ease. In the seventeenth century, land assessed at thirteen million *koku*—more than one-third of the country—was reassigned. *Tozama* daimyo decreased in number and new *fudai* daimyo were created. The accompanying chart indicates the scale of these changes. It thus becomes evident that daimyo held their domains in trust and not as private possessions. The shogun invested each daimyo at the time of his majority, and on the accession of each new shogun all the daimyo swore private oaths of obedience and service.

As the Edo period went on and reassignments and confiscations diminished, however, tenure became more secure. It is customary to focus on the fact that hundreds of daimyo were moved in the first century and a half, but closer examination shows that with the exception of postwar settlements approximately half of those moved received domains larger than those they lost, that almost half experienced no change in assessed productivity, and that in many cases of confiscation or attainder the action was taken because of issues of succession (failure to produce a male heir—something that became

Confiscations and Changes in Daimyo Holdings, 1601–1705

Shogun	No. of daimyo	*Tozama/fudai*	Confiscated land
Ieyasu	41	28/13	3,594,640 *koku*
Hidetada	38	23/15	3,605,420
Iemitsu	46	28/18	3,580,100
Ietsuna	28	16/12	728,000
Tsunayoshi	45	17/28	1,702,982
Total	198	112/86	13,211,142

Source: John Whitney Hall, "The *bakuhan* System," in *Cambridge History of Japan*, vol. 4: *Early Modern Japan*, ed. Hall (Cambridge: Cambridge University Press, 1991), p. 152.

rare after permission for deathbed adoptions was granted) or personal misconduct and unconscionable behavior, often listed as "madness." In such
cases, the bakufu was clearly concerned with the maintenance and appearance
of public order.[19]

The Tokugawa collateral house of Matsudaira in Echizen (modern Fukui)
provides an example. In view of its strategic location as a possible avenue for
invasion of the Edo plain from the northwest, Ieyasu installed there a son,
Hideyasu, had him take the older family name of Matsudaira, and consolidated nearby domains into a formidable integrated realm rated at 680,000
koku. Hideyasu's son performed valiantly, though impetuously, in the siege
of Osaka, but soon thereafter began to behave erratically. Tales of his dissipation and wanton cruelty filtered into Edo. Worse, from the shogunal point
of view, was his display of a cavalier attitude toward his obligations in attendance at Edo. Edo representatives were sent to Echizen, and the young daimyo's principal vassals were warned of the possible effects of his behavior,
but to no avail. The daimyo next became infatuated with the beautiful wife
of one of his principal vassals. When she sought to evade his attentions by
taking refuge in a Buddhist convent, the daimyo ordered her son and heir to
commit suicide and confiscated the land (15,350 *koku*) the family had been
assigned. The rest of the family responded by joint suicide in the flames of
their residence. Hidetada, the shogun, now banished the daimyo to Kyushu,
appointed the son as successor, and reduced the domain by 130,000 *koku*.
Derangement continued to plague the ruling house, until Tsunayoshi, the fifth
shogun, reduced the domain again to 225,000 *koku*. This time a bakufu elder
was attached to the house to suspend it; ceremonial privileges—the use of
the Matsudaira name, the Tokugawa crest, the use of gilt as decoration of
saddle trappings, and use of the term "lord" *(tono)*—were withdrawn, and
the daimyo was excluded from attendance at the New Year's Day ceremonies
in Edo. At the daimyo's mansion in Edo the main gate was ordered closed
and sealed, and access was limited to the side gates. Moreover, the land that
remained to the house was now highly fragmented, much of it taken from
other daimyo. Thus public humiliation was combined with drastic diminution
of geopolitical power.[20] It was generations before the house was restored to
bakufu favor. By late Tokugawa wiser leadership had restored the Matsudaira
house honor, with the result that its daimyo was able to play an important
role in the politics of late Tokugawa bakufu reform.

The early shoguns also saw to it that daimyo military prowess was kept
under control. In 1615 the bakufu decreed that there should be only one castle
in each domain. At the same time it did not want military skills to diminish,
and standards of preparedness were issued for all domains. In 1649 regulations

tried to spell this out. A domain of 100,000 *koku,* for instance, was to have 2,155 men under arms; of these 170 were to be mounted, 350 armed with guns, 30 with bows, and 150 with spears, while 20 were to be trained in signal flags. Farther down the scale, a samurai with the rating of 200 *koku* was supposed to maintain 5 men: himself with his horse, a horse leader, spear bearer, armor bearer, and a porter.[21] As the system of alternate attendance at Edo became structured, standards were also set for the size of the military entourage that daimyo could bring with them; once again the criteria were set by the *koku* productivity of the domain, but this time the purpose was to lessen competitive display and extravagance.

The centerpiece of bakufu control over daimyo was its codification of rules for deportment. In 1615, shortly after the fall of Osaka, the daimyo were summoned to receive the Code for the Military Houses *(Buke shohatto).* Revised and augmented over time, these injunctions became the center of bakufu-daimyo relations. As Harold Bolitho has put it, these laws "served notice to all *han* that they were to surrender their independence in certain vital areas."[22]

Daimyo were not to admit "criminals" or "traitors" within their borders, they were prohibited from adding fortifications, or repairing old ones—"crenelated walls and deep moats are the causes of anarchy," one clause read— and they were to request official permission before arranging marriages for family members. Suspicious activities in a neighboring domain were to be reported without delay; but on the other hand, "since the customs of the various domains are all different," there should be no unnecessary contact between neighboring jurisdictions. In its concluding admonition, the bakufu ordered the daimyo to select men of ability for office. "If there are capable men in the administration the domain is sure to flourish; if there are not it will surely go to ruin." Thus the bakufu was claiming for itself the right to define and enforce standards of proper rule by which its vassal daimyo could be judged.

The second version of these laws, issued by Iemitsu in 1635, strengthened and extended these controls. In 1622 daimyo had been ordered to leave family members as hostages with the bakufu (it will be remembered that Ieyasu had spent his youth as a hostage). Many daimyo had been wise enough to send hostages or come personally to Edo to pay their respects before this; Maeda of Kanazawa, for instance, brought his mother shortly after Sekigahara. Hidetada formalized this as an obligation for *fudai* daimyo in 1622, but in the 1636 regulations of Iemitsu it became institutionalized and structured for all the daimyo as a form of military service. The *sankin-kōtai* "alternate attendance" system structured daimyo life. They were assigned plots of land in Edo appropriate to their status. Most maintained three spacious mansions there. They staffed them with service corps and samurai attendants, and maintained their personal family and their principal vassals' families at the shogunal capital. They themselves were to come in alternate years—or, for some, alternate half-years—to pay homage to the shogun. Begun as a system of hostages, the system became the basis of a rotating service life for the elite. By its workings future daimyo were born and raised at the metropolitan center and never visited their domain until they were invested as daimyo, after which they rotated between Edo and their fief. Within a generation or two the system had transformed the military leaders of Sengoku times into cultured urban aristocrats trained to appreciate the finer points of the tea ceremony, cuisine, culture, and costume.

Next came requirements for the registration of commoners. The bakufu and individual domains conducted registers of population and livestock from an early date, but methods for combining this with guarantees against religious—Christian—subversion were worked out as the drive against Christianity intensified. The bakufu instituted registration of all residents of its own domains at Buddhist temples beginning in 1614. As the persecution of Christians increased in Iemitsu's years the bakufu tightened requirements in its own territories, and a few decades later, in 1665, domains were ordered to carry them out as well. The following year this was strengthened to require that registrations be carried out annually. The implementing agency was the Buddhist temple, which was co-opted in the service of state security. Henceforth temple registers were submitted by village headmen and city elders to certify there were no Christians among their numbers. The *shūmon aratame-chō*, "sect investigation registers," served as powerful measures of central government intervention in private life throughout Japan. The *Buke shohatto* also specified that domain laws should follow those of the bakufu in broad outline. The twenty-first regulation in the 1635 code stipulated that "in all matters the example set by the laws of Edo is to be followed in all provinces and places." As this took effect there was a further resonance between the content of major bakufu codes and those of major domains.

The bakufu thus took it upon itself to issue orders for the whole country, as with the proscription of Christianity. Its claim to represent *kōgi*, the public interest, gave it the right to oversee and interfere. It issued and mounted sign-boards, *kōsatsu*, which appeared at conspicuous locations—intersections and bridges—throughout the country, in daimyo as well as bakufu lands. Originally renewed when era names changed and at the accession of a new shogun, these remained constant from the eighteenth century on. It is significant that the issuing authority declined in rank. They were originally issued over the name of the bakufu *rōjū*, but later over the name of the bakufu *bugyō*. The signboards were written in simple language for the commoners, and constituted the commoner equivalent of the rules for the military houses. Some enjoined readers to observe the civic virtues of filiality, respect, and compassion; others warned against the false teaching of Christianity and the dangers of arson and included promises of reward for information against any who violated such prohibitions. The *kōsatsu* came to be used as basic texts in parish schools (the *terakoya*), and they acquainted commoners everywhere with the existence and will of the bakufu.

In 1633 the bakufu showed its power again by appointing a corps of some thirty inspectors who were to monitor developments in han that seemed to merit observation. To help them in their work the han were ordered in 1644 to submit detailed maps to the bakufu.

Sometimes these inspections could be formidable affairs. When bakufu inspectors visited Okayama in 1764 prior to approving the succession of a new daimyo, they ordered the domain administrators to provide them with detailed accounts of the laws, administration, and economic conditions of Okayama. The domain elders submitted a report whose headings, greatly condensed, fill four pages of a modern study. In submitting it they assured the bakufu inspectors that their daimyo ordered them to obey the shogunate's laws; he maintained high standards of frugality, and he was tireless in the investigation of possible Christian subversion.[23] So too with transfers and moves of daimyo; they were expected to report in full their holdings and equipment, rather like servicemen being transferred from one unit to another.

As time passed, however, many of these requirements became more formal than real. Mention has already been made of the charade the domain of Satsuma prepared to prevent the inspectors to that distant area from learning much about that realm. In 1651 the bakufu permitted deathbed adoptions, thereby removing what had been the most frequently cited reason for confiscation: failure of the daimyo to provide a male heir. The hostage system at Edo was given up in 1665 to commemorate the fiftieth anniversary of Ieyasu's death, though by then the attractions of life at Edo had so far outweighed the torpor of life in most castle towns that "voluntary" hostages were probably almost as numerous as those that were there earlier under duress. Demands for labor and materials for massive construction projects diminished. The call to the daimyo for the provincial maps that had been made in 1644 was repeated only once again, in 1697.

Although some small domains changed hands frequently, transfers of major domains became less frequent. By the nineteenth century a good many daimyo seem to have regarded the shogunate as not so much the instrument of a powerful hegemon as a bureaucratic council of their peers. In 1840 a shogunal effort to force a single *fudai* daimyo, the lord of Shōnai, to exchange his seat for another half its size in order to benefit the son of one of Ienari's consorts proved unenforceable. As will be discussed below, protests against the transfer ensued from leading commoners, local merchants, daimyo retainers, and even twenty-seven *tozama* lords. Ultimately the order was canceled.[24] Seventeenth-century daimyo and others beneath them would have known better than to take up such concerns with the bakufu.

The pages above have concentrated on ways in which the bakufu inhibited the freedom and performance of the domains, but it must be remembered that the bakufu-han relationship was a two-way street and not a zero-sum game. The two needed each other, and the relationship was more symbiotic than antagonistic.

The bakufu *kōgi* provided a context of stability for the han. They no longer had to fear one another, for the bakufu set the rules of interaction and provided the court of appeal in the Hyōjōsho when that judicial body was established in 1635. The Tokugawa overlordship also provided guarantees against disruption from below by peasant rebellions and sectarians. As these grew in scope in the eighteenth century the bakufu frequently authorized, and often ordered, neighboring domains to help suppress the insurrections. All feudal authorities shared an interest in keeping the countryside under control.

The bakufu and the han needed each other. Shogunal lands were scattered throughout the length and breadth of the country, and the bakufu frequently farmed out administration and taxation rights to han whose location made it easy for them to play a supervisory role. In turn bakufu exactions on han for assistance in building projects gradually came to be replaced by bakufu assistance to han in meeting emergency food shortages that resulted from failed crops. Loans were extended by the eighth shogun, Yoshimune, in the early eighteenth century, in a pattern that continued thereafter. The bakufu was supposed to claim all mines producing precious metal for itself, but these too were frequently best left to domains to run. The northern domain of Akita provides a startling case in point. Its mines were the source of copper ore that was smelted in Osaka refineries and shipped to Nagasaki for foreign trade payments to Dutch and Chinese merchants. The bakufu set stiff quotas for production in Akita, but when the han pleaded inability to meet its obligations the bakufu relented with loans to help the domain manage the mines and meet its quotas.[25]

6. The Tokugawa "State"

For all its imposing presence, however, the Tokugawa state was far from all-powerful. It controlled foreign affairs and foreign trade and legislated against foreign subversion like Catholic Christianity, but it had no central national treasury or tax codes. Its Hyōjōsho functioned to some extent as a court of final appeal in disputes between rival domains, but the institution was only one of the many duties of the *rōjū* and there was no national judiciary. Public justice was imperfectly administered, particularly among the samurai class, who were responsible to their domain authorities. Private justice was permissible, indeed honorable, for those who applied through the proper channels. Blood feuds were permitted to settle outrages that crossed domain borders. One source lists 113 instances in which private vengeance was authorized, carried out, and properly reported; of these 30 were carried out by nonsamurai, 4 of whom were merchants.[26] The bakufu established five major national highways over which it asserted authority and laid down rules for support from villages along those routes, without regard to daimyo authority, but it had no national communications system and no national constabulary.[27] Even the bakufu army was only one, admittedly large, force among others, and bakufu efforts to coerce depended upon the cooperation of its vassals' armies. When that cooperation was withheld in the 1860s the bakufu gradually declined to the status of a regional power. Economic change and internal commerce led to a great increase in the integration of the economy, particularly in central Japan, but no political advances accompanied this. The great lords, *tozama* and cadet houses alike, were systematically excluded from participation in national affairs. Trade between major domains was discouraged by the bakufu and by domains that strove for mercantilist self-sufficiency.

As a result it is not surprising that attempts to classify the Tokugawa state by historians continue to differ. One student of early Tokugawa, focusing on the first half century with its strong shoguns, argues that even then, although power was concentrated, it was in the collective body of daimyo and not at the center. "The Tokugawa shogunate was not conspicuous in public life," she argues; there was no police force, no general levy for war, no organized concern with social welfare, nor for schooling or health. There was no central code of law. The bakufu created no judiciary, assembled no bureaucracy, and opened no public treasury. It capitalized on medieval forms of personal political attachment, utilized marriage and adoption as instruments of alliance, and continued the familial pattern of a prebureaucratic order. Gift giving, more than law giving, characterized interpersonal relations at the level of the elite.[28]

Others differ. Basing himself on the longer perspective of the entire Edo period, James White reminds readers that the "absolute" states of early modern Europe were themselves only relatively so. What was unique about Japan was the lack of imperatives for strengthening central power beyond what had been necessary to achieve the goals of the seventeenth century. Japan was not part of a competitive state system and not subject to military threat. It faced no requirements of increasing its central power beyond the modest incentives of preventing insurrection by unarmed peasants. Consequently its central power waned in centuries of peace despite the growing centralization of the larger political economy.[29]

With time, however, the peasantry became more of a threat than it had been in the seventeenth century. By the middle of the eighteenth century the bakufu became increasingly concerned with popular protest and ordered neighboring domains to cooperate in suppressing it. In the middle decades it issued a series of regulations for handling and reporting incidents along with new bans on unauthorized gatherings. With this came a greater interest in law and a new structuring of procedures for housing and representing litigants at the Edo courts. These matters will be taken up after further discussion of social and economic change, but can be mentioned here as evidence that the bakufu became more conspicuous than it had been.

The two positions that have been sketched here, the one doubting and the other affirming the validity of addressing the Tokugawa structure as a "state," say something important about the problem of perspective or point of reference. For a historian judging the Tokugawa period from the perspective of its antecedents and its establishment, the crisp and confident categories of power in which it can be described at the time of its fall will seem anachronistic and misleading. The late Tokugawa state was significantly different from that political order at its birth: things looked different, they were spoken of in a different way, and they were in fact different. Something very important had taken place in the eighteenth century.

It has already been noted that the term *han* is one of late Tokugawa use and that it did not become standard until the late Tokugawa days. But recent studies by Japanese historians extend this caution to the other terms that have been used here: *bakufu* was seldom used before the Tokugawa state began to near its end; "court" *(chōtei)* was not restricted to Kyoto but used of Edo also; and "emperor" *(tennō)*, which had fallen out of use in the thirteenth century, made its reappearance in the early nineteenth century.[30]

Most Tokugawa period writers spoke of authority as *kōgi* (imperfectly rendered here as "public matters"), and that centered in Edo so clearly that it was frequently used almost interchangeably with the *chōtei* later reserved for "imperial court." That entity itself, without a political role and as much place as person, was a mysterious and forbidden entity referred to as *kinchū* or *kinri*.

These studies make it clear that terms like bakufu, court, and emperor convey a clear definition of subordination that was the creation of late Tokugawa Confucian scholarship associated with Mito ideologues, of whom more will be said later. Their scholarship laid the theoretical basis for the "imperial" ideology with which the modern state was launched. Uncritical use of these terms to describe Japan before the nineteenth century, it is argued, risks distortion by making clear what were in fact quite indistinct outlines of power and prestige. Worse, they risk perpetuating the emperor-centered, praise-and-blame history that dominated the textbooks of prewar Japan. In terms of the discussion at hand, these points, by reminding us that Edo period contemporaries thought of the shogun's system as authority and were less conscious of the court-bakufu dualism than later historians, would strengthen judgments about a Tokugawa state.

The historian, however, needs terms to serve as pointers for the journey through Japan's early modern period. What is needed is the realization that the landscape of that passage is in the process of gradual but steady change. The thrust of terms will change with time, and they must be made to serve analysis but kept from distorting it.

Whatever the changes in terms we use to describe power relationships within Japan, there can be no question that Japan's protected position on the fringe of the East Asian world had profound consequences for the development of its political order. It is now necessary to turn to the international dimension of the Tokugawa system.

3

A Tokugawa period wood-block map of Nagasaki, printed for popular sale, shows one of the world's most beautiful harbors (see illustration 4). The city itself is shielded from ocean storms by low mountains that enclose the bay to the north and west. The map's legend indicates distances to other centers: Kyoto, 120 *ri* (*ri* = 2.44 miles) by land and 248 by sea; Edo, 332 by land and 470-plus by sea; Kumamoto, 35 by land, 46 by sea. The mapmakers add ships in the harbor to make things more attractive: one Dutch ship is at anchor, another, towed by a line of small Japanese ships, fires its guns in salute; one Chinese junk is identified as "Nanking," another as "Fukien." There are also guard ships, identified as part of the fleet of the lord of Hizen, who was charged (in alternation with the lord of Fukuoka) with the security of the port; many smaller scows are for freight. At the center right of the map, and quite out of proportion, is a curious, fan-shaped island connected to the mainland by a curved bridge. This is the artificial island of Deshima (see also illustration 5), prepared for the Portuguese and inherited by the Dutch in 1641. It is the center of Nagasaki lore, and the mapmaker/artist has expanded its dimensions out of deference to its importance. To the south is a second artificial fill that served as loading area, also connected to the mainland by a stone bridge that leads to a walled and moated area designated as *tōjin yashiki,* or the Chinese quarter.

These two foreign enclaves, the center of Tokugawa foreign trade, were what made Nagasaki unique in Japan. As the early-eighteenth-century Confucian scholar Ogyū Sorai wrote, "Nagasaki is a place where eastern barbarians [Japanese] and Chinese associate, where ocean-sailing ships come to port; it is the port of a myriad goods and strange objects, where people from the five directions gather, abandoning their homes and coveting profit; it is the first place of our land."[1] Ogyū, Confucianist that he was, thought poorly of those who worked for money and profit, but he was in the minority in that respect. Ihara Saikaku, whose prose writings were the rage among townsmen at the turn of the century, thought better of financial drive. He rhapsodized about the overseas ventures possible in the early Tokugawa years and argued that "to turn from Japan to risky speculations in the China trade, sending one's money clean out of sight, needs boldness and imagination. But at least a Chinese merchant is an honest man, and keeps squarely to his promise: the insides of his rolls of silk are the same as the outsides, his medical herbs are not weighted with worthless ballast, his wood is wood, his silver is silver, and none of it changes as the years go by. For sheer duplicity one need go no farther than Japan."[2] Nagasaki was where it all took place, and the exotic center to which one could come to see foreigners, Dutch and Chinese, albeit at a distance.

The system within which the Tokugawa bakufu kept out most foreigners has highlighted most accounts of the period. Many writers have described Tokugawa Japan as a country hermetically sealed off from the rest of the world, and in consequence exaggerate the importance and achievement of the nineteenth-century "opening." Textbook titles like *Japan before Perry* and *Japan since Perry* contribute to this misconception. One would think there were no foreigners and no foreign policy in Tokugawa Japan.

In fact there was a foreign policy, and it is because it was concerned more with Asia than with the West that Western writers have used terms like "seclusion" and "isolation." It was also a policy in constant change. Throughout the period, although limitations on foreign trade became more exacting, policymakers focused their fears more on the West than on Japan's Asian neighbors. It can be argued that the famous decrees that closed the country were more of a bamboo blind than they were a Berlin wall.

1. The Setting

The Tokugawa rise found Japan vitally affected by the process of empire and nation building of the maritime states of western Europe, by the Reformation and counter-Reformation in Europe, and by the tides of dynastic change in Asia.

It began with the maritime explorations sponsored by Henry the Navigator of Portugal. His ships rounded the coast of Africa to find the sources for the riches of the spice islands of the East that had previously been brought by Arab ships to Venice for transshipment to the West. In the mid-sixteenth century the Portuguese established themselves at Malacca and then at Macao;

Magellan's Spanish fleet entered Philippine waters shortly afterward. The wealth in bullion the conquistadors seized from the mines of Central and South America justified ever wider probes.

The Chinese economy was as eager for silver as was that of the Iberian peninsula, for China was in the process of shifting to a tax system based on silver. Trade was stimulated by the exchange of textiles. Ships from England and the Low Countries sought markets for their woolens and returned with spices and silks; the fine silk thread that came from China was keenly sought by the tailors who prepared the gorgeous costumes of the wealthy who stare at us from Renaissance paintings. Together Iberian and northern European ships broke the monopoly of Arab traders who had supplied the merchants of Venice with these goods. European guns that bested Arab navies, as the Portuguese did at Diu in 1509, were soon turned against one another as well. Freebooters from northern Europe like Francis Drake seized what they could not purchase. The revolt of the Protestant Netherlands against Catholic Spain brought with it Spanish efforts to subdue all of Protestant Europe and added ideological and religious sanction for violence and greed. During the English war against Spain more than one hundred privateers plied the oceans in search of prey.

This maritime competition soon extended to the seas of Southeast Asia. There a trading network had been developed by Chinese junks. After the Ming dynasty lifted its ban on travel overseas in the 1560s, close to a hundred large vessels, containing some 20,000 tons of cargo space, sailed to Southeast Asia every year. In the words of one authority, "they brought thousands of pieces of silver back from Manila as well as tropical products. At Jakarta (which the Dutch renamed Batavia) the Chinese fleet in the early seventeenth century had a total tonnage as large or larger than that of the whole return fleet of the Dutch East India Company."[3] With the goods came Chinese immigrants, and as the colonies grew a network developed into which Japanese traders, and after them the Europeans, could fit. The Chinese chain of trading posts throughout Southeast Asia thus served as the basis for Portuguese, Japanese, and Dutch trading activities in the area. Much of the activity that took place can be understood as the securing and maintaining of access routes for the transport of Japanese and New World silver to China and Chinese silks to Japan: more and finer silks for Japanese merchant princes, who supplied the warlord armies of Japan; more richly embroidered garments with family crests for the affluent warriors, and the glories of Momoyama design for the ladies at the daimyo courts. European ships competed with these junks. They frequently assaulted them and stole their cargoes, but they also utilized the network of bases and shipping lanes that had grown in response to the needs of the Chinese traders.

In the sixteenth century the Protestant Reformation shook the Christian order in Europe and combined with the personal and political goals of monarchs to shatter what had once been Christian unity. Catholic Counter-Reformation monarchs struggled to regain and enlarge the ground that had been lost, and after mid-century they made spectacular gains in Asia. In 1540 Loyola's Society of Jesus, manned by committed and able priests who were frequently drawn from restless and adventurous members of the minor nobility, began an advance that led it to the portals of India, China, and Japan. The knowledge and technology of early modern Europe contributed to this growth. Portuguese ships brought with them new instruments of navigation and of warfare as well as agents of the Counter-Reformation. Missionaries, trade, and war led to bases on the edge of the great states of Asia—Goa, in India, Malacca, in Malaya, and Macao, in China—from which probes could be launched to test the classic centers of Asian civilization.

Enthusiasm for conversion intersected with political change in Europe. Marriage politics joined the Portuguese and Spanish thrones in 1580. Soon succession to the Holy Roman Empire combined Iberian with Habsburg expectations. All of this found echo in East Asia. Spanish Franciscans and Dominicans contested the Portuguese Jesuit monopoly, and Anglo-Dutch Protestants stood prepared to profit from Japanese rulers' fears of becoming a base for struggles not their own. A glance at the chart of principal dates and events will show how direct an impact world politics had on Japan.

In the sixteenth century commercial and political ferment also brought a renewed rise of trade and piracy in Japan. Fleets of buccaneers based on islands off the coast of Kyushu ravaged the coasts of China and Korea. Private shipping ventures sponsored by Japanese feudal lords and wealthy temples began to participate in the trading network established by Chinese ships in Southeast Asia. After the middle of the century the guns the Portuguese had brought helped to speed the process of unification in Japan. More powerful central governments were gradually able to put an end to the freebooting of neighboring coasts. Then, at the century's end, the conqueror Hideyoshi added a new dimension to the violence as his armies ravaged Korea in their failed effort to invade China. At the same time Hideyoshi did his best to encourage foreign trade by granting permits to merchants for overseas voyages. The first of these authorizations, the *shuinjō*, were issued in 1592, the year his armies attacked Korea; they authorized voyages that ranged from Taiwan to Thailand and Macao to Manila. Hideyoshi thus replaced unorganized piracy with organized warfare, and piecemeal trading by ships bearing the unifier's vermilion seal *(shuin)*.

Hideyoshi also turned against the missionaries, and ordered them out of Japan after he conquered Kyushu in 1587. His edict announced that Japan was the "land of the gods," and that the diffusion from a *kirishitan* country of a "pernicious doctrine was most undesirable." The fathers (*bateren,* padres) were to leave within twenty days. But trade, he made clear, was a different matter. "As years and months pass, trade may be carried on in all sorts of articles." As before, all "who do not disturb Buddhism" could continue to travel freely.[4] Some of the missionaries left; but most did not. At Nagasaki some Jesuits considered organizing daimyo followers for an uprising, but it fortunately never came to light. By 1597, however, an increasingly exasperated and unpredictable Hideyoshi had become obsessed with fears of political difficulties arising from Christianity; converts, who included several prominent daimyo, might prove responsive to claims other than his, and Franciscans,

	Principal Dates in Foreign Relations, 1497–1648
1497	Vasco da Gama rounds Cape of Good Hope
1509	Portuguese victory over Arab fleet at Diu
1540	Society of Jesus founded
1542–1643	Portuguese land at Tanegashima south of Kyushu
1557	Portuguese established at Macao
1567–1648	Revolt of the Netherlands
1580	Union of Portuguese and Spanish thrones under Philip II
1588	Defeat of Great Armada
1600	Arrival of *Liefde* (Will Adams, pilot) in Japan; English East India Co. (EIC) founded
1602	United Dutch East India Co. (VOC) founded
1609	Dutch factory established at Hirado; Ieyasu grants trading rights
1609	Japanese-Korean treaty reestablishes trade
1613	EIC establishes factory, also at Hirado
1620	Date (Hasekura) mission returns from Europe
1623	EIC abandons Hirado factory
1623	Portuguese limited in residence
1634, 1635, 1636	First three seclusion decrees; Deshima prepared for Portuguese
1635	Chinese restricted to Nagasaki
1637	Shimabara rebellion
1640	61 Portuguese put to death
1641	Dutch ordered to Deshima
1648	Treaty of Westphalia ends European war

Dominicans, and Augustinians, who preached to ordinary Japanese instead of associating with the military elite, were finding a good response to their teachings. That year twenty-six Franciscan missionaries were executed at Nagasaki, their bodies left to rot on their crosses. After Hideyoshi's death a year later, however, all major daimyo were preoccupied with the problem of succession. For a time Christians enjoyed a respite and their numbers even seemed to grow, but the grounds for political and ideological assault against the imported faith were being laid.

Hideyoshi's invasions of Korea also speeded the political and military disintegration of Ming China, which was soon to be tested by new invasions from the north. Manchu armies began to threaten first Korea, and then China itself. As Manchu armies subdued the heartland of Ming dynasty China, holdout forces on Taiwan and the southern coast sought help from Japan. The years in which Tokugawa rule developed thus saw enormous changes in world affairs. Communications were slow, of course, and no country was fully informed about events far beyond its borders. Nevertheless the new technology and navigation brought an end to the isolation that had prevailed. Europeans knew of warlord politics in Japan, church leaders followed the progress of Christian emissaries in Asia, and the Tokugawa founder Ieyasu struggled to secure the benefits of foreign trade without letting it enrich his rivals or undermine his own security. Western and Chinese traders were in Japan, Japanese trading ships were in Southeast Asia, and groups of Japanese settlers and adventurers could be found as far away as the Thai capital of Ayuthia. "Chinatowns" appeared along Japan's coasts. Japan's new rulers had need of a foreign policy.

2. Relations with Korea

In late Tokugawa times shogunal officials spoke as though it had from the outset been a cardinal point of shogunal policy to repulse Western overtures for trade and professed their inability to change it out of respect to the sainted founder who had established the great Tokugawa peace. In fact nothing could be further from the truth. The Tokugawa years began with energetic efforts to encourage trade and international relations. It was only after Ieyasu's death in 1616 that things began to tighten up.

Ieyasu's first problem was to undo the results of Hideyoshi's disastrous adventure in Korea. As the leading daimyo in Japan, second only to Hideyoshi, he had to be aware of the ghastly toll in men and treasure the Korean invasions had taken. Of the approximately 158,000 men who crossed over to the peninsula, probably one-third failed to return. For the Korean side, of course, the cost was higher still due to the ferocity of Hideyoshi's orders for vengeance after he was undeceived about the peace negotiations with China.

After his victory at Sekigahara Ieyasu thus indicated a wish to negotiate. Peace was declared in 1605. Two years later a Korean mission of 504 men came to honor the accession of Hidetada as second shogun, and then went on to Sunpu to visit Ieyasu. Now came talks that resulted in the Treaty of Kiyu in 1609. By its terms Japan was permitted to resume trade with Korea, but while trade had previously been permitted at three ports it was now restricted to Pusan. There the Japanese were kept in a special quarter, the *wakan*, living under conditions somewhat comparable to those that were to be experienced by the Dutch and Chinese at Nagasaki later in the century. Japanese were closely monitored and denied permission to leave the quarter, and they could never venture closer to Seoul.

The bakufu delegated the management of these relations to its vassal Sō, the daimyo of Tsushima. For Tsushima, Korea was the foundation of its wealth and importance. The domain was rated at only 5,000 *koku*, and the greater part of that income derived from its monopoly of trade with Korea. Studies of that trade by Tashiro Kazui make clear that the trade was lucrative for Tsushima and important to the bakufu.[5] Initially the Japanese traded silver bullion for Korean shipments of white Chinese silk thread. Even after the export of bullion from Nagasaki was prohibited, an exception was made for the Tsushima-Korea exchange. Naturally the trade was vital for Tsushima. The daimyo's vassals derived their chief income from the trade, and one even forged a bakufu letter to Korea to help it along. Tsushima's sponsored merchants operated sales centers in Nagasaki, Kyoto, and Edo. As urban culture and wants developed in Japan, the import of ginseng, a medicinal root, played a large part in the shipments, and when the cultivation of ginseng developed in Japan in the latter part of the eighteenth century it had distressing effects on the Tsushima economy.

There were no formal Japanese missions to Korea, although Tsushima was ordered to send one in 1629, but twelve major Korean missions came to Japan during the Tokugawa years. Most of these, and all of those after 1655, came to mark the accession to rule of a new shogun. The bakufu made much of these visitors, parading them the length of the land to Edo and often on to the shogunal tombs at Nikko. By this means it showed daimyo and commoners alike that it was an important regional power with its own distinctive world order, and not a satellite orbiting within the Chinese world.[6]

Major Korean embassies, the *tsūshinshi*, were imposing events involving three hundred to five hundred people. The Koreans took these very seriously, for they were cultural as well as diplomatic in purpose. There are thirty-four

travel diaries written by Korean members of these missions. Cultural credentials were as important as diplomatic formalities. A diary written by a member
of the mission in 1764 describes his audience with the Korean king, who interviewed candidates and had them compose lines of Chinese poetry within a
fixed time limit to make sure that they would be able to hold their own when
exchanging, and competing, with their Japanese hosts.

In fact they more than held their own, for the Koreans were closer to the
Chinese cultural tradition than the Japanese. The Koreans tended to disdain
their vernacular *hangul* writing system in favor of classical Chinese, while for
their Japanese hosts Chinese was an acquired literary language that supplemented writing in Japanese *kana* syllabary. Consequently one finds even accomplished Tokugawa scholars like Arai Hakuseki (1657–1725) eager to have
the Koreans think well of his Chinese poems. When a Korean embassy visited
Japan in 1682, Arai wrote that he sent to ask the "three leaders of the embassy,
who were fine scholars, to write an appreciation of a collection of a hundred
verses of occasional poetry I had composed"; the Koreans courteously asked
to meet the poet, and the young Arai was gratified to have one of the visitors
send him a foreword he had written for the collection.[7] Some years later the
daimyo Maeda Tsunanori, a formidable scholar in his own right, noted that
after a study group working on Ming law got into trouble they found it necessary to consult Koreans; "no one," he wrote, "had any idea what it meant,
but the question was put to Koreans, among others, and at length some understanding was gained."[8]

Koreans also served as transmitters in Tokugawa studies of the neo-Confucian scholarship of China. The works of the Korean scholar Yi Hwang (1501–
1570), better known by his honorific Yi T'oegye, circulated widely among Japanese scholars and acquainted many with what was to become a principal
strand of Tokugawa thought. Korean medicine also attracted wide interest in
Japan. From the first it was usual to include doctors with each Korean mission,
and question-and-answer sessions with the physicians were held along the
routes of travel. Nor did it end there. As has been mentioned, many of the
daimyo who invaded Korea at Hideyoshi's orders brought back with them
groups of potters, a craft in which Koreans had excelled since medieval times.
In the domain of Saga, Korean potters brought knowledge of the clays and
glazes that made possible Japanese production of blue slipware porcelain that
rapidly became highly prized and widely used. The simple blue-and-white
designs called *karakusa,* "Chinese grass," were soon shipped to all corners
of Japan, and the secret of its production, rigidly guarded by the domain
government, became a significant share of the cash income of the domain.
Before long this ware made its way (via the port of Imari, for which it became

named) to Nagasaki, whence Dutch merchants brought it to Europe. By the eighteenth century Delft, Meissen, and Worcester kilns were offering European versions of its glazes and patterns. In Satsuma, too, a smaller group of Korean potters located at Naeshirogawa performed a similar function in the production of earthenware ceramics; as late as the 1860s a visiting samurai wrote of his surprise at finding a community of potters set off by language and costume from the villagers who lived around them.

Thus it is clear that relations with Korea remained an important thread throughout the Tokugawa period. The volume of the trade declined, to be sure, and as bakufu finances worsened the regime became less enthusiastic about hosting major embassies. The last embassy sent, in 1811, did not get beyond Tsushima. But that slowdown affected Tsushima finances more than it did the formal Korean-Japanese ties.

Over time the intense hostility and fear of the early years, when the *tsūshin-shi* were charged with making sure that Japan was not planning another invasion, gradually gave way to equanimity and moderate good feeling. Mention has been made of Arai Hakuseki. A contemporary of his was Amenomori Hōshū (1668–1755), who studied Korean in the Japanese community at Pusan and prepared a language textbook that was used into the nineteenth century. On the Korean side there was Sin Yu-han, who visited Japan in 1719 as part of the mission that was sent to congratulate the shogun Yoshimune on his accession to rule. He noted in his travel diary that "a rush of people wanted to have my poetry; they piled papers on my desk to ask me to write something, and although I wrote for everyone who asked the papers continued to pile up like firewood." Requests were particularly numerous in Osaka; "sometimes I could not sleep until dawn, or I was kept from eating, by these people. Japanese respect our writing as though we were gods, and keep them as treasure. Even a miserable palanquin bearer is happy to have a Chinese character written on a piece of paper by a Korean envoy." Sin was not, however, impressed by what he saw of Japanese classical scholarship, and he was disturbed by a lack of formal reverence for Confucius. He found no shrines for the worship of Confucius at schools, and he deplored the absence of formal funeral dress to observe the death of parents or of monarchs, noting sadly that "they are born with good natures, but they do not know the Way." On the other hand, he was overwhelmed by the evidence of urban prosperity he saw. In Osaka the road was "full of spectators. I am dizzy with its splendor, so dazzled that I cannot count the number of villages through which we have passed." In Kyoto he found the Tōji temple "decorated with gold and silver" and described his emotions on traversing "miles of streets with beautiful street lamps." He fancied himself "in a dream paradise." In Edo, where missions were paraded through the heart of the city, "long buildings along the road are shops of merchants. Spectators' clothes are so colorful that I think Edo is much more prosperous than Osaka and Kyoto." As a good Confucian Sin felt obliged to deplore this as materialistic, but as an observer he concluded that even Japanese villagers were rather well-off.[9]

It would be pleasant to conclude that old enmities and complexes had been put aside and that the two countries now saw each other as equals, but there are disquieting signs that suggest that old attitudes lived on. Sin Yu-han recorded a conversation with Amenomori Hōshū in which each complained about the other's view of his country. We have been friendly with Korea for some time, Amenomori said, but Korean books still refer to us as pirates; how can this be? Well, said Sin, those books were probably written after the Japanese invasion of Korea, so it's quite understandable. Still, how is it that Japanese refer to us as *Tōjin* (Chinaman)? Well, responded Amenomori, by law we are supposed to call you *Chōsenjin* (Koreans). But because of your similarity to Chinese, we usually call you Tōjin; this means that we respect your culture. Unfortunately, Amenomori was disingenuous, for Tōjin had become a generic term for foreigner, which ordinary Japanese applied even to Westerners. Worse still, only a few years before this the diary of the Dutch mission head in Nagasaki notes of a summer day that "this day commemorates their victory over the Koreans, whose country they turned into a tributary nation."[10] In other words, in Nagasaki the Japanese were explaining to the Dutch that they were celebrating Hideyoshi's "victory" over the Koreans and that Korean missions were those of a tributary state.

3. The Countries of the West

Ieyasu was no less eager to continue and expand trade with the West. His options had increased with the coming of the Dutch and English, who brought with them the rivalries and hatreds of seventeenth-century Europe. Will Adams, a Cornishman who arrived as pilot of the Dutch ship *Liefde* in 1600, remained in Japan until his death in 1620. He was the beneficiary of favorable treatment from Ieyasu and Hidetada, and enjoyed relatively high status: a small fief, a family, and the opportunity to profit from *shuinsen* (vermilion seal ship) voyages. Meanwhile he also supported his wife and family in England, and in his will divided his estate between the children of the two families. Ieyasu seems to have found him interesting and useful, for Adams broke the monopoly on news about the Western world previously enjoyed by Iberian missionaries and the interpreter Rodrigues.[11] The English East India Company (EIC) was formed that same year of 1600, and for a time Adams was in its employ as a consultant. The Dutch United East India Company (VOC) was chartered two years later through the union of a number of smaller trading companies.

The companies were virtually independent principalities. Their directors were empowered to wage defensive war, build forts, conclude treaties of peace and to enter into alliances, all in the interest of expanding their trade. In its early years the VOC became a particularly formidable power. By 1648, the year the war for independence against Spain ended, Holland was in fact the greatest trading country in the world, carrying three-quarters of the trade in Baltic grain, the same proportion of the trade in Scandinavian timber that made Dutch shipbuilding possible, and much of the trade in Swedish metals; then there was salt from France and Portugal that went to the Baltic, and cloth that was finished in Holland and sold throughout Europe. Soon the VOC became the largest importer and distributor of spices, sugar, and porcelain as well. In so doing it ran into direct competition with Portuguese ships that came from Macao and Spanish ships that came from Manila. In the seventeenth century Dutch trading stations and maritime power saw the United West India Company, the counterpart of the VOC, establish forts and bases in Brazil, the Caribbean islands of Curaçao and Surinam, and the east coast of America with New Amsterdam, while the VOC extended its network of trade and power to South Africa, Ceylon, India, Australia, Java, and Taiwan, where the factory (as trading posts headed by a chief factor were called) of Zeelandia, established in 1624, was planned as a stable base that could rival Macao and guarantee steady trade with Japan.

The union of the Portuguese and Spanish thrones in 1580 came at a time when the United Provinces of the Netherlands were waging their war of independence from Spain. Followed soon by the threat Philip II's Great Armada posed to England in 1588, this union made possible Dutch and English cooperation and occasional alliance against Iberian power in the Pacific. Dutch and British companies established nearby bases at Surat, in India; on Java, where Batavia (Jakarta) was founded in 1619, and in Japan, where both companies settled on Hirado, a port north of Nagasaki, the Dutch in 1609 and the English in 1613. Dutch and British ships used Hirado as their base for several assaults on Spanish power and shipping outside Manila, and the Dutch also struck against Portuguese Malacca and gleefully raided the larger and more unwieldy Portuguese carracks wherever they intercepted them. Piracy and privateering were the expected manner of procedure. Chinese junks were also inviting targets, especially if they were plying between ports controlled by Spain or Portugal; they were spared only if they carried *shuinjō* issued by the shogunate, which took a dim view of violence where its own profits were concerned.

This was the setting in which Ieyasu had to make decisions about foreign policy and trade. The great Portuguese ships that came from Macao had long been the most important sources of trade, and they remained so until the expulsion of Portugal in 1639. Missionaries and Christianity, however, were another matter. The bakufu inherited Hideyoshi's edicts and actions against missionaries and Japanese Christians. The union of Spain and Portugal complicated enforcement of that edict, however, for the union was followed by missionary rivalry between the Jesuits and the newer orders that came on Spanish ships. In 1593 free-wheeling Franciscans arrived from Manila; they came as emissaries and stayed as missionaries. Imperfectly aware of the setting into which they had come, they scouted the cautious approach the Jesuits had followed in the hope of delaying or evading enforcement of the prohibitions, and proceeded to carry out public preaching. Their success seemed to confirm their charge that the Jesuits were pusillanimous. Meanwhile bakufu officials were also becoming aware that communities of expatriate Japanese in Southeast Asia were attracting Christians fleeing from persecution, and they were suspicious that religion and politics, in the following of some of Hideyoshi's former partisans, might intersect. It was disconcerting for them to see that the state documents that came from Manila and Macao in response to bakufu suggestions said more about propagating the faith than they did about trade.

English requests for trade were somewhat less threatening. James I identified himself as "defender of the faith," but he did speak of commerce. Consequently an English request carried by representatives of the EIC in 1613 was honored with a permit to come to "any port" in Japan. The Dutch, on the other hand, reinforced Japanese fears of Catholic missionaries and offered trade without any ideology at all.[12] A letter from Mauritz of Nassau of 1610 warned that "the Society of Jesus, under cover of the sanctity of religion, intends to convert the Japanese to its religion, split the excellent kingdom of Japan, and lead the country to civil war." To emphasize the point the Dutch sent as gifts items likely to appeal to the old warrior—lead and gunpowder—instead of playthings for the rich and aristocratic.

Ieyasu's response was predictable. To Manila he sent a warning that Japan had been considered a Divine Country from ages past, and that he was not about to reverse the stand of previous generations. The Dutch, however, received so formal a permit to trade that it came to stand as a state-to-state agreement, the only one so issued. The result was that the Dutch chief factor could in future years come regularly to pay homage to the shogun as though he were a feudal lord and not the representative of a merchant company.

As it worked out all parties to these agreements found their hopes of profit dashed. The English were the first to become discouraged. After some years of trading at Hirado they discovered that their permit had to be renewed by each successive shogun. Under Hidetada its new wording limited their purchasing privileges to the port of Hirado, thus denying them the leverage to exploit different markets. In 1623 the EIC, convinced that its representatives were skimming the trade to their personal advantage, closed its factories at Hirado and at Batavia to concentrate on the richer profits of India.[13]

Shogunal officials who profited personally from the Portuguese trade also saw their chances fade as the association of that trade with Catholic Christianity became more firm. The bakufu strengthened its monopoly on trade by narrowing and then closing the opportunities for the *shuinsen*. Under Ieyasu these were frequently extended to daimyo and temples, and also to foreign merchants (Will Adams among them) and ships, many of them Chinese; not a few were used as cover for high bakufu officials. The daimyo were the first to be frozen out. In 1631 an additional guarantee came to be required that could be issued only by the *rōjū*. Now the permits were restricted to a select group of seven families or individuals, each with a particular tie to the Tokugawa. In 1633 overseas travel was ruled out for all Japanese.

The Dutch watched these developments with satisfaction, expecting that they would end by monopolizing the trade with Japan. Their emissaries confirmed the Japanese in their fear of Iberian duplicity and encouraged doubts about overseas Japanese. "Let us do your trading for you," they seemed to say. In the end they proved successful, but hardly in the way they had anticipated. An artificial island in the harbor of Nagasaki that had been prepared for the Portuguese instead became their home. In 1641 they were ordered to move from Hirado to Deshima, where they inherited all the misgivings official Japan had developed about foreigners and where their chances of profits through free trading privileges were constrained by regulations that limited them to dealing with merchant groups sanctioned by the bakufu. The Dutch achievement of peace with Spain in 1648 even raised bakufu doubts about their former enmity, while the political cooperation that had marked Holland's earlier economic competition with England was replaced by wars with England from 1652 to 1654 and again from 1657 to 1667.

4. To the Seclusion Decrees

Hideyoshi had ruled against Catholic Christianity in 1587 and moved to execute the first missionary martyrs in 1597, but the fate of Christianity was still not entirely clear in the early Tokugawa years. Ieyasu was eager to increase the volume of foreign trade, and he had more important political problems facing him with the need to reduce Hideyori's castle and followers at Osaka.

Numbers of highly placed feudal lords were also in doubt about the future of *kirishitan,* as Catholic believers were called. Some, perhaps impelled by desire for the wealth brought by trade, made wrong guesses. In 1582 three Kyushu daimyo had sponsored a mission of promising young samurai to Europe. They were greeted enthusiastically as harbingers of a Christian future, and requested, and were promised, more missionaries in the years to come. By the time they returned to Japan in 1590 Hideyoshi had issued his first orders against propagandizing Christianity, and the mission had come to nothing. But almost a quarter century later, in 1613, Date Masamune, the powerful lord of Sendai, sent his vassal Hasekura Tsunenaga to Rome by way of Mexico and Spain. Hasekura was accompanied by a Franciscan priest, Luis Sotelo. He accepted baptism in Madrid, and took as his Christian name Don Philip Francisco. It was his mission to negotiate for additional trading arrangements and mission exchange, but by his time churchmen, including Pope Paul V with whom he had an audience, were more on their guard. Hasekura returned in 1620 to find that the fall of Osaka in 1615 had been followed by stronger measures against *kirishitan.*

The principal decisions against Christianity were made in the years around 1614–1615, and they bore little relation to the mistaken expectations of Date Masamune. They had their origins in a number of political, economic, and administrative considerations. Uppermost among these was the bakufu's need to know that samurai, and especially daimyo, believers would have no higher loyalty than the one they bore their Tokugawa overlord. Ieyasu was receiving counsel from two Buddhist advisers, men who could have been expected to perceive the missionaries as their enemies. They were able to find arguments for their case against real or alleged Christian converts in a number of incidents that angered Ieyasu. In one, a Christian daimyo named Arima tried, through bribery at Ieyasu's court, to win restitution of lands that he had lost. When exposed he hurriedly apostasized, but it did not save him from an early banishment. Next a bakufu official responsible for finances proposed a scheme for increasing the productivity of mines for precious metal and meanwhile added to his own wealth through dishonest reporting. He was accused, probably wrongly (since his twenty-four concubines denounced him), of being a Christian, but in any case further allegations that he was conspiring with missionaries heightened the scandal.

These events were followed by an edict of 1614 once again ordering all Christian missionaries out of the country. This marked the start of a general persecution. Now too began measures requiring all residents in Tokugawa-held territories to register as parishioners of Buddhist temples; priests were to make regular reports to political authorities of the names and numbers of their communicants. In the mid-1680s this directive was made nationwide and annual. Buddhism was thus co-opted into the service of the Tokugawa state.

It is probably not surprising that Christian daimyo, their numbers already drastically reduced by this time, by and large chose to maintain their rank and abjure their faith. For some, conversion must have been a matter of commercial and perhaps social convenience. What was striking, however, was the fortitude and perseverance of ordinary converts, most of whom had been evangelized by Augustinian preachers. It is undoubtedly a measure of the hardship of their lives as well as the tenacity of their hope that public executions of *kirishitan* who refused to apostasize frequently attracted large throngs of believers who seemed indifferent to the danger they were courting by singing hymns and offering prayers.

It now became incumbent on suspected or formerly *kirishitan* daimyo to begin persecution of Christian sectarians in their domains in order to demonstrate their dependability to the shogunate. No area had been more evangelized than the rugged Kyushu countryside around Nagasaki. The city itself was now under direct shogunal rule. No area was more immediately subject to dragnet searches and tortures designed to force repudiation of faith in Christianity. As the intensity of persecution mounted it combined with social and political distress on the part of yeomanry and declassed samurai, now *rōnin*, former vassals of lords whose punishment had cost them their income and following.

In 1637 these forces came together in an uprising on the Shimabara Peninsula near Nagasaki. It was an area that had experienced frequent changes of governance and misrule by cruel and rapacious feudal lords determined to extract more income from the impoverished peasantry. The Shimabara rebellion was a major test and shock for the bakufu and the third shogun, Iemitsu. Initially the uprising was far from being entirely Christian in makeup, but soon its most important leaders, including a young fighter named Amakusa Shirō who became a legendary figure, were believers. Christianity had put down deep roots in the infertile soil of the Shimabara Peninsula. By 1637 the greater number of commoner believers throughout Japan, whose numbers are estimated to have approached 300,000, had been hunted down, executed, or had apostasized. Those who rebelled in 1637 and 1638 fought with the desperation of people who had nothing to lose. To the bakufu's dismay they fought extremely well. The final result could nevertheless have been predicted; the rebel force found itself surrounded in Hara Castle, short of food and short of weapons. The end of the resistance was followed by the grisly slaughter of all who had survived.[14]

The series of decrees that are considered to have "closed" Japan represented a gradual tightening of political controls over the daimyo. The bakufu had reason to be particularly alert where the large daimyo of the southwest— particularly Kyushu—were concerned. To that end it began with restrictions on their access to *shuinjō*, first limiting and then closing such opportunities. In 1609 it forbade them to have ships with a capacity exceeding 500 *koku*. After Ieyasu's death in 1616 Hidetada, the second shogun, showed himself more hostile to Christianity and more suspicious of the foreign presence. The EIC experienced this in the limitation of the privileges it had previously enjoyed, and missionaries were ordered out. When the English factor Richard Cocks journeyed to Edo to remonstrate with the new authorities, he found himself grilled about his monarch's profession to be "defender of the faith"; the Japanese demanded that he explain the difference between the faith of English and that of Iberian Catholics. At the same time that the English were being forbidden to trade outside Hirado, the daimyo of western Japan were forbidden to trade within their domains and ordered to see to it that all foreign ships that came to their ports be sent to Nagasaki or to Hirado. It did the hapless English no good to try to show their dependability by informing on the presence of Catholic missionaries known to them. Richard Cocks wrote in 1621:

> Yestarnight I was enformed that Francisco Lopas and a semenary priest were com to towne, and lodged in the house of the capt of the friggot taken the last yeare; of which I advised Torezemon Dono to tell the king [i.e., daimyo] thereof by Coa Jno. our jurebasso [interpreter]. It being late, and to give order noe strangers should passe out. And this morning I sent the same jurebasso to Torezemon Dono secretary, to know the kinges answer; which was, I might speake of these matters when Gonrok Dono came. Unto which I sent answer, it might be that then these pristes would be gon, and then it was to late to speake. Yet, for all this, there was noe eare nor respect geeven to my speeches.[15]

Cocks persevered until he was called, with other witnesses, to identify the priests, and the matter ended with the daimyo forced, perhaps reluctantly, to send local Christians who identified them under duress, after which they were sent off in chains.

The five principal decrees came in the six years between 1633 and 1639. In the first, a seventeen-article decree, forbade the sending of Japanese ships overseas, except for those properly certified, decreed death for Japanese who, having been overseas, returned (articles 1–3), ordered the reporting and offered rewards for identification of *kirishitan* (articles 4–8), limited trade in objects from abroad to channels of the authorized five guilds, and ordered that all ships be sent to Nagasaki (articles 9–17). Two years later, a second decree removed the exception of certification for overseas travel, made the ban all-inclusive and ordered punishment by death for any who disobeyed. Foreign ship captains had frequently employed Japanese seamen, but that too was now forbidden.

The next regulations strengthened prohibitions on Japanese *kirishitan* and any missionaries who might be found. Now the count of prosecutions of believers found in violation of the decrees grew steadily. The Portuguese, as prime source of the infection, were exiled. In 1636 Portuguese and 287 of their offspring were sent to Macao. In 1639 a fifth and final decree settled the matter. When officials in Macao attempted a final remonstrance by sending a ship in 1640, the point was driven home by executing the captain and sixty others and allowing thirteen survivors to return to Macao with the story of what had happened to the others.

The seventeenth century did not show examples of religious tolerance or freedom of conscience in many parts of the world. Within Japan fears of sectarian insurrection made for extirpation of *ikkō* Buddhism in the domain of Satsuma into the nineteenth century.[16] The other countries of East Asia remained hostile to Japanese visitors. Korea limited the Japanese to Pusan, Ming China maintained its ban on commerce with Japan, and memorialists at the Chinese court argued for laws against the construction of ships large enough to sail to Japan. From this one might almost argue that Japan's was not the first, but in a way the last, *sakoku* (closed country) policy in East Asia. Nor were things very different in Europe. The fires of the Inquisition had not yet been banked. The long war of independence the Dutch fought with Spain came to an end in 1648, but that raised doubts in Edo about the wisdom of contact with even Protestant Europe. Nor was freedom of religion popular in the West. The Treaty of Westphalia of 1648 resolved the Protestant-Catholic standoff with a Latin formula that called for the acceptance of the ruler's faith by those under his governance. *Cuius regio, eius religio*—the ruler's faith prevails—as the formulation had it, left no room for individual decision.

What was probably unique about the Tokugawa persecution was its ferocity. Japan's insularity made escape impossible. In Kyushu sectarians went underground and maintained their community through ingenious devices, utilizing Buddhist images that opened to reveal Madonna and child. This pattern of indigenization made the *kirishitan* survivors almost a folk religion. For most, however, the inquisitor's tortures brought death or apostasy. Captured priests were subjected to tortures so ingenious and fiendish that six European fathers renounced their faith. Several of these became authors of pamphlets that proved particularly telling in the inquisitors' attempts to battle Christianity on the ideological level.[17]

These measures may have owed something to the character of the third shogun. Iemitsu was a ruthless and paranoid ruler, and his leading inquisitor, Inoue Chikugo no kami Masashige, was able to prey upon his depraved tastes with particular skill.[18] The terror which their methods could inspire in victims has left its mark on historical and fictional accounts of those years.[19]

5. The Dutch at Nagasaki

The departure of the English, followed by the expulsion of the Spanish and Portuguese, left the Dutch as the only Europeans in Japan. This had been the hope and purpose of their drive to monopolize the Japan trade. They had taken pains to assure the Japanese that their form of Christianity was very different from that of their Iberian rivals, and a Dutch ship had even obliged its Tokugawa hosts by lobbing shells into Hara Castle during the Shimabara rebellion. Nevertheless in 1641 the taste of victory turned to ashes when they were ordered to vacate their factory at Hirado, where a new building had carried the offensive date "1640 A.D.," and move into the man-made island of Deshima in Nagasaki harbor.

Deshima had been prepared for the Portuguese, its costs levied against Nagasaki merchant wards that stood to profit from foreign trade. It measured about 600 feet by 200 feet in a fan-shaped pattern. It was surrounded by a high board fence on its stone embankments, posted with signs warning people to stay away. It was connected to the mainland by a stone bridge with guards stationed on it. The Dutch were charged a yearly rental. Within the fence were a few warehouses, housing for twenty or so Dutch residents, and quarters for Japanese interpreters and guards. There was also space for a vegetable garden and a few cows, sheep, pigs, and chickens. Water came from the mainland through a bamboo pipe, and it was paid for separately.

The contingent of VOC personnel was headed by the chief factor, called *opperhoofd* by the Dutch and *kapitan* by the Japanese. The group included a doctor, a bookkeeper, assistants, and usually personal black slaves for the ranking Dutchmen. None of them was free to cross the bridge without special permission, which was rarely given, and then usually for visits to the Nagasaki pleasure quarter; more often women from that quarter were permitted to cross to visit the Dutch.[20]

Around this was a Japanese bureaucracy whose costs were charged against the Dutch; a headman and his deputy, five secretaries, fifteen laborer supervisors, and thirty-six treasurers, five gate guards, night guards, cooks, and grooms, and other hangers-on typical of a status society that was based upon the support of a large underemployed and nonproductive class. Samurai income, it will be remembered, was often phrased as "rations" for two or four or more servants. In street scenes in genre paintings and prints one always sees attendants carrying things for their betters, and "betters" was and remains a highly relative concept.

Special mention must be made of the corps of interpreters. Portuguese remained the lingua franca of Western trade into the mid-seventeenth century, but with the narrowing of contacts to the VOC the study of Dutch became necessary. Nagasaki trade also required a corps of interpreters for Chinese and Southeast Asian languages for the China trade that is discussed below. To meet the needs of contact with the VOC some twenty families were given hereditary jobs as interpreters. They maintained their guild by co-opting successors, usually through adoption as family members. The patriarchal principle that characterized Tokugawa society meant that they would be arranged hierarchically under family heads as "major" and "apprentice" interpreters. It was Japanese policy to discourage the Dutch from studying Japanese lest the outsiders get too close to those they would contact. On a number of occasions representatives of the VOC were told to leave Japan because their knowledge of Japanese was becoming too good. The Japanese wanted to keep the contact on their own terms.

The rhythm of life at Deshima was boring in its regularity. Ships arrived in July with the summer monsoon. Their approach would be announced by Japanese coastal lookouts, and they were signaled at the harbor entrance from Papenberg ("Pope hill," named for *kirishitan* martyrdoms); the captain would then order his crew to unload the guns and lock all Bibles and other Christian literature into barrels. In at least the early years the crew was obliged to tread on images of the Madonna and child *(fumie)*, a test that had been found particularly effective for interrogation of *kirishitan*.

Crews remained on board as Japanese laborers unloaded the cargo. In the seventeenth century, when the trade was at its height, Chinese silk thread led the list of valuables. War-related raw materials—tin, lead, saltpeter, borax— came next, and curios and luxury items ranging from deer pelts to spices to tropical woods, and European-origin curios like eyeglasses, clocks, and mirrors came last. Once on land, the cargo was displayed for inspection by representatives of the merchant guilds authorized to deal with the foreigners. The most important of these guilds, the *itowappu*, literally "thread allocation," represented merchants in the principal shogunal cities. Bakufu officials had first choice of objects and of course kept the materials of war for themselves. They could also give the Dutch order lists for the next year's delivery.

In return, the Dutch obtained bullion, first silver and, after mid-century, copper. Japan was a major exporter of silver in the seventeenth century, and remained a major exporter of copper. In addition, as direct access to China became difficult because of the wars that ended with the victory of Manchu invaders over the Ming dynasty in 1644, Japanese porcelain, blue-and-white slipware first produced by the emigré Korean potters in Saga, became an important item of trade, ideal for ballast and soon keenly desired in Europe and in the Near East. Japanese lacquerware and chests completed the list of items salable in a Europe experiencing the tastes of "Chinoiserie" that had grown out of Jesuit contact with Ming China.[21]

VOC ships sailed back to Batavia with the fall monsoon in November. Their profits depended only in part on Japan-Java-Holland trade; what mattered was the carrying trade all through Asia and the Near East, and it is no accident that some of the major collections of Japanese ceramics survive in the Ottoman palaces of Istanbul.

The details of this commerce make for dreary reading in the daily register kept by the Deshima chief factor and forwarded to Batavia and on to Holland. His successor normally came the following year, and with the exception of Hendrik Doeff, who was marooned on Deshima during the Napoleonic years, few factors spent very long in Japan. Actually the factor's most important official duty came in the form of a November trip to Edo for a ceremonial audience with the shogun that took place after the departure of the ships for Java. The court trip (*hofreis,* as the Dutch called it) changed the chief factor's status from merchant head to feudal lord. In this he stood above Korean ambassadors and Chinese captains, for he alone came there by virtue of Ieyasu's permit to Mauritz of Nassau.

The trip took place a total of 116 times in Tokugawa years; annually after 1633, biennially after 1764, and then every four years from 1790 to 1850, the last such trip. The round trip averaged 90 days, and the longest required 142. It began by boat to Shimonoseki, went on by procession to Osaka, and then moved along the Eastern Sea Route (Tōkaidō) to Edo. It involved low-level haggling as well as high-level encounter. Costs were borne by the Dutch (as they were by feudal lords), and the *opperhoofd* was anxious to keep his entourage as small as possible. The Japanese wanted it as large as possible, to permit more attendants and the possibility of combining private with public business. Throughout the operation the Dutch felt that the Japanese did their best to maximize featherbedding. One purpose of the daily diary of the mission was to have evidence of precedents with which the Dutch chief factor could argue his case for economy.

This regular look into a Japan that was increasingly remote and inaccessible made service at Batavia attractive for some remarkable and curious Europeans whose accounts provide invaluable pictures of Tokugawa Japan. The best known of these is Engelbert Kaempfer (1651–1716), who was at Deshima as doctor in 1690 and accompanied the chief factor on his journey to Edo in 1691 and 1692. His *History of Japan*, first published in English translation in 1727–1728, provides a rich storehouse of information. Kaempfer was able to gain information through the help of a young student interpreter who remained with him for two years and provided him with much information that he was not supposed to obtain. Although it is by no means the most important contribution of the book, Kaempfer's account of the audience with the fifth shogun Tsunayoshi makes clear that Europeans had become little more than exotic and amusing creatures by the end of the century.

> Soon after we came in, and had after the usual obeysances seated our selves on the place assign'd us, Bingosama [the Lord of Bingo] welcom'd us in the Emperor's [shogun's] name and then desir'd us to sit upright, to take off our cloaks, to tell him our names and age, to stand up, to walk, to turn about, to dance, to sing songs, to compliment one another, to be angry, to invite one another to dinner, to converse one with another, to discourse in a familiar way like father and son, to shew how two friends, or man and wife, compliment or take leave of one another, to play with children, to carry them about upon our arms, and to do many more things of like nature. Moreover we were ask'd many questions serious and comical; as for instance, what profession I was of, whether I ever cur'd any considerable distempers, to which I answer'd yes, I had, but not at Nagasaki, where we were kept no better than prisoners; what houses we had? whether our customs were different from theirs? how we buried our people, and when? to which was answr'd, that we bury'd them always in the day time . . . Whether we had prayers and images like the Portuguese, which was answered in the negative . . . Then again we were commanded to read, and to dance, separately and jointly, and I to tell them the names of some European Plaisters, upon which I mention'd some of the hardest I could remember. The Ambassador [Opperhoofd] was asked concerning his children, how many he had, what their names were, as also how far distant Holland was from Nagasaki . . . We were then further commanded to put on our hats, to walk about the room discoursing with one another, to take off our perukes . . . Then I was desired once more to come nearer the skreen, and to take off my peruke. Then they made us jump, dance, play gambols and walk together, and upon that they ask'd the Ambassador how old we guessed Bingo to be, he answer'd 50 and I 45, which made

them laugh. Then they made us kiss one another, like man and wife, which the ladies particularly shew'd by their laughter to be well pleas'd with. They desir'd us further to shew them what sorts of compliments it was customary in Europe to make to inferiors, to ladies, to superiors, to princes, to kings. After this they begg'd another song of me, and were satisfy'd with two, which the company seem'd to like very well. After this farce was over, we were order'd to take off our cloaks, to come near the skreen one by one, and to take our leave in the very same manner we would take it of a Prince, or King in Europe . . . It was already four in the afternoon, when we left the hall of audience, after having been exercis'd after this manner for four hours and a half.[22]

The Japanese began to limit the number of VOC ships, banned the export of silver, and imposed restrictions on the export of copper, the item the Dutch were most eager to obtain. The diary the chief factor submitted to his superiors in Batavia and Holland is full of complaints about the cost of presents to Japanese officials, haggling with Nagasaki authorities about prices and the volume of goods, the quality of lacquer and porcelain that came in, and the efforts of Japanese officials to take advantage of them. Over time the physical restrictions imposed in the early Deshima years eased somewhat, although the Dutch were never permitted to step out of their role as merchants working through interpreters. But the trade, so profitable in the early decades when conditions were most difficult, declined steadily in bulk and in value.

Despite restrictions, a number of remarkably astute observers left accounts of their experiences. Kaempfer remains the best known, and his achievement was a considerable one; he even managed to map the route to Edo secretly with his compass. A Swedish scientist, Carl Peter Thunberg, a student of the botanist Linnaeus, was at Deshima in 1775 and collected over eight hundred species of Japanese flora. The Hollander Isaac Titsingh was in Japan three times during the 1780s. By his time Japanese interest in the Dutch language had increased sufficiently for him to be able to correspond in Dutch with studious daimyo after his return home. Titsingh too prepared a massive study of Japan, but he retired to Paris and his materials were scattered and lost in the upheavals that followed the French Revolution. Hendrik Doeff, as mentioned, was marooned at Deshima from 1804 to 1817; he worked toward a dictionary of Japanese and left memoirs describing his experiences. The German Philipp Franz von Siebold, who was in Japan from 1823 to 1828, was an army doctor, and was permitted to establish a school for medicine in the city of Nagasaki. He had his students prepare essays about their country, and collected material for an important study of Japan before he was expelled for espionage after managing to obtain a map of northern Japan. In addition, there were a number of Dutch doctors who served at Deshima much longer than the famous men whose books informed the Western world about Japan, but few of their records survive.

Why, then, did the Deshima station, with its dwindling quantity of trade, continue to exist? For the Dutch it was an extension of the Batavia station that became, as Netherlands East Indies, the country's profitable colony and claim to continued great power standing.

On the Japanese side, the Dutch contact provided intelligence about the outside world. Each arriving captain was obliged to submit a *fūsetsugaki*, or account of what had happened since the last ship's arrival. Indeed Kaempfer, in his closing chapter, opined that this was the reason Japan maintained the system even in his day. Japan could easily provide for its own needs, he wrote, and it lacked nothing of importance. Why then had Japan not expelled the Dutch as well? His answer was that "it was not thought advisable to oblige them also to quit the Country, and yet dangerous freely to admit them. For this reason they are now kept, little better than prisoners, and hostages under the strict inspection of crowds of overseers, who are obliged by a solemn oath narrowly to watch their minutest actions, and kept, as it seems, for scarce any other purpose, but that the Japanese might be by their means informed of what passes in other parts of the world. Hence, to make it worth their while to stay, and patiently to endure what hardships are put upon them, they have given them leave to sell off their goods to the value of about 500,000 Crowns a year. It is certainly an error to imagine, that the Japanese cannot well be without the goods imported by the Dutch. There is more Silk and other Stuffs wore out in the Country in one week's time, than the Dutch import in a year."[23]

6. Relations with China

Ieyasu's efforts to heal the relationships that Hideyoshi had broken with Asia extended also to his concern for China. Chinese goods, especially textiles, were after all the most important import in the seventeenth century, and the possibility of getting them directly at the source had to be attractive. Chinese artisans and traders had long evaded the Ming dynasty's rules against trade with Japan. Indeed, "Chinatowns" were to be found everywhere along the coasts of Kyushu and as far east as Kawagoe and Odawara on the main island of Honshu. Chinese artisans had helped design the tiles for Nobunaga's castles, and Ieyasu and his contemporaries recruited skilled Chinese for their capitals. Some were rewarded with land and residence. As order improved under Tokugawa rule and declined under late Ming rule many of those Chinese chose to remain in Japan and assume Japanese names and nationality. Then as trade became concentrated in Nagasaki most overseas Chinese found it necessary to move to that city; in the first decades of Tokugawa rule resident Chinese there came to number over two thousand.

Ieyasu's success in reestablishing relations with Korea in 1609 was followed by discussion of reopening trade relations with Ming China. Ming authorities were less forgiving than their Korean counterparts, however, and they showed little interest in Japanese overtures; memorials to the court argued that Japanese "pirates" were not to be trusted under any circumstances. In 1609 these doubts received substantiation when Satsuma, with bakufu knowledge, seized control of the Ryukyu islands, disarmed their inhabitants, and installed a shadow government that maintained the ruler in his Okinawan capital in an effort to continue, under the pretense of independence, a tributary relationship with China. In years to come it was easier for all parties to pretend that this had not taken place; when missions from China came to invest Okinawan rulers the Japanese supervisors kept a discreet distance. Satsuma thus had access to Chinese goods, and the bakufu gained in self-esteem from Ryukyu embassies that were paraded in Edo when they came to mark the installation of a new shogun. Late Ming memorialists were not taken in by this, however, and warned their emperor of new dangers from Japan. Since, moreover, the Chinese merchants most eager to travel to Japan were from the southern Chinese coast and farthest from the control of Peking, it is not surprising that memorialists also called for laws forbidding the construction of ships large enough to sail to Japan.

Nevertheless, between 1611 and 1625 the bakufu addressed several letters to Fukien Province authorities concerning the possibility of reopening direct trade and commerce with the Ming. The letters, however, failed to meet the protocol requirements the Chinese court set for documents from its tributaries; they did not conform with standards of terminology and form, and they were not dated by the era names of the Chinese calendar. Worse yet, they made no apology for the seizure of Ryukyu but asserted that the island king now called himself Japan's vassal.[24] Despite this, responses from provincial officials seemed to hold out the possibility of an arrangement. By the time these arrived, however, Osaka had fallen, Ieyasu had died, and the bakufu was very much more confident of its ability to have its own way. The same officials who had planned the original approach to China now dismissed the Chinese responses as impertinent and directed that future correspondence be routed through Tsushima, as was the case with Korea. Both regimes, in other words, chose to stand by principle and dignity and rejected any arrangement that did not bring protocol as well as commercial advantages. In the 1640s, when Chinese officials sought Japanese help against the Manchus, the Edo authorities were in a position to assert their full authority and respond with scorn. The Chinese, one daimyo wrote a retainer, "won't allow Japanese ships to approach their shores; they even post picket ships. Therefore it is hardly proper for them to come, now that their country has fallen into civil war, and say, 'We are having some trouble, so could you please send some troops?' "[25]

Thanks to private Chinese traders, however, the bakufu found it possible to have it both ways. On the state-to-state level it maintained a haughty arrogance, while the VOC, Tsushima, Satsuma, and private Chinese merchants more than fulfilled its commercial needs. As conditions in Asia changed it seemed wise to cut off Japanese traders from sources of contamination in Southeast Asia and, after the 1630s, make them stay home altogether. But that did not by any means involve the sacrifice of goods, intelligence, or even technology from the outside world.

Japan's "seclusion" was thus aimed principally at the West. It is Western ethnocentrism to think that a country that chooses to cut itself off from Westerners has cut itself off from the world. Most bakufu trade policies were designed for access to Chinese goods, and in this regard they were highly successful. Foreign trade and the Nagasaki system were so important to the bakufu that it subsidized domains that produced copper for export in order to keep them going and to prevent them from selling it on the domestic market, where it brought higher prices. The "Dutch" trade was actually trade in Asian, chiefly Chinese, goods. And Chinese and Koreans brought more of those than the Dutch. The Nagasaki trade, as Ōba Osamu has put it, was really China trade.[26]

The Chinese had no headman and no formal authorization as the Dutch did, and they too experienced a gradual narrowing of freedom of movement and of commerce, but they were far more numerous. The Chinese quarter in Nagasaki, the *tōjin yashiki* that was established in 1689, harbored thousands of people when the fleet was in; in its first year it housed 4,888 Chinese. It occupied an area larger than seven acres, double that of Deshima. In the 1740s, when things were going badly for the Dutch, Deshima was patrolled by over thirty Japanese guards; the Chinese quarter was administered by over three hundred officials, guards, and inspectors. Things were on a dramatically different scale. At Nagasaki interpreters were divided into two groups, one for the Dutch, and a far larger company for the Chinese. The "Chinese" interpreters were really responsible for all of Asia, with subcategories assigned to "other" countries beside China. In the seventeenth century this meant specialists for Thailand, Vietnam, "Luzon" (Manila), and India. For the most part ships from those areas were sent by colonies of overseas Chinese. The interpreters maintained a rather familial establishment, and their students and successors were normally relatives by blood or adoption. Chinese specialists received higher pay than those for Southeast Asia. As time went on, and the bakufu became more wary of representatives of areas beyond what one scholar calls a "Luzon-Macao," or Catholic, line, they also became fewer.

The trade assumed significant proportions, especially during the seventeenth century. It was in 1635 that the Chinese were ordered to come only to Nagasaki. Their numbers grew rapidly; in 1640, 74 ships came; a year later there were 97. After the Manchus seized Taiwan in 1683 the traffic became so heavy (193 ships came in 1688) that it became necessary to establish the Chinese quarter for their crews and to institute regulations to limit their number. The eighteenth century consequently saw a decline; in 1720 there were 30 ships, and in 1791, only 10.

It is, however, the cultural role of the Chinese, at least prior to the late Tokugawa development of interest in the West, that provides the most striking contrast to the role and treatment of the Dutch. Kaempfer and his companions were obliged to humiliate themselves with several hours of silly pantomime to amuse the shogun Tsunayoshi, but that same shogun tried hard to be a serious student of the higher culture of China. He laughed at Kaempfer, but he treated visiting Chinese monks with the greatest deference. The Dutch were well advised to keep their faith under wraps, and they sealed whatever religious books they brought with them while their vessels were in port. But at Nagasaki the Chinese were permitted to build branches of their temples in Fukien and Chekiang, and shogunal officials accompanied captain and crew to these temples in processions of thanks for safe arrival. Three temples were established before the decrees of the 1630s; one to provide for the needs of provincials from Chekiang, Kiangsu, and Kiangsi ("Nanking"), and two more added for sailors from Fukien, Foochow, and Changchow-Ch'uanchow. In 1678 a fourth temple was established for men from Canton (Kwangchow). For over a century priests and abbots came from China to staff these temples.

The "Nanking" temple also served as the avenue of introduction for Chinese monks who moved on to central Japan to found the Ōbaku Rinzai Zen temple of Manpukuji at Uji. The first abbot was Yin Yüan (Japan's Ingen), who brought a revised ordination procedure. He was soon put in touch with the (Kyoto) Myōshinji abbot Ryōkei, who saw to it that he was invited to Kyoto for an audience with the retired emperor Go Mizuno-o; he also enjoyed the patronage of Tokugawa Ietsuna, the fourth shogun. Until 1740 all Manpukuji abbots were from China. Thereafter they alternated with Japan-born abbots for sixty years, and only after that were they all Japanese.[27]

Ingen and other Chinese Rinzai monks were honored guests at the court of the shogun Tsunayoshi. Tsunayoshi prided himself on his knowledge of the Chinese classics. He presided at 240 seminars on the *I Ching (Book of Changes)* at which monks, officials, daimyo, and Confucian scholars were expected to be present.[28] His chamberlain Yanagisawa Yoshiyasu organized groups for the study of spoken Chinese, and the court Confucianist Ogyū Sorai went to great effort to try to master spoken colloquial Chinese. Sorai's letters to these learned Chinese are full of almost cloying respect and flattery.

> Yesterday I visited a Buddhist place and for the first time I met your compassionate and gracious person. We had a marvelous conversation on various subjects. It was like the playing of bells: when they [i.e., you] sounded high inquiries were answered; when they [i.e., I] sounded low, there were gasping sounds. The brushes flew over the paper [i.e., as we communicated in writing] creating a wind, the ink came down on paper producing flowers . . . Now, untiringly and diligently you presented me with your beautiful teaching. The spirit of harmony could be felt. Having returned home, I felt close to fainting and I was filled with memories . . . I have just tasted the sweetest taste of sweets, it still sticks to my teeth and cheeks, and I cannot get it rinsed from my mouth . . . if at your leisure, after practising your *Zen* meditation you would trouble your august brush, and if I could attach it to my simple hut, a word from an eternally connected, it would shine there for ever and ever [i.e., could I persuade you to send me some calligraphy I could display?].[29]

In short, the contrast between the treatment of these Chinese prelates and the dragnet that was out for Catholic priests brings home the fact that although for a century and more the seclusion system tried to exclude Western thought and religion, during the same period the Japanese elite was struggling to master the Chinese cultural tradition. That same respect was extended to Chinese goods. The bakufu saw to it that the best of Chinese silks came into its own hands and that the best of Chinese books were available to its scholars.

In some ways this respect extended to Korean scholars, partly because they could help in the transmission of Chinese texts and thought. Amenomori Hōshū struggled to master Korean, but before that he went to Nagasaki to study spoken Chinese. Members of Korean missions exchanged more than poems, paintings, and calligraphy with their hosts. Japanese were also keen to learn of medicine as it was practiced in Korea, and sought out the doctors who accompanied each mission; question-and-answer sessions with the visiting physicians were held along their route of travel. In addition, as has been mentioned, Korean potters brought knowledge of the clays and glazes that made possible Japanese production of blue slipware porcelain, in patterns and shapes so closely identified with Ming dynasty Chinese pottery that Ming dates were often stenciled on the bottom, and the result, as Japanese Imari, was exported by the Dutch to the Near East and Europe for further emulation by Dutch, German, and English artisans. In some respects, in other words, "closed" Japan was a transmission point for international cultural and technological exchange. Studies of bullion flows also show that seventeenth-century Japan was a major player in economic exchange as well.[30]

In the time of the eighth shogun, Yoshimune, the study of Chinese precedents extended to institutional patterns with particular emphasis on Ming administrative law. The Six Maxims of Shun-chih, the first Manchu emperor, were forwarded from Ryukyu by Satsuma. Yoshimune, who saw that these simple moral exhortations could have direct application to Japan, ordered a simplified translation of a popular text containing the maxims for use in lower schools. There are records of daimyo who ordered village leaders to explain the importance of the maxims on the first day of every month. The influence of the document extended into modern Japan. In the Meiji period the Imperial Rescript on Education of 1890, which served as the chief ideological text for prewar Japan, drew on the use of this document as a precedent.[31]

In addition to all this, Tokugawa period contacts with China had room for popular culture also. We have the names of about 130 Chinese painters who came and stayed at Nagasaki for a time. They were not the great artists of their day; most of them were priests and merchants who were sufficiently skillful for Japanese to admire their work. The ablest of these men enjoyed enormous fame in Japan. Shen Nan-p'in, the best known, came in 1731 and again in 1733. After his return to China he continued to send his paintings to Japan for sale; about two hundred of them survive. He and three others became known as the "four great teachers" who introduced late Ming and early Ch'ing styles of bird and flower painting. Theirs was a pleasant, bourgeois style that was easy to live with. It was popular with the urban residents of central China, and it quickly became popular with the townsmen in Japan. The Chinese painters also introduced Chinese "literati" painting, which found echo in the Japanese *nanga* and *bunjinga* styles of Buson, Ike no Taiga, and late Tokugawa eclectics. Ming period prints also played a role in the development of Japanese printmakers' skills, skills that led to the burgeoning production of prints that were eagerly sought by townsmen in Japan's fast-growing cities. Meanwhile the formal art patronized by Japan's feudal elite, of course, drew on the examples of earlier and greater schools of Chinese art.

By Yoshimune's time in the early eighteenth century the bakufu's interest extended to practical imports from China in the hope of reducing what was becoming a serious trade imbalance. As Japanese mines ran out, restrictions were put on the export of bullion in 1685, in 1715, and once more in 1790. Both the Dutch and Chinese were now sharply limited in the number of ships they could send and the amount of copper they could export. New measures to control smuggling came into effect, with drastic punishments carried out publicly in order to intimidate any who might be bold enough to try.[32] More interesting, however, was the bakufu's eagerness to encourage the production of things like silk, sugar, and pharmacopoeia that had figured high on the list of imports. This brought with it the hiring of specialists from China to help in the search for useful plants and appropriate locations in Japan.

In other words, during the years of "seclusion" there was a continuous process of change in Japan's international trade. As the need for, and interest in, raw materials for war such as gunpowder and saltpeter diminished, the Dutch too found themselves sending different kinds of goods to Nagasaki. Sugar was high among these, and it was a crop whose domestic production Yoshimune did his best to encourage. When the sugar available to the Dutch dried up after a Chinese insurrection on Java resulted in destruction of refining facilities there in the eighteenth century, it endangered the whole arrangement with Deshima; bakufu administrators provided less copper, and the Dutch threatened to break things off altogether. Significantly, they knew they had the inhabitants of Nagasaki on their side, for the city lived for and on foreign trade. So did the officials lucky enough to be appointed to deal with the Dutch and Chinese, as they were able to improve their income many times through quiet peculation.

7. The Question of the "Closed Country"

The Japanese term *sakoku*, "closed country," was coined by a Japanese scholar who translated the chapter in which Kaempfer discussed the "closed country" and, incidentally, argued its benefits. The translation circulated privately and was not published until the 1850s. It became, and has remained, a standard term. As we shall see, in the last decade of the Tokugawa period *kaikoku*, or "open country," served as the antithesis to *jōi*, "expel the barbarians!" in fevered political discourse. Commodore Matthew Calbraith Perry was serenely convinced that he was bringing civilization to a benighted land that lived in flagrant violation of all norms of international society.

From the account above, however, it seems clear that we should pause before accepting the verdict of Kaempfer the way his translator did. The seventeenth century should be judged by seventeenth-century standards, and a number of qualifications are in order before we accept Perry's nineteenth-century view of the matter.

Japan itself, as we have seen, was far from fully "closed." For Japanese, forbidden on pain of death from leaving and trying to return to the country, the fact was clear enough. These draconian rules were relaxed a bit toward the end as the regime saw utility in the news and skills that returnees might bring with them, but they held good through most of the period. Nineteenth-century English and American captains who thought they were ingratiating themselves with the Japanese government by bringing shipwrecked sailors and fishermen back to their home country were helping neither the castaways nor their own cause. Europe was far more multinational and international. Korea, however, was if anything more secluded.

Yet the world of the Japanese was far from closed mentally, culturally, or even technologically. Chinese scholars, artists, and priests came to Nagasaki throughout the Tokugawa years; educated Chinese received cordial hospitality from their Japanese hosts, and even Chinese commoners who had skills and ability were able to make an important contribution to Japanese culture.

As the eighteenth century went on the same was true of the Dutch; they were gradually exempted from the humiliation of being displayed like Martians at the shogun's court. As Japanese scholars began to develop the ability to read Dutch, the books Dutch ships brought to Nagasaki became more important than the copper they took back with them. In the 1820s Dr. Philipp Franz von Siebold, as mentioned, was even permitted to open a school for Japanese students in Nagasaki.

At the same time the Japanese paranoia about Christianity was never relaxed. In Nagasaki even Chinese books that entered were checked for references to Christianity. In 1704 a courageous Sicilian named Giovanni Battista Sidotti made his way to Manila, where he studied Japanese with expatriates, and in 1708 managed to land on the island of Kyushu with the hope of evangelizing for his faith. He was speedily intercepted and transported to Edo, where he spent the remaining seven years of his life in the dungeon ironically referred to as the "Christian residence." There he was interrogated by the shogunal scholar Arai Hakuseki, who admired his intelligence and courage but professed dismay at his credulity. Sidotti then confirmed Japanese views of the danger of his creed by converting his jailers. Soon interpreters were sent to inform the Dutch that Sidotti and his converts had been confined in small square boxes from which they would not emerge again. This took place in 1715. Over a half century later the diary of Dr. Sugita Ganpaku, a pioneer specialist in Western medicine, noted that ordinary villagers had been seized, tortured, and executed on the basis of charges that they were secret Christians. Allegations of belief in Christianity remained one of the most effective ways of dealing with political enemies and demonstrating personal vigilance. It was not that Christians were necessarily evil; quite to the contrary, wrote the samurai Aizawa Yasushi in 1825; rather, they were able to mislead stupid commoners by kindness and thereby prepare them to become traitors to their country.

One can grant that what are now called "civil rights" were nonexistent without dismissing Japan as "closed." To be sure, after the awareness of Russian advances on the Kurils and Hokkaido from the north and English advances on China from the south, Japanese authorities tightened their guard and closed their minds anew. National security was now at stake. By that time Ieyasu had been credited with the design for national isolation, and it had become an apparently inviolable part of Tokugawa tradition. Foreign trade had also run its course; fewer ships came to Nagasaki, and what they brought—except for books—was far less important to the Japanese economy, which had now matured in production of silk, of cotton, and of sugar.

It was precisely in eighteenth and early nineteenth centuries that the West had changed most dramatically. The long interval of peace in Japan contrasted with an almost unbroken series of wars in the West. In the process dramatic changes in military technology made the weapons Japanese carried as obsolete as the class structure of those who carried them. Intellectual, political, and economic transformation in America and Europe had led to the participatory state with its citizen soldiers, while in Japan ordinary people took little interest in the activities of samurai.

The relative standing of the Western powers had also changed dramatically. At the start of the Tokugawa period Holland was becoming one of Europe's great powers, with stations in all parts of the world, but by the nineteenth century it had been transformed into a small trading state that minded its own business almost as quietly as Tokugawa Japan did. Japanese students sent to Holland in the 1860s concluded with dismay that they had been studying the wrong Western language and country. Matsuki Kōan, the future Terajima Munenori, spoke for them in a letter he sent in 1862. "Many scholars in England and France raised their eyebrows when they heard that we read Dutch books," he wrote; "even the Hollanders themselves all read their books in French or German . . . Beyond the borders no one knows Dutch. I must honestly say that the country is so small and mean as to startle one."[33] He might, of course, have said the same things about a Japan in which scholars read books in Chinese and in Dutch.

It is this feeling of having made the wrong choice, and having fallen behind in consequence, that helps to account for the large literature modern Japanese have produced about their "closed" country. Additionally, they began to study world history at a time when European writers emphasized the primacy of interstate relations and war as formative in the creation of modern states.[34]

What "history," then, had an isolated Japan experienced? It became the more natural to highlight the "seclusion" laws, and blame them for Japan's failure to achieve international standing in early modern times. In the closing days of World War II the philosopher Watsuji Tetsurō described *sakoku* as the "tragedy" of Japan, responsible for most of the problems the country had experienced in modern times. It forced, he thought, the rushed modernization under state control that followed, and contributed to the drive to compete and excel with its disastrous end in the Pacific War.

A half century later, however, the Edo period has come to look very different to Japanese historians. This generation has not, of course, been frustrated by its cruelties or preoccupied with its failings in the way their forebears had been. Generations of research have made it clear how much things actually changed during the Edo years. Contemporary Japanese are no longer obsessed by Japan's "backwardness" in comparison with the West. The disasters that dominated Watsuji's consciousness are now far behind them. Consequently they show a calm and dispassionate willingness to equate Japan's experience with that of other countries. For some liberal, even internationalist, scholars, the entire system of seclusion needs to be rethought and reevaluated. They prefer to see it as the normal, or at least reasonable, response of an early modern state that was defining itself and its boundaries. They draw on the evidence of vigorous intellectual life in Edo times to deny that seclusion choked off intellectual curiosity and variety. One scholar indeed has been quoted as saying, no doubt with tongue in cheek, that "the country was far more open to new currents during the *sakoku* period than it is today . . . foreign goods and information flowed in abundantly." If one followed this, it would be necessary to conclude that the generalizations of the textbooks have been badly overblown, and that the heroic mold in which Western writers have cast the achievement of Commodore Perry is ill deserved.

It is not necessary to take so benign a view of the Tokugawa system to suggest that the issue has been badly overdone. What if the Tokugawa founders had taken a less restrictive view of Japan's place in the international system? Things probably would not have been so very different. China and Korea, after all, were part of a world order that was closed to Japan unless it was willing to make substantial modifications in its professions of sovereignty and autonomy. Tributary status would have had its costs, and rejection of close ties with the West would have been one of them. But in any case those ties remained unlikely. The English had left of their own accord in the 1620s, and thereafter found themselves increasingly involved in the subcontinent of India, where profits and glory were far greater. The Iberian empires of Spain and Portugal were already in decline by the seventeenth century, hardly capable of threat to Japanese policymakers. That left the maritime holdings of the Dutch in Southeast Asia, holdings that were consolidated with full political control only in the late nineteenth century.

Things might not, in other words, have been very different. With one exception: the ferocity of the Christian extirpation, though an internal matter, was what led to the external restrictions. That control over sectarians, in turn, was central to the bakufu's assertion of control over its feudatories. In that sense "seclusion" and bakufu "power" were interchangeable.

4

Most early societies have arranged people in groups for purposes of order and of honor, but few have calibrated that status with the nice precision that distinguished Tokugawa Japan. In the latter half of the nineteenth century that precision was galling to young men who had escaped it. Tokutomi Iichirō (usually known by the pen name Sohō), in a best-seller entitled *Youth of the New Japan,* argued that Japanese had lived in compartments:

> Who was the actual authority or ruler of feudal society? Discerning and clear-minded individuals would certainly say the ruler of society was not the Emperor, the nobles, the warriors, peasants, or merchants. Authority lay somewhere else. The ruler of society, the repository of authority, was *custom, usage,* and *tradition.*[1]

The distinction between *fudai* and *tozama* feudal lords that was described in Chapter 2 suggests something of what Tokutomi meant, but it did little more than scratch the surface of what is perhaps the most interesting aspect of Tokugawa Japan—the *mibunsei,* or system of status. Since early modern times Western society has known an increasing degree of social mobility, and the United States has probably carried this to its farthest point. Imperial China assigned special privilege and status to the scholarly and educated, but it combined this with the myth of social mobility in which the farmer's son could, by demonstrating his learning in the civil service examinations, rise to high estate.

Japan, however, began with the myth of a divine emperor whose authority derived from his relationship to the sun. No higher appeal could be imagined. Buddhism diluted this by denying its substantive reality, but in practice many of the highest places in the Buddhist hierarchy came to be restricted to men of high status. Confucianism in turn added criteria of performance, morality, and ability, but these were added to, and seldom substituted for, considerations of birth.

Some scholars have pointed out that Tokugawa compartments of status could in a sense be considered protection for people who had until then known the harshness of capricious injustice and casual brutality of earlier days.[2] In the nineteenth century some romantics were prepared to go considerably farther by suggesting that Japan's society of fixed status produced a desirable stability in human relationships. That, at any rate, is the way Lafcadio Hearn appraised the system:

> Conditions tended toward general happiness as well as toward general prosperity. There was not, in those years, any struggle for existence—not at least in our modern meaning of the phrase. The requirements of life were easily satisfied; every man had a master to provide for him or to protect him; competition was repressed or discouraged; there was no need for supreme effort of any sort—no need for the straining of any faculty. Moreover, there was little or nothing to strive after: for the vast majority of the people there were no prizes to win. Ranks and incomes were fixed; occupations were hereditary; and the desire to accumulate wealth must have been checked or numbed by those regulations which limited the rich man's right to use his money as he might please. Even a great lord—even the Shōgun himself—could not do as he pleased . . . Every man's pleasures were more or less regulated by his place in society, and to pass from a lower into a higher rank was no easy matter.[3]

There is some common ground here on major points, except that Tokutomi, who remembered what things had been like, was restless in his compartment, while Hearn, who did not, was more complaisant about the thought of a life spent "at the length of one's chains." But both spoke in hyperbole, and the system needs to be investigated more closely.

The principal status divisions of the period were codified in the occupational distinctions—samurai, farmer, artisan, merchant (*shi-nō-kō-shō*)—that are still rooted in textbook generalizations about premodern Japanese society. Before taking them up, however, it is well to consider those who were above these categories.

1. The Imperial Court

There were thirteen sovereigns during the period between 1586 and 1866. Two were women; the restriction of the line to males did not come until the codification of the imperial household succession rules on European lines in the nineteenth century. During the years of Tokugawa peace the income and amenities of life at court improved greatly from what they had been during the uncertain days of the warring states period. But they remained fixed at a modest level; it will be recalled that the total income land set aside for court and nobility was less than 150,000 *koku*.

As in earlier times many sovereigns abdicated relatively early, and as a result the income available to the court often had to support a former emperor with his own establishment. There were also collateral families to maintain. A standard device for the support of excess males was their placement as abbots and priests for court-related *(monzeki)* temples, of which there were sixteen. Palace daughters were often sent as brides for the most important feudal lords; others could be placed as nuns. The emperor was the responsibility of the shogunal deputy in Kyoto, the *shōshidai;* his permission was required for any visits the sovereign might plan, even to the imperial gardens near his residence in Kyoto. This important office was at first entrusted to the head of the Itakura family, one of Ieyasu's most trusted vassals. The court itself retained the administrative hierarchy of an earlier day. Communication with the shogunal representative was entrusted to a noble with the title *buke densō*. Each "government" thus kept the other at arm's length and little was left to chance. Appointments to all court posts, from regent, the title Hideyoshi had claimed for himself, on down were cleared with the bakufu representative. But it would probably be wrong to imagine a court seething with indignation and frustration over domination by warriors in Edo. In a Kyoto setting where office, lineage, and function had atrophied for centuries, structured warrior control was merely one additional fetter that was added to the endless restraints accumulated by precedent over the years.

The training of members of the imperial family bred habits of docility and rigidity, and any who became restless under this regimen could be expected to seek early exit from formal responsibilities through abdication. Even that, however, required careful preparation, negotiation, and approval from Edo.

At court, life was centered around some 180 ceremonies that were scheduled with mathematical precision on the calendar. These ranged from poetry festivals to ritual invocation of favor from the deities of the Shinto and Buddhist pantheons. Ieyasu's injunctions to the court and nobility, prepared with great care after an exhaustive study of precedents, directed that they specialize in the world of culture. The court became and remained the most authoritative source of precedent and rigor for the entire range of Japanese culture, from poetry to flower arrangement and incense burning.

Politically powerless though he was, the emperor nevertheless symbolized tradition and legitimacy; as Herschel Webb has phrased it, he was the center of a group whose collective power far exceeded that of any member.[4] Bakufu and court honored each other. By the end of the seventeenth century, ceremonies that had gone into eclipse could be funded and staged again through bakufu generosity and courtesy. The enthronement ceremony, the Daijōsai, was restored to the place of honor it had once known, and ceremonies that had not been held since medieval times were restored to the court calendar. As scholarship flourished and customs and texts of antiquity received their due, the bakufu, especially under the shogunate of Tsunayoshi, did its best to identify and honor tombs of former emperors; sixty-six of seventy-eight tombs were researched and maintained in this manner.

In turn the court's honors were important to the bakufu. Each shogun was appointed by the emperor. Court approval was required for the designation of Ieyasu's tomb at Nikkō as a major shrine. Each shogun was designated "Chief Abbot of the Junna and Shogaku Monasteries" and "Captain in the Right Division, Imperial Palace Guard"; he was also named head of the military houses *(buke no tōryō)*, and named Minister of the Right in the nonfunctioning court bureaucracy.

The honors the court could confer on military houses were eagerly sought by the daimyo, and the bakufu controlled and monitored this carefully. An elaborate calculus was worked out for eligibility for the special ranks (fourth and above) in the nine-step designations of rank that had been introduced from China centuries before, for these designations were the basis of precedence for seating in the audiences held at the shogun's castle in Edo. Tokugawa branch houses naturally fared better than other daimyo in such allocations.[5]

Court titles appropriate to position were also parceled out to bakufu functionaries. These too harked back to the age of court governance, and usually brought designation as "ruler" or "governor" or "general" of some geographic area. However distant or irrelevant such a title might be to the official's job or actual location, those so designated would use, and would be referred to, by that designation from then on.

The court also designated era names *(nengō)* by which the calendar years were numbered and known. Era appellations (like "Genroku," 1688–1704) were selected by scholars and astrologers who searched for auspicious two-character phrases in the Chinese classics. The eras so designated were never more than twenty and frequently as short as four or five years long. The *nengō* were considered to have important consequences for fortune and success, and usually required extensive negotiation with the bakufu.

Despite its political powerlessness the imperial court remained and increased in importance as a source of legitimacy and honor throughout Japanese society. The bakufu did its best to isolate the court from contact with the military houses and tried to rationalize and control its significance for commoners and shrines, but there is no question that a rather shamanistic awe continued to surround it. Nor were court titles restricted to the military elite. Honorary titles of lesser distinction (for example, "Secretary in the Provincial Government of . . .") were also issued to honor outstanding commoner craftsmen, or artists who had attracted the notice of the court. Once so designated, the honored families tended to continue to use such titles. When the bakufu tried, in 1707, to put some order into this system by mandating that these titles be registered and thereafter issued for one generation only, its survey turned up 521 such for the city of Edo alone.[6] The imperial court, by virtue of its special relationship to the Sun Goddess and the great shrine at Ise, also conferred designations of rank on (Shinto) shrines all over the country.

Warrior statesmen sometimes disparaged court nobles as "long sleeves" (*nagasode*) to indicate that they were impractical, inexperienced in the real world, jealous, and petty, and no doubt they often were. But their status and prestige made daughters of court nobles ideal marriage partners. This, too, was regulated by the bakufu, for the Code for the Military Houses warned against contracting marriage privately. Nevertheless over time major daimyo houses developed marriage ties with major aristocratic families. The Shimazu of Satsuma, for instance, and the Konoe often intermarried, as did the Yamauchi of Tosa with the Sanjō, and a number of others. This was no less true at the very highest level. The marriage tie which Hidetada, the second shogun, formed with the court by sending a granddaughter as bride for an emperor was followed in each generation thereafter as wives and consorts were selected from the imperial line or high court nobility. Tokugawa collateral houses also followed this example. As a result by late Tokugawa times, as Bob Wakabyashi points out, a genuine feeling of kinship formed among the members of Japan's highest class.[7] In the 1860s the marriage of an imperial princess to an Edo shogun became highly controversial, as we shall see below in connection with the Meiji Restoration.

References to "the court" usually refer to the Kyoto nobility as well as to the imperial families, and the court nobles, or *kuge*, formed a separate and uniquely insular society. There were 137 noble families at Kyoto. They too were arranged in a strict pattern of hierarchy. *Kuge* families sprang from the cluster of aristocratic houses that began to assume their historic place from the time of Fujiwara no Kamatari (614–669). It was he who masterminded the Taika Reform of 645 that installed the emperor as a Chinese-style monarch surrounded by the panoply of a bureaucratic system. From him descended the numerous branches of the great clan that dominated court and national affairs until the assumption of political power by the military in the eleventh century.

The Kyoto nobility were headed by five families, designated as *sekke,* that constituted the principal branches of the Fujiwara. One of the greatest of these was the Konoe. Each *sekke* house was allotted the income from lands producing 1,500–2,000 *koku.* From them came the principal appointees in the court bureaucracy, including the post of *kanpaku.* Below them were nine families (the *seika)* whose income stood at 300–700 *koku.* The villas (often modest enough) of the court nobles were clustered around the emperor's palace in Kyoto. Many of the court families supplemented their modest income by reigning over house specialties *(kagyō)* like incense, flowers, tea, poetry, music, and traditional dance. In these skills they functioned as the highest expression of *iemoto,* the hierarchical, hereditary, and house-centered pattern of secret tradition and transmission of skills that followed a prescribed, orthodox path.

Life in the rarified society of the Kyoto court nobility was stilted and desiccated. Although there was constant infusion of new blood through regular and furtive sexual unions, the principal lines were inevitably highly inbred. During the centuries of peace that the Tokugawa dominance made possible, however, the arts of war receded in importance and the needs and interests of a more civil society came to the fore. As this happened the Kyoto court gained steadily in respect and prestige. In the eighteenth century currents of intellectual change added additional currents of antiquarian study that helped to rekindle interest in the emperor as the center of what was truly "Japanese." The imperial institution and its traditions, long the center of cultural nationalism, then lay ready at hand to serve as the center of a new political nationalism as well.

2. The Ruling Samurai Class

It was the samurai caste that gave the Tokugawa years their distinctive character. Samurai served as ideal ethical types, theoretically committed to service and indifferent to personal danger and gain. They received special and separate treatment in criminal procedure. Everything set them aside from commoner culture. Two swords, one long and one short, were thrust through the waist sash but not attached or supported; a special hip-forward posture and stride were required to compensate for the swords. Their hair was done in a special topknot. Samurai wore distinctive, stiff-shouldered jackets *(kataginu)* and trousers *(hakama)* that resembled a divided skirt. Their swagger and swords set them off from ordinary people. A possibly authentic "Legacy of Ieyasu" authorized the use of the swords on a commoner unwise enough to be rude (*kirisute gomen,* license to cut down). Prestigious samurai houses could pride themselves on their ancestor's suit of armor, and manuals illustrating the proper procedure for donning it were increasingly necessary as the years passed.

These perquisites of status were to some degree balanced by the proprieties of death. The samurai was supposed to have a fatalistic preparedness to redeem his name and honor by the excruciatingly painful self-immolation of *seppuku* or, more vulgarly, "hara-kiri" to which his lord might sentence him. The memoirs of the nineteenth-century Christian pastor, Ebina Danjō, provide a graphic reminder of the way such standards survived into the 1860s.

> I was thirteen when drill in the English manner was introduced. Only fifteen-year-olds were supposed to be included and I should not have been, but I exerted myself and managed to be included. One day, at the peak of the gunfire, I somehow pulled the firing pin on my gun without having removed the priming rod. When the gun fired the rod went flying and wounded one of the officers. Not knowing what to do, I crept home towards evening. On the way I encountered father. He confronted me, saying "You have done a terrible thing. You will have to commit suicide! But wait until I get home before you carry it out. Meanwhile resign yourself to what you have to do." Having resigned myself, I waited, testing the sincerity of my warrior determination. When father returned home around midnight I was still waiting, but he cried out, "It's not bad enough for suicide."[8]

An early-seventeenth-century primer of samurai morality, *Hagakure,* written by Yamamoto Tsunetomo, a Saga samurai, is often cited as the classic exposition of the samurai value system. The book was revived as a classic during Japan's fevered prewar ultranationalist years, and it enjoyed a postwar afterglow in the writing and *seppuku* of the author Mishima Yukio in 1970. It is a curious work with at least three aspects that deserve comment. The first is its insistence on the total subordination of the samurai to his lord, a commitment that is almost religious in character. Second is its espousal of a fatalistic resignation, indeed a renunciation of life, as the samurai is enjoined to prepare himself for death. A third and more surprising feature of this work is its anticipation of the anonymity of a subsequent bureaucratic world of suspicion and backbiting by its warnings against confiding in others. The proper samurai, it suggests, keeps his mouth shut and concentrates on himself. This insistence on the observation of proper form and bearing does little to prepare one for the more colorful world of the Edo samurai. The author, however, was already lamenting that the standards he extolled were being lost in times of peace.

> Bushidō [the Way of the Warrior], I have found out, lies in dying.
>
> When confronted with two alternatives, life and death, one is to choose death without hesitation. There is nothing particularly difficult; one has only to be resolved and push forward.
>
> While some say "Death without gaining one's end is but a futile death," such a calculating way of thinking comes from conceited, citified bushidō. Pressed between two alternatives, one can hardly be sure of choosing the righteous of the two. To be sure, everybody prefers life to death; he tends to reason himself into staying alive somehow. But if he comes out alive without gaining his righteous end, he is a coward. Therein lies a crucial point to consider.
>
> Conversely, as long as one's choice is death, even if he dies without accomplishing his just aim, his death is free of disgrace, although others may term it as a vain or insane one. This is the essence of bushidō. If one, through being prepared for death every morning and evening, expects death any moment, bushidō will become his own, whereby he shall be able to serve the lord all his life through and through with not a blunder.[9]

It was in the Tokugawa years that the articulation of bushidō as a code of morality was perfected. Samurai moralists had to explain how it was that they, alone among their countrymen, performed no productive labor. Yamaga Sokō (1622–1685) asked, "How can it be that the samurai should have no [productive] occupation?" His answer was that "the business of the samurai consists in reflecting on his own station in life, in discharging loyal service to his master if he has one, in deepening his fidelity in associations with friends, and, with due consideration of his own position, in devoting himself to duty above all . . . The samurai dispenses with the business of the farmer, artisan, and merchant and confines himself to practicing this Way; should there be someone in the three classes of the common people who transgresses against these moral principles, the samurai summarily punishes him and thus upholds proper moral principles in the land."[10] In other words, the samurai was the only one who, by not having to "work," was free to concentrate on virtue and to embody it in society. This made for a stern ethic, and it is not surprising that not all samurai lived up to it.

Japan had received from Chinese classics the notion that in the well-ordered society classes were arranged in order of the nature of their service. Under the administrator-scholars came the agriculturalists, whose nurture of the five grains sustained society. Both they and the next group, artisans who made useful objects, ranked higher than merchants. Merchants not only failed to produce anything, but also risked contributing to materialism and selfishness by their role in the exchange of goods.

In Japan the "administrator-scholar" who led in importance to society now became the warrior-administrator, as the term and character "saburau," to serve, became "samurai" instead.[11] The samurai order was never given a fully legal basis, however, and it remained to some degree artificial and imprecise. Yet the idea of a hierarchy of specialization served as the accepted norm of social organization.[12] Acceptance of such an idea was spread throughout society by a number of media, particularly the theater. Popular culture, as will be seen, reinforced and diffused these attitudes throughout the Tokugawa years.

Warriors had been set aside as a social, and a closed, class by the decisions separating them from agriculturalists that Hideyoshi made in the 1580s and 1590s. Historians credit his edicts with trying to end the kind of social mobility that had made his own rise possible. The countryside was disarmed, and samurai, with a monopoly on violence, became full-time specialists in keeping the peace. Military overlords were warned against giving shelter to samurai from other areas that could destabilize society,[13] and samurai were gathered at their lords' headquarters. In the process families could divide. The first Tosa daimyo, Yamauchi Kazutoyo, was the younger brother of an Owari grandee who, staying in place on his acreage, continued to be considered head of the main branch of the family despite his surrender of warrior status, while his younger brother, who went off to Hideyoshi's wars, became head of a branch house.

Each daimyo army of course had a range of ranks from general to private, and each lord maintained duty rosters of his retainers. In our histories the higher ranks naturally receive much more attention than the lower, although foot soldiers were far more numerous. It is useful to examine one domain, that of Tosa, to see how the principal retainers were ranked and rewarded. As was true throughout Japan, samurai were divided between "upper" (jōshi) and "regular" (hirazamurai) ranks in this pattern:

11 *karō*, "house elders," granted lands with a tax base of 1,500–11,000 *koku*. Headed major military formations; frequently intermarried with daimyo family. In effect, the Tosa equivalent of the Tokugawa *fudai* daimyo.

11 *chūrō*, with tax base of 45–1,500 *koku*, "hands-on" administrators of the most important functions.

Tosa "regular" samurai included

> 800 *umamawari*, mounted guard with tax base of 100–700 *koku*, field-grade officers who furnished the bulk of the administrative personnel.
>
> *koshōgumi*, with lands producing 70–250 *koku*, not fixed in number, who staffed most magistracies.
>
> *rusuigumi*, also not fixed in number, with lands producing 50–200 *koku*, who staffed lesser offices.

Far below these were the

> *ashigaru*, foot soldiers, who served as labor battalions and foremen for construction and lumbering.

These *koku* figures reflect assessment and not samurai income, which might average half the total. Office normally brought an additional supplement.

Discussions of "samurai" usually focus on the upper and middle ranks, which produced the men who qualified for domain housing, had armor, swords, horses, and followers, and were eligible for office. Their claim to domain standing and income could count for "property." Farther down the line, men moved into and out of petty rank and burdensome duty with some frequency.

If so, how many Japanese should we count as samurai? The first careful attempt at a national tally came in the nineteenth century, when the Meiji government tried to calculate its burden in entitlement for former samurai. Its figure came to 408,823 households, with a total of 1,892,449 people when dependents were included.[14] This represents about 5 or 6 percent of the population of Japan, and constituted an extremely large privileged class. In prerevolutionary France, for instance, the clergy and nobility combined numbered 0.5 to 0.6 percent of the population. The French nobles lived on their own land, however, while the Japanese armies, which included hosts of privates and foot soldiers, were paid by their daimyo.[15]

In the Edo period the complexities between "upper" and "lower" were enormous. Sendai had 34 ranks, Yamaguchi had 59, and the Meiji educator Fukuzawa Yukichi, in his memoirs of the tiny Kyushu domain of Nakatsu, spoke of 100 ranks. He noted that sometimes men managed to cross the barriers that separated "upper" from "lower," but wrote that there had probably not been more than four or five such who succeeded in the entire 250-year period. In Nakatsu men of lower rank had to prostrate themselves before those of higher rank; even a casual encounter on the road would involve removal of footgear and prostration in the dust. "The lower samurai," Fukuzawa wrote, "were thus ill-versed in literature and other high forms of learning, and not unnaturally came to have the bearing and deportment of humble workmen," while their superiors, "their manners . . . naturally elegant and aristocratic . . . could be considered most cultured and refined gentlemen."[16] Comparable barriers of class within those of warrior status could be found in all parts of Japan. But movement into and out of the class at lower levels, where perquisites were few, were much more common. John W. Hall's analysis of the domain of Okayama concluded that there was a surprisingly high turnover through adoption and recruitment, and that the farther down in the hierarchy one went the more numerous the recent entrants. Of the 527 Okayama *kachi*, a petty officer rank, 354 joined after 1632.[17]

Samurai entered the Tokugawa period as fighting men, and within a few generations they found themselves charged with civil administration. As this developed the arts of peace and the requirements of education gradually came to the fore. In areas known for scholarship and daimyo patronage of learning there might consequently be somewhat more latitude for recognition of ability. In the Tokugawa domain of Mito, an area that prided itself from the seventeenth century on historical scholarship, Fujita Yūkoku (1774–1826), the son of an old clothes dealer, and his son Tōko became major political and intellectual influences through the patronage of a lord eager to surround himself with learned advisers.[18] But it was rare for ordinary commoners to have the opportunity to enter into substantial samurai ranks, and more rare still for it to be recognized.

In times of peace it was no less difficult for soldiers to demonstrate qualities that would justify advancement into higher ranks. In wartime valor and quick response could win reward, but after the Shimabara rebellion Japan's samurai knew nothing more threatening than a confrontation with large bodies of discontented commoners who had been deprived of their swords. In consequence the samurai class was like an army of occupation that stayed in place from generation to generation. Divisions of status and perquisites of rank are notoriously obvious in garrison life in time of peace. The proportion of samurai to commoners, and hence the intensity of military occupation, varied from area to area, and older, more peripheral domains like Satsuma had a much higher count of samurai than domains to which Tokugawa vassals were promoted in the early years of the shogunate, but within the samurai class precise gradations of rank and status were everywhere the rule.

Overall, the retention of jurisdiction over a parcel of counties, villages, and land best served to distinguish "upper" from "lower" samurai. Subinfeudation of this sort was more usual in *tozama* domains than it was along the Pacific coast heartland where Tokugawa *fudai* predominated. In most areas a pattern of administrative rationalization gradually led domains to substitute stipends for fiefs. The majority of samurai, and certainly all lower samurai, received their income from the domain warehouse in the form of bales of rice. This placed them at the mercy of rice dealers who could convert those bales into money for goods they could not produce themselves; the larger the castle town in which they found themselves, the more they needed to buy.

It is difficult to imagine the limitations of a life in which income was determined by the awards granted one's early-seventeenth-century ancestors. Kozo Yamamura's study of the personnel files of 4,956 Tokugawa bannermen—the *hatamoto*—for the entire period suggests how unlikely things were to improve for these "upper" samurai.[19] The bannermen were the center of the bakufu's military and administrative structure. Most were enfeoffed with small grants in the Kantō plain in the early years, "lords" over territory so minute that a village might find itself carved into two or even three administrative taxing areas.

Throughout the Tokugawa years 55 percent of those studied remained in the classification the founder of the house had received. Only 4 percent experienced a promotion of status and income. Slightly more than half (53 percent) of the group ever had an official post, and of that number 41 percent succeeded their parent in the identical job. Demotions were handed down for 464 men for personal profligacy: excessive drinking, flagrant immorality, and ruinous debt. Of those 23 were banished, 5 executed, and 8 were permitted to take their life "honorably" by *seppuku*. Forty family lines died out, presumably for lack of an heir, but in 1,124 cases house heads were permitted to adopt their successors. Through all this the income of most bannermen remained constant, but as the commoner society around them was gaining in affluence their real, and certainly their psychic, income declined. As Yamamura sums it up, their "modal income was sufficient to classify them as poor by almost any standards applying to a ruling class."

The chief hope for improvement within any generation would be appointment to a post in which one might at least feel useful, and be able to improve the conditions of life through the additional office salary provided or the peculation that would be possible. A number of diaries indicate how difficult it was to win appointment to a post to which one's ancestor's precedence had not entitled one. One diary of an Owari samurai reveals a frantic and frustrating search for a post that is so disheartening that he makes a spectacle of himself by dashing up to the daimyo's procession in a futile effort to present him with an anguished petition.[20] By and large rigidification of rank became worse as Tokugawa rule progressed. Katsu Kokichi, an early-nineteenth-century *hatamoto*, wrote disconsolately, "Every morning I put on my *kataginu* and *hakama* and made the rounds of the powers that be. I went to the home of Commissioner Ōkubo, Kōzuke no suke [an honorific court title] in Akasasaki Kuichigaisoto and begged him to recommend me for a post. I even submitted a list of the misdeeds I had committed, adding a request that I be considered, now that I had repented . . . but not once was I given a post."[21] It is not surprising that for many (and certainly for Katsu Kokichi, as his diary shows) the frustration of an empty life found an outlet in antisocial behavior. In Katsu's case he became so consistently erratic that his adoptive family, despairing of his reform and afraid that he would commit some deed that would bring dishonor to them all, had a wooden cage installed for him inside their house.

In essence, then, the maintenance of so large a samurai class in unproductive idleness put a premium on underemployment. At higher levels this worked against excessive accumulation of personal power; at lower levels it spread the work and maintained dependency. At the very highest levels of the bakufu bureaucracy in which most posts had multiple appointments, men served on a system of monthly rotation. At middle and lower levels the expectations of status and society made for a lavish use of retainers as personal servants. In Tokugawa prints the samurai is never shown carrying anything, even his umbrella; that is the function of someone lower in status. And since those persons too were the concern of a regime determined to maintain its standing forces in peacetime at as low a cost as possible, bakufu and domain legislation prescribed such service as appropriate. An increase in stipend, whether reward or emolument for office, was usually expressed in terms of "rations for two (or more) men." In 1712 the bakufu used *koku* income as a basis for prescribing the minimum number of attendants that should be maintained at the daimyo residences in Edo. *Hatamoto*, too, were ordered to maintain a fixed complement of retainers. In theory the rationale for this was the possible needs of military service, but since the land was at peace most such individuals functioned as little more than domestic servants.[22]

Social order also made it desirable to keep up appearances appropriate to status. The retainer should not go into debt with merchant lenders, but it was also improper for him to scrimp in order to fatten his personal account. His security lay with his superior's benevolence. Bakufu directives enjoined all retainers to "reflect upon your station and practice frugality so that you will not do things which smack of extravagance." But, as the *Buke shohatto* of 1710 pointed out, "In clothing and houses, provisions for banquets, and articles of gifts, some are extravagant and others are too frugal. Both of these are at variance with the rules of propriety." Ieyasu himself was reported to have warned that "there are also people who misunderstand frugality and believe that they are being frugal even when they carry it to the point of not doing what they should do, and when they fail thus in their obligations, they are greatly in error."[23]

For lower ranks this balance was not easy to maintain. By the eighteenth century many samurai came to the conclusion that it was less expensive for them to employ commoners to keep up appearances, even as bearers and attendants at official audiences. Consequently the lower level of "samurai" society faded off into that of the nonsamurai with no neat or clear distinctions. In Edo administration the magistrate had under him assistant magistrates, or *yoriki,* who in turn were served by many more *dōshin,* or "helpers," who wore only one sword and wore no formal *hakama;* they in turn had assistants who were nonsamurai altogether. Writers concerned with military preparedness and samurai discipline frequently complained of the trend to hire *dōshin* for routine guard duty at barricades and bridges.

In many large castle towns, and particularly in Edo, commercialization and materialism thus came to water down the stern ethic of the much-quoted warrior moralists. In smaller castle towns and in poorer areas, however, samurai often faced a real struggle for existence on their income. This could particularly be the case if the local daimyo was a martinet determined to "reform" his local economy to restore military preparedness. In such cases the real burden was borne by the samurai wife, who had to make a slender income stretch to cover basic needs. It was up to her to extend herself in the weaving, sewing, and cleaning of clothes. It was also she who had to take responsibility for the education of her children. Her primary duty was to continue her husband's line, and a barren wife was likely to be sent home.

No doubt economic conditions worsened over time, but Yamakawa Kikue's recollections of her nineteenth-century childhood as the daughter of an "upper" samurai family in the Tokugawa domain of Mito provides a startling picture of genteel poverty and hardship. Her childhood came during a period of particularly severe "reform" under a daimyo (Tokugawa Nariaki, 1800–1860) who was determined to prepare his domain for the crisis he saw coming with the West. Of the thousand-odd Mito samurai, she writes, about seven hundred had stipends of less than 100 *koku.* They received less than half that amount in income, however, and so the domain permitted those at that level and below to supplement their income, usually by having their wives do weaving on the side. In some cases men, too, might make umbrellas or weave baskets for additional change, but the real burden fell on the women. The highest-ranking retainer, who had the hereditary designation of Keeper of the

Castle, enjoyed an income of 5,000 *koku* and kept as many as thirty retainers. Most samurai, however, did their best to economize by keeping fewer and fewer retainers and hiring peasant second and third sons as part-time retainers instead. In Yamakawa's youth the han reform program was so stringent that rules prohibited even samurai girls from developing skill in the traditional arts of music, tea ceremony, and flower arrangement. They went to school (where students were grouped according to their fathers' incomes) for basic literacy in Japanese syllabary, but once that was achieved their time went to household arts and weaving. Sumptuary regulations forbade dressing in silk, and the han developed fields of cotton; this kept the samurai women busy at their spinning wheels. Family clothes were turned and resewn, repaired and reused constantly. Frugality extended to the care of the body and hair; professional hairdressers existed, but they were not allowed to work on samurai wives. "Women normally washed their hair no more than twice a year, in midsummer and at year's end, and men, too, washed their hair only very rarely. In the early Tokugawa period life in Mito was very stark and primitive, and until the 1690s even the daimyo, it appears, did not use hair oil."[24] Cushions *(zabuton)* were never used in Yamakawa's family, even for meals and "banquets" of the humble foods available; the only one in the house was reserved for the house head's desk. Children reluctant to eat their food were lectured with reminders that a samurai could never know when duty would call him to battle and when he would need all possible strength.

In other words, two centuries after the fighting had stopped in Japan the military ethic and language of the early seventeenth century was being invoked to prepare young retainers for future crises. Pitiful reminders of a heroic past were adapted to a mundane present. One Yamakawa relative, a family whose income had slowly dropped from 500 *koku* to 200 *koku,* and whose ancestor had once served as Captain of the Vanguard, was now charged with duty as fireman. When a fire broke out he would don his special jacket with spark protection, rally his platoon of twenty foot soldiers, and sally forth to meet the "enemy." During his absence the members of the house were no less busy warming the sake and preparing the food with which to welcome the firefighters upon their return. Yamakawa writes that by the nineteenth century the Mito retainer houses like the one in which she grew up had assumed a dark, neglected, and desolate character. Samurai families could no longer afford to keep their properties up. The spacious grounds were covered with weeds, and the rush-covered floor mats *(tatami)* were bare, soiled, and worn. It is clear that by her time life for the "upper" samurai of a domain came far short of what might be posited for a "ruling class." These mid- and late Tokugawa realities are in particularly striking contrast to the sumptuary legislation with which busy Edo bureaucrats tried to curb excessive spending and bring appearance into conformity with status.

3. Village Life

Farmers ranked second, after samurai, in the traditional fourfold division of honor and function. The food they produced made everything else possible. In the Tokugawa years some 85 percent of all Japanese were agriculturalists, and their productivity, welfare, and discontent mirrored the success or shortcomings of government.

Climate, geography, and tradition differed a good deal from one part of Japan to the other, but a concern with status makes it possible to blur some of these differences. There were approximately 63,000 villages in Japan in Tokugawa times. The Tokugawa village was to some degree the product of the great surveys which the unifiers, especially Hideyoshi, undertook during the Sengoku period. Although the effective date of that stabilization differed from one part of Japan to the other,[25] most accounts cite the Hideyoshi survey as the central point of departure. It was these surveys that broke up, or finalized the break up of, the medieval pattern of administration privatization of large tracts *(shōen)* usually referred to as "estates." The late-sixteenth-century surveys made it possible to put an end to overlapping rights. They removed warrior-farmers from the picture and substituted for them full-time warriors or agriculturalists. They were carried out with a nationwide, largely standard measure of land. The focus of the surveys was on the village and not on individual agriculturalists, but in each village fields were identified with their tillers. Those so named were presumed responsible for the village's *nengu,* or produce tax. The surveys extended to residential and upland plots as well as paddy rice fields, but all assessments were calculated in rice equivalents by *koku* yield.

Premodern village life was a community enterprise. It required the cooperation of the group to level land for paddies that could be flooded, to channel the water course and to allocate it during the growing season. Rice planting was also a communal exercise. Particularly favorable locations were set aside as seedbeds, and the seedlings were planted in villagewide cooperative patterns that were followed by festivals to celebrate the work and invoke shrine blessings for its success. Cooperation was also required to raise the roof for new buildings and repair the old. Access to compost taken from the common lands or uplands was overseen by cooperative measures as well.

Life in isolation thus became virtually impossible for farming families. Deviance from village norms could be punished by exclusion *(mura hachibu),* and the problems this raised for individuals were so severe that it was usual for them to submit a petition for reinstatement to favor. Exclusion from group activities was a powerful sanction throughout rural society. In most areas young men were organized in Young Men's Associations (and in some areas young women in Young Women's Associations, *musume gumi*) that disciplined their members by ostracism. Readmission to society would usually involve assurances of contrition, as shown in this apology for getting into a drunken brawl after a wedding:

Apology

My two younger brothers and I, from the beginning unruly, have in the past committed excesses in the eyes of all of you. So on this year of the Tiger second month, 26th day, at my wedding, we three brothers, when a slight disturbance occurred as Asakichi came to observe, chased him into the fields and beat him with our farmers' tools. Not only that, but we dragged him into the house, and with our parents we slandered and bad-mouthed him and also beat him up. For these reasons, the Young Men's Association expelled us; and since we were charged with being evil persons, it has touched us deeply. Since being expelled from the association we have had no one to consult with, and we finally asked a mediator to implore you for reconciliation. The collective consultations were difficult for you because of all this, but thanks to your charity the matter has kindly been settled, and we are most grateful.

It has been decided that we will never hold any offices in the Association. At the *sake* celebration we will of course never occupy honored seats, and we will be treated as junior members. At all points we will accept advice without talking back, and we pledge to be quiet and change our behavior. If by any chance we should have a change of heart and fail to live up to this, then you may hand down any penalty you wish. Furthermore, as we have now reformed, and presented this apology, we do not harbor the slightest ill will or resentment. Anyōji Village, Kurita County, Ōmi province, 1866.[26]

The village produced more than rice. Upland, dry fields were used for coarser grains, sweet potatoes, soy beans, and hemp. Local conditions might permit the production of more unusual items like cotton, indigo, sugar cane, and salt in coastal beds. As time went on and urban markets developed "luxury" crops like tobacco (which was, with potatoes, a sixteenth-century import) were added to the list. Initially domain authorities wanted full concentration on food crops, but the commercial possibilities of such yields made them attractive for merchant groups that developed. By the eighteenth century domain merchants often took the lead in urging the advantages of producing, rather than importing (from other domains), such commodities, and helped to lessen and finally remove the distaste the samurai directors of han finance had for such production.[27]

The core of the village social structure in the early Tokugawa period was to be found in the farmers identified with fields in the early surveys. These *honbyakushō*, "principal," as opposed to ordinary, farmers *(hyakushō)* were in many cases derived from the privileged, half-samurai caste of early Sengoku days; they might have exclusive rights to forest land, direct local water projects, and maintain large establishments. At no time did villagers constitute an undifferentiated group. Registers show astonishing variations in holdings that range from, as Thomas Smith has put it, mere garden plots to estates of 100 and more *koku*.[28] Those in the upper categories clearly had superior access to education and to favor from administrators, and they usually chose their spouses from comparable families. Only they possessed full "membership" or shares *(kabu)* in the village, and as village leaders it was up to them to determine the allocation of the tax burden which the village collectively owed its lord. They alone participated in the village assembly. In time their fields would be known as *honden*, the original *(hon)* paddies recorded in the early surveys.

Village leaders might be hereditary, appointed by samurai officials, or elected from leading village families. The names of the office they held varied from place to place, but their function was everywhere the same; to mediate between the village *hyakushō* and the samurai district official whose headquarters were in the nearest town of any size. The village head's responsibility was a heavy one, for he stood between the village and the local "state." He was held responsible by either side if things went wrong. In early Tokugawa years options were relatively scarce, and it was up to him to remonstrate with the authorities if duty became too burdensome. Peace and relative prosperity brought gradual change, however, and by the middle and later parts of the period villagers were to be found asserting the desire for greater say in the selection of their leaders and their own affairs.[29]

Below the *honbyakushō* were the landless, many of them tenants and many more serving as part of the establishment of the social leaders. Tenantry in the Japanese countryside was not something that developed with capitalism, but it had its origins in the inequality of premodern times. The nature of the Japanese countryside in most areas meant that holdings took the form of small paddies and fields scattered through a valley instead of single contiguous units, and for most households this meant a more desirable arrangement than a single contiguous unit, since it provided a measure of security against weather, pestilence, and drought. Even when the lay of the land did not dictate such an arrangement, however, tradition encouraged it. In many areas flood plains were redivided periodically in a process reminiscent of the allocations system specified in the codes of earlier days. Divided holdings, however, required frequent, indeed almost constant, movement between the plots. If they were sizable it became more efficient and profitable to sublet activities to men whose names were not listed with the owners of land in the early registers. The tenant, however, shared few of the public rights and duties of his landlord, and he lived under severe economic dependence. His plot was usually too small to give him the opportunity of accumulating anything, and the house in which he lived, and the tools he used, were probably not his own. Paternalism, vital for his life, was expressed in language, deportment, and deference summed up in his status as a *mizunomi*, or "water drinking," farmer. The landlord was his "parent person," *oya-kata*, and he the landlord's *kokata* or child.[30]

Rural families were organized in five-household units, the *goningumi*, under a system of communal responsibility. Punishment could be inflicted on the unit for the misdeeds of any of its members, and a tax shortfall from one could be imposed on those who remained. The unit of rural life was the family, or house, and not the individual. In the seventeenth century stern rules forbade movement in or out of the village, and every individual could have been expected to have an unspoken but sure knowledge of the relative standing of households, their history and record in that locality, and their resources.[31]

Our understanding of the nature of status and well-being in the Japanese countryside has benefited tremendously from historical research carried on in the last fifty years. Prior to World War II most historians concentrated their attention on the history of Japan's samurai rulers. From that perspective the countryside was seen through the lens of hortatory and minatory edicts that came down from the castle towns. Alarming tales of oppression and victimization of the countryside created the impression of early modern agriculturalists as severely oppressed, a largely undifferentiated and faceless body of peasants stooped to their labor. Official documents left little doubt of the purpose with which the authorities viewed the peasants; they should be squeezed like seeds, one statement had it, in order to extract as much as possible from them. Another held that farmers should be worked so that they would neither live (to consume) nor die (and stop producing). Major edicts, especially those of the seventeenth century, bear this out. A Tosa document of 1612 indicates the fear of absconding peasants by warning that "the main thing is to keep [peasants] from leaving the province"; harboring a runaway "probably deserves the death penalty, but if we become too severe the result would only be to make them flee all the way to the next province." Again,

"It is a very serious offense to desert to another province. Those who assist in the getaway are equally guilty. Both ears and nose must be cut off." However, "If a person is a fugitive, his offense is less serious if he hides within the borders of this realm. But fleeing to another province must be absolutely forbidden."[32] Clearly the focus here was on retention of productive labor. The classic statement was probably the bakufu's ordinance of 1649, a schoolmasterish document of thirty-two articles that spoke of neat planting, careful weeding, early rising, and evening work "to be done with great care," and warned farmers not to buy tea or sake. "However good-looking a wife may be," it went on, "if she neglects her household duties by drinking tea or sightseeing or rambling on the hillsides, she must be divorced." Peasants should eat millet and other coarse foods instead of rice, they should wear only cotton or hemp and never silk, and "they should not smoke tobacco. It is harmful to health, it takes up time, and costs money. It also creates a risk of fire."[33]

These are gloomy indications of a life of consistent oppression and hardship, and they suggest that the Tokugawa village resembled a well-regulated concentration camp. It is however wise to regard these injunctions as the products of samurai officials who had a very low estimate of farmer diligence and intelligence, and at some variance from the life that farmers actually lived. The officials were anxious to keep peasants from profiting from their labor. Their sumptuary laws made clear that farmers should not wear cotton rain capes or use umbrellas, which were reserved for village headmen. Leather-soled sandals were prohibited, and the use of hair combs made of tortoise shell could bring punishment of thirty days' confinement. In some areas farmers were forbidden to ride a horse or ox within a mile or two of the castle town. Farmers were ordered to uncover their heads and bow when samurai passed. Still other laws spelled out the limits of consumption permitted for wedding and feast days, specified proper limits for housing, and ruled out sliding door panels and *tatami* floor mats. Clearly the authorities were on the lookout for excessive consumption, and determined to keep the rural surplus for their own use.[34]

After World War II Japanese specialists submerged themselves in the minutiae of village life and economy anew. From their work emerged a much more interesting village, one with complex strata of status and privilege, and in many ways a microcosm of the larger national hierarchy of status. As a leading student of this literature summed it up, "The peasants were not the homogeneous class depicted by the Confucianists. Peasant society itself was a pyramid of wealth and power and legal rights that rose from the tenant and *genin* [servants] at the bottom through small and middling landholders to what might be called a class of wealthy peasants at the top."[35]

In recent years interpretations have shifted in emphasis once more. The discussion now is on the change from the severe picture presented by seventeenth-century administrators who were trying to get things under control to the varied forms of growth in eighteenth-century Japan. For one thing, the degree of village autonomy meant that while samurai might fulminate they did not necessarily dominate. Most of them lived in castle towns, and in some domains they were actually forbidden from entering the countryside, where they might disrupt things. Consequently the likelihood and frequency of a farmer's encountering a samurai before whom he had standing orders to prostrate himself were not very great. Furthermore the countryside became more productive and more of that product, as we shall see, stayed in the countryside. Land reclamation, improved agricultural technology for seeds, irrigation, and fertilizer increased yields and opened new opportunities for private accumulation. Commercialization brought with it shifting fortunes; large family holdings tended to break up as branch households made their way from total dependency to partial and then virtual independence. Samurai administrators in the towns, it is clear, failed to extract much of the new agricultural surplus; tax rates seem to have remained largely unchanged, probably kept there by the certainty of peasant protest.[36] As more of that surplus remained in the countryside, cash crops for Japan's growing cities made possible, and required, artisan specialization and periodic markets in the countryside. A new type of rural elite discovered the advantages of investment in agricultural improvement, and began to chafe under the arbitrary pattern of village governance that relied on old families exclusively. Books on agronomy appeared, and began to circulate in hundreds of copies for the growing number of literate farmers. As farmers got to keep more of what they grew, they worked harder to produce even more. In the words of the economic historian Hayami Akira, an "industrious revolution" was a rural equivalent of the West's "industrial revolution."[37] Texts began to speak of *hyakushō kabu*, or "farmer shares," that indicated the possibility and practice of sale of land and movement into the privileges of village assembly, water allocation, and governance that went with that designation.[38] The term *kabu* is one we shall encounter again, and its prevalence suggests a congruence of terminology and of status divisions.

4. Townsmen (*chōnin*)

The third and fourth ranks of the social order, artisans and merchants, were residents of cities and towns, and may be considered together. Bakufu and domain legislation referred to them undiscriminatingly as "townsmen," or *chōnin*. Yet there were important distinctions to be drawn. In theory the artisans contributed to society by providing it with its needs for housing and goods, but merchants and tradesmen concentrated on exchange and profited from things they had not themselves produced. Orthodox social theory therefore put them last. In a zero-sum view of society anything that noncontributing merchants accumulated came to them at the expense of other, more productive groups; consequently they were portrayed as parasitical, self-interested people.

Artisans and merchants had grown enormously in number and importance during the Sengoku years. The burgeoning needs of the unifiers were provided by their agents in the port city of Sakai (today a suburb of Osaka), Kyoto, Nagoya, and Nagasaki. Sakai was particularly important as a center of trade and manufacture. Its wealthy merchant princes were leaders in culture and in the tea ceremony. Sen no Rikyū, who served as chief tea master to both Nobunaga and Hideyoshi (and whose suicide was mentioned in Chapter 1), was a figure who combined considerable personal wealth with a cult of simplicity and modesty that he codified in the tea ceremony of his day. Contemporary paintings of Sakai show its waterways lined with shops and eating places catering to a lively urban culture. As Ieyasu's daimyo developed their own castle town culture in the early Tokugawa decades, many prevailed upon merchants from the urban centers of the Kyoto-Sakai area to accompany them to their domains in hopes of re-creating on a smaller and provincial scale some of the splendor of the Kinai metropolis. The Yamauchi daimyo of Tosa, for instance, persuaded a merchant house named Harima to come to Kōchi. Frequently such merchants, functioning in something of a quartermaster role, were able to cross the status line and enter the samurai class. Great Sakai and Osaka merchants like the Suminokura also played important roles in the international trade that was possible until the bakufu put an end to overseas voyages.

City life in the early decades of the seventeenth century presented a colorful picture of ferment and consolidation as bakufu and daimyo administrators struggled to put things to rights. The large number of daimyo transfers and demotions displaced many vassals and created large numbers of ex-samurai *rōnin* who were desperate for employment. Daimyo who were rewarded with larger territories might take some of them on, but many more had to live by their wits and swords. Their distress came to a head in a plot that was unmasked in 1651. Yui Shōsetsu, a teacher of martial arts, organized a number of *rōnin* with the intent of detonating the bakufu arsenal in Edo and starting massive fires in the city. A subsidiary plan was to burn Ieyasu's former retirement town of Sunpu. The plot was discovered, apparently through the boastfulness of Yui's chief lieutenant Marubashi Chūya, and ended with the execution of thirty-four plotters and their relatives. Yui, getting wind of the crackdown, committed suicide before his arrest and left a note explaining that it had been his purpose to bring the hardships of dismissed samurai to the authorities' attention. Perhaps because of a subsequent decline in the rate of confiscation of daimyo domains—and the departure of the Sengoku generation of fighters—*rōnin* problems thereafter diminished in importance.

For some years the towns were plagued by large numbers of raffish youths who, perhaps in anger or despair that there were no longer military and social prizes to win, affected a contempt for ordinary social and personal morals. Loud-mouthed braggarts sporting unusually long swords, long haired and outrageously dressed, they swaggered along the streets of Kyoto as well as other cities and dared others to challenge them. They became known as *kabu-kimono* from the verb "kabuku"—to lean—and prided themselves on their nonconformity. This was a passing phenomenon, but its prevalence posed a major problem for urban authorities and helps explain the flood of stern and humorless injunctions to morality and order of the first half century of Tokugawa rule.[39] Although they were a social problem, in a perverse sense the *kabu-kimono* also laid claim to a heritage of bravado that later became institutionalized in the kabuki theater. This form had its origins in Kyoto in early Tokugawa years, and was associated with an informal troupe of women whose dances delighted commoners and scandalized the respectable. In later years some of the most popular theatrical pieces served to commemorate this spirit of resistance and gave theatergoers the vicarious thrill of watching daring supermen who supposedly stood for justice and challenged authorities. This was also true of the *rōnin* plot, which was immortalized in seventeenth- and eighteenth-century plays.

The bakufu's desire to control such phenomena coincided with its persecution of the *kirishitan* movement and relates to the series of registration measures that it developed. From an early point separate surveys of households and draft animals had been used as a basis for the conscription of corvée labor. As noted earlier, the bakufu in 1614 instituted in its own territory measures that were extended to the whole country a half century later, to combine this with registration at Buddhist temples. In the countryside the surveys were combined in a tally that included the name of the household head, household members, ages and relationships, household *kokudaka,* and draft animals. Thus the entire population came to be recorded in temple registers. These were submitted for the entire village or other administrative unit. This network of interconnected controls worked for the classification of all inhabitants.

The same meticulous concern for categorization extended to craft specialization. That there were many such can be seen from a seventeenth-century illustrated book by the Kyoto artist Kaihō Yūsetsu (1598–1677), which depicts 120 specialists.[40] Their work ranged from clothing, food, housing, and tools to entertainment, gambling, religion, and magic. In an age when access to the occult seemed believable soothsayers and fortune tellers were as legitimate as clothiers and doctors. In some areas documents indicate a highly structured productive system in which carpenters, for instance, were required to work for the lord twenty-four days a year, in return for which their status as craftsmen was formally recognized, with a subsistence allotment of rice and housing spelled out.

It is not surprising that in the burst of building that accompanied the development of the shogunal cities and daimyo castle towns artisans were regarded as important elements of domain wealth. The modern term for carpenter *(daiku)* has its origins in reference to what might better be called contractors. Ieyasu attracted the services of Nagai Masakiyo, "Lord [*kami*] of Yamato," whose predecessor had worked at the Hōryūji (temple) before Hideyoshi took him on to construct the Hokōji in Kyoto, and he kept him busy with castles at Fushimi, the Kyoto Nijō, the Chiyoda Castle at Edo, and his retirement castle at Sumpu in Shizuoka. Nagai was given responsibility for the organization of carpenters in a number of provinces, and with so many official commissions he came to bear the title of *daiku no tōryō,* "head of the builders," in evocation of the shogun's title as head of the military houses.[41] Thus the hierarchy that characterized other branches of Japanese society was reproduced, at least in the higher circles, in crafts and professions. In castle towns craftsmen were initially housed together in specialty sections or *machi.* In the countryside carpenters and toolmakers were also important, but the village registers persisted in labeling them as *hyakushō,* in deference to the strictures against mixing groups and classes.

Merchant activities were too important to the authorities to be left to chance. In late Sengoku times the unifiers had done their best to open the closed ranks that characterized medieval society by declaring an end to specially privileged groups that, in effect, operated in constraint of commerce for the profit of local warlords. By the Tokugawa years priorities changed once more as the authorities concerned themselves with structure and order. The most important device was the licensed guild, or *kabu nakama,* "share [*kabu*] holders," groups of traders authorized to monopolize their part of the market, in return for which they paid a license fee "in gratitude" to the authorities.

Each merchant enterprise was itself a hierarchy, from house head to clerks and servants. The house of Mitsui, for instance, which developed the great Echigoya textile store in Edo that spawned the modern Mitsuikoshi department store empire, made a point of bringing in boys between the ages of eleven and thirteen from communities just outside the range of the store as servants in order to be sure their loyalty would be to the enterprise. After ten to fifteen years, they might be promoted to head clerk, and a small percentage might advance beyond that rank. After decades of loyal service a clerk might be favored with a permit to open a branch house of the main enterprise, but by the time this was granted he could be expected to have internalized the values and ethos of the master's establishment. Each major house had its own system of branch, related, and affiliated houses, and each saw to it that no single branch or executive was likely to accumulate enough power to imperil the harmony of the whole. In cities, enterprise organization stretched up to great houses that enjoyed special privileges and opportunities through their relations with domain and bakufu governments. Their family codes resembled those of the warrior houses and showed the greatest care for continuity of house management and direction. Many of the greatest, including Kōnoike, Sumitomo, and Mitsui, in fact began as samurai houses whose heads changed to merchant status after the extinction of their feudal lords. In so doing they brought many of the principles of administrative organization to the world of commerce. Most, certainly those who survived to prosper, took considerable care to avoid the dissipation of funds by an unworthy successor. Frequently their family codes also warned about the dangers of becoming unduly familiar with samurai authorities; great profits could be gained through such favoritism, but the dangers of political setbacks were even greater. "Never forget that you are merchants," the Mitsui head Hachirōemon warned his descendants in his will. Occasionally the bakufu gave point to such warnings by confiscating the property of a merchant house whose extravagance had become too striking. The Osaka lumber contractor house of Yodoya gained the confidence of the bakufu in 1615 at the time Osaka fell to Ieyasu's armies. Subsequent house heads acted as fiscal agents for several daimyo, assisted in the development of central Osaka's Nakanoshima, the city's financial and commercial center, and were favored with the permit to establish the Osaka rice commodity market. In 1705, however, the house fell afoul of the shogun Tsunayoshi's desire to rein in merchant wealth and display and suffered the expropriation of its properties and enterprise.

Great houses like the Mitsui and Yodoya stand out in any discussion of merchant organizations, but they were of course far outnumbered by smaller and less spectacular houses. Tradesmen ranged from part-time itinerants who appeared at the periodic public market days established in country towns to men who hawked potatoes and trinkets in the streets, to the heads of great urban establishments.

The formal categories of status, however, leave little room or preparedness for the fact that the *chōnin* of the castle towns and cities included large numbers of laborers who came in from the countryside in hope of improving themselves by finding a job. In number they probably constituted around one tenth of the total urban population. They too ranged in standing from those who caught on as pages for upper samurai households and served as attendants and sandal-bearers, some of whom might hope to elevate their status by being permitted to wear silk clothing and carry one sword, to bearers, household servants, and ordinary clerks. At the beginning of the period degrees of servitude were expressed in the word we have already encountered for hereditary daimyo. A *fudai* servant began the period less than free, but in 1616 the bakufu issued its first ban on trade in people.[42] Hideyoshi, anxious to stabilize long-term loyalties, had warned against using day laborers, but with the wave of construction that followed the Tokugawa peace the substitution of day laborers for *fudai* servitude for labor construction became increasingly common, as daimyo tried to avoid interruption of the agricultural cycle that corvée labor caused. *Hōkōnin,* a term that originally indicated a samurai, came gradually to "indicate the range of occupations that 'servant' implied in early-modern Europe."[43] The prevalence of labor in bakufu cities is shown by the frequency with which regulations addressed the length of service time; Gary Leupp's study lists twenty-seven laws in the first century of Tokugawa rule. Gradually the length of contract permissible grew from three years, to ten, and then to indefinite periods of time. But in addition wages tended to rise, making it more difficult for lower-income people, whether samurai or commoners, to keep more than the minimum number of servants. Here again, the contrast between the enormous clusters of attendants maintained in daimyo residences, by merchant princes, and the small number maintained by ordinary householders, not to speak of renters, illustrated the hierarchical pattern of social relations.

5. Subcaste Japanese

Tokugawa Japan also had a system of built-in discrimination for a large number of Japanese who constituted in effect additional status groups. Throughout society, as David Howell puts it, status meant membership in a group which had particular obligations. The samurai provided service and leadership, farmers provided rice and taxes, artisans goods, and merchants trade. The borders of groups might be porous, with movement up or, more often, down, but the core of each group was distinct, largely self-regulating, and to a degree autonomous. Japan's was not a caste society, but the body of Japanese outside these status groups was sufficiently large and important to merit the term subcaste.[44]

The largest of the subcaste groups was known as *eta*. Physically indistinguishable from other Japanese, they were firmly associated in the popular mind with defilement and death. In violation of Buddhist precepts against the taking of life, their diet included animal products (tripe), and their occupations were in areas repugnant to Buddhist sensibilities: slaughtering and disposal of animal carcasses, tanning and fashioning items from leather, and executions and disposal of the corpses. Disapproval of such activities and discrimination against those who practiced them antedated the Tokugawa years, but a formally structured pattern of separate identity grew out of the social distinctions decreed in the age of unification: the separation of farmers and samurai, pacification of unruly remnants of lost causes, and registration of the populace as Buddhist communicants to guard against Christian or illegal Buddhist sectarians all combined to rearrange and classify social groupings.

One product of this discrimination and contempt was that the *eta* were, collectively, invisible. Their residences clustered outside normal villages and towns. The early land surveys presumably treated them as branches of the nearby village, but quietly, and throughout the Tokugawa period maps discreetly ignored their existence. They were mustered in population registers to make sure they were not Christians, but the registers were kept separate and handled differently. In the larger communities they lived lives that were kept as separate as possible to spare others the dangers of being defiled. At the same time they were a significant fraction of the population and knew a degree of autonomy. Their headmen were recognized as such by the authorities, and they were held accountable for their people. On occasion the headman of a subcaste community could approach the authorities to complain about infringement by "outsiders" on occupations like leatherwork conventionally reserved for his group. The boundaries of the headman's jurisdiction, as Howell shows, did not necessarily coincide with those of other status groups, particularly in the parcelized holdings of the Edo (Kantō) and Osaka-Kyoto (Kansai) region, where it might in fact represent authority over *eta* communities in several otherwise distinct domains.

Not all *eta* were occupied exclusively in activities designated for them; many farmed plots in areas on the fringes of other villages, of which theirs was then considered a sort of branch, or on the outskirts of cities and towns. In such cases they were expected to pay their tax in produce—though it brought them none of the privileges of village membership—and perform, as their substitute for the corvée labor other villagers had to provide, tasks like the removal of animal carcasses. Under such conditions, as Howell points out, *eta* specialties were almost a form of by-employment for the agricultural-ists concerned, but their status membership remained distinct and neigh-boring villagers could be expected to give them a wide berth. The relationship was not, in other words, a simple one. *Eta* communities and roles were, one might say, essential to the material and moral functions of society—as others saw it, at any rate. They also had designated roles in popular festivals in many areas. Thus they offer one more, and a particularly striking, example of the workings of a status society.

The "despised" communities *(senmin)* included another and quite distinct category, the *hinin*, or "nonhuman." These were associated with despised pro-fessions: lower forms of entertainment, fortune telling, prostitution, and beg-ging. *Eta* status was hereditary, but *hinin* status was not, and might perhaps be classified as "achieved" by drop-outs and transients. The common bond that related *hinin* activities was that of physical mobility; in an orderly and structured society people who lived, however badly, by their wits could not be thought respectable. The authorities nevertheless recognized their utility and granted them monopoly privileges, of which the most common was beg-ging. Landless peasants down on their luck who came to the cities hoping for a living were supposed to be sent back to their villages by *hinin;* failing this, they might be able to "join" the ranks of beggars.

Hinin might be "despised" in theory, but some contributed to the few areas of levity and indulgence possible in a society ruled by samurai. There were traveling troupes of actors who presented folk kabuki and other plays at festivals, others from street entertainers to those who managed and plied the trades of prostitution, and incorrigible misfits as well as the floating tide of beggars. Similarly, the licensed quarters of cities and even castle towns be-came areas of permitted pleasure. They also became the center of the larger entertainment world of kabuki theater, and provided the setting for Tokugawa popular culture with its literary and artistic expression. Consequently there could be a mix of contempt and admiration involved in the judgment of these themes; samurai moralists and commoner realists did not by any means make the same judgments, but members of both status groups rubbed shoulders in the entertainment quarters.

6. Status and Function

From what has been said it becomes clear that the division of Tokugawa soci-ety into *shi-nō-kō-shō* categories was no simple matter. The arrangement has no place for those above and those below the categories, the court and the depressed classes. Nor does it make allowance for the complexity of major categories. Confucian scholars, doctors, and priests, for instance, might come from modest origins, although their need for learning restricted their number to those from relatively favored circumstances. In each of these categories there was also a range of people, from relatively unlearned to those who had the education and well-being of daimyo in their hands.

Doctors, for instance, had no formal accreditation. They might be specialists in Chinese medicine like acupuncture, or they might have some knowledge of Western surgery that had come via the Nagasaki trade. They might be specialists in obstetrics or offer treatments in moxa (cauterization through the insertion and burning of small amounts of mugwort), which was thought to cure a hundred ills. Those attached to daimyo were usually men of some consequence, conscious of their responsibilities to their betters; others might be unlettered quacks. Many made additional profit from medicines they developed. Shibue Chūsai (1805–1858), for instance, a doctor of impressive attainments, developed a potion that was part opium. He was introduced to his daimyo at the age of ten, and given appointment as an apprentice at seventeen. Gradually he won his lord's confidence, called on him each day, and accompanied him into retirement. He thus represented a member of a relatively class-free group, able to indulge itself in learning and art, and able to mingle with others for whom formal status was relatively unimportant. Indeed, literature and the arts developed with scant regard to the niceties of formal status, and particularly in Edo, salons of many sorts had regular meetings of highly cultured men of many specialties who gathered for poetry, art, and tea.[45]

Rather than seeing Japanese society as layered with the samurai on top, then, it would be better to think of Tokugawa status society as consisting of a series of complementary hierarchies, each of which had its own upper, middle, and lower classes. The warrior rulers, of course, enjoyed clear predominance, but one did not have to go very far down in samurai (bushi) ranks to reach forms of financial and personal insecurity. Agriculturalists ranged from village leaders whose sturdy dwellings with proud walls and massive beams were light years away from the dark and dirt-floored cabins of tenants and landless laborers. The life of artisans could range from that of contractors and specialists who purveyed by appointment to the political elite to those who cobbled together an existence from waxed-paper umbrellas and utilitarian baskets. The category of merchant included proud houses of wealth and influence like the Mitsui and Sumitomo as well as peddlers who eked out a living by hawking boiled potatoes. The upper ranks of each hierarchy knew the advantage of wealth and education and prided themselves on a mastery of the arts of tea, poetry, and garden, but Fukuzawa's description of low-ranking samurai in Nakatsu as little different from deferential and scruffy workmen underscores the humble circumstances in which the numerical majority passed their days.

If Japan's society was not one of layered castes, how then might it best be understood? Bitō Masahide has argued that it should be seen as a series of interdependent services *(yaku)*. In considering how it was that the radical social upheaval that separated soldiers from peasants worked as smoothly as it did, and lasted as long as it did, he points to the necessity of considering the "function" an individual filled in society and the responsibility that came with this function, and suggests that the many nuances of *yaku* provide some of the answers.

Warriors were expected to justify their stipend, whether in land or rice, by maintaining an appropriate number of men and quantity of equipment for service in battle. Thus *gunyaku* was their equivalent of the rice tax the farmers, and the labor service or corvée *(buyaku)* that ordinary Japanese were expected to provide. This might range from thirty working days a year, as was common in early Tokugawa, to a money payment, as it became, or the provision of horses and men for travel on designated highways. The *eta*'s grimy work of cleaning the countryside of carrion was his *yaku*. Peasant laborers were often referred to as *yakuya;* warriors were often *yakunin*, the term still used to designate "officials" in Japan. Responsible, established farmers *(honbyakushō)* were also *mura* (village) *yakunin*. Their management of the village tax rate and delivery brought substantial tax exemption for them, because their administrative duty was a form of *yaku* also. Similarly, for the townsmen, inhabitants of the *chō*, qualification brought responsibilities in the form of specialized labor in their craft and unspecialized labor in the form of public labor; for some, administrative burdens as elder of the *chō* had the same connotation that it did for the village heads. These responsibilities began as privately held feudal governance, but as peace generalized them throughout the country they became public as well as private, bureaucratic as well as feudal.

Bitō thus writes that "the overall aim of the rulers in this period was to develop the system of 'yaku' for society, and maintain it through the strength of great military might and rule by law. Such a policy would succeed because it answered the needs of the entire populace, and achieved a political stability."[46] He goes on to argue that the shogun's codification of duties for the emperor and court should be seen as articulation of the "yaku" for the sovereign and his entourage, just as the regular entrustment of rule to the shogun by the emperor amounted to a reverse "yaku" for the military hegemon.

Central to the understanding of the entire system is the fact that things became less and less "private." All but a very few daimyo houses received their domains as assignments from the shogun. The assignment could be shifted or terminated; the domain was not the daimyo's own. The duties that came with the post were returned as gratitude and acknowledgment for that favor. The samurai with his hereditary stipend, whether large or niggardly, owed thanks and service to his superior as he owed fidelity to the ancestor whose merit had earned him that reward. As the years of peace lengthened, the peasant and the townsman learned to praise the rulers whose valor and merit had replaced the insecurity of Sengoku times with the even tenor of Tokugawa days. We may grant that this set of interdependent services was particularly favorable to the rulers who inherited a relatively docile and cooperative people. Poor administration or capricious irrationality, however, would usually bring grumbling, petitions for redress, and find the subservient commoner transformed into a litigious, sturdy fellow whose complaints called for a return to things as they had been. Acceptance of status did not mean acceptance of injustice. Relations and duties were reciprocal, and there was a generalized concept of a covenant even though it was not articulated clearly.

The opening pages of this chapter presented contrasting views of Tokugawa society; Tokutomi's abhorrence of the restriction of its "compartments," followed by Lafcadio Hearn's estimate of those arrangements as largely conducive to the well-being of the whole. The system can be contrasted to the dynamism of a modern industrial society, as Tokutomi did, but also to the capricious injustice and insecurity of the years of violence that preceded the Tokugawa "Great Peace." The historian must also be concerned with the system's capacity for growth and change, a task which lies ahead.

URBANIZATION
AND COMMUNICATIONS

5

By the end of the seventeenth century measures taken by the Tokugawa regime to maintain its control over its feudatories had changed the face of the land. The concentration of samurai in castle towns led to the development of a large service class of townsmen—merchants and artisans—in all but the most insignificant domains. As peace came to the land the shogun substituted service in the form of residence and attendance for military duty, and required the presence of the feudal lords at his capital in Edo. Now those vassals found themselves obliged to maintain a schedule of regular rotation between their domain and the distant capital, and that duty became the center of their lives. Provisions for it dominated the administration and economy of their domains. They brought with them what they could and purchased what they lacked, and the flow of men and goods from country to capital made a country out of what had been a congeries of fiefs.

Communication routes, in turn, required measures to regulate, monitor, and control: mileposts indicating the distance from the Japan bridge in Edo, runners for official business, checkpoints and barriers, relay stations and designated villages for the provision of men and horses. Commoners required permits and passports to cross those stations; wherever they went they found, at intersections and bridges, signboards warning them against the proscribed worship of Jesus and exhorting them in their duties. National highways had precedence over local jurisdictions, but within those borders most domains reproduced this system on a smaller scale. The feudal lords also maintained their vassals and samurai at their castle towns; they too needed the help of merchants, and they too regulated and restricted travel. But the feudal lords had one problem the central regime did not, and that was the need to maintain and fund parallel administrative structures for the lands allocated to them in Edo and their own castle town; arrangements for absentee governance followed from the periodic absence of the governors.

Edo became the central hub for the powerful, and Osaka grew as a national market center, but Kyoto and Nagasaki were no less centers of commerce, crafts, and travel. By the 1690s Engelbert Kaempfer, who traveled twice from Nagasaki to Edo, marveled at the scale of movement on the roads. Japan was being knit together; the military class by its duties of residence and service, the domains by their need to provide links between castle town and distant captial, and status groups by the need of each for the others. Conflict had given way to ceremony and consumption, and commoner culture flourished in the interstices of the urbanization that resulted.

1. The *sankin-kōtai* System

Of all the institutions established by the Tokugawa regime none was more central than the requirement that the daimyo spend alternate years at the shogun's capital of Edo. The *sankin-kōtai* system, as it was known, had momentous consequences for Japan's future. It fixed the attention of the ruling class on life at the capital; after the first generation of feudal lords, daimyo were born in Edo and did not visit their domains until they attained their majority. The system also drained the economies of provinces in all parts of Japan. It required the development of a system of national communications that did more to unify the country than Ieyasu's victory at Sekigahara. As commodities of every sort were funneled to the center, regional economies grew to cross domain political boundaries. The provision of materials needed for life at the capital and transporting them there provided economic opportunities for commoners, and as the merchant and artisan classes grew in size and importance a new popular culture emerged. Gradually a national culture grew out of what had been provincial variants. Edo became the nerve center for the ruling class, and information gained there was quickly spread to the ends of the land. In the nineteenth century awareness of the approach of the West quickly made the samurai a strategic elite convinced of the necessity for political change.

The system was not without its precedents in East Asia. Prior to the creation of the Chinese empire in the second century B.C. classical texts spoke of seasonal visits by the feudal lords to the Chou dynasty emperor. In Japan, the brilliant culture created at the imperial capital by Ashikaga shoguns drew daimyo from all parts of the country to establish residences at Kyoto, and it was their concentration on matters at the center that created the competition among provincial warlords from which Nobunaga, Hideyoshi, and Ieyasu emerged as unifiers. Hideyoshi too gathered vassal daimyo around his head-quarters during the round of warfare at the end of the sixteenth century, and his concern with the prevention of insurrection in the countryside behind their backs had led him to demilitarize the villages and separate samurai from farmers in the 1590s. But those measures had been taken during times of tur-bulence and war. The new Tokugawa institutions were designed to preserve the peace that had been won on the battlefield.

Those efforts began shortly after the victory at Sekigahara, when Maeda, the lord of Kanazawa, journeyed to Edo to pay his respects to the victor. Ieyasu's principal vassals had long been at his side, but the appearance of Maeda, nearly his equal, suggested the formalization of a new hierarchy. Be-fore long other lords from the west made their appearance at Edo; their pres-ence was not yet compulsory, but it was highly politic. Soon many sent family members to Ieyasu in Edo as hostages as well.

Iemitsu, the third shogun and the first born to the rule, formalized this pattern and made it compulsory. His 1635 revision of the Code for the Military Houses made this clear: "It is now settled that the *daimyō* and *shōmyō* are to serve in turns [*kōtai*] at Edo. They shall proceed hither [*sankin*] every year in summer during the course of the fourth month." Military service that had been required in time of war was now transformed into attendance in time of peace. The 260 feudal lords were expected to present themselves at the shogun's court in audience in alternate years. Some, petty *fudai* vas-sals, might be put on six-month, practically full-time, duty. Others might have their terms adjusted in compensation for other military service that was required. The lords of Saga and Fukuoka, who took turns in the defense against the West by providing guard service at Nagasaki, were compensated in that way, as were the lords of Tsushima and Matsumae, at the extremes of the country, responsible for Korea and for Hokkaido respectively. From 1622 to 1665, a hostage system intensified these requirements of attendance. Daimyo and their chief retainers were expected to have their immediate family—wives, children, and sometimes even mothers—in permanent resi-dence at Edo.[1]

Attendance in Edo was no substitute for help with the immense engi-neering and construction projects the regime mounted in the seventeenth century. Assessments were made in terms of hundreds of workers, boatmen, lengths of giant stones, and shipments of timber, all required to build the great castle in Edo and rebuild the keep in Osaka. Local specialties (as with lumber from Tosa) were set for some areas, while other lords were assessed workers in ratios calibrated per *koku* rating of their domain. The giant blocks that undergird the Chiyoda Castle, the shogun's (and today the emperor's) residence, for instance, were transported from all parts of Japan, but especially from the rocky cliffs of the Izu Peninsula, where evidence can still be seen of cutting and quarrying.

In turn, the bakufu allotted land to the daimyo in Edo. The location and size of the estates were, predictably, appropriate to past merit (for *fudai*) and prestige (for *tozama*). These estates came to distinguish the topography and layout of the shogun's capital.

The implementation of this system required the services of a large bakufu bureaucracy. Daimyo processions to and from Edo began as military operations, and to the end they could involve the movement of as many as several thousand men. Samurai guards surrounded and guarded the daimyo, whose litter (*kago,* an enclosed palaquin) was carried in the center of the procession. The rank and splendor of the retainers in the procession rose to, and declined from, the center that was its heart. Since so many of the lords were on the road in the spring months, care had to be taken to avoid competition for facilities and resources along the way; rival forces whose members viewed their lord's prestige as an extension of their own could not be permitted to upset the public peace. Already in 1635, Iemitsu's instructions noted that "lately the numbers of retainers and servants accompanying [the lords] have become excessive. This is not only wasteful to the domains and districts, but also imposes considerable hardships on the people. Hereafter suitable reductions in this respect must be made." Yet cutting corners too much would have constituted disrespect to the feudal overlord the daimyo was theoretically coming to serve. Rule of thumb ratios of men to domain *koku* rating were worked out in 1648 (fifteen horsemen per 100,000 *koku*), and in 1660 limits were set on the number of porters and horses that could be requisitioned without cost, but everything conspired to make daimyo exceed these guidelines. Consequently there was a premium on precise and elaborate scheduling. Emissaries moved between the lord's castle and the shogun's capital, setting departure dates and reporting safe return. The most distant *tozama* were often the greatest and most powerful feudatories, and they traveled with the greatest pomp. From Kagoshima, the castle town of Satsuma, it took the Shimazu lord some fifty days to make his way to and from Edo. For some lords part of the journey might be made by water, and we possess illustrations of the fleets that could be marshaled by a lord like that of Kumamoto. The last leg, however, was usually by land along the great highways leading into Edo, where the procession was greeted by the shogun's officials at the outskirts of his city. The passage of a feudal lord, with a small army of samurai, under arms, with all their accoutrements, also posed a political and security problem for daimyo through whose territories the procession wound its way. Punctilio and courtesy required that official representatives greet the procession as it entered the realm and accompany it until it departed its borders, where it would be met by a new contingent of officials. Given the checkerboard pattern of *fudai* fiefs along the principal routes of communication, this constituted a formidable and time-consuming burden.

Late Tokugawa printmakers like Hiroshige have acquainted us with the sight of such processions moving in single or double file along the twisting narrow roads. These were formidable affairs and they must have created unforgettable impressions. The lord of Tosa came with an entourage that numbered 2,775 men in 1690.[2] These processions were subjects of immense interest to nineteenth-century Western observers. The nineteenth-century American Francis Hall, watching the progress of the Tokugawa lord of Owari toward Edo from a slight eminence above the road, was aware that if it had been a century earlier the samurai who scowled at him from below would have made short work of his little group for such a violation of ritual courtesy. The train, he wrote, "was scattered at irregular intervals and the white hats [of its members] could be seen for two miles in length moving like a great snake with white scales along the winding Tokaido . . . The procession had been filing along slowly in this manner for nearly an hour when the train began to move in a more compact mass, for the lord of Owari himself was approaching." A year later, when the "young Prince of Owari" had been selected as shogunal successor, Hall saw his progress once again. "All the morning long the baggage carriers and menials of the train passed on and a little past noon the Prince himself and his guard of several hundred armed men came on. A babe of some four years old lolling his head out of the window of his elegant norimon [palanquin] in infantile undergarment and supported by his nurse represents the sprig of royalty for whom all this parade was essential."[3] Kaempfer, whom we have encountered before, saw the system at its height in the 1690s, and took part in it twice himself as a member of the small party that accompanied the Dutch chief factor, who was expected to lead his own procession annually to offer thanks for the favor of trading at Nagasaki. His description of a daimyo procession they encountered remains a classic. He notes the heraldry with which the procession moves: the nonsamurai bearers carrying giant cases labeled with the daimyo crest, the variety of warriors, arranged from low to highest rank as the daimyo palanquin nears, and then tapering off again in reverse sequence. As it enters a village an advance man, reveling in the importance of his role, shouts "Down!" *(shita ni!)*; commoners are expected to turn their faces to the ground rather than look upon the face of the daimyo. As the procession enters a community, its most humble members adopt the kabuki theater version of a goose step to show the gravity of the occasion. Here is how he describes it:

> What appears still more odd and whimsical, is to see the Pages, Pikebearers, Umbrellas and hat-bearers, Fassanbak or chestbearers, and all the footmen in liveries, affect a strange mimic march or dance, when they pass through some remarkable Town, or Borough, or by the train of another Prince or Lord. Every step they make, they draw up one foot quite to their back, in the mean time stretching out the arm on the opposite side as far as they can, and putting themselves in such a posture, as if they had a mind to swim through the air. Mean while the pikes, hats, umbrellas, Fassanbacks, boxes, baskets, and what ever else they carry, are danced and toss'd about in a very singular manner, answering the motion of their bodies.[4]

Protocol and grandeur thus counted for everything. For those at the center of the procession, however, it was a rather comfortable camping trip. Some extracts from a description of such a trip made in 1858 by the Dutch representative van Polsbroek, who accompanied the Nagasaki station chief on a mission to secure the Netherlands' equivalent of the treaty Townsend Harris had just worked out for the United States, will illustrate how important travelers fared.

> The bannerman, dressed in black with Dutch insignia, carried the Netherlands flag on a black lacquered pole topped with a gilded lion. I was seated in a *norimon* with a Japanese officer and servant walking on each side. The *norimon* was carried by four bearers in black, with the Dutch coat of arms on it. The Netherlands Commissioner was seated in a *norimon* with six bearers, flanked by two Japanese servants. Some 20 Japanese functionaries, the officers and interpreters in their *norimon*. Some sixty chests, all the same size, all painted black, each carried on a bamboo pole by two men. The chests contain the food, drink, and clothing not needed immediately ... It was almost possible to sit in the *norimon* with legs outstretched. Mine had a beautifully brocaded mattress, my chief's was yellow satin. There were arm rests on both sides. In front, at the foot end, three holes, contained a bronze comfort, a bronze box for cigars, and one for tobacco ... Fit as I then was, I could stand barely an hour in my *norimon* before I warned my servants that I preferred to walk. It was then lowered to the ground in front, the rear maintained at an angle, to make it easy to exit, after a servant had put on my shoes for me ...
>
> Each of us had his life goods in a beautifully lacquered chest with a

wooden frame around it . . . at night we found our sleeping clothes; in a word, we lacked nothing, not even a snifter . . . Among our servants were six cooks, three charged with lunch and three with dinner; when we finished a meal and moved on, the black lacquered table and table service were packed up and swiftly carried to the place where we were to have our next meal; we arrived there to find it set up and everything in order. Food was perfection, and the best that could be provided; delicious fresh- and salt water fish, tender wild fowl, wonderful fruits, all prepared by the Commissioners' cooks, men who had served in that function, father to son, for centuries . . .

We stayed in great hotels called *Honjin,* that are reserved for high Shogunal officials, daimyō and princes. Seen from outside they could not be distinguished from palaces. Inside they were beautifully laid out; fine mats on the floors, golden leather finishings. The bathrooms most tasteful, towel racks and fixtures black lacquer with gold. In short, everything tastefully done . . .

When we entered a town the head official together with the eldest of the counselors greeted us at its borders and walked in front of the bannerman, in turn preceded by four police agents with great iron staves equipped with iron shackles at the end. With each step they stomped these on the ground, making the shackles ring as they shouted *"Shita ni!"* Not that it was necessary, for the inhabitants kneeled quietly in front of their residences in their best clothes and looked at us with the greatest amazement. As we left the town the head official saluted us again and we moved on.

The road, beautifully maintained, led through a plain that showed, as far as one could see, fields of rice, taroot, grain, and rapeseed . . . In towns where we stayed people had spread clean white sand in front of their homes in our honor, just as they were accustomed to doing for the passage of their lord.[5]

The high-ranking traveler was thus insulated from the country through which he passed by his countrymen and comforts. If foreigners in late Tokugawa received this courtesy, one can imagine the protocol that was involved in the passage of the train of a major daimyo.

By the mid-eighteenth century the western domain of Chōshū had over two thousand samurai stationed in Edo. The problem of provisioning so large an establishment constituted a drain on han finances that used up all available funds. But while on the one hand the bakufu tried to set limits on domain extravagance, on the other hand it enforced the performance of duties as indications of loyalty. In addition, it was to bakufu advantage, at least in the early decades, to have daimyo strain their resources in meeting their obligations of vassalage. This could also create strains within the daimyo's retainer band; those in Edo wanted to keep their end up in the competitive world of comparison there, while those at home wanted to limit the outflow of scarce resources.

Daimyo failure to meet the obligations of compulsory attendance—the usual excuse was illness—could be met with sharp reproof and measures that ranged from disgrace to expropriation. Thus in 1686, as has been noted, the bakufu took note of repeated infractions of duty on the part of the feudal lord of Echizen, a collateral house *(shinpan)*, with punishment that ranged from ritual disgrace—revocation of permission to use of the Matsudaira name, the hollyhock crest, and his seat at audiences—to loss of almost half of his territory. In addition, he was ordered to close the front gate of his Edo mansion and restrict himself to the smaller gates beside it.[6] These drastic curbs on display and hauteur, with their attendant loss of pride for the daimyo house and its retainers (several of whom had committed suicide in vain attempts to remonstrate with their daimyo), say a good deal about the desperation that loss of public recognition, or "face," was expected to bring in a society of status.

2. Communication Networks

From an early point Tokugawa land travel was regulated and regularized by the bakufu with concerns of security and control in mind. Before long those concerns were secondary to economic considerations, and by the last century nonofficial commerce and travel loomed no less important than official needs. Japan had developed a communication system that knitted the country together to a surprising extent.

At first the road system was designed for security.[7] After Sekigahara, Ieyasu moved quickly to make national the system he had worked out in his own provinces. Two of his vassals were instructed to survey the principal coastal highway linking Kyoto and Edo (the Tōkaidō) and make post stations official. Soon the system was expanded to include other main roads, until there were five national highways (the Gokaidō). Of these the most important ran along the eastern coast; another provided an alternate route through central Japan, while others crossed Honshu to the Japan Sea and ran northeast to the Straits of Tsuruga.

After the *sankin-kōtai* system was formalized in the 1630s it became government policy to regulate a national network. Private, or domain, barriers and interference with national networks were ruled out. Post stations were established along all the major routes in addition to the five major roads. The five national highways, the principal focus of attention, had a total of 248 stations, usually spaced four to twelve kilometers apart. The Tōkaidō, the most traveled route of all, had 53, made familiar by the series of wood-block prints of the nineteenth-century artist Hiroshige.

Post stations were simultaneously rest stops, transport centers, and information centers. They had a station manager or head, who was assisted by a staff of subordinates to dispatch porters and horses, keep accounts and records, and maintain the *honjin*, the accommodations reserved for official travelers. Before long inns of varying degrees of elegance and cost sprang up to service nonofficial travel and transport. The stations in turn became entrepôts for local souvenirs, merchandise, foods, and entertainment.

Although these stations were for the most part within the domains of *fudai* daimyo, whose territories had been spread along major communication routes, this was by no means true of all. Consequently bakufu regulations establishing them and regulating their conduct and costs constituted a significant infringement on domain autonomy by the bakufu and clearly established its national primacy. The bakufu established a Magistrate of Roads *(dōchū bugyō)* in 1659, and with the passage of time the responsibilities and importance of the post increased. For a time local bakufu representatives reported on road conditions and upkeep, but after the early eighteenth century everything came under the supervision of the central government's magistrate. From the establishment of the system of alternate attendance, it became essential to the administrative calendar and domain rhythm of life that the stations should run smoothly. Travelers and processions might have wished to bypass some for reasons of economy and time, but bakufu regulations ruled that out. To permit it would have risked overloading the more popular ones and rendering the less interesting irrelevant.[8] People, processions, and goods thus moved along a relay system, with each post guaranteed more or less equal access and income.

A station was supposed to maintain a minimum of thirty-six pack horses and an appropriate number of bearers; this was increased to one hundred horses and as many bearers in the 1640s, but few stations found it possible to achieve this state of preparedness; an early-eighteenth-century survey found that only 9 of the 53 Tōkaidō stations were up to that standard. The station's costs were largely defrayed by the income from land that was set aside for its support. Householders in station towns were also assessed according to their frontage in an effort to provide some balance between commercial opportunity and obligation. This was a general principle of commoner urban taxation; at Nagasaki merchant frontage had been the basis for exactions to pay for

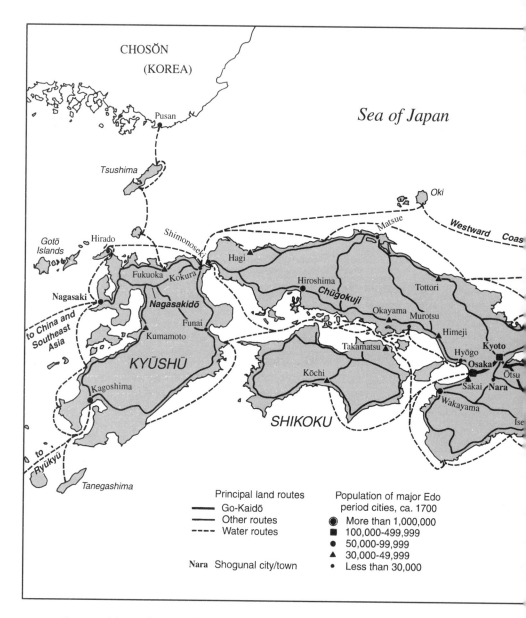

3. Largest cities and principal land and coastal communication routes in the eighteenth century.

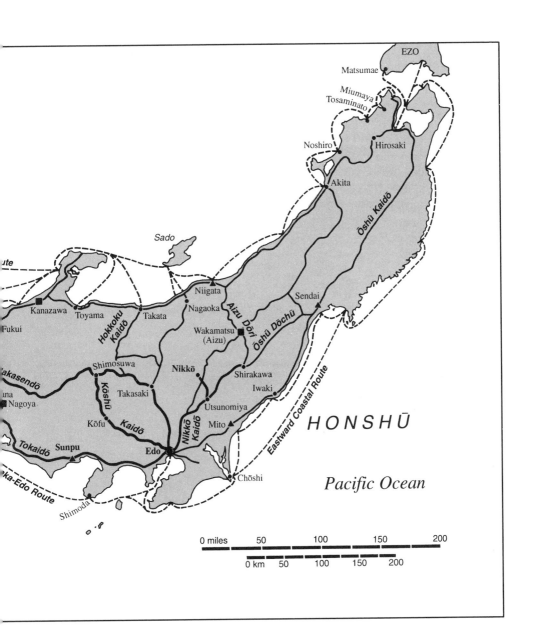

construction projects like Deshima. A domain that experienced particularly heavy traffic along its highways, as was true of those along the Tōkaidō, was thus deprived of substantial income as well as autonomy. The growing need for porters and horses brought the bakufu to reserve even more land in order to increase the capacity of the stations to service traffic.

More onerous for ordinary people was the requisition of horses and men from villages within a radius of the stations designated as "assisting villages" (sukegō). Despite bakufu instructions, daimyo processions tended to grow larger; in the 1690s Kaempfer noted that "the train of some of the most eminent among the Princes of the Empire fills up the road for some days," and the largest domains, as we have seen, were also the most distant. In 1694 the bakufu regularized these demands on villages without reference to the territorial jurisdiction within which they were located. Thereafter villages under several—in one, extreme, case, twenty-seven—lords could be assigned to provide labor in men, horses, or boats and bearers according to the village's koku income. The rule of thumb was two porters and two horses per 100 koku, but special needs could create special demands. As traffic increased, the radius within which villages were ordered to "assist" grew larger. Peasants so conscripted received less remuneration than regular porters. Worse still, since spring and fall were the peak seasons for daimyo travel, farmers could be left short handed during the most critical months for planting and harvesting their crops. Wealthy farmers might, since assessments were based on koku ratings, try to hire poorer peasants to do such work, and in some cases entire villages tried to shift their obligations in this manner. The arrangement was a frequent source of protest. As the economy developed, growing shipments of commercial goods of high value and low bulk complicated things further; merchants with access to impecunious daimyo sometimes managed to include their goods in daimyo chests for a fee, thereby taking advantage of the favorable handling rates reserved for the "princes" of the land.

Costs were also met by fees levied on travelers. Those on official business traveled free of charge, and a staggering list of seventy-nine exemptions was set up for men on official business relevant to bakufu, court, and foreign relations. Next were seventeen categories of travelers entitled to fixed-rate charges. Daimyo processions qualified for these rates up to the size of the entourage to which their status entitled them. Attendants and baggage in excess of those numbers, and all unofficial and private traffic, were at full charge—not fixed, however, but set by negotiation in a free market system. Now packhorse owners and bearers were able to recoup some of the cost and inconvenience they incurred by having their labor requisitioned. To protect bearers and packhorses, and to provide for some equality of income, additional regulations about loading specified the amount that men and horses could be asked to carry. No doubt such provisions were often flouted in practice, and the pitiless exaction of labor at peak agricultural seasons constituted a serious burden for ordinary farmers. It is probably no accident that Tanaka Kyūgu (1663–1729), a writer whose descriptions of rural poverty at a time of hardship are often cited by historians, was the manager of a post station.

Most bulk transport moved by boat along the coasts, and consequently the roads did not have to serve the needs of carriages or carts. Wheeled vehicles were, however, used in large communities. As virtually everything moved on backs—animal and human—the roads were not churned into muddy morasses in spring as was the case in Europe. For other than bulk traffic, the bakufu preferred that things move overland. It was easier to control that way, and it maximized the revenue at post stations. Consequently major highways were thronged; as early as the 1690s Kaempfer registered his astonishment at the volume of travel. Urgent official messages were sent by special runners (*hikyaku*, "flying legs"), who could bypass most restrictions. For everybody else, however, overland traffic was slow, expensive, and sometimes dangerous. A number of rivers, easily passable in dry season, came rushing down the mountain slopes in spring, providing steady income for rafters and bearers who carried travelers across at points where the streams could be forded. Some rivers were bridged, but the largest and most famous, the Ōi along the Tōkaidō route, never was. It is not entirely clear whether this was because it formed a convenient natural barrier or whether the problems were technological. Whatever the reason, the Ōi crossing served throughout the Tokugawa period as a symbol of the thrills and dangers of travel.

No aspect of the Tokugawa road system has attracted more notice than the checkpoint barriers (*sekisho*) on major highways. There were fifty-three of these on the five major highways, largely concentrated in a circle around Edo. Sengoku unifiers, beginning with Nobunaga, had abolished independent barriers, and the Tokugawa continued this practice. The bakufu did not permit daimyo to erect barriers on major highways that passed through their territories, but on other roads within their own territories and at their borders major domains usually had their own barriers, called *bansho* in deference to the prohibition on *sekisho*. From an early point Tokugawa concerns were with security, and encapsulated in the prohibition phrased as *de onna-iri teppō*, or "women leaving, guns entering," Edo. Either phenomenon could indicate an incipient plot against the shogunate; daimyo might be removing their hostages, or smuggling guns. Yet daimyo processions were not examined, although in theory barrier guards could do so; smaller parties that included samurai women, on the other hand, were carefully checked to make sure their passes were in order and their members were as described. The forces maintained at *sekisho* were modest, ranging from a handful to several dozen guards, though they might be augmented in the event of an important crossing. The barriers were closed at night, and passage was forbidden. The barriers thus slowed traffic considerably. Commoners who traveled needed passports as well as barrier crossing permits. Their documents were carefully (and tediously) checked, and frequently supplemented by physical examinations to make sure no women disguised as men, or young boys dressed as girls, were trying to slip through. Anyone with wounds was also well advised to have his travel papers specify their location and cause. Applications for travel documents were also time consuming. Barrier crossing permits usually required the approval of the Commissioner of Chiyoda Castle in Edo or a comparable magistrate. Samurai of course applied to their superior officers, while commoners could file applications with temples, village heads, or household-group heads. The travel document identified the traveler's sponsor and guarantor, and falsification of such information could cost all concerned dearly.

By the eighteenth century, the problem of security against daimyo family-hostage defection or firearm entry was no longer of any consequence. Firearms had given way to swords once more as the weapon of choice, and daimyo and retainer families accustomed to life in Edo were not likely to try to sneak out in order to return to the provinces. These institutions came to represent institutional inertia, time-honored customs begun by the sainted founder. They also provided rather congenial busywork for an underemployed samurai caste. But in a more basic sense, as Vaporis shows, they should be seen as expressions of the Tokugawa assumption of a fixed, land-based society in which people were not really supposed to travel.

Nevertheless in fact travel became more and more popular. Guidebooks and popular prints brought illustrations of famous places and intimations of distant delights to more and more people who could read. At all times visits to famous temples constituted good excuses for travel requests, though the real object might as frequently be the pleasures of the road and pilgrimage site. Pilgrimages combined sight-seeing with piety. Visits to the Shinto shrines at Ise were periodic phenomena. At approximately half century intervals—1650, 1705, 1771, and 1830—hundreds of thousands and then millions of ordinary people thronged the roads to Ise in festival fervor that sometimes bordered on the millenarian, many throwing themselves on the compassion and goodwill of villagers along the way. The timing of these movements was loosely related to the sexenary zodiacal cycle of the Chinese calendar, but the *okagemairi,* as they became known, seem to have provided intervals of release

1. Detail, screen commissioned by Tokugawa Ieyasu showing his victory at the battle of Sekigahara. Troops of a daimyo who changed sides fire at fleeing soldiers; others fight with swords, spears, and lances.

2.
Detail of a screen painting showing how Nobunaga's foot soldiers, equipped with firearms, withstood a cavalry attack to win the battle of Nagashino in 1575.

3. Himeji Castle, built in 1600, is the largest redoubt of the early Tokugawa period to survive intact.

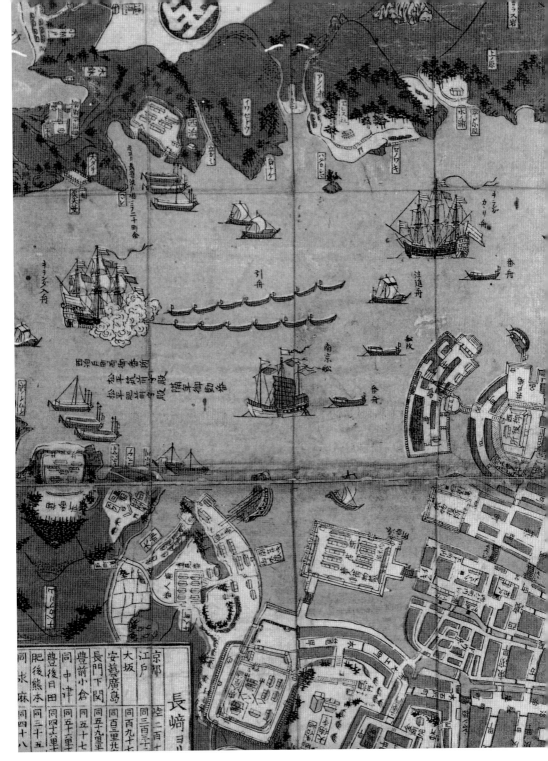

4. An 1802 wood-block map of Nagasaki, looking north from the legend, which gives distances to other cities. Off Deshima the artist depicts a Dutch (above) and a Chinese ship, the latter just off the Chinese quarter.

5. Deshima as depicted in a painting of Nagasaki harbor by Maruyama Ōkyo (1733–1795) in 1792.

6. A sacred image designed to be desecrated: *fumie*, Madonna and child, worn smooth by the feet of those forced to trample it to show they were not Catholic Christians.

7. Samurai in fighting gear.

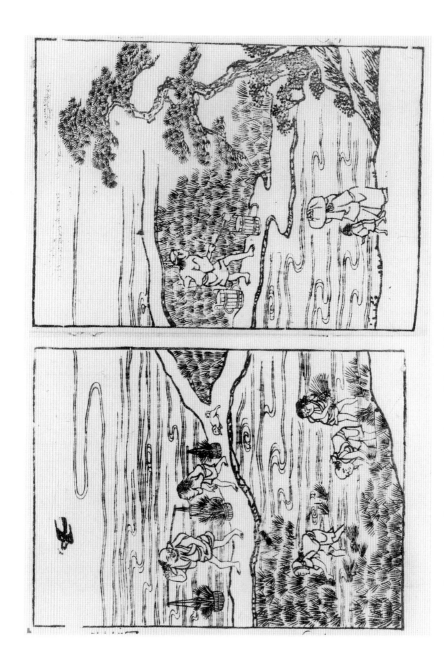

8. The *Nōgyō zensho*, an agricultural manual first published in 1697, was an important handbook that circulated widely. Paddy cultivation was a cooperative communal enterprise. Here young women are planting seedlings brought from a common seedbed.

9. Years of peace and access to urban entertainment soon led to less martial types, as in this seventeenth-century depiction of a young fop leaning on his long sword without impressing the bored ladies.

10. The fish market at Nihonbashi, or "Japan Bridge," the center of Edo commerce.

11. Engelbert Kaempfer's sketch of the Dutch procession bound for Edo. The entourage of a daimyo on *sankin-kōtai* duty would of course have been many times larger.

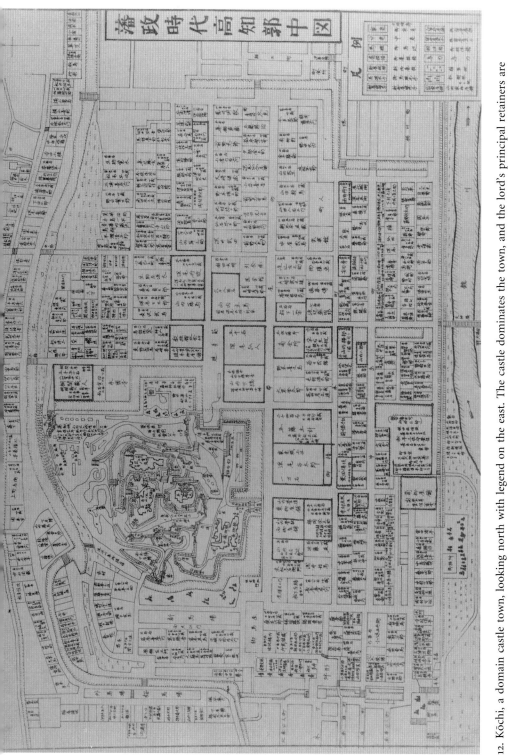

12. Kōchi, a domain castle town, looking north with legend on the east. The castle dominates the town, and the lord's principal retainers are allocated lots appropriate to their rank and status in size and location. Merchant shops cluster in less salubrious areas near and across the river.

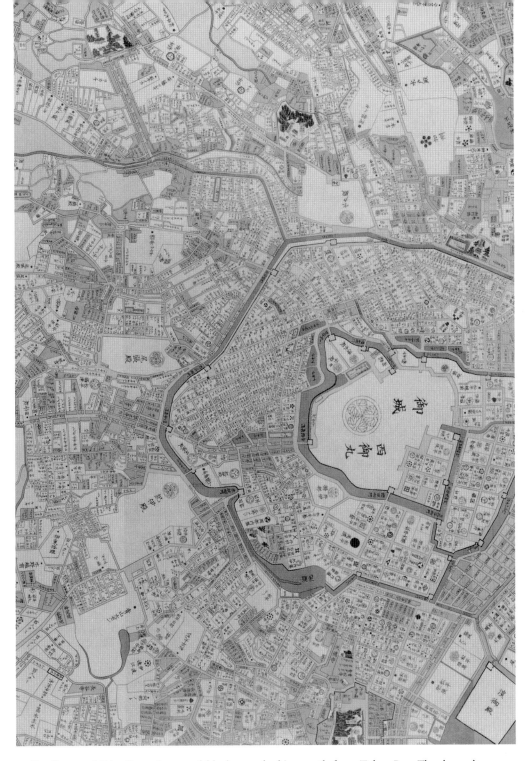

13. Detail, central Edo, from 1843 wood-block map, looking north from Tokyo Bay. The shogun's Chiyoda Castle, now site of the imperial palace, dominates the city. Waterways around it were used for commercial and private transport. The largest *yashiki* (five-leaf clover) is that of Kaga, also the largest daimyo; today it is the campus of the University of Tokyo. Cadet houses of Mito, Owari, and Kii, their insignia *(mon)* resembling medallions, ring the castle.

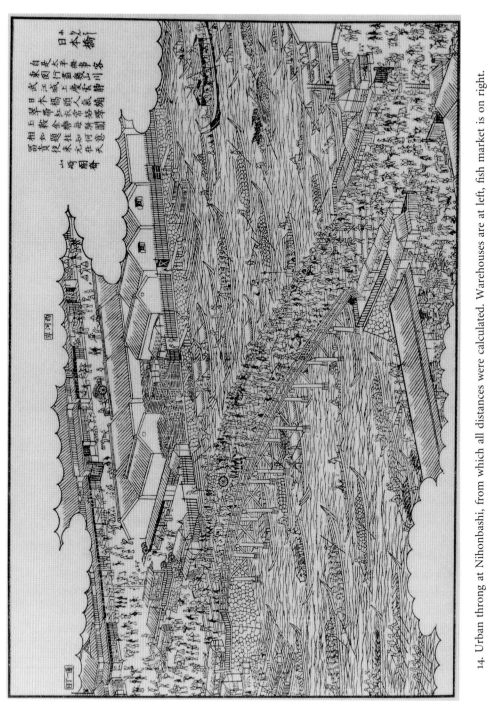

14. Urban throng at Nihonbashi, from which all distances were calculated. Warehouses are at left, fish market is on right.

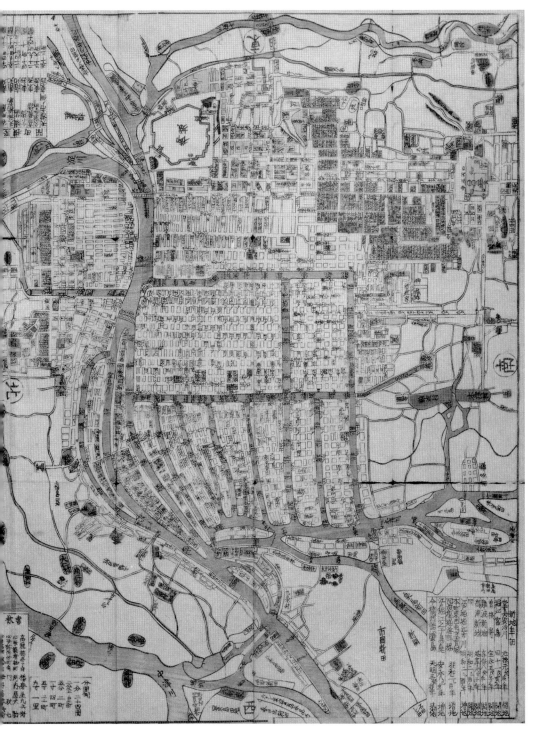

15. Wood-block map of Osaka, 1847. The lords' warehouses, lined up along the moats for ease in unloading, provided the basis for a national rice commodity exchange.

16. Delights of an Edo festival in the mid-seventeenth century, as depicted in a screen painting. Revelers move by boat to entertainment centers that line the shore.

17. Edo book and print shop, early nineteenth century.

18. Unloading rice at Osaka. A samurai oversees the operation.

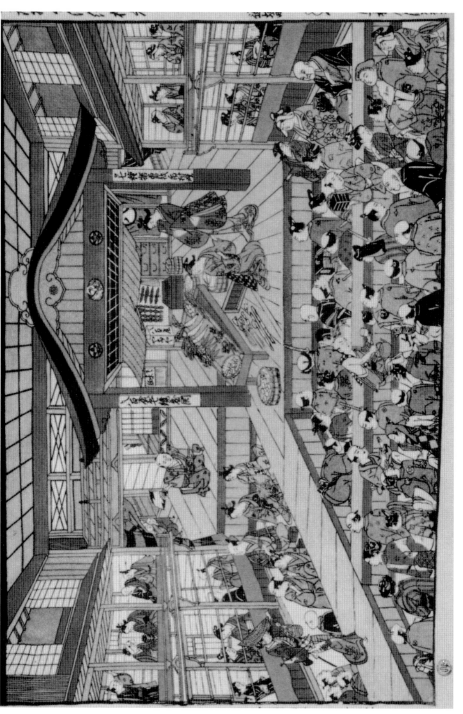

19. Wood-block print of *kabuki* theater, Okamura school, Genroku era. Entrances and exits on the *hanamichi*, which runs through the pit, increase audience participation.

and experience of other worlds for poor peasants who slipped past guard stations without permits. In such cases barrier restrictions were inadequate to their task, and side roads and night crossings led people to "break the barrier." Nevertheless sporadic crackdowns made violations of this sort dangerous, and could sometimes lead to draconian punishment. Despite this, nothing sufficed to lessen the enthusiasm for travel as diversion. To an astonishing degree Tokugawa society, ruled as if it were altogether static, gradually became a society of movement and variety. The *sankin-kōtai* system helped make it so.

It remains to say a word about the bulk transport of foodstuff that was required to provision a great city like Edo.[9] This, too, became highly structured. Although the seclusion edicts had included injunctions against the construction of ships of more than 500 *koku* capacity, these were soon obsolete as coastal transport grew in volume. By the 1670s a Western Circuit brought ships from northern Japan along the Japan Sea coast, and through the Straits of Shimonoseki to Osaka. Usually these were loaded with the rice surplus of domainal lords who wanted it marketed there in order to finance their travel to and stay in Edo. A second, Eastern Circuit, developed to do the same thing for domains along the Pacific coast. As cities grew, both routes served to bring tax rice, rape-seed oil, raw cotton, vinegar, sake, and other goods to Osaka (and later, Edo), and returned with dried sardines, fish-based fertilizers, and handicraft products of the two great cities. Throughout the seventeenth century Edo was largely dependent on Osaka for its goods, but as that dependence lessened shipping procedures grew more varied and sophisticated. Keen competition between two groups of shippers developed; one was controlled by ten major trade organizations licensed by the bakufu, another by sake brewers. Gradually specific cargo was allocated to each line. Capital accumulation was central to these enterprises; the Western Circuit shippers tended to purchase their cargoes and market them themselves, while others charged for freight. As commerce increased ships became larger, often becoming three and four times the legal 500-*koku* limit. In time, as bakufu reformers tried to control prices and merchant profits, these organizational devices changed again; exclusive guild relations were relaxed, and free contracts replaced the shipper-dominated organizations of the seventeenth century.

3. Domain Castle Towns

Sankin-kōtai processions began and ended in castle towns, and Tokugawa highways knitted the provincial capitals together. The route of every procession would lead through such a town. Van Polsbroek, the Dutch representative whose 1858 trip has already been mentioned, described the castle town of Saga, from which the province of Hizen was governed, as follows:

> A handsome, well kept city, surrounded by water with well built gates and bridges. A broad street led through the city, from gate to gate. It took us almost an hour to traverse the city. The inhabitants, formally dressed, had decorated their houses and kneeled in front of them.[10]

Saga was relatively isolated and few processions would wind through its streets; the Nagasaki envoys may have provided a welcome change. But along the Tōkaidō the passage of daimyo processions would have been a common sight in spring and fall.

Castle towns represented an unusual form of urban development. They were laid out as administrative centers and created, rather than derived from, commercial centers. Many daimyo invited merchants from larger metropolitan areas to come to their towns. The towns held a monopoly position in their area, as the bakufu had limited daimyo to a single castle per domain. They also served as physical reminders of the division of social classes. Most of the area, and all its desirable space, was given over to samurai residences and temples, leaving artisans and merchants squeezed into what remained. Nevertheless castle towns served to accelerate urbanization in Japan, for by the eighteenth century some 10 percent of the average domain's inhabitants, including virtually all its samurai, were to be found residing there.

The castle town as center of military power had its origin in Hideyoshi's edicts disarming the countryside and separating samurai from commoners. During the intermittent warfare of Sengoku times daimyo had to keep their fighting forces at the ready, and as peace returned to the land their military headquarters became administrative centers. In medieval warfare castle sites had been selected for defensive strength and were usually on strategic heights, but as larger units of control became common the new warlords built their fortresses in the centers of alluvial plains to control the population and profit from its labor.

The castle town of Kōchi, in the Shikoku domain of Tosa, illustrates a pattern that was reasonably standard. The town was located where river valley met ocean harbor, so that it was at once an avenue of contact with other centers and master of the plains. The castle, with its gleaming white *donjon* or keep, was set on massive granite rocks; around it were clustered the mansions of the daimyo's major vassals and related houses on spacious lots arranged in a regular grid. Those in turn were flanked by the villas of the ranking samurai arranged in blocks of ever smaller plots according to income and rank. It was a planned city, a premodern "company town."

Topography required adaptation, especially on coastal sites, but everywhere the upland and more salubrious locations were reserved for the upper class. Samurai areas constituted well over half of the available space. Another 10 to 15 percent of space went to Shinto shrines and Buddhist temples. Of these the largest and most imposing, with rows of massive memorial lanterns and tablets to commemorate the daimyo's forebears, reinforced the message sent out by the castle.

What remained, usually in low-lying and less desirable locations, were the artisan and merchant quarters. Except for a few merchants specially favored for their importance to the authorities, townsmen houses were crowded into narrow lanes. Artisans were frequently clustered together by trade and specialty, but shopkeepers and peddlers carried on their trades everywhere. Lanes were often too narrow to permit the passage of ox- and horse-drawn carts returning the inhabitants' waste to the neighboring paddies that first provided their food, and when that was the case bearers carrying buckets on bamboo took them to those carts or all the way to nearby fields of rice. Residential quarters had often been reclaimed from agricultural fields along the river banks. At flood season, and in times of sickness and pestilence, they were the first to suffer loss. Major disasters of fire and storm did not respect class or status, but they were most certain to destroy the crowded townsmen quarters.

Within the castle walls, and in the lives of retainers who mattered, life was dominated by the rhythm of the annual trip to and return from Edo. For a time Tosa processions moved through neighboring Tokuyama and thence by ship to Osaka, but after the eighteenth century the route led over the mountain passes to the north, where the travelers took ship for passage to Osaka through the Inland Sea. By bakufu regulations of 1658 daimyo were allowed 90 men per 10,000 *koku* (the minimum for daimyo rank) rated income, so that Tosa, which was rated at 200,000 (although its real product grew to more than double that) was entitled to 1,800 people. In 1645 1,477 men made the trip; their number rose to 1,799 in 1680 and 2,775 ten years later. The breakdown shows 50 horses, 46 boats, 1,313 boatmen, and a thousand or more samurai. Leading samurai families could expect their heads to make this journey regularly. In nine generations of the Mori family, for instance, among samurai with the rank of Mounted Guard *(umamawari)*, only two family heads failed to make the trip at least once. Moreover, the family records show that many went in smaller groups without traveling in the daimyo's train. Such trips must have been more interesting, for they were judged more worthy of diary record and description. A man traveling alone or with a small party had the opportunity to sightsee and buy souvenirs, something not possible for procession members intent on station and dignity.[11] With the head of the family absent for such long periods of time and, in many families, so regularly, responsibility for management of the household and bringing up the children inevitably devolved upon the women. Japanese literature is rich with stories of stoic samurai wives who set a stern example for the young.

Once the daimyo's family was established in the Edo residence on a permanent or at least long-term basis, it could not of course be left there alone. For a time the daimyo's principal retainers' families were there as hostages too, but even after those regulations were relaxed residence in Edo remained the pattern for many. Life in the Edo mansions was played out in a separate world of ritual and ceremony centered on the lord, his consort, and usually his concubines. After the first generation future daimyo were normally born and brought up there. For the heir this was an enervating aristocratic life, and it is not surprising that the majority of daimyo who became strong leaders were brought in from collateral families as adopted sons. The maintenance, staffing, and provisioning of the Edo residence was of major importance. Tosa, like other domains, developed two bureaucratic structures, one exclusively concerned with its responsibilities in Edo.

In turn the domain's economy and administrative problems were often dominated by meeting the costs of the system. Rice surpluses and any salable specialty products were shipped to Osaka, where they were marketed in what became a national commodity market. All major daimyo maintained Osaka warehouses and agents, and even today the "Tosa moat" *(Tosabori)* area in that city serves as reminder of the early modern economy. The daimyo needed cash to defray travel and living costs. Life on the road was often expensive, since so much had to be purchased at station stops where a seller's market prevailed. Travel in proper pomp took time. And the trips could be long, and the trips could take time; as mentioned, the lord of Satsuma, in southern Kyushu, took fifty days for his journey to Edo. To this had to be added the cost of gifts appropriate to station and prestige of the recipient. Japan's was a society of gifts. The gifts that were exchanged ranged from fine porcelains and other luxuries to horses. Daimyo consorts were expected to exchange gifts with their peers, and daimyo senior vassals with the bakufu's *rōjū*. This process was monitored, and not optional by any means. "It has come to our attention," the bakufu announced in 1692,

> that the gifts prescribed for presentation to the *sobashū* and other officials concerned with public affairs by the daimyo upon arrival at the capital and on different other fixed occasions during the year have fallen off in quantity, declined in quality, or ceased altogether. These gifts are not merely personal courtesies but duty offerings to superior authorities . . .

Henceforth each daimyo will see that his gifts are in keeping with the established status of his house and that they are not of inferior quality.[12]

Of course gifts had to flow in both directions. In that exchange the shogun, as the superior, had to do his part, and that posed no small burden for the finances of the Edo regime, which was heavily outnumbered by the daimyo with which it dealt.

In all large domains the crushing costs of the Edo system led in time to programs to encourage exports of products to the central markets and efforts to restrict imports from across their borders. This produced a form of mercantilism that was argued as of "national" (= provincial) benefit, *kokueki*.[13] The production of crafts, as with ceramics in Saga or lacquer in Kaga, was so central to domain finance that a domain commissioner was put in charge of what was in effect a state enterprise. Production secrets were carefully guarded from possible competitors. Official control made it possible to keep production prices low, since market opportunities were an official monopoly, and wherever possible import substitution and protectionist measures were pursued to keep the profits at home. Since major domains also issued their own paper (and frequently coin) currency for use within their borders, thus monopolizing the means of exchange, enterprises in the provinces grew slowly, bonded as they were to the political authorities. Outstanding craft leaders, however, were extremely important to their patrons, who honored them with special privileges. The great ceramicists of Saga who produced the exquisite porcelains the daimyo presented to his peers, the Kakiemon and Imaemon lines, were favored citizens whose genius made natural the adoption of outstanding students in the creation of dynasties of specialists who served from generation to generation. Unlike their warrior "superiors," in fact, those lines live on into contemporary times; their skills proved even more valuable in the free market of modern times. In areas closer to metropolitan centers, however, the smaller size of domains and larger opportunities for commercial outlets made mercantilist policies impractical. Especially on the great plains around Edo and Osaka, private interests had a better chance to develop ties with urban distributors and contributed to the development of a regional economy with less regard to samurai interests.

The setting was thus one of considerable variety. Throughout Japan, however, urbanization developed rapidly—perhaps by a factor of four—during the first century of Tokugawa rule. The domain system with its castle towns meant that the distribution of local cities was relatively even in proportion to the productivity of the area. Everywhere there was a gradual diffusion of urban influence from metropolis to castle town and from castle town through

market towns and periodic markets. Some modern city names reflect the Tokugawa antecedents of contemporary urbanization.[14]

4. Edo: The Central Magnet

The shogun's capital, Edo, was the largest castle town of all. A large Tokugawa
map shows the complexity of its design (see illustration 13). Situated at the
tip of the Musashino plateau overlooking a natural bay, the site had been used
by a minor lord before Hideyoshi transferred the area to Ieyasu in 1590. Ieyasu
began the construction of his castle shortly afterward, but it was not until his
victory at Sekigahara and his investment as shogun that he was able to order
the great lords to contribute labor and materials to the building of the great
Chiyoda Castle. The construction of Edo was practically a task of national
proportions, as feudatories were called upon for thousands of tons of rocks,
forests of timber, and thousands of workers to provide the labor, transport,
and shipping. Giant engineering projects altered the flow of rivers to drain
the flood plain into the Sumida River and on to Edo Bay. Part of that bay
was reclaimed as a port; Kanda mountain was leveled to provide fill and partially replaced by a deeply recessed river highway (Ochanomizu, "Tea Water");
a network of canals and waterways provided a supply of water from the west
as well as the means of transportation throughout the city.[15]

The city's commercial and amusement areas developed along the banks
and at the base of bridges that spanned these waterways. Freight and passenger
traffic moved along those arteries. Eighteenth-century popular prints show
parties of revelers bound for restaurants, theaters, and the brothels of the
licensed quarters in evening excursions on pleasure barges. Waterfront areas
were public space, and administered by the bakufu. At first their slopes were
grassy and muddy, but as the city grew they were buttressed with substantial
stones and lined with warehouses, shops, and markets. They became areas
where official and popular life could intersect. The greatest of the bridges was
the Japan Bridge, or Nihonbashi, completed in 1604. Two years later official
notice boards (kōsatsu) posted official decrees and instructions; much later,
the same boards came to carry satirical verses that criticized a sluggish government. Nihonbashi was soon the center of a great fish market and commercial
center. It was considered the center of the realm, and all distances were measured from it.

Tokugawa era block-print maps show the centrality of the city's waterways
to its life. In modern times the canal and river routes have provided inviting
routes for rails and roads, and much of the old network has disappeared. The
area within the inner moat describes the circumference of modern Tokyo's

"High City" *(yamanote)* rapid transit line, and the Japan Bridge, an arched eminence in Hiroshige prints with splendid views of Mt. Fuji, is buried in insignificance beneath the modern highway system.

The map centers, as the city did, on the enceinte, the line of fortification, around the shogun's (and presently emperor's) residence. Around it, to the west and north, were clustered the residential sections for daimyo and for Tokugawa samurai; these occupied almost 70 percent of the city's land. Temples and shrines had approximately 15 percent, and the remaining 15 percent were listed as the *machi* or *chō*, the so-called towns for the *chōnin*, the townsmen or commoners. The most desirable heights were reserved for the daimyo estates *(yashiki)* the bakufu set aside for daimyo obliged to take up residence by the *sankin-kōtai* system. Most of these were in the high city to the west of the castle. It is an area divided into three sectors and dominated by seven hills, intersected by five valleys, and was by far the most salubrious and desirable residential quarter of the city. Ridge roads ran along the summits, ring roads connected them, and branch roads marked the development of smaller hills that protruded from the larger ones. This same hierarchy characterized the arrangement of the daimyo mansions, which dominated the heights, the quarters for the Tokugawa bannermen *(hatamoto)*, and for ordinary foot soldiers. Vagaries of topography made it impossible to be completely consistent, but what seems a jumble of patchwork arrangements was in fact laid out with measurements for everything, including the daimyo mansions, along a grid pattern measuring 360 × 480 × 720 feet, one that had been used to divide the capital of Kyoto at the dawn of imperial history.[16]

Daimyo estates could be very large, and some became veritable municipalities. Their size and location were appropriate to the domain's assessed rice productivity and the daimyo's status within the Tokugawa hierarchy, and that, for *fudai* at least, had been determined by the ancestors' valor in the wars of unification. The greatest of the lords, Maeda of Kanazawa in Kaga, was assigned an area which in the nineteenth century became the sprawling campus of the government university, today's University of Tokyo. These areas passed into imperial hands at the time of the Meiji Restoration, and other great estates shown on the map became government offices, detached palaces, and homes of the powerful and wealthy. Bakufu sumptuary regulations indicated the daimyo's status by specifying appropriate dimensions for central and supporting gates. The gates too were designed along set patterns in unit measurements by master carpenters who were veritable lords among craftsmen, directing squads of workers.[17] The entire estate was walled, many of the walls doubling as "long house" residences for domain samurai. In contrast to the great mansions fronting on public squares with which aristocrats tried to impress one another in early European cities, the Edo daimyo, if they could afford it and had the space, developed bucolic parks within their walls. Frequently elaborate landscaping reproduced in miniature famous spots of natural beauty in China or Japan. Consequently much of upland Edo was an area of greenery and parks, a restful space from which ordinary people were, of course, excluded.[18] Within the daimyo compound life went on as though it was a branch of the province from which the daimyo hailed, and, since the Edo *yashiki* were gatherings of provincials, the local dialects of Satsuma, or Tosa, or Niigata prevailed. The lord's residence, often of great elegance, was supplemented by buildings for his staff and required offices, storehouses, stables, a school, gymnasium, quarters for servants, and sometimes even, since the lord's people were subject to his jurisdiction only, a prison.

The lords' life in Edo was punctuated by shogunal audiences at set intervals. These were not individual meetings, however, but calls to pay homage through obeisance. In the audience chambers daimyo in residence in Edo were arranged by status within seven categories, each assigned a hall and place; the seventh and last, naturally a large and numerous category, was for those rated at less than 30,000 *koku*. This accomplished, the lords and their retinues returned to the splendid isolation of their *yashiki*. There the lord could receive *his* vassals and carry on ancestral rites and ceremonies appropriate to the season. Some socializing took place between them (we read of the Tosa daimyo summoning a potter from Kōchi to display his skill for one of his peers) but it was profoundly unlike the glittering seasons and salons staged by their counterparts in Europe. Some *fudai* found themselves serving as bakufu administrators, but charts of official appointments show a high preponderance of the same families generation after generation. The daimyo highest on the status ladder, the *tozama* of western Japan, however, were systematically underrepresented in bakufu councils. Domain administrators might seek marriage partners for their lords from other mansions if bakufu officials approved; on the whole, however, there seems to have been surprisingly little interaction among the lords. Instead they tended to create within the walls of their estates as satisfactory and familiar a world as possible. Retired lords were often likely to remain in Edo, sometimes residing in a secondary mansion. Most han developed additional mansions after the mid-seventeenth century; by the eighteenth century the average domain had three, designated as "upper," "middle," and "lower."[19] Not infrequently additional space might be purchased to house domain functions or functionaries. Most major domains located their "lower" mansion on the waterfront for convenience in importing foodstuffs and other materials. Parts of holdings designated as "lower" might be adjacent to, and not even within, the walled enclaves.[20] As restrictions loosened, domains came to buy, sell, and exchange plots of land that had been granted to them. Some establishments were so large that requirements for space must have been formidable; Mōri of Chōshū, for instance, maintained an entire community, some 5,000 people, in Edo.

Interaction with men from other areas became more possible and probable as one went down the scale of ranks. Domain administrators had to deal with comparable problems of mansion maintenance and bakufu relations. When the daimyo was away from Edo an absentee alternate, a *rusuiyaku*, was responsible for matters at the capital. There was even a fledgling council of such men that might have been thought to hold promise for some sort of future representative assembly, but it is known to us chiefly through bakufu scoldings that its members did more partying than planning. At the lowest, samurai, level, interaction with men from other areas was more likely. Schools of martial arts, concerns of household economy, and centers of entertainment and amusement were all there to fill the empty hours.

To nonsamurai the mansions were spheres of gentility and luxury, and service there, while difficult to arrange, was eagerly sought. Francis Hall, the nineteenth-century diarist we have encountered earlier, wrote that "the Edo yashikis, or palaces of the hereditary nobles, employ a large number of female servants and each mistress of such yashiki is surrounded by a bevy of maids whose idle and luxurious life is the coveted position to which many a simple country maid aspires, knowing in what arts and accomplishments she will here be educated, to the better adornment of her position."[21] Not that entry was easy. Mori Ōgai tells of a girl of fourteen who applied for duty in a daimyo mansion. She was examined "in calligraphy, writing Japanese poetry in the classical thirty-one syllable mode and music. The examiner was a senior woman attendant. An inkstone, a writing brush and a piece of formal, patterned paper were put in front of [the candidate] . . ." On being accepted, "She was immediately made a *chūrō* (a term we have encountered in the feudal hierarchy of officials), or female attendant of the middle rank, assigned to the lord's quarters, with the additional responsibility of being private secretary to [his lady] . . ." In that status she "had an apartment of three rooms, and kept two maids." Her salary, however, was modest in the extreme, and she herself paid the maids; she was there, really, at her father's expense, to be educated and to prepare for living a refined, upper-middle-class life.[22]

House plots for the bannermen and ordinary bakufu soldiers, who were of course far more numerous, were also far more modest. A recent study notes that "nearly all the roads running through the warrior areas have quietly remained exactly as they were. What is most noteworthy about these areas is their beautifully planned character. Examples abound of uniform neighborhoods and lot divisions created by the straight roads through these basically complete and independent units."[23] These samurai, unlike the rotating service elite, were permanent residents of Edo. Of course their homes varied by rank and stipend. A high-ranking *hatamoto*'s mansion might rival that of a minor daimyo in size and ambience, but humbler castes were housed in group compounds in which a street or block *(chō)* had some twenty or thirty residences on each side. Such a *chō* was a unit of municipal administration. For most of the period entrance and exit were restricted by wooden gates at both ends that kept outsiders out and were closed at night. Since Edo was both a rural and a relatively spacious area for the privileged, gardens and green were possible, and only the lowest of ranks would fail to have room for at least a few vegetables.

Protection of the city was provided for in sites set aside for sacred use, selected by Taoist geomancy about direction and fortune. Three great protective temple complexes took shape in the northeast, the most dangerous direction (Ueno); a shogunal temple (Zōjōji) guarded the southwest quarter in Shiba; and Sensōji, in Asakusa, centered on a great temple of Kannon to the north. These precincts and the river and canal banks were as close as Edo came to "public" or "common" land, and the Asakusa temple area, at least, became associated with a vast commercial and entertainment zone surrounding the compassionate figure of Kannon in the central temple.[24]

That left 15 percent of Edo's territory for the greater half of its inhabitants. Commoner concentrations might be found in some of the valleys and defiles that separated the high city hills of the elite, and in these areas service trades quickly took shape. Modern highway development and high-rise housing has brought an end to most of these, but one that survives is at the confluence of a river, Second Bridge, and a road near Shiba where a cluster of merchant shops provided goods for the daimyo mansions on the "Shrine Hill" (Torii-zaka) of Azabu that rose around it. In more recent times its merchants have catered to the hotels, apartments, and embassies that inherited the land once reserved for daimyo mansions.

Most commoners were crowded into narrow lanes in the low-lying areas of Fukagawa and Nihonbashi that were reclaimed from Edo Bay or developed from agricultural fields. This became the "low city" *(shitamachi),* where the thousands of craftsmen, artisans, peddlers, and merchants thronged. Lots were fairly standard. Two-story merchant houses lined the main streets, and the lots behind them were relatively long. Behind the houses with frontage were rows of tenement houses, divided into two- or three-, or sometimes a single, room accommodation, where poorer artisans and laborers were to be found. Outside was a communal latrine, a source of water (well or access to the water supply), and a place for refuse. The back street might also be jammed with shops. The owner or renter of the building with the frontage collected rents from those within. Frontage space conferred membership or "share" *(kabu)* in the *chō*, and a degree of responsibility for what went on inside. Frequently gates closed off the street for ease in enforcing curfews and security.

In one aspect of security the government was, however, quite helpless: that of fire. The wooden construction of all of the city and the narrow lanes of commoner quarters made fire a devastating experience, and it came sufficiently frequently to be called "the flowers of Edo." Fires were no respecters of status and rank, and when driven by winter winds in the dry season they roared through the city. For the domains, this multiplied the costs of maintaining the Edo mansions, which had to be restored and rebuilt with materials purchased locally or shipped by sea. In the 268 years of Tokugawa rule the Tosa "upper" *yashiki* (at "Blacksmith Bridge") suffered eighteen fires, and the Shiba middle residence burned twelve times. Four of these were citywide conflagrations. Merchant areas burned thirty-one times in two centuries, and even the shogun's castle suffered major damage seven times.

The greatest of the fires was probably that of 1657, the Meireki era fire, which ranks with the 1923 earthquake and 1945 B-29 firebomb raids as pivotal in the city's history. James McClain describes it well:

> The first fire began early on the eighteenth afternoon of the new year of Meireki 3, 1657, at Honmyōji, a small, inconsequential temple located in Hongō, on the northern rim of the city. By late afternoon flames had burned through Hongō, charred Yushima. Carried by flying sparks, the blaze jumped across moats and canals, wiped out dozens of daimyo estates clustered to the north of the castle, made short work of hundreds of bannerman compounds, scorched merchant housing in the thickly settled districts that lined the Kanda River. In the early evening the treacherous winds shifted and hurried the flames into the merchant quarters along the banks of the Sumida River . . . Several hours later a carelessly tended cooking fire in a samurai residence in Koishikawa ignited a second day of terror. The wind, still fierce, quickly fanned the flames into another major conflagration. First lost were several large daimyo estates, and then the blaze leaped into Edo Castle, consuming large portions of the central residential keep and swallowing up the great donjon, towering symbol of the shogun's wealth and power.[25]

The author goes on to quote a seventeenth-century writer, Asai Ryōi, who wrote that people poured out of the residential quarters, hoping to escape the rapidly spreading fire. Discarded family chests clogged street crossings . . . Tongues of raging flames shot into the crowds of jostling people, pushing and shoving against one another . . . bridges fell, reduced to ashes. Hemmed in by flames, the crowd first surged to the south, then came back to the north. Struggling helplessly, they tried the east, the west.[26]

When it was over more than 100,000 had died. Lying in ashes were 160 daimyo estates, 3,550 temples and shrines, more than 750 residential compounds of *hatamoto* and samurai, and perhaps 50,000 commoner houses.

After the fire the city was quickly rebuilt. A half century of peace had brought increased standards of prosperity and comfort, and the daimyo mansions tended to be more splendid than before. Additional residences were built by domains that had not yet supplemented their primary residence. The bakufu did its best to reorder some arrangements to prevent a recurrence of the fire. Many temples were moved from the center to relatively suburban positions, and the city grew outward to the north and west. In the crowded commoner quarters the government tried to institute clearings along waterways and bridges to create firebreaks. As McClain's study of Edo Bridge shows, however, these efforts were not long successful. The first to petition for exceptions to the rule were wholesalers anxious to establish warehouses for the goods that arrived by boat. In their wake came temporary shops that gradually became less temporary and tutelary temples that provided protection against disaster; restaurants and houses of entertainment soon multiplied, and with them came theaters, entertainers, and beggars. What was happening, as McClain describes it, was a gradual shift, over time, in which the commoners were gaining at the expense of elite status groups in respect to the appropriation of space despite the fact that the inequality of space remained largely as it had been.

This was to be seen in two additional areas. Fire fighting in the broad expanses of samurai Edo was at first a warrior prerogative; daimyo were responsible for their compounds, and bakufu vassals for their zones. But as fires knew no jurisdiction, the inefficiency that divided responsibility produced led daimyo to petition for permission to pursue fires before their compounds were endangered. In the early eighteenth century the bakufu tried to establish a citywide authority structure under which clearly defined zonal responsibilities were established. Fire-fighting technology consisted largely of pulling down houses that were expected to be in the line of fire rather than trying to pump water. This led to a combination of authoritarianism and privatization: commoner units were conscripted as a form of taxation, and merchants, who protested unsuccessfully against this, tried to hire substitutes. Gradually specialist corps emerged. By the early nineteenth century these showed considerable élan and laid claim to the tradition of urban toughs *(kabukimono)* of early Tokugawa days, and annual displays of gymnastic virtuosity became a festival tradition. Equipped and authorized to pull down houses in the line of fire, they also possessed the means for social intimidation of uncooperative house owners.[27]

Another area in which commoner interests gradually became distinct from those of their samurai betters was water supply. In laying out Edo Ieyasu's engineers had followed the pattern of daimyo castle towns, giving first priority to defense and security with a system of waterways that served chiefly the interests of samurai defenders. As additional supplies were needed enclosed culverts carried drinking water from desirable locations in western Edo and the Kanda River, while commoners were restricted to neighborhood wells that were located in the back of their narrow alleys. They were maintained communally with periodic cleaning to keep them usable. As the "public" samurai system became overloaded and brackish, however, the upper-status groups turned to wells they could sink on their more extensive grounds, while commoners increasingly came to rely on the less desirable but relatively plentiful "public" supply. Gradually the burden of maintaining the public system shifted from the samurai to the merchant and artisan neighborhoods. In a process that was coordinated by the city magistrates, commoner property owners were taxed and conscripted for the system's maintenance. As with protection against fire, security of the water supply became interwoven with the routine and complexity of commoner social life. As people tired of the heavy work involved in dredging the lines, those who were able to increased the levies for local needs so that they could hire day laborers to do the work.[28]

The complexity of Edo's social fabric was reflected in its patchwork administrative structure. Daimyo were responsible for their estates and their retainers. Commoner *chō* administration was entrusted to a pattern of headmen that resembled the countryside from which the urbanites had come. Policing was relatively light and informal, though the watch stations and barriers and gates made it unwise to challenge the curfew. Through it all, however, the direction of change was toward greater integration and consolidation under the direction of the city magistrate. This pattern tells a great deal about Japanese society, and it is important to note some points. Just as the city grew and changed with time, the bakufu's response to problems of order and efficiency changed. The mid-decades of the seventeenth century, centering on the great Meireki Fire, provide one period. In the early eighteenth century, Shogun

Yoshimune's reform administrator Ōoka Tadasuke, styled Lord of Echizen, left his mark on the city by struggling to organize a castle town that had become a metropolis.[29] The early-nineteenth-century decades of rethinking society that preceded the tumultuous period of the Meiji Restoration mark the third.

A consistent pattern was the fact that the bakufu, despite its plethora of underemployed retainers, did as little as possible itself and wanted individual categories of inhabitants to run their own affairs. Shogunal courts were reluctant to interfere in disputes that did not directly concern the government and urged litigants to work out their own settlements.[30] The bakufu wanted information about the way people were doing things, and it wanted local officials to report its laws and warnings to those below them, but it was not prepared to establish a functioning bureaucracy. Daimyo establishments, like the domains that supported them, were substantially autonomous. "Outside" samurai, as from Satsuma or Tosa, enjoyed virtual extraterritoriality in Edo, though severe infractions of order by troublemakers would, when reported, bring consultations between shogunal and domain administrators. No police official attached to the City Magistrate was empowered to apprehend anyone within a daimyo quarter or even within the areas set aside for bakufu vassals. The senior councillors (*rōjū*) dealt with the daimyo, who in turn were expected to enforce regulations reasonably congruent with those of the bakufu itself. Bakufu vassals, the *hatamoto* and ordinary samurai, were the province of the Junior Council. Temples were under the administration of the Magistrate for Shrines and Temples, while townsmen were the preserve of the City Magistrate. Since the townsmen constituted so large a sector of the population, it will be useful to examine that administrative grid more closely.

In the fourth decade of the seventeenth century the bakufu, alarmed by the number of persons being cut down on the streets, ordered that guardhouses be set up in its samurai areas, and before long over nine hundred such were established. Several hundred of these were staffed and financed by daimyo, and the rest by bannermen. From these centers (which might be seen as the antecedents of the modern Japanese police box), guards issued forth to patrol the neighborhood and detain suspicious types or ruffians. In merchant quarters the City Magistrate set up several hundred more stations, staffed by constables, who usually inherited their positions. They were supposed to report on the public mood, encourage virtuous conduct, and in general make up for the fact that Edo was so lightly policed. Commoner residential quarters in turn set up guardhouses and gate houses to look after things and make sure the gates to *chō* were closed at night and during searches for criminals. The commoner quarters gradually developed additional functionaries. At the very top were three elders *(machitoshiyori)*, who were permitted swords and were received in audience by the shogun at the New Year. Although not salaried, they received plots that they normally rented out. Each neighborhood had a chief *(nanushi,* the word also used for village heads). This office too became hereditary. By the middle of the eighteenth century about 250 men held this position. At the lowest level, families were organized into five-family *(gonin gumi)* groups headed by substantial people (that is, owners of houses with street frontage), who were responsible for the compliance of their tenants and hangers-on with bakufu laws. These groups were given oversight of street maintenance; they collected levies for fire fighting and water system maintenance, expenses for festivals, guardhouses, gates, and the like. Each group had a chief, who served by rotation. He was the one to approach with petitions (as for travel permits), investigations, and so on.

Thus there was a complex process of devolution of responsibility downward from the city magistrate to ordinary city dwellers. The bakufu seems to have hoped, as one author puts it, "that with so many people involved, all would feel heavier weight of accountability, all would take a hand in enforcing the laws of the realm and the city."[31]

Withal, Edo, no doubt like other castle towns, remained a city in which one proceeded with caution, especially after dark. This was partly because rank made it possible to intimidate those of lower status. The diary of a *hatamoto* wastrel, *Musui Dokugen*, describes his ability, by standing on his rank, to organize fellow toughs, start fights, and generally terrorize his neighborhood. In part this seems to have developed from his frustration at never finding employment. "Once," he writes, "while waiting in one of the rooms at the court, I got into a big argument with Kamiue Yatarō, a senior policeman in the service of Ōkusa Noto-no-kami. It took three men—the custodian of the court, Kamio Tōemon, his inspector-aide, Ishizaka Seizaburō, and a policeman, Yuba Sōjūrō—to convince me to let him off without reporting it to his lord. The altercation lasted about two hours." Lower orders fared still worse: ". . . We picked fights along the way and went as far as Ryōgoku Bridge. That evening, with nothing special to do, I went home."

Families of some status with such a troublemaker on their hands had to provide their own restraints.[32] Musui at one point found that

> on returning home, I saw that a cage the size of three tatami mats had been set up in the middle of the sitting room. I was thrown in. Inside the cage I jiggled the bars and in less than a month had figured out a way to remove two of them. I also reflected on my past conduct and came to the conclusion that whatever had happened had been my fault.[33]

Privatization of punitive or preventive measures of this sort could hardly be a substitute for a well-policed society. In late Tokugawa days, when the fabric of authority became frayed, the Meiji period educator Fukuzawa recalled making his way home in the dusk after a pleasant evening with a group of fellow students of Western learning. All the guests forgot the time. Antiforeign feeling was on the rise, and they felt themselves in danger. Swords were kept at the ready.

> Our host came to the emergency and hired a covered boat for us on the neighboring river. In this unsuspected craft we were to be carried to various parts of the city along the rivers and canals. Those who lived nearby got off first, and one by one as the boat came to the vicinity of a home, someone landed. Finally, an old doctor named Tozuka and myself were landed at Shimbashi. Tozuka went in the direction of Azabu, and I was to walk to my place in Shinse.
>
> It was a walk of a little less than a mile. The hour had already turned an hour past midnight—it was a cold and clear winter night with the moon shining brightly overhead . . . I walked along the broad, vacant street—no one in sight, absolutely still. Yet I remembered that strolling ruffians had been appearing every night, cutting down unfortunate victims at dark corners. I tucked up the wide ends of my *hakama* in order to be ready to run at any signal and kept up a very fast pace.

Suddenly he saw a fellow coming toward him, who "looked gigantic in the moonlight . . . nowadays there are policemen to depend upon, or we can run into someone's house for protection," but not then. Fukuzawa decided there was no way for it but to tough it out, and moved to the center of the street. To his consternation the other man did the same. They were on a near collision course.

> Every step brought us nearer, and finally we were at a striking distance. He did not draw. Of course I did not draw either. So we passed each other. With this as a cue, I ran. I do not remember how fast I ran. After running a little distance I turned to look back as I flew. The other man was running too, in his direction . . . He must have been frightened; certainly I was.[34]

This story speaks, of course, of unusual times of uncertainty and danger. But it illustrates a number of points: the absence of police protection, particularly in samurai quarters; the use of boats for transportation throughout Edo; the curfew. We are familiar with Tokugawa wood prints showing covered ships, cheerful with their lanterns, inebriated passengers, and colorful inamorata, festival fireworks in the background, heading for an evening of sport in the licensed quarter. Fukuzawa's route, however, led to the other side of Edo.

Violence and lawlessness, privatized imprisonment, post stations, and assisting villages, sporadic and frenzied pilgrimages that encouraged license and levity as much as they did piety, all provide color in the panorama of early modern Japanese society. Beneath the whole, however, was the development of a pattern of interrelationships that set Japan off from most other countries.

The first was the sheer scale of urban growth. The political measures that forced samurai to take up residence in castle towns and cities resulted in the concentration of the elite in administrative centers throughout the land. They in turn required the presence of service trades, and thanks to that the cities and castle towns speedily became local, regional, and national centers of manufacture, trade, and commerce. By the turn of the first century of Tokugawa rule virtually every domain had close to one tenth of its population in such an urban center.

Second, the system of alternate attendance transformed the upper reaches of the samurai elite into a circulating or rotating service class and built a never-ending round of travel and preparation for travel into their lives. Hostels and business enterprises sprang up along the main traveled roads to service and profit from that travel. In response to the demands of the Edo government a communications network developed; Edo became the nerve center of the country, its stories and concerns diffused by every procession that filed out of the walled estates to return to its point of origin.

Third, this had a telling effect on domain, regional, and national economies. The urban centers with their large populations required food, raw materials, and constant reinforcement of their numbers. Daimyo needed to sell part of the rice tax their agents collected, greengrocers had to scour the countryside for supplies, and peasants needed the urban waste to fertilize their fields. From village to domain, Japan became less self-sufficient and more attuned to exchange.

Fourth, the interaction of regional with metropolitan culture speeded the development of a national culture. The system of alternate attendance acquainted the thousands who traveled with the state of affairs in the provinces through which they passed, providing a basis for comparison and evaluation. They returned home with the goods and learning they had acquired at the capital. Metropolitan center teachers of everything from swordsmanship to

Confucian learning came to have disciples in the provinces and attracted students who could come. The descendants of the Sengoku daimyo became by degrees urban aristocrats who prided themselves on their mastery of the arts of tea and calligraphy. Like the Korean court's care to select worthy cultural ambassadors for missions to Japan, they began to see to it that their Edo mansions did not lack the presence of men able to hold their own in cultivating the arts of peace.

THE DEVELOPMENT
OF A MASS CULTURE

6

In the seventeenth century there was a top-down spread of literacy and culture, as there had been of urban settlements. In the case of cities the concentration of the warriors at their lords' capitals was followed by the recruitment of servants, artisans, and merchants to meet their needs, and that sequence of settlement helped give the castle towns their distinctive topographical arrangement. In literacy and culture the development was broadly similar; the average samurai, poorly schooled and barely literate at the time of Sekigahara, was enjoined by early shoguns and lords to follow the path of letters as well as that of arms; urban life gave point to this, and by the end of the century most samurai had acquired at least some literacy. The new society of cities, with the flow of men and goods they brought, made literacy possible and gradually essential for many more. Block-printed texts of religious and ethical precepts, proper manners and deportment, and the efficient conduct of trade and agriculture spread throughout the land. Requirements of periodic registration for religion and for census, for tenant shares and taxes, spread the most basic skills of syllabary literacy even farther. As these needs were earliest felt and became most pressing near the great cities of Osaka and Edo, it was also there that a commoner mass culture had its birth. By the century's end new forms of poetry, new tastes in reading, and new diversions in theater marked the dawn of a modern people's culture.

1. Civilizing the Ruling Class

For the first century of Tokugawa rule the shogunal capital of Edo and the castle towns that dotted the communication routes were dominated by the warriors whose residences took up most of the urban area. After decades of warfare that had brutalized the samurai it required some time to change them into useful agents of civil government. Most of the major generals were literate, but some were barely so. An early daimyo of Tosa, for instance, drew ridicule for his fondness for the Confucian *Classic of Filial Piety,* and had difficulty explaining its utility as a tool for ruling the country. Ieyasu himself was conscious of the importance of civilizing his samurai, utilized existing libraries for studies of precedents, and thought it desirable to encourage the diffusion of literacy among his retainers. Even so, as late as 1715 only twenty of the domains had established official schools for their samurai. Early education was for the most part carried out by private tutors for the high-ranking, or sometimes in small groups by Buddhist monks. By the end of the century, however, the writer Saikaku could point out that a samurai unable to read was sadly behind the times, and permitted himself the sweeping statement that "there is nothing in the world as shameful as being unable to write."[1]

The material the young samurai was expected to read and write began with edifying excerpts from Chinese classics about morality and loyalty. Besides basic calligraphy in Chinese characters and the Confucian Four Books (*The Analects of Confucius, The Book of Mencius, Great Learning,* and *Doctrine of the Mean*), he was taught deportment, the tea ceremony, and some elementary Nō chanting and drums. With adolescence he was tutored in fencing, swordsmanship, horse riding, and archery. By the age of eighteen or nineteen the young warrior–turned gentleman was supposed to be competent in Chinese and Japanese verse, chess, backgammon, and military administration. In other words, with allowance made for the zone of civilization, the young man's accomplishments were similar to what might have been expected of his upper-class counterpart in western Europe.

Civilization also involved pacification. The early shogunate had to curb random violence in city streets by *kabukimono,* the young toughs who had proved to be a dangerous nuisance. It was better to have young bloods working at their books than swaggering around the towns making life dangerous for ordinary people. The Meireki era fire of 1657 marked something of a divide in problems of this sort, for the Edo that was rebuilt was far more attuned to patterns of peace.

In castle towns samurai youths were subject to fewer of the civilizing influences that prevailed at the shogun's capital, but by and large there was a parallel, albeit slower, trend in the same direction. Anticipation of duty and residence at Edo can have been expected to provide incentives for achievements of this sort. By the end of the century private tutoring and fencing academies in which rank counted for less than accomplishment gradually began to change the nature of samurai society.

Tokugawa Japan provided sponsorship and patronage for architecture, painting, sculpture, calligraphy, and theater to a degree previously unknown. The explosion of activity involved in developing warrior-sponsored temple complexes, castle town residences for high retainers, and daimyo mansions in Edo all created a setting for the development of virtuosity of artisans and artists. Artists and architects enjoyed a level of support they had never known before. Painters adorned the walls of temples, palaces, and castles with paintings and screens that still stand as markers of upper-class taste and refinement. Landscape architects too could test their skills in gardens that were commissioned for temples that were restored and new mansions.

In the paintings for private quarters of the new residences convention favored scenes from Chinese life, as imagined in the classics used in education. The leading exponents of these themes were the artists of the Kanō school, which had come to the forefront in late Muromachi (Ashikaga) and Sengoku years. Nobunaga and Hideyoshi were both patrons of Kanō artists, and with the Tokugawa victory the Kanō school became virtually the official school of art. Kanō Tanyū (1602–1674), the patriarch of the line, received private audiences from Ieyasu and Hidetada, was given an Edo residence outside the Edo castle gate, and received an imperial court rank appropriate to a daimyo. A large number of artists worked in Kanō workshops, and the master provided the finishing and legitimating touches.[2] Tanyū and his brothers furnished sliding-door *(fusuma)* paintings for Tokugawa palaces in Edo, Nagoya, Kyoto (Nijō), and the imperial palace, Ieyasu's mausoleum at Nikko, and a number of the great Buddhist temples in Kyoto. In old age he was given the Buddhist honorary title of *hōin*, the highest title bestowed on a painter. Since the Kanō school was patronized by the shogun, its works and style were favored by the daimyo and upper retainers as well. Another line of painters, the Tosa school, owed less to Chinese style (and nothing to the province of that name) and featured a clearer sense of line and motion. Accomplished artists sometimes combined the two or worked in both separately. These two schools set the standards for the artistic preferences of the elite.

Architecture too profited from the sponsorship made possible by a country at peace plentifully provided with ruling-class patronage. Almost all major Buddhist temples were rebuilt in the early Tokugawa reigns. In most cases the slavish commitment to Chinese style that had characterized the Muromachi era with its emphasis on Sung-era gates (*Karamon*, "Chinese gate") was replaced by a more sober and less flamboyant approach. Two exceptions perhaps prove the rule. In Uji, near Nara, a branch of a Chinese Zen sect brought in through Nagasaki was responsible for the great Ōbaku Manpukuji temple, which was constructed in almost purely Ming dynasty style. For the first half of the period, it will be remembered, it was headed by abbots brought from China. The other exception, and far more famous, is the Nikko mausoleum/temple dedicated to Ieyasu after he was deified as the "Shining Deity of the East" by his grandson Iemitsu. Here the urge for rich sculptured decoration was expressed in dazzling color quite in contrast to the normal Japanese preference for unpainted wood. The Nikko shrine, given imperial honor equal to that accorded the Ise shrine dedicated to the sun goddess Amaterasu, was approached by a special highway lined with cryptomeria trees contributed by daimyo. Along it wound processions of successive shoguns, emissaries from the imperial court, and Korean ambassadors. At Nikko itself "the efforts of the architect and the wood-carver to reach maximum richness in a whole group of buildings have been complemented by an equal emphasis on color, inside and out. The key is almost barbarically high, hot red, intense light blue, gold accents, a contrabass of black lacquer; the ultimate visual shock is given by key areas painted a dazzling white." Yet even here the Chinese-style magnificence was subdued by its setting. In China this striking group of temples would have been left open to the sky and surrounded by marble pavements, but at Nikko a setting of towering cryptomeria provides a depth of shadow into which the tumult of the group of buildings sinks, almost without an echo.[3]

Ceramics too made great headway. The tea ceremony, an essential accomplishment for the cultured, brought with it opportunity for potters whose ware complemented the rustic simplicity of the artfully simple setting in which the great found respite from the formality of official life and duty. Each of the Sengoku unifiers played a part in the immense respect that was paid to water jars and tea bowls of particularly subtle and quite natural beauty; not a few carried names and became objects of desire and intense competition at the very highest ranks of society. Some master potters developed works of quiet and exquisite elegance. The early-seventeenth-century potter Nonomura Ninsei, perhaps the first to sign his work, indicated an awareness of craftsman-as-artist that marked a new sophistication. His tea jars and incense burners, done in a boldly decorative style, complemented the magnificence of the new ruling class.

The surge of urban needs and travel that has been described also brought the opportunity to market nationwide the products of humbler kilns. Many areas developed local glazes and clays that made it possible for commoners to shift from wooden to ceramic bowls, with consequent benefits for health and longevity. Porcelain complemented earthenware. In the northern Kyushu province of Hizen the Saga daimyo, Nabeshima, had the advantage of groups of Korean potters his armies had commandeered and brought back to Japan after the Hideyoshi invasions of the 1590s. In the early seventeenth century Saga potters discovered a rich vein of kaolin that permitted experimentation with porcelain. Production became a domain enterprise, and it was carried out under careful supervision and control. Slightly removed from the main Arita kilns, a very special porcelain ware, known to the daimyo as Nabeshima, was produced under conditions of military security to protect its secrets and used for gifts the daimyo needed to make to his overlord in Edo. Meanwhile the main ware produced at Arita, modeled on dishes produced in Ming China in its patterns of blue and white, became exported through the port of Imari to Nagasaki whence it was diffused through Europe. Far greater amounts were shipped around the coastal trading routes of Japan to serve as noodle bowls and dishes in all major urban centers.

The diffusion of such wares, albeit of more modest quality, for large-scale markets gradually produced a congruence in pattern and taste throughout Tokugawa society. It is somewhat misleading to speak of "popular" culture as something quite distinct from "high" culture. To be sure some pastimes, among them Nō theater, were restricted by edict to the ruling caste, as were, by cost and practice, the finest porcelains and paintings. But what was shared and diffused was more important than what was set apart. As the period progressed, a truly mass culture began to take shape.

2. Books and Literacy

In a country at peace samurai were not the only ones who needed to be literate. Heads of five-family units had to know the rules and report on their enforcement, village leaders had to keep records and file reports on population and temple registers, merchants had to keep books, and the simple warnings (*kōsatsu*) that were posted at traffic intersections and bridges had no point unless people were able to know what they said. After the early decades of the seventeenth century Japanese had access to a steadily growing volume of books—devotional, entertaining, and practical—and grew up surrounded by print in a society that valued the ability to master that medium.

At first authorities did not have much reason to encourage literacy among commoners, and in some parts of the country they never did. But they seldom discouraged it. As those authorities themselves gradually became more imbued with Confucian values, they usually came to realize that literacy in the basic collections of homilies would make those they ruled easier to rule. After the first century of Tokugawa rule literacy among commoners, reflected in the establishment of commoner schools (*terakoya*), accelerated rapidly. Even before that it was important for local notables. By end of the century, when the poet Matsuo Bashō went on pilgrimage to outlying corners of the land, he was welcomed everywhere he went by village leaders who knew of him and often did their best to match the poetic skills of their famous guest with their own, more humble, efforts. The effects of reading could also go far beyond the circle of those empowered to read. Local notables and village leaders were expected to enlighten their people on what was expected of them, somewhat in the way Chinese village heads were expected to gather their charges for readings of the imperial edicts on morality.

Movable type printing was introduced to Japan—or, as Henry Smith puts it, stolen—from Korea by Hideyoshi's armies.[4] It was also utilized by the Jesuit press at Nagasaki, which published translations of works as varied as devotional writings and Aesop's fables. Some three hundred titles are known to have been published in wooden and metal movable type in the first decades of the seventeenth century. By 1626, however, publishers had reverted to the older technology of wooden printing blocks. Japanese had long been familiar with that method; indeed what are probably the world's oldest printed documents survive from devotional blocks done in seventh-century Japan. Block printing seems to have been more congenial to the needs of a language coded in the formidably complex writing system of Japanese, which makes use of Chinese characters and supplements them with two systems of phonetic symbols. Blocks made it possible to include cursive script and illustrations. Japan's publishers came to produce works in purely Chinese characters, mixed Sinico-Japanese, and purely Japanese syllabary. These skills developed first in the older cultural centers of Kyoto and Osaka. For much of the Tokugawa period Kyoto led in the production of Buddhist and Confucian material, both of which were most heavily "Chinese" in composition. Commercial publishing grew rapidly in Kyoto. By mid-century it had developed in Osaka, and in the eighteenth century it spread to Edo and the larger castle towns. One authority estimates that the total volume of titles produced in the seventeenth century came to 7,200, perhaps something over 100 per year; by the mid- and later years of the Tokugawa period, it probably rose to five or six times that number.

Block printing required skills different from those used in movable type, and its problems were human rather than technological. A skilled calligrapher was first needed to write on a block. The next and more difficult step involved the carver who prepared the block. Artisans came to specialize in cursive style, in various styles of formal script, and in illustrations. The completed block was inked and readied for the moistened sheet of paper that was applied by the printer. With little of the heft required for the binding and endpaper that distinguished Western books, the final process of assembling and stitching was relatively simple, often performed in-house by female labor. The final product was something far more fragile than its European counterpart. The rice paper used was subject to destruction by insect predators, but the process permitted rapid production. The number of copies that could be gained from a single set of blocks varied with the complexity of the design of the page of print and the quality of the wood used. Cherry was considered ideal because it was so hard. A formal work of Chinese characters could be reproduced many hundreds of times from the same block, while a delicately carved block of cursive type with illustrations was less serviceable over time. Used blocks might be planed smooth and used again, or they could be stored for later printings, though not without danger of warping. The skills and capital required, as Smith observes,[5] were dramatically different in Japan and in the West. The Western printer needed machinery and fonts of type, but once things were in place his skills were relatively easily obtained. His Japanese counterpart required little capital, but he did need an extended period of tutelage, which was usually organized along guild lines. Blocks and knives might be plentiful, but those capable of etching a fine and beautifully pointed line were not always easy to find.

It is worth noting that printing was a private enterprise. The shogunate was reasonably vigilant to make certain that publications did not endanger its security and did not offend public morals too dramatically, but it made no attempt to control things closely or to license what was published. There were, however, taboos that became more explicit as the reading public grew. Ordinances issued periodically, especially during periods of "reform," were especially firm in warning against works dealing with Christianity, which had of course been under the ban from the first. Inspection of books imported from China was motivated by the need to prevent Jesuit translations from coming in Chinese dress. A second category concerned anything that might be considered harmful to the public order. Contemporary politics were off-limits, as was discussion of the Tokugawa house. A third category concerned public morals and focused on pornography. There was no censorship, but publishers and authors could be charged with violation of these concerns after books appeared. Typically, punishments consisted of destruction of blocks and other capital equipment to cow the publishers, and use of the cangue, a wooden stock for neck or hands, to keep authors from producing more. These latent dangers were expected to intimidate the enterprise. It seldom proved necessary to invoke them, and outstanding incidents came only during the three periods (1729–1736, 1787–1793, and 1837–1843) when reform and regeneration were heralded as shogunal policy.[6]

Textbooks used in teaching young people to read were usually didactic, as in the West; in Japan they contained a mixture of Confucian homilies and

Buddhist moralisms. By the late seventeenth century, a more practical manual, or primer, appeared. *Ōrai,* as they were called, often provided terminology and know-how for commerce. Similar *ōrai* appeared to provide competence in everything from farming to household needs. By the end of the period, about 7,000 books of this sort had appeared. By the late 1600s another category, *chōhōki* ("accumulated treasures"), became common. These contained instructions for personal and social skills in many walks of life, for women as well as men. Still other collections of *Setsuyō* prepared the reader for life in a Japan at peace; there were sample forms for letter writing, lists of famous places, maps of the three major cities, outlines of Japanese history, and calendars of annual events. In short, they were close to the household encyclopedias common in the West.[7]

3. Osaka and Kyoto

Edo did not become Japan's greatest city until the eighteenth century. Until then two cities of the west, Osaka and Kyoto, were far more developed and advanced. Even after Edo caught up the three were usually referred to as *santo,* "the three metropolises" or capitals. Kyoto and Osaka were radically different from castle towns, of which Edo was the greatest, in the arrangement and allocation of space. The castle towns were military centers in which over half the space available was reserved for samurai. In Kyoto and Osaka the samurai presence was very slight; aside from a small number stationed there by the bakufu or domains, other groups came first.

Kyoto was the ancient capital, and throughout the Tokugawa period it remained the home of the imperial court and the old aristocracy. The *kuge* residences clustered around the imperial palace, which looked south down the central north-south avenues that echoed the arrangement of Chinese imperial capitals. The edges of the city were dominated by the grounds of the great temples. Two imperial gardens, the Katsura and the Shūgakuin, were located to the west and the north, but the emperor required bakufu permission for visits even to them. The great Buddhist temples, many of which had suffered partial or total damage in the wars of the sixteenth century, were restored. Craftsmen's and traders' residences and places of business were to be found in geometrically arranged streets south of the aristocratic quarter. They were often concentrated by craft, in streets that still indicated their original specialty, but more often there was a mix of products and specialties. Long periods of political instability had created a crazy quilt of patronage in which areas were responsible for, and contributed toward, their shrine, temple, and noble protectors. The unifiers, especially Hideyoshi, who virtually made Kyoto his capital, leveled this confusion out and made things uniform. Kyoto was known for the refinement of its citizens and of its products. Elaborate brocades and other textiles, fine lacquer and metal work, were among its specialties. A census report of 1593 for the northern, commercial center of Reizen-Muromachi listed fifty-nine workplaces and shops in which skilled workers produced oil, silver, copper, tin, needles, silk and woven cloth, gold-flecked lacquer ware, sword sheaths, armor, leather goods, blades, bamboo blinds, brushes, fans, umbrellas, tea scoops, paintings, medicine, and rope. The city had long been a center for luxury goods, and it remained that.[8]

It was even more a center for Buddhist establishments. The bakufu divided the great popular-faith, Amida-centered sects of Shin Buddhism into an Eastern and Western Honganji, "Temples of the Original Vow," and each was centered in a complex of massive buildings that dominated its area in the central city. The Pure Land (Jōdo) Sect, no less committed to invocation of the name of Amida, matched the great Honganji temple in the city center with its giant Chion'in complex in the Higashiyama hills. These had an interior magnificence borrowed from the Momoyama palace style—indeed, the celebrated Kanō Eitoku ceiling panels in the western Honganji had originally been done for Hideyoshi's Jūrakutei palace, which, like other structures associated with the Hideyoshi era and legacy, had been dismantled by the bakufu after its victory at Osaka. Monumental and impressive columns supported massive roofs. Worship services that were held in these temples grafted on to the simple repetition of the name of Amida an impressive theatricality that owed much to the magnificence of its setting. The whole was designed for the edification of large-scale congregations. "Beyond the seated priests, the lamps twinkle on the pure gold surfaces of the altar furnishings. The air prickles with incense, and seems to throb with the responses chanted by a hundred throats. In the imagination of the faithful, the scene must stand as a convincing promise, wonderfully close and real, of the beauty and majesty of the Western paradise."[9] These temples had no equal elsewhere in Japan.

Construction and maintenance of these structures required the talents of very large numbers of skilled craftsmen. It is small wonder that Kyoto became and remained a pilgrimage center long after it ceased to be a power center. Its streets were crowded with samurai, priests, acolytes, students, and pilgrims. Class lines counted for less than they did in castle town administrative centers. The bakufu realized the importance of the experienced commoners from these cities. So did daimyo, many of whom did their best to attract residents from the old centers for their castle towns. In 1634 Iemitsu remitted the land taxes of Osaka, Sakai, and Nara; those in Kyoto (and Edo) had been canceled earlier. The bakufu put relatively few restraints on commerce. It did away with the cumbersome imposts and levies of the sixteenth century and took advantage of the traditions of self-rule that townsmen had developed during years of military confusion.

The bakufu had a presence in Kyoto, one that was essential to its control and manipulation of the imperial court. The great Nijō Castle in the western quarter projected power in the stonework of its foundations, the defenses of its moats, the dimensions of its gates and interior, and the majesty of the paintings of massive pines that first greeted visitors important enough to be admitted within its portals. This was the headquarters of the bakufu resident, the *shōshidai,* who was its official for contact with the court. In early Tokugawa decades shoguns came to Kyoto, but after Iemitsu's great descent with 300,000 men in 1634 no shogun came until the 1860s. There were samurai guard posts, but there was no samurai residential quarter. Eighty-six daimyo maintained stations or offices in Kyoto to have access to its luxury goods for themselves and for exchange with their peers, but they were never in residence themselves.

Kyoto was an early center of publishing, and it remained the leader in works in Chinese. Sometime around 1650, as travel picked up and curiosity about other parts of the country grew, a boom of map publishing began. Maps of Kyoto became immensely detailed, with woodblock prints that combined identification of each of the many merchant districts *(chō)* with current information about the capital.[10] Publishers competed with rival versions of ever more detailed and colorfully done products. Similar maps began to appear for other cities, particularly for Osaka and Edo. It is seldom noted, but important, that these maps were available for sale and distribution. Across the waters in China, officials of the Manchu garrison state would have been aghast at the thought of providing such convenient guides for insurrectionary forces. The Tokugawa regime had no such fears long before the Manchu conquest was complete.

Osaka, the third of the "three metropolises" *(santo),* was quite unlike Kyoto and Edo. It had always played a central role in Japanese history through its port and commerce. To it came ships from China and Ryukyu, and from it the goods of that commerce moved along river routes to the early capitals of Nara and Kyoto. Japan's first Buddhist temple, the Shitennōji, was established there. In the sixteenth century Honganji Buddhist sectarians had resisted Nobunaga from their Osaka headquarters and, until Hideyoshi brought them to heel, they maintained a doughty tradition of commoner defiance. Hideyoshi used the city as his military headquarters. The giant castle he erected there, though burned in the final Tokugawa victory of 1615, was rebuilt by the bakufu as a symbol of its power.

In the first century of Tokugawa rule Osaka quickly became the center of the Japanese economy. Feudal lords from all parts of Japan were able to ship their surplus rice to Osaka for sale in what became a national commodities market. With their profits they were able to finance the obligations they incurred under the *sankin-kōtai* system. The city's flourishing markets had earned it the name "Kitchen of Japan" even before the Tokugawa years, but that title became firmly fixed within a few decades of the bakufu's establishment. The city's numerous moats, some named for their most important provincial shipper (for example, Tosabori), were lined with warehouses. The city was famous for the hundred and fifty bridges that crossed its rivers and moats; construction and maintenance was an important part of the local residents' duty. At first domains had stationed a samurai officer there as their agent, but those duties were soon taken over by commoner warehouse managers, the *kuramoto*. Some of them handled affairs for several domains. There might be a domain samurai attached to the enterprise, but due to the intricacy of the rice exchange professional agents were essential. For many samurai, numbers and calculations were denigrated as "shopkeepers' tools," and men brought up in those values were no match for commoner merchants.

The Osaka domain storehouse agents had three functions; they sold domain surplus rice and other exports, they purchased items like arms, clothing, and luxuries for the domain elite, and they became domain agents for borrowing money through loans from other merchants. Rice was shipped to Osaka in the fall, and offered for bids on a market in which authorized brokers, who numbered more than five hundred, had permits to participate. Bidders made a deposit in silver and paid the remainder later; meanwhile they were given vouchers for the rice held in the storehouses. These vouchers began as promises of payment within thirty days, but before long they became promises of future delivery and could be transferred, and sold, as commodity shares. They had the backing of the shogunate against default, and became marketable commodity securities. The Osaka agents thus became essential to the domains. They could provide advances in anticipation of revenue, and those in turn developed into long-term loans that bore interest of 10 percent to 20 percent a year. Out of all this a futures market developed; buyers could gamble on movements in the future price of rice as a "hedge" against weakness in their present position. The present, or "spot" market, and the futures provided the material for capitalist exchanges of very great complexity.[11]

The Osaka market set the standard for the national rice price. Market quotations were sent around the country by pigeon and by fast runner. By the middle of the seventeenth century bakufu officials indicated discomfort with some market functions and became aware that they could lead to price manipulation, or to large personal profits. It was in the bakufu's interest to keep the price of rice stable and high, for that was the *koku* currency in which its retainers were paid. At the century's end, Tsunayoshi's reform program sought out particularly wealthy traders as subject for confiscation. In 1705 the confiscation of the accumulated wealth of the house of Yodoya revealed with startling detail the kind of riches a commoner house could accumulate. Officials were confused and even alarmed by the evidence of merchant wealth, and did what they could to keep it within bounds. Edicts sometimes warned against the acceptance of *tegata*, or options and futures contracts, but largely in vain.

Osaka was a merchant town without a samurai residential quarter, and the bakufu wanted it kept that way. Like Kyoto it was under direct bakufu jurisdiction, administered by commissioners who reported to the Edo *rōjū*. Tax income from the countryside around the city was assigned to bakufu *hatamoto*.

Kyoto and Osaka led in the establishment of giant mercantile enterprises. Most of these stores concentrated on textiles; in the case of Mitsui, this was combined with a currency exchange house. As transfers of funds from Osaka, where the economy was based on silver, to Edo, where the gold *ryō* was the standard, were necessary for bakufu and domains alike, authorized exchange houses provided essential services.

The Kyoto or Osaka store was often the headquarters for branches elsewhere, ideally in Edo. In this way these establishments contributed to the diffusion of goods from centers of production to those of consumption. These giant stores were very probably the world's largest at that time, and they constituted prominent features of urban life recorded by contemporary printmakers. In time the Mitsui Echigoya, established in Kyoto, became the modern Mitsukoshi chain of department stores; Shirokiya, Matsuzakaya, Ebisuya, and several others have similar histories.

The largest of these were giant establishments in space as well as staff. Employees or *hōkōnin* were typically young, single men who boarded in; they sometimes numbered over one hundred, and in one case close to five hundred.[12]

In structure and organization establishments of this scale can be seen as a bridge between warrior houses and civil society. Founders left house codes to guide their successors, they specified succession procedures, and they enjoined them to keep the interests of the house in mind. There were also interesting differences. Samurai family codes stressed the importance of public service and duty, but the merchant was more inclined to be wary and remember his proper status and private interest. Succession could at times devolve on a woman, though adoption of an male heir was more likely. Occasional acts of

- The descendants shall forever observe these rules without fail.
- The members of the House shall with one accord promote the common benefit. Those in authority should treat subordinates with kindness, while the subordinates should in turn respect those in authority. The House will be more prosperous when its rules are observed with courtesy. Even if one is friendly with outsiders, if he maintains only his own dignity and does not think of the other members of the House, there will be no peace at home, and disorder and chaos may arise. If one lives in luxury and neglects his business, there will be no prosperity for the House.
- When a merchant's efforts and intentions are loose, his business will be taken over by others. Care must be had.
- It is the will of [the head] that the family of Hachiroemon shall remain at all times as the Senior Main Family. Therefore even if the son of Hachiroemon should not be old enough, if he is sufficiently capable, he shall succeed his father and become the Head of the House.
- When there are no children to succeed the head of the main family, a son may be adopted from other members of the House. When there is no male issue, a female may succeed.
- Although the eldest son is to succeed his family in principle, if his conduct causes harm to the family, he shall be expelled even if he is the only son, and sent into the priesthood, and an adopted successor from among the other members of the House shall be chosen. If the other members of the House should not be sufficiently capable to maintain their families or if their conduct should be immoral, such members shall also be sent into the priesthood.
- Should any member of the House be prevented from attending to his business duties due to ill health, the quota of his living expenses shall be reduced by twenty percent. The accumulation of this shall be laid aside for distribution as a bonus among other members of the House who worked with great diligence.
- Persons in public office are not, as a rule, prosperous. This is because they concentrate on discharging their public duties and neglect their own family affairs. Do not forget you are a merchant. You must regard dealing with the government always as a sideline of your business. It is therefore a great mistake to cast the family business aside and consider government service as a first duty . . .
- To believe in the gods and Buddha and to follow the teachings of Confucianism are the duties of a man. Nevertheless, it is not good to go to extremes. Extremists in religion will never be successful merchants . . .
- The gods and Buddha lie within one's heart. Therefore, you should not offer gold and silver to them and expect some special grace in return . . . contributions should be made to the poor and the suffering and the return will be ten thousand times as large.

Adapted from Eleanor M. Hadley, "Concentrated Business Power in Japan" (Ph.D. dissertation, Radcliffe, 1949), app.

charity could bring benefits, but religious fervor could be as dangerous to the house as government service. At the same time, the Buddhist priesthood could provide a useful repository for incompetents.

The Mitsui house was founded with dry-goods stores in Kyoto and Edo in 1673. A decade later it added services in money exchange and money lending; an Osaka branch appeared in 1691. That year, "by appointment to the shogun" *(goyō shōnin)*, Mitsui was authorized to send bakufu receipts of funds from Osaka to Edo. This role as fiscal agent of government could be, and was, turned to good advantage; funds could be transferred in the form of goods sold at a profit in the consumption center of Edo.

As the house interest and activities grew, a governing council made up of heads of branch families was established in Kyoto. Family heads were brought up to place the good of the lineage ahead of personal considerations. Like the heads of warrior houses, generations of Mitsui family chiefs were drilled in the importance of the house and taught to regard themselves more as stewards than owners of the properties they administered.

One expression of this was the house instructions *(kakun)* and laws *(kahō)*. These had always been standard for aristocrats in the Heian period, and great warrior houses also prized them from an early point. Asakura Toshikage (1428–1481), who fought his way to dominance in the province of Echizen, for instance, left seventeen articles to guide his descendants. He warned them to value ability more than seniority in the selection of aides, and went on to stress sobriety, frugality, and the avoidance of ostentation. House heads were to carry out systematic observation and inspection of the domain, and they were warned that "public opinion" mattered. "When passing in front of monasteries, shrines, or dwelling houses, rein in your horse," he counseled; "if the place is pretty, praise it. If it is in poor condition, express your sympathy. This will have a good effect."[13]

The Mitsui rules and procedures were formalized in the early eighteenth century by descendants of Mitsui Takatoshi (1622–1694), who headed the house during its formative decades. In old age he dictated his recollections for his grandson, Takafusa (1684–1748), who, as head of the "northern" house, played a central role in regularizing Mitsui house management. Takafusa reworded and wrote out the stories he had been told as *Chōnin kōken roku,* "Some Observations on Merchants." The collection was copied by hand for heads of each of the nine branch families and not published until the nineteenth century. These observations concern the rise and fall of about fifty wealthy Kyoto merchant houses. It was the fall of those houses that most interested Takafusa, and he posed their cases as guides for future Mitsui heads. Over half of the houses he wrote about failed because they made the mistake of lending to daimyo. Other houses had sons who lived extravagantly and thought they were gentlemen, forgetting their place as merchants. "We know from our own observation," he wrote, "that notable merchant houses of Kyoto generally are ruined in the second or third generation and disappear from the scene." Example after example drove home the point. "When great men are extravagant," he went on, "they lose their territories, but lesser folk lose their livelihood."[14]

The Mitsui founder's recollections of others' disasters also led him to formulate a house code or law. This was worked over by his eldest son and successor, Takahira (or Sōchiku, his Buddhist name, 1653–1737), and established as the house code in 1722. The document stood as the house code until the Mitsui incorporation as a modern enterprise in 1900. Its overwhelming concern was to stress the need for unity among the branch houses, but its more general warnings, based upon the family founder's experience and recollections, are so telling for what they show about merchant values that the document deserves quotation at some length. With allowance made for merchant concerns, these instructions put one very much in mind of warrior codes. They specify the rules of succession and indicate that ability should count for more than seniority. They warn against ostentation and excess of any sort, including expensive piety. Properly publicized gifts to the poor are a better investment than gifts to the temples and shrines. Mitsui successors are warned not to become too involved with government, for that could be costly and dangerous. The code is perhaps best summed up in a trenchant sentence: "Never forget that we are merchants; dealing with government is a sideline of our business."[15]

There are many testaments like Takatoshi's from other merchant family founders. Like elderly men everywhere, they were prone to stress the intensity of their application and commitment in youth and hold it up as an example to those who followed, but they all show a staunch conviction of merchant integrity and importance.[16]

In large enterprises like Mitsui a structured bureaucratic organization took great care to ascertain the quality of personnel before entrusting them with responsibility. The Mitsui archives detail the case histories of enterprise employees. Like the rosters of samurai service records, these track each man's career and show the care that was taken to train him. For one example: in 1810 Ichikawa Chūsaburō entered Mitsui service as a youngster of fourteen. He came with the backing of his parents and several sponsors, who provided a written affirmation of his quality as well as payment for his initial expenses. As he caused no problems after a five- or six-month period of trial, he was formally admitted to *hōkōnin* status, with the lowest (114) grade of company

Excerpts from the Will of Shimai Sōshitsu (1610), Hakata Merchant

- Some clerks, it is said, are going out at night. It should hardly be necessary to repeat the rules against this . . . nocturnal excursions are strictly forbidden.
- Apprentices . . . are important to a merchant house and should be treated kindly so they too will be loyal to the house.
- Until you are forty, avoid every luxury and never act or think as one above your station in life . . . Do not cultivate expensive tastes; you should avoid such things as the tea ceremony, swords, daggers, and fine clothes. Above all, do not carry weapons. If you own a sword or some armor that someone gave you, sell it and carry the money instead.
- Never wander about outside the shop or visit places where you have no business being . . .
- You should pick up all trash inside and behind the house, and chop up the pieces of rope and short bits of trash to use in plaster, and use the long pieces to make rope. Collect and clean pieces of wood and bamboo longer than five *bu* and use them as firewood . . . Do as I have done, and waste absolutely nothing.
- Bargain for the items you need and pay as little as you can, but remember the range of possible prices for each item . . . you can then give the maid only the precise amount she will need.
- . . . If you provide your servants [a hodgepodge], you and your wife should eat it as well. Even if you intend to eat rice, first sip at least a bit of [the hodgepodge], for your servants will resent it if you do not . . .
- Those with even a small fortune must remember that their duty in life is to devote themselves to their house and to its business . . . Although a samurai can draw on the produce of his tenured lands to earn his livelihood, a merchant must rely on the profit from his business, for without that profit the money in his bags would soon disappear . . .
- No matter at what meeting you are, if a fierce argument breaks out, leave at once . . . If people call you a coward for avoiding a fight, tell them that to violate [this] would be tantamount to breaking an oath.

Adapted from J. Mark Ramseyer, "Thrift and Diligence: House Codes of Tokugawa Merchant Families," *Monumenta Nipponica*, 34 (1979).

servant. At eighteen, with *genpuku* ceremonies of maturity, he had moved up to grade 91, and after three years in that category he was a "regular" *(hei).* Having reached a man's estate, his rank and responsibilities slowly rose; foreman (20) at age thirty-one, section head (*kumi gashira,* 15) at thirty-four, and manager (*shihai,* 8) at thirty-seven. He married in 1839 at the age of forty-three and then moved to the top; deputy treasurer (*kanjō myōdai,* 4th rank) at forty-seven, and finally first rank at sixty-one, by which time he could make decisions and held the seal *(kahan)* for the firm. He held this position of trust until his death at sixty-nine in 1865, after fifty-six years of service.[17]

Organizations the size of Mitsui were of course the exception in Tokugawa Japan; family-run shops remained the norm. The great houses dwarfed other enterprises by their scale. The typical enterprise was contained within the bounds of one *machi,* or block, organization. The *machi,* like the village, was normally administered in a collegial fashion by the close integration of its leading members, who reached decisions on a face-to-face basis. This was clearly impossible with organizations the size of Mitsui, which stood out in terms of ground space, resources, and personnel. Their owners were not long-time residents in the blocks, and were in fact absentee figures. So too with the large staff of service people, who tended to be drawn from home areas—in the case of Mitsui, the Yamashiro province around Kyoto. Nevertheless the rise and fall of these titans of commerce, as of more modest fortunes, was a fact of life. It also became a favorite topic for popular fiction.

4. Genroku Culture

The Genroku era was the interval between the years 1688 and 1704. It signaled such decisive changes in Japanese culture that the term is used interchangeably with Tokugawa popular culture. These were the years in which Kaempfer visited Edo as part of the Dutch mission. They were also years in which the fifth shogun, Tsunayoshi, tried to ameliorate social conditions through laws for the protection of animals, laws that in turn became crushing burdens for the populace of Tokugawa cities. They were years in which the Edo elite, under Tsunayoshi's guidance, deepened its knowledge of Confucianism. For commoners there was both hardship in laws that put animal rights above human rights—and prosperity—reflected in the merchant fortunes and the pleasure quarters of the great cities—so striking that Genroku became a metaphor for economic growth centuries later. But it is the outpouring of poetry and prose and the flowering of wood-block prints and of theater that most typify the age.

One can begin with the development of *haikai* (or *haiku*) poetry, a genre that made use of ordinary vocabulary and great brevity. The poet Matsuo Bashō (1644–1694), born the second son of an impecunious samurai, grew up on the fringes of the upper class without its benefits or income. Friendship with one of superior rank helped him for a time; when that ended, he moved to Edo and took a minor position in the water department. In 1680 he moved to a modest cottage; a disciple planted an ornamental banana *(bashō)* tree outside his door; the house, and then its resident, became named for it, as he changed his name to Bashō. In Bashō's early days there was lively debate and competition among different schools of poetry. Together with his friends he relished the challenge of linked-verse *(renga)* competitions in which two and three line offerings were pieced together in a somewhat meandering but meaningful progression. Gradually he settled on the three-line segment, of five, seven, and five syllables, using it as a single statement. Within this extraordinarily brief compass, the polysyllabic Japanese language could do little more than sketch a scene and suggest an emotion. It was thus all the more remarkable to produce, as Bashō frequently did, a Zen-like flash of universal significance in the presence of the daily and the ordinary. Accompanying this was a striking simplicity of vocabulary and setting. The sound of a frog leaping into an old pond, the sight of a crow on a naked branch, or summer's grasses on a legendary battlefield could provide the setting in which the reader or listener's emotions did the rest. Often there was a transference of the senses, as emotion was reinforced by sight and sound.

In 1684 Bashō began a series of five journeys, each of which resulted in a poetic narrative. For months at a time he wandered through distant parts of Japan, describing the setting and producing compelling verses telling of his loneliness and dread or sadness and serenity. He moved on foot and on horseback and took no supplies. He accepted no students for pay, something that was commonly done, though he occasionally sold examples of his calligraphy. Nevertheless by now his fame preceded him. Everywhere he went he was welcomed by leading local residents who outdid themselves to honor their distinguished guest. Evenings were usually devoted to the exchange of verses as the locals did their best to match their more modest skills against Bashō's. One might have expected this in an urban, middle- or upper-class setting; that it took place in remote mountain villages tells a great deal about the accomplishments of the local elite and channels of information.

Poetry has always held a central place in Japanese culture, and Bashō's is of course one chapter in a great tradition. He himself expressed it well in a famous passage; "one and the same thing runs through the *waka* of Saigyō, the *renga* of Sōgi, the paintings of Sesshū, the tea ceremony of Rikyū. What is common to all these arts is that they follow nature and make a friend of the four seasons. Nothing the artist sees but is flowers, nothing he thinks of but is the moon. When what a man sees is not flowers, he is no better than a barbarian. When what he thinks in his heart is not the moon, he belongs to the same species as the birds and beasts. I say, free yourself from the barbarian, remove yourself from the birds and beasts; follow nature and return to nature!"[18] A few decades later the scholar Motoori Norinaga, of whom more will be said below, stated this commitment to poetry by saying flatly that people who were not able to convey their feelings through *waka* were imperfect, inferior even to animals. "Even birds and insects" he wrote, "on occasion chirp songs with a tune of their own. Is it not shameful for man not to be able to compose a single *waka?*" And again, "Every man has to have the sense to appreciate elegance. Without this one will not be able to appreciate *mono-no-aware.*"[19]

Motoori's term, *mono no aware,* is at once simple and complex and it has received attention as the essence of what is at stake. Literally "the awareness of things," George Sansom preferred "lacrimae rerum, the pity of things"; others suggest "the pity of things" or sensitivity to the emotional or evocative power of things. Nothing evokes this better than the everyday images Bashō endowed with haunting depth. Small wonder, then, that he was idolized by his contemporaries, honored wherever he traveled, and surrounded by disciples on his deathbed. His life shows how literacy and culture had penetrated even rural Japan by Genroku days.

In prose writing, a new realism in the description of everyday life can be considered comparable to the release of poetry from formal standards and vocabulary. This was a gradual process, and it expanded with Japanese readership.

Kana zōshi, books published in the Japanese *kana* phonetic syllabary and far easier to read than books in Sino-Japanese, began to be published in the early Tokugawa years. Some old-fashioned romances were even published in small editions by movable type. But gradually wood-block editions took over as a medium. At first moral exhortations outnumbered other kinds of books; the authors tended to be court nobles or physicians, and then impecunious samurai, some of whom had become Confucian teachers or Buddhist priests. The most prolific author of *kana zōshi* was the son of a Buddhist priest who had been dismissed from his temple. Asai Ryōi (1612?–1691) lived on his writings, and has been called Japan's first professional writer.[20] He produced twenty or more titles, books ranging from treatises on moral guidance to fiction and travel accounts. His most famous work, *Ukiyo monogatari* (Tales of the floating world), was written sometime after 1661. Its title is important for the shift of meaning attached to *ukiyo,* the "floating world." The term had been used as a Buddhist synonym for the impermanence and transiency of the temporal world. Asai now used it to designate instead a "floating world" with the overtones of "delightful uncertainties of life in a joyous age when people lived for the moment, merrily bobbing up and down on the tides of uncertainty like a gourd on the waves."[21] Transiency, which had been associated with sorrow and pain, now became translated to the shifting pleasures of the up-to-date. This is the meaning that has stuck to the literature and popular art of the Genroku period and after.

In 1682 Ihara Saikaku (1642–1693) published *The Life of an Amorous Man*, an account of a young rake who makes the rounds of brothel beauties and finally sails off to an island populated exclusively by women. The book is credited with the introduction of a new style of fiction, *ukiyo zōshi*, or tales of the floating world. Saikaku was the son of a townsman, but had no interest in the family trade. For some years he wandered around the country. He studied poetry and achieved fame for virtuosity that led to astounding feats of speed and endurance in poetic competitions. But it is his fiction for which he is known, and his first work is often hailed as opening an entirely new concept in Japanese fiction. It combined an elegance in vocabulary and style with themes addressed directly to townsmen of the Genroku era. He wrote in a terse, enigmatic prose in the colloquial of the day, and his book sold more than one thousand copies in its first Osaka printing. Saikaku produced books at almost the same speed that he had produced poetry. He is sometimes held up as the first truly popular writer of Japanese fiction. He regaled his readers with accounts of rakes' and harlots' progress with a cool irony and detachment supplemented by comic effects by the score. Works that circulated in such numbers naturally drew the attention of outstanding artists, who provided the illustrations. Saikaku illustrated the first version of his book himself, but the Edo edition that appeared shortly afterward was illustrated by Moronobu (d. 1694), an artist who played a pivotal role in the development of *ukiyo-e* prints. Virtuoso printmakers illustrated the *ukiyo zōshi*, as this genre became known, and in some cases the text was printed within the borders of the illustration. There was consequently an intimate relation between word and image in Genroku culture. Like the prints, Saikaku's characters are two-dimensional, remarkable not for depth or development but as line drawings, pen portraits from the demimonde. Most of them have a single-minded concentration on the pleasures of the licensed quarter with its brittle beauty and transient pleasures. The author himself is never far from the reader's ear, interspersing ironic commentary and feigning disapproval of the activities of his characters. Fiction had now reached the commoners, but it undoubtedly appealed no less to samurai with time on their hands.

Saikaku also turned to tales of merchant life. The message of works like *The Japanese Family Storehouse* and *Some Final Words of Advice* is the importance of money, and the difficulty succeeding generations seem to have in keeping the resources the founders of family fortunes have accumulated. It would be possible to take his message as a documentation of the (much more serious) advice that Mitsui Takafusa offered his successors in "Some Observations on Merchants."

The foibles of rich men's sons made inviting topics for many who came after Saikaku. Ejima Kiseki (1667–1736), whose lifetime saw the center of the publishing world begin to shift from the Kyoto-Osaka area to Edo, spent his career working with, then competing with, and finally cooperating again with his publisher. His characters, Howard Hibbett writes, "are shaped by satirical and descriptive tendencies . . . Kiseki was not a portrait-painter: his forte was the intimate scene, of the kind familiar in *ukiyo-e*. In his sketches of the floating world, he preferred to group his rakes, actors, courtesans, and ordinary townsmen in casual tableaux of the sort one finds in the picture-books of [the printmakers] Moronobu and Sukenobu."[22]

An additional measure of the times was the development of the Tokugawa masters of the wood block. The *kana zōshi* were usually illustrated, frequently by men whose names have not come down. In the course of the seventeenth century an ex-samurai artist, Iwasa Matabei, developed a novel style of painting, employing elements of both the Tosa and the Kanō schools to record the life of the licensed quarters and also ordinary folk going about their daily tasks. These became known as *ukiyo-e,* or pictures of the floating world. Later artists, among them Moronobu, mentioned above, found a new outlet for their art in book illustration. Soon a market developed for pictures that could be hung up for display, like the more dignified hanging scrolls *(kakemono),* or pasted to screens; artists were now liberated from the limitations of book illustration. Broadsheets began to be produced for the urbanites who wanted decorations for their homes. Scenes depicted could be of many sorts; a striking print usually attributed to Moronobu, for instance, shows Korean horsemen (who were part of a 1682 embassy) performing for their ambassadors and Japanese officials. Wood-block artisans provided decorations for poetry and classical tales, but their preference (and largest market) was for the denizens of the licensed quarter and theater. By the latter half of the eighteenth century they were producing work of an elegance and perfection that has seldom been equaled and never surpassed.

The *ukiyo-e* delighted townsmen in Edo days and inspired collectors in the nineteenth-century West. Impressionist painters were fascinated by their clarity and color, as were Western art historians—somewhat to the surprise of

Victorian-era Japanese and Japanese classicists, who had thought them rather vulgar. Our museums and contemporary tastes permit careful study of these pictures of Edo types and styles. The best combine magnificent precision of line and elegant decorative design. The ladies they portray are not full faced, something the carver could not provide, but minimalist sketches; they return our stares unblinking and uninvolved. We admire them but do not relate to them, somewhat the way Saikaku's readers regarded his characters. We sample, admire, and often relish the beauty and the exquisite virtuosity of those whose talents—artist, carver, and printer—brought them to us.

If the merchant's danger was to lend money to samurai and daimyo, his son's proclivity was to spend it on the women of the licensed quarter. These quarters exerted an extraordinary influence on the popular culture of the Edo period. Each of the major metropolises had its own: Kyoto the Shimabara, Osaka its Shinmachi, and Edo its Yoshiwara. In the early years of the period authorities established them under samurai administration, and they were patrolled carefully to keep samurai, who provided the customers, from resorting to violence when in their cups. In Kyoto and Osaka, where samurai were few, order was less of a problem, but in Edo thousands of samurai were away from their families for months at a time, and they made up the majority of men frequenting the area. In Edo the bakufu first located the quarter near the center of the city, but after the Meireki era fire it was moved to the city's outskirts. As the city grew those "outskirts" were closer by, and the great Asakusa temple area of Sensōji became something of a staging area for revelers bent on an outing of pleasure and dissipation.

Houses in the quarter varied immensely in splendor and cost; teahouses, drinking spots, and restaurants were nearby. The women involved also differed sharply in quality, ranging from country girls who were sold into a life of degradation by villagers desperate for survival to magnificently costumed and educated beauties who could be selective with their favors. Japan's was a hierarchical society, and there were formal rankings of women in the quarter; four in Kyoto, where they totaled 308, five in Osaka, where there were 760, and seven in Edo, where the same survey (of about the year 1700) gave the figure of 1,750.[23] Even these totals, however, cannot begin to suggest the total numbers involved in the many minor *akusho,* "bad places," to be found in the metropolis.

At the highest rank was the *tayū,* trained from childhood by her proprietor in deportment, dignity, and elegance, and usually accompanied by younger and lower-ranking girls who seemed virtually her retainers. Her favors were reserved for the great and the wealthy, and Saikaku and his followers chronicled disasters of finance as great merchants engaged in rivalries of conspicuous ostentation in which these women played a central role. Few samurai could afford to compete with the great merchants. Famous (and expensive) beauties were the cynosure of printmakers' attention. In the gorgeous sweep of women shown by Kiyonaga and printmakers of the Kaigetsudō school we sense the haughty self-possession of these "daimyo" among courtesans. Other printmakers, and writers of rating (hyōbanki) and guidebooks, give some idea of the ideals of female beauty that suffused commoner and samurai society.

Confucian morality frowned on dissipation and particularly on unregulated "bad places," but Tokugawa society overall attached little moral opprobrium to this trade. For farm girls submission to parental authority and need could make self-sacrifice an act of virtue, while for those more fortunately placed work as entertainers might provide the opportunity for eventual "independence" in a managerial role or placement with a patron-master. It was a male society, and although in the countryside and merchant quarters commoner family structure was not as firmly male-dominated as it was within the military caste, in which the eldest son inherited his samurai rank and income, in the cities the samurai code set the norm of social expectations for many nonsamurai. The tradesman's wife might be essential to his enterprise and even in the effective control of its finances, but social standards of respectability required at least formal adherence to the primacy of the husband. Marriage was arranged. Public displays of affection with intended or present marriage partners were improper, but male resort to the licensed quarter might reflect taste and discernment. Attachment, however, could lead to disaster.

In Genroku theater one finds these relationships displayed most clearly, and domestic dramas provide some of the best insights into the web of obligations that bound Japanese in all walks of life. Allowance has to be made for the exaggeration that makes for melodrama, but the plays nevertheless constitute invaluable materials for social history. Genroku kabuki theater had its origin in the dances of a woman named Okuni in the first years after Sekigahara. The root meaning of kabuki referred to wild or deviant behavior; it was, after all, attached to uncontrollable gangs of kabukimono, young blades who sauntered around the streets of Kyoto with outrageous clothes and very long swords. Okuni's dances mimed the part of a young man visiting a brothel and caused a sensation. She is supposed to have gone on to Edo to perform at the castle there in 1607. Soon brothel owners were setting up stages on the banks of the Kamo River in Kyoto for performances designed to draw customers to their houses. For a time even tayū, the stars of the quarters, appeared on stage.

As dances grew in popularity the performances became marred by samurai brawls, often with serious consequences. As a result the bakufu banned women from the stage and ordered them confined to their quarters in the licensed section. Next came troupes of young boys in their stead. Homosexuality was prevalent among samurai during the wars, as it was among Buddhist priests, and before long samurai were no less rambunctious at stage performances, fighting over the youths. The shogun Iemitsu invited command performances of kabuki particularly toward the end of his life, but after his death in 1651 the bakufu banned all kabuki for a time. It also, less successfully, forbade homosexuality among samurai.

The notion of male entertainers was not limited to the stage. In Genroku times male specialists in dancing, music, and repartee were common, and it was only in the mid-eighteenth century that women who were trained in these arts, tutored from an early age and organized by house, became known as geisha, persons of talent. There were initially several terms denoting such entertainers, but the term "geisha" seems to have become standard in both Kyoto and Edo after the 1750s. Geisha were prepared for their craft through years of apprenticeship and drill in singing, dancing, poetry, witty conversation, and party games. These were in a sense upper-class accomplishments, and women so prepared commanded skills that could equip them for many years of service and, frequently, liaison with clients or patrons. In practice a host, planning an evening of entertainment, would make reservations for space, food, drink, and entertainment with one of the many meeting houses that were to be found in pleasure quarters like Gion in Kyoto or Akasaka in Edo. These handsome houses in turn sent out to specialist restaurants for food and drink and summoned the entertainers. This would be an expensive evening, for after the party the host was expected to leave a generous gratuity in addition to payment. Geisha charges became calibrated in terms of sticks of incense, which burned about four to one hour. The system thus became highly structured, and employers and teachers set and maintained high standards of achievement. Late-eighteenth-century masters of the color print delighted in portraying these entertainers. By then women had come to play a central role in entertainment, spicing evenings of food and drink with their clever repartee.[24]

The Genroku stage, however, became and would remain a male world. When kabuki reappeared all roles were played by men. Specialists in women's roles were required to shave the front part of their head in samurai fashion in hopes of making them less sexually desirable, but printmakers showed this did not succeed either. Guidebooks with rankings of actors were closely modeled on those for courtesans. By the 1680s actors were graded in three to six ranks according to skill. Now came plays adapted from military tales, puppet drama, and the classic Nō drama of an earlier day. By Genroku times a few actors of superior ability transformed kabuki and produced stage dramas that captivated samurai and commoners alike.

Actor worship came to dominate the people. Kabuki itself became dominated by actors, and stories of their extravagance, ostentation, and scandals became the stuff of daily talk and print. Scripts were sketched out and left for the actor to define. Stage preferences varied from the warrior's excesses, (*aragoto,* "tough stuff") to the sentimental (*nurigoto,* "wet stuff") more popular in the nonsamurai world of Kyoto and Osaka. In a search for personal satisfaction authors increasingly turned to the puppet *(jōruri)* theater, where fidelity to the script could be expected. Now it was the chanter, strumming his *samisen* (which had been imported from Okinawa) in cadence with the sonority of the prose and intensity of the action, who became the star. Authors wrote with a particular chanter's strengths in mind, somewhat in the way a nineteenth-century Italian composer might write for a particular soprano. More and more kabuki themes were drawn from the puppet theater. These in turn ranged between *jidaimono,* or historical dramas, and *sewamono,* or domestic dramas.

In Genroku days it was Chikamatsu Monzaemon (1653–1724) who brought the Tokugawa theater to its full potential. His domestic dramas document the claims of obligation *(giri)* that warred against human emotions *(ninjō)* in the lives of ordinary people. Not that there was a simple polarity between them, for *giri* to one person or claim could conflict with that to another. The merchant had an obligation to meet his business agreements, but he faced other obligations as well. The dramatists' skill was to show how difficult it could be to live in conformity with moral principles and traditions as they were defined by social expectations. The structure of obligations in social relations was so comprehensive that it served as the basis for the ethical code, rather than an abstract concept of good and evil. *Giri,* in its broadest sense, could encompass the total social environment of the individual.[25] Escape from dilemmas this might create was usually possible only through flight, from society, or from life, through suicide. For a merchant trapped in a hopeless love with a young woman from the brothel, an attachment that made him neglect bonds of family and creditors, a double suicide, or *shinjū,* with his love might constitute a "happy" ending in the hope that the two would be reborn together in paradise. The tension in the plays was thus the pull of obligations, often themselves in conflict, and of love. In the process Chikamatsu's characters usually seem to lack individuality; they struggle hopelessly with their bonds in the web of society, with no more chance of escape than that of a moth in a spider web.

Chikamatsu's characters—one hesitates to call them heroes—try mightily to keep their names unsullied in the eyes of society, and their wives are no less anxious to protect their mates from the consequences of errors of their ways. *Giri* to their husbands can impel them to heroic acts of sacrifice. An Osan pawns her wedding clothes to cover up her husband's prodigality at the licensed quarter, hiding even from her parents, whose loan made it possible for her husband to start his shop in the first place, the fact that they are in trouble. The husband, in turn, desperately unhappy but unable to break his attachment to his illicit love, sees his reputation, family, and living disappear before his eyes. Nor is the prostitute less miserable; her guilt is compounded by compassion for the wife, to whom she has an obligation as a fellow woman, and remorse for her parents, from whom restitution will be required of the sum they first received from the brothel owner or his contractor. It is in every sense a no-win situation; double suicide may offer one, albeit poor, solution for the principals, but everybody else will suffer.[26]

The alternative, one might think, might be a conscious act of will and remorse on the part of the shopkeeper husband. Instead Chikamatsu's male characters, aware of the impossibility of living up to the most fundamental *giri* and maintaining a fair name in society, yield to *ninjō*, human emotions. More often than not the men seem spineless and weak, in contrast to the sure compass with which women live out their obligations. One is struck by the fact that in this male society it was so often the women who proved stronger. Perhaps self-sacrifice built character. Tokugawa society made severe and total claims on Japanese. Even in the moment of supreme truth when lovers prepared a double suicide, society was present in their consciousness of what people would say and think, and what the morning broadsheets that announced this latest scandal would have to say about them.

Double suicides for love were a new phenomenon in Japan, and they became common only after the 1660s. The bakufu issued decrees threatening punishment for survivors in 1712 and declared it illegal to discuss them in novels or plays, but these orders were never effectively enforced. There was published, in fact, a *Shinjū ōkagami,* or *Great Mirror of Love Suicide,* that listed seventeen such; in these the males included one *rōnin,* one peasant, seven artisans and eight merchants. Townsmen were avid for news of such affairs and Chikamatsu was often prompt with a stage version. In the case of *Sonezaki shinjū* in 1703, the suicide took place on the thirteenth of the fourth month and was made public the next day. Chikamatsu's play was on the boards within a few months. He often exercised considerable license in altering the facts for dramatic effect, but it is clear that he was closely responsive to the social events of his day.[27]

Chikamatsu's domestic dramas probably exaggerated the impact of social restraints on civil society. Kabuki historical pieces, in contrast, had the effect of diffusing and glorifying warrior ideals among the commoners by describing superhuman deeds of loyalty and courage. This is famously shown by the story of the forty-seven *rōnin*, "The Treasury of Loyal Retainers" *(Chūshingura)*.[28] It is based on historical fact. In 1701 the young daimyo of Akō, a small (35,000 *koku*) domain near Hiroshima, was being instructed by Kira Yoshinaka, a bakufu official, in etiquette appropriate to the reception of an envoy from the imperial court. Kira had apparently considered Asano's gift too insignificant, and humiliated and insulted him. Infuriated, the young daimyo drew his sword and wounded Kira slightly before he was restrained. The shogun Tsunayoshi, enraged that anyone should dare to draw a weapon on one of his officials within the precincts of the Chiyoda Castle, ordered Asano to commit *seppuku*, terminated his lineage, and transferred the domain to someone else. Asano's faithful samurai, now *rōnin* and without prospects for the future, resolved to take revenge on Kira. To throw him off guard they pretended to have lost all sense of honor; they led lives of dissipation in the licensed quarter and ignored their families. When the opportunity came on a snowy night in the last month of the last year of Genroku, they encircled Kira's mansion, broke through his guard, took his head, and marched off to their lord's tomb in the Sengakuji Temple with it. After that they turned themselves in to the authorities for punishment.

This spectacular demonstration of feudal loyalty came at a time when urban and commercial interests seemed to be replacing the stern code of the warrior. All Japan was moved. Traditionalists, who had been deploring the decline in feudal values, were divided as to a proper punishment. The bakufu consulted leading Confucian moralists for their opinions. The *rōnin* had clearly broken the law, spectacularly so; even vendettas were supposed to be announced and registered. They had murdered a shogunal official. Should they be punished, and how? On the other hand they had given a demonstration of purest self-sacrifice for an age that lacked these qualities. Should they be praised, and how? A Solomonic solution was worked out: they would die, but not at the hands of an executioner but as honorable samurai, through *seppuku*. In death their tombs were arranged around their lord's in the grounds of the Sengakuji.

Dramatists were soon at work with versions of this story. Contemporary events were off-limits, however; an initial attempt which placed matters in the eighth century was transparently topical and banned; its text has not survived. In 1706 Chikamatsu had a try at it with a play in which he carefully assigned roles to fourteenth-century figures. This survived, and provided the backbone for a far greater piece done by later dramatists in 1748. It immediately became the most popular item on the puppet and kabuki stage. It is traditionally staged on the day of the *rōnin* attack on Kira's mansion, a day when many also visit the Sengakuji to place incense on the retainers' tombs. There have been numerous modern versions for film and television.

The tale thus became a textbook summary of martial virtues. The *rōnin* are paragons of loyalty determined to avenge their lord. They are also totally obedient to his chief retainer, who is in charge of the vendetta. They are self-less and make themselves family-less through their neglect of ordinary domestic considerations. Their families and merchant associates, however, far from resenting this, sense what is at stake, beg to be of help, and esteem them for their virtue. Another and essential appeal of the tale is not necessarily warrior-centered at all: the beauty of each character's fidelity to the larger group of which he is a part. This determined demolition of self in the interest of community spoke to readers and viewers of any persuasion and calling, and it has continued to do so.

Genroku culture, then, marked the point at which a new and larger national cultural awareness was beginning to form. Large-scale literacy provided a market for floods of printed books and wood prints. Page and stage made it possible for commoners to empathize with samurai brought low, and samurai to understand something of commoner distress as well. In addition, currents of commercialism made it possible for some samurai and many merchants to compete in consumption on almost equal terms.

EDUCATION, THOUGHT,
AND RELIGION

7

The eighteenth century in Japan brought little political change.
The country was at peace; the large-scale transfers of land carried out by the first five shoguns came to an end, and bakufu
and domains consolidated and structured their administrative
machinery. Vassals lost the opportunity to win reward through
valor in war, and resigned themselves to the status and honor
their forebears had earned for them; ritual and precedent took
priority over courage and initiative, while performance in administrative position—or personal favoritism—provided the
only avenue to recognition and reward. The samurai now had
need of different skills, and many had difficulty squaring those
new requirements with their sense of identity as members of a
military caste.

For commoners the growth of urban concentrations and
the rise of commercial farming brought new opportunities and
challenges that also called for skills acquired by literacy. When
the Tokugawa years began, relatively few Japanese, even among
the samurai, had been literate. By the end of the eighteenth century this had changed radically. Outwardly Japanese society
seemed unchanged, but in fact it had been transformed. The
fruits of an intellectual renaissance had penetrated downward
through society. A new civic religion bound society together in
patterns of values and belief; a nation was emerging from the
groupings of earlier days.

1. Education

Before the Tokugawa years members of the aristocracy, the
Buddhist priesthood, and the upper reaches of the warrior class
had access to private tutors, but most Japanese did not. Early
rulers made little effort to change this, but by the Genroku pe-

riod Tsunayoshi, the fifth shogun, styled himself a Confucian sage and Buddhist ruler and did everything he could, by precept and example, to encourage learning as the central element of the arts of peace.

A quarter century later the eighth shogun, Yoshimune, who was determined to restore the spirit and attitudes of the samurai class, also realized the importance of education. The nativist scholar Kada no Azumamaro, who will be discussed below, petitioned successfully to establish a school for Japanese studies. A group of merchants petitioned for shogunal support of an academy in Osaka. The Kaitokudō, which developed as a result, became a powerful source for rational analyses of problems of political economy.[1]

A third period of concern with education came at the end of the century in the Kansei era (1789–1801), when a reform administration reorganized the bakufu school, ruled out contrary or possibly subversive teachings, and campaigned extensively for the selection of men of ability in important offices instead of accepting the incumbency of well-born incompetents.

Education efforts began with attention to the samurai. Domain, or han, schools usually restricted entrance to the sons of the ruling class. They were for the most part a development of the eighteenth century, and they grew rapidly in number. Forty were established before 1750, 48 between 1751 and 1788, 78 between 1789 and 1829, and 56 between 1830 and 1867. In most schools leadership was in the hands of Confucian scholars. About 60 schools had Confucian shrines on the grounds and carried out regular services dedicated to Confucius, designed to impress students with the importance of learning, on the half-yearly observance of the equinox. Administrative control was usually provided by a senior retainer, who might or might not be a scholar himself. Instruction was seldom stimulating, and concentrated on learning to read Chinese texts; the purpose was simply to construe the text by "reading it off" in a clumsy mixture of Chinese and Japanese. There was a heavy weight of ceremonial and formal bureaucratic regulation, all designed to heighten the student's sense of the seriousness of learning. The teachers have been described as "retailers of packaged knowledge, not participants in a developing branch of inquiry, and one could hardly expect them to convey a sense of intellectual excitement."[2] Students took their seats strictly in order of age seniority, regardless of rank, and older students tutored those who were younger. In some respects these samurai schools showed a curious ambivalence toward book learning, for the military calling took precedence. Teachers were not of very high rank, and instruction in the military arts was usually rated more highly than that in book learning.

Private academies *(shijuku)* also proliferated.[3] Most were the creation of an individual, often a rather charismatic scholar who inspired his young students with ideals of perseverance and managed to instill a sense of discipleship and loyalty. Popular fiction, then and later, was full of examples of influential figures of this sort: beloved, often eccentric, and invariably demanding of their young charges.[4] Private academies might specialize in one or another of the several schools of learning that are detailed below.

Last but not at all least were commoner schools that are usually grouped together as "parish" or "temple" schools *(terakoya)* and village *(gōkō)* schools. The former were by no means Buddhist in sponsorship or staffing, though they sometimes met in village temples; indeed it seems probable that the identification with "temple" came after the Meiji government, anxious to replace them with its own network of schools, saw the term as pejorative. These commoner schools did not concentrate on the Chinese classics that were the stuff of the samurai schools, but concerned themselves with practical skills at the same time that they inculcated simple morality.

Some Terakoya *Precepts*

- To be born human and not be able to write is to be less than human. Illiteracy is a form of blindness. It brings shame on your teacher, shame on your parents and shame on yourself. The heart of a child of three stays with him till he is a hundred as the proverb says. Determine to succeed, study with all your might, never forgetting the shame of failure.
- At your desks let there be no useless idle talk, or yawning or stretching, or dozing and picking your nose, or chewing paper, or biting the end of your brush. To imitate the idle is the road to evil habits . . .
- One who treats his brushes or his paper without due respect will never progress. The boy who uses carefully even the oldest, most worn-out brush is the one who will succeed. Treat your brushes carefully.
- Luxurious habits begin with the palate; eat what you are given without fads and complaints. Any child who buys food in secret is guilty of unworthy conduct and can expect to be expelled.
- Keep seven feet behind your teacher and never tread on his shadow, as the saying goes. Every letter you know you owe to him. Never answer back to your parents or your teacher. Observe carefully their admonitions and seek their instruction that you may walk ever more firmly in the Way of Man.

From R. P. Dore, *Education in Tokugawa Japan* (Berkeley: University of California Press, 1965), pp. 323f.

Changes in Japanese society made education important for commoners. The complexity of merchant management and the responsibilities that village leaders carried produced the rise in literacy and publishing that has already been discussed. Private academies, commoner schools, and village schools came in response to those needs. By the early decades of the nineteenth century Japan had become one of the most highly literate countries among agricultural societies. It is not possible to quantify this with meaningful figures. In early modern England, for instance, the criterion of literacy usually used by scholars is the ability to sign one's name, an act that assumes further acquaintance with the entire range of alphabetic symbols. In the case of Japan, however, "signing" has been done by the use of a small name stamp. It is not possible to use the criterion developed in England, for the nature of the Japanese writing system rules it out. A "name" usually consists of two or three Chinese characters, and few who tried can have been so dull as to be unable to give evidence of so small an accomplishment. In any case, surnames among commoners did not become universal in Japan until the reforms of the Meiji (1868–1912) period. R. P. Dore's landmark study instead uses estimates of student numbers and extrapolates them against the entire population. He estimates that by the end of the Tokugawa period some 40 percent of boys and 10 percent of girls were receiving some sort of education outside the home. On that basis, it is probable that Japan was behind only two or three Western countries, and well ahead of all other countries, in the percentage of its people with access to education and literacy. It is to be noted, moreover, that, as the chart indicates,

Numbers of Schools by Date of Establishment

Year	Shijuku	Terakoya	Gōkō	Han schools
pre-1750	19	47	11	40
1751–1788	38	47	11	40
1789–1829	207	1,286	42	78
1830–1867	796	8,675	48	56
Totals	1,076	10,202	118	225

Source: Richard Rubinger, *Private Academies* (Princeton: Princeton University Press, 1982), p. 5.

the figures and percentages were steadily on the increase as the period went along.

2. The Diffusion of Confucianism

The political scientist Maruyama Masao once characterized Confucianism as "a set of categories through which people saw their world." In Tokugawa times those categories began with loyalty. They went on to include filiality, obligation, duty, harmony, and diligence. These values were not, of course, exclusively Confucian—few civilizations think poorly of those qualities—but for Japanese they were phrased in Confucian terms and examples. They spoke in terms of the "five relationships" (ruler-subject, father-son, husband-wife, elder-younger, and friend-friend) and struggled for a "rectification of names" that would enable the individual to live up to the responsibilities that accompanied the realization of his position in this structure of relationships. "Self-cultivation" was essential to the moral life, and the key to social order and harmony.

These teachings were imbedded in the Confucian classics and reinforced by primers of moral guidance that came flooding from the printing press. As they made rulers better rulers and the ruled easier to rule, they undergirded the authority structure of society and had the full support of Tokugawa administrators. Even so, it was not an exclusively one-way process, for there was also assumed a basic reciprocity involved. Some have even described this as a "covenant." The moral posture of those above, shown in "benevolence," would evoke an obligation (*on*) from those below; but in turn the respectful cooperation of the ruled imposed the obligation to be just on those above. The network of relationships that resulted extended throughout society and included ruler and ruled, master and servant, landlord and tenant, and of course lord and vassal. There were obligations on both sides.

Teachings of this sort were basically this-worldly and rational. They did not require, and did not receive, sanctions or rewards of supernatural forces for their implementation. Yet there was also a spiritual cultivation involved. Self-cultivation and the search for morality, like that for Buddhahood or for Zen illumination, struck a responsive chord in Japanese tradition and expressed a truth that was common to the Buddhist and Shinto traditions as well as to Confucianism.

Confucian thought had entered Japan much earlier as part of the stream of Chinese influence that included Buddhism. One of the first documents, the seventh-century "Constitution" of Prince Shōtoku, contains a mixture of both teachings, and is in fact almost a dialogue between them. Learning for court aristocrats was based on Confucian texts at the same time the Buddhist world view dominated the court. During the medieval centuries learning had survived chiefly in monastic establishments, and it was Buddhist scholars who preserved the Confucian tradition. Then and later Buddhist pilgrims to China brought back the Sung scholarship of the twelfth-century Confucian scholar Chu Hsi. Chu Hsi, a contemporary of St. Thomas Aquinas in the West, had encased Confucian teachings in Taoist and Buddhist metaphysics to found a powerful synthesis. Moral principles were now described as the reflection of higher, universal principles that led up to the "Supreme Ultimate" of a cosmic metaphysics. New emphasis was placed on the "investigation of things," for study of the particular could lead the seeker to comprehend universal principles. By extension, this could also be extended to the principles of the authority structure; self-cultivation, requisite to sincerity, would best equip ruler and subject alike to fulfill their proper relationships. Adherence to them produced harmony between the individual and the cosmos. It was a demanding search, and Neo-Confucianism sometimes developed a religious and confessional dimension in the search for and attainment of truth. For many the encounter with the writings of Chu Hsi marked a pivotal point in personal development that approached Zen enlightenment.

Sung dynasty Confucianism provided a powerful synthesis and ideology for early modern China and Korea. In China the civil service examinations offered social and political reward for demonstrated talent, and the writings of the Sung scholars became official truth. In Korea too, although admission to the examinations was increasingly limited to the special social ranks of so-called *yangban*, similar sanctions and rewards obtained. It is significant that the writings of the Korean scholar Yi T'oegye became known and influential in Japan in the wake of the cultural treasures brought from the continent by Hideyoshi's generals after his invasions of Korea.

Japan, with its restrictions of a fixed status system and assumptions of the priority of heredity, could not have been expected to conform to this Confucian ideal, nor did it. Nevertheless, after the Sengoku wars came to an end the Tokugawa peace provided a setting conducive to the support that elements of this scholarship provided for the authority structure. But it made its first appearance in Buddhist dress, and it required time to give Confucian teachings a role independent of monastic establishments. Hayashi Razan (1583–1657), progenitor of a line of Confucian scholars who served "by appointment" *(goyō gakusha)* to the shoguns, was ordered by Ieyasu to take the Buddhist tonsure, but his successors succeeded in placing some distance between themselves and institutional Buddhism. Indeed, it was said in praise of Nakae Tōju (1608–

1648) that his filial piety was so strong that he read Buddhist sutras which he personally deplored to his ailing mother.

At the upper reaches of warrior society "Confucianists" (*jusha*) became part of the elite establishment as advisers and educators. In 1630 a school for samurai was established in Edo with the Hayashi family as rectors. Daimyo followed shogunal policy, and by the mid-seventeenth century Confucian advisers were to be found at most castle towns.

Jusha were usually men of modest and even low status. The list of Chu Hsi specialists includes a smattering of commoners, a good many doctors, and more sons of *jusha,* but the majority were samurai of modest rank. They were able, but also rather marginal men in warrior society, and their advocacy of the importance of scholarship and rule by ability must often have reflected personal frustration as well as intellectual conviction.[5]

As adviser to the daimyo the Confucian teacher felt himself responsible for grounding him in classical learning as a way of developing his moral, and hence political, potential. By the second century of Tokugawa rule, shoguns and daimyo were more symbols than figures of authority, and they were trained very much the way modern Japanese emperors have been. They developed a stoic patience to show their respect for the classics and for learning. Arai Hakuseki (1657–1725) wrote that he lectured to his lord 1,299 times in nineteen years and praised both his demeanor and his endurance. To show respect for the classics that Arai was expounding, the future shogun Ienobu sat motionless despite the cold of winter and the mosquitoes of summer.[6] Some daimyo became such splendid representatives of Confucian principles that they became lauded by scholars as "sage rulers" (*meikun*). Tokugawa Mitsukuni (1628–1700), lord of Mito, established Confucian temples and transferred to them the duty of personal registration normally carried out by Buddhist temples. He gave shelter to a refugee Ming dynasty loyalist scholar and installed him as the central figure in a long-term project for the compilation of a massive "dynastic history" that followed Chinese models, the *History of Great Japan (Dai Nihonshi).* Its emphasis was on imperial loyalty, and the sponsors prudently stopped their account short of the Tokugawa rise. Ikeda Mitsumasa (1609–1682), daimyo of Okayama, weakened Buddhism by disestablishing half of the temples in his domain and ordered people to register with Shinto shrines instead of Buddhist temples. He set stern standards for himself, announcing that "the ruler must regard his own filial behavior as the most important thing . . . [he] treats samurai and farmers with benevolent love, and causes the country to prosper . . . The truly learned man . . . cultivates himself before trying to rule others." Mitsumasa followed Chinese Confucian example by honoring outstanding instances of filial piety; in a three-year period he issued official commendations to 1,684 people of all classes for praiseworthy demonstrations of filiality, loyalty, truthfulness, and exemplary service.[7] In cases like these, daimyo acted almost as propagandist for Confucianism, somewhat in the pattern of Ming magistrates and Korean *yangban*. Still, although many established Confucian rites and temples, most remained within the patterns of sectarian Buddhism.

The shogun Tsunayoshi's enthusiasm for Chinese studies, especially those of the *Book of Changes,* has already been noted. It was natural for him to consult Confucian scholars when the problem of the proper response to the emergency created by the case of the forty-seven *rōnin* came up. Some sternly argued the need to punish the assault on a bakufu official as rebellion, while others argued that the extraordinary loyalty displayed by the *rōnin* could serve as justification for something short of dishonorable execution. The solution, it will be recalled, was honorable self-immolation. Arguments from Chinese precedents were often compelling, but selecting and applying them in complex circumstances was not a simple matter. Arai Hakuseki provides a case in point.

Arai Hakuseki was called in for his advice in a case in which a wife reported her husband missing. On investigation it proved that he had been murdered by her father. This proved a problem in filial behavior: had she, by a report that ultimately brought judgment on her father, violated the tenets of filial piety? The Hayashi family head held that she should be executed, arguing from the *Lü Shu* that those who informed about their parents' crimes deserved death. He cited a passage in which "Chi Chung of Cheng asked her mother, 'Which is dearer, father or husband?' and had been answered, 'Any man can be the husband; only one man can be the father.'"

Not so, argued Arai; the woman was a victim of circumstances, and had not realized that her father and brother had killed her husband; this was very different from informing against them. He argued that "There is absolutely no reason to put this woman to death. If, on the day that her father's and brother's crime in murdering her husband was revealed, she had killed herself at once, she would have been faithful to her husband, filial to her father, and sisterly to her elder brother. We would have had to say that she had shown great virtue in a case which was an extreme example of abnormal morality." But perfection, alas, eludes us all, and Arai's more "reasonable" counterproposal carried the day: "If it is privately suggested to her that she should become a nun for the sake of her father and husband, and if we send her to a convent, have her take the tonsure, and offer the property of both her father and husband to the temple, we will be saving her from the danger of destitution and protecting both the law of the country and women's chastity."[8]

The *jusha* were an interesting and important group. They took themselves very seriously as the carriers of scholarly morality. They carried out literary projects for their daimyo and compiled genealogies, codes of law, and administrative precedent. Many studied and classified local flora, something highly appropriate to the "investigation of things." Not a few left personal accounts of their accomplishments. It is natural that their activities, scholarly and educational background, and personal records have received a great deal of study. Nevertheless, despite all this it is important to remember that they were never part of the real power structure they served.

3. Scholars and Scholarship

Tokugawa Confucianism developed in a setting of eclectic variety and profited from the efforts of extremely able and independent specialists. Because they were not tied to the power structure of any particular band of retainers, they could profit from the ability to seek guidance from several sources and respond to offers from other domains. Collectively, they struggled with a sense of crisis and frustration. The crisis was the result of the disjunction between the ideals of an earlier, no doubt imagined, past that had known a direct correspondence between morality and action, and the far more complex society of ritual and status of which they became a part. Commercialism seemed to be shredding the values of frugality and simplicity they espoused, and domain and bakufu government were simultaneously at war with, and dependent upon, the rising power of merchants and tradesmen. The scholars' frustration derived from the awareness that they were marginal to the decision centers of warrior society and often irrelevant to the concerns of the ruling figures. Despite this, or perhaps because of it, Tokugawa Confucian scholars made distinguished contributions to the wisdom they inherited and ended by changing the discourse of politics and policy so drastically that their achievements deserve to be considered a Japanese intellectual renaissance. Space does not permit extended treatment of the vitality of that setting, but its principal features and figures require mention.

Yamazaki Ansai (1618–1682) was born the son of a *rōnin*, and spent some years as a novice in several Buddhist temples. Beginning in Kyoto, he moved on to Tosa, where he encountered Sung scholarship as taught by that domain's line of Confucianists, before opening his own school in Kyoto. Later he moved once more to Edo. There he encountered powerful influence from a school of Shinto studies, and he spent the rest of his life advocating and teaching a blend of Confucianism and Shinto that was very much his own. Nationalist urges, one might suggest, had come to temper his fervor for imported thought. Perhaps seeing himself as a Japanese Chu Hsi, he wrote an "Elementary Learning for Japan" (*Yamato shōgaku*) for a daimyo. In this he based himself on an earlier text of loyalism and imperial history. He went on to work Japan into the cosmological charts of Sung scholarship, and devised elaborate proofs for the superiority of ancient Japan.[9] During his years of activity Ansai is credited with having had some six thousand students; his advocacy of the unity of Confucianism and Shinto helped spark the revival of studies of ancient Japan.

> Once Yamazaki Ansai asked his students a question: "In case China came to attack our country, with Confucius as general and Mencius as lieutenant-general at the head of hundreds of thousands of horses, what do you think we students of Confucius and Mencius ought to do? The students were unable to offer an answer. "We don't know what we should do," they said, "so please let us know what you think about it." "Should that eventuality arise," he replied, "I would put on armor and take up a spear to fight and capture them alive in the service of my country. That is what Confucius and Mencius teach us to do."
>
> Later his disciple met [the Sinophile] Itō Tōgai and told him about it, adding that his teacher's understanding of Confucius and Mencius was hard to surpass. Tōgai, however, told him smilingly not to worry about the invasion of our country by Confucius and Mencius. "I guarantee that it will never happen."[10]

Kaibara Ekken (1630–1714) sprang from distinguished samurai vassals of important daimyo, but this did not keep him from experiencing during his life the sort of ups and downs of official favor that characterized the lives of many Tokugawa samurai. His father was trained as a doctor. The son began to follow in that path, but moved successively from Buddhism to Chu Hsi Confucianism. As a member of the retainer band of Fukuoka he had duty opportunities in Nagasaki (where Fukuoka alternated with Saga in defense responsibilities), in Edo on *sankin-kōtai* duty, and in Kyoto, where he was sent for seven years of study as a domain-sponsored scholar. By the time of his maturity he had known a period of drift as a *rōnin* in addition to the opportunity to experience the widest variety of educational breadth that was available in seventeenth-century Japan. Ekken became and remained an orthodox adherent of Chu Hsi scholarship, and his medical training and personal predilection invested his "investigation of things" with great rigor. Medical studies led to concerns with herbal remedies and botany as well as the compilation of what became a classic study of the flora and fauna of the Fukuoka domain. Ekken was also known for studies of local history and topography, essays on farming, travelogues, and genealogies of the (Kuroda) Fukuoka daimyo house. In addition, of course, he lectured and taught and established so sound a reputation that the German physician Philipp Franz von Siebold, who served at the Dutch station in the early nineteenth century, hailed him as the "Aristotle of Japan."[11] Like every good Confucian scholar Ekken was a moralist as well, and author of influential books of precepts that became standard texts for filial piety. A discourse on the education of women that is credited to him remained influential into the nineteenth century. Though designed as guidance for upper-status daughters, *Onna daigaku* (The great learning for women) prescribed so drastic a bondage to the family system that it has caused its author's name to be execrated by twentieth-century feminists.

Seeing that it is a girl's destiny, on reaching womanhood, to go to a new home, and live in submission to her father-in-law and mother-in-law, it is even more incumbent upon her than it is on a boy to receive with all reverence her parents' instructions. Should her parents, through excess of tenderness, allow her to grow up self-willed, she will infallibly show herself capricious in her husband's house, and thus alienate his affection, while, if her father-in-law be a man of correct principles, the girl will find the yoke of these principles intolerable . . .

More precious in a woman is a virtuous heart than a face of beauty . . . The only qualities that befit a woman are gentle obedience, chastity, mercy, and quietness . . . From her earliest youth, a girl should observe the line of demarcation separating women from men; and never, even for an instant, should she be allowed to see or hear the slightest impropriety . . . Even at the peril of her life, must she harden her heart like rock or metal, and observe the rules of propriety . . . A woman has no particular lord. She must look to her husband as her lord, and must serve him with all worship and reverence, not despising or thinking lightly of him. The great life-long duty of a woman is obedience. In her dealings with her husband, both the expression of her countenance and the style of her address should be courteous, humble and conciliatory, never peevish and intractable, never rude and arrogant . . . Let her never dream of jealousy. If her husband is dissolute, she must expostulate with him, but never either nurse or vent her anger. If her jealousy be extreme, it will render her countenance frightful and her accents repulsive, and can only result in completely alienating her husband . . .

The five worst maladies that afflict the female mind are: indocility, discontent, slander, jealousy, and silliness. Without any doubt these five maladies infest seven or eight out of every ten women, and it is from these that arises the inferiority of women to men . . .

Parents! teach the foregoing maxims to your daughters from their tenderest years! Copy them out from time to time, that they may read and never forget them![12]

It is probably true that most eighteenth-century educators in Europe with advice for parents preparing young women for marriage would have had more or less similar advice to offer, but what is special and Japanese about Ekken's strictures is the bondage to the family system. Still, it may be encouraging to note that he laments the fact that seven or eight out of ten fall short of his goal of perfect docility.

Among all the *jusha*, Ogyū Sorai (1666–1728) was probably the finest and most influential scholar. His thought has been analyzed with great care by a line of intellectual historians and political scientists, including the distinguished Maruyama Masao, and is relatively accessible in English.[13]

Sorai's career straddled the Genroku and Kyōhō eras and the shogunates of Tsunayoshi and Yoshimune, a time when the social changes produced by urbanization—higher standards of living for the fortunate, an increase of luxury, and a rise in warrior indebtedness—were becoming obvious. His life also illustrated the uncertain fate that could befall even the most distinguished of scholars. Born the second son of a doctor, he spent much of his youth in rustic exile that had been brought on by his father's political reversals. After he had founded a small school in classical studies attended by Buddhist monks, Sorai came to the attention of the shogun Tsunayoshi's counselor, Yanagisawa Yoshiyasu. Soon he was the central figure in a coterie of China-oriented scholars at the capital. His salary increased from rations for fifteen followers to 300 *koku*, and then to 500. He was one of those consulted in the case of the forty-seven *rōnin*, and it was his proposal for the middle path of *seppuku* for the *rōnin* that eventually carried the day.

With Tsunayoshi's death Sorai's sponsor fell from favor. For some years he was again in relative obscurity, overshadowed by Arai Hakuseki. When Yoshimune took office as shogun in 1716 things changed once more as Sorai became a member of the shogun's brain trust. He renewed his contacts with Ōbaku Zen monks and directed studies in the Ming dynasty statutes. He wrote at length about contemporary problems in political economy. In addition he was able to steep himself in studies of philology that were his passion; treatises on literature, thought, law, history, military science, and music also came from his brush. Sorai was an unabashed enthusiast for things Chinese. Once, when he moved his house in Edo, he expressed his pleasure at being that much closer to China, and on another occasion he referred to himself as an "eastern barbarian." Later nationalist detractors did not forgive him for that, but the context of the statement was his desire to express his satisfaction that he, a non-Chinese, was the equivalent of China's best scholars. Despite all this, however, Sorai, for all his talent, never received high samurai status. The humility he expressed in his correspondence with learned Zen monks from China may not have been altogether artifice.

Sorai was leader of a new school in Confucian scholarship, one that had profound significance for Japanese culture. The Sung Neo-Confucianists had staked their position on the existence of an ultimate principle which was in turn reflected in all things and spirits. The spirit (*li;* Japanese, *ri*), or principle, of all things material and immaterial had its origin there. Human nature, the spirit of interpersonal relationships, the political order—each and all of these were reflections of this cosmic principle. So too with the "thingness" of inanimate and animate objects—table, plant, or beast—all were emanations or reflections of that higher, cosmic Supreme Ultimate. Consequently to investigate anything thoroughly was to begin to apprehend the whole. Nature, as Tetsuo Najita has put it, was all encompassing, and ultimately one. "A timeless and absolute norm drawn from outside historical time and transcending the chaotic warfare of the recent past was called on to establish the *baku-han* structure of non-centralizing governance as being 'principled.' "[14] By Genroku times Sung scholarship, while not the ideology it became in the late Tokugawa decades, and indeed never as prescriptive as it was in China and Korea, was nevertheless gaining in favor and seemed to be becoming dominant.

Sorai and his followers took powerful exception to these ideas. He argued that Chu Hsi Neo-Confucianism distorted history; Sung learning was based on later accretions to the Confucian canon. Worse still, Japanese scholars were getting it at third or even fourth hand. In good measure the problem was one of language, and it could only be attacked through meticulous philology. The twelfth-century texts of Sung scholars were distanced by a millennium from the classical Confucian canon. Worse, Japanese scholars were reading those texts in the peculiar version of Sino-Japanese *(kanbun)* in which signifiers and markers were distorting the grammar to make it conform to Japanese rules. The result was a poor mishmash of translation rendered in a sort of gibberish, "what language I do not know."[15] "Chinese," Sorai went on, "is different in nature from the Japanese language. And even within the Chinese language, there are differences between the ancient and modern varieties." Sorai set himself to unravel this by serious study of contemporary Chinese and careful study of ancient Chinese. He compiled dictionaries and glossaries that gave definitions in modern, contemporary Japanese. In that sense he might be thought of as a philological equivalent of Saikaku's commoner prose and Bashō's diction.

Yet Sorai was not content to stop there. Ultimate comprehension of the classics required an effort to return to the source by reading the canonic texts the way men would have read them almost two millennia earlier. "Ancient Learning," as it is often called, or *kobunjigaku,* went "behind" Neo-Confucian talk of "principle" and "nature" in an attempt to meet the ancients on their own ground and terms. From this Sorai derived the view that what had been achieved by the system builders or "sages" of the remote past, the ritual and music that ordered society, was not so much the reflection of a moral principle, as the Sung scholars would have it, as it was the product of their genius and invention. The same was true of the institutions of the shogunate; Ieyasu, no less a "sage" than those of ancient times, had devised them.

Sorai thus restored will and initiative to politics. What Ieyasu had done others, building on his work, could continue. Modern men could tap into this well of wisdom by direct contact with the ancients through the words those ancients had invented. Sorai's "amoral modernism," to use Sumie Jones's term, gave the past an immediacy and reality, and his Confucian texts were records of objectified and standardized historical reality. The moral exegesis of the Chu Hsi school was quite beside the point.

Philological wrestling with the works of antiquity required confidence and often produced arrogance. The wordy battles of scholars like Lorenzo Valla in the Italian Renaissance were echoed in the assurance and aggressive exposition that Sorai and his disciples gave these ideas.

From this it is possible to understand the leading role that Sorai could take at the court of the shogun Tsunayoshi, with its enthusiasm for the study of Chinese and deferential reception of Chinese Buddhist abbots, and his preparedness to prescribe remedies for social and political maladies for Yoshimune a few decades later. Unfortunately those proposals assumed it was possible to look back to the institutions and time of Ieyasu. Daimyo and samurai on *sankin-kōtai* duty in Edo spent their time and income like travelers at an inn, he argued; they should be returned to the countryside, thereby reversing the trends toward urbanization and merchant growth that had overtaken Japan. Rites and music, too, should be re-formed; Ancient Learning could be the guide to a reconstruction of politics.

In fact none of this took place. Scholars can turn to more ancient texts, but governments cannot reverse social trends. Tokugawa institutions had been designed to ensure shogunal control over daimyo and daimyo control over vassals, and they could not be lightly set aside.

Consequently Confucianism served the realities of Japanese society imperfectly. Confucian scholars and advisers writing for posterity usually exaggerated their impact on the warriors they served. At the outset of Tokugawa rule Ieyasu showed intense interest in precedents of earlier regimes and institutions in China as well as in Japan, and specialists in Chinese studies frequently found employment. Hayashi Razan, whose descendants served as educators and court Confucianists, was awarded his post after an interview with Ieyasu in which—according to his own account—he demonstrated unusual command of Chinese history and precedents. He served Ieyasu for the next eleven years. But Ieyasu relied more on the counsel of Zen priests Sūden and Tenkai, and Hayashi himself was obliged, as we noted, to shave his hair in accordance with Buddhist practice. He was, as one scholar puts it, involved in many bakufu activities, but he helped and did not originate; on occasion his counsel was not even requested.[16]

Despite the attractions of Confucianism for rulers and educators, it was not equipped to be a state ideology. Moreover, there was a consistent anti-intellectualism in warrior society, and loyalty and valor received higher marks than book learning and benevolence. Sorai's assertion that ancient sage-kings had invented the rites and music with which they ordered society made it possible to praise the Tokugawa founders as social planners, and to that extent it could be deemed constructive, but the Edo rulers were not likely to follow the suggestions of Arai Hakuseki or Ogyū Sorai and his followers that they reform and establish rites and music as the basis of their rule.[17]

The school of Ancient Learning enjoyed tremendous intellectual prestige during much of the eighteenth century, but the wrangles between its partisans and their opponents confused things so much that warrior rulers with little tolerance for complexity ruled against it. In 1790 Matsudaira Sadanobu, a grandson of Yoshimune who served as the bakufu's first minister, warned against "heterodox teachings." "The teaching of Chu Hsi," the edict read— not altogether accurately—"has had the full confidence of successive shoguns since the Keichō era . . . Not only in your own school [the Shōheikō, the bakufu's school], but in all others as well, you are advised to see to it that the orthodox doctrine alone is taught as the basis for the training of men for public service."[18] Thereafter the educational establishment, beginning with the bakufu's own Shōheikō, concentrated on Neo-Confucian explanations of nature and morality. By late Tokugawa times, when Sorai's writings enjoyed a revival, they had come to be considered almost subversive by bakufu scholars, some of whom wrote to describe the sense of daring with which they perused them.[19] In private life, however, the newly proclaimed orthodoxy never completely closed the door to alternate forms of expression. Many a Shōheikō teacher managed to compartmentalize his life, giving public adherence to Sung scholarship while maintaining a private interest in other schools of Confucianism.

4. The Problem of China

It is natural that men whose standing derived from their command of traditional Chinese culture would be sensitive to criticism from their countrymen that they were praising a foreign civilization. It would be tedious to trace in close detail the dialogue that resulted, but a glance at the response of some leading Tokugawa Confucian scholars to this problem shows that it was one they struggled with themselves.

An early stage, as Kate Wildman Nakai shows,[20] was to claim that Japanese and Chinese traditions were entirely congruent. Hayashi Razan, who served Ieyasu, went into eclipse under Hidetada, and reemerged after the second shogun's death, identified Shinto with the Confucian "kingly way," and tried to establish a correspondence between Confucian and Shinto ideas, even to the point of working Japanese mythology into the cosmological theory of Neo-Confucianism. The steps advocated by the sages of China, in other words, had already been realized in the Japanese past. He could also argue that it was only by chance that the canons had been composed in China, for the ideas they espoused were universal and applied to all humankind. "One may say it is the way of the *kami* [gods] of Japan," he wrote, "while at the same time it is the way of the sages in China." Elsewhere, he wrote that "There are people among the Japanese who are superior to the people of China. Superiority does not lie in teaching nor inferiority in learning. Superiority lies only in the exemplification of the virtues of knowledge, benevolence, and valor."

It was also argued that classical China should be distinguished from the China of the eighteenth century. Even Ogyū Sorai, who styled himself an "eastern barbarian," vaunted himself on his mastery of texts that were becoming difficult for contemporary Chinese. In that sense, China was no longer China; the place called China had fallen under the rule of barbarian Manchus. Moreover, China had always known tides of rebellion and dynastic upheaval. In one sense the "Way of Japan," which combined religion with government, represented a better parallel to the wisdom of the ancients than China's dynasties of conquest did. Sorai's disciple Dazai Shundai (1680–1747) carried this a step further with a discussion of political economy in which contemporary

China came out second. China, he pointed out, had moved from feudal to central government, while Japan's progression since the eighth century had reversed this sequence. China's centralization, with its rotating magistrates, men who were never assigned to their own areas, had no provision for a bond between officials and people; Tokugawa domains did. Was not Japan's order, with its built-in localism, more conducive to virtue, and was it not closer to the institutions Confucius had known and praised?

Other Confucian scholars worked out a proud affirmation of Japaneseness. Yamaga Sokō (1622–1685) moved from the Neo-Confucianism of his early education through Taoism and Buddhism and on to a final position in which he reconciled Confucianism and Shinto. He was an immensely influential teacher; the forty-seven *rōnin* considered themselves followers of his strategy. Yamaga set himself the task of explaining the justice in a system in which one class, the samurai, lived on the labors of another, the farmers. "The samurai," he wrote, "eats food without growing it, uses utensils without manufacturing them, and profits without buying or selling. What is the justification for this?"

He found that justification in the higher morality of the samurai's calling. The work of the samurai, as he saw it, was to reflect on his station in life, give loyal service to his master, deepen his fidelity with his friends, and "devote himself to duty above all." In short, in a world in which others were out for themselves, the samurai should stand as a moral ideal for the three classes of the common people who respected him and took him as an object lesson. "By following his teachings, they [commoners] are enabled to understand what is fundamental and what is secondary."[21] Yamaga Sokō's was the most satisfactory exposition of these ideas, and from his time *bushidō*, the "Way of the warrior," became a standard term.

And yet the problem of China remained. China-centrism was built into Chinese civilization. China was referred to as the "Central Country" or the "Central Efflorescence," and dynasties styled themselves as "Great." What were Japanese Confucianists to do about this? Sorai simply denied the applicability of "Great" to any fallen dynasty, and thought it better to use it for his own country in "Great Japan" *(Dai Nihon)*. Yamaga Sokō re-arranged the basic Confucian virtues to Japanese advantage by grouping valor with knowledge and benevolence. From that perspective, he argued, it was Japan and not China that deserved designation as the "Central Country."

In the nineteenth century a blend of Confucian and nativist scholarship that developed in the domain of Mito prepared the way for a final, rousing affirmation of this. By then China was being bested by a new and stronger West. Aizawa Seishisai (or Yasushi; 1781–1863), when he wrote his *Shinron*

("New Theses") in 1825, flatly named Japan as *Chūka*, the central efflorescence. He began with the ringing affirmation that "our Divine Realm is where the sun emerges. It is the source of the primordial vital force sustaining all life and order. Our Emperors, descendants of the Sun Goddess, Amaterasu, have acceded to the Imperial Throne in each and every generation, a unique fact that will never change. Our Divine Realm rightly constitutes the head and shoulders of the world and controls all nations."[22]

New and important notes are being struck here. Confucianism has been warped to emphasize imperial loyalty. Japan's uniqueness no longer derives from samurai nobility but from dynastic continuity, and myth and religion are in the service of, in fact united with, government and politics. In line with Confucian "rectification of names" the ground is beginning to shift to the advantage of the imperial court and at the expense of the bakufu. "Mito scholarship," as it became known, pointed to an imperial future.

It is clear that advocacy of Confucian solutions to Japanese problems, by scholars somewhat marginal to the power structure of their society, resulted in significant psychological strains. Those strains were worsened by the erosion of samurai self-confidence and autonomy under the restrictions of bakufu and domain centralization, an erosion that made it necessary to argue the case for samurai and for Japan. As Nakai has put it, Tokugawa Confucians tended to become involved in a game of one-upmanship played with the invisible opponent of China, and this lent a certain quality of shadowboxing to much of the eighteenth-century dialogue.[23] In the crisis that lay ahead affirmation of national identity would outweigh the impulse for national apologetic.

That in turn was affected by the fact that in the eighteenth century China-centered scholarship was facing additional problems as a vigorous anti-Confucian and anti-Chinese polemic was mounted by a new school of nativist scholars.

5. Ethnic Nativism

Kokugaku, "National Learning," provided another thread in the rich tapestry of scholarship and thought that distinguished the eighteenth century. It developed in a setting of conscious opposition to the "Chinese Learning" (Kangaku) in which Confucianism was encased, and affirmed the superiority of Japan and Japanese culture. It began with antiquarian literary study in the seventeenth century, but by the early nineteenth century it carried a powerful political message as well.

Intellectually *kokugaku* should be seen as ancillary to the other movements of its time. The passion of Ogyū Sorai and others for the "ancient learning" of China could have been expected to have its parallels in scholars concerned with Japanese antiquity, and the sort of Confucian loyalism shown by the Mito domain's sponsors of the *History of Great Japan* could be expected to have its impact on evaluations of the role of the Japanese emperor in antiquity. Tsunayoshi, the Genroku shogun, made it part of his civilizing mission to encourage the study of ancient Japan, and sponsored renovation and identification of imperial mausolea. Many leading scholars of national learning received sponsorship from shogunal or Tokugawa-related houses. It would be quite wrong to restrict the study of nativism to its bearing on later loyalism and insurrection, for it found resonance with many other trends in the intellectual life of its day.

The first concern of the founders of *kokugaku* was with early Japanese literature, especially poetry. The evocation of nature and praise of emotion that they found there seemed to them to be far removed from the formal didacticism of much of the Confucian teaching as they came to know it in Japan. Normative "forms" seemed to stand in direct opposition to "nature," as different as the often lengthy Chinese poem was from the evocative simplicity of Japanese poetry. Japanese poetry best captured the spirit of Japan; its only standards were those of beauty and emotion. Motoori Norinaga wrote that questions of morality and duty had no relation to those of aesthetics. As he put it, "Poetry . . . attempts neither to trespass on the teachings of Confucian and Buddha nor to pass moral judgments. Its aim is merely to express a sensitivity to human existence." For a scholar or holy man to admire the tinted leaves of autumn, but to pass by a beautiful woman pretending not to notice her, he argued, was insincere and dishonest; "It is as if a hundred ounces of gold were desirable but not a thousand."[24] Beauty was its own excuse for being, and made all moralizing superfluous.

The focus by nativist scholars on ancient Japanese literature in the context of a revival of Japanese tradition inevitably brought them into conflict with the Sino-centric world of most Japanese Confucianists. Kada no Azumamaro (1669–1736) was a Shinto priest influenced by Sorai's call for return to the language and texts of the past. In his studies of the *Manyōshū* (A.D. 759), the first Japanese poetic anthology, Kada argued that its poems were quite free of Chinese influence; they were "the natural expression of our ancient heritage; they are the voice of our divine land." This was the beginning of a lifelong battle he waged against syncretism and multiculturalism. While Sorai struggled to undo the influence of medieval texts that stood between the scholar and a true understanding of Chinese antiquity, Kada and his student Kamo tried to throw off the accretions of the entire Chinese tradition.

In 1728 Kada petitioned the shogun Yoshimune for permission to establish his own school in Kyoto. It was needed, he thought, because Japanese learning was being overwhelmed by Chinese and Buddhist learning. Confucian terms had become household words, but "the teachings of our Divine Emperors are steadily melting away, each year more conspicuously than the last. Japanese learning is falling into ruin." Almost no one was conversant with the terms of antiquity any longer, and therein lay a danger: "If the old words are not understood the old meanings will not be clear. If the old meanings are not clear the old learning will not revive . . . The loss will not be a slight one if we fail now to teach philology."[25] This sounds very much like Sorai.

Kokugaku teachings spread rapidly, and the ever wider circle of students these men attracted provides evidence of the cultural integration of Japan. Kada's best-known student was Kamo no Mabuchi (1697–1769). Like his teacher, Kamo was the son of a Shinto shrine priest. In 1738 he opened his own academy in Edo, where he attracted many students and lectured to important Tokugawa family members. The vow of loyalty his students took exemplifies the almost religious nature of the influence his teachings exerted. Each student signed a pledge assuring the master that he had a "burning desire to learn the way of former days in the sacred land of the Tennōs, which Master Kamo is good enough to teach . . . I will not whisper what I am taught to others until the time comes when it fills me and when I am given permission. Nor will I conceive an unwilling or contrary thought to the Master. If I fail to keep this faith, may the earthly and heavenly *kami* punish me."[26]

Kamo closed his school in 1760 and began travels to Ise and other places sacred to the Shinto tradition. In so doing he attracted more students, among them Motoori Norinaga, who was to become the best known of all the *kokugaku* scholars. In 1765 Kamo wrote his most important work. *Kokuikō*, "A Study of the Idea of Our Country," was not published until 1806, but it circulated widely in handwritten copies. This represented a frontal attack on the Chinese tradition, from Confucianism to the writing system. Kamo argued that the Chinese history so esteemed by his contemporaries was fraudulent and designed to cover up rebellion and deceit; the changeovers of dynasties stood in startling confrontation to the purity of Japan's tradition of an unbroken imperial line. He found merit only in the Taoist canon of Lao Tzu, with its rejection of formalism and structure. He contrasted Chinese rationalism with Japanese commitment and belief. The human mind, he argued, was limited in its power to understand and explain, and men should be willing to trust and accept. "The acts of the gods are illimitable and wondrous." Faith was more powerful than reason.

Motoori Norinaga (1730–1801), like most of the nativist scholars, was from nonsamurai stock; he was born the son of merchants near the great Ise shrine to the sun goddess Amaterasu. His life passion was the study of poetry and of ancient texts. Study of "The Record of Ancient Matters" *(Kojiki)* of 712, Japan's first text to chronicle the origins of the gods, the creation myths, and the sun goddess's commission to her descendants to rule the Japanese islands, occupied thirty years of his life. He went on to a detailed study of Lady Murasaki's tenth-century masterpiece, *The Tale of Genji.*

Motoori was more concerned with the individual than with politics. *Kokugaku,* he argued, accepted man as he was instead of trying to remake him as Buddhism and Confucianism did. Moral exhortation was ultimately vain and insincere. The goal of literary study was something he termed *mono no aware,* a term that, we have noted, conveys sympathetic awareness of the pathos or sadness of things. This required an intuitive, aesthetic empathy conveyed as a simple, heartfelt expression of sentiment. Any deep emotion—happiness, joy, or sorrow—could be classified as *aware.* To try to control it, or discipline it, or conceal it with samurai rigidity or "Chinese" rationalism, was simply dishonest. *Genji,* for instance, had long been interpreted as allegory, or denounced altogether as immoral. But the book, like all real literature, was not concerned with good or evil, but simply with *mono no aware.* And no branch of literature was more expressive of awareness than poetry. A further point was that women, who were less indoctrinated in the repression of emotion than men, were usually truer judges of real emotion. Poetry was in fact essentially feminine. And if Japanese poetry was the heart of Japanese expressiveness, then the Japanese "spirit" overall, especially that part of it that related to the *tennō* (emperor), was also feminine.[27]

Norinaga was a master of rigorous philological study, but he also held a highly irrational belief that the *Kojiki* mythology was historically authentic. He argued that what was recorded in that classic had to be true, and that adherence to its teachings constituted the "Way." For this term he used the Japanese *michi* rather than the Sino-Japanese *dō;* and rather than accept the usual reading for "The Record of Ancient Matters" as *Kojiki,* Motoori insisted on avoiding Chinese phonetic derivations and substituting purely Japanese words to read those characters as *furu koto bumi.* To succumb to innovations that had been introduced into the Japanese language together with Chinese characters was to lose the "pure Japanese heart" *(yamatogokoro)* in favor of an "errant" *magokoro,* thereby running the risk of accepting a foreign tradition of formalism, dishonesty, and insurrection. The stories about the gods had to be true, he argued; no one could have made them up.

Harry Harootunian has argued that this obsession with the Chinese tradition on the part of Tokugawa nativists was more metaphor than literal fact, and that they used "China" as a shorthand signifier for rationality and logic.[28]

There is room for agreement here. It is also true that the Confucianists the *kokugaku* scholars warred against were Japanese Confucianists, who often lived up to their reputation as fastidious bores. Nevertheless the close identification of China with everything that was wrong with Japanese culture had important ramifications for the future.

By the time of his death, Motoori is credited with having had five hundred disciples in forty provinces. But even this impressive network was dwarfed by the influence of Hirata Atsutane (1776–1843), under whom nativism became firmly associated with Shinto and spread throughout the countryside. With Hirata *kokugaku* became more religious and also more political. There was new emphasis on ancient prayers and affirmation of the ancient ideal of *matsurigoto,* a union of worship and politics. In this ancient concept it was the emperor who linked the aura that was his by virtue of descent from the gods with the governance of his people. He served the gods, and they in turn joined him to share the burdens of rule. This revival of ancient, indeed primitive, ideas was one of the dubious contributions of the nativist revival to the Meiji state in the nineteenth century. Nativism was by its very nature intensely parochial and particular. Indeed, one *kokugaku* assertion had it that other countries were assembled from the less worthy materials rejected in the original generation of the Japanese islands.

At the same time, Hirata's preparedness to accept whatever might be useful in other traditions was somewhat contradictory to this. The nativists, no longer bound to the Sino-centric focus on Chinese antiquity, were prepared to see merit in other traditions. Hirata in particular was out for arguments that contributed to Japan's superiority. He himself had been trained as a physician, and he had some knowledge of Western medicine that had filtered in through books imported by the Dutch at Nagasaki. He found it easy to justify this; the gods had taught medical lore to all countries, but virtuous Japan had not produced as many cures as had medicine in more polluted countries. But after Japan became damaged by its acquaintance with pernicious foreign doctrines, it had need for their healing too. And in any case, whatever was useful in "foreign" countries was ultimately Japanese. When Hirata learned of the Copernican revolution in astronomy, he argued that it provided proof of the greatness of the sun goddess. The story of Noah's flood, which he learned through some Jesuit translations that had made their way into Japan, went to show that Japan, which had experienced no flood, was on higher ground than other countries. He even found a creator god in the Shinto divinity, Takami-musubi. "These truths," he wrote, "are by no means confined to Japan. In many other countries it is believed that the seed of man and all other things owe their existence to the powers of this god."

Ultimately, then, Japanese learning was superior to all others because it represented a sea in which many rivers joined. As he put it, "We may properly speak not only of Chinese but even of Indian and Dutch learning as Japanese learning: this fact should be understood by all Japanese who delve into foreign studies."[29]

Even so, it should not be thought that his ability to co-opt foreign learning made Hirata think better of foreigners. He was virulently anti-Chinese and contemptuous of the Dutch at Nagasaki. "As everybody knows who has seen one," he assured his readers, "[the Dutch] shave their beards, cut their nails, and are not dirty like the Chinese . . . [but] Their eyes are really just like those of a dog. Apparently because the backs of their feet do not reach to the ground, they fasten wooden heels to their shoes, which makes them look all the more like dogs . . . [this] may be the reason they are lascivious as dogs . . . Because they are addicted to sexual excesses and to drink, none of them lives very long."[30]

It would nevertheless be wrong to dismiss Hirata on the ground of his hyperbole in polemics. One feature of nativism in Hirata's work, and a very important one, is the extent to which his influence took root in rural Japan. He and his disciples developed an emphasis on productivity—originally of the cosmos in the *Kojiki* mythology—that grew into highly practical discussions of the cultivation of rice. Ritual and prayer that had always been part of folk festivals focused on the well-being of the community or common folk. Agriculture was becoming more productive than it had ever been, in part through the writings of agronomists like Ōkura Nagatsune (1768–?). Ōkura, born the son of farmer-merchants in Kyushu, first planned a life of scholarship, but changed directions in conformity with his father's warning that book learning would divert him from farming and lead to ruin. "Even if I could not study the classics and thus learn the secrets of ruling a country," he consoled himself, "I refused to spend my life doing nothing of value; so I concentrated my ambition on learning the art of farming and studied it for many years."[31] Ōkura was one link in a line of influential writers that began with Miyazaki Yasusada (Antei, 1623–1697), whose classic *Treatise on Agriculture* went through numerous editions. Ōkura's writings emphasized ways to make farming more efficient and productive: timely cultivation, better seeds, better equipment, supplementary crops, and the care and culture of silkworms. Nor was he alone in this. The spread of literacy and opportunities for commercial farming as city markets grew larger resulted in a reading public of rural leaders that encouraged publishers to issue first editions of two and three thousand copies of relevant books for village readers.

Hirata propagandists for nativism worked their way into this readership and their ideas into journals and books. Their almanacs and calendars combined Shinto observances with practical advice. They also produced a flood of practical and pseudoscientific counsel that made such learning popular among village headmen.[32]

The nativist tradition of eighteenth- and nineteenth-century Japan is full of paradoxes. It found its intellectual beginnings in the surge of scholarship concerned with antiquity and it produced studies that are monuments of philological exactitude, and yet its leaders also advocated uncritical acceptance of wildly improbable assertions. It deplored the pollution of primitive Japanese sincerity by foreign, especially Chinese, ideas, while calmly laying claim to any strain of foreign thought that seemed useful. Co-optation of foreign thought was combined with contempt for foreigners. The Tokugawa peace and, frequently, Tokugawa sponsorship made possible work that was ultimately used to buttress the claims of the imperial court and the construction of the modern state religion of Meiji Japan.

6. Dutch, or Western, Learning *(rangaku)*

By this time it should be clear that the intellectual trends that have been discussed were seldom mutually exclusive. All educated men had a good knowledge of the Chinese classical tradition, for that was the medium in which scholarly literacy was transmitted. The practical needs of communication, on the other hand, naturally put the emphasis on Japanese. Ogyū Sorai, the most formidable scholar of Chinese learning of his day, wrote his memorials on statecraft for his shogun in Japanese. The eighteenth-century development of nativist learning added dignity and depth to work in that language, but even so Kada wrote the petition in which he asked permission to open a school for native learning in classical Chinese. Popular culture and folk tradition was of course couched in Japanese, as were the numerous handbooks and manuals of daily use that circulated in town and country; so were domestic records and the diaries so many people kept. What mattered for them was practicality and utility. In the eighteenth century an additional school of specialization developed in response to the apparent practicality and rationality of Western learning that filtered in through Nagasaki.

It began with medicine. Seventeenth-century European medicine was not always scientific or reliable, but it was grounded in study of the body. Dutch paintings of a class gathered over a dissection for the study of anatomy represent a direct observation that was less common in East Asia. Classical Chinese texts of medical lore were based on theories of balance and cosmology, and treatments followed from this. Physicians worked to maintain a proper bal-

ance of the five elements and the negative and positive (*yin* and *yang*) principles in conformity with the same normative expectations that were applied
to maintenance and restoration of the social order. Surgery was a basic of
Western medicine from its early days, but it was neglected in East Asia, where
invasive techniques ran the risk of doing damage to a body inherited from
the ancestors.

The little Dutch station at Deshima played a role in the transmission of
medical techniques, particularly surgery, from early on. Although chief factors
at Deshima rotated annually, many doctors attached to the station were there
for years. Unlike Kaempfer, they did not leave ethnographic descriptions or
compile histories; their names have come down to us but not, unfortunately,
their correspondence. Nevertheless they surely exchanged information with
Japanese curious to learn about their skills.[33] Thus there was a "Casper" (von
Shaumbergen) school of surgery, known as *Kasuparuryū*. Then paradoxically,
as Dutch trade diminished in the early eighteenth century, interest in Dutch
(= Western) techniques increased.

In the 1720s the shogun Yoshimune, eager to increase domestic production
of goods that had to be imported, relaxed restrictions on books that could
be imported at Nagasaki. The shogun's curiosity about Western ways extended
to horses and horsemanship, which was demonstrated by a Hollander ordered
to come to Edo. In the same years he was inviting botanists and doctors from
China. Yoshimune also wanted to know more about the Western calendar,
and commissioned several young scholars to go to Nagasaki and study with
the Dutch. As the century advanced such interests grew.

The study of Dutch gradually became fashionable among a small coterie
of educated Japanese. Toward the end of the century the Dutch station head,
Titsingh, on his return to Europe, was able to exchange letters in Dutch with
several daimyo he had come to know during his stay in Japan. The daily record
kept by the Dutch station indicates that during the stay of the Dutch in Edo
on *sanpu* visits, as they were known, more and more questions were being
asked by Japanese doctors who were permitted to see them.

The story of the struggle of Japanese to learn more about the West from
the Dutch is one of the most extraordinary chapters in cultural interchange
in world history. There were two groups of Japanese involved. One was in
Nagasaki, where the interpreters guild was headed by four families. Under
them were another dozen or more families that enjoyed hereditary rights
in this occupation. Each, in turn, had junior members, and in the 1690s
Kaempfer estimated that there might be as many as 140 enrolled altogether.

In Edo a much smaller group, mostly physicians, worked in almost complete isolation from the men at Nagasaki. The Edo doctors were mostly of

modest rank, but they were interested in adding some of the skills of Western surgery to their knowledge of Chinese medicine. There was very little contact between the two groups, for the Nagasaki experts were not eager to see their monopoly on language broken. Moreover, there was no private system of internal mail, and communication was possible only through access to men attached to processions or shipments for other reasons. Consequently the Edo scholars had to work entirely from books. Those fortunate enough to be personal physicians to daimyo, however, could urge their patient to purchase items for them, either books already in Japan or titles that could be added to the "order list" that bakufu officials gave the Dutch. Fulfillment of an order required at least a year, however, and the process must have been maddeningly slow. The Edo doctors could hope to see a real Hollander only on the visits of the Dutch to the capital, and these were biennial after 1764 and every four years after 1790.

On one occasion one of the doctors, Ōtsuki Gentaku, found himself unable to get the floor with a question and noted ruefully that he would have to wait four years for another chance.[34] The books available became the more precious, and they were frequently copied out by hand.

Deciphering them, however, was harder because there were no language tools. An early effort used a French-Dutch dictionary in which Japanese words were substituted for the French. But even this was available in handwritten copy only in 1796, and it was not published until 1855. On rare occasions an Edo scholar received permission or orders to study at Nagasaki. Such an opportunity was tantamount to the chance to "study abroad" and usually marked its fortunate recipient as a future leader.

In 1771 a milestone event took place: a little group of Edo scholars was permitted to be present at the execution of an old woman and allowed to direct the executioner, who was a member of the ostracized subcaste community, to dismantle the corpse. There had been a few dissections earlier, but they had been conducted without a reliable chart at hand and represented undirected curiosity. On this occasion, however, the scholars had with them a Dutch book on anatomy (which in turn had been translated from the German) entitled *Anatomical Tables*, which had charts showing and identifying the parts of the body.

The man who organized this gathering was a doctor named Sugita Genpaku (1733–1817), whose name and career became closely identified with the development of Dutch learning. His life also illustrated the interdependence of the intellectual trends that have been discussed, for he had been influenced by Ogyū Sorai's call for careful preparation in all study. Sugita's autobiography provides the standard account of that occasion, and it is probably not an overstatement to describe this as a pivotal day in Japanese intellectual history and science.

> The corpse of the criminal was that of an old woman of about fifty years, nicknamed Aocha Baba, born in Kyoto. It was an old butcher who made the dissection. We had been promised an *eta* named Toramatsu, known for his skill in dissection, but because he was sick his grandfather came instead. He was ninety years old, but healthy, and he told us he had been doing this since his youth. According to him up until this time people had left it up to him, and he had not shown them where the lungs, kidneys, and other organs were. They would pretend that they had studied the internal structure of the body directly. But the parts naturally weren't labeled, and they had to be satisfied with the way he pointed them out. He knew where everything was, but he had not learned their proper names . . . Some of the things turned out to be arteries, veins, and suprarenal bodies according to our [Dutch] anatomical tables . . . We found that the structure of the lungs and liver and the position and shape of the stomach were quite different from what had been believed according to old Chinese theory.[35]

On their way home Sugita and his friends reflected on how shameful it was that they had tried to serve their lords as doctors without first having a true knowledge of the human body. They vowed, he writes, that thereafter they would seek facts only through experiment. "I suggested," he went on, "that we decipher the *Tafel Anatomia* (the book they had used) without the aid of interpreters in Nagasaki, and translate it into Japanese. The next day we met and began . . . Gradually we got so we could decipher ten lines or more a day. After two or three years of hard study everything became clear to us; the joy of it was as the chewing of sweet sugar cane."

This began a new age of translation. Long ago there had been another project to translate from Chinese, but this time it was Dutch science and technology that was the focus. The earlier effort to translate the corpus of Chinese learning, Sugita noted, had the backing of an imperial court that sent student monks to China, but this time a much smaller number of men had to work things out on their own. Sugita and his associates thus had a consciousness of themselves as partners in a venture of historic importance. At the same time, he granted, the earlier tradition "probably prepared our mind" for the task at hand. By the time Sugita wrote his memoirs in 1815, he could marvel at the spread of *rangaku* (Dutch learning; the "ran" from "Oranda," Holland) and looked back on a career that was rich in reward and interest. Private practice and official recognition had given him an income the equivalent of an upper samurai. He took delight in his grandchildren, his students, and his success. "In the beginning," he wrote, "there were only three of us . . . who came together to make plans for our studies. Now, fifty years later, those studies have reached every corner of the country, and each year new translations seem to be brought out . . . And what particularly delights me is the idea that, when once the way of Dutch studies is opened wide, doctors a hundred or even a thousand years from now will be able to master real medicine and use it to save people's lives. When I think of the public benefits this will bring, I cannot help dancing and springing for joy."[36]

In time this new wave of foreign learning would reinforce the ideological assault that *kokugaku* was making to challenge the dominance that Chinese learning had enjoyed. Nativist scholars could argue that Chinese learning was foreign and spiritually harmful to Japanese "purity," but Sugita and his friends could prove that Chinese wisdom was occasionally wrong, as in the morphology of the body, or impractical. And of course each persuasion seemed personified by its representatives; in late-eighteenth-century Japan "China" began to be associated with conservatism and even obscurantism. In a dialogue he wrote in 1775 Sugita had an interlocutor protest,

> "Look here! Korea and Ryukyu are not China, but they at least received the teachings of the same sages. This medical learning you are teaching, though, comes from countries on the northwest frontier of the world, 9000 *ri* from China. Their language is different from China's and they don't know anything about the sages. They are the most distant of all the barbarian countries; what possible good can their learning do us?"

Sugita's alter ego answered this as follows: it was all very well for the Chinese to profess scorn for barbarians, but notice that it was the barbarian Manchus who were ruling them now! More important, though, people were the same the world around, and China itself was only one country in the Eastern Seas. Real medical knowledge had to be based on more universal grounds than on the wisdom of a few. Experiment proved that the sages' ideas about anatomy were not correct, and one simply could not dismiss the Dutch or their learning out of hand.[37]

Dutch studies spread rapidly in the last quarter of the eighteenth century. Sugita could count 104 men from thirty-five provinces as disciples by the time of his death. Nor was his case as isolated as he wanted his readers to believe, for many others were at work.

Medicine led in this, but not to the exclusion of other disciplines. Nagasaki served as entry port for artistic inspiration as well. Vanishing point perspective came to characterize prints and maps, and experiments with copperplate engraving added to the eclectic nature of mid- and late Tokugawa art. Many were, in other words, prepared to act on Hirata Atsutane's assertion that ultimately everything was "Japanese learning." The common element here, whether in art, medicine, or, in the nineteenth century, mathematics and physics, was accuracy and practicality. What was true to life began to compete with what was in conformity with the universal principles of the Neo-Confucian universe.

Even so, it is too much to argue, as some have, that the rise of Dutch studies sounded the bell for the demise of Tokugawa feudal institutions. Scholars of Dutch learning were dependent on their superiors for the resources that made their studies possible. Far from imagining a revolutionary role for themselves, they saw their new specialty as helping them personally and strengthening the society of which they were a part. In some cases their authorities granted them the ranking of *jusha*, "Confucianist," indicating how varied an assemblage of talents that term could cover. At first almost none of their writing circulated among the general public.

The first generation of Dutch scholars did not overturn tradition. Nor, for that matter, did they modernize Japanese medicine as rapidly or as profoundly as Sugita thought they had. It was not a matter of an either-or contrast. Most doctors added aspects of Western medical lore to the mix of Chinese and Japanese therapies they used. Moreover, the process of selection for translation was far from scientific and in fact quite random. In any case medicine was changing rapidly in eighteenth-century Europe. Translators sometimes spent months on works that were already dated.

Rather, the importance of the first generation of scholars of Dutch learning lies in the attitude and mind-set that they showed. *Rangaku* brought a delight in the new, the different, and the difficult. It was new, for it opened windows onto a body of learning that was radically different from what had been available and, in its assumptions, often farthest removed from the classical knowledge of the China-centered world. And it was difficult, difficult beyond the imagination of scholars in our day who have access to instruction, learning tools, and dictionaries. It added important strands to the rich tapestry of Tokugawa intellectual activity; it also had profound consequences for the future.

7. Religion

The importance of the intellectual currents in eighteenth-century Japan should not be allowed to overshadow the beliefs that had meaning for the millions of Japanese in countryside and city. Japan's earlier religious traditions lived on in Buddhism and folk religion, but both underwent significant change in response to the direction of the state and the diffusion and dilution of the ideas of the scholars who have been discussed.

Buddhism had been the religion of Japan long before the Tokugawa unification, and it remained so in Tokugawa years. At the turn of the seventeenth century Christianity had offered a serious threat in some areas, but although it lived on in southwestern Japan as a secret underground sect, the Tokugawa suppression of Catholic sectarians ended its ability to compete with Buddhism. Throughout Japanese society Buddhist doctrines of karma, rebirth, and denial of the reality of corporeal existence became and remained basic to the worldview of millions of Japanese.

Buddhism was also intimately related to the power structure. At the highest reaches of society court nobles were closely intertwined with the priestly hierarchy. Younger sons of the imperial family were routinely assigned to selected *monzeki* (court-related) temple establishments. Among the samurai elite the stern intellectual and physical discipline of Zen influenced many men. Learned Zen statesman-priests were central to diplomatic intercourse with the continent and found sponsorship for some of the most celebrated and beautiful temple and garden monuments to austerity and contemplation in the population centers of Kamakura and Kyoto. In early Tokugawa the new land settlement cost most temples their land and political influence, but the kind of systematic horror that Nobunaga had brought to the Enryakuji complex gave way to daimyo patronage and subsidies for the reconstruction of buildings that had been damaged or burned. Ieyasu himself relied on several canny Buddhist monks for counsel, and the Tokugawa family tombs remained with the popular faith Jōdo-Shin sect temple of Zōjōji in Edo.

Jōdo-Shin itself, however, having been battered by its struggles against Nobunaga and Hideyoshi, was now absorbed into the administrative structure by charging it with the requirement of registering communicants in the *shū-mon aratame* surveys to certify their hostility against Christianity. The "temple guarantee" *(terauke)* system came full cycle in the eighteenth century. From then on the family, rather than the individual, had to register with a parish temple. The temple's attestation was required for marriage, employment, change of residence, and travel permits. In this way the Buddhist organization became an arm of state control. In some domains even Buddhist sects with a history of insurrection were also outlawed; the bakufu discriminated against some branches of Nichiren, and the Satsuma domain, which required all commoners to wear wooden identification tags, forbade Ikkō Buddhism as well.

The bakufu did its best to control, as well as use, the Buddhist establishment. Temples of each sect were organized along hierarchic lines to facilitate supervision by the commissioner for temples and shrines *(Jisha bugyō)*. The great Honganji sect was divided into an east and a west branch to make it more manageable. Temples were ordered to simplify and purify their doctrines and to avoid feuding with one another.

Such close relations with despotic government did not make for moral fervor or spiritual depth. Guaranteed adherents and discouraged from competing with one another, Buddhist temples and priests seldom enjoyed respect or high prestige. Popular writers and printmakers of the cities often lampooned their eccentricities, while samurai intellectuals scorned their doctrines. The seventeenth-century Confucian scholar Kumazawa Banzan wrote that "from the ordinance banning Christianity on, a faithless Buddhism has flourished. Since throughout the land everyone has his parish temple, unlike in the past, monks can freely indulge in worldly affairs without concern for either discipline or scholarship . . . The freedom with which they eat meat and engage in romantic affairs surpasses that of even secular men." There were outstanding Buddhist reformers and scholars of quality who did their best to reverse these trends and change that image, but they had to battle against the main current. It is noteworthy that such individuals usually offered teachings that reflected aspects of the intellectual atmosphere that has been considered. Jiun Sonja (also known as Onkō, 1718–1804), for instance, combined a scholarly command of Sanskrit with restorationist views of Buddhist law with affirmation of basic Confucian morality like filial piety. He was a distinguished calligrapher and painter, studied Confucianism with Itō Tōgai, and practiced Zen meditation. He was above all a pioneer in the study of classical Sanskrit. Before him the Japanese had relied chiefly on Chinese translations, but Jiun pushed beyond and behind this screen; he thus provides a Buddhist variant of the enthusiasm for antiquity and philology that animated Sorai and Norinaga.[38]

But while Buddhism remained the religion of the Japanese, it was losing a good deal of its vitality. For the great majority of the villagers who made up most of the population it was closely intermingled with folk religion that pieced together ancestor worship, portents, directions, and concern with a beneficent though capricious nature. In late Tokugawa days much of this became structured into something called Shinto, but it was long in getting out from under the wide, though porous, umbrella of Buddhism.

At the end of Tokugawa rule in 1868 there were 87,558 temples and 74,642 shrines.[39] Since there were about 70,000 villages (mura), this averaged out to one of each. Yet they were seldom separate. Most shrines were small and lacked a full-time priest. More often than not the shrines were close to or within a temple complex and controlled by Buddhist clergy. This mix held true even at Ise, the ancestral imperial shrine dedicated to the sun goddess Amaterasu, which had almost 300 temples connected with it. For the most part "Shinto" priests were subject to the Buddhist registration laws and were technically "Buddhist."

There was also a plethora of popular cults. Many were regional in focus, centering on sites that drew pilgrims. Mt. Fuji, Kumano on the Wakayama Peninsula, and Iwashimizu were the outstanding examples of this. Their regional focus could nevertheless encompass a considerable area; the Mt. Fuji cult, for instance, had a complex system of traveling circuit priests *(oshi)* who organized and visited groups of believers *(kō)* on a regular rotation. Itinerants in a world of status and stability, these priests constituted a special category, and it was understandable that officials might be wary of them.

Government regulations for Shinto were necessarily rather loose due to its amorphous character. Major shrines usually had hereditary priesthoods, and sometimes confraternities organized for pilgrimages. Tutelary shrines connected with daimyo lineages also had hereditary priesthoods. In an effort to regulate this confusion the bakufu, in 1665, decreed that all priests and shrines were to apply to the Yoshida house, descendants of an ancient ritualist clan, for approval of vestments with indications of ranks and titles.

Within this complex pattern the Ise shrines were special in the range and breadth of organization and support, for their network of *oshi* circuit priests and the village confraternities *(kō)* on which they drew were to be found all over the country. The circuit priests moved constantly along major communication networks, and might come through once or twice a year. One man might supervise as many as ten thousand households. *Oshi* were intimately related to the cycle of agricultural life. They distributed almanacs with the all-important agricultural calendar and information about the progress of the sixty-year cycle with its zodiacal referents, as well as simple emblems or talismans for health, good harvests, good fortune, and purification. They were supported by a modest sum appropriate to the village's tax assessment. The Inner Shrine at Ise had 309 *oshi* related to it, and the Outer Shrine, 555.

The sixty-year cycle (based upon the interrelationships of the five elements and twelve horary animals) had entered Japan from China and had been used as early as the seventh century to back-date the inauguration of the ruling family to 660 B.C. Completion of a cycle, whether in an individual life or larger era, was an auspicious event that signified a renewal. In Edo this became associated with pilgrimages to the Ise shrines. The *oshi* received the pilgrims at an Ise lodge; sacred dances *(kagura)* would be performed, and the pilgrims were then free for sight-seeing and relaxation. Pilgrims returned with magic slips or talismans *(fuda)* that brought good luck. Sometimes affairs took on a carnival nature; rumors of magic appearances of talismans implying promises of health and harvest could bring a rush to acquire one. Joyous celebration and dancing could become lubricated by sake provided by the rich, whether in generosity or, more often, an urge for self-protection from the crowd. The almanacs the *oshi* distributed kept people informed of approaching dates, guided their route, and directed them to rustic hostels ("Iseya") along the way. With the spread of travel that has been described it gradually became accepted that an Ise pilgrimage was a once-in-a-lifetime experience. Not everyone waited for the festival year; indeed the timing of the major pilgrimage "happenings" showed only a loose correlation with what should have been banner years. By the eighteenth century upwards of a half-million pilgrims came to Ise annually. Intimation that a festival year was at hand could bring astonishing numbers on the road: in Genroku an estimated three and a half *million*, in 1771 two million, and in 1830, three to four million. It should be noted that there was little specifically "Shinto" about this, except that the sun goddess was the focus of the ceremonies at Ise.

For most people the Ise pilgrimage was a rare interval of joyous, even delirious, passage from the familiar. In every corner of Japan festivals, *matsuri*, were the opposite, a regularly scheduled form of collective piety that served to reaffirm ties with person and place. Carried out at appropriate points in the agricultural calendar, these shrine-centered events were occasions of local jubilation and pride; their preparation and execution absorbed the cooperation of every age group, from the village leaders and adults who organized and contributed support for food and costume, to the boisterous young men whose strength carried the ponderous *ujigami*, or local *kami*, from and to the shrine, to the excited children who ran behind.

Another mix of Buddhism, folk religion, nature worship, and pilgrimage could be seen in the phenomenon of Shugendō, a religious order active throughout rural Japan.[40] Mountains had religious significance in Japan from very early times. Emperors and aristocrats made pilgrimages to mountainous areas, particularly Kumano and Yoshino, and the same sites attracted ascetics who purified themselves by entering the mountain in a symbolic transition from a profane to a sacred world. The consecration of Zen temples was also referred to as "opening the mountain." The mountain ascetics were credited with magical powers of endurance to heat and cold, and levitation and transport to heaven. When they came down from the mountains and returned from their purifying rites they could function as shamans, with power to overcome the spirits that caused sickness. With the institutionalization of these practices both Kumano and Yoshino became centers for Shugendō. They were fiercely competitive, but both were associated with the esoteric practices of Shingon Buddhism.

Here, again, the bakufu entered to tidy things up. In 1613 all *yamabushi* ("mountain priests") were ordered to affiliate with one or another of the Shu-gendō lines, in order to structure and legitimize the cult. At the same time Shugendō was now free to widen its links with ordinary people, and its influ-ence. As the *yamabushi* gained authority they also abandoned much of their asceticism. They married and ate meat; instead of remaining itinerant mendi-cants they settled in villages and performed rituals for a regular clientele. The rationale for mountain asceticism also changed, from personal mysticism or repentance to services of healing for nonascetic villagers. Parish populations in turn were organized into confraternities that launched pilgrimages and sponsored the worship of specific deities.

Shugendō practitioners became a large group of men and women; one study estimates that there may have been 170,000 by the nineteenth century. Leaders often doubled as clergy of Buddhist temples or of local shrines. Some-times they operated parish schools, and in many respects became close to or part of the upper level of landowner village society. Not infrequently, members of that elite engaged in Shugendō discipline themselves in the belief it could contribute to the order and discipline of village life.

Like the new religions of nineteenth- and twentieth-century Japan, Shu-gendō had a place and role for women. In temple records they were sometimes registered as priests' wives, but they usually functioned like partners. A female medium *(miko)* worked with the *yamabushi* in healing rites; he, the stern, unbending chief, gave the orders, but she, the yielding, empathetic part of the team, entered into a trance in which the spirit spoke through her, revealing what was required as compensation or correction. *Miko* had their own bounded territories, and they trained under female mentors who taught them their craft. Some (the *itako* of northern Japan) were blind.

Shugendō rituals were vitally connected with pregnancy, childbirth, the location of lost articles, healing, the exorcism of malevolent spirits, ancestral rites, and pilgrimages.[41] Services were usually communal events in which the sponsoring family had to provide refreshments for the community, and they could constitute a considerable burden for all but wealthy villagers.

All this illustrates both the variety but also the harmony of ritual and religious thought. The language and the imagery owed everything to Bud-dhism, but the elements of nature worship and shamanist practice clearly had more ancient roots.

8. Popular Preaching

The syncretic nature of the teachings that attracted villagers in the countryside was also present in the popular preaching and lecturing in local towns and castle cities. There were long traditions of popular preaching in Japan; storytellers had acquainted commoners with the heroism of medieval warriors, and Buddhist reformers of the Kamakura period had made their way through the country attracting great crowds. Yet it is safe to say that preaching had never been so accessible or so tuned in to the practical problems of daily life. It was not unusual for lecturers to speak to hundreds of listeners. Hosoi Heishū (1728–1801) wrote that after his tour of a domain in northern Japan the "villagers were all choked with tears, and especially the older men were so sad to see me go that when I left for Yonezawa 700 or 800 of them prostrated themselves in the snow and wept aloud."[42] Hosoi's message was one that must have pleased authorities who invited him to speak: sincerity, frugality, modesty, and diligence were essential to life, and if villagers only knew how careful their superiors were about their finances they would gladly reciprocate by paying what was due them. Nevertheless, even if one makes allowance for the lack of alternative forms of education or diversion available to the villagers, these figures speak to the driving urge for self-improvement on the part of those who came.

Lecturers included popularizers of Zen Buddhism who reached to lay audiences or wrote in easily understood vernacular Japanese. They tried to reduce Zen teachings to their essentials, and spoke directly to the concerns of their auditors. Suzuki Shōsan (1579–1655), who had fought as a samurai in the battles of Sekigahara and Osaka, argued that in the life of commoners ordinary, daily work could lead to enlightenment. What mattered was internal attitude; when this was properly adjusted and focused, all trades could become the roads to spiritual emancipation. Enlightenment involved a focus on attaining one's "true mind," a concern that was shared, to differing degrees and different but related terms, with Neo-Confucian idealism.

Ideas of this sort received powerful expression in the teachings of Ishida Baigan (1685–1744), a farmer's son who was apprenticed to a Kyoto merchant family. After studying what he could of Buddhism, Shinto, and Confucianism, Baigan began a series of lectures in Kyoto in 1729 from which his movement, Shingaku ("Heart study"), can be dated. Basing himself principally, though not explicitly, on the teachings of Chu Hsi, he regarded learning ("gaku") less as an intellectual activity than as a challenge to investigate human nature through personal experience and reflection. Becoming convinced of the universal nature of morality, Baigan argued that when it came to moral practices the merchant, supposedly the lowest in the status order of society, should in no wise be thought inferior to anyone else. This in effect postulated a merchant ethic, "the Way of the townsman," that deserved equality with the Way of the samurai (bushidō).

These ideas were further developed by a number of disciples, principally Teshima Toan. Baigan's thought was "less a philosophical system than a type and method of spirituality directed to townsmen and merchants."[43] Shingaku grew through the multiplication of reading and study groups which were conducted under the guidance of a certified master who would test the spiritual advancement of his charges. Meetings were held in utmost simplicity, and masters usually declined to accept gifts or payment. This was entirely congruent with the emphasis on merchant values of frugality and diligence.

Shingaku was in no sense political or subversive, although its valorization of the traditionally scorned merchant class might have been deemed so. Quite the reverse: it was said of Teshima Toan that when he passed in front of a government proclamation board (the *kōsatsu* described earlier) he would take down his umbrella, bow, and keep from using his walking stick (lest he seem to raise it against authority). In periods of reform bakufu administrators tended to exempt Shingaku preachers from their bans on public gatherings and performances, and it was in fact this seeming compliance with feudal authority that guaranteed that with the Meiji Restoration and abandonment of status restrictions Shingaku too would come to an end.

Its importance, however, is to be found in the way that it once again showed the way the quest of ordinary Japanese for spiritual cultivation characterized commoner, perhaps even more than samurai, society in Edo Japan. Whether searching for one's "original mind," or attempting to "attain Buddhahood" or become like a (Shinto) *kami,* Japanese of many stripes strove to restrain their "selfish" desires and calculation, and they were endlessly patient in listening to expositions of and exhortations to *makoto* (sincerity). Notwithstanding the bounds of a feudal status system and rule that was frequently arbitrary, the values of all groups within Japan's society had become congruent, each group persuaded of the importance of its contribution to the larger whole.

8

On February 19, 1837, Ōshio Heihachirō, a samurai bureaucrat who had abandoned government for Confucian philosophy, set fire to his Osaka house as the signal to his followers to rise in revolt. Farmers were to seize and burn tax records, and the urban poor were to seize the property of the wealthy merchants and distribute it. It was not clear what was supposed to happen after that, but there was no doubt that the evils of Tokugawa rule were contrasted to the absolute purity of the sun goddess and her descendant, the emperor. The fires raged for two days through the merchant centers of Osaka, and the poor sacked the homes and storehouses of the wealthy until bakufu troops put down the rebellion. Ōshio had abandoned Neo-Confucian orthodoxy for the rival (and prohibited) school of Wang Yangming, which preached the unity of knowledge and action. He had come to see himself as a sage who would court death to "save the people," the slogan on his banners. His memory, ideals, and thought survived him and moved Japanese of many sorts to direct action in later years: loyalist activists in the Meiji Restoration, samurai like General Nogi struggling against the perversion of warrior purity by selfishness, young military radicals in the years before World War II, and their successors, student radicals in the 1960s as well as the author Mishima Yukio who ended his life with a spectacular suicide in 1970. Like them, Ōshio acted from moral rather than political impulses. His ill-fated revolt served as the climax to the Tokugawa tradition of protest, and it foreshadowed later expressions of nihilistic violence. It therefore serves as an introduction to the forms of crisis and response to crisis in Tokugawa society.

All discussions of political economy and changes in religious belief during the Tokugawa years took place against a background of steady change in authority and society. Outward forms of deference and hierarchy remained as they had been, but this often masked almost continuous change. That change also varied by place and time, for Japan was far from monolithic. Economic change around the great metropolitan areas outsped that in relatively backward provinces, but even so there were few areas in which life retained its early Tokugawa patterns in all respects. Contemporaries often record their regret at the way things were going; as Conrad Totman has put it, "eighteenth and nineteenth century rulers glorified the age of the founders, urban people recalled the wonders of pre-1657 Edo, and merchants enshrined Genroku as an era of unparalleled opulence."[1] There was a gradual shift in the balance of forces between bakufu center and domain periphery, another in the balance between rulers and ruled, and still another in the balance between village leaders and villagers. Each of these had its impact on the events that accompanied the mid-nineteenth-century collapse of the bakufu, and each contributed to the dynamics of the modern Meiji state and society.

1. Population

If economic and social hardship was often sufficient to spark protest, consideration of the root causes involved has to begin with the balance between people and land. The relation between population growth and economic development presents important problems. The underdeveloped world of the twentieth century is full of cases in which population growth consumes the resources of agricultural societies without leaving a surplus for investment, and the urban blight accompanying that population growth often seems to prevent economic development.

Until recent decades scholars usually described Tokugawa Japan in comparable terms. They argued that rapid growth in the seventeenth century brought the population to a Malthusian limit, exhausting possible resources and leaving a countryside heavily taxed and incapable of further growth. Tokugawa authorities were understood to have squeezed agriculturalists to the limit of what was practicable, and farmers seemed taxed to the point that they could neither live nor die. Early-twentieth-century Japanese historians, often heavily influenced by Marxist assumptions, found convincing substantiation in the writings of contemporary observers who recorded the desperate conditions that accompanied periods when famine stalked the land. Yet this view accorded poorly with other descriptions; foreign travelers who came to Japan in the 1850s and 1860s described a smiling and apparently prosperous countryside. The Malthusian emphasis was also difficult to reconcile with the dynamic growth of the later nineteenth century.

More recently demographers who work with village records and the na-

tional surveys of religious affiliation required by the shogunate come to different conclusions. They begin with the contention that the earlier picture erred
in overestimating the size of Japan's population at the time of Sekigahara;
earlier studies estimated the 1600 population at twenty million. It now seems
probable that some twelve million would be a more reasonable estimate. A
group of demographers led by Hayami Akira go on from there to discern
extremely rapid growth in the seventeenth century. Figures remain estimates,
for records omit many of the elite and urban floaters, but Japan's population seems to have tripled during the entire Tokugawa period. A major element in that growth relates to the shift from extended and patriarchal families to nuclear families among the peasantry; smaller units made for more
rapid growth. The land filled out, new fields were opened, and before long
even unpromising slopes were exploited for step-paddies and dry fields.
Seventeenth-century daimyo encouraged such developments by offering tax
advantages and, in some cases, conferring status (*gōshi,* country samurai) on
men for undertaking agricultural expansion. From 1720 on the central government also interested itself in such developments by ordering land surveys every
six years. The eighteenth century brought a slowdown of such expansion, one
that seems at first glance to justify discussions of a more or less Malthusian
stagnation. Now the demographers discern important regional differences.
Some areas, particularly those around Edo to the northeast, grew particularly
rapidly at first and later began to exhibit a net decline; others, previously
"behind," continued to grow, although more slowly. Thus the most urbanized
and economically advanced areas showed a stabilization or even a decline,
while less "developed" provinces continued to grow. Later, in the nineteenth
century, growth was resumed in most areas.

Other scholars, notably Kozo Yamamura and Susan Hanley,[2] have made
important contributions to our understanding of checks on population
growth. At times natural disasters provided severe checks. The domain system
of regional autonomy made it difficult to fight famine by importing grain
from other areas. In the Kyōhō years of 1732–1733 climatic disturbances supplemented by insect infestation destroyed almost half of the rice crop in some
areas, and authorities reported many deaths and several millions struck by
undernourishment. In 1783 (the Tenmei era) volcanic eruptions showered ash
that destroyed productive fields and engulfed villages through entire districts,
and bad weather followed to bring crop failures for almost all of the harvest
in northeastern Japan; this disaster inevitably led to large-scale starvation and
population decline in the areas affected. Then, in 1837 and 1838 (the Tenpō
era) cold weather once again led to crop losses, and in the city of Osaka epidemics carried off one-tenth and more of the population during the Tenpō

famine.[3] Nevertheless demographers contend that specific disasters of this sort (like astounding civilian casualties in modern wars) tend to be made up within a generation. On the other hand the ecological damage that followed from erosion, and the substitution of commercial crops like cotton for food grains, clearly left villagers less able to survive severe climatic setbacks.

In another sense the relative stability of Japan's population left the country fortunately situated for the demographic developments of the latter nineteenth century. China's population very nearly doubled during the eighteenth century, but Japan's did not. By the early years of the twentieth century Japanese publicists were worrying about overpopulation and discussing possible loci for emigration and settlement, but it had required almost a half century for things to reach that point.

Recent studies also focus on means of population control that were practiced in Tokugawa years. Marriage in Japan was relatively late, and as a result women faced fewer child-bearing years. In many parts of Japan young men were sent off for out-of-season employment in urban centers, a process that continues in modern times under the classification of *dekasegi* ("going off to work"). Hayami argues that by the eighteenth century bakufu five-family units (the *goningumi*) and prohibitions on the sale and division of land were virtually dead letters with very little practical meaning for the way people actually lived.[4] Inheritance was, however, unequal, with the result that many younger sons and daughters were sent off into service. Early forms of abortion were common. In famine and hardship years contemporary moralists deplored the practice of infanticide, but recent scholarship challenges assertions that it was common.[5] Rulers, who saw the practice as an implied reflection on their morality as governors, frequently warned against it. In any case, whatever its prevalence, the practice varied by area, and within area by class and income, which established the dividing line between those who could afford to raise all their children and those who could not. One would expect infanticide (*mabiki*, an agricultural term used for "thinning out" seedlings to ensure better growth) would be more common among the desperately poor than among the well-off, and Thomas Smith bears this out. His study of a village gives the picture of constant movement in and out of economic categories (defined in terms of possession of land) and provides eloquent refutation of theories of "stagnation" and torpor.[6]

2. Rulers and Ruled

Another aspect of structural change in the Edo period was a blurring of distinctions within the elite. In the seventeenth century the bakufu had been at pains to wall off the imperial court from contact with daimyo, and in the early years the distinction between *fudai* and *tozama* lords was also of critical importance. As years of peace followed those of war, and the ceremonies of civil life and status replaced those of violence, the court had new attractions for the heads of military houses. Marriage alliances were eagerly sought. Bakufu approval was required for them, but the central government too began to concern itself with attention to the imperial tombs. Daimyo, whether *fudai* or *tozama*, were increasingly preoccupied with the management and economic health of their domains. High bakufu appointments tended to be monopolized by a relatively small number of *fudai* houses, leaving other lords free to pursue their own interests and advantage. So too with alliances formed by marriage and adoption. Shogun Ienari's progeny by his numerous concubines led him to place sons wherever he saw an opening. He himself chose as his consort a daughter of the (Satsuma) Shimazu *tozama* lord, a lady who was first "naturalized" by adoption into the Konoe family of court nobles. The dual court-military elites of Ieyasu's day were beginning to merge. In the 1880s the new Meiji government made that official in creating the new class of peers, though subtle distinctions of "old" and "new" aristocrats remained and the "new," former daimyo, peers usually had more money but less prestige.

In the Tokugawa system, however, status and honor carried a high price. In the ranking of domains and their lords the *koku* rice assessment brought its appropriate honor and ceremonial reward. As time passed there was less and less congruence between the real, or "inside" yield of areas as reflected in *koku* assessments and their original, or "surface" rating. The fine distinctions of honor and hierarchy that the system required were, of course, relative. As a result the alteration of one ranking would have an immediate impact on others. Although two centuries of economic growth and agricultural expansion gave many a lord a tax base almost double that with which he was credited, formal *koku* rankings of domains were left much as they had been in the days of Ieyasu. In the southwestern domain of Tosa, for instance, the daimyo's "inside" or real yield was at least one-quarter greater than the 202,600 *koku* with which he was credited. But since the "outside" rating was factored into the daimyo's court rank, the size and location of his mansions in Edo, his seat when in audience in Edo castle, the size of retinue he was permitted, and his ceremonial obligations, it would have been difficult to change his ranking without changing many others. During the shifts of daimyo and domains in the seventeenth century, many houses experienced dramatic changes in their gradations of honor, but they usually did so in inheriting another house's position or losing their own. At times a strong shogun might catapult a particular favorite over the heads of his betters, and young and ambitious daimyo or their vassal mentors sometimes lobbied for elevations in the gradation of honor. Success could be expensive, however, and conservative advisers seldom thought the game was worth the candle.

What is more surprising, though, is that in most domains the *koku* assessments of villages tended to remain unchanged as well. Thomas Smith's study of tax data for eleven villages found that, despite the increase in acreage under the plow and improvements in agronomy that surely brought village productivity to higher levels, village assessments showed no change at all for long periods between the years of 1700 and 1850. Furthermore, land was not surveyed systematically after 1700; by the "middle of the nineteenth century, therefore, taxes were based on assessments a century to a century and a half old."[7] If this is so, then the benefits of good farming—improvements in irrigation, in seeds and fertilizers, recourse to books on agronomy that circulated widely—stayed, at least in part, in the village. There were other taxes, to be sure, levied in money, produce, and labor, and these could be extremely burdensome. Matsudaira Sadanobu, of whom more will be said below, noted that "it is difficult to recite the different types of taxes and miscellaneous exactions in existence. There is a tax on vacant lots and gardens, a tax on buildings, a tax on doors and windows, and there is even a tax on girls who have reached a certain age. Taxes are also imposed on cloth, *sake*, herbs, and sesame seeds."[8] Nevertheless the basic produce tax, the *nengu*, remained at or near its original level in the cases Smith studied. It is difficult to explain this moderation and abstention on the part of samurai administrators who have so often been credited with pitiless severity. One element, though surely a minor one, may have been deference to the wisdom and rulings of the past. A more important reason is likely to have been the cost and difficulty of a large-scale regional reassessment. In the annals of peasant revolt to which we refer below, even the threat of a reassessment often brought complaints and protests.

The village world, however, was largely self-regulating, administered by landholding families who often had considerable pride of name and background. They intermarried with one another in preference to forming alliances with "ordinary" peasants, and they were often permitted the dignity of (family) name and sword. They were also the ones who stood to gain, and retain, the growing surplus of their land. The ability to retain part of that surplus must have provided good incentives to increase it by diligence and planning. Good farming brought its own reward. Hayami is probably not far off the mark when he observes that although Japan did not experience an "industrial revolution" *(kikai kakumei)*, it did produce an "industrious revolution" *(kinben kakumei)* that prepared those situated to profit from it admirably for a longer future.

If leading peasants and village leaders stood to gain and increased their share of the pot, as did prosperous urban merchants, the same could not be said of most samurai. The lucky ones, to be sure, could afford to relieve their boredom by entering the Edo equivalent of café society. In the 1770s Edo culture developed a select circle of writers who produced a playful and satirical *gesaku* genre that encoded some of the changing styles and values of their day. Young samurai—those who were sufficiently attuned and could afford to—mingled with theater and merchant connoisseurs to form a brittle and witty circle of brilliant dilettantes in search of variety and pleasure. For many samurai it must have brought relief from the suffocating life of barrack and punctilio, and for merchant sons this represented freedom from diligence and the search for profit. The pen names these samurai writers used were often full of self-mockery that revealed their frustrations; "Troubles with curfew," "Drunken indiscretion," and, for one daimyo son, "Monkey with rusty bottom."

Equally striking was the section on sartorial advice for samurai in a handbook ("The Essence of Current Fashions") for young men about town written in 1773 by an "undercover" samurai from the northern domain of Akita at the time it was negotiating for bakufu favor. The work is full of worldly advice on attire, with sections appropriate to each social status group. Samurai are told how their *kamishimo* trousers should be stiffened with whalebone, with the outermost folds stitched down. The *obi* sash, they are advised, should be worn on the level of the navel with the front slightly elevated. Done right, it is known as a "Bye-bye Obi" or "Cat Teaser." "Curve your back a little to get the right effect," goes the advice. Fashion extends to the sword; "When you are wearing *kamishimo*, pull the narrow sword a little forward to keep the tip pointed upward. But when you are wearing only *haori*, wear the sword straight down for casual chic." Illustrations supplement the text. As for kimono, "black silk with crests. Lining in chic brown. Hem linings should show about seven *bu*; revealing too much is vulgar . . . Since the general principle of formal wear is elegance, stick with the classics. Don't overdo it, though, or you'll end up being stuffy. The trick is in balancing the classic and the contemporary . . . in the manner, so to speak, of *bun* and *bu*."[9] This is tantamount to sacrilege. The long-sacred warrior values of sword and brush, *bun* and *bu*, stressed in every Code for the Military Houses since the Tokugawa founders, were now whimsically suggested as guides for proper dress for a night on the town.

But those pleasures were reserved for the few who could afford them. Samurai lucky enough to have petty fiefs could try to squeeze more out of the farmers who worked their lands, but the majority had to live on fixed incomes measured in rice from the lord's warehouse. For them good harvests that were accompanied by modest prices for rice were not good news. Urban residents, forced to purchase items of daily need, they might encourage their wives in the production of salable handicrafts, but this seldom made up for their disadvantage relative to successful tradesmen and landholding farmers. Thousands, in the words of Yamamura, "were motivated by the painful necessity of trying to live from day to day and not get further into debt . . . It is important to realize that the traditional samurai class was a heterogenous group of men whose modal income was only sufficient to classify them as poor by almost any standard applying to the ruling class of most societies."[10]

The problem was, however, that a bannerman had to maintain a certain standard of living appropriate to his honor. In 1855 one writer complained that Edo samurai "treat those who are fresh from the country as bumpkins, and the latter are anxious to become men of the world." Another writer noted that it was increasingly difficult to live on the income of a bannerman. "with a stipend of 300 *koku*, in accordance with the law of 1633, the *hatamoto* must keep two samurai, one armor carrier, one spear carrier, one traveling-case carrier, two stablemen, one carrier of sandals, and two porters for military services . . . Then the living expenses of the family of four or five, including a maid servant, require an additional thirty *ryō* . . . if a *hatamoto* with an annual stipend of 300 *koku* owes 600 *ryō*, his annual net income is reduced to an equivalent of seventeen *ryō*, since he must pay an annual interest of thirty *ryō* for his debt."[11]

The Yamamura study focused on the shogun's bannermen, the *hatamoto* from whom many bakufu functionaries were recruited, and provides numerous examples of their difficulties. The bannermen did what they could to reduce the number of dependents they had to support, sending younger sons off for adoption and resorting to abortion and even infanticide as their economic position relative to those they ruled declined over time. Daimyo tried to reduce their costs by "borrowing" from retainers' stipends, and the retainers in turn tried, when possible, to borrow against future taxes from those below them. Yamamura provides the response made to a bannerman of 700 *koku* rating by three village leaders under his authority in the mid-1850s:

> 1. Because of your promise to reduce expenditures, we have, during the past years, advanced tax rice and made loans. However, we see no sign of any efforts to achieve necessary reductions in your expenditures.
>
> 2. Your brother is an immoral idler. As long as such a person is supported by your household, there is little chance of reducing expenditures. Last winter, we asked that some actions be taken against your brother. What is your plan?

3. You have more than six servants including maids and horsemen. Some should be dismissed.

4. Your representative asked us if we could assist in negotiating a further loan. Even if a low interest loan were to be made to you, it would be of little use as long as you have your useless brother. The temple from which you hope to borrow does not know that you already have 200 *ryō* in debt, but you know that you already have a large debt.

5. What is the purpose of your debt? As far as we can determine, you are sufficiently provided for; and

6. To keep your brother is uneconomical. If no action is taken, we intend to resign our post as village leaders.[12]

Not long before this, the bakufu itself discovered that its command relationship with even *fudai* daimyo had changed. As mentioned earlier, in 1840 the lord of Shōnai, on the Japan Sea coast, was ordered to change his seat for another half its size to make room for the son of one of the shogun's favorite consorts. The Shōnai retainers, expecting to have to move with their lord, started collecting funds from major merchants and landowners. They, in turn, were disturbed because the daimyo family to which the shogun's son had been assigned had earned an unpleasant reputation for extravagance—perhaps understandably, since it had been forced to move eleven times in two centuries. Meanwhile the shogun, Ienari, died, but bakufu officials, their prestige at stake, let the order stand.

Leading commoners went into action. Petitioners singing their lord's praises were sent to Edo, only to be rejected. Then groups got up their courage to go to Edo to press petitions on high officials. The punishment they received was unexpectedly light and encouraged others to try. Petitioners were sent to neighboring daimyo to ask their help; still other groups headed for shrines and temples to seek divine assistance. Conveniently, the young lord who had been designated beneficiary of the switch died. At this point twenty-three powerful *tozama* daimyo who shared audience privileges in one of the Edo castle galleries intervened by sending a joint query to ask what was going on. "As we have had no notification from [the bakufu] and have not been given any information," they asked, "we humbly offer this communication . . . since Sakai [Tadakata] Saemon-no-jō [the daimyo slated to be moved] comes from a line of hereditary officials, why has he now been ordered to move and take over Nagaoka Castle? We hereby inform you that we wish to be told."[13] The order was canceled.

One can imagine how preposterous this upshot would have seemed to the shogun Iemitsu, a century earlier. The daimyo interference, the protests of leading commoners, the preference of local merchants for the continuation of familiar problems rather than risking new overlords: all signified corrosive weakness at the center and dramatic changes in authority relationships.

3. Popular Protest

If authorities failed to extract most of the surplus from the countryside it was not for lack of trying. Despite their best efforts, however, attempts to do so were thwarted more often than they were successful. A great deal of writing about Japan emphasizes a "consensus" model that would lead one to anticipate a smoothly functioning social organism, one lubricated by deference on the one side and paternalism on the other. The facts do not bear this out. Dispute was endemic throughout the country in the Tokugawa period. A modern scholar, Aoki Kōji, has tabulated a total of 7,664 instances of social conflict and political protest between 1590 and 1877, and more recently James White, eliminating 333 that were wholly within-channels petitions, has classified the remaining 7,331 to see what conclusions can be drawn.[14] In a brief comparison he finds Japan slightly less contentious than Europe with respect to peasant, manorial, and other popular protests in selected periods, but probably more contentious than China was during the Ming (1368–1644) era.[15]

It has to be stressed that the vast majority of Tokugawa protests were nonviolent. They had little "revolutionary" content, and they were not designed to secure basic changes in the way Japan was governed or the way Japanese society was structured. There was little talk of "rights" that inhere in a "just" society that were being violated by officials. But there was, nonetheless, a broader and less legalistic concept of "justice" and reciprocity.[16] Cooperative and deferential conduct deserved "compassionate" regard from those above.

Most disputes were brought on by the efforts of those in authority to extract more than they were getting from those they governed—by a proposed reevaluation, by the imposition of new monopoly controls in marketing local products, or by failure to check on an unusually abusive or capricious official. Disputes could focus on unfairness shown by village authorities (who allocated, after all, the basic land tax), or they could represent a communal protest against excessive demands for additional taxes or corvée labor. "Assisting" villages along the major highways could resent demands for men and horses to accommodate unusually heavy traffic.

Village headmen were responsible for remonstrating with higher offices as representatives of their people, and failure to do so could earn them the wrath of their constituents. Theirs was not an easy role. They were the links between villagers and samurai officials, and they frequently faced the uneasy choice between "representing" their villagers—a role likely to bring on punishment—or becoming themselves the focus of popular anger, and risking destruction of their property by the crowd. Still other disputes could be between villages; there could be arguments about village boundaries and about villagers' rights of access to woodland for compost for fields and building materials. In extreme cases, disputes might become regional and reflect shared indignation of villagers along highways or, as the period went along, economic zones. In such cases outsiders, little-known individuals, could come to rally enthusiasm and discontent. Such "entrepreneurial leaders," as White calls them, might help create or intensify an ethos of rebellion.

The Tokugawa village was relatively autonomous, and as long as taxes were forthcoming, protests few, and order maintained, the authorities left its elders and headmen to run things their way. Preventive coercion was difficult to exercise. On the other hand, in those instances in which large-scale protests were being mounted the first concern of the authorities was getting the farmers to go back to work. The typical pattern of response began with conciliation; exactions would, authorities promised, be studied, and rethought. Frequently they were even reversed. Then, once order had been restored and there was time to investigate, the allocation of blame was possible. Those judged to have been in the lead of the protests would be punished harshly.

The village headman faced a dilemma that had no easy solution. If he resisted the crowd he was likely to lose his reputation and the honor essential to successful implementation of his role, and if he cooperated and "led" the crowd he was likely to lose his head.

For honorable men desperate conditions frequently made the latter choice the preferable one. It could also bring posthumous renown. Sacrificial figures sometimes became the subjects of tales of heroism and even deification as a merciful and self-sacrificing *daimyōjin,* commemorated by a local shrine. Peasant narratives praising such men provided the text for memory of social wrongs and individual self-sacrifice.[17] The classic case is that of Sōgorō, a headman who tried to intercede with his lord for his oppressed villagers. When this failed he is said to have tried to intercept a shogunal procession in Edo with a petition, and for that presumption he was crucified together with his wife and children. Sōgorō was honored with a shrine at the present town of Sakura, the site of the National Museum of History. His story became the stuff of legend and was performed on the popular stage. It also provided inspiration for modern-day farmers who stoutly resisted the inclusion of their fields in the nearby Narita International Airport. In this manner *gimin,* "virtuous men," became associated with a tradition of protest, punishment, and ultimate triumph in peasant memory.[18]

As traced by White, the rhythm of protest movements provides an important insight into the health of the Tokugawa political economy. In early Tokugawa years protests were importantly affected by the sweeping changes that accompanied the urbanization of the samurai, disarmament of the countryside, and retainers' upheaval related to daimyo transfer. Some early protests were led by farmer-soldiers, but shifts in authority were not easy for farmers who had to pay the price. On occasion large bodies of peasants would simply defect and move across the border of the neighboring domain and negotiate from there. When the population was still low daimyo were helpless without agriculturalists, and many lords, recently moved to larger jurisdictions, were themselves understaffed and unable to apply coercion. Early-seventeenth-century codes often showed their predicament. In Tosa a code noted that harboring a runaway "probably deserves the death penalty, but if we become too severe the result would only be to make them flee to the next province . . . the main thing is to keep them from leaving the province."[19] When they did leave the domain peasants sometimes applied for residence, as though for sanctuary; more often the "host" daimyo, who could be expected to side with his peers, would send a vassal to broker some kind of settlement. Then, once the runaways returned, it would be possible to exact vengeance on the presumed ringleaders.

After the daimyo domains were settled and adequately staffed there was less likelihood of a large group's absconding, but instances can still be found in the eighteenth and nineteenth centuries. In Tosa in the 1780s, rural papermakers struggled against the fixed price at which the domain forced them to sell their product to chartered guilds. Over five hundred villagers moved across the mountainous border to Matsuyama. Their initial wish was to stay there, but when that desire was denied they negotiated their return with Tosa authorities. Matsuyama granted them sanctuary during the negotiations, and a temple served as intermediary. The Tosa administration gave way on seventeen complaints, after which the protesters moved back for a "final" agreement. That was followed by the execution of three peasant leaders. A few years later the paper monopoly was reinstated.[20] Again, in 1853 several thousand peasants in the northern domain of Nambu decamped to neighboring Sendai. They protested onerous corvée for public works, being forced to support too many officials, and having to pay excessive supplementary taxes. As usual, they demanded amnesty for the protesters. After the domain gave way on the issues under contention they returned to their villages. The domain then hunted down the leader, a headman named Miura Meisuke, and executed him.[21]

There were also disputes within village communities, usually against village authorities for unfair allocation of labor and taxes, arrogance, and dishonesty. There were disputes between communities, about rights to irrigation water, forest products, and borders. Undoubtedly, though, most protests concerned taxes; there were appeals against existing taxes, against additional taxes, and against planned reassessments. The reassessment process was almost sure to arouse contention, both for its probable results and for the cost to villagers who had to house and entertain the official parties making the reassessment. Again, a new and unknown lord could inspire fears of change for the worse. So could new samurai officials at the county office, the point at which farm life encountered officialdom.

Collectively these protests are termed *ikki*. The word is sometimes used to signify rebellion, but it would be more accurate to say it constituted an agreement to seek redress. White defines the term as a "spontaneous, special-purpose organization created contractually among (or between) either elites or people designed for the pursuit of goals impossible to achieve through ordinary channels or by individual striving."[22] *Ikki* represented explicit compacts and oaths, based on a relatively egalitarian principle in which those subscribing—something usually done by signing names in a circular ("umbrella") pattern—shared responsibility equally.[23]

Some idea of proportional frequency can be gained by one classification of 2,051 disputes: categories of *ikki* included 552 *osso*, in which complaints were addressed to higher officials, typically by village leaders who could get no satisfaction from those immediately responsible (White characterizes these as "end runs"); 783 *gōso*, in which villagers presented complaints without going through their village heads; 230 cases of flight; 78 *hōki*, or protests that led to violence; and 408 urban *uchikowashi*, or "smashings." It goes without saying that all of these were illegal. Indeed, Tokugawa edicts warned against unauthorized gatherings of any sort; they were termed *tōtō*, or rebellious group. (This was not without its problems for modern political parties *(tō)*; in the nineteenth century members were careful to describe their organizations as "public" parties, or *kōtō*).

White's figures show that, from the first quarter of the eighteenth century to the end of the Tokugawa era, contention gradually increased in frequency and magnitude. In the mid-eighteenth century bakufu officials responded to this with warnings to all daimyo that they were to cooperate if necessary to suppress revolts. By then, clearly, the population had increased dramatically, agriculture had reached some sort of limit of productivity in central Japan, and urban developments made integrated economic zones of what had been separate localities. The old rules against daimyo cooperation had to be sacrificed in the face of this greater danger from ordinary Japanese. Each period of natural disaster, of crop failure and famine, punctuated this steady rise of contention with spectacular increases: the 1780s, 1830s, and 1860s produced waves of *ikki*.

Within this pattern, however, one looks in vain for truly "revolutionary" purpose. There was little real thought of devising a different social order. Two exceptions are sometimes posed. In the last few decades of Tokugawa rule "world renewal" *(yonaoshi)*, vaguely millenarian, movements swept major urban areas. But their net total was as often ludicrous and carnival as it was purposeful. On such occasions rumors flew that divine signs had been seen to fall mysteriously, usually on the homes of the wealthy. This would spark rejoicing, dancing, and celebration. The wealthy so favored by the gods usually found it prudent to share their goods, particularly drink, with the throng; the resultant enthusiasm could sweep an entire region. Yet the "world"—*yo*—of those who rejoiced was more a cosmos than a society, and most participants seem to have assumed the imminence of a more just and moral society than the one they knew. A better case for revolt can be made for the intended rising of Ōshio Heihachirō, the samurai official whose abortive 1837 rising in Osaka opened this chapter. His was a special case, however, and it will receive more attention below. Even he achieved little more than a conflagration that destroyed much of a city that was central to the national economy and distribution system.

Cumulatively, suppression worked poorly. Popular narratives of insurrections indicate a massive incompetence and often pusillanimity on the part of samurai officials. These accounts are often based on fact. At Ueda in 1761, for instance, the samurai officials retreated behind their defenses and communicated with the crowd by dangling messages from poles rather than risk a confrontation that might turn violent. Elsewhere authorities might show sporadic vengeful brutality in the suppression of a particular protest, but the coercion was seldom consistent or sustained. The parcelized sovereignty of the bakuhan structure also made possible gross discrepancies in tax burdens between even nearby domains. As a result sources of dissatisfaction rose as respect for samurai declined. In any case, bakufu and domain officials were aware of the tide of protest, worried about it, and looked for solutions that would solidify their control.

4. Bakufu Responses

The contrast between the urban opulence of the Genroku and later eras and the rural hardship punctuated by protest, and between the comfort of successful merchants and the discomfort of indigent samurai, left few observers in doubt that something was out of balance. For the samurai well-being depended on getting a good price for the income they received in rice. Crop failure brought high prices, but also made it difficult to collect taxes, while abundant harvests drove prices down. Yamamura has argued that during the first century or more land was relatively more valuable than labor; reclamation and paddy construction accompanied the rise in population. Then, as commercialization brought new markets for indigo, oils, sesame, and other products, labor rose in value relative to land. Small landowners began to lose land to large, prosperous farmers *(gōnō)* and became tenants, wage earners, or joined the urban poor. Commercial agriculture brought with it expensive fertilizers. An entire industry, financed from Osaka, developed ground fish from the far north in Hokkaido for the fields of central Japan.[24] The expansion of cotton, tobacco, and textile production increased the possibilities for by-employment. Writers now began to complain about arable land lying unused, and about insubordinate and presumptuous landless farmers. In turn the poor grumbled about the new agricultural elite. These changes came at different rates of speed in different areas, of course, and benefits were unequally shared. Japan's rulers and those who advised them put the well-being of the samurai first, but few of them were confident they knew how to further that.

Japanese historians distinguish three periods of shogunal rule as "reforms," and then refer to the Meiji "restoration" of 1868. In many respects, however, it would be more meaningful to refer to the "reforms" as attempted "restorations," since each of them tried to bring about a return to the remembered fiscal and administrative health and vigor of the seventeenth century. The Meiji changes, on the other hand, better deserve the term "revolution," for they brought permanent change to Japan's institutional life. Not one of the "reforms" succeeded in its goals, but each added institutional innovations in its attempts to deal with the increasingly complex problems of Japanese society.

KYŌHŌ

The rule of the eighth shogun, Yoshimune (1716–1745), has become known for the reforms of his "Kyōhō" era. By the time Yoshimune came to power the direct shogunal line had run out, and his position as Ieyasu's great-great grandson and the last surviving grandson of Iemitsu won him the succession. What mattered, however, was the fact that the new shogun was already mature and experienced as the daimyo of Kii (Wakayama), one of the "three great" cadet houses. Time and again the adoption of a vigorous "outsider" into ruling lines, whether shogunal or daimyo, made for vigor greater than that shown by pampered favorites who had known only the bloodless ceremonies of the sheltered elite in youth. Yoshimune provides a case in point, for he did what he could to breathe new life into the institutions of samurai society. We have already noted the vigor with which he sponsored Chinese and Dutch learning.

Bakufu administration reflected the hands-on direction of a leader who knew his mind. Although he owed his appointment to the decision of the *rōjū*, Yoshimune allowed that institution to atrophy through attrition.[25] He instituted a system of office salary so that able men whose income level was too low to qualify them for office could serve. He also developed an inspection or intelligence agency to inform him of the activities of the daimyo. In an effort to improve communication, he set up a "petition box" *(meyasubako)* in 1721 to encourage suggestions and complaints, a device that was soon adopted by many of the daimyo.[26]

In an effort to regularize administration and make it more efficient, the shogun paid particular attention to administrative and law codes. In 1742 the government worked out a comprehensive code of procedure and precedents that became the basis for all subsequent jurisprudence. This was not made public, but it remained the preserve of officialdom. Provisions limiting the use of torture in interrogation and exempting relatives of those found guilty from punishment represented steps toward a more rational legal system. At the same time Yoshimune's bakufu had no intention of being deflected from its work by commoner squabbles; the government washed its hands of commercial suits and ordered complainants to work things out for themselves.[27] Commoners were expected to keep their place. Yoshimune ordered the diffusion of precepts used in China through commoner schools *(terakoya)* that were beginning to dot the land, and children were coached in the importance of Confucian familial relations. Useful plants and methods were imported from China, and a number of specialists came to teach as well. In 1721 an edict permitted the import of Chinese translations of Western books. Confucian scholars like Ogyū Sorai were put to work preparing memoranda on political economy.

In all this, the watchword was practicality. Tsuji Tatsuya goes so far as to suggest that Yoshimune's rule helped to change the direction of Japanese thought from speculative philosophy toward areas of natural science, classical study, and textual analysis, a "shift that helped clear the way for the intellectual revolution of the eighteenth century."[28] Yoshimune also encouraged the establishment of the Kaitokudō, a merchant academy, in Osaka. Its scholars stood out for the practicality and rationality with which they approached problems of the day. One outstanding figure, who wrote under the name Yamagata Bantō, was in his business incarnation the commercial agent for the lord of Sendai and thus deeply experienced in the complexities of Osaka trade and finance.[29]

The economic problems Yoshimune's administration faced were complicated by a crop failure in 1732. The next year this was followed by the first urban riots Edo had known. In the years that followed the bakufu's determination to get more out of the countryside even led to a once-only levy on all the daimyo. For commoners, tax assessments were changed from an annual inspection of the crop to a levy based on average yields over a period of years in the hope of providing a better basis for planning. While this avoided the expenses involved in annual surveys, it also left farmers helpless in years of natural disasters. In 1721 Yoshimune banned all presentation of petitions and took steps to deter agriculturalists from mass flight, thereby cutting commoners off from the few measures of recourse they had known. Draconian severity on the part of tax collectors produced bumper tax yields for a time, but the result was a rise in Osaka warehouse inventories and the decline in price that resulted damaged samurai interests. In addition attempts to produce a higher-quality currency by recoinage and to ban the issuance of paper money within domains meant that there was less coinage in circulation, further lowering the price of rice. In trying to control this process the bakufu ordered money changers to organize themselves within licensed guilds, and in 1721 it extended this policy by requiring the formation of guilds for ninety-six categories of merchants.

The Kyōhō reforms, in short, reflected the changes that had come over Japan's political economy with the rise of commercialism. Samurai administrators had no sure recourse for dealing with this. The measures attempted indicated a new solidarity between daimyo and bakufu; at one point the bakufu even borrowed money from the Kaga domain. Gradually the old problems of security against daimyo disloyalty were beginning to seem moot; the desire for frugality led Yoshimune to substitute a screen of evergreens for what had been a formidable, but expensive, wall around the great shogunal castle in Edo. It was gradually becoming more important to cooperate with daimyo against commoner opposition to excessive levies.

Toward the end of his reign, Yoshimune seemed to retreat from some of his measures. The bakufu canceled its prohibition of paper money in domains, and it vacillated in its policies on merchant guilds as well. In 1736 the bakufu gave up on the sound coinage it had worked so hard to strengthen by lessening the proportion of precious metal in coins. Gold and silver mines had been exhausted. No further gold coins were minted until 1818, and silver coins were minted again only in 1820. New copper mines, however, were coming on stream, and in a period of less than a decade the bakufu minted more than half the copper coins issued during the entire Tokugawa period. The Kyōhō "reforms" did, however, result in a stronger administrative structure as the bakufu tried to influence and regulate. Yoshimune's measures showed that bakufu officials had come to realize that changes in administrative procedures were necessary to deal with economic changes that had taken place, and in that sense his rule stands out as one of vigor and innovation. Unfortunately Japan's problems had grown beyond the capacity of the regime to deal with them by administrative measures, and deep-seated contradictions remained to frustrate bakufu reformers. For a time the bakufu managed to extract unprecedented amounts of rice in tribute from its domains, but those measures fell far short of the institutional changes that would have been required to bring a real solution. Ogyū Sorai advised Yoshimune that daimyo should be released from the "hotel existence" which found them at the mercy of the urban, commercial economy, but it was no longer possible to re-create the conditions of an earlier day.

TENMEI

Tokugawa policies were characterized by broad swings between austerity and consumption. Yoshimune's Kyōhō measures were followed, a few decades later, by a new wave of extravagance in the Tenmei (1781–1789) era. It is not surprising that when this in turn was followed by one of the most severe famines of Tokugawa times, there was a new interval of administrative and policy change. The chief policymaker was now Tanuma Okitsugu, a shogunal favorite whose meteoric rise from page to grand chamberlain and member of the rōjū earned him the envy and dislike of bakufu traditionalists. Tanuma had his son appointed a member of the Junior Council, and built up a faction of officials within the finance office that gave him leverage over every request. He himself became the center for favoritism. There was a good deal of gift giving built into the administrative system, but Tanuma seems to have carried this to new heights. He undoubtedly deserved the charges of corruption that were directed against him, but it is also true that any attempt like his to increase shogunal power at the expense of that of traditionalist *fudai*, particularly by a relative parvenu, would have stirred opposition and would have required extraordinary measures.

To some degree the tug of war between bakufu and daimyo, center and periphery, had become a zero-sum game in which one side could gain only at the expense of the other. Daimyo, especially the lords of major, integrated domains, responded to financial pressure by developing mercantilist measures for "national" (that is, provincial) profit, *kokueki*, by maximizing exports to central (that is, shogunal) cities. The bakufu, in contrast, was trapped by its responsibility for the national markets that surrounded the great cities, but the points of origin of such products were beyond its reach. The bakufu, with its consumption centers, relied upon these "sending" areas, but they were able to concentrate on exports and restrict imports in the interest of their domain economy. A century and more of economic as well as political autonomy had accustomed administrators and merchants to think of the domain as countries, *kuni*, as opposed to the larger "realm" of Japan.[30]

In trying to resolve this problem Tanuma was not afraid of innovation. Earlier reforms had focused on the allocation of existing resources, which were regarded as fixed, but he envisaged increasing them through policies of economic growth. He took steps to increase foreign trade, and went so far as set quotas for production for Akita copper mines with the purpose of channeling their product into the Nagasaki trade, even though the domestic market brought higher prices.[31] Tanuma's officials went on to grant monopoly patents, usually for a fee, for iron, brass, sulphur, camphor, cinnabar, ginseng, lamp oil, and other products, actions which placed the bakufu in direct opposition to daimyo interests.[32] He also invested major resources in a massive public works drainage program designed to increase agricultural acreage. When this failed, and when it was followed by crop failures that led to serious famine, and as drought was followed by floods, the country was swept by protests and peasant rebellions and urban riots so serious that Edo was practically without a government for three days in 1787. Traditionalists had ready explanations for this sequence; the "voice of Heaven" had been followed by the "voice of the people."[33] Tanuma's influence did not long outlast his years in office. The death of the shogun who had been his patron and the assassination of his son brought a swift fall in his status, and he ended his days in disgrace.

The Tanuma years brought a new flowering of urban and middle-class culture. They witnessed the medical experimentation under the influence of Dutch sources that has been described. Urbanized samurai and affluent commoners shared in the new wave of playful, satirical, and cynical writing of *gesaku*. This was accompanied by a great flowering of the multicolored *(nishiki-e)* wood-block prints that conveyed the delights of travel, theater, and licensed quarter to townsmen who could afford them. Inevitably, traditionalists also associated this cultural flowering with the political corruption and moral shortcomings they ascribed to those in power, and a new wave of austerity was in prospect.

KANSEI

The "Kansei" (1789–1801) reforms were under the direction of Matsudaira Sadanobu (1758–1829), a grandson of Yoshimune who had been daimyo of a domain in northern Japan before being appointed to his bakufu post by the young shogun Ienari. Ienari, who was born in 1773, served as shogun from

1787 to 1837, and remained the final authority until his death in 1841. His fifty-year incumbency was the longest of the Tokugawa shoguns. It was a half century that marked a further blurring of lines within the ruling elite, for Ienari's consort was the daughter of a great *tozama* daimyo; to become eligible she was first adopted into the Konoe family of aristocrats at the imperial court. Ienari cultivated that court aggressively. He had himself appointed to a series of honorific posts that ended with his designation as minister of state *(dajō daijin)*. He accumulated a large harem that produced fifty-five children, and these became his pawns in marriage politics with daimyo from all parts of the country, and that in turn contributed to the development of a cosmopolitan and largely undifferentiated aristocracy. The neat designations of an earlier era no longer had much meaning.

Matsudaira Sadanobu's period of influence was actually short, for he fell out with his strong-willed master and resigned after a little more than four years.[34] He was determined that relations between the Edo and the Kyoto courts be based on the primacy of Edo and that appropriate terminology be maintained. In a famous dispute with Kyoto the emperor, who had been adopted, tried to give his natural father the status of ex-emperor—but Sadanobu had his way and put a stop to it. Unfortunately in the next dispute he ran afoul of his shogun, for Ienari too had been adopted from a cadet house and decided to try to get his natural father the protocol due a retired shogun. Sadanobu succeeded in blocking this too, but the standoff that resulted led to his resignation.

Sadanobu was at the helm of shogunal policy for only a few years, but steps he took proved so lasting and important that they can be seen as pivotal for early-nineteenth-century Tokugawa administration. He began with measures to curb the corruption and ostentation of the Tanuma years. Frugality was once again the order of the day. A vigorous purge replaced many officials. District administrators were instructed to prepare injunctions to villages stressing the importance of diligence, self-denial, and filial piety. Publishers once again had to look out for censors, on pain of confiscation of their equipment. Several authors of material judged indecent found themselves in stocks and manacles. All reformers were sticklers for propriety in such matters, however, and these concerns were not in any sense new.

Sadanobu's efforts to strengthen the economic position of Edo in the national economy are more interesting. The city that had begun as a consumer of products from the western cities of Osaka and Kyoto had now become the center of economic life in eastern Japan. The currency was revalued to diminish the price advantage enjoyed by Osaka, where the economy was based on silver. Sadanobu wanted to make the area around Edo more self-sufficient and lower its imports from western Japan. In a sense, he was adapting the mercantilist policies developed by major domains to bakufu purposes. Local sources for sake, cotton, oil, and paper, commodities traditionally imported from western Japan, were developed. To reduce needs for food Sadanobu ordered recent migrants to return to their villages. The city itself became the focus of administrative reforms. Sadanobu established a Town Office to oversee social services and surveillance. He set aside a portion of land taxes for the construction of granaries as a device to regulate prices. He ordered officials to direct more attention to systematic record keeping, fire control, and roads and bridges. Urban problems were now beginning to receive the attention they required.

In struggling to deal with the effects of urban commercialism Sadanobu resorted to rather crude measures. The bakufu announced that loans to samurai were canceled, and rates for house rentals were to be controlled. This was not very effective, for if samurai had become dependent on merchants it did not really help them to try to punish the merchants.

Sadanobu, a student of Confucianism, was particularly intent on ways to tidy up the educational and intellectual scene. Here he had more success. The "Kansei prohibition" of dissident teachings proclaimed for the first time that Chu Hsi Confucianism was the orthodox teaching. Earlier shoguns had been relatively indifferent to ideological distinctions between schools, and Sadanobu himself had written that for practical administrators what mattered was the way one lived and not one's philosophical preferences. Once in power, however, he was concerned with order and convinced that the growth of competing philosophical schools created confusion. From this came the proscription of heterodoxy *(igaku no kin)* of 1790. "Novel doctrines" of recent times, he decreed, threatened the order of the realm; there was to be a "return" to a central doctrine. This campaign began with appointments to the bakufu's central academy. Daimyo and domain schools, which were experiencing their most rapid period of growth, soon followed the shogunal pattern. By the mid-nineteenth century the writings of Ogyū Sorai had come to be considered almost subversive reading in the bakufu's Shōheikō academy. Not that other schools of thought and interpretation died out. Many teachers maintained a compartmentalization between what they could teach and what they thought. In addition nativist teachings continued to grow in popularity and volume, and *kokugaku* (National Learning) was becoming diffused throughout much of rural Japan. Dutch studies grew apace; Sadanobu sponsored them and saw to it that the bakufu itself began to collect Western books. He also tried to contain them and restrict such learning to official channels. "The barbarian nations are skilled in the sciences," he wrote, "and considerable profit may be derived from their works of astronomy and geography, as well as from their military weapons and their methods of internal and external medicine. However, their books may serve to encourage idle curiosity or may express harmful ideas."[35] The solution was for the government to collect useful works at the point of entry at Nagasaki and make sure that they did not fall into unauthorized hands. Sadanobu also reduced the volume of foreign trade that was permitted, and he lengthened the period between Dutch visits to Edo. Many of these steps were extensions of earlier moves, though they were also reversals of the policies of Tanuma.

In many respects the Kansei years stand as a symbol of an impressive increase in education and the importance placed on it in Japan. Sadanobu's concern with orthodoxy was related to his desire for a more educated and responsible officialdom. He recruited scholars from many areas for the bakufu's Shōheikō academy. Daimyo too paid more attention to education in their domains. Throughout Japan the steady increase in the number of schools showed that new expectations and requirements were at hand.

The bakufu, meanwhile, had now taken a stand on its "tradition" and tried to define it. Henceforth the term "as in earlier years," *jūrai no gotoku,* was applied in areas as different as foreign trade and philosophical inquiry to discourage experiment and innovation, and it came to stand as a powerful and negative warning. In retrospect it can be seen that the regime had become more rigid, less resilient, and less adventurous.

KASEI: BUNKA (1804–1818) AND BUNSEI (1818–1830)

The first three decades of the nineteenth century, sometimes referred to as the Kasei eras, encompassing Bunka (1804–1818) and Bunsei (1818–1830), are often described as something of an Indian summer for Tokugawa rule. There were no crop failures. Peasant protests took place, but they were not of the scale or intensity of late-eighteenth-century uprisings. School building continued to expand; there was now truly large-scale development of private academies and commoner schools. The "Indian summer" extended to include harvest time for many of the trends that have been described, and it brought them into focus.

At the highest level of society the fixation on loyalty that had made daimyo categories so important in the seventeenth century had given way to a much more undifferentiated aristocratic class that had never known war and was deeply rooted in the urban culture to which bakufu policies had directed it. At lower levels, and particularly in urban areas, there was less differentiation between the more affluent commoners and most sectors of the ruling samurai class. This was partly the result of increasing differentiation *within* the previously monochromatic village. Commercialization and developments in agronomy had brought with them an increasingly visible village elite whose white-plastered storehouses, heavily timbered residences, and carefully tended evergreens and gardens left little doubt of economic well-being. Many village disputes originated in resentment against the favored status of the wealthy who dominated village affairs, and had as goals alternation of or election to the office of village headman. Some aspirations of the commoner elite overlapped with the needs of indigent samurai. Purchase of samurai commissions became common. In Morioka, in northern Japan, there was even a price list for status. Full samurai standing required 620 *ryō*, and 50 *ryō* got the purchaser the privilege of wearing a sword. But at the same time youth organizations *(wakamono gumi)* were resentful of such pretensions. They corralled their members by ritual and coercion to maintain a different hierarchy. In 1827 the bakufu attempted to ban such organizations, but its success was limited. Nevertheless the reasons cited in the ordinance are revealing: edicts warned against harassing prosperous villagers and suggested that the motive was envy of their wealth; they warned against organizing an end to village litigation, and urged more respect and gratitude for "the benevolence of the shogun."[36]

Most injunctions of this sort fell on deaf ears. Japan's feudal administrators were operating in a system of parcelized sovereignty, and they were unable to affect the root causes or areas of trends that influenced the areas they governed. The bakufu could devise policies that would be helpful to its urban centers, but vassals and daimyo who controlled the hinterland often had different ideas. Lords of great domains like Tosa and Chōshū had their own problems extracting exportable goods from their villages and limiting imports from "abroad," but they could at least control their borders. The bakufu could even run into trouble within areas under its own jurisdiction. In the early nineteenth century the metropolitan hinterlands were well on their way to developing rural industrial and finishing techniques that were beyond the control of the bakufu-licensed guilds in the big cities. In the 1820s villages in the plains around Osaka became restive when bakufu orders forbade them from pressing their own oil from rape seeds and ordered them to sell to and buy from metropolitan processors instead. Petitions from over a thousand villages repeatedly asked for a free market, and the bakufu gradually loosened its controls to avoid violence.

As the economic role previously restricted to official urban guilds became shared with rural enterprises, the importance of the metropolis diminished somewhat, but only because it had become an engine of growth in surrounding areas. By 1800 Japan had five of the world's cities with over 100,000 inhabitants, three of the world's twenty cities with more than 300,000 inhabitants, and probably, in Edo, the world's most populous city, one with more than one million inhabitants.[37]

As northern Japan developed, Edo's importance as a transportation and market center grew. Travel and pilgrimage continued to develop, and with this came even closer integration with other metropolitan areas. From its early days the bakufu had designed its system of highways and post stations to provide speedy and reliable communications. The standard time for official runners to reach Edo from Osaka, a distance of 500 kilometers, was six days. Then private operators in Edo and Kyoto began to supplement and compete with the official network. With improvements in security and economic development private operators in Edo and Kyoto provided express messenger service, shortening the time to five, four, and then three and a half days. Skilled operators managed to infiltrate the official communications network and increase its productivity by purchasing the right to acquire, affix, and display official insignia for commercial shipments. By the early nineteenth century express communication service between Kyoto and Edo broke the two-day barrier. Additional private express and freight shipping operators also spread their networks into the rural sending areas that surrounded the major cities. Private as well as official travel grew proportionately.[38]

With additional advances in literacy, the role of publishers also grew. Guidebooks held out the pleasures of distant places for readers and told of some three hundred temples in Kyoto. Other, more worldly booklets told of the joys that awaited travelers to the restaurants, local products, and brothels of Osaka. Santō Kyōden and Takizawa Bakin, two leading authors of popular fiction, had readers waiting anxiously for publication of the next section of their works. Bakin, in fact, used his profits to secure samurai status, something his family had once enjoyed, for his grandson. Books were relatively cheap, but the cost was brought even lower by the spread of book-lending shops. Edo had eight hundred of such lending libraries, and in all parts of the land circuit lenders traveled to even distant villages with packs of printed material on their backs.

One would expect social commentators to note, and usually deplore, such shifts, and so they did. In 1816 an otherwise unknown writer, perhaps a *rōnin*, used the pen name Buyō Inshi to produce a long jeremiad that provides a useful summary of the changes we have mentioned. Daimyo, he wrote, were infatuated with the splendor of their Edo mansions, and once frugal samurai were living lives of idle luxury like that of the Kyoto aristocrats. Those who competed in this desperate race for consumption frequently stooped to the adoption of merchant sons and to renting out space to commoners in their Edo homes; they sold their valuables and nevertheless incurred staggering debts at ominous rates of interest. Their military skills were long forgotten, and they performed almost no soldierly service. Conditions in the countryside were equally deplorable. The poor were poorer, the rich were putting on airs. Their wealth made it possible to bribe officials, avoid taxes, and take even minor personal matters to court. Happiness for the few had come at the cost of misery for the many. Things were worst near the great cities. Prosperous farmers in the vicinity of Edo, he wrote, had no hesitation in heading for the courts, and they were not in the slightest fear of the magistrates who presided there. The peaceful, relatively prosperous years of Bunka and Bunsei, in short, were not without their Cassandras.[39]

TENPŌ

In 1833 a new series of natural disasters seemed to prove that these warnings had been correct; Japan was once again in crisis. Reform attempts revealed deep cleavages between bakufu and even *fudai* daimyo, between urban residents and inefficient administrators, and within the central bureaucracy itself. The reforms of the Tenpō (1830–1844) era clearly failed to achieve their purpose, and the era itself is frequently described as the point at which the end of the bakufu began to be in sight. Harold Bolitho has written that "despite its auspicious opening, its reforms, and its cultural achievements, the Tenpō era was to prove calamitous for both the common people of Japan and those who ruled over them . . . for damage inflicted on Tokugawa Japan's system of government, the Tenpō era had no peer."[40]

That damage centered first of all on public order and satisfaction with government. The bakufu cannot be blamed for all of this, for the crop failures that began in 1833 and reached a height in 1836–1837 were caused by climate, though it is true that the bakuhan system made it difficult to move grain from one area to another. By 1836, however, years of unnaturally cold weather that destroyed the delicate balance of warmth and water needed to produce a rice crop had spread the damage from northeastern Japan, where it began, to central and western Japan as well. Famine was widespread. In Mito officials removed corpses from the roads so that the daimyo, Tokugawa Nariaki, would not have to see them on his trips to Edo. In the cities the price of rice reached levels it had never known before.

These hardships produced waves of popular protest. The yearly average was even higher than it had been in the 1780s, which marked the previous peak. The most careful tabulation registers 465 "disputes," 445 uprisings, and 101 urban riots for the Tenpō years. The peak of violence coincided with the peak of crop failures in 1836. The riots and insurrections were large-scale; they took place in many areas, and involved more people than had ever been the case before. Bad weather, hunger, and anger knew no political boundaries; entire economic districts and communication networks rose in protest.

It was in this context that the Osaka revolt planned by Ōshio Heihachirō took place. Ōshio was a moral, rather humorless and conscientious samurai administrator who withdrew from his official duties in disgust at what he saw as the immorality and indifference of Tokugawa administrators. He then set up a school to which he admitted students from all social classes. Himself a stern samurai taskmaster, he did not hesitate to use the rod on his pupils. He taught chiefly through historical analogy, and his lectures were replete with examples of Ming dynasty loyalists. His intelligence, honesty, and learning won him wide esteem.

In his teaching Ōshio followed the Confucianism of the Ming dynasty scholar-official Wang Yang-ming (1472–1529), the most famous exponent of a Confucian school that argued the unity of knowledge and action. In early Tokugawa times several distinguished philosophers had taught this; Nakae Tōju (1608–1648), revered as a saint in his lifetime, had abandoned an earlier commitment to Chu Hsi for Wang Yang-ming, and Kumazawa Banzan (1619–1691), his student, had incurred bakufu displeasure for the severity of his criticism of misgovernment. Gradually implications of subversion had become attached to these teachings, however, and Sadanobu's designation of Chu Hsi Confucianism as bakufu orthodoxy in 1790 had seemed to end its influence altogether. But Ōshio was not concerned with orthodoxy. On the contrary; he found the assertion that thought and action were inseparable a compelling mandate to correct the ills of his day, and he traveled to Nakae Tōju's home as a pilgrimage. He saw himself as a sage-hero destined to reform society.[41] The sage-hero's mission was to "save the people" *(kyūmin)*, and that is the slogan Ōshio had on his banners for revolt. He lived what he preached. He sold his extensive personal library and used the proceeds to buy food, which he distributed. It was never enough, of course. He also managed to acquire some firearms and a small cannon. He then prepared a *gekibun*, or manifesto, which he quietly distributed in the area around Osaka. Ōshio's manifesto read in part:

> To the village officials, elders, farmers, peasants and tenant farmers in the domains of Settsu, Kawachi, Izumi and Harima:
> From the time of the Ashikaga the emperor has been kept in seclusion and has lost the power to dispense rewards and punishments; the people therefore have nowhere to turn with their complaints . . .
> If the four seas suffer destitution, the beneficence of heaven cannot long survive . . .

. . . We who are confined to our homes find it is no longer possible to tolerate the existing conditions. We lack the power of King T'ang and King Wu [of ancient China]. We do not have the virtue of Confucius or Mencius. For the sake of all under heaven, knowing that we have no one to depend on and that we may bring on punishments to our families, those of us who are of like mind are resolved to do the following: First we shall execute those officials who torment and harass those who are lowly. Next we shall execute those rich merchants in the city of Osaka who are accustomed to the life of luxury. Then we shall uncover gold and silver coins and other valuables they hoard as well as bags of rice kept hidden in their storage houses. They will be distributed to those who do not own fields or gardens in the domains of Settsu, Kawachi, Izumi and Harima, and to those who may own lands, but have a hard time supporting fathers, mothers, wives and other members of the family. The above money and rice will be distributed. Thereafter as soon as you hear that there is a disturbance in the city of Osaka, mind not the distance you must travel, but come immediately to Osaka.

What we do is to follow the command of heaven to render the punishments of heaven.[42]

In this statement Ōshio pointed to the natural disasters as sure signs of Heaven's discontent with the government. It was in the hands of arrogant bureaucrats who were indifferent to the misery of the people. It was vital, he wrote, to "respect heaven's command and carry out its wrath." He called on farmers to break into government offices to destroy tax records. Others were to seize control of the city's great warehouses in order to distribute rice to the needy.

Ōshio's Confucian certainty was supplemented by Shinto belief and incipient imperial loyalism. Saving the people went hand in hand with restoring the moral government of the legendary dynastic founder, Emperor Jimmu. Famine, ignorance, and suffering for the people, who were fundamentally good, was related to the bakufu's disregard for the court; Ōshio spoke in the name of the great Ise shrine to the sun goddess. Yet while he spoke often of "Heaven," he was concerned with the three provinces he knew, and his program did not go far beyond killing the evil and distributing their riches.

The revolt, when it came, was a fiasco for all concerned. Ōshio and the few hundred confederates he had prepared for action had to advance their timetable because treachery by an informer alerted the authorities. Ōshio then set fire to his own house as a signal to his followers, who sallied forth with banners marked "Save the People!" and "Amaterasu the Sun Goddess." They proved poorly trained in the use of the few weapons they had assembled, but their incompetence was matched by the commanders of the bakufu's force, who fell from their horses and temporarily demoralized their troops. They soon became subjects for popular ridicule. Before long, however, bakufu strength prevailed. In the end all that Ōshio achieved was a raging fire that destroyed over 3,000 houses and 30,000 to 40,000 *koku* of rice. He himself fled to the mountains, and his followers committed suicide or took flight. Before long Ōshio was hunted down, his hiding place surrounded by his pursuers. Before they could take him he set fire to the building and perished in the flames together with his son. Predictably, the government exacted savage vengeance. Of twenty-nine conspirators who remained to be condemned, only five survived incarceration and interrogation. They were pickled in salt so that their bodies could be mounted on crosses for the crucifixion to which they had been sentenced.

Despite all this, it is quite unclear what Ōshio's political program and strategy were. He based his objection to the stratification of society, and the betrayal of morality, on Confucian universalism. By implication he can be made to seem a genuine revolutionary, and later dissidents wrote in his praise. On the other hand there is no evidence of planning beyond his desire to make a moral statement. His complaint was with the "immoral" excesses and evil administrators of his day. It was a pattern that recurred in Japanese history, and in this he resembled the leaders of most protests.

Even so Ōshio's revolt marked something quite new. It had been led by a samurai official of outstanding rectitude. The fires Ōshio started devastated part of a metropolis that was central to Japan's distribution networks, and virtually every domain had some sort of station or warehouse there. Consequently the affair was soon known to people all over Japan. Ōshio's manifesto also had an afterlife of its own, for it circulated widely in handwritten copies. The evils of which he complained were recognized by people in all parts of Japan. Moreover the country was being drawn increasingly into international politics once again, and it seemed vital that its social and economic problems be addressed.

In the Tenpō years reform became a matter of urgency for most domains of any size. The Edo bakufu was slow to address them, for Ienari, the former shogun, was still in charge and not inclined to sacrifice his comfort. Yet it was widely recognized that domains and their lords were in trouble. Honda Toshiaki, in a document he was too wise to publish, had written earlier that "in recent days there has been the spectacle of lords confiscating the allocated property of their retainers on the pretext of paying back debts to the merchants. The debts do not then decrease, but usually seem rather to grow larger

... there is not one [daimyo] who has not borrowed from the merchants. Is this not a sad state of affairs? The merchant, watching this spectacle, must feel like a fisherman who sees a fish swim into his net. Officials harass the farmers for money, which they claim they need to repay the daimyo's debts, but the debts do not diminish. Instead, the daimyo go on contracting new ones year after year."[43]

Domain administrators did not have many options. They could "borrow" from retainers by lowering or even confiscating their stipends, but only at the risk of ruining morale or losing followers. For many samurai the advantages of status, accompanied as they were by marginal income and boring routine, were becoming marginal, and the prospect of personal freedom and possible economic opportunity could lead them to give it up altogether. Administrators could also try to get more out of their people. Every regime tried to increase the taxes borne by its farmers, but here the risks of protest were obvious. Moreover, there was frequently not very much more to be had. Even Matsudaira Sadanobu had written, when he was still a daimyo, that "farmers fear officials like tigers and foxes." Nevertheless the effort had to be made, and most domains did their best. The "reform" invariably began with attempts to limit consumption through sumptuary regulations and exhortation. As had been the case with each earlier reform, austerity was expected of rulers and ruled alike. The next problem was that of debt and interest costs. Daimyo could try to announce cancellation of debts to their own merchants, but debts to metropolitan merchant agents, who were under bakufu jurisdiction, were more of a problem. Often they were renegotiated on better terms. The danger here was that once a domain lost its credit it could expect to have even more difficulty, and higher interest rates, in borrowing more money. And everywhere there were efforts to increase han income. Methods varied with the degree of imagination on the part of the domain, the means of coercion available, and the resources that could be exploited. Some domains put an end to monopolies in the hope of stimulating producers and of selling permits to new economic actors, but others established monopolies in order to keep the profits from commercial crops out of the hands of merchants. Some programs were clearly successful; others equally clearly failures. The programs in Satsuma and Chōshū, southwestern domains that were to play a large role in future politics, were relatively successful; in Tosa and in Saga reforms achieved little. In Tosa the domain took steps to strengthen official control of exports to Osaka, but much of the drive was lost in partisan wrangling within the han bureaucracy. Saga was perennially in debt; on one occasion in the early nineteenth century its lord was unable to leave for his domain because debtor Edo merchants were camped around his estate. In the Tenpō "reforms" the domain proposed renegotiating its debts with Edo creditors over a 250-year period, and in effect tried to declare bankruptcy.

In view of their future military and political importance, however, the reform measures in Satsuma and Chōshū deserve closer attention. Both areas, it will be recalled, were large and integrated areas with a high proportion of samurai, which were populations that provided the potential for coercion. Both also had coastal locations that made it possible to exploit maritime trade. Satsuma had the many islands south of Kyushu and its tribute system with Okinawa, while Chōshū had control over the Straits of Shimonoseki through which much commerce moved.

Satsuma began with its debt of nearly five million *ryō*. A domain administration under Zusho Hirosato cut that Gordian knot with military ruthlessness. On the ruse of conducting a survey he ordered all debtors to submit their promissory notes, and once they were in his hands he burned them and declared the problem solved. Merchants had little recourse against so determined and large a domain; a number of Osaka houses went bankrupt, but Zusho was never called to account. Further, the Satsuma administration deprived them of future leverage by seeing to it that no more debts needed to be negotiated. Meanwhile the han also took steps to take advantage of its geographic location. Its Ryukyuan connection and control of Okinawa made it possible to increase trade with China, and in time a trading station facilitated the import of weapons from the West through Nagasaki. Satsuma's southern location and warm climate proved even more advantageous, for the domain had long enjoyed a virtual monopoly on the growth of sugar cane. Zusho ordered that all paddies on the islands south of Kyushu be drained and planted in cane. Food had to be imported, and the zone became a giant sugar plantation that was frequently referred to as a "sugar hell" *(sato jigoku)*. Draconian measures established quotas for production and made it a punishable offense for even children to lick their fingers for the sweetness of the cane; adults caught smuggling or diverting cane could be executed. Zusho also made major efforts to improve quality control of other commodities Satsuma could export. Monopolies were established over lacquer, rape seed, wax, medicinal herbs, saffron, cinnabar, paper, and livestock. The result was that by the 1840s Satsuma showed a surplus. As a result the domain could afford to begin to develop military strength.[44]

Chōshū too had a large samurai class that should have made coercion possible. By one estimate samurai, rear vassals, and family members numbered 50,000, over 10 percent of the domain's 470,176 commoners. The domain was wracked by very large-scale uprisings in 1831 and 1836 that must have sharpened the administrators' awareness of problems. They proved themselves remarkably inventive and systematic in their response. A government bureau for savings and investment, the *buikukyoku*, had been set up as early as 1762, and it was now directed to investment in income-earning projects like land reclamation and harbor works, the latter in order to be able to attract shipping from western Japan that came through the Straits of Shimonoseki. The domain was remarkable for its meticulous and systematic planning; an inventory of the domain foodstuff production capacity of 1841, for instance, provided detailed figures for each subdistrict. This kind of bureaucratic planning, combined with a location reasonably remote from Edo and its distractions, made it possible to whittle down indebtedness and bring the domain into late Tokugawa days in relatively stable financial condition.[45]

The bakufu's Tenpō reforms had to wait until the death of the former shogun Ienari in 1841. This time the leading figure was the *rōjū* Mizuno Tadakuni. The reforms were deliberately cast in the tradition of earlier programs. In 1842 a bakufu edict announced that "we are re-creating the policies of the Kyōhō and Kansei eras," and like the earlier efforts those policies began with calls for frugality, sobriety, and rectitude. In contrast, however, to the martinet Yoshimune and the moralist Matsudaira Sadanobu, whose concern with personal perfection reached religious proportions,[46] Mizuno was a "known glutton, debaucher, dilettante, and taker of bribes."[47] One might have expected calls to reform to have a hollow ring when coming from such a source.

Nevertheless the minister lived up to his role. The bakufu warred more vigorously than ever before against unseemly mores and morality, arresting performers charged with lewdness, regulating areas of prostitution, banning licentious wood prints, and making examples of popular authors of off-color tales by placing them in manacles and stocks. Frugality was enjoined as seldom before; a stream of edicts warned against luxurious living and tried to regulate deportment with rules affecting Edo hairdressers, commoners' clothing, specialty foods, and festival toys. Once again officials were subject to searching inquiry and purged if found delinquent. Farmers were warned against moving to cities. Everyone, in short, was ordered to resume or maintain a proper station and status.

In addition to striking against urban frivolity the bakufu looked for ways to curb merchant profits and lower prices. Mizuno ordered dissolution of the great guilds that had been licensed to control internal commerce. Here he miscalculated badly. The guilds had operated to suppress producer prices in order to maximize profits, but with a free market those prices now rose instead. Mizuno's campaign against monopolies also extended to daimyo enterprises, and in this his administration broke new paths. A year after ordering dissolution of commoner monopolies, a bakufu order noted that daimyo of Kinai, Chūgoku, Saigoku, and Shikoku have been, by various methods, buying up the products not only of their own domains, but of other domains also; . . . sending them to their warehouses, and then selling them when the market price is high . . . This is most irregular, particularly bearing in mind our frequent instructions to reduce prices.[48]

With attempts like this Mizuno was reversing the precedents of Yoshimune and other reformers who had interpreted the tradition left by Ieyasu to mean relative autonomy for the great daimyo. The concentration and rationalization of national commerce had now created a contradiction between the needs of the bakufu and those of domains with "national profit," kokueki programs. To the degree that Mizuno had his way, domains were hurt; in Chōshū the reform administration of Murata Seifū was soon out of power.

Mizuno's efforts to increase bakufu income came at daimyo expense in two other respects. In 1843 the bakufu tried once again to drain the Inbanuma swamp along the Tone River, north of Edo, to reclaim it for paddy agriculture. It was an effort that had been attempted by Yoshimune in 1714 and Tanuma Okitsugu in 1785. Five daimyo were ordered to shoulder the expenses. Mizuno's stay in office, which ended the following year, was too short to see the project through. It failed a third time, and was to succeed only after World War II in 1946.

By all odds, however, Mizuno's most ambitious and controversial plan was one that alienated fudai daimyo and led directly to his dismissal. In 1843 the bakufu sent out orders to daimyo and hatamoto to surrender lands within a radius of Edo and Osaka. The argument could have been cast in terms of political efficiency and centralization, but instead it stated simply that "it is inappropriate that private domains should now have more high-yield land than the bakufu." Had this been successful, the bakufu would have benefited from an income increase of major proportions. This effort marked the most direct challenge to daimyo autonomy since the seventeenth century. Moreover it was to come at the expense of the shogun's closest vassals, hatamoto and fudai daimyo. Unfortunately they were also the ones best situated to intrigue and protest within bakufu councils and channels, and within the year Mizuno was out of his post. He was brought back briefly a few months later to deal with a crisis in foreign policy, but his power within the bakufu was at an end. By then he was widely detested, and after he left office commoners stoned his Edo residence.

How should we evaluate these alternating cycles of prosperity and protest? What do the events we have considered tell about the fundamental health or contradictions of Tokugawa society?

When seen in retrospect, in the knowledge that the bakufu was to fall in the 1860s, it is easy to class the recurrent crises as handwriting on the wall. Peasant protest and urban riots, complemented by contemporary descriptions of commoner misery and maladroit samurai response, surely suggest an early end for the bakuhan order. And yet, as harvests improved, towns rebuilt, and order returned to the land after each cycle, the system seemed to renew itself. Social change was continuous, but there was a remarkable dearth of suggestions for changing society.

Devices to cushion change were everywhere. The village was largely autonomous, and at its best it operated in a communal manner. Agriculture was constantly more efficient and productive. Gradations of status and well-being outlined an organism that functioned smoothly. Notions of reciprocity, obligation and tolerance were diffused by every public function. Perhaps because there was in any case no real possibility of exit or escape, the Japanese tolerated inequality and inequity, thankful that they were not worse. It would thus be incorrect to think the countryside simmered with discontent. But it would be equally erroneous to mistake its placidity for contentment. Outward deference masked substantial distrust and tension that broke easily in emergency.

It is clear that each period of reform showed that problems were more intractable and options fewer. Central Japan—the Osaka-Kyoto and Edo plains that were the bakufu heartland—was steadily less "feudal"; government pronouncements were dangerously close to becoming empty bombast. Popular culture was full of mockery that lampooned pompous formality and hollow pretension. A commercialized countryside was no longer as willing to subsidize urban guilds. Petty daimyo and bannermen were unwilling to bear the cost of administrative rationalization and centralization, and a government desperate for income could have met that need only by decreasing the support it owed its samurai retainers. Samurai, except for the fraction that found public office, were becoming irrelevant and superfluous, consuming but not producing wealth.

It was somewhat different in southwestern and northeastern Japan. Commercialism and urbanism were less advanced. A larger proportion of the population was samurai; and their efforts, if successfully enlisted by their superiors, could make meaningful reforms designed to strengthen the domain economy. Granted, their task was also less complex; the problems of administering Kagoshima or Yamaguchi were not as intractable as those their bakufu counterparts faced in Osaka and Edo. But although those domains remained more military than did the Tokugawa lands, they were not therefore more "feudal." Reform governments turned their attention to surveys and plans designed to meet the domains' fiscal and military problems.

For this reason the Tenpō reforms have long been the center of debates about their meaning. Many historians contend that the sort of government leadership that was shown—successfully in Satsuma and Chōshū, unsuccessfully in the bakufu—marked a new and more intrusive regime, prepared to sweep away status divisions and restraints in the construction of a new and proto-modern absolutism.[49]

It is also clear, however, that the system seemed quite able to continue, perhaps through sheer inertia, until a shock administered from without made it clear that changes so basic that the institutional structure could not sustain them were required if Japan was to retain its sovereignty and integrity.

During all this internal change an awareness of Japan's lack of preparedness to face problems from without added to the concern of informed Japanese. Mizuno Tadakuni had shown a somewhat greater willingness than his colleagues to discuss this and listen to men who had made a study of world affairs and modern armaments, but effective action would have required more central power than even he had tried to exert. In the process the bakufu had proved, as Bolitho puts it, too weak to offer protection for domains that were trying to strengthen themselves, and too strong to allow domains to prepare for their own defense.

9

By the nineteenth century Japan had become more isolated and insular than it was in early Tokugawa times. Dutch studies had made progress and Western books were imported, but there was little or no personal contact with outsiders. Commercial trade with the outside world had dwindled as Japan's economy had diversified sufficiently to meet domestic needs. The Dutch had continued their trade as much from inertia as from interest; so long as it was a monopoly there was no reason to give it up, but there were also few expectations of growth or profit. Within Japan the richness of cultural developments in the great urban centers combined with the effects of censorship as it was applied to all discussion of national and international affairs to create something of a cocoon seldom penetrated from without.

From 1800 on, however, the national consciousness was periodically punctuated by the knowledge or appearance of outsiders whose effect was great. Some were substantial intrusions, others were mere pinpricks; some were from near and others from great distances, but because isolation allowed so little distinction between what was near and what was far each could seem formidable and even menacing. A maverick Hungarian nobleman who came with tales of Russian invasion plans, a Russian emissary seeking permission for trade, a shipwrecked sailor, a British frigate from the south, a chartered merchant vessel bringing back some castaways; ships more often sighted from the shore, shipwrecked whalers; a sudden letter from the king of Holland, and then more warnings from the Dutch at Nagasaki; all this came to a climax with great black ships from across the Pacific, many times the size of anything in Japanese waters, contemptuous of Japanese practice and demanding far-ranging changes. All of this was interspersed with the social and political events already discussed, to create complementary vibrations that were to doom the Tokugawa ship of state.

1. Russia

It began with encounters to the north, where boundaries were very indistinct. That became a problem for both Japan and Russia as the issue of sovereignty of the Kuril Islands arose in the nineteenth century, and the debate has intensified since the island chain came into Russian possession in the aftermath of World War II. In Tokugawa times, however, things faded into the mists that shrouded the islands.

The northernmost Tokugawa feudatory was the domain of Matsumae, a rather bizarre land grant made by Ieyasu to a warrior who had joined him at the battle of Sekigahara. Because the northern climate made rice cultivation impossible, there was not even a formal *kokudaka* rating. Matsumae authorized his vassals to meet their needs by trading with the indigenous Ainu for pelts and fish. This was done by allocating special spots *(basho)* where Ainu came to barter. That procedure grew out of a highly structured and largely ritual exchange, usually of goods of approximately equal value, that had its roots in Ainu tradition. Gradually Ainu chiefs began to make regular, usually annual, appearances at Japanese settlements in order to obtain the Japanese commodities—sake, rice, tools, cloth—that became important to them, in return for the fish, fur, and seaweed in which the islands abounded. The Matsumae vassals, who had neither aptitude nor appetite for trade with Ainu villages, soon began to delegate the management of that exchange to merchants from Osaka and Sendai. This in turn generated enterprises, soon fueled by Osaka capital, eager to exploit not only the Ainu trade but also the coastal fisheries. These yielded rich returns of herring which, ground and dried, provided highly prized (and priced) fertilizer for the paddies of central Japan.

Hokkaido itself, which was then known as Ezo, was not much prized or inhabited by Japanese; late-eighteenth-century Japanese writers still thought of it as a separate land. The southern fringe, where the Matsumae "capital" was located, was considered "Japanese land" *(wajinchi)* because it was controlled by "wajin," or Japanese; in contrast, the far larger reaches of "Ezoland" *(Ezochi)* were inhabited by Ainu. As the fish fertilizer industry grew it provided the impetus for quiet moves farther north. Small-scale fishing was done by immigrants who fled the poverty of their home. More and more, however, they found themselves in competition with larger and more complex organizations funded from Osaka and manned by contract workers. Commercial exploitation of the area's marine resources became steadily more intense.[1]

Then, just as Japan's northern reaches were becoming important to financiers of central Japan, they also became known to Russians probing southward from the Pacific bases that had been established in the course of the long process of expansion in north central Asia.

Russian exploration in Central Asia began in the Urals and ultimately extended to North America. As the pioneers reached Kamchatka and the northern Kurils they traded with Ainu for the pelts of sable and fox. These barren outposts had continuous need for food resources, however, and this led to moves to the south toward Japan and ultimately east toward the coast of northern California. It was a development that had its origin in the energetic sponsorship of geographic and ethnological inquiry by Peter the Great. These efforts continued after Peter's death in 1725, though the contact was for the most part fortuitous. In 1728 a 1,000-*koku* grain ship bound for Osaka from Satsuma was driven off course and shipwrecked on the southern point of Kamchatka. Fifteen of its crew of seventeen were killed by a troop of Cossacks, but one merchant and an eleven-year-old boy serving as pilot's apprentice were spared. Five years later they found themselves in St. Petersburg, where Empress Anna questioned them about their country sometime around 1734. Residence in Russia required conversion to Russian Orthodoxy; the lad, Gonza (now Damian Pomortsev), after further study for which he had government support, received the patronage of Andrei Bogdanov of the Russian Academy of Sciences and ended his days as instructor in Japanese and author of several books about Japan.[2] This arm's length contact was not accompanied by much first-hand experience in the northern islands. Aside from their fur trade the Kuril Islands had little attraction for settlers from Russia, however, nor did they for Japanese. The few who ended there tended, as John Stephan phrases it, to be "reluctant pioneers, forgotten victims of circumstance."[3] Japanese castaways, moreover, faced possible prosecution and execution if they managed to return home. Thus, although shipwrecked Japanese and Russian pioneers, sailors, and furriers were clearly in contact by the latter part of the eighteenth century, neither government showed very strong interest in this development.

So few were the contacts that those that can be documented have received inordinate attention. Current Japanese and Russian historiography makes much of these early attempts, partly in order to score points in the dispute about sovereignty over the "northern islands," but there is little justification for attributing twentieth-century concerns to avaricious Cossack fur traders or Japanese castaways. The most interesting of these is the Japanese sailor Kōdayū, who spent four years in Russia between 1788 and 1792 and is sometimes considered to mark the beginning of Russian interest in Japan. Kōdayū managed to return to Japan, where he was sentenced to house arrest until his death in 1828. He was of course subjected to close interrogation about his experience in Russia and his knowledge of the outside world.

In the time of the Kansei reforms at the end of the eighteenth century, however, the bakufu began to obtain more scientific knowledge of the north. This resulted from the work of the great geographer Inō Tadataka (Chūkei, 1745–1818), who began as a student of an official astronomer named Takahashi Yoshitoki, father of the better-known Kageyasu. Armed with his master's knowledge of mathematics and science, Inō was commissioned by the bakufu in 1800 to conduct a serious geographic exploration of Hokkaido. With this beginning, he produced a series (214 sheets) of excellent maps of all of Japan. Inō worked out latitudes and accurate distances between points in a system that used the imperial capital of Kyoto as base for his meridian zero, and his maps were so accurate that many of them continued to be used by the Japanese army well into the twentieth century. With Inō's work as a start, additional first-hand probes of the southern Kurils were made by Mogami Tokunai, a surveyor who had been attached to Inō's mission.

In the years around 1800 Russian probes south to the Kurils and to Japan became more purposeful. In 1799 they were delegated to a new company, the Russian-American Company. Like the British and Dutch East India Companies two centuries earlier, it was authorized to administer territory as well as to trade. Because it was so difficult to supply distant posts across the land mass of Central Asia there was a new priority on developing Pacific coast sources; this also held the possibility of trade with China and, secondarily, Japan. Out of this came an expedition commanded by Nikolai Rezanov, carrying a letter from Alexander I to ask for privileges of trade, which entered Nagasaki harbor in 1804. Rezanov cooled his heels at Nagasaki for six months before bakufu officials returned from Edo with a flat no. This so angered him that, assuming the Japanese would respond to force, he authorized two subordinates to stage nuisance raids on Japanese settlements in the southern Kurils and Sakhalin during 1806–1807. The result was hardly what he had expected; the Japanese became more vigilant. When a Russian survey vessel entered the northern waters in 1811 the Japanese managed to capture its commander, Vasillii Golovnin, and held him for two years before repatriating him via the Dutch at Nagasaki.[4] At first Golovnin's detention, which he described in a *Narrative of a Captivity* that became famous, was unpleasant, but after he was able to convince his hosts that the earlier raids had not been authorized by Moscow, his conditions improved to the point that he was permitted to teach his curious keepers something about mathematics and astronomy. But the Japanese made clear they had no interest in trade. "Our countrymen wish to carry on no commerce with foreign lands," their response read, "for we know no want of necessary things"; this was true also of the trade with the Dutch, which "we do not carry on for the sake of gain, but for other important things." Actually the decline in interest was mutual; Russia had been drawn into the Napoleonic Wars in Europe, and its Pacific efforts did not revive until the 1840s.

Reports of these attempts circulated among intellectuals at the capital. Sugita Genpaku, the doctor whose translation efforts we met earlier, was alarmed to think that in the Rezanov affair Japan had affronted a vigorous young power like Russia. He saw no alternative between granting the Russians' requests and preparing for war with them, but he also thought the prospect of victory was slim. This was because the fighting spirit of the samurai class had deteriorated. *Bushidō*, the cult of the warrior, was dead even among the shogun's direct vassals, bannermen and house samurai, who should be its first line of defense. As he put it in an 1807 dialogue, "seven or eight out of ten [samurai] are like women. Their spirit is mean, like that of merchants"; they could not make an arrow fly two feet, and "they cannot stay in the saddle even if the mount is more like a cat than a horse."[5]

Japan's concern with its northern borders naturally led to ideas about the defense of Ezo. Interest in the Russians, described as "red-haired Ainu" by some writers, led to a work by the Sendai doctor Kudō Heisuke, who memorialized the Tanuma government in 1783 urging that defensive measures be taken against the Russians. The innovative mood of the Tanuma years also stirred interest in commercial possibilities in the north. In 1785 the bakufu authorized the survey that produced Inō's careful maps; other men compiled inventories of flora, fauna, and natural resources. Now, for the first time, the strange nature of practices that had developed during the years of Matsumae control, with the *basho* system of delegated trade, became apparent. This intersected with awareness of the Russian approach. Tanuma's fall brought an end to this active interest, but in 1799 the bakufu, reconstructed during the Kansei reforms, decided to place the eastern part, and in 1807, all, of Ezo under its direct control. The Matsumae lord was given paltry (9,000 *koku*) compensation in northern Honshu. Now attention was given to communications and administration; a simple code of legal procedure was laid out, and barter with the Ainu for local products replaced the exploitative system Matsumae retainers had delegated to merchant entrepreneurs.[6] Bakufu officials summoned Ainu chiefs to annual *uimamu* ceremonies, which now took on the nature of tribute missions, at Matsumae and Hakodate. At these points of contact assimilation to Japanese mores became the norm. Northern domains were ordered to contribute military force for the defense of the northern reaches.

Surveys were conducted to confirm the fact that Sakhalin was an island and not part of the Manchu-dominated mainland, and reached as far north in the Kurils as Urup, which had also become the southernmost extension of Russian activity.

Before long the bakufu, like the Russians, became more concerned about the impact of the Napoleonic Wars than it was with affairs to the north. As the impact of the European wars affected Holland and Java, and hence Nagasaki, the misty northern boundaries declined in importance. In 1821 Ezochi was returned to Matsumae once again. The domain inherited the gains of the bakufu interlude, but it was not equipped to maintain the economic reforms. Trade was soon delegated to merchants through the *basho* system once again, under conditions increasingly exploitative. With the increase of Japanese inhabitants communicable diseases ravaged the Ainu population, and by the time the bakufu took the area over again in 1854 a population that had numbered 27,000 had shrunk to 19,000.

The intellectual response to these matters was more noteworthy than their political impact, and centered on the writings of two men whose life stories serve to underscore many of the discussions above. Hayashi Shihei (1738–1793) was born the younger son of a low-ranking bakufu official. When his father lost his samurai status after incurring the displeasure of the authorities, Hayashi and his siblings were adopted by an uncle who was a country doctor. When an elder sister was taken on as a concubine by a high-ranking Sendai samurai, Hayashi's elder brother managed to get samurai status there, but as the samurai soon died the family did not prosper; Hayashi found himself with paltry status and income. But this did bring freedom from duty, and he used it to travel widely in the Sendai domain; he even managed to make three trips to Nagasaki. He was fortunate in forming friendships with leading experts on the West: Kudō Heisuke, whose warnings about the Russians have already been mentioned, scholars of Dutch learning like Katsuragawa Hōshū and Ōtsuki Gentaku, and Nagasaki interpreters from whom he managed to get world maps. Hayashi was of course also educated in Chinese learning, and he seems to have been partial to the teachings of Ogyū Sorai. Convinced that Japan faced danger, he now presented three memorials to the Sendai daimyo urging military and structural reforms to prepare for the trouble he saw coming. Not content with this, he wrote an account of Korea, Ryukyu, and Ezo which he titled *Sankoku tsūran zusetsu* (An illustrated survey of three countries), and went on to a major work, *The Military Defense of a Maritime Country (Kaikoku heidan)*. In this he warned of the dangers Japan might face, not only from Russia but also from China, which had fastened its rule on

Inner Asia in the great military campaigns that established the borders of modern China. Japan might once again face the danger it had known from Mongol fleets in the thirteenth century, he warned, and it should look to its defenses.

Unfortunately the bakufu was more concerned with its internal defenses. In the Kansei reform crackdown on publications Matsudaira Sadanobu targeted Hayashi for his temerity in writing about current affairs in defiance of censorship laws. His book and the printing blocks that had been carved for it were burned, and Hayashi was sentenced to house arrest in Sendai. Disconsolate, he died there the following year. An individual of ability could not, one concludes, overcome the restrictions imposed by place and status to challenge the wisdom of political authorities. At least he could not do so openly; Sadanobu was, as we have seen, doing something to sponsor Dutch studies and taking direct control over Hokkaido, but he wanted no open discussion or advice.

The case of Honda Toshiaki (1744–1821) provides an equally appealing instance of someone who tried desperately to penetrate the official wall of silence to learn and think about Japan's problems. Very little is known of Honda's antecedents on the Japan Sea coast of Japan, where he was born. He arrived in Edo at the age of eighteen, studied mathematics and geography, and gradually steeped himself in such Chinese translations of Western books as he could obtain. His philosophical leanings were away from Neo-Confucianism; he preferred the writings of Kumazawa Banzan and Ogyū Sorai, and after seeing the effects of the Tenmei period famine, he did his best to determine how Japan might increase its wealth to overcome the pressure of people on land. What was required, he decided, was some of the *sakui*, artifice or innovation, praised by Ogyū Sorai. The development of explosives could lead to techniques to open channels for rivers and also lead to the discovery of precious metals through mining; the precious metals produced should no longer be exported from Japan at Nagasaki but instead become the basis for a flourishing foreign trade that brought to Japan the goods it could not produce itself. Japan had the opportunity to expand its lands to the north where the climate might approximate the stimulating air of the maritime countries of western Europe; indeed, by moving its capital north to Kamchatka, it could develop its trade and wealth to become the mistress of the East, comparable to England in the West. Thus a vague presentiment that Russia might preempt Japan combined with poorly digested geographic knowledge to produce the proposal to center a new Japan in the supposedly salubrious climate of the mist-shrouded land to the north. Honda was wise enough not to publish his treatise, and thus escaped the punishment that was Hayashi Shihei's fate.[7]

2. Western Europe

Although the bakufu was able to dismiss its fears of danger from the north, this was not the case with western Europe. The flames of the French Revolution soon spread to Holland, where the conservative political structure was overthrown in 1794 and a new Batavian Republic took its place. This had immediate impact on Java and the Deshima trading station at Nagasaki. In 1798 England went to war with the Batavian Republic and seized Holland's colonial outposts in South Africa and Indonesia. Holland's republic became a monarchy in the shadow of Napoleon, who placed his brother on its throne. When Holland regained its independence with the fall of Napoleon, the descendant of the former *stadhouder*, who had taken refuge in England, returned to become king.

These events impinged directly on the Nagasaki trading system. The Dutch East India Company's autonomy had already been curtailed by administrative changes in 1766 and 1791 that made it more nearly official, and when Holland regained its sovereignty under the monarchy the company became a colonial office.[8] During the period in which direct contact with Holland was cut off, however, Batavia (present-day Jakarta) authorities had to negotiate with trading ships of neutral countries to supply Deshima. Then, when Thomas Stanford Raffles took over as British proconsul in Java, Deshima became the last outpost that still flew the Dutch flag, and contracts for supplies were made directly by the Deshima station head. Rotation of station heads became impossible. One *opperhoofd* died on duty in Japan, and after Hendrik Doeff took over command of the Deshima station in 1798 he and his compatriots were marooned there until the resumption of Dutch control. In the meantime, from 1797 to 1817, a period of twenty-three years, Deshima was minimally supplied by chartered ships from neutral countries; of those eight were American, one of which made two trips.[9] In each case the Dutch instructed the captains to fly the Dutch flag and to conceal their Bibles and their weapons, and tried to pretend that everything was normal.

As a result Nagasaki authorities were not immediately aware that something was up. The Deshima station chief, who was supposed to report on events in the outside world, was slow and evasive in his accounts, hoping to conceal the fact that he was chartering foreign ships. There had been riots in Paris, the Japanese were told, but things had been brought under control. In 1808, however, Raffles wanted to add the Deshima station to his Java command, and dispatched a ship, the *Phaeton*, to Nagasaki. Its captain demanded supplies, and when these were denied, seized what he could and made off, leaving behind a distraught bakufu official who committed *seppuku* to atone for his failure. The Japanese then began asking hard questions. American sailors in port resembled English; were they part of a larger scheme? They now learned by interrogating Doeff that the American Revolution had resulted in independence from England, and that tumultuous events were taking place in Europe. New heroes, dimly seen, filtered out to Japan from these inquiries. One was Napoleon, a giant of will and strength. Another was George Washington, who had raised an army to drive out the foreigners, declined to serve as king, and instead established a "country of peace and concord," *kyōwa koku*, the literal meaning of the characters selected to render "republic." At first dimly seen, one was a modern warlord, the other something of a Confucian sage.

In response to these discoveries the bakufu took up Western knowledge as a project for itself, hiring and co-opting the specialists who had worked under a variety of separate sponsors or on their own. Its first instrument for this was the Bureau of Astronomy. Foreign knowledge was important for astronomy and revisions of the calendar, and that was why Yoshimune had relaxed rules for the import of books in the eighteenth century. The bureau had prepared revisions of the calendar in 1754 and 1798. It now found itself charged with work in geography, and indeed was responsible for the explorations to the north in 1785 and after. That in turn led to efforts to study the history, institutions, and military science of the foreign countries. The bureau was naturally able to have its needs recognized in the preparation of the book order lists when Deshima regained communication with Holland. But in 1811, even before that system was restored, astronomy bureau scholars were ordered to translate an encyclopedic work by a French scholar named Noel Chomel that had come into Japan in a Dutch translation published between 1778 and 1786. It was to be reordered time after time, and appeared on order lists regularly between 1819 and 1849. Chomel's work contained a vast miscellany of entries helpful for everything from personal health and household management to manufacture and merchandising. "Everyone," its preface assured readers, "can convince himself of all the verities, in looking for whatever he wants, in entries that are arranged alphabetically the way they are in dictionaries."[10] The bureau added many linguists to its rolls for this effort. By the time the project came to an end in 1846, enough entries had been translated to fill 164 stitched Japanese volumes. They were never published, however; this was official business and classified knowledge. Still, from the frequency with which orders for the encyclopedia were filled, it is obvious that many daimyo were getting sets in response to requests from their own scholars.

During all this, Japanese knowledge about the West and competence in Western languages improved. The Dutch station at Nagasaki became the transmission point for the rudimentary study of French, of Russian, and of English. From a Japanese perspective these languages, all of them written horizontally and not vertically, seemed related. Moreover the fact that Europeans dressed similarly—unlike the case with Chinese, Japanese, and Koreans with their distinctive national dress—suggested a pattern of envelopment by a single superpower, one the more dangerous because its nationals were devious and pretended to be from different places.

Against this background the bakufu issued an order in 1825 to make no distinction among Westerners but to expel them without thinking twice.

> We have issued instructions on how to deal with foreign ships on numerous occasions up to the present. In the Bunka era we issued new edicts to deal with Russian ships. But a few years ago, a British ship wreaked havoc in Nagasaki, and more recently their rowboats have been landing to procure firewood, water, and provisions. Two years ago they forced their way ashore, stole livestock and extorted rice. Thus they have become steadily more unruly, and moreover, seem to be propagating their wicked religion among our people. This situation plainly cannot be left to itself.
>
> All Southern Barbarians and Westerners, not only the English, worship Christianity, that wicked cult prohibited in our land. Henceforth, whenever a foreign ship is sighted approaching any point on our coast, all persons on hand should fire on and drive it off. If the vessel heads for the open sea, you need not pursue it; allow it to escape. If the foreigners force their way ashore, you may capture and incarcerate them, and if their mother ship approaches, you may destroy it as circumstances dictate.
>
> Note that Chinese, Koreans, and Ryukyu can be differentiated by physiognomy and ship design, but Dutch ships are indistinguishable [from those of other Westerners]. Even so, have no compunctions about firing on [the Dutch] by mistake; when in doubt, drive the ship away without hesitation. Never be caught off guard.[11]

This policy, ostensibly consistent with Iemitsu's decrees two centuries earlier, was actually far more sweeping. Earlier policy would have been to mobilize coastal daimyo to intercept a foreign presence; now watchers were to shoot on sight without hesitation or without thinking twice, *ni-nen naku*. Yet it was not a product of ignorant obscurantism, but drawn from the advice of an outstanding intellectual and student of foreign languages. Takahashi Kageyasu (1785–1829) was the son and successor to the astronomy bureau scholar who had organized the surveys of northern Japan. His reading had taught him that the coasts of foreign countries were not open to casual entrance; ships requesting entrance approached ports with proper protocol, but "when ships from a nation with whom diplomatic relations are not maintained tries to enter, blank rounds are fired from the nearest cannon on shore. It is customary for those ships to leave the harbor after thus being informed that entry is not permitted."[12] In Takahashi's mind the policy he proposed for the bakufu was a bit strict, but since foreigners were becoming such a nuisance, gathering "like flies to a bowl of rice," stern measures were justified. He and his like assumed that the foreigners so challenged would learn their lesson and sail away, leaving Japan at peace.

Takahashi was by no means "antiforeign" in a visceral sense, as can be seen from the friendship he developed with Philipp Franz von Siebold (1796–1866), a German savant mentioned earlier who was attached to the Deshima Dutch station between 1823 and 1828. The Dutch alerted their hosts to Siebold's unusual qualifications, and gave him the title of "surgeon major, authorized to conduct a survey of the natural history of the realm." The Japanese in turn permitted him to set up a school on the outskirts of Nagasaki where he taught a total of fifty-six students.[13] Siebold made major contributions to Japanese medical science, and made it possible for Takahashi to acquire Dutch translations of English explorers' accounts as well as the work of the Russian Krusenstern. While in Edo, where he accompanied the Dutch mission's quadrennial trip, Siebold also met daily with Mogami Tokunai and informed himself about Ainu life, culture, and language. As he was preparing to leave in 1828, however, it was discovered that Takahashi had given him in exchange a copy of Inō Tadataka's map. The bakufu reaction was harsh; twenty-three of Siebold's students were taken into custody; Siebold himself was arrested and expelled. Takahashi, despite his distinction and achievements, died under interrogation. His corpse was preserved in salt for transport to Edo and a proper beheading.

A decade later things became even more discouraging for specialists in Western studies, thanks to the *Morrison* affair and the *bansha no goku,* or "purge of barbarian scholars." As with Sugita's alarm about Rezanov's rejection, this was based on misinformation with dark expectations of a danger that had already passed. But the alarm was real enough. In 1838 an American-owned merchant ship, the *Morrison,* arrived with seven shipwrecked Japanese on board in the hope of winning trade privileges in return for this demonstration of compassion. The effort failed; in line with the 1825 "don't think twice" order, shore batteries at Edo and again at Kagoshima fired, and the ship returned to Canton with its cargo of castaways. After the Dutch reported, mis-

takenly, that the vessel had been English, a group of scholars who called themselves the "bansha" began to meet to discuss the possible significance of that
event. At the center was Watanabe Kazan (1793–1841), a high-ranking retainer
in the small *fudai* domain of Tawara. His interest began with the study of
Western painting, and he went on to concern himself with matters of national
defense by reading widely and consulting with specialists in Western studies.
Among them was one of Siebold's prize students, a man who had gone underground after Siebold's expulsion. It was as able and cosmopolitan a group as
could be found.

Takano Chōei, the Siebold student, wrote "The Story of a Dream," in
which he revealed his fear that the bakufu policy of unthinking repulse of
foreigners would make an enemy of England and tarnish the name of Japan
in world affairs. For this he was sentenced to life imprisonment, but managed
to escape and support himself for a time by translation. A colleague, Kozeki
San'ei (1778–1839), committed suicide rather than run the risk of capture,
interrogation, and torture.

Watanabe himself became an inviting target for denunciation and slander.
Investigators discovered an essay he had written in which he argued that, given
the power of the West, stubborn resistance by Japan could only lead to disaster; "one may call them barbarians," he wrote, "but they will not resort to
arms without an excuse." In all Asia, he argued, Japan was the only country
that had managed to retain its sovereignty, for even China had fallen to the
Manchus in the seventeenth century. The West, however, was a more potent
predator than Asia had ever known, for its strength in science and technology
and its open class structure and effective political institutions gave it a dynamic
that other rivals lacked.

Watanabe's pamphlet discovered, he was denounced, convicted, and sentenced to permanent confinement in his Tawara domain. Two years later,
when he was caught in violation of the terms of his sentence by sending paintings to Edo for sale, he committed *seppuku* to spare his daimyo further difficulty, leaving a poignant and celebrated lament, "disloyal, unfilial!" (*fuchū,
fukō!*).[14]

It is impossible not to sympathize with the men who paid a heavy price
for the knowledge they had of the Western world. Sugita Genpaku's descendant Sugita Seikei, employed as a Dutch translator by the bakufu, could not
get the word "freedom" out of his mind after encountering it in his work. A
contemporary who compiled a history of Dutch studies, wrote that

> when he heard that Takahashi, Watanabe, Takano, Takashima and others
> had been seized for spreading foreign ideas he feared he too was asking

for trouble. He held himself in check and was very careful not to let [the Dutch for "freedom"] slip from his mouth.

The only way he could find solace for the heaviness of his spirit was by drinking, but when he was drunk he could not keep from shouting "*Vrijheit!*"[15]

And yet it would be wrong to conclude that these men were necessarily "pro-Western," as their enemies often charged, or intent on changes in the society they knew. Some, to be sure, envisaged changes to strengthen Japan that would have constituted radical innovations in the closed social system by valorizing ability. Many more, however, were eager to place their knowledge at the disposal of the authorities and thereby strengthen Japan's defenses. They were virtually one in dreading the newly intrusive West; metaphors like "flies on a bowl of rice" and "ravenous beasts" convey the revulsion with which they saw the Westerners who disturbed the tranquillity of Japan's coasts.

Probably the most influential writing of these years was Aizawa Seishisai's "New Theses," written in 1825 (but not yet published) by the Mito retainer we have mentioned earlier. Aizawa himself was learned in Chinese philosophy and by no means ignorant of Western knowledge, but it will be recalled that he was also dedicated to the superiority of Japan's "Divine Realm," which "rightly constitutes the head and shoulders of the world and controls all nations." Its superiority inhered in its unbroken imperial line. The barbarians, however, "unmindful of their base position at the lower extremities of the world, have been scurrying impudently across the Four Seas, trampling other nations underfoot. Now they are audacious enough to challenge our exalted position in the world. What manner of insolence is this?"[16] Aizawa also warned against dangers that inhered in studies of the West:

One source of harm that has appeared of late is Dutch Studies. This discipline grew out of translation work—the reading and deciphering of Dutch books by specially trained interpreter-officials. There is no harm in Dutch Studies itself; the harm comes when some dupe with a smattering of second-hand knowledge of foreign affairs mistakenly lauds the far-fetched notions spun out by Western barbarians, or publishes books to that effect in an attempt to transform our Middle Kingdom to barbarian ways. There are, moreover, many curiosities and concoctions from abroad that dazzle the eyes and entice our people to glorify foreign ways. Should the wily barbarians someday be tempted to take advantage of this situation and entice our stupid commoners to adopt beliefs and customs that reek of barbarism, how could we stop them? [The *Book of Changes* tells us,] "The lining of frost on which we tread [in early winter soon] turns into a hard sheet of ice." We must adopt appropriate measures to thwart them now before it is too late.[17]

3. News from China

A few years after the bakufu crackdown on Watanabe Kazan and his friends, shattering news came into Nagasaki. The British government, having succeeded to the place of the long-compliant East India Company, had refused to accept Chinese destruction of opium stocks in Canton, insisting on the sanctity of property. War had broken out in 1838 and the treaty of Nanking, which followed in 1842, had forced China into a new set of institutional relationships that were to become known as the treaty port system. What this meant for Western countries, led by England, which was tired of its trade deficits in the tea trade and anxious for markets in which to sell the products of its new mills, was full access for trade in selected ports. Its goods were guaranteed a low fixed tariff when entering and leaving those ports. Individuals engaged in that trade would enjoy protection under Western law, in the form of extraterritoriality administered in consular courts by British judges. "Free trade" on these terms was thus to be carried out on Western terms. This constituted a loss of sovereignty for China. The most-favored-nation clause extended privileges gained by any Western power to all other Western powers.

It was some time before the full dimensions of this settlement became apparent to the Japanese, but distance and isolation heightened the sense of shock and crisis. Mizuno Tadakuni, still in office despite the failure of his Tenpō reforms, wrote that "This concerns a foreign country, but I think it should provide a good warning for us."

Nagasaki provided two channels for transmission. One was the Dutch. They were soon questioned closely, but the results of such interrogations could to a large extent be kept under control. This was not the case with books from China, for all educated Japanese could read them. Moreover, the very system of supervision of imports the bakufu had installed at Nagasaki served to alert officials at the center. News traveled as though through a central nervous system.

The circulation of works by the author Wei Yüan provides a case in point. His book describing Chinese military problems with rebellions and border conflicts was written in 1842, reached Nagasaki in 1844, and was soon in the hands of members of the Senior Council including its new head, Abe Masahiro. An even more influential work, *Hai-kuo t'u-chih*, an illustrated geography of maritime countries, was first published in China in 1844. When three copies reached Nagasaki in 1851 the censor, thinking it might be considered dangerous, alerted his superiors and requested instructions. In a short time three members of the Senior Council had copies. A few years later another seven were in the hands of other bakufu authorities and eight went on sale. Before long a Japanese edition edited by a specialist in Chinese studies, Shionoya Tōin, was circulating. Japanese editions put these books in the hands of leading officials as well as samurai intellectuals, who learned about Western expansion from them.[18] The samurai intellectual Sakuma Shōzan, who submitted a memorial urging more attention to coastal defense, wrote that when

> the English barbarians were invading the Ch'ing empire . . . I, greatly lamenting the events of the time, submitted a plan in a memorial . . . Later I saw the *Sheng-Wu Chi* of the Chinese writer Wei Yüan. Wei had also written out of sorrow over recent events . . . while Wei wrote only four months before I submitted my memorial, the two of us, without having had any previous consultation, were often in complete agreement. Ah! Wei and I were born in different places and did not even know each other's name. Is it not singular that we both wrote lamenting the times during the same year, and that our views were in accord without our having met?[19]

Shionoya Tōin, who edited (in Chinese) Japanese editions of Wei's books, went on to write his own account deploring the lax preparation China's rulers had shown; for him China's fate underscored the cultural and political threat posed by the West. Like Aizawa Seishisai, he warned of attempts by Westerners to infiltrate Confucian society and subvert ignorant commoners by devious tactics. As a scholar who had devoted his life to mastering and applying the wisdom of China, he was left without moorings as he witnessed the inability of his ideal state to respond effectively to the West, and his distress finds eloquent echo in his loathing of even Western-style writing.

Important as Wei Yüan's work was for intellectuals, however, popular accounts reached many more readers. Mineto Fūkō's *Kaigai shinwa*, written in 1849, was an illustrated popular account based almost entirely on Chinese sources and presented in the style of Japanese classical war tales. Bob Wakabayashi notes that the work "enjoyed a broad circulation in late Tokugawa times," and "helped create a whole genre of fictionalized or semi-fictionalized accounts of the Opium Wars and Taiping Rebellion" in late Tokugawa and early Meiji Japan as well.[20] From this work readers could follow, with some inaccuracies, the successive encounters of the war. According to the *Kaigai shinwa* account, moreover, the war had not by any means been as sweeping a victory for Western technology as the West (and Japanese leaders) thought it was. Ordinary Chinese soldiers had fought with courage, only to have their cause betrayed by cowardly Chinese officials who feared their own people as much as they did the foreigners. (This explanation that valiant soldiers had been betrayed by cowardly officials would return to haunt bakufu negotiators a decade later.) Mineto initially failed to get approval for publishing his book and spent two years in prison, but by then the damage had been done; the book was out. Tōin, who had edited the Japanese edition of Wei Yüan, provided striking evidence of the way China's fate could distress Japanese intellectuals:

> The Chinese say: "Foreign countries are separated from China by a distance of sixty or seventy thousand miles. They will not come and rob us." But the Chinese do not know that the foreigners have made their beds on the waves and that their colonies are very near . . . they do not realize that armoured ships are like mountains and that Chinese traitors are as multitudinous as flies: . . . Now the foreign barbarians are very clever at conquering people's hearts. For they scheme in such a way: if soldiers are used to conquer the land, then this does not imply that the population has submitted itself . . . It is far better to lead the people on by means of the Christian Faith . . . If then, afterwards, we seize some good opportunity for invading the country, then, without losing a single soldier, and without spending one single gold piece, we will make the people our faithful servants. [Nevertheless] That the foreigners can conquer the hearts of our people is because we ourselves have alienated our people from us. For, if we ourselves had not lost the heart of our people then, even if the foreigners tried to allure them with a hundred means, they would not have a chance of conquering them . . . [Worst of all, the foreigners are now infiltrating by learning our language] . . . Except for our country, there are only Annam, Korea, and a few other countries that employ the Chinese script. As the others do not know the characters how can they understand the teachings [contained in them]?

Shionoya now went on to contrast Western with East Asian scripts, a difference that seemed to symbolize the gulf between Western depravity and Eastern elegance:

> Now as regards the shape of foreign letters, they are confused and irregular, wriggling like snakes or larvae of mosquitos. The straight ones are like dog's teeth, the round ones are like worms. The crooked ones are like the fore legs of a mantis, the stretched ones are like slime lines left by snails. They resemble dried bones or decaying skulls, rotten bellies of dead snakes or parched vipers. In the construction of their dots and lines, one misses

the balance of the pictorial characters, the significance of the suggestive compounds, and the deep meaning of the indicative [Chinese] characters . . . [characters] are evenly balanced and well-proportioned, their shape is luxuriant and graceful, their demeanor is like that of correct literati, they seem to look backward and aside like beautiful women, they are deftly constructed like golden palaces or sacrificial vessels . . . [Because they realize this] the Russians sent students to Peking, and the English asked to be allowed to follow their example . . . Here is an ominous sign.[21]

Bakufu officials supplemented the reports they received from China with a questionnaire addressed to the Dutch at Nagasaki. From them they learned the size of the English force in China, and the capabilities of ships powered by steam. "Why have the Tartars [Manchus] lost," one question read, "since they are said to be brave enough?" The answer was direct: "Bravery alone is not sufficient, the art of war demands something more. No outlandish power can compete with a European one, as can be seen by the great realm of China which has been conquered by only four thousand men."[22]

In the face of such discouraging news, Mizuno Tadakuni, who returned to head the Senior Council for a brief period, came to the decision that the "don't think twice" edict of 1825 would have to be abandoned. A circular addressed to officials and domains, and read to the Dutch station chief at Deshima, explained that compassion had led the shogun to revert to procedures of earlier periods. "It is not thought fitting to drive away all foreign ships irrespective of their condition, in spite of their lack of supplies, or of their having stranded, or their suffering from stress of weather. In accordance with the ordinance of 1806, after investigating the circumstances of each case, you should, when necessary, supply them with food and fuel and advise them to return, but on no account allow the foreigners to land . . . If, however, after receiving supplies and instructions they do not withdraw, you will, of course, drive them away, adopting such measures as are necessary." His purpose was not to abandon the seclusion system, but rather to avoid the likelihood of war at a time when Japan was woefully unprepared.

Japan was as unprepared for decisions as it was for war. This was shown by the reaction to a formal proposal addressed to the shogun by King William II of The Netherlands in 1844. This document, announced by the *opperhoofd*, was brought to Nagasaki by a special warship, the *Palembang*. The king's letter expressed his appreciation of the bakufu's relaxation of the exclusion policy. It then went on to speak of the vast increase in manufacture and trade since the Napoleonic Wars had ended; all governments were now at pains to further their trade. England's eagerness to do so had led to war with China, a war that had led to the death of thousands of Chinese, the devastation of many cities, and the expenditure of millions in indemnity payments to the victors. William went on warn that similar dangers now threatened Japan; there were many more ships in Japanese waters than there used to be; the world, in fact, was being knit together by the new technology.

> This process is irresistible, and it draws all people together.
>
> Distance is being overcome by the invention of the steamship. A nation that tries to hold itself aloof from this process risks the enmity of others. We are aware that the laws laid down by Your Majesty's enlightened predecessors limit exchange with foreign people severely. But, as Lao Tzu says, "where wisdom is enthroned, its product is the maintenance of peace." When ancient laws, by strict construction, threaten the peace, wisdom directs that they be softened.[23]

When the Edo authorities replied to the Dutch commander waiting for a response at Nagasaki, the Senior Council wrote King William that his suggestion was quite impossible, and asked him not to write again. Soon Mizuno was out of office once more, his place taken, as we have noted, by Abe Masahiro.[24]

The Dutch warning proved accurate. By the time the bakufu had responded to King William's letter, foreign ships had come ashore at several places. Soon the Satsuma daimyo was reporting that a French ship stood into Naha harbor on Okinawa with the explanation that it was there only to anticipate the British. In 1846 a Protestant missionary began work there.

In the event, the principal push for opening trade with Japan came not from England but from the United States. Under the pattern of most-favored-nation privileges, all powers inherited the gains won by any one. The British, conscious of a certain amount of unpleasantness attached to forcing China open for Western-carried opium, were quite content to be second in Japan. Britain already had a substantial stake in China. Trade prospects with Japan seemed modest, and the London foreign secretary informed the commander of England's Pacific forces that his government "would think it better to leave it to the Government of the United States to make the experiment; and if that experiment is successful, Her Majesty's Government can take advantage of its success."[25]

4. The Perry Mission

American interest in Japan was twofold. Until the discovery of oil in Pennsylvania in 1858 the country was illuminated by whale oil lamps; Pacific waters were busy with fleets of whalers, some of whom inevitably ended up on the shores of Japan. At that time Americans were more eager to protect whalers than they were whales, a priority that has been reversed more recently. Accounts of the mistreatment of shipwrecked sailors and the failure to help ships in need fired public indignation. Americans had also entered the competition for the China trade. Speedy clipper ships bound for China by the Great Circle route had long moved close to Japanese shores, for Japan lay astride that course. The advent of steam navigation brought with it need for a Pacific source of coal, and hopes of a coaling station en route to China added importance to contact with Japan. Entrepreneurs began to dream of routes that would circle the globe. American victory over Mexico and the acquisition of California strengthened the American position on the Pacific coast, and the gold rush that followed brought many more Americans to the far west. Slogans of manifest destiny stirred popular imagination and led easily to Pacific adventures. For all these reasons Japan was more important to Americans than it was to English.

In 1832 President Andrew Jackson directed steps to bring America into the China trade that had been opened by Great Britain, and the 1834 Treaty of Wanghsia brought America benefits the British had won by force. At the same time relations were opened with Siam. Naval commanders at the time were instructed to open talks with Japan if it could be done without risk, but the only action that followed was the private voyage of the *Morrison* in 1837. Significantly, the missionary on board that vessel was from the China coast, a pattern that would be repeated in future contacts.

In 1845 the United States representative in China was instructed to send a mission to Japan. Captain James Biddle arrived in Edo Bay in 1846 with two ships and the hope of opening relations, but when the Japanese explained that foreign relations could be carried out only at Nagasaki he withdrew, since he had no authorization to use force. At one point he was rudely jostled by a guard, and his failure to demand some concession in return seemed, to some Japanese, to justify their refusal to bend their rules.

The Perry expedition that followed in 1853 was more carefully prepared and forcefully managed. Its story has been told often and well. It is one replete with ironies. Commodore Matthew C. Perry, who would win fame as the man who "opened" Japan, accepted the assignment reluctantly, for he feared that it would bring him little honor; he would have preferred the Mediterranean command. Then, making the best of a bad situation, he prepared with great care, insisting on enough strength to guarantee the success of his mission, arming himself with what was known of Japan and taking counsel with others who had traveled in Japanese waters. The New York Public Library contained only a handful of books for him, drawn from the Dutch experience, and from these and from the example of Biddle he resolved to insist on his dignity. The Dutch subservience, as he saw it, and indeed Nagasaki itself were to be avoided; he would deal only with the highest authorities. Noting this, the Japanese "promoted" officials sent to deal with him and presented them as worthy of their guest. The system of honorary imperial titles under which a man could be "Lord of Dewa" without having been there provided a convenient cover.

Perry was resolved, as his official account put it, to "demand as a right, and not as a favor, those acts of courtesy which are due from one civilized nation to another." He was well aware that "the more exclusive I should make myself, and the more exacting I might be, the more respect these people of forms and ceremonies would be disposed to award me." The lofty tone to be adopted was indicated by the instructions he carried, which he certainly influenced and perhaps wrote:

> Every nation has undoubtedly the right to determine for itself the extent to which it will hold intercourse with other nations. The same law of nations, however, which protects a nation in the exercise of this right imposes upon her certain duties which she cannot justly disregard. Among these duties none is more imperative than that which requires her to succor and relieve those persons who are cast by the perils of the ocean upon her shores. This duty is, it is true, among those that are denominated by writers on public law imperfect, and which confer no right on other nations to exact their performance; nevertheless, if a nation not only habitually and systematically disregards it, but treats such unfortunate persons as if they were the most atrocious criminals, such nations may justly be considered as the most common enemy of mankind.

(Then, after specifying Perry's objectives—protection of seamen and property, permission to obtain supplies, if at all possible a depot for coal, and permission "to enter one or more of their ports for the purpose of disposing of their cargoes by sale or barter"—the instructions continued that)

> If, after having exhausted every argument and every means of persuasion, the commodore should fail to obtain from the government any relaxation of their system of exclusion, or even any assurance of humane treatment of our ship-wrecked seamen, he will then change his tone, and inform them in the most unequivocal terms that it is the determination of this government to insist, that hereafter all citizens or vessels of the United States that may be wrecked on their coasts, or driven by stress of weather in their harbors shall, so long as they are compelled to remain there, be

treated with humanity; and that if any acts of cruelty should hereafter be practiced upon citizens of this country, whether by the government or by the inhabitants of Japan, they will be severely chastised.

Actually Perry did not wait until he had "exhausted every argument" before changing his tone. At the very outset of the talks he sent some white flags to the Japanese negotiator together with a harsh personal letter. Failure to meet his demands, he warned, would bring on a war that Japan would most assuredly lose, and in that case the white flags of surrender would be useful. In this bit of bravado he was probably acting beyond his instructions, and since it gives a rather different picture of his achievements than he might have wished, he quietly omitted all mention of this letter from his official and personal reports.[26]

Perry entered Edo Bay on July 2, 1853, with four ships mounting sixty-one guns and carrying 967 men. As Chinese interpreter he had the missionary S. Wells Williams, who had been aboard the ill-fated *Morrison* sixteen years earlier, but while Williams was of help in translating documents the actual interpretation was carried on in Dutch.[27] Perry had made a stop at Naha on Okinawa. He credited the fear that the Americans sensed there to tyrannical misrule, and recommended to Washington that the United States give thought to taking the Ryukyus for itself. Now and on his return he insisted on being taken around the island, demanding the porters and supplies required. But of course his mission lay to the north. The American warships were six or more times the size of any ship in Japan, and their dark hulls earned them their "black ships" *(kurofune)* name in Japanese lore.[28]

After the inevitable orders, and then requests, that he go to Nagasaki, Perry made it known that he had been ordered to present a letter from the president of the United States to the emperor of Japan and that he would not deviate from those orders. By the time arrangements had been worked out for ceremonies at Kurihama at which he would deliver his letters, the shore was lined with thousands of troops that daimyo in central and northern Japan had been ordered to send. Perry's ships, their decks cleared and crews ready for action, were drawn up so that their guns could sweep the beach. Interpreters quoted Perry as having warned that he could call on fifty more ships from Pacific waters, and as many more in California. Neither side trusted the other, and each side did its best to overawe the other. The Japanese had built a special pavilion for the reception, and the American landing party moved between long lines of Japanese, many of them armed with seventeenth-century flintlocks. Perry himself marched between two flag-carrying black stewards, the tallest in his command, followed by his officers. Two cabin boys carried rosewood boxes with gold hinges that contained the official letters with their seals, boxes that were opened by the black stewards for presentation.

The ceremonies were formal and labored, with statements translated from English to Dutch to Japanese and in return order. Perry was eager to return to Chinese waters to replenish supplies that were running low, and announced that he would return in April or May to receive the Japanese response to the letters he had delivered. Then, to underscore his indifference to Japanese prohibitions, he had his ships move toward (but not as far as) Edo to survey the coast.

Perry returned in February, sooner than he had thought and certainly sooner than the Japanese had expected. He had learned that a Russian mission under Admiral Putiatin was in Nagasaki anxious to negotiate a treaty, and he was determined that he would not be anticipated or held to conform to terms others had worked out. His squadron was stronger this time: each of three steamers had a sailing ship in tow. Again there were long debates about where the shore meetings would convene. The Japanese wanted them at Uraga, as far as possible from Edo, or at Kamakura, while Perry held out for Kanagawa, near present-day Yokohama. Perry had his way. Once again no element of pomp that could be managed was left out. The Americans again marched between rows of Japanese guards, Perry now in the rear, followed by six black stewards. Once begun, the talks went better; the Japanese had determined they had no hope of resisting some kind of treaty.

Actual negotiations were delegated to Hayashi, head of the shogunal Shō-heikō academy. Negotiations went on for twenty-three days, and Hayashi played a weak hand with considerable skill. Perry maintained a heavy-handed stance.[29] When Perry pressed for trade privileges, asserting that China was finding them extremely profitable, Hayashi chided him with confusing profit with humanity; had it not been his aim to seek help and supplies for those thrown up on Japan's shores? Finally it was agreed that Japan would provide two harbors, Shimoda, at the entrance to Edo Bay, and Hakodate, on Hokkaido. Naha, on Okinawa, remained unspecified, but ships were already stopping there at will. At the two designated ports American ships would be able to receive supplies and coal, and shipwrecked sailors were to be helped and returned. Americans would be permitted to pay for supplies they received, something Perry saw as an opening step for trade, and a formula that permitted the Japanese to maintain they had denied trading privileges. The Americans were convinced a consul was to reside at Shimoda; the Japanese were less clear on that, but in the end the American reading prevailed. Both sides had reason to be pleased; Perry that he had achieved his minimum objectives, and the Japanese that they had so far managed to avoid the fate that China had encountered in its subjection to the unequal treaty system.

That, however, was not long in coming. Townsend Harris, who came to Shimoda as American representative, brought stories of new wars in China and warnings that Japan would do well to submit voluntarily to what it could not hope to avoid by resistance.

5. The War Within

Japan's military backwardness and the example of China's defeat might seem to have left few alternatives to abandoning the policy of seclusion, but in fact responsible officials in the Tokugawa power structure were subject to a wide range of advice and criticism. At the center, Mizuno Tadakuni had been replaced as head of the Senior Council in 1845 by Abe Masahiro (1819–1857), daimyo of Fukuyama. Abe held that post for a full decade, but as problems multiplied no successor was likely to stay in office that long. The bakuhan structure was so balanced and checkmated that in the absence of an unusually strong and able shogun, decisive acts of statesmanship were unlikely, and in the years after Abe's death in 1857 policies followed a zigzag pattern that was destructive to careers. Officials who had to deal with foreign countries were in constant jeopardy at a time when success was impossible to attain. Self-preservation dictated caution, hesitation, and postponement, all of which the Americans took for dishonesty and evasion. Things were particularly unstable at the level of implementation. A new magistracy, *gaikoku bugyō*, Commissioner for Foreign Countries, was established in 1858, and five men were appointed to serve in a collegial capacity. In the decade that followed no less than seventy-four men moved through its revolving doors. New heads brought new policies and new teams, and aside from a very few foreign affairs "experts" who became essential because the foreigners were accustomed to working with them, tenures were short.

When Honda Masatoshi replaced Abe Masahiro as head in 1857 the Senior Council of *rōjū* experienced a 100 percent turnover. Ambassadors sent to the United States in 1860 to ratify the Harris treaty, of which more below, disappeared into obscurity when they returned to Japan. Japan had rediscovered politics in addition to rediscovering diplomacy.

When he came into office in 1845, Abe had moved swiftly to undo many of the Tenpō policies that had made Mizuno unpopular, and the daimyo Mizuno had alienated by his programs to centralize holdings around Edo were initially mollified. Abe's aims were to inform and conciliate the daimyo, but that very decency soon got him into serious trouble. Bakufu decisions had long been reached through collegial agreement among the members of the *rōjū*, rather than through broad consultation or unilateral action. In the aftermath of the crisis presented by Perry the Edo government changed tactics to try consultation and, after that failed, unilateral decision. In so doing it opened the way to criticism, controversy, and violence.

Abe knew that the daimyo of the cadet house of Mito, Tokugawa Nariaki, had remonstrated with the bakufu for not informing him about the letter the Dutch king had sent. Abe was not going to make the same mistake. In 1849 he asked daimyo of coastal domains if they thought it would be wise to reinstate the "don't think twice" edict for expulsion; they did, but nothing came of it.

The arrival of Perry's squadron presented a far more urgent problem, and Abe decided to circulate the American demands to all daimyo, all high officials, and even some commoners. More striking still, he also informed the imperial court at Kyoto. Perry had, in effect, "opened" Japanese politics, an area that had been as closed as Japan's ports.

Abe hoped to establish a consensus by this measure, but found there was none. Of the daimyo responses that have survived, only two favored accepting the American demand. Two more thought it would be a good idea to do so temporarily, and three favored letting the United States trade long enough to give Japan time to prepare its defenses before going to war; four suggested prolonging the negotiations so that the Americans would give up, and three confessed that they could not make up their minds, and eleven wanted to stand and fight. It must be remembered that the daimyo themselves had first consulted their own senior vassals, so that these responses mirrored the uncertainty and confusion of a broad sector of the ruling samurai class. There simply was no satisfactory solution to the problem.

Abe's most active critic was one who advocated war, the strong-willed lord of Mito, Tokugawa Nariaki, whom he alternately conciliated and ignored. Nariaki (1800–1860) had succeeded to the rule of his domain in 1829 after a lively succession dispute, and his readiness to express strong opinions cost him bakufu displeasure several times. On becoming daimyo he had immediately instituted stringent standards of frugality, reflected in the earlier discussion of samurai women. In Mito he also inherited the domain's tradition of imperial loyalism, and he soon patronized a reform faction of able men committed to that cause. The "Mito learning" of his day based itself on an ethnic nativism (as we saw in the writing of Aizawa Seishisai) that affirmed the superiority of Japan's imperial institution. In 1841 Nariaki established an academy, the Kōdōkan, to foster practical Western learning; its charter, carved on a stele in Nariaki's elegant hand, first combined as one term the phrases that were to be a rallying call, "revere the emperor, drive out barbarians." As foreign warships came closer Nariaki tried to militarize his domain, melting down temple bells to manufacture cannon. In 1844, immediately before Abe's rise, the bakufu tired of Nariaki's advice and removed him as daimyo, ordering him to keep to his residence. One of the first things Abe Masahiro did was to lift this order. In 1849 he appointed Nariaki as adviser on maritime defense, and let him resume direction of domain affairs from retirement. Not surprisingly, when he received the bakufu's request for advice in responding to Perry Nariaki opted for war. Japan might well be unprepared, he admitted, but war would galvanize resolve and raise morale:

> . . . When we consider the respective advantages and disadvantages of war and peace, we find that if we put our trust in war, the whole country's morale will be increased and even if we sustain an initial defeat we will in the end expel the foreigners; while if we put our trust in peace, even though things may seem tranquil for a time, the morale of the country will be greatly lowered and we will come in the end to complete collapse.
> . . . the Americans who arrived recently, though fully aware of the bakufu's prohibition, entered Uraga displaying a white flag as a symbol of peace and insisted on presenting their written requests . . . They were arrogant and discourteous, their actions an outrage. Indeed, this was the greatest disgrace we have suffered since the dawn of our history.
> . . . I hear that all, even though they be commoners, who have witnessed the recent actions of the foreigners, think them abominable; and if the Bakufu does not expel these insolent foreigners root and branch there may be some who will complain in secret, asking to what purpose have been all the preparations of gun-emplacements.
> . . . But if the Bakufu, now and henceforward, shows itself resolute for expulsion, the immediate effect will be to increase ten-fold the morale of the country and to bring about the completion of military preparations without even the necessity for issuing orders.[30]

Of the daimyo responses that advocated concession, the most important came from Ii Naosuke, the powerful *fudai* daimyo of Hikone who was fated to carry the responsibility for implementing what he advocated. Japan should accept the American demands, he wrote; it should in fact return to the kind of merchant-sponsored trade it had abandoned in the seventeenth century, and thereby buy time to prepare for a future confrontation with the Americans:

> . . . Careful consideration of conditions as they are today . . . , leads me to believe that . . . it is impossible in the crisis we now face to ensure the

safety and tranquillity of our country merely by an insistence on the seclusion laws as we did in former times.

. . . We must revive the licensed trading vessels that existed [in the
early seventeenth century], ordering the rich merchants of such places as
Ōsaka, Hyōgo and Sakai to take shares in the enterprise. We must construct new steamships, especially powerful warships, and these we will load
with goods not needed in Japan . . . these will be called merchant vessels,
but they will in fact have the secret purpose of training a navy. Forestalling
the foreigners in this way, I believe, is the best method of ensuring that
the Bakufu will at some future time find opportunity to reimpose its ban
and forbid foreigners to come to Japan . . . And since I understand that
the Americans and Russians themselves have only recently become skilled
in navigation, I do not see how the people of our country, who are clever
and quick-witted, should prove inferior to Westerners if we begin training
at once.[31]

Although his advocacy of resistance was not followed, Nariaki did not
flag in his efforts to provide the bakufu with counsel. He peppered Abe with
suggestions, many of them critical and dangerously impractical. Perhaps because he was trying to conciliate him, Abe made an additional concession that
brought into prominence a young man who was to be a key player for the
next decade: he approved the adoption of Nariaki's seventh son into the Hitotsubashi line, a position from which he would become eligible for selection
as shogun. The young man in question, Tokugawa (or, now, Hitotsubashi)
Yoshinobu (or Keiki, as his name is usually read, 1837–1913) was able and
highly regarded; he soon came to be a major figure in national politics.

In 1858 the death of the young shogun Iesada, who was quite incompetent,
opened a succession dispute, and almost immediately this became intertwined
with foreign policy. The Edo authorities who had difficulty reaching one decision now had to face two. The new shogun had to be adopted from a cadet
line. One possibility was from the house of Kii (Wakayama), but since Japan
faced critical times and a national emergency was at hand there was also a
compelling case to be made for selecting the twenty-one-year-old Keiki over
the candidacy of the twelve-year-old lord of Kii. On the other hand Keiki's
quarrelsome parent guaranteed that the matter would be politicized, however,
and bakufu traditionalists carried the day for the boy from Kii, the future
shogun Iemochi. This time Ii Naosuke was with the majority; somewhat disin-
genuously, he argued that derivation was what counted, and that that was the
Japanese way. These arguments carried the day for the future Iemochi. The
bakufu went on to penalize those who had tried to interfere, and Nariaki was

once more put under domiciliary confinement. His position as head of one of the three great cadet houses made him difficult to ignore, and his strong advocacy of an antiforeign loyalism helped make Mito thought and Mito samurai dynamic forces in the politics that lay ahead.[32]

What raised the stakes in these disputes was the issue of a full commercial treaty with the United States. Townsend Harris had arrived in Shimoda as American consul in 1856.[33] It had already become clear that other countries would demand what Perry had received. The British were first; an admiral who arrived at Nagasaki after the outbreak of the Crimean War planned to ask Japan not to harbor Russian ships, and was instead offered, and accepted, a convention like Perry's. The Russians were not far behind; Admiral Putiatin tried several times for trade concessions, but had to settle for an agreement in the Perry pattern early in 1855. The two parties discussed Sakhalin Island without results, but they did agree on a division of the Kuril Islands.

None of this constituted a formal agreement for the exchange of representatives and the conduct of trade, and those were the goals Harris had set for himself when he arrived at Shimoda. It was his goal to open four ports to trade and secure residence rights for American representatives in each as well as in Osaka and Edo. Hotta Masayoshi (1810–1864), daimyo of Sakura (the domain of the peasant martyr Sakuma Sōgorō), had succeeded Abe (who was to die two years later at the age of thirty-eight) as head of the *rōjū* in 1855, and now became the chief negotiator on the Japanese side.

Bakufu representatives did everything they could to stall Harris and throw him off track, but he held his ground and insisted on presenting his proposal personally to the shogun. Harris's journal finds him lamenting the fact that he had no warships to back him up; his treatment, he thought, showed that "no negotiations could be carried on with them unless the plenipotentiary was backed by a fleet, and offered them cannon balls for arguments." But in fact he had something as good or better: news that England was inflicting even greater humiliation on China in warfare that France had joined. Canton fell in 1858, and by the time the second round of wars was over Peking itself was in allied hands. In this context no bakufu negotiator could expect Japan to be able to resist successfully. The Dutch added their advice. They had already secured improvements in the conditions under which they traded, and now advised the bakufu that it concede with negotiations rather than having a treaty forced upon it. Harris was further spurred on by news that the Dutch and Russians had worked out limited agreements for trade at Nagasaki. Harris felt this inadequate and denounced the agreements as "disgraceful," but they further strengthened his resolve to have things done his way. By the fall of 1857 he was in Edo, where he had an audience with shogun Iesada (who was to die shortly afterward), and lectured Hotta on the dangers of the trade in opium, which the British were likely to protect as they had in China. Harris argued that the United States would not tolerate such practices, and would thereby set an example that might restrain European imperialists. A treaty with the United States would be in Japan's self-interest. By early 1858 Harris and Hotta had worked out a treaty under whose terms Japan would open five ports between 1859 and 1863 to American residence and trade.

Up to this point the Americans had assumed that the shogun's approval was all that was required, and Harris was now startled to have Hotta tell him that he would have to travel to Kyoto to have the emperor's authorization for what had been done. He assumed initially that this was only another way of temporizing. It was not, however, for the court was suddenly to become the focus of lobbying and controversy.

Leaders opposed to the new commercial treaty, above all Tokugawa Nari-aki, sent representatives to urge xenophobic court nobles to deny Harris's request for approval of the treaty. Hotta, by his trip there, brought the bakufu influence to bear, while several important Tokugawa daimyo sent agents to urge the court to recommend the succession of an "able" shogun. By this they meant twenty-one-year-old Keiki rather than the Kii lad. Nariaki himself, of course, could have been expected to favor his son's candidacy too. The Kyoto scene that Hotta entered was extremely complicated. Both sides had tried to involve the imperial court. The foreign crisis thus precipitated abandonment of traditional reserve and caution. Abe Masahiro had indirectly contributed to this by the alacrity with which he responded to an imperial query about coastal defense, and by his request for court advice in responding to Perry's demand, but no bakufu official would have envisaged court interference in matters of Tokugawa house succession. Now Hotta's request for formal sanction of the treaty took this a step farther, and provided the opening Tokugawa Nariaki needed. That worthy had been increasingly alarmed by what he heard about Harris's demands. A few months before, in December 1857, he had proposed to the *rōjū* that the bakufu send him to America—with a goodly company of *rōnin* and younger sons ("always unwanted") "and that you should let me act as middleman for the goods in which the Americans want to trade." Even if they were all killed, it would not be as dangerous as letting foreigners reside in Edo. He went on to argue that if the bakufu had delegated Ezo to his care earlier there would have been no trouble with the Russians.[34] Thus when Hotta headed for Kyoto Nariaki was ready with messages for the poorly informed and antiforeign court nobles, most of whom had no contact with the world of politics, to have them delay and finally deny the approval Hotta was seeking.

The court kept Hotta waiting four months, after which he got his reply: he should consult the daimyo again, paying particular attention to the opinions of the three great cadet houses (of which Nariaki's Mito, of course, was one), and to the views of the *tozama* lords who had always been excluded from policy matters. Hotta, a failure, resigned. To the east, Townsend Harris's impatience grew.

During all this wide fissures opened in bakufu and daimyo politics. The matter became complicated by the jockeying for succession to the office of shogun; a number of major daimyo, acting through vassals they sent there, worked to have the court endorse the candidacy of an "able," that is, mature, successor. Bakufu leadership was being challenged at its very core.

Upon Hotta's fall, leadership in the bakufu passed into the hands of Ii Naosuke (1814–1860), who took command of the *rōjū* with the special title of *tairō*, or Great Elder. Consultation as a tactic had failed, and the bakufu now shifted to dictatorial commandism. After Townsend Harris convinced negotiators that Japan faced real danger because of the hostilities in China, and that it should procrastinate no longer, Ii Naosuke resolved to sign the treaty on his own. At court Emperor Kōmei was furious that his orders had been flouted, and communicated this anger to Nariaki's Mito representatives. The bakufu sternly, but unsuccessfully, ordered Mito to keep that knowledge to itself.

At this point Ii moved to restore strong central leadership in national affairs and equally strong *fudai* domination in bakufu councils. The emperor was pressured to give his approval to the treaty, and did so reluctantly on grounds that it was too late to change things. Shogunal succession went to the boy Iemochi, from the traditional house of Wakayama (Kii), rather than to Hitotsubashi (Tokugawa) Keiki. In a letter to his man in Kyoto, Nagano Shuzen, Ii Naosuke put the matter very simply: it was more important, and more consonant with traditions of the realm, to follow the line of descent than it was to select a model ruler *(meikun)*, for that would be "completely in the Chinese fashion."[35]

Next the powerful lords who had lobbied in Kyoto were punished. Nariaki was ordered into domiciliary confinement. A number of daimyo, including those of Tosa, Fukui, and Owari, suffered the same fate. So too with the court nobles who had been involved. In each case their underlings became politicized by the punishment of their lords; ripples at the center spread rapidly throughout samurai society.

What followed was a purge that has become known for the era name, "Ansei"—which, ironically, translates as "peaceful rule." Lower-ranking men who had been stationed in Kyoto to lobby there were hunted down and sent to Edo in prisoners' cages. It made no difference that some had been carrying out their lords' orders; they should, the judgment read, have tried to change their daimyos' minds. Over one hundred men were sentenced to punishment, eight to death with six of those beheaded like ordinary criminals. Japan had not seen so severe an assertion of bakufu supremacy and power since the seventeenth century. It would soon cost Ii his life.

6. Defense Intellectuals

Daimyo could dispose, but others proposed, and a group of extremely interesting samurai scholars, who may be thought of as defense intellectuals, set the lines for the internal debate that now took place. Their ideas began as proposals by vassals to their lords, but in the years of turmoil that lay ahead they became the focus of passionate belief and action.[36]

Nariaki's chief adviser was Fujita Tōko (1806–1855), who was, with Aizawa Seishisai, whose "New Theses" have already been discussed, the major representative of Mito scholarship in his generation. Fujita was punished when his lord was, though his conditions were considerably less comfortable, and he returned to the fray with him with undiminished enthusiasm. It was Fujita who wrote the charter for Nariaki's academy with its invocation sonnō-jōi, which called for reverence to the throne and expulsion of the foreigners. Fujita began with an undifferentiated image of a hostile West. Because the Hollanders he saw were dressed differently from pictures of seventeenth-century Dutchmen and in fact just like Rezanov's Russians at Nagasaki in 1804, he concluded that Japan was threatened by a devious West that was trying to envelop it from all directions. He wrote numerous memorials for Nariaki advocating stronger defenses; Ezo, they proposed, should be delegated to Mito. The domains, at least the great domains and certainly the three great cadet houses, should be permitted to build oceangoing ships and encouraged to develop better armaments. Like Aizawa, Fujita was an irreconcilable foe of Christianity, the "evil teaching" foreigners used to subvert and subjugate credulous commoners. Mito issued an anthology of Ming dynasty anti-Christian writings in 1855 to ward off the foreign cult. Fujita approved of training people in foreign studies, but they in turn should be prevented from disseminating that learning among the people. Every step taken should reinforce the superiority of the native; in educational institutions salaries should reflect the intellectual hierarchy of Japanese over Chinese, and of both over Western studies.

Japan should, he thought, avoid war with the West if it could be done in a manner consonant with national dignity, but while Japanese should prepare themselves with foreign learning, Westerners should under no circumstances be allowed to enter Japan. Better, indeed, to put closer controls on the Dutch at Nagasaki. When Perry's letter was circulated among the daimyo Nariaki, who bridled at the insult offered by the white flags, urged that the proposals be rejected and that Japan prepare for war, arguing that once the Americans landed, death-defying samurai in overwhelming numbers could surely exterminate them. Even if things went badly for a time, he argued, morale would increase tenfold and the whole country would prepare for war. "Only by doing so will the shōgun be able to fulfil his 'barbarian-expelling' duty."[37]

The Mito advocacy of Western exclusion at the same time that Japan improved its defenses on Western lines was not without contradictions. Other advocates of rearmament were more consistent, and since the circle of such "experts" was relatively narrow, it soon produced a special corps of defense specialists.

Takashima Shūhan (1798–1866) came out of the Nagasaki environment. As a boy of ten he was startled by the impertinence displayed by the *Phaeton* in seizing the supplies it was denied. His family members were municipal officers of Nagasaki and apparently of some means, since Takashima began his studies and experiments more or less on his own. From his reading he concluded that the defenses of Nagasaki were quite inadequate and that the 1825 bakufu "don't think twice" edict could not possibly be enforced. Through Deshima he managed to get Western weapons—field guns, mortars, and up-to-date firearms—as well as manuals for their use, which he had friends and disciples translate. In time he had two companies of infantry and a small artillery battery, an achievement that is the basis of his reputation as the first serious student of Western-style weapons. The Mito men, on the other hand, had also favored buying or making modern weapons, but their basic reliance had been on the superiority of Japanese swords and spirit in hand-to-hand fighting. By 1841 Takashima's writings and activities had brought him to the attention of a forward-looking bakufu official named Egawa Tarōzaemon, who arranged for a demonstration for his fellow samurai officials. Takashima came with a group of 125 men, and gave an example of close-order drill on a parade ground. The maneuvers they conducted had been learned from Dutch books, and the commands to which they responded were also in (what passed for) Dutch.

Predictably, this provided material for critics, some of whom derided the drill as child's play and denounced the idea of using Dutch. The bakufu, however, commissioned Takashima to train more men, and, after first restricting him to bakufu retainers, permitted him to teach young men from other domains in a new school he set up. His enemies now trumped up charges of subversion and treason, and managed to have him put under house arrest between 1846 and 1853. The Perry arrival brought him back in favor, and a number of important students continued his work. What should be noted is the political infighting that put men as varied as Tokugawa Nariaki, Fujita Tōko, and Takashima in periodic danger of disgrace and punishment. It was difficult for those who saw their whole identity threatened by the adoption of Western methods to reconcile themselves to such changes, and this made for turbulent politics. What was true on the national level was no less true on the local. Before long groups who styled themselves "righteous" were at odds with those they derided as "vulgar" or "conventional" in domain after domain. Samurai intensity did not always have room for fine distinctions of motivation.

This was also the experience of Sakuma Shōzan (1811–1864), a person who died for having the courage of his convictions; he was murdered by antiforeign zealots because he was riding a horse with a Western saddle. Sakuma was a maverick with great ability and equally great self-confidence. He was born in the mountainous domain of Matsushiro, but studied in Edo and became thoroughly versed in classical Chinese learning. He was also an accomplished painter and calligrapher. When he studied gunnery with Egawa Tarōzaemon, he was astonished to discover that modern firearms could be used in the rain. He repeatedly showed impatience with the status system as it affected him personally, a trait that got him into trouble with higher authority. Yet almost everyone was convinced of his ability and he prospered as a result. This was particularly the case with his lord, who, a son of Matsudaira Sadanobu, had been adopted into the Matsushiro daimyo line. When that worthy was appointed a member of the *rōjū* in 1844 and placed in charge of maritime defense, Sakuma, who followed him to Edo, found himself strategically placed to influence others. Able to mix easily with scholars of Dutch learning, he undertook the study of Dutch and persuaded his lord to order and collect for him books that came to constitute a major collection of foreign learning.

From his reading he derived material for experiments. Using the Chomel encyclopedia that was attracting so much attention in Japan, he tried making glass; he cast cannon, looked for silver, copper, and lead deposits, and even experimented with new items in his diet. He tried and failed to get permission to publish a translation of the Dutch-Japanese dictionary that the chief factor Doeff had developed during Deshima's long Napoleonic interlude. Then, in what must have astonished his lord, Sakuma petitioned to return his subfief to the domain in exchange for money with which he wanted to establish a school in Edo. Permission nevertheless granted, he operated an academy within the precincts of the Matsushiro estate in Edo and welcomed students from all parts of the country—in all, he claimed, five thousand. Sakuma was clearly an inspirational teacher, and numbers of his students went on to become important figures in late Tokugawa and early Meiji politics and intellectual life. When the Perry mission arrived Sakuma was, predictably, prepared with advice for the defense of Edo Bay, all of which was ignored by the bakufu. He was outraged by the agreement to permit Townsend Harris to reside in Shimoda because of its strategic position on Edo Bay.

Long convinced of the importance of "knowing the enemy," Sakuma now conceived plans to accompany the enemy to his lair and study at first hand the sources of Western strength. One of his students was the young Chōshū samurai Yoshida Shōin, who will be discussed below. Yoshida, having broken out of han discipline, was now a *rōnin,* and Sakuma encouraged him to try to travel abroad. He went first to Nagasaki, only to arrive just after Russian ships had left; the Perry expedition provided another opportunity nearer the capital. Yoshida Shōin approached Perry's *Mississippi* at night in a rowboat, but Perry, not wanting to prejudice his larger goal, refused to take him. Discovery of the rowboat led to Shōin's arrest, and the path led to Sakuma when it turned out that the would-be traveler had been carrying a farewell poem by his teacher. Sakuma too was arrested, and when he was interrogated he boldly advocated the wisdom of travel and study abroad. Respect for Sakuma's ability led bakufu underlings to limit punishment to a relatively light sentence of house arrest. Even so, Sakuma spent the next eight years in confinement in Matsushiro. Now he composed a famous work, "Reflection on My Errors," in which he discussed his own difficulties and the dangers that Japan faced. It is a work that justifies quotation at some length.

All learning is cumulative. It is not something that one comes to realize in a morning or an evening. Effective maritime defense is in itself a great field of study. Since no one has yet thoroughly studied its fundamentals, it is not easy to learn rapidly its essential points . . .

. . . Last summer [when] the American barbarians arrived in the Bay of Uraga . . . their deportment and manner of expression were exceedingly arrogant, and the resulting insult to our national dignity was not small. Those who heard could but gnash their teeth . . . A certain person . . . suffered this insult in silence, and, after the barbarians had retired, drew his knife and slashed to bits a portrait of their leader [Perry] which had been left as a gift.

. . . The principal requisite of national defense is that this prevents the foreign barbarians from holding us in contempt. The existing coastal defense installations all lack method; the pieces of artillery that have been set up are improperly made; and the officials who negotiate with the foreigners are mediocrities who have no understanding of warfare. The situation being such, even though we wish to avoid incurring the scorn of the barbarians, how in fact, can we do so?

. . . I have wished to follow in substance the Western principles of armament, and, by banding together loyal, valorous, strong men of old, established families not in the military class—men of whom one would be equal to ten ordinary men—to form a voluntary group which would be made to have as its sole aim that of guarding the nation and protecting the people.

. . . Mathematics is the basis for all learning. In the Western world after this science was discovered military tactics advanced greatly, far outstripping that of former times.

. . . Learning, the possession of which is of no assistance and the lack of which is of no harm, is useless learning. Useful learning on the other hand, is as indispensable to the meeting of human needs as is the production of the light hemp-woven garment of summer and the heavy outer clothing of winter.[38]

By this time many domains were on the hunt for experts who could help them to strengthen their defenses, and when Sakuma was pardoned in 1862 Tosa and Chōshū were among the domains that requested his services. He chose to stay at the capital, and rose in bakufu circles as Japan found itself increasingly enmeshed in problems with the West. Sakuma was sent to Kyoto as an emissary of the shogun Iemochi. By now Sakuma had worked out the formula he believed appropriate for his times. Japan should adopt Western learning and Western technology, but remain grounded in the moral values of its tradition. *Seiyō no gei, Tōyō no dōtoku;* Western science, Eastern morals: this combined rationality with morality.[39] He maintained a stubborn indifference to the rising tide of antiforeign emotion around him. As he wrote his concubine,

Whenever I go out on horseback, I always use my Western saddle . . . I have not once used a saddle made in this country ever since my arrival here, and there are those foolish enough to criticize me for this. Yet I have deliberately used only the Western saddle, for I believe whatever is good must be adopted by this country . . . this belief of mine is based on what is in the eternal interest of all Japan; . . . Since there is such a thing as the Way of Heaven, I do not think that others will raise their hands against me.[40]

He was wrong. Today a small marker in the precincts of Kyoto's Myōshinji temple complex indicates where he was cut down.

Of Sakuma's many students none was more important, or more interesting, than Yoshida Shōin (1830–1859), the young man who tried and failed to travel to America with Perry's squadron. Yoshida was a serious scholar of Confucianism, a splendid teacher, and an impetuous activist. At the age of three he succeeded to the headship of the Yoshida family into which he had been adopted, and by the hidebound hereditary strictures of the day he was soon given the family assignment and appointed lecturer in the military teachings of Yamaga Sokō. No doubt this contributed to his precocity, and though we can smile at the hagiographic tradition that has the boy soon impressing his lord with his command of the texts there is little doubt that he became an accomplished scholar at an age when most samurai children were playing with bamboo swords. When he was twenty years old he was permitted to travel to Kyushu, and during that trip he first absorbed Aizawa Seishisai's "New Theses." In addition to contacting the major castle towns, he visited Nagasaki, where Dutch sailors invited him on board their ship. On his return he wrote the first of many memorials to his daimyo on the importance of upgrading education in the arts of war and peace.

A few months later the daimyo took Yoshida to Edo as part of his *sankinkōtai* entourage. He now met many well-informed scholars, including Sakuma Shōzan. "This Sakuma," he wrote home, "is an extraordinary man of really heroic proportions . . . Those who enter his school to study gunnery he compels also to study the Chinese classics, and those who enter to study the Chinese classics he compels also to study gunnery."[41] Not content with this, Shōin was now determined to see the rest of Japan. When his permit was delayed he went off without it anyway, a serious offense for a military man. In Mito he visited Aizawa Seishisai and other scholars and then crossed Japan to visit Sado Island, where he entered the shafts of the gold mines, and on to Ezo. His meticulous journal records his dismay at the sight of foreign ships in Tsugaru Straits. Then, after his return to Edo, Shōin turned himself in for his violation of travel rules. He was quickly remanded to the castle town of Hagi. Despite this, so great was his reputation that his punishment was light; his name was removed from the samurai roster and he was stripped of his paltry stipend, but then given ten years for study at any place of his selection.

He returned to the stimulation of life at Edo, and it was now that Sakuma spoke to him of the importance of trying to go overseas to study the West at first hand. He tried first at Nagasaki, as we saw, and returned to Edo on the eve of Perry's arrival. His attempt to board Perry's warship was unsuccessful and he was soon detained in an outdoor cage. His plight moved American naval officers of the mission who happened to see him so confined. He managed to hand them a thin piece of wood on which he had written, "Regarding the liberty of going through the sixty [Japanese] provinces as not enough for our desires, we wished to make the circuit of the five great continents . . . Suddenly our plans are defeated . . . Weeping, we seem as fools; laughing, as rogues. Alas for us! we can only be silent."[42]

After several months in an Edo prison (Sakuma was in the next cell for a time) Shōin was remanded to his domain authorities, as Sakuma was to his. As with Sakuma's "Reflections on My Errors," Shōin's "Record from Prison" (Yushūroku) was more concerned with reforms than with penitence. Among his suggestions were to move the bakufu to Kyoto, and there establish a new academy for Western learning and technology. After being returned to Chōshū he spent fourteen months in prison. During this period his determination hardened, and his thought became far more focused. Upon his release he began to teach, and soon opened his own school.

The Shōka Sonjuku—village school under the pines—as he called his school, attracted an extraordinary group of future leaders—some seventy— who drank in his stern lectures about the dangers of regarding learning as an accomplishment instead of moral guidance for practical action. Death, he taught, was unimportant; the moral man should keep death ever in mind in contemplating what his contribution was to be, and this would endow his effort and his memory with honor and ultimate success. "Otherwise," he wrote, "one's life will be devoid of grace and skill." Unfortunately the great of his day were intent on comfort and weak in resolve, and it would require the intensity of "grass-roots heroes" to save the country:

> What is important in a leader is a resolute will and determination. A man may be versatile and learned, but if he lacks resoluteness and determination, of what use will he be? . . . Life and death, union and separation, follow hard upon one another. Nothing is steadfast but the will, nothing endures but one's achievements. These alone count in life.
>
> . . . In relations with others, one should express resentment and anger openly and straightforwardly. If one cannot express them openly and straightforwardly, the only thing to do is forget about them. [Not to do so] can only be called cowardice.
>
> . . . Those who take up the science of war must not fail to master the classics. The reason is that arms are dangerous instruments and not necessarily forces for good.
>
> . . . First we must rectify conditions in our own domain, after which conditions in other domains can be rectified. This having been done, conditions at the court can be rectified and finally conditions throughout the whole world can be rectified. First one must set an example oneself and

then it can be extended progressively to others. This is what I mean by the "pursuit of learning."

. . . As things are now the feudal lords are content to look on while the shogunate carries on in a highhanded manner. Neither the lords nor the shogun can be depended upon, and so our only hope lies in grassroots heroes.

. . . If one is loath to die at seventeen or eighteen, he will be equally reluctant at thirty, and will no doubt find a life of eighty or ninety too short . . . Man's life span is fifty years; to live seventy is a rarity. Unless one performs some deed that brings a sense of gratification before dying, his soul will never rest in peace.[43]

These were stern directions, but they were firmly in both the Confucian and the samurai tradition. What made them memorable was the burning intensity and idealism with which Yoshida carried out his plans and inculcated his disciples. It was the crisis Japan faced that gave this its meaning.

As he learned of the bakufu's determination to force a reluctant imperial court to approve the Harris treaty of the Ansei era, Yoshida, who was no longer free to travel, wrote memorials, proposals, and letters to his students as they entered the field of political action. He deplored the superficiality of upper samurai life at a time of national danger, and proposed that the domain ignore rank, and even status, in its appointments. If the country was to be opened he wanted the bakufu to do it actively and purposefully, rather than, as it seemed, cravenly and hesitantly. Students should be sent abroad to each country; Japan should have a fleet, and trade, and become a presence on the world stage instead of remaining a victim.

And he plotted a spectacular act of virtuous terrorism to alert, and ultimately transform, society. To this end he proposed that his followers waylay a high bakufu official, Manabe, who was being sent to Kyoto to deal with the court and Emperor Kōmei's anger. The plot miscarried—all of Shōin's did—and when the bakufu reasserted itself under Ii Naosuke, the Ansei purge began. Chōshū was ordered to send him to Edo, where he was beheaded.

His judgment read that he had been guilty of having tried to go to America, he had presumed to advise the government on defense while still in prison, he had opposed hereditary succession to office, he had been planning to give advice about foreign policy to the bakufu, and he had done all these things while still under house arrest; he had, in short, shown disrespect to higher authority. In death he became a martyr and a hero, proof of his teaching that death was not to be feared.

10

The Tokugawa bakufu fell a decade after Townsend Harris had his treaty. Its fall meant the end not only of the early modern bakufu-han system but of seven hundred years of warrior rule. The agreements Perry and Harris had wrung from reluctant bakufu negotiators made it necessary for Japan to abandon policies of seclusion and enter the international order on terms defined by the West. The struggle to regain its sovereignty then forced Japan to embark on policies of centralization and institutional innovation in order to build a modern nation-state, and involved the basic restructuring of domestic society. These developments were important for Asian and in fact for world history because they brought a new and dynamic player onto the stage of nation-states. Japan's domestic reconstruction led to the restructuring of the international order; what began as defensive steps to head off a perceived Western threat was soon followed by membership in, and then challenges to, the military and economic order that had first challenged Japan.

Historians have grouped these developments under the term Meiji Restoration. Taken as a whole, the Meiji Restoration constitutes a pivotal step in Japanese history. One's judgment of that restoration affects, and is in turn affected by, every aspect of the history of modern Japan. Each persuasion, and each period, has had its own narrative of those tumultuous events. Nostalgia softens contemporary judgments of the actors on that stage, but the appraisal of their achievements remains contentious to this day. In discussing these momentous events this chapter begins with a brief consideration of the political narrative and chronology, and then looks at the role of the outside world, the transvaluation of ideas and slogans, the program on which unification of the polity was resolved, and the question of the participation of ordinary Japanese in the Meiji Restoration.

1. The Narrative

Ii Naosuke's triumph was of short duration. He was brought down by the bitter opposition his policies had roused in Mito samurai. It will be remembered that Tokugawa Nariaki, their lord, had played a prominent role in opposition to the way Japan had responded to the demands of Perry and of Harris. "Mito learning," as represented by Aizawa Seishisai's "New Theses," had argued the importance of developing a national polity based upon the purity of Japan's imperial tradition, and it was Nariaki, more than anyone else, who had linked opposition to the Harris treaty with the imperial court. He did his best to get the emperor to express his opposition to that treaty, and through the complicity of court nobles word of that opposition was sent to Mito with instructions that other domains be informed. The Tokugawa bakufu, getting wind of this, forbade further circulation of that message, and Ii Naosuke went on to consolidate his power in the Ansei purge. Nariaki, forbidden to involve himself again in national affairs, was one of the daimyo punished in that purge. His death in 1860 removed his polarizing influence.

Those in Mito who knew, samurai and commoners alike, were indignant that their superiors had been indifferent to the fact that the emperor was opposed to the treaty. When han officials prepared to abide by bakufu instructions to prevent circulation of the imperial message and instead sent its bearers back to Kyoto, indignant samurai resisted and tried, unsuccessfully, to block the party charged with its return. Others, caught between conflicting loyalties to domain and court, committed suicide. A few decided to strike back. On a snowy day in March 1860, Ii's entourage was on its way to the shogun's Chiyoda Castle. The guards' swords were covered to protect them against the sticky snow. Suddenly the little group was attacked by Mito samurai. While some took on the guards another managed to pull Ii out of his palanquin and take the *tairō*'s head, and then dashed off with it to the gate of another *rōjū*'s mansion, where he disemboweled himself.

This daring act inaugurated a decade of violence. A few decades earlier Sugita Genpaku had remarked on the weakness of bakufu retainers; they were quite incapable of fighting, he thought, and they seemed to have lost all sense of the warrior's mission. What happened now proved him wrong. In the last decade of warrior rule warrior spirit revived. The sense of danger from an intrusive West roused an ethnic consciousness that quickly came to center on the Kyoto emperor. It also came to outweigh more particular loyalties to daimyo and domain. Men were quick to charge their fellows, and particularly their superiors, with criminal negligence and misconduct. The simpler matters seemed, the more immediate the violence.

Ii Naosuke's assassins had prepared a statement of their purpose. It was couched in the heavily Chinese, formal *kanbun* used by all educated men in Tokugawa Japan. These were not ruffians. They were well aware, they wrote, that with the coming of the American barbarians to Uraga the shogun, as "Barbarian-Subduing Generalissimo" had found it necessary to make some changes. Nevertheless to grant as many concessions as had been made—commercial relations, reception of foreigners into the very castle, relaxation of the prohibitions on the "evil religion," permission for foreign representatives to reside in Japan—was "truly to set aside the military traditions that had guided the country from ancient times. It constituted pollution of the national polity [*kokutai*], and ignored the wise precepts the ancients had left for their descendants."[1] The document made frequent appeals to emperor, court, sun goddess, and Ise shrine, but as yet there was no derogation of the bakufu as such. The problem rather centered on Ii Naosuke, a willful autocrat who had ignored the court's opinion, censored lords who had tried to guide him, and dishonored the wise guidance exemplified by Tokugawa Ieyasu.

This shocking event was soon known everywhere. Word of Ōshio Heichachirō's rebellion in Osaka had spread quickly too, but Edo, even more than Osaka, was the nerve center of samurai society. Censorship could delay diffusion of the news for a brief period, but it was impossible for the bakufu to contain knowledge of the murder of its first minister at the very gate of the shogunal castle.

The bakufu showed itself demoralized and puzzled. Its first reaction was to try to smooth things over by backing away from Ii's punishments of leading daimyo. The next step was to seek a new tie with the imperial family, and the third to permit relaxation of controls of daimyo in a series of moves known (for the era name) as the "Bunkyū" reforms of 1862. Leadership passed to the very forces that Ii Naosuke had opposed. Rotation in office became more frequent, and resolution in the implementation of policy weakened.

National leadership now shifted to some of the daimyo Ii Naosuke had tried to punish. Nariaki, who had died while still under domiciliary confinement, was out of the picture, but his son Hitotsubashi Keiki (Yoshinobu), who had failed to win the nod for the shogunal succession, now became steadily more prominent. So too did Matsudaira Shungaku (Keiei), daimyo of the collateral house of Fukui, who had lobbied for Keiki as shogun. It also seemed important to restore relations between Edo and Kyoto. The young Kii heir, who had succeeded to the shogunate as Iemochi, was not yet a player in the game. In Kyoto Emperor Kōmei was still smarting from the way Ii had ignored his wishes but he was also startled by the audacity of the attack on Ii and conscious of the need to work out some relationship with Edo in face of the

danger from the West. The Western pressure soon increased. The fishing village of Yokohama, near Kanagawa, was being developed as a port for foreign
trade; it "opened" in 1859. Townsend Harris, however, led the group of foreign
ministers who insisted on implementation of the right to reside in Edo that
was granted by the treaty.

It was becoming more important to build strength against the West than
to maintain the cumbersome measures that had been developed for control
of the daimyo, but the turbulence of national politics was beginning to be
reflected in domains. The Tosa daimyo, Yamauchi Yōdō, had proposed a
seven-year moratorium on *sankin-kōtai* alternation to give domains a chance
to develop military strength. In the southwest Chōshū, Satsuma, and Saga had
inaugurated crash programs of remilitarization. The Ansei purge had dis-
rupted some of this, and Yōdō, for one, had been ordered into retirement by
Ii Naosuke. During his absence from the scene a group of samurai had gathered around a charismatic figure named Takechi Zuisan. Their charter, which
they signed in blood, justified the formation of such a secret group on grounds
of loyalty to emperor and to daimyo. In view of the humiliation that "our
divine and magnificent country" had suffered at the hands of the barbarians,
"our former lord [Yamauchi Yōdō] was deeply grieved and talked and debated
about it with those in power, but instead of getting action, he himself was
accused and punished." What were men of spirit to do? The answer was simple: "We swear by the deities that if the Imperial Flag is once raised we will
go through fire and water to ease the Emperor's mind, to carry out the will
of our former lord, and to purge this evil from our people."[2] Tosa's first minister, who was maintaining a prudent course of acquiescence to the bakufu
while trying to restructure the domain's economy, became their initial target
and suffered Ii Naosuke's fate. A few months after the *tairō*'s demise the first
minister of Tosa lost his head to assassins. They mounted it at the execution
grounds over a wooden sign that detailed his crimes. In this, the first stage
of what we shall call a loyalist movement, there was still no conflict of loyalties.
There was evil in high places, and cowardly ministers should be struck down,
but it could be done in the name of the domain lord and the Kyoto emperor
whose will the daimyo had been trying to advance.

When the "wronged" lord was returned to favor, however, and proved to
be angered or alarmed by assaults on his ministers, the loyalists began to face
a conflict of loyalties. The daimyo who returned from shogunal disfavor to
the center of politics were still in a difficult position. They did not want to
overdo their role, for to do so would awaken the jealousy and suspicion of
their peers in and out of the bakufu establishment. Moreover it was always
possible that bakufu regulars might be able to reassert their control, and that

mandated caution. They also found themselves presiding over an increasingly turbulent cauldron of samurai opinion. In many cases they were creatures of their leading vassal handlers, men who had the long-term interests of the house and domain in mind. Yet they also had to maintain appearances in the interests of samurai "public" opinion, for by now participation had extended well down the social hierarchy. In 1853 the bakufu's distribution of Perry's letter had requested daimyo response; in preparing they had consulted their upper vassals, and the participation of domain *rōjū* had activated still others on the fringe of the power structure. Lower samurai, the most volatile, were also the most poorly informed on details, but intensely aware that Japan was in trouble. Village headmen and station masters along communication routes received demands for ever greater contributions and resources. Throughout the countryside a growing network of nativist enthusiasts produced volunteers eager to establish their status as participants. Thus daimyo were not, in other words, free agents; they had to keep an ear to the ground and their officials had to watch their backs.

Ideology and politics intersected in several major southwestern domains in plans to influence national affairs. Han statesmen worked with court nobles in devising schemes that would increase the court's—and, not incidentally, their domains'—leverage in national affairs. Chōshū led in this, only to have its proposal trumped by one submitted by Satsuma, and while that was still on track a third and even more sweeping scheme was advanced by Tosa. The daimyo themselves were often cool to ideas of court participation in national affairs, for the court nobles they knew personally were as often as not poorly informed, impractical, and xenophobic. Yamauchi Yōdō of Tosa, for instance, often dismissed them as "long sleeves." Their vassals, with points to score against competing domains, were more likely to see merit in forming working relationships with court activists, and ordinary samurai, especially those tinged by loyalist thoughts of imperial revival, were enthusiastic at the thought of cooperation with elegant representatives of ancient lineage whose proximity to the emperor lent an almost religious element to their planning. Not a few samurai absconded from their domain to take up service with court nobles in Kyoto. As emotions rose and stakes became greater, failure could lead to disgrace and often death. Nagai Uta, who formulated the first Chōshū plan, was condemned to suicide when it failed. Takechi Zuisan, who organized the Tosa/court mission to Edo, suffered the same fate when his lord, secure once again in control of han affairs, decided that Takechi had overstepped his bounds. Indeed, his "crime" illustrated the way loyalist enthusiasm could threaten feudal hierarchy. The judgment against Takechi noted that he had affixed his lord's name to a memorial circulated at court proposing that the entire Kyoto-Osaka plain be given over to the court to manage, and that Osaka merchants be required to provide the resources to fund the security guard that would be required. That done, presumably, it would be possible to drive out the foreigners.

KŌBU-GATTAI

Historians (and nineteenth-century contemporaries) refer to the next stage of politics as the period of *kōbu-gattai,* or union of court *(kō)* and camp *(bu),* Kyoto and Edo. Both sides tried to pull back from the impasse Ii Naosuke had created between the two power centers. *Fudai* daimyo who had traditionally staffed the bakufu's highest posts now took a back seat to men who were strangers to high office. Since the problem was relations with Kyoto, these newcomers spent much of their time in Kyoto, creating something of a division within the bakufu. Matsudaira Keiei (Shungaku), head of the Fukui collateral house, had been disciplined by Ii in the Ansei purge. In the summer of 1862 he was called from retirement and named *seiji sōsai,* or Supreme Councillor, an imposing title that masked a poorly defined office established in the hope of conciliating the aggrieved court. Hitotsubashi Keiki (Yoshinobu), whose candidacy for shogunal succession had so alarmed Ii, was named *kōken,* or Guardian, of the young shogun Iemochi.

Matsudaira Shungaku came prepared with many ideas, most of which had been worked out by his adviser Yokoi Shōnan, perhaps the most brilliant of the defense intellectuals of the decade. He began with a general pardon for all those who had been disciplined by Ii and a call for punishment of the officials who had helped set those sentences. It is not difficult to imagine the consternation of the Edo *fudai* who had directed the Ansei purge. This time it was Nagano Shuzen, Ii's right-hand man in Kyoto, who was ordered to commit *seppuku.* Next came implementation of a step that bakufu leaders had designed before the appointment of the new team. Andō Nobumasa, a lieutenant of Ii Naosuke whose career ended when he was grievously wounded by a would-be assassin, had argued that a marriage connection between the court and the young shogun was the best way to cement relations with Kyoto. In fact it was to have almost the opposite effect. Princess Kazu ("Kazu no miya"), an imperial princess, was proposed as consort for the young shogun Iemochi despite the fact that she was already affianced to Prince Arisugawa. Princess Kazu was carried to Edo in the winter months of 1861–62. Her enormous procession, preceded and followed by supplies and baggage of every sort, took eighty days for the three-hundred-mile trip. The bakufu took massive security precautions, and travel stations along the route found themselves forced to provide thousands more porters than usual.

The proposed match increased anti-bakufu pressures at the court, for it was known that Emperor Kōmei objected to sending his younger sister off to Edo. As tempers rose, court nobles who had helped engineer the match in hopes of increasing political leverage for Kyoto found themselves in danger. Iwakura Tomomi, a future builder of the modern state, was one. He and five associates were reviled as "four scoundrels and two matchmakers," and as the court grew increasingly radical he was dismissed from his posts and took shelter outside the capital. It was now that emissaries from Kyoto, accompanied by strong forces of samurai from southwestern domains, began to arrive in Edo with demands for expulsion of the foreigners. The first of these, in which eight hundred Satsuma men accompanied the court noble Ōhara Shigetomi, was on its way back to Kyoto when it encountered a party of English who remained mounted as they watched it pass. An indignant Satsuma samurai cut down one of them, a merchant named Richardson, an event which had portentous consequences for bakufu foreign relations.[3]

Activists were beginning to refer to the emperor as a "jewel," possession of which could be the ace card in future politics. The bakufu, with his security in mind, appointed the young head of its vassal house, Matsudaira Katamori of Aizu, to a new post, Protector of Kyoto. His assignment was to keep other and possibly hostile forces from getting control of the court. He fulfilled that role ably, and, despite one assassination attempt, held the post from the day of his appointment to the fall of the bakufu, managing to avoid alienating either it or the court. In addition to the 1,500 Aizu samurai he kept in Kyoto he could call on the resources of his younger brother, who was also a daimyo. Few figures in late Tokugawa times were more effective, something the future Meiji leaders could never manage to forgive.[4]

Late in 1862 the bakufu relaxed its regulations for *sankin-kōtai* so that daimyo could look to their defenses for the anticipated war with the foreigners. They now needed to be in attendance at Edo only one year in three, and they were permitted to remove their families from Edo. This change produced hundreds more processions as family dependents, military entourages, and baggage horses moved slowly along the major arteries. The strain on highway stations that were expected to deal with this, and on surrounding villages from which they drew their porters, grew apace.[5] Even worse was to come.

Traffic reached its height when the young shogun himself traveled to Kyoto in 1863 to pay his respects to a newly confident court. Not since 1634, when Iemitsu had traveled with a mighty host, had a shogun visited Kyoto. But while Iemitsu had gone with strength to overawe court and daimyo, Iemochi went from weakness to conciliate in hopes of gaining strength.

The young shogun was treated with courtesy in Kyoto, but what had been expected to be a short visit grew longer as more ceremonies were scheduled, culminating in a grand imperial progress to the Kamo Shrine accompanied by the shogun and large numbers of court nobles, daimyo, and samurai, to pray for divine assistance in driving out the foreigners. It was clear that the court was in charge, and not the bakufu. Ironically, this was probably best shown by a clear authorization of civil rule issued by the emperor to the shogun—one the shogunate had never felt necessary in earlier years. Indeed, if one follows the arguments presented earlier about the Tokugawa state, this "commission" was a late Tokugawa concept that owed a good deal to the diffusion of Mito scholarship and ideology. Iemochi was to visit Kyoto two more times. In 1864 he joined a group of daimyo for a ceremony in which a court chamberlain read a document quoting the emperor to the effect that "I cannot sleep at night, nor can I take nourishment at the state of the realm." The shogun was to die in Osaka on his third visit to the Kansai area in 1866.

Even the "authorization" to rule carried its price; Tokugawa Keiki accepted, on behalf of the bakufu, a court directive to drive the foreigners out of Japan by June 1863. This was of course patently impossible, and most of those involved knew that it was. But it seemed wise to show "sincerity." Bakufu leaders hoped they would be able to delay implementing that, and also that they could persuade the powers to accept some delay in opening the ports. They tried the latter first, with a mission to Europe that tried, by an agreement known as the London Protocol, to secure acceptance of a delay in opening Edo, Osaka, Kobe, and Niigata for five years, but instead of cooperating, England and France, worried about the safety of their nationals in Japan, landed a force of 1,500 men to guard the foreign settlements in the summer of 1863. This was an increasingly unreal world. Keiki dutifully promised on behalf of the shogun that the bakufu would drive out the foreigners, with no intention of trying to do so, while the bakufu implored the powers to delay without much expectation that they would do so. It might, one supposes, have stood as evidence that they had done their best. With delaying tactics of this sort, the bakufu was now using tactics that had been used in dealing with Perry and Harris in an attempt to hold off antiforeign extremism. This temporizing did not bode well for the future.

The swings of policy now became particularly complex. A series of intertwined narratives makes it easier to follow developments from regional or ideological perspectives than to see the whole process in perspective. Those narratives include struggles for the control of domain politics in Satsuma, Chōshū, and Tosa; for control over and manipulation of the court and nobles in Kyoto; over the direction of bakufu politics and policies; and among the foreign representatives to realize the privileges they had been promised in the treaties. "Loyalists" who linked emperor with expulsion attacked their opponents as "bakufu supporters," but the Tokugawa ranks themselves were far from united, and even the little group of foreign representatives, although they took a hard line on diplomatic issues, had deep fissures as European rivalries reappeared in Japanese waters. It will be useful to chart events in order to show how they conspired to accelerate the change in court, domains, and bakufu.

For a period it seemed as though *kōbu-gatai* cooperation between a cooperative bakufu and a more reasonable court might bring results. In the sum-

---

Last Days of the Bakufu

1860   First bakufu mission to the United States to ratify treaty. Ii Naosuke assassinated ("Sakurada Gate" Incident).

1861   Chōshū's Nagai Uta, in Kyoto, opposes expulsion (subsequently condemned to *seppuku*). Russians occupy Tsushima, retreat at English demand. Princess Kazu leaves Kyoto for Edo.

1862   Assassination attempt on *rōjū* Andō ("Sakashita Gate" Incident). Appointments of Matsudaira Shungaku, Hitotsubashi Keiki; "Bunkyū" reforms. Matsudaira Katamori assigned to Kyoto defense. Relaxation of *sankin-kōtai*.

1863   Court authorizes emissary to Edo to order expulsion. Shogun Iemochi travels to Kyoto. Chōshū, "obeying" order, shells foreign ships in Shimonoseki Straits. Aizu and Satsuma troops drive Chōshū out of Kyoto. English shell Kagoshima in retaliation for Richardson's death.

1864   Chōshū units try, and fail, to seize control of court. Bakufu orders campaign against Chōshū. British, French, Dutch, U.S. ships shell Shimonoseki.

1865   Chōshū submits to bakufu; internal coup reverses policy, and bakufu orders second punitive expedition.

1866   Satsuma-Chōshū alliance against bakufu. Bakufu-Chōshū war halted on death of emperor and shogun. Hitotsubashi Keiki named shogun. Urban riots; *ee ja nai ka* movement. Bakufu launches sweeping reforms with help of France.

1867   Shogun, in Kyoto, resigns office. Proclamation of Restoration of Imperial rule. Satsuma-engineered coup brings on Toba-Fushimi battle and "Boshin" civil war.

mer of 1863 Aizu forces that had been commissioned to guard the court combined with Satsuma units in seizing control of the palace gates. Satsuma and Chōshū had their own legacy of suspicion and rivalry. Domain administrators were alarmed by the insubordination shown by antiforeign zealots; and the daimyo of all the southwestern domains except Chōshū were taking steps to suppress their radicals. Satsuma regulars routed a group of loyalists they surprised at a Fushimi inn in 1862, and Yamauchi Yōdō, the Tosa lord, broke up the Tosa loyalist league and condemned Takechi Zuisan to *seppuku*.

The warships of the foreign powers also played their part in bringing the Japanese together. The bakufu found that it was held responsible for every antiforeign act of terrorism, despite the fact that its control over daimyo and their samurai was not total. On two occasions, however, the foreign powers did their part in showing that expulsion of the foreigners would not be a simple matter and punished the offending domain instead of the bakufu. In response to the murder of the merchant Richardson in 1862, English warships shelled and burned the Satsuma castle town of Kagoshima in 1863. And when Chōshū, where a strongly radical party had taken control, decided to carry out the imperial order for expulsion on its own by shelling foreign shipping in the Straits of Shimonoseki in 1863, its gun batteries were destroyed by a flotilla of British, French, Dutch, and American warships the following year. At Kyoto the court was also shaken by evidence of radicalism and insubordination on the part of its alleged adherents. Young court nobles joined forces with antiforeign radicals in several quixotic attempts to raise the imperial flag. Then in the summer of 1864 Chōshū radicals went so far as to challenge the Aizu-Satsuma protective cordon that had been thrown around the imperial palace. They suffered a bloody defeat, and the most radical court nobles fled the city for exile in Kyushu. The emperor was indignant at this clear insubordination and the damage done to his capital, and Chōshū was branded an "enemy of the court." Not content with that, the court demanded that the bakufu take steps to punish Chōshū for its temerity and intemperate conduct.

THE TOKUGAWA RALLY

The Bunkyū program of reform had at its center the hope for cooperation between bakufu and the great lords, especially the daimyo of Satsuma, Tosa, and Chōshū, in the interests of preparing Japan for the opening of the ports. The presence of those lords, who had previously been excluded from participation in national affairs, was supposed to deter the bakufu from self-centered, "selfish" direction. Unfortunately daimyo, each a petty emperor within his realm, were not accustomed to collegial cooperation. When things went badly they tended to return to their domains from Kyoto, and from that base they were likely to think and bargain with parochial interests in mind. It began with Matsudaira Shungaku, an architect of the program, who resigned his post of Supreme Councillor and returned to Fukui, where he was followed by an order to enter domiciliar confinement. By the summer of 1863 he had been pardoned, but the distrust that had been building between Edo regulars and outside meddlers deepened. Shimazu Hisamitsu of Satsuma and Yama-uchi Yōdō of Tosa were equally prone to register dissent by departure, and proved quite as "selfish" as the bakufu they were out to restrain. The unrealistic discussion of expulsion of the foreign powers distorted plans for cooperation and alarmed Edo administrators who had to deal with the outside world, and the domination of a group of radical antiforeign zealots in Chōshū removed that domain from the conference table and earned it condemnation as an "enemy of the court."

Under these circumstances the apparent triumph of reason in Satsuma and Tosa, where domain administrations had turned against their radicals, and the clear evidence that Chōshū loyalists had overplayed their hand encouraged Edo administrators to think about a restoration of bakufu authority. Even more compelling arguments for the restoration of discipline were closer to hand in Mito, where an insurrection broke out in 1864. The movement had its origins in ideological and factional lines that had formed in Nariaki's time. Embittered samurai and *rōnin* gathered in the area around Tsukuba, refused to disband, and then grew in number and potential. The bakufu ordered fourteen daimyo to mobilize against the insurgents, whose pronounced aim was a descent on Yokohama to drive out the foreigners. The Mito administration was in total disarray and only gradually responded to the crisis. As disorder grew the bakufu found its own military seriously deficient and called for assistance from more daimyo. Then, just at the time that Chōshū insurgents were being routed in Kyoto, the pacification of Mito began to make headway; daimyo who had wavered decided to support the bakufu orders, and the Mito force, defeated in full battle, shrank to several hundred *rōnin* who tried to make their way to Kyoto. When they finally gave in to vastly greater forces, bakufu retribution was ruthless; hundreds were beheaded.[6]

This insurrection, and the events that had embroiled the Kyoto-Osaka area, helped to convince conservatives that it was time to reassert Tokugawa authority. The defeat of radicalism in the Kansai and Kantō coincided with the chastening of antiforeignism in Satsuma, where the English had shelled and burned Kagoshima, and in Chōshū, which now found itself quite isolated.

The bakufu moved to exploit its advantage. Twenty-one daimyo were ordered to mobilize against Chōshū. The expedition was to be led by the lord of Owari, and even Satsuma cooperated fully with it. It proved unnecessary to fight. Within Chōshū the crisis brought on factional battles that finally ended in the victory of a conservative group that was willing to accept bakufu conditions. The three domain elders who had led the attack on Kyoto were ordered to commit suicide and their heads were sent to bakufu commanders, together with assurances that four lesser staff officers had been executed. The radical court nobles who had fled Kyoto with the Chōshū forces were removed to Kyushu for confinement.

Not content with this, the bakufu had decided a few weeks earlier that *sankin-kōtai* regulations would be restored; daimyo who found it difficult to travel were offered transport on steamships the bakufu had acquired. Some domains had rented space to commoners, and now daimyo were warned that they were not to let their Edo residences be used by others. The attempt was not a success. Small daimyo near at hand responded, but many larger domains remained silent. Early in 1865 the bakufu reminded them that they were expected to come. In 1866 bakufu administrators sent questionnaires about the residences and their staffing that were designed to show their state of compliance. But most daimyo, and all large domain daimyo, ignored these messages. The court, as was increasingly the case, also interfered, sending instructions to Edo that daimyo should be permitted to concentrate their resources on rearmament. It was clear that this time it was the bakufu that had overreached.

Bakufu conservatives were also dissatisfied with the disposition of the case against Chōshū. They wanted the domain reduced in size, and demanded that the daimyo and his son be sent to Edo in formal and public penance. Nor were they content with things at court. In 1865 Edo dispatched two *rōjū* with 3,000 troops to Kyoto with the goal of exerting more direct control over the court. Hitotsubashi Keiki, who was considered unreliable and too moderate, was recalled to Edo. They also backed away from other cooperative ventures. At Hyogo Katsu Kaishū, an innovative young official (and former student of Sakuma Shōzan's) who had been in charge of the first steamship sent across the Pacific, had established a naval training school that enrolled spirited and able young men from all parts of the country, even *rōnin*. Katsu's assistant was a young *rōnin* named Sakamoto Ryōma, who had fled his native Tosa to join the many young activists eager to take part in national politics; he had set out to assassinate Katsu only to be persuaded that military preparedness made better sense than antiforeign heroics, and helped Katsu recruit others like him. This sort of thing looked suspicious to Edo conservatives; Katsu was soon out of his job and Sakamoto a refugee in Satsuma.

Each of these retreats carried a price. The court was not impressed by these measures, and let it be known that the system of alternate attendance should not be reestablished. The "united front" of Satsuma, Aizu, and Edo that had brought Chōshū to heel broke up over the new round of bakufu demands, for few were comfortable with the idea of calling the Chōshū lord and his son to Edo.

It then proved that the Chōshū problem had not been solved after all. Before its concession the Chōshū radical government in that domain had been recruiting irregular military units that included commoners. In practice these were usually sons of the village elite, headmen and the wealthy farmers, men whose social standing had given them near-samurai status and whose literacy had made it possible for them to be passionately aware of the national and domain crisis. The Chōshū surrender government now ordered them to disband, but instead they rose in revolt to strengthen the radical faction and force another change in domain political leadership. This insurrection, for that is what it was, did not involve disrespect to the daimyo, for that worthy, something of a political cipher, simply changed his position once again and continued to head the domain.

In view of these developments bakufu administrators had to rethink their course once more. Reform-minded men argued the importance of national unity and military growth and advocated lenient treatment for Chōshū and close consultation with the other great domains, while conservatives argued the case for a second expedition against Chōshū, one led by the young shogun himself. They were confident that the domain would submit a second time once it saw that overwhelming force was being arrayed against it.

They were wrong. The radicals who had seized power took a firm stand against the bakufu; they knew they had their backs to the wall and that no compromise was possible. The bakufu had difficulty getting cooperation from other domains a second time. Satsuma leaders, who had helped work out the terms of the original compromise settlement, now saw themselves threatened by the possible subjugation of Chōshū and wondered whether they themselves would be the next targets for a victorious bakufu.

There were also alarming indications that Edo leaders had found promising sources of support for military modernization from the France of the Second Empire. Léon Roches, a diplomat who had won his spurs in Algeria, arrived in Japan in the spring of 1864; before long he had become the senior member of the foreign representatives. Roches saw opportunities for his country in the Tokugawa eagerness to obtain technology, training, and equipment. A bakufu military mission was dispatched to France. Sweeping reforms envisioned a commoner conscript army. At Yokosuka French technicians were beginning work on an iron foundry and armory. Since a victorious and united bakufu would be able to command resources far superior to those available to any of its vassals, it is not surprising that leaders of Satsuma were anxious to prevent Edo from becoming too strong. Satsuma leaders were working more closely with court nobles, and it is probable that they had their hand in some of the decrees that countered bakufu policy.

Unfortunately for Edo, Chōshū refused to buckle, and a military advance became necessary. Many elements of the bakufu-led alliance were half-hearted in their participation, while the Chōshū defenders, fighting on their home territory and for their very lives and honor, were far more motivated. Bakufu attempts to invade Chōshū were unsuccessful at every point. The bakufu was saved from its embarrassment by the death of the shogun Iemochi, which made a truce inevitable. Tokugawa Iemochi died at the age of twenty in Osaka, where he had come to "lead" the campaign, as the news of military reverses came in.

This time it was clear that there was no real alternative to Hitotsubashi Keiki as shogun; he was promptly named successor and invested early the following year. Approval of this succession was one of the last acts of the Emperor Kōmei, who died late in 1866.

THE TOKUGAWA FALL

Keiki was shogun for less than a year. How was it that the man generally thought to be the most promising political figure of his time had so short a tenure? Granted, he was not eager for the appointment, realizing its problems; granted also, he was, by general agreement, indecisive; and granted further that he was distrusted by many of the Edo "regulars." Nevertheless problems remain. Within a few months of his accession things seemed to be going better with the foreign powers. He had plans for a cooperative council of sorts in which all the great lords would have a voice. The program of military modernization undertaken with French help was on schedule, and he dispatched his younger brother to France to represent Japan at an international exhibition with the expectation that he might succeed him after further seasoning. Yet within months all this was in ruins and Keiki was on a warship headed for Edo in retreat from his pursuers.

Bakufu miscues in the attempted suppression of Chōshū gave strength to a new program contained in the slogan *tōbaku*, "overthrow the bakufu!" Exclusion was clearly no longer possible, but *tōbaku* could be combined with loyalism, *sonnō*, quite as well as *jōi* exclusionism had been. There was now a new perception among men who had been animated by antiforeign sentiment that the bakufu, while sobered by its setbacks, was turning to cooperate with the foreigners; consequently they themselves shifted their animosity from the foreigners to the bakufu. The brief rally in which bakufu conservatives had shown signs of trying to reassert their control then served to coalesce disparate domain forces into a united front against the bakufu.

This was not an easy or an obvious choice. The disputes of a decade had raised provincial and domain consciousness and distrust, and if bakufu leaders found French military advisers less threatening Satsuma leaders were no less impressed by the British guns and ships that had devastated Kagoshima. Chōshū was still beleaguered behind its borders, under sentence from the court. Yet somehow the changing image of the bakufu began to unite men and forces that later fell apart.

It will be useful to see these events through the eyes of one unusual figure whose career cuts across all the barriers of status, ideology, politics, and geography that have been discussed. Sakamoto Ryōma was born a *gōshi* (country samurai) in Tosa in 1835. He was a youth when the crisis of Perry's black ships

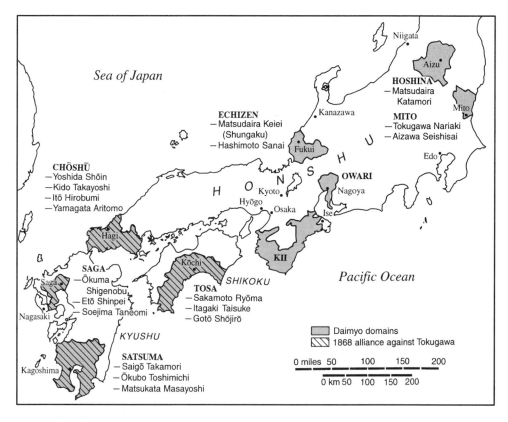

4. The Meiji Restoration: the four leading domains (Satsuma, Chōshū, Tosa, Saga), their leading figures, and others who mattered.

broke the tedium of life in a status-bound society. This provided incentive for study in fencing schools in Edo, and from that came contacts with young braves from other areas. After he returned home he became one of the young loyalists who collected around Takechi Zuisan in 1861. A younger son without family responsibilities, Sakamoto felt himself free to break the samurai code. He left Tosa illegally and secretly by a mountainous route to savor the excitement of participation in national affairs. His first goal, direct action, took the form of trying to assassinate Katsu Kaishū, the bakufu *hatamoto* charged with setting up a naval training school. Katsu's cool response to his youthful would-be assailant was to argue with him about the things that had to be done to make Japan secure against the foreigners. Converted from enemy to disciple, Sakamoto became a staunch follower, helping to recruit other *rōnin* for the school. After Katsu lost his job, Sakamoto, who narrowly escaped an assassination attempt, took cover in Satsuma, together with a courageous young woman who had helped save his life and now became his wife. With Satsuma help Sakamoto was now able to launch a small commercial operation. His Kaientai was something between a primitive navy and cargo company, and it carried contraband from Nagasaki to Chōshū and to Satsuma.

As bakufu leaders stumbled into the second expedition against Chōshū, Sakamoto worked to mediate the political chasm between Satsuma and Chōshū. His *rōnin* wanderings had won him credentials in both camps, and in the early days of 1866 he brokered an alliance between the two military powerhouses. By its terms Satsuma promised not to join the bakufu in the second expedition and to intervene with the court to restore Chōshū to favor. Clearly, the bakufu was now the enemy and had to be replaced or at least restructured.

Sakamoto's own domain of Tosa saw new merit in this *rōnin* with such good connections; Katsu Kaishū intervened with Yamauchi Yōdō to get him restored to duty. The next step was a Tosa-Satsuma agreement. Its text stressed the shameful nature of a land with two governments. "Our first great duty," it read, "is to seek out the national polity and structure of the Imperial Country of old so that we may face all nations without shame . . . There can not be two rulers in a land, or two heads in a house . . . is there anywhere else that there is a national polity like this? We must reform our regulations and return political power to the court, form a council of feudal lords, and conduct affairs in line with the desires of the people in this manner; only then can we face all nations without shame and establish our national polity . . . Let us elevate the wisdom of the ruler and loyalty of subjects, seeking out the great peace and carrying out for all the people of the realm a governance of generosity, humaneness, wisdom, and compassion."[7]

This brief examination of one individual's awakening can suffice to show the speed with which consciousness changed in a decade of crisis. What began as outrage against intrusive foreigners had become anger directed at a polity that did not conform to international standards. The agreement's references to a "council to be established in Kyoto" show that Sakamoto had also become aware of ideas of representative government and collegial cooperation through his contacts with progressive figures in Edo. Central to this was a proposal he made to the Tosa *rōjū* Gotō Shōjirō that the Tosa daimyo be persuaded to submit to the shogun a proposal whereby he could achieve peace with honor in a new structure that would replace Tokugawa with imperial hegemony. Under its terms a council of lords would provide a firmer basis for a unified political structure.

Sakamoto Ryōma's Eight-Point Plan was the basis for the Tosa petition on which the last shogun surrendered his powers.

1. Political power of the country should be returned to the Imperial Court, and all decrees issued by the Court.

2. Two legislative bodies, an Upper and a Lower house, should be established, and all government measures should be decided on the basis of general opinion.

3. Men of ability among the lords, nobles, and people at large should be employed as councillors, and traditional offices of the past which have lost their purpose should be abolished.

4. Foreign affairs should be carried on according to appropriate regulations worked out on the basis of general opinion.

5. Legislation and regulations of earlier times should be set aside and a new and adequate code should be selected.

6. The navy should be enlarged.

7. An Imperial Guard should be set up to defend the capital.

8. The values of gold, silver and goods should be brought into line with those in other countries.[8]

This maneuvering came to a head in November of 1867. Edo modernizers were pushing their reforms to produce a more effective bakufu, and Satsuma and Chōshū were readying their troops for a military confrontation. In Kyoto Tosa representatives presented the shogun with their daimyo's proposal that he resign his office and titles. The court would rule, but a two-house council made up of daimyo and court nobles would direct new treaties, the building of an imperial army and navy, and correct the errors of the past.

Yoshinobu (Keiki) agreed. He announced his decision to the daimyo who were on hand; their images remain bowed in respect and loyalty in the audience chamber of Kyoto's Nijō Castle. He did not consult people in Edo, but it is clear that he saw this course as a way of escaping the predicament of responsibility without power. Under the new conciliar system, after all, he would remain first among his peers, his position strengthened by the success of the modernization steps under way in Edo. But this does not lessen the importance of his decision. The Tokugawa polity was at an end. Gotō, the Tosa domain elder who had been summoned to Nijō Castle to hear the announcement, wrote Sakamoto in elation: "The shogun indicated to us his intention of handing over his administrative powers to the throne, and tomorrow he will petition the Court to this effect. There will be a council chamber with an upper and a lower house . . . This is the event of a millennium. I could not delay in telling you, for nothing will cause more rejoicing in the country."

THE MEIJI RESTORATION

The Satsuma leaders had been quite willing to propose that the shogun surrender his powers, but they did not regard this as a solution, for they had more sweeping aims in view. Unlike Tosa, which had sponsored the resignation request, Satsuma and Chōshū were large enough and strong enough to see themselves as central to a new structure. Satsuma leaders Saigō Takamori and Ōkubo Toshimichi had been working with the court noble Iwakura Tomomi, newly restored to favor after he had fallen into disgrace for favoring the marriage of Princess Kazu to Iemochi, to secure a court authorization for striking down the bakufu. A letter from Ōkubo to Iwakura argued that "if everything is allowed to proceed as it is, and the great issue of how to govern the country is delegated merely to the hard work of the Imperial Court and to the consensus reached by the three highest positions within the [long ineffective] Council of State, then war is to be preferred . . . We urge you to think through the matter carefully and consider all the alternatives. It is most important that the first step in the new government is not a mistaken one . . . At the present time, regardless of whatever arguments may be advanced, it is necessary to demote the *shōgun* to the position of an ordinary daimyo, reduce his official rank by one degree, let him return his domains, and let him ask for the pardon of his crimes."[9] In other words, nothing short of an abject confession of error and surrender of all Tokugawa territories would provide the basis for a new system. Iwakura secured for them an order from the new boy-emperor to chastise the Tokugawa.

It is possible to argue that two, in fact three, programs were under way in the waning weeks of 1867. Edo administrators were rushing the modernization of the bakufu military structure. Satsuma and Chōshū were preparing to have their way by force of arms. The Tosa lord, aware of both alternatives, tried to head off violence and secure a resignation in the hope that this would bring a peaceful and equitable solution.

Keiki's resignation had created a void. The court ordered nearby daimyo to stay in place. It seemed likely that the rescript authorizing an attack on the bakufu would be withdrawn. Satsuma, Tosa, and Chōshū leaders cajoled their daimyo and rushed their preparation. On January 3, 1868, the court proclaimed the Restoration of Imperial Rule of Old (*Ōsei fukko no daigorei*).

That same day a little group had met at the residence of Iwakura Tomomi to set in motion plans for their units to seize control of the palace gates. Keiki was ordered to surrender his lands as well as his powers. Unsure of his course, he retreated to the Osaka Castle to attend a meeting previously arranged with representatives of the foreign powers. By then Kyoto was securely within the control of the coalition headed by Satsuma. After some hesitation Keiki yielded to the pleas of his indignant vassals; he remonstrated to the court, and then decided to contest the issue by force. A battle on the approaches to Kyoto, at Toba-Fushimi, followed on January 27. In sharp fighting bakufu units were subjected to withering fire along the way. Unprepared for battle and poorly led, they fell back on Osaka. Keiki returned by ship to an Edo he had not visited during his brief reign as shogun. The Restoration War (*Boshin sensō,* so named for the zodiacal cycle) had begun. It would continue until the surrender of the last bakufu naval units in Hokkaido in the spring of 1869.

2. The Open Ports

This political narrative does little justice to the complexity of the 1860s, for at each step the story was affected, and sometimes determined, by the presence and problem of the foreigners. It was they who provided the figured bass against which the complex counterpoint in Restoration politics was played out. Bakufu efforts to delay opening of the ports were undone by violence directed against Japan's unwelcome guests, and bakufu concessions to the powers in satisfaction of such violence drew greater charges of shame and cowardice. From the opening of Yokohama on, issue after issue—currency exchange, channels of trade, violations of security—found the bakufu losing round after round. Every concession opened the door a little farther and alarmed an often xenophobic imperial court. Bakufu officials did their best to rein in or at least delay the schedule of opening that had been set in Harris's treaty of 1858 at the same time that they found it necessary to prod the court to cancel its sweeping orders for expulsion. At the very end Keiki had just won an expensive victory by forcing the court to agree to the opening of

Hyōgo (modern Kobe) when the Restoration drama came to its climax, thus defining the "crimes" for which the bakufu was held to account.

There were also ways in which the bakufu could gain by the open ports. If Japan was to stand off the West at all remilitarization was urgent, and modernization of the military could be best carried out by importing up-to-date equipment. Of all Japan's political units the bakufu had the first and best chance to gain by a program of import, and it had the most resources as well.

Dutch naval officers developed a naval training school at Nagasaki immediately after the coming of Perry, and the domain of Saga, responsible for the defense of Nagasaki, provided over one-third of the student body. The Saga daimyo, who was welcomed on a visit to a Dutch warship, invited the Dutch instructors and bakufu students to visit the Saga school of Western learning, only to have the bakufu superintendents *(bugyō)* veto the idea out of fear that bakufu and Saga men would grow too friendly.[10] They had some reason to be careful, for of all the Tokugawa rivals Satsuma and Chōshū were the best positioned to acquire modern technology thanks to their proximity to Nagasaki.

Throughout the 1860s the foreign representatives were concerned chiefly with trade, while their Japanese counterparts were focused on politics. "The West," as W. G. Beasley puts it, "saw the system in terms of commercial advantage, [but] both Chinese and Japanese were preoccupied with the political disabilities it imposed on them. They made economic concessions almost without thought."[11]

England and France took the lead in the struggle to implement the treaties. The United States was torn by civil war, and Russia, weakened by the Crimean War, turned to internal reform. As a result most of the diplomats involved in the decade had served on the China coast before coming to Japan. It must be granted that their frustrations were real enough, but to them they brought attitudes that had taken shape in China. Conciliation, they thought, would be construed as weakness, and successful diplomacy depended upon the willingness to use force whenever necessary to win a point. One finds this well stated in the writing of Rutherford Alcock, Britain's first minister to Japan from 1859 to 1861:

> It is weakness, or the suspicion of it, which invariably provokes wrong and aggression in the East . . . Hence it is that all diplomacy in these regions which does not rest on a solid substratum of force, or an element of strength, to be laid bare when all gentler processes fail, rests on false premises, and must of necessity fail in its object—more especially, perhaps, when that end is peace.[12]

When Yokohama was opened to foreign trade in 1859, the first problem that came up was that of currency to be used in commercial transactions. Harris demanded the exchange of silver coins by weight, but bakufu officials realized that the silver content of their coins was greater and resisted this. But this problem was soon eclipsed by a greater one. Not only were there major discrepancies between Japanese currency used in the Edo and in the Osaka areas, but an even greater disparity concerned the ratio between silver and gold; in Japan the silver ratio was approximately 1 to 5, but the world level was closer to 1 to 15. Foreign traders quickly realized the profits to be gained from exporting Japanese gold *ryō* to Shanghai, converting them to silver there, and returning to begin again. This "gold rush," as one author describes it, forced the bakufu to realign its entire currency, something probably desirable in view of the fact that there were an estimated sixteen hundred issues of paper money and multiple issues of coinage in circulation in the 1860s. While this was taking place, however, a galloping inflation complicated life for urban Japanese; in 1862 the Edo city magistrate reported that living costs had risen by 50 percent.

There was also a consistent undertone of danger and violence for foreigners outside the enclave of the treaty ports. Many of the terrorists were trying to provoke war with the foreigners; others wanted to make a political point by embarrassing the bakufu, and still others were simply xenophobic swordsmen. The bakufu felt it had little alternative to yielding to foreign demands for monetary satisfaction for attacks on foreigners; political concessions in the form of more ports would have cost it more. As a result a good deal of currency left Japan. In 1861 Townsend Harris's interpreter, Henry Heusken, was cut down in Edo. Harris's response was relatively measured, but when the British legation at Tōzenji was attacked by Chōshū samurai six months later Britain called for satisfaction. The most expensive case of all was the murder of the English merchant Richardson. Britain demanded not only monetary satisfaction but execution of those responsible in the presence of British observers. The bakufu paid the naval commanders for each day they were in Japanese ports. When the bakufu could not force Satsuma to produce those responsible a strong detachment of British warships sailed into Kagoshima harbor to seize Satsuma warships; in the gunfire that resulted much of the city was burned. Chōshū's attempt to carry out the expulsion edict by itself in June 1863 brought down on it the wrath of each of the powers who had ships at hand as they joined in shelling the Shimonoseki batteries. Each of these incidents became the basis for a demand for satisfaction for which the bakufu, though not primarily involved, was held responsible, and the major sums—one hundred thousand British pounds, paid as three million dollars

Mexican for the Richardson incident—had to be paid over in hard currency that was secretly loaded at night to ward off more violence. At that, the Satsuma and Chōshū people sometimes charged the bakufu with being in collusion with the foreigners, "striking them with foreign hands."

Against this background of danger, bakufu requests that the schedule of port openings be delayed fared poorly. An early effort led to a London Protocol of 1862 that was undone by the violence, and a second mission sent to Europe to ask for a delay was so poorly timed that the emissary found himself agreeing to advance the schedule, only to return, be dismissed, and denounced. Life was often difficult and dangerous for foreigners and the merchants who dealt with them, and the attacks that resulted provoked the Western powers into additional measures that fastened the treaty port system on the country. In 1864 a regiment of soldiers was brought up from Hong Kong and stationed in the capital to protect the foreign representatives.

At the very last an additional element of competition between England and France came into the picture in the persons of Léon Roches, minister from France's Second Empire from 1864 to 1868, and Harry Parkes, British minister from 1865 to 1883. Both men were experienced colonialists; Parkes had begun as an interpreter in Canton, and Roches had spent several decades in North Africa. In the major disputes concerning opening and terrorism, the foreigners stuck together, but as bakufu power began to wane the two men saw different opportunities for their countries. Parkes remained ostensibly aloof from political involvement, but a visit he paid to Satsuma, added to his consistent pressure on the bakufu, led to the impression that English policy favored the southwestern domains. A pamphlet written without authorization for a treaty port paper by Ernest Satow, his able interpreter (and, much later, successor as minister), entitled "On English Policy," circulated widely in Japanese translation and was taken as a statement of British intentions. Satow argued that the shogunate and the powers should work together to get a formal authorization of the treaties from the imperial court, as it seemed to be gaining power. Roches, on the other hand, saw an opportunity for France in providing the bakufu assistance for development and arms. The Japanese would be able to pay for this through a large-scale export of silkworm egg cards to France, where silk production had been afflicted by a deadly blight. A French military mission was sent to train a new bakufu army, and French engineers began the construction of the naval base and arsenal at Yokosuka. Both ministers' efforts helped to speed political change: the perception of British favor lent support to advocacy of unification around the emperor, and the fear of a bakufu stronger because of France's assistance made it more urgent to act against it while there was still time.

The 1860s also provided opportunities for individual Western businessmen, and their activities sometimes had political consequences. Dealers in arms stood to make handsome profits from trade at a time when bakufu and domains were rearming frantically. Some, like the Scottish merchant Thomas B. Glover (whose Nagasaki residence is shown to tourists as the "Madame Butterfly House"), ingratiated themselves sufficiently with the southwestern domains to become the subject of legend. Glover arrived at Nagasaki in 1859 and began as something of a subcontractor to the great China coast firm of Jardine, Matheson & Company. By 1862 he had established his own firm, beginning with the export of Japanese tea, an enterprise he directed through a largely Chinese work force. By 1864 the political turmoil in Japan offered larger profits in arms and ships, and Glover opened branches in Yokohama and Shanghai. In 1862, as part of its movement to encourage daimyo to rearm, the bakufu had rescinded its ban on the purchase of foreign ships by daimyo, and thereafter small steamers, many of which had seen better days in service on the China coast, were eagerly purchased by bakufu and daimyo alike. In the decade of the 1860s 167 ships were imported, 116 of them via Nagasaki.

Much of this trade was on long-term credit at high rates of interest. Glover managed to get capital from Jardine (which held itself aloof from the surreptitious arms trade) and other providers. He played a major role in the import of more than a half-million rifles imported at Nagasaki and Yokohama between 1865 and 1868, 7,300 of them purchased by Chōshū in preparation for its war on the bakufu. Glover was also involved with the development of the Takashima coal mine near Nagasaki; its output was used by American, French, German, and Russian naval ships. Currency exchange between Yokohama, where the Mexican dollar was strong, and Nagasaki, where Japanese currency was stronger, and Shanghai, where rates of exchange were different again, offered further opportunities. Glover was often dangerously overextended, as when he loaned Satsuma Mexican dollars which he had received as bakufu contract payments for Armstrong guns without receiving permission from Jardine, to which it was due. In later days Glover boasted of his contributions to the Tokugawa fall, but the record indicates that his loyalty lay with his ledgers and that he dealt gladly with any authority whose requests promised rapid profits. The times, as one British consul at Kanagawa reported, "brought into the commercial field a large number of adventurous men with little or no capital, eager to make rapid fortunes and quit the scene. These imported into business a sort of gambling spirit, which soon gave rise to a degree of competition and reckless speculation which the trade could not possibly sustain."[13] In time Glover lost his firm, but he did not quit the scene; he died in 1911 while serving as consultant to Mitsubishi.

A final observation to make concerning the role of foreigners is that they contributed significantly to the demolition of Japan's status society in the areas where they were to be found. Japanese entrepreneurs were not slow to set up places of amusement for sailors, and the prints of Sadahide provide colorful documentation of partying in the Yokohama Gankirō and other brothels. Ordinary merchants and visitors may have played even larger roles. The journal of Francis Hall, who was at Kanagawa and Yokohama between 1859 and 1866, makes absorbing reading for its unintended illustrations of the way curious and even well-meaning foreigners could change the quality of life. No one can question the advisability of men's providing themselves with pistols, but picnic excursions to islets in Edo Bay that ended with target shooting had to constitute disruptions of the moral order to ordinary Japanese, who were puzzled by these self-confident outsiders. So too with innocent but determined ethnographic curiosity that could lead to booted foreigners marching through ordinary people's houses. On the one hand commoners' discovery that the samurai, for all their vaunted bravery and courage, seemed helpless to do anything about this, had to speed the realization that Japan's social structure no longer made much sense. For sworded samurai and *rōnin*, on the other hand, such unconscionable behavior must have been an infuriating reminder of inferiority. Add liquor to such rage, and another careless foreigner was likely to be in danger of his life.[14]

3. Experiencing the West

There was intense opposition to the entry of outsiders into Japan, but few Japanese leaders had qualms about going to the West themselves. Some thought that Westerners in Japan would threaten the body politic through the diffusion of Christianity, and others felt that their presence stained the sacred soil of the Divine Country and constituted an implied threat to the emperor; most feared that tolerating their entry invited a form of colonialism. China seemed to offer an object lesson; its government had been unable to keep the foreigners out; it had lost sovereignty over sections of its coast, and a bizarre form of Christianity had resulted in the disasters of the Taiping Rebellion. But none of these dangers were attached to sending Japanese abroad. Even Tokugawa Nariaki had proposed that, if trade was what the Westerners wanted, he be sent to trade with them, and no less a nationalist than Yoshida Shōin had tried to sail with Perry. To learn from the West, and master the secrets of its strength in order to repulse its advance, meant traveling to the West.

An initial step was to undertake serious study of the West. With the coming of Perry forward-looking bakufu officials proposed the establishment of an institution that was to become the Bansho Shirabesho, or Institute for the Study of Barbarian Books. The principal focus, they agreed, should be on military matters, but these related to other disciplines. As Katsu Kaishū put it in a memorial, the institute should deal with

> military matters and gunnery. Within the school orders [should be given] to set up faculties for the study of astronomy, geography, science, military science, gunnery, fortification, and mechanics.

His proposal was seconded by Tsutsui Masanori, who argued that

> It is urgent that we know more about the West; by studying the truly useful things like the strength and weakness, the semblance and the reality of each country, the state of its army and navy, the advantages and drawbacks of its machinery, we can adopt their strong points and avoid their shortcomings . . . [We should translate] books on bombardment, on the construction of batteries, on fortifications, books on building warships and maneuvering them, books on sailing and navigation, books on training soldiers and sailors, on machinery, books that set forth the real strength and weakness, appearance and reality, of these countries."[15]

The growing awareness of the utility of such studies was reflected in the institute's name; within a few years it became the Institute for Western Books, and then the Institute for Development (Kaiseijo). The center was soon crossing domain barriers and hiring men from all parts of Japan. Many domains, Saga and Satsuma among them, did their best to organize similar schools. Experts in foreign studies were soon in great demand.

Such studies soon led to study and travel abroad. The first opportunity came with a mission to the United States in 1860 to ratify Townsend Harris's treaty. The 1860 embassy included a total of seventy-seven men, and a number of the travelers left journals of their impressions. To judge from their diaries, the leaders did not have much curiosity; they were concerned more with maintaining their dignity. The chief ambassador's account has little interest in technology; its author shows a fastidious distaste for bizarre features of American society like the presence of women at state occasions, and he was particularly unimpressed by the unseemly disorder of the United States Senate session he witnessed. "One of the members," he writes, "was on his feet haranguing at the top of his voice, gesticulating wildly like a madman. When he sat down, his example was followed by another, and yet another." After a reception at the White House he proudly recorded his hope that the "barbarians would turn their faces upward" to contemplate "the glory of our Eastern Empire."

Others saw it differently, as when Walt Whitman, after watching the procession that marched down Broadway in honor of the embassy, exulted "Superb faced Manhattan / Comrade Americans!—to us, then at last, the Orient comes." These flights of national exultation aside, the mission had great importance as the first fully authorized voyage abroad by a Japan about to reorient itself toward the wealth and strength it sensed in the Western world. The ambassadors realized the importance of their role; their forebears had traveled to China a millennium earlier, and they themselves were following in that tradition, albeit in the opposite direction.

The ambassadors' lack of curiosity was only part of the story, for some who were selected to go with them learned much more. The American ship on which the Japanese embassy traveled was accompanied by a small steamer the bakufu had received from Holland. The *Kanrin maru*, which had reached Nagasaki in 1857, was 163 feet long and powered by a 100-horsepower engine. Although an American advisor was on board, the Japanese crew, commanded by Katsu Kaishū, managed on its own and its members exulted on the success of Japan's first trans-Pacific journey. Moreover, not all the members of the mission were equally fastidious about keeping to their rooms. Several young men who served as interpreters were full of curiosity about the things they saw, and went on to become some of nineteenth-century Japan's most important intellectuals. Several of them got to travel again two years later, as members of the mission instructed to seek a delay in the opening of the ports. It failed in that purpose, as would yet another in 1864, but each time the Japanese learned more about the West. The 1860s saw a steady advance in the pace of missions; they were more frequent, more purposeful, and their members were increasingly sophisticated in the information they brought back. Successive ambassadors worked harder than the first group; they saw more, and reflected more. They soon realized that it was industrial development that distinguished strong nations from weak nations. Paris might be more beautiful than London, but England, for all its dirt and noise and the squalor of its urban poor, generated more power. "When it comes to trains, telegraphs, hospitals, schools, armories and industries," one account stressed, "England must have twenty times what France does."[16] Mission followed mission; a sixth was abroad at the time of the bakufu fall in 1867, and shogun Keiki's younger brother was in Paris being groomed for future leadership.

Recognition of the need for modernization of Japan's military institutions meant that the bakufu and large domains undertook programs of Western-style armament. It was quickly apparent that traditional samurai fighting tactics, in which officers were responsible for providing their own retainers, porters, and equipment, had to be replaced. But this, in turn, involved institutional changes. Close-order drill for units armed with modern rifles required uniformity and discipline, and for this sturdy commoners could serve as well or better than a pampered hereditary samurai class. A number of domains developed units that included nonsamurai. Chōshū, where Yoshida Shōin had advocated such moves as early as the 1850s, led in this; in the fighting to seize control of domain leadership and to resist the bakufu's punitive expeditions Chōshū's "special units" *(kiheitai)* performed well. Other domains followed suit; by the late 1860s the bakufu, in its final reform phase, was developing plans by which samurai could utilize their stipends to hire commoners to enter the ranks.

The dispatch of students overseas also brought changes in its wake. The bakufu led here as well, and an initial party of eleven was sent to Holland by way of Java in a Dutch ship in November 1862. Their orders were to study navigation, law, and medicine, but it was difficult to restrict curious minds. Nishi Amane, one of their number, wrote his Leiden tutor that "I should also like to investigate the field of knowledge which is called philosophy or science, yet distinct from religion, which is not allowed by the law of our land—that field which in former times was represented by Descartes, Locke, Hegel, Kant, and others. This subject seems to be very difficult to learn but . . . would, I feel, contribute to the civilization of our country." On his return Nishi was assigned the task of drawing up a constitution to incorporate decision sharing between bakufu and domains.

Two great domains were not far behind the bakufu. In 1863 the Nagasaki merchant Thomas Glover helped five young Chōshū men to travel to England for study. Two of them, former students of Yoshida Shōin, were to go on to become leaders of the Meiji government. On hearing that a foreign force was preparing to shell the Chōshū batteries at Shimonoseki, Itō Hirobumi and Inoue Kaoru rushed back to try to head off this disaster, but their compatriots refused to listen to their advice and the bombardment went off as scheduled. A third member of the group, Yamao Yōzō, remained abroad until 1870, working at a shipyard and studying at a technical college in Scotland. On his return he would become head of a the Meiji government's Technological College (Kōbu Daigakkō), an institute with six faculties that would employ forty-seven foreign teachers between 1873 and 1885. Satsuma too worked through Glover at Nagasaki. In 1865 fourteen young men, ten of whom had been attached to the domain's own Kaiseijo, or Institute for Development, were sent off for study in England and France. This was part of an ambitious plan that contemplated shipping Okinawan and Satsuma products to Shanghai in English ships in order to build economic strength for the purchase of armaments. Five of the students later became distinguished figures in Japan. They traveled widely and drank deeply at the fountains of Western strength. One, Mori Arinori, entered a utopian community and returned after the Restoration to become a diplomat and the architect of the Meiji education system. Another, the future diplomat Terajima Munenori, utilized a visit to Holland to warn his countrymen that Holland was no longer an important country. Future efforts, he wrote, should concentrate on the truly great powers.

And one made it on his own. Niijima Jō, assigned the study of Dutch and then of navigation by his domain authorities, made his way to Hokkaido and managed to be taken on as cabin boy on a ship bound for America in 1864. Thence he made his way a decade later to become one of the founders of the Meiji Christian church and Dōshisha University in Kyoto. Once they were abroad, these young men were particularly convinced of the need for basic changes in Japan. The outside world became less threatening and its achievements more inviting. They also became more conscious of their nationality as Japanese, and of the need for centralization and unification. Within a decade of their departure they were back in Japan, forming the inner cadre of a remarkable generation of modern-oriented specialists for the new government.

Of all the travelers, none took his task more seriously than a young interpreter and student of Western learning who became his generation's leading intellectual and educator. Fukuzawa Yukichi was born in Kyushu in 1835. He studied Dutch in Osaka, and entered bakufu service in the Institute for the Study of Barbarian Books before being assigned as interpreter to the first two embassies to the Western world. He proved a young man of inexhaustible curiosity and energy, and spared no effort to collect books and information about the countries he had visited. On his return he set about writing a volume that became his generation's textbook about the West. *Seiyō jijō,* or *Conditions in the West,* circulated so widely that mention of it is encountered in the diaries and correspondence of virtually every major figure of the day. The first section, which appeared in 1866, sold an estimated 150,000 copies, and pirated editions probably provided readers as many more. Writing in a lucid, simple style that was accessible to anyone, Fukuzawa relayed exactly the kind of information which the Japanese at that time were needing to substantiate their shadowy vision of the Western lands—namely, simple, concise accounts of everyday social institutions such as hospitals, schools, newspapers, workhouses, taxation, museums, and lunatic asylums.[17]

For people of this stamp, the return to a Japan seething with fear and resentment of the foreigners was often traumatic. Fukuzawa tells of his trepidation sitting in a barber's chair while the barber, gesticulating with his razor, railed against specialists in foreign learning; he breathed a silent prayer that his identity would not be discovered. Nishi Amane, freshly home from his studies in Holland, wrote in despair to his Leiden tutor after the proclamation of imperial restoration to prepare him for the likelihood that he would not hear from him again, for antiforeign zealots had seized control of his country. Instead, with the realization of what it was that Japan had to do to become strong, the zealots' cries for death to foreigners gradually gave way to enthusiasm for "civilization and enlightenment," and both Fukuzawa and Nishi found themselves in an almost oracular position. Fukuzawa wrote in his autobiography:

> During this mission in Europe, I tried to learn some of the most common-place details of foreign culture. I did not care to study scientific or technical subjects while on the journey, because I could study them as well from books after I had returned home. But I felt that I had to learn the more common matters of daily life directly from the people, because the Europeans would not describe them in books as being too obvious. Yet to us those common matters were the most difficult to comprehend. So whenever I met a person whom I thought to be of some consequence, I would ask him questions and would put down all he said in a notebook . . . After reaching home, I based my studies on these random notes, making the necessary research in the books which I had brought back, and thus had the material for my book, *Seiyō jijō*.[18]

Between the voyage of 1860 and the time of his death in 1901 Fukuzawa earned recognition as nineteenth-century Japan's foremost modernizer. Founder of Keiō, destined to become Japan's first private university, commentator on cultural and public matters in a never-ending series of essays and books, his influence permeated every aspect of Meiji life.

4. The Other Japanese

The Restoration drama is usually treated largely from the point of winners and losers; both samurai, supplemented by a few adventurous court nobles. To leave it there, however, is to treat their countrymen as inert—or, as Confucian writers often put it, as *gumin*, "stupid commoners." In actuality "commoners" came in many varieties, and few of them were stupid. Throughout the country there was a stratum of families, usually of some property and tradition, who served villages and districts as intermediaries between samurai authority and village reality. They bore different titles in different areas—village heads (*shōya*) and *nanushi* in western Japan, district chief (*gunchū sōdai*) in bakufu territories, station master (*honjin*) along highway communication routes, and many more—but these were the people who made the system work. They were invariably literate and usually responsible; respected and sometimes distrusted by those they represented and usually claimed to "protect," and essential to but also distrusted by those whose income they collected as tax.

Although there were no ordinary newspapers or routes of information, these people were often surprisingly well informed about national affairs. They were also drawn into the fringes of intellectual controversy and change. Nativist thought, especially Hirata-school *kokugaku,* found a receptive audience among them; its romantic view of an archaic past in which rural patriarchs served the village shrines and ordered the village fields described their self-image, and its reminder of a sacral ruler free from the restrictions and hierarchies of a military bureaucracy spoke to their aspirations and discontent. As the Tosa *shōya* league of 1841 phrased it, "we can see that we were once commissioned directly by the Imperial Court, and if we look at it this way, is not our work anything but humble? Should we not say that the *shōya,* who is the head of the commoners, is superior to the retainers who are the hands or feet of the nobles?" With pride there was also prudence: "Since ours is work which easily incurs the suspicion of the *han* administration on the one hand and of the people we rule, who are quick to point out our weaknesses on the other, we must always be on the alert."[19]

Shimazaki Tōson's epic novel *Yoake mae* (Before the dawn) embodies all these themes in treating the era through a (lightly disguised) picture of his father, a *honjin* station master on the central mountain highway between Edo and Kyoto.[20] A network of nativist scholars provides linkage to the intellectual trends of Hirata *kokugaku;* a pride of ancestry in service animates the station master in his response to the needs of the domain authorities, and a certainty of place and identity separates the stratum of station masters from the farmers and tenants of their village. Strains of the 1860s place almost unbearable burdens on the station, as it has to commandeer hundreds of bearers from surrounding villages, far beyond what was usually required, to man the imposing entourages of daimyo, bakufu emissaries, the eighty-day journey of Princess Kazu to Edo, the pursuit of the Mito *rōnin,* and bakufu and daimyo forces. The opening of the ports brings additional traffic as silk merchants transport their goods to Yokohama. There was no hope of keeping knowledge of what was afoot from people along these communication routes. Nor was there doubt that lines of authority would become frayed, and break at times. Hanzō, the station master, trying to interrogate his tenants about a disorder during his absence, is asked a question that had resonance for all in authority; "Were you actually expecting someone to tell you how things really are?"

Men of this stratum were essential to every move of rearmament that domains and bakufu undertook. Their sons joined the ranks of special units that trained with modern arms. They were the ones who corralled the enormous amounts of labor that a samurai army required, and they were the ones who had to manage the quartermaster functions of movement and supply.

Merchants also played a role. The support of provincial businessmen like the Mitajiri merchant Shiraishi in housing and supporting Restoration activists in their ceaseless travels provides one case. Bakufu and domains alike responded to the extraordinary needs for rearmament and security by pressuring their merchants to subscribe with special contributions optimistically described as *goyōkin,* "money needed for official purposes"; samurai found their stipends reduced with similar euphemisms. More than ever before domains tried to husband their resources by eliminating imports from other areas at the same time that they tried to organize monopolies for their own exports.

To make things worse, the last decade of bakufu rule was marked by a number of events that further reduced the margin of adequacy for normal life. The first was a cholera epidemic that struck Japan shortly after the opening of the ports, a disaster that carried off many lives and reduced birth levels for several years. This was a worldwide pandemic, but its virulence in Japan— where it spread northeast, beginning at Nagasaki—was clearly related to the opening. The massing of bakufu and daimyo armies around Osaka for the lengthy period that preceded the second expedition against Chōshū was also a factor in a ruinous outbreak of illness; Emperor Kōmei was among those claimed by smallpox. To make matters worse, rice crops were poor in the last years. It may have been partly in response to this widespread uneasiness and sense of change and doom that the last of the great mass frenzies, the *ee ja nai ka* ("isn't it grand!" or "isn't it O.K.?") movement of 1867 broke out. Its character, all observers agree, quickly produced a carnival atmosphere in the great cities. Outbreaks began in the Kyoto-Osaka area, which had also been the center of the mobilization for the Chōshū campaign, with rumors that amulets from the Ise shrine were falling from the skies; commoners interpreted this as a sign of better things to come. It soon spread along the Tokaido to Edo, and constituted a significant obstacle to bakufu attempts to keep order. Some bakufu supporters suspected that activists of the imperial cause were somehow involved.

That commoners were aware of the momentous events of the decade can also be proven from other evidence. Despite prohibitions to the contrary, there was a pervasive spread of wall scribbling commenting on the disruptions of society and the ineffectiveness of those in charge. Scholars point to the diffusion of *kawaraban,* crudely printed pictures with text that relayed information, though often distorted and inaccurate, to commoners; these served as news broadsheets into the Meiji period. Such evidence provides valuable indications of the way urban commoners reacted to the events of the times. Some were imaginative reconstructions of ships, people, and events, others gave a fanciful description of defense installations in anticipation of the war that many expected, and still others, though humorous in tone, were bitterly satirical and critical of the bakufu and its efforts. Not a few were antiforeign. For example, a depiction of Perry as a Buddhist devil was glossed by a text that described the image as having

> an arrogant crown; in its right hand is a gun and bayonet; from its left hand hangs a depth-sounding rope; from its mouth pours great praise of its own country, but its chest is so full of evil spirits that it has a smoke stack coming out of its back to expel fire and smoke . . . The image lands here and there on islands where it reveals its true nature as the wild and fearsome sword-wielding Myōō. Its esoteric words are: "I have given you the letter twice; hurry up and reply." Its gang of wild men are far off, so you can come and see the black ships.[21]

Not all popular representations were this nationalistic, of course. English seamen who landed at Shimonoseki to spike the Chōshū batteries that had caused the mischief were surprised to have villagers who had been watching the cannonade come down to give them a hand. Kagoshima natives who watched the English flotilla sail away after starting fires that destroyed much of their city were impressed by the shipboard band that serenaded and celebrated their achievements. But everyone, or almost everyone, knew, and had to know, that things were out of joint.

5. The Restoration Remembered

Interpretations and memories of the 1860s dominate the historical memory of modern Japan. The stirring story of the plotting and fighting between Restoration activists and bakufu supporters grips the historical memory of the present, and fiction and television serials combine to keep it fresh. As was the case with the American Civil War, partisanship in evaluation has receded as time has passed. There was an abundance of heroes on both sides; duty, courage, and idealism were not exclusive to either side. Much of the plotting had taken place in restaurants and inns, where loud conviviality might have been expected to arouse little suspicion. In that setting women also played their part. Repeatedly high-spirited, courageous, and intelligent hotel maids and entertainers entered the story to warn and save their lovers. Kido Takayoshi and Sakamoto Ryōma both married young women whose courageous action saved their lives.

After the Restoration, to be sure, the leaders of the Meiji state saw to it that succeeding generations would see things their way: the decade was to be a story of the battle of courageous young men determined to free their country from the shackles of semicolonial status to which it had been reduced by Tokugawa feudalism. The historical commissions that sponsored official narratives had advisory boards on which each of the great southwestern domains was represented. Meiji government leaders have been commemorated by multivolume, authorized biographies that guard the subjects' memory and contribution for the future. Collectively, these accounts focus on the struggle, centered in Kyoto, to restore the emperor to rule, something that was prerequisite to national unification and salvation. Histories of the Tokugawa fall, on the other hand, focus on events in Edo, where bakufu officials did their best to protect government and state from the consequences of the violence of antiforeign extremists and win time desperately needed for rearming and modernizing the country's institutions. As a result there are two narratives, which seem to intersect only at points of conflict.[22] Neither is incorrect, but each needs to be considered in full awareness of the other.

An additional complication derives from the fact that no one, however affiliated, would disavow respect for the emperor, and that by the time the builders of the Meiji state had done their work all actors remembered that they had been second to none in wanting to shelter and strengthen the throne. This "Meiji bias," as Conrad Totman has called it, tended to distort the past as well as the present and future. The era of warrior rule was redrawn in line with Mito teachings to emphasize shogunal dependence on the moral authority of the court, the Meiji rule became a long-deferred return to moral certainties, and adherence to those values held up as the inescapable duty of every true Japanese. This bias in turn tended to deprecate bakufu efforts, and encouraged historians to overlook the violence of the decade and the depth of disagreements that divided Japanese in the 1860s. Losers in those struggles tried to restore their honor by professions of loyalty, while winners could sublimate their ambition to the imperial banner.

The Restoration years were remarkable for a transformation and transvaluation of ideas that were dimly conveyed by militant slogans. These sometimes seemed personified in men whose courage and ideological "purity" made them proper candidates for canonization by the modern imperial state. In many cases untimely, tragic death kept memory from being contaminated by the compromises that practical politics required of those who survived.

Japanese associate the Restoration process with the activities of a colorful

group who styled themselves, and have been known to posterity, as *shishi*—
men of high purpose. These activists tended to be young samurai of modest
rank and income. Their world was less structured by ritual than was the world
of their betters; with less to lose they felt free to bond closely with friends,
to party and to plot. Unencumbered by the obligations that were attached to
high status, they were relatively free to cross domain borders. They mingled
in the fencing schools that sprang up as samurai rediscovered their calling and
in heated discussions of national affairs. They began as impulsive hotheads,
imperfectly informed about the context of foreign affairs and prone to quick
judgments and simplistic solutions. They were not afraid to die and not afraid
to kill, and their participation in national politics introduced an explosive
element to the tangled debates of the 1860s.

Self-interest and self-image could enter in. For some participants the political scene provided a welcome release from the tedium of daily life in a status-
bound society. The Tosa activist Sakamoto Ryōma wrote his sister contrasting
the excitement of his *rōnin* life with that at home, "where you have to waste
your time like an idiot." Takechi Zuisan experienced a brief moment of triumph as part of the Tosa escort for a court mission to Edo, and wrote his
wife that "I'll get to enter the castle, and see the shogun"; hardly able to believe
his new standing, he went on to say that "I'm followed everywhere I go by
these fellows: it's like something on the stage." Others, like Maki Izumi, who
died by his own hand after the disasters that struck the loyalist cause in 1864,
responded to national affairs with a continuous sense of rage.

It was the imperial cause that legitimated, or required, setting aside normal
standards of morality and duty. When Sakamoto entered the Tosa loyalist
league in 1861 he joined in the pledge that "if the Imperial Flag is once raised
we will go through fire and water to ease the Emperor's mind," and he wrote
his sister to stress the fact that that was what had to matter most. "The idea
that in times like these it is a violation of your proper duty to put your relatives
second, your domain second, to leave your mother, wife and children—this
is certainly a notion that comes from our stupid officials . . . one should hold
the Imperial Court more dear than country, and more dear than parents."[23]
The official reading that was given to the violence of the Restoration days by
the Meiji government endorsed these sentiments fully. Extremism in defense
of loyalism was virtue. Two of the men who took part in the murder of Henry
Heusken, Townsend Harris's interpreter, and five others of the "Tiger Tail
Association" to which they belonged were posthumously awarded imperial
court rank.[24]

The era and its movements is also remembered by its slogans. After Perry
jōi and *kaikoku*—expulsion and opening—seemed to polarize opinion. In

fact, as Totman has shown, the two could overlap in many ways.[25] It was possible to recognize the inevitability of opening and nevertheless object strongly to the manner and degree of the bakufu's capitulation to Western demands. There was an ethnic revulsion against foreign presence on Japanese soil, but particular dread of foreign proximity to the imperial court and the Kansai area. One is struck by the frequency with which the loyalists vowed to "relieve the emperor's mind" and charged the bakufu with causing that mind to be "disturbed." The court had a sacral quality that grew in importance as the debate intensified.

After the *kaikoku* "opening" was a fact, the phrase *sonnō*, "revere the emperor!" became a powerful and amuletic term. No one opposed reverence for the throne, but this did not necessarily become advocacy of an active political role for the emperor. High Edo officials and many daimyo had reservations about entrusting matters of practical detail to court nobles whose existence was dominated by empty ceremony; in contrast, starry-eyed *shishi* vied to attach themselves to the household of activist courtiers. Two such nobles were killed in connection with impractical putsches, and another five fled with Chōshū troops when Aizu and Satsuma took control of the palace gates; their disposition was one of the issues in the bakufu expedition against Chōshū. One of them, Sanjō Sanetomi (1837–1891), later played an important role in the early Meiji government.

After the violence of 1864 a new polarization came to the fore, expressed in the terms *sabaku* and *tōbaku,* calling for the preservation or overthrow of the bakufu. It was still several years before men in high places would admit complicity in plans to overthrow the shogunate, but on lower levels *shishi* showed no compunction. The discourse was most vocal in Chōshū, which found itself having to choose between submission and defiance. The years 1864 and 1865 were critical in this regard. Once it was clear that the bakufu itself might be in danger, some who had been vocal in criticism backed away from their more youthful admirers. This was the case with Aizawa Seishisai, whose "New Theses" had won a steadily wider readership among young radicals. The growing intensity of ideological disagreements in Mito reinforced his conservative sentiments. By 1862 he was drawing examples from China to argue that "if we refuse to enter into friendly relations, we will make all foreign states our enemies and will not be able to maintain independence among them,"[26] but shortly after his death in 1863 the Mito civil war showed that many of his compatriots had drawn other lessons from his earlier writings.

Tōbaku, "overthrow the bakufu!" required an alternative, and that came increasingly to be expressed in the term *fukko,* "restore the old!" The term carried romantic nostalgia for a more pure past that surrounded the imperial court. Restoration of the purity of antiquity was an important theme in *koku-gaku* politics, but it was not limited to that. In the domain of Kaga a combination of practical motives—the han's desire to stop having to import—and local patriotism produced a *fukko-kutani* school determined to rediscover the techniques of a style of ceramics that had atrophied centuries before.[27] Artists also tried to recapture the painting style of schools that had been important at the very dawn of Tokugawa times. A school known as *fukko Yamato-e* also related to politics. It centered in Kyoto, where Tanaka Totsugen (d. 1832) tried to recapture tradition in screens he did for the imperial palace in 1790. Ukita Ikkei (1795–1859), his disciple, was himself imprisoned in the Ansei purge. Okada Tamechika (1823–1864) was determined to study the Heian period Ban Dainagon scroll. In his eagerness to see the original, he cultivated Tokugawa officials who could arrange it, thereby angering Chōshū radicals who tracked him down and murdered him in 1864.

The Restoration years provided many heroes but few villains for modern Japanese memory. Military campaigns against the northern domains in the warfare of 1868–1869 to some degree resemble those of the American Civil War, with a nostalgia of romance and intensity shrouding winners and losers alike. The fight was "for" the emperor and "about" the commoners, though both were assumed to want their thinking done for them and neither was much involved. Those who gave their lives in the Restoration (Boshin) War were soon enshrined in what became the Yasukuni Shrine in Tokyo, where their spirits were later joined by the millions sacrificed in Japan's modern wars. The official account of the Boshin War, the *Fukko ki* (Annals of the return to antiquity), had an editorial board with representatives of the southwestern domains to guarantee the acceptability of the its heroic narrative.

Few of the losers in that war were "wrong" in popular memory; a number of Tokugawa commanders who held out to the end were soon co-opted to serve the modern state. An exception must however be noted for the daimyo of Aizu and his samurai. Matsudaira Katamori's determined stand as Protector of Kyoto ended with the defeat of his troops at Toba-Fushimi in the opening rounds of warfare, but thereafter he withdrew to his castle town of Wakamatsu and prepared to resist the enemy from the southwest. He had the moral support of a league of large northern domains whose leaders distrusted the purposes of the newly "imperial" army of Satsuma, Chōshū, Tosa, and Saga and tried to negotiate the submission of Aizu. When push came to shove the larger units of that league offered only perfunctory resistance to the "imperial" armies, but in Aizu the domain's resolution was matched by the ferocity of the attacking force of some 30,000 men that advanced through mountain passes and river valleys. The castle was besieged for more than two weeks; its supplies and manpower gradually weakened, and then it was subjected to a withering cannonade from the best guns that had been imported from the Western world. The siege and fall of the castle became the closing epic of samurai warfare. Domain commanders, with their usual indifference to commoners' lives, ordered the city put to the torch to facilitate the fighting. A group of several dozen samurai youths, known to history as the White Tigers, thought that all was lost and committed *seppuku* on seeing the flames. Aizu lost close to 3,000 of its samurai before the daimyo surrendered. The domain was confiscated, and a year later the Matsudaira remnants were offered a niggardly patch to the far north so impossible to cultivate that many of the 17,000 samurai and dependents who "followed" their lord there soon had to plead with the new government for help in burying their dead.[28] Aizu remained under the cloud of designation as an "enemy of the court" until 1928, when the union of a Matsudaira granddaughter with Prince Chichibu, Emperor Hirohito's brother, took place; the event was greeted with joy as the long-awaited "restoration of honor to Aizu."[29]

Different times, different heroes. In imperial Japan Sakamoto Ryōma received only modest honor; its Victorian codes of dutiful sons and proper deference had limited tolerance for an individualistic, self-willed youth who deserted family and lord to pursue ambitions that seemed suspiciously personal. After World War II, however, those same qualities set him apart from the Meiji leaders whose "success" had brought Japan its modern wars. Sakamoto came to enjoy genuine popularity. His image, bolstered by popular fiction, television serials, and posthumous endorsements of every sort, has far outsped those of his more orthodox contemporaries.

6. Why Did the Tokugawa Fall?

The sudden and largely unanticipated collapse of the Soviet Union in our day provides a new departure for consideration of the question that has beggared much discussion of the history of nineteenth-century Japan. The bakufu had more experienced people, access to better resources, and better advice than its rivals. If its military commanders had conducted themselves more adroitly than they did at Toba-Fushimi in 1868, the insurgent Satsuma-Chōshū forces would have been hard put to continue. Shake-ups in some castle towns, accompanied by the ritual suicide of leaders of the resistance, could well have papered over fissures in Tokugawa governance for some time. Instead that failure started a bandwagon effect in the domains along the line that doomed the effort to maintain the old order.

In some sense, however, the old order was unsustainable when confronted by the crises of foreign affairs. The bakuhan construct did not have enough unity to become a modern state. Yet at the last serious efforts were under way to make it one. The reforms of Keiki's closing year might have gone far to provide a new, at least a regional, structure. Fear that they would, in fact, gave urgency to the bakufu's enemies. The British interpreter Ernest Satow wrote that in talks with a Satsuma leader in 1867, "I hinted to Saigō [Takamori] that the chance of a revolution was not to be lost. If Hiōgo [Kobe] was once opened, then good-bye to chances of the daimiōs."[30]

One nevertheless wonders whether reconstruction was a viable option. Modernizing regimes seldom survive to reap the benefit of their work; cautious openings and relaxation of controls, as the Soviet leaders found, can all too readily create an irreversible momentum. The bakufu discovered this when it tried to reinstate regulations for alternate attendance. Initial reforms can alienate stalwarts (in this case the Edo *fudai* daimyo) and activate their opponents. The *tozama* daimyo, so long excluded from participation in affairs, had proved themselves incapable of playing a constructive collegial role; their first thought was of their own relative advantage. Tokugawa *fudai*, no less than their "outside lord" contemporaries, were preoccupied with details of provincial budgets and reforms. All daimyo in the 1860s were conscious of the fragility of their hold on the saddles of power. Samurai bred to dismiss the wisdom and worth of commoners had to keep one eye on those below them. Some of the bakufu's best units never saw action, partly because they were on watch against ordinary Japanese.

Bakufu leadership was also badly divided between men who had spent enough time in Kyoto to know the political realities there and others in Edo who had their eyes on the foreign threat. The last shogun was himself reluctant to undertake a thankless and unpromising assignment. From shogun on down, there was a lack of will and determination, brought on by suspicion that the existing order could not long be perpetuated.

The aura and charisma of the Kyoto court made new coalitions possible. This was quite independent of the wishes of the sovereign; Kōmei, for all his indignation at the signing of the treaties, seems to have preferred the bakufu to the alternatives in sight, and Mutsuhito, who succeeded him and "authorized" the coup that brought an end to the bakufu, was too young to be a player in the game at all. But at the same time the court as institution or society contained enough able men whose discontent and discernment provided the legitimacy and leverage the Restoration leaders needed. Even so, one is struck by the degree to which the power of those in charge had eroded. Shoguns Iesada and Iemochi were never in charge, while Keiki was at best a troubled, uncertain actor. At court Emperor Kōmei was uneasy with those who strove to "serve" him, while Mutsuhito was too young and new to participate. In virtually every domain leadership lay with bureaucrats who set the tone for policies, eyed their counterparts in other principalities with caution and suspicion, and "handled" their lord in national affairs. Within this group strength of character, access to military support, and resolution carried the day.

The "Restoration" itself was a coup, and the revolution was still to come. It was the crisis of the foreign presence that provided the explosives for the bakufu's demise.

11

The fall of the bakufu and the emergence of a new, professedly imperial government left everything for the future. Some who had taken the rhetoric of antiforeignism at face value expected the men now in charge to institute sweeping xenophobic measures that would reverse the steps toward westernization that the shogunate had begun. It will be recalled that the young Nishi Amane, a bakufu student newly home from study in Holland, wrote his Leiden professor that he should not expect to hear from him again. A group of Tosa samurai, on guard in the port city of Sakai, felt free to murder eleven French sailors. They were wrong; Nishi was soon an important figure, and the Tosa samurai were ordered to disembowel themselves in the presence of French representatives. As soon as the most urgent matters had been taken care of, almost half of the leadership group departed on a lengthy mission to learn the secrets of Western wealth and power.

Others, schooled in the rhetoric of *kokugaku* that had become so prevalent among advocates of restoration, thought they saw the dawn of a fundamentalist and theocratic state that would return Japan to the imagined purity of antiquity. Early ritual made use of those precedents, but it was not long before Shinto enthusiasts realized that practicality and rationality ruled that option out. A group of reform leaders, intent on building a state capable of holding its own in the modern world, bent Shinto to their purposes without allowing it to distract them from the work at hand.

There were differences on dealing with the West and on ideology, but there was substantial agreement on the need to extricate Japan from the incumbrance of late Tokugawa feudalism, which could safely be denigrated as the "evils of the past." The new regime began with consensus on this point. It experi-

mented with governmental institutions of antiquity and found them impractical. It offered prestige and place to representatives of the old elite before rele-
gating them to the sidelines. It experimented with a campaign for cultural
unity that did little more than alarm its countrymen. By trial and error, with
little fanfare and firm suppression of disgruntled samurai, the new reform
leaders led in what became the Meiji revolution.

1. Background

For the fifteen years that followed the overthrow of the bakufu the principal
drive of Japan's leaders was to bring order and unity out of the divided sovereignty of Tokugawa days. One can date the "restoration" of imperial rule from
the edict of January 3, 1868. The first step was to change the palace guard with
Western-armed troop units of the domains and lords that had emerged as
leaders: Satsuma, Owari, Aki (Hiroshima), and Fukui. Chōshū was still under
the ban. In Tosa the lord, Yamauchi Yōdō, hesitated, suspecting that the ex-
shogun, who had acceded to his advice, was going to be betrayed. His chief
vassals, however, alarmed at the thought that delay would cost their domain
a place at the council tables, saw to it that Yōdō was there and kept their
troops nearby.

Next came the edict announcing a "renewal of all things" and an end to
warrior misrule that had saddled the country for so long. The wording for
this had been worked out for the court noble Iwakura Tomomi by his Shinto
adviser and ghostwriter, Tamamatsu Misao. With additional input from Satsuma leaders, particularly Ōkubo Toshimichi, they worked out language that
combined grandiose pronouncement of renewal with excoriation of past leadership. This was then put into the hands of the fifteen-year-old (by Japanese
count) emperor Mutsuhito. This coup, for that is what it was, led to the anguished protest of the ex-shogun Keiki and the military campaign of the
Boshin War against northeastern domains.

Alternatively, the "restoration" can be dated from the five-article Charter
Oath that was prepared for the young ruler. He proclaimed this on April 5,
1868, before a gathering of nobles and daimyo. This is in many ways a better
date to select, for its propositions, while phrased in extremely general terms,
proved sufficiently prophetic of what was to come for Emperor Hirohito, after
Japan's defeat in World War II, to cite them as evidence for the continuity
of national and dynastic purpose. We shall turn to these shortly.

What matters at the outset, however, is the fact that Japan, which began
the Meiji period as one of the modern world's most fractured polities, emerged

within a generation as one of its most centralized states. In the 1860s Karl Marx was telling his readers in the columns he wrote for the New York *Herald Tribune* that it was only in Japan that a truly feudal state, with all its irrationalities and divisions, was still to be found, but by the 1890s the Chinese scholar-diplomat Huang Tsun-hsien was writing from Tokyo to describe to his countrymen a central order and control far superior to that of China.

How was this possible? The change came far more rapidly in Japan than it had in the West. The United States managed to combine a regulatory state with its federal system only toward the end of the nineteenth century. England, France, Russia, Italy, and Germany had an ever harder time establishing unity throughout the century, and never eradicated pockets of localism as successfully as Japan did. Yet those countries knew a crisis of foreign war and the competition of adjacent countries that stimulated competition for strength and greatness. Japan's wars came only after the centralization had been brought about. China and Korea, Japan's neighbors on the continent, were the centralized empires to which Japanese analysts had traditionally contrasted their system of division. In early Meiji years the Chinese example still seemed to offer possibilities for emulation, but not for long.

There was, however, Japan's burning determination to join the company of the "Great Powers" that had encircled it and restricted its sovereignty. The powers' haughty—as the Japanese saw it—condescension and disdain served as spurs to Japanese response quite as effectively as direct confrontation might have. Erwin Bälz, a German doctor who spent his career ministering to the Meiji elite and to Westerners in Japan, noted with distress that the German minister's wife, on proudly showing him her newly furbished parlor, assured him that "no Japanese will ever sit in it." For other Japanese the European example stirred admiration and accommodation. We are told that Itō Hirobumi, the principal maker of the Meiji Constitution of 1889, was so impressed by the carriage and bearing of Otto von Bismarck that he habitually held his cigar the same way. The Victorian sideburns of British minister Sir Harry Parkes were mirrored on many a Meiji leader's face. Admiration, as well as irritation, could serve to strengthen the awareness Meiji Japanese had of a "class" distinction among nations and leaders; together they stirred the determination of Meiji Japan to break free of its second-class standing in the world of nation states.

Determination, however, would not have sufficed to explain the speed of Japan's transformation. It is important to remember the peculiar nature of the landed settlement of Tokugawa centuries that went before. Of all the feudal lords who headed Tokugawa domains very few—Satsuma's was the most conspicuous—knew tenure that went back to medieval times. The great majority had come to prominence as the result of the Sengoku wars and the centripetal institutions of Tokugawa feudalism that accompanied the peace. The lords did not "own" their domains, but held them in trust. By the end of the period the shogun himself was only first among equals, grateful to the imperial court that commissioned his temporal authority. Legitimacy lay elsewhere, conferred by the secluded emperor. And if the entire realm could be said to be the emperor's, as petitions would soon make clear, that was the equivalent of saying that no one else could lay claim to any part of it. The ruling class was not really "landed," but held land in stewardship and lacked any base from which to protest.[1] Since, in addition, it was also compensated rather generously for its willingness to step aside, struggles came with dispossessed samurai but not with their lords. This order was in decided contrast to that in Europe, where many princes and petty sovereigns had enjoyed a tenure that far exceeded that of the national monarch to which they were expected to become subservient.

It now becomes possible to describe and understand the process of Meiji centralization.

2. Steps toward Consensus

Since the Meiji Restoration began as a coup organized by domain officials and court nobles, their first problem was to establish confidence on the part of other domains that the regime they proposed to construct would be something more than a new bakufu under Satsuma domination. This was particularly necessary during the opening year, dominated as it was by the war carried out against northeastern domains, where Sendai had taken the lead in forming a counterleague. There was talk there of using an imperial prince as evidence of loyalty. Nor was distrust limited to the north, for even Tosa men set about organizing a league of Shikoku domains with contingency plans to kidnap the boy emperor and keep him as their "jewel" for use in the political wars of the future. But the fact that even dissidents planned to focus on some aspect of the imperial line in establishing the legitimacy of their enterprise shows that the use of the emperor would provide the key to a solution. The "restoration" team had him securely in their control, and their skillful use of him provided the route to consensus. In the early months of the Meiji period the modernity of centralization and reform was cloaked in the antiquity of the court. A few generations later, when Japanese society was outgrowing the new institutional pattern that had been worked out and was beginning to struggle toward more substantial change, the technique was reversed; the now centralized state utilized the antiquity of the throne in an attempt to choke off further modernization.

The Restoration edict of January began by declaring an end to all previous administrative structures, civil (court) as well as military (shogunal), and instead named a triumvirate of imperial princes. The central figure named was Prince Arisugawa, the younger brother of the late Emperor Kōmei and the once-intended spouse of Princess Kazu in the earlier years of the decade. He was also nominal commander of the Satsuma, Tosa, Saga, and other military units that marched to the east in "obedience" to the imperial command. In November, once it was safe and practicable, the young emperor himself was carried to the north to enter and occupy the shogunal castle at Edo, which was renamed Tokyo (Eastern Capital) in September. A foreign reporter described the way the great palanquin was carried on a frame that raised it a full six feet above the ground. Carried by yellow-robed bearers, it was at the center of a procession of several thousand men. As the palanquin approached, he wrote,

> a great silence fell upon the people. Far as the eye could see on either side, the roadsides were densely packed with the crouching populace . . . As the phoenix car . . . with its halo of glittering attendants came on . . . the people without order or signal turned their faces to the earth . . . no man moved or spoke for a space, and all seemed to hold their breath for very awe as the mysterious presence, on whom few are privileged to look and live, was passing by.

This in turn was followed by other circuits through various parts of the country; the young emperor was literally held aloft as a talisman, a kind of wand, or in Maruyama Masao's term, a festival shrine *(omikoshi)* with which to awe his people.

In 1868 a similar visit to the sun goddess's Ise shrine was prepared by instructions replete with the taboos of Shinto folk religion; those in mourning and women in menstrual period were to refrain from viewing the emperor, lest death or blood bring ritual impurity near his sacred person.

One finds a perfect example of this blending of tradition with intended change in the famous Charter Oath that was issued by the young emperor in April of 1868. It was drawn up by men from the southwestern domains, with Chōshū's Kido Takayoshi and Tosa's Fukuoka Takachika playing particularly important roles. It was designed to allay the fears of non-Restoration domains that they were being excluded from decisions, and held out the prospect that future policies would be based on consensus.

The Charter Oath

1. Deliberative councils shall be widely established and all matters decided by public discussion.

2. All classes, high and low, shall unite in vigorously carrying out the administration of affairs of state.

3. The common people, no less than the civil and military officials, shall each be allowed to pursue his own calling so that there may be no discontent.

4. Evil customs of the past shall be broken off and everything based upon the just laws of Nature.

5. Knowledge shall be sought throughout the world so as to strengthen the foundations of imperial rule.[2]

Read today, this seems an entirely progressive pledge. In the context of its formulation, however, it constituted a shrewd blending of points of view. Yuri Kimimasa, an Echizen (Fukui) samurai who had profited from the thought of Yokoi Shōnan (assassinated in 1869) and Sakamoto Ryōma (killed the year before), first suggested a draft that began with the need to "unite the hearts of the people," spoke of rewarding "men of ability," and ended with working out "all matters" on the basis of "general opinion." Yuri's draft spoke of terms of office of appointees and the importance of giving way to "men of talent." All the Meiji leaders, born to modest rank, had experienced the frustration of service under hereditary incompetents, and they were determined to make openings for "talented" men like themselves. Fukuoka Takachika, a Tosa samurai to whom Yuri showed this, preferred language that would be less alarming; his council was to be one of "feudal lords"; "the people" became "high and low," and opportunity would be provided for *chōshi*, (the *chō* later used for conscripts), "designated" or "appointed" samurai. Kido in turn reworked this once more into its final form, with language broad enough to embrace both readings; officials would be able to "pursue their callings," and "evil" (hereditary) practices would be discarded.

There is something else to note here, and that is the ability of men of like mind from different areas to work together. Yuri Kimimasa, retainer of Matsudaira Keiei (Shungaku), Fukuoka Takachika, whose lord Yamauchi Yōdō had been so ambivalent about the treatment given the last shogun, and Kido Takayoshi, with ties to the military powerhouse of Chōshū but sobered by awareness that his countrymen did not fully trust him—each had different weaknesses, but together they worked toward a future for themselves and for their country.[3]

The final product of this should be seen as a promise of gradualism and equity. "Deliberative councils" and "public discussion" were, after all, terms that had been applied to cooperation between lords of the great domains. That "all classes" were to unite indicated that there would continue to be classes. Even "commoners" were to be treated decently by "civil and military" officers, the privileged ranks of the recent past. No one was likely to be in favor of the retention of "evil customs"; a rather Confucian "Nature" would indicate the path to be chosen. Only in the promise to "seek knowledge throughout the world" was there a specific indication of change; but here, too, late Tokugawa activists had deplored the irrationality of Japan's two-headed government as the only one in the world. Moreover, the search would be selective and purposeful, designed to "strengthen the foundations of imperial rule."

It is the mark of a successful document of state that, phrased in general terms, its meaning can expand with changing circumstances. American readers, with their distinction between the "original intent" of the country's eighteenth-century lawgivers and the expanded role of government required in a modern society, should have no difficulty in understanding that the Charter Oath's generalities, worked out in compromise drafts by a few samurai members of the leadership group, grew rapidly in significance as circumstances changed. Only four years after helping word the oath, the Chōshū leader Kido Takayoshi found himself stalled in Washington, D.C., while two of his colleagues were sent back to Tokyo for additional credentials. As the mission scribe was filling his time by translating the United States Constitution, they discussed the utility of such a statement for Japan. Reminded of the Charter Oath—which he had helped draw up—Kido clapped his hands and said, "Of course! That was in there!" The next morning he said that he had re-read it, time after time; "it is a superb document; we can never allow that spirit to change." Even more striking was the use Emperor Hirohito made of the Charter Oath in the rescript he issued January 1, 1946, in which he renounced the "false conception that the Emperor is divine and that the Japanese people are superior to other races and fated to rule the world." Instead, he reiterated the Charter Oath as "the basis of our national policy." "We have to reaffirm the principles embodied in the charter [oath]," he said, "and proceed unflinchingly toward elimination of misguided practices of the past . . . we will construct a new Japan through thoroughly being pacific, the officials and the people alike obtaining rich culture and advancing the standard of living of the people."[4]

In that April of 1868, disagreement extended to the kind of ceremony that should mark the issuance of the oath. Should it be a contract between lords and sovereign, as Fukuoka preferred, or a sacred pledge by the emperor in the presence of the spirits of his divine ancestors? This time it was Kido who held for sacralization of the ceremony. Shinto ceremonies were worked out to emphasize the fact that the emperor stood at the precise point of unity between the present, or seen, world and the unseen world of the gods.

> The Emperor began the ceremony by performing the *heihaku teijō*, a "presentation" of a folded-paper offering to the myriad deities that is then used as a divine "cloth" *(haku)* to clear away the "defilements" *(hei)* of the assembly. The representative from the Office of State . . . then intoned the verses of dedication *(norito)* to the kami. Finally, the members of the Office of Rites arranged and carried out the offerings and other ritual performances for dedication and worship. The simultaneous presence and cooperative performance of the Emperor and the government, as mediated by the Office of Rites and the ceremonial of dedication, first physically articulated here in the promulgation of the Charter Oath, was to serve as the paradigm for one of the basic tropes of the Meiji system: the Unity of Rites and Rule, *saisei itchi*. After this Sanjō Sanetomi, a court noble recently returned from exile in Kyushu, read the Oath to those assembled.[5]

These promises of participation in government decisions were particularly important during the first stage of military consolidation. There was as yet very little substance to the new "government" at Kyoto, where the boy emperor, the court noble Iwakura, Kido, and a little group of nobles and daimyo were to be found. A military headquarters, located at Edo, was under the control of the Satsuma samurai Ōkubo Toshimichi and a few confederates; this was the command center for the campaign in the northeast, but it was desperately short of resources. It also administered the lands that had been under bakufu control, in effect the only part of the realm where authority had changed hands. In some areas the new government was embarrassed by rash promises of a 50 percent reduction of taxes that had been made by overzealous officials anxious to win popular support. These promises of "virtuous government" impelled members of the local elite to organize fund-raising campaigns for the new dispensation that was at hand, but there was never enough.[6] In the northeast the "imperial" armies consisted of Satsuma, Chōshū, and Tosa units; as other domains came aboard they were expected to contribute troops and munitions; Hizen (Saga), for one, contributed generously to make up for its failure to join at the outset. The field commanders of these units were to become the leaders of the Meiji state after peace was restored. The "home base" of the regime, as Albert Craig has put it,[7] was the southwestern domains of Satsuma, Chōshū, Tosa, and Hizen, that gave the government its muscle and its money. These were in the hands of associates of the samurai leaders in Kyoto, Edo, and with the armies. Their daimyo were still very much a factor, and domain elders were jealous of their institutional and parochial interests. Local and national loyalties were frequently at odds. No one felt this more keenly than the Chōshū samurai Kido Takayoshi, whose diary is full of introspection:

> In the early part of the year [1868] gossip circulated in Yamaguchi [Chōshū] castle town that I was so preoccupied with affairs of the Imperial government that I was neglecting my own country of Chōshū, or else that I was disloyal to my Lord. Certainly I usually concerned myself with problems of the central government; but in doing so I was repaying my obligation to my Lord to soothe the souls of our fallen samurai. Still those vicious rumors were in circulation everywhere . . . I was so overwhelmed with anxiety that I pressed for leave from the Imperial Government to return to Yamaguchi. There I made clear how I had always felt, so the controversy was settled to some degree . . .
>
> Now once again people misunderstand me. Their discussion of my views tends to be murky and irrelevant. This situation in my domain impinges on my thoughts constantly. If I am so ineffective in dealing with my own [Chōshū] countrymen, how can I be effective in the Imperial Government?[8]

Similar concerns plagued the Satsuma leader Ōkubo Toshimichi; those at home might expect national leadership or at least total autonomy, but because it was important to keep other domains from joining the northeastern lands that resisted, it behooved the regime to sound, and be, generous in its early months. The Charter Oath was the central product of this.

In June 1868, a few months after its promulgation, this mood was incorporated into a new structure of government, the Seitaisho, that had a legislature of two houses—the upper stocked with appointed officials, and the lower containing representatives sent by the domains. Meanwhile the young emperor was used as much as possible. When he traveled from Kyoto to Edo between November and January 1869 messengers were sent to shrines along the way to announce his coming, rewards and alms were distributed to filial children, chaste wives, the old and the unfortunate, and a festival was held in Edo: a public relations enterprise that consumed almost one-fifth of the new government's regular budget for the first year.[9] The army units in the field, meanwhile, were maintained by the domains.

As victory neared, the government had less need to be generous. The upper house of the legislature was abolished, leaving the members of the lower house without an upper to advise. In April the Council of State was moved from

Kyoto to Tokyo, over the protests of court nobles who saw themselves losing ground. Even before that, meetings had shown that the nobles, elegantly attired and carefully seated, had less of substance to talk about than samurai advisers who sat on straw mats on the gravel outside the council chambers; not infrequently, one participant recalled, "those who discussed policy were mainly the [samurai] councilors, so the nobles crowded out onto the veranda to participate in the talk."[10] The role of daimyo soon diminished as well. The new government, desperate for income and determined to control, next began to interest itself in the governance of the domains. Two days after the last of the Tokugawa holdouts at Hakodate surrendered, the first and last election promised under the Seitaisho was held. The "electorate" consisted of the top three grades of officials, who voted to decide which of their number should remain in government. Of twenty senior councillors only three survived; junior councillors fell from sixteen to six. Military consolidation had made it safe to begin to push court nobles and daimyo figureheads out of the way.

On the other hand, the early months were not characterized by a desire for vengeance. Ruling houses of domains that resisted were not extinguished, though their chiefs were obliged to stand down and be replaced. Daimyo for the most part escaped unscathed, and they would shortly be compensated for their losses. Nor was daily life of ordinary Japanese changed very much. The transfer of power in Edo was arranged without bloodshed between Katsu Kaishū for the bakufu and Saigō Takamori for Satsuma; when a group of Tokugawa holdouts made violence necessary citizens expected the worst, but the educator Fukuzawa Yukichi noted with surprise that "even in this skirmish, it seems the soldiers were very mild. They did not attempt to molest any civilians or harm other men not engaged in the fight. Some of the officers actually went around and spread the report that the populace need not be alarmed, as there was strict regulation and perfect control of the troops. So, contrary to what most people expected, there was really nothing to fear."[11] He himself saw little to choose between the two forces and chose to stay aloof. In this he undoubtedly spoke for most Japanese. Itagaki Taisuke noted with astonishment that during lulls in the fighting between the Tosa units he commanded and Aizu defenders local farmers tried to sell fresh fruits to both sides. It was that indifference that military leaders of the new government were determined to correct in the future.

The liberal promises of the Charter Oath had little relevance to ordinary Japanese. At an early point the notice boards were repainted and commoners told to go about their business as before—with the important addition, however, that

the Imperial Court has made known its desire to maintain friendly relations with foreign countries. All such matters relating to foreign countries
are to be handled by the Imperial Court . . . if a willful murder of a foreigner or an indiscreet act is committed, it will be deemed an act against
this specific Imperial command, calculated to bring about a national crisis.
Furthermore, if such an act is committed, this Imperial country, which
has entered into friendly intercourse with foreign nations, will suffer a loss
of prestige. Deplorable indeed is such an act.[12]

As long as the outcome of the war remained uncertain, special efforts were
made to attract the support of commoners, and Saigō Takamori had advocated promising that taxes would be halved. During the early days of the
military campaigns some units, notably one led by a Sagara Sōzō, spread
promises of full tax remission to draw popular support. But before long Sagara
and his successors were chided and prosecuted with orders denouncing them
as "ignorant of the very art of governing society; you simply offered petty
charity in order to please the local people."[13] Activists, too, were thanked for
their contributions and told to return to their domain authorities. The time
for governing was at hand.

3. Toward Centralization

It was clear to Japan's leaders that the threats posed to the country by foreign
expansion, foreign trade, and diffusion of foreign culture could not be countered without centralization. But it was also the case that Japan's peculiar
institutions—division into feudal domains, lord-vassal relations within the
samurai elite, and separation of social classes—posed difficult problems for
centralization. It was fortunate that Japan's historical memory included an
era of unification under a central government headed by the emperor, and
that the Tokugawa years had spurred economic and cultural integration.

The first problem was therefore to bring political institutions into line.
This took place so swiftly that the difficulties can be forgotten much too easily.
Leaders of the early Meiji government had to maintain their standing with
their domains, whose military clout was essential to whatever took place, ac-
custom themselves to working with colleagues from other domains who were
suspicious of their purposes, and cooperate with court nobles who struggled
to find breathing space so that they would not seem mere puppets of their
samurai associates from the southwestern domains. It was clearly in the interest of each group to magnify the role and persona of the boy emperor Mutsuhito in order to deflect suspicion.

It was also fortunate that personal relations had usually been established during the dangerous years that preceded the Restoration and by cooperation in the military campaigns against the bakufu and hold-out domains. Nor did it hurt that a high level of education and social skills helped to lubricate and cement friendships.

One sees this clearly in the diary of someone like Kido Takayoshi (1833–1877). He narrowly escaped death in Kyoto in the 1860s, and was so often a target of assassins that he once startled a company of friends by turning up just as rumors of his death had spread. But he was also a bon vivant, skilled in calligraphy, a connoisseur of art, and assiduous in cultivating friendships. Men of this stamp moved easily amid the mighty of the old society. Most Restoration *shishi* were as capable with poetry as with polemics and famous for dismissing their cares at well-lubricated evenings. Thus in February 1869, with everything left to be done, Kido's diary notes an invitation from a daimyo's son;

> on leaving the Palace I, with Lords Higashikuze and Ōhara, went directly to his mansion. Lord [Yamauchi, former Tosa daimyo] Yōdō was already there. We drank and made merry almost until dawn. More than ten geisha from Imado, Yanagibashi, and Shimbashi came to help serve the sake. Each of us took the brush in hand to do calligraphy and ink painting as it pleased him. Today Lord Yōdō and I discussed the main trends of the future; and we agreed on the need to establish the Imperial foundations, and to make clear the proper relations between sovereign and subject. In my heart I rejoiced.[14]

More color than content, one might think, but that would be erroneous. Not even Kido trusted his diary to say how the "Imperial foundations" were to be established. Instead there is vague talk of consultation with his counterparts from Satsuma and Tosa and travel by steamship between the castle towns, which bore fruit two days after this entry in a petition to the court submitted by the lords of Satsuma, Chōshū, Tosa, and Hizen asking that they be permitted to "return" the registers of their domains.

> The undersigned subjects petition with reverent obeisance. We respectfully opine that what the Imperial Government should not lose for a single day is its great Polity . . . The great Polity is . . . that, within the realm, there is no territory which is not owned by the Sovereign and no person who is not subject to him. The great Authority is: that [the Imperial Government] has the sole power to give and to take; that it maintains its servants by means of ranks and emoluments; and that no one shall presume

privately to own a single foot of land or privately to possess as single person.

. . . Now that [the establishment of] a new regime is being sought, [it is essential that] what the great Polity consists in and the great Authority depends upon should not in the least degree be loaned . . .

The abode where we the undersigned dwell is the Sovereign's land; the people over whom we rule are his people. Why should we privately own them? Now therefore, we respectfully restore our domains to the Sovereign. We pray that the Imperial Government, according to its judgment, give what should be given and take what should be taken away; that then an Imperial command be issued that the domains all be reorganized; and also that all the regulations, from the ordering of laws, institutions, and military affairs, even unto the fashioning of uniforms and instruments, issue from the Imperial Government, and that the conduct of all the affairs of the realm, whether great or small, be placed under unified control.[15]

These fascinating phrases deserve close study and thought. There is no mention or suggestion of "rights," except those of the sovereign which have been impinged upon by history. Nor is there apology or self-abnegation. These are great barons whose authorization for holding registers of their population requires new validity, presenting them to the sovereign and assuring him of their confidence that he will "give what should be given and take what should be taken away."

What Satsuma, Chōshū, Tosa, and Hizen had done others could not long delay. "Should it not be we, guilty of having sided with the Bakufu, who should return our fiefs before anybody else?" read a petition circulated by samurai in a northern domain.[16] Three centuries earlier Satsuma leaders had shown the same alacrity in conforming with Hideyoshi's sword hunt edict, and for the same reason. By the time the court formally accepted the four-domain petition on July 25, 1869, and made it compulsory, most of the three-hundred-odd domains had submitted similar requests.

All daimyo were now appointed governors of their domains, but without hereditary succession privileges. The immediate effect of this was slight, but the change in status provided cover for cautious feelers with which the central government began to issue orders. The most important of these specified that the former daimyo could retain one-tenth of the tax revenue of their domains for household expenses. There was now the assumption that the central government could concern itself with fiscal policies that had so far been out of its control.

The "Return of the Registers" (*hanseki hōkan,* as Japanese term it) thus marked a first step toward centralization. More dramatic was the reform of governmental institutions at the center. The Council of State, now renamed the Dajōkan, represented a much more powerful executive than the new government had known. The senior post, Minister of the Right, went to Sanjō Sanetomi. Beneath him were three Great Councillors, of whom Iwakura Tomomi (1825–1883) was the most important, and then a group of councillors, all from Satsuma, Chōshū, Tosa, and Hizen. The number of court nobles and former daimyo now decreased remarkably. The court nobles involved did not change the Satsuma-Chōshū balance. Iwakura had developed close ties with Satsuma, and Sanjō had taken refuge in Chōshū a half-decade earlier.

Despite these gains, things remained at a standstill for a year. The "government" controlled little more than the Tokugawa lands, which had been reclassified as prefectures (ken). The leading Restoration domains found themselves saddled with heavy expenses incurred by their programs of militarization, and key figures left the central government to take up reforms within their domain. In Chōshū steps to prune the swollen military establishment produced a revolt from the units demobilized in October of 1869, but Kido succeeded in putting it down. In Satsuma Saigō Takamori (1827–1877) was the leader in revising relative ranks of hereditary status groups, and worked for the formation of a lower-samurai military state. In Tosa the military leader, Itagaki Taisuke, led an impetuous program of modernization. Permits for private enterprise were made much more accessible. Foreign "experts" were brought in to advise on reforms in codes of law. Old handbooks of domain administration were ordered burned, and even portraits of former daimyo were destroyed. In Wakayama (Kii) progressive samurai struggled to strengthen the domain's leverage in future politics by undertaking military reforms that included a nascent conscription system and hiring German military instructors. Commoners were placed in administrative positions and able young samurai, among them the future foreign minister Mutsu Munemitsu, were sent abroad. That former Tokugawa domain was not about to be caught unprepared again. "We were determined," the *rangaku* specialist Tsuda Izuru later recalled, "to make our domain the pioneer in reform for all Japan." On the Japan Sea coast, Fukui, the former domain of Matsudaira Keiei, hired William Griffis to direct education in Western learning.[17] Similarly, the Kyushu domain of Kumamoto did not limit its changes to military reforms, but set up a new school for Western learning for which it hired an American Civil War veteran, Captain L. L. Janes, as head. The results were not always those anticipated. Under Janes's influence the first class produced the "Kumamoto band," or fellowship, of earnest young Christians who dedicated their lives to spiritual rather than martial modernization.[18]

There was, in short, some danger that centripetal forces might be pulling Japan apart. It seemed so to some. The Tosa leader Sasaki Takayuki lamented that the new central government was not popular and no one wanted to serve in it. No one would heed his argument that it would serve Tosa interests for Tosa men to serve at the center; instead, he wrote, "men of samurai rank tend to detest the idea, believing that working in the Imperial government means serving more than one overlord. Consequently they despise us."[19]

Nor was there unity at the center. Iwakura and Sanjō, both of them well down in the peer ranks of the fossilized court, naturally incurred the jealousy of the old status families they had replaced. They knew better than most the tensions within the southwestern domains that had led in the Restoration. Sasaki Takayuki noted in his diary that Satsuma and Chōshū men did not trust each other, that the Tosa and Hizen leaders tended to lean to one or the other, and that "Sanjō and Iwakura are greatly worried. They avoid talking with persons from Satsuma, Chōshū and Saga, and speak secretly with me instead." "Only Ōkubo," he noted later, "can be relied on; without him we could not carry on . . . The troubles of these days are beyond description."[20] Ōkubo, for his part, wrote that "Satsuma and Chōshū are the foundation stones of the imperial country; its life depends on them. If they do not cooperate, its life will be shortened . . . If at present the imperial country faced no foreign threat, a few internal disturbances would be no cause for alarm."[21] Diaries like Kido's speak opaquely about "great achievements" that are called for; instead men wondered where the other stood. No one could be sure he was safe or trusted, and yet a consensus was at hand.

It is probably fortunate that most men believed that the imperial country did in fact face a foreign threat, and it is certainly the case that they agreed on a prescription for unity, however doubtful they might be about its ingredients or leadership.

Those at court worked out a way out of this morass of distrust. In January of 1870 Iwakura, accompanied by Ōkubo of Satsuma and Yamagata of Chōshū, was sent as Imperial Messenger to prevail upon the daimyo of Satsuma and Chōshū, ordering them, and the Satsuma military leader Saigō, to come back to Tokyo. They then went on to Tosa. All three domains complied with these instructions.

Three months later the three domains were ordered to detach 10,000 men from their armies and send them to Tokyo to constitute an Imperial Guard. Saigō, Kido and Itagaki saw to it that the troops were on the scene soon. The government now had some clout. It was also in receipt of petitions from thirteen domains—most of them small, but including Morioka in the north, who petitioned that they could no longer make it on their own and asked to be taken under the government's protection as prefectures. By mid-August, talks among young, progressive Chōshū figures found them discussing the need for further consolidation. Itō Hirobumi and Inoue Kaoru had been members of the little group sent to England in the 1860s, and Yamagata Aritomo was freshly back from Europe. They now began to lobby their seniors, especially Kido Takayoshi. There were surprising abstentions; Iwakura Tomomi, for one, seems to have been told about this only a few days before the August decision to abolish the domains. Always alert to the danger of seeming to be a Satsuma-Chōshū puppet, Iwakura quickly recruited Owari, Fukui, and Kumamoto. On the other hand Michio Umegaki discerns a gradual decline in influence for the military leaders Saigō and Itagaki. Whatever the case, in August 1871 the domains were declared abolished and replaced by prefectures. *Haihan chiken,* "dissolution of the domains and establishment of prefectures," was soon hailed by Yamagata as a "Second Meiji Restoration." In some ways it was the first, for only now would the structure of Tokugawa fragmentation be abolished. The court announcement made clear what was happening:

> We deem it necessary that the government of the country be centered in a single authority, so as to effect a reformation in substance as well as in fact . . . All this is for the purpose of doing away with superfluity, for issuing in simplicity, for removing the evils of empty forms and in order to avoid the grievance caused by the existence of many centers of government.[22]

William Griffis, who was teaching in Fukui, recorded the astonishment of men in that province.

> The thunderbolt has fallen! The political earthquake has shaken Japan to its center. Its effects are very visible here in Fukui. Intense excitement reigns in the homes of the samurai of the city today. I hear that some of them are threatening to kill Mitsuoka [Yuri Kimimasa], who receives income for meritorious services in 1868, and who has long been the exponent of reform and of national progress in Fukui.

Next the former daimyo/governors were summoned to Tokyo, as once they were summoned by the shogun. Griffis's account continues:

> Tomorrow Fukui bids farewell to feudalism. On the next day we shall be in a province without a prince. The era of loyalty is passed. The era of patriotism has come . . .
>
> From an early hour this morning, the samurai in *kamishimo* [ceremonial dress] have been preparing themselves for farewell, and have been

assembling in the castle . . . I shall never forget the impressive scene. All the sliding paper partitions separating the rooms were removed, making one vast area of matting. Arranged in the order of their rank, each in his starched robes of ceremony, with shaven-crown, and gun-hammer top-knot, with hands clasped on the hilt of his sword resting upright before him as he sat on his knees, were the three thousand samurai of the Fukui clan . . . It was more than a farewell to their feudal lord. It was the solemn burial of the institutions under which their fathers had lived for seven hundred years.

And then, within weeks, Griffis's students melted away.

My best friends and helpers have left Fukui, and now my advanced students, their support at home being no longer sufficient, are leaving to seek their fortune in Yokohama or Tokio. My classes are being depleted. Fukui is no longer the capital of a prince. It is simply an inland city . . . The military school has been disbanded, and the gunpowder works and rifle factory removed . . . Three companies of imperial troops, in uniform of French style, with the mikado's crest on their caps . . . now occupy the city barracks. The old local and feudal privileges are being abolished.[23]

As Griffis discovered, central planning would now replace local devising; from seeming to be in danger of flying apart Japan would suddenly become ever more centralized. The new governors were samurai, but they were seldom natives of the provinces to which they were assigned. Even Chōshū received a former Tokugawa bureaucrat as governor. A process of experimental juggling of borders reduced the three-hundred-odd domains to fifty. Only a very few of the largest domains retained their boundaries, and nine represented consolidation of eight or more domains. With this came a remarkable consolidation of posts as well. Griffis was told that the number of local officials in Fukui was to be reduced from five hundred to seventy. Under the bakufu the problem had been one of employing as many of the domain samurai as possible; now the priorities were those of efficiency and economy.

4. Failed Cultural Revolution

Revolutions often bring with them sweeping assaults on traditional ways of thought and belief. Like the shifting of tectonic plates, they unsettle, at least momentarily, everything that had hitherto seemed fixed and firm. In France revolutionary enthusiasts warred on the Catholic church, expropriated its wealth and frequently its buildings, and tried to supplant it with a Religion of Reason. The reaction of the population, part stunned and part disoriented by the seismic shocks of change, ranged from silence to vociferous support before subsiding to something closer to traditional attitudes.

This was true also in the early Meiji years, except that the substitute proposed for traditional religious outlooks, the revival of the spirit world of primitive Japan, was closer to a religion of unreason. There was, however, more involved than a retreat from modernity. The symbiotic relationships between the Tokugawa bakufu and Buddhism made it easy to characterize that as one of the "evils of the past" the Charter Oath had promised to undo. There was also the pull of antiquity in *fukko*, a driving ideological force of late Tokugawa days. The invocation of the theocratic pretensions of a state headed by a ruler descended from the sun goddess provided important support for consensus and centralization. And there was cultural politics involved, in terms of the proper ideological foundations for the new state.

Once the bakufu had fallen it was inevitable that the political upheaval would involve the role of Buddhism as well. It will be recalled that registration with Buddhist temples was compulsory, and that the reports of sectarian affiliation were a central aspect of Tokugawa controls on Christianity and subversion. The leaders of the new regime thought no more highly of Christianity than their predecessors had. Despite the resumption of foreign intercourse in the 1860s the notice boards continued to warn against the "worship of Jesus," and the early Meiji government retained this injunction in its version of the notice boards that were to be found everywhere. In 1865 the French built a church at Nagasaki. To the astonishment of the curate, Father Petitjean, a large proportion of the nearby fishing village of Ōura, which had retained the "hidden Christian" (*kakure kirishitan*) faith, took advantage of the opportunity to attend the first mass accessible to them since the early seventeenth century.[24] Startled bakufu prosecutors had seized the communicants and remanded them to daimyo in all parts of the country for isolation and observation. Meiji officials saw nothing wrong with this, and stoutly resisted the complaints of foreign diplomats who saw it as a violation of human rights and civilized behavior.

Nevertheless restrictions on belief were one thing, support of a Buddhist institution that had grown political and corrupt under Tokugawa favoritism another. There were also Tokugawa precedents. Confucian thought in Tokugawa times had grown steadily more critical of Buddhism as superstitious and irrational.[25] Outstanding Confucian daimyo like Ikeda Mitsumasa of Okayama and Tokugawa Mitsukuni of Mito had warred on Buddhism in their domains, disestablishing hundreds of temples and ordering their monks to return to lay life. These trends were particularly evident in domains that led in Restoration thought and action. In Mito Tokugawa Nariaki ordered the confiscation of temple bells and bronze objects that could be melted down and used for cannon, defrocked hundreds of monks, and destroyed temples. Indeed, the bakufu's indictment of him in 1844 noted that he had destroyed temples and forcibly converted the Nikko shrine to Ieyasu into a purely Shinto place of worship. In Satsuma too reformers charged Buddhist monks with contributing nothing to the defense or economy of the domain. The administration amalgamated and closed temples, confiscated bells and gongs, and expunged Buddhist traces from Shinto shrines. Both Satsuma and Chōshū seized Buddhist temple lands. Similar feelings were at work in Tosa, where the reforms that followed the Restoration very quickly focused on temples and their wealth. If Confucian statesmen had their doubts about the utility of Buddhism, *kokugaku* thought, with its explicit advocacy of the national deities and criticism of the Buddhist import, promised to provide an alternative.

Buddhism had become almost inextricably intertwined with Shinto. Virtually every temple included a Shinto shrine, and monks frequently served them both. Ideological fervor of the day called for a rigid separation of the two, *shinbutsu bunri*, in which the national gods would reassert their sovereignty just as Japan was resolved to restore its own integrity. This was foreshadowed by the way Restoration leaders worked with Shinto intellectuals to formulate the basis for imperial autonomy and superiority. Iwakura Tomomi worked closely with the Shinto theorist Hisamatsu Misao and with Fukuda Bin and Ōkuni Takamasa, leading *kokugaku* figures. These men found themselves in a strategic position, for they had history on their side. The eighth-century state structure that was theoretically being restored had added a Bureau of Divinities to the bureaucratic structure that Japan had imported from the mainland.

The administrative structure that implemented these measures began with the establishment of an Office of Rites in 1868 as one of seven departments of the Council of State. (Buddhism, in contrast, was directed from an office in the Department of Home Affairs.) As the government began to flex its muscle this bureau was elevated above the council, in the theory that Japan would at last achieve a true "unity of rites and government" *(saisei itchi)*, long advocated by *kokugaku* theorists. This high-water mark of Shinto political influence continued until 1871. After the abolition of domains in that year further bureaucratic juggling brought the Office of Rites back into line as one of the ministries, and in time it was further downgraded to be added to the functions of the Ministry of Education. These shifts were the product of intense bureaucratic infighting in which reform bureaucrats like Kido Takayoshi and Iwakura Tomomi managed to free themselves from the convulsive grip of Shinto ideologists.

They were helped in this by divisions among the Shinto backers. Ōkuni Takamasa and his disciples wanted to have Shinto play a central role in politics and serve as a religion of unification. At the highest level, state rites would serve to expand and consolidate the authority of the new regime, while at the popular level Shinto control of pastoral functions and funerals would enable it to replace completely the function of Buddhism in popular life. Disciples of Hirata Atsutane, on the other hand, argued that Shinto could only be cheapened by associating it with the pollution traditionally identified with death, and they fought against anything that would seem to make it possible to classify Shinto as an organized religion. As the arguments raged reform bureaucrats realized it would be necessary for them to separate themselves from both camps; Japan had more urgent problems with the Western world that had fastened unequal treaties onto it.

For the first few years, however, the Shinto enthusiasts had their way. Separation of Buddhism from Shinto was ordered in 1868. Shinto objects of worship were to be removed from Buddhist temples, and all shrine priests and their families were to have Shinto funerals. These orders evoked popular enthusiasm and excesses on the part of Shinto priests and believers who had long resented the Buddhist primacy. Under the slogan *haibutsu kishaku* (eradicate Buddhism!), ferocious and vindictive destruction of temples and religious objects took place. Since centralization had only just begun, the intensity of this campaign varied by domain. In part it represented the sort of abandon with which crowds have always greeted political overturn. From Fukui Griffis wrote in December 1868 that "the Buddhist theological school has been broken up by orders from Tōkio," but went on to say that

> many old yashikis of ancient and once wealthy families have been torn down and converted into shops. The towns-people and shop-keepers are jubilant at getting a foot-hold on the sites hitherto reserved to samurai. Old armor, arrows, spears, flags, saddlery, dresses, norimonos [palanquins], and all the paraphernalia of the old feudal days can now be bought dirt cheap. The prince's mansion has been demolished, and everything left in it sold . . . Everything pertaining to feudal Fukui is passing away.[26]

The campaign against Buddhism was more purposeful and more vengeful than this. In some cases organized bands led by Shinto priests burst into major temples and destroyed priceless sutras and works of art. In Satsuma an order of 1869 specified that only Shinto observances would be permitted. An 1872 survey reported that all 1,066 Buddhist temples had been abolished, their monks ordered to return to lay life, their buildings confiscated for military expenses, and their statues, sutras, and ritual objects destroyed. In Tosa the persecution was only slightly less severe. In Kyoto and Nara, traditional centers of Buddhism, temples and artworks were destroyed and in one instance, reminiscent of the *fumie* test for Christians, teachers and students were required to step on Buddhist statues to prove that no harm would befall those who did so.[27] One leading Buddhist prelate gloomily wrote that "provincial temples are being destroyed, people are withdrawing their memberships; priests are gladly returning to secular life . . . there probably has been nothing to compare with this situation in the fourteen or fifteen centuries during which Buddhism has been in Japan. In my opinion, there will be an Imperial Rescript eradicating Buddhism within five to seven years."[28]

This destructive impulse could extend to individuals in the countryside. Shimazaki Tōson's protagonist in *Before the Dawn*, Aoyama Hanzō, a true if simple-minded Hirata follower, is caught by his fellow villagers as he goes off with some combustibles to set fire to the village Myōshinji temple, explaining in all seriousness, "Well, we don't need that any more." The villagers beg to differ, however, stop the conflagration, and incarcerate Hanzō to prevent further mischief.

As was to be expected, mindless destruction aroused popular indignation and even violence in some areas. Shinto enthusiasts who had done their best to stir up the trouble were sometimes denounced as possible Christians. The great majority of Japanese continued to adhere to traditional customs of their family sect and temple graveyard, and Buddhist solemnities of funeral and All Souls *(obon)* observances. Much of the worst unrest was Shinto-led and not government authorized, and within a year or two the tide began to ebb.

The principal aim, the separation of Shinto from Buddhism, was nevertheless achieved. Government edicts clarified gray areas; Shugendō mountain priests were forced to declare themselves Buddhist or retire, and Fugendō and smaller Buddhist mendicant sects were banned. The once-mixed divinities of shrines like Ieyasu's Tōshōgu tomb at Nikko were declared Shinto, and Hachiman reverted from being a Boddhisatva to resume his career as Shinto God of War.

At the same time that Buddhist prelates were being deprived of the insignia of rank they had enjoyed in Tokugawa years, Shinto shrines were being structured in a hierarchy that stretched up to the sun goddess Amaterasu's home at Ise. Heretofore shrines had been virtually autonomous, representing only the natural gods and folk religion of the countryside, but henceforth they were the objects of government policy. Shrine lands were confiscated, as the much larger Buddhist patrimonies had been. There were now promises of state support for major Shinto, which were named National or Imperial, shrines. The role of registration, previously performed by Buddhist temples, was now transferred to Shinto. Japanese were to be organized as "parishioners" *(ujiko)* of shrines, and to be registered by them. Parishioners were to receive a talisman at birth which would be returned to the shrine at death. In this manner the deities of the Ise shrine were to be installed in every household; with each house a "branch shrine" of Ise, all Japanese would be related to the cult center.[29] Thus ambitious plans proposed to use Shinto to unify the population in a single cult, headed by the emperor as head priest; his ancestral (Ise) shrines and a new shrine that was established (the future Yasukuni Jinja in Tokyo) for those killed in the Restoration War, now declared "national deities," would be the center of this national religion.

Although its main contours were never renounced, the extremity of this potentially totalitarian structure was soon moderated. One factor was clear evidence of popular distress over the attacks on familiar centers of Buddhism. A second was the impracticality of the Shinto and *kokugaku* enthusiasts, who proved xenophobic and badly out of touch with the realities of the political situation; they irritated and then alienated their erstwhile supporters among the Restoration leaders. Perhaps most important was the long arm and clear disapproval of the Western powers, who advocated rights for Christianity in Japan and whose approval was requisite to the success of efforts to amend the treaties.

The final stage of the Restoration cultural revolution thus took a milder stance. The Great Promulgation *(Daikyō)* campaign, which was inaugurated in 1870 and sputtered to a close fourteen years later, enlisted Buddhist as well as Shinto and new religion (Kurozumikyō and Konkōkyō) preachers as Proselytizers or Missionaries for a synthetic "Great Teaching" to produce patriotic and ideologically malleable subjects. Ostensibly nonsectarian and national, the Great Teaching was more Shinto-centered than not. It focused attention on three rather bland instructions to (1) revere the gods *(kami)* and love the country, (2) clarify heavenly reason and the Way of humanity, and (3) revere the emperor and respect the court. A Great Teaching Institute served as seminary for the training of the evangelists who were to expound these platitudes. Preaching guides focused on paying taxes, complying with rescripts, education, the (new after 1873) solar calendar, military buildup (*fukoku-kyōhei,* or "rich country, strong army"), and the importation of Western learning and modern civilization. This could be seen as a modern version of the Sacred Maxims that Ming and Ch'ing dynasty emperors had directed village leaders to read to their communities, and also a forerunner of the 1890 Imperial Rescript on Education. Much effort went into it. In 1876 there were over 10,000 registered National Evangelists. In that same year it came under the direction of the Ise shrine authorities and took on a more frankly Shinto appearance.

And yet the campaign failed, and badly. Its ubiquitous propagandists with their bland teachings and slogans were the butt of satirists and wall scribblers. Japanese for the most part bent with the wind and waited it out. There were to be significant carryovers of these attempts in national Shinto, attempted regulation of shrine Shinto, and state exhortation to civic virtue, but this did not take clear shape until later Meiji. By then the emperor's aura had grown, and Japan's modern wars would soon produce thousands of *kami* for the Yasukuni shrine.

5. Wisdom throughout the World

The Charter Oath ended with a pledge to seek wisdom throughout the world in order to strengthen the foundations of the imperial state. Nothing distinguishes the Meiji period more than its disciplined search for models that would be applicable for a Japan in the process of rebuilding its institutions. The Tokugawa bakufu had, to be sure, begun this process. Members of missions abroad spent increasing amounts of time in observation while carrying out the specific duties for which they had been dispatched. Still, there are no precedents in world history for Japan's decision to send its government—fifty high officials—accompanied by as many students and high-born tourists, to the Western world on a journey that kept them away from their jobs for a year and ten months from 1871 to 1873. That Japan did so is remarkable, and that the travelers returned to find their jobs waiting for them is more remarkable still.

The idea for such a learning mission originated with the Dutch-American missionary Guido Verbeck in suggestions he sent from Nagasaki, first to Ōkuma Shigenobu and later to Iwakura Tomomi. Verbeck proposed that the mission visit only five countries; "if these are well understood," he wrote, "the others are not worth spending time upon," but the Japanese were far more thorough. The embassy circled the globe to visit twelve countries, making comparative studies of governmental organization, industrial development, trade, and education. Inclusion in the embassy was a plum for all its members. It was headed by Iwakura Tomomi as ambassador plenipotentiary; Kido Takayoshi and Ōkubo Toshimichi were vice ambassadors. Recent feudal lords of Chōshū, Saga, Fukuoka, and Kanazawa came, each accompanied by retainers. The Hokkaido Colonization Office added representatives. With a court noble its head, and a reasonable Satsuma-Chōshū balance, official members included three nobles, five Chōshū, three Hizen, and one Satsuma; other slots went to former bakufu men with experience in modern administration. At middle and lower levels membership was not firmly fixed, as some joined and others left the embassy during its long stay abroad. Many leaders in the Meiji period wanted to travel. The future intellectual and political leader Nakae Chōmin laid siege to Ōkubo to get himself included as a student bound for France; and many government leaders, including Ōkubo, saw to it that their sons were attached. More remarkable still, five women, the youngest only seven, were sent to be educated in the United States.[30] Itō Hirobumi, one of the Chōshū group sent to England a decade earlier, and in the United States Japanese minister Mori Arinori, a charter member of the Satsuma group abroad in that same era, were the only seasoned travelers in the group.

A famous painting depicts the ambassadors' departure from Yokohama for San Francisco in 1871. At the same time that they studied and observed they also served as evidence of Japan's determination to modernize, and throughout their travels they were state guests, accompanied by the diplomatic representatives stationed in Japan and wined and dined by civic, industrial, and governmental leaders. The San Francisco *Daily Evening Bulletin,* for instance, hailed the ambassadors as representatives of what "is today, all the circumstances of her previous condition considered, the most progressive nation on the globe." The Western world was in an expansive, confident mood in the 1870s. World fairs and industrial expositions provided settings for competition in achievement. Peace had been restored in the United States and in Europe, and industrial and rail development was reaching unprecedented heights. Pride in accomplishment went together with expectations of future commercial gain to make for receptions designed to inform and impress the Japanese visitors. They held to an exhausting schedule. The embassy scribe, Kume Kunitake, carefully recorded the details of their visits in fact-studded narrative that alternated description with observations about its significance for Japan.[31]

The progress of the embassy can be followed in Kido's daily diary notations and in the voluminous correspondence he maintained. Nothing impressed him more than education in the United States. "Nothing has more urgency for us than schools," he wrote, and "unless we establish an unshakable national foundation we will not be able to elevate our country's prestige in a thousand years . . . Our people are no different from the Americans or Europeans of today; it is all a matter of education or lack of education."[32] Minister to Washington Mori, for his part, did spadework for the embassy by inviting leading American educators to submit their views on how Japan

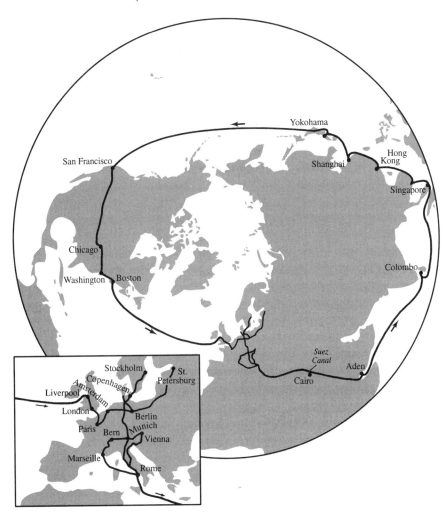

5. Route followed by the Iwakura embassy of 1871–1873.

might best enhance its material prosperity and commerce, develop its agricultural and industrial interests, build up the social, moral, and physical condition of its people, and improve its laws and government. He published these replies in 1873. A reply that David Murray prepared for the president of Rutgers, which argued that a Japan situated in respect to Asia as England was to Europe could be built into "an equally colossal commercial power," so impressed the Japanese that Murray was invited to Japan as adviser to the new Ministry of Education, where he served until 1878. Mori concluded that while in the United States applied science received great attention, higher and theoretical science stemmed from Germany. Within a decade this would be reflected in the structure of Japanese higher education, which, like the new graduate schools in the United States, found its model on the Continent.

The embassy was authorized to discuss, but not to negotiate, changes in the unequal treaties which, beginning with the American treaty negotiated by Townsend Harris, came up for reconsideration during its stay abroad. Itō and Mori, however, brashly assured their senior colleagues that it would be a good idea to negotiate with the United States. The discovery that they lacked proper credentials to do so made it necessary to send Ōkubo and Itō back, producing a four-month delay while the others cooled their heels in Washington. By the time the two returned from Tokyo, where they had encountered strong opposition from colleagues who were already worried that they were arrogating power to themselves, Iwakura and Kido had become convinced that treaty reform would have to be negotiated on an across-the-board rather than bilateral basis, and so informed a surprised Secretary of State Hamilton Fish. Kido was irate with his confident young colleagues, castigating Itō and Mori as "clever young men who aspired to a moment of fame," and described the last session with Fish as "indescribably more difficult than facing enemies coming from all sides on the field of battle."[33]

Thanks to this delay the embassy ended up spending more time (205 days) in the United States than in England (122 days), Prussia (23), France, Russia, or other European countries. Kume's journal reflects this in its distribution of coverage. Nevertheless the industrial might of Britain, and the lessons of the United States as a developing country, would probably have given the United States and Great Britain priority in any case. As it happened the long delay in Washington, added to an unanticipated delay in Salt Lake City, where the mission was marooned by a snowstorm that closed the Union Pacific for a time, made the visit to America a long one.

There was never much doubt that Japan's models would be found in the West. "There are strong and wealthy nations which are called mature civilizations," Fukuzawa Yukichi wrote in 1872, and "there are also poor and weak nations which are primitive or underdeveloped. In general the nations of Europe and America illustrate the first category, those of Asia and Africa the second."[34]

The ambassadors returned with the conclusion that the immediate danger to Japan's independence was less pressing than they had thought. The superiority of the West was in any case of relatively recent date. Rather than prepare for military defense, Japan should inaugurate a program of "defensive" modernization, setting its house in order so that it could work its way up the international hierarchy of respect and prestige. The West had not always led the way: as Kume's journal pointed out,

> The wealth and prosperity that one sees in Europe date to a considerable degree from the period after 1800 . . . In 1830, steamships and trains made their first appearance. This was a time of abrupt change in the trade of Europe, and the English were the first to devote their entire energies to making improvements.[35]

Japan was not, in other words, hopelessly behind; careful planning and hard work could bring it up to the mark.

The ambassadors also became convinced that Japan would have to do something about representative institutions in order to build consensus for government actions. It will be recalled that a hesitant step in this direction had been taken with the short-lived institutional pattern of June 1868, but the experience of the West suggested a direct correlation between representative institutions and national wealth and power. On his return Kido argued from the experience of Poland to make the case that lack of popular participation would be fatal to national independence. The Charter Oath's language about deliberative councils, he had decided in Washington, could be considered as "the foundation of our Constitution." Constitutions provided a way for "the people of the whole country" to "give expression to their united and harmonious wishes"; in turn, those who held office "respect the wishes of the whole nation and serve their country under a deep sense of responsibility, so that even in extraordinary crises they take no arbitrary step contrary to the people's will." Japan might not be quite ready for parliamentary governance, but basically "it is no different from those countries of Europe and America the conduct of whose governments embodies the will of the people."[36] On the other hand the embassy's travels showed that choice within Western institutions was not only possible but in fact necessary. Kido was somewhat put off by American democracy, and relieved to learn from Japanese resident in Germany that other patterns were available.

The Meiji government's continuing ban on Christianity drew disapproval wherever the embassy traveled. It is no accident that the notice boards forbidding Christian worship were pulled down in 1873, the year of the mission's return. The ambassadors also developed a respect for the importance of religion in American and European life. The Bible, Kume Kunitake noted, seemed to be Confucian classics and Buddhist sutras rolled into one. Conversely, since the Japanese did not have a similarly rigorous code, it behooved them to move with care and discernment lest society come unraveled.

The travelers were steeped in Confucian values, of course, and it was inevitable that Kume's thoughtful commentary should compare the Ten Commandments of the West with the Five (Confucian) Relationships; the one prescriptive, the other more accommodative and humanistic. The West seemed acquisitive and assertive, the Orient was structured on moral principles of family-style rule under a ruler with benevolence and concern for his people. Kido was astonished by one elderly American "philosopher," as he characterized him, who expressed surprise when he heard that he would put his parents before his wife; each seemed immoral to the other, and Kido wondered whether it would be possible to modernize and retain the values of the Way of humanity. These musings came in Western Protestant countries whose worth and duty ethic seemed accessible. On the other hand, institutionalized Christianity in Catholic and Eastern European countries was something else again. "I was astonished," Kume wrote, "at the extent to which Western religions squander the people's wealth in churches." He was quick to relate this to the new hierarchy of nations he was forming; "the more backward a country, the more powerful is the influence of religious superstition and the more likely the people are to worship idols and animals."

What mattered, though, was that the new international society Japan was entering was based on these "Western" values; intensely competitive, participatory, and constantly developing new colonial bases for further expansion. Western nations seemed engaged in a ceaseless competition characterized by unrelenting suspicion and distrust. "Even though the diplomacy of all Western nations outwardly expresses friendliness, secretly there is mutual suspicion," Kume wrote; "the small countries of Belgium, Holland, Sweden, and Switzerland, like porcupines bristling their quills, shore up their defenses . . . they are not able to loosen the straps of their helmets."[37]

It would be difficult to imagine a more thoughtful and informed discussion of Japan's present state and future course than that provided by the embassy's journal. The lessons were clear. Japan had entered a highly competitive world in which victory went to the educated and united. It should choose carefully from among the models before it. Initially American education, British industrialization, French jurisprudence, and German representational institutions held particular promise. It would have to modernize those institutions to establish its qualifications for release from the inequality defined by the unequal treaties, thus postponing immediate gratification for the sake of long-term gain.

Some junior members of the mission could be spared for longer periods of study in the West. The future general Katsura Tarō and Prince Saionji Kinmochi, who as prime ministers were to alternate in power the first decade of the twentieth century, stayed on, the one in Germany, the other in France, for long periods of conditioning. A small army of students, perhaps the first of modern times, also descended on the West. Between 1868 and 1902, 11,148 passports were issued for study overseas. Within five years of the Restoration private efforts to promote study abroad were beginning to compete with public, and students headed overseas in large numbers. In the first decade of Meiji one-third of these (293) headed for the United States, one-tenth (178) for England, and another 69 for Germany.[38] Iwakura and Kido already had sons studying in the United States (at Rutgers) at the time of the embassy.

6. The Breakup of the Restoration Coalition

In 1873 the ambassadors received an urgent summons from Tokyo to return home. During their absence things had been left to an absentee government whose principal members were Saigō Takamori, Itagaki Taisuke, Etō Shinpei, Soejima Taneomi, and Ōkuma Shigenobu. Sanjō Sanetomi, the court noble who had fled to Chōshū a decade earlier, provided the aura of the imperial court. The absentee leaders were bound to an agreement that they would not undertake major changes in government policy until the return of their colleagues. In fact important steps were undertaken in education, conscription, and taxation, but it could be argued that those had already been sketched out before the departure of the Iwakura embassy. The Tokyo government was frequently divided by difficulties in financial policy, a field in which Ōkuma (who had his doubts about Chōshū-Satsuma dominance) held inflationary views while others were more cautious. They were also bedeviled by corruption and scandal. Yamagata Aritomo, in charge of the army, had entrusted matters to a friend-turned-merchant who proved to have made himself a fortune with public funds, and not even his suicide kept the others from being critical of Yamagata. Inoue Kaoru had an equally rocky ride in and out of office. Domain rivalry was alive and well, turning every infraction into a wider charge of clique or clan dishonesty.

But some problems would not wait for Iwakura's return. Japanese and Russians contested quietly for control of Sakhalin (Karafuto) and the Kuril (Chishima) islands, until an exchange (Kurils for Japan and Sakhalin for Russia) was worked out by the former bakufu official Enomoto Takeaki in St. Petersburg in 1875. Japanese also worried about Hokkaido itself; an "Ezochi Development Office" was replaced by the Hokkaido Colonization Office, under the command of the Satsuma Kuroda Kiyotaka, who pursued vigorous measures of immigration and development. All this cost money, however, and limited possibilities in foreign and military affairs.

The most powerful leaders of the absentee government, Saigō and Itagaki, had come to prominence as military commanders. They could be expected to show particular concern for, and be under pressure from, their old comrades in arms, samurai who were struggling to make ends meet under the pension plan that had been worked out for them. Yamagata and other "modern" military thinkers were convinced of the superiority and malleability of peasant conscripts, but some old soldiers were not so sure. The uncertainty of foreign policy developments raised concern about Russian ambitions to the north and on the nearby continent, and it was probably inevitable for them to think about measures that might utilize the energies of restless former samurai and simultaneously win public support.

By 1873 the argument had come to focus on Korea. There was a striking element of belligerency in Japanese attitudes toward Korea, perhaps in compensation for the frustration rooted in weakness. Late Tokugawa figures, among them Yoshida Shōin, had held out prospects of Asian conquest, and a number of Tsushima youths who had studied with Yoshida hoped for direct action in which they might have a role. Kido Takayoshi before his trip to the West had also wanted to find grounds for war with Korea. The Koreans did their part by rejecting Japanese proposals for diplomatic relations with some hauteur. In its closing days the Tokugawa bakufu had tried to place relations with Korea on a modern basis, but the Koreans, used to dealing through Tsushima and suspicious of Japan, rebuffed the attempt. Once in power, the early Meiji government tried again, explaining its adoption of "modern" state-to-state relations and proposing to establish normal ties with Korea. It too was rebuffed in terms that promised to provide the grounds for a "punitive" expedition. *Sei Kan ron,* the argument for punishing Korea, now became an issue that divided the absentee government and the Iwakura ambassadors upon their return.

The historian has to be astonished by the alacrity with which Meiji leaders suggested strong steps. Japan itself was still struggling for unity, the new government controlled little more than part of the Tokugawa domains, and yet Kido Takayoshi and others suggested threats of force to admonish Japan's closest neighbor on the continent. Kido had written on January 25, 1869, that

> we should determine without delay the course our nation is to take, then dispatch an envoy to Korea to question officials of that land about their discourtesy to us. If they do not acknowledge their fault, let us proclaim it publicly and launch an attack on their territory to extend the influence of our Divine Land . . . If this be done, the reactionary traditions of our nation will be altered overnight . . . we shall make advances in developing all sorts of practical skills and technology; and we shall wash away our

undesirable practices of spying on one another, criticizing and reproaching each other . . . the advantages of this policy to the country are incalculable.[39]

In other words, war would bring unity and promote modernization. A few months later Kido thought he had worked things out:

I do not mean that we should invade the nation without good reason. I want to put forward a rationale that will be universally accepted. The rationale which I wish to advance is that we shall bring our superior national policies to that land.[40]

It would be difficult to find a more obtuse and parochial "rationale." The expectation that this would be "universally accepted" in 1869 is no less staggering, though by the twentieth century many Japanese labored under that illusion. Kido got himself named special emissary to Korea in July 1870, but the order was never implemented.

During the absence from Japan of the Iwakura ambassadors the absentee government, notably Saigō Takamori, Itagaki Taisuke, and Etō Shinpei, continued to struggle with the problem of Korea policy. The abolition of the prefectures of 1871 had removed the daimyo of Tsushima from the stage, and some new arrangement had to be worked out. The government sent a number of missions of investigation to Pusan, where the Tsushima trade had been carried out; they returned strong advocates for the use of force. Korean productivity would make it worth the price, they argued. China, where Foreign Minister Soejima had been the first foreign diplomat received in audience by the T'ung-chih emperor, was unlikely to intervene, as it had just been trounced by the Anglo-French expedition sent to avenge a massacre at Tientsin. Russia should be satisfied with the Sakhalin-for-Kurils exchange, and even if it tried to take advantage of the occasion by moving on Hokkaido Britain and France would probably join to prevent it. The coast seemed clear for action on Korea; Saigō was to be sent as emissary. Imperial approval had been given, but before taking action a nervous court wanted the participation of the Iwakura ambassadors. Hence the urgent call for them to return home.

Their return put the project on hold for a period of vigorous debate in October 1873 that ended with reversal of the decision to send Saigō to Korea. The records of the discussions are still imperfect, but little or nothing of this was known to the public at the time. Not even Yamagata, who headed the modern military, or Katsu, who headed the infant navy, were made aware of the debate until it was nearly over. Saigō argued vehemently that the decision to send him could not be reversed. If he failed to bring the Koreans around and was instead assassinated in Korea, he said, that itself would provide Japan with a perfect excuse for war. "I cannot claim to make as splendid an envoy as Soejima," he wrote Itagaki, "but if it is a question of dying, that, I assure you, I am prepared to do." Moreover, war would utilize disgruntled samurai and "divert abroad the attention of those who desire civil strife, and thereby benefit the country." On the other side of the argument, Ōkubo and (a newly converted) Kido spoke from their knowledge of the international situation to argue the insanity of creating a situation that would invite the intervention of China and the European powers. The collapse of an increasingly nervous Sanjō Sanetomi, who had been chairing the meetings, and his replacement by Iwakura sealed the decision.

An indignant Saigō left Tokyo and the government for Kagoshima, together with his closest followers and elements of the Konoe Imperial Guard, which was largely made up of Satsuma soldiers. Itagaki Taisuke, Gotō Shōjirō, Etō Shinpei, and Soejima Taneomi also left the government, first preparing a petition for an elective council so that the decision process would not again breed dispute and anger. The Meiji leaders had broken up after a decade of remarkable and civilized accommodation of differences. Numerous imponderables about individual positions and motivation in this debate remain, but it is probably reasonable to argue, as Inoue Kiyoshi does, that the argument was really about who would rule Japan: Saigō, Itagaki, and the military-minded, or reform bureaucrats of the Ōkubo Toshimichi and Kido Takayoshi stamp.[41]

7. Winners and Losers

This chapter has focused on the activities of the men who led in the Meiji changes. The core leadership, a cluster of samurai from southwestern domains who had gained military and bureaucratic experience in the 1860s, worked through their daimyo and court aristocrats to gain consensus for steps of centralization before setting out on a search for foreign models for their country's new institutions. Within a few years they had moved from the wings to the center of the political stage to replace their former superiors. What of the other, more numerous, Japanese? Who gained and who lost?

In terms of centrality to the political process, the former daimyo and court aristocrats were soon irrelevant. But most of them had long been ciphers as individuals. Of the few who might have had the best chance to survive, Shimazu Hisamitsu of Satsuma grumbled angrily from the sidelines. Yamauchi Yōdō of Tosa commented mournfully that daimyo were a thing of the past before drinking himself to death. Date Munenari of Uwajima played a role in early Meiji diplomacy. Ōkōchi Teruna of Takasaki cultivated friends in the

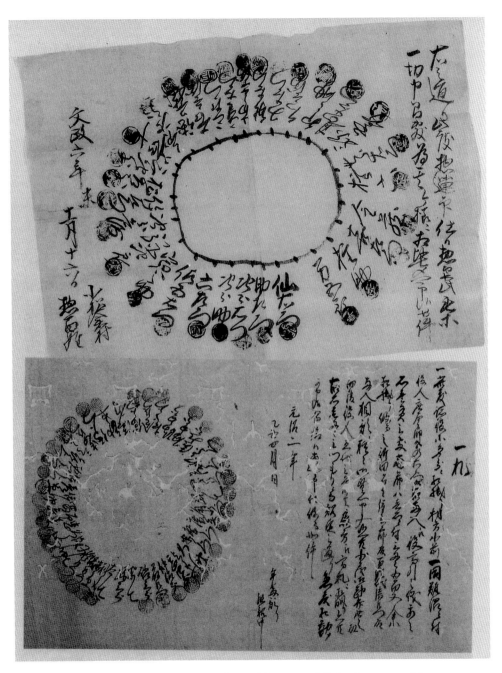

20. Circular ("umbrella") petitions submitted in 1823 and (below) 1865 promising cooperation in return for abatement of additional demands.

21. American troop formation ordered by Commodore Perry at Shimoda, June 8, 1854.

22. Tokugawa Keiki (1837–1913), the last shogun. The English diplomat Ernest Satow thought him "one of the most aristocratic-looking Japanese I have ever seen . . . such a gentleman."

23. Artist's conception of procession carrying the young Meiji emperor across the moat into the shogun's castle, thenceforth imperial palace grounds, November 1868; painting by Kobori Tomone (1854–1931).

24. In this early Meiji print, "Bustling Crowds at Nihonbashi," the scene (see illus. 10 and 14) has been changed by the presence of Westerners in a horse-drawn cart and several Chinese. The hawkers, jugglers, and shoppers remain unchanged.

25. Painting by Yamaguchi Hōshun (1893–1971) showing departure of the Iwakura embassy for the United States and Europe on December 23, 1871.

26. The embassy leaders. Iwakura, still in Japanese dress, flanked by vice ambassadors (left to right) Kido Takayoshi, Yamaguchi Naoyoshi, Itō Hirobumi, and Ōkubo Toshimichi.

27. The Meiji leaders in their prime: Matsukata (top left) in 1905, robed for an honorary degree at Oxford; Itō (top right) in 1885, when he organized his first cabinet in preparation for the constitution; Itagaki (center), leader of the Freedom and People's Rights Movement; Yamagata (bottom left) as home minister in 1887, when he laid out the lines of local government; and Mori (bottom right) in 1872, when he headed the Meiji legation in Washington.

28.
Advocates of the Freedom and People's Rights Movement spoke to large and enthusiastic audiences despite police efforts, as in this newspaper caricature, to intimidate them.

29.
The 1890 Imperial Rescript on Education, with its emphasis on loyalty and traditional values, was the centerpiece of moral instruction in lower schools. A reverential reading of the rescript was followed by three banzais for the emperor and patriotic song. In this classroom the teacher stands between the characters for loyalty (left) and filial piety (right).

30.
The Meiji emperor in 1879,
when he was twenty-seven.

31.
In time the animosities of
early Meiji gave way to
cooperation and self-
congratulation. Here Ōkuma
Shigenobu (left) and Itō
Hirobumi, at Itō's Ōiso villa,
show the eclectic mix of
dress Meiji gentlemen preferred when not on stage.

32. During the Sino-Japanese War of 1894–95 wood-block prints celebrating military triumphs were often patriotic fabrications, but they were vastly popular illustrated news sheets, focusing on ordinary (though heroic) soldiers and contrasting Japanese modernity to Chinese inefficiency. Here a soldier, "risking certain death," scouts the enemy at the Taedong River. Print by Toshihide.

33. "Brave Japanese fighters rout enemy at Fenghuangcheng" (in South Manchuria) in a charge allegedly scheduled for the emperor's birthday. Print by Toshikata.

34. The taste of empire: Japan's Konoe Division, under the command of Imperial Prince Kitashirakawa, enters the north gate of Taipei on June 11, 1896, in a campaign to "pacify" the Taiwanese. Painting by Ishikawa Toraji (1875–1964).

35. Meiji wood-block prints served to convey news, though not always accurately, as in this depiction of reluctant Koreans presenting an agreement to "reform" to a stern Japanese minister Ōtori Keisuke in 1894.

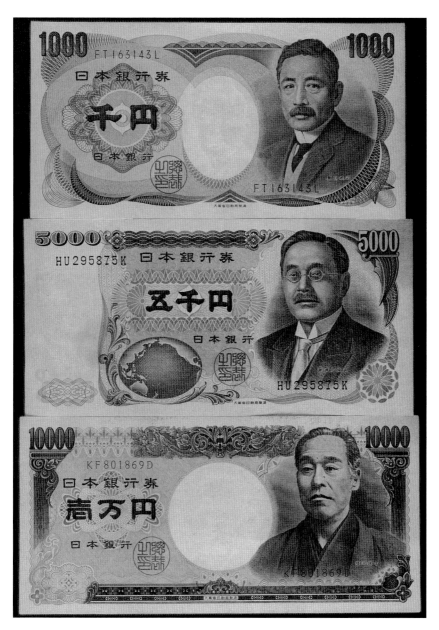

36. Contemporary Japan, determined to substitute heroes of culture for those of war and empire, has placed figures of cultural distinction on its currency. Figures who loom large in cultural change are (top) the writer Natsume Sōseki (1867–1916), 1,000 yen; the educator and internationalist Nitobe Inazō (1862–1933), 5,000 yen; and the educator and westernizer Fukuzawa Yukichi (1835–1901), 10,000 yen.

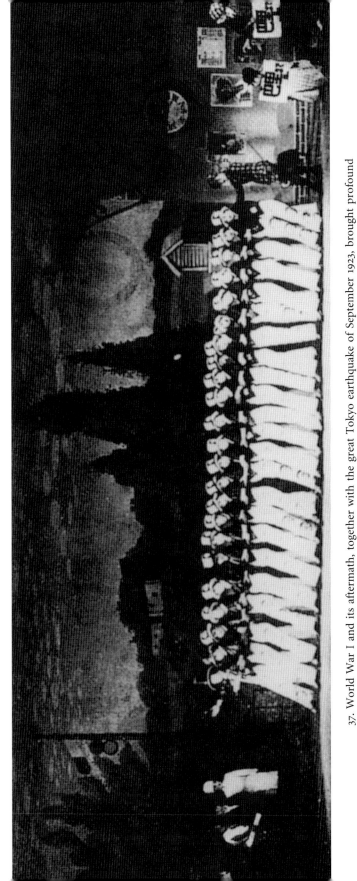

37. World War I and its aftermath, together with the great Tokyo earthquake of September 1923, brought profound changes in the outlook of urban Japanese. One aspect of this was the enormously popular all-girl Takarazuka revue. This "train dance" is from the 1927 production *Mon Paris*, which contrasted Japan-centered "internationalism" and modernity with quaint orientalism in the countries traversed en route to Paris.

38. Artistic traditions lived on in a school of gifted painters whose work carried on the gentle humor of *nanga* painters of Tokugawa times. This detail of a scroll by Dōmoto Inshō (1891–1975) expresses the nostalgia of cultured men for the leisurely pleasures of the scholar's life in traditional China. (Griffith and Patricia Way Collection; photograph by Eduardo Calderón, courtesy of Seattle Art Museum)

39. Empire offered investment potential and encouraged popular saving. This hundred-yuan bond, issued by the "Empire of Manchukuo" in 1937, guaranteed the holder a 4 percent return through the five twenty-yuan coupons attached.

new Chinese mission in order to exchange poems and parties, the meanwhile deploring the excesses of Japan's turn to the West and execrating Ōkubo and other leaders. As individuals, however, the daimyo had few causes for complaint. Together with the court nobles, they were classed as *kazoku*, a rank above former samurai, and they were later named to a new peerage *(kizoku)* established in 1884. They were handsomely rewarded with pensions appropriate to their former domains, so that the largest lords remained extremely wealthy. The new government took over the foreign debts domains had accumulated, and summoned daimyo and nobles to live in Tokyo. It established a special bank to guide them in their investments and to have access to the capital they had gained in the settlement.[42]

Samurai had, of course, always known a different universe; structured by rank and marred by factional insecurity, it ranged from relative affluence to genteel poverty. The few who emerged as leaders in the Meiji period experienced great power and security. We shall turn to the many who did not shortly.

The commoners concern us first; in what way were they gainers or losers? The evidence, as Stephen Vlastos shows, is mixed.[43] Peasant protests totaled 343 between 1868 and 1872, and rose to a peak of 110 in 1869. There were three successive years of crop failures beginning in 1867, however, and most of these incidents continued a pattern of petitions for tax reduction that had become established in Tokugawa times. Hopes of tax reduction had been encouraged by the new government, as we have noted, and when these proved illusory farmers protested the more. In some areas they objected to the departure of feudal authorities who had shown compassion and understanding in administration, preferring to trust old authorities to new promises. New administrators, working within a new administrative structure, could be particularly indifferent to long-established communal practices and customary rights. Before long the new government had the services of troop units without local ties who showed little of the compunction peasants had grown to expect from local samurai forces.[44]

The new government also issued a number of edicts that stirred confusion and indignation. In 1871 bans on intermarriage between commoners and samurai were lifted. In the nature of things this did not affect very many farmers; fewer, certainly, than the declaration that same year that the subcaste class was to be raised to commoner *(heimin)* status. This change sparked a number of protests. Even for those "liberated" it was at first a mixed blessing, as the occupational monopolies (like that in hides) and self-government to which they were accustomed came to an end and they became subject to the new tax structure.

There were also clear gains. Farmers were permitted, indeed required, to adopt family names. Freedom of cultivation constituted an important gain for peasants whose crops had been dictated by domains' desire for self-sufficiency, and a new freedom to move and to sell formalized capabilities that had had to be carried out overtly. Also in 1871, a new Registration Law stipulated that households should be listed as units in a new district system, and that household heads be held accountable as responsible for the actions and obligations of household members. Where the old countryside had focused, in theory at least, on the community as unit, now the household head, with his new family name and dependent family members, was to take on something of the nature of the Tokugawa samurai who inherited and held his commission.

In 1873 two additional ordinances brought basic change to all commoners. The conscription law of January of that year required four years of service in the army to be followed by another three in the reserves. Exemptions were possible for those able to pay 270 yen, but as this was beyond the means of most agriculturalists the new requirement bore most heavily on the poor. The new law produced a number of protests, some sparked by misinterpretation of the "blood tax" (the French term used by the government) and others by smoldering suspicion that the new order favored the rich.

Similar ambivalence characterized rural response to the most important reform of all, the land ordinances that were announced in 1873. Farmers would now receive legal title to their land, and imposts that had been levied on the village were now to be the responsibility of the owner. While the old tax had been based on estimated productivity, with rates and details varying from domain to domain, the new system required a uniform 3 percent of what was thought to be the commercial value of the land, paid in cash. Land value in turn was worked out by a complicated formula.[45] In practice, most authorities agree, the tax due was usually not very different from what it had been. The process of assessment and issuance of certificates of title required time, of course, and in some parts of Japan, notably Satsuma, it was not completed for years. What matters is that a system to which people had become accustomed, worked out with authorities who were at least occasionally amenable to negotiation in years of hardship, was now replaced by one that was far more inflexible and impersonal. Taken overall it was probably more equitable, although to farmers in areas where tax rates were relatively low under the old regime it would not have seemed so. Payment in money meant that the benefits of inflation would accrue to the owner-taxpayer, but people in some parts of Japan were at a disadvantage in dealing with a distant commodities market. Under the reforms of the prefectural system new administrators, less familiar with local conditions, were likely to have their eyes fixed on higher authority.

All this conspired to produce a rash of protests, some of which became violent. Where local administrators directed the process or where the new tax rate seemed reasonable things went well, but when the Tokyo government ordered a speedup in 1875 protests rose sharply in response to perceived injustice. Those protests were usually futile, for the Meiji government, unlike its daimyo predecessors, had ready access to military units. Intent on maintaining a fragile unity, it had no hesitation in squelching revolt. In 1877, however, the regime felt sufficiently constrained by its pressures to lower the tax to 2.5 percent, work out agreements for reduction in years of crop failure, and permit payment in kind for farmers far from marketing centers.

Did ordinary Japanese, especially agriculturalists, benefit from the reforms? In some areas traditional leaders and headmen provided such continuity that awareness of those reforms may have been slow in coming.[46] Within the space of a few years, however, a new local elite—overlapping with, but not identical to, the old—began to take form. Its members were established, landowning farmers, men Japanese historians class as gōnō (wealthy farmers); they were the ones who organized the new village schools and had the resources and initiative to undertake protests in cases of glaring misgovernment. They were also astonishingly free with petitions, memoranda, and suggestions for improving the state of affairs. A massive set of printed volumes indicates the range and vigor of their proposals.[47] These men thought of themselves more as New England selectmen than as humble and downtrodden peons. On the other hand the changes affected adversely the less able, the disadvantaged, and the poor. The advantage lay with the landlord, the employer, and the petty official who knew the rules, knew those who applied them, and enjoyed the backing of the new codes for free exercise in areas where customary rights and mutual obligations had served to moderate the opportunity for self-advancement. But for every successful farmer-turned-entrepreneur there was probably a "water-drinking" (mizunomi) tenant pushed closer to the line of destitution. The question of relative benefit from the changes has generated a large amount of important scholarship, and is one to which we shall turn again.

Samurai surely experienced the greatest change of all, and most of them were clearly losers. The military leaders in the new government had become convinced in late Tokugawa days of the superiority of civilian conscripts to samurai units. The latter had dash and pride, but those same qualities went poorly with discipline and routine. Equally important, the structure of life-stipends for this hereditary class absorbed so much money that governments could do little else.

Immediately after the Restoration reform began in the southwestern domains. Satsuma reduced stipends, Chōshū simplified its rank structure, Hizen launched a search for "men of ability" for office, and in Tosa sweeping reforms suggested an early end to hereditary status divisions. In the autumn of 1870 the central government issued orders designed to produce uniformity in rank structures; domains, too, were classed "large," "middle," and "small," according to their *kokudaka.*

Once the abolition of domains and establishment of prefectures was announced in 1871, the central government found itself responsible for all samurai income. The first problem was to identify "real" from "almost" samurai, after which middle- and higher-level men were termed *shizoku,* lower, *sotsu.* Soon the bottom category was abolished; single-generation *sotsu* became commoners, the others, *shizoku.* The government, pressed for funds, next turned its attention to the Tokugawa vassals whose domains were being reclassified as prefectures. Incomes were cut drastically, and monetary rewards offered for those who resigned their commissions altogether.

But that still left most of the country and most of the samurai. Tokugawa vassals, and samurai from the northeast domains that had lost in the civil war, were not a great problem; they knew they had lost the war, and their expectations were low. It was not so with the newly militarized southwestern domains that had led in the Restoration movement. Their men were flushed with victory, their expectations were high, and they had powerful friends at the center. Incomes were reduced, and the new government was pinning its hopes on a conscript army. Attempts to streamline the army in Chōshū caused one rebellion. Worse, the government was finding even reduced pensions for an unemployed class an intolerable burden. It had already permitted samurai to enter trades and productive activities, but few had the aptitude and preparation to do so successfully. "Bushi shōhō," warrior business management, became a byword for incompetence. In 1874 the government tried to encourage samurai to exchange their pensions for interest-bearing bonds. Two years later, despairing of this program, the government made commutation into bonds compulsory. Like the earlier pensions, the bonds were scaled to former income; great daimyo might emerge as plutocrats, but for most samurai the bonds represented pitifully small nest eggs. In many cases they were soon lost to speculation or incompetence.

In this context talk of war for Sakhalin, or of an expedition to avenge the murder of Okinawan fishermen by Taiwanese aborigines, or of avenging perceived insults from Korea was understandably popular. Samurai were supposed to be indifferent to gain or loss, but they were also supposed to value honor more than life.

Consequently the breakup of the leadership group over the argument about Korea in 1874 was soon followed by violence. In Hizen a group of firebrands persuaded Etō Shinpei to act as their leader in an enterprise that was doomed from the start. Ōkubo personally directed the suppression of the Saga rebels. Etō fled to Kagoshima to seek help from Saigō and to Tosa to try to recruit Itagaki, but he failed, was captured, and was executed. Next Maebara Issei raised the flag of revolt in Chōshū in 1876. The chief effect was destruction of the castle town by fire and anger of the commoners that the *shizoku* had brought them so much grief. In Kumamoto a "Divine Wind" (*Shinpūren* or, read differently, *kamikaze*) zealot group was so opposed to the government's modernization attempts that they refused to use firearms and relied on swords, which simplified the problem of suppression.

The grand finale of these protests came in Satsuma, where Saigō Takamori took to the field, avowedly in an attempt to persuade the emperor of the villainous conduct of his ministers. Since his withdrawal from the government Saigō had lived quietly and in relative isolation, but the province itself had become an armed camp. "Private schools" (*shigakkō*) that were thinly disguised training camps were everywhere. Saigō was the young warriors' hero and to some degree, sponsor; the prefectural governor, fully in sympathy with local discontent, also cooperated. Tokyo, becoming suspicious, dispatched spies to investigate; soon captured and interrogated, one confessed under torture that his real mission had been to assassinate Saigō. Next the government tried to remove the supply of arms it had in the Kagoshima arsenal; young hotheads blocked that move. At this point, in 1877, Saigō agreed to lead a march to Tokyo to remonstrate with the emperor. Wanting to protect his flank, he first laid siege to the Kumamoto castle garrison. When it withstood his attack the revolt was doomed, but it went on for the better part of the year. The government's response had been to appoint Prince Arisugawa once more as nominal general of an army of suppression.

The Satsuma Rebellion may be considered the real war of the Restoration. It took six months to crush the southerners. The government was stretched to the limit, recruiting former samurai from other domains as well as sending units of its own police. In all it mobilized 65,000 men, and its armies suffered 6,000 deaths and 10,000 casualties. Saigō professed loyalty to the throne throughout and wore his Imperial Army uniform, but his force was destroyed; some 18,000 rebel troops were killed or wounded.

The samurai rebellions failed in part because they were limited to samurai and utilized commoners only as beasts of burden. Drawn from different domains, their leaders proved unable to coordinate plans or work together. As a result the government was able to deal with them one by one. After Saigō had failed, moreover, it was clear that no further samurai revolts would have a chance of succeeding. Saigō was a Protean figure, large in life and larger in death, with a legacy for would-be populists as well as militarists. After some years his posthumous pardon by the emperor restored him to his position as national hero.

Kido Takayoshi died on May 26, 1877, of tuberculosis and some form of brain disorder. Saigō died by his own hand on September 24, 1877, before the final charge. The following May 14, 1878, Ōkubo Toshimichi, the third member of the powerful triad of the first decade of Meiji, was assassinated in Tokyo by a group of samurai who resented his monopolization of authority.

The three principal leaders of the Restoration thus died within a year of one another, after a decade in which the power of the new state had been consolidated. It would fall to their successors to complete the institutionalization of the Meiji state.

12

The deaths of Kido, Saigō, and Ōkubo at the end of the first decade of the Meiji period moved the next group into leadership slots. The Meiji leaders were by any measure a remarkable assemblage. If we take 1880 as the date by which the leadership had become firm, some interesting facts emerge. Iwakura Tomomi, at fifty-five the senior figure, was a survivor of the original team, but he was to live only three more years. The others averaged forty years of age and were young men in the prime of life. They had been born as samurai of modest rank in the domains that led the Restoration movement. Two (Itagaki Taisuke and Gotō Shōjirō) were from Tosa, and one (Ōkuma Shigenobu) from Saga, but they were soon muscled out by those from Chōshū and Satsuma. It was the military strength of those domains that brought about the Restoration, and the new leaders had, without exception, participated in those wars. Itō Hirobumi and Inoue Kaoru were members of the original group of *sangi* (councillors) of the infant Meiji government; the others soon joined them, and they kept their seats as its numbers shrank from 106 to 26 and finally to 7 when the modern cabinet system replaced that designation in 1884. Key members of the group had been overseas; Itō Hirobumi and Inoue Kaoru were members of the little group that Chōshū sent to England in the 1860s, while others like Yamagata Aritomo (Chōshū) and Matsukata Masayoshi (Satsuma) were soon abroad investigating military and financial systems. They were given lower bureaucratic posts in the initial round of assignments, but the 1870s saw them move up rapidly as Satsuma and Chōshū control asserted itself. In their early twenties when the boy-emperor Mutsuhito assumed his role in 1867, they remained his councillors and servants as he matured in his twenties and thirties. Beginning in 1889 he expressed his debt by a series of proclamations designating them his *genkun,* "meritorious elders," a title China's emperors had sometimes granted ministers at the founding of dynasties. In common usage this became *genrō.* The throne also honored them with titles in the new aristocracy that formed, and with monetary gifts; those benefits, though hardly nominal, were eclipsed by the advantages that came to them in a nascent and fast-growing capitalist economy. Intermarriage, adoption, and honorary posts put the little oligarchy at the center of Meiji society, key figures in a web of influence and power. By the 1890s a new generation of ambitious young publicists began to decry the conservatism of the "men of the Tenpō era." The departure of Yamagata (1922) and Matsukata (1924) ended the sway of the original group, but it was not until the death of the court noble Saionji Kinmochi in 1940 that their quiet, unobtrusive guidance from behind the throne came to an end.[1]

No one of the Meiji leaders gained exclusive ascendancy in one area. Specialization was particularly marked in areas like finance and arms, but their backgrounds were so similar that specialized bureaucracies did not emerge until the successor generation took over. The Meiji leaders considered themselves all-purpose authorities and expected to participate in foreign as well as domestic decisions and in national as well as local institutions. Despite this, what emerged became so closely identified with individual contributions that it is convenient to take them up under such headings.

1. Matsukata Economics

Economic problems were so central to the concerns of the Meiji government that it would be quite wrong to credit everything that was done to the work of Matsukata Masayoshi (1835–1924), but his long tenure of more than ten years as finance minister beginning in 1881 has understandably resulted in terms like "Matsukata Economics" and the more dubious references to "Matsukata deflation" and "Matsukata depression." As a young Satsuma samurai Matsukata was befriended by Ōkubo Toshimichi, who would be his mentor until he was assassinated in 1878. By that time Matsukata had already held a number of important posts, often simultaneously. Immediately after the Restoration he was charged with holding Nagasaki for the new government; after a period as governor of Hida Prefecture he moved to the central government. His recommendations were central to land tax reform. Subsequently Ōkubo, before leaving as a member of the Iwakura mission, put him in charge of a new Bureau of Industrial Production and called on him to oversee relief for destitute former samurai. At the time of the Satsuma Rebellion Matsukata's family was still in Kagoshima, but they managed to make their way to

Tokyo after escaping the flames that destroyed the city.[2] The longest-lived of the Meiji *genrō*, Matsukata was not as adroit in politics as his Chōshū counterparts—Ozaki Yukio's autobiography, in fact, deprecates him as the slowest and most obtuse of the Meiji prime ministers—but his personal staying power and the clout of the financial web that formed around him—referred to as the "Matsukata zaibatsu" (financial conglomerate)—guaranteed immense influence throughout his life.

"The major preoccupation of the Meiji government," E. Sydney Crawcour has written, "was to create a sound fiscal base for its needs."[3] The economy over which Matsukata came to preside in 1881 was anything but that. The government had assumed debts of all the domains that acceded to its rule in 1871. It then took on the crushing burden of providing income for a samurai class that was being displaced by its land and conscription policies. Samurai stipends consumed almost one-third of the new government's revenue, and the swift steps to reduce them and permit and finally force the substitution of interest-bearing bonds helped to bring on the samurai rebellions. Suppression of those, particularly the Satsuma uprising of 1877, forced the government to print increasing quantities of yen, the unit that replaced the Tokugawa *ryō* in 1871. Government efforts to operate the monopolies that domains had begun failed, and newly instituted trading and finance companies operated by substantial Tokugawa-era merchant firms under government control took their place. These were ordered to hold in cash the equivalent of the notes they issued, and when the government abruptly ordered them reconstituted as national banks in 1872 a number of Osaka houses were driven into bankruptcy.

Inflation of the note issue brought a decline in real income for urban workers and samurai who tried to make do with their bonds, until by 1880 the market value of 7 percent bonds was less than two-thirds of their face value.

Meanwhile the land tax reform, announced in 1873 and implemented over the next six years, changed life for the large majority of Japanese living in the villages. Land became a capital asset that could be freely sold, and with taxes fixed in money terms and a government note issue growing by one-third in the three years prior to 1881, farmers stood to profit as the yen value of their crops increased.

Government leaders tried desperately to ward off foreign investors. The example of Egypt, brought to colonial status through foreign loans, was constantly held up as a counter to the proposals of Ōkuma Shigenobu of Saga, who was most inclined to inflationary policies. The international order of the day did not in any case favor developmental efforts through institutions like the World Bank; foreign aid was a thing of the future. The Meiji leaders ventured only a single foreign loan, and that to finance the beginning of the railway network with an eighteen-mile line from Tokyo to Yokohama. By 1877 only sixty-four miles of track were in place, and those on British narrow gauge for reasons of economy. British example also contributed to the decision to have traffic keep to the left and not to the right. The long-standing bakufu system of land transport through packhorses maintained by post stations and "assisting villages" was discontinued in 1871 and delegated to private management. In the process entire mountain routes that had been established for and maintained by men and horses gradually lost their meaning and income, and local elite—like Shimazaki Tōson's Hanzō—who could not maintain their primacy on the basis of their holdings in land became as obsolete as the samurai to whom they had reported.

Coastal trade continued as vital as before, but government leaders worried about inroads by faster and better foreign shipping. A semigovernmental shipping company designed to use bakufu and domain vessels soon failed, and in 1875 the regime presented thirty of its ships, free of charge, to the Tosa domain official Iwasaki Yatarō, whose Mitsubishi company also received a generous operating subsidy. Mitsubishi services to the government during the Satsuma Rebellion resulted in further benefactions, and gave the company the ability to compete favorably with the American Pacific Mail and British P & O lines that had grown up with the treaty ports. Telegraph communications were cheapest and fastest of all, and contributed importantly to the government's ability to overcome the Satsuma Rebellion. By 1877, 2,827 miles of line had been installed.

The government also invested heavily from its slender resources in industrial development. It inherited and retained title to all mineral and modern industrial plants that had been begun by the bakufu and domains. Ironworks, munitions plants, and shipyards existed in a narrow band of coastal and pro-Restoration areas. The country's forests and major mines were now the state's, often to the distress of local residents whose customary rights were no longer of interest to new officials. To these were added the few cotton-spinning plants that had been started in unsuccessful efforts to reverse the growing deficit incurred through foreign trade. Late Tokugawa Japan had profited from European demand for silkworm eggs and tea, but as the European silkworm blight was conquered and the superior quality of foreign textiles and thread became apparent the trade surplus of the past was soon reversed. Government efforts to counter this through the import of cotton-spinning plants enjoyed only modest financial success, but served, it was hoped, to familiarize Japanese managers and workers with factory methods and standardize export products.

The government ordered sweeping surveys of production in 1874 and again in 1884, and tried urgently to categorize and catalogue the country's resources with an eye to finding some sort of plan for economic development. A major problem was that posed by the unequal treaties, which limited Japan's power to protect infant industries. One finds this awareness made explicit by Itō Hirobumi in a memorandum he wrote for his fellow ambassadors in the Iwakura embassy. British hosts and statesmen, he warned, would champion free trade in their talks, but it was important that the Japanese be prepared to counter their arguments. Itō here extended the "national profit" long sought by domain administrators to the needs of the larger entity of a central-ized Japan, but still found it necessary to argue the case for setting aside Con-fucian morality in working toward the goal of modern "civilization":

> Unless domestic products are cheaper than foreign products one's own people will not buy them, so one increases import tariffs in order to put up the price of foreign goods . . . such a tariff is called a defensive tax . . .
>
> Countries like our own that have not yet attained full development will delay the arrival of civilization if they do not apply this method. For example, we should keep the tax low on domestic goods such as books and machinery and make it high on goods such as silk textiles, alcohol and tobacco, thus helping to stimulate our own production. A country such as America, by using solely this method in relation to alcohol and tobacco has already reached a stage where the people have greatly increased production . . .
>
> From the point of view of morality this favoring of one's own [coun-try] looks like seeking one's own profit and one's own advantage and aban-doning the usual principles of justice. But for enriching one's country, making one's country prosperous, it is in fact an indispensable means . . . use of the protective tariff is how Britain reached its present prosperity and came to dominate the world's manufacture.[4]

This fascinating document illustrates perfectly the problem the early Meiji government faced. Itō's logic is incontrovertible; developing countries, he thought, needed to protect their industries, but the unequal treaties made it impossible for Japan to do so. It could, however, also be argued that Japan was fortunate in its inability to put up tariff walls, and that what it was forced to do was ultimately more healthy. What it now had to do was to launch a bootstraps-operation of self-help, and that is what Matsukata and his associ-ates undertook in the 1880s.

In 1877, immediately after the suppression of the Satsuma Rebellion, Matsukata went to Paris to head the Japanese exhibit at the Paris Exhibition of that year. While there he took as his mentor the finance minister Léon Say, the grandson of a well-known exponent of free trade. Say himself, however, had raised French tariffs sharply in order to pay off the indemnity incurred through France's defeat at the hands of Prussia, and Matsukata, like Itō before him, was convinced of the necessity for Japan to regain the freedom to adopt protectionist policies at the earliest possible date. Meanwhile the only course to follow in order to lower Japan's foreign trade deficit was one of austerity. Government income was reduced because of inflation, government bonds were being discounted, and the value of land was rising rapidly. As Matsukata later recalled, "farmers, who were the only ones to profit from these circumstances, took on luxurious habits . . . imports from foreign countries were increased. Merchants, dazzled by the extreme fluctuations in prices, all aimed at making huge speculative profits and gave no heed to productive undertakings."[5] The solution for this "bubble economy" was austerity.

What followed was the "Matsukata deflation." Government expenditure was drastically reduced, and government industries were sold off to private interests. New taxes were imposed and the note issue was brought back to pre–Satsuma Rebellion levels. The results were disastrous for many small farmers who found creditors and tax men seizing their assets, and rates of bankruptcy and tenancy rose sharply. In terms of purely economic rationality, the process transferred resources to the government, to the banking system, and to stronger and more competitive elements of both urban and rural economy. In human terms the decade was nevertheless one of wrenching difficulty for many small farmers.

It is not surprising that problems of the "Matsukata economy" have generated a vast quantity of scholarship of great importance to the interpretation of Japan's subsequent history. Studies of tenancy and rural immiseration have related trends discerned there to sharp economic differentiation in the modern Japanese countryside and a depressed and apathetic peasantry susceptible to manipulation by a capitalist and militarist government. Some studies are more hesitant to ascribe a straight-line process to rural differences of the twentieth century, however,[6] while one study goes so far as to reject the thesis altogether.[7]

A second area of dispute concerns the sale of government enterprises. The conglomerates, or zaibatsu, that emerged constituted industrial concentration so striking that many have credited this to collusion and charged it with making impossible the growth of democracy in Japan. Thomas Smith, however, concludes that the sales were dictated by government difficulties and that those fortunate enough to have vision and, especially, capital to buy them, were so few that better bids were not forthcoming.[8] Whatever the case, it is certain that the concentration that resulted gave firms like Mitsui, Mitsubishi, Sumitomo, and Yasuda a commanding position that led to an oligopoly in control of markets. The rural and industrial solutions both combined to reduce the development of consumer orientation, a pattern not unfamiliar in other late-developing countries after World War II. Neither arguments based upon classical economics, which stress the positive impact for future economic growth, nor those on Marxist economics, which stress immiseration and a static countryside, do justice to the variety that characterized Japan as its economy stabilized, for the proportion of winners and losers differed by place and time. What is certain, however, is that the decade saw the Meiji leadership commit itself to modern economic growth.[9] The drive was encapsulated in the slogan *fukoku kyōhei* (rich country, strong army), a goal that had already been held up by late Tokugawa domains. Modern scientific thought and technology began to be applied to production, per capita productivity accompanied population growth, and the changes were made in full consciousness of the pressures and possibilities posed by international contacts. The Matsukata decade did not bring striking improvements in industrial efficiency or individual well-being, but it did see the development of a substructure that was probably essential for later economic change.

2. The Struggle for Political Participation

These same years saw the inception and intensification of a struggle for political participation that began as a movement of disgruntled samurai, but soon engulfed the political and social scene. Its opening stages are inseparably associated with the career of the Tosa military figure Itagaki Taisuke (1837–1919), who left the Meiji government at the same time as Saigō Takamori. Many of Itagaki's followers wanted to revolt against the new regime as Saigō did, but Itagaki saw a different path of resistance. "Saigō fights the government with arms," he told his men, "but we will fight it with people's rights *(minken)."*

In 1874 Itagaki and Gotō Shōjirō, with the cooperation of Soejima Taneomi and Etō Shinpei of Saga, submitted a petition that argued that the handling of the Korean issue, on which the leadership group had parted company, proved the need for the council chamber that had been promised in the Charter Oath. It had been assumed, they wrote, that after the Iwakura mission members had observed the workings of Western governments, plans would be set in motion for representative government in Japan, but "although several months have elapsed since the return of the embassy to this country we do not learn that any measures have been adopted." The 1874 memorial calling for an assembly continued:

[T]he decrees of the government appear in the morning and are changed in the evening, the administration is conducted in an arbitrary manner; rewards and punishments are prompted by partiality, the channel by which the people should communicate with the government is blocked up and they cannot state their grievances . . .

The people whose duty it is to pay taxes to the government possess the right of sharing in their government's affairs and of approving or condemning. This is a principle universally acknowledged and it is not necessary to waste words in discussing it . . .

How is the government to be made strong? It is by the people of the empire becoming of one mind . . . The establishment of a council chamber chosen by the people will create a community of feeling between the government and the people, and they will mutually unite into one body. Then and only then will the country become strong . . .

Gradual progress has not been the case with council-chambers only; all branches of knowledge and science and art are subject to the same conditions. The reason why foreigners have perfected [council chambers] only after the lapse of centuries is that no examples existed previously, and these had to be discovered by actual experience. If we can select examples from them and adopt their methods, why should we not be successful in working them out? If we delay the use of steam machinery until we have discovered the principles of steam for ourselves, or wait until we have discovered the principles of electricity to construct an electric telegraph, our government will be unable to work . . .

By establishing such a council chamber public discussion in the empire will be established, the spirit of the empire will be roused to activity, the affection between governors and governed will be greater, sovereign and subject will be brought to love each other, our imperial country will be maintained and its destinies developed, and prosperity and peace will be assured to all.[10]

Several themes pervade the fascinating document Itagaki and his friends prepared. One is that of rights, an assumption that requires no defense. A second is that participation will bring unity and a common purpose; far from becoming partisan, politics will be single-minded. The third is the note of progress that pervades the document; Japan can do things more rapidly than the West did, since it can profit from that example. "Latecomers" to modernity and civilization can leapfrog over experimentation.

The debate over Korea had divided the Restoration coalition, and the disgruntled losers resigned from the government and returned to their provinces.

In Saga Etō Shinpei was soon drawn into the leadership role in the Saga rebellion; his attempts to get help from Saigō and from Itagaki were, it will be remembered, unsuccessful, and he himself was executed. In Tosa things went differently. On returning home Itagaki and his followers organized a society they named the Risshisha. Its name was adapted from the (1870) translation of Samuel Smiles's *Self-Help* (*Saikoku risshi hen,* "Tales of men who achieved their aims in Western countries"). This curious little book was made up of a series of inspirational stories of men who had overcome difficulties by struggle and determination, and it was meant to inspire workers in England to do their best. It became and remained immensely popular in Japan, where many readers undoubtedly transferred its moralisms to the nation; Japan, a poor boy in the company of competitors, could achieve its goals of wealth and strength if it persevered. The Risshisha arranged its activities through representative elections of the sort its leaders urged on the government, and they also sponsored mutual aid and education for the former samurai, now *shizoku,* who made up the group's members. But a class-bound movement had little future, and Risshisha statements embodied the ambivalence of condescension and compassion that characterized so much early Meiji rhetoric.

More important, the government, worried about *shizoku* discontent, did everything it could to checkmate the movement by persuading Itagaki to accept political office again, as it did through a meeting in Osaka in 1875. There was new talk of an elective chamber, but when the progress seemed to slow he withdrew once more. New press laws and a steadily more effective police organization exerted enough pressure on those advocating representative institutions for them to adopt names like that of Risshisha's successor, which called itself the "Public Society of Patriots" to make it clear that it was not a secret group of violent subversives. It has to be added, in the government's defense, that it was not unreasonable to associate *shizoku* disaffection with violence. A group of Itagaki's Tosa supporters did plan to support Saigō's efforts in the Satsuma Rebellion, but the police uncovered the plot before anything came of it. Ōkubo Toshimichi himself, it will be recalled, was struck down by assassins in 1878. It was natural for the government to monitor the activities of dissident former samurai.

Prior to that, in 1876, the government requested the members of the Genrōin (a consultative body established in 1875 at the time the government persuaded Itagaki to rejoin the government, and not to be confused with the oligarchs, or *genrō*), to prepare a possible draft for a constitution, something it did two years later. Key figures, particularly Itō and Iwakura, rejected the result as unsatisfactory because it seemed to divide authority between emperor and legislature and had no provision for imperial ordinances that would have the force of law. Government leaders now turned to the task themselves. Elective institutions were clearly in the air.

Enthusiasm for them soon broke out of the narrow social base with which Itagaki's movement had begun. *Minken,* people's rights, became linked with *jiyū,* freedom, to give its name to the *jiyū-minken* movement that dominated and very nearly transformed Japanese life in the early 1880s. These were new words, now encased in the four-Chinese-character format that was so common in Meiji years. They emerged as part of a series of translations of Western thought that began to flood the country. Each part of the slogan had its problems in the East Asian context, and the memoirs of numerous contemporaries describe a confused but genuine conversion experience as people struggled to fathom the meaning and significance of the words. They conveyed genuinely new ideas, and it required time for them to be appropriated in a "Western" sense. As their priorities and understanding changed individuals could often exhibit puzzling changes. For some, *jiyū* had overtones of a Taoist formless but freely moving spirit, something rather foreign to Confucian categories. For some, it suggested self-indulgence and selfishness. Fukuzawa Yukichi, in his seminal book about the West, apologized for the use of the characters he appropriated for "freedom," and warned that they should not be misinterpreted. *Minken,* "people's rights," also had an uncertain derivation, but probably entered Japan through translations into Chinese of Western books on international law. It followed that it was more easily understandable in the mass—the national rights of sovereignty or the rights of all people against autocratic government—than as something to which the individual was entitled. Add the fact that early translators of John Stuart Mill sometimes confused "society" with "government," and the overtones of Western liberal thought could vary widely.

In 1881 the Itagaki partisans again presented a petition, and shortly afterward they took advantage of a sake brewers' convention in Osaka to organize a national Jiyūtō, "Liberal" or "Freedom" political party. New local tax laws, including a levy on sake, that were part of the Matsukata deflation, angered regional entrepreneurs and gave meaning to calls for participation in decisions. The Tosa leaders were soon moving around the country on speaking tours. Reporters for the rapidly growing urban press were drawn into the movement, frequently making as well as reporting news as they addressed regional gatherings. The government responded with harsher press and police provisions, but could not succeed in dampening the eagerness of rural and town audiences to hear the new evangel. Itagaki, stern warrior leader, became an effective public speaker and symbol of the movement. The role was not without its dangers. In 1882 he narrowly escaped death at the hands of a police officer assigned to a meeting he was addressing in Gifu. Legend has it that he had the foresight to shout, "Itagaki may die, but liberty never!" as he collapsed. The emperor ordered a government physician, the future political leader Gotō Shinpei, to take care of him, and later he received a monetary grant as well.[11]

By then there was a second political party in the field. The Saga councillor Ōkuma Shigenobu (1838–1922) had survived the narrowing of governmental leadership in the 1870s, but as the sole "outsider" in a Satsuma-Chōshū group his days proved to be numbered. For a time he was seen as a possible competitor for power with Itō. His chance, and his downfall, came in response to a request by Prince Arisugawa for ministers of state to submit their ideas for a constitution. The drafts were to be submitted in confidence, so that the government could make its decisions without the intervention of outside opinion. Ōkuma waited till the other drafts were in, and then submitted to Prince Arisugawa a draft that was much more radical than the others. His draft had been prepared for him by Ōno Azusa, a student of English constitutional practice. The other ministers' drafts offered only limited degrees of participation, but Ōkuma's proposed a British system of majority rule based on party strength. Worse, he proposed almost immediate implementation.[12] The emperor had just left on an inspection tour of the island of Hokkaido, and in his absence politics came to a boil. Itō denounced Ōkuma for proposing a draft that weakened imperial sovereignty, and threatened to resign if it were adopted.

Ōkuma's bold attempt to bypass the Satsuma-Chōshū group brought on a governmental crisis. There were other elements at work. The sale of government assets in Hokkaido, undertaken as part of Matsukata's decision to sell off early investments in industrialization, had been carried on by cronyism at considerable loss to the treasury. Press and politicians were vocal in denunciation, and Ōkuma too made his objections known. The other leaders, particularly Itō, were furious with Ōkuma and suspected him of wanting to gain primacy. In hurried meetings during the emperor's absence they reorganized the government and drove Ōkuma from office. Modifications were announced in the contractual arrangements for the Hokkaido assets. Most important, a rescript was prepared for the young emperor to issue upon his return. In it he announced that a constitution would be drawn up at his command, with elections to be held for a Parliament to meet in 1890. "Systems of government differ in different countries," the rescript went on, "but sudden and unusual changes cannot be made without great inconvenience . . . We perceive that the tendency of Our people is to advance too rapidly, and without that thought and consideration which alone can make progress enduring, and We warn Our subjects, high and low, to be mindful of Our will, and that those who may advocate sudden and violent changes, thus disturbing the peace of Our realm, will fall under Our displeasure."[13] It was not the last time the Meiji leaders would maneuver the emperor to slow political change.

A considerable number of Ōkuma's friends and followers, some of them, like Ozaki Yukio, destined to play distinguished roles in Japan's constitutional movement, left office with him. Ōkuma himself, undaunted, proceeded to organize a second political party, the Rikken Kaishintō (Constitutional Progressive Party; hereafter, Kaishintō) in the spring of 1882.

The two parties proved to be quite different. Ōkuma's group was strongly influenced by English constitutional thought and practice. The Jiyūtō was more strongly influenced by the language and enthusiasm of the French Revolution. Nakae Chōmin, one of its intellectual lights, was trained in French legal and political thought, having begun as a Tosa student in Nagasaki (where he also met Sakamoto Ryōma) and continued his study of French in Edo. He served as interpreter to French minister Léon Roches before succeeding in having himself attached to the Iwakura embassy as a student, and returned three years later to set up his own academy in Tokyo. Appointed to the staff of the Genrōin, he soon left government service out of discontent with the leisurely progress on a constitution. He was the translator of the French Legal Code and, more famously, of Rousseau's *Social Contract.* Together with the young court noble Saionji Kinmochi (who had also studied in Paris) he launched the *Asian Liberal Press (Toyō jiyū shinbun),* a newspaper that was almost immediately banned, and thereafter, as a member of Itagaki's Jiyūtō, became its most influential publicist. The Jiyūtō was headed by Itagaki, and much of its leadership was made up of former *shizoku.* Sake brewers and rural notables made up a good deal of its membership. Nakae Chōmin was prominent, together with Ueki Emori, another Tosa intellectual who became Itagaki's brain trust and also prepared his own version of a constitution. The Jiyūtō was thus by no means made up of country bumpkins and unruly samurai, as its urban opponents often claimed.

The Kaishintō, in contrast, drew many more urban interests to its cause. Much of its leadership, while no less *shizoku* in origin, could be traced to Fukuzawa Yukichi's Keiō academy, and it also had strong support among publishers and newspapermen. The government, not to be outdone, thought it useful to fund its own counter with the Teiseitō (Imperial Party), and *Nichi-nichi* newspaper, but their influence and circulation were small by comparison with that of the opposition.

The gulf between the party men was often personal as well as ideological. Ozaki Yukio's memoirs tell of an incident during the period the Jiyūtō and

Kaishintō were trying to work together to best the government. A joint dinner meeting was well attended, though violence was in the air. It came to a head in a row between Numa Morikazu of the Kaishintō and Hoshi Tōru of the Jiyūtō. Both were trained in Western studies, law, and language; Hoshi had studied in England, and Numa, better born, had served both the bakufu and new government before leaving service to enter journalism. On this occasion Numa drank too much and started baiting Hoshi by calling him a country bumpkin. Hoshi, no less lubricated and long contemptuous of Numa, ordered his entourage of toughs to douse the lights, after which they belabored Numa with brass candlesticks. "Hoshi," Ozaki writes, "had every intention of beating Numa to death and throwing him out of one of the upper windows into the Sumida River. Fortunately the police arrived in time to rescue Numa from the brink of death."[14] Government leaders could be more discreet and had their own opportunities for intimidation, but it is not hard to see why they distrusted and monitored these advocates of freedom and people's rights carefully.

It is nonetheless astonishing to see that within fifteen years of the Tokugawa fall, and at a time when there were no functioning parliaments outside of Europe and the United States, the dispute in Japan was not over whether there should be a constitution but over who should draw one up and what it should contain.

Indeed that conviction extended well beyond the men and movements that have been described. The struggle of former samurai leaders with their recent colleagues was only part of the story, for there was a far more widespread and pervasive search for new governmental forms abroad in the land. In 1968 a Japanese historian leading a field trip with his students in a search for Meiji documents came upon a long-abandoned storehouse that provided material for a fresh look at the Freedom and People's Rights (jiyū-minken) Movement. Itsukaichi, on the western edge of the Tokyo plain, is today a rather remote mountain village. One hundred years ago it would have been a journey of at least a day from the then borders of Tokyo. The walls of the deteriorating storehouse yielded a rich trove of materials that indicate the intensity with which the villagers followed and tried to participate in the national debate. There was a petition urging the establishment of a parliament at the earliest possible minute, the draft of a 204-article constitution, and several hundred books and copies of books relating to national affairs. There were memoranda and by-laws for the discussion group that had debated these subjects, and copies of the unequal treaties Japan was struggling to revise: evidence, in other words, of a lively and articulate political consciousness in remote mountain villages. "The men who drafted that constitution," Irokawa

Daikichi, whose party discovered the documents, points out, were "hitherto unknown to history, were without exception family men: farmers, merchants, and school teachers—in other words—'commoners' with deep ties to the life of the people."[15]

The condescension with which most *shizoku*—and many historians who were limited to their accounts and records—regarded ordinary Japanese of the early 1880s was thus misplaced. A modern consciousness was advancing steadily among responsible members of rural communities in Japan. The impact of the West provided the catalyst for that movement, but in its essence it included a reformulation of older and earlier moral and political traditions of benevolence and fairness. Nor, it proved, was the village of Itsukaichi unique in this; further investigation revealed the existence of more than sixty associations like that of Itsukaichi in the greater Tokyo countryside alone, and local historians (among whom Japanese high school history teachers play a leading role) can be expected to continue to look for and find more such treasure troves of documents.

As the spotlight narrows to Itsukaichi itself, the cast of characters proves extremely interesting. The schoolteacher, who was also the center of the discussion group and whose hand drafted the constitution in question, was a young man who called himself Chiba Takusaburō. Born into the lower fringe of samurai status in the northern domain of Sendai, he began as a student of medicine under the tutelage of a well-known advocate of opening the country, a man who in addition to studies in Chinese prose and poetry had knowledge of Dutch medicine and a smattering of information about artillery that he had gained from Sakuma Shōzan. Ōtsuki Gentaku had advocated alliance with Russia to ward off the Anglo-American threat and helped negotiate the alliance of northeastern domains that resisted the "imperial" armies at the time of the Restoration. As a youth, Chiba had taken part in that war, and as a loser and in fear of prosecution he went underground and began a quest for spiritual and personal guidance in a time of chaotic change. His first stop was a discipleship with a learned student of medicine who had served the shogun, but the arrest of his teacher soon drove him elsewhere. Next he took up the study of nativist *kokugaku*, but its ties to the early Meiji state made this an unlikely home for long. Next came a short period of study with a Pure Land Buddhist priest—just about the time, it will be remembered, that Buddhism was under intense attack. This too failed to meet the young man's crisis, and he next turned to Orthodox Christianity, which he came to know through association with a group of disciples of the remarkable Russian pioneer Father Nikolai, who had first arrived in Hokkaido in 1861. Nikolai's mission found the Sendai area a rich field for converts in the confusion and disorientation that followed the failed war against the Meiji government. In 1872 his new convert followed Father Nikolai to Tokyo, where Soejima Taneomi, then in charge of foreign affairs, had provided government start-up money for the establishment of a school and seminary. Letters from the Iwakura ambassadors had the proper effect, and the bans on Christianity were replaced with tolerance and even welcome for the access missionaries provided to foreign language study. Within a few years, however, Chiba Takusaburō abruptly changed direction to enroll in the academy of Yasui Sokken, an anti-Christian polemicist, Confucian scholar, and poet whose despairing lines caught the mood of a generation's dislocation. To no purpose: Yasui soon died, and Chiba, once again thrown upon his own resources, found shelter and meaning with a Catholic missionary he assisted in evangelizing tours through the western Tokyo plains and mountains.

The personal record Chiba filed in applying for his position in the Itsukaichi school indicates a brief period with a Methodist missionary. He took a position as schoolteacher in the mountain school in 1879, became its head in 1881, and died in Itsukaichi of tuberculosis in 1883. Under his direction the school was clearly a lively place; his successor complained that Chiba had turned it into a branch of the People's Rights Movement, and Chiba threatened to resign when the prefectural government issued a ban on the political activities of schoolteachers in 1881.

This glimpse of the spiritual pilgrimage of a loser—indeed, by most Meiji standards, a failure—is important because it had its parallels in the life histories of hundreds, more likely thousands, of confused, intense young men who embraced foreign teachings and became political activists in a search for meaning and direction.[16]

Chiba ended his wanderings in the town of Itsukaichi, an area he had probably come to know during his periods of service to his missionary masters. He was welcomed by a group of local notables who were anxious to better inform themselves and improve their country by helping to form a political discussion group. For Chiba the *jiyū-minken* movement provided an outlet of hope for the regeneration of Japanese politics and society in an age of confusion and decay, and an escape from the increasingly autocratic control of the institutional life of his country by the small clique from Satsuma and Chōshū. His friends and sponsors were men of some property and standing in the village, literate, astonishingly well read given the materials then available, and fond of registering their opinions in Chinese poetry, which they found more satisfactory than its Japanese counterpart for expressing complex arguments.

The thrust of the constitution drafts of groups like that at Itsukaichi is often ambivalent. In the case of Chiba Takusaburō's draft there is a fair amount of ambiguity and a rather naive utopian view of the reciprocity of people and ruler in accordance with the will of Heaven—ideas clearly drawn from traditional thought. Of course Chiba and his counterparts in other societies had none of the advantages of government officials who were able to consult their foreign advisers. Nevertheless there is a rather clear sense of restrictions on imperial sovereignty, grounded in conceptions of morality and justice. One need not see this as revolutionary; it was assumed that the emperor, in his promises of a constitution, shared these ideas, and that the Itsukaichi planners were giving voice to the long-held intentions of the throne. Chiba's draft is one of a number that have survived.

What is clear, then, is that the constitutional movement gathered headway at an astonishing rate of speed. When Itagaki's Society of Patriots addressed a petition to the government preparatory to the founding of the Jiyūtō in 1880, they claimed to speak for 100,000 petitioners from twenty-two prefectures. In another instance 23,555 petitioners in nearby Kanagawa Prefecture begged the popular Fukuzawa Yukichi to draft for them a petition calling for a national assembly.

As the Matsukata deflation tightened its hold on the country, the People's Rights Movement began to be associated with rural distress. In several minor incidents government forces suspected political party participation, and in 1884 a force variously estimated as between 5,000 and 10,000 people revolted in the Chichibu district of Saitama Prefecture, near Tokyo. In sharp fighting the rebels briefly had the upper hand over local forces, but after the government moved in more troops they had little difficulty in suppressing a ragtag body armed with hunting rifles, bamboo spears, and wooden cannon. After the roundup of participants 4,000 were found guilty, 300 convicted as felons, and 7 executed. The rebels, who had styled themselves the Debtors' and Tenants' Party, were derided as troublemakers and rioters. A study of the 161 participators who can be traced, however, shows that the rebels were broadly representative of the countryside population. Two-thirds were literate. The largest group were in their thirties, with the others spread on both sides of that age level. They were almost all middle- and lower-ranking farmers, though there was also a scattering of landlords and merchants. Contemporary critics seized on the fact that seven were former convicts and gamblers. One can consider this rebellion as a Tokugawa-style uprising that was dealt with in non-Tokugawa ways. People accustomed to the moderation of earlier domain movements, suddenly subjected to the merciless strictness of the new legal and tax structure, protested in the only way they knew. They were also, however, people who had come, however briefly to entertain hopes of a new order, no doubt somewhat messianic and utopian in transmission. This seemed to be promised by the institution of representative government. The *jiyū-minken* movement, which had originated in the discontent of a disestablished samurai elite, spread to lower orders of society and revolutionized for a time ordinary people of the countryside—not only debtors and the poor, but also middle-strata men whose puzzling over the word *jiyū* had produced expectations of quick and total relief.

The mainline Jiyūtō and Kaishintō leaders wanted no part of this nonsamurai rebellion. Both parties took steps to dissolve their organizations in 1884. Cynicism and despair caused some to give up on large-scale action altogether, while obedience to the emperor's 1881 rescript announcing that Japan would be given a constitution stilled others. In addition, the parties had fallen into bitter infighting and accusations that brought an end to the optimism and enthusiasm of the day of mass petitions. In July of 1882 Itagaki, recently recovered from the assassination attempt, made it known that he and Gotō Shōjirō were planning a trip to Europe. His explanation was that foreign observation and study of the comparative merits of political systems should not be left to government figures.

Many of his fellow Jiyūtō leaders opposed this vehemently. The party movement was in full swing. Itagaki was its most popular figure. He had developed the ability to sense the emotions of his audience and stir them, and he seemed to be awakened to the economic and social issues that were animating many Jiyūtō meetings. Consequently his departure seemed inexplicable. Baba Tatsui, a Tosa follower who became increasingly radical, later blamed the entire downfall of the movement on its leaders; he eventually moved to exile in America, from which he lamented the "election of a leader who was utterly incapable of the management of a political party."

Worse still, rumor had it, correctly as it proved, that the government had played a role in this; Inoue Kaoru, close to Mitsui interests, had arranged for that firm to provide the money to fund the trip. It has never been made clear that Itagaki realized this, but he could certainly have been more curious about the source of his ticket. His defection at this juncture seemed comparable to his brief return to government in 1875 immediately after the original petition for a constitution. Perhaps the heady experience of a central role in the early leadership group, combined with the impressions of imperial solicitude after he had been struck down, combined to make him think it natural that he should receive special treatment at a time when his associates of earlier days were seeking wisdom in Europe. After his return from Europe Itagaki decided that the party had been precipitate in its demands, and lent his prestige to those who proposed closing down the party movement for a time. Itagaki's motives in this episode remain obscure; he was not corrupt personally, but famously poor at a time when government figures were assembling rich rewards, yet he let his followers down badly. In years to come both he and Ōkuma chose cooperation with their former associates over frontal opposition. One suspects that the aura of the throne played an important role in this.

Nevertheless the party leaders' trip to Europe is full of interest. When Itagaki and Gotō reached London Japan was represented by the Satsuma leader Mori Arinori, who had returned to government service after a period in a utopian community. Mori had represented Japan in Washington when the Iwakura embassy came through, and in China. Through Mori, Itagaki was able to meet with Herbert Spencer, a system builder whose imposing scheme of social development dazzled most Meiji, indeed most nineteenth-century, readers. The encounter was not a success. Mori's report to Tokyo said that "[Itagaki] went into [the meeting] as though approaching the Emperor, but in the actual discussion master and pupil traded places, with the disciple doing all the sermonizing and putting forth his usual empty and unfounded theories. Finally the central idol lost his patience, got up in the middle of the conversation muttering 'no, no, no' and took his leave of Itagaki, just like that."[17]

The anecdote is significant, for it reminds us that most observers thought it rash for a country at Japan's stage of development to even think of constitutional government. Disparities of evolution and development combined to suggest caution. When former President Ulysses S. Grant visited Japan on his world tour in 1879, he too warned government figures against offering, prematurely, liberties they would not be able to take back. Spencer himself had warned of Japanese social fragmentation under rapid modernization, and sent, via Kaneko Kentarō, his advice that Japan should keep foreigners at arm's length except for such trade as was essential. The reason, he explained, was discrepancies of strength; "let one of the more powerful races gain a *point d'appui* and there will inevitably in course of time grow up an aggressive policy." As to the other question he had been asked, concerning intermarriage between Japanese and non-Japanese, he was emphatically negative: "It should be positively forbidden . . . It is at root a question of biology. There is abundant proof, alike furnished by the intermarriages of human races and by the interbreeding of animals, that when the varieties mingled diverge beyond a slight degree *the result is inevitably a bad one* in the long run."[18]

Perhaps it should not be a surprise that Itagaki returned from England chastened in his expectations of early constitutionalism. He accepted, though reluctantly, a title (Count) in the new peerage that was set up in 1884, stipulating only that it not be passed on to his heirs. He served in several cabinets, and grew gradually more conservative. His final position on the franchise was that, in the interest of maintaining social solidarity, it should be extended only to heads of households. Curiously, the same idea had been advanced in confidence by Spencer to Mori Arinori. Clearly, the Itsukaichi villagers had more confidence in their fellow citizens than did this *shizoku* leader.

A number of observations emerge from this brief summary of political competition. The first relates to the virtually universal agreement that there should be a constitution, and hence a representative system, of some sort. This conviction pervaded society from the Itsukaichi villagers to the men who wrote "council chamber" into the Charter Oath. Can it be said that the Tokugawa parcelized jurisdiction, with representation, however tenuous, at the center, contributed to this? It is also true that the powerful nations of the world, as the Iwakura ambassadors discovered, had representative institutions. The central government in Tokyo saw a parliament as a device for deflecting suspicion of its Satsuma-Chōshū narrowness, while those not at the center saw it as a way of sharing in that power.

Second, one is impressed by the speed with which these convictions spread through Japanese society. At every point they intersected with the Japanese context, to be sure; the power structure saw a constitution as insulating the throne from partisanship, Tosa and Saga dissidents saw it as an avenue back to the influence they had lost, villagers as protection from arbitrary administrators, and tenants as justification for peasant revolt. Few, one can say, approached this with the same concerns, and none with the assumptions that pervade the Philadelphia meetings of the American constitutional convention. Nevertheless the momentum that carried things forward made Itagaki, the original standard bearer, virtually irrelevant by the time of his death. What slowed and then almost stopped that momentum was the codification of the Meiji Constitution.

3. Itō Hirobumi and the Meiji Constitution

Of all the Meiji leaders Itō Hirobumi (1841–1909), as a farmer's son, had the most modest parentage. Through adoption into the Itō family and the patronage of Chōshū leaders like Kido who recognized his ability, he was from the first a junior member of the leadership group. After the death of Ōkubo he emerged as the most talented and many-sided figure of the club. More inclined to collaboration and compromise than Ōkubo, he probably enjoyed, more than any other person, the trust of the young emperor. When he was assassinated by a Korean nationalist in 1909 Emperor Meiji's eulogistic rescript, unlike the more formal pronouncements made for the death of other statesmen, expressed genuine grief.

Itō and his lifelong associate Inoue Kaoru were sent to England by Chōshū in 1863—Itō had just been promoted to samurai—and rushed back in an unsuccessful attempt to ward off the cannonades at Shimonoseki. Itō was a central member of the Iwakura embassy, able to respond to welcomes with speeches in English. Together with Mori Arinori, then minister to Washington, he showed sufficient independence and confidence to annoy Kido, his senior. Everything prepared for his emergence as a central figure after the death of the original triumvirate of Kido, Saigō, and Ōkubo. He was the central figure in the ouster of Ōkuma from the government in 1881.

The year after the emperor's promise of a parliament, an imperial rescript commanded Itō to head a commission to study the governmental institutions of other countries. Together with Itō Myōji, an able younger bureaucrat from Nagasaki, he left Japan in March 1883 and returned the following August. In Europe he was able to consult with Mori Arinori, now minister to London, and Aoki Shūzō, minister to Berlin. His principal investigations were carried on in Germany, where he consulted with the scholar Rudolph von Gneist, and Vienna, where Lorenz von Stein gave him a crash course in constitutional theory in a little classroom attached to his house, one in which he later taught other Japanese, including the peer Konoe Atsumaro. These preparations did not take place in a vacuum. The German state was taking form under the direction of Otto von Bismarck, who impressed Itō so much that he was later chided for trying to mimic his mannerisms. Faced with vigorous competition from social democrats and warned by assassination attempts on the newly invested ruling house, Bismarck had devised a series of measures designed to safeguard state prerogatives from popular control. One can imagine that the German scholars, who doubted Japan's preparedness for constitutional government, would in any case propose caution in extending rights to an Asian people.

Itō did not work alone. A leading German scholar, Herman Roesler (1834–1894), had been recruited to come to Japan as adviser to the Ministry of Foreign Affairs in 1878; by 1881 he was first legal adviser to the government, and he earned such trust from the leadership group that from then to 1893, when he left Japan, there were few major decisions on which his advice was not requested. This was preeminently the case with the constitution. Roesler became special counselor to Inoue Kowashi (1843–1895), a Kumamoto man whose intellectual lineage reached back to Yokoi Shōnan. It was this Inoue who had prepared the draft constitution for Iwakura Tomomi in the first round of ideas submitted to the old Genrōin, and his views on the centrality of the emperor were now of critical importance. The correspondence between

Itō and Inoue during Itō's absence from Japan makes it possible to trace the elements that came together in the Meiji Constitution. Another person involved was Kaneko Kentarō, a long-lived (1853–1942) Fukuoka man who graduated from Harvard in 1878. These three—Inoue Kowashi, Kaneko Kentarō, and Itō Myōji as scribe—worked as Itō's principal assistants, and Roesler's memoranda and commentaries were vital to the whole.

Although a number of constitutional provisions in the final product followed the example of the Prussian constitution of 1850, it should not be concluded that the goal was to create an East Asian Prussia. Roesler was highly critical of Prussian statism. He argued the case for what he called a social monarchy, and wrote that the voting and taxing rights were the central features of a constitutional order. At the same time he was equally opposed to the separation of powers incorporated in Western European and especially English practice, and thought ultimate power should be united in the monarch. Gneist and Stein were also relatively moderate in the German spectrum of constitutional thought, and their vision of a *rechtsstaat,* or government of laws, was by no means unchallenged by more reactionary contemporaries. Yet they were united on the dangers involved in leaving matters entirely to representatives of the people, and argued that disparities of wealth and irresponsible individualism could combine to create irreparable fissures in the body politic. Roesler's idea of a "social monarchy" sought to counter both factionalism and autocracy. Ultimately, though, his preference for a simple statement of monarchical primacy lost out to his employers' insistence on invoking monarchical divinity.[19]

Every move that Itō made upon his return to Japan can be seen as the product of his determination to protect the imperial institution from popular radicalism—and, to be sure, the central role he and his colleagues occupied in the power structure. The first step was to formalize a divide between emperor and commoners by the creation of a new peerage. This was announced in a decree of July 1884. Under its terms 11 daimyo and 7 court nobles *(kuge)* were designated Prince *(kōshaku)* or Duke; 24 daimyo and 9 nobles were named Marquis *(shishaku);* 73 daimyo, 30 *kuge,* and the inner core of government leaders became Count or Marquis *(kōshaku,* written with a different Chinese character); 325 daimyo and 91 nobles were named Viscount *(shishaku,* again with a different character); and 74 daimyo, but no nobles, were named Baron *(danshaku).* Thus a total of 507 former daimyo joined the 137 court nobles to form the new peerage as *kizoku* (peers). To be sure there were additional distinctions between the "old" (noble) and "new" (warrior) peers in snobbery and status, and nine court ranks, each of two degrees, of ancient Chinese provenance, provided additional differentiation. Nevertheless the top of the old Tokugawa elite had now been absorbed into the old *kuge* houses. At the very summit, the Tokugawa were ranked with the illustrious house of Konoe, suitable for imperial consorts and other honors. Princes of the Blood (*shinnō*) were above the throng altogether.

Many thought it strange to institute a peerage in the age of modernization, but Itō was perfectly frank about the reasons. There was a danger that people might slip into the spirit of republicanism, he wrote; although it might seem contrary to the trend of the times and against people's sentiments, the peerage provided the opportunity "to take advantage of the fact that the last flow of feudal reverence for the Emperor has not died out." He was sorry that in coining rank titles it seemed necessary "to bring out the Chinese system," and invited his associates to come up with alternatives if they could do so. It has to be pointed out that the only function of this new peerage was to people an anticipated House of Peers in the future Diet. The newly appointed peers were not counts or barons of anything in particular, and although modest financial provision was made for them they enjoyed little more than prestige. When that was withdrawn after World War II they disappeared into Japanese society almost without a ripple.

Itō's next step was to separate the Emperor from the rather Heian-period Council of State (Dajōkan) that had been set up. As it had been worked out the emperor was directly above three ministers (Left, Internal, and Right); there were councillors below them, and special responsibilities were allocated to a lower rank (*kyō*, used today for the English "sir"). There were two problems about this; the councillors had shrunk steadily in number and responsibility was diffuse, and there was no provision for the emperor's special advisers—elders and court figures. Put differently, the emperor was dangerously close to public responsibility for governing.

In place of this came a cabinet system that was announced in December 1885. This move brought Japan into line with the Western countries whose favor it needed for treaty reform, but there were also sound internal reasons for the change. Under the cabinet system the court was protected by separate bureaucracies, that of the Imperial Household and the lord keeper of the privy seal, both safely removed from the realm of politics. Political direction derived from an appointed prime minister, under whom functional ministries took shape. There was some awkwardness about relocating Sanjō Sanetomi. After the death of Iwakura in 1883 he had, as senior noble, been minister of state (*dajō daijin*). With due negotiation the solution arrived at was to have Sanjō himself propose the change in a memorial prepared for him by Inoue Kowashi, after which a safe berth as lord privy seal combined honor with proximity to the palace.

Itō himself emerged in 1885 as Japan's first prime minister. Around him he collected cabinet ministers evenly divided between Chōshū and Satsuma, with one slot each for Tosa (Tani Kanjō) and the former bakufu official and diplomat Enomoto Takeaki. Surrounded by men of the caliber of Matsukata, Yamagata, and Mori, to name only three, he was first among equals. From now until 1900 prime minsters came from the Satsuma-Chōshū group represented in Itō's first cabinet; they served almost in rotation between Satsuma and Chōshū, with the exception of a brief interval when Itagaki and Ōkuma were permitted to form a (short-lived) cabinet in 1898.

Work on the constitution could now be speeded. It proceeded in strict secrecy; Harvard graduate Kaneko Kentarō pointed out, if justification was needed, that the United States Constitution had also been worked out without public input. Once again, the central problem was the way power should be reserved for the emperor. The rescript of 1881 announcing that a parliament would be promulgated had indicated this; "with regard to the limitations upon the Imperial prerogative, and the constitution of the Parliament, We shall decide hereafter and make proclamation in due time." Easier said than done. Roesler's drafts and memoranda advocated Western formulations for declarations of monarchical authority, while Itō and the others sought shelter in the greatest possible emphasis on antiquity and divinity. Itō repeatedly said, and wrote, that while Western countries had a bedrock of civic responsibility and conservatism in religion and values, Japan did not. As he put it in presenting the final document to the Privy Council, "In Japan the power of religion is slight, and there is none that could serve as the axis [alternatively pivot, foundation, or cornerstone] of the state. Buddhism, when it flourished, was able to unite people of all classes, but it is today in a state of decline. Shintō, though it is based on and perpetuates the teachings of our ancestors, as a religion lacks the power to move the hearts of men. In Japan, it is only the imperial house that can become the axis of the state. It is with this point in mind that we have placed so high a value on imperial authority and endeavored to restrict it as little as possible."[20] He had come to this conclusion earlier, and writing about it from Europe he expressed his satisfaction with "I can die a happy man."

In April 1888 Itō was able to report to Privy Seal Sanjō that the draft of the constitution and Imperial House law had been completed. Now it was necessary to legitimate it through discussion and imperial ratification. To this end a Privy Council was created later that month. Itō stepped down as prime minister, vacating that spot for Kuroda Kiyotaka of Satsuma, to head the new council, which was the guardian of the new constitution. Discussions began in May and concluded in January 1889. Forty-one regular and three special meetings were held in the presence of the emperor. Woodblock artists capture the solemnity of the council's work, portraying its members resplendent in uniform and decorations arranged around an enormous council table. The work continued to be secret, and council members were not trusted with copies of the documents under discussion.

There were special reasons for this secrecy. In 1886 the political parties, after several years in dissolution, had begun the organization of what was to become their Grand Alliance (Daidō Danketsu). The popular pulse was inflamed by an unruly encounter at Nagasaki in which Chinese sailors had rioted against Japanese police in a row that left casualties on both sides. The popular press and mood was also highly critical of the government's abject (as they saw it) efforts to win foreign favor to speed treaty reform. Ōkuma, who had been recalled as foreign minister and whose proposals to improve extraterritoriality seemed inadequate, very nearly lost his life, and did lose a leg, in an assassination attempt. The atmosphere was highly charged, and the party stalwarts would have seized on any governmental slip to increase their hold on public opinion.

Discussions began with distribution of Roesler's opinion of the proposed constitution. More than a month was devoted to the Imperial House law. Only now was succession limited to a male heir, a step in the Europeanization of the throne. After this, in June, Itō introduced discussion of the constitution itself with his explanation of the need to bolster the imperial institution as the fulcrum, or foundation, of government. If they failed to build such a rampart, he warned, "politics will fall into the hands of the uncontrollable masses; and then the government will become powerless, and the country will be ruined. To preserve its existence and to govern the people, the state must not lose the use of the administrative power . . . Because imperial sovereignty is the cornerstone of our constitution, our system is not based on the European ideas in force in some European countries of joint rule of the king and the people. This is the fundamental principle of this draft constitution, and it will become evident in every article."[21]

Debate found Itō defending his draft from others, some no less "modern" and well traveled, who feared that Itō had gone too far in proposing phrases like "with the consent of the Diet"; would not, Mori Arinori asked, this weaken the sovereign power of the throne? Mori argued for a Diet that was merely advisory, but Itō held his ground in defense of the draft; "if we want to establish a constitutional government," he said, "we have to give the right of decision to the Diet. Without the consent of the Diet, budgets or laws cannot be determined. This is the essence of constitutional government."

After vigorous discussion the draft was approved with minor changes. It was then made official by an imperial promulgation on February 11, 1889. The date selected, for the ascension to rule of Jimmu, the sun goddess's grandson, became a national holiday (National Foundation Day), and conveyed the solemnity with which the occasion was designed as both inauguration and continuation. As in 1868, modernity and change were presented as a renewal of antiquity. Nothing illustrates this in more striking fashion than the mythology that was invoked in the constitution's opening paragraph:

> Having, by virtue of the glories of Our Ancestors, ascended the Throne of a lineal succession unbroken for ages eternal; desiring to promote the welfare of, and to give development to the moral and intellectual faculties of Our beloved subjects, the very same that have been favored with the benevolent care and affectionate vigilance of Our Ancestors, and hoping to maintain the prosperity of the State, in concert with Our people and with their support, We hereby promulgate, in pursuance of Our Imperial Rescript [of 1881] a fundamental law of the State, to exhibit the principles, by which We are guided in Our conduct, and to point out to what Our descendants and Our subjects and their descendants are forever to conform.

Itō's greatest work had been accomplished. He would serve again and frequently, as prime minister, as designer of the peace after Japan's victory over China in 1895, as emissary to the courts of Europe (and recipient of an honorary degree from Yale) before losing his life as Resident General in Korea. He probably had the broadest vision of the Meiji leadership group. It is for the constitution that he is best known. His picture, together with the Diet building, appeared on the basic thousand-yen note of post–World War II Japan.

4. Yamagata Aritomo and the Imperial Army

Yamagata Aritomo (1838–1922) was, after Itō, the most important of the Meiji leaders. If Itō's successive posts—from chairing the constitutional preparation committee to prime minister four times to chief of Privy Council to Resident General in Korea—shadowed critical points in the political power structure, Yamagata's career—commander in Restoration wars, commander of the Konoe Imperial Guard, vice minister, then minister, of the army, chief of the new General Staff, councillor, home minister through much of the 1880s, always concurrently general, and twice prime minister—indicated the locus of power in the state control structure as it took form. In some ways Yamagata's shadow was longer than Itō's; he outlived him by more than a decade, and left behind a more powerful faction group in the army and the bureaucracy. Chōshū domination of the army lasted much longer than Satsuma-Chōshū domination of the government. Yet Yamagata and Itō also shared many experiences. Both came from modest beginnings in Chōshū—Yamagata from a samurai foot soldier family—and both studied in Yoshida Shōin's village school. Both participated to the full in the excitement and danger of Restoration days. Itō's experience of foreign countries began earlier, but Yamagata lost no time in requesting a foreign tour of inspection and spent six months abroad with Saigō Tsugumichi (brother of Takamori, and a navy leader) immediately after the Tokugawa fall. With this shared background each exercised an influence beyond his specialty; Itō demanded and received full participation in army decisions in the two decades before his death, and Yamagata, though army-centered from the first, left a strong imprint on domestic government and police organization during periods as home minister and later as prime minister. They were very different in person, Itō affable and garrulous and Yamagata stern, private, and silent. They were frequently in disagreement, but their shared background and Chōshū interest made cooperation possible.

Satsuma-Chōshū domination in the army and navy lasted as long as it did in part because of the prestige associated with the role of the two domains in the Restoration. More recently the longevity of Yenan veterans in the People's Liberation Army of China provides something of a parallel. Historians refer to the Meiji government as a *hanbatsu*, a "domain clique" of Satsuma and Chōshū. As with zaibatsu, the economic royalists, the term was one of criticism and reproach. Yet the group was far from monolithic. There were sharp bureaucratic clashes between Satsuma and Chōshū, and divisions within Chōshū, over the question of military direction. The group was united, however, by a shared determination to prevent the erosion of what they had achieved by "outside" political partisans. Party politicians frequently called for national unity and decried "selfish" *hanbatsu* tactics, but the *hanbatsu* leaders saw their leadership as merited and essential to the imperial cause, and since they largely controlled access to the emperor they seldom lost out.

Most countries in the West were restructuring their military at the time the Japanese were building theirs. In Japan, however, the military's newness was one of its strongest features; European militaries were sometimes charged with being backward or conservative, but "Japan's new army considered itself to be the *embodiment* of the spirit of a new age."[22] At the time the Meiji leaders took over, every country in the West with the possible exception of the United States, which had just demobilized after the Civil War, was rebuilding and rethinking its military system on the basis of the lessons of the wars of Italian and German unification, the American Civil War, and especially the Franco-

Prussian War. Industrial development and population growth made for new possibilities in the movement, equipment, and direction of mass armies of citizen-soldiers. It would have been strange if Meiji leaders, themselves so recently samurai, had failed to absorb this lesson on their missions to the West and apply it to their own country.

In immediate post-Restoration days many men continued to look to French officers and tactics for guidance. Despite the French defeat at the hands of Prussia, the Meiji government regarded French theory and structure of military as preeminent. Moreover, substantial moves in the direction of French guidance had been begun in late Tokugawa, and it was logical for the regime to order, as it did in 1870, all domains to follow the French model for their land forces and the English model for their navies. Land forces turned to German models in the 1880s. This was largely under the leadership of Yamagata's principal disciple and future *genrō* Katsura Tarō (1847–1913), who spent a total of almost eight years in Germany. In 1878 a separate General Staff headquarters was established; Katsura had followed, and anticipated, German plans for a similar organization. Katsura was also responsible for the invitation to the military theorist Klemens Wilhelm Jakop Meckel to come to Japan. Meckel served as consultant from 1885 to 1888, and among the military his influence was comparable to that of Roesler among the jurists.

The fall of Saigō Takamori gave Chōshū a commanding lead in army control, but in the navy Satsuma leadership continued strong, though less dominant than Chōshū's with the army. The list of seventy-two full generals down to 1926 shows 30 percent from Chōshū; while of the forty full admirals 44 percent were from Satsuma. In the central bureaucratic and command structure that preponderance was stronger still. No navy builder, however, dominated the scene to the degree that Yamagata did the army during his lifetime.

For the navy the model had from the first been British, and it continued to be so. Promising naval officers were sent to England for study and often served ten years or more on English ships, and the bulk of the early navy was ordered from the great English shipyards. For some years the navy resisted pressures to bring its command structure into line with that of the army, but in the late 1880s army and navy general staffs, independent of their respective ministries, were brought under a General Staff; this brought both command structures into line.[23]

Yamagata's opinions played an important role in the conscription act that was issued in 1872. He had commanded the Chōshū mixed commoner-samurai units in the Restoration warfare and, himself of insignificant status in the samurai hierarchy, was convinced of the merit of peasant soldiers. He also saw conscription as a way of educating future generations in citizenship.

Give a boy six years in lower, and six in middle school, he argued, and "in due course the nation will become a great civil and military university." It required a generation for this goal to be achieved. The first conscription law permitted exemptions for those who could pay and for first sons, and consequently recruited a plebeian and largely illiterate cohort. Moreover those called up were relatively few, since the government could not afford more; on the eve of the Satsuma Rebellion the army numbered only about 33,000 men. At the bureaucratic level a series of experiments and changes slowed, but ultimately improved, efficiency as work on the training of an officer corps began to take shape.

In barrack and officer academy the theme constantly invoked was that of loyalty to the emperor. The Imperial Army and Navy were the emperor's. He himself was moved into military uniform in the 1880s. This represented an enormous change for the long-secluded monarchy, which, in contrast to the European tradition of rulers on horseback, had always been associated with the arts of peace. It followed that Princes of the Blood were also expected to take up military careers, and for some years the offices of chief of staff were designated for members of the ruling family. The tie between ruler and army was seen as the best defense against localism, class antagonism, and disruption, as in 1878, when a rebellion within the imperial guard had to be suppressed. At the same time it was important that the emperor refrain from exercising his power and delegate it to experienced professionals. The "solution," which gave the high command direct access to the ruler, strengthened the hand of the military in domestic affairs. Ordinances stipulated that the chief of staff should be the emperor's major adviser, with direct access to him on policy and strategy. The right of "direct command" might not be exercised very often by the sovereign himself, but it prevented interference in decisions affecting the military from the civil government and so gave military advisers a powerful weapon in internal political disputes.

With the advent of the political party movement and memories of *shizoku* insurrections still fresh, Yamagata was explicit in instructions to the military to stay out of politics. In 1882 the emperor transmitted to Yamagata the Imperial Precepts to Soldiers and Sailors, a rescript that had been prepared at his direction. Designed to serve as moral guidance for the modern armed forces, it reminded soldiers and sailors that it was not impetuous bravery that counted, but prudence, self-control, and disciplined loyalty. "Soldiers and Sailors," it read in part, "We are your supreme Commander-in-Chief. Our relations with you will be most intimate when We rely upon you as Our limbs and you look up to Us as your head." It went on to discuss at some length loyalty, respect for superiors, valor, faithfulness, righteousness, and simplicity. Values that had become the core of samurai *bushidō* were prescribed for the commoner recruit. Having abolished the samurai class, Japan now needed a nation of samurai. "These five articles should not be disregarded for even a moment by soldiers and sailors. For putting them into practice, the all important thing is sincerity . . . If only the heart be sincere, anything can be accomplished. Moreover these five articles are the 'Grand Way' of Heaven and earth and the universal law of humanity, easy to observe and to practice."[24] The bond between emperor and armed services was symbolized by his uniform and his attendance at military exercises and the graduation ceremonies of the army and navy academies.

The military was by no means completely united, however, and men from "outside" domains frequently proved restive under the domination of the mainstream *hanbatsu* factions. Military expansion and new training institutions increased the supply of officers, and the new men found themselves up against the old guard at every point. General Miura Gorō, director of the Military Academy and himself from Chōshū, criticized his seniors repeatedly. "The high-ranking commanders in Japan's army," he wrote, "are peculiar to our nation. They were irregular soldiers who fought battles at the time of the Meiji Restoration without any knowledge or experience of modern techniques for commanding troops, unlike the officers of today, who are well-versed in modern strategy and operations."

In the 1880s there were several tests of the ability of the high command to resist the emperor's wishes while professing to be his "limbs." Apparently uncomfortable with Chōshū dominance, the emperor made clear his desire for a reshuffle of posts following a military reorganization in 1885, and let it be known that he favored higher posts for four outsiders, one of them Miura, who had become estranged from the mainstream faction. The emperor's suggestion had the support of Itō and Inoue Kaoru, but the issue became entangled with a budget wrangle in which the army was resisting Matsukata cutbacks. Itō and Inoue, powerful as they were, found it necessary to back the high command in order to get its approval for budget restrictions. In the compromises that resulted the four "outsider" generals lost their chance and retired from the army. The emperor's cautious approaches were thus set aside by his generals, who thought they knew better. Yamagata, however, also responded by moving army leaders into civilian posts, thereby giving himself additional support in other areas.

There was more at stake in this than personality and money, for the four outsiders favored a smaller and defensive military force. Katsura Tarō and

Kawakami Sōroku, deputy chief of the General Staff, prevailed with a joint memorandum that put it starkly:

> Nations maintain an army for two reasons. First, to defend themselves against enemy attack or to preserve their independence. The armies of most second-class European nations are of this kind. Second, to display the nation's power, resorting to arms when necessary to execute national policy, as in the case of first-class European powers. Japan's aim in maintaining armed forces is not that of the second-class nations but that of the first-class powers.[25]

In other words, the army was destined for greater things than national defense alone.

Yamagata's importance was not limited to the military. In 1883 he added the responsibilities of the Ministry of Home Affairs to those he held as chief of staff, and in the first cabinet Itō organized in 1885 he continued in that post. Now he turned his attention to organizing institutions of local government and a national police system. It is easy to see why. The People's Rights Movement was growing in power, and the countryside was resisting the new tax structure imposed by the Matsukata deflation. Nothing seemed more urgent than establishing institutions that could be insulated from and counter expressions of popular discontent. It must be remembered that even Itō, in his correspondence, was afraid that radical sentiments were rising. For a soldier like Yamagata, the "enemy" had to be isolated and checked. Time, he thought, was working against the government, and it was important to stabilize things while it could still be done.

Yamagata's approach to structuring local government derived from his military preoccupations; control, order, and uniformity were the goals. Similar concerns and restructuring were going forward in Germany in the 1880s, and Albert Mosse was invited to come to Japan for four years beginning in 1886. Local self-government was an important part of Yamagata's plans. In his mind, Roger Hackett has written, "conscription and local self-government were clearly related: both represented service to the state; both bound the people to the central government, strengthening unity and contributing to stability."[26] To this end he advocated and secured the election of lower-echelon officials, while at the same time he ruled out their participation in political parties. City mayors, district heads, and prefectural governors, however, were to be appointed directly or indirectly by the government. These regulations were completed in 1888, and issued as Law No. 1 of the nation.

Police matters were no less important. A *kempeitai*, or gendarmerie, was established in 1881; originally restricted to military concerns with added functions like the censorship of books permitted in barracks, it would exercise increasing power over civil life in the militarist Japan that lay ahead. The larger Meiji police system had initially taken the French system for its model, and the centrality of the Tokyo Metropolitan Police structure retained many of these features. Yamagata, however, turned his attention to the German model more in line with the political and legal models that were being followed in the 1880s. Once again a German adviser was brought in. More important was the emphasis on training institutes that were set up in every prefecture, with instructors chosen from the graduates of a national academy. As in the army, formal training and a sense of professionalism were emphasized. Furthermore the police system, theretofore concentrated at the center, was extended into the countryside. Police posts throughout the country increased from 3,068 in 1885 to 11,357 five years later, and the ubiquitous presence of police boxes in village centers as well as urban intersections dates from these years.[27]

Yamagata's concern with order also produced legislation that extended the power of the police in daily life. In 1886 regulations forbade the petitioning of public officials. Those planning any kind of public meeting had to provide the details, reasons, and names of those attending to the police. More striking still was the Peace Preservation Ordinance of 1887 that was designed to rid Tokyo of its political troublemakers. The home minister now forbade all secret societies and assemblies. He could halt any meeting or assembly, and he received authority to expel from a seven-and-a-half-mile radius of the imperial palace anyone judged likely to create a public disturbance or disrupt public tranquillity. After the order was issued on December 26, 1887, 540 political party members classed as dangerous were expelled in an operation carried out with military precision. Ozaki Yukio, among those banned from the capital, later wrote that he was not to have a police escort again until he was appointed a cabinet minister a decade later. In conversation with his guardians, who were sobered by the prominence of the man they were escorting out of town, he learned that they had instructions to cut him down on the spot if, as it was hoped, he tried to resist.

In 1888 Yamagata made a tour of Europe to study other systems of local government at first hand. In 1889 he formed his own cabinet for the first time, serving simultaneously as premier and home minister. Throughout all this he retained his military status and importance. There was a consistency about his work and career and tactics, an emphasis on discipline, but also caution. He and his generation had experienced Japan's weakness and unpreparedness, and he was determined that no internal foes or foreign adventures would be allowed to threaten the safety and stability of the imperial state.

5. Mori Arinori and Meiji Education

We have encountered Mori Arinori (1847–1889) at several points in this narrative. As a young Satsuma samurai he was assigned to the study of naval matters
and sent to England in 1865. There, while studying chemistry, physics, and
mathematics, he became the disciple of a religious teacher named Thomas
Lake Harris, the founder of a utopian group called the Brotherhood of the
New Life. Mori became a Christian and followed Harris and his community
to New York State. When the bakufu fell, Harris convinced Mori that his duty
lay with the new Japan, and he returned home to serve in the new government.
His command of English made him an ideal minister to Washington, where
he was also charged with a study of education. After a special mission to China
he was assigned to London, where he introduced Itagaki Taisuke to Herbert
Spencer in the Athenaeum.[28]

Mori was curious, impressionable, rash, and supremely self-confident. His
premature advocacy of the banning of samurai swords cost him his position
for a time, he angered conservatives by a suggestion that Japan substitute
English for Japanese, he favored equal rights for women in marriage, and he
asked Fukuzawa Yukichi to arrange a marriage ceremony with contractual
equality. In 1889 light-hearted disrespect for the sun goddess's shrine at Ise
cost him his life at the hands of a true believer.

Mori was appointed minister of education in the first cabinet that Itō
Hirobumi organized in 1884. Although he was by no means a clan-centered
authoritarian, his brief tenure in that post left Japan with its pre–World
War II education system: the lower schools rigidly centralized and emperor-
centered, the upper reaches less controlled, focused on scholarly inquiry, and
struggling for autonomy.

The education system Mori inherited had begun with a Fundamental Code
of Education in 1872 whose preamble carried the enthusiasm of early Meiji
reform in language that combined the respect for education of homilies used
in commoner schools in Tokugawa years with denunciation of the old society:

> Learning is the key to success in life, and no man can afford to neglect it.
> It is ignorance that leads man astray, makes him destitute, disrupts his
> family, and in the end destroys his life. Centuries have elapsed since schools
> were first established, but man has gone astray through misguidance.
>
> Because learning was viewed as the exclusive province of the samurai
> and his superiors, farmers, artisans, merchants, and women have neglected
> it altogether and do not even know its meaning. Even those few among
> the samurai and his superiors who did pursue learning were apt to claim

it to be for the state, not knowing that it was the very foundation of success
in life . . .

The Department of Education will soon establish an educational system and will revise the regulations relating thereto from time to time;
wherefore there shall, in the future, be no community with an illiterate
family, nor a family with an illiterate person . . .

Hereafter . . . every man shall, of his own accord, subordinate all other
matters to the education of his children.[29]

These were ambitious goals, but they would require centralization and
money, and neither was as yet at hand. In implementing them the builders
of the Meiji education system had three major ingredients: the centralization
of a single system for what had been a great variety of regional and local
institutions, the replacement of domain schools oriented toward samurai by
newly established official schools that fostered and rewarded talent wherever
it was found, and the substitution of a single national grid for the discontinu-
ous and unpredictable public and private schools.[30]

The Fundamental Code set ambitious goals for what was to be a national
system; it envisioned a grid of 8 university districts, each of which would
divide into 32 middle school districts, each in turn would have 210 primary
schools. Here France provided the model of administrative organization. It
is not surprising that resources fell short of achieving these goals and that the
decade that followed saw discontinuity in detail, though never in commitment
to mass education. The underlying intent was clear: popular education was
to be a major goal of state policy. Financial limitations made for attempts at
local support and local variety, but within a remarkably short time even
mountain villages found schooling centered around village schools. An 1875
survey of the roughly 20,000 primary schools then in use found that 40 percent were housed in Buddhist temples (reminiscent of the old *terakoya*), 33
percent in private homes (as with the old *shijuku*), and 18 percent in new
buildings. Those structures, built when possible in Western style with elaborate touches like porticoes and towers, were harbingers of modernization and
centers of civic life. Their towers housed bells or drums that signaled the hours
of the day and served as watchtowers for fires, and the buildings often saw
additional service as centers for police and public health functions like vacci-
nations. Meiji literature conveys numerous tributes to the significance of these
imposing buildings, and contemporary Japan has singled out the best of those
that survived for immortality on postage stamps.

The real story is that of the diffusion of literacy throughout the Japanese population. "For most local officials," Richard Rubinger writes, "the essence of the new school law boiled down to establishing public elementary schools and increasing attendance in them."[31] Enrollment grew steadily, though in some areas, slowly, until by 1905 it was virtually universal. Analysis of local data shows a dramatic leveling process. In more "developed" parts of Japan, where a variety of schools already existed, progress was slow, but in more remote and "backward" domains rates of attendance—and hence of literacy—rose dramatically. Male pupils at first outnumbered females, as could be expected, but that distinction too was gradually lost. Nevertheless army figures provide a sobering check. Granted that educated, urban, and affluent sons were a minority among conscripts, an 1892 army survey showed that almost 27 percent of all new army enlistees were still illiterate, while another 34 percent were rated as marginally literate. Even on the eve of World War I, only some 4 percent of conscripts had reached a level beyond middle school.[32] In comparative, world terms Japan was somewhat, though probably not seriously, behind the progress of major Western nations.

The exhortation of early Meiji calls to education echoed the language of goals of achievement and self-realization of American and English educators. In lower schools books by the educator Fukuzawa Yukichi were so ubiquitous that the term "Fukuzawa books" acquired a generic ring, while middle school materials gave a prominent place to works like Francis Wayland's *Elements of Moral Science* and the study of English. The government established numerous schools for foreign-language instruction, and private educators and missionaries started more. In the 1870s 156 English-language schools were training over 6,000 students.

For a decade and more the scene was one of considerable confusion. There was a tug of war between central authorities and communities in which village schools, like that in Itsukaichi, had developed with the support and allegiance of the local elite, and communities resisted and negotiated with the new agents of centralization.[33] Many able young men looked anxiously for guidance and direction in the welter of new cultural influences that were sweeping into Japan. The journalist and historian Tokutomi Sohō (1863–1957), for instance, began as one of Captain Janes's students in Kumamoto, but attended seven schools in as many years, encountering Confucian, English, and Christian principles, and his writings show impressive familiarity with each.

In the 1880s Meiji government planners became concerned about content and control. Not a few educational institutions were set up as a result of the People's Rights Movement; Chiba Takusaburō, the author of the "People's Constitution" drawn up in the mountain village west of Tokyo, it will be remembered, was a former Tokugawa partisan who found employment in a village school. Conservatives like Motoda Eifu, Confucian tutor to the Meiji emperor, deplored such schools as "political discussion groups," and extended their fears to the general reliance on foreign learning.[34] The Education Ministry, together with most branches of the executive, was devoting impressive proportions of its budget to hiring foreign teachers and sending students abroad.

These misgivings began to come to a head just as the Meiji government was rocked by the crisis of 1881, in which Ōkuma Shigenobu challenged the Satsuma-Chōshū main line through his advocacy of an early constitution and his public criticism of the sale of government-funded developments. Motoda had provided the opening salvo in what he saw as a war for the soul of Japan with an imperial rescript the Emperor Meiji issued in 1879 as "The Great Principles of Education." "The essence of education, our traditional national aim, and a watchword for all men," it read,

> is to make clear the ways of benevolence, justice, loyalty, and filial piety, and to master knowledge and skill and through these to pursue the Way of Man. In recent days, people have been going to extremes. They take unto themselves a foreign civilization whose only values are fact-gathering and techniques, thus violating the rules of good manners and bringing harm to our customary ways . . . For morality, the study of Confucius is the best guide. People should cultivate sincerity and moral conduct, and after that they should turn to the cultivation of the various subjects of learning in accordance with their ability.[35]

Even before this, official enthusiasm for foreign language instruction had begun to ebb as more emphasis was placed on ethics and Japanese literature in order to build a nation of soldier-subjects.

The polarities of the debate that ensued can be suggested (and perhaps exaggerated) by the view held out by some army leaders who felt that the main business of the schools was to prepare ordinary people to become the emperor's soldiers. Lt. Col. Tōjō Eikyō, father of the prime minister who led Japan into war with the West in 1941, addressed an educational association in 1897 with the ringing assertion that

> it is vital that you Educators of the People know the educational methods used by the army, which is the main school. It is the duty of the preparatory school to educate the people in such a way that they can be educated easily when they arrive at the main [army] school. You are the mothers who bear the army.[36]

Not everyone would have agreed with so stark a military mission for the schools, though everyone did agree that the health of the new state depended upon the development of patriotic participation.

At the other extreme was the educator and publicist Fukuzawa Yukichi, who argued the need for an education that would build independence and foster practicality, in contrast to what he considered the impractical and uneconomic moralities of Confucianism and nativism. The enormous popularity of Fukuzawa's books in private and school use concerned Motoda and other Confucianists. During the 1870s educational policy had been delegated to Tanaka Fujimaro, the author of the Fundamental Code of 1872, and it was the "excesses" of those policies that Motoda deplored.

A practical statesmen like Itō Hirobumi was understandably wary of educators like Motoda, who sought to prescribe learning for the country, and leaned toward a more open and varied course, but during the preparation of the constitution he had other and larger concerns on his mind. Itō responded to the rescript Motoda had prepared for the emperor with sharp criticism, and saw to it that Motoda's post of Confucian tutor to the emperor was abolished. But his victory was short-lived; direction of the Ministry of Education changed to conservative hands; morals were put at the head of the curriculum, and a new directive for elementary school teachers issued in 1881 made it clear that "Loyalty to the Imperial House, love of country, filial piety toward parents, respect for superiors, faith in friends, charity toward inferiors, and respect for oneself constitute the Great Path of human morality." Translations of Western textbooks on morality were ruled out for use in schools, central control was strengthened, and the new concern with Confucianism led to the appointment of Nishimura Shigeki as head of a Compilation Board of the Ministry of Education. Henceforth Nishimura's writings on training in morals became the basis for courses on "ethics," or *shūshin*, that were regarded as the center of the curriculum.[37] Schools were to be walled off from the agitation for political rights that was spreading, and in 1880 an ordinance made it illegal for teachers to attend political meetings or lectures. In this assertion of control financial concerns were also involved. Early plans for education had been premised on support from local taxes, but in the years of the Matsukata deflation local resistance to taxation made it necessary for the central government to increase its share of the funding. With greater central input it was probably inevitable that central direction should increase as well.

While Itō was in Germany to study foreign constitutions Mori Arinori, then posted to London, traveled to the Continent to visit him, and the two discovered that they were in basic agreement on the subject of education. Itō had been impressed by the educational thought of his Austrian mentor Lorenz von Stein, and indeed invited him to Japan to direct the Japanese effort. Mori had devoted much of his time in his Washington tour of duty in the early 1870s to study of the American education system, and took advantage of his time in London to familiarize himself with leading educational authorities in the major states of Western Europe. He had retained much of his youthful enthusiasm for a well-rounded educational program that produced strength of body as well as mind. He was also increasingly dismayed by what he regarded as the superficiality of Japan's early political party movement. Increasingly, he thought it important for Japan to base institutions and practice on its own tradition. (It may not be irrelevant that most of his Western counselors agreed enthusiastically.)

Itō, having failed to attract the services of von Stein, asked Mori to undertake the direction of Japanese education, and promised him the portfolio of education when he organized his first cabinet in 1885. Mori returned to Japan well read, well informed, and well connected with leading spokesmen for education. Nevertheless he was not in the first instance an educator so much as he was a statesman and an administrator. He was concerned with the role of education in nation building, and with the primacy of state over personal interests. He was also more of a nationalist than he had been before his trip—a common phenomenon among Meiji leaders who returned from the West—and was convinced of the importance of the imperial institution for education in Japan of the future. On this point he was more pragmatist than believer, convinced of the utility and centrality of the institution. What mattered was the state; "the best way," he insisted, "is to focus on the state alone." Education was not only for the pupils, but for the "sake of the country." Continental and English education combined to persuade him that a multitrack system that trained an elite for state service was the path Japan should follow, and Spencerian visions of competition between nations made this essential. "Anyone who is the least bit Japanese," he said at one point, "must try to advance Japan from the third rank, where she now stands, to the second; and when she achieves the second rank, then to the first; and finally to the foremost position in the entire world." Nevertheless Mori also retained a belief in the values that his Christian sponsor, Thomas Lake Harris, had espoused in his utopian community. Harris's emphases on "Discipline, Friendship, and Obedience [to God]," now secularized, became the Mori's slogan for Japan's new normal schools.

Conservatives who feared Mori's Western leanings and reputed Christianity did their best to block his appointment to the education post, but Itō was determined and he had his way. "No other education minister in modern Japan," writes Mori's biographer, "comes anywhere near Mori in the extent of his personal imprint upon the entire school system."[38]

Shortly after Mori's investment as minister a group of three ordinances gave the Japanese school system the form it was to retain until the end of

World War II. It is appropriate to take these from the top down, beginning with the Imperial University. Tokyo University, as it would become known, had emerged from a congerie of educational institutions that went back to the Tokugawa School of Western Learning, but in attraction and quality it was hard pressed by a number of private schools. First among these were Fukuzawa Yukichi's Keiō and a rival, Waseda, that was established by Ōkuma in 1882 after he had been driven out of the government. The graduates of these schools, and of additional private institutions set up for the study of modern law and foreign languages, many by missionaries, played important roles in political agitation, journalism, and private enterprise.

Mori distanced the university from such competition by naming it the "Imperial" University. Its graduates qualified for posts in the bureaucracy without having to stand for the examinations that winnowed out competitors from other schools. A second national university was established at Kyoto in 1897, but Tokyo Imperial University, as it now became, stood at the pinnacle of the education system. Its top graduates were honored by the emperor and assured of prestigious careers. Its costs were born entirely by the central government. In makeup the student body was drawn for the most part "in fact if not by statute to the sons of upper- and upper-middle class families (of civil bureaucrats, military officers, landlords, rich farmers, businessmen, and industrialists), except for a very small number of students holding scholarships provided by former feudal lords and other rich people," as Masamichi Inoki puts it. His study of the *Jinji kōshin roku* (Who's Who) for 1937 shows that 73.6 percent of the higher civil servants and 49.7 percent of judicial officials were graduates of the Imperial University (or, after the establishment of Kyoto University, "Tokyo Imperial University").[39] Appointment to bureaucratic office was frequently followed by the opportunity to study abroad. The university's faculty was in overwhelming measure drawn from its own graduates and frequently interrelated to a startling degree. Section heads were direct imperial appointees, and the university president was usually honored with an imperial appointment to the House of Peers.

It should also be noted, however, that Imperial University students were not drawn from the Restoration centers but instead represented a new and national meritocracy that would govern Japan after the passing of the early Meiji generation.

Mori's second major change came in the structure of middle schools. Here too he was instrumental in finalizing a trend toward elitism that had begun before his administration. The original grid of schools laid out in 1872 had proved impractical and beyond the government's means. As a result a division developed between an elite track, in "Special Higher Schools," which prepared students for the Imperial University, and ordinary secondary education.[40] The first-named were directly under the supervision of the ministry and financed entirely by the central government, while the ordinary schools were the charge of prefectures in which they were located.

Primary education, in Mori's view, should be devoted to strengthening pupils' awareness of and support of the state, and it was reasonable to expect patriotic parents to pay the costs. Parents were expected to pay tuition, an innovation first begun by Fukuzawa at Keiō in an attempt to escape from the structured gift-giving of earlier days. Any deficit was to be made up by local communities. Until 1900, when attendance at four years of lower school became compulsory but also free for all children, rural communities found education burdensome; in some areas attendance declined during the Matsukata deflation.

There remained a desperate need for teachers, and here Mori's imprint was particularly strong. In the first Meiji decades former samurai and local teachers of many sorts had staffed the schools, but the results were uneven and in some cases unwelcome to the government, with its fear of political involvement. The ordinance of 1880 forbidding teacher and student attendance at political meetings represented one response to this. To counter politicization Mori now provided for a structure of normal schools; one elite institution, situated in Tokyo, trained teachers for provincial normal schools, while in those schools graduates were obligated to serve ten years as teachers after graduation. Admission procedures were tightened; political recommendation—from governor, ward head, or mayor—led to a three-month probationary period.

Mori's imprint included steps that emphasized a distinction between the relative freedom of "scholarship" at higher levels and the uniformity of "instruction" at lower. He was convinced (as were many of his contemporaries in England and America) of the need for physical as well as mental training. Unfortunately he chose to meet this need through the use of army drill masters, who had the additional attraction of coming free of charge. To quote Hall again, this training "was calculated to produce not only a new generation of teachers with a new dispensation of authority but also a whole new disciplinary framework for everyday school life." In Mori's mind this seems to have been a way of using the military, but in the military mind it resulted in an atmosphere that stifled freedom of inquiry under regulations that were designed to give teachers and school heads sweeping authority. Ultimately, "the ethos of the parade ground was deliberately extended to the dormitory, refectory, and study hall of the normal school, whence it eventually spread to infect the classrooms of an entire nation." Consequently "Mori's normal school policy may be viewed as his most profound and permanent and distinctive legacy to future generations."[41]

Mori's statist emphasis also influenced his participation in the Privy Council discussions on the draft of the Meiji Constitution. There he fought unsuccessfully against every clause that might in the future strengthen the hand of the Diet. That body, he argued, should be purely consultive and have no power to legislate. Nothing should be allowed to weaken, even by inference, the charismatic aura of the emperor. Itō often had to cut Mori's flow of rhetoric short.

In one of the major ironies of Meiji times Mori was nevertheless assassinated by a fanatic who charged him with disrespect to Shinto and national traditions. The Meiji Constitution was to be promulgated on February 11, 1889. As Mori, resplendent in his official uniform, stood waiting for his carriage, he was suddenly stabbed by a rather seedy youth who had requested, and been denied, an interview to discuss student dissatisfaction. The youth was killed on the spot by Mori's bodyguard (who was tried and exonerated for possible complicity), but doctors attending the ceremonies were so long in reaching Mori that he did not recover. The young man proved to be carrying a manifesto that charged that "Education Minister Mori Arinori, while visiting the [Ise] shrine, mounted the steps of the sanctuary without removing his shoes, in defiance of the Imperial prohibition, lifted the sacred veil with his walking stick to peer inside, and retired without performing the customary obeisance."

Mori's opposition to Confucian character building in the schools did not long survive him. On October 3, 1890, Motoda Eifu and his associates had their way with an Imperial Rescript on Education that became the cornerstone of Meiji ideology. Yamagata had become Japan's third prime minister and agreed that something comparable to the rescript for soldiers and sailors was desirable; the emperor himself informed the new minister of education that since Japanese were "easily led astray and confused by foreign doctrines, it was essential to define the moral basis of the nation for them."[42]

The result was a document that was popularly thought to have been written by the emperor himself. Until 1945 it was distributed to every school in Japan together with the emperor's likeness so that all could make obeisance to it. Teachers and principals risked their lives to rescue it from burning buildings, and students committed it to memory. In form the document was a compromise; Motoda's wish that it make explicit reference to Confucius was rejected, but the Confucian relations were enumerated and credited to Japanese tradition. To the modern reader the document seems rather innocuous and platitudinous. Its power derived from the way it was used, and examination of its wording will show how the tone of paternal omniscience and authority could awe those who heard and read it.

Know ye, Our subjects:

Our Imperial Ancestors have founded Our Empire on a basis broad and everlasting, and have deeply and firmly implanted virtue; Our subjects ever united in loyalty and filial piety have from generation to generation illustrated the beauty thereof. This is the glory of the fundamental character of Our Empire, and herein lies also the source of Our education. Ye, Our subjects, be filial to your parents, affectionate to your brothers and sister; as husbands and wives be harmonious, as friends true; bear yourselves in modesty and moderation; extend your benevolence to all; pursue learning and cultivate arts, and thereby develop intellectual faculties and perfect moral powers; furthermore, advance public good and promote common interests; always respect the Constitution and observe the laws; should emergency arise, offer yourselves courageously to the State; and thus guard and maintain the prosperity of Our Imperial Throne coeval with heaven and earth. So shall ye not only be Our good and faithful subjects, but render illustrious the best traditions of your forefathers.

The Way here set forth is indeed the teaching bequeathed by Our Imperial Ancestors, to be observed alike by Their Descendants and the subjects, infallible for all ages and true in all places. It is Our wish to lay it to heart in all reverence, in common with you, Our subjects, that we may all attain to the same virtue.[43]

One might conclude, with Hirakawa Sukehiro, that where the Meiji Revolution began with a turn to the West in the Charter Oath's promise to "seek wisdom throughout the world," and posited that "just laws of nature" had theretofore not been followed in Japan, the Imperial Rescript on Education brought that process to an end with its assertion that a "national essence," whose values had been manifested in Japan's antiquity, should be the foundation for future action and belief.[44]

6. Summary: The Meiji Leaders

Evaluations of the Meiji leaders have undergone sharp changes over the years. In prewar Japan their role as builders of the imperial state brought praise for their loyalty and wisdom, and their achievements were marked by statues and memorials that kept their memories green. In wartime Japan most of the statues fell victim to the desperate shortage of materials for the war machine, and postwar writing often reversed the judgments of imperial history.

Today a half century of peaceful reconstruction permits a more balanced view. Their achievements, and Japan's, were real, though often built on the sacrifices of ordinary Japanese and at a cost to other Asians. Still, in the face of what the Meiji leaders accomplished it is interesting to reflect on the nature of that leadership. The first thing to note is that, although they specialized, they were also generalists. Yamagata doubled as interior minister, Mori and Itō as diplomats, Itagaki as general, Matsukata as local official. No one of them was essential to the process we have described; the assassin's dagger or political eclipse cannot be shown to have made a tremendous amount of difference. The Meiji leaders were a disparate group—Yamagata's dour methodical plans contrasted with Itō's more casual and almost breezy approach—but they were agreed on essentials and pulled together when their collectivity was threatened.

These were men whose image of the international world into which their country had been drawn was threatening and almost demonic. They traveled abroad to learn about that West, and returned with first-hand knowledge and impressions. Each of the men whose lives we have followed here, and many more we have not, found it essential to their careers to have been abroad. The foreigners they met on these travels invariably warned them about what they were trying to do; modern institutions had taken centuries to develop in the West, they said, and no oriental country could appropriate them overnight. The Meiji men were out to prove them wrong. At the same time they held tenaciously to national traditions, and no adviser from abroad found his expectations of his own work fulfilled; the Germans expected the peerage to provide a self-perpetuating hereditary elite assisting a powerful sovereign, the Americans an irreversible march toward democratic individualism.

It is also clear that the political parcelization of the Tokugawa times in which they came to maturity produced an oversupply of young men steeled by danger and experienced in responsibility. The Satsuma and Chōshū group at the helm never allowed anyone to challenge their primacy, but they also never hesitated to reach out and down to qualified outsiders for help at critical points. It is particularly striking to note how often former Tokugawa bureaucrats, men with experience who no longer posed any political threat, were recruited by the new team.

The Meiji leaders were pragmatists, and the design of the Meiji state took form as it grew. At every point the historian is impressed by the vigor of debate and the readiness of men to speak their minds. In this respect the Meiji men were rather different from those who followed them, for their successors' formative years came in structured bureaucracies and they came to the table with a deep consciousness of the importance of the military or political group they represented.[45]

No Meiji leader ever wrote or spoke of what had been accomplished without crediting it to the virtues of the sovereign. Mutsuhito was at the center of the plans as they developed; protected from the future politics of the lower house of the Diet by the new peerage, from the cabinet by the powers accorded by the Privy Council, lord privy seal, and imperial household minister, from civilian interference by the direct command he had over the armed services, from Diet squabbles by sweeping grants of land and securities that created immense wealth and independence, from representative institutions by his prerogatives to appoint the cabinet, from popular disorder by the ubiquitous presence of his police, from disloyalty by rescripts that identified his rule with morality and justice, and, no less important, from himself by a protective screen of officials who spoke and acted in his name and saw in him the ultimate justification for their role.

Emperor Meiji began his reign as a callow youth whose predilection for ease worried Kido Takayoshi and the others, but grew to manhood as a functioning member of the leadership group. No other Japanese ruler ever experienced such sweeping change. His life began in the shadowy penumbra of a court beyond which the ruler's voice was never heard, heir to a tradition of civil grace, art, and poetry. He was supposed to move in patterns far removed from the din of politics, one in which structured hierarchies of ancestry and blood suppressed the petty jealousies and xenophobia of a shadow court. Suddenly he was paraded throughout his realm, his aura used to win support when the consensus was most fragile. Heir to the world's oldest civilian traditions, he found himself clothed in a general's uniform, photographed with his awkward sword; the calligraphic grace of his poetry, now carried out in privacy, gave way to the sturdy Chinese characters for *kokka* ("state") with which his subjects now associated him. He developed a grumpy acquiescence in the essentials for a modern general and king, condescending to have his empress at his side for garden parties he detested for foreign dignitaries. Within the leadership group his preferences gradually became apparent; more with Itō than with Yamagata, more with traditional character-building goals than with the modernism Mori espoused, and more with caution than with adventure. Then, as Meiji institutions took root and prospered, he was credited with their success, and after Japan's armies defeated first China and then Russia he became the symbol of everything that had been done, his picture in remotest mountain village houses and his sacred edict on the lips of schoolchildren.

13

In July 1890 Japan carried out its first national election under the Meiji Constitution. Japan's was the first attempt to inaugurate representative government outside the narrow band of countries bordering on the Atlantic, and Japanese were well aware that many Western observers doubted that a country little more than two decades out of warrior rule could do so successfully. Constitutional government was the monopoly of industrialized and "advanced" countries of the West, and it seemed absurd to think that a country so recently "primitive," a country whose people still had "thongs between their toes," as one Japanese diplomat in Europe scornfully dismissed traditional footwear, could carry it off. Thus the grant of the constitution, and the election that followed, were solemn occasions that represented the hope for a different future.

Yet it was not the first election for those who took part. Prefectural assemblies had been elected since 1875 as part of the compromise with which the Meiji leaders lured Itagaki back into their ranks, and local councils of many sorts followed the same route. Most such, like the prefectural assemblies themselves, had powers that were sharply limited, and they were often designed as advisory bodies to cloak the authority of the appointed governors. Even so, this did not keep them from becoming thorny problems for those governors, and the adversarial nature of their responses to those governors mirrored the discontent that had surfaced in the political party movements of the 1880s.

The Meiji Constitution, drawn up during those same years, was designed as a generous gift of power sharing by a compassionate sovereign. But the sovereignty that made it possible to share was not lessened by that generosity, and the language of the constitution left little doubt that the throne remained paramount. The constitution had been worked out by Satsuma and Chōshū leaders who had accumulated towering prestige as founders of the regime and servants of the throne during careers in which they had developed strong ties of patronage across palace, official, business, and political circles. Prime ministers chosen from their number would have it within their power to suspend Diet sessions and dissolve the House of Representatives, issue ordinances limiting political expression and association, and appoint governors and lower officials who could manipulate elections. At the same time the members of the two houses could embarrass or disrupt government functions by withholding approval for increases in government expenditures and impeaching their leaders in direct appeals to the emperor. The constitution was phrased in language that was frequently imprecise and general, and its meaning was to become clear only by working within the parameters it set up. To a large degree, future characteristics of parliamentary government in Japan were to be seen in the politics of the period between 1890 and the end of the Meiji period in 1912, and that justifies a closer look at the first election and the early cabinets.

1. The Election

In its determination to minimize the possibility of rootless radicalism, the Election Law limited the franchise to men who paid a direct national tax of 15 yen. In 1890 the land tax provided 60 percent of government revenue, and this provision meant that landlords would be well represented in the electorate and those it chose.[1] The number of those qualified to vote numbered 450,365, a figure rather close to the total membership of the old samurai class. But most samurai had long since parted with their pensions, and the new electorate was geared to men of property. This was even more apparent in the provision for representation of very high taxpayers in the House of Peers; the fifteen highest taxpayers of each metropolitan city and prefecture could select one of their number every seven years, but the same rule stipulated that their wealth had to be in land, industry, or commerce. Securities, bonds, and stocks did not qualify as "property."

More than one thousand candidates competed for the three hundred seats in the House of Representatives. The Jiyūtō and Kaishintō, political parties that had sprung back to life by combining to campaign against "weak-kneed" government diplomacy in the late 1880s, provided the majority of these. But by 1890 it proved impossible to maintain the unity of the Grand Alliance, or united front, and the two parties were prepared for vigorous combat. There was also a broad spectrum of small and splinter groups. All election manifestos reflected the impassioned objections to the treaty reform proposals of the

1880s and stressed the importance of maintaining national dignity. There were also calls for party, or at least for "responsible," cabinets, for greater freedom of speech and association, and for the reduction of taxes and government expenditure, with an underlying assumption that Japan stood at the threshold of a new age of participation and decision. Several groups, among them one led by the former general Tani Kanjō (Tateki), called for a leaner military that would be geared toward defense, and coupled this with calls for a return to the morality and hierarchy of an earlier day. Tani had been named a member of the new peerage and was to sit in the House of Peers until his death in 1911, and it is interesting to note that this new "peer," now and later, campaigned, though not very successfully, for the votes of ordinary citizens. It is also worth noting that a conservative like Tani attacked the expansionist and ultimately military policies of the "modernizers" who were setting state policy. Oddly, though, it was nowhere indicated how these programs were to be carried out, or that the decisions of the electorate would be central to the inauguration of a new administration. The election was carried out under the administration of a cabinet headed by Yamagata Aritomo, and it was not at all clear that that Chōshū general could be expected to change his spots or be replaced. The constitution specified (in Article 55) only that "the respective Ministers of State shall give their advice to the Emperor, and be responsible for it"; presumably they were to be appointed by the throne.

Election campaigning was accompanied by a fair amount of generosity; the return of favor for favor was deeply built into concepts of public morality. There was also some intimidation; strong-arm tactics were familiar to those engaged in party warfare of the 1880s. Opponents criticized the Jiyūtō for its widespread use of "toughs" (sōshi), and party leaders were often well advised to take them on as bodyguards, but this nowhere led to fatalities.

The turnout on that July day was, predictably, high. Of those eligible to vote, 97 percent did so. Of those elected 191 were commoners and 109 were former shizoku, an indication of the speed with which the class and status assumption of centuries had changed. Of those elected 125 listed agriculture as their profession and may safely be considered landlords. The next highest group (33) came from trade and commerce, followed by law, government officials, and journalism in that order. Two-thirds were less than forty-three years old. It is not surprising that from their numbers could come figures who would dominate electoral politics and the Imperial Diet until (and in the case of Ozaki Yukio, who had become well known as a journalist, throughout) the years of World War II. One recognizes in these figures, and those who elected them, the trend of social change that had been transforming the countryside in Tokugawa times; the leading village figures, landed and prosperous *(gōnō)*, local leaders and officials, the kind of people who came together in the Itsukaichi school to discuss regional and national affairs. These were the men whose petitions and suggestions had come flooding in to the early Meiji government, *meibōka*, "local notables," who had emerged as the pillars of influence in rural society. Their favor and cooperation enabled many a political leader of the future to establish a firm base in his political turf. In the cases of particularly successful and long-lived individuals—Inukai Tsuyoshi, repeatedly returned from his district in Okayama until his murder in 1932, and Ozaki Yukio, returned twenty-five consecutive times from Kanagawa— the favor of such groups provided an "iron constituency," one that could frequently be inherited upon the member's death in a bond that survived depression, war, and generational change. As recently as the 1990s over 40 percent of members of the Japanese House of Representatives were second- and third-generation representatives.

"What motivated them?" asks R. H. P. Mason, before going on to provide the answer: "Basically, their objection to arbitrary taxation, coupled with their dislike of centralization and the *Satsuma-Chōshū* monopoly of power."[2] The economic power and local influence these voters had acquired under the old order gave them the confidence, self-interest, and potential for political action. Not infrequently, this was accompanied by a smug provincialism that saw the whole process as proof of the validity and superiority of Japanese society. The conservative *Japan Newspaper (Nihon shimbun)* congratulated its readers on the successful completion of the election by noting that "our country is indeed superior to any other, and is the one that produced the system of making the Monarch sacred and the Prime Minister responsible [to the elected representatives], which has recently become common to all constitutional countries . . . in the final analysis what has been made manifest must be attributed to the Imperial Way and to the character of the people from the time of the foundation of the Empire."[3]

2. Politics under the Meiji Constitution

The editorialist was somewhat premature in celebrating the fact that the prime minister would henceforth be "responsible." The Meiji Constitution said nothing about the prime minister or cabinet, but spoke of "Ministers of State." Executive authority remained ambiguous, no doubt because it might be interpreted to interfere with the emperor's powers. It was not explained how prime ministers were to be selected. In practice the senior statesmen decided on the rotation to be followed, after which the emperor charged the designee to form a government in what became known as the great command. It was unthinkable to disobey such a command, but there is also a remarkable record of indisposition, illness, and protestations of unworthiness as those designated met difficulty in forming their cabinets.

The constitution guaranteed many rights, but with the exception of the right to property they were invariably conditioned by the phrase "within the limits of the law"; property, of course, was central to a modern capitalist society. "Every law," said Article 37, "requires the consent of the Imperial Diet." Diet members were free from arrest "unless with the consent of the House" during the session, "except in cases of flagrant dereliction or of offenses connected with a state of internal commotion or with a foreign trouble."

What turned out to be central to the Diet's clout was the power of the purse. "The expenditure and revenue of the State require the consent of the Imperial Diet by means of an annual Budget," said Article 64. Article 71 went on to allow that "when the Imperial Diet has not voted on the Budget, or when the Budget has not been brought into actual existence, the Government shall carry out the Budget of the preceding year." Authors have sometimes cited this as a fatal qualification of the budget power, but they are surely mistaken.[4] From the very first session the sharpest conflicts between Diet and government centered on the budget. The House of Representatives would consider it first, and next the House of Peers. As Japan entered its modern century of war and expansion, the Meiji state needed ever more revenue. Andrew Fraser notes that "yearly government expenditure rose steadily from 82 million yen in 1890 to 464 million yen in 1905; successive cabinets each demanding heavier taxes than the last had to resort to all measures, fair or foul, to get their budgets passed."[5] The government could dissolve the Diet and call for new elections, as it did several times, but it could be no more confident of besting the political party–dominated House of Representatives thereafter, for too often the same men were returned. In 1892 it tried to interfere in elections with direct intimidation through police and roughneck *sōshi* violence; estimates of fatalities range from ten to twenty-five, and of those wounded from sixty to three hundred, but without appreciably changing the results. Another tactic was bribery: members of the House of Representatives with money, and peers with prestigious positions or personal favors. When Yamagata formed his first cabinet he was rumored to have received almost a million yen from palace funds, from which a generous subvention brought the Jiyūtō's Hoshi Tōru and his group around. The difficulties and embarrassment prime ministers experienced in getting budgets approved helps explain the frequency of cabinet changes. Itō himself, for instance, was hissed and booed shortly before throwing in the towel on one occasion.

The Diet had no say, however, in the formation of cabinets. Throughout the remainder of the Meiji period the continuity of the original group that had formed the institutions they now had to direct provides a remarkable study in what anthropologists might describe as "village governance." The persistence of Satsuma-Chōshū domination in turn guaranteed the intransigence of the political party leaders who had experienced repression in the 1880s while being kept out of the drafting process. They had now been given an arena for combat, and made good use of it. All too often, they saw it as their mission to bring down governments made up of their enemies. The memoirs of Ozaki Yukio provide eloquent testimony to this determination. He recalls with relish his ability to skewer more than one prime minister, and cites with pride the popular description of one of his efforts as "Minatogawa," after the last-ditch stand of a medieval loyalist hero.

The data in the chart repay study and thought. The first thing to note is the careful alternation between Satsuma and Chōshū interests and, after the Satsuma decline, Chōshū civil (Itō) and military (Yamagata) prime ministers. This should occasion no surprise, given the fact that these men had argued, worked, and struggled together for a full third of a century. Their careers,

Prime Ministers, 1885–1912

Name	Year	Domain	Held cabinet posts	Highest rank	Named *genrō*	Died
Itō Hirobumi	1885–1888	Chōshū	4 times	Prince/Duke	1889	1909
Kuroda Kiyotaka	1888–1889	Satsuma	3 times	Count	1889	1900
Yamagata Aritomo	1889–1891	Chōshū	5 times	Prince/Duke	1889	1922
Matsukata Masayoshi	1891–1892	Satsuma	7 times	Prince/Duke	1898	1924
Itō (2nd cabinet)	1892–1896					
Matsukata (2nd)	1896–1897					
Itō (3rd)	1898					
Ōkuma Shigenobu	1898, 4 mos.	Saga	5 times	Marquis	1922	1922
Yamagata (2nd)	1898–1900					
Itō (4th)	1900–1901					
Katsura Tarō	1901–1905	Chōshū	6 times	Prince/Duke	1912	1913
Saionji Kinmochi	1906–1908	Court aristocrat	6 times	Prince/Duke	1912	1940
Katsura (2nd)	1908–1911					
Saionji (2nd)	1911–1912					

plans, and even families were linked in so many ways that no outsider had much of a chance to join the inner circle. Ōkuma, who had been forced out of the government by Itō in 1881, lasted, as will be noted, six months when he finally got his first chance.

The *genrō* were, broadly speaking, equal, and served in one another's cabinets; consequently the prime minister was seldom more than a first among equals. It was only late in life, and in some cases after their death, that they became national heroes. Indeed, they have probably enjoyed more respect from historians than they did from their contemporaries. Most of the group entered the peerage as counts, and received rapid promotion as the Meiji state grew in strength. Japan's victories over China and Russia provided particular occasions for congratulation and promotion. At first, however, the principal cabinet ministries, particularly when posts were held by members of the first team, or inner core, tended almost to develop the characteristics of autonomous units. Early on efforts were made to institute a liaison and coordination office within the cabinet, but nothing came of it because members were unresponsive to the suggestion. Even Ōkuma, when he came to hold the helm for those six months in 1898, found himself hard-pressed to control his associates. He had particular difficulty with Hoshi Tōru, who was then stationed as minister in Washington, D.C.; Hoshi thought he was entitled to the post of foreign minister, and insisted on returning to Japan against his instructions. It follows that there was not, as yet, or perhaps no longer, a true hierarchy of generally accepted status.

The usual reaction of the prime minister to an unpleasant impasse with the Imperial Diet was to resign and challenge his successor to do better. This made the Meiji emperor long for the days when, as he put it to the court chamberlain Sasaki Takayuki, Ōkubo Toshimichi had been willing to face the opposition head-on. Why couldn't the others just take turns heading the government? he wondered. But in fact, as the chart shows, they did, though with excessive speed. Moreover Ōkubo had paid for his straightforwardness with his life, and his successors preferred to cultivate their interest groups and return to fight another day. Certainly there was little tolerance in this system for arbitrary, much less dictatorial, power.

The oligarchs, as we may now call them, were frequently in disagreement as to how the government should treat the Diet. Yamagata began things with a lofty announcement that the government should be *above* party politics in the Diet, and that it was the Diet's duty to provide the legislation and money that was needed. When in trouble, he was not slow to use money or the threat or actuality of dissolution to try to bring the Diet to heel. Itō, determined to make the constitution he had created work, took a milder line and tried for cooperation with the Diet. Indeed, as early as 1891 Itō began thinking about forming his own party, one that could deliver the Diet votes that were required for effective government. The next year he asked for permission to form such an organization. His colleagues' reaction ranged from surprise to indignation, and Matsukata responded with the strong-arm interference in the 1892 elections already mentioned. That failure brought the end of Matsukata's brief tenure.

Another tactic was to manipulate the emperor in such a way as to bring the parties around. Itō, who was the most trusted of the emperor's ministers, used this tactic several times. When the Diet was withholding funds for naval expansion in 1893 an imperial rescript lowered all official salaries by 10 percent for six years and announced an annual palace contribution of 100,000 yen. Faced with this austere example, the House of Representatives complied. On another occasion members of the lower house, indignant with Hoshi Tōru, submitted a memorial to the throne impeaching him as speaker of the House. Itō's manipulation once more doomed this effort. Was their action, the emperor asked, designed to apologize for their own error in having elected Hoshi to his post, or did they expect him to correct their mistake by dissolving the Diet? Chastened and outmaneuvered, the representatives explained that they had wanted to show their remorse.

From an early point military-civil relations were also at issue. The constitution reserved all functions of command to the sovereign, and the military officials who sat as ministers were quick to use this in their attempt to sway the government on the issue of increases in budget allocations. In 1892, when war and navy ministers refused to attend cabinet meetings and submitted their resignations, Matsukata was prepared to step down as prime minister, but the emperor told him there was no need to do so. In the end Matsukata resigned after all because of his difficulty in persuading the services to provide successor cabinet members. The question of military autonomy remained in the forefront of attention until 1900, when Yamagata secured imperial ordinances limiting service as war and navy minister to generals and admirals on active duty. From that point on the services had an important weapon at hand for the coercion of cabinet cooperation in service expansion. Military expenditure was indeed the fastest-growing part of government expenditure, and foreign war played a major role in this. Until 1895 only about 5 percent of young men of military age were taken as conscripts, but with the war against Ch'ing China of that year that proportion doubled, and additional security needs and continental concerns thereafter guaranteed a continued rise. Diet debates about budgets showed a lively awareness that Japanese taxpayers were being asked to provide a far higher percentage of their income than were their counterparts in Europe, where industrial and consumption taxes had long since passed land taxes as the principal source of government income.

It is clear that the inauguration of the Imperial Diet constituted a basic change in the rules of Japanese politics. It was little more than two decades since the fall of the bakufu, and yet the reader finds himself or herself in a different world. In rural Japan change in the conditions of life was still slow, but at the center the clash between new interest groups struggling for the control of new institutions made the structured ritual of bakufu and domain government seem centuries earlier. The *genrō* were frequently at odds as to how best to respond to the new challenge they faced, and their disunity provided openings for political party and splinter groups. The disunity of those groups in turn provided opportunities for the Meiji politicians. Throughout the first decade the importance of the House of Representatives grew, and by mid-decade Itō had found it advisable to offer a cabinet post to Itagaki of the Jiyūtō. Matsukata, not to be outdone, brought Ōkuma on board, and in 1898 the oligarchs even experimented with the short-lived Ōkuma-Itagaki cabinet. It soon failed, but the need for cooperation with political parties in the Diet nevertheless became more pressing. Two years later Itō finally had his way and organized a party of his own, the Rikken Seiyūkai, or Friends of Constitutional Government, into which he lured most of the Jiyūtō Diet representatives. By that time party and tax battles had turned on the issue of rural-urban competition, each claiming the other should pay more of the bill for building the modern state. Economic change and developing industrialization guaranteed the outcome. The 60 percent of government revenues borne by Japan's farmers in 1890 had changed to half that percentage in 1900, with consumer (37 percent), business (8 percent), and customs fees (6 percent) steadily becoming more important.

These same issues drove the debate in the House of Peers. Studies show that at the outset the peers were only slightly less difficult for the government than the lower house, and probably better informed and more eloquent as well. Debates on the justice of tax allocation in 1898 dominated those proceedings. Andrew Fraser's conclusion is worth citing:

> Were the Diet debates on land tax anything more than theatrical outpourings? Not entirely; at least they enabled views for and against the increase to be put at length by informed and able speakers. Even if the outcome was never in doubt, the losers had their full say. The ideal of parliamentary government, vitiated though it often was by bribery, violence, and manipulation both inside and outside the Diet, somehow seems to shine forth in such debates, with their touching appeals to the best in Japan's past and passionate concern for its future.[6]

After 1900 cabinet leadership shifted to a successor group with alternation between Saionji Kinmochi (1849–1940), Itō's chosen successor as Seiyūkai leader, and General Katsura Tarō (1847–1913), who could usually count on the support of the urban-based Kenseitō representatives. A modus vivendi had been worked out between the government and opposition groups. By now elements of future political life were firmly in place: a specialist bureaucracy, selected by merit and removed from party politics, military service specialists who regarded themselves as members of a selfless elite devoted to the emperor's cause, firmly based political parties with strong constituency support in countryside and growing industrial sectors, and a top-level elite of senior statesmen who found it increasingly difficult to maintain control of the ship of state but who were hard to attack because they were, in institutional terms, invisible. The political parties had, in a sense, been co-opted, but they had also shown themselves essential to the operation of constitutional government. The process had not been without its problems, but Japan had emerged as the first non-Atlantic country to make a go of constitutional government and representative politics. Japanese had reason to be proud.

3. Foreign Policy and Treaty Reform

Japan entered its era of constitutional government with its major problems in foreign affairs still unsolved. Treaty reform had not been achieved, and relationships with Japan's Asian neighbors, particularly Korea, were not yet defined.

Others, however, had been met. The borders had been defined, and areas left ambiguous in the decentralized nature of premodern statecraft had been made firm. To the north an agreement with imperial Russia in 1875 had exchanged Japanese interests in Sakhalin for unquestioned ownership of the entire chain of the Kuril Islands. Border relations once delegated to feudatories like Tsushima (with Korea) and Satsuma (with Okinawa) were no more tolerable than the shadowy jurisdiction Matsumae had managed with the North. In 1874 the murder of Okinawan fishermen by Taiwanese aborigines had been avenged by a lackluster expedition to Taiwan, whose settlement brought Chinese acknowledgment of Japanese control over Okinawa. That done, Okinawa had been integrated into the Japanese polity in 1879, its royal line ended, and its reluctant king summoned to Tokyo and oblivion.[7] Throughout, the early Meiji government's obsession with centralization drove policy. Participation in national affairs was still limited to former samurai, but their restlessness made it essential to counter discontent with action. At critical junctures the early Meiji leaders argued that, as Kido put it in 1869, vigorous steps would "instantly change Japan's outmoded customs, set its objectives abroad, promote its industry and technology, and eliminate jealousy and recrimination among its people." Using strong-arm methods overseas would make it unnecessary to use them at home. The Taiwan expedition was far from heroic—all but 12 of its 573 casualties were incurred by tropical disease—but it unified national opinion and bolstered the regime's prestige. It also helped to define individual preeminence. Leaders competed for overseas assignments because success would translate into power. That was one reason the core group blocked Saigō's proposal for Korea, why Kido was first an advocate and then an opponent of that policy, and why each step in Korean policy came under the personal responsibility of one of the inner core or first team. Foreign policy, as Akira Iriye puts it, "was but a context in which domestic rivalries were played out."[8]

Korea provided the best example. After the departure from the government of Saigō, Itagaki, and other dissidents in 1874, their policies were carried out by other hands. A combination of gunboat diplomacy in the interests of "free trade imperialism" showed how aptly the Meiji government had mastered the lessons Commodore Perry had brought two decades earlier. Koreans fired on Japanese gunboats in Korea waters in 1875; Kuroda Kiyotaka was sent as emissary with military support the following year, and managed to hammer out a treaty quite as unequal as those which Japan had been forced to accept in late Tokugawa times. Three Korean ports were opened for trade, consular jurisdiction brought extraterritoriality, and Korea was declared fully independent from Chinese hegemony. Other trading nations quickly followed to profit from Japan's action, and Korea too had now been "opened." China, however, was the loser. A treaty had been worked out with Peking on a basis of equality in 1871, and two years later Foreign Minister Soejima had been first among the Great Power diplomats received in audience with the Manchu emperor, but the humiliating settlement of the Taiwan expedition (for which China reimbursed Japanese costs and "improvements"), forceful annexation of Okinawa, and denial of Korea's tributary status had come at the cost to China's trust.

The treaty of 1876 did not solve the Korean "problem" for long. Instead it set the stage for intense political rivalry within sectors of the Korean Confucian *yangban* elite and a small group of young reformers, for whom Meiji Japan provided a model of modernization, in the interests of preserving national sovereignty. The struggle ultimately destroyed that sovereignty, as its partisans attracted the sympathy and support of China and Japan in what became a duel for control of the Korean peninsula that culminated in the Sino-Japanese War of 1894–95. In turn, the euphoria generated by that victory proved the catalyst for solution of the Meiji government's relations with the political parties and obstreperous Imperial Diet.

The standoff in Korea developed in three stages. After the opening of Korea, Japanese firms quickly took a commanding position in its foreign trade, exporting its early products such as matches and serving as intermediary for Western goods and as agent for the export of Korean rice and soybeans to Japan. In 1881 a Japanese military mission arrived to help train a modern military. Private groups in Japan were enthusiastic about these developments; educators like Fukuzawa Yukichi patronized students from Korea, and activists of many stripes called for close relations with the peninsula. Within Korea, however, the changes, sponsored by a court group around Queen Min, alarmed factions of the elite who had held power during the decade that a wily regent, the Taewon'gun, had maintained an exclusionist policy while trying to restore the regime to its earlier vigor.[9] In 1882 the Queen's faction was ousted, traditional army units rioted against the Japanese advisers, and the Japanese representative narrowly escaped alive. China sent troops to prevent further disruption and abducted the regent to China to keep him from stirring up more trouble. From then on, backers of the regent and the queen would roil the waters in a search for support against their rivals. As in preconstitutional Japan, politics did not stop at the water's edge.

Conservatives having overplayed their hand, Korean reformers now had their chance. A mission of apology came to Tokyo. Ōkuma and his followers had just been driven from the government and the political party movement was in its first bloom; many of the young Koreans were welcomed with open arms by opposition groups who charged the Meiji government with a weak and craven foreign policy.

The second stage came in 1884. It was now the turn of Korean reformers and their Japanese sympathizers to overplay their hand.[10] The party of the queen had become identified as hostile to reform (and therefore to Japanese) interests, and in that year the radicals attempted a bloody coup d'état in Seoul. Japanese Minister Takezoe Shin'ichi, who was forewarned, had requested instructions from his government, but its reply telling him to keep out of it came too late to dissuade him from providing covert support, which soon became obvious. To no avail. Chinese troops, urgently requested by the conservatives, arrived to overthrow the pro-Japanese government that had been formed, and angry Korean mobs killed forty Japanese officers and residents. This crisis brought even the most urgent business of the Meiji state to a halt. Foreign Minister Inoue Kaoru turned from problems of treaty reform to head for Seoul in an attempt to patch things up and save face. The Koreans agreed to apologize for the deaths of the Japanese who had been killed and to prosecute their assailants, and also promised to rebuild the Japanese legation, which had been sacked. Itō Hirobumi interrupted his preparation of the Meiji Constitution to travel to Tientsin for a meeting with the Ch'ing official Li Hung-chang. The Tientsin Agreement that resulted had as its terms a mutual withdrawal of forces from Korea and an agreement that in the future each country would inform the other prior to reintroducing armed units. Thanks to their "superior" status in their treaties with Korea both China and Japan were entitled to station legation guards at their Seoul headquarters, but the Chinese, having just ousted the reformers, were in a stronger position.

Meanwhile leaders of the Korean reform group had fled to Japan, which refused to extradite them despite Korean demands that it do so. The Tokyo government leaders kept them at arm's length, but private enthusiasts, some of whom enjoyed the support of highly placed Japanese, nurtured and protected them as possible harbingers of a future era of Japanese influence. In fact, however, an era of Chinese ascendancy had now begun. Li Hung-chang dispatched an able young disciple, Yüan Shih-k'ai, to Seoul; there he proceeded to erect the structure of an "informal empire" protectorate. To many Japanese the situation seemed quite hopeless. The Matsukata reforms were keeping the government too strapped to allow more military muscle, and efforts for treaty reform made it important to cultivate Western opinion. The Taewon'gun returned from his exile in China, though not to power. The Korean court tried to avoid the too-friendly Chinese embrace by intriguing for Russian support, but without success.

"Koreans," complained a puzzled Japanese diplomat to Seoul in 1894, "seem to regard the Japanese as wild beasts,"[11] but in trade the situation was quite different. Iriye notes that "it was from the 1880s onwards that foreign trade established itself as a serious objective of the Meiji state."[12] The Matsukata deflation had made Japanese goods more competitive, and exports to Korea rose rapidly. Cotton yarn, piece goods, and transshipped Western goods combined to make Korea better known and more strategic for Japan.

The same years saw large-scale emigration of Japanese overseas. Meiji writers were convinced from the example of the West that trade and expansion were related aspects of a vigorous and healthy state, and the word *hatten*, with its twin meanings of expansion and development, combined these aspects perfectly. There was much writing about "wars" of commerce, and the movement of Japanese overseas, whether to Korea or Hawaii, provided evidence of such health. Indeed, professional immigration companies would soon spring up, funneling settlers to Thailand as well as to Hawaii and North America.[13]

Although political relations with Korea had suffered disastrous setbacks, the Meiji government continued to give first priority to efforts to secure treaty reform with the West. The treaties, through their limitations on tariffs, made it difficult for Japan to encourage industrial development, and the humiliations of extraterritoriality (to which Japan had just subjected Korea) were, when applied to Japan, constant reminders of inferiority. The problem was becoming more acute. By the 1880s the Western powers were extending their tentacles to hitherto unthreatened parts of the globe, exploiting their riches and closing their markets. It was important for Japan, Fukuzawa Yukichi wrote in 1885, that it should not be associated in Western minds with a decrepit and backward "Asia"—one that, as in Korea, seemed to resist change and modernization. Japan should "part with Asia" and go its own, Western-style, way. In a memorandum to his colleagues, Foreign Minister Inoue wrote that it behooved Japan to set up a Western-style empire on the edge of Asia, and to do it while it was still possible, before the growth of Western hegemony ruled it out. This could not be done without regaining diplomatic equality, and that in turn would require reassurances for the West that Japan was able to live by Western rules. Everything would have to be adjusted; there had to be a spread of Western-style customs and behavior. And if there were no longer treaty ports, foreigners would have to be granted unrestricted residence. But this was highly controversial. For many Japanese, the one thing about the unequal treaties that was bearable was that they kept Westerners in their (treaty port) place. Inoue, however, argued that contact with Westerners everywhere in Japan, on a daily basis, would speed Japan's modernization and that the contact with "advanced" races this produced would have more benefits than dangers. He was also willing to phase in legal equality on a gradual scale and prepared to accept the presence of foreign judges on panels resolving issues arising from mixed residence and internation trade. His proposals took form after a year (May 1886–April 1887) of meetings with foreign representatives of all the treaty powers. In these he reluctantly agreed to provisions under which, pending a complete reformulation of the Japanese legal code, there would be a majority of foreign judges in cases affecting foreigners. When this became known there was widespread indignation. Nor was it limited to those out of power, for important members of the ruling oligarchy drew on the counsel of the French jurist Gustav Boissonade, adviser to the Ministry of Justice, to register their disapproval. Minister of Agriculture and Commerce Tani Kanjō resigned in protest. All of this coincided in time with the full-scale program of efforts to obtain foreign approval by sponsoring social events symbolized by a costume dress ball staged for foreign representatives in 1887 at the Rokumeikan, an ornate Victorian social center that gave its name to an era of, as Japanese critics charged, appeasement of the West.

Publicists and politicians, eager for useful ways of attacking the administration, seized on this to charge the government with toadying to the West. This was the context in which Gotō Shōjirō of the old Jiyūtō and others joined to form a united front (Daidō Danketsu) movement that has been mentioned; they had been kept from participating in the framing of the constitution, but no one could question their right to demand that Japan receive full equality, sovereignty, and dignity.

After Inoue resigned in despair the task of treaty reform devolved on Ōkuma Shigenobu, who was selected in good measure to still the torrent of criticism Inoue had received from party leaders. The government also sought to deal with its critics; prefectural governors were summoned to Tokyo and instructed to prevent public discussion of treaty reform proposals. In December 1887 the government issued the peace ordinance, under which over five hundred political party leaders (including, as we have noted, Ozaki Yukio) were banished from the Tokyo metropolitan area. Nothing helped.

Ōkuma took on the task early in 1888 and tried to avoid the mistakes Inoue had made. He kept the details of negotiations confidential and failed to brief even his government colleagues until his plans were far along. Instead of across-the-board negotiations in which the powers could combine against Japan, he chose a series of bilateral meetings and concentrated on Great Britain as the most important treaty power. Unfortunately the London *Times* printed the gist of his proposals in a dispatch from Tokyo, and the revelation that the use of foreign judges was to be phased out only when Japan's new law codes were complete once again enraged the political opposition.[14] Protests came from every part of Japan, and the Genrōin received over three hundred memorials protesting the plan. The Kuroda cabinet, mired in indecision, held an extraordinary meeting at the palace in the emperor's presence. This proving insufficient, the debate continued for days. In October Ōkuma finally agreed to put the whole issue of treaty reform in abeyance for a time. On his way home from the meeting, however, a member of a patriotic society threw a bomb that cost Ōkuma a leg and led to his resignation a few weeks later. Kuroda resigned and was succeeded by Yamagata, who had opposed the Ōkuma draft.

The point of this detail is to show how popular interest, enthusiasm, and outrage were becoming a factor on the eve of the inauguration of constitutional government. This added significantly to the pressure on government leaders, who felt themselves harassed quite as severely as the political party figures whose problems have received a more sympathetic hearing from modern historians. The revival of political opposition in the united front movement and the successive treaty reform attempts coincided exactly with a cabinet shift and the sensational trial of an activist, Ōi Kentarō, who had plotted to raise men and money for a guerilla movement in Korea,[15] with the final discussions of the Meiji Constitution in the Privy Council, and with the promulgation of that constitution (and, on the same day, the murder of Mori Arinori). In addition to all that, administrative changes that finalized the general staffs of the armed services were being worked out. It is not surprising that the government leaders felt themselves beleaguered, and rather impressive that they functioned as well and as consistently as they did.

The inauguration of constitutional government improved the situation but it did not solve it. Yamagata, in his first cabinet, rejected plans for treaty reform that his foreign minister, Aoki Shūzō, worked out. Under Matsukata, who followed as prime minister, the issue became tangled with discussion of new law codes. By 1892, when Matsukata was followed in office by Itō, the House of Representatives submitted directly to the throne a call for unilateral abrogation of the treaties if suitable reform was not achieved. When representatives proposed legislation to that effect, Itō first prorogued, and then dissolved, the House of Representatives. This provided breathing space during which the government could set its course.

This time Foreign Minister Mutsu Munemitsu, one of the most interesting and able of the government group, prepared his measures carefully.[16] Finally in July 1894 a new treaty with Great Britain did away with consular courts. Tariff autonomy was to follow in five years. By separate agreement Japan agreed to keep the treaty in abeyance until its new codes of law had become effective. Even under the constitution, the government had found it necessary to insulate its moves from public discussion in order to get the flexibility it needed for foreign approval. When the House of Representatives, after spirited debate about its constitutional right to be informed on treaty negotiations, voted a bill demanding that right, Mutsu and Itō had prorogued, and then dissolved the Imperial Diet to quiet their opposition. In the interim they had the privacy to make the concessions that were necessary; provisions that would have been denounced had there been public debate, but which made it possible to work out arrangements acceptable to England. With the most important of the treaty system powers under control, comparable agreements with the others followed rapidly. In the case of the United States full agreement on tariff autonomy came only in the 1911 Treaty of Commerce and Navigation, a year before Emperor Meiji's death. The treaties also brought to an end the long debate about the desirability of unrestricted residence for foreigners in Japan. Thus the unequal treaties imposed inferiority on Japan for a full half century, and they were not completely outgrown until the very end of the Meiji period.

4. War with China

From the first, the political parties had discovered that their demands for a strong and, as they put it, independent foreign policy gave them a powerful issue. Their objections to higher taxes for military expansion were often at odds with their oratory about putting an end to Western privileges and expansion, but the government's cautious course in foreign policy was not popular. Once the issue of treaty reform was out of the way, however, the government precipitated a confrontation with China over the issue of Korea.

This cause was taken up with remarkable unanimity. The Imperial Diet voted the sums required immediately. War headquarters were set up at Hiroshima and the Diet convened there to show its support. The emperor himself was also moved to Hiroshima, where he lived in what were described as spartan conditions, to emphasize his leadership. Soon the rancor and bitterness of internal division gave way to jubilation over the victories in the field and on the sea. In this Japan's experience was probably not significantly different from that of other countries, except that the wartime unity, preceded as it had been by centuries of relative isolation and long decades of humiliation and frustration, was the more striking. Fought for the "independence" of Korea from China, the war seemed to presage a new sense of national purpose. The journalist Tokutomi Sohō wrote that he now suddenly realized, for the first time, that the government he had savaged so successfully was in fact *his* government. He was not the only one to make this discovery.

In the decade since Itō and Li Hung-chang had worked out an agreement on Korea in Tientsin, China had enjoyed political ascendancy in Seoul. Li's agent, the able Yüan Shih-k'ai, had managed to work out something approaching a protectorate for China. He was more concerned with control than with reform, however, and on a number of occasions he blocked the efforts of Korean reformers to bring about steps toward administrative modernization and efficiency. In the early 1890s the Korean government found itself preoccupied with the suppression of a sectarian, millenarian movement known as Tong-hak (Eastern Study).[17] Its difficulty in doing so led it to request help from China, which dispatched forces in response. In accordance with the agreement reached at Tientsin, Japan was informed of this.

That same year the shocking murder of a Korean inflamed Japanese opinion. Kim Ok-kyun was a well-born youth who had visited Japan as a member of a mission sent to apologize for the anti-Japanese rising of 1882. Two years later he was also involved in the unsuccessful coup d'état in which pro-Japanese advocates of change brought on the Chinese intervention that led to the Tientsin Agreement. Kim then fled to Japan, where Asia-firsters and activists saw in him hope for a future role in Korean modernization. Government leaders were more cautious; they turned down Korean demands that he be extradited, but after some hesitation they exiled him to the Ogasawara (Bonin) Islands. He tired of that, and when he was given reason to think that he could contact friends and followers he made his way to Shanghai. The encouragement proved to be a trap; he was struck down in his room in a Japanese inn in the International Settlement. After some hesitation, the British authorities concluded that rules against extradition did not apply to a corpse and turned him over to Chinese authorities. They in turn sent his body to Korea, where it was cut up and distributed to all provinces as a lesson to other putative "traitors." Kim's brutal end became something of a cause célèbre in Tokyo, where it was portrayed as a betrayal by Li Hung-chang and a setback for Japan's stature and dignity, and evidence of Korean barbarity.

As indignation rose the Meiji leaders, after satisfying themselves that the new treaty with Great Britain would not be threatened, concluded that the time had come to cut the Gordian knot of Korean "reform" and eliminate the Chinese influence. When the government was advised of Korean requests for military assistance against the Tong-hak rebellion, it concluded that the Tientsin Agreement entitled it to send its own forces. By the time the Japanese troops arrived the rebellion was no longer a problem, but the presence of Chinese and Japanese units in Korea did present a problem—and an opportunity—that could not be ignored. After long discussion the Tokyo government decided to ask the Chinese to join in demanding that the Koreans carry out governmental reforms. They did so in the full expectation that such a request would be denied, and with the determination that such a denial could be construed as justification for hostilities.

The reforms proposed, or rather demanded, were, all things considered, rather like those Japan had carried out after the Meiji Restoration. They called for the establishment of a specialized bureaucracy in a newly rationalized government structure, a new judiciary, a more rational accounting for government finances, with a regular budget and reformed tax system, and a modern military. The Tokyo leaders were convinced that the Korean monarchy and sovereignty were doomed unless such changes were made, and that it was only a question of time before some outside power would force the issue anyway. They wanted to be first in line. At the same time they wanted economic primacy for themselves in terms of trade, raw materials, and concessions for communication lines. That economic primacy may have been uppermost in mind, but it was conditioned on political change. At the highest level, leaders saw the issue in terms of power politics. As Foreign Minister Mutsu put it in his account of his stewardship, it did not make sense that Japan should extend itself for the benefit of Korea. "I never thought there was any reason for internal reform in Korea beyond our political interest," he wrote, "and I thought that there was little use in trying to see ourselves as a chivalrous, crusading army. Our political interest was what mattered, and nothing was to be sacrificed to it."[18] But of course it made sense to pose as the sponsor of progressive change for a corrupt and deteriorating Korean government, and many Japanese responded to that.

On receiving the Japanese demands, for that is what they were, the Koreans hesitated. They were encouraged to do so by the Chinese. Then the Chinese declined to join the Japanese in forcing modernization on the Koreans. On July 12, 1894, Tokyo had decided on war and instructed its minister in Seoul to "use any pretext available" to justify action.[19]

In the fighting that followed Japanese forces were successful on every front. The principal land battle took place at Pyongyang. The Japanese navy secured its communications by defeating the Chinese fleet in the Yellow Sea, and after the remainder of the Chinese ships took shelter at Weihaiwei in Shantung they were outflanked by Japanese landings that made it possible to shell the harbor from land positions. The Chinese admiral committed suicide; his body was treated with full military honors by the victors, who admired this samurai death. China was not to have a blue-water navy again for the next century.

Japan's victory over China could be credited in good measure to its greater speed in modernizing its society and armed services. That conclusion was the one drawn by outsiders, many of whom had expected China to prevail, and it was central to Japan's rise to membership in the (curiously misnamed) "concert of powers" thereafter. Japanese military units were uniformly armed, in contrast to the variety of weapons with which Chinese soldiers were outfitted; they were highly motivated, in contrast to the lackluster units of semi-trained forces the Chinese mounted, and their commanders showed dash and imagination that contrasted with the more conservative demeanor of their opponents. Both navies had been purchased from European shipyards. China had the larger ships, but Japanese commanders used their rapid-firing guns to sweep the decks of their opponents' vessels; agility, speed, and tactics prevailed. By the time Li Hung-chang arrived at Shimonoseki to sue for peace in the spring of 1895, Japanese units had occupied Port Arthur and the Liaotung Peninsula, Weihaiwei in Shantung, and shattered the Chinese fleet, and Japanese publicists were enthusiastically calling for an advance on Peking. Prime Minister Itō Hirobumi came to Shimonoseki to represent Japan. There was little doubt that the terms would be severe.

The Treaty of Shimonoseki was the most damaging that China signed in the nineteenth century. It included transfer of territory, economic privileges, and a large monetary payment, and was to serve as the springboard for a new round of imperialist advances that seriously threatened Chinese sovereignty. Japan seemed to have achieved membership in the line of Western imperialists, and the concessions it now extorted from China were immediately extended to all other powers through the provisions of the most-favored-nation clause which was at the center of the system of unequal treaties. China agreed that Korea was independent. It ceded the island of Taiwan to Japan, and in addition transferred the Liaotung Peninsula, with its fine port of Dairen (Dalien) and fortifications at Port Arthur. Japan fell heir to the full range of privileges earlier granted to Western powers under the unequal treaty system. To these were added new rights to navigate the Yangtze River and to establish factories in Shanghai, which guaranteed Japan a larger financial stake in the future. A large indemnity of 2 million *taels,* approximately 3 million yen, payable over seven years, would in large measure defray Japan's war costs.

At this point, European interference came in to remind the Meiji state that there was more to do. Germany, Russia, and France combined in notes advising Japan that "for the peace of Asia" it would be best to return the Liaotung ("South Manchurian") territorial concession that had been promised, and the Tokyo government saw little choice but to comply. The indemnity was increased in partial compensation, but no amount of payment could make up for the sense of outrage and humiliation that was left by the "Triple Intervention." An imperial rescript exhorted Japanese to remain calm and diligent in adversity.

It is often noted that the war marked some sort of divide in Japanese public opinion and nationalism. One casualty was the respect in which China had long been held. This was the first time there had been large-scale, personal contact between Japanese and Chinese. It came under abnormal conditions, of course; the "China" that had been imagined by intellectuals, a land of learning and sages, came to grief in the observations and letters of the country boys writing home. The Japanese violence against Chinese ex-soldiers and civilians that followed the fall of Port Arthur helped harden mutual dislike. At the same time the Japanese, in print, press, and song, denigrated and often demonized the enemy. Prints showed Japanese soldiers looking rather Western and perfectly disciplined, coolly facing an undisciplined rabble. The veteran statesman Li Hung-chang was reviled as crafty and untrustworthy, credited with utilizing European patrons—who were soon "rewarded" by new concessions—to rob the Japanese of gains their soldiers and sailors had won.[20] Respect for Koreans declined even more rapidly as Japanese armies, inadequately served by the laborers they brought with them, commandeered Koreans as coolies.

The war was broadly popular in Japan, where intellectuals accepted the argument that Japan was freeing Korea from China and exulted in success. Fukuzawa Yukichi saw in it "a war between a country which is trying to develop civilization and a country which disturbs the development of civilization," and the Christian leader Uchimura Kanzō characterized the struggle as a "righteous war." A 1994 study[21] nevertheless shows that in the Japanese hinterland, still poorly served by rail, where young men often plodded long distances to board the trains that would take them to recruiting centers, there was a good deal of ambivalence. There was widespread profiteering, and not a little draft evasion.

The government was highly successful in using the war to raise the aura of the emperor, but Mutsuhito himself seems to have had little enthusiasm for the conflict. It was later revealed that he grumbled that it had not been his idea, and rejected the suggestion that he report to the ancestors at the Ise shrine. At the end, when the terms of the Treaty of Shimonoseki became known, some of the euphoria changed. Uchimura now lamented the fact that his "righteous war" had proved after all to be a "piratical war." Conservatives like former general Tani Kanjō, who had argued for a small military, thought the territorial gains unwise and counterproductive. In fact the "pacification" of Taiwan took years and required 60,000 troops and produced more casualties than the war itself. Yet critics were very much in the minority. The emperor's real thoughts could never be known, and the misgivings of people like Uchimura and Tani were outweighed by the enthusiasm of the many that Japan had shown its mettle. The emperor's soldiers were the heroes of the day, and congratulatory imperial awards of peerages went to the victorious commanders. If one adds to this the new willingness of the Imperial Diet to vote war credits and Itō's decision to offer a cabinet post to the political party leader Itagaki Taisuke, it is clear that the war had a major impact on politics within Japan.

But it failed to solve Japan's Korea "problem." When the war began the Japanese seized control of the royal palace in Seoul. Since the issue was ostensibly Korea's "independence," it would have been disconcerting to have the king flee to Chinese protection to escape the Japanese embrace. But that left the problem of what should be done in the palace. There was little help to be expected from the Korean government. A rather bizarre first step was to form a puppet government around none other than the Taewon'gun, recently extricated from Chinese exile. He, however, had little trust in the Japanese and proved an unwilling and unreliable partner. In August 1894 an agreement calling for considerable increases in Japanese economic and political influence was designed to strengthen the "reform" faction of Korean ministers. A joint

Japanese-Korean commission was to "meet and decide upon those matters necessary to consolidate Korea's independence and autonomy,"[22] but these words had a very special meaning for Japanese: "independence" and "autonomy" meant elimination of Chinese influence. Next, the Korean government signed a treaty of alliance with Japan promising Korean help in moving troops and supplies. Reform moved slowly, however, and in the Japanese press exasperation mounted over the fact that Koreans seemed to be dithering while Japanese were fighting, supposedly for Korean independence.

Tokyo now sent Inoue Kaoru, a formidable member of the first team who had considerable experience in Korea, as representative to Seoul. The selection was not without political significance: Satsuma commanders had won a disproportionate number of the battles, and now it could fall to a Chōshū man to win a battle of peace.

Inoue adopted a high-handed position. He told the Korean king that the emperor had personally sent him to advise him, and that he had to begin by cleaning out the pockets of conservatism at the court. The Japanese seem to have seen Korea through the lens of their recent experience, and thought that a revitalized court, directed by knowledgeable and experienced reformers, could turn the country around. They were of course wrong: the Meiji reformers had not let themselves be mired in Kyoto politics, but they had brought the emperor to Tokyo. More important still, the entire direction, while motivated in good part by the need to win foreign favor, had been in the hands of Japanese nationals determined to build and strengthen their country against any and all comers.

Inoue's confidence soon began to falter. "What Koreans do is not always what they say and they cannot be trusted," he cabled Foreign Minister Mutsu. The Taewon'gun, once again deprived of his office, soon intrigued against the Japanese, while the queen's faction was more hostile still. Pak Yong-hyo, a maverick reformer Inoue next recruited, proved no more dependable. Outwardly, the program of reform continued. By the spring of 1895 some forty Japanese advisers were in place in the royal household, ministries, police, and postal services, and their power and influence grew steadily. Further gains were dependent on a program of loans that would give Inoue leverage and influence in reinforcing the base for Japanese economic control.

But people in Tokyo were less enthusiastic about raising money for Korean reform. The government's submission to the Triple Intervention had once again made it unpopular, and allocation of the sums Inoue promised the Koreans would have required approval of the Imperial Diet. Consequently there was an increasing gap between paper reforms and actual deeds. A blizzard of decrees affecting everything from topknots to rules of commerce was produced, but alarmed conservatives were usually able to delay implementation. After eleven months of work a discouraged Inoue returned to Japan in September 1895.

His successor, retired General Miura Gorō, was made of sterner stuff. He had no specific instructions from Tokyo, but he went along with plans for a coup against the Min faction that was to have the support of the Taewon'gun, who was once again intriguing from the sidelines. To guarantee a margin of victory Miura collected members of two Japanese patriotic societies; dressed as Koreans, they joined the plotters on the day of action. On October 7, 1895, a mixed group of Koreans and Japanese invaded the palace, stabbed the queen in her bedchamber, and went on to kill several members of the royal household staff. This brutal act shocked observers of all ranks and nationalities. Miura was quickly recalled to Japan, where he was tried (but not convicted) for complicity. This time the Tokyo Foreign Ministry dispatched a career diplomat, Komura Jūtarō, to try to patch things up with the foreign representatives in Seoul. Inoue returned with a letter of apology for the Korean king.

In the meantime Russian influence had been on the rise in Korea. On February 11 (ironically enough, Japan's "National Foundation Day" once more) the Korean king and crown prince fled to residence-in-exile in the Russian legation in Seoul. Thanks to strong-arm tactics and bungling on the part of Tokyo, and consistent distrust on the part of the Koreans, Japan had succeeded in little more than replacing Chinese with Russian influence in Korea.

5. The Diplomacy of Imperialism

In the years after the Treaty of Shimonoseki imperialist pressures increased in East Asia. Expansion driven by industrialization seemed to be the destiny of modern states. Some might decry its costs in men and money, but more accepted those burdens as the price of national greatness. The United States, its westward expansion having reached the Pacific shore, went beyond it to take a share of Samoa, responded to a staged coup by occupying Hawaii, and after defeating Spain in 1898, extended its domination to the Philippines. The decision to take over the Philippines was not made easily or lightly, but largely for the same reasons that led the Japanese to take Korea; if the islands were left for the picking, some other power would claim them. The enthusiasm of the press before and during the war against Spain was comparable to that in Japan during the war against China. Annexation of the Philippines also brought America face to face with Japan in a new way. In Japan, no less than in many Western countries, imperialism came to occupy a central place in politics, economy, and culture.

Theorists of world politics, the geopolitical seers of the age, emphasized the importance of defense in depth. "Defense," wrote Admiral Alfred Thayer Mahan, "means not merely defense of our territory, but defense of our just national interests whatever they be and wherever they are." In Japan Yamagata Aritomo expressed similar views in important state papers in which he distinguished between Japan's line of defense and its line of interest. Korea was well within the second. Imperialism also coincided with industrialization and seemed a natural by-product. A large part of the Chinese indemnity went to fund Japan's Yawata Iron and Steel Works, and that in turn increased Japanese concern for coking coal and iron ore from China. National pride was central to this process; the Tokyo *Asahi* editorialized that imperialism was an expression of basic national energy made manifest through the organization of the state. It might not require seizure of neighboring territory, but it did mean denying to others the exclusive appropriation of resources that were seen as vital to the economy.

These trends found expression in many ways. "Militarists" might limit their vision to political control, and many asserted that Korea and part of China were fated to come under Japanese rule. Others, "Asia-firsters" who were more sensitive to the needs of neighboring countries, deplored crude aggression, argued for closer relations with neighboring Asia, and encouraged activists who provided help to refugee reformers from Korea, China, and Southeast Asia. Enthusiasm for this position knew no barriers of class. Konoe Atsumaro, who was president of the House of Peers from 1895 to 1904 and the scion of a family whose interrelationships with the imperial house extended from the seventh century, was in this group. He sponsored a "Common Culture" (Dōbun) Association to foster study and contact with China, championed Korean independence, and criticized swollen military budgets. He was also vehemently opposed to granting foreigners unrestricted residence, as well as being a committed Russophobe, heading a People's Alliance demanding Russia's withdrawal from Manchuria.[23]

A number of activists, survivors of the idealism of the *jiyū-minken* movement of the 1880s, busied themselves with plans to help people like Kim Ok-kyun and Sun Yat-sen, hoping that they would lead their countries in what they termed the "regeneration of Asia." Their need for political and financial support in those efforts might drive them into strange and unpromising alliances, but confidence in their own sincerity usually blinded them to the dangers of compromising their cause by accepting army money.[24]

Soon after the Japanese defeat of China, a new stage of imperialist penetration began with "concession diplomacy." Now fully aware of Chinese military weakness, the powers began to seek primacy in the areas most important to their strategic and economic interests.

The new threat to Asia that alarmed these Japanese began with moves by the countries that had participated in the Triple Intervention, each of which claimed its reward from China: France in the South Chinese province of Kwangtung and Germany in Shantung. Russia, most objectionably of all, demanded and received a twenty-five-year lease on the Liaotung Peninsula, territory Japan had been obliged to give up three years earlier. Together with this came rights for a railroad running north to connect with the Trans-Siberian Railway, the future Chinese Eastern and South Manchurian Railroads, and rights along their right-of-way. To counter the Russians, Britain occupied the Shantung port of Weihaiwei after the Japanese vacated it, while to the south it added the Kowloon area, on a ninety-nine-year lease, to its Hong Kong colony.

Japan joined in this to the extent of securing guarantees that no part of Fukien, the province opposite Taiwan, would be alienated to another power. This precaution proved worthwhile when the United States expressed interest in a port there shortly afterward. Still, Japan came off poorly in this sudden burst of concession grabbing. There was much talk and writing about an impending breakup of China, and the Tokyo leaders did not have to be paranoid to find all this alarming. Ōkuma Shigenobu became known for speeches and articles advocating the "Preservation of China."

Chinese too were alarmed. In 1899 an antidynastic movement that had long been underground broke out in Shantung, coupling virulent antiforeignism with opposition to the ruling Manchus. As it spread through North China, xenophobes at the Peking court saw the possibility of combining with it to resist the foreigners. Antiforeign terrorism that had been directed principally against missionaries now spread to the capital and culminated in the siege of the legations in the summer of 1900. This brought on international intervention. Japan played a major role in the suppression of the "Boxers," as Westerners termed them; the 10,000 men it sent were as many as the forces of all the other powers combined. At the same time Russia occupied the three northeastern provinces collectively known as Manchuria, and its forces stayed in place after the Boxer fall. Despite the alarm of "open door" powers—Britain, the United States, and Japan—that had interests in North China and regarded the Russian occupation as a violation of treaty rights, Russia insisted that the issue was merely a bilateral problem with China.

The response to this in Japan vacillated between efforts to work out an agreement with the Russians and determination to build strength against them. There were several exchanges proposed whereby Japan would grant Russian primacy in Manchuria in return for a free hand in Korea, but the Tokyo government was unable to reach an agreement; worse, it began to suspect the Russians harbored plans for North Korea as well. Itō Hirobumi, on a trip to Europe, was the last to make the effort for an agreement with Russia, but in his absence the Katsura government worked out the terms for an alliance with England that settled the issue.

The Anglo-Japanese Alliance, signed in 1902, became the mainstay of Japanese diplomacy for twenty years in much the same way that the American alliance became the pivot of Japanese foreign policy for a half century after 1945. Under its terms Japan and Great Britain committed themselves to joint action in the event any fourth power joined with Russia. This meant that Japan need have no fear of a new Triple, or Double, Intervention if it went to war with Russia. The alliance marked the final and full "arrival" of Japan in international society; it now became a player in world diplomacy.[25] For the next decade the international system was characterized by alliances, often with clauses that remained secret for years. These gradually enmeshed all the Great Powers except the United States in a system that, ostensibly meant to strengthen their security, actually deprived them of freedom of choice in intervention. Yet for Japan the tie with Britain had few dangers and obvious advantages. Japan limited its involvement in world affairs to issues concerning its security, and limited its contributions to the allied cause in World War I to the seizure of German holdings in China and the Pacific.

With its back protected, Japan could now enter into serious negotiations with imperial Russia.[26] Once again most of public opinion favored standing up to the Russians. Politicians, writers, and intellectuals organized movements urging the government to take a strong stand. The Russians, however, assumed the Japanese were bluffing; let the tsar mobilize one division, his minister to Tokyo was reported to have said, and the Japanese would back down. Rather than negotiate seriously with a small Asian country, Russia expressed its preference for a conference of interested powers. And things moved slowly. The tsar was away from his capital between August and Christmas, and the interminable delay in responding to Japanese proposals seemed a deliberate insult. In Japan the genrō, including Yamagata Aritomo, tended toward caution, while the second generation of diplomatic and army leaders chafed under their delay. Itō Hirobumi was the last to abandon hope for a peaceful settlement and come aboard, and he became convinced of Russian intransigence only in 1903.

The Katsura cabinet decided for war in February 1904. The warfare of the

Russo-Japanese War, though dwarfed in cost and horror by World War I a decade later, was in many ways prophetic of what was to come. Trench warfare, barbed-wire entanglements, and machine gun nests took a formidable toll of life. In the grinding battle for the Liaotung base of Port Arthur General Nogi Maresuke lost 58,000 men and the Russians 31,000, and in the final gigantic battle for Mukden Russian casualties were estimated at 85,000 to Japan's 70,000. At sea the Russian losses were even more staggering. Japan opened the conflict with a surprise assault that bottled up the Russian Pacific fleet at Port Arthur and Vladivostock, and the following spring at Tsushima Straits (in what Japanese refer to as the Battle of the Japan Sea) Admiral Tōgō Heihachirō's ships sank virtually the entire Russian Baltic fleet, which had sailed halfway around the globe in a vain attempt to right the balance. These victories provided the epics of modern Japanese military and naval lore. Future discussions of Manchuria would be phrased in terms of the sacrifices the Meiji generation had made at Port Arthur, and the reverence the Meiji emperor inspired as spiritual leader of his country was in no small measure due to his presence at the helm of his country at the time of a great crisis.

Japan also enjoyed international approval and even acclaim. The opening assault on the Russian navy, which came before a declaration of war, was described by the London *Times* as "an act of daring which is destined to take a place of honor in naval annals," and the stoic and disciplined courage General Nogi's conscripts demonstrated as they marched to their death at Port Arthur won the attention of the world. Russian pogroms made it possible for Japan to raise large sums of money in New York and London, and Kaneko Kentarō and Suematsu Kenchō, senior figures who were dispatched to court American and British opinion, enjoyed great success. In the United States President Theodore Roosevelt seized the opportunity offered by the exhaustion of both contestants to sponsor a peace conference that met at Portsmouth in New Hampshire in 1905.

The Portsmouth Treaty of Peace transferred to Japan the Russian lease of the Liaotung Peninsula and the South Manchurian Railroad rights in Manchuria. The southern half of the island of Sakhalin became Japanese territory. Perhaps most important of all, Russia was forced to recognize Japan's paramount interest in Korea. Not only was Japan now a major world power, but its performance had excited the admiration of the world. In England, where the Boer War had left memories of incompetence, there was a "Learn from Japan" movement that called for a rebirth of patriotism and loyalty. Throughout Asia the fact that Japan had defeated a major imperialist power attracted the admiration of nationalists of many stripes. Sun Yat-sen, the first president of the Chinese Republic, later recalled how, in going through the Suez Canal, he had encountered an Arab who asked him if he was Japanese. The Arab had "observed vast armies of Russian soldiers being shipped back to Russia from the Far East," which seemed to him a sure sign of Russia's defeat. "The joy of this Arab," wrote Sun, "as a member of the great Asiatic race, seemed to know no bounds."[27]

6. The Annexation of Korea

Not everyone shared the joy that Sun Yat-sen's Arab expressed. Even in Japan the dangers and costs of the conflict had raised doubts. The Christian leader Uchimura Kanzō, chastened by the "piratical" outcome of the war with China, had adopted a pacifist position. Uchimura and other intellectuals published their views in a liberal daily, the *Yorozu chōhō,* before its management changed its policy to support of the war. Others went even further; the founders of a fledgling socialist movement managed to publish a *Commoner's Daily (Heimin shinbun)* for two months before it fell victim to censorship for publishing a translation of the Communist Manifesto. Much support of the war was more fatalistic than enthusiastic, and the songs and ballads that emerged stressed the separation and hardships of the troops ("Ah! The red soil of Manchuria, hundreds of miles from home" was a classic song that has remained popular) in contrast to the euphoria of the war with China.

If there was some ambivalence in Japan, there was none in Korea, where the government had long been aware that its independence depended upon maneuvering in the competition for control between China, Russia, and Japan. Japan, the most insistent of the three, now faced no further competition. Japanese influence had gone into temporary eclipse when King Kojong took refuge in the Russian legation, but it was not long before the Russians in turn had overplayed their hand. In the same years conservatives at the Korean court had organized a petition campaign to raise the prestige of the king by terming him Emperor. This change took place in October of 1897, and from then on, terminologically identical with the Chinese and Japanese emperors, Kojong could claim equality with them. The surface attributes of a modern nation-state followed, with a national anthem, flags for monarchy and for the army, and vastly greater powers for the throne. The ruler could now overturn cabinet decisions, and he was given control over all mines in the country and monopoly rights over valuable ginseng and consumption taxes. This meant that Japanese attempts to control change would have to focus more than ever on the palace.

Nevertheless the underpinnings of this centralization were very shaky. Officials rotated in office at bewildering speed; in seven years there were twenty-seven prime ministers, leading the American minister Horace Allen to report to Washington that there was "practically no central government in Korea." Few had much hope for Korean independence.

Korean cooperation was essential to Japan for success in the war with Russia. Japan rushed troops to Korea before war was declared, and on February 23 the Japanese minister cajoled the Korean government into signing a "Protocol" that permitted the Japanese to undertake operations on Korean soil, in return for which Japan would guarantee "the independence and territorial integrity" of Korea. The principal anti-Japanese leaders were soon spirited out of the country to Japan. Resentment against this bullying inflamed Korean opinion and produced many kinds of sabotage; the Korean government did not completely choose sides until the Japanese defeated a Russian force at Pyongyang in May. Emperor Kojong then broke off diplomatic relations with Russia.

As the war situation improved Japan began to define its aims for Korea, and in May 1905 the Katsura cabinet reached a formal decision on Japan's goals there. Japan should have permanent army and navy bases, it needed supervision over Korean foreign policy and finances, and it would have to direct Korea's mail and telegraph communications and in general supervise economic reform.[28] This decision left little doubt about Japan's future path, and as the war proceeded Japanese control intensified.

None of this surprised or upset foreign observers. On the contrary: the disparity between Korean and Japanese power made it seem inevitable. American acquiescence seemed assured by the Taft-Katsura Agreement of July 1905 that implied a trade-off for control over Korea with the American annexation of the Philippines, and Great Britain's misgivings were met in 1907, when the Anglo-Japanese Alliance renewal added coverage for India. More to the point, however, was the fact that Japan enjoyed the favorable opinion of most observers, while Korean politics emphatically did not. As Minister Horace Allen wrote to Washington,

> We will make a serious mistake if we allow sentimental reasons to induce us to attempt to bolster up this "Empire" in its independence. These people cannot govern themselves . . .
>
> I am no pro-Japanese enthusiast, as you know, but neither am I opposed to any civilized race taking over the management of these kindly Asiatics for the good of the people and the suppression of oppressive officials, the establishment of order and the development of commerce.[29]

Similarly, the American journalist George Kennan expressed sympathy for Japanese advisers who were being frustrated by the velocity of men in high office.[30] He asked,

What are you going to do with a government which . . . avoids action and evades responsibility by allowing its Ministers to resign at the rate of one or two a week? The Korean Emperor has a set of twenty or thirty men who may be compared with the court cards in a whist pack . . . Every time the cards are shuffled and dealt the same old knaves turn up, but in new places.

Like many others, Kennan was more than willing to see what the Japanese could do. "It is a gigantic experiment," he wrote, "and it may or may not succeed, but we, who are trying a similar experiment in the Philippines, must regard it with the deepest interest and sympathy."

The Tokyo establishment, however, was by no means united on the steps that should be taken. Army leaders despaired of Korean cooperation and competence and wanted annexation, but Itō Hirobumi, who was concerned about overseas reaction and less pessimistic about Korean ability to respond realistically, was not so sure. Consequently an intermediate step was taken by working out a Protectorate in November 1905. Japan would now exercise full control of Korean foreign relations "until the moment arrives when it is recognized that Korea has attained national strength." A Japanese Resident General, with the right of access to the Korean throne, would be in Seoul, and Japanese would be in charge at other points as needed.

The nature of this "agreement" continued to provide material for Japanese-Korean confrontation into the 1990s, when conservative Japanese government leaders asserted that the document conformed to all legal requirements and was fully valid. Not so in Korea, where scholars in 1992 charged that the document carried neither Kojong's seal nor his signature. The dispute is essentially a quibble, for there is no doubt that the "agreement" was forced on a reluctant Korean government by Itō, who warned the Koreans of dire consequences if they resisted. He himself professed confidence in the future;

I am not insisting that your country commit suicide, nor do I believe that your country cannot progress to a position similar to our own. I expect that if you thrust forward boldly, the day will come when you will advance to a position of equality with us and we will cooperate with one another.[31]

Itō was given the opportunity to prove his case. He was appointed Japan's first Resident General in Korea in December 1905. It would burden this narrative to describe the way this Meiji leader undertook the last assignment of his career. Prior to accepting the post he saw to it that he would have full authority, with control over military as well as civil policy. Only the greatest of the genrō could have managed this; by the 1930s it would be unthinkable. Itō seems to have been bemused by the events of his youth. He compared the achievements of the Meiji Restoration with what was required for Korea, and saw parallels with the steps he and his fellows had taken at home four decades earlier. Resistance, he thought, was as wrong-headed and hopeless as the samurai rebellions of early Meiji had been. He tried to separate the Korean throne from politics, and wanted to place implementation in the hands of bureaucrats who would be responsive to their Japanese advisers. He spent an inordinate amount of time and effort at the court. That court, however, resented his presence, and throughout the government the advisers he brought met even greater resistance. Policies of "wealth and strength," when sponsored by unwelcome Japanese, could hardly have been expected to evoke the support they had received in Meiji Japan, where they had been designed to secure national independence. The Japanese do not seem to have recognized this, and Itō himself was strangely obtuse on this point.

Events now moved rapidly toward the extinction of Korean independence. The Korean monarch, increasingly desperate for foreign support, managed to send an English journalist to America, where he received no hearing, and to the Hague Conference in 1907, where he failed to receive diplomatic accreditation. By now Yamagata was firmly in favor of annexation, but Itō had the backing of the Saionji cabinet for one last intermediate step. A new Protectorate Treaty gave the Resident General the right to approve all laws and administrative decisions, including the selection of all high officials, thus extending Itō's control to domestic as well as foreign affairs. In July 1907 Kojong was obliged to abdicate in favor of his son. He was to become more successful in retirement than he had been on the throne, for he now became a symbol of Korean nationalism. Throughout the country resistance flared. "Righteous armies," as they styled themselves, had risen earlier to protest the power exchange, but they now grew in number and size. Koreans resented the increasingly overbearing attitude of Japanese nationals and of the many Japanese who had come thronging in, in search of employment, land, and fortune. The Korean armed forces were disbanded. This provided a large supply of disaffected, trained, and armed reinforcements for guerrilla movements. Itō might have thought of these as disgruntled samurai, but in fact the insurgents' support extended throughout Korean society, and they warred against the collaborationist government as well as against the Japanese. With tens of thousands of guerrillas in the field pacification required extensive Japanese counterinsurgency measures, and these, though ultimately successful, often took a heavy toll of villagers suspected of aiding the resistance. There were other Koreans who saw a future for themselves in collaboration. A large-scale organization, the Ilchinhoe (Unity and Progress Society, which was for a time sponsored and funded by Japanese, carried on a "popular" campaign calling for full annexation that added further to social instability.

Itō resigned his post in the early summer of 1909, probably in frustration because his methods were not achieving results. He had never ruled out annexation, but expected that the reforms he was sponsoring would bring about voluntary cooperation and compliance. When a stable collaborative structure did not materialize, he withdrew his objections. In August of 1910 a cabinet of Korean collaborators quietly signed a treaty of full annexation at the Residency General. The act was not made public for a week to give the Japanese time to prepare for the Korean public's indignation and protest. The Meiji emperor's rescript, issued later that month, made it official. It explained that

> We, attaching the highest importance to the maintenance of permanent peace in the Orient and the consolidation of lasting security for our Empire and finding in Korea constant and fruitful sources of complication . . . have now arrived at an arrangement for permanent annexation . . . All Koreans, being under Our direct sway, will enjoy growing prosperity and welfare, and with assured repose and security will come a marked expansion in industry and trade.

By then Itō was no longer alive. He had been killed in October of 1909 at Harbin, where he had gone to meet with Russian representatives. His assassin was a young Korean named An Chung-gun. An had begun as a scholar of Chinese studies before forming his own academy; as annexation neared he had slipped over the Manchurian border and returned to form a group of guerrillas fighting for independence. One might almost compare him to Itō's old mentor, Yoshida Shōin. Today a statue of An stands on the site of Itō's old Residency General in Seoul. There must be few other cases in which the assassin of a neighboring country's leading modern statesman has been elevated to the status of national hero.

7. State and Society

By the time the Meiji period came to an end in 1912, Japanese imperialism was firmly established. The acquisition of Korea met with little resentment elsewhere in the world. Agreements with the United States (Taft-Katsura, 1905), Great Britain (the restructured Alliance, 1907), and Russia (agreements firming up continental borders and treaty rights, in 1907, 1910, and 1912) seemed to have brought security. Japan was raised to the level of equality by the other powers. In 1905 the British Legation in Tokyo was raised to embassy status, and similar changes with other Great Powers followed swiftly. It was

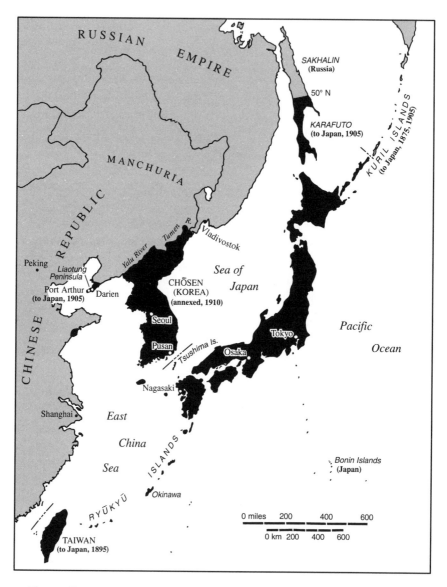

6. The Meiji Empire, 1910. Japan secured possession of the Kurils in 1875, asserted full control over Ryukyu in 1879, acquired Taiwan after the Sino-Japanese War in 1895, obtained the south Manchurian leasehold in 1905, and annexed Korea in 1910.

pleasing to Japanese that diplomats assigned to Tokyo now had the rank of ambassador while those accredited to China remained ministers. All foreign representatives had left Korea.

New problems replaced the old. The growth of continental responsibility brought with it heavy defense expenditures. The circle of "interest" that Yamagata had extended to Korea two decades earlier grew ever larger, and the Imperial Army and Navy required larger budgets. Yesterday's friend could be tomorrow's foe. Heavy industry began with iron- and steelworks funded by the Chinese indemnity; industry and imperial growth fed upon each other. Japan began to build its own ships. An enlarging merchant marine related to exports, and a new navy was required by the development of the dreadnought, which suddenly rendered previous warships obsolete. Japan entered this new competition as a near equal with its rivals. Future Diet debates would continue to be focused on the degree and allocation of assessments for more divisions and more battleships.

The early twentieth century brought a new balance between rural and urban Japan, for the distribution of population was changing rapidly. Early post-Restoration estimates indicate a population of 35 million in 1873. By 1891 the count stood at 41 million, and in 1913 it was 52 million. With better fertilizers and strains of rice agriculture grew more productive, but by 1900 some sort of ceiling had been reached and Japan began to import food. Theretofore much of the government revenue had come from agriculture, but as mentioned earlier, after 1900 the balance shifted as consumption, income, business, and commerce taxes carried the load. The population growth was to a large degree in cities. New commercial and industrial cities were arranged along the Pacific coast that Tokugawa daimyo had traveled on their trips to Edo; Kobe, Osaka, Nagoya, Yokohama, and Tokyo were the centers.

Japan's electorate, however, remained disproportionately rural. Since the franchise had been extended to property-owning taxpayers with a minimum of 15 yen tax annually, landlords and established farmers provided the bulk of the votes, and this remained the case even when the tax qualification was lowered to 10 yen in 1900.

The growth of population and the need for foodstuffs naturally led to talk of emigration. For many years it was thought that Korea was relatively underpopulated and would be able to support many settlers, and hopes were also high for Taiwan. Enthusiasts wrote of this as a natural form of national expansion. The bulk of emigrants, however, were attracted by the dream of land and wealth in Hawaii and the United States. Until well after the Russo-Japanese War the United States and its possessions attracted the largest number of overseas Japanese, more even than Taiwan and Korea. "The movement was sustained," Iriye writes, "by the confident psychology of expansionism and by an image of that country as Japan's friend."[32] After the victory over Russia confidence in Japanese expansion in all directions, westward as well as eastward, was striking. As one journal editorialized, "Peacetime war has already begun. The trumpet has sounded, and the war cry has been heard. Are our people ready to rush to the enemy camp?" Expansion overseas seemed to some the nation's most urgent business. Journalists vied with one another to call for courageous Japanese to step forth and show their mettle and ability. The movement of settlers began with naive assumptions of welcome and partnership: Japanese and Americans, one journalist wrote, were the two most progressive peoples on the globe, and the vast spaces of the American West were a logical site for joint endeavor. Unfortunately Americans were less convinced of this, and the result was an impending crisis in Japanese-American relations.

The first decade of the century was also the time that talk of a "Yellow Peril" filled world journals. Japanese government leaders were alarmed by this and took a cautious position, but some, like Ōkuma Shigenobu, wrote that the country's response should be to assert the nation's rights boldly. The performance of Japanese settlers, he was confident, would provide proof that they were closer to Westerners than to Chinese and other Asians. When immigrants began to meet hostility and discrimination, however, the mood changed to one of hurt and indignation.

The Russo-Japanese War thus left a mixed legacy in Japanese-American relations. On the one hand American loans had played an important part in helping to finance Japan's tremendous effort, and President Theodore Roosevelt's role in arranging the Portsmouth Peace Conference won the gratitude of the Japanese authorities, who realized that the nation had reached the limits of its abilities. But this was not at all the case with ordinary Japanese. Poorly informed by a government that had not bothered to keep them posted, confident that further struggle would bring the Russians abjectly to heel, and determined that their hardships would be rewarded, Japanese were indignant when they discovered that the Portsmouth treaty had no provisions for indemnification. The Japanese press, their chief source of information, had expressed its reservations about the peace conference as premature, and greeted it in terms of humiliation and disgrace. The meeting of an organization dedicated to opposition was called at Hibiya, in central Tokyo, on September 5, 1905, the day the peace treaty was signed in Portsmouth. A good part of the crowd moved to the bridge leading to the imperial palace to urge rejection of the treaty and to call on the army to continue fighting, only to be repelled by a clumsy and maladroit police response. Soon rioting spread all over Tokyo, continuing for several days, and from Tokyo it spread to other cities. The government found itself forced to declare martial law to restore order. By then the wrath of the crowd had resulted in the destruction of 250 buildings in Tokyo alone, including the residence of the home minister and the offices of the sole pro-government newspaper. Nine police stations and hundreds of police boxes were burned; government and crowd casualties exceeded 1,000, with 17 dead. This popular fury, directed at a government people did not trust, was far removed from the response that might have been expected by a paternalistic government from a grateful people. In Andrew Gordon's thoughtful analysis,

> While the high degree of control maintained by a narrow elite that promoted capitalism and created a modern nation has seemed distinctive to many historians of modern Japan, the history of the crowd reveals a more complex, ironic distinctiveness; elite control was limited, and the revolution from above in fact fueled the popular response.[33]

Contemporary observers saw traces of anti-American feeling in the Hibiya riots, although it is clear that their root cause was the disaffection of the urban crowd. Yet they added an element to a growing uneasiness in Japanese-American relations, had their own implications for future naval costs, and thus helped to fuel mutual distrust. That distrust seems to have sprung up most quickly in the United States, where it resonated with racist fears of immigration to Hawaii and the West Coast. Some military authorities responded to perceived Japanese sensitivity with surprising alarm; a Japanese student found with a sketch pad near San Diego, for instance, or Japanese seen with maps near the mouth of the Columbia River, could prompt reports to the War Department of suspected espionage. An army major reported that 10,000 to 20,000 Japanese on the West Coast were ex-soldiers, armed, and poised for conflict. United States Navy authorities were less paranoid, but in 1907 an "Orange" (for Japan) war plan was worked up at the request of President Roosevelt. Intrinsic to that plan was the capability of moving the entire battleship fleet to the Pacific coast from its Atlantic bases, and out of that grew in turn the world cruise of the American navy that was hailed as the "White Fleet" on its visit to Japan in 1908. Somewhat to American surprise, the fleet was warmly welcomed there. The Japanese Imperial Navy, in turn, now considered the United States its possible future enemy, and in 1907 war plans that targeted Russia, the United States, and France as putative enemies were prepared. Japanese authorities doubted that conflict was inevitable, and they were dismayed by reports from the United States, but in the international flux that followed the Russo-Japanese War they emphasized the need to build defenses and maintain precaution. Tokyo authorities were far less concerned than their journalists and commentators with the fate of indigent farmers who migrated to distant shores. In 1907 Foreign Minister Komura, in his address to the Imperial Diet, deprecated the intensity of the immigration crisis; it was more important, he argued, to direct future emigration to northeast Asia, for that was where future Japanese interests lay. During the same period Japanese development of exclusive interests in "Manchuria," as the three northeast provinces of China became known, alarmed and angered American officials like Willard Straight. In short, Japan's sacrifices in the defeat of Russia were not followed by a slackening of effort; to the contrary, new and larger burdens awaited Japanese taxpayers.

The Meiji leaders had come to maturity in full consciousness of Japan's weakness relative to Western powers, and the lesson they drew from those years was the need for caution. Unlike Japanese journalists, most of them placed much greater importance on good relations with the American and Western elites than they did on the treatment of the farmers who had left Japan. Yamagata, Itō, and the others had predicated much of their action on Western approval, and experience had convinced them of the vast gulf in national strength between Japan and America.

This was less the case with their successors. By the late Meiji years they were beginning to bridle under the restraints of discipleship, tired of being told about the great deeds of the past and eager to take their own place in the front rank. It was difficult to keep the aging *genrō* out of decisions and impossible to keep them uninformed, but diplomats like Katō Takaaki (1860–1926) and Komura Jutarō (1855–1911) struggled for autonomy and in doing so incurred the dislike of their seniors. So too in the armed services, where Katsura Tarō and especially Tanaka Gi'ichi (1864–1929) became vigorous advocates of larger armies and national expansion.

The same generational shift can be followed in politics, where a second generation of leaders emerged from the fledgling institutions of early Meiji to express impatience with the "old men of the Tenpō Era." By 1900 Itō, tired of trading cabinet posts for Diet support, had formed his own political party, as noted earlier. What he had in mind, when he announced the formation of the Friends of Constitutional Government (Rikken Seiyūkai), was a party made up of established and responsible people: the bureaucracy, wealthy businessmen, landed rural leaders, intellectuals—a party of "haves" with which the government could withstand the attacks of the jealous "have-nots." But for the most part what emerged was not so much a "new" party as it was an addition of new men and leaders to the old Jiyūtō. Senior figures like Itagaki disappeared from party politics, and a new generation of aggressive and ambitious younger men took their places. Hoshi Tōru was one of these, and his attitude on working with Itō was perfectly frank: "We won't let the old men lead us for very long," he said; "once the foundations have been laid, let's expel them, beginning with Itō, and do as we please." In the event neither man found his expectations fulfilled. Yamagata remained hostile to Itō's plans, and without waiting for Itō to finish his preparations he resigned to make way for him. Itō saw through this device, and grumbled, "It's just like Yamagata to launch a surprise attack before the enemy has prepared his positions."[34] On taking office as prime minister in 1900 Itō found the House of Peers implacably hostile to his ideas of party government. An imperial rescript brought that chamber to heel, but when he continued to have difficulty marshaling army support Itō decided to resign once more.

As successor he proposed Inoue Kaoru (1835–1915). his associate since they were both sent to England by Chōshū. Inoue, the only *genrō* never to form a cabinet, found everyone he approached indisposed or ill, including Katsura, whom he asked to continue as army minister. When he returned to tell his colleagues of his failure, they persuaded him to ask Katsura to accept the prime minister's post despite his health problems; Katsura then overcame his feigned reluctance and accepted, a complex plan that Yamagata had scripted in advance.

The second line of leaders now took over. Itō was removed from politics by a post as head of the Privy Council (from which he emerged to his final assignment in Korea), and turned over the Seiyūkai to the young aristocrat (and last surviving *genrō*) Saionji Kinmochi. For the rest of the Meiji period Katsura and Saionji maintained a reasonably harmonious alternation, the former serving almost five years, Saionji for three and one-half, Katsura another three, and Saionji a final year. Hoshi Tōru, however, did not live to "expel the old men," but was assassinated in 1901. His assailant, the head of a private academy, explained that while he bore Hoshi no personal dislike he had found his willingness to take bribes an unconscionable "disgrace to the nation, from His Majesty the Emperor down to the mass of the people."[35] Actual leadership of the party then came into the hands of Hara Takashi, a man who would emerge two decades later as the first professional politician and party leader to head a cabinet. It is worth noting that in the course of these developments the survivors and once eloquent spokesmen of the Freedom and People's Rights Movement showed a realization that access to power depended on relations with the political elite. One of the contributing causes of the Hibiya riots, in fact, was the crowd's unawareness that a quiet agreement had been reached between Hara and Saionji with Katsura for Seiyūkai support for the government in return for agreement to turn over the prime minister's post to Saionji. As a result opposition of Diet members to the treaty, which had been expected, was not forthcoming.

Generational change within the military was muted by the continued dominance of Yamagata's Chōshū clique, but it was no less real. Bureaucratization of the Imperial Army came full circle with the institutionalization of the "big three": the army minister, chief of General Staff, and inspector general of military education (a post created in 1898) formed the troika that determined policy. That same year the army secured a special imperial command for the war and navy ministers to serve in the Ōkuma-Itagaki cabinet to make it clear they were not working for civilian politicians, and in 1900 Yamagata worked out the imperial ordinance formalizing what had been the practice; thereafter war and navy ministers had to be chosen from the active list of generals and admirals. The provision was relaxed in 1913 but reinstated in 1936, and it gave the armed services a potent weapon to secure dissolution and prevent the formation of cabinets unless their demands were met.

This was the more serious because military education began to provide an officer corps with an outlook and background that was quite different from that of their civilian contemporaries. The usual path of education for military officers involved leaving the regular sequence of public schools after lower school. Middle and high school years found the future officers steeped in military instruction and discipline. Successful completion of that schooling could be followed by the Military Academy *(Shikan gakkō)* and, for the fortunate few, War College. Those who emerged from this were remarkably different from their fellow Japanese, all too often with simple solutions to complex problems in national policy.

The military professed to follow the Imperial Precepts to Soldiers and Sailors with its warnings about avoiding politics, but since virtually every political decision had military consequences (and vice versa) their leaders, who thought of themselves as the "emperor's soldiers," enjoyed a protected refuge from which they could challenge their civilian counterparts. The first generation of leaders had developed before the specialization of the twentieth century, but it was unlikely future statesmen would be able to demand overall control the way that Itō did in Korea. The victories over China and Russia added to the prestige and strength of the military; new peerage titles followed each war, and popular press and education focused on the military's valor and commitment. The same press fanned popular disapproval of civilian politics. Allegations of scandals and corruption were often on target, and in the popular mind political corruption was easily contrasted to the professed selflessness of the professional military.

By late Meiji the civil bureaucracy had also taken its twentieth-century form, and within it generational distinctions were no less remarkable. In early and mid-Meiji offices had been dominated by former samurai bureaucrats, and patronage counted for much. By the turn of the century, however, the proportion of bureaucrats who had entered government service through the Imperial University was growing in number and importance. In 1895 a Civil Service Appointment Ordinance laid out the lines of future procedure, and thereafter selection was to come through open and competitive examinations. Public service became a permanent, professional career, and a system of grades and ranks structured all ministries along consistent lines. If education was to provide the key to bureaucratic careers, graduation from Tokyo (and, later, Kyoto) imperial universities became the preferred route. The makers of the Meiji state considered partisan politics and a political spoils system a sure path to ruin, and took measures to protect the autonomy and security of bureaucratic elites. In 1899 Yamagata secured an amendment to the Civil Service Ordinance to rule out political appointments. As party influence grew in later years the civil service began to display some response to cabinet changes, but it was always by shift of personnel within the bureaucracy, and never from without.

Internally, the bureaucracy was structured by seniority that was shown by year of entrance. Examinees of a given year constituted a cohort; in the Imperial Army graduation from the Military Academy worked much the same way. Since these cohorts were small throughout the Meiji period, they served to define high-level groupings in later decades. In the Foreign Ministry, for instance, the examination for diplomats and consuls was first offered in 1894. Ranks and ratings were regularized by an ordinance of 1897. In 1906, when Yoshida Shigeru (1878–1967), Japan's leading post-surrender statesman, took the Foreign Ministry examinations after graduating from Tokyo Imperial University, the examination was offered for the twelfth time; the successful cohort numbered exactly eleven. The group included Hirota Kōki, who was foreign minister when the war with China broke out in 1937; the next year's yield included Matsuoka Yōsuke, the architect of Japan's alliance with Nazi Germany and Italy in World War II. Performance and evaluations of the examinations varied (Yoshida's rating was in a tie for last, and Hirota's the highest).[36] Those who entered that narrow gate would rub shoulders as section heads, consuls general, ambassadors, and ministers in years to come. The system thus produced a corps of public servants that was at once hierarchic and open to talent. The ministries of Foreign Affairs and Finance were the most prestigious of the specializations, but similar patterns could be found in all other cabinet ministries. Late Meiji entrants, whether in diplomacy, finance, or commerce, were "present at the creation" and dominated Japan's bureaucracies until World War II.

Discussion of economic change must wait for a later chapter. Here it is enough, but also important, to suggest the nature of the social change that accompanied it. Until the end of the Meiji period domestic and export productivity, traditional and modern industry both grew rapidly, and the relationship between them was complementary rather than competitive. Growth from above and growth from below, to put it differently, proceeded together. Until the 1890s the traditional sector—agriculture, fisheries—provided food for the populace and, in the form of silk, exports to pay for needed imports. The wars with China and Russia marked, and speeded, changes in this pattern. During those periods government expenditures rose dramatically, and the Chinese indemnity and American and British loans received in 1905 accelerated the process of industrialization. Consequently a clearly defined business interest grew in influence and power. At its highest level of management of the industrial conglomerates that had begun to form in the 1880s, leaders were full-fledged members of the power elite, joined in a network of investments and personal contacts. The *genrō* Inoue Kaoru was associated with Mitsui interests, Mitsubishi helped fund and profited from urban political movements associated with Ōkuma, the banker Shibusawa Ei'ichi could affect government policy, and Matsukata's ties with peerage wealth incorporated in the Fifteenth ("Peers'") Bank led to funding for shipbuilding and railroad development. Priorities in development and distribution were undoubtedly warped by this, with national goals taking precedence over personal consumption.

Nevertheless the increasing scale of urbanization, strengthened by the move of landlords to towns and cities, had its impact on parties and politics and helps account for the fact that the bitter hostility between parties and government during the first decade of the Meiji Constitution gave way to the compromises and horse-trading of the second decade with its alternation of Katsura and Saionji cabinets. With the exception of a few mavericks, of whom Ozaki Yukio was the chief, politicians fell in line, supported wartime budgets while criticizing the military between wars, criticized governments when their policies did not seem sufficiently assertive, and accepted, and dispensed, favors.

Life-styles and standards of living were also in the process of change. Here the introduction of the new was much slower. Most of the events discussed above had their origin among the power elite and played themselves out in Japan's cities; in the countryside, among ordinary people, things went on much as before for most of the Meiji period. Life for Japan's tenant farmers remained difficult and penurious, and a well-known fictional account makes it clear that for many life was lived at its lowest possible level: simple houses with dirt floors, bare feet or straw sandals, and a diet that featured coarser grains than rice and little or no fish or meat.[37] For independent, land-owning farmers conditions of life changed noticeably only by the turn of the century. The changes that did come, Susan Hanley shows, represented as much a downward diffusion of what had been upper-class or samurai life-styles as they did borrowing from abroad. Houses became better, mat floors were raised above the dirt, wide eves swept around the building, and sliding paper panels, sometimes upgraded to glass, made for a brighter and cleaner home. Tiles, long forbidden for commoners, brought color in the monochrome villages of earlier times. Around the turn of the century oil lamps, and then gradually electricity, made it possible to be up after dusk. Hulled rice became the staple of every diet that could afford it, and soy and other sauces to supplement its taste became common. Fish, and sometimes meat, became more common in the diet of ordinary people. In the cities horse trams appeared along with swarms of rickshaws, and by late Meiji, street cars and rail made it possible to travel to the cities to work and to shop. By mid-Meiji years a Tokugawa-style top-knot was a rarity in cities, and by late Meiji men all over Japan wore their hair short. The head then began to be covered, with cap or hat. Leather shoes were expensive and frequently uncomfortable, but the straw-shod and bare-footed commoners of early Meiji turned to wooden clogs. One sees the marriage of new and old in numerous photographs of Meiji men: bowler hat, kimono, and wooden clogs. The opening of the Diet, where representatives were expected to be dressed in Western style, brought a rush of business to tailors in the cities. Here too, the late Meiji wars played a major role. For most Japanese "the impetus for the eventual diffusion of new life styles and of a preference for the new goods can be attributed to the military. Just as the Sengoku wars transformed life in the sixteenth century, it was the Sino-Japanese and Russo-Japanese wars at the turn of the twentieth century that transformed life in the Meiji period."[38]

14

Histories of Meiji Japan usually follow a periodization derived from the construction of the modern nation-state. The process of institution building, followed by its implementation in politics, economics, and foreign policy, leads to war, empire, and international recognition at the end of the half century. Meiji culture, in contrast, is much less chronicled, but its study provides a vital dimension of the process of transformation that was going on.

Meiji literary history has been well studied. Magisterial studies by Donald Keene and translations by a number of gifted specialists have made its chief monuments accessible to Western readers. Meiji art has been less noted, nor has religion received its due. It would require more space than is available to do justice to these themes, but they loomed so large in the mentality of Meiji contemporaries, and have such compelling interest, that they require discussion here.[1]

There are broad congruities between the periodization acceptable for the development of Meiji culture and those for Meiji modernization. They are seldom identical, but both find their wellspring in the flood of Western influence to which Japan had to respond. One can use the metaphor of the Dutch historian Johan Huizinga, who noted that a wave might break at different points along the shore in response to the topography and resistance it encountered, but that it was nevertheless one single tide. And that tide was overwhelming. As Irokawa Daikichi has phrased it, "The influence of European and American civilization on Japan during the 1860s and 1870s was traumatic and disruptive to a degree that is rarely found in the history of cultural intercourse . . . For a time any thought of defending traditional culture was scorned as an idle diversion from the critical need to respond to the urgency that faced the country.

What had to be done was to penetrate the enemies' camp, grasp their weapons of civilization for use against them, and then turn to use them in the national interest."[2] When put this way the process can seem vengeful and even melodramatic, but it is important to remember the element of national striving that went into the formation of Meiji culture.

One finds this dichotomy encapsulized in the two four-character slogans that suffuse the age. *Bunmei kaika* (civilization and enlightenment) signified the need to grasp the new, but *fukoku kyōhei* (rich country, strong army) pointed to the desired outcome.

Although the Restoration was described as a return to the patterns of antiquity, it was soon clear that the international competition in which Japan found itself required the acquisition of the tools of the contemporary, modern world. The question then arose of selecting these, and of locating those elements of tradition that could best converge with them. By the middle and late years of the Meiji period there was a pervasive awareness of the need to develop a culture that would be new, modern, and yet also Japanese. In the process tradition itself had to be defined, selected, and structured. To some degree this has been true for other traditions abruptly challenged by the West. No two resolved them in the same way, but Japan's experience, as the first in the non-Western world, can offer insights into the larger clash of civilizations. Meiji writers themselves were deeply conscious of their task. In 1902 the novelist Natsume Sōseki noted in his diary that "people say that Japan was awakened thirty years ago, but it was awakened by a fire bell and jumped out of bed. It was not a genuine awakening but a totally confused one. Japan has tried to absorb Western culture in a hurry and as a result has not had time to digest it. Japan must be truly awakened as regards literature, politics, business, and all other areas."[3] This was the task that Meiji intellectuals, artists, and thinkers set themselves.

1. Restore Antiquity!

It is necessary to begin with the reminder that many aspects of late Tokugawa culture prepared the way for the Meiji effort. It is also convenient to characterize movements by utilizing the slogans that were used. The first of these, *fukko*—restore antiquity!—it will be remembered, was the drive to free Japanese culture from its encumbrances of Chinese and Confucian import. The great *kokugaku* scholars like Kamo no Mabuchi and Motoori Norinaga wrestled with the problem of what it was that was truly, intrinsically Japanese, and they were determined to define and restore what they saw as primitive purity and the honesty of simple, romantic affirmation. The political dimension of this was the ideal of restoration of imperial rule and abandonment of warrior usurpation.

In a sense the nativist scholars were already redefining Japanese culture. In art the narrative tradition of the Yamato paintings was to be substituted for the formal Chinese elegance of the Kanō school; in ceramics enthusiasm for old styles intensified; and when the Kyoto imperial palace was restored in the 1860s the goal was to restore what had been lost.

The *fukko* movement had other aspects. Emphasis on the native deities and mythology produced a world in which nature was somehow sacred, and the natural was restored as the criterion of the true and the good. Emphasis on Shinto generation (as opposed to creation) brought with it vitalism, acceptance, and also pragmatism; the final stand of nativist thought found Hirata Atsutane prepared to accommodate, and to claim for the Japanese tradition, whatever might be useful from other traditions. Praise of antiquity also brought reminders of Japanese borrowing from the past in that antiquity; the ancestors, many said, might have overdone it with their reliance on the imported culture from the continent, but they had seized on what was useful and practical without hesitation. By the same token, foreign borrowing in nineteenth century could also be justified. Mori Arinori's debate with the Chinese leader Li Hung-chang in 1876 expressed this perfectly. Li, looking disdainfully at Mori's Western suit, asked if Mori's Japanese ancestors had dressed that way. No, Mori had replied, they had adopted Chinese dress, but it was no longer practical; Japan had always taken the best of other civilizations for itself, and it was doing so once more. (He then went on to remind Li that Li's ancestors had not worn the official robes prescribed by China's Manchu conqueror either; Japan, by inference, had at least made its own choice.)

In practice, as we have seen, the attempt to restore the institutions of antiquity in their entirety and to adopt Shinto theocracy once more was soon rejected by the Meiji leaders. Antiquity could be invoked and put aside. But not entirely, and not at all where the imperial institution was concerned. The ritual and aura of a vanished past was put to work in the task of modernizing the country, as when the promulgation of the Charter Oath in April 1868 was surrounded with the panoply of the past.[4] Historians have usually emphasized the "progressive" elements involved in its promises of "deliberative assemblies" and abandonment of "evils of the past," but it is equally important to see it as a ritual in which the centrality of the throne was affirmed in a manner laying claim to the power of the legendary first emperor Jimmu. Sanjō Saneomi recited the articles for the young emperor, and the 411 nobles and daimyo present pledged their obedience. The effect was to politicize and engage the throne. In John Breen's words, "The one-way ritual dialogue was designed to engage the *gijō* [councillors'] group to the emperor in a new relationship: to pry the daimyo away from their own agendas and obsessions, to dislodge the courtiers from the premodern, conservative court, and to declare themselves as his loyal subjects." Within the drama, in turn, these events marked the decisive emergence of the early Meiji leaders and signaled their access to power through utilization of the sovereign.

In terms of culture, the affirmation of antiquity offered remarkably little resistance to material modernization. With the exception of the ideological supports for the throne and emperorism, antiquity was something of a void into which modernity could be inserted; the "evils" of the recent past, warrior rule and a China-oriented worldview, meanwhile, fitted neither antiquity nor modernity. The vigorous persecution of Buddhism had its roots in the campaign to restore Japanese antiquity, but was comparatively brief. It brought with it a number of popular rebellions as villagers voiced dismay and fear at the proscription of an important part of their life. For thousands of villagers, the action of the government in promoting the "old" deities and reviling the practices to which they were accustomed constituted issues for resistance. In 1873, for instance, a major uprising of 20,000 Popular Faith Buddhists broke out in Echizen on the Japan Sea coast. Leaders denounced government measures for the cutting of topknots and religious reform as covert expressions of Christian subversion. Small wonder that there were objections to measures like those prohibiting observance of the new year, village dancing, and observation of the August Buddhist *bon* festivals.[5] By decree in 1871 the new government also moved to "liberate" the suppressed class of *eta*. This brought temporary joy to those affected, but often resulted in vicious protests and riots from their neighbors who felt a loss of status and threat from these new "commoners" *(heimin)*. In addition, the former subcastes now found themselves subject to the full range of civil duties and tax, something from which they had been to a degree sheltered by the semiautonomous governance under which their communities had lived; their new authorities were not likely to take a particularly sympathetic attitude toward them. Nor were villagers the only Japanese affected negatively by the new order. In all samurai-dominated cities a large service class had become dependent upon the warrior class as their employers and customers, but with the end of special privilege and income for the samurai the advantages of urban life quickly disappeared. In Edo-Tokyo alone the population fell from approximately 1.3 million to 600,000 for a time, and the large numbers of rickshaw pullers that characterized the Meiji proletariat constituted a pressing social problem until the end of the century.

2. Civilization and Enlightenment! Be a Success!

Important as the trappings of antiquity were for political symbolism and ritual, for most young Japanese the modernization of their country along Western lines and personal advancement were stronger motivations. These goals were expressed in two slogans that expressed the reform enthusiasm and optimism of early Meiji: *bunmei kaika*, civilization and enlightenment, and *risshin shusse*, be a success! The two were not in any sense contradictory, for Japan was seen, correctly, as a disadvantaged latecomer to the goods of the modern world, in effect a poor boy among the wealthy. Japan had to "achieve its place," and it could best do so if its citizens achieved theirs. "For the sake of the country" *(kuni no tame)* was a phrase that was in everyone's vocabulary, from businessmen to intellectuals and writers.

The early Meiji decades were a time of great optimism. Farmers were worried about new patterns of local administration and samurai grumbled about their lot in the new order, but intellectuals shared a determination to remake their society with an idealism that would not reappear until the immediate post–World War II era in 1945. The world seemed to be at its beginning. "We have no history," a young student protested to Erwin Bälz, the German physician who ministered to the foreign community and the Meiji elite; "our history begins today." Intellectuals with Western experience or training found themselves in an extraordinarily strategic position. The same was true of foreign advisers and teachers brought in by the government to organize everything from lighthouses to educational institutions. They were housed in Western-style houses constructed especially for them. They were paid handsome salaries.[6] They taught in English, with the result that the first generation of students drank directly from the classics of nineteenth-century England and America and mastered English in a way that would not be true for their successors, who could profit from the flood of translation that followed.[7] History has seldom seen a time when people threw themselves into the tasks of learning and mastery with such intensity.

Fukuzawa Yukichi (1835–1901) was of course the major figure in this rush to self-improvement. His study of the West had been widely—one might almost say universally—read in late Tokugawa days, and in early Meiji "Fukuzawa books" became a general term. In 1869 his *Introduction to the Countries of the World (Sekai kunizukushi)* was arranged in metrical patterns suitable for recitation on the lines of Buddhist catechism for use in schools. *The Encouragement of Learning (Gakumon no susume)* became the textbook of an age, and in 1875 his *Outline of a Theory of Civilization (Bunmeiron no gairyaku)* provided a world-historical perspective on the task that faced a Japan that had to advance toward civilization from its present status of "semicivilized."[8] He was also Japan's most prominent educator. Keiō Specialty School, which he had established in a former daimyo estate in Tokyo at the time of the Restoration, would grow to become Japan's premier private university. Fukuzawa also broke through the tradition of gift-giving and sponsorship to charge tuition and regularize administration. Not content with this, he established an influential newspaper in which he wrote regularly, inveighing against the evils, as he saw them, of dependence on the government and preaching the necessity of individual responsibility. What was needed, he wrote, was for the Japanese people to be imbued with the "spirit of civilization"; it was that, and not the material trappings of the West, that distinguished the modern world.

Nakamura Masanao (Keiu) was another major figure in the drive for civilization and enlightenment. Born in 1832, he received a traditional education in Tokugawa academies and was appointed a Confucian scholar (*jusha*) before being sent to England to study in 1866. By the time of his return to Japan two years later he had become an enthusiast for Western learning and Christianity. He too began a private school, but soon went on to pursue a career as an educator and government official. Together with Fukuzawa, Mori Arinori, and other "enlightenment" figures, he founded the Meiji Sixth Year Society (Meirokusha), an elite group that met regularly to discuss ways to advance modernization in Japan. Many of the talks given at its meetings were published in its magazine, a journal that was short-lived because its sponsors discontinued it in protest against the government's press laws of 1875.[9]

Nakamura's most influential contribution, however, was his translation of Samuel Smiles's *Self-Help*, which he published as *Tales of Men Who Achieved Their Aims in Western Countries (Saikoku risshi hen)*. It would be difficult to exaggerate the influence and currency of this curious work, for it became the textbook for a generation. Smiles was a "success story" writer, for whom the nineteenth-century gospel of rugged individualism was best represented by the locomotive builder George Stephenson, who encouraged workers to emulate him with the challenge, "Do as I have done: persevere!" *Self-Help* was one of a trilogy, grouped with *Character* and *Thrift;* its chapters represented talks that the author gave to youth and worker groups to help them along the road of success. Its pompous warnings about the dangers of dreaming, romance, and idleness found a responsive echo in a land where samurai duty and merchant thrift were worn like badges of self-respect.[10] And while Smiles's aim was to activate, his Japanese readers must have sensed some continuity with the calls to frugality with which Tokugawa village preachers had tried to win their hearers. In Meiji Japan, however, Smiles's homilies also resonated with national goals. What was true for individual workers struggling to achieve their aim in life was even more true for a Japan struggling to make its way in an unfriendly international environment. We have already noted that the early stages of the democratic movement found Tosa samurai organizing themselves as a Self-Help Society, the Risshisha.

Enlightenment and self-improvement were efforts which Japanese embraced enthusiastically. At the same time that government leaders were trying to restore the aura of premodern mystery for the throne, intellectuals were prepared to jettison much of tradition, and their efforts went largely uncriticized because they worked for the larger purpose of building the new society. Mori Arinori suggested that it might be wise to abandon the Japanese language itself—for official purposes, at least—and utilize English instead. Fukuzawa proposed with tongue in cheek that it might be a good idea to declare Japan a Christian country; even if only a minority took the new creed seriously, the mere affirmation would impress the West. There were arguments about the feasibility and utility of Japanese as a medium of oral communication. Confucian society was suspicious of verbal agility and prized the written word; could spoken Japanese cut through the layers of education and refinement required for written transmission? Fukuzawa settled this at a Meirokusha meeting by standing on a chair to discuss the proposed expedition to Taiwan. After he finished he asked his neighbor if he had understood what he had said, and on being assured—with some scorn—that he of course had, Fukuzawa pointed out that that settled the question about spoken Japanese as a medium of communication. Fukuzawa in fact went on to become a formidable orator, and lectured regularly in the assembly hall built on the Mita campus of his school.

Private academies and schools mushroomed in the early Meiji years. Many were personal, one-man enterprises that closed their doors when the founder died or moved on to other things, but others survived to become private schools and ultimately colleges. Protestant missionaries were important sponsors. The urgency of learning English and learning Western law, sometimes separately and sometimes on the same site, and the restless ambition of Meiji youth determined to make a name for themselves in the new society produced a never-ending supply of eager young students. Most schools were located in Tokyo, the center of the new age, but in one instance a fervent young Christian, Niijima Jō (1843–1890), selected the old capital of Kyoto as the site for what became Dōshisha University as a direct challenge to the Buddhist establishment of the ancient capital. Niijima himself had managed to get away from Japan in late Tokugawa times to study in America. He was still in the United States when the Iwakura mission arrived in 1872, and his sturdy independence so impressed Kido Takayoshi that he persuaded him to join the group as an interpreter. Upon his return to Japan Niijima and the school he founded became a major force.

3. Christianity

It will be recalled that it was the Iwakura embassy, which encountered reproach and criticism of Japan's laws against Christianity, that was responsible for ending the ban on what was considered the "Western" religion in 1873. The early Meiji government had not only refused to release those seized by bakufu authorities in 1865, but it had extended the search in 1870, when almost 3,000 suspected adherents in Urakami were shipped to various parts of Japan for incarceration. Despite the protests of foreign representatives this impasse continued until the Iwakura ambassadors advised their release; in 1873 the prisoners were finally returned to their homes, but over 600 had died in exile.

Despite this, there had been significant steps toward the toleration of Christianity by then. Guido Verbeck, a Dutch-American clergyman, arrived at Nagasaki in 1859. Missionary work was still illegal, but it was possible to minister to the needs of the foreign community. James Hepburn, a Princeton-educated doctor and clergyman, arrived at Kanagawa (Yokohama) that same year. Yokohama was next door to the center of bakufu power, but in Nagasaki Verbeck, farther from the center, was able to work with young samurai from Satsuma, Chōshū, Tosa, and Saga, some of whom went on to become leaders in the future Meiji government. They studied English with him and plied him with questions. After the Restoration it was Verbeck who first suggested the dispatch of an embassy overseas, and the Iwakura mission owed much to his advice. Moreover, Verbeck's ties with the Dutch Reformed community and Rutgers in New Brunswick, New Jersey, made him a strategic figure in the recruitment of additional teachers.

Captain Leroy L. Janes, a Civil War officer, was probably the most important and interesting of those recruited and placed by Verbeck. He owed his invitation to the desire of the domain of Kumamoto to build modern military strength. On his arrival in 1871 Janes was supplied with an impressive Western-style house built for him, and put in full charge of his group of young samurai students. Those students were growing up in an era when the received wisdom of their parents' day seemed mistaken, and their insecurity and determination combined to give Janes, as instructor, an oracular quality. Janes desired that they learn of religion as well as science and mathematics, and affected them powerfully in optional evening sessions at his house. It was not long before a group of thirty-five of his finest students gathered on a small mountain overlooking Kumamoto to affix their names to a document in which they asserted

> In studying Christianity we have been deeply enlightened and awakened. The more we have studied it, the more filled with enthusiasm and joy we have become. Moreover, we strongly desire that this faith might be proclaimed over the whole Empire in order to dispel the ignorance of the people . . . It is consequently our duty as patriots to arise with enthusiasm, and with no concern for our lives, to make known the fairness and impartiality of this teaching. It is to this goal that we dedicate all our energies, and it is for this purpose that we have gathered here . . . Since at the present time the majority of our people are opposed to Christianity, the lapse from faith of even one of our number not only invites the scorn of the multitude, but frustrates the very purpose for which we are banded together.

This group of young men has become known as the "Kumamoto band." They included some of modern Japan's most important intellectuals, publicists, and preachers. As the language of the oath to which they subscribed shows, they considered themselves patriots; indeed, Christian samurai, prepared to sacrifice and suffer in order to enlighten their countrymen. Their sense of solidarity—"banded together" in the words of the oath—is also clear, for they had prepared their steps with painstaking care worthy of the forty-seven *rōnin* a century and a half earlier. They were prepared for criticism and persecution, and soon met both. Their fellow students first ostracized them and then debated them, and in many cases their families resorted to house arrest and other pressures to dissuade them from their new faith. But the most stouthearted stood their ground. Kozaki Hiromichi, the future pastor of Tokyo's largest congregation, wrote that "in proceeding from Confucianism into Christianity" he had "not rejected the one to replace it with the other, but "embraced Christianity because we believed that it fulfills the spirit and real import of Confucianism."[11] At the same time, the students' determination to "serve the country" through espousal of their faith, and affirmation of martial valor, contained the possibility, and in fact the development, of a future nationalist orientation. It goes without saying that these developments were unwelcome to the Kumamoto authorities who had wanted a Western, modern military school. The domain dismissed Janes at the end of his appointment in 1876 and closed the school. Janes's students moved on to Kyoto, where Niijima Jō had established the future Dōshisha University with the assistance of the American Board of Foreign Missions.

Another group of Christian leaders developed in an educational institution far to the north. As was the case in Kumamoto, it was the personal influence of an American teacher that affected student lives at a time when they were most impressionable. "The arts of philosophical defense which might have presented [the traditional Japanese viewpoint] convincingly," John Howes has written, "were no more equal to the emergency than were the defenses of Tokyo Bay equal to the emergency posed by Perry's gunboats. Knowledge of the West ultimately bred insecurity about themselves."[12] Janes was not a "missionary" and in fact soon fell out with the church mission establishment, but as a self-confident Christian layman he was the more influential. This was also true to the north.

In 1876 the Japanese government hired William S. Clark, then head of the Massachusetts Agricultural College, to direct studies at a new institution slated to be set up in Sapporo as part of the Development Office *(kaitakushi)* plan for the development of Hokkaido. It was understood that Clark would stick to his teaching, but no barriers were placed on his private contacts with his students. Clark was in Hokkaido very briefly, and in fact returned to the United States the following year, but during that period he, like Janes in Kumamoto, exercised immense influence over his students. They were soon convinced that the teachings of Christianity were central to Western civilization and hence to Japan's rebirth. Janes's students had all been from Kumamoto, but in Sapporo a government program brought able youths from a number of northern domains together. Clark won for himself a place in Japanese legend by reining in his horse as he left the campus and calling to the boys who accompanied him to its gate, "Boys, be ambitious like this old man!"[13] In Japanese memory the final two words were soon forgotten, and the challenge has lived on as inspiration for a generation of modern Japanese who took it to heart.

In the Sapporo school there was soon a religious awakening that was speeded by an almost coercive social pressure exercised by the first group of converts. Out of this tumultuous setting came two giants of modern intellectual and religious work, Uchimura Kanzō (1861–1930), founder of the "nonchurch" movement, and Nitobe Inazō (1862–1933), a Quaker educator and internationalist. Both men studied in America. Nitobe returned to serve his government as agronomist in Taiwan before heading the preparatory college for the Imperial University in Tokyo. After World War I, when Japan as a world power joined in the League of Nations, Nitobe served as its under secretary-general.[14]

Uchimura provides the most arresting figure among these Christians. First won to Christianity through the pressures of his peers, he immediately sought to persuade his parents, infiltrating the defenses of his father, who was a scholar of Chinese learning, with a biography of St. Paul written in Chinese. Study in the United States in the 1880s brought him face to face with what he had thought of as a promised land. "My idea of the Christian America," he wrote in his autobiography *How I Became a Christian,* "was lofty, religious, Puritanic. I dreamed of its templed hills, and rocks that rang with hymns and praises. Hebraisms, I thought, to be the prevailing speech of the American commonality, and cherub and cherubim, hallelujahs and amens, the common language of its streets." The reality was something else. "Yes," he went on ruefully, "Hebraisms in one sense at least I found to be a common form of speech of piety. Instead, the words which we have never pronounced without the sense of extreme awe are upon the lips of workmen, carriage-drivers, shoe-blacks, and others of more respectable occupations. Every little offense is accompanied by a religious oath of some kind." Equally startling, he was repeatedly taken for Chinese. "A well-dressed gentleman sharing the same seat with me in a car asked me to have my comb to brush his grizzly beard, and instead of a thank you which we in heathendom consider as appropriate upon such an occasion, he returned the comb saying, 'Well John, where do you keep your laundry shop?'" It is not surprising that, as he writes, his native Japan began to seem newly dear and beautiful in his memory. Uchimura retained and deepened his faith, but he also retained his pride in his nationality. In talks to church and mission groups he felt that his hearers expected him, as he wrote, to look like a "tamed rhinoceros." Soon nothing short of an independent, Japanese type of worship would satisfy him, and in a spiritual struggle with his Creator he worked out an agreement whereby he would remain a Christian so long as he did not have to become a "professional preacher." Upon his return to Japan he accepted a teaching post at the preparatory college for the Imperial University for his livelihood, while organizing informal Bible reading and study groups for evenings and weekends. In this Uchimura's, like Nitobe's Quaker, activities, found a resonance with the lay Buddhist organizations, or *kō,* familiar to all Japanese. Uchimura was particularly determined to avoid any dependence on foreign church mission boards.

Uchimura's independence was soon put to a different test. When the Imperial Rescript on Education, surrounded by the aura of imperial divinity and calling for an education grounded in Confucian ethics, was read in a school ceremony, Uchimura's colleagues bowed in recognition of its authority, but he himself hesitated, uncertain whether he could accede to any authority higher than that of his Creator. Later he decided that it would not have been a violation of his faith to bow, but by then his hesitation had become controversial, and he became the object of criticism so harsh that it led to his resignation. Thereafter his was a career as a freelance writer and ethical teacher.

Books, articles, and columns poured from his pen. Discussion and study groups he founded became the core of a "nonchurch" *(mukyōkai)* movement that continued to have influence in urban intellectual circles into the mid-twentieth century. Exponents of traditional ethics, however, seized upon Uchimura's case to argue the incompatibility of Christianity with loyalty and patriotism, and soon the Education Ministry lifted the exemptions from military service for students in Christian schools. There was never any doubt about the patriotism of men like Uchimura, whose tomb bears witness to his love for "two J's," Jesus and Japan. Under pressures of this sort many Japanese Christian institutions, notably Dōshisha, struggled to free themselves from the control of foreign mission boards lest they disadvantage their students.

A third current of Christian influence emanated from the foreign presence at the port of Yokohama, where the medical missionary Joseph Hepburn had begun work earlier. After the 1880s, however, the most influential Japanese Christians faced steady pressure to demonstrate freedom from foreign direction in order to protect themselves and their students from native xenophobia. It was after the promulgation of the Meiji Constitution, as Japanese nationalism was stirred by successful foreign wars and conservative intellectuals were developing a new ideology of imperial divinity and national superiority, that these issues began to come to a head. Since Christians advocated spiritual autonomy and freedom of conscience, they were an important stimulant in Meiji intellectual life, with leading roles in social reform and political change. In the 1880s the tide of enthusiasm for Christianity ran strong, and newspapers frequently carried the names of prominent political and social leaders who had received baptism, but a decade later the tide was running in the opposite direction.

Meiji Christianity was predominantly urban and Protestant, although there was also an Orthodox community in eastern Japan as the result of the work of a remarkable Russian, Father Nikolai (Dmitrievich Kasatkin, 1836–1912), who reached Hakodate in Hokkaido in 1861,[15] and Catholic missionaries were active in many rural districts. The Protestant leaders were predominantly former samurai, educated, able, and articulate. Their early successes also related to the international setting in which Japan found itself, for the United States, England, and Germany seemed predominant. Verbeck's proposal for an Iwakura mission itinerary, for instance, did not include any Catholic countries, but on that point he was ignored. Christians played important roles in social reform and in the early socialist movement. For a time Christian leaders were confident and jubilant. "Old Japan is defeated," Niijima wrote; "new Japan has won its victory. The old Asiatic system is silently passing away, and the new European ideas so recently transplanted there are growing vigorously and luxuriantly . . . [Japan] has shaken off her old robe. She is ready to adopt something better . . . Her leading minds will no longer bear with the old form of despotic feudalism, nor be contented with the worn-out doctrines of Asiatic morals and religions."[16]

His optimism was premature. In the late 1880s a growing tide of conservatism began to check and then reverse these trends. The government's failure to achieve treaty reform led to bitterness and disillusion. The excesses of fashionable Westernization produced inevitable countercurrents of national affirmation. Completion of the network of institutional devices to reify the imperial aura made it desirable and often necessary to compromise with the state and its supporters. By the 1890s newspapers sometimes noted the names of men who had left the Christian church. Buddhist leaders too regained their voice and drew comfort from the Darwinian thought that challenged creationism. By the time of world religious conferences around the turn of the century Japanese Buddhists, who had been maligned by Shinto enthusiasts a few decades earlier, appeared as representatives of the national tradition. The dangers and indignities of the early Meiji persecution had been put behind them, and for all practical purposes ceased to exist.[17] Under such conditions the determination and ability of Christian leaders like those from the Kumamoto and Sapporo groups to maintain the essentials of their belief stands as striking evidence of the problems involved in balancing individual autonomy and affirmation of universalism in the particularist society of imperial Japan.

4. Politics and Culture

A conviction that political life would change was an important part of the optimism of the early Meiji years. The government leaders intended the Charter Oath's language about "deliberative assemblies" to reassure their fellow members of the elite, and planned to build on the aura of the throne to maintain public order, but many of their countrymen hoped for a different kind of political order. In recent years scholars have assembled eight stout volumes of petitions and proposals for change in every aspect of Japanese society. The early Meiji scene was far more dynamic, and local leaders were far more outspoken and independent, than they were to be after the central government had established its sway.[18] The degrees of local autonomy permitted by the fractionalized administration of feudal rule had helped develop confidence and courage. In the decade beginning in 1871 alone 130 petitions were submitted to the government demanding some form of popular representation, and we have seen how enthusiasm for such ideas led to a snowballing of expectations in the Freedom and People's Rights Movement.

This enthusiasm had its cultural expression. The local elite was well schooled in traditional learning and versification in Chinese *(kanshi)*, and many among them chose to register their sentiments in lengthy, thoughtful poems. In the 1880s it was common to form associations for composing poetry; recognized masters could support themselves by charging for corrections made to efforts submitted by village leaders in the countryside. As was to be expected, Fukuzawa Yukichi, as the leading "modernizer," was often urged to play a leading role in the expression of political hope. He was asked by 23,555 residents in nine counties of what is today Kanagawa Prefecture to draft their petition for a representative assembly.

When the government, in 1881, issued the emperor's promise that a constitution would be ready at the end of the decade, and the nascent political parties found it wise to disband in 1884 and 1885, the yearning of Japanese for political change and liberalization produced a remarkable outpouring of fiction, much of it by ambitious young politicians who took as their model English political novelists like Edward Bulwer-Lytton and Benjamin Disraeli. Many such tales were placed incongruously in ancient Greece or the more recent West, but they shared the theme of noble and ambitious youths determined to make their way in the world of politics by courageous espousal of liberalism. These works appeared in a literary setting in which translations from Western literature, from *Self-Help* to Shakespeare to *Robinson Crusoe,* were immensely popular.[19] The political novels were for the most part written in a complex mixture of Sino-Japanese vocabulary that was appropriate to their romantic and frequently bombastic style. Probably the best-known of these works, *Kajin no kigu* (Strange encounters with elegant females), by a young Aizu samurai who graduated from the University of Pennsylvania and returned to Japan in 1884, begins with its hero in Philadelphia musing on the significance of the Liberty Bell; there he encounters the daughter of a Spanish struggler for constitutional government and an Irish beauty whose father died as a political prisoner. Soon a Chinese butler, not to be outdone, turns out to be a rebel against Manchu tyranny. The book is in essence a catalogue of democratic movements and resistance to oppression. Significantly, it adds to this a promise of a democratized Japan leading modernization in Asia; "Korea will send envoys and the Luchu [Ryukyu] Islands will submit to your governance. Then will the occasion arise for doing great things in the Far East." The book was immensely popular. In Sansom's words, "it is said that there was not a remote mountain village in Japan in which some young man had not a copy in his pocket, and the Chinese verses that so freely stud its pages were recited everywhere with great relish."[20]

One reason that themes of individual achievement and ambition were so popular in Meiji Japan was that in a rapidly developing society and economy, one in which a structure of status had not yet developed, they often had a resonance in real life. Two brothers from the Kyushu domain of Kumamoto may serve as examples. Tokutomi Roka (Kenjirō, 1868–1927) was a novelist who sprang to fame with the publication of *Omoide no ki* (Things remembered)[21] in 1901 after appearing serially in a newspaper for twelve months. Clearly modeled on *David Copperfield,* the work sees the struggles of the early Meiji decades through a nostalgic regret for the generosity and decency of precapitalist Japanese society. The hero's background matches that of the Tokutomi brothers, whose father was a country samurai. His father is poorly equipped for the competition of the modern society. After his early death, the hero, still a schoolboy, falls in with village ne'er-do-wells from whom he is rescued by the rigor and courage of his mother, who threatens him with suicide at his father's tomb unless he resolves to restore the family status and honor. "Thousands of young men in the first decade of the century," Tokutomi's translator writes, "found it easy to identify themselves with him, not merely for his endurance and cheerful energy, but because of more specifically Japanese elements in his story: the ambition to restore the independence and honor of the fallen House of Kikuchi as a filial duty to his widowed mother, the intoxication with Western literature and Western ideals of freedom, and the passionate patriotism and longing to modernize and 'improve' Japan, crystallizing in the romantic vision of a Utopia to be ushered in with the establishment of representative government." The author achieved relatively little of this for himself, for he was dominated most of his life by his far more prominent and successful elder brother.

Tokutomi Sohō (Iichirō, 1863–1957) was one of the youngest members of Captain Janes's students to join the Kumamoto band. After the Kumamoto school was closed he enrolled at Dōshisha, but left before graduation to return to Kumamoto, where he founded a private school. He worked to instill in his students the ideals of liberty and individualism. Years later a student described the excitement of that school:

On the one hand white-bearded Kisui, Iichirō's old father, would be seated on a shabby floor-mat lecturing on Spencer's *Principles of Ethics;* on the other our Iichirō-san was getting more and more exited talking about the French Revolution. As his lecture reached its climax, the students would involuntarily break into wild approval, jump up and dance around, swing their swords and strike the pillars.

all students were required to join a Speech Club, and this posed problems for the writer:

> I was really taken aback by their eloquence . . . But I, a self-defined advocate of freedom and people's rights, was put to shame by the knowledge of these speakers, who went on and on lauding Robespierre and Danton, quoting Washington and Cromwell, and arguing about Cobden and Bright with confident enthusiasm.[22]

In 1885 Tokutomi published *The Future Japan,* a book in which he expounded his Spencerian views of the future for his country. He saw a future in which military might would be replaced by mercantile, and envisioned a central role for Japan in that future. "Japan," he predicted,

> will become a pier on the Pacific, the great metropolis of the Orient and emporium for international trade. The smoke coiling up from thousands of chimneys will obscure the sun. Ship masts will be as numerous as trees in a forest. The sound of drills, levers, and hammers will be orchestrated with the echoes of steam engines, and the sound of the horses and vehicles will be heard as a roll of thunder on a fine day. How delightful it will be![23]

This cheerful view of future environmental degradation hit a responsive chord with Meiji readers, and the book catapulted Tokutomi into prominence. In 1887 he established the Minyūsha Press and produced the periodical "The Nation's Friend" *(Kokumin no tomo),* Japan's first modern periodical, and followed that with the newspaper *Kokumin* (The Nation) in 1890. It would be pleasant to record his consistent advocacy of the ideals of his youth, but Japan's fate in international affairs intervened. At the end of the Sino-Japanese War the forced retrocession of the Chinese peninsula of Liaotung made him rethink his hostility to his government. He became an intimate of the future prime minister General Katsura Tarō, and grew very close to the political establishment. When the author of these pages interviewed him in 1951 he had been purged from public activities by the Allied Occupation of Japan because of his enthusiastic support of World War II as head of National Writers Union. His literary skills, which were formidable, were reflected in some of the language of Japan's declaration of war. By then he had given his editorial talents to the authorized biographies of many of the leaders of modern Japan, and he had written a multivolume history of Tokugawa Japan which remains of importance and value to students today.

Tokutomi's press, the Minyūsha, attracted young, optimistic, and Western-oriented writers and intellectuals. In the latter half of the 1880s it began to be challenged by the Seikyōsha, a press that warned of excessive Western orientation and argued the virtues and importance of Japan and Japanism. Its organs were magazines called "Japan" and "Japan and the Japanese" (*Nihon, Nihon to Nihonjin*). Tokutomi and his group argued for the need of reform in society to foster individualism and end the worst aspects of family tyranny, and pointed with alarm to the increasing regimentation of education. The Seikyōsha writers, in contrast, stressed the importance of retaining a clear sense of traditional values in filial piety and loyalty and warned of the moral disintegration of a society that did not retain its prime values. The Imperial Rescript on Education, issued at the inception of constitutional government in 1890, put the state squarely on the side of conservatism and tradition in its affirmation of filiality and loyalty as "the glory of the fundamental character of Our Empire," and placed the full weight of the imperial house in the balance. With the encouragement of the Ministry of Education the philosopher Inoue Tetsujirō, who had studied in Germany, began to write commentaries on the rescript and morality. It was also Inoue who led the attack on Uchimura Kanzō when he failed to bow in reverence at the first public reading of the Rescript on Education. The government's success in securing treaty reform and defeating China in 1895 provided powerful advantages for the Seikyōsha cause.[24] During the 1890s a controversy over the nature of the new Civil Code further roiled these waters. An early version was attacked as weakening the bonds of family loyalty that, it was argued, were preliminary to imperial loyalty; when a final version was issued in 1898 it was clear that the samurai family system with its strong paternal powers had emerged as the model for all Japanese. The Minyūsha was never stilled, but as already noted Tokutomi himself veered into a strongly nationalist position after the Sino-Japanese War to become a stalwart of support instead of independent critic of his government.

What we have seen, in public policy, private lives, and the larger climate of opinion, all reinforces Huizinga's metaphor of wave with which this chapter began. In the first stages of response to the flood of Western thought, ideals, and models there was an urgent program to refashion and transform thought and opinion. The government, determined to activate the nation, was adventurous in its encouragement of rapid change. And then, on second thought, it seemed that the ocean swell might become a tidal wave that ought to be resisted, lest it wash old Japan away. The basic program of *fukoku kyōhei,* wealth and strength, suggested the need to draw some lines and preserve what could be kept. The Western world, on closer examination, was by no means entirely benign or uni-directional. And so the pendulum of change swung back. Japan would be forever changed, but still Japan.

5. The State and Culture

The state was an important player in Meiji culture. It based its legitimacy on the imperial house, and to that effect nurtured the *fukko* movement with its aura of ritual and mystery. But it also stood to profit from, and indeed helped sponsor, the *bunmei kaika,* civilization and enlightenment, movement for internal rationalization and modernization and for external approval.

The reform bureaucrats showed a pressing desire to regiment, classify, centralize, and ultimately to control. The abolition of the domains and the assumption of samurai obligations led, as we have seen, to inventories of samurai, weapons, and resources. Domains were divided into three categories by size, their inhabitants registered, and productive capacity and resources became the subject of careful surveys. This was also true of the arts. In 1874 all musicians, dancers, and actors were registered and divided into three grades by income. Heads of all schools of music, crafts, and the arts were to report to the authorities. Private schools were inventoried as a prelude to abolishing them in favor of state-run schools. Temples and shrines were classified and inventoried. Society was gradually leveled out, and the arts, newly categorized and inventoried, were judged for their utility to the modern state and frowned on if they seemed irrelevant or inappropriate to its purposes. It will be useful to consider several categories more closely.

LANGUAGE AND TRANSCRIPTION

Official interference may have been relatively slight in the development of a standard language, but it did play a role. In the early years there were numerous expressions of doubt about the efficiency of retaining the use of Chinese characters in transcription. Already in Tokugawa days, scholars of Dutch learning had praised the practicality of the Western alphabet. In early Meiji Maejima Hisoka was prepared to go a step farther, and called for the abandonment of "inconvenient ideographs imported by our ancestors as part of their indiscriminate importing of the culture of China." In 1875 Nishi Amane,[25] an important Tokugawa and Meiji bureaucrat-intellectual, argued for the abolition of Chinese characters in an article written for *Meiroku zasshi.* He predicted a future in which "even children will be able to read the writing of men, even the ignorant will be able to record their opinions . . . All things of Europe will be entirely ours . . . we can boast to the world that it is the beauty of our people's character thus to follow the good. This will leave them dumbstruck." Some years later, Mori Arinori went so far as to suggest the adoption of English as Japan's national language.

The median path, of course, was to retain Japanese, but to simplify its transcription and utilize the colloquial instead of the stiff Sino-Japanese *(kanbun)* in which Tokugawa youth had been schooled. In Meiji terms, this was to be a middle path between the elegant and the vulgar, and its development and finalization required the better part of four decades. Writers sometimes visited music and story halls to ascertain what was comprehensible to ordinary citizens, and a short-hand transcription *(sokki)* utilized by, among others, the police to monitor political meetings, played its part.[26] It required decades to work out the final solution. The novelist Futabatei Shimmei wrote two versions of his classic novel *Ukigumo* (Floating clouds)[27] between 1887 and 1889, the second in more "modern" and colloquial style. Thereafter, as compulsory education in the state-run schools took over, the educational system standardized transcription and vocabulary.

MUSIC

The distinction between "elegant" and "vulgar" was particularly sharp in music. A government that was, on the one hand, determined to orchestrate a return to the proper "rites and music" of antiquity also had to make allowance for the possibility of utilizing music to mobilize its people and especially their children. The Meiji government did its best to organize and tidy up the lively setting of late Tokugawa entertainment. Izawa Shūji, who played a major role in the reform of music, was very clear on the fact that much of Edo popular culture was part of the "evil customs" of the past that the Charter Oath proposed to end. "The popular music of Japan," he wrote,

> has, neglected by the educated, remained for many centuries in the hands of the lowest and most ignorant classes of society. It did not advance moral or physical culture, and it was altogether immoral in tone . . . it damages the prestige of the country.[28]

Consequently entertainers and those who patronized them were subjected to moralizing from the Meiji Victorians. Schools of dancers, musicians, and actors were classified and registered. "Martial songs" *(heikyoku)*, which had enjoyed bakufu protection, went down with its patrons and the leading master ended his days as a masseur. Consistency, however, eludes all governments; many popular Satsuma and Chōshū songs, sung to the accompaniment of a stringed *biwa*, now came into vogue with the new bureaucrats from western Japan. Much of this music had been considered rather country-bumpkin by sophisticated Edo samurai, who occasionally referred to their sponsors condescendingly as *imo-zamurai* "potato[-eating] samurai."

At other points music that had been restricted to the old elite received a new lease on life and became more widely diffused. Music of the *nō* theater seemed endangered for a time, but Iwakura Tomomi returned from his embassy with the idea that it might become a Japanese-style opera. He invited the young emperor to a concert at his residence, and soon many of the new aristocrats followed his lead. Commoners, previously excluded, were now permitted to cultivate *nō* as well.

The ancient court music, *gagaku*, gained, though at the cost of a measure of codification and stultification of its repertory. *Gagaku* musicians, as favorites of the court, were able to wield a good deal of influence from their sanctuary within the Imperial Household, and even gained power over early bands and Western music.

Western music entered Japan in the form of martial strains. The band that celebrated the success of the English squadron that shelled and burned Kagoshima in 1863 seems to have made as strong an impression on those who heard it on shore as had the ships' guns. As Satsuma officials turned to modernize their military structure, they requested an English bandmaster at Yokohama to instruct Satsuma militiamen. By 1871, after the Satsuma victory in the Restoration warfare, they formed the core of a national military band. Six years later the Englishman was replaced by a German who orchestrated and harmonized verses of loyalty from the ancient *Kokinshū* poetry anthology to produce the *Kimi ga yo*, a solemn ode to imperial rule that came to serve as the national anthem.

Military songs and marches had become popular during the Restoration military campaigns. As public schools developed, school songs soon adapted the melodies of Stephen Collins Foster, as with *Tobe tobe tonbi sora* (Fly, little falcon, high in the sky!), a tune in Japanese mode that was a version of "Way, down upon the Swanee River."[29]

The Ministry of Education turned to music as part of the public school curriculum as early as 1871. Izawa Shūji was sent to the United States in 1875. There he met the Boston educator Luther W. Mason, and urged his appointment to reform Japanese popular music. Mason, he wrote, had done wonders with the Boston school system since his arrival from Cincinnati; when he arrived

> The people were not familiar with the benefits of music . . . in some schools classical music prevailed, in others vulgar, and bad street songs were used . . . [Mason had] invented an original system in formulating the best music

and songs, old and new, of the countries of Europe and assimilated them with those existing in the United States, thus establishing good music in schools, or in short nationalizing it.[30]

This was exactly what Meiji bureaucrats wanted done. Mason came in 1880 and stayed for two productive years. In books prepared under his direction about half the songs were foreign in origin. Western melodies were fitted with Japanese words; for others *gagaku* or *koto* melodies were utilized. Education authorities, however, insisted on some additions, like the "Song of the [Five Confucian] Relationships," to the first book. By 1891 the Education Ministry guidelines made it clear that "setting the beauty of music apart, the cultivation of moral character is to be made the fundamental principle." In this Japan did not differ greatly from the United States and other nineteenth-century countries, for in the Victorian age the thrust of public education was highly normative and moralistic. In France, for instance, the Third Republic had a Ministry of Fine Arts and Public Education that was justified by the argument that works of art could provide the entire population with a common vision of a productive and self-ordered life.

ART

The Meiji government's program in art had a substantial Tokugawa background on which it could build. The Dutch had done little or nothing to introduce Western music, but their influence in art had become increasingly important in the nineteenth century. What impressed Japanese artists like Shiba Kōkan was the accuracy and practicality of the pictures he saw in Dutch books; compared with that, he wrote, traditional Chinese and Japanese painting seemed child's play. The need to prepare fortifications against possible invasion brought the government to employ artists to sketch sites and trajectories. The Tokugawa Institute for Barbarian (and later, Western) Learning included instruction in painting as a utilitarian discipline, related to map making and descriptive drawing.

The Meiji government carried this a step further. Its program was directed by a Chōshū samurai who had been sent to England to study together with Itō and Inoue. After a seven-year stay, Yamao Yōzō (1837–1917) returned as a graduate of Anderson College, a technical school in Glasgow. Entrusted with responsibility for a new Kōbu Daigakkō, or technological school, he recruited a fellow graduate of Anderson, Henry Dyer. Together they built an institute modeled on that of the Zurich Polytechnical Institute. The Kōbu Daigakkō had six faculties, one of which was architecture. A technical art school was added in 1878 with divisions for painting and sculpture. Its key instructors were from Italy; Antonio Fontanesi in painting, Vincenzo Ragusa in sculpture, and Giovanni Cappellati in architecture. Between 1873 and 1885 it employed a total of 47 foreign teachers, a significant proportion of the 500-odd foreign employees hired by the government in those years. Students were from all parts of Japan, with admission slots doled out according to the category (large, middle, small) assigned their domain in the first Meiji years. This scrupulous concern for equity should not go unnoticed. The Meiji leaders were careful to keep central control in their own hands, but their concern for representative participation in all aspects of building the new institutions was not unrelated to their agreement on the need for a representative assembly. The Kōbu Dai-gakkō was regarded as a vital part of the program that Ōkuma Shigenobu's Department of Public Works had launched for the development of railways, mining, iron foundries, lighthouses, telegraphs, and shipbuilding.

Government planners may have been preoccupied with practicality, but the teachers and their students inevitably had their own interests. Fontanesi's rather moody canvases used somber pigments and his forms were often indistinct, and his students followed his lead. As we have seen, the pace of Westernization had begun to arouse nativist reactions by the 1880s, and charges of disloyalty we have noted in other areas began to repeat themselves in art. In 1881 a leading Western-style painter, Kawakami Tōgai, was accused of passing rumors and selling maps to foreigners—a striking evocation of the Siebold case of the 1820s. In an act that can be considered symptomatic of the larger conservative shift of the tide, Kawakami committed suicide. In other fields, however, experimentation continued. In architecture the buildings of the English architect Josiah Conder, notably the Rokumeikan social center of 1883, became monuments of the decade.[31]

Foreigners played a major role in the development of early Meiji culture, but it is important to remember that they were under Japanese, usually government, control. Left to their own devices they would have implanted their own ideas of an exotic Orient; Saracenic themes and evocations of temples and pagodas in architecture, kimonos at court. But in most cases the Japanese would have none of this and wanted to have their Westernization be honest. Itō rebuffed the suggestion of the German expert on court protocol that the imperial family remain in Japanese dress, and the art critic Okakura Tenshim (Kakuzō) warned his son that he should never appear before Westerners in kimono unless his English was flawless. Government committees turned down more Western plans for buildings than they approved, on grounds that they were too "oriental."

Before long Japanese specialists, graduates of the new institutions, were prepared to carry on without foreign help. Then, as Japan gained international stature after its successful wars against China and Russia in 1895 and 1905, a new taste for imperial magnificence developed. In 1908 the Akasaka Palace was built to house the crown prince and Western visitors of state. It was a granite evocation of Versailles. At the end of the Meiji period Tokyo Central Station, a giant red brick structure completed in 1914, was often erroneously compared to the Amsterdam station. In fact the differences are more important than the surface similarities, for while Amsterdam's opens to the central business area and port as a symbol of its merchant life, Tokyo's was placed on a bias with the palace, and its elaborate central waiting room served the emperor rather than the city.[32]

Western employees and visitors often deplored what they considered excesses of Westernization and pleaded for retention of the native tradition. The prime instance of this is in the work of Ernest Fenollosa (1853–1908), a Harvard graduate who came to Japan in 1878 to teach philosophy. Once there he became an enthusiast of traditional Japanese art and deplored what he regarded as excesses in the program of modernization. He thought it wrong to teach drawing with pencils instead of brushes, and did his best to help artists who were still painting in the traditional style. Together with his student and colleague Okakura Tenshin (Kakuzō, 1862–1913), he founded an art school and association. He returned to direct the East Asian program of the Boston Museum of Fine Arts in 1890, and continued his crusade in several influential books. Fenollosa has been credited with a major role in "saving" traditional art. Important as he was, the attributions are probably overgenerous, and reflect political currents as much as cultural. Fenollosa personally amassed a large collection of traditional art which he sold to collectors and museums, and his writings were welcomed by Japanese conservatives who found it convenient to use a foreign voice.[33] But the Japanese art tradition was never in danger of extinction. Japanese collectors and aesthetes like the Mitsui executive Masuda Takashi had seen to it that the government was already declaring major works national treasures and banning their export. The posthumous repute of Fenollosa illustrates the convenience of being able to cite an articulate foreigner in support of trends already under way. In post–World War II times Japanese often mistakenly ascribed the salvation of Kyoto from bombing to the Harvard art historian Langdon Warner. Similarly, the management consultant W. Edwards Deming was credited with transforming Japanese management thinking, although industrial management had long been attuned to Western developments.

After the confusion of the 1880s Japanese artists went on to develop in several directions, each rather neatly separated from the others and moving in relative isolation. A neo-traditional art known as Nihonga (Japanese painting) pursued traditional themes but did so in a new dimension, and the annual expositions mounted in evocation of the Paris *concours* attracted the attention and effort of a notable group of artists. Because of the conservatism of art historians who, like Fenollosa, deprecated deviation from the classical canons of the Kanō school, these paintings have only recently begun to be fully appreciated.[34] Meanwhile a parallel school of Western painting, working in oils, took its models directly from Europe and developed a lively tradition of its own, one that is also only now beginning to receive serious attention.[35]

LITERATURE

It is in literature that we would expect to find the most articulate and sensitive record of the struggle for new cultural forms, and it is no accident that this area has received the most attention from Western scholars.[36] Here limitations of space make it impossible to do more than provide a cursory introduction.

By late Tokugawa times the cultural achievements of the Genroku age lay far behind. Growing literacy and urbanization had created an impressive market for popular entertainment, but it was for the most part pitched to the lowest common denominator of taste and quality. Kabuki plays dealt increasingly with figures of evil and perversion, and may have helped account for the preoccupation with practices like tatooing. Popular tales like *Hizakurige* (translated as "Shanks Mare") followed the adventures of two rascals along Japan's major highway. Overall, fiction seemed to have reached a low ebb. It was certainly scorned by Japanese of taste and breeding.

Consequently, although Japan's early experiments with modernity provided opportunities for humorists and storytellers, it came as something of a surprise to Meiji Japanese to discover that in the West the novel had become a major form of social and psychological commentary. The political novels that have been mentioned owed a good deal to the example of Disraeli and Bulwer-Lytton. Increasing familiarity with other European traditions brought the Russian novel to the attention of writers, particularly through the work of Futabatei Shimmei, whose *Ukigumo* has been described as Japan's first modern novel. The great works of the Meiji period, however, novels which have spoken to all twentieth-century Japanese, came at its close in the early decades of the twentieth century. They are associated with the names of Natsume Sōseki (1867–1916), Mori Ōgai (1862–1922), and Shimazaki Tōson (1872–1943). Each left behind a distinguished body of work, and each struggled conscientiously with the problems of creating a new culture.

Sōseki was born the son of a commoner Edo municipal official. An unwanted child, he was passed off to another couple and then returned, and grew up thinking that his parents were his grandparents—a misperception that they, somewhat embarrassed by this last-born child, did nothing to correct. Nevertheless he was able to follow the main path to success by graduation from the preparatory school of the Imperial University, which he entered in 1884, and the university itself. He was well schooled in English, something that was essential for his generation in a day before translations were widely available. He had some thought of becoming an architect, despite the warning of a brother that "there was no glory in being an architect in such a poor country as Japan, where there would never arise the opportunity of building a great monument of the order of St. Paul's."[37] After graduating from the university in 1893 Sōseki was appointed to a post in English at Tokyo Normal College. Soon he showed his indifference to the anticipated "road to success" by accepting an offer from a high school in the town of Matsuyama. Next he moved to the Special Higher School in Kumamoto. Then, in 1900, the government sent him to England for two years of study.

Sōseki went without introductions or preparation and had to live on a meager stipend. He had nothing to do with the better-funded Japanese community of diplomats and merchants, and lived a reclusive and deeply unhappy life in London. Upon his return to Japan he was obliged under the terms of his contract to accept a post in literature at the Imperial University, where he succeeded to the position Lafcadio Hearn had made famous.[38] To the consternation of his friends, Sōseki resigned as soon as he could. He accepted employment with the newspaper *Asahi* under contract to write a novel a year to appear serially in its pages.

This casual disregard for the accepted values and goals of Meiji society marked Sōseki as a nonconformist. He had also begun to show signs of a nervous breakdown during his stay in London. He was contemptuous of Japanese jingoists, but also scornful of people who accepted the dominance of Western culture slavishly. "It would be a pity," he wrote in 1905, "to lose one's own and one's country's special characteristics through too much adoration of the West . . . Writers must imitate literary techniques simply to develop those qualities peculiar to ourselves." Sōseki abandoned his academic post in English literature to write Japanese literature, and he developed a personal, and by extension national, idiom. To some extent, as critics have written, he was writing "for the sake of the country," but he was also scornful of the wave of self-satisfaction and nationalism that swept Japan after its successful wars in which everything was attributed to unique qualities of Japanese spirit. "Do we go to the toilet or wash our faces for our country?" he asked in one talk, and in another, "My Individualism," he argued that "as long as Japan is not in such a state that it is likely to collapse at any moment or meet the misery of destruction, it is not necessary to run around shouting 'Nationalism! Nationalism!'"

In the novels of his mature years Sōseki's characters are depicted with remarkably realistic psychological insight. They suffer from a compelling loneliness and a usually futile struggle against egotism; they are people living in times of rapid social and moral change. By Sōseki's time the problems of transcription had been sufficiently solved to permit the emergence of a supple prose free of the florid and often bombastic turns of phrase of earlier prose, and the language he and his peers utilized reads well as modern Japanese.

Kokoro (The heart) is probably Sōseki's most compelling book, and it is widely known thanks to Edwin McClellan's sensitive translation. It is placed at the juncture of Meiji and twentieth-century Japan, and centers on problems of loneliness and isolation. Its central event is the death of the Emperor Meiji in July 1912. At the moment that cannon announced the funeral rites, General Nogi Maresuke, whose victory at Port Arthur had cost so many thousands of lives, followed the emperor in the medieval samurai tradition of *junshi*, partly to atone for having lost his regimental banner flag in the Satsuma Rebellion decades before, and more particularly to call his countrymen back to a code of morality that seemed to be waning. His wife in turn followed her mate in death. On learning of this, Sōseki's protagonist, Sensei, also commits suicide, leaving a long letter of explanation for a young friend which makes up the core of the book. The slender volume is in one sense an elegy for an age that has past. "I felt as though the spirit of the Meiji era had begun with the Emperor and had ended with him," Sensei writes his young friend; "I was overcome with the feeling that I and the others, who had been brought up in that era, were now left behind to live as anachronisms . . . Perhaps you will not understand clearly why I am about to die, no more than I can fully understand why General Nogi killed himself. You and I belong to different eras, and so we think differently. There is nothing we can do to bridge the gap between us."[39] It is impossible to read this without feeling, as McClellan has put it, that these men were "very much children of Meiji. They were uprooted people, intellectually and socially; and as novelists their major concern was to depict the conditions of those who had to pay a price for having been born in a time of great change."

Mori Ōgai's trajectory of life was quite different. He was educated as an army medical officer and had four years of study in Wilhelmine Germany. He returned conversant with current literary criticism, which he introduced through a number of journals. He was party to debates about the modernization of Japanese culture, and ultimately came to agree that "the adoption of an alien culture was to set up stresses and threatened to leave a spiritual vacuum." That vacuum became one of Ōgai's major preoccupations in later life. He set himself the problem, as Bowring puts it, of deciding "to what extent could the importation of Western culture and thought continue before it caused a fatal break with the past."[40] Ōgai too was a nonconformist in his relations with military superiors, but he nevertheless had a distinguished career in army and public health and medicine. He managed to balance science with an equally important role in literary circles. As with Sōseki's Sensei in *Kokoro,* however, the startling news of General Nogi's *seppuku* in order to follow the Meiji emperor in death brought Ōgai to reconsider his writing and indeed Japanese history. There followed a series of graphically naturalist historical tales, scrupulously researched, dealing with incidents of violence in Japanese history.[41]

Ōgai is one of modern Japan's most respected intellectuals and writers. As a novelist, however, his rigid and almost academic concern with accuracy has probably made him less important than Shimazaki Tōson. If Sōseki stands out for the psychological depth of his depiction of loneliness and egotism and Ōgai for his historical works, Tōson's contribution was closer to the Japanese tradition in its concern with self. Much of his work, in fact, prefigures the popular twentieth-century form of the "I novel," in which authors have laid bare their struggles and uncertainties. Tōson's best-known work, however, is probably the novel *Before the Dawn (Yoake mae),*[42] a semiautobiographical account of the changes and tragedies that overcome a simple-minded and rather naive believer in the teachings of late Tokugawa *kokugaku.* We have alluded to its principal figure, Hanzō, at many points in the Restoration narrative above. Tōson himself was the son of just such a station chief, whose fortunes and standing declined with the disestablishment of the great Nakasendō highway of Tokugawa days, and the work that emerged was one that combined grandeur with tragedy.

IDEOLOGY AND HISTORY

Meiji ideology developed throughout the era in a zigzag pattern that engaged the efforts of private scholars and thinkers as much as it did the concern of government bureaucrats. In the field of history, particularly in the treatment of Japan's antiquity, however, the influence of the state was marked.[43]

The whirlwind pace of political and institutional innovation in the Meiji period had an important impact on the historical consciousness of the Japanese. History had always been one of the principal branches of letters in the Confucian tradition, and Tokugawa scholars made important contributions to historical writing.[44] With the growth of respect for facts and evidence under the influence of scholars like Ogyū Sorai, standards became more rigorous. Writers like Arai Hakuseki had developed a periodization that accounted for and justified the primacy of warrior rule, and in so doing treated the flaws of dominance by earlier emperors and courtiers with a dispassionate detachment. Confucian rationalism found further support in European knowledge transmitted by the Dutch. By late Tokugawa times writers like the Osaka merchant-scholar Yamagata Bantō (1748–1821) were able to refute as nonsense the attempts by Motoori Norinaga and other nativist scholars to give new life to the ancient Shinto mythology about the sun goddess and the founding of Japan.

There was a great deal of continuity between the work of the best Tokugawa Confucians and the development of modern historical writing in Meiji. This is seen most clearly in the work of the historian Shigeno Yasutsugu (1827–1910). Shigeno was born the son of a country samurai in Satsuma, where his ability won him a rapid rise in status and honor. He was an instructor in the domain samurai school at sixteen, and went on to teach Chinese poetry and prose at the bakufu's Shōheikō academy at twenty-five. After the Satsuma victory in the Meiji Restoration he came to head the Historiographical Bureau, lectured before the Meiji emperor, and became known as the finest scholar of Chinese learning and evidential research in the Ogyū Sorai tradition. Shigeno was emphatic on the desirability of fostering closer relations with China, and advocated sending students to China for long periods of study. He also argued that it was a necessity of learning to speak and read Chinese as Chinese did, and deplored Japanese use of grammatical markers as semitranslation attempts in traditional *kanbun* reading.[45] But Shigeno was also impressed by the techniques of Western history. After an English diplomat, August H. Mounsey, published a history of the Satsuma Rebellion in 1879, Shigeno noted that its approach seemed to be quite different from the East Asian tradition of annalistic records. He and his colleagues in the Historiographical Bureau had been gathering documentary sources on that event, but he noted that Mounsey's book did more: "Unlike Japanese and Chinese histories which confine themselves to factual statements," he wrote, "Western histories inquire into causes and consider effect, [and] provide detailed accounts of their subjects and vivid pictures of conditions of the time with which they are concerned. There can be no doubt that their form and method embody many points of value to us."[46]

In 1888 the Imperial University established a Department of Japanese History, and the two leading figures in the Historiographical Bureau became professors. Along with Shigeno there was Kume Kunitake, the Confucian scholar who had served as annalist of the Iwakura embassy to the West of 1871–1873. Both of them set out to free Japanese history from the myths that dominated the treatment of antiquity, and before long a number of traditional attributions and figures became suspect. In 1890 Shigeno gave a lecture in which he refuted long-current belief in the existence of a Kojima Takanori, long hailed as a loyalist stalwart in the fourteenth-century wars in which opposing warlords supported rival (Northern and Southern) imperial courts. Shortly afterward he did the same for Kusunoki Masashige, long venerated as a paragon of imperial loyalty. All this attracted a good deal of attention, and Shigeno became known as "Dr. Obliteration."[47]

To the Chinese school of evidential research which Shigeno represented there was added the authority of Western, Germanic historical science. In 1887 Ludwig Riess, a student of the great Leopold von Ranke, was invited to come to Japan as professor in the newly established department of history. Riess, who was Jewish and unable to secure a chair in a German university, was at the Imperial University until 1902. In addition to teaching world history he played a major role in the development of historical science as an academic discipline in Japan.[48] The German influence supplemented the Japanese zeal for the compilation of sources, and it was the move of the Historiographical Bureau to the Imperial University that launched academic history with Shigeno and Kume as historians. The Ranke influence had an additional by-product. Working from the European example, Ranke was convinced that foreign relations were central to the creation of the modern state. Despite the contrast offered by Tokugawa Japan's relative seclusion, it could be argued that Japan's emergence as a modern state was the result of the nineteenth-century opening, and as a result an ambitious plan to collect documents relevant to foreign relations was soon under way.

The Meiji surge of Western influence and optimism for a new day of "civilization and enlightenment" thus carried the Confucian zeal for evidence and reason a step further. Popular writers like Fukuzawa and Taguchi Ukichi, the author of a history of Japanese development, did their best to fit Japan into a larger multinational perspective. At the same time, however, the architects of *fukoku kyōhei* were reaching back to earlier beliefs in their efforts to construct a strong state by utilizing and augmenting the aura of imperial power and divinity. So long as scholars and intellectuals were writing for one another and speeding the modernization that was necessary for Japan's international repute there was no problem, but once the new institutional structure was in place and commoners were educated participants in a growing and increasingly open society, "history," writ large, would become a matter for public debate.

This debate took some time to develop, and in a sense it had been anticipated by the appearance of conservative and nationalistic journals in the late 1880s, but it came into the open only in the 1890s. By then the constitution was in place, and the Imperial Rescript on Education had committed the state to a normative role in customs and morals. Private and semiprivate philosophers and educators were beginning to lay out what were supposed to be the "right" positions and beliefs that their fellow citizens should hold. Japan was also at the threshold of the nationalist self-satisfaction that would accompany its victories in wars against its Asian and European competitors.

In 1892 Kume Kunitake published an article entitled "Shinto Is an Outdated Custom of Heaven Worship" in the principal academic historical journal. It was soon republished in a popular historical journal, *Shikai*. "By itself," Kume argued, "Shinto cannot meet modern needs and must be stripped of its useless elements like a tree shedding its dead branches and leaves."[49] The problem was, however, that the builders of the modern state, far from considering Shinto "useless," had decided that it was essential to their task. Many conservatives and Shintoists were outraged by Kume's public disavowal of the historic link between the imperial family, the sun goddess, and the Ise shrine. Kume was soon under vigorous press criticism; his cause was not helped by the *Shikai* editor, Taguchi Ukichi, who relished controversy. Before long Shinto partisans were demonstrating in front of Kume's house, and self-styled experts barged in to interrogate him. They debated with him for five hours, and they were little mollified by Kume's explanation that he had wanted to demonstrate the common origin and nature of all primitive religions. In the end Kume decided to retract or at least modify his position "pending further study." His retraction appeared in the press, but the harm had been done. His opponents complained to the Imperial Household Ministry and the Ministry of Education, which dismissed him from his teaching post. Kume was able to move to Waseda, the private institution founded by his fellow Saga clansman Ōkuma Shigenobu. The curriculum vitae he submitted with his application for appointment at Waseda provides laconic evidence of the swift change in his fortunes:

1889	February 23	Promoted to First Grade official.
	February 27	Awarded Fifth Order of Merit.
		Awarded Order of the Sacred Treasure.
1892	February 29	Awarded Junior Fifth [Court] Rank.
	March 4	Ordered to resign position.
	March 30	Resigned as ordered.[50]

Kume continued to teach and write, but his tie with the government-sponsored Historiographical Bureau was at an end. The scribe of the Iwakura embassy, sent to the West to "seek wisdom throughout the world" two decades earlier, thus fell victim to charges that he had shown sacrilegious disregard of Japan's mythic past.

The 1997 study by John Brownlee points out that Kume was silent about his dismissal. In 1903, when he was invited to contribute a chapter on Shinto by Ōkuma for the collection *Fifty Years of New Japan,* he was considerably more circumspect and respectful. Even when the government, in 1925, decided to censor parts of an earlier book in which he had discussed early accounts of imperial misadventures to illustrate the shortcomings of premodern history, he remained silent. Part of this can probably be ascribed to the increasing conservatism that came with age, but more to a patriotic acceptance of the need to support official ideology and the emperor.

What is more surprising is the fact that none of Kume's colleagues in the Historiographical Bureau or at the Imperial University chose to say a word in his defense. This may be because of long-lingering disputes between schools of interpretation of the national myths, or because of fear of personal involvement. Shigeno too was sidelined for a time, though never dismissed. This silence on the part of people who knew better probably had its origins in an unspoken agreement that the interests of the state should come first, and that while specialists ought to be able to carry on their work in seminars and professional journals, the larger public should be protected from possible confusion and doubt. As that larger public became more literate and capable of participating in the debates, censorship became more appealing an option. A book by Kume acceptable in 1887 could require censorship in a few decades later.[51]

The most effective controls, however, were social and internal. Before the 1930s the Japanese state required few coercive tactics because elements within the Japanese society and conscience did its work for it. Elite professionals preferred to remain silent while Shinto fundamentalists monitored debate, so long as their silence worked to preserve their freedom within the walls of the academy. Before long the Historiographical Bureau resumed its work of collecting and classifying documents but not controversies. In Brownlee's words, "the brief era of Dr. Obliteration and his killer colleagues passed. The Age of the Gods and the early Emperors got a reprieve from scholarly execution."[52]

In 1911, at the end of the Meiji period, the government involved itself even more directly in the interpretation of history by telling specialists what they could write in textbooks. The issue was that of the Northern and Southern courts in the fourteenth century. Remarkably, during that same period there were also rival papacies in Rome and Avignon. In Japan the debate over which of the imperial lines should be considered legitimate had deep roots in social and ideological change, and those require comment first.

Meiji Japan had, in every sense, "arrived." Two wars had found its arms victorious. The government had seen to it that the emperor received the credit. During the Sino-Japanese War of 1894–95 he moved, together with the Imperial Diet, to Hiroshima, the headquarters for the military effort, so that he could be credited with an active role of command despite the fact that he personally showed little enthusiasm for that war and declined to report it to the putative ancestral spirits at the Ise shrine. In 1900 Japan had strengthened its image of modernity by playing a major role in the relief of the missions at Peking from Chinese "Boxer" fanatics. In contrast to the looting by other elements of the allied force, Japanese troops behaved in exemplary fashion. The Anglo-Japanese Alliance provided a partnership with the world's greatest naval power. But it was particularly the stoic heroism of the farm boys who marched to their death at Port Arthur in the Russo-Japanese War that won the attention of the Western world. The contrast with the performance of British forces in the Boer War a few years earlier produced the "Learn from Japan" movement in Britain. Once again the aura of the Meiji emperor profited from success and sacrifice. In Japan the senior generation exulted in this fresh evidence of the importance of Japanese spirit *(tamashii)*, and it is not surprising that the memoirs of many Meiji figures provide striking evidence of this self-satisfaction.

Former liberals and doubters also came aboard. One exception was provided by the Christian leader Uchimura Kanzō, who had, as we have noted, declined to bow before the Imperial Rescript on Education. Disillusioned by the land grab that had followed the victory over China, in a war he had originally characterized as "righteous," Uchimura had become a pacifist and opposed the war with Russia. Not so his generation. Tokutomi Sohō had cemented his ties with Prime Minister General Katsura, and his *Kokumin* newspaper trumpeted the need for victory. In article after article Tokutomi called on his countrymen to accept the sacrifices necessary to maintain Japan's status as a Great Power. The Quaker Nitobe Inazō, Uchimura's old friend from Sapporo days, had published *Bushidō*, which explained and praised the warrior cult, in 1899. The book came into its own by the time of the war with Russia, was translated in many languages, and was so congenial to President Theodore Roosevelt that he ordered copies for all his children. "What won the battles on the Yalu, in Korea, and Manchuria," Nitobe was persuaded, "were the ghosts of our fathers, guiding our hands and beating in our hearts. They are not dead, those ghosts, the spirits of our warlike ancestors." Nitobe saw *bushidō* as a counter to the materialism and utilitarianism of modernity; "the seeds of the Kingdom, as vouched for and apprehended by the Japanese mind, blossomed in Bushido." He saw it dying, however, and hoped for its replacement by Christianity, but he was sure that while "Bushido as an independent code of ethics may vanish, . . . its power will not perish from the earth; its schools of martial prowess or civil honor may be demolished, but its light and its glory will long survive their ruins."[53]

Most Japanese shared in this satisfaction, and even Uchimura wrote that he could not refrain from sneaking into a closet to utter a few banzais. Nevertheless the enormous costs of the war, and the need for ever larger levies to support more divisions and more battleships after its conclusion, heightened strains that would in any case have accompanied industrialization and urbanization. It was possible to cheer the victories and venerate the emperor while objecting to the failure of the government and bureaucracy to spread the benefits of victory more widely. The mobilization of support for the war with Russia, and the lantern processions that were organized, contained potential for politics as well. There were countless marches through Japan's great cities; hundreds such received police permits, and thousands more, avowedly nonpolitical, did not. All this could lead to demands for social instead of psychological reward once the guns were stilled.

There were a number of major riots in Tokyo between 1905 and 1918. The first and greatest of these, the Hibiya riots, were in protest against the Portsmouth Treaty of Peace that concluded the war with Russia. Rioters, as we have noted, felt that Japan had been shortchanged in failing to get an indemnity to cover the crushing burden of debt the country had incurred, blamed this on the government, and wreaked havoc on the city, destroying 70 percent of the police boxes in Tokyo. Violence in Kobe and Yokohama followed.[54] Later riots focused on a rise in streetcar fares, opposed a tax increase, demanded a stronger China policy, opposed the government's resistance to majority opinion in the Imperial Diet, protected profiteering in naval construction, and demanded universal manhood suffrage. Then, in 1918, spiraling prices for rice led to riots in which 178 people were arrested in Tokyo alone. The causes of these disturbances thus varied, but they added up to discontent and bitterness in the growing cities, and that alarmed conservative Japanese.

Governing cabinets, led by nonpoliticians selected by the aging survivors of the Meiji leadership group, usually showed themselves slow-moving and often maladroit in their response to such expressions of discontent. In 1908, for instance, protests against a tax increase were answered by a Local Improvement Movement that was designed to help reform village life. The Home Ministry set out to rationalize and centralize the administration of village Shinto shrines, thereby alienating supporters of rural autonomy. Credit unions were set up, and Young Men's Associations were supposed to offer "spiritual guidance." Not to be outdone, the army established a nationwide organization of former soldiers, the Imperial Military Reserve Association, as one sponsor put it, "to protect the *kokutai* [national polity] and keep evil and materialistic foreign ideas from flowing into Japan." This had the capability in some cases of threatening established village hierarchies by pitting valorous veterans against wealthy landlords, but it was meant to firm up village structure with a focus on imperial service.[55] The capstone of the campaign, however, was an imperial exhortation to thrift and diligence. "All classes of Our people" were told to act in unison, to be faithful to their callings, frugal in the management of their households, submissive to the dictates of conscience and calls of duty, frank and sincere in their manners; they should abide by simplicity and avoid ostentation, and inure themselves to arduous toil without yielding to any degree of indulgence. These sentiments would have sounded familiar to the Tokugawa period villagers who listened to popular preachers like Hosoi Heishū, but those villagers had not been asked to give their lives in war. Certainly nothing could be further from the language of the 1868 Charter Oath, which had pledged that "the common people, no less than the civil and military officials, shall each be allowed to pursue his own calling so that there may be no discontent."

But there was discontent, and there were good reasons for it. Too exclusive a focus on government and urban modernity risked overlooking the disparities that were developing in the course of Meiji social change. Opportunities for urban investment attracted the capital of many rural landlords just as education and employment attracted their sons. In the process many villages became less "healthy," to use the government's term, and social cohesion was weaker. Novelists working within the new pattern of realism provided graphic descriptions of rural poverty and misery; Nagatsuka Takashi's *The Soil*, published in 1910, stands as an important ethnographic document. Its portrait of rural life rather repulsed Natsume Sōseki, whose introduction for a 1912 publication noted dryly,

> The characters in *The Soil* are the poorest of farmers. They have no education, no dignity. Their lives are like those of maggots hatched out of the soil ... [the author] portrays every detail of their almost beastly, impoverished lives.[56]

In northeastern Japan hardship was made worse by disastrous crop years. In 1905 unusually cold weather made for the smallest harvests since the famines of the 1780s and 1830s, the Tenmei and Tenpō years that witnessed so many peasant insurrections. "In Miyagi Prefecture the crop registered only twenty percent of a normal year's production, and as a result approximately 280,000 of the people in the prefecture became destitute."[57] In afflicted areas loss of land and employment, vagabondage, and a desperate search for sustenance at the lower levels of drudgery in mines and among the urban proletariat changed the face of rural life.

It is not difficult to find expressions of deep concern for the direction Japanese society seemed to be taking. Kitamura Tōkoku was a talented poet and essayist, active in the Freedom and People's Rights Movement and a convert to Christianity. He too struggled with the themes of individualism and authority, only to take his own life in 1892. He was depressed by shortcomings in the Meiji dream. "On the surface," he wrote in 1891,

> Meiji civilization manifests truly immeasurable progress, but do the majority of the people enjoy it? Go and carefully examine the actual condition of each house. On a cold day, when it is snowing, how many households contain families with rosy cheeks sitting by a warm fire? It is impossible to count the number of young girls without color in their cheeks and young boys without books who wander about the roadside . . . Although society seems outwardly splendid and gradually approaches grandeur, on the other hand we see conditions of gradual deterioration, weakness due to illness, and destitution . . . Nothing is more disastrous to a country than having its poor despised more and more while the rich become more and more arrogant and extravagant.[58]

The vast majority of Japanese accepted their society stoically; and many, of course, were in fact better off or had hopes for improvement. The memoirs of the novelist Yoshikawa Eiji (1892–1962), who grew up in grinding poverty in a household cursed by the inability of his (ex-samurai) father to make his way in Meiji commerce, show how it seemed to a child:

> While preserving intact in their domestic lives these customs reminiscent, in their austerity and traditionalism, of the samurai style of life, people were at the same time ashamed of appearing poor to the outside world. In a sense, people in those days never thought to trace the causes of poverty to politics or the social system; poverty was a personal trait, and there was a strong tendency to discriminate against the poor as, by definition, inferior human beings. Thus families were scared to death of going under. Even if you were in real trouble, you tried to hide it and keep up appearances . . . In those days when welfare systems were unknown, it was quite possible for a whole family to starve to death without their neighbors realizing it. It is also true that my parents were the kind of people who, finding them-

selves in that dire condition, were incapable of devising any way to save themselves.[59]

But there were some who did protest. A small socialist movement in which Christians played an important role got under way. An early study group was formed in 1898, and in 1901 a Social Democratic Party was formed, though it was quickly banned by the police. Kōtoku Shūsui (1868–1911), whose life span was almost exactly that of the Meiji period, was a young partisan of the Freedom and People's Rights Movement who became active in these study groups. In 1901 he published an attack on imperialism, which he labeled the "specter of the 20th century," and a book on the essence of socialism. As war with Russia neared he joined with the Christian leader Uchimura Kanzō in advocating pacifism in the columns of a liberal newspaper until it abandoned its opposition to the war. Kōtoku then joined with others to found a weekly, *Heimin shinbun* (The Commoners' Press). It too was banned, but not before it had published the first Japanese translation of Karl Marx's *Communist Manifesto*.

After a brief imprisonment, Kōtoku left for a six-month stay in San Francisco. There he experienced the earthquake of 1906, something that strengthened his views on the possibility of society without a government. He returned to Japan convinced that it was futile to try to work for social justice through existing institutions, and began to advocate a general strike and direct action. His insistence on this speeded the break-up of a socialist party that had formed once more in 1907. Kōtoku now became the acknowledged leader of the radical left, and was on the fringes of a group, which included his common-law wife, that prepared a plot on the life of the Meiji emperor. The police arrested him with the other members of the group in 1910. The "High Treason Trial" that followed was conducted in secret and its records have never been made public. In 1911 Kōtoku and eleven others of the group were hanged. This became a shattering event for many liberal intellectuals. The novelist Tokutomi Roka delivered a famous lecture at the First Special Higher School in which he told his young hearers that

> one should not fear the rebel. One should not be afraid of becoming a rebel himself. To do something new has always been called rebellion . . . What is to be feared is the death of the spirit. To believe only what one is taught to believe, to say only what one is told to say, to do only what one is asked to do, to find security in life by existing formally like a doll poured from a model, to lose completely the idea of self-confidence in one's independence and the belief in self-improvement—this is the death of the spirit. To live is to rebel.[60]

This was the voice of the early Meiji period, but it had become anachronistic in the conformity of the late Meiji days. Most intellectuals seem to have seen the incident as proof of the impracticability of individual opposition to the state. It confirmed them in what was probably their inclination: withdrawal, retreat, or indifference to political issues.

For historians and writers of textbooks the High Treason Trial had other and unanticipated reverberations. Uniform textbooks had come to play a role in intellectual homogenization. In 1903, after a series of scandals involving bribery in the adoption of privately prepared books, the Ministry of Education introduced a series of national textbooks. A course in ethics *(shūshin)* was central to this system; it stressed civil virtues of loyalty and patriotism, and portrayed Japan's as a "family-state" in which the myriad family hierarchies reached up to and were crowned by the imperial family, which in turn had its links to the mythic gods. History, geography, and language received definitive treatment in this pattern. The books were revised in 1910, after the annexation of Korea; in 1918, after World War I; in 1933, after the establishment of the puppet state of Manchukuo; and in 1941, on the eve of World War II. Except for the edition of 1918, each of these revisions tended to strengthen the nationalist content of the textbooks. Description of other societies and accounts of distinguished non-Japanese diminished, to be replaced by increasing emphasis on Japan, its heroes and its beneficial social order.

In 1911, at the time of the High Treason Trial, a relatively obscure period of Japanese history suddenly became the center of intense controversy. Shortly after the Russo-Japanese war patriotic organizations among schoolteachers had begun to campaign for a uniform and orthodox treatment of the years between 1336 and 1392, the period of the Southern and Northern Courts in which rival emperors held forth in Kyoto and in Yoshino. In January 1911, one of the major Tokyo dailies raised the alarm that the 1910 textbooks left it unclear which governance was legitimate and which was not, despite the fact that the government supposedly favored the claims of the Southern, or Yoshino, line. Politicians and public intellectuals soon joined the fray. The Kōtoku anarchists, some argued, showed the dangers of education in a fact-oriented, valueless history. It was after all a cardinal point of Japanese belief that there could not be two suns in the sky or two sovereigns in the land, and yet the textbook suggested that this had not been the case during this period of rival courts. Before long the matter was taken up by the cabinet, which was nearly unseated by the dispute. Prime Minister General Katsura, who probably did not find the issue one of compelling interest, later wrote that nothing had given him as much difficulty.

The upshot of the uproar was a Ministry of Education decision that the period in question should be termed the era of the Southern Court to make it clear that the Northern Court had lacked legitimacy. The course dealing with the problem at Tokyo Imperial University was relabeled "The Yoshino Court Era." Ministers and warriors of the Southern Court, especially Kusunoki Masashige, whose very existence had been threatened by Professor Shigeno, were lionized in print and sculpture. One of the authors of the offending 1910 textbook was suspended from his post for two years, and many other leading authorities were publicly criticized for having placed facts ahead of public morality. For the most part, Japan's historians remained silent, and distinguished, as Brownlee puts it, between education (*kyōiku*), under which the people of Japan were to be taught useful and inspiring fictions appropriate to a sacerdotal state, and scholarship (*gakumon*).[61]

Meiji culture thus had its contradictions: on the one hand there was the urgency of a program of modernization that took the West as its model, and on the other was the commitment to adapt Japan's oldest myths to modern uses in order to bolster the authority of the emperor—and, of course, those who stood at his elbow. When the two were in conflict, the authority and legitimacy of the state took precedence, for in the minds of officialdom, professors at the Imperial University were cultural officials.

But there are other things about the Meiji drive to create a new culture that deserve mention. In trying to create and define the new culture Meiji Japanese were also creating and defining tradition. T. S. Eliot has written that "what happens when a new work of art is created is something that happens simultaneously to all the works of art that preceded it," and this is no less true of institutions and of letters. The institutions and rites of rule were in large part re-created to serve new purposes. In the case of *gagaku* court music, what had in origin often been improvisational and entertaining became solemn and awe-inspiring, and in many ways "tradition" itself was declared finalized.

In order to depart from, or to emphasize, tradition it became necessary to define what it was that Japan had been. The models of warrior rule and culture had been rejected, but what was to replace them? This process was most apparent on the part of men of letters, some of whom were the most articulate and interesting of their generation. Sōseki and Ōgai were determined to build a new literary tradition that would be worthy of comparison with that of the West and would win Western respect. They succeeded in this, but in their mind it was clear that the old tradition could not play this role.

What, then, were to be the most important and enduring monuments of the past? What was to be the literary canon? It may be that their task was lightened because eighteenth-century nativist scholars like Motoori Norinaga had anticipated some of these questions in trying to set the Japanese tradition off from that of China. Motoori, however, was intent on purification and "return," and not on building the new. Building the new meant locking off the old. Add the fact that the Meiji men lived in the Victorian age, and were in fact Victorians themselves. Their concern with what the West would respect and understand strengthened this, and they blended Victorian and Confucian standards of propriety. To some degree questions of this sort have plagued every developing society in modern times. Japan's experience, as perhaps the first of the "latecomers" to wrestle with these problems, thus has lessons of profound interest for these themes.

The half century of determined effort made for an additional periodization in which "Meiji" as definitive change became standard in writing and thought. By the second decade of the twentieth century the consciousness of Meiji as a turning point was universal, and not limited to writers who articulated it. Two monuments stand as symbols of this consciousness. The first is the Heian Shrine in Kyoto, a copy of an eighth-century Chinese-style administrative building, that was built in 1895 to mark the eleven-hundred-year anniversary of the designation of Kyoto as capital, and dedicated to the Emperor Kammu in whose reign that took place.

The second is the Meiji Shrine in Tokyo, built in 1920 with the labor of more than 100,000 volunteers. Its wide and graveled path leads through majestic trees to an imposing Shinto *torii* and on to a simple purification font and traditional shrine. Nearby a pictorial gallery contains giant murals in Western style that depict the principal events of Meiji times. The shrine is a symbol of the worship of Emperor Meiji, whose memorabilia, including the taxidermists' preservation of his faithful steed, dominate the scene. In this setting one can appreciate Natsume Sōseki's selection of the emperor's death and the self-immolation of General Nogi, the last samurai, as symbols for the end of an era. Yet the shrine also points to the future, for it is most crowded during New Year holidays when families bring their children, usually dressed in colorful kimonos, to worship at the font.

15

The Meiji era was not followed by as neat and logical a periodization. The Emperor Meiji (his era name was conflated with his person posthumously) symbolized the changes of his period so perfectly that at his death in July 1912 there was a clear sense that an era had come to an end. His successor, who was assigned the era name Taishō (Great Righteousness), was never well, and demonstrated such embarrassing indications of mental illness that his son Hirohito succeeded him as regent in 1922 and remained in that office until his father's death in 1926, when the era name was changed to Shōwa. The 1920s are often referred to as the "Taishō period," but the Taishō emperor was in nominal charge only until 1922; he was unimportant in life and his death was irrelevant.

Far better, then, to consider the quarter century between the Russo-Japanese War and the outbreak of the Manchurian Incident of 1931 as the next era of modern Japanese history. There is overlap at both ends, with Meiji and with the resurgence of the military, but the years in question mark important developments in every aspect of Japanese life. They are also years of irony and paradox. Japan achieved success in joining the Great Powers and reached imperial status just as the territorial grabs that distinguished nineteenth-century imperialism came to an end, and its image changed with dramatic swiftness from that of newly founded empire to stubborn advocate of imperial privilege. Its military and naval might approached world standards just as those standards were about to change, and not long before the disaster of World War I produced revulsion from armament and substituted enthusiasm for arms limitations. Japan's political leaders broadened popular representation in government that would have been welcomed in Meiji years, only to have expectations outrun those advances in response to newer impulses of revolution and radicalism abroad. Government vigilance and police eagerness to repress that radicalism all but vitiated what were genuine steps in the direction of representative government. World War I and its aftermath, together with the great Tokyo earthquake of 1923, brought profound changes in social, intellectual, and urban consciousness. In some ways these years brought a growth in democracy and a setback in civil rights, and both found support within Japanese society.

1. Steps toward Party Government

The Meiji Constitution was deliberately vague on the subject of executive responsibility. Sovereignty and final authority in all matters rested with the throne, but at the same time the ruler had to be protected from active participation lest he be found fallible. What resulted was a curious sort of pluralism in which many participated and no one was ultimately responsible. The prime ministers were relatively weak, especially in the early years when they sat with ministers who were their equals. Cabinet ministers presided over relatively autonomous organizations; the Home and Justice ministries, with responsibility for local government and the national police, were particularly powerful. Since the emperor was in theory commander of all armed services, the ministers of the army and navy reported directly to him, but they in turn were selected from the generals and admirals on the active list by their respective general staffs. The lifting of this requirement between the years from 1913 to 1936 marked a significant, though temporary, step forward, but the services remained vital to the political process. Powerful bodies were beyond the control of the elected members of the House of Representatives. The Privy Council, made up of imperial appointees, had to be invoked for key decisions of constitutional interpretation and national policy. The House of Peers, a mix of hereditary aristocrats (many newly created) and imperial appointees, was susceptible to influence by government figures who, like Yamagata Aritomo, had the opportunity to nominate members. After each successful war its lower ranks had been swelled by titles granted members of the armed services. In later years leading industrialists also took their place with other leading taxpayers and imperial appointees who included distinguished academics. In other words the House of Representatives, itself elected by voters who qualified for suffrage by a direct tax, was one contender for power, and badly outmatched except for the constitutional requirement that it approve the budget.[1]

Thanks to this provision, cabinets had found it steadily more necessary to work out arrangements with the lower house, and in their struggles with it the Satsuma-Chōshū oligarchs had to a large extent had to submerge the differences that divided them in order to present a solid and seemingly harmonious front. At first they had thought of political parties as a source of partisan disunity and tried to adopt a posture of transcendence or superiority, lecturing the representatives on their responsibility to cooperate. When this failed a special imperial statement or rescript usually carried the day, but overuse of this tactic had its own dangers of cheapening the currency of Imperial Otherness. The throne was surrounded by a sacerdotal awe, and misuse of its numinous power, especially for personal political advantage, was a form of blasphemy. After the Sino-Japanese War in 1895 the oligarchs found it wise to add party leaders with impeccable Restoration credentials to their cabinets. Itagaki Taisuke and Ōkuma Shigenobu came to hold seats under Itō and Matsukata respectively. In 1898 the *genrō*, at Itō's urging, even experimented with a cabinet jointly led by the two party leaders, but it soon failed because of internal disunity. Itō now got the idea of organizing his own party. He was tired, he wrote, of the horse-trading necessary for cooperation with the lower house, and he needed his own army instead of having to deal with mercenaries. His colleagues, particularly Yamagata, had been firmly opposed to this at first and blocked it. It was Yamagata who followed the Itagaki-Ōkuma cabinet, and it was then that he secured an imperial ordinance that restricted the service posts to commanders on the active list in order to safeguard governments from party control. Thus the services, by refusing to approve, or withdrawing, a minister, could block or bring down the cabinet.

It was in 1900 that Itō had his way and organized his party, the Friends of Constitutional Government (Rikken Seiyūkai). Most of its members were former Liberal Party adherents, drawn to the new organization by the lure of power and patronage under the leadership of the author of the constitution itself.

Yamagata remained hostile to the idea. He promptly nominated Itō as his successor prime minister before the latter's preparations were complete, and then quietly sabotaged the new cabinet that Itō formed. Shortly afterward he managed to have the emperor appoint Itō to head the Privy Council, forcing him to end his role in party politics by ceding control to Saionji Kinmochi. Not long after that Itō's assignment to Korea removed him from internal politics altogether.

The *genrō* were thus far from united. For the early years of constitutional government the prime minister's chair alternated between leaders from Satsuma and those from Chōshū. After 1900 Satsuma was out of the running for over a decade, but a new alternation took place between Katsura Tarō, an army protégé of Yamagata's, and Saionji, as heir to Itō's political party. It was now to some extent a Chōshū world. But within that world rivalries remained: two powerful men, foreign policy alternatives, and civil-military priorities. What distinguished this last decade of Meiji was a rather patterned, gentlemanly competition of a sort possible only between men who had worked together for half a century and who had begun to be aware that other, new forces might threaten their ascendancy. No one was ever allowed to "fail," and exquisite care was taken to avoid loss of face. We have earlier noted the way Inoue Kaoru was blocked from forming a cabinet in 1901; Katsura, when invited to continue as army minister, professed illness, and was free to accept the prime minister's post only after other members of the gentlemen's club prevailed on Inoue to ask him to put national above personal considerations.

Katsura experienced a remarkable recovery. It was on his watch that the alliance with England was formed, the decision taken to stand up to Russia, and the Russo-Japanese War carried to its successful conclusion. The great Hibiya riots against the failure of the Portsmouth treaty to include a Russian indemnity forced Katsura's resignation. He now recommended Saionji as his successor. In 1908, when disputes over the size of military appropriations brought Saionji down, he in turn recommended Katsura as his successor. This time the annexation of Korea stood as Katsura's accomplishment, with the result that he was elevated in rank to duke or prince (kōshaku). Saionji, descended from a distinguished aristocratic lineage, held that rank by birth.

What had made this alternation in power possible was a working agreement between Katsura and Saionji's Seiyūkai. Katsura needed their votes, and they needed his willingness to forgo dissolution of the Diet (which was the prime minister's prerogative), as that would have plunged them into expensive election campaigns. Katsura was far from a free agent, in other words, and his restiveness under these restrictions led him in turn to think about organizing his own political party, as Itō had done before him. His old mentor Yamagata still objected. In 1911 it was Saionji's turn once again. He was in office during the Meiji emperor's final illness, but shortly after that a dispute with the army once more brought him down. Saionji, the only court aristocrat (kuge) among the oligarchs, was now asked to serve as genrō, and the last to be so honored. After the death of Yamagata in 1922 and Matsukata in 1924 it fell to Saionji, until his death in 1940, to advise the court on the selection of new prime ministers.[2] Katsura, for his part, was quietly removed from politics by being elevated to the imperial court as lord privy seal and grand chamberlain. Yamagata had not changed his mind about political parties.

Saionji's eminence had given the Seiyūkai access to power, but the most important political figure of the party was not Saionji, who was a rather languid aristocrat, but Hara Takashi (Kei, 1856–1921), who was to form a political party cabinet, the first to be structured and headed by a party politician, in 1918. Hara's career and character provide a good illustration of the sort of qualifications necessary for a successful party politician in a Japan in which many of the reins of power were still beyond popular control.

Hara showed little doubt about his commitment to representative government and in particular the House of Representatives. Early on he voluntarily gave up his classification as "former samurai," and he consistently resisted offers of a peerage that would have forced him out of the House of Representatives. For this some contemporary observers hailed him as "the great commoner." In fact, however, his origins were more distinguished than those of most of his colleagues and competitors, for his forebears had been of the highest rank in the northern domain of Nambu. What was distinctive about him was his place of origin, for Nambu and the northeast in general had fared very poorly in the Meiji order. Hara made no particular effort to ingratiate himself with the ordinary people whose cause he was supposed to champion. A genuinely popular following would have made him seem a dangerous competitor in the eyes of leaders whose approval was vital to his rise to power. Far from participating in the Freedom and People's Rights Movement of the 1880s, he had begun as a government official; he held a number of important diplomatic posts, and worked particularly closely with Foreign Minister Mutsu Munemitsu. His background also included a period as editor of the Osaka *Mainichi* as well as business posts. He was, in other words, very much part of the establishment and he had a record that inspired confidence. In addition, however, he was an adroit participant in political decisions. He had played an important role in the establishment of his party in 1900. Thereafter he helped keep its members in line in Diet negotiations. More important, probably, was his skill in pork barrel politics. Under his leadership a broad-gauge railroad the length of the land that the military wanted was given up in favor of politically popular projects of local lines, roads, bridges, ports, and other improvements that gratified electoral supporters. At the same time Hara kept a careful eye on Yamagata, now easily the single most powerful of the oligarchs, and did his best to develop a position of trust with him. He made little headway in this for many years, but when he finally came to power he was rewarded by the old soldier's frank admiration of the hard line he took on maintaining social order.[3]

The orderly alternation of political power that characterized the last decade of the Meiji era broke down at the very inception of the next. Katsura had assumed his court positions and taken on the role of the new emperor's political tutor a few months after Emperor Meiji's death and a few months before Saionji, refusing to agree to the army's demand for two additional divisions, resigned in December of 1912. The wrathful resignation of the army minister, General Uehara Yūsaku, brought down the cabinet, and there was no hope that the army would nominate a successor unless its demands were met. What followed became known as the "Taishō political crisis," and it became an important step toward political party cabinets.

The council of *genrō*, now much depleted despite the addition of Saionji, met repeatedly in search of a successor prime minister. A number of men, most of them Yamagata disciples, were approached, but none of them wanted to inherit Saionji's problem. In December Katsura offered to break the deadlock by resigning his court offices to form his third cabinet. There was widespread shock and resentment, particularly on the part of politicians who had thought the day of party cabinets was finally at hand. They charged that Katsura had violated his word, forsaken his responsibilities to the young emperor, and dragged the court into politics. A political coalition was formed to "Protect the Constitution." Katsura, meanwhile, had begun work on a new political party, the Rikken Dōshikai, that drew its strength from the non- and anti-Seiyūkai strength in the Diet, but he had become the focus of long pent-up anger. A fiery and independent legislator, Ozaki Yukio (1859–1954) sealed his fate with one of the most memorable speeches in Japanese Diet history. During a Diet interpellation he skewered Katsura by charging that he and his bureaucratic allies were cowards who hid behind the aura of the emperor. "The throne is their rampart," he said in his peroration, "and Rescripts their missiles." Katsura, unable to sustain the opprobrium, resigned and died shortly afterward. Ozaki's speech symbolized the opening of a new parliamentary era.

Despite this the process of party governments was a slow one, and it was not to be won on the floor of the Diet. Katsura was followed by Admiral Yamamoto Gonnohyōe in a "Satsuma" and "navy" cabinet. That cabinet, however, was soon brought down by discovery of corruption and kickbacks in naval contracts with foreign, especially German, suppliers.

The *genrō*, disconcerted once again, turned a last time to one of their own generation in the hope for stability and chose Ōkuma Shigenobu. Ōkuma was now close to senility and in no sense the maverick of his youth. He accepted the office of prime minister in the expectation of Diet support from the Dōshikai, the party Katsura had launched, since many of its members could trace their political lineage to Ōkuma's career. The real leadership of the cabinet, however, came from Katō Takaaki (Kōmei, 1860–1926), who held the post of foreign minister. Katō's influence on all aspects of the administration was so great that some of Ōkuma's most trusted lieutenants were dismayed. Inukai Tsuyoshi (Ki, 1855–1932) declined to accept a cabinet position, and Ozaki Yukio, although he did take the post of minister of justice, feared it would become a "Katō cabinet." Ozaki later wrote that Ōkuma "was past eighty, and beginning to show signs of senility . . . he now added indifference to his character. It was not infrequent for him to support two incompatible sides of an issue at the same time."[4]

Katō had served as ambassador to Great Britain, and his fondness for things English was legendary. Yamagata sometimes referred to him disparagingly as "Our Englishman." From Yamagata's perspective Katō's real failing, however, was his effort to keep control of foreign policy in his own hands. He failed to consult or even inform the senior statesmen in the way that had become usual; in the matter of the Twenty-one Demands, as will be seen below, their caution would have been preferable to his headstrong tactics. This mattered, for diplomacy played a central role in Ōkuma's administration. The relatively close coordination that had characterized Japanese policymaking during the rule of the oligarchs was now becoming slack and sometimes clumsy.

After taking office Ōkuma dissolved the Diet and called for new elections; in those the Dōshikai gained a solid majority, thereby ending the absolute majority the Seiyūkai had enjoyed since its formation in 1900. In politics the government held a solid Diet majority. After Ōkuma dissolved the House of Representatives, the Dōshikai managed to end the absolute majority the Seiyūkai had enjoyed since its formation in 1900. The garrulous old prime minister spoke in resounding generalities, but he was probably more popular than his silent predecessors.

But not for long. In 1917 army and Chōshū leaders managed to replace Ōkuma with General Terauchi Masatake. Yamagata too pinned his hopes on Terauchi as a return to orthodox leadership, but he was soon disillusioned. Terauchi tried to govern without securing the support of either party group in the House of Representatives, but this attempt to turn the clock back failed badly. Nature and economics conspired against the government when rice riots broke out in 1918. These began in July in fishing villages on the Japan Sea coast, where women gathered to protest the shipment of rice to the Osaka market, and followed communication lines to the great industrial cities of eastern Japan. The country was wracked by demonstrations, strikes, and riots that were directed against the rich and the police. Desperate to restore order, the government bolstered the police presence with armed troops; some 25,000 people were arrested, and 6,000 convicted, with sentences ranging from fines to execution. The social paroxysm of the *kome sōdō*, rice riots, was an important element in the emergence of the Hara party cabinet. The government's response was neither effective nor successful, and Japan needed a new prime minister once again.

By this time there were grounds to expect the elders to endorse a political party cabinet, but bureaucrats, peers, *genrō,* and the military were still reluctant. Nevertheless in the aftermath of the rice riots there seemed no real alternative. Hara, who had played his cards very carefully, finally had his chance. He had avoided open rupture with Terauchi and quietly lent him his support, and he had even won the grudging respect of Yamagata. His cabinet, which lasted until his assassination in 1921, marked the real dawn of political party governments. Even so, after Hara's death conservative forces still dreamed of a system in which "independent" cabinets would be able to negotiate with a divided Diet without becoming dependent on the electorate. Selecting a career bureaucrat seemed a middle path, and a cabinet was formed under Kiyoura Keigo. This, however, lasted just six months. By then, experiments with generals (Terauchi) and admirals (Yamamoto, Katō Tomosaburō) and octogenarian survivors (Ōkuma) had failed to attract the popular support that was increasingly necessary to govern. The hapless Kiyoura government provoked a massive "Protect the Constitution" opposition movement that brought Seiyūkai and Kenseikai (the new name adopted by the Dōshikai in 1916) together into a powerful front that led to the appointment of Katō Takaaki as head of a coalition government in the summer of 1924. Political party cabinets now seemed certain to govern Japan in the future. Powerful bureaucrats like Wakatsuki Reijirō and Hamaguchi Osachi (Ministry of Finance), leading bankers (Takahashi Korekiyo), career diplomats (Shidehara Kijūrō), and even leading generals (Tanaka Gi'ichi) "descended from heaven" (*amakudari,* reminiscent of the sun goddess's commission to her grandson to rule the island's kingdom) to pursue new careers as political party leaders.

The chart of prime ministers and cabinets suggests some interesting things about the politics of Japan between the wars. One is the frequency of cabinet transfers. Meiji cabinets changed frequently, to be sure—there were eleven between the inception of the cabinet system in 1885 and the Russo-Japanese War—but only six prime ministers, as the leaders of factions, tended to serve in rotation. Between the Russo-Japanese War and the Manchurian Incident the velocity of rotation continued—there were eighteen cabinet changes— but now there were fourteen prime ministers. The search for stability was never very successful. Those who proposed candidates for succession never worked out a system that could combine acceptability to the plural institutions that the constitutional order had created with responsibility to the increasingly vociferous electorate. If different prime ministers came and went with such frequency, more and more of the everyday decisions had to lie with the bureaucracy, for that was where legislation originated.

There was also an impressive mortality rate among prime ministers. Both

Katō Tomosaburō and Katō Takaaki died in office from natural causes, but in addition there were three assassinations—those of Hara, Hamaguchi, and Inukai, and of these Hara and Hamaguchi possessed particularly vital and virtually irreplaceable talents.

Ozaki Yukio, who had his own brushes with violence without having become prime minister, later reflected on this in his memoirs. Military men, he remarked, liked to be thought of as men who put their lives in danger for the sake of the nation, and derided civilian leaders and politicians as power hungry, selfish, and often corrupt. But in fact, he thought, the cases were quite opposite. In the military, the higher one's rank the less the likelihood of personal danger, for top commanders were usually kept at a prudent distance from the violence of the battlefield. It was quite the reverse with civil leaders; the higher the post, the greater the individual's personal danger. The office of prime minister was perhaps the most dangerous of all.

The assassination of the three prime ministers in office was in each case related to problems of foreign policy. Hara fell victim to a rightist who ob-

Cabinets between the Russo-Japanese War and the Manchurian Incident

Prime minister	Diet support	Fall
Saionji Kinmochi, 1906–1908	Seiyūkai	Army budget demands
Katsura Tarō (2nd cab.), 1908–1911	Seiyūkai	Funding priorities
Saionji (2nd), 1911–1912	Seiyūkai	Army budget demands
Katsura (3rd), 1912–1913 (2 mos.)	Dōshikai	"Taishō political crisis"
Adm. Yamamoto Gonnohyōe, 1913–1914	Seiyūkai	Navy procurement scandals
Ōkuma Shigenobu, 1914–1916	Coalition	*Genrō* decision
Gen. Terauchi Masatake, 1916–1918	Seiyūkai	Rice riots
Hara Takashi, 1918–1921	Seiyūkai	Assassinated
Takahashi Korekiyo, 1921–1922 (6 mos.)	Seiyūkai	Stand-in
Adm. Katō Tomosaburō, 1922–1923	Seiyūkai	Died in office
Adm. Yamamoto (2nd), 1923 (3 mos.)	Seiyūkai	Attack on Crown Prince
Kiyoura Keigo, 1924 (6 mos.)	None	United front opposition
Katō Takaaki (1st-2nd), 1924–1925, 1925–1926	Coalition/Kenseikai	Died in office
Wakatsuki Reijirō, 1926–1927	Kenseikai	Bank crisis
Gen. Tanaka Gi'ichi, 1927–1929	Seiyūkai	Hirohito displeasure
Hamaguchi Oschi, 1929–1931	Minseitō	Assassinated
Wakatsuki (2nd), 1931 (8 mos.)	Minseitō	Manchurian Incident
Inukai Tsuyoshi, 1931–1932 (5 mos.)	Seiyūkai	Assassinated

jected to the way the prime minister had forced compliance with the naval limitations being worked out at the Washington Conference, Hamaguchi too had overruled navy opposition to reductions worked out at the London Naval Conference, and Inukai was murdered by young naval officers newly returned from the violence at Shanghai that the government had managed to stop. The flash point of violence was particularly low whenever civilian interference with military prerogatives was involved.

It is not surprising that as the party leaders came closer to political power they changed. In the early days of the Freedom and People's Rights Movement their constituency was smaller and made up of substantial citizens and local leaders. It was easy to denounce Satsuma and Chōshū men who monopolized power, especially when the emperor himself had promised institutions of representative government. But in the Meiji institutional pattern the leaders became part of the palace system, or managed to draw the palace into their system; "hiding behind the throne," in Ozaki's words. In the early days demonstrations and public forums had drawn the participation of leading politicians; as late as the Hibiya riots against the peace with Russia the lead had been taken by stalwarts of the Freedom and People's Rights Movement. But in the interwar years the crowds were larger, rowdier, and less interested in speeches; urban workers and the poor began to predominate, and the politicians increasingly saved their rhetoric for one another on the Diet floor. The original leaders had been "popular," but popular with their peers; they had less in common with the new urban crowd, and that crowd had its doubts about them as well.

CENSORSHIP AND REPRESSION

The absorption of party political leaders into the institutional pattern of the state may explain the fact that there was not more concern with the institutions of civil society and individual rights on the part of parliamentarians. Intelligent and responsible political leaders felt it vital to extend the franchise in order to hold the allegiance of the larger crowds that now took part, but on the fringe of those crowds there were already figures who argued the need to change the entire system instead of tampering with the rules for voting. The secrecy that surrounded the High Treason Trial of Kōtoku Shūsui and the other anarchists who were executed in 1911 showed the fear with which radicalism was viewed by the government. The echoes of the Bolshevik revolution alarmed conservatives and liberals alike, and prepared the way for repression. As the 1920s moved along there were warning voices raised against repressive legislation in the Diet. This was particularly the case with some leaders of the urban-based party: Katsura's 1913 Dōshikai had become the Kenseikai in 1916, and that in turn spawned the Minseitō in 1927, although its makeup changed very little in the process. In the 1920s its leading Diet figures often warned that excessive vigilance could be counterproductive, but when faced with the rise of nonparliamentary radicalism few doubted that the Home and Justice ministries should take a strong line.

Interference with public meetings intensified, most strikingly during the Seiyūkai cabinet of General Tanaka in 1927. Legislative restraints on "dangerous thought" increased in severity. To be sure, publication had never been without restrictions, and press laws were invoked shortly after the Meiji Restoration. The Peace Police Law of 1900 was designed specifically to hamper the organization of radical groups and the diffusion of radical thought. A Book Section in the Police Bureau occupied itself with details as "literary" as the new tides of realism and naturalism that were increasingly important among men of letters, and few authors escaped brushes with the police censorship apparatus. "They started looking for Naturalism and Socialism in everything that appeared," Mori Ōgai wrote in 1910, "and men of letters and artists were looked at askance in case they might be Naturalist or Socialists. Then some of them discovered the phrase 'dangerous Western books' . . . [T]o translate was to retail the dangerous goods themselves."[5] It was to be expected that the High Treason Trial of Kōtoku Shūsui and the appearance of a group of anarchists around Ōsugi Sakae (1885–1923) would create appropriate settings for the intensification of such concerns. Ōsugi Sakae noted how easy it was to be arrested. He tells about walking home with friends late one night. As they passed the Yoshiwara brothel district they came upon a commotion caused by a drunk who had broken a window; soon a small crowd gathered around the culprit and his accuser, who was demanding that someone send for the police, with the idea of forcing him to pay for the damage. Ōsugi got the facts and then took over:

> This man hasn't a penny on him now. I'll pay the damages. That should be the end of it. It's no good to go calling the police every time something happens. As far as possible we shouldn't call the authorities. Most things can be settled this way by the people who are on the spot.
>
> The people from the bar agreed to that. The neighborhood patrol also agreed. The onlookers too agreed. The only person who could not agree was the policeman. He had been staring at me from the beginning with a sullen expression and now challenged me.
>
> "The gentleman was talking socialism, aren't you?"
>
> "I am. So what?" I challenged him back.
>
> "It's socialism, so you're under arrest. Come with me."

"This is humorous! I'll go wherever you want." I shoved the police-man's hand away and rushed into the Nihonzutsumi police station, which was just across from us. There, an assistant inspector ordered the police-man to take me to the detention hall along with the others who had fol-lowed us. This incident was reported in one newspaper at the time as 'ŌSUGI AND OTHERS ARRESTED.' "[6]

In this case higher authorities apologized for the absurdity, but Ōsugi's list of incarcerations, which totaled six years for two violations of the press ordi-nances, two violations of peace preservation ordinances, and "seditious riot-ing" in the streetcar fare disturbances, probably help explain his untimely end.

In 1909 the Katsura cabinet responded to perceived radicalism with a new Press Law under whose provisions it became easier for police to monitor and detain left-wing radicals like Ōsugi. Editors and publishers found it wise to be cautious about what they produced. One device adopted was for authors or their editors to omit one or more elements [Chinese characters] in words that might attract police attention. They could manipulate this by leaving out different elements of the same word in sequential use, thereby retaining intelligibility and, no doubt, adding a mild thrill of danger for the reader. The police, it had to be assumed, were either too obtuse to realize what was going on or content to have only formal compliance with the law.

Another device was sarcastic straight-faced prevarication. The handling of a 1921 story about the murder of a Korean collaborator provides an example. Min Won-sik, a Korean newspaper man who advocated cooperation with the Japanese occupiers, was murdered, presumably by a Korean nationalist, in Tokyo's Imperial Hotel; his body was returned to Korea with the honor due a friend of Japan. *Hōchi* took no chances in reporting his departure. "Bin Gen Shoku" (as Japanese readers would have Japanized Min's name), it said,

suddenly decided to return to Korea . . . The Premier, Home Minister, Minister of Communications, and the Minister of Railways said goodby to Mr. Bin. Escorted by the station-master, Mr. Bin entered a second-class compartment especially reserved for him, and decorated with wreaths. When the train was about to start, Dr. Mizuno, chief of the civil service of Korea, advanced a few steps toward the compartment where the Korean gentleman was, and greeted him without a word.[7]

The capstone of police repression in imperial Japan was provided by the provisions of the Peace Preservation Law of 1925. A Special Higher Division of the police had been established in 1911; this unit, charged with monitoring Koreans, labor, foreign thought, censorship, and arbitration, provides an indication of government priorities. The 1925 legislation, which accompanied the passage of the universal manhood suffrage law, was clearly intended as a step designed to checkmate whatever dangers the broader suffrage might produce. The awareness of an incipient communist movement resulted in provisions targeting "anyone who had organized an association with the objective of altering the *kokutai* [national polity] or the form of government or denying the system of private property and anyone who has joined such an association with full knowledge of its object . . . [anyone found guilty] shall be liable to imprisonment with or without hard labor for a term not exceeding ten years."[8] Other provisions went on to forbid discussion or encouragement of such activities. Three years later, the law was revised to make it more severe. Discussion of altering the *kokutai,* which meant questioning the imperial system, could now be punished with the death penalty.

Draconian as these provisions were, it would be an exaggeration to describe interwar Japan as a police state; that distinction had to wait for the intensity of the militarist era that lay ahead. It made a difference which party held power. The Seiyūkai governments were on the whole more prone to authorize police power, and this reached a peak in the police sweeps authorized by the Tanaka government on March 15, 1928. In these 1,600 were arrested, and political organizations of workers and tenant farmers were ordered dissolved. A few months later many more were "detained" because of a security paranoia at the time of the coronation of the young Emperor Hirohito. On the other hand, while it is undoubtedly true that a number of lives were lost to prison coercion and interrogation, in terms of formal executions the death penalty was used only once, and that in the extirpations of the spy ring developed by the Soviet agent Richard Sorge in the early 1940s. Implementation of these harsh codes tended to be less stringent during periods of Kenseikai/Minseitō rule, and the tactics of the Tanaka government drew harsh rebukes from Minseitō Diet members who warned that excessive violence would solve nothing and probably bring on more subversion in a setting in which only political reform could provide a genuine answer to social unrest.

THE POLITICAL AGENDA

What were the practical results and achievements of what is often called "Taishō Democracy" in the interwar period? It would be wrong to expect a checklist of specific goals and proposals, for the object was to gain control of government for the people, the *kokumin.* Since the lower house of the Diet was the only elective organ of the national government, that meant control of the Diet by the House of Representatives, and since the political parties contested control of that house, "democracy" meant in practice governments elected and run by the political parties. The obstacles—senior statesmen, peers, Privy Council, military—were real, and this meant that tremendous effort had to be expended in wresting final authority from those groups. The memoirs of the veteran politician Ozaki Yukio, a man who won reelection continuously from 1890 to 1953, illustrate this; he conceived it his duty to try to oust every cabinet as long as they were selected from behind the scenes; only so could constitutional government become a reality. Since it was the emperor who had granted the constitution, moreover, this was the people's right, and any obstruction of it by elements claiming to represent the emperor was in violation of the imperial pledge. The widespread popular support for the "protect the constitution" movements of 1912–1913 and 1924, when Katsura and Kiyoura cabinets seemed a clear contravention of "constitutional government," shows that this view had spread beyond the circle of politicians.

This in turn led to demands for a wider, indeed a universal (manhood) suffrage to make it possible for the people's will to be known. The tax qualifications for voting rights at the outset of parliamentary government meant an electorate of approximately half a million males. Even before the end of the Meiji period efforts were under way to broaden this. A league to petition for universal manhood suffrage was first formed in 1897. It is interesting to see that from the very beginning its goals were preventive—heading off the social dislocation its leaders saw in Europe—and positive—the realization that popular opinion would count for more if there was more of it. As had been the case from the first days of Itagaki's petition in 1874, there were also implications for nationalism and foreign policy. Popular indignation against Japan's submission to the Triple Intervention would, the league's founders felt, have been more effective if it could have been expressed by ballot. The Hibiya riots of 1905 in opposition to the Portsmouth treaty showed the same potential.

A petition for universal manhood suffrage was first presented to the Diet in 1900, and bills calling for that step were introduced several times before the House of Representatives voted for such a measure by a narrow majority in 1911. The House of Peers refused to agree, thus killing the bill. "The extension of the suffrage and the strict enforcement of electoral laws," Professor Yoshino Sakuzō wrote in 1916, "are the most pressing matters facing Japan." As Japan found itself allied with democratic powers in World War I this view gained support, and by 1919 the Kenseikai had endorsed universal suffrage despite the opposition of the majority Seiyūkai. Tax qualifications for the vote had been lowered in 1900 (from fifteen yen to ten) and again in 1919 (to three yen), but it remained obvious that rural landowners were disproportionately advantaged in comparison with unpropertied urban workers.

In the years after World War I public expressions of support for universal suffrage seemed to wane, partly because significant numbers of urban work-ers—the most likely supporters of demonstrations—began distancing them-selves altogether from elective politics. This made the issue more urgent than ever to its proponents, who saw it as a way to stem the advance of radicalism. With the appearance of the Katō Takaaki coalition government in 1924 Kensei-kai supporters of universal manhood suffrage had their way, and the bill passed in 1925. The legislation had been drafted with care. Suffrage was limited to men, although by this time a women's suffrage movement had also been launched. The vote was restricted to males twenty-five years of age or over, but only if they had not been recipients of private or public welfare. In the years that followed reformers proposed lowering the age qualification, but no further action came until after Japan's surrender in 1945, when the Allied Occupation ordered the enfranchisement of all men and women.

Despite the shortcomings of the 1925 legislation, the change was the most important political achievement of the era and it proved successful and sig-nificant. Up to this point general elections had usually been called by cabinets newly installed in power, and the voters' discontent with the predecessor gov-ernment, combined with election "management" by patronage and money, produced a Diet majority for the newcomers. As a result elections functioned rather like plebiscites, and more often than not served to endorse the ruling cabinet.

The first election held under the new rules was called in 1928 by Prime Minister General Tanaka Gi'ichi, who clearly expected this tradition to con-tinue. The electorate had now quadrupled, from roughly 3.25 to 12.5 million. To Tanaka's surprise his government eked out only a narrow victory. His Seiyūkai won 219 seats, and the opposition Minseitō 217, with the remaining 30 seats going to splinter (24) and "proletarian" (6) candidates, who drew 190,000 votes.

What were the political parties? In one sense they were groups of profes-sional politicians, some of whom shifted back and forth with dismaying indif-ference to principle. Loyalty, name recognition, and habit could make some constituencies very safe for the incumbent. Ozaki Yukio on one occasion la-mented that Japan had no real parties, but only factions. Certainly he himself never stayed with a party very long, and he did organize his own faction for a time. On the other hand the parties were far from authoritarian, and even the Seiyūkai, in Hara's prime, had an elective board of councillors that dis-cussed important matters that were referred to it by the executive staff. The parties were no more subject to individual or personal hegemony than any other element of Japan's political pluralism. As the electorate grew in size and the parties became more powerful leadership, as has been noted, began to be drawn from men who had gained administrative skill in civil and military bureaucracies. Those individuals saw that the parties offered paths to influence and power, while parties, locked in their own struggles for power, looked to such outsiders as men who could lead them to political victory. The Seiyūkai's election of General Tanaka as its president provided a perfect example of this; he needed support for his political and foreign policy goals, while his new followers wanted a powerful advocate.

Hamaguchi Osachi (1870–1931), the last Minseitō premier, provides an example. Born in a remote Tosa village in 1870, he became an adoptive son of a Hamaguchi family in 1889, graduated from the Imperial University in 1895, and stood for the examinations for the Ministry of Finance. He advanced rapidly, heading tax offices in various parts of the country. In 1917 he resigned to enter the Dōshikai at the recommendation of Gotō Shinpei, whom we first encountered as a young doctor sent to watch over Itagaki, and who went on to a varied career as diplomat, administrator, and empire builder. Hamaguchi first stood for election (from a Tosa district) in 1915, held subcabinet posts in the Ōkuma administration, and emerged as minister of finance under Katō Takaaki in 1924. Under Katō's successor, Wakatsuki, he was appointed minister of home affairs. By now he was a recognized party and governmental leader and the logical head when the Kenseikai reorganized as the Minseitō in 1927. When the Tanaka government fell Hamaguchi received the imperial command to form a cabinet, in the process becoming the first prime minister to have been born in Tosa, where the democratic movement had first begun. Japan's was not a system that produced or required silver-voiced orators— Hamaguchi's Tosa constituency was remote and small—but it could produce men of courage and ability.

One might have thought that universal manhood suffrage would stir great enthusiasm. The prospect did activate the crowds during the 1912 governmental crisis, and it was an announced goal of the second "Protect the Constitution" movement in 1924. It was a subject on which many could agree, from left-wing leaders who retained hope for democratic reforms to right-wing leaders who were confident that popular support for a strong foreign policy would help swing Japan out of its internationalist pose. But there were also opponents. Yoshino Sakuzō could write in 1916 that "among many Japanese intellectuals there is an incredible misunderstanding of and violent antipathy to universal suffrage." Among urban workers enthusiasm was high for a time, but it waned as the climate of opinion became more radical. For other groups disaffection with Japanese politics, from behind-the-scenes control to political corruption, led not so much to enthusiasm for reformist candidates as to withdrawal into privatism, a trend that will be discussed below. And no doubt for even the most optimistic the speed with which the Tanaka government moved against liberals and the left after its setback in the 1928 election, and the way it crushed the incipient proletarian parties, must have served to weaken faith in the effectiveness of the popular voice and mandate.

Despite this the achievements of political party cabinets deserve respect. Each strong prime minister—Hara, Katō Takaaki, Hamaguchi—showed a willingness to try the issue of civil-military relations, Hara after the Washington Conference, Katō in military retrenchment by four divisions, and Hamaguchi after the London Conference. Unhappily each died in office; two by assassination, and Katō from natural causes. Each of the three also showed awareness of the need for changes in the power structure if Japan was to follow what seemed to be the world currents of postwar democracy. These measures would have required changes in the powers and makeup of the House of Peers and of the Privy Council, both of which lagged behind liberal and even moderate opinion. Liberalism and democracy also required a willingness to treat Japan's two new monarchs as constitutional kings rather than "living gods" as chauvinists of the 1930s preferred.

At the end of the decade the appearance of the Hamaguchi government offered hope for the realization of goals that intellectuals like Yoshino Sakuzō had set out a decade earlier. Before the Minseitō came to power a "shadow cabinet" had mapped out a striking agenda that included legislation for reforming labor-management relations, improving tenant-farmer relations, extending the vote to women in local elections, and lowering the voting age. In foreign affairs the return of the career diplomat Shidehara Kijūrō to the Foreign Ministry seemed to promise a firm commitment to international cooperation and reason in relations with China, which was beginning to experience national (and nationalist) unity after two decades of intermittent civil war. Unfortunately a combination of economic disaster and military insubordination combined to defeat that program, and Hamaguchi's death at the hands of an assassin in 1931 marked the end of an era. For all its shortcomings, it had brought significant change.

2. Japan in World Affairs

After the Russo-Japanese War Japan was the strongest power in Asia. In the next two decades it increased its stature and emerged as one of the five Great Powers, with a permanent seat on the Council of the League of Nations. It was not long before this remarkable transformation had led to an equally remarkable change in world, and especially Asian, perception of Japan. Meiji Japan had projected the image of a young, vigorous country determined to free itself from restrictions imposed by imperialist powers, but it went on to impose its own colonialism on Taiwan, Korea, and South Manchuria. The disruption of the international order during World War I brought tantalizing possibilities. Some Japanese wanted their country to serve as a role model in reviving East Asian reform and reconstruction; others continued to hold the West as a model for national expansion. As Japan's Meiji leaders aged, the polity they had created also began to seem curiously old-fashioned in a world intent on self-determination, international cooperation, and popular participation. Throughout the world monarchy and empire came crashing down; Ottoman Turkey, Germany, Austria-Hungary, Russia, and imperial China all broke up within a decade. One cannot fault Japan's leaders for finding it difficult to respond to such cataclysmic changes in the world order. In some cases it is possible to contrast the advocates of a "small Japan" to those of a "big Japan," but most Japanese were more ambivalent, intent on the dignity and importance their country should be accorded, but uncertain how best to cope with new challenges they faced in Asia.

"CHINA FIRST"

The problem of China was clearly uppermost. Its imperial polity, which had endured for centuries, dissolved under the attacks of imperialism, governmental incompetence, and some of the bloodiest insurrections of modern history. Throughout history Japan's stability had been related to that of China; secure from invasion from the mainland and protected by its Pacific remoteness, Japan had flourished in peace. The violence of fifteenth- and sixteenth-century Japan was related to the disintegration of Ming rule and uncertainty about the intentions of the new Manchu regime, and the Western incursion against China in the Opium War had created the crisis that brought forth the Meiji Restoration. Meiji Japan drew on imperial China for some of its institutions; the identity of the era with the monarch, the development of civil service examinations, and the grandiose imperial pronouncements with their normative and moral thrust all had their roots in Chinese precedent.[9] When, at the end of the nineteenth century, it seemed possible that European powers might partition China, Japanese statesmen and opinion leaders had warned of the importance of "preserving China." The Japanese victory over Russia, and the diversion of European attention to the mutual destruction in World War I, created a new situation. Reform-minded Chinese statesmen and eager Chinese students saw in the example of Japan a lesson for their country.

During the late Meiji decades a number of idealistic Japanese felt it their country's destiny and their personal responsibility to work for reform and revival in China. Many had political roots in the Freedom and People's Rights

Movement, and held a rather naive view of a China that would respond to the finest in Meiji modernization. They believed passionately in the urgency of revitalizing the Asian tradition and saw China's restoration as central to this. Some wanted Japan to lead, while others sought only to serve in what they saw as a turning point in history.

Miyazaki Tōten (Torazō, 1870–1922) can serve as an example of this determination. He was born in Kumamoto, where his early schooling included a period in the private academy set up by Tokutomi Sohō. This brought a heady exposure to half-understood theories of Western democracy and revolution. A period of spiritual wandering in Tokyo found him a Christian convert, until, astonished by the competitive jealousy of rival missionaries, he turned his attention to the "salvation of Asia." He and a brother set out to enter Chinese society and find a hero to whose work they could commit their lives. He became acquainted with the Korean reformer Kim Ok-kyun, worked with commercially recruited Japanese immigrants to Thailand in hopes of encountering China there, and ultimately found his hero in Sun Yat-sen, who had taken refuge in Japan after an unsuccessful revolt timed to coincide with the Japanese victory over Manchu China in 1895. Now came immersion in the wanderings and plots of Chinese revolutionaries in Southeast Asia (where the suspicious British authorities locked him up in Singapore), recruiting arms and money for Sun Yat-sen wherever they could be found in Japan, and then devoted service in the cause of revolt as Sun Yat-sen organized a revolutionary party (that would ultimately become the Kuomintang) among the thousands of Chinese students who poured into Tokyo in hopes of learning there the secrets of nationalism and revolution. Inukai Tsuyoshi, at that time an Ōkuma lieutenant, patronized him to learn what was going on in China, and Japanese army figures—some with less than altruistic purposes—helped him find weapons. Miyazaki had full power of attorney for Sun Yat-sen's organizations, gloried in his hero's successes, and despaired at his reverses. He and his fellow activists saw themselves as the idealists (shishi) of a new and greater, Asia-wide, Meiji Restoration, and their Chinese friends (who, like Sun, often posed as Japanese on travels on the fringe of China) had no doubt of their idealism and sincerity. The thousands of Chinese students who came to Tokyo after the Russo-Japanese War (in what was one of the modern world's first large-scale student migrations) offered an unprecedented opportunity for cultural exchange and future political friendship.[10]

JAPAN FIRST

The "China rōnin," as they have become known, were on the fringes of the Japanese political structure. Senior and more powerful Japanese felt their country was achieving its goals the European way, through compromise with the West and empire in Asia. They were more intent on claiming and safe-guarding privilege than they were in sponsoring liberation. Sun Yat-sen was quietly encouraged (and funded) to leave Japan. The gains Japan had scored at Shimonoseki and Portsmouth were secured against nationalist recovery by a series of agreements. The Anglo-Japanese Alliance was renewed in 1905 and strengthened in 1907, agreements with Russia were worked out in 1907, 1910, 1912, and 1916, France came into line in 1907, and the United States (with the Root-Takahira Agreement) in 1908. Far from sponsoring change in the system that surrounded China, Japan was making every effort to perpetuate it. In each of these agreements Japan received assurance that its "special position" would be recognized, and it in turn had no intention of challenging the impe-rialist order from which it now stood to benefit. As Hata Ikuhiko puts it, advocates of "Greater Japan" were winning out over those of a "Lesser Ja-pan,"[11] and the Tokyo government had little confidence in plans enthusiastic amateurs were working out for the "revival of Asia."

Revolution broke out in China in October of 1911, and within weeks the world's oldest imperial polity collapsed. The faltering Manchu regime turned to the leader of its modern Peiyang Army, Yüan Shih-k'ai, for help, but that worthy instead counseled surrender to the revolution and abdication for the infant emperor, later known to the West as Henry Pu Yi. That done, Yüan negotiated a settlement with the revolutionaries that brought him to power as first president of the Chinese Republic.

Yüan was anathema to Japan because of the role he had played holding off Japanese advances in Korea, and he soon made himself equally unpopular with the Chinese revolutionaries by violence that removed important leaders from the scene. The Saionji government opted for caution. Liberal supporters of the revolution were initially jubilant and did what they could to provide the revolutionaries with supplies of arms, but as the larger drama unfolded they were helpless to affect it. Japanese military figures oscillated between support for cooperative international moves to restore order in China and quiet sponsorship of more adventurous steps. The aging Yamagata felt that the West was ultimately hostile to Japan and that it therefore behooved Japan to cultivate good relations with China. "Manchuria," however, the term Japa-nese used for the Manchu homeland in the three northeastern provinces, was another matter. When it was clear that Manchu power would collapse, Yama-gata felt that Saionji's caution had missed a "God-given opportunity" to ex-pand Japan's sphere in northeastern China by consolidating its privileges there. Other army officers sponsored small-scale efforts to expand Japan's continental power in several attempts to set up pro-Japanese "autonomous" regimes in Manchuria and Mongolia. The army General Staff, led by General Tanaka Gi'ichi who would later head the Seiyūkai, thought it urgent to expand the military in a time of crisis and maneuvered Saionji's ouster over the war minister's demand for two additional divisions. The reemergence of Katsura in the Taishō political crisis has already been described. What needs to be noted is the speed with which instability in China reverberated in Japan to complicate politics and policies that were already in transition from the control exerted by the council of *genrō*.

By the summer of 1913 discontent with Yüan's regime led to a "second revolution" in which Sun Yat-sen's partisans tried and failed to unhorse the Peking government. More serious for Yüan, provincial governors and military leaders in all parts of China signaled their discontent. Events had moved from centralization to provincial rule and from civilian hands to military figures who would later be known as "warlords." Sun Yat-sen was soon back in Japan, more desperately in need of Japanese assistance than ever before, and more likely to seek help wherever it could be found.

This was still unsettled when war broke out in Europe. Ōkuma Shigenobu was prime minister, and Minister of Foreign Affairs Katō Takaaki was the chief formulator of Japanese policy. Japan was committed by the Anglo-Japanese Alliance to join the allies, but was not inclined to participate in areas where its interests were not involved. Some destroyer-escorts were sent to do duty in the Mediterranean, but otherwise Japan limited its contribution to seizure of German holdings in the Chinese province of Shantung, occupation of German-held islands in the South Pacific, and sweeping Eastern waters clear of German raiders.

The "Twenty-one Demands" came out of this setting. There was first of all the refusal to treat what was perceived as a rogue government under Yüan Shih-k'ai with trust and cooperation; it seemed essential to tie things down while the opportunity was at hand. Second, the South Manchuria leases taken over from Russia in 1905 had a limited time to run, and if they were to be properly exploited they needed to be extended. Third, although the concessions taken from the Germans in Shantung province were destined for an "ultimate return" to China, the details and dates of that return were not yet clear, and meanwhile it seemed important to have formal Chinese approval of Japanese management. Fourth, Yawata, Japan's first iron and steel complex, which had been financed with the Chinese indemnity, had proved dependent on Chinese raw material since it came on stream in 1901. Japanese industrialists wanted to firm up commercial relations with the Hanyehp'ing works at Hankow, and hoped for joint, Sino-Japanese control of those resources. Fifth, China was to promise not to make further grants of rights to third powers.

Each of these five points was summed up in a separate group and transmitted to the Peking foreign office with suggestions of confidentiality. The last, fifth, group was something of a grab-bag wish list of items that had been added after it was known that negotiations were in the offing. Technically they were only "requests" and not "demands"; nevertheless they would have added up to substantial infractions of Chinese sovereignty, and went so far as to suggest employment of Japanese advisers responsible for aspects of finance and administration.

The Ōkuma-Katō government bungled badly in its tactics. Its representatives were overbearing and even insulting to Chinese sensitivities, and dishonest in their bland denials to other interested powers. Years later the Chinese Republic continued to withhold its approval for Japanese diplomats involved when Japan proposed sending them as emissaries. The Chinese, in contrast, had a good case, a youthful administration that had the enthusiastic support of Western, particularly American, representatives, and handled their case adroitly. In Tokyo Foreign Minister Katō tried to keep matters in his own hands, but as the Chinese rallied foreign opinion to their side the indignant *genrō,* who had been kept out of things, insisted on acquainting themselves with the details and did what they could to salvage practical gains and national prestige. In the end the Tokyo government issued an ultimatum that secured Chinese agreement, but omitted Group V altogether. The day of China's final capitulation became memorialized as a "National Humiliation Day" in China.

World War I had diverted the attention of the European powers, but that was not the case with the United States, still at peace, and inclined to welcome the developments of "young China," which was, many thought, the product of American missionary and education work. This was particularly true of President Woodrow Wilson and his secretary of state William Jennings Bryan. Wilson's minister to China, Paul Reinsch, worked closely with the Chinese. Bryan issued a stern warning that the United States would not recognize any actions that "violated Chinese sovereignty," a formula that Secretary of State Stimson would revive after the establishment of Manchukuo in 1933. Japan thus gained its minimal objectives during World War I, but at considerable cost. It had lost whatever opportunity there was to exert leadership in China, and it had awakened—or, for some, confirmed—distrust of its policies in the United States. In the final period of the war Japan joined the United States, England, and France in sending troops to Siberia; the motives announced were different in each country, but ultimately were anti-Bolshevik. There was widespread suspicion that the Japanese units, which were far larger than the others committed there, were designed to seize and hold an area in eastern

Siberia, and they did in fact remain there until 1922, long after the other nations had withdrawn their forces.[12]

MARCH 1 AND MAY 4, 1919

The image of Japan that was held by its Asian neighbors suffered lasting damage at the end of World War I. The hopes of Chinese liberals, not to say revolutionaries, declined as Japan pursued Great Power politics in the matter of the Twenty-one Demands. Japan's intervention in Siberia was motivated in part by fears that Bolshevism might spread south of the Amur River border, and the Terauchi government invested substantial sums of money (the "Nishihara loans") in efforts to stabilize the northern border by backing conservative northern military leaders. The "modern" forces equipped in response were however soon crushed in the civil wars that now began to plague China. But nothing did damage to compare with the suppression of the March 1 independence demonstration in Korea and the May 4 demonstrations in China.

In the aftermath of the Allied victory in World War I there was widespread hope throughout Asia—certainly among students and intellectuals—that a new and more just world order was at hand. Some of this was poignant and naive, as in rumors in Korea that Woodrow Wilson would appear to restore the country's sovereignty, but a more literate generation in China had every reason to expect that bases seized from the Germans would be returned by the Japanese. The Twenty-one Demands had shown this would not be simple, but the Paris conference, Treaty of Versailles, and League of Nations might still correct this matter, as indeed Wilson had hoped they would. Unfortunately the Japanese, having been forced to abandon their demand for a statement of racial equality at Versailles, were in no mood to give way on matters of economic and territorial interest to them, and in this they had the support of agreements they had worked out with their European allies.

Korean nationalist leaders were equally distressed that the League and the war settlement contained nothing for them, and resolved on a nonviolent demonstration calling for national independence on March 1, 1919. The date was set to coincide with funeral ceremonies for the last King/Emperor Kojong, who was regarded as a martyr to his country's independence. Representatives of major religious communicates had been planning an appeal to the outside world since 1918, and the funeral date found Seoul crowded with mourners in white attire. The leaders signed their declaration of independence and waited quietly to be arrested. Japanese colonial authorities were startled and responded with extraordinary brutality and fury. Japanese records admit to some 500 killed and 1,500 wounded, but post-Independence Korean estimates run far higher, to more than 7,000 killed and 145,000 wounded. As late as the

1980s Japanese textbook references to the slaughter of nonviolent protesters as the suppression of "riots" poisoned relations between Japan and Korea.[13]

These events drew protests throughout the world, but also affected Japan, where they provided fuel for antimilitarist sentiment. The Hara Seiyūkai cabinet moved to lessen the authority of the army in selecting colonial administrators and setting policy, and a "policy of culture" *(bunka seisaku)* tried to undo some of the harm the pointless violence had caused. Despite this the handling of the Independence declaration remained as a stain on Japanese rule and an ugly refutation of Japanese rhetoric of leadership in Asian modernity.

Japan fared only slightly better in Chinese opinion. Two months after the Korean independence movement was suppressed, the May 4 demonstrations marked the dawn of modern Chinese nationalism. The cause was disillusion that the peace treaty signed at Versailles had no provision for the return of the German concessions in Shantung to China, but left them in Japanese hands. The Chinese officials who were blamed for accepting the Paris accord became objects of popular fury in Peking. Everywhere in China the discovery that Chinese hopes had been betrayed produced great demonstrations, and in May students from thirteen colleges and universities gathered to denounce the treaty and then converged on the residence of Ts'ao Ju-lin, a minister who was considered pro-Japanese, and put him to flight. The "May Fourth movement" is taken as shorthand for the larger cultural revolt against tradition and conformity. The birth and growth of the Chinese Communist Party took place in the atmosphere of alienation from Chinese society and culture of those years. What matters for the purposes of this discussion is that Japan, which had been for a time the seedbed of the Chinese revolution and the exemplar of a modern national response to the threat posed by the West, was now coming to be seen as the single most important element of the imperialist threat that China faced. Complementary vibrations between anti-Japanese demonstrations in China and Japanese disrespect for China contained ominous potential for future disputes.

Fortunately these events were not by any means the sum total of Chinese-Japanese and Korean-Japanese interaction of the interwar period. Relations were too close, too complex, and too varied to be summed up in a single rubric of nationalist distaste. Japanese men of letters who traveled to China could find themselves warmly welcomed, and Chinese students trained in Japan could bring back equally warm memories of friendly and helpful teachers. Even in Korea, where the wounds were greatest and most personal, the interwar years saw the development of a new generation of students oriented to Japanese institutions and opportunities, and entrepreneurs eager to cooperate with Japanese enterprises in bringing modern institutions to Korea.[14] The fact that such contacts and emotions could survive should probably be seen as measure of how great the opportunity for solidarity and friendship in East Asia might have been if it had not been weakened by Japanese imperialism.

Japan occupied a place of honor in the new League of Nations, which now replaced the Anglo-Japanese Alliance in Japanese diplomacy. It was a mark of Japan's growing status that Nitobe Inazō, the Sapporo student and Tokyo educator we have encountered earlier, was named under secretary-general, thereby symbolizing an era of internationalism. A new generation of intellectuals, teachers, and students shared fully in the worldwide hope that this new era would find Japan taking its rightful place at world conference tables.

Others, and perhaps most, of the Meiji generation found the new international order badly flawed and regretted that in the absence of the Anglo-Japanese Alliance there was no secure special place for Japan. Even so optimistic and committed and internationalist as Nitobe noted that the new League of Nations might be of little help in addressing the problems of Asia. He pointed out that neither the United States nor the Soviet Union, Japan's most important neighbors, were members, and that the organization provided a forum for the weak and querulous that seemed to limit the influence of Japan, which was the only major power in Asia.[15] Even before this, however, there had been voices urging caution before subscribing to an Anglo-American view of the world.

Konoe Fumimaro (1891–1945), scion of Japan's most distinguished aristocratic house and descendant of the Fujiwaras, was invited by Saionji Kinmochi to accompany him to the Paris Peace Conference. To Saionji's consternation the young prince, who had recently graduated from the Philosophy Faculty of Kyoto Imperial University, published a short essay in which he voiced his misgiving about the prospect of an "Anglo-American peace." He raised the distinction between "have" and "have-not" powers. The Western allies now so intent on peace, he pointed out, already had everything they wanted and were chiefly interested in sustaining the status quo. It was easy for them to blame everything on German aggression, for that had come later than their own. A disconcerted Saionji warned the young man to keep his views to himself, but the fact is that many Japanese were full of doubts about the benefits of the new international system. Doubts had already been raised by nationalists about the benefits of the Anglo-Japanese Alliance, but the new organization seemed to remove from Japan whatever protection that alliance had conveyed. It was not that much could be expected of the old alliance in the future, for the increasingly close cooperation between the United States and Great Britain raised doubts about the utility of the English alliance. It was clear that Britain would not support Japan in a possible struggle with the United States, but it was also clear that Japan lacked the strength to challenge both powers.

Other voices resisted this parochialism and spoke for internationalism, and the Washington Conference on naval limitations was one result. First, and most important, was the fact that all participating nations had embarked on massive programs of naval buildup during the war; none could sustain these in peace, but each needed the assurance that limitations on building would not disadvantage it in future competition. Second, the Anglo-Japanese Alliance came up for renewal or replacement in 1922. It was obvious that Britain would never join Japan in a war against the United States, and therefore some new structure of security was required to replace it. And finally the turbulent state of Chinese politics made it incumbent on the powers to agree on cooperative steps in dealing with the floundering Chinese republic. Military equipment, so recently plentiful in Europe, was now flooding into Asia. There was thus every reason to convene a conference to address these problems.

Ozaki Yukio, a confirmed political maverick, had returned from a postwar trip to Europe convinced that security could not be maintained without a cooperative agreement for arms retrenchment. A motion he filed in the House of Representatives was defeated by a crushing vote, but he then took the issue to the people by traversing the country to address large audiences about disarmament. In a crude public opinion poll he distributed postcards at all his meetings, and of the 31,519 that were returned to him, 92 percent favored his proposals. Clearly many Japanese were in favor of international cooperation.

At the Washington Conference, Japan was represented by Ambassador to the United States Shidehara Kijūrō, Tokugawa Iesato, and Admiral Katō Tomosaburō. The conference produced a network of interrelated agreements that can be described as the "Washington Conference system"; it set the parameters of Pacific policy and security for the rest of the decade.

A Four Power Pact, with the United States and France included, replaced the Anglo-Japanese Alliance. Its members pledged themselves to respect the status quo in the Pacific and to consult if the security of any one power was threatened.

Naval limitation was at the center of the negotiations that followed. In Japan a "fleet faction" had advocated the construction of eight battleships and eight cruisers. The Anglo-American counterproposal was for a moratorium on all construction of capital ships—battleships and heavy cruisers—and adoption of a tonnage ratio of 10 for the United States and Great Britain to 6 for Japan. Japanese negotiators argued vainly for a 10/7 ratio, but accepted the smaller figure under the condition that substituted several newer ships for others to be decommissioned. The essential security for Japan, however, lay in the guarantee that additional bases would not be built in the Pacific Ocean sites, with exceptions made for Hawaii, Singapore, and Japan itself. Japan's fleet faction was discontented with this, but Admiral Katō's prestige was great enough to quiet vocal naval opponents (though not, it will be noted, Prime Minister Hara's assassin). These arms limitation agreements had no real precedent and seemed to bring an assurance of peace in the Pacific. It has to be remembered that they affected capital ships only, and that the extension of this to smaller ships at the London Conference in 1930 was far more rancorous. Aircraft carriers were still things of the future and not regulated, but the Japanese, who had more confidence in the future of air power, managed to refit several battleships under construction and slated for "scrapping" as aircraft carriers.

The last treaty signed, the Nine Power Treaty, was designed to protect Chinese sovereignty. The powers profiting from "unequal treaties" with China pledged to respect China's territorial sovereignty, maintain the "Open Door" in trade, and cooperate in helping China achieve unity and stability.

In the early 1920s Japan moved to live up to the commitments it had made at Washington. The former German holdings in Shantung were returned to China. Japanese troops were withdrawn from Siberia and Northern Sakhalin, and under the leadership of Gotō Shinpei normalization of relations with the new Soviet government was worked out. Japan lived up to the commitments it had made with respect to naval limitations, and it was for some time a full participant in cooperative efforts to work out new tariff and customs arrangements for China. In each of these cases, however, opinion within Japan was far from united; Prime Minister Hara lost his life to an assassin, the armed services had factions that sought a larger army and navy, and some argued the case for expansion, but there were reasons to think that Japanese leaders would be able to see the advantages of the new international order.

THE IMMIGRATION IMBROGLIO

Arms agreements seldom survive distrust and suspicion, and the promise of the Washington agreements was soon marred by the resumption of immigration issues in the United States. The matter seemed to have been settled by the "gentlemen's agreement" (not unlike the "voluntary export restrictions" worked out for automobiles in the 1970s) in which the Japanese "voluntarily" restrained immigration. In the 1920s the issue came up once more. Nativist sentiments in the eastern United States had been raised by the scale of immigration from eastern and southeastern Europe, while in the west anti-Oriental agitation had led to a series of Alien Land Laws making it difficult for immigrants to own or even lease land. In 1922 the United States Supreme Court ruled that Japanese were ineligible for citizenship because of prior legislation. California had adopted an Alien Land Law in 1920, and similar legislation was quickly adopted by fifteen other states. All this set the stage for congressional legislation.

To understand the indignation with which Japanese greeted the Immigration Act of 1924 it is necessary to realize how unnecessary it was. Congress had adopted a quota system based on national origins in 1921; it was heavily weighted in favor of the countries of northern Europe, where quotas were so large that they were seldom filled. The baseline of residence for those quotas was 1910 (with 3 percent admissible); in 1923 the baseline was advanced to 1920, but the percentage lowered to 2 percent. One group now advocated moving the baseline back to 1890, reducing the Japanese quota to 246, but even that failed to satisfy nativists who wanted total exclusion. The legislation that emerged excluded immigrants ineligible for citizenship.

In an effort to prevent so egregious an affront to Japanese sensibilities, the secretary of state encouraged Japanese ambassador Hanihara to stress Japan's adherence to the gentleman's agreement. This he did, but ended his statement by expressing the fear that the proposed exclusion could have "grave consequences" on the otherwise happy relations between Japan and America. This phrase was then denounced by Senator Henry Cabot Lodge as a "veiled threat," and it virtually ensured passage of the act. The legislation was deplored by much of the American establishment and by major United States newspapers, but it did lasting damage to the influence of some of Japan's foremost internationalists. Nitobe Inazō, probably the most distinguished of these, vowed that he would not set foot on American soil until the offensive act was repealed, and went to considerable inconvenience in making his way to and from Geneva. Nitobe had dedicated his life to being a "bridge across the Pacific," but in this instance the bridge broke down.

THE EMERGENCE OF NATIONALIST CHINA

The Washington Conference system ultimately fell victim to disagreements among the powers over the proper response to the rise of Chinese nationalism. Japanese were divided on the issue, but its consequences for Japan were so far-reaching that the diplomatic policy adopted became a major issue in domestic politics.

There were reasons to expect a sympathetic response to Chinese nationalism in Japan. The two countries shared a commitment to East Asian civilization, and both had felt the injustice of the unequal treaties imposed by the

West. No country had more people in China, more China specialists, or more knowledge of Chinese culture and civilization than Japan. Unfortunately the "China first" men who had worked with Sun Yat-sen were outnumbered by others. Some prominent scholars argued that "China" was more civilization than nation, and that the Chinese, focused on family and village to the exclusion of nation and state, were unlikely to make the kind of response to the modern world that Japan had made. This was the contention of a best-selling work by a distinguished China specialist, Professor Naitō Konan, *Shina ron* (On China).[16] This position had only limited tolerance for the facts that Manchu rule, imperialist intervention, and foreign example had begun to produce a new generation of Chinese. The May Fourth movement with its advocates of democracy and science as alternatives to the Confucian tradition that had left China defenseless in the face of outside aggression was leading to a social and cultural revolution. There was also a political change, encouraged by Soviet example and backing that helped transform a small Nationalist Party (Kuomintang) at Canton into a potent force. A military school (headed by Chiang Kai-shek) with modern weapons and tactics was supplemented by programs to train propagandists and activists to work with Chinese workers and students.

In North China the major warlords destroyed themselves in suicidal conflicts that raged in 1924 and 1925.[17] In South China the Kuomintang and Communist groups merged in a national united front and prepared to seize on this opportunity by launching the "Northern Expedition" in 1926. When the troops reached Nanking, antiforeign feeling and disorganization resulted in a number of acts of violence against non-Chinese. Foreign Minister Shidehara came under attack for refusing to join other powers in countermeasures. Shortly after, when the Kuomintang forces reached Shanghai, Chiang Kai-shek turned on his Communist allies in a bloody coup; the left-wing survivors retreated to Wuhan—where they, too, soon dismissed their Soviet advisers—while Chiang Kai-shek prepared for advancing north to Peking and national unification.

This political turbulence in China had a direct impact on Japanese politics; China policy became a potent issue. Japan's failure to respond forcefully to the episodes in Nanking, it was charged, had weakened its prestige and honor. Shidehara, with an eye to Japan's long-range relations with the commercial centers of central and southern China, stood firm. Chiang's break with the Communists in Shanghai seemed to bear out Shidehara's estimate of the Kuomintang promise, but the rival Seiyūkai had found an issue for attack.

Appropriately, the attack was led by a war hero and senior general who had resigned from the army in 1925 at the request of Seiyūkai leaders that he lead them out of the political wilderness. General Tanaka Gi'ichi (1864–1929) had served in Russia and considered himself an authority on Japan's northern border. During the Russo-Japanese War he had provided help for a bandit leader, Chang Tso-lin. As imperial unity gave way to provincial warlords Chang was to emerge as the strongest force in Northeast China thanks to his Fengtien Army, which enjoyed Japanese favor and occasional advice. Chang's proximity to Peking gave him a stake in national politics. Within Japan, Tanaka had been instrumental in the establishment of the nationwide network of reservist associations. He had served as army minister under Prime Minister Hara, and as Yamagata weakened—and died in 1922—he emerged as head of the "Chōshū faction" at army headquarters. Now, as head of the Seiyūkai, he brought with him an imposing set of qualifications to head a government. In 1927 a bank crisis (which will be discussed below) was responsible for the fall of a Kenseikai government and left a political vacuum into which Tanaka led his Seiyūkai.

A month after Tanaka took office, he ordered the transfer of Japanese forces to Tsinan in Shantung in order to protect the lives of Japanese residents—and, incidentally, deter Chiang Kai-shek's progress north to Peking. The situation was full of ambiguities. Some civilians and diplomats thought it wise to prevent the sort of attacks that had been directed against Japanese in Nanking earlier, while Tanaka's successors in the General Staff were unenthusiastic about risking involvement in continental politics. As yet no lasting harm had been done, and before long the Japanese troops were withdrawn. Chiang Kai-shek (who had been trained in Japan) resigned his political offices temporarily and traveled to Tokyo for talks with Tanaka. Both men thought they had reached an understanding. Chiang pointed out that it was important for Japan to avoid the appearance of support for the northern warlords, while Tanaka emphasized the need for Chiang to maintain an anti-Communist position and concentrate on political stability in central and southern China.

This was all well and good, but Chiang's Northern Expedition was soon headed for Peking again. That city was temporarily under the control of Chang Tso-lin, who, like all the major warlords, saw himself as head of a national government. If things were allowed to take their natural course, and Chiang's Northern Expedition defeated the Fengtien Army and Chang Tso-lin was unhorsed, it could be anticipated that Chiang Kai-shek's forces would follow him over the mountain pass that separated the Manchurian province of Fengtien from Peking. Japan would then face a Nationalist presence in an area it considered vital to its interests. Even Foreign Minister Shidehara, internationalist that he was, had made a distinction between Manchuria and China; Tanaka, militarist that he was, thought that it was essential to have Chang Tso-lin in Manchuria as a buffer against Chinese nationalism.

In the summer of 1927 Tanaka convened a Far East Conference of Foreign Ministry, Ministry of Finance, and army, navy, and General Staff representatives to try to work out Japanese priorities. One of the unexpected results of this gathering was a spurious document that became known as the "Tanaka Memorial," which purported to lay out a program of systematic expansion in China. Its origins have never been fully traced, but theories about its authorship have ranged from Chinese Communists to Japanese critics of Tanaka. Unfortunately the document proved in some sense prophetic of future Japanese moves, and thus, understandably, contributed to belief in its authenticity.

In contrast to a plan for expansion the conference produced a welter of conflicting opinions. In the end a rough consensus emerged to the effect that the emerging Kuomintang regime was likely to meet Japan's standards for a stable and non-Communist government that Japan would be able to work with, but also that the Chinese should be assured that Japan would support Chang Tso-lin's efforts to hold on to his position in Manchuria. To Tanaka, this meant getting Chang Tso-lin out of Peking and out of harm's way beyond the mountainous barrier to Manchuria lest the Kuomintang forces pursue him there.[18]

This danger was soon at hand. When Chiang Kai-shek returned to China he resumed command of the Northern Expedition and prepared to move on Peking. In December 1927 Tanaka decided that the possibility of conflict in the area made it wise to send troops to Shantung again to protect Japanese nationals and Japanese interests. He hoped that if he sent them to Tsingtao they would be out of Chiang Kai-shek's path of advance, while nevertheless available if needed. The division commander thought he knew better, however, and moved to Tsinan as the northern forces retreated. As might have been expected, a clash between Japanese and Chinese Nationalist forces broke out in May. Attempts for local settlement of whatever had prompted the clash failed when the Japanese military decided the national honor was at stake; when the Chinese would not accept the demands they made, Japanese troops occupied Tsinan. The Japanese now took over the area, imposed martial law, and held on until 1929.

Worse was to come. After Chang Tso-lin agreed to vacate Peking and return to his capital in Mukden, staff officers of the Japanese Kwantung Army, which had the mission of security for the Liaotung (Port Arthur and Dairen) Peninsula and South Manchurian Railroad, decided the time was ripe to precipitate a crisis that would, they thought, force their superiors to take steps to seize control of Manchuria instead of continuing to work with Chang

Tso-lin. Within the Japanese military there was increasing talk of a "China problem" and a "Manchuria and Mongolia problem." Impatient and restless young military officers thought they had the opportunity to hurry history. Colonel Kōmoto Daisaku arranged to have the railway car in which Chang Tso-lin was riding blown up as his train was entering Manchuria. Kōmoto's hope that higher echelons would respond to take advantage of his rash act proved misplaced; there was no follow-up. Chang Tso-lin's son took over command of his father's Fengtien Army, and after his position was stabilized, announced his commitment to the new Kuomintang government that had been set up in Peking. Chiang Kai-shek, in turn, designated him commander of the "Northeastern Frontier" Army. For Japanese obsessed with the "Manchurian-Mongolian problem," things were if anything worse than they had been before Chang Tso-lin's departure from the scene in June of 1928.

THE EMPEROR AND THE GENERAL

Prime Minister Tanaka himself, however, was in trouble. The government had announced that the cause of the explosion that killed Chang Tso-lin was an as yet unsolved act of terrorism, but opposition Diet members wanted to know how this could have happened in an area guarded by Japanese troops, and demanded an investigation. More serious, the young Emperor Hirohito asked Tanaka what had happened. Tanaka promised to look into the matter and punish the perpetrators if it turned out that army men were involved. When Tanaka tried to keep that promise, however, he ran into opposition from his former army associates who now saw him as part of the political establishment; they insisted that disciplining Kōmoto would do irreparable damage to the image of the Imperial Army and compromise Japan's position in continental and international affairs. Better by far, they thought, to cover things up.

Tanaka thus was unable to keep his promise to the emperor. To his astonishment and dismay, Hirohito took him sharply to task. He resigned in July 1929 and died soon after. The incident took its toll on Hirohito as well as Tanaka. Shortly after World War II, when it still seemed possible he would be charged as a war criminal, the emperor dictated some recollections to palace officials. In these he described his dismissal of Tanaka as a pivotal event in his understanding of the limits of his personal role. As he put it,

> Tanaka again came to me and said he would like to settle the matter by hushing it up. Well, then, I answered in an angry tone, what you say now is completely different from what you said before. Don't you think you ought to resign?

Soon complaints were making the rounds to the effect that unnamed senior statesmen were acting like a behind-the-scenes palace cabal; senior advisers took alarm and remonstrated with the emperor about what his role should be. He continued,

> I now think it was my youthful indiscretion that led me to talk that way. In any case, I expressed myself in those terms. Whereupon Tanaka submitted his resignation and the Tanaka cabinet resigned en masse. According to what I heard, Kōmoto said that if he was put before a court-martial and interrogated, he would have revealed everything about Japan's plot. So, I understand that the military court martial was canceled . . . Ever since this incident, I resolved to approve every report that the cabinet laid before me although I personally might hold an opposite opinion.[19]

It will be seen from this that Kōmoto was not acting alone, and that the murder of Chang Tso-lin expressed the wish for direct action that came three years later.

"RENOUNCING WAR AS A SOVEREIGN RIGHT"
During all this Tanaka was in trouble on another front. This discussion has brought out some of the differences between the Seiyūkai and Minseitō, usually to the latter's advantage. But the Minseitō members were also politicians who needed public support, and in 1928 they took a leaf from their opponents' book to charge Tanaka with derogation of the imperial prerogative. It is worth tracing the dispute over the Kellogg-Briand Pact, because the wording at issue returned in the postwar Japanese constitution as Article 9, in which "the Japanese people forever renounce war as a sovereign right of the nation."

The Kellogg-Briand Pact had its origins in negotiations between the French foreign minister Aristide Briand and United States secretary of state Frank Kellogg about an agreement to renounce war as an instrument of national policy. What began as a plan for a bilateral agreement became a convention between sixty-two countries, including all the major powers, that their governments, "in the names of their respective peoples," would outlaw war "as an instrument of national policy." Japan, represented at what became the Pact of Paris by Count Uchida Yasuya, was one of the original fifteen signatories. For a time it seemed clear that this commitment would win universal approval.

The rival Minseitō, however, still smarting from its treatment at the hands of Seiyūkai nationalists, launched an attack that the phrase "in the names of their respective peoples" was a violation of *kokutai* and an unconstitutional infringement of the emperor's prerogative to make war and declare peace.

Elements of the right-wing press supported this, but responsible commentators endorsed the proposal and realized that Japan would suffer in world opinion if an agreement endorsed by its representative at Paris failed to receive endorsement by the Imperial Diet. Nothing daunted, the opposition carried the battle to the Privy Council, and particularly its deeply conservative president Itō Miyoji.[20] After heated debate in the Privy Council the pact was ratified with the declaration

> The Imperial Government declares that the phraseology "in the names of their respective peoples" appearing in Article I of the Treaty for the Renunciation of War . . . viewed in the light of the provisions of the Imperial Constitution, is understood to be inapplicable in so far as Japan is concerned.[21]

Uchida, who would reemerge in the 1930s as a hard-liner, resigned in protest in response to all this; he felt it called into question his own role as negotiator and damaged the prestige of his country. After the matter was resolved the Minseitō returned to power and Shidehara Kijūrō took over the Foreign Ministry again.

The Pact of Paris affected Japanese history in two ways in later years. First, when the International Tribunal convened after World War II to render judgment on Japan's war responsibility, it ruled that the Kellogg-Briand Pact had made aggressive war illegal, and consequently a nation's leaders could be brought to justice for planning such a war.

The second, however, is of greater importance. In 1946 a group of American officers was convened in General Douglas MacArthur's headquarters to prepare a new constitution for Japan. One of the few specific instructions the general gave them in handwritten notes was that the document should prescribe a pacifist polity. Uncertain how to word this, they resorted to the Pact of Paris and used its wording for Article 9 and the renunciation of war. No provision of that document has generated more discussion and debate than these famous phrases renouncing war as a sovereign right, which earned the document the description "Peace Constitution."

3. Economic Change

The Japanese economy was transformed during the interwar years. The institutional changes of the Meiji period had prepared the way; many changes had been made in advance of the necessity for them. The banking structure, for instance, was complete by 1900. There were hundreds of small banks formed by public subscription that served the needs of ordinary citizens. Organized on the lines of public stock companies and among the first institutions to use Western business methods, these banks played an important role in daily life. There were others, however, government directed, that were established to meet the needs of future imperial expansion. These included the Industrial Bank. Like the Fifteenth (Peers') Bank established to provide access to and direction for the generous financial settlements made with daimyo after the abolition of the domains, these could guarantee profitable returns on items of national importance like railroad and shipbuilding development. What was distinctive about Japan's modern economic growth was that it not only took place without jeopardizing the traditional economy, but benefited from it. Unlike colonial economies in India or Indonesia in which unfinished goods were exported in exchange for consumer goods that had previously been produced by traditional means, Japan continued domestic production for domestic use. This had been foreshadowed by a lengthy "Report on Manufactures" (Kōgyō iken) worked out by Maeda Masana in 1884, a document that has been compared to Alexander Hamilton's proposals in the early United States. Imports, he argued, should be restricted to items essential for Japan's growing strength, while traditional manufacturers, suitably improved and modified to fit the contemporary scene, should provide the needs of the populace. Until the Russo-Japanese War, only a modest proportion of Japan's workers—perhaps for the most part those in the government, security, and education— were employed in the "modern" sector. It grew rapidly, to be sure, but its growth was made possible by the much larger number of workers involved in small enterprises utilizing traditional methods. As late as 1910, 87 percent of cloth looms were still hand powered.[22] Modest and small-scale technological change proved more manageable than expensive imported machinery of the sort used in the early government-established mills, and because patterns of daily life changed little until the twentieth century the traditional sector was able to supply Japan's needs. Over one-third of workers employed in "factories" were in establishments that had no more than ten workers. This extended to the production of silk, preeminently a household product in which one in five farm families participated, but also "modern" export goods like matches. These could be produced by teams of households organized by manufacturers who borrowed from local banks to organize material and equipment; groups or teams of households worked separately to split the wood, dip the heads, make matchboxes, paste labels, and pack the final product. "The 'makers,'" E. Sydney Crawcour writes, "might employ several hundred people working in their own homes at rates of pay so low that often the whole family needed to work long hours to make a living."[23]

The two economies, traditional and modern, moved in tandem until at least the twentieth century. As the modern sector grew in size and importance its gains, and those for Japanese who worked in it, outsped those in the traditional sector, and the resulting pattern, often described as a "dual economy," characterized twentieth-century Japan until the economic growth that followed World War II.

Crawcour and other authorities suggest that Japan's economic growth differed from the sequence experienced by the early industrializers in the West because of the government's active role in favoring developments important to its "rich country, strong army" *(fukoku-kyōhei)* policy. Those priorities and goals were acceptable to most Japanese. A long view to future needs justified investment in enterprises that were initially unprofitable and frequently managed by ex-samurai government bureaucrats. Once the enterprises became profitable, however, there was no shortage of nonsamurai businessmen who saw opportunities and joined in. This was early the case with textiles, in which country girls recruited by agents were kept in factory dormitories and received treatment so harsh that many tried to run away.[24]

The government saw to it that trunk railway lines and arsenals were in its hands. More impressive is the pattern of administrative guidance provided to promote standardization, quality, and hence profitability. Village cooperatives, universal by 1914, spurred improvements in agronomy with short-maturing strains that permitted double cropping, communal seedbeds and planting in rows to permit improved tillage, massive increases in fertilization, and better paddy drainage. Trade associations were formed under government direction, first on a local, and then on a prefectural, and finally a national, basis. Throughout all this the links to traditional guidance previously provided by Tokugawa period guilds *(nakama)* and social organization were recognized and utilized.

After the Matsukata deflation of the 1880s Japan's economic growth included a number of cycles of downturn, but overall the trend was steadily favorable. Between 1886 and 1920 national output rose by a factor of six; thanks to the growth of population during the same period, however, per capita productivity averaged a more modest 1.8 percent annually. Moreover national (governmental) expenditure rose a good deal more rapidly than personal consumption, helping to account for the slow pace of change in daily life.

Each of the wars sparked an economic boom and government expenditures rose, as did wages. In each case the war economy gave way to a postwar recession as a slackening of demand coincided with continued high or higher military costs that were deemed necessary to provide for occupancy and security for the new territorial gains and to cover Japan's larger role in Asian and world affairs. There was never a "peace bonus" for the Japanese taxpayers.

The mood after the Sino-Japanese War was one of sullen resentment at the Triple Intervention (expressed in the phrase *gasshin shotan,* a reference to the hero's patient wait for revenge in a famous Chinese novel), but it was in part compensated for by the large indemnity exacted from China in the peace settlement. The government had tried repeatedly to get a Diet budget allocation for a steel plant, but without success. The needs of war finally brought approval, and the bulk of the Chinese indemnity was used to defray the cost of the Yawata steel plant, which marked an important step in heavy industry. The Yawata works came into operation in 1901. Even this, however, brought new needs, for as we have seen its dependence on imported coke and iron ore was reflected in the inclusion of China's Hanyehp'ing works at Wuhan in the Twenty-one Demands.[25] The Russo-Japanese War, however, produced no indemnity—that was why the Tokyo crowd was so indignant—and it was followed by even greater military costs in Korea and South Manchuria and naval modernization. The government tried to counter this, it will be recalled, by the Local Improvement Movement and the emperor's injunctions to diligence and frugality.

Yet it would be an exaggeration to conclude, as some have, that the Japanese were victimized by the "rich country, strong army" slogan to inherit a poor country, strong army fate. Both wars speeded the growth of the modern sector dramatically. Japan was no longer dependent on outside suppliers of military and peacetime machinery. There were massive subsidies for ship and weapon production. During the war with Russia, some European shipyards that had provided warships for Japan pleaded neutrality, but Japan was increasingly able to proceed on its own. Of seventy-seven ships commissioned by the Imperial Navy between 1905 and 1915, all but seven were built in Japan. By 1914 Japan was one of only five countries (with France, Germany, England, and America) to be self-sufficient in the production of steam locomotives.

All this helped prepare Japan for the commercial opportunities offered by World War I, which was by far Japan's most profitable war. Its costs in lives and treasure were insignificant. The developed economies of the West were fully occupied in mutual destruction, unable even to exploit the colonial markets from which Japan had been excluded. Japan's modern sector was prepared to fill this gap. The balance of payments with the West, long dominated by loans contracted during the Russo-Japanese War, was rapidly reversed, and Japan's status changed from debtor to creditor. Japan's national product rose at a rate of 9 percent a year, growing more than 40 percent during the war. Iron and steel, vital areas in which Meiji Japan had been import-dependent, became profitable. Textiles grew apace and Japan was able to capitalize on arrangements built into the Treaty of Shimonoseki to expand investment and production in China, where Japanese-owned spindles increased tenfold.[26] Within Japan private investment in modern industry became more profitable than it had ever been, and the confidence and success of the new industrialists was symbolized by the establishment in 1917 of the Industrial Club, where the makers and shakers of the new economy met to dine, socialize, and plan.

There was now a shortage of labor. Wages rose steeply, and with them the general price level. Soaring costs of food, made worse by profiteering and speculation, were an important element in the outbreak of the rice riots of 1918. In industry there was a rapid rise in the use of electricity as a source of power, though the total remained modest by Western standards. In 1919, for instance, one-quarter of plants employing five to fourteen workers relied on electric power, but even so that represented a fourfold increase since 1914. "In contrast with the industries producing military or investment demand," Crawcour writes, "those producing for domestic or foreign consumption re- mained mainly labor-intensive, small in scale, and slower to accept technolog- ical innovation."[27]

If the wartime boom was greater than had been the case with the earlier wars, however, so was the post–World War I depression that resulted from a return of international competition. Japan was left with a high rate of infla- tion that made it difficult to retain the markets developed during the war years. The government had encouraged rice imports from Taiwan and Korea in an attempt to counter the inflation of food costs that led to the rice riots of 1918, and as a result, with the return of peace, agriculturalists found themselves forced to compete with imports during the postwar depression. The economic turndown of the 1920s was severe, worsened by the earthquake that struck the Yokohama-Tokyo metropolis in 1923 and exacerbated by a bank crisis in 1927. In considering the decade-long struggle for political liberalization it is important to remember that perceptions of deflation, depression, and eco- nomic crisis accompanied (and for some probably caused) the steps toward continental adventures.[28]

The importance of the international economy to Japan was now greater than it had ever been. Japan was far more self-sufficient in chemicals and heavy industry than had been the case, but was also more reliant on exports of textiles and small, low-cost consumer goods than it had been. This made it important to end the inflation of costs and wages and return to a competitive price level. For some time business continued its scale of wartime investment and expansion, only to have the "bubble" burst in 1920 as orders dried up. The imbalance of imports over exports that had been stopped by the war soon returned, and stock prices tumbled dramatically. It was particularly the new and speculative enterprises that did poorly. The older giants of the economy, the zaibatsu, were usually able to weather the storm. Indeed, their ability to shop selectively among the newer enterprises that were now in trouble built up their power within the economy to the point that they became targets of abuse. In September 1921 Asahi Heigo, member of the "Righteousness Corps of the Divine Land," assassinated Yasuda Zenjirō, founder of the great Yasuda conglomerate. He left a statement excoriating the corruption of the day. The poor, he wrote, had no hope, while malefactors of great wealth could twist the judicial system to their own protection and even reward. It was important to try to stage a new, Taishō, Restoration; but meanwhile "the punishment of the traitorous millionaires is the most urgent of all these [measures], and there is no way of doing this except to assassinate them resolutely." "Just sacrifice your life," he concluded, "and work out your own way of doing this. In this way you will prepare the way for the revolution."[29] This lethal terrorist diatribe was still an isolated act and a decade in advance of the anticapitalist violence ultranationalists would mount against politicians and businessmen in the 1930s, but indicated strains in the polity that would worsen as economic conditions became more serious.

The Hara government was searching for ways to curb and reverse the wartime inflation in order to return Japan's fiscal policy to the gold standard, whose adoption in 1897 had been one of the triumphs of Meiji era direction. Together with its trading partners Japan had to abandon that standard during the war emergency; the United States, increasingly important to Japanese trade, had returned to it in 1919, but the Japanese depression of the following year forced delay. Worse disasters lay ahead. On September 1, 1923, the Tokyo-Yokohama area was devastated by an earthquake that led to fires that raged for forty hours. An estimated 120,000 buildings were destroyed and 450,000 burned. Casualties were estimated to number 140,000, and 250,000 people lost their jobs. The national wealth had been estimated at 86 billion yen in 1909, but estimates of earthquake-incurred losses ran as high as 10 billion yen. A disaster of this scope ruled out early measures for deflation and devaluation. Instead large-scale government support was raised in the form of "earthquake bonds," and these continued to complicate fiscal policy for many years thereafter. Reconstruction brought a new surge of imports. Mitsui, for instance, having lost its headquarters building in the Nihonbashi financial center of Tokyo, immediately engaged American architects (Trowbridge & Livingston) and builders (Steward & Co.) to undertake construction of a palatial and imposing temple of commerce that was dedicated in 1929.[30] Under such pressures an early return to the gold standard was impossible.

The exuberance of the postwar speculation had given way to a minor panic before the earthquake struck, but what came in 1927 was a genuine banking crisis. The Suzuki Trading Company, its sugar dealings involved with the Bank of Taiwan, declared bankruptcy and took in its train the Bank of Taiwan and a number of other banks. These included the Fifteenth (Peers') Bank whose administrators, often referred to as Matsukata zaibatsu, had stubbornly retained its investments in shipbuilding despite the development of a worldwide glut of shipping; business was made worse by the program of naval disarmament that involved the discontinuation of some planned ships. The death in office of Katō Takaaki had brought a successor cabinet headed by Wakatsuki Reijirō, and it was his government that was brought down by the banking crisis. The crisis could have been avoided or at least mitigated, for it had its roots in political antagonisms related to differences over China policy. The Bank of Japan required Privy Council authorization to shore up an ailing bank, but the Privy Council delayed for quite unrelated reasons because of its discontent with Foreign Minister Shidehara's determination to avoid inflaming sentiment against Chiang Kai-shek's Kuomintang antiforeign acts in Nanking. In the final analysis, Thomas Schalow concludes, the crisis was brought on by "the Privy Council's refusal to authorize the Bank of Japan to move sufficiently quickly to forestall the run on banks," and that refusal in turn had its roots in "the Privy Council's adamant opposition to the 'weak kneed Shidehara' approach to Japan's foreign policy in China."[31] When the Fifteenth National Bank declared bankruptcy, the reduction in the fortunes of former daimyo families was striking. The Satsuma Shimazu, for example, saw their estimated worth of 6.5 million yen shrink to less than 180,000, and major firms like Kawasaki Shipbuilding, which had looked to the Fifteenth Bank for funding, suddenly found themselves in desperate financial plight. Losses extended to the Imperial Household itself, which had made the Fifteenth Bank its official depository in 1913. The Wakatsuki cabinet was helpless. The run on banks, estimated to have claimed 11 percent of deposits nationwide (and almost one-third of deposits in the Tokyo Fifteenth Bank branches), was so severe that the Ministry of Finance, in a desperate attempt to restore depositor confidence, hurriedly printed one-sided banknotes and stacked then ostentatiously in tellers' cages. Thirty-two banks suspended operations.

It was under these circumstances that the Wakatsuki cabinet resigned and was replaced by General Tanaka Gi'ichi's Seiyūkai. Tanaka appointed a veteran financial bureaucrat, Takahashi Korekiyo, as minister of finance. Takahashi declared a twenty-day bank moratorium, during which time his ministry reorganized the Bank of Taiwan. New government regulations set higher standards of deposit reserves for banks and encouraged bank mergers, and as a result the number of banks declined by one-third. As before, the stronger firms, zaibatsu and zaibatsu-allied, emerged in health, but in the process the great firms, their tentacles extending through all branches of Japanese society, also became intensely unpopular.

The problems Tanaka incurred in his "correction" of the Shidehara China policy have been better chronicled than his efforts to restore confidence to the economy. Takahashi was an advocate of expansionist economic policies, and returned to the pattern of "pump priming" in the interests of economic growth that the Seiyūkai had followed under the leadership of Hara earlier in the century.[32] Relatively liberal government expenditures created a favorable setting for business. Small, secondary supplier plants grew rapidly in number. There was fierce competition between them, and this helped to keep prices low. The government did not try for direct control, but it did support many cartels, and its protectionist policies helped to restrict imports, from agriculture to steel.

With Tanaka's fall in 1929 the opposition Minseitō returned to power under the leadership of Hamaguchi Osachi. The party had preached fiscal responsibility and advocated an early return to the international gold standard. Hamaguchi was, it will be remembered, a veteran of extensive service in the Ministry of Finance. He had contested Takahashi's liberal government spending during the Hara cabinet, and served as minister of finance under Katō Takaaki and home minister under his successor Wakatsuki. As his minister of finance he selected Inoue Junnosuke, a banker who had studied in England and served in the United States. Inoue had been president of the Bank of Japan before becoming finance minister in 1923, and it fell to him to keep the system going in the tumultuous days that followed the earthquake in 1923. After service in the House of Peers he had returned to head the Bank of Japan after the panic of 1927 broke out, and then resigned that post to join the Minseitō and resume service as finance minister.

This time the world depression that began in 1929 undid all plans. Inoue, intent on sound fiscal policy, was resolute about a deflationary policy, and he took Japan back on the gold standard in 1930. As it turned out his timing could hardly have been worse. Great Britain abandoned the gold standard that same year, and the United States was to do so soon. In the years of growing economic crisis, free trade was seldom any country's highest priority. The Hamaguchi cabinet, through its appointment of Shidehara Kijūrō as foreign minister, hoped for a policy of international cooperation and trade. Japan extended formal recognition to the new Nationalist government of Chiang Kai-shek in 1930. That same year Hamaguchi stood his ground against objections from the Imperial Navy to force acceptance of the decisions reached at the London Naval Conference, which extended the quotas worked out at the Washington Conference to smaller warships.

Both men failed. Shidehara's policies were doomed by new violence precipitated by the military in Manchuria, and Hamaguchi, fatally wounded by an ultranationalist, was succeeded after a brief interregnum by a new Seiyūkai cabinet headed by Inukai Tsuyoshi. Takahashi returned to the Ministry of Finance and resumed expansionist policies. Inukai was to be murdered in 1932, and Takahashi three years later.

We shall turn to those events shortly. For now it is important to note that throughout the world managed currencies signaled a decline of the internationalism that had characterized the post–World War I era. For Japan, where foreign trade to pay for raw materials was so important, these changes were particularly traumatic. They brought on an isolation that was intensified by the military steps that brought the country little honor. Nakamura describes the economic dimension of that isolation in this way:

> The relationship of trust and cooperation between Japan's financial circles and those in Britain and the United States gradually cooled [after 1931]. This relationship, cultivated by Japanese financial circles since the Russo-Japanese War of 1905, had made it possible for Japan to raise foreign capital after the Kantō earthquake and to float local bond issues and electric power company bonds repeatedly during the 1920s. But with the Manchurian incident, the founding of Manchukuo and the outbreak of the Shanghai incident, Thomas Lamont of the Morgan Bank began to take an unfriendly view of Japan. This cooling of international financial relationships meant that when Japan faced a balance of payments crisis, it could no longer look abroad for help.[33]

There was, however, another and more cheerful side to interwar Japan, and to that we turn next.

16

The Taishō era lasted a bare fifteen years before the emperor's death in 1926, and as an era it has little of the cogency of Meiji that preceded or of the militarist era that followed it. Despite this the sense of newness and change that accompanied the movement toward parliamentary democracy was palpable. "Taishō Democracy" remains a symbolic designation for new currents of cosmopolitanism, discontent, and reform that found expression in the years during and after World War I. All contemporary Japanese were conscious of those changes. Some welcomed and others feared them. But no one could be unaware that there was a new climate of change. The sense of liberation that followed the desperate urgency of the rush to build a modern state was widespread. With the growth of higher education, industry, and urban population a new society began to take shape, with new divisions and differentiation within government, business, and gender.

1. Education and Change

The new Japan was far better educated and more literate than the old. By 1898 attendance rates for the four years of compulsory education had reached 69 percent, and by the end of Meiji it was virtually universal. In 1907 compulsory education was extended to six years. A network of girls' and vocational schools prepared young people for useful jobs in the new society. At higher levels specialty *(senmon)* schools, many of which had begun as foreign language schools, mushroomed, especially in Tokyo.

The most distinctive and important unit in the education system was to be found in the eight Special Higher Schools *(kō-tōgakkō)* which functioned as the preparatory level for the imperial university. Of these the First, the most important, popularly known as "Ichikō," was in Tokyo. Like so much in prewar Japanese education, this system came out of the work of Mori Arinori as minister of education in the 1880s. The schools' students ranged from grade-grubbing careerists to dandified playboys. The schools placed great emphasis on Western languages and learning, and for many years the teaching in those subjects was quite unpredictable and erratic in quality. A good deal of the teaching was done by foreigners, some of them poorly qualified for their task.

Many of the Meiji elite, themselves the products of domain and private academies, worried about the future of their country if it had to be left to a generation without sound training in values. Mori's solution for this had been to work out a two-track system. Ordinary five-year high schools, open to those who could afford them, would provide schooling to produce useful citizens able to help build the new state. The Special Higher Schools, on the other hand, were designed to provide a broad humanistic and general education in two (soon extended to three) years, to prepare students for university training. The object was to develop a Japanese counterpart to the American undergraduate college, but the result was more centralized and hierarchic, frankly designed to produce an elite capable of leading the country to its goals of loyalty, wealth, and strength. Structure and purpose would replace the anarchy that had prevailed before, with a system which would nurture a responsible elite for leadership in government and society.[1]

Among the educators who pioneered in planning these schools there were some who had deep personal experience of education in other countries. Orita Hikoichi, who directed the Kyoto Third Higher School, was the first Japanese to graduate from Princeton, from which he returned full of admiration for the mix of moral, intellectual, and physical training that had been worked out there by President James McCosh. Nitobe Inazō, who headed Ichikō in Tokyo for seven years, had degrees from Johns Hopkins and from Halle in Germany. But the mix of values and ritual that characterized the Special Higher Schools was uniquely Japanese. In the closing decades of the Meiji period the ethos of domain samurai schools, at least as the students understood that code, produced a distinctive environment and student culture, boisterous in rowdy masculinity, suspicious of guidance, intolerant of outside interference, and tyrannical in suppression of privatism and individual exceptionalism. It also promoted intense bonding that resulted in lifelong friendships.

Students were usually contemptuous of the capitalist materialism in the society around them. "From our vantage atop Mukōga Hill," went the Ichikō song, "we stalwarts of the five dormitories, Our ambitions soaring to the sky,

Gaze down upon a vulgar world, which is addicted to the dreams of ordinary life."[2] Dormitories were usually "self-governing" and autonomous, and the campus was closed to outsiders. School administrators were remarkably tolerant of adolescent exuberance and assertiveness; demonstrations and riots to protest disciplinary measures were common, and teachers and even school heads might be targets of criticism in student convocations. On one occasion Nitobe, charged with cheapening his school by writing essays on morality for popular outlets, turned the tables on his critics by reading a prepared statement of resignation as headmaster; this shocked the students and brought them around to beg him not to submit it. Dormitories were famously unclean, and so were the students who lived in them. Clattering about on high wooden clogs, they were shaggy and unkempt, latter-day invocations of Edo *otokodate* and Restoration *shishi*. "Have you seen," Nitobe asked in *Bushidō*,

> many a young man with unkempt hair, dressed in shabbiest garb, carrying in his hand a large cane or a book, stalking about the streets with an air of utter indifference to mundane things? He is the student to whom the earth is too small and the heavens are not high enough. He has his own theories of the universe and of life. He dwells in castles of air and feeds on ethereal words of wisdom. In his eyes beams the fire of ambition; his mind is athirst for knowledge. Penury is only a stimulus to him to drive him onward; worldly goods are in his sight shackles to his character. He is the repository of loyalty and patriotism. He is the self-imposed guardian of national honour. With all his virtues and his faults, he is the last fragment of Bushidō.[3]

Nitobe's picture of a lonely seeker for the grail should not be allowed to obscure other aspects of student life. The Special Higher Schools produced a bonding process that was enforced by ritual, sometimes brutal when applied to nonconformists. Sport club heads and dormitory chiefs were campus leaders. Institutionalized riots ("storms," as they were called) pitted half-naked participants against one another. Homosexuality might be tolerated,[4] but evidence of dalliance with women could bring the perpetrator a "clenched-fist" ritualized thrashing from student leaders, conducted by candlelight on the playing fields in the middle of a silent circle of observers.[5] With the passage of time the more brutal aspects of this code were moderated, especially during Nitobe's years as headmaster at Ichikō (1906–1913), and new space was found for interior and intellectual life. "By 1910," Donald Roden observes, "the debates [about the essence of the school experience] had subsided and the importance of culture and the inner self to the uniqueness of the higher school was widely acknowledged."[6] The curriculum had always focused on foreign languages, often devoting a third or more of class time to them. Now literature and study clubs, frequently with their own informal journal or pamphlet-magazine, flourished, and student essays and poetry reflected and helped form the Taishō intellectual scene. Elitism was in no sense weakened, but status and prestige were now accessible to brains as well as bullies.

Taishō writers explored the reaches of the inner self, and student readers eagerly followed their example. Twentieth-century radicalism also entered the campus gates, and provided, in German philosophy and Marxist theory, more sophisticated weapons than samurai asceticism for criticism of bourgeois materialism. What resulted was not a simple East–West or tradition–modern dichotomy, but something at once Japanese and international in origin.

What stood out was the compulsive interest in philosophy. The writer Akutagawa Ryūnosuke remarked that Ichikō students were "more philosophical than Kant," and observers familiar with the student song that satirized their own preoccupation with "Dekanshō" (for Descartes, Kant, and Schopenhauer) might have been led to agree. Through all this a commitment to the production of an elite continued. Student numbers grew rapidly in the interwar years. After the expansion of 1918 the number of Special Higher Schools, theretofore numbered one to eight, quadrupled as new institutions were set up. The new schools, established in and named for provincial towns throughout Japan, were relatively isolated from the great metropolitan centers. They did their best to carry on the traditions of their older rivals, but they could never match their fame. If anything, the inflation in the number of new schools increased the prestige of the old. Ratings of school and university mattered in careers, and competition was intense.

Each Special Higher School graduate was, in theory, guaranteed admission to an imperial university. As the student population grew, more universities were needed to fill this need. The Imperial University in Tokyo was chartered in 1886, again on Mori's watch, out of a consolidation of institutions founded earlier. As the first created, and closest to the capital city, it was the pinnacle of the education system. Its initial mission was to transmit foreign learning and train government officials. An analysis of Japan's basic *Who's Who,* the *Jinji kōshin roku,* shows that the majority of the Meiji elite had not attended a university, but that among those who had the majority were graduates of the Imperial University. For the next generation of bureaucrats, however, university education was a must. Kyoto Imperial University was established in 1897, and subsequently institutions were established at Sendai (1907), Fukuoka (1910), Sapporo (1918), Seoul (1924), Taipei (1928), Osaka (1931), and Nagoya (1939). In that process the prestige of the older imperial universities, and especially of Tokyo Imperial University, rose.

All professors had the status of government officials, and consequently had to be sensitive to the direction and funding provided by the Ministry of Education. Despite this many faculties, especially those of law, established a certain autonomy from state control. Once ideas and teaching reached beyond the campus gate to influence the broader public, however, there was less tolerance and freedom; education officials, and especially self-styled private monitors of orthodoxy, sometimes brought pressure to bear that could lead to resignation or dismissal. Nevertheless this was quite unusual, and the principal cases stand as landmarks in the construction—or destruction—of Japan's civil society. In response to such incidents, faculties, which were in any case frequently divided, tended to place institution above individual, and hew the line rather than imperil the larger university.[7] As with the Special Higher Schools, the proliferation of imperial universities enhanced rather than diminished the stature of the first and most powerful, the Imperial University, which now became Tokyo Imperial University. Its faculty members were instrumental in the formation and leadership of other imperial universities. The university also provided the avenue for employment of government officials and bureaucrats. Major ministries were staffed to an astonishing degree by Tokyo Imperial University graduates. In addition, the university gained from the fact that Tokyo, as the capital, drew the country's finest writers and most discriminating readers. Japan was becoming an increasingly centripetal society.

The years of World War I also brought a major expansion of education opportunities in private institutions. In 1918 the University Law liberalized the criteria for university charters and made it possible for many of the specialty schools to gain university status. By 1930 Japan had thirty universities which enrolled approximately 40,000 students and produced 15,000 graduates a year.[8] Formal education counted much more than it had in the Meiji period, when regional origin or personal recommendation could often suffice to secure employment in official or civil society. Now that was no longer the case. Indeed, one of the consequences of this expansion was that even a degree from a first-line school might no longer guarantee a good job; graduates from newer and lesser schools were particularly hard-pressed to find employment. Japanese society in general and government in particular were gradually falling into the hands of a new kind of elite, more open to talent though by no means indifferent to favoritism.

The imperial universities thus constituted a clear hierarchy of power and prestige, one directly related to the order of their establishment and location. They were state-founded and metropolitan-centered, designed from the first to serve the state as well as society. Tokyo and Kyoto each had seven different faculties. They were organized on the German pattern of chairs, each with a professor with a retinue of assistants who did much of the teaching. Collectively, the student bodies of these two universities constituted as much as one-third of Japan's entire student body.

It was the Law Faculty of Tokyo Imperial University that gave the institution its particular cachet, and its graduates constituted the principal pool of talent for government officials. The result was a curious mix of meritocracy and ascription. Admission was open to all and governed by examination, but once the gates of opportunity had been entered they became gates of privilege. The graduates' rise, particularly in government, was determined largely by the label of the school attended. Consequently what remained, in some sense, unchanged from earlier times, was "the conviction throughout the great part of society that certain people were destined to stand out above others and that this natural elite should lead society."[9]

2. The Law Faculty of Tokyo Imperial University

All this gave professors in the Tokyo Imperial University Faculty of Law an extraordinary position and importance. They were well funded, and virtually certain of extended periods of study abroad. They stood at the crossroads of education and government, for their best students manned the most important ministries. They were public as well as academic leaders, consulted by government bureau chiefs—often their former students—to serve on study commissions. They were sought out by publishers to give leadership and tone to debates on issues of the day. On retirement, still in the prime of life, they were eagerly sought out by leading private universities to teach and continued their careers another decade or more.

In Taishō years three men stood out. The first of these was the constitutional scholar Minobe Tatsukichi (1873–1949). Minobe, who had studied in Germany, developed an interpretation of the Meiji Constitution in which the emperor was an organ of the state. This view became dominant during the thirty-two years Minobe taught at the Imperial University; he was widely honored, the books in which he laid out his views became standard texts, and Minobe was appointed to a seat in the House of Peers. As we shall see, Minobe's views were sharply contested by others who held for imperial autocracy. He was to fall victim to right-wing hysteria, but during most of the interwar period stood as a symbol of Taishō Democracy.[10]

Yoshino Sakuzō (1878–1933) was a far more visible figure and emerged as the chief theorist and exponent of what became known as Taishō Democracy. Yoshino became a Christian during his student days at the Second (Sendai)

Higher School. Together with the Christian socialist Abe Isō, he was an active member of the Tokyo congregation of Ebina Danjō of the early Meiji "Kumamoto band." After graduating from the Law Faculty he accepted a teaching position in China during the brief presidency of Yüan Shih-k'ai and developed a warm interest in the revolutionary movement of Sun Yat-sen. He returned to a post at Tokyo Imperial University, was sent to Europe and America for several years of additional study, and came back to his post in 1914 convinced that Japan needed political reform to equip it for the new world order that he saw emerging.

Christianity was an important element in Yoshino's conviction of the importance of morality in political leadership and citizenship. He was also influenced by his study of Hegel. The moral order he worked toward was grounded in his belief in the goodness of man. He believed that the Meiji leaders, however important their contribution, had, in their rush to build the modern state, created a narrow nationalism. What was needed now was a more universal goal, and that could be attained through education and greater popular participation. Yoshino did not concern himself with what he considered the myths of Christianity, and he also looked beyond the imperial myths of Japan and assumed that they too would be outgrown in time. What was needed was leadership by men of character and quality.[11]

Yoshino did not limit his teaching to his classes. He lectured widely in a university extension movement and became particularly known for thoughtful articles in popular liberal monthlies. In these he argued the need to make government more responsive to the people by a larger franchise, better protection for individual rights, and a stronger representative assembly. He also thought it important to limit the powers of the House of Peers and eliminate or curb the Privy Council. He was central to the organization of liberal student groups, and became their hero when he withstood the attack of ultrarightist ideologues in public debate. He also participated in the formation of the Social Mass Party (Shakai Minshutō) in 1926. His scholarly achievements were equally impressive. He was a leading figure in projects to preserve and publish historical sources on the early Meiji period. That area had drawn mostly official, and therefore partisan, attention, but little systematic scholarship. Yoshino was, in short, an exemplar of the qualities he sought in Japanese leaders: moral commitment, lofty goals, and personal courage.

An advocate of democracy in imperial Japan had first of all to face the fact of imperial sovereignty as it was proclaimed in the Meiji Constitution. For Yoshino personally this was not a problem; at one point, as Peter Duus writes, he suggested that the imperial institution would some day be stripped of its magical aura the way primitive conceptions of Jehovah had been. He himself regarded the emperor as a human and civil monarch. At the same time, he felt that his readers and students might not as yet be ready for this. The standard translation for "democracy," *Minshu shugi,* conveyed the idea of popular sovereignty. Yoshino preferred the translation *minponshugi,* literally "people centered," or "people based." Popular sovereignty, he wrote, was "inappropriate to a country like ours, which from the beginning has been monarchical." In contrast *minpon,* the term he preferred, could apply to steps to make monarchical rule more people centered. (It also had Confucian overtones, although Yoshino did not stress or discuss these.) At present, Yoshino felt, the elder statesmen and bureaucrats seemed to regard the people as a problem, and tried to manage rather than lead them. Prosperity brought by the world war had produced a new plutocracy, and Japan now seemed to have a new privileged class, whose interests were unfairly protected by law. "In recent times," he wrote, "capitalists have gained strength and with their huge financial power are finally on the point of wrongfully trampling upon the public interest." Japan's politicians, for their part, were responsive to these interest groups and did not inspire much confidence either. He was scathing in his criticism: "The frequent occurrence of corrupt behavior among legislators is probably a peculiarity of Japan." The problems Japan faced were moral and personal, but they could be met by increased participation and a better sense of responsibility. "Most of the civilized countries of the world," he pointed out in 1916, "have seen fit to adopt universal manhood suffrage." Only Russia and Japan, in fact, lagged behind. Yoshino's basic optimism about human nature led him to believe that once this reform was achieved, education and responsibility would hold out hope for a better future. He also realized, however, that it would require more years for Japan to make that move. In fact, as we have seen, it required nine years for universal manhood suffrage to be enacted.[12]

Yoshino himself practiced what he preached. He resigned his university post to write for the *Asahi Shinbun,* and when that paper ran into problems of censorship he returned to work with students as a lecturer. His writings illustrate some of the limitations of what was possible in his day. They are not free of contradiction,[13] but they represent one of the most thoughtful attempts to carry further the political reforms that had begun with the Meiji Constitution.

Yoshino was a charismatic figure and the principal intellectual and academic sponsor of the Shinjinkai (New Man Society) that was formed at Tokyo Imperial University in 1918. This grew out of informal meetings that Yoshino had with students interested in the campaign for universal manhood suffrage.

The Shinjinkai was the product of rising student concern with social problems and international affairs. The ferment of the first decade of the Taishō era included the capitalist boom of the war years followed by the rice riots of 1918, the collapse of empire in China and in central Europe, rising interest in anarchism and communist materialism brought to focus by the Russian Revolution, and the lofty rhetoric of Wilsonian internationalism. Yoshino met informally with groups of particularly able students to discuss these matters. This in turn led students from different campuses to meet; those at Tokyo and Kyoto imperial universities, and their counterparts at leading private institutions like Waseda, where Yoshino's friend Abe Isō had a student following. At the Special Higher Schools debating clubs and social science study clubs took up the task. On every hand there was a consciousness of change in the air, enough of it to lead people to break out of their parochial units and reach out to their counterparts.

The first stage of this, as Henry Smith shows,[14] was romantic, idealistic, and quite unfocused. The handful of students who organized the New Man Society in December of 1918 proposed to "advance the new trend towards the liberation of mankind" and further the "movement for the rational reform of contemporary Japan." They committed themselves to work for universal (manhood) suffrage, but as part of a broader dedication to "the people." The task they set themselves was one of educating and ultimately leading those people, but the first steps required recruiting more students like themselves.

During its ten years of activity the Shinjinkai never claimed more than three hundred members, but, centered as it was in the Tokyo Imperial University Faculty of Law, it was an impressive and influential group. Its ranks were made up of alumni as well as student members. The son of Miyazaki Tōten, Sun Yat-sen's leading Japanese disciple, was a leader, and it is not surprising to find the organization taking stands that were critical of Japanese foreign and colonial policy. Akamatsu Katsumaro, who had won his spurs leading student strikes, was there. In future years both he and Miyazaki would be influential leaders in the socialist movement. From Waseda University came student disciples of Abe Isō.[15]

As Japan entered the 1920s liberal and radical students had no lack of complaints. The depression that followed the war years tightened job opportunities. Worker strikes mirrored social discontent. The massive environmental degradation caused by Ashio copper mine effluent, which poisoned rivers and threatened the livelihood of hundreds of thousands of farm families, produced governmental controls that were not enforced, and ultimately the entire flood basin was condemned. The problem and the protests had begun as early as 1877, but it festered almost a century until 1974, when a class action suit was successful.[16]

There was grinding poverty in industrial cities, some of it the target of Christian socialists like Kagawa Toyohiko. Worst of all, the Diet was temporizing regarding the issue of universal manhood suffrage. There were also antimilitarist movements. A national organization of students that was formed in 1923 took as one of its targets an army program to introduce military training in high schools in order to provide employment for officers rendered redundant by budget cuts. Large-scale student protests proved unsuccessful, but they succeeded in working up enthusiasm.

Conservatives, of course, found it deplorable that students should heckle and disrupt, as they did, speeches by the army minister. They were even more alarmed by indications of student interest in the fledgling communist movement.

The Japan Communist Party was formed in 1922. It was dissolved in 1924 as its leader, Yamakawa Hitoshi, concluded that the situation called for education and preparation for mass organization rather than plotting by a small elite.[17] The party was reconstituted in 1925, but in that year the apparatus of state suppression had been strengthened by the Peace Preservation Law. Consequently its activities were necessarily limited to conspiratorial work by a small and dedicated minority. This time leadership came from a group of intellectuals led by Fukumoto Kazuo. Radical students found this challenge stimulating, but it also brought their organization under official suspicion. For some time the government was remarkably tolerant of student-organized disorder (as it would be again in postwar days), but in March 1928 the great police sweeps carried out by the Tanaka government brought an end to student agitation and to the Shinjinkai itself.

From the first, right-wing enthusiasts did their best to combat what they defined as radicalism. The two persuasions were mutually reinforcing. The formation of Shinjinkai grew in part out of student enthusiasm for Yoshino's response to a challenge by an organization (the Rōninkai, or Rōnin Society) that was sponsored by the right-wing Amur (Black Dragon) Society. Left-wing student activity found an echo in right-wing student groups. These too could be found in the corridors of the Tokyo University's Faculty of Law. Their faculty hero and sponsor was Uesugi Shinkichi (1878–1929), a leading critic of Yoshino and especially Minobe Tatsukichi. Uesugi's early path was remarkably similar to that of the men he criticized. He too began as a Christian, won the favor and attention of his mentors at Tokyo Imperial University, and was appointed to its faculty. In early works his positions on imperial power and the emperor's relation to the state were not unlike those of Minobe. In 1906, however, Uesugi was sent to Germany for study, and there he encountered the statecraft teachings of Georg Jellinek. He returned to Japan a firm advocate of an imperial sovereignty that knew no limit, and altered his constitutional interpretation and teaching sharply as a result. Before long he was taking public issue with his colleague Professor Minobe's stand that the emperor was an organ of the state. When the Ministry of Education invited Minobe to address a convention of middle school teachers, Uesugi was aghast that theories developed for academic discussion should be spread among teachers responsible for instructing the young, and with apparent bureaucratic endorsement at that. The Katsura cabinet, it may be recalled, was already struggling with demands for greater orthodoxy in teaching about the Northern and Southern courts, and now it had to confront a new problem concerning the role of teachers and learning: Uesugi charged that Minobe had no business accepting the invitation to speak, and that by accepting and speaking as he had he was crossing the line between academics and politics. The Uesugi-Minobe debate served to polarize opinion on the issue and politicized what had, until then, been an academic discussion of constitutional interpretation into a debate about ideology. Uesugi became a favorite of the right, and toward the end of his life he was receiving respectful attention from military leaders. His adamant advocacy of imperial power prepared the way for the assault on Minobe and his books by militarists a few years later.

Uesugi was no more partial to Yoshino Sakuzō's youthful Shinjinkai admirers. He encouraged conservative students to form a "Seven Lives" Society dedicated to the fourteenth-century warrior Kusunoki, who was said to have vowed to sacrifice his life seven times for the imperial cause. These enthusiasts did their best to disrupt meetings and inform on liberal and left-wing student groups. The Meiji historian Shigeno Yasutsugu had dismissed the Kusunoki story as unfounded myth-making, but now that the ideology of the emperor-centered family-state was in place that sort of (in Shigeno's case) Confucian rationality was no longer welcome.

Uesugi was by no means alone in his stance. He was popular with many students—some said because his grades were lenient—and he was not averse to mobilizing support on and off his campus to enforce his points. One such occasion was the case of Professor Morito Tatsuo, who published articles on the anarchist thinker Peter Kropotkin. In 1920 the authorities filed charges against Morito. The first verdict was in his favor, but higher education bureaucrats, cheered on by a student faction responsive to Uesugi, reversed the verdict and secured a three-month jail sentence for Morito, who was also dismissed from his position. Shinjinkai members protested, but to no effect. Uesugi also had numerous off-campus admirers. One such, Minoda Mineki, himself a graduate of the Tokyo Imperial University Faculty of Law, taught at Keiō University for some years before turning his full attention to the politics of orthodoxy. Officious monitoring of this sort mattered. Government bureaucrats preferred to avoid controversy, but when the issue was forced on them by public criticism and picked up by the press they felt their hand was forced.

These paragraphs have dealt with major figures in the academic firmament. There were of course other and estimable members of the Faculty of Law. An American banker named Hepburn endowed a chair of American constitutional law that was held provisionally by Nitobe while its future occupant, Takagi Yasaka (1889–1984), prepared himself by study in the United States. Takagi, like Yoshino a Christian, was a man of unfailing integrity who refused to bend with the wind of public controversy. But on the fringes of academe things could be quite unpredictable. Some academics hardly deserved the name of educator or intellectual. One student's description of the head of the Department of Colonial Economics at Japan University (a private university), remembered him as a xenophobic rabble rouser. "He'd say in class, 'I've been to Shanghai, where signs say 'Dogs and Yellow People: No entry!' . . . He'd ask us, 'What are you going to do to knock down this structure?' He had studied in America and he was a professor of current events, but he devoted himself to rousing speeches like this."[18]

3. Taishō Youth: From "Civilization" to "Culture"

New Man Society liberals and Seven Lives Society rightists may have been preoccupied with social reform and ideology, but many more students, particularly in the Special Higher Schools, were focused on problems of identity and personal development. In Meiji times young men occupied themselves with success, for themselves and for their new country; *kuni no tame,* "for the sake of the country," was, as we have noted, an amuletic phrase that accompanied almost every act.

In the interwar years this wore thin. The nation-state had been built, Japan had taken its place among the powers, and people began to think about the structure and justice of society. Meiji youth had been brought up on Fukuzawa's theory of civilization, in which societies were arranged in hierarchic order by degree of "civilization"; the challenge was to climb another rung on that ladder of development. Japan had done this. Now what began to matter was "culture," being rather than doing, and feeling rather than achieving. The sense of collective national crisis was replaced by a sense of individual and existential crisis. Introspection and doubt replaced the formulaic invocation of the previous generation. Veterans of the Meiji struggle, no longer young, looked on this change with distaste and disdain. Tokutomi Sohō, whose *Youth of the New Japan* had electrified its readers in the 1880s, deplored the change. Taishō youth, he wrote, were self-indulgent, soft, and lacked character and purpose.[19]

The undergraduate years of the future elite in the Special Higher Schools provide a tableau on which this is seen most clearly. It is in adolescent years that questions of identity and purpose become most pressing, and it is then that signals are most informative for what lies behind and what points to the future. Sakamoto Ryōma's age cohort awoke to a rage at foreign penetration of Japan and indignation at the inability of its leaders and institutions to respond. In the next cohort, Tokutomi Sohō resolved to duplicate the deeds of the West while Miyazaki Tōten vowed to undo Western control by assisting in what he called the salvation of Asia. The early Taishō cohort looked within instead of looking outside itself.

Japanese had become aware of what were known as "anguished youth" since 1903, the year a promising and well-connected First Higher School student named Fujimura Misao threw himself over the Kegon waterfall at Nikko, leaving, carved into a tree trunk, a "Meditation on the Precipice" that testified to his existential anxiety. Suicide was not uncommon in Japan, but the story of Fujimura was first-page news, and the words of his poem became a legacy to students who celebrated it in song, wept over it, and, in some cases took his act as a model for themselves. It is the more noteworthy that the incident caught so much attention just when Japan was gearing up for the war with Russia and manly courage was the order of the day. There were more than the usual reasons for student distress, but the prevalence of concern with identity and purpose indicates that the Meiji cult of effort and success was losing its attraction for young men.[20]

That the new atmosphere of the Higher Schools centered around the study of philosophy and identity says something about student culture. Two of the books most avidly read by students were highly personal ruminations on life and purpose. Abe Jirō's *Santarō's Diary* and Kurata Hyakuzō's *Setting Out with Love and Understanding* enjoyed tremendous popularity for many years, and they tell a great deal about the young men who read them so compulsively. Both books were close to stream-of-consciousness reflections on life, and both were studded with the names and ideas of Western, usually German, writers. Abe's Santarō broods "at his desk for hours while his 'inner voice' berates him for worldly thoughts." Kurata's book was a highly personal collection of short essays that discussed his inner struggles and changing philosophical perceptions. These books, published in 1914 and 1917 respectively, provide a window on student life and concerns.

The ready reference to men and ideas in such books, and the authors' confidence that these would resonate with their readers, provide testimony, if more is needed, to the cosmopolitanism of the interwar years.[21] (The students' grandparents, to be sure, had grown up with books equally pretentious with references to classical Chinese literature.)

By the Taishō years Japanese had ready access to inexpensive editions of translations of virtually all of the major works of European philosophy. The publisher Iwanami Shigeo (1881–1946), himself a graduate of Tokyo Imperial University's Faculty of Philosophy, began with a used bookstore and won the friendship of Natsume Sōseki. Sōseki's *Kokoro* was the first large-scale success of the publishing house he founded, and from there he went on to publish major works of philosophy before carving out for himself a new market in paperback editions of major works. The logo of the house he founded, Millet's *Sower,* symbolized its role in the diffusion of current Western thought.

Many did not have to rely on translations, but studied Western thought first hand. For those on the elite track in university, government, or business, a period of study abroad was financed by their employer. Hundreds of Japanese, perhaps over one thousand, were sent to study in the West, most of them to Germany, in the interwar years. Cosmopolitan internationalism was everyone's goal. Nitobe Inazō devoted his life to becoming a "bridge across the Pacific," and major academics did their best to bridge the worlds of Eastern and Western philosophy.

First-hand familiarity with Western thought was also available at home. Professor Raphael Koeber (1848–1923), who taught philosophy at Tokyo Imperial University from 1893 to 1914 and remained in Japan until his death, was immensely influential as a representative of German idealist philosophy, and he is memorialized in the writings of many leading men of letters.

The most impressive product of this philosophical inquiry is to be found in the life and work of Nishida Kitarō (1870–1945), modern Japan's most influential philosopher. His *Study of the Good,* published in 1911, was so popular despite its formidable difficulty that it was often ranked with the works by Abe and Kurata described above as "must" reading for students.

Nishida's career shows that Special Higher School culture could produce lifelong intellectual friendships as well as boisterous bonding. He attended the Fourth Higher School in the Japan Sea city of Kanazawa, where his classmates, an unusually gifted group, included Suzuki Daisetsu (1870–1966), a man who would introduce Zen Buddhism to the Western world.[22] Nishida left school abruptly before graduation, probably because of a disagreement with new administrators from Satsuma sent out by the Ministry of Education, but sustained the entrance examinations for Tokyo Imperial University nonetheless. There he found himself placed in a "special" track because of his failure to have graduated from a Special Higher School, and barred from access to the library or other study facilities. His problems continued when he searched for a post after the completion of his studies. Despite this he persevered and immersed himself in his reading. Professor Koeber encouraged him to master classical and European languages in order to engage Western thinkers directly. While unemployed after graduating, Nishida studied Zen and began work on an individual outlook, emphasizing experience, that bridged much of what he had read with what he had gained from Zen discipline. After teaching at the Fourth Higher School for a decade, he was able to secure a post at Kyoto Imperial University through the enthusiastic recommendation of a former teacher. At Kyoto Nishida made his career, and gathered around himself a group of like-minded colleagues who became known as the "Kyoto school" of philosophy. In later years many criticized this group, with its emphasis on experience, will, and national distinctiveness, as having provided intellectual support for idealistic and romantic nationalism. It is true, as Isaiah Berlin has pointed out, that neo-Kantian thought, through its emphasis on the inner realm of spirit and the autonomy of conscience, created possibilities that were exploited by later and lesser men in arguments for an incarnate national spirit,[23] but it would be an exaggeration to credit these philosophers with a causal role in the tragedy that lay ahead.

The cultural kaleidoscope of Weimar Germany presented additional attractions for Japanese studying abroad. Murayama Tomoyoshi (1901–1977), who went to Germany to study Christian theology and philosophy, turned instead to avant-garde art as a result of what he encountered there. He returned to Japan and espoused a "constructionist" art, leading a group that styled itself MAVO. The MAVO members were contemptuous of academic art and the establishment that supported it. They found in the chaos of post-earthquake Tokyo conditions somewhat comparable, they thought, to those of postwar Europe, and worked to construct a new and revolutionary culture. Abstract decorations on the ugly barracks built for the homeless provided one target, and trendy cafés another. MAVO members cultivated eccentricity in dress and appearance as a form of freedom. Disillusioned with politics, they were deeply alienated from the state and the bourgeois culture around them. As a movement MAVO was short-lived, but it had considerable influence on graphic design. Murayama went on to work for reform of the theater and dance. The group and movement were provocatively "modern" in life-style and affirmation of freedom of the body. It was a time when the erotic and the grotesque were also becoming faddish in literature, and all this combined to startle conservative contemporaries.[24]

The most compelling basis for cultural and philosophical criticism in Taishō Japan, however, was that provided by Marxism. Marx's writings had been introduced earlier—Kōtoku Shūsui's *Heimin shinbun* had published a translation of the *Communist Manifesto* before the Russo-Japanese War—but in the depression years, when politics seemed corrupt, capitalists greedy, and government stodgy and repressive, it had a new resonance. Intellectually, Marxism held out an integrated view of what was wrong and, through its institutional support from the communist movement, a program of action. From fastidious idealists who scorned the materialism they saw around them to philosophy students who had encountered Hegel, the all-encompassing alternative offered by Marxism was attractive and often overpowering. We have noted that the Shinjinkai students were increasingly drawn to it in the mid-1920s, and that it was precisely in those years that the government turned to new legislation and institutions to combat "dangerous thoughts."

It is not an overstatement to say that the main trends of social science analysis became predominantly Marxist in the 1920s. Student leftists, a Ministry of Education survey found, were predominantly of good background, the majority of them "modest," "decent," "sober," and "diligent"; what was worrisome was that they were of exactly the quality that should have been on the ladder of success through careers in government, business, and academe.

Meiji socialists had been moralists, many of them Christians, who objected to the injustices of early capitalism and looked to a socialist order as the promise of twentieth-century improvement. The new generation of Marxist intellectual leftists, many of them the recipients of government grants for graduate study in Europe, often returned to their universities to take up positions in economics or political science, and became pillars of the academic establishment.[25]

Some figures caught in this vortex of the new and foreign turned instead to study to preserve a set of values they saw disintegrating around them. The ethnographer Yanagita Kunio (1875–1962) was the founder of folklore studies in Japan. Yanagita's varied career—government official, newspaper writer, poet—centered in ceaseless travels in which he recorded the beliefs and life patterns of ordinary people. He tried to collect and systematize tales and customs that would explain Japan's distinctive national character. In over 100 books and 1,000 articles, he showed a love for particular detail in a timeless pattern that he felt was being destroyed by the uniformity imposed by the centralizing government he had once served.[26]

A quite different approach was taken by the Kyoto Imperial University professor of philosophy Kuki Shūzō (1888–1941). After a lengthy period of study in Europe, he returned to reappraise Japanese tradition and taste. Following in the tradition of several Meiji figures who had tried to distinguish Japanese culture and sense of beauty as intrinsically different from—and superior to—that of the West, Kuki focused on a moment in the Tenpō era of the nineteenth century as exhibiting, in its culture and chic, the essence of what was truly Japanese. In an extraordinarily influential essay, "Iki no kōzō" (The structure of taste), he built an argument for cultural exclusionism and social distinction that became and remained influential for many years. Remarkably enough, the taste *(iki)* Kuki lauded was that of the well-to-do townsman of the great cities and especially Edo. Nitobe, in the work he wrote to further foreign understanding of Japan, had centered on the samurai ethic, but Kuki, an aristocrat writing for his own people, preferred to concentrate on the townsman whose fastidious taste in dalliance and food seemed to offer such a contrast to the capitalists of his day. Both were, of course, exercises in nostalgia.[27]

4. Women

The air of liberation among members of the urban middle class in the years around World War I included a women's movement. It is not surprising that such a movement developed in Japan. Japanese women faced greater obstacles in their struggle for equality than did their counterparts in most developed countries, but it is noteworthy that a movement for woman suffrage was under way as early as 1918 at a time when only Sweden, New Zealand, Australia, and the United Kingdom had given women the vote. Future feminist leaders naturally expected to share some of the benefits men were gaining from increases in the suffrage, but not many crumbs fell from that table. Fundamental reform, in fact, was not to come until the years after World War II, when the Meiji Civil Code was abandoned. That code had been based on the samurai family ideal, and it emphasized patriarchal authority and perpetuation of the household *(ie)* line. Inheritance was by primogeniture, the wife had no share in her husband's property (although hers became his), and she had no legal rights over her children. To be sure, the Meiji wife, like the samurai wife, was in practice usually more important than this would indicate; she was central in her children's lives and normally managed the family finances, but she enjoyed little security. The philosopher Nishida Kitarō, for instance, recorded glumly in his diary (in German) his distress when his father sent his daughter-in-law, Nishida's wife, packing.

With industrialization the number of women who joined the work force rose steadily. Since most women workers did so on contract in the textile mills, however, they were not likely to have the background or opportunity to express themselves. Many more women in remote villages and depressed areas worked along with, and as hard as, their men in coarse and heavy labor, but they too did not provide promising material for a feminist movement. At the same time, however, women became increasingly important in the modern sector, with jobs like telephone operators, ticket collectors, and clerks.

The feminist effort can probably be dated from 1911, the year Hiratsuka Raichō (1886–1971) launched a movement with its journal, called "Blue Stocking" in evocation of a contemporaneous group in Great Britain. "I am a new woman," its manifesto began. "It is my daily desire to become a true new woman. What is truly and forever new is the sun. I am the sun." In the years that followed "new women" often startled their contemporaries by kicking over the traces of decorum. Hiratsuka first came to public attention with plans for a double suicide with a novelist. He later changed his mind and wrote a novel about their affair. "Byakuren" (White Lotus) was the pen name of a daughter of the nobility, a famous beauty and poetess, who freed herself from a loveless marriage with a Kyushu coal magnate by eloping with Miyazaki Ryūsuke, Shinjinkai leader and son of Sun Yat-sen's old friend Miyazaki Tōten. Given the number of upper-class women locked into unhappy marriages, it is probably remarkable that there were not more such escapes.

Before long the Blue Stocking movement lost its momentum, but other organizations continued the campaign for women's rights. In 1920 a New Woman's Association was announced. Two years later changes in the 1900 Peace Police Law made it possible for women, who had previously been forbidden from engaging in any sort of politics, to begin to attend political meetings. Publishers now responded to the opportunity with women's magazines, and it became possible to launch a campaign for women's suffrage.

The lead in this was taken by Ichikawa Fusae (1893–1981), who was prompted to enter the women's movement by witnessing her father's cruel treatment of her mother. Ichikawa was a true pioneer, and entered employment as the first female reporter for a Nagoya newspaper. In 1918 she moved to Tokyo, where she met Hiratsuka Raichō. In 1921 she left for two and a half years of study in the United States. On her return she founded the Women's Suffrage League, which remained in existence until 1940, when wartime restrictions made further efforts impossible. Women's suffrage had to wait until it was mandated by the Allied Occupation of Japan, and shortly afterward Ichikawa ran successfully for the Diet.[28] Although prewar suffrage efforts proved unsuccessful, it is worth noting that the ill-fated Hamaguchi Minseitō cabinet prepared a Women's Civil Rights Bill that would have extended the franchise to women in elections for city, town, and village officials.

The women's movement should thus be seen as one part of the larger Taishō period expression of change and liberation. In 1919 *Kaizō* (Reconstruction), a general interest liberal monthly, expressed in its name and content the spirit of the age. Its management arranged lecture tours of Japan for Albert Einstein and Margaret Sanger, the latter at the urging of Ishimoto (later Katō) Shizue, who had become an admirer of Sanger and a proponent of birth control for Japanese women. This, however, was directly contrary to government policy, and bureaucrats did all they conveniently could to block Sanger's tour. They finally relented and allowed her ashore on condition that she not discuss birth control in her public lectures. This in turn provided excellent publicity for the tour, which attracted immense attention.[29]

5. Labor

The urban labor force grew rapidly during the interwar years. Lives were increasingly centered around the routines of school and factory. Employers looked for ways to encourage stability and order in their labor force, and workers struggled for better remuneration and better conditions of work. The particularities of Japanese development give this effort great interest for comparative study as well as for Japanese history.

The problems Japanese workers faced in the interwar years were real enough. The galloping inflation that accompanied the boom years of World War I helped ignite the rice riots of 1918, and the steps the government took— permitting the import of rice from Taiwan and Korea—in turn brought problems for the countryside, where landlord-tenant disputes increased in number. Industrialists were not convinced that there was a real labor problem, however, and found it easier to speak grandly of Japan's "beautiful customs" (bifū) of kindly paternalism in the land of the "family state." Legislation and administrative snooping, they argued, could only sour the familial intimacy that made the workshop such a pleasant place for their employees. Government officials knew better, however, and carried out surveys that revealed the extent of exploitation. They were also aware that Japan had to take into account the existence of new interwar institutions like the International Labor Organization (ILO). Japan was now a world power and recognized as such in the League of Nations. Who was to represent Japanese labor?

It has sometimes been thought that the "permanent employment" and "seniority pay" systems that contributed to stable labor relations in post–World War II Japan were products of the Japanese cultural tradition; status relationships and (fictive) familial relations, it seemed, might have bridged the transition from traditional to modern society. In the Tokugawa period economic and political relationships had usually been expressed in familial terms, and the "parent" was expected to do the right thing by his inferiors, in exchange for their loyalty.

This interpretation no longer suffices. Japan's contemporary labor relations may well have proved congruent with some cultural assumptions and preferences, but on examination it is clear that they were worked out after a good deal of experimentation in a setting marked by contention and dispute.[30]

One must first of all note the high concentration of Japan's urban labor force, which might have been expected to encourage organization. Japan's population grew from some 44 million in 1900 to 56 million in 1920. The urban growth that followed World War I was concentrated in and near the great port cities along the Pacific coast. There were good reasons for the fact that these cities led in foreign trade. The unequal treaties had limited that trade to those centers when they were "treaty ports," and by the time those provisions had been outgrown at the turn of the century internal shipping routes, communications, and port facilities operated to maintain and increase the importance of those cities.[31] Kobe and Yokohama were new port cities adjacent to the great metropolitan centers of Osaka and Tokyo. The urban sprawls that resulted made them the first to be served by modern public transportation and suburban railroads that carried urban waste to fertilize the paddies, suburban commuters to their jobs, and shoppers to their stores. By the end of the interwar years the great plains around Tokyo and Osaka were becoming among the most congested in the world. It was a process that accelerated during the rapid economic growth of the post–World War II years. Today the Tokyo plain, with some 35 million inhabitants, contains more Japanese than the entire country did at the time of the Meiji Restoration.

Most urban workers came from villages where, as younger sons, they had little future. The countryside was already fully settled by the eighteenth century; indeed, restrictions on movement between domains in Tokugawa times resulted in overcrowding that frequently forced farmers to develop unproductive upland areas or hack out tiny paddies that climbed the hillsides. Even in fertile valleys, however, younger sons were disadvantaged. The Meiji Civil Code supported primogeniture, and it was natural for younger sons to head for the cities in search of work. Eldest sons would normally remain in place near the ancestral tombs. In boom times the move to the cities threatened to become a flood. In recessions workers frequently returned to the temporary security of the village, but many stayed to work at minimal wages for artisans or managed to start small enterprises, hanging on until the economic climate changed. Small and marginal producers were to be found in towns of any size, but they were particularly numerous in and around large cities as suppliers to larger firms.

There were important differences between "labor" in small firms and in large, capital-intensive firms, many of which were established in connection with the government's program for "wealth and strength." Those dockyards, arsenals, and heavy industries were unprofitable for many years and required taxpayer support in subsidy or orders. After Japan caught its stride and expanded its markets, however, private entrepreneurs rushed to share the profits. The Russo-Japanese War marked a first stage in this transition, but it was the boom of World War I that made the real difference.

Things were different with light industry for consumer goods. The early Meiji government had experimented with government enterprises but not for long, and thereafter production for the home market was entirely in private hands. Firms varied greatly in size, though most were small, and they were less closely tied to population centers. For many years textiles were at the core of this private economy.

The two structures had different labor needs. Textile workers included country women and girls recruited by contractors who scoured the countryside. They were frequently unscrupulous and devious in their methods and promises. The workers lived under spartan conditions, and their hardships were legendary.[32] Since they were under contract for a limited period of time and had little opportunity to socialize, much less organize, however, these workers made poor material for would-be labor organizers; their discontent was more usually shown by flight than fight.

Government officials concerned with public health and welfare were aware of labor conditions, and the surveys they authorized provide a baseline for labor reform. In 1903, a comprehensive survey of factory workers, *Shokō jijō* (Conditions among factory workers), detailed practices and abuses. In time this led to a Factory Law, enacted in 1911, that set safety standards for factories that employed twelve or more workers. Under its provisions workers were to be at least twelve years old, and the workday for women and boys under fifteen was not to exceed twelve hours. These restrictions might be seen as moderate, but the vocal opposition of industrialists delayed implementation of the law for another five years.

Larger factories with significance for national defense presented a different problem. Here the need was for training in the use of imported technology and maintaining a reasonably stable labor force. The Meiji government had inherited a number of arsenals and shipyards from its Tokugawa and daimyo predecessors, and the most successful of these were taken over by the new government or government-related industrialists. The shipyards and arsenals that are the focus of Andrew Gordon's study typically began by hiring Western technicians who left after training their successors.[33] Ordinary workers were usually recruited by labor bosses who, styled *oyakata* (parent) by those they recruited, stood between the enterprise and its workers. The problem for the enterprise was to get these men to shift their loyalty from the workers they recruited to the firm, perhaps as foremen. The novelist Yoshikawa Eiji, whose ex-samurai father's incompetence brought the family to destitution, recalled his boyhood experience when he was able to get a job at the Yokohama Dock Works to provide some income for his long-suffering mother:

> When I turned up at the Dock Company with his letter of recommenda-
> tion I found to my surprise that I was given no examination; all they did
> was ask me how old I was. Mr. Naito had warned me not to give my real
> age, seventeen, the minimum age set by the company for dockhands being
> nineteen, so I said I was nineteen. I was immediately sent to join the sundry
> parts section. Of all the sections into which the workers were divided—
> the others included electrical, mechanical and metal divisions—ours
> ranked the lowest, the miscellaneous tasks assigned to it requiring physical
> fitness primarily and no skill to speak of.

Yoshikawa's section had a sort of foreman:

> There were more than a hundred workers in our section, divided into six
> teams of seventeen or eighteen men each, the purpose presumably being
> to encourage competition. Each team had a leader and assistant leader.
> First thing in the morning, the leader would go to the foreman's office
> and come back with assignments for the day: to paint the ship in such
> and such a dock, for example, or to go out on a launch to a foreign vessel
> moored offshore and ready it for docking.[34]

As Yoshikawa describes it, his work was always gritty, often extremely danger-ous, and poorly paid; yet a kind of camaraderie developed within the section. Its members were as likely to squander their meager pay in self-indulgence as they were to use it to support the families who waited anxiously for their return. Their sense of loyalty, much less obligation, to Yokohama Dock was understandably minimal.

It was not long before technological developments made the kind of ar-rangement described above obsolete. Rationalization in patterns of produc-tion replaced the rather chaotic picture Yoshikawa describes, but it also broke up the camaraderie, if only of shared misery, that was part of worker morale. Factory workers in the Meiji period, as Thomas Smith notes, were considered extremely low class and enjoyed little respect. A worker's letter to a newspaper in 1913 deplored the fact that "because our countrymen despise us, we try to avoid their contempt by dressing outside the plant gate as merchants or stu-dents. If all of us were to walk down the street at the same time in work clothes, people would be astonished not only by our numbers but also by our good behavior."[35]

Within the enterprise there were also likely to be very sharp distinctions of status and respect. The novelist Matsumoto Seichō gave up his job at the great *Asahi* newspaper for the army, and later wrote that

> army life was a revelation to me. It turned out just as they told me when I arrived there: "Here social position, wealth, and age count for nothing. Everyone is on absolutely the same level." The equality I found among the new recruits gave me a curious sense that life was worthwhile. At *Asahi* I was not just a cog in a wheel but a cog of no value . . . At the newspaper my very existence was not recognized. Here I counted. Discovery of a human condition not present in the factory enlivened me in a strange way.[36]

Armies are not on the whole known for an absence of status distinctions, and Matsumoto's discovery that it was more egalitarian than his workplace speaks volumes about that workplace.

In late Meiji and early Taishō years workers in Japan's largest industrial enterprises began to demand more respect, more consideration, and more money. Factory workers made up a significant proportion of the urban demonstrations and protests that have been mentioned. They were beginning to demand that they be considered part of the *kokumin*, "the people," a new, inclusive, and value-laden term.[37]

Early Japanese labor fraternities did not develop along craft lines as they had in the West, probably because the political fragmentation of Tokugawa Japan had inhibited the development of more than local guilds. When unions did make their appearance they tended to be enterprise-specific. In the years before World War I there were a total of seventy-five disputes at heavy industrial plants, but none of these involved unions. Nevertheless, thoughtful industrialists and early labor leaders realized the desirability of having some sort of overarching organization that would contribute to labor peace.

The Yūaikai, "Friendship Society," that was organized in 1912 represented such an effort. It began with moral and ameliorative goals. Its platform called for mutual aid through friendship and cooperation, the improvement of character, furthering of knowledge, development of skills, and cooperation in the interest of improving workers' status. Small wonder, one might think, that sympathetic capitalists like Shibusawa Ei'ichi supported it. Yūaikai members grew from a few thousand at the outset to 30,000 in 1918.

World War I sharpened labor expectations and discontent. Inflation kept real wages low even though enterprises were extremely profitable. More private entrepreneurs entered the field of heavy industry; the labor force grew in size and its choices also widened. In 1917 alone the Friendship Society was involved in seventy labor-management disputes, almost as many as Japan had experienced in the years since the Restoration.

Under these circumstances both government and business turned hostile, and many Yūaikai branches were forced to close. In 1921 the Yūaikai changed its name to General Federation of Labor (Sōdōmei), but its stand remained moderate. In time it became the conservative wing of the labor movement. In its early years, however, its success in organizing workers subjected it to constant pressure from the police.

Law enforcement agencies had a potent weapon at their disposal, for Article 17 of the 1900 Peace Police Law, which had been enacted in the aftermath of labor disputes during the Sino-Japanese War, made it a punishable offense to incite others to join unions, engage in collective bargaining, or strike. This provision was not repealed until 1926, though its implementation went through many phases as its provisions became increasingly archaic. Nevertheless it constituted a formidable threat to labor organizers.

In 1921 the postwar depression idled shipyard workers at the Kawasaki and Mitsubishi shipyards and produced the largest labor dispute Japan was to experience until after World War II. Sōdōmei organizers led some 35,000 workers through the streets of Kobe in a massive demonstration to demand the right to organize and bargain collectively. They also announced plans to seize the plants and control production; at this the government sent soldiers to reinforce the police. Owners, for their part, sent in strikebreakers prepared to do battle. Several hundred arrests, and at least one death, resulted from the suppression that put an end to the strike after a month and a half of struggle. The strike failed, but it had important results. Firms previously tolerant of labor organizations became more hostile to them, and many labor leaders began to doubt the possibility of peaceful protest.

A small group of anarcho-syndicalists lost all confidence in proposed reforms like universal manhood suffrage and concluded that it would be necessary to overthrow the entire system. The Japan Communist Party, as has been mentioned, was formed in 1922, and although it was broken up by police the following year some of its members, previously engaged with the Yūaikai and Sōdōmei, carried on to pursue more radical solutions. The strike thus hardened positions on both sides. Ōsugi Sakae, a leading anarchist, was brutally killed while in police custody immediately after the earthquake in 1923, and at least ten others were murdered in December 1923 by police and army men who took the law into their own hands and became, in effect, vigilantes.[38]

Management and police did their best to stifle labor organization, but help now came from government bureaucrats.[39] The concerns of officials in the

Ministry of Agriculture and Commerce had been shown in the surveys of labor conditions, and their first conclusions had been reflected in the Factory Law of 1911. In addition private reformers, among them many Japanese Christian socialists, had long argued the need for government laws to protect workers. The evidence and scale of worker discontent in large firms prompted a new examination of labor-management relations by government bureaucrats.

Japanese academics and officials had been aware of measures taken in Europe, particularly in Wilhelmine Germany, to deal with the "social problem," and they were eager to forestall conflicts that they felt were sure to come.[40] After World War I Europe had additional examples of social policy to offer as the Labor Party grew in England, while in Russia the Bolshevik revolution of 1918 added urgency to measures to head off radicalism.

This coincided with the emergence of a new cohort of officials in Japan. The Satsuma-Chōshū generation was giving way to a new university-educated group, many of whom had direct experience of the West as part of the flood of students who went abroad. This inevitably had a strong impact in a country where government planners mattered, and its influence was particularly direct in the Ministry of Home Affairs, which took over responsibility for these matters from Agriculture and Commerce and established a Social Bureau in 1922. The implementation of government policy was affected by bureaucratic competition for jurisdiction. The Social Bureau of the Home Ministry thought in terms of reforms, while the Justice Ministry, with its control over the police, was more likely to use strong-arm tactics. In addition the question of which side would prevail, the Social Bureau with its carrot of reform and suffrage, or the Justice Ministry with its stick of police repression, was affected by the larger political struggle involved in the movement toward political party government.

In the 1920s Japan was coming close to a two-party system of politics with the balance of power held by splinter and independent groups within the Imperial Diet. The main strength, as will be remembered, was divided between two groups whose roots were to be found in the Freedom and People's Rights Movement of the 1880s. The core of the Jiyūtō had found its home in the Seiyūkai, and a good deal of the original Kaishintō had been absorbed by (Katsura's) Dōshikai, whose name changed to Kaishintō and finally, in 1927, to Minseitō. These were not so much "parties" as they were combinations of politicians. Independent-minded men with safe constituencies moved frequently. Ozaki Yukio, beginning as an Ōkuma follower, moved in and out of the Seiyūkai before becoming a confirmed independent and head, for a time, of his own "Enlightenment" faction. Inukai Tsuyoshi, no less an Ōkuma follower at the beginning of the parliamentary movement, ended years of independence by moving into the Seiyūkai. There were no real issues of ideology or philosophy involved, except how best to force the political establishment to accept the idea of political party cabinets. Both main groupings were "bourgeois," imperial, and imperialistic. Nevertheless there were differences of emphasis that divided them, and Sheldon Garon's study has shown that it made a difference who held power.

The Seiyūkai constituency was more predominantly rural, and it maintained that support by programs of public works, but its upper echelons were oriented toward heavy industry, strong foreign policy, and strong armed services. The mainstream of the Kaishintō/Minseitō, however, was more likely to be urban and commercial in its support and emphasis. Periods of Seiyūkai rule, with Takahashi Korekiyo in charge of finances, tended to see an expansive, growth-oriented economic policy, while the opposition Minseitō preached fiscal responsibility and worried about getting and staying in balance with international trading partners. The ascendancy of particular officials and agencies could be affected by which party held the reins of power, and issues and differences were particularly clear with respect to labor problems. Garon documents those differences, and finds Kenseikai/Minseitō leaders voicing outrage at the repressive tactics pursued by the Tanaka Seiyūkai cabinet, and articulating a more liberal alternative with significantly greater respect for civil rights and labor. The alternative to such liberal moves, they argued, would encourage the very radicalism that the opposition was intent on rooting out. Yet it would be a mistake to carry this distinction too far, for the Peace Preservation Law of 1925 came during the cabinet headed by the Kenseikai's Katō Takaaki.

The Seiyūkai mainstream was hostile, and the Kenseikai/Minseitō partial, to labor legislation. As parties alternated in power the pendulum swung to some degree between the obsession of the Justice Ministry with repression and the willingness of the opposition leaders to back the views of the more enlightened bureaucrats of the Ministry of Home Affairs' Social Bureau.

In the Katō coalition cabinet the post of Home Affairs was in the hands of Wakatsuki Reijirō, a former bureaucrat who instructed the Social Bureau to prepare a bill on labor relations. The bureau's draft was toned down in the cabinet, where Seiyūkai members objected to many of its provisions. Prime Minister Katō's death catapulted Wakatsuki into the premiership just as the legislation was being prepared for submission to the Diet. There, the Seiyūkai, which had now seceded from the coalition and gone into opposition, resisted forcefully. The government then sought the help of splinter and independent groups, only to fall victim to the bank crisis of 1927 that has been discussed. At this point Wakatsuki was succeeded by General Tanaka and a Seiyūkai cabinet, and that had little comfort for advocates of labor legislation. Tanaka called for elections in February of 1928. They were, as we have noted, the first to be conducted under provisions of universal manhood suffrage, and in the aftermath of the results—a draw with the opposition that left control with splinter parties—Tanaka staged the great police raids in March. The prospects for the recognition of labor's rights to organize were now dismal, and instead the Justice Ministry prepared the revisions that strengthened the Peace Preservation Law of 1925, and then went on to fund a major increase in police surveillance with the Special Higher ("Thought control") Police. Opposition spokesmen berated the government's clumsy attempt to suppress dissent, and warned that only participatory democracy could be effective in preventing the spread of radicalism. Despite the opposition's efforts, the harm done to labor—and tenant—organizations and their leaders was real and lasting. The principal organizations were destroyed and with them the Labor-Farmer Party, which had gained 190,000 votes in the previous month's general election.

But as we have seen Tanaka's days too were numbered. His failure to retain the confidence of the young Emperor Hirohito by violating his promise to prosecute any army officers guilty of the death of the Manchurian warlord Chang Tso-lin resulted in his resignation. The field was once again ready for new efforts to institute labor legislation by a new Minseitō government led by Hamaguchi Osachi.

Hamaguchi's team was prepared for reform on several fronts. The Social Bureau chief Yoshida Shigeru (who should not be confused with the diplomat and postwar prime minister of the same name) again prepared a labor relations bill. The provisions of the proposal would have given unions more legal protection than that provided by any previously proposed legislation. Their specialists prepared proposals for an agricultural tenancy reform law to strengthen cultivators' rights. Plans were ready to introduce legislation extending the vote to women in local government. When the cabinet came into office Shidehara Kijūrō returned to the Ministry of Foreign Affairs, and Japan extended formal recognition to the nationalist government of Chiang Kai-shek against which Tanaka had intervened. There were areas of friction: the Chinese refused to agree to the appointment as Japanese minister of a diplomat who had been involved in the negotiation of the Twenty-one Demands, and the Seiyūkai nationalists wanted to make an issue of this.

Worse conflicts lay ahead. Japan reluctantly accepted the conclusions of the London Naval Conference; Hamaguchi overrode objections, and himself took the Navy Ministry chair during its incumbent's absence. There followed a fight over ratification of the treaty. Hamaguchi, charged with violating the emperor's "supreme command," was fatally wounded by a rightist assassin. There were other disasters. Finance Minister Inoue Junnosuke, a fiscal conservative, insisted on returning Japan to the gold standard on the eve of the world depression that virtually destroyed the international market for silk, with disastrous consequences for Japan's agricultural sector.

When the proposed labor legislation was introduced in the Imperial Diet it faced sharp opposition, and Shidehara had to take over its defense from the dying Hamaguchi. Next Shidehara, as foreign minister, inherited the storm brought by the Kwantung Army's precipitation of the Manchurian Incident. The labor bill was soon sacrificed to the larger crisis.

The labor movement failed in most of its objectives. Police and private violence struck down some of its most effective leaders and silenced more. Legislation prepared by relatively liberal bureaucrats gave way to more authoritarian state leadership during the war years that lay ahead. Nevertheless, the movement's strength and promise and its stand between submission and radicalism gave substance to the quiet transformation that the growth of industrialism brought to interwar Japan.

6. Changes in the Village

Change came more slowly to the Japanese countryside, but the interwar years nevertheless saw impressive changes in rural society. The basic causes were the same: people were tired of being told their sacrifices were for the sake of the country, they were tired of seeing those more privileged than themselves gain at their expense, and they were sufficiently educated and literate to realize that other people, in other areas, were demanding more justice. In addition, their rent—a share of the crop—might be sold at great profit by their landlord.

Japan was still overwhelmingly rural after the Russo-Japanese War; rapid as urban growth had been, the vast majority of Japanese lived in hamlets and villages. There was widespread agreement that the spiritual and social health of the country depended upon the stability of the countryside. Agriculture was ultimately the basis, and this view, codified as *nōhon shugi*, "agriculture as the basis," harked back to physiocratic Confucian thought. Some antimodernists deplored the fact that Japan was forsaking its roots for the false glitter of the West, but everybody thought of a healthy countryside as the real bulwark against the corrupting influences of the city.

Unfortunately that countryside was far from healthy, and most of its inhabitants had shared poorly in the benefits of modernity. By the years after World War I about 40 percent of all agricultural land was tenant farmed. This percentage fluctuated over time, but it remained relatively stable until the reforms that followed World War II. Rent averaged about 50 percent of the yield and was paid in kind; the tenant was obliged to carry it to the landlord's storage granary. Tenants were also expected to be of service to the landlord in a variety of ways when help was needed. The relationship was supposedly paternal, expressed in the landlord's status of *oyakata* (parent), a term encountered earlier with reference to labor contractors, but it could often signify submission rather than affection. The tenant had no security of tenure, and he risked his landlord's displeasure at his peril.

Nevertheless the tenant-landlord relationship was one of considerable variety. Landlords might be absentee. This category could range from school-teachers or other expatriates from the village who were reluctant to part with the family holdings, to professional money lenders who did their best to add to their holdings and who managed their lands through agents or representatives. More landlords were resident in the village. These in turn ranged from a handful of truly large landowners—the biggest were along the Japan Sea coast—who contacted their tenants through a senior tenant-lieutenant who in turn lived better than the others. Here the relations were hierarchic and structured. An ordinary tenant would no more presume to enter his landlord's main gate than a low-ranking samurai would have tried to use his lord's. Things were run in a businesslike manner. Several old landlord residences near Kanazawa, transformed into museums, permit the visitor to see the mounds of account books, chits, and receipts for rent received. The great majority of landlords, however, were owner-tenants, farmers whose holdings were so small that they found it profitable to rent additional land. Sometimes these plots, owned and rented, could be very small indeed; they testify to the narrow margin of solvency for most agriculturalists.

Tenancy arrangements were typically oral, and left the tenant with no security in the event the landlord chose to exploit or evict him. Where contracts were drawn up, their language gave eloquent evidence of the tenant's weakness. In one the tenants asked that "in years of bad harvest through natural causes you will on inspection of the crop, make such reduction in rent as seems to you fit. In the case, however, of a fall in yields resulting from my own management and affecting myself alone, I undertake to ask for no reduction in rent . . . I undertake to raise no single word of complaint should you, as your convenience makes necessary, decide to terminate my tenancy."[41]

By the end of the Meiji period several aspects of modern society had come to affect rural social structure. One was education. The landlord's son sat in the same schoolroom as the tenant's, and if he was a dullard and the tenant's son promising, that awareness could not fail to enter into later attitudes. Another was the military. The Imperial Reservists organization whose branches blanketed the country could also make a difference, as the display of valor in battle by a tenant could come into play in status relationships in the reserves.

The years of World War I helped bring these problems to the fore. The inflation of food prices profited the landlord, who could keep his storehouse full until the price went up, but not the tenant, who paid his rent in rice and could not afford to wait for a market to dispose of whatever he did not need for himself. The 1918 rice riots, it will be remembered, began in fishing villages on the Japan Sea coast and quickly spread to other parts of Japan.

Tenant-landlord disputes became common in the interwar years. Villagers knew that they were not participating in the prosperity; their rent remained as it was, while the landlord's profits rose steeply along with the wartime inflation. Figures for the growth of tenant disputes show a startling rise. In 1917 there were 173 tenant unions. In 1923, after the boom times of the war years had given way to depression, there were 1,530, and in 1927 they numbered 4,582 with a membership of 365,322. In those years the movement was concentrated in central Japan, the area most influenced by urbanism, education, and best served by progressive leadership. Leadership in most unions, Ann Waswo notes,[42] came from the ranks of upwardly mobile and profit-oriented tenants, but the membership was provided by small, economically distressed tenants.

Nineteen seventeen marked a significant stage in tenant protest. The harvest that year was below normal, and tenants asked for appropriate reductions in rent. In Aichi Prefecture, not far from Nagoya, a dispute involving 800 tenants and some 70 landlords began with requests for rent reduction and gradually spread to issues of labor for paddy maintenance and drainage, and security of tenure. Extensive mediation found the courts and local police involved. As the dispute escalated, a Kyoto University professor provided leadership in legal action designed to secure permanent tenure for tenants. When the date for the hearing approached so many tenants demonstrated that the authorities thought it best to postpone the meeting. A full settlement was not worked out until 1923, and then through the intervention of the Nagoya magistrate.[43] Disputes of this sort, which grew during the war years, showed how fragile the fabric of consensus had become in the countryside. Landlords, in self-defense, formed their own unions, and bureaucrats worried about the prospects of radicalism.

Dore notes that intellectuals played a significant role in stimulating the organization of tenants. The surge of liberal and left-wing thought that has been discussed encouraged it, and international trends reinforced it. The International Labor Organization passed resolutions upholding the right of tenants to bargain collectively. The fledgling Japan Communist Party advocated expropriation of the landlords. The JCP was soon outlawed, but Christian socialists, among them Kagawa Toyohiko (1888–1960), who had become famous through his work in the slums of Kobe, also advocated socialization of land as a long-range objective.

As was the case with labor, government bureaucrats understood the problem and tried to work out a tenancy law, but their efforts ran afoul of landlord representatives and lobbyists in the Imperial Diet. Politicians from both major parties were involved with this, but on the whole it was the Seiyūkai that had the stronger ties to rural notables, and in the election campaign of 1928 it was the Minseitō candidates who argued the need for a tenant relations law. There was thus a ferment in the air; in Waswo's words, "Tenants were clearly and in many cases consciously in revolt against the institutions and etiquette of status inequality."[44]

Despite this the tenant movement began to fade in the late 1920s. The great majority of tenant unions were organized at the hamlet level. It was much more difficult to build a union encompassing the entire administrative village, and to go beyond that was more unlikely still. Strong government repression might have produced such a result, but although the state monitored and discouraged tenant unions in many ways it did not resort to strong-arm tactics. That treatment was reserved for leftist organizers, particularly in the great round-up of 1928. In addition some efforts were made to head off greater conflict. In 1924 a Tenancy Conciliation Law established formal machinery for handling disputes, and legislation passed in 1926 provided low-interest loans to enable qualified tenant farmers to buy land. The government also revised an earlier Industrial Cooperative Law to provide machinery for cooperative action of the sort many tenant unions had advocated.

Tenant and worker power might have been more effective if there had been more cooperation between the two. The Labor-Farmer Party that formed in 1926 tried to bring this about, but in spite of the best efforts of its leaders most agriculturalists had little stomach for a class struggle, as they saw no resemblance between their lives and those of urban laborers. In any case, the Tanaka government's proscription of the Labor-Farmer Party in 1928 put that possibility to rest.

The impact of the world depression on Japanese agriculture brought a change in the distribution and frequency of tenant disputes. The surge of tenant unions, coming as it did in Japan's most developed areas, seems to have reflected a state of rising expectations. In contrast, in the late 1920s those expectations were replaced by a desperate attempt to ward off disaster. Tenant disputes now multiplied in less developed, peripheral areas in Japan, while in the central prefectures there was a slow decline. The impact of the Great

Depression, however, was felt throughout the country. With the collapse of the international silk market prices for silk cocoons fell by 47 percent in one year. The price of rice also fell sharply. Using 1926 as an index of 100, rural income declined to 33 in 1931, and it recovered only to 44 by 1934. Amid general agreement that there was a "crisis of the villages," government relief measures increased.

The shortages that developed during the years of crisis that began with the Manchurian Incident of 1931 brought relative prosperity for farmers. As Japan became more isolated the government increased its control over the distribution of what was now a limited supply of food. Landlords' control over their lands and produce gave way to government directives to deliver rice to newly established cooperatives. Landlords became relatively separated from their holdings and they were no longer as free to dictate terms. Small farmers and tenants, their pockets somewhat heavier for the money sent home by conscript sons, found themselves in a stronger position for the first time in modern Japanese history. The country was thus ready for the land reform mandated by the Allied Occupation after World War II.

7. Urban Culture

During the interwar years Japan developed a new popular, or mass, culture. The great cities of Osaka and Edo had earlier enjoyed a vibrant popular culture in Tokugawa times, one increasingly fashioned by and for commoner townsmen. It was their taste and fastidious expertise in leisure activities that Kuki Shūzō held up as an ideal in his "Structure of Taste." The Meiji march to modernity had little space for this, and the combination of nation building and Japanese Victorian standards made frivolity and consumption seem wrong. We have noted that after the Restoration city populations actually declined for a time, as the unproductive samurai consumers lost their incomes. By the time of the Russo-Japanese War, however, a new pattern of urban life had developed; city populations grew rapidly, but the newcomers were workers who moved from the countryside. The new generation of consumers was far more plebeian than the fastidious dandies of Tokugawa times, but they were also far more numerous. What they needed was not the near-professional appreciation of pleasures available to the man of leisure, but relief from the rigors and boredom of labor in office and factory. Far less self-sufficient than the relatives they had left behind in the countryside, they needed clothing, food, and diversion that they could afford. Prostitution was widespread; the costly pleasures of the talented geisha were reserved for the wealthy and the powerful, but endless chatter with bar girls and café hostesses over beer occupied many more. Beer, it should be added, was to some extent a product of Japan's seizure of German holdings in China; the brewers and equipment came to Japan.

There was, as contemporaries termed it, a "massification" *(taishūka)* of culture, consumption, and taste. This process was set in motion in late Meiji days. It advanced with the prosperity of the years of World War I, and it accelerated after the great earthquake. The products of technology and industrialization began to shape the lives of ordinary people. Photography, recordings, and movies became accessible to ordinary people. Newspapers grew as the rotary press of late Meiji developed into rotogravure, color, and offset printing. The *Asahi Graph* first appeared in 1923. Despite the ubiquity of state control, the new mediums offered a lively and relatively free rein for the growth of commerce and entertainment.

The great earthquake of September 1, 1923, marked a significant divide in this process. The disorientation and destruction it caused offered a free field to MAVO constructionists and other radicals, but not for long. Reconstruction was swift under the direction of Gotō Shinpei (1857–1929), one of the most important bureaucrats of the twentieth century.[45] Major avenues cut through the rubble of once-intimate streets, and ambitious plans for reconstruction were being drawn up while the city was being rebuilt in only slightly less haphazard fashion. The old merchant quarters, the "Low City" *(shita-machi)*, were particularly devastated, and the center of urban life moved closer to what had been the "High City."

After the earthquake Tokyo residents lived in a quite different environment. Pre-earthquake Tokyo was dotted with islands of green that remained from the gardens of daimyo estates. It was much smaller than it would become; the interior rail commuter (Yamate) circle described the arc of settlement. Shibuya and Shinjuku, now the vortex of commuter lines, were still relatively rural and occasional paddies and truck gardens retained touches of rural life. Postearthquake Tokyo was a quite different city. The moats that had provided transport and evening entertainment gave way to road, rail, and subway. Green space became rare, and it would disappear almost entirely in the aftermath of the destruction of the city a second time in 1945.

The Ginza, named for the silver guild in Edo years, became the showplace of the city. The central, Nihonbashi area was dominated by the great banks that took their place as temples of the new capitalism. From Kyōbashi to Shinbashi department stores, trendy shops, and cafés lined the main and side streets. The first subway to be built brought customers and workers from Shibuya to Ginza in fifteen minutes. A consumer culture for ever larger urban masses took shape.

Those masses were now almost fully literate, for by 1930 almost 90 percent of adult Japanese had at least the six years of elementary education behind them. There was an immense outpouring of print to catch their attention. Newspapers achieved mass circulation. Between 1918 and 1932 the number of journals registered under the Newspaper Law rose from 3,123 to 11,118, and the circulation of the great metropolitan daily the *Osaka Mainichi*, long the leader, climbed from 260,000 in 1912 to 670,000 in 1921 and 1,500,000 in 1930.[46] Newspapers also changed in character. In Meiji the newspaper was often a one-man or one-group effort to espouse a cause. With vastly more money involved newspapers now became a branch of big business, with boards, editors, and platoons of reporters. Entrance into the major dailies for college graduates was by examination; at first there were few takers, but by the late 1920s applicants outnumbered openings by a factor of fifty or more. With large sums of money involved the major dailies could ill afford suspension by the police, and since they knew how broadly press directives could be interpreted they tended to adopt a cautious stand on national affairs. The result was a certain uniformity, one that characterized the Japanese press in the less repressive days of the latter part of the twentieth century as well. Even so, the interwar press took up the cudgels for popular reforms like universal manhood suffrage, and it was much less circumspect than it would become in the 1930s, when militarism and imperialism provided popular rallying points.

Interwar publications included hundreds of magazines addressed to special audiences. Serious readers found in monthlies like *Chūō Kōron* (Central Review) a range of materials, from Yoshino Sakuzō's thoughtful expositions of democracy to discussions of contemporary policy and politics to serialized novels. *Kaizō* (Reconstruction) was bolder and sufficiently more critical to bring it to the attention of censors in the 1930s. *Fujin Kōron* (Women's Review) and *Shufu no tomo* (The Housewife's Friend) reached large audiences. Noma Seiji (1878–1938) was founder of the Kōdansha Publishing Company. It took its name from traditional tellers of historical tales—who were fast disappearing—and began with historical narratives that established its finances. Before long the firm was one of Japan's largest. "Kōdansha culture," as it became known, was mass culture. The house was (and remains) particularly sensitive to the existence of special interests and markets, and its success gave it a commanding position in providing materials for popular reading. If the Iwanami publishing company provided inexpensive editions of important books, Kōdansha provided material of every description. In both cases success was built on small inexpensive paperbound volumes, a tactic soon copied by other houses.

Japan thus took long steps toward becoming a consumer society. New products like Shiseido cosmetics and Lion toothpaste were advertised in the press and available on the shelves. Department stores, however, became the symbol, indeed the temple, of the new era of mass consumption. In the Meiji era the large stores followed the Edo tradition of specializing in dry goods. Gradually their offerings grew in variety, and by the 1920s new multistoried buildings along the Ginza offered so great a display of domestic and imported goods that they were objects of pilgrimage and family entertainment. Amusement areas and often small zoos to entertain the children were on the roof, restaurants and art galleries found their place below, while basement delicatessen and specialty food shops catered to urbanites in search of snacks or attractively packaged gifts. For a time the wealthy could arrange to have salespersons come to their homes or, if they came to the store themselves, had respectful clerks bring them items while they sat in comfort on rice straw mats. As the store displays grew in splendor, however, and the inventory was spread out for all to see, customers had to come to the goods. For years entrance was in the traditional manner, with store slippers provided in exchange for customers' shoes, which they found neatly arranged on their departure. After the earthquake it was the department stores that led in permitting customers to keep their shoes on. Wood and marble replaced rice straw mats, and the masses could enter freely.[47]

Urban pleasures multiplied and diversified. In 1913 Kobayashi Ichizō, a politician and talented producer, introduced an all-girl revue at Takarazuka, then a resort town near Osaka, as an attraction for his development. The Takarazuka revue grew to develop its own school for talent and enjoyed a popularity that survived World War II and reconstruction. It billed its stars as "beauties in male dress" and became famous for spectacularly staged musicals and revues. These were at once international (as in "Mon Paris," a journey through quaintly oriental countries of Asia to Paris), and parochial, with a subtext of Japanese modernity and empire. The organization grew to add a Tokyo theater in 1934. So great was its success that a rival group, the Sōchiku Girls Opera Company, was formed in 1922. Takarazuka featured singing and Sōchiku dancing, but both staged sumptuous productions, some of which might have several hundred girls on stage, on the scale of Hollywood extravaganzas. These drew large audiences, and they were particularly popular with throngs of youthful female patrons in addition to a middle-class clientele. Kabuki and Nō were all male, and Takarazuka, with an official motto of "clean, proper, and beautiful," struck a shrewd note of middle-class propriety.[48]

As the city and its population grew, a new scale of commercial development appeared. Private railroads knit suburban areas together, developing residential districts and carrying their occupants to places of employment and shopping in the metropolis. Their terminals were stops along the central commuter circle, the Yamate line, and at those stations department stores owned by the developers became new palaces of consumption. What was true of Tokyo was also the case with Japan's other large cities; Kobe, Osaka, and Nagoya become hubs for private railroad lines that brought the countryside ever closer to the city. Of Tsutsumi Yasujirō, perhaps the largest and most successful developer of modern Japan, a recent study notes that he "was much affected by the rise of Taishō democracy during 1912–1926 . . . He foresaw a huge increase in the number of middle-class consumers and invested in tertiary-sector businesses in the 1920s to cater to them: railways, suburban housing and mountain resorts."[49]

Cafés blossomed everywhere and served as recreation, drinking, and meeting places. Edward Seidensticker notes that the number of drinking spots doubled along the Ginza during the 1920s. The cafés were, Gennifer Weisenfeld notes, fashionable. They had a slightly decadent air about them, not unrelated to the ready attention of the waitresses, but they were a new way of telegraphing culture.[50] Popular authors frequented them, described them, and used them as settings for their stories.

Amid this kaleidoscopic change there was also growing nostalgia for what had been lost. In the Meiji ethos there was little space for Edo and its culture, but now there was sufficient distance to permit it to take on a rosy hue. Sometimes there was a linkage to more recent history. The vogue for tales of nihilistic swordsmen who struck down men they encountered were, one author suggests, a by-product of the crushing in the High Treason Trial of Kōtoku and the anarchists.[51] Forerunners of the Meiji Freedom and People's Rights Movement were lionized. A play about the Tosa loyalists Takechi Zuisan and Sakamoto Ryōma was so well received that it traveled to all parts of Japan. "No one," Tsurumi Shunsuke suggests, "did more for the cause of Taishō Democracy than this fictitious hero of the Edo period." Films, which entered Japan in late Meiji years, became enormously popular. More often than not they focused on loyal samurai. The description of Restoration politics was no longer a simple morality tale; there were heroes on both sides, and in depictions of the violence Tokugawa adherents frequently held their own. The great leaders of the Meiji period were gone, and their immediate successors, the cautious old men who dominated the Privy Council and House of Peers, had little claim on popular affection. Ironically, although these films, many with a consistent antiestablishment message, could be shown during Japan's war years, they were banished by the Allied Occupation as dangerously militarist.

Mass culture included cartoonists and comic strips. The *Asahi Graph* first appeared in 1923 with versions of popular American comics, but others soon drew on the brilliant graphic traditions of Hokusai and other Japanese artists. Major cartoonists like Okamoto Ippei (1886–1948) recorded for the masses important cultural events like the visits of Albert Einstein and Margaret Sanger. Future consumers of what became a burgeoning comic industry had their training in the portable picture shows narrated for neighborhood children on street corners and in empty lots by storytellers who appeared on bicycles each day. This tradition survived World War II, though not for very long.

Mention has already been made of the role of Yanagita Kunio, the father of folklore studies, who collected, classified, and preserved the customs of the past still living in the present. Other ethnographers were determined to record the present for what it might show about the future. These scholars, who took the city as their text, were fascinated by the interplay of the classes, genders, artisans, and white-collar workers who thronged the streets and amusement centers of Tokyo. They studied and recorded, as one student puts it, the "rupture in social relationships through discourse preoccupied with mores and customs and in the process exhibited a profound awareness of the ongoing construction of a new culture shared by all, but at the same time differentiated by gender and class."[52]

Still others, no less aware of the importance of ordinary people and objects, reached back to save aspects of everyday life that were being lost in a mass-production industrial society. The folkcraft movement, led by Yanagi Muneyoshi (Sōetsu, 1889–1961), was one more expression of the awareness that society and culture were changing irrevocably. Yanagi began as an art historian and member of a literary group known as the White Birch Society. In 1916 he traveled to Korea and fell under the spell of the beauty of ceramics produced by and for ordinary people. Some of the best of these pieces had long had the attention of Japanese tea masters and the potters who produced wares for them. Yanagi sought to restore dignity and appreciation for the beauty inherent in simple implements used in daily life in traditional Japan. He rallied to his cause two of Japan's greatest contemporary potters, Hamada Shōji (1894–1978) and Kawai Kanjirō (1890–1966). Together these men, with those they attracted, brought about a new awareness of the artistic and, as they saw it, spiritual importance of a tradition that was in danger of being lost to the products of modern mass production. A folkcraft museum in Tokyo, housed in a simple but sturdy country building, became the symbol of their efforts. Earthenware produced in country kilns for daily use took on new dignity, and the blue-and-white ceramics from Saga that had once flooded the Tokugawa market became collectors' pieces. The leaders of the folkcraft movement were men of courage as well as taste. Yanagi founded a museum in Seoul and espoused the cause of Korean independence. Hamada attached importance to the textiles and designs of Okinawa and encouraged the use of its dialect at a time when Japan's militarist leaders were making strenuous efforts for full Japanization. In these cases admiration of simple products of the past was related to distress for the forced centralization and homogenization of twentieth century Japan.

8. The Interwar Years

The years between the wars exhibited a remarkable pluralism in politics and thought. The rapid course of industrialization, spurred by the Russo-Japanese War and climaxing during the years of World War I, brought to focus changes initiated by the Meiji reforms. Those changes had as their goal the creation of a Japan able to hold its own with the Great Powers and a Japan dominant in Northeast Asia. The forces they unleashed, however, brought dislocation in every part of Japanese society. Women began to tire of the "good wife, wise mother" role to which they had been assigned. A labor movement began to challenge the undisputed dominance of the members of the Industrial Club, and a tenant movement gave evidence of dislocations in village life. The diffusion of education brought with it ready access to outside thought, and modern transportation brought premodern Japan to the new industrial centers and cities. Urbanization brought with it a new mass culture. Japan had become a land of far greater social variety than before. It was more open to the world than it had been. The products and tensions of the modern world had rendered it more internationalist and cosmopolitan. But because more and more of Western literature and thought was available in translation, and Japan's academic and cultural institutions had developed their own structure and mechanisms, Japan's intellectuals were in some ways more parochial than their Meiji predecessors, who had had to meet the West on its own terms and not in Japanese translation.

Japan's picture of the world, so clear and graded in Meiji times, also became less distinct and more complex. Japan was now one of the Great Powers, but the clarity of the model it had held up for emulation gave way to a multiplicity of images. The imperialist goal that had energized developed states in the nineteenth century gave way to talk of self-determination and cooperation. In China, in Russia, in Austria-Hungary, in Germany, and in Turkey monarchy was replaced by republicanism, and Japan—the struggling youth of the imagery of the 1880s—found itself an uncertain and rather fearful senior.

Within Japan the political consensus of the Meiji period, long moderated by the founding fathers of the modern state, was also giving way. The Meiji state structure had divided responsibility by reserving it—ostensibly to the emperor—to separate institutions charged with responsibility for military, diplomatic, and political affairs. The original *genrō* had been able to coordinate the institutions this created; their collegial tactics made it work, but their successors had not been bonded by youthful struggle in the same way. Katsura's disastrous attempt to work behind the imperial screen was the signal that a new day was at hand and that new actors or instrumentalities were required. Economic difficulty imported from abroad and foreign policy crisis generated from within warped this growth to produce a decade of instability.

17

At first glance the course of Japanese history in the 1930s differs so radically from that of the decade before that it presumes a profound discontinuity. Terms like "military takeover" or "fascism" have been employed to emphasize that gap. Other considerations come in to complicate interpretation and understanding. Which was the main course of modern Japanese history, that of the "democratic" period of party government or that of the militarist 1930s? What was the aberration? Earlier writers have tended to emphasize one or the other; the 1920s represented only a temporary interlude in modern Japan's rush to strength and empire, or the militarist era came in response to what was becoming an irreversible course toward a democratic modernity. These positions in turn had policy consequences for the second half of the twentieth century. If Japan's polity and psychology had indeed been fatally flawed by militarism, then reconstruction after defeat would require an almost total reorientation; if not, reforms in which the influence of forces making for imperialism were blocked or eliminated would make it possible for trends of the 1920s to continue.

In the narrative that follows it will become clear that neither case obtains. Many of the developments of the 1930s would in fact have been impossible without the development of mass culture and participation that had come before, and it is no less true that the military buildup and domination had powerful roots in the institutional pattern of the modern Meiji state. At first there was a shift in priorities and in weighting. There was no longer the influence of the original state builders to moderate and referee change. The measures they had adopted, from ideology to army, now assumed a momentum of their own. The institutions they built had generated powerful and frequently antagonistic bureaucracies and interest groups.

Generational change also played its part. Although there was remarkable carryover in the highest echelons, where Prince Saionji, now a frail old man, tried to find a middle path, a new generation of leaders who had not experienced the chastening fact of Japanese weakness proved capable of arrogance of a sort the Meiji leaders had not shown.

Japanese readings of the outer world also underwent drastic change. The impact of the great world depression weakened forces for internationalism abroad as they did at home. In the face of the drawbacks of capitalism new forms of state-led economy and polity seemed everywhere ascendant. As fascist leaders seemed successful in Germany and Italy the orderly hierarchy of world powers to which Japanese had looked for guidance changed. In neighboring China new forces of nationalism threatened to disrupt the leadership Japan had exercised in southern Manchuria since the Russo-Japanese War. The return of Russian influence in Northeast Asia alarmed Japanese planners who had never ceased to fear a replay of the contest of a quarter century before. These and other issues divided men of every stripe. There was no consolidated and unified "military," nor was it opposed by a uniformly pacifist "civilian" government. Linkages of many sorts produced partnerships in aggression, and the mass media developed in the "Taishō democratic" era trumpeted the new challenges of expansion and of war.

1. Manchurian Beginnings: The Incident

The three northeastern provinces of China—Liaoning (or Fengtien), Kirin, and Heilungkiang—were the homeland of China's ruling Manchus. Non-Chinese often referred to the area as "Manchuria." Manchu legislation had tried to prevent Chinese immigration into this area, but those restrictions had become a dead letter in the nineteenth century. The area, together with the province of Jehol, lay immediately north of the Great Wall, and the Shanhaikuan mountain pass served as entry to the province of Hopei, in which the capital of Peking was located. In the twentieth century Japanese references to the "Manchurian-Mongolian problem" (Man-Mō mondai) referred also to the Manchu dependency of Inner Mongolia, of which the most important part was the province of Chahar. After the fall of the Ch'ing in 1911 it was common to speak of the area as though it had become a political vacuum, unstable, underpopulated, and poorly defended against the new Soviet state to the north. As early as 1823 the political economist Satō Nobuhiro (1769–1850) wrote that Japanese expansion should begin with "the place we can most easily take, Manchuria, which we can seize from China. It will not be difficult for us to take advantage of China's decline."[1] In his time this was blustery expansive rhetoric, but a century later there was more to the argument.

The Japanese presence in Manchuria had been won from Russia in the Treaty of Portsmouth of 1905 and bolstered by extensions of the lease won under the Twenty-one Demands a decade later. South Manchuria, as it was known, consisted of the Liaotung Peninsula tip of Liaoning Province with the defensive site of Port Arthur and the port of Dairen (Dalian) and that portion of the former Chinese Eastern Railway extending south from Changchun to Dairen, henceforth known as the South Manchurian Railroad.

The administration of this area was divided into a complex pattern of overlapping jurisdictions. Beginning with general Foreign Ministry primacy, the structure changed to the advantage of the military during and after World War I with a largely unified military command, only to revert to civilian leadership during the administration of Prime Minister Hara. The leased area of Liaotung Peninsula was administered by a bureaucracy headed by a governor appointed by the throne. In some ways, however, the most strategic position was that of head of the South Manchurian Railroad (SMRR), an organization capitalized by impressive government and private sources but government-controlled. Its first head was Gotō Shinpei, earlier an architect of empire in Taiwan. (Later, as we have noted, Gotō was charged with the reconstruction of Tokyo after the 1923 earthquake.) The SMRR became the economic engine of imperialism in Northeast China. It controlled coal mines at Anshan, Fushun, and Yentai in addition to other mining, electrical, and warehousing enterprises. Along the railway Japan controlled police, taxation, public facilities, and education. Its generous funding included provision for research activities that grew constantly in importance and enrolled the talents of some of Japan's best scholars.[2] In the cities there were also police, responsible to the consuls. The consulates established in the principal cities and particularly ports were under the control of the Foreign Ministry. Manchuria was testing ground for the careers of many future leaders. The future diplomat and postwar prime minister Yoshida Shigeru won his spurs as consul in Manchuria. Matsuoka Yōsuke (1880–1946), a diplomat whose flamboyant style distinguished Japan's crisis years, and who entered the Foreign Ministry within a year of Yoshida, served as executive and president of the SMRR before becoming foreign minister. He was credited with coining the phrase that Manchuria and Mongolia were Japan's "lifeline" (seimeisen), a term that came into wide use.

Security was entrusted to the Kwantung Army, literally "east of the barrier," in reference to the Shanhaikuan pass between China proper and the eastern provinces. This force also experienced a number of changes in administrative accountability, but by 1931 its commander was responsible to the army minister and the Imperial Army General Staff. Its strength was calculated on a ratio of men per mile of railway track. The Kwantung Army consisted of one division that was rotated from regional regiments in Japan every two years, and six independent garrison battalions. The army had shrunk slightly during the military retrenchment carried out under Army Minister General Ugaki Kazushige in 1925, but Prime Minister Tanaka Gi'ichi had restored its strength in consequence of the return of Soviet forces to Eastern Asia.[3] Kwantung Army staff officer Colonel Kōmoto Daisaku had engineered the murder of the warlord Chang Tso-lin in 1928. It will be recalled that Tanaka had promised Emperor Hirohito to investigate that incident, and that his government had fallen because of his failure to keep that commitment. Kōmoto had meanwhile been succeeded by two quite extraordinary officers; they, in turn, were due for rotation back to Japan in 1931.

Colonel Itagaki Seishirō (1885–1948), like his colleague Lt. Colonel Ishiwara Kanji (1889–1949), was far removed from the old Chōshū mainline of army leaders. He was born in northern Iwate, and Ishiwara in Yamagata. Both excelled in the Military Academy and the War College. Itagaki, somewhat senior, headed the Kwantung Army's Staff Planning section; later he was posted to commands in China before Prime Minister Prince Konoe Fumimaro called him back to be his war minister in 1937. Later, now promoted to general, he returned to China as chief of staff of the China Expeditionary Force. After Japan's surrender he was listed as a major, Class A suspect by the International Tribunal that met in Tokyo and, after the trial, executed in 1948 as a war criminal.

His younger colleague Ishiwara was a more interesting nonconformist. He had graduated second in his class at the War College and received the cherished "imperial sword." His commitment to Nichiren Buddhism may have been a factor in the apocalyptic vision of war he developed. Personal knowledge of the destruction caused by World War I in Europe moved some civilians like Ozaki Yukio to call for disarmament and internationalism, but other Japanese, army students of war, came to sharply different conclusions. In three years of study in Germany Ishiwara drew on the writings of Frederick the Great, Napoleon, and von Moltke to work out views that he delivered as lectures in the Army War College upon his return. What he saw coming was a series of ever greater wars that would culminate in a final, titanic struggle between Japan, as hegemon of Asia, and the United States as leader of the Western world. That, however, would not come until technology had advanced to the point where airplanes could circle the globe without refueling. In the meantime the need was for the conquest of Manchuria in order to develop it as a resource base in preparation for war with the Soviet Union. In 1937 Ishiwara, then on duty in the General Staff, opposed the China War as a diversion from this larger strategic plan. His nonconformist demeanor and crusty independence blighted his army career, but that in turn probably helped save him from greater responsibility. After the war was over, and he was being questioned by interrogators for the International Tribunal, he lashed back by lecturing his questioners with the reminder that it was Commodore Perry, whose opening of Japan to the dangers of a pitiless international system, who was to be blamed for Japan's war with America.[4]

The Manchurian Incident was by no means the product of insubordination on the part of free-wheeling military activists. It was the product of meticulous planning and preparation, carried out in a context of complex personal and group affiliations. To begin with, Soviet announcement of a Five-Year Plan in 1928 brought with it fears of a resurgent enemy to the north. Chinese Communist forces contributed to this insecurity by restructuring party control in parts of Manchuria. Chang Hsüeh-liang had inherited the power of his father, Chang Tso-lin, in Fengtien, and his accession to Kuomintang rule in 1928 and Shidehara's recognition of the Kuomintang government of Chiang Kai-shek the following year added fears of erosion of Japanese autonomy in the leased area of Liaotung. Along the Korean border, in the Chientao region, hostility between Chinese and Korean settlers, many of them refugees from Japanese rule, provided room for charges of "outrages" against Japanese subjects. Japanese settlers in South Manchuria, particularly a Youth League, were vociferous in calling for protection.

In the summer of 1929 Itagaki and Ishiwara convened a study group and organized reconnaissance tours for Kwantung Army staff officers. Ishiwara lectured them about his theories of coming war. Out of this came a full proposal, printed by the Kwantung Army, for Japanese takeover of Manchuria in three stages. Other military officers, however, were at work with more sweeping plans to revamp the central government. Prime Minister Hamaguchi had selected General Ugaki, who had carried out retrenchment a half-decade earlier, as his army minister, and he, in turn, set out to strengthen his control of army policy by a series of personnel shifts. As the rotation date for Kwantung Army staffers approached, junior officers in Tokyo misread Ugaki's position, and began to see him as a possible leader for a military takeover of the central government. In the 1931 March Incident, a group of field-grade officers (members of a "Cherry Blossom Society"), and General Staff figures (Koiso Kuniaki and Tatekawa Yoshitsugu), encouraged by civilian right-wing theorists (Ōkawa Shūmei), hoped that by attacking the prime minister's office (occupied by Shidehara, Hamaguchi having already been fatally wounded) and headquarters of the political parties and organizing a crowd of thousands, they would be able to get the army to declare martial law as prelude to the appearance of Ugaki, as the man on horseback, to restore order. It was not to be. Ugaki held back, military leaders thought Manchuria more urgent, and the crowd did not materialize. The affair remained a secret; the planners were reassigned, and some to the Kwantung Army, whose turn came next.

In April Prince Saionji had to propose a new prime minister to succeed Hamaguchi, who had succumbed to his assassin's bullet. Fearful that a complete turnover might lead to additional violence, he secured the appointment of Wakatsuki Reijirō as prime minister. Shidehara was still foreign minister, but he too was experiencing difficulties. Negotiations with the Kuomintang government at Nanking had been going well until Saburi Sadao, Shidehara's emissary who was trusted by the Chinese, died under mysterious circumstances, either suicide or, more probably, murder. Ugaki, the failed hero of the March Incident, was succeeded by General Minami Jirō as army minister, and he in turn began to struggle with additional budget cuts ordered by Finance Minister Inoue Junnosuke. Rumors of army restiveness alarmed the Foreign Ministry, and Prince Saionji made it clear to Army Minister Minami that the palace expected discipline and restraint. On the other hand Mori Kaku, a Seiyūkai leader, was in full sympathy with Manchurian agitation and advised all party representatives to utilize the Manchurian-Mongolian "problem" in their rhetoric.

Plotters had better success in Manchuria. In the days preceding the explosion that triggered the Manchurian Incident an unsavory group of Japanese had collected at Kwantung Army headquarters. Amakasu Masahiko, who had murdered Ōsugi Sakae in 1923, was there with money sent by Japanese rightists. Even better financed was Colonel Kōmoto Daisaku, who had arranged for Chang Tso-lin's murder. Arrogance, avarice, and dishonesty found shelter under the claims of crisis. Kwantung Army officers were in touch with associated figures in the Tokyo General Staff, but those men, doubting the timing though personally favoring the coup, dispatched Tatekawa Yoshitsugu, freshly disappointed that March, to the scene to urge caution and delay. Kwantung Army plotters, aware of Tatekawa's mission, deflected him when he arrived with a round of partying that delayed his appearance at headquarters. When he was ready to resume his mission the next morning, a bomb had already gone off on the South Manchurian tracks at Liutiaokou, just north of Mukden; and a few bodies in Chinese uniforms bore witness to the vigilance of Kwantung Army guards charged with policing the SMRR right of way. The dead Chinese soldiers, it would be said, had imperiled Northeast Asia by planting the bomb. The damage was slight, for the next southbound train managed to arrive in Mukden on schedule. Nevertheless the "Incident" had taken place. Ishiwara had been worried about the reaction of Kwantung Army commanding general Honjō Shigeru, fearful that he might, despite his personal desires, be receptive to orders for caution from Tokyo. He need not have been. Honjō had just completed inspection trips to Kwantung Army posts, but Ishiwara had managed to insulate him from contact with Foreign Ministry officials at Mukden, for Honjō's cooperation was essential to the plan. Chang Hsüeh-liang, who had a much larger Fengtien Army force under his command, was also a possible problem, but in the event Chang helped the cause by issuing orders to his commanders they were under no circumstances to return Japanese fire, in order to avoid provocation. When Ishiwara pressed Honjō for action pleading the need for resolution, the commander reflected briefly and then said, "Yes, let it be done on my responsibility."

Within hours the Kwantung Army had achieved its initial military objectives against the Fengtien Army. Once the forces were engaged, pleas of military necessity were used as justification for additional moves, giving the lie to promises from the Tokyo civilian government that these were steps taken to preserve order and that no further expansion was contemplated. Those in positions of responsibility were anxious to limit the Incident and regain control of events, while the field and junior grade officers that peopled the General Staff and Army Ministry were jubilant that the Manchuria-Mongolia "problem" was finally being addressed. In Tokyo the atmosphere was electric with rumors of plots to take on the home government. A nervous government did its best to hush things up to avoid destabilizing the situation, but this had the effect of magnifying rumors. The reality was bad enough. A few weeks after violence broke out in Manchuria Lieutenant Colonel Hashimoto Kingorō of the Second Division, General Staff, and stalwarts of the Cherry Blossom Society conceived a bizarre plan to wipe out the entire government by aerial bombardment of a cabinet meeting; a crowd of rightists would then surround the War Ministry and General Staff headquarters and demand the creation of a military government. For this "October Incident," which never took place, Hashimoto received twenty days' confinement from superiors who did their best to deny that anything untoward had taken place. Hashimoto's name was to surface again later in the decade in connection with the shelling of an American ship, the *Panay,* on the Yangtze.

It is remarkable that indiscipline and terrorism on this scale could threaten Japan's stability so suddenly. But one has to factor in deep currents of underground dissatisfaction that characterized Japanese society in the 1920s. We have noted sporadic violence against individual capitalists, and military insubordination in Manchuria in 1928. The Imperial Army had deep fissures between those who conceived and carried out retrenchment, like General Ugaki, and others who deplored such steps. Right-wing ideologues feared a rise in social radicalism as a result of rapid industrialization at the same time that they justified their own direct action as measures to "save" the villages. Constant talk of a "China problem" and criticism of the government's "weak" diplomacy prepared many for relief that something was finally being done to address those matters. Young hotheads like Hashimoto could get nowhere without the support of staff officers like Ishiwara and Itagaki, and they in turn needed at least tacit approval from their superiors. Fear of even worse violence combined with military bonding to produce quiet approval or at least tolerance. Demands for "reform" at home reverberated with calls for "solution" abroad. Army activists served as point men for widespread doubts about the health and direction of Japanese society and polity. Guardians of that polity, the aging *genrō* Saionji and colorless senior statesmen who were struggling with problems of economic depression and international opprobrium, retreated while giving as little ground as possible, hopeful that the tide would turn their way again in days to come.

These tactics, if they can be so described, led to bizarre confrontations. On September 8, 1932, General Honjō and his staff were treated like conquering heroes at the imperial palace. Horse-drawn carriages provided by the Imperial Household met them at the station and carried them across the famous "Double Bridge" onto the palace grounds. After lunch, in the unstructured questions that followed Honjō's report on military matters in Manchuria, Emperor Hirohito startled his guests by asking whether there was any substance to stories that the "Incident" was actually a plot by certain individuals. A silence fell on the gathering; Honjō rose, bowed, and then stood at attention. "I too," he said, "have heard it said that this had been engineered by some army men and divisions, but I assure Your Majesty that neither the Kwantung Army nor I were involved in anything of the sort." Ishiwara, who was among those present, is said to have muttered, "Someone's been talking out of turn to His Majesty."[5]

In Manchuria the Kwantung Army continued its advance; aerial bombardment and rapid advance brought all three eastern provinces under Japanese control. Japan was now in clear violation of the Nine Power Pact and the Kellogg-Briand Pact of Paris. Other developed economies were reeling under the impact of the world depression, however; readers were inured to stories of civil war and banditry in China, and condemnation of Japan was by no means certain. What made it so was the steady series of failures by civil officials to get the military to abide by the assurances they offered other governments, the drumbeat of violence within Japan as well as overseas, and the pointless truculence and hyperbole of Japanese officials in international contexts. Civilian and diplomatic spokesmen sensed that acceptability to the army was gradually becoming a criterion for selection, and this resulted in rhetoric designed for Japan as much as for the outer world.

By the time General Honjō received his welcome in the imperial palace momentous steps had been taken for the Northeastern Provinces. On December 13, 1931, the hapless Wakatsuki government was replaced by a Seiyūkai cabinet under the veteran Inukai Tsuyoshi. On January 3, 1932, the Kwantung Army took Chinchow, which it had earlier promised not to occupy. A few days later representatives of the Foreign Ministry, army, and navy agreed on the establishment of an independent state in Manchuria. The next day a Korean threw a bomb at the emperor's carriage outside the palace gate, bringing Prime Minister Inukai's offer—which was rejected—of resignation. The following week several Japanese Buddhist priests were killed in Shanghai, leading to hostilities between Japanese naval and marine forces and the Chinese Communist Ninth Route Army that was withdrawing from the Peking area. Prime Minister Inukai called for elections to the House of Representatives. Seiyūkai speakers were urged to emphasize the importance of reaching a solution to the Manchuria-Mongolian issue, and won a solid majority over the Minseitō. There was additional violence. Inoue Nisshō, a Nichiren priest, organized a Blood Brotherhood Band on January 31, recruiting volunteers to assassinate prominent persons as symbols of the capitalist-internationalist order. Former minister of finance Inoue Junnosuke (on February 9) and Mitsui chairman Baron Dan Takuma (on March 5) fell victim to its members, others of whom went on to collaborate with navy officers returned from the fighting at Shanghai to gun down Prime Minister Inukai in his residence on May 15. During all this the Kwantung Army tightened its grip on Manchuria by taking Harbin on February 5. On March 1, just after the arrival of the Lytton Commission, which the League of Nations dispatched to make an on-the-scene investigation of the affair, the announcement of the "independent" state of Manchukuo was made. The capital of the new state was to be at Hsinking (the former Changchun), and the head of the new state was to be Hsuan T'ung, the last Ch'ing emperor (known in the West as Henry Pu Yi), who had taken refuge in Tsinan after being expelled from the Forbidden City by warlord conflict. On September 15 Japan extended diplomatic recognition to the new state. In the Imperial Diet the House of Representatives had gone on record with a unanimous vote advocating such recognition three months earlier, and Uchida Yasuya, who had been Japanese representative to the Pact of Paris and was now appointed foreign minister, had assured the Diet that Japan was prepared to carry out a "scorched-earth diplomacy" against those who stood in its way. Japanese internationalism, the Shidehara China policy, and indeed the entire Washington Conference order that had structured East Asia for a decade were thus seemingly at an end. A Japan that had warred against the Ch'ing empire in 1894 as a representative of modernity and progress was now proposing to re-create that rule under its own auspices in northeastern China.

By the time the Lytton Commission submitted its report on October 2, in other words, Japan was well committed to an independent course and matters were no longer negotiable. Matsuoka Yōsuke returned to Geneva; also there, largely to monitor him, was Lt. Colonel Ishiwara, who had organized the entire "Incident." The Lytton Commission had visited Japan and China and spent six weeks in Manchuria trying to sort things out. Its verdict, while damaging to Japan's case, was by no means completely hostile to the Japanese cause. Matsuoka, however, would broke no criticism and led his delegation out of the hall when he saw the certainty of a defeat in the League's General Assembly. Before doing so he astonished his hearers by depicting Japan as crucified by world opinion, and predicted that verdicts on Japan would change just as they had on Jesus of Nazareth.[6] Japan announced its withdrawal from the League, although its representatives continued to work with the many specialized agencies of that organization. In a matter of weeks the goals that Japanese diplomacy had pursued since 1868—gaining equality through cooperation with the largest of the Great Powers—were thrown to the wind.

It is not difficult to understand the dilemma that faced liberal and conservative leaders who had come to maturity under the goals of the old order. Most of them hesitated, hoping that the climate of opinion would change once again. To this end it was important to persuade the West that Japan had not completely or permanently abandoned its policies of international cooperation, and simultaneously to assure Japanese that the Western condemnation did not mean a permanent severance of ties. A group of distinguished diplomats with wide foreign contacts sent reassuring messages to the London *Times* and other organs of opinion. The ailing Nitobe Inazō, once under secretary of the League who had vowed never to visit America so long as the Immigration Law stood, changed his mind to embark, despite ill health, on a lecture tour from which he never returned. When the government's hasty translation of the Lytton report seemed stark and provocative to a group of liberal academics, they worked throughout the night with George Sansom, the distinguished English diplomat and scholar, to rework it in the vain hope that milder wording would help their cause. At every point, however, the military seemed to carry the day. In January 1933 Japanese forces seized the mountain barrier of Shanhaikuan that controlled the Peking plain, and a month later Chinese forces evacuated the province of Jehol in response to an abrupt Japanese ultimatum. The borders of Manchukuo were not yet clearly defined, but Japan was committed to its creation and defense.

2. Manchukuo: Eastward the Course of Empire

Once the Kwantung Army had occupied all of Manchuria, the question arose of what to do with it. Kwantung Army planners had made up their minds and prepared plans for a semiautonomous state before they precipitated hostilities. A "colony" on the lines of Taiwan or Korea would be needlessly provocative, and it would furthermore be under the control of the colonial bureaucracy of the Tokyo government. A semiautonomous state, on the other hand, could be billed as "independent" and allied with Japan. Ishiwara saw this as essential to his larger strategic goals, and at one point even speculated about abandoning his Japanese citizenship to accept that of the new Manchurian state. He himself might have voted for a republican arrangement there, but the advantages of having a Manchu ruler were compelling. The last Manchu ruler, Pu-yi, who had reigned as a child from 1909 to 1912, was prevailed upon to return as head of state of Manchukuo in 1932. Two years later he was enthroned as emperor of the "Manchukuo Imperial Government" (Manshū teikoku seifu) with the reign title K'ang-te (Prosperity and Virtue). Full imperial status for Pu-yi might have seemed a challenge to that of Hirohito, but when he visited Tokyo in June 1935 the two were seated side by side in the royal carriage as they reviewed Imperial Army formations at Yoyogi.

Manchuria provided a new frontier for Japan, the first it had known since early Meiji Hokkaido, but far more promising. Taiwan was fully populated and the Korean polity older than Japan's, but Manchuria was (incorrectly) thought of as relatively open space. From the first the Incident was wildly popular in Japan. Depression had impoverished many and party politicians labored under images of corruption and self-seeking, but the lightning victories of the Kwantung Army caught the national mood. There was a great deal of cheap chauvinism celebrating heroics that, considering the fact that the Fengtien Army had initially been under orders not to resist, must have been rather hard to document. The Shanghai Incident, in which well-trained and highly motivated Chinese soldiers were involved, served that purpose better. Still, the speed with which the Kwantung Army, a force of 10,000 men, had driven a Fengtien force many times its size from Manchuria could be expected to bring approval.

What made that approval count was the diffusion of mass media that had developed between the wars. No doubt much of this was market driven, but its impact and significance is none the less for that. The great dailies *Osaka*

Mainichi and *Asahi,* with their metropolitan editions and suburban satellites, blanketed the country with exciting headlines and jubilant extras. As their circulation grew they developed into joint stock companies, handsomely capitalized and capable of buying airplanes that could carry correspondents to the front and rush copy and photographs back. Until paper shortages and rationing prevented it, magazines without number detailed the opportunities of the new frontier, and the popular Kōdansha house "turned its string of magazines into cheering sections for the Kwantung Army." Radio supplemented this, and in an era of rapid electrification of the countryside supplemented the staccato rattle of infantry fire.[7]

The army had only recently suffered from currents of antimilitarism, and in seeking to reverse those it launched what was probably the first drive to contact ordinary Japanese. Officers back from the front were sent on lecture tours, symposia on Manchuria enlisted knowledgeable scholars and travelers, and surveys revealed the impact of these tactics on even hitherto skeptical university students. What was most effective was a campaign to show the need for a "national defense state" *(kokubō kokka)*. The whir of the printing press and the rhetoric from lecture podiums drove home the dangers of a Soviet Russian resurgence on the continent, the facts of Japan's resource-poor state, its disadvantage in a world of unfairly critical "have" nations, and the history of Western aggression and exploitation that began with Perry's black ships.

Intellectuals were not left out of this campaign; in many ways they helped to lead it. Prospects for employment for university students, so recently darkened by depression, rose with the prospect of challenges in the new empire. The tide of explicitly Marxist analysis in social science that had been prominent in the 1920s changed under the pressures of orthodoxy and intimidation, but assumptions of state and bureaucratic leadership in economic development fit smoothly with the army's drive for planned growth in Manchukuo. A Five-Year Plan was announced in 1936 in a backhanded compliment to that of the Soviets in 1928. There were new challenges and new opportunities. Moreover the facade of Manchukuo independence seemed to offer a path by which to transcend the old imperialism. It was as modern as Soviet planning, Italian corporatism, German state socialism, and the American New Deal.

Planning involved close study of society and economy, and research institutes proliferated at home and abroad. Graduates of reputable institutions were sure of employment. More surprising, in some ways, was the fact that Manchurian institutes, particularly the enormous enterprise sponsored by the South Manchurian Railroad, were hospitable to Marxist and left-wing scholars who were being targeted by the thought control police at home. Until those purges extended to Manchuria after the opening of the Pacific War in 1941, many who were advocates of revolutionary change and social planning at home found employment on the continent.[8]

Manchuria held out a role for every talent. Urban planners cramped by Japan's narrow space and crowded streets laid out boulevards and parks in the new capital. Academic builders had their chance in the new *Kenkoku daigaku,* the "Nation-Building University" in Hsinking. Transportation experts could lay out new broad-gauge lines to supplement the South Manchurian and Chinese Eastern (which was purchased from the Soviet Union in 1934). Tourist hotels, beginning with the luxurious Yamato in Dairen, sprang up along the major lines, and the "Asia Express" with its up-to-the-minute rolling stock, much of it more elegant than anything to be found in Japan itself, carried Japanese tourists along routes that had once transported Manchurian soy beans and little else.

Manchuria absorbed immense quantities of capital investment in the drive to develop a heavy industry base. It became, in Louise Young's words, a sink-hole for capital, and resources at a time when immense armament programs were also being carried out in Japan. Much of this capital was in the form of state-guaranteed bonds; private enterprise regarded the new equities more warily. The major zaibatsu firms had to carry a heavy part of this load, but "new" zaibatsu, especially Nissan, whose head Ayukawa enjoyed close relations with the military, were particularly active in the growth of iron and steel works. Inevitably there were contradictions and conflicts along the way as well. Textile exporters relied heavily on the Chinese market, but anti-Japanese boycotts reduced them to the much less important sector of Manchuria. Here their interests conflicted directly with those of Kwantung Army planners; the Japan-based firms wanted low tariffs to maximize their exports, while Manchukuo authorities were in desperate need of tariff income to finance heavy industry. As the continental planners had their way what began as a favorable trade balance became a drain instead, and the businessmen were frequently and openly critical and even contemptuous of the programs produced by military planners.

Behind the orderly ports, sleek trains, and luxurious hotels the visitors saw there was also a harsher reality. The Kwantung Army advance took care of organized resistance, but the struggle for security of the interior lay ahead. A "Manchukuo" army and police force was organized, but for most of the decade that followed it required continual effort to control guerrillas and "bandits," many of them Communists from across the border. To combat this the Japanese organized secure and "purified" villages with road and telephone contact with local constabulary units, and also emphasized propaganda about the benefits of the "kingly way" (*wang tao,* Japanese *ōdō*) that was supposed

40. In 1935 the last Manchu emperor of China, Pu Yi, who had been installed as "emperor" of the new Manchukuo, was brought to Tokyo, where he and Emperor Hirohito (left) reviewed troops on June 9.

41. Barricades thrown up in downtown Tokyo by insurgents in the February 26, 1936, Young Officers' Revolt.

42. As the war intensified, the ties between nationalism and State Shinto became more compelling. In this 1941 ceremony at Yasukuni Shrine 14,975 *katsura* branches were presented, each the spirit of a casualty the previous year.

43. In the great fire raids of March 1945 most of Tokyo was destroyed. In this picture of the Kanda area, everything combustible has burned, leaving a wasteland.

44. The lives of Hirohito, Emperor Shōwa: (top) examining
    bomb damage in his destroyed capital; (bottom left) as
    generalissimo reviewing his troops; and (bottom right)
    encountering ordinary Japanese after the surrender.

45. May Day riots in 1952 at the imperial palace plaza, immediately after Japan's resumption of sovereignty, revealed the social and political tensions in post-Occupation Japan.

46. Yoshida Shigeru was not popular when he stepped down, but in retirement he soon assumed the mantle of postwar *genrō*.

47. Nihonbashi, the Japan Bridge, so striking and busy in Edo and Meiji times (illus. 10, 14, and 24), now lies hidden beneath the elevated roadways of the contemporary metropolis.

to be the answer to nationalism and radicalism. As the 1930s wore on these efforts were increasingly, though never completely, successful; the harsh climate made it possible to separate guerrillas from their food supply in winter, and Japanese organizational efficiency, with its plethora of reports, charts, and surveys, gradually overcame the problem of security.[9] The porous borders that made it possible for insurgents to obtain arms served Japanese purposes to the west and south in the form of opium distribution methodically pursued as a source of income. It was a pattern developed by splinter warlord regimes and Chinese rightists under the protection of treaty port extraterritoriality (which had itself, of course, come into being through the Opium War), but Japanese rule made possible a new scale, with official protection, that covered routes from Inner Mongolia to North and Central China. Meticulous records published only recently make it possible to trace the orderly flow of opium from the new territories as well as from Iran, the latter in Mitsui and Mitsubishi steamers.[10]

There was heavy Japanese migration to Manchukuo, almost all of it urban. Jobs in administrative and transport facilities were tempting, and the Japanese population in the urban areas grew steadily. Kwantung Army planners, however, wanted settlers who could build a wall of defense villages, particularly along the northern border. Early Meiji settlement of Hokkaido had been based on similar *tondenhei*, or militia, units. But it was not as easy to persuade farm families to go north as it had once been to attract them to Hawaii and America's West Coast. Propaganda campaigns worthy of Jay Hill's blandishments about a northern plains "banana belt" along the Northern Pacific Railroad sought out tenant and landless farmers. Visions of a "paradise" with ownership of farms and woodlots adequate to support family and animals were held out, with subsidy for travel provided. Those who accepted found themselves on land their new government had taken from Chinese, frequently at an extortionate price or by mislabeling it as untilled, unaccustomed to the climate and terrain and unable to obtain the mechanized tools they had been promised. Many resorted to hiring Chinese farmers as laborers or even tenants. Agricultural production grew, but far more slowly than had been hoped. As the war situation worsened and a Soviet invasion became probable the government callously drafted able-bodied male settlers while leaving their families defenseless along the border. Remarkably, bureaucratic inertia kept the program going long after it had no chance; groups from Nagano Prefecture were still coming as late as May of 1945. Agricultural settlers made up only 14 percent of the Japanese in Manchuria, but they accounted for almost half of the civilian casualties there when war came in August 1945.[11] When they were finally encouraged to flee, most families had no transport and little food. Postwar Japan has been visited by scores, perhaps hundreds, of Japanese who speak no Japanese in a vain search for relatives and roots, people who were left behind as infants with friendly Chinese families by desperate mothers who knew they had no other chance for survival.

3. Soldiers and Politics

The Meiji leaders' concern for their own position as the emperor's chief advisers resulted in provisions that put him in personal command of the armed forces. The 1882 Imperial Precepts to Soldiers and Sailors had warned them to steer clear of politics, but the institutional structure made it even more certain that civilians' decisions would not interfere with the military. The exception, and it was an important one, concerned budget allocations, which were in the hands of the Imperial Diet; demands for funding additional divisions and warships became constantly more pressing as Japan expanded its strategic interests.

The emperor could not, however, be trusted with military decisions, and an elaborate structure of advisers developed. They reported to him, but he was expected to legitimize their decisions and not to direct them. This structure included first of all the army and navy chiefs of staff who, after reporting to the emperor, transmitted his orders to the cabinet through the minister of the army and the minister of the navy. An additional advisory body was the Supreme War Council, made up of field marshals, fleet admirals, the service ministers, the chiefs of staff, previous holders of those posts, and additional military councillors selected by the emperor from the generals and admirals. There was also a Conference of Field Marshals and Fleet Admirals that came into play in times of crisis. After decisions had been reached, a Liaison Conference between army and navy chiefs prepared the agenda for an Imperial Conference. Throughout all this the emperor traditionally remained silent. Despite all the talk of "direct command," authority and responsibility were fragmented. No single person was really in charge, for the Meiji Constitution, by giving supreme command to the sovereign, denied it to anyone else. This was satisfactory only as long as a small and reasonably cohesive group of senior advisers was in the background to coordinate opinion, but by the 1930s that was no longer the case.

Civilians were not involved at any point in this process of military decision making until they reached the very highest level, but military men, through outside "politics," played a major role in politics through their ability to break cabinets. The 1900 ordinance had seen to it that service ministers would be professionals on the active duty list, but it did not end there, and even when that requirement was relaxed in the 1920s military men and issues remained important. Between 1885 and 1945 there were 43 cabinets headed by 30 prime ministers, of whom half were military figures: 9 generals and 6 admirals. Again, of the 494 civilian posts in those cabinets, 115 were occupied by generals and admirals. The military proportion was high in Meiji, lower in Taishō, and up again in presurrender Shōwa, with 62 of 165 posts. The Ministry of Finance, however, was never infiltrated by the military.[12]

A list of cabinets between that of Inukai Tsuyoshi and Suzuki Kantarō, who presided over the decision to surrender, illustrates this growing military influence. The chart gives evidence of instability rooted in insubordination, errors in judgment of the international system, and inability to build a dependable base of support in the Imperial Diet. Inukai was murdered. Okada escaped his would-be assassins, but his position was hopelessly compromised by the disgrace of the revolt. Saitō and Hayashi were unable to handle a Diet that felt it was being denied its due, Hirota and Hayashi incurred the wrath of the army, and Konoe gave up in frustration, first when his policies in China were failing, and then when he was unable to stop or even slow the drift toward the war that his rhetoric had helped encourage.

Until his death in 1940 it fell to Saionji Kinmochi, the last *genrō,* to suggest

Cabinets, 1931–1945	
Prime minister	Cause of fall
Inukai Tsuyoshi, 1931–May 15, 1932	Murdered
(Adm.) Saitō Makoto, 1932–1934	Charges of corruption
(Adm.) Okada Keisuke, 1934–1936	Young Officers' Revolt, Feb. 26
Hirota Kōki, 1936–1937	Army minister claimed Diet insult
(Gen.) Hayashi Senjūrō, 1937 (4 mos.)	Election defeat
Konoe Fumimaro, 1937–1939	China war fatigue
Hiranuma Kiichirō, 1939 (8 mos.)	Unprepared for Nazi-Soviet Pact
(Gen.) Abe Nobuyuki, 1939–1940	Party, service opposition
(Adm.) Yonai Mitsumasa, 1940 (6 mos.)	Army opposition
Konoe (2nd cab.), 1940–1941	Drop Foreign Minister Matsuoka
Konoe (3rd), July–Oct. 1941 (3 mos.)	Failure of Washington negotiations
(Gen.) Tōjō Hideki, 1941–1944	Fall of Saipan
(Gen.) Koiso Kuniaki, 1944–Apr. 1945	Okinawa invaded
(Adm.) Suzuki Kantarō, Apr.–Aug. 1945	Surrender

prime ministers. Saionji was now in his eighties, and made a point of consulting with senior court officials, among them Privy Seal Makino Shinken and Kido Kōichi, whose steady advance through appointive posts brought him to palace prominence. In this he was dealing with the true political elite of the modern state; Makino was the son of Ōkubo Toshimichi while Kido was the grandson of Kido Takayoshi. Other senior court officials came in for consultation, as did, in less direct ways, former prime ministers, collectively thought of as "senior statesmen" (*jūshin*), the ministers of the army and navy, and heads of political parties. The Seiyūkai had won a decisive victory in elections Inukai had called in February 1932. When the prime minister was murdered in May the party selected Suzuki Kisaburō as his successor as party head, and it had every reason to expect that he would be named prime minister. Saionji, however, neither liked nor trusted Suzuki, whom he considered extreme in his views, and the service ministers were opposed to another party cabinet altogether. The Minseitō, now the opposition party, was also unenthusiastic about a Seiyūkai cabinet led by Suzuki. Saionji moved toward an alternative: a retired admiral, Saitō Makoto, a former governor general of Korea, was asked to form a "national unity" cabinet. He would have reasonable Diet support from elements of both parties, and politics would be less partisan at a time of national crisis. The decision to form a nonparty cabinet proved to have momentous consequences, for there would not be another until after World War II. Yet at the time, in view of the crises occasioned by Manchuria, Shanghai, assassination, and international opprobrium, Saionji's decision seemed reasonable to most Japanese.

One can thus conceive of Saionji and other members of the "old guard" giving ground, but slowly and reluctantly, to the demands of the military. They were also determined to avoid more direct imperial intervention in the process. At the outset, at least, Hirohito was upset and concerned by what was being done and probably willing to utilize his prestige and aura. There were two problems about this for Saionji: the first was adherence to his understanding of the role of a constitutional monarch; imperial intervention, he argued, would be contrary to the spirit of the Meiji Constitution. The other was Saionji's awareness of currents of radicalism in the army. He did not like what he heard about disrespectful mutterings among young officers, and feared for the preservation of the monarch, or even the monarchy itself. This was a factor that would have absolute priority for him.[13]

Strong tides of factionalism, sectionalism, and ideology made the Imperial Army contentious and problematic. A regional faction centered on Chōshū and led by Yamagata Aritomo had dominated the high command since the early Meiji period. Yamagata lived until 1922; he remained powerful to the last, but the men who seemed to be his chosen successors fared poorly. Katsura Tarō died after his attempt to form a third cabinet in the first year of Taishō, and Terauchi Masatake, who seemed next in line, proved a dismal failure as prime minister and died in 1919. Leadership then passed to Tanaka Gi'ichi, who had, as has been mentioned, Russian experience before serving in Manchuria during the Russo-Japanese War. Tanaka led in organizing the army reserve and youth groups and served in the General Staff and as army minister in the Hara cabinet before assuming the presidency of the Seiyūkai in 1925. He was associated with the planning of continental policy, but died in 1929 after incurring Emperor Hirohito's displeasure for failing to keep his promise to investigate the murder of Chang Tso-lin. Leadership of the faction now passed to Ugaki Kazushige (Kazunari, 1868–1956). Ugaki was actually from Okayama and not from Chōshū, but carried on Tanaka's pattern of cooperating with the political parties, in his case the Kenseikai/Minseitō, serving as army minister in the cabinets of Katō Takaaki and Hamaguchi Osachi before withdrawing to become governor general of Korea. The plotters in the March 1931 Incident had expected him to support their efforts and emerge as prime minister of an emergency government, but by failing to follow through he alienated them permanently. When he was authorized to form a cabinet in 1937 he was blocked by army opposition. The next year Ugaki served briefly as foreign minister under Prince Konoe, but resigned in protest against bureaucratic changes that weakened and compromised the Foreign Ministry.[14]

The long ascendancy of the Chōshū faction aroused the antipathy of outsiders who rejected its dominance and condemned it as conservative and politically partisan. If resentment of Chōshū monopolization of senior posts was one source of army factionalism, disagreement about spending priorities also divided army from navy. After the Russo-Japanese War navy leaders reconditioned some of the ships that had been captured from the Russians, but they soon realized that with the appearance of the British *Dreadnaught* more basic steps would be required and demanded a large-scale building program. The army's counter was to demand two additional divisions to handle its new responsibilities on the continent, a demand that brought down the Saionji cabinet in 1912 and lay behind the "Taishō political crisis" that brought down Katsura. The scandals in navy procurement that brought down the Yamamoto cabinet in 1914 gave the army new advantages, and World War I, which opened new continental opportunities (the Twenty-one Demands, Terauchi's "Nishihara" loans to northern warlords, and especially the Siberian intervention), marked the end of the old pattern of cautious *genrō* control.[15]

In 1914 Prime Minister Admiral Yamamoto secured relaxation of the requirement that service ministers be selected from generals and admirals on the active list, making it possible to appoint retired officers to those posts. In response the army high command strengthened the powers of the General Staff to offset possible political interference in military affairs. World War I, however, brought defections at the center as well as a weakening of support throughout Japanese society. The international currents of antimilitarism and demobilization in which Japan shared have already been described. These might unite army factions, but internal disputes centered around the issue of army modernization to bring it up to standards that had been developed by the combatants in Western Europe. Tanaka Gi'ichi, who had strongly supported the army's demands for two additional divisions and the Siberian intervention from his post in the General Staff, now realized that Japan would have to make choices in the troubled interwar years. His choice was for modernization combined with manpower limitations to make it possible to fund growth, and his alliance with the leadership of the Seiyūkai—as the party became more favorable to heavy industry—followed the logic of that situation. Ugaki, though he cast his lot with the opposition political party, shared those goals. In 1922 the Army Ministry carried out economies by streamlining existing army divisions, in 1924 Ugaki demobilized four divisions altogether, and when he became army minister again in 1931 Ugaki proposed demobilizing the Konoe Imperial Guard Division. These moves were strongly resisted by opponents, who argued that since Japan's continental enemies did not have technological superiority they should be opposed by conventional forces steeped in Japan's indomitable spirit and trained for sudden attack. Advocates of modernization had their way, but carried the day by only a single vote in the Supreme War Council in 1924. One of the most powerful opponents was General Uehara Yūsaku, a Satsuma man who had held office for more than a decade and gathered a strong following. Those who placed their hopes in "spirit" rather than in modernization formed the nucleus of what became known as the Imperial Way *(kōdō ha)* faction. Araki Sadao (1877–1966), whose obscurantism muddied the waters throughout the 1930s, became a spokesman for this persuasion.

Another issue that divided army leaders concerned the policy Japan should adopt toward nationalist China. Most viewed Shidehara's willingness to recognize the Nanking government of Chiang Kai-shek as a threat to Japan's position in Northeast Asia, and advocated full control of that area instead. These views were naturally strongest in the Kwantung Army staff, but those who held them had numerous allies in the General Staff. Intelligence on China was available from many sources. Major Chinese warlords had Japanese officers at their headquarters, sometimes as advisers. The center for processing this intelligence was the Second Bureau of the General Staff. While this post went to able graduates of the War College, its heads were unlikely to advance to positions directly charged with policy-making. Nevertheless they were far more strategically placed than their colleagues in the Army Ministry, who were somewhat constrained by that ministry's relations with the civilian cabinet ministries.

In the late 1920s a new and frequently lethal form of factionalism developed through associations formed by classmates of the military academy. These horizontal groupings, nurtured in nights of discussion lubricated by drink, produced men impatient with the caution of their superiors and committed to simple solutions based on the assumption that direct action to eliminate symbols of the old order would bring to power men more likely to be willing to take risks through decisive policies. These terrorists, for that is what they were, had no clear-cut program; as one of Inukai's assassins explained to the court, "We thought about destruction first. We never considered taking on the duty of reconstruction. We foresaw, however, that once the destruction was accomplished someone would take charge of the reconstruction." General Araki Sadao, army minister for the first half of the 1930s, was their hero. The vision of a spiritual and resurgent Japan he held up, blurred and indistinct, was exactly the sort of rhetoric they mistook for wisdom. He, in turn, saw them as admirable, if sometimes somewhat flawed, exemplars of the Japanese spirit; they were selfless patriots, and had no hesitation in committing their lives to the cause in which they believed so passionately. Unfortunately they also had no hesitation in committing other people's lives, and their rashness must have made many conservatives think twice before warning their countrymen about the course Japan was taking.

These currents of perverted ultranationalism and factionalism merged in the half-decade between the Manchurian Incident and 1936 to make Japan a dangerous place for moderates. At the highest army level General Araki used his influence as war minister to have his ally Mazaki Jinzaburō appointed vice chief of staff, and together they managed to send members of the Chōshū (that is, Tanaka and Ugaki) factions off to the hustings in retaliation for their agreement on streamlining and modernizing the army, cooperation with the political parties, and eagerness to keep from provoking the Anglo-American powers. Japan, these men felt, should rely on its traditional values and not put its faith in modern machinery; indeed, some even decried modern weaponry as inhumane.

Araki's emphasis on ideology and "spirit" lent a rather unreal character to his years as army minister. He felt that conflict with the Soviet Union was inevitable, and even opposed purchase of the Chinese Eastern Railway in 1934 on grounds that it would inevitably be booty after Japan's victory over the

Soviets. He retarded military modernization to favor subsidies for "the villages," and his confidence in the superiority of Japanese spirit was so strong
that he was indifferent to gains in Soviet air power.

During these days Japan's policies continued to provoke anger in the West.
When the Kuomintang regime added the province of Jehol to the responsibilities of Chang Hsüeh-liang, the Kwantung Army seized it for its own as essential to the defense of Manchukuo. Everything north of the Great Wall was now
under Japanese rule or protection. This was followed by skirmishing south of
the Great Wall. The Nanking government's Central Army, conscious of its
continuing problem with warlord forces in the area, and bullied by Kwantung
Army commanders, reluctantly agreed to a cease-fire (the T'angku Truce) in
May 1933 whereby the area north of the Peking-Tientsin plain was demilitarized. In a sense the fighting with Chinese forces that had taken place since
the Manchurian Incident was now ending, and had Japanese army field commanders abided by their own conditions peace might have been restored. The
Nanking regime retained residual sovereignty over the area, but authority was
delegated to local forces that were in no position to stand up to the Japanese.
It was a pattern the Japanese would later try to extend to central China; there
was, in James Crowley's words, a relentless army expansionism at work, led
by field commanders, but basically condoned and approved at higher army
levels.[16]

In April 1934 Amō Eiji, a Foreign Ministry spokesman, asserted that relations between China and Japan were solely the responsibility of those two
countries, and that any interference in or assistance to China either politically
or economically could only harm the situation. In effect, Japan was declaring
a kind of Asian Monroe Doctrine and announcing the end of the entire structure of the Washington Conference system. The disarmament, cooperation
in approaches to China, and mutual guarantees of that system now lay in
ruins. James Crowley writes, "The Japanese government was by December
1933 committed to a policy which proposed to neutralize the influence of the
Soviet Union, the Nationalist government of China, and the Anglo-American
nations by a diplomacy rooted in the arrogance of Japan's military forces."[17]

When Admiral Saitō was followed by Admiral Okada as Prime Minister
in 1934, it was Araki's turn to go. He had trumpeted the coming "Crisis of 1935"
with the Soviet Union so insistently that he had alarmed men who thought it
urgent to build strength for a longer struggle in the future. Nagata Tetsuzan,
an advocate of military modernization who had been exiled to command of
an infantry regiment by Araki, was now promoted to general and returned
to the center as director of military affairs in the Army Ministry. The ministry
declared the importance of a total national defense state in a pamphlet that

contained the arresting phrase that war was "the father of creation and the mother of culture."

When Okada's foreign minister, Hirota Kōki, nevertheless seemed interested in the possibility of discussions of an agreement with the Nanking government, army figures were quick to warn of probable Chinese "impertinence" if talks were initiated, and moved to head off that possibility by agreements between Japanese field commanders and local Chinese leaders. The Ho-Umezu (10 June) and Ch'in-Doihara (23 June 1934) agreements were designed to ward off the danger of Kuomintang authority in North China.

These events were, however, overshadowed by revolt in Japan: the largest, perhaps, since the Satsuma Rebellion of 1877. General Nagata Tetsuzan, who had taken decisive action against participants in a plot against the government, was hacked to death in his office by a sword-wielding Colonel Aizawa. The public trial Aizawa received became a circus for ultranationalist emotionalism, as propagandists extolled the morality and patriotism of the defendant. Currents of emotion seethed so erratically the Foreign Ministry gave up any attempt to work things out with Nanking. At home Professor Minobe Tatsukichi, whose "organ theory" of the emperor's role had long been accepted, suddenly became the target of a campaign that ended in his resignation from the House of Peers and the burning and banning of his books. To a large extent, Minobe was the innocent victim of internecine strife among professional patriots who were out to redress the ouster of Generals Araki and Mazaki.

In this atmosphere of hysteria a group of civilian extremists conspired with young officers to stage a rebellion that broke out on February 26, 1936. The army's First Division was slated for transfer to Manchuria; this, like the impending transfer of Ishiwara and Itagaki from the Kwantung Army five years earlier, triggered the timing of the insurrection. In a late winter snowfall assassination squads moved out to remove the principal conservative members of the authority structure. The recent prime minister and now Lord Privy Seal Admiral Saitō (age 78), Inspector General of Military Education General Watanabe (62), who held one of the army's "big three" posts, and Finance Minister Takahashi Korekiyo (82) were awakened from their sleep and gunned down in their bedrooms. Admiral Suzuki Kantarō (69), grand chamberlain, was severely wounded but survived because his wife pleaded for the privilege of dispatching him herself. The captain in charge of the assailants explained to her that the admiral was dying for the good of the country, saluted the old man on the floor, and left. Still another group of soldiers attacked the inn in Yugawara, in the foothills of the Hakone mountains, to deal with Saitō's predecessor as lord keeper of the privy seal, Count Makino Shinken (75). Policemen on guard exchanged shots with the surprised attackers, and Makino, together with his daughter, a nurse, and a policeman, made his escape from the back door. The most important squad was assigned to eliminate the prime minister. The soldiers quickly took possession of the official residence, only to err by shooting Admiral Okada's brother-in-law, who resembled him somewhat, instead of the prime minister, who escaped by hiding in a closet. Okada was declared and assumed to be dead, but he managed to slip out of the residence in disguise a few days later. Nevertheless his political career was clearly at an end.

While the assassination squads were doing their work, officers of the Imperial Guard Division led their men to take over the gates to the imperial palace. Possession of the emperor was nine-tenths of the game, they thought, and they prepared to separate Hirohito from his "evil advisers." They saw the sovereign as a bespectacled and nervous young man who could be persuaded by their own righteous integrity to appoint a military government, led by General Mazaki Jinzaburō as prime minister and Araki Sadao as home minister, to carry out a "Shōwa Restoration." Should he hesitate, one young officer was prepared to disembowel himself on the spot to drive home the point.

The conspirators' plans to enter the palace, however, miscarried badly. They had hoped to gain access to the palace with reasonable decorum by presenting counterfeit orders, but the palace guard commanders on duty already had word of the murders that had been carried out and managed to block their entry. The rebels had reason to believe that sympathizers in the army high command were on their side, but after some initial waffling on the part of Imperial Way faction leaders, Emperor Hirohito's personal outrage swung the balance against them. For a few days Japan witnessed something the Meiji founders had tried to avoid, personal and direct imperial rule. By not appointing a successor to Admiral Okada immediately the court, in effect, became the cabinet. In communiqués the high command initially described the rebels as an "uprising" but gradually, with subtle changes of terminology, they became a "rebel" force. Additional and more dependable units were called into Tokyo to surround and doom the First Division core. The rebel leaders expressed satisfaction with initial statements that granted the purity of their motives, but to their consternation these never extended to approval of what they had done. It is clear that the personal opposition, even fury, of young Emperor Hirohito was central to this shift. The surviving members of the Saionji court faction maneuvered skillfully; they prevented the appointment of a successor cabinet, left the rebels in uncertainty and doubt, and finally ordered their commanders to give in.

This time there was no tolerance for the brazen action of the rebel terrorists. Of those who had participated 1,483 men were interrogated, and 124 were prosecuted and tried in secret courts martial. Nineteen officers, 73 noncommissioned officers, 19 soldiers, and 10 civilians faced the court in separate trials. Secrecy prevented any of the histrionics that had marred earlier trials, and the courts' refusal to entertain discursive explanations about motives made it possible to complete the proceedings in two months. Thirteen officers and four civilians were sentenced to death and another fifty to lesser sentences. Only three high officers, among them General Mazaki, were prosecuted; Mazaki was acquitted, and the others received light sentences. Right-wing leaders Nishida Zei (Mitsugi) and Kita Ikki, of whom more below, were executed, but financiers who had helped provide support were interrogated but not prosecuted. Most Japanese were puzzled by this outcome; press and many spokesmen had praised the young officers' "sincerity," and even the initial army announcement had seemed to suggest approval.

Some, closer to the facts, felt the young officers had been used and then abandoned by their sponsors. General Ugaki indicated this in his diary:

> How disgusting it is to watch these rascals, holding in one hand the matches and in the other the water hoses, setting fire and putting it out at the same time, inciting and purging young officers, pleading their cause and then claiming credit for having put them down.

Much has been written about the insurrection and its leaders; it, and they, should not be dismissed out of hand. Many of the young officers were well connected, including one who was son-in-law of General Honjō, who was now the emperor's aide-de-camp. Honjō pleaded his case for the leaders' "sincerity" with his ruler, but to no avail. Had the insurgents managed to take and control the palace, moreover, the ambivalence of the high command might have gone the other way.

With this chapter, insubordination and violence on this scale now came to an end. The army high command became dominated by members of the faction dedicated to control and efficiency, bureaucrats and no longer ideologues. Abashed civilian ministers and the Imperial Diet granted the army huge budget increases, and within a year the China War turned attention abroad. Insubordination and rebellion appeared once more, but only at the very end of imperial Japan a decade later when young officers opposed to the surrender once more invaded the palace and seized radio stations in hopes of blocking the broadcast and reversing the decision to surrender. That, too, failed.[18]

The years of murderous insubordination were few, but they left their mark on Japan. There was a hysteria abroad in the land that seems difficult to reconcile with the methodical bureaucratic leadership we have come to expect. That may be one reason why the courage and idealism, however misplaced, of the young officers made them appealing figures for contemporary observers and even for postwar romantics like the novelist Mishima Yukio.[19] As late as 1988 the discovery of court records previously unknown fastened popular interest once more on this strange era.[20]

In army politics the suppression of the rebellion brought a moratorium on the kind of factionalism that had caused so much bloodshed. A group that has become known as the Control (*tōsei*) faction now did its best to end controversy by getting rid of both the Imperial Way and the Ugaki partisans. Political affiliation of any sort (Ugaki, after all, had worked closely with political party leaders) was now to be avoided. When the emperor commanded Ugaki to organize a cabinet in 1937 the army blocked his efforts. As Professor Kitaoka puts it, sectionalism now replaced factionalism; the office of the army minister lost influence in relation to that of the chief of General Staff. Army budgets, which had been kept in some sort of check by Finance Minister Takahashi, suddenly increased by a dramatic 33 percent as new officials embarked on massive spending programs designed to lessen internal squabbling as much as to prepare for greater war. The future lay with cool-headed, bureaucratic figures like General Tōjō Hideki.[21]

4. The Sacralization of *Kokutai* and the Return to Japan

The "purification of the army" that was carried out by the surviving members of the high command after the shake-up that followed the bloodletting of the February 26 revolt did not by any means end the careers of the targets or proponents of the violence that had taken place. The Ugaki, "Chōshū" mainliners, and Araki "Imperial Way" leaders lost their places in the high command, but they reappeared in other posts. Ugaki, who had served as Hamaguchi's war minister (and was the hope of the plotters of the March 1931 Incident) then followed the Admiral Saitō as governor general of Korea from 1931 to 1936; the army vetoed him as nominee for prime minister after the 1936 revolt, but he followed Hirota Kōki as foreign minister under Prince Konoe. After a few months he resigned in protest over the downgrading of the Foreign Ministry that followed the establishment of an Asia (Kōain, later Kōashō) ministry, and retired from public service altogether.[22] The reemergence of Araki, who was to have become prime minister after the October 1931 plot and who took a fatherly view of the February 1936 rebel officers, was more startling and fateful, for Konoe resurrected him to serve as minister of education. In that post he presided over a crusade of spiritual rearmament designed to make sure that every Japanese would, as he put it, have as the first and major element of his identity the consciousness that "I am . . . a Japanese." What this required was gratitude in the heart of every schoolchild and subject that the polity of *kokutai* centered in the "family state," a myriad of familial hierarchies in a pyramidal structure with the compassionate figure of the emperor, at once parent and divine descendant, at its apex. It was something to inspire awe and gratitude, devotion and a fierce but also protective resolve.[23]

The distillation of this narcissistic view was necessarily ambiguous, bolstered by invocations of mythic tradition and documented by evidence of Japan's martial and moral superiority. In 1937 the Ministry of Education issued *Kokutai no hongi* (Cardinal principles of our national polity), with which it blanketed schools and media. The first draft was from the brush of a distinguished Tokyo Imperial University scholar of Japanese literature, but by the time it appeared special committees and bureaucrats had added to its obscurity. Replete with invocation of elaborately named deities from the texts in which eighth-century Japanese had recorded oral transmission of ancient lore, the book seemed at once mysterious and profound.[24] Although it was the Meiji court officials who had resuscitated much of this in an effort to provide a ritual basis for the modern national state, by 1937 the invocation of ideas couched in such language represented a retreat from Japan's embrace of Western culture and institutions and a "return to Japan," albeit one that had never existed. In the 1880s Fukuzawa had advocated "Departure from Asia and Entry into the West" *(datsu A, nyū Ō);* now voices sought to reverse that slogan.[25]

This was the culmination of a process that had been under way since the late 1920s, and its chief components were agrarian culturalism and ethnicity. Self-appointed spokesmen for the virtues of Japan's rural past had decried the impact of capitalism, the luxury of urban life, and the corruption of politics that had followed. Gondō Seikyō (Seikei, 1868–1937) and Tachibana Kōzaburō (1893–1974) wrote widely to deplore Japan's departure from its rural roots to follow the false gods of capitalism. Western-style representative government, they argued, institutionalized partisan conflict and corrupted the familial patterns of Japanese social organization. The makers of the modern bureaucratic state had tried to throw off the village values that lay at the core of Japanese tradition. Tachibana went a step farther to identify virtue and country with the emperor, and called for the establishment of a brotherhood of men prepared to lay down their lives to carry out his presumed wishes. Gondō saw the imperial house as the center of a national tutelary shrine, and felt it had been disfigured and dishonored by the trappings of modern Western-style royalty. The Nichiren Buddhist priest Inoue Nisshō (1886–1967), it will be remembered, had organized a Blood Brotherhood Band (Ketsumeidan) of youths prepared to take responsibility for the death of individual leaders of the capitalist elite. Ōkawa Shūmei (1886–1957), a student of Islam and Asian philosophies, also believed it necessary to purge society of capitalist and bureaucratic leaders so that Japan could become the center of a renaissance of Asian peoples who would look to it for moral guidance and physical liberation from the imperialist West.

It is beside the point that these spokesmen for the scorned and disinherited were themselves educated representatives of the modern society who turned away from or, in Ōkawa's case, utilized "modern" prestigious attainments as a platform from which to denounce modernity. They were intimately involved in the plots and terrorism of the early 1930s. Their instigation was particularly attractive to young navy and especially army officers, who were at once commanders of recruits who followed their orders unthinkingly and yet trapped by the bureaucratic structure of the armed forces. They could deplore the "state of the villages" whose young men they led and the process and privilege of bureaucracy which they themselves exemplified. Ben-Ami Shillony has shown that for all the talk of "villages" the young officers who led the insurrection in 1936 were for the most part well connected with army families in higher echelons; they were, as R. P. Dore has put it, more interested in villages than villagers.[26]

Disapproval of capitalist political institutions found support from a quite different perspective. Kita Ikki (1883–1937), an advocate of national socialism, was a true outsider to the social elite. Born on the Japan Sea island of Sado, he audited courses at Waseda University and immersed himself in socialist writers. An early result was a slender volume entitled *Kokutai oyobi junsui shakaishugi* (Our national policy and pure socialism) that was quickly banned. He was acquainted with Kōtoku Shūsui and other socialists, and then turned his attention to revolution in China. When that broke out in 1911 he was sending regular and voluminous reports to Japanese Asianists, especially the Kokuryūkai (Amur or Black Dragon Society) leader Uchida Ryōhei. Kita attributed the failure of revolution in China in good measure to the greed of Japanese capitalism, which failed to supply the revolutionaries with resources of which they were critically short. Japan's future in Asia, he concluded, was limited unless it carried out a decisive social and institutional renovation of its own. A return to China during the May Fourth movement of 1919 gave him personal experience of anti-Japanese sentiment. The problems of Asia thus had their roots in Japan.

From this background Kita worked out a proposal for a corporate state. Private greed and power would be replaced by state-led enterprises; even the emperor would be a "people's emperor," living on an annual salary instead of being able to draw on private resources.[27] Kita was clearly not an agrarianist; he was far more in tune with contemporary national socialism than with the virtues of premodern Japan. The book in which he outlined these plans was censored so heavily that whole sections—notably on the emperor—were reduced to empty pages by his publisher. For all his criticism of capitalist corruption, however, Kita accepted a subsidy and an automobile from businessmen who may have regarded this as a form of insurance. But his brand of radicalism also commended him to young officers. Documents discovered in 1988 show that the 1936 rebels planned for Kita to be named minister without portfolio in the Mazaki government that would take power. He was one of six civilians charged and executed for plotting rebellion after the February 26 uprising. Kita was one of the few accused who refused to shout "Long live the emperor!" (Tennō heika banzai!) when they faced the firing squad.

Currents of nationalism and cultural ethnicity also reached into higher levels of society. Among academics the leading voice calling for reverence for the emperor as the sole criterion of value was that of Hiraizumi Kiyoshi (1895–1984), who came to play the role of theoretician or theologian for matters of kokutai. His interpretation of history, known as "imperial history" (kōkoku shikan), became a force academic skeptics had to contend with. A graduate of Tokyo Imperial University's Faculty of Japanese History,[28] Hiraizumi became known as a specialist on the religious and cultural life of medieval Japan. In 1930 he traveled to universities in Germany, England, Austria, and Italy to better prepare himself in the practice and history of historical scholarship, and on his return the following year he published an influential work on the attempted ("Kenmu") imperial restoration of 1333. That failed effort, it will be recalled, had ushered in the competition between rival imperial courts that had caused so much controversy in interpretation two decades before. Hiraizumi seems to have immersed himself in those issues and factored in a disapproval of trends in the Japan of his own day, He became an advocate of a "Shōwa Restoration" and began to delegate some of his university teaching to disciples. The historian Irokawa Daikichi, who entered the university as war clouds were breaking, describes these men as follows:

When I entered the National History Faculty of Tokyo Imperial University, we were told by disciples of Hiraizumi Kiyoshi that "The leaders of the Japanese navy are secretly pro-American and pro-British, and advocate peace; they will have to be dealt with when the time comes." Those men saw everything in black and white, and talked like fanatics. But they provided no data or evidence of any sort, and so I half believed and half doubted what they said.[29]

Hiraizumi himself lectured in a private school he established near the campus. Before long he had a following of young military officers who were glad to have one of Japan's foremost historians espousing the cause of ethnic nationalism and imperial sovereignty. As Japan's armies advanced, so too did Hiraizumi, invited to lecture to Henry Pu Yi, head of state of the new Manchukuo. He may have been implicated in the planning for the attempted coup of February 26, but if so, drew back and added his voice to others dissuading the emperor's brother, Prince Chichibu, from showing sympathy for the rebels. Hiraizumi's highest reward was an invitation to assist in drafting the emperor's declaration of war in 1941.

A final element that should receive mention is that of ultranationalist organizations. Though oriented more toward action than thought, patriotic societies were numerous and everywhere. They seemed to thrive at the intersection of the respectable and disreputable, the legal and the illegal, exhorting and intimidating as the occasion demanded. The parent, and strongest, of these was the Kokuryūkai or Amur Society. It won fame in the West through a literal translation of its name as Black Dragon, as the Amur is written in Chinese. Its manifesto asserted, long before the establishment of Manchukuo, that the Amur River should be Japan's northern border, but its efforts went well beyond agitation for a strong foreign policy against Russia. The organization traced its genesis to participation in the Freedom and People's Rights Movement, and worked for freedom—in collaboration with Japan—for Asian nationalists like Sun Yat-sen and Kim Ok-kyun. It was sharply critical of Japanese capitalist society and active in calls for a "Shōwa Restoration." It warred against an education system slavishly copied from those of the West. A purified polity, centered on the divinity of the imperial line, could then extend its compassionate governance to Asian lands burdened by Western imperialism. The career of the leading figure in these activities, Tōyama Mitsuru (1855–1944), illustrates continuities in Japan's modern history. Born to samurai parents in Fukuoka, his imprisonment for antigovernment activities prevented his participation in the Satsuma Rebellion. After being released he formed a Kyushu branch of the *jiyū-minken* movement, but soon turned to lead opposition to the government's slow progress on treaty reform. He was implicated in the attack on Foreign Minister Ōkuma in 1889, and then busied himself in efforts to strengthen Japanese policy in Korea, the while trying to organize help for Sun Yat-sen—in anticipation of cooperation with China—as well. For some decades after that he was a behind-the-scenes manipulator and funder with growing influence, on the fringes of politics and business, and by the years of World War II, always pictured in his native dress and flowing beard, he was the grand old man of patriotism, writing newspaper columns calling for united national effort. At the last Tōyama's rival columnist was Tokutomi Sohō. The two nonconformists of the 1880s, different as they were, thus ended as pillars of the nationalist establishment.

5. The Economy: Recovery and Resources

Japanese aggression in China, the political fallout of the early 1930s, the murderous vendettas of army factionalism, and agitation for a "Shōwa Restoration" all took place during the years of the world depression. They were years in which the international trading system broke down as countries pursued goals of economic nationalism. The collapse of the international silk market devastated thousands of Japanese villages, and also handicapped the country's need for export earnings with which to finance the import of raw materials. The international capitalist order seemed to have broken down; trade preferences, protectionism, and currency crises that resulted in bank failures brought investment to a halt. Agrarianists could call for return to an imagined Eden of the past, reformers could argue for an increase of bureaucratic state controls, but all had to agree that the current system seemed to have run its course.

Yet Japan also proved to have advantages relative to other capitalist countries. Its banking crisis came earlier with the events that brought down the Wakatsuki government in 1927; consolidation and mergers left the system better prepared to weather future storms of international competition. The government's brief dalliance with the gold standard was followed by a deflation so severe that, while it further distressed the agricultural sector, made exports more competitive. Japan was in crisis before its competitors among developed countries, and its steps toward recovery also preceded theirs.

Dimensions of control advanced as cartels and mergers came to dominate markets that had been competitive. A new combine produced 97.5 percent of iron and 51.5 percent of steel production, and a new trust controlled 90 percent of newsprint. All along the line new combinations in banking, machinery, electric power, and consumption items like beer, each centered around a larger and more powerful zaibatsu bank, dominated the economy. This did not, to be sure, endear the zaibatsu to the Japanese people. Zaibatsu banks were accused of profitable currency speculations during the brief experiment with the gold standard. Every writer who deplored the devastation of the villages contrasted it with the prosperity of the new economic royalists, and the murder of politically connected industrialists like the Mitsui head Baron Dan Takuma could bring a chorus of praise for the purity of the assassins' motives. The contrast was greatest in agricultural districts within range of the great metropolis; the single prefecture of Ibaraki, on the outskirts of Tokyo, had the dubious distinction of producing the murders of Baron Dan, Finance Minister Inoue, and Prime Minister Inukai.

In this period of economic emergency the Ministry of Finance was headed by Takahashi Korekiyo (1854–1936). No modern Japanese leader has had a more striking career or better deserves a full biography. Born in Edo and adopted by a Sendai samurai, Takahashi studied English as a houseboy for a foreigner (and later also worked for Mori Arinori), attended what was to become the Imperial University, dabbled in speculation and in an unsuccessful attempt to develop a silver mine, and then found his niche in finance. He advanced steadily in the Bank of Japan and the Yokohama Specie Bank, worked in government at Matsukata's elbow, and then joined the Seiyūkai, headed the Finance Ministry under Hara Takashi and briefly succeeded him as prime minister. Takahashi returned to head the Ministry of Finance under Tanaka Gi'ichi, a role in which he resolved the banking crisis, and served again under Prime Ministers Inukai, Saitō, and Okada, serving from 1931 to 1936 except for a six-month interlude, before he was shot on February 26.

Nakamura Takafusa describes Takahashi as an early Keynesian.[30] During his years at the helm government spending rose markedly, and steps to spur production combined with economic nationalism to accelerate industrialization. He allowed the yen to find its market valuation, resulting in a devaluation of some 40 percent. Spending for agricultural relief and military expansion increased, much of it financed by government bonds. Low interest rates, low exchange rates, and higher government spending for public works, relief, and armament brought a rapid improvement. A revival of exports and government spending combined to expand the economy. Terms like "national emergency" and "national defense state" became popular as justification for measures to restore prosperity at home and permit expansion abroad. Tariffs were raised to protect industries, and as the exchange rate worsened the higher cost of imports further contributed to domestic investment and capacity in chemical and heavy industries. Low interest rates were made available for village reconstruction, and public health insurance and other social legislation built confidence and welfare. Military spending was an important item in this renewal of growth, but not, it seems, as central as many have thought. In heavy machinery and chemicals the percentage of outputs devoted to military needs was at its highest at the beginning of the decade, and then declined by 1936. It may, of course, have played a particularly important role in the start-up stage of economic recovery.

In this context the enthusiastic responses to the military moves in Manchuria and North China that the media and their readers showed is probably understandable. Many people felt they were better off. Some were, none more so than urban laborers in the modern sector of the economy. Years later one man recalled how good things seemed, especially after war broke out with China in 1937:

> Machinists welcomed the munitions boom. We'd been waiting anxiously for a breakthrough. From that time on, we got really busy. China news was everywhere. Even my father subscribed to *Asahi Graph* since every issue carried lots of pictures of soldiers in China. By the end of 1937, everybody in the country was working. For the first time, I was able to take care of my father. War's not bad at all, I thought. As a skilled worker I was eagerly sought after and earned my highest wages in 1938, '39, and '40. There were so many hours of overtime! I changed jobs often, each new job better than the one before. In 1940, a draft system for skilled workers was introduced to keep us from moving around.[31]

By the time Takahashi was murdered in 1936, his policies had succeeded in creating full employment and reflating the economy. He now thought it desirable to rein in the agents of inflation, but those who followed him instead approved expansion plans for the army and navy to extend five and six years respectively. The government's 1937 budget was almost 40 percent higher than that for the previous year, but even that percentage paled after the outbreak of the war with China in July 1937, for in the three months that followed military spending rose to consume practically the entire national budget for that year. The inevitable result was a spiral of inflation that drove up further the cost of the imports of raw materials essential to the industrial sector. Business leaders stockpiled imports in anticipation of future price increases, and the balance of trade worsened day by day.

In the analysis of Bai Gao this led to an increasingly "managed economy" that became at the last a command economy.[32] Government leaders created new boards, notably the Cabinet Planning Board (October 1937), the Diet passed laws designed to control some industries (beginning with the Important Industries Control Law, 1931) and control imports (Temporary Capital Adjustment Law and Temporary Export and Import Commodities Law), culminating in the National Mobilization Law of 1938. Under its provisions the government was empowered to establish firms, issue directives relating to the manufacture, distribution, transfer, and consumption of materials related to imports, and issue directives for the management of labor, working conditions, and the administration, use, and expropriation of factories and mines.

By the mid-1930s Japanese leaders saw the world becoming divided into dollar, sterling, and yen blocs. One notes the absence of a Soviet bloc; the USSR's external trade was not yet a significant factor, and in any case the Japanese army was deeply committed to the view of a coming struggle with the Soviet Union once the Soviet Five-Year Plan was completed in 1936 (the so-called crisis of 1936). Ishiwara Kanji's vision for Manchukuo now became formalized in a series of plans to prepare for what he considered a certain war with the Soviet Union that would precede Japan's struggle with the West. Plans envisioned the creation and consolidation of a Northeast Asia bloc centered on Japan, drawing on the resources of Manchuria (iron, coal, aluminum, gold, industrial salt, and agricultural products, chiefly soybeans). Korea would contribute coal, iron, aluminum, magnesium, cotton, and wool, and North China coal, cotton, wool, salt, and meat. China, however, was not yet completely in the fold, and that is why army leaders preferred working with local leaders of splinter regimes, where the disparity of strength with Japan was greatest, to trying to deal with the national government at Nanking.

All well and good, but this "yen bloc" was a dream of the future, based on hopes of rapid industrialization through the expenditure of vast sums, particularly in Manchukuo. In the meantime precious gold reserves were being drained away to pay for essential raw materials, particularly petroleum, for which the bloc could make no provision. Out of this came complaints of unfairness on the part of the United States and the European imperialist powers in South Asia; by virtue of getting there first they found themselves in control of impressive resources in what is now Vietnam, Malaysia, the Philippines, and Indonesia, the while presuming to lecture—and gradually to strangle—Japan in its search for a place in the sun.

At this point ironies abound. The skilled machinist quoted above felt better off and saw his life as one of prosperity brought about by war, but many more workers, particularly those in textiles, suffered from the shift of national priorities to heavy industry. Moreover Japan was shifting to an area in which its need for imports placed it at a comparative disadvantage. The decline of Japanese exports and the worsening of the trade balance, together with the inflation this spawned, began to reduce real wages. Yasukichi Yasuba summarizes these contradictions particularly clearly:[33] Japan was emerging successfully from the depression on the basis of exports of light industry, when the military buildup shifted weight to chemical and heavy industry, in which Japan was poorly equipped. "Since military build-up and the resultant expansion of heavy industries tremendously increased demand for natural resources, the previously non-existent shortage of natural resources eventually became real, and the terms of trade started to deteriorate" at that point. The military buildup and imperialistic expansion started to look necessary. Warnings of impending economic crisis became self-fulfilling and the imagined problems had become real.

Many who observed this taking place had their doubts about the wisdom and practicality of political and military policies, but no sector of society protested. Leaders of export industries and zaibatsu banks were unenthusiastic about the prospect of wartime taxes, but they profited from the government loans and guarantees that financed increased expansion of capacity and conversion.

The crisis that resulted from the dispute with China helped bring labor leaders into line. Labor was by this time divided between right- and left-wing organizations; the right led, and the left followed, to support the state in time of perceived crisis. Government measures to promote order and productivity improved working conditions and stifled worker organizations. Home Ministry bureaucrats worked to improve standards of safety and thereby efficiency in the workplace. The same years that saw the end of internal army violence brought an end to open disputes between labor and management. The outbreak of hostilities with China shortly afterward served to firm things up. The military were eager to curb radicalism in the union movement, and in this they had the enthusiastic support of big business. Soon the unions pledged not to strike. After the China War began Sōdōmei leaders resolved that "our task is to protect the rear base of the nation as soldiers who fight in the industrial front in thus time of emergency." They went on to propose the establishment of a council representing labor and industry, but the government had its own ideas. In 1938 preparatory work began on what would become the *Sangyō hōkoku kai* (Patriotic industrial organization), which was under state control. Five million workers in more than six thousand firms were enrolled. In 1940 labor unions were banned. Regulations designed to prevent worker mobility became an ironic forerunner of the much-praised "life time employment" of postwar Japan, and a free labor movement was ruled out until after the surrender in 1945.

6. *Tenkō:* The Conversion of the Left

The sense of national and international emergency that animated the "return to Japan" in the intensity of ethnic nationalism that was shown in the homiletics of *kokutai* and imploded in army factionalism was equally compelling for the left, as a campaign for *tenkō*—conversion, or apostasy—brought radicals back to the fold. In the 1920s categories of Marxist analysis had become overwhelmingly popular in the study of social problems and political economy. State guardians of public morality, alarmed by this, had launched the great police drives that resulted in the large-scale arrest of real and suspected radicals in March 1928. These arrests broke the back of the labor movement and extinguished the underground Communist Party, but prosecutors continued to puzzle over the fact that so many of those contaminated by Marxist cosmopolitanism were intelligent and indeed outstanding young people. Manchuria, and the sense of international crisis, came to their rescue.

In 1933 Sano Manabu (1892–1953), who had joined Yoshino Sakuzō's Shinjinkai as a student at Tokyo Imperial University and subsequently became a leader in the Japan Communist Party, and who had been arrested in Shanghai in 1929, issued a statement from prison together with Nabeyama Sadachika, who was also a member of the party's Central Committee. The two announced their defection from the Communist Party. They withdrew their opposition to the events in Manchuria, and said they no longer believed self-rule was necessary in Korea and Taiwan. Most important, they no longer believed (as the Comintern's thesis issued that year had specified) that the "emperor system" *(tennōsei)* was an impediment to institutional reform in Japan.

This defection of two top Communist leaders had an electrifying effect on Japanese who were in police custody, and it was followed by what can only be called mass apostasy. Within a month 45 percent of those not yet convicted (614 out of 1,370) and 34 percent (133 out of 393) of those who had been convicted of radical thought or activities followed suit and defected. Within three years 74 percent (324 out of 438) of those convicted of subversion were ready to announce that they, too, had returned to the fold.

These defections were of great interest for psychology and for theory. Although coercion in various forms was undoubtedly exercised, interrogators were warned to avoid the resistance that argument or duress would provoke. The radicals, most of them still young, were, after all, better educated than most of the police. Instead every effort was made to get them to "return" to the values of home and hearth that had now been threatened by the clouds of war and crisis. A workbook prepared for interrogators suggested that they begin by providing a bowl of chicken and egg on rice (*oyako dombori*, lit. "parent-child" bowl) which would remind the prisoner of the parental bond. The policemen should say nothing about ideology, but offer a reproachful reminder that "your mother is worried about you." He should by all means avoid mention of the father, as that might trigger defiance of authority.[34] There was something distinctively Japanese, almost soft and cloying, about these tactics. Determined recalcitrance, to be sure, brought worse food and harsher treatment.

The impact of the *tenkō* movement in terms of social science scholarship and Marxist theory was even more important. In the early 1930s a group of outstanding historians and social scientists battled over theoretical issues that had immediate relevance for political action. These concerned the nature of the Meiji Restoration: was it a revolutionary development, in which case Japan might be ready for the next move and stage of democratic-socialist revolution, or was it an incomplete, "from-above" reform that had to be transcended before Japan could enter a stage of modernization in which presocialist democracy was to be sought? Was Japan, in effect, ready for revolution or not? These debates, published by Iwanami Shigeo's publishing house in multiple volumes entitled *Lectures on the Historical Development of Japanese Capitalism (Nihon shihon shugi hattatsushi kōza),* set the parameters for private thinking before 1945 and public debate thereafter so solidly that a multivolume bibliography of the controversy bears testimony to the earnestness with which this debate was carried on.

Tenkō apostates gave up their communism, but not by any means their Marxism. They did reject the standard thesis that capitalism was a system under which the ruling class held power by its exploitation of the surplus value created by oppressed workers. They also rejected the cosmopolitan aspects of Marxism, under which an international bourgeoisie exploited an international proletariat. Japan's was a different case. Calls to class conflict should end; real social reform could be achieved only through cooperation among all classes in Japan. This was because nationalism had merged with theory. If Meiji readers of Samuel Smiles saw Japan as a poor boy in the family of nations, the Shōwa scholars, chastened by their personal and Japan's national experience, saw Japan as a somehow exploited, "proletarian" land, exploited by international capitalism. Its own imperialism was of a different sort, motivated by a shortage and not a surplus of capital, and necessary to its survival.

In some instances this position had been anticipated by liberal and radical writers before the large-scale apostasy from the Communist line. Takahashi Kamekichi, for instance, a member of Prince Konoe's Shōwa Research Association, found it possible to argue that Japanese domination of Korea, Taiwan, and Manchuria was transitional, forced upon it by the competitive international system, unlike the imperialism of the more exploitative West. Expansion, in fact, was historically progressive and furthermore necessary for Japan's mission.[35]

There was frequently a continuity of underlying assumptions in much writing in the 1930s. Japan was disadvantaged by lack of resources. It suffered from population pressure. It had somehow been victimized by its historical lateness, and by racial prejudice that made it impossible for foreign critics to understand its problems.

And yet this should not be taken to mean that there was no opportunity for dissidence among intellectuals. Right-wing critics certainly had no difficulty in finding men and ideas they could deplore; when they had institutional backing, as in the persecution of Professor Minobe's interpretation of the imperial role, selected individuals might be stifled. But there was also a tradition of university autonomy that survived a number of crises. The rise of student interest in social questions had naturally drawn the attention of educational authorities, who suspected that their teachers were at fault, and this led to a number of confrontations between faculties and educational bureaucrats. Unfortunately, as the example of Uesugi Shinkichi's vendetta against Minobe Tatsukichi showed, the resistance of university faculties was frequently weakened by a factionalism that was personal as well as ideological. University administrators tended to strive for compromise when crises arose, as they were aware that direct confrontation with educational bureaucrats would bring down on them the criticism of self-appointed zealots outside the university whose ties with military and civilian rightists found them better prepared for combat.

The more impressive, then, to note that when Professor Takigawa Yukitoki of Kyoto Imperial University drew criticism in 1931 for a lecture he had given at a private university, his colleagues in the Faculty of Law submitted resignations in protest against proposals of the Ministry of Education that he be dismissed. Despite this, the ministry ultimately had its way. After intense pressure and prolonged negotiation the ministry agreed to accept three resignations, one of them Takigawa's. Academics, clearly, were fighting rearguard actions and were anxious to avoid direct battle in a conflict they knew they could not win. There are additional things to note. One is that the spread of education and inflation of institutions had served to weaken the position of the university professor as compared with his more exalted Meiji predecessors, and another is that it was unusual for embattled faculty members to enjoy the united support of their colleagues. After the outbreak of the China War the opportunity for the free exchange of ideas and speaking out on public issues diminished sharply. Those opposed to national policy had a choice between silence and speaking in obscure indirection. At the Tokyo Imperial University Faculty of Economics, which was already polarized between Marxist and non-Marxist instructors, a number of able young faculty members were taken into police custody in 1938. A first trial acquitted all but Arisawa Hiromi (of whom more below) and Abe Isamu; the government appealed; new trials were held two years later with much the same result, only to have the case reopened once more. The case of the "professors' group," as it became known, dragged on, and it required six years before Arisawa and Ōuchi Hyōei, and four years before Kawai Eijirō, were fully cleared.[36]

The events best chronicled concern cases in which freedom of speech and thought was challenged in a particularly striking manner by bureaucrats anxious to avoid public criticism of their lack of vigilance. What is probably more striking, however, is the lack of public discussion and examination of the basic premises that underlay Japanese policy and aggression. By the 1940s, as will be seen, this was clearly impossible. The question of when it became so, and why so few raised their voices to protest or warn, has had its effect in the compulsion Japanese intellectuals have felt to exercise that freedom in postwar Japan.

7. Planning for a Managed Economy

It is ironic that this pursuit of suspected subversives freed some of Japan's finest young economists from the tasks of teaching and enabled them to offer their services to research groups of the South Manchurian Railroad and other think tanks in Tokyo. Men who were suspended from their duties, sometimes with pay, could not speak or write openly, but neither could they be kept from thinking. Some published under others' names and others did not publish at all, but all of them turned to wrestle with problems of Japan's economic predicament.

Some of the most important of these figures found employment in the Shōwa Research Association, a study group established by Prince Konoe Fumimaro (1891–1945) in 1936 to study options for national policy. The organization was headed by the influential Tokyo Imperial University political scientist Rōyama Masamichi, and his mandate was to organize a group prepared to plan for whatever structural changes might be required for Japan in the uncharted waters that lay ahead. Politics, diplomacy, economics, and education; no area of investigation was to be overlooked. The capitalist order seemed to be disintegrating everywhere in the developed world; in America the New Deal, in Germany national socialism, in Italy corporatism, and in the Soviet Union a Communist economy—all seemed to indicate permanent change in the international order. Konoe's brain trust had the task of deciding what changes would best apply to Japan's situation. Konoe himself, an aloof and moody figure whose intentions were rarely made explicit, had, it will be remembered, won prominence with warnings about the preference of "have" countries and an "Anglo-American peace" he published immediately prior to the Paris Peace Conference.

The Soviet model, with its ruthless demolition of the social order, must have seemed least useful, but the announcement of five-year economic plans were already being taken up in Manchukuo. The mass movements focused on charismatic leaders of the fascist states offered even less relevance for Japan, but the notion of structured economies and economic planning, rooted in the experience of World War I, was another matter. Nevertheless it seemed possible and in fact necessary to achieve much of what was worthwhile in the foreign examples within Japan, and to do so from above by bureaucratic direction that would transcend the sectionalism of the administrative state that had taken form. "Reform bureaucrats," as some of Konoe's followers became known, and reform planners of a nonviolent "Shōwa Restoration" might produce a more effectively guided and united polity. The Meiji Constitution might remain inviolable, but its nonspecific generality could cover differences in direction to rejuvenate a Japan that seemed to have come to a dead end. It was a vision that enthused young intellectuals no less than it did President Franklin D. Roosevelt's young planners on the other side of the Pacific. By the time Konoe came to power in 1937 his chief cabinet secretary, Kazami Akira, was armed with plans his committees had drawn up.[37]

It is useful to show how these trends intersected in the life of Arisawa Hiromi (1896–1988), a young member of the group who went on to become one of the chief planners of Japan's postwar economy. Arisawa began his study of economics at a time when the rice riots of 1918 seemed to foreshadow a crisis in the Japanese economy, and the post–World War I depression suggested there were structural flaws that required attention. As a young instructor in the newly established Faculty of Economics at Tokyo Imperial University, Arisawa had as colleagues young scholars who would become known as some of Japan's most able and also most radical intellectuals.

In 1926 Arisawa left for two years of study in Germany, where his understanding of Marxist thought deepened. He also read widely on problems the German economy had encountered during World War I, and became something of an authority on the theories of "total war" worked out by German thinkers. Arisawa returned to Tokyo just as the police sweeps of 1928 were netting many of his friends and colleagues, but he went on to organize a series of seminars devoted to what he saw as the impending crisis of capitalism in Japan. After the outbreak of the Manchurian Incident, he turned his attention to the need to prepare for wider, indeed total, war. It would, he concluded, require state intervention in many areas of production to provide the basis for total national mobilization. His interests now began to draw closer to those of army planners like the future prime minister Koiso Kuniaki, who had organized a study to determine the measures required to achieve the ideal of a "national defense state." Contrasting the experience of the United States and Germany during World War I, Arisawa argued that it was particularly important for a resource-poor country like Japan to control and allocate resources effectively. Then, as Japan entered the China War, Arisawa prepared a comprehensive framework of steps that would be required for the larger war. What was needed, he thought, was a "state capitalism" that would eliminate the waste of unnecessary duplication and competition, and allocate capital where it was most needed. Many of his studies, though not the last, were published in monthly magazines as he developed his analysis.

Arisawa was arrested in 1938 in the "professors' group" incident mentioned earlier, and through the long period of litigation that followed he was not free to teach or write openly. This did not prevent him from writing influential articles and books that were published under the names of his friends. He now prepared plans for a state-managed economy that would separate capital from management and provide a more efficient economic structure.

The conclusion Arisawa reached in his study was that Japan could not possibly prevail in a war with the more developed and productive democracies of the West. That was not what army planners who had encouraged his study wanted to hear, however, and his report was quietly suppressed. Even so, a number of his recommendations saw action as the Japanese economy girded itself for a larger war, and others saw implementation in postsurrender days when his gospel of managing scarce resources for economic growth was even more badly needed. The young scholar who had been purged as subversive ended his days with Japan's highest imperial decoration as one of the key planners of postwar industrial policy.[38]

8. War with China and Konoe's "New Order in Asia"

In North China Japanese field commanders had bullied Chinese authorities into agreements that protected their forces from interference by units of the Nanking government, but until 1936 Japanese government policy had been relatively cautious. Chiang Kai-shek, embattled with problems of military unification, had temporized in his response to the creation of Manchukuo. The T'angku Truce that demilitarized the Peking area could be, and by some critics was, read as acquiescence in Japanese domination of northeastern China. Chiang was determined to solve his internal problems of unification by defeating the Chinese Communist regime that had fallen back to positions in the southeastern province of Kiangsi after Chiang's coup in Shanghai. After surviving a series of "extermination campaigns" in which Chiang had the help of German military advisers, the Chinese Communist armies undertook the famous Long March that enabled them to resettle in Yenan in the northwest. Chang Hsüeh-liang, the defeated commander of the Manchurian Fengtien

Army, had been given a title and nominal command in exchange for his acceptance of Kuomintang primacy. In Japan the generals of the Imperial Way (*kōdōha*) faction had propounded a "crisis of 1936" that would require a preventive strike against the Soviet Union, and that would not by any means have been unwelcome to Chiang. There seemed to be a tacit agreement between Chiang Kai-shek and the Japanese generals that suppression of the Communists had first priority. The events of 1936 changed all this, and permanently. The failure of the February 26 revolt in Japan was followed by eclipse of the leaders of the Imperial Way faction and their fixation on war with the Soviet Union. Then the Sian Incident of 1936, in which Chang Hsüeh-liang and Communist leaders kidnapped Chiang Kai-shek—just as he was planning a final campaign against Yenan—and forced his agreement to a United Front against Japan, changed the entire situation.[39]

In Japan, as has been noted, the Hirota cabinet agreed to accommodate the increased budgetary demands of the armed services. It also restored the provision, in abeyance for two decades, that the army and navy ministers be chosen from generals and admirals on the active list, thereby giving the services veto power over nominations of men (like General Ugaki) considered unreliable. Later that spring and summer Hirota and his foreign minister, Arita Hachirō, made it clear that Japan would no longer feel bound by the interlocking network of treaties that made up the Washington Conference system. A new military view required a new military buildup, and during the summer months Imperial Army and Navy staffs prepared contingency plans for possible war with China, the Soviet Union, and the Atlantic powers and submitted them to the cabinet for approval. It was the first time that a formal state document, as opposed to military plans, had begun to lay out conditions of what would be needed for Japanese domination of East Asia.

It was also the first time that the turbulence of European politics intruded on Japanese decisions. It has been argued that the outbreak of World War II can be treated with the virtual exclusion of Japan, but Japan's policies and politics were inextricably intertwined with its perceptions of developments in the West. Fear of the Soviet Union and of communism led in this. In November 1936 Japan and Germany agreed to form an Anti-Comintern Pact which Italy joined a year later. The three agreed to exchange information on Comintern activities and consult together in the event of attack by Russia. This agreement, strengthened a few years later, provided the bond for what became known as the Axis powers. Japan was thus backing away from its ties with the Anglo-American powers and associating itself with the "revisionist" states of Europe. Army leaders backed the new arrangement, and saw it as useful in negotiations with the United States, but it had the opposite effect on the

Roosevelt administration. In the United States suspicion of Japanese intentions and disapproval of Japanese moves in China were growing; at the same time Japanese dependence on outside, and especially American, resources was increasing. Therein lay a crisis far greater than the 1936 crisis with the Soviet Union that Japanese army leaders talked about.

Japan had now committed itself to an international anti-Comintern stand just as the Comintern was encouraging the formation of a United Front against Japan in North China. At Sian Chou En-lai, as representative of the Yenan government, prevailed upon Chang Hsüeh-liang to release Chiang Kai-shek on the condition that he give up his campaigns to crush the Communist regime and instead join with it to lead a United Front against any further Japanese advance. Chiang was now able to stand as leader of Chinese nationalism and appeal for world opinion and support. Recent events had improved his position considerably. Monetary reforms worked out with American advisers had strengthened China's economic position, and army assistance provided by German advisers had improved Chiang's military capability. In an astonishing transformation Chiang, rescued from incarceration and possible death at Sian, emerged as a national hero and effective leader just as Japanese generals were prepared to dismiss him as an ineffective nuisance. Anticommunism was their sole criterion. Japan prevailed upon Berlin to have it withdraw the German military mission to China, and prepared to concentrate on developing the gains it had made.

These events set the stage for what was to follow, but even so contingency played its part. The war that followed was unplanned by Japan, and unwanted. In the spring of 1937 a short-lived cabinet headed by General Hayashi Senjūrō, a former army minister, brought in as foreign minister a professional diplomat, Satō Naotake, who tried to regain control over Japan's China policy. He emphasized the importance of trade with China, and did his best to lower the pitch of Japanese rhetoric. Unfortunately the Hayashi cabinet, which lacked a single political party representative, was denounced as rigidly bureaucratic and proved unable to win cooperation from the Imperial Diet. Although there had not been a political party cabinet for the six years since Inukai's death, the political parties were still powerful, and their cooperation was essential for any government. After setbacks in national elections the Hayashi cabinet resigned. It had lasted only three months.

Saionji now turned to Prince Konoe Fumimaro. He had long had doubts about his judgment. But Konoe was acceptable to political party leaders, and that seemed to promise a smoothly functioning government. Konoe had been asked and declined to serve in the aftermath of the February 26 military revolt, but he now accepted the challenge, albeit somewhat reluctantly.

Modern Japanese history has not known a more enigmatic man that the prince who now became prime minister.[40] Scion of one of Japan's most aristocratic families, one intertwined with that of the imperial family since the dawn of recorded Japanese history, Konoe was the only one of Hirohito's councillors and ministers who could relax and be casual in his conversation with him; he even scandalized others by crossing his legs when seated in the emperor's presence. Konoe was at once a pampered aristocrat, thoughtful intellectual, and ambitious politician. He had studied philosophy at Kyoto Imperial University with Nishida Kitarō and Japan's most eminent group of neo-Kantian and idealist philosophers. While still a student he was given a seat in the House of Peers, a body his father had chaired. As a young man he became a member of Saionji's delegation to the Paris Peace Conference, as already noted. He had thought of becoming a university professor, only to be warned off by guardians afraid lest he involve himself in controversy. He did not shrink from politics and had a wide circle of acquaintance with men of many stripes. After the outbreak of the Manchurian Incident he was cultivated by middle-rank military figures. Like his father, who had sponsored Asia firsters and refugee Asian nationalists, Konoe cultivated Asianists and came to head an organization his father had helped found, the East Asian Common Culture Association (Tōa Dōbun Shoin). In 1933 he became president of the House of Peers, and three years later he gathered around himself a group of stellar bureaucrats and intellectuals in the Shōwa Research Association. He was deeply interested in all forms of state polity, without completely committing himself to any one, and he encouraged those around him to think that he might be willing to take the lead in a new, super-party national structure. Konoe was personally popular, though aristocratic and remote, and he seemed to project ideas of reform and social progress. Nor was he parochial. In 1933, when he took his eldest son to America to enroll him at the Lawrenceville School preparatory to his enrollment at Princeton, he visited with President Roosevelt to discuss American-Japanese relations. He told his eldest daughter that if she had been a boy he would have wanted her to study in Moscow. He himself responded to the suggestion of his brain trust to ponder the advisability of a new kind of nonparty structure. The ultimate product of this was the Imperial Rule Assistance Association, of which more below, which was supposed to eliminate all partisan bickering and "money power" (kinken) to promote true national unity. Far younger in years but superior in rank to Saionji, the last of the genrō, he was uncomfortable when the latter addressed him as "your excellency" and suspected ridicule behind the courtesy. In fact Saionji did harbor doubts about Konoe's judgment, a distrust that began with the essay the young prince wrote attacking the British-American peace as hypocritical and unfair, in 1918. At one point Saionji headed Konoe off by having him named to head the Privy Council, but by 1936 Saionji, in his eighties, no longer saw an alternative to Konoe. As Japan's political crisis deepened it became inevitable that Konoe, acceptable to the armed services, well connected in the party system, a handsome and rather charismatic young aristocrat, should be named as prime minister, and he took that office on June 4, 1937. A month later Japan was at war with China.

The China "Incident," as both sides preferred to call it in order to head off any stoppage of supplies under neutrality legislation, began as what seemed a skirmish on the Marco Polo Bridge just west of Peking on July 7. A Japanese soldier was missing from his formation; his commanders demanded the right to search the area, and the Chinese countered with a proposal for a joint search. By the time the soldier returned (from having relieved himself) small-scale violence had broken out. Hardly, one might think, an event that could lead to years of battle and millions of casualties, but it marked the beginning of the China War.

The area in question was designated as "demilitarized" under the T'angku Truce. Some Chinese security forces were under Japanese command, and others were under the command of the most pro-Japanese of Chinese generals, a man who attended the funeral services when his Japanese counterpart died unexpectedly, and who was prepared to offer his personal apologies for the outbreak of hostilities. Initially both sides hoped for a speedy local settlement, but within a month both sides were rushing reinforcements to the scene.

There was more at stake, however, much more; a match had been struck in a highly combustible environment. Commanders of Japanese field armies in southern Manchuria, including the new chief staff officer of the Kwantung Army Tōjō Hideki, had been urging that Japan take stronger steps to control the resources of North China in preparation for battle with the Soviets. The fear of Russia responsible for the Anti-Comintern Pact had as a corollary fears of Communist cooperation with Chiang Kai-shek in the new United Front. So long as Chiang had concentrated on what he called "extermination campaigns" of "Communist bandits" there was some good in the man and his cause, but after he turned to cooperate with Mao Tse-tung's Yenan government, Japanese army figures, Tōjō among them, saw their cause endangered. Suddenly there was a clear explanation for anti-Japanese boycotts and propaganda throughout China, and the solution was for Chiang to renounce the bargain he had reached at Sian and go back to fighting Communists.

On the China side patience was also wearing thin. Since first becoming foreign minister in 1933 Hirota Kōki, who held that post until 1937 (with the exception of his brief period as prime minister after the February revolt), had become increasingly peremptory in his statements to the Nanking government demanding cooperation in anti-Soviet policies. Kwantung Army leaders had taken steps to create buffer Mongol regimes west of Manchukuo; the Chinese thought they saw new signs of Japanese designs on the entire Peking area, the province of Hopei, as well.

In the Tokyo General Staff Ishiwara Kanji, obsessed with the larger struggle ahead with the Soviet Union, was convinced that a war with China would be the wrong war at the wrong time. The Army Ministry, however, saw things differently, and divided councils contributed to the dispatch of larger forces. Violence increased as the Japanese tried to oust Chinese forces from the demilitarized zone, with Chinese losses reaching 5,000 in one day. As violence increased additional divisions sailed for China. At the end of July a Chinese "Peace Preservation Corps" under Japanese command rose up, killed their Japanese officers, and went on to kill several hundred Japanese civilians. Pressure for all-out war became stronger. Chiang moved his best, German-trained divisions to the north, and Tokyo civilian and army leaders thought they saw the opportunity for a swift strike that would "solve" the China problem for some time.

Calamitously, the new Konoe government, despite its civilian leadership, adopted a stronger position than its predecessor, under General Hayashi, had. Konoe was no warmonger, but he seems to have seen himself as checkmating army firebrands by giving them responsibility. This made for some very strange appointments indeed to his cabinet. His initial choice for minister of the army was General Itagaki Seishirō, the fomenter (with Ishiwara Kanji) of the Manchurian Incident, and his preference for the post of navy minister, Admiral Suetsugu Nobumatsu, had championed the fleet faction in opposing the decisions of the London Naval Conference. Wiser heads in the Supreme War Council blocked both appointments, but Konoe later had his way with Itagaki, while Suetsugu emerged as head of the Home Ministry. Even more startling was the appearance of General Araki Sadao, idol of the young officers in 1936, as minister of education, a post from which he could work for the diffusion of *kokutai* thought throughout the educational network. Against such leadership the more practical officers in the General Staff faced an uphill fight.

Japan's descent into the quagmire, as it is rightly called, of the China War was neither expected nor desired by Tokyo.[41] Japanese army planners were confident that a show of force would suffice to secure a new and more advantageous position for them. Chiang Kai-shek, on the other hand, had been crowned as national leader of the new United Front at Sian, and thought a strong stand on his part, backed by the signatories of the Nine Power Pact to which he appealed, would serve to deter further Japanese aggression. In this setting it was the arrogance and overconfidence of Japanese leaders that led them into a maze from which they found no exit. While field commanders were working out a local solution in the immediate aftermath of the clash in July, Tokyo fulminated against the impertinence and lack of "sincerity" displayed by China in calling for outside assistance. Chiang, sensing the need to live up to his new mission, declared North China in danger and moved in some of his best, German-trained divisions, thereby violating, as the Japanese saw it, the T'angku Truce. Three divisions sent from Japan, the first of many to follow, quickly established military superiority in the north and encouraged

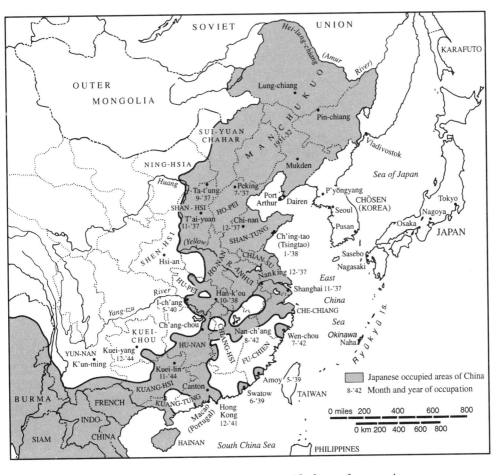

7. Japanese-occupied areas of China, 1937–1945, with dates of occupation.

a march to Shanghai and the Yangtze Valley. As Chinese resistance seemed temporarily broken, the Japanese advanced on Nanking, which was vacated by the Kuomintang government as it retreated up river to Wuhan before moving on to Chungking.

The fall of Nanking to Japanese armies in December 1937 was more rapid than expected. General Matsui Iwane's armies found themselves encumbered by thousands of Chinese soldiers, many taking refuge as civilians, for whom they had no preparation. A house-to-house search throughout the city by soldiers drunk with victory and vainglory led to days of murder, rapine, and looting that has to this date never been acknowledged and will stain forever the honor of the Imperial Army. Far from receding into the past, the horror has come to take on a life of its own. The "Rape of Nanking" has advanced to the present, utilized by the People's Republic as an issue in Sino-Japanese relations, fueled by controversies over Japanese textbooks' treatment of the war, and finally memorialized in a museum inscribed, in the calligraphy of Chinese leader Teng Hsiao-p'ing, "300,000 victims."[42]

Matters were also complicated by the difficulty Japanese leaders had in reading world political trends. Tokyo leaders considered the Washington Conference system a dead letter, but Chiang Kai-shek's attempt to breathe life into it by calling on the signatories of the Nine Power Pact resulted in a meeting of Western signatories in Brussels which, however inconclusive, emphasized Japan's isolation. The Anti-Comintern tie forged with Germany seemed to offer alliance with a strong and growing power; when Italy joined as well, the self-proclaimed "have-not" powers were aligned. The Soviet Union remained the major threat. Buffer regimes in Inner Mongolia were designed to secure that border, but the Kuomintang government's acceptance of a United Front with the Chinese Communist Party brought new imagined dangers.

A first idea was to ask for German help in bringing the war with China to an end. Foreign Minister Hirota indicated that Japan would be agreeable to a buffer regime in Inner Mongolia, a larger demilitarized zone in China to be administered by Nanking through pro-Japanese forces, China's cessation of anti-Japanese activities, and cooperation with Japan in opposing communism. Chiang Kai-shek was first scornful. Then, as his military situation worsened, he seemed to show interest, only to have the Japanese raise their demands as appropriate to their new military position. Now Japan added an indemnity as the cost of peace, in effect demanding that China surrender. Small wonder those efforts too collapsed. Next Hitler, who had maintained good relations with both Japan (the Anti-Comintern Pact) and China (through a large military mission), decided to remove his military mission from China in the interests of closer cooperation with Japan. To do so, he reasoned, might help tie down the United States, England, and the Soviet Union while Germany had its way in Central Europe. Tokyo took comfort from this display of anticommunism, only to be caught short by the German-Soviet Non-Aggression Pact in 1939. This had immediate repercussions in Japan and brought the fall of the short-lived cabinet of Hiranuma, who had succeeded Konoe in January 1939.

While Tokyo groped for ways to end the war, the field armies carried on in China, looking for an enemy to defeat or a mission to carry out. By the end of 1938 most major cities in China had fallen into Japanese hands, and major rail lines connecting them were also reasonably secure. But the vast hinterland of China was in good measure under the control of Communist and other guerrilla forces. The Kuomintang government had retreated to Chungking, but aside from bombing runs the Japanese had no thought or resources to occupy the interior province of Szechuan. Far too much of Japan's military machine was already tied up in China. Worse, Japan remained dependent on its Western, and especially American sources, for resources, especially petroleum, that were essential to its ability to carry on its war. Short of a complete collapse or surrender by Chiang Kai-shek's government, there seemed no end to it.

When, despite Japan's military successes that culminated in the fall of Nanking in December 1937, Chiang Kai-shek showed no sign of willingness to negotiate a peace on Japanese terms, the Konoe government decided to try new tactics. In a remarkably arrogant statement issued on January 16, 1938, Konoe announced that Japan would no longer deal or meet with the Nanking government. This famous "we will not meet" *(aite ni sezu)* position closed off any hope of peace with the Nationalist regime. It was now clear that Japan was in for a longer war. The government presented to the Diet the National Mobilization Law and took steps to institute controls over electricity and other resources. Konoe tried to strengthen his cabinet by bringing General Ugaki and the financier Ikeda Seihin on board. There was the usual talk of bringing about a fundamental solution to Sino-Japanese relations, but Japan's actions had made such an outcome extremely unlikely. This had been the context in which gropings for Western support through Germany to deprive Chiang Kai-shek of the German military mission had taken place; when Chiang, despite the loss of that assistance, persisted, Japanese military leaders began to suspect that the help he received from Great Britain and the United States must be propping him up.

In November 1938 Konoe announced a "New Order" *(shin taisei)* in East Asia, and planning began for the creation of a collaborationist government in Nanking. Sun Yat-sen's disciple Wang Ching-wei fled Kuomintang authority in the expectation that, as head of a substitute Kuomintang, he would have the opportunity to establish a regime of some legitimacy in Nanking. At each step, however, the commanders of the Imperial Army raised their requirements for even a limited withdrawal, with the result that Chinese separatist movements were quickly unmasked as collaborationist puppets. Frustrated and weary, Konoe resigned in January 1939. He would return to office the following July with new hopes for China policy and domestic reform. China would be promised a reconsideration of Japanese policy with hints of troop withdrawal, while in Japan political restructuring in the form of the Imperial Rule Assistance Association was supposed to end political divisiveness and bring about unity of purpose. Some observers saw this as a harbinger of a new totalitarian structure, but in fact it achieved few of those goals. In retrospect it can be noted that, although Japan's problems centered in controlling and curbing its military, these plans for a "New Structure" focused on the civilian sector instead.

The Konoe administrations led Japan into a war with China in which it won the battles but could never prevail in the war. Ever larger numbers of men and resources were tied up in the China quagmire. The high command worked desperately to extricate enough strength to permit it freedom of action elsewhere in Asia, but it also ruled out meaningful concessions and withdrawals that would have permitted negotiators to work out some face-saving settlement with a Chinese regime. There can be very few precedents in the annals of war and diplomacy in which a power, considering itself victorious but unable to have its way, announced that it would no longer recognize its foe. The celebrated *aite ni sezu* proclamation thus portrayed a peace-loving Japan as unwilling to meet with the only party with whom a peace could have been arranged, and it stands as a curious legacy of a failed regime. The next step was to conclude that Chungking survived only because the United States and Great Britain were propping it up, and to take the matter up with them. Work also began on planning for a new Nanking government that would be in more friendly hands.

18

The naming of periods carries with it differences in interpretation, and it is not surprising that what is commonly referred to as "World War II" seldom gets that designation in Japanese writing. The Japanese war was somewhat apart. It is possible to write about the war against Germany and Italy with little reference to East Asia. It is not possible to write about Japan's war without reference to events in the West, for too much depended on Japanese leaders' readings of those tumultuous events. The Japanese saw the Anti-Comintern Pact of 1936 as reinforcement for their own expectations of war with the Soviet Union, and when Hitler and Stalin reached an agreement instead the government in Tokyo resigned to atone for its error. A new government tried to adjust to this, and Foreign Minister Matsuoka bravely negotiated with Stalin to work out a Japanese-Soviet Non-Aggression Pact. The ink was hardly dry on this before Hitler reversed his field once more by invading the Soviet Union. Matsuoka now tried to show his mettle by proposing that Japan join in that war by attacking the Soviet Union from the East. Instead he lost his job.

The Japanese thought of the alliance formed with Germany and Italy in 1940 as a deterrent to interference from Great Britain or the United States, and had little plans for joint action with the Nazis. In this the pact seemed a modern version of the tie forged with England in 1902, which served to checkmate the Germans and the French. Its effect was the opposite of that, for it led the democratic powers to see Japan and Germany as a single entity and threat. German victories in western Europe seemed to create a power vacuum in the Dutch and French colonies in Southeast Asia, and impelled the attack on those resource-rich areas. To be sure, there were miscalculations on both sides. President Roosevelt thought that stationing the Pacific Fleet in Hawaii would make it more of a deterrent to the Japanese, but they instead saw it as an opportunity to improve their chances of success in war such that it impelled them to attack.

The two wars—Atlantic and Pacific—were not really one. There was minimal cooperation between the Axis powers and Japan, and the German military attaché to Tokyo learned of the attack on Pearl Harbor while walking his dog. As Japan gradually lost its access to sea lanes there were a number of efforts to transfer German technology, including a shipment of uranium for atomic experimentation, by submarine to Japan, but neither partner ever thought of coordinating activities; distance, and the greater naval strength of England and America, would have worked against the effort in any case.

Wartime Japanese spokesmen termed the conflict the "Greater East Asian War." The overtones of this were that Japan was freeing Asia from the oppressive domination of the West. Colonies were expected to respond positively to this chivalrous crusade carried out on their behalf, and the fact that China held back and instead resisted illustrated its obtuse faith in the doomed Western cause. When China somehow stayed in the conflict this could be explained only by the fact that it was receiving help from England and America.

In the International Military Tribunal that convened in Tokyo to assess responsibility for war, the prosecution argued for a consistent, purposeful plan of aggression in Asia in the interest of a new Japanese hegemony. A variant of this in Japanese historiography uses the term "Fifteen-Year War": one that began with the Manchurian Incident in 1931 and ended with the surrender in 1945. The hidden baggage of this designation is its focus on Japan's attack on China. It downgrades the naval conflict and instead follows the soldiers on the ground. There are, however, problems here: there was an interlude of four years of relative quiet between the T'angku Truce of 1933 and the Marco Polo Bridge and the China Incident. The Japanese high command did not want the war with China at that time and rather stumbled into it from arrogance, and after 1941 the China fronts became almost a backwater as the overwhelming focus of Japanese effort was on the army bases that had been developed for the use of the U.S. Fourteenth Air Force. In a technical sense, the China War, another designation, began only with the full onslaught in 1937 after which Japan's government dedicated itself to the establishment of a "New Order" and ruled out dealing with the Nationalist government of Chiang Kai-shek.

This chapter is entitled the "Pacific War," a name probably first coined by Shidehara Kijūrō in the memoir he published shortly before his death in 1951. It has become the preferred term for mainstream historians in Japan. A magisterial collaborative effort that has been translated in four volumes, *Ja-*

pan's Road to the Pacific War, begins with the Manchurian Incident, but all is prologue to the naval strike that initiated the bloody Pacific battles. This appellation also has its problems. To some degree it becomes a war with the Western powers, especially the United States, and downgrades the China War. Nor can anyone overlook the China background that brought the United States and Japan into conflict.[1]

1. Reading World Politics from Tokyo

Every turn in the road Japan took toward the Pacific War was taken on the basis of perceptions of change in the international system. The apparent success of state planning as a way of dealing with the problems of the Great Depression brought home the advantages of government leadership. Japan's awareness of its dependence on imported resources had as an understandable corollary a determination to work out a pattern of autonomy. As Western democracies responded to the Japanese advance with the imposition of sanctions, the awareness of that dependence became more acute.

For Japanese army leaders the tie with Germany seemed to offer one way out of the isolation that loomed ahead. The Anti-Comintern Pact of 1936 moreover seemed in harmony with the government's determination to resist the spread of Communist power in Asia. It was to be expected that military commanders in Manchuria, where boundaries were fluid, were eager to test the mettle of the Soviet forces they faced. In August of 1938 Kwantung Army units in northeastern Manchuria, where Manchukuo, Soviet, and Korean borders met, tried to push Soviet forces back to what Japanese thought was the proper border. When they were unsuccessful in this they wanted to escalate the contest by calling in more troops, but Tokyo leaders, not ready for more war, ruled them out.

A year later Kwantung Army units contested the borders of the area they controlled on the opposite, western border, where they were trying to augment their control between Inner Mongolia and Outer Mongolia. The center of this struggle was an obscure spot called Nomonhan, where a contest became a full-scale, though unacknowledged, war.[2] This conflict was little noted in the outside world. The Soviet Far East was closed to outside observers, and the Kwantung Army had its own reasons for keeping the confrontation quiet. Yet during the summer months of 1939 both sides committed everything they had available on the spot as the Soviet forces rallied to resist the Japanese advance. The difficulties experienced by the Japanese helped serve to swing the balance of government and army planning from *hokushin,* "northern advance," to *nanshin,* "southern advance." The Imperial Way faction, it will be recalled, had emphasized the priority to be accorded to the war against the Soviet Union, but the success of Russian air and tank forces commanded by General Georgi Zhukov, later hero of the battle against invading German forces, forced the Japanese to accept a truce after the loss of more than 17,000 men either killed or wounded. During the last month of the fighting the Germans invaded Poland to begin World War II, and that same August whatever expectations Japanese had of cooperation with Germany against the Soviet Union turned to ashes with the announcement of the German-Soviet Non-Aggression Pact. Both sides, Japan and the Soviet Union, continued a military buildup in expectation of a possible full-scale war, and Kwantung Army supplies were of such impressive dimensions that many of them remained unused when the war ended in August 1945. In Tokyo the cabinet of General Abe submitted its resignation. A fractious Diet speeded Nobuyuki's departure; the unity born of crisis and sacrifice was wearing thin; the China War showed no sign of solution; military opinion was divided among those advocating establishment of a substitute Nationalist government under Chiang Kai-shek's long-time rival Wang Ching-wei, pursuit of Chiang until he was forced to surrender (a commitment of resources that would limit other choices), or prolonged occupation of the area Japan already held. The "holy war" (seisen) was no longer above criticism, and the Japanese people were becoming tired of the growing shortage of materials required for normal civilian life. Japan was without a government when war broke out in Europe, and after some hesitation the elites responsible for political decisions temporized by selecting as prime minister Admiral Yonai Mitsumasa.

The struggle now lay elsewhere. It was probably speeded, though not determined, by the United States' informing Japan in July that it would not renew the commercial treaty of 1911 (which had constituted implementation of Japan's breakout from the unequal treaties), and that it would no longer be applicable after January 1940. Within months the startling German victories in western Europe opened new possibilities for demanding access to the resources of Dutch, French, and British colonies in Southeast Asia. In Indochina French authorities were answerable to the pro-German regime that had been set up at Vichy, but Dutch authorities in the future Indonesia, responding to a government that had taken refuge in England, chose to side with British and American policy designed to restrain Japan. The result was what the Japanese referred to as "ABD encirclement," a nefarious combination designed to deprive them of the resources they needed. No resource was more critical than oil, and Japanese planners saw their hand forced by the knowledge that agreement with Washington carried a deadline beyond which they could not procrastinate. Ironically, in their determination to avoid complete dependence on the United States they took steps that ultimately brought them precisely to that state. Washington, in turn, confident in the defenses of Hawaii and sure that it had the upper hand through its control of materials essential to the Japanese war machine, and urged on by supporters of China and by a British government that saw its survival dependent on American participation in the European war, held the line.

These considerations began to bring a change in the balance of forces in Tokyo decision centers. The navy had opposed commitment to a full alliance with Germany, aware that its resources for a contest for control of the seas were inadequate to the task. As Nazi victories in Europe opened up possibilities of access to resources in Southeast Asia, however, and as stockpiles of oil in Japan began to dwindle navy leaders reluctantly came around to army advocacy of the Axis alliance, which was formalized in 1940. The die was not yet fully cast, but plans for military action if diplomacy should fail now accelerated.

2. Attempts to Reconfigure the Meiji Landscape

The Manchurian Incident began as a case of military insubordination, but in the years that followed every step in the designation and implementation of national policy was taken in full compliance with the underlying structure set in the Meiji period. The one possible exception to this was Emperor Hirohito's assumption of personal control during the February 26 army revolt. It can be argued that in the absence of a functioning government—Prime Minister Okada in hiding until he escaped from his official residence—there was no real infraction of the constitutional order.[3]

The discussion so far has made little reference to the political parties. Their leaders had been displaced by individuals Saionji and others hoped would serve as symbols of national unity—distinguished admirals, generals, and a scion of the nobility—but that unity proved elusive. The Imperial Diet remained essential to effective government, and there the contest for political influence between Seiyūkai and Minseitō continued as before. The representatives in turn, elected in a system that grossly overrepresented the agricultural interest, spoke to traditional constituencies of local notables.[4]

On a number of occasions the Diet exerted its displeasure by refusing to back government policies, thereby causing the fall of cabinets. This was particularly the case with army leaders (Hayashi, Abe), who lacked experience in manipulation and compromise. At the same time, the services did not hesitate to unseat cabinets that were unsatisfactory to them. The Yonai cabinet, in an attempt at full cooperation with the political parties, had included six leading party members, but as events showed this did not solve the problems of unity. The leverage for the fall of the cabinet, which lasted a bare four months, was provided by a speech by a Minseitō leader who rose to deliver a trenchant critique of army inconsistency. He noted that as the China Incident dragged on Tokyo alternated between talk of establishing a rival government under Wang Ching-wei and sending feelers for peace talks to Chiang Kai-shek. Given this kind of dishonesty, he asked, how could the struggle possibly be characterized as a "holy war"? How could the government expect to preserve national unity? Army leaders charged that this constituted disrespect to the thousands who had given their lives in battle and demanded that the remarks be stricken from the Diet record. After some struggle the issue was resolved not merely by that act of censorship, but also by expulsion of the offending member from the Diet. The result was a flurry of organizations and groups dedicating their names to prosecution of the "holy war."

With national mobilization and unity more and more the problem in the face of discontent, many speculated on ways of consolidating the multiple interest groups that characterized Japan's plural politics into a more effective union. There were "reform" elements in the bureaucracy and politics who tired of the constant bickering and logrolling of Diet politics, and many political party leaders, despairing of a return to the "normal" party governments of the 1920s, were themselves willing to think about an alternative arrangement that would suit their needs. Army leaders were particularly keen on the development of a stable political structure that they would be able to work with. The drive lacked only a reasonably popular and nonpartisan leader, and for this signs seemed to point toward the return to politics of Prince Konoe Fumimaro. He had been on the sidelines since the resignation of his cabinet in January 1939; he had the advice and plans of the intellectuals who staffed his Shōwa Research Association, and he was acceptable to army leaders. He, in turn, thought that he could ride the tiger without having it devour him. This was the situation when Konoe was given the imperial command to form his second cabinet in July 1940.

It was probably logical for Konoe, who had proclaimed the "New Order in East Asia" earlier, to return to power amid talk of a "New Structure" in Japan. The Shōwa Research intellectuals and reformist bureaucrats had agreed on the desirability of working out some system to end the partisan bickering and selfish manipulation that seemed to lie behind so much of Japanese politics. There had been reformist influences for several decades as Japan struggled with the plural elites without the central moderation provided by the original oligarchs. In the Imperial Diet backbenchers in the two major political parties often combined with self-styled reformers in splinter and independent groups, all of whom hoped to have a larger say in politics than they had in recent years. Similarly, reform bureaucrats hoped for the rise of a new political party structure that would substitute efficiency and mobilization for the patterned influence peddling that characterized the prewar system. Leaders of these groups centered their hopes on Konoe, and he in turn was determined that the divisive influences of mass society and culture should not be permitted to work against the stability of Japanese society and politics.

When he returned to power he thus saw himself as the symbol of a New Order movement. He now drew upon the counsel of a number of leading intellectuals, among them Yabe Teiji of Tokyo Imperial University. Konoe thought that a solution to the China War was close at hand through some kind of negotiated settlement, and his advisers placed high hopes on the final text of the statement they had prepared at his direction. To their astonishment and disappointment, however, pledges to withdraw troops were removed from the final form of the statement, probably in response to army pressure.[5] Konoe seems to have judged that the timing was right for a new political order, and during the summer of 1940 he had representatives of all major interest groups meet to work out proposals for such a structure.

The result of this was the Imperial Rule Assistance Association (Taisei Yokusan Kai, hereafter IRAA) that was launched in October 1940. Designed to penetrate and coordinate Japanese society by organizing from village hamlet to metropolis, this was to be Japan's answer to the mass political parties of the fascist states. A preparatory commission of thirty-seven members represented all important interest groups. Konoe's intent was a structure that would replace the existing political parties, have representative organizations on both regional and national levels, and thereby dominate the administrative and legislative organs of the state. Institutionally the chief gainer of this institutional change would be the office of the prime minister; long ineffective and unable to coerce or to coordinate, it would now be at the center of the new structure, able to represent Japanese from city to hamlet and draw on every constituent body and interest group.

That was not, however, the way things worked out. The interest groups present at the creation worked to defend their territories. Those in the Home Ministry, particularly, saw the new organization as a way of increasing their control, and the military, working through the reservist associations and affiliated youth groups, saw it as a device for the further militarization of society. Business was not prepared to surrender its prerogatives, and rightist groups expressed suspicion of anything that might seem to overshadow or threaten the imperial aura. Faced with this struggle Konoe, as he usually did, backed away. Ultimately an IRAA structure that established a grid of "participatory" units spread throughout society did emerge. In cities its "neighborhood associations" were organized on a block-by-block basis. They coordinated everything from ration permits to fire-fighting efforts, and in the hands of self-important leaders they reduced considerably the amount of freedom that Japanese civil society had developed. The IRAA, although it had some utility in responding to wartime emergencies, activated the citizenry less than it repressed it, and rather than becoming a way of curbing or democratizing the Home Ministry it served that organization's purposes. Konoe too seems to have concluded that things were not working well. He replaced the reformist ministers who had placed their hopes in him with senior and almost honorary appointees, among them (recently prime minister) Hiranuma, men who were more "Japanist" than "reformist" and who were suspicious of IRAA activities. After the general elections in 1942 practically all Diet members found it wise to join the political wing of the new Imperial Rule Assistance Association. Thereafter it was this organization that selected candidates for political office, but this kind of political monopoly was far from what the idealistic theorists of the New Structure had hoped for. The IRAA became simply one more designation or attribution for what was already present; especially in the countryside, local notables added one more title and continued to do what they had long been doing.

The Meiji system, in short, remained as it was, albeit somewhat more centralized and authoritarian. The old system proved to have sufficient flexibility to enable Japan to deal with its wartime emergency. The next attempt to reshape the modern institutions would come from the headquarters of General Douglas MacArthur.

3. The Washington Talks

One reason that Konoe did not persist with plans for an internal new order was the pressing nature of foreign affairs. He chose as his foreign minister the mercurial former diplomat Matsuoka Yōsuke, who had served more recently as head of the South Manchurian Railroad. Matsuoka Yōsuke (1880–1946), educated in Oregon, was sure of his understanding of the United States. It was he who had led the Japanese delegation out of the League of Nations when that body accepted the report of the Lytton Commission; he was highly acceptable to army leaders, and a strong advocate of revisionist foreign policies. At the time of his appointment, he prepared a document for Konoe laying out what he thought should be Japan's policies. The war in Europe, as he saw it, made it urgent to tighten Japan's relationship with Germany by converting the Anti-Comintern Pact into a full military alliance. China, cut off from

Western assistance, should be made to see the importance of cooperation with Japan in the construction of the new Asia, and the southern colonies, cut off from their European home countries, should be thought of as part of a "Greater East Asia." (It was Matsuoka who first coined the term "Greater East Asia Co-Prosperity Sphere.") The United States, Japan's natural adversary in the Pacific, would have to learn to respect Japan's sphere as it expected Japan to respect its own; all other paths would lead to confrontation. Finally, Japan's energies and resources should be concentrated by reaching a nonaggression treaty with the Soviet Union, as Nazi Germany had done, to give Japan breathing space for five or ten years during which it could build up its strength.[6] Konoe was expected to offer the Nationalist regime of Chiang Kai-shek a new opportunity to work out peace, with Japan adding its assurances of its intent to withdraw its troops.

Matsuoka's document is a curious mixture of wishful thinking and arrogance. Events in Europe were moving so fast that a five-year grace period was unlikely, and Japan's image and record in China made it unlikely that Chungking would place much confidence in any promises. That Konoe was hardly in full charge was shown immediately. When the Konoe statement on China was made public, as we have noted, however, the language about troop withdrawal from China was left out, no doubt at the insistence of the military, and Wang Ching-wei, who had grounds for expecting better treatment, was left waiting on the doorstep. Matsuoka proved a treacherous guide to international politics. He was impetuous and self-important, and on occasion fond of hyperbole, as when he asserted that it was sometimes necessary to "be prepared to jump from the Kyomizu Temple." As crisis approached he became more vehement, leading at least one colleague to wonder about his sanity.

That, however, lay in the future. In 1940 Matsuoka embarked on a whirlwind tour of diplomacy that produced the Axis Pact, now a formal alliance, with Germany and Italy, and a nonaggression pact with the Soviet Union. His own truculence in speech was paralleled by that of his military counterparts, who increased pressure on China in an attempt to bring Chiang Kai-shek to the conference table. Konoe meanwhile revived the Liaison Conference, in which top cabinet ministers combined with the General Staff in an attempt to improve coordination of planning and priorities. There were serious differences between the Imperial Army and the Imperial Navy, the latter understandably nervous about its ability to withstand the combined fleets of Great Britain and the United States.

The United States policies of deterrence and sanctions, by forcing navy leaders to make decisions, brought the two services closer together. The United States Pacific Fleet had been moved, despite some misgivings, from the West Coast to Pearl Harbor at Hawaii, presenting the Imperial Navy with a threat and a target. The United States decision against renewing the 1911 Treaty of Commerce and Navigation with Japan helped bring home Japan's dependence on American scrap steel and petroleum. Matsuoka had seen the Axis Pact as providing Japan with leverage against the United States, but its actual effect was quite the opposite. The United States regarded the survival of Britain as essential to its own security, and that priority colored every decision about Japan. When the 1911 commercial treaty was abrogated in January 1940, the United States directed an embargo on aviation gasoline and lubricants and restraints on scrap metals. Under these circumstances attention to the rich colonies of western European countries would become more compelling unless an agreement could be worked out with Washington. This was the more so as the Japanese began to blame their failure to bring an end to the China War on Chiang Kai-shek's ability to get help from Great Britain and the United States via Southeast Asia.

To deal with these problems Tokyo now selected as ambassador to the United States a distinguished retired admiral, Nomura Kichisaburō (1877–1964). Nomura had been acquainted with Franklin D. Roosevelt years before during World War I, when he served as naval attaché in Washington and Roosevelt was under secretary of the navy. Before taking up his task, Nomura consulted with Japanese field commanders on the continent and with the service general staffs to assure himself of their cooperation in any agreement he might reach. His task may have been an impossible one, but Nomura was unfortunately not the best choice for the post. He was a genial elder citizen, but he had no diplomatic experience. He was also very hard of hearing, so much so that stories about his errant replies to questions were numerous. He wanted desperately to succeed, and to that end led his Tokyo superiors to believe that the American position was more flexible than it was, in order to keep them from taking obdurant positions too quickly. When they found him wrong in November 1941, their disappointment and anger boded ill for the talks.

Perhaps most serious of all was the fortuitous intervention of some well-meaning Maryknoll missionaries, with backdoor access in both Tokyo and Washington, who inserted themselves into the diplomatic exchanges by suggesting language for possible compromises. The result was confusion over what was and what was not the "Tokyo" position, with Washington formulating responses to proposals that had never been authentic, heightening distrust and suspicion. When these early misapprehensions of the American position were transmitted to Tokyo Matsuoka was jubilant, assuming that his belief about the value of the Axis Pact had been proved sound, but he then lost much of his enthusiasm for the Nomura embassy when he discovered his error.[7]

Nomura's task was made more difficult for him by clear evidence of Japanese preparation for moves in Southeast Asia. The Japanese high command had secured approval for moving troops and air strength into northern Indochina in July of 1940—before, in fact, the Axis alliance had even been finalized. Then, after the Germans invaded the Soviet Union in June 1941, Matsuoka began campaigning for a strike to the north in order to give meaning to the Axis Pact. His impetuous advocacy of this angered the high command, which had recent evidence of Soviet strength at Nomonhan, and annoyed Emperor Hirohito; Konoe finally found it necessary to ditch his foreign minister. He did this by a general cabinet resignation on July 16, 1941. Two days later he reconstituted the cabinet, without Matsuoka on board.

In the interim there had been heated debates in Tokyo about whether priority should be given to moves to the north or to the south. The Imperial Navy, with its eye on oil supplies, favored the south, while many army leaders were attracted by the possibility of combining with Germany to deal the Soviet Union a death blow. These and other deliberations were followed closely by a master Soviet spy, Richard Sorge, who came from the Volga German community, posed as a German correspondent, and soon had full access to the German embassy in Tokyo. He developed warm friendships with a number of Japanese, of whom one, Ozaki Hozumi, was a member of Konoe's Shōwa Research Association and enjoyed access to the highest levels of the government elite. Sorge was able to transmit the contents of thousands of secret documents and files to Moscow, and until his arrest and execution in 1941 he was perhaps the most successful intelligence agent of the age. Ozaki too was arrested and executed, the first to receive the death penalty under the provisions of the Peace Preservation Law of 1928. The unmasking of this subversion in high places in turn led to new police sweeps against left-wing intellectuals and writers. Many questions about the participation of men like Ozaki remain unanswered, and some scholars argue that the motives were grounded in a desperate attempt to head off war or at least a Japanese militarist victory.[8]

In Washington President Roosevelt and his advisers also faced the choice of giving priority to the Atlantic world or the Pacific. The Axis Pact had helped to resolve this question by making it seem a single struggle, with Japanese hegemony in Asia almost as dangerous to United States security concerns as German hegemony in Europe. One group of officials, among them the secretaries of war (Henry Stimson), treasury (Henry Morgenthau), and interior (Harold Ickes), favored a very hard line against the Japanese advance. On the other hand it was desirable to buy time, as United States readiness for conflict was at a relatively early stage. In the State Department Secretary Cordell Hull favored a milder stance, though Stanley Hornbeck, political adviser and former head of the Far Eastern section, was confident that the Japanese were bluffing and offered odds against a showdown. It was clear that time favored the United States, which was gearing up for war, and not Japan, which was searching frantically for resources that its war machine required.

Nor was it a simple Japan-America clash. As the Japanese pushed harder, Washington took counteractions in China. The move into northern Indochina had brought sanctions, and when, in July 1941, the Japanese high command insisted on the occupation of the rest of Indochina as well, the United States froze all Japanese assets. The firmness of this stand then encouraged doubters elsewhere to make up their mind. The Chungking government of Chiang Kai-shek, which had shown some signs of willingness to negotiate an end to the war, took heart from the prospect of having powerful support and turned its back on overtures from Japan. The Japanese, in turn, went ahead with plans to establish a puppet Kuomintang government under Wang Ching-wei at Nanking. In England the Churchill government, focused on the importance of getting American assistance in its struggle with Germany, reversed a decision to close the Burma Road that had carried supplies to Chungking and reopened it. The stakes in the Washington talks became daily more crucial.

The pace of the Washington negotiations was driven by the demands of the Japanese military. Konoe had opposed the move into southern Indochina, because he knew that it would affront the United States, but to no effect. The armed services, aware that time was not in Japan's favor, insisted on an October deadline for an agreement with the United States. Failing that, Japan would have to give up its hopes for regional hegemony, or launch an attack, or at least occupy Indonesia, with its oil fields, before its supplies of oil ran dangerously low. What did not change was the conclusion that if Japan was not given access to resources for war it would have to fight to get them.

In Tokyo decisions were now worked out, or reported, in Liaison Conferences with armed services and cabinet representatives present. The records of these conferences show fateful, even fatal, decisions being made in phrases of numbing generality. Documents were prepared in the offices of the various bureaus of the Army and Navy ministries and General Staff divisions and then passed on to superiors; in an April Liaison Conference meeting, General Sugiyama, army chief of staff, made it clear that the discussion should be nonbinding because he had not yet seen the document in question. Liaison Conference decisions were passed on to Imperial Conferences, which met in the presence of Emperor Hirohito for legitimation but very little discussion. The weight of the decision, and parameter of the discussions, lay with the document. It will also be noted that everything was done in strict conformity with established procedure; there was no more opportunity for impetuous, unauthorized action by field commanders. It was the military who had from the first the dominant role in these discussions, however, and even more so after the elevation of Tōjō Hideki to head the government in October.

By mid-summer an inertia of slow but insistent movement toward war had become apparent. At an Imperial Conference held on July 2, devoted to ratification of a document entitled "Outline of National Policy in View of the Changing Situation," it was formally agreed that Japan would contribute to world peace through the establishment of a Greater East Asia Co-Prosperity Sphere and through speedy termination of the China Incident; it would also, however, be prepared to solve its "northern problem" with the Soviet Union if the world situation made this advisable. In other words, the basic decision was to move (that is, attack) to the south, but in the event the German-Soviet war offered a tempting opportunity the northern border too could be secured. "In order to achieve the objectives above," the document continued, "preparations for war with Great Britain and the United States will be made. Our Empire will not be deterred by the possibility of being involved in a war with Great Britain and the United States."[9]

As the situation grew more critical Prime Minister Prince Konoe Fumimaro decided on an attempt at personal diplomacy with the president he had visited in the White House eight years earlier. On August 8 he had Admiral Nomura propose a personal meeting between Konoe and President Roosevelt. If he was able to gain some satisfaction from the president, Konoe reasoned, he would be able to have the emperor intervene to save the peace. Roosevelt had just returned from the meeting with Churchill at which they worked out the Atlantic Charter. He could not leave for Alaska, the side proposed, immediately, but expressed some interest and asked for more details of the Japanese plan. The Konoe request had come with a general statement in which he explained that the Japanese move into Indochina had been motivated by the desire to solve the China conflict, and that it should not be understood as a desire to expand into Southeast Asia. Roosevelt, who also believed in personal diplomacy, thought he would like several days of meetings, and suggested a meeting sometime in mid-October. The president's advisers, however, particularly Secretary of State Hull, were deeply suspicious of the Japanese and their proposals and advised against the meeting unless some guarantees could be worked out in advance. Nothing came of the proposal. Konoe later argued that he had selected the military representatives who would have accompanied him, and that he would then have had the ability to bring the emperor's influence to bear to force acceptance of any agreement. American leaders regarded the chance of success as so remote that it could not justify the risks involved. Neither the Chinese, who feared such an agreement, nor the British, who saw the Pacific conflict as America's door to participation in the Atlantic war, regretted the abandonment of Konoe's plan.

Almost a month later, on September 6, an Imperial Conference marked a turning point. The conference met to ratify a document entitled "Essentials for Carrying out the Empire's Policies." Its contents showed that military leaders had concluded that the Washington talks would not be successful, and were prepared to go to war. The "main points" were that Japan would complete its preparations for war in the interests of self-defense and self-preservation, and to that end would not avoid war with the United States and Great Britain. It would continue to negotiate, but against a late October deadline and with specific goals. Those were spelled out in an annex to the document: the U.S. and Great Britain were to refrain from interference with Japan's settlement of the China War, close the Burma Road and end military support for Chiang Kai-shek, recognize the "special relations" of Japan with Indochina, refrain from further buildup of their forces and from making military agreements with Thailand or others of Japan's neighbors to the south or north, and agree "amicably" to economic cooperation between Japan, Thailand, and the Dutch East Indies, the meanwhile resuming commercial contacts so that Japan could acquire necessary goods and materials. In turn Japan was prepared, as its maximum concessions, to refrain from further advance in Southeast Asia and to withdraw its military from Indochina after a "just peace" was established, with guarantees of the neutrality of the Philippines. Japan would, however, insist on living up to the responsibilities it had incurred by membership in the Axis Pact.

This was not a very promising position, for it would have given Japan everything it could conceivably want in exchange for a promise not to attack the Philippines. This truculence, along with the imposition of a deadline, seems to have alarmed the lord privy seal, Kido Kōichi, and the emperor himself, for Hirohito broke his silence to read a poem by the Meiji emperor expressing a wistful longing for brotherhood among nations.

The actual negotiations, fortunately, focused on issues less sweeping than this document proposed. The Japanese wanted the United States to resume trade in commodities of strategic importance, and the Americans wanted the Japanese to indicate some kind of schedule for withdrawal from China. Distrust, however, had corroded relations, and Japanese negotiators had the pressure of their military leaders at their backs. In Tokyo Admiral Nagano Osami, chief of the navy General Starr, warned his colleagues that time was running out; if oil were not made available, Japan would have to alter its goals. In July

Nagano warned that "there is a chance of achieving victory now, but it will diminish as time goes on." In October he pointed out that "the navy is consuming 400 tons of oil an hour. We want it decided one way or the other quickly." And in the final conference he summed the situation up as follows: "The government has decided that if there were no war the fate of the nation is sealed. Even if there is a war, the country may be ruined. Nevertheless, a nation that does not fight in this plight has lost its spirit and is doomed."[10] One has the impression, then, that there was more gloom than euphoria in the meetings that preceded the final decision for war. Japan had worked its way into a corner, and Japanese leaders were determined that war and possible defeat were preferable to accepting the role of a second-class power. It made no difference that they had worked themselves into this problem; retreat would be weakness, and that was unthinkable.

After a discouraged Prince Konoe gave up and resigned, Army Minister Tōjō Hideki succeeded him as prime minister on October 18. For a time he took the posts of army minister and home minister in addition to serving as prime minister. Japan had rarely seen as much institutional power vested in one man. Documents that came to light several decades later attributed this to his determination to maintain public order over extremists who might try to block a possible diplomatic settlement, but since there was no settlement and no problem with extremists, he passed the home ministry post on, though he kept the army ministry for himself. Tōjō's choice for foreign minister was the veteran diplomat Tōgō Shigenori, and he and Finance Minister Kaya Okinori were the chief civilian spokesmen as the deadline neared.

In commissioning Tōjō, Emperor Hirohito instructed him to go back to the beginning and study the entire matter once more, and in order to allow time for this the deadline for war—if no agreement could be reached with the United States—was moved from October to late November or early December. The conclusions of this study, and the recommendations presented to the throne, remained unchanged. The armed services set the end of November as the date by which some agreement with the United States would have to be reached. On Japan's side the need was for resumption of trade, particularly oil, and on the American side the insistence was that Japan present a schedule for withdrawal of its forces from China.

Early in November, Admiral Nomura was given two proposals to present to Secretary of State Cordell Hull as possible paths to an agreement. Of these, Proposal B, clearly the Japanese preference, would have had the United States agree that Japan might have to maintain its troops in China until 1955 while working out a peaceful solution, while trade would return to the level it had reached before abrogation of the Treaty of Commerce. Japan would have had supplies of oil and scrap, the meanwhile working on a solution to the China problem on a rather leisurely timetable. This was not a very attractive option, and Hull, who was weary of the way the negotiations had dragged on, responded on November 16 with an unequivocal demand that the Japanese withdraw from Indochina as well as from China.

Many Japanese, then and since, have characterized the Hull note as an ultimatum, but it is difficult to see the logic of that. Hull, and indeed, the Japanese negotiators, assumed that it would be followed by further talks; Nomura and Kurusu Saburō, a foreign ministry professional who had been sent to Washington to help the aging admiral, both thought of the Hull response as offering some grounds, albeit poor, for further talk. In any case, the ultimatum, if such it was, was Japan's and not Hull's. The Imperial Army and Imperial Navy had set a deadline, but Washington had not. Other writers speak of the freezing of Japanese assets by the United States as an act of war, but it could be seen as such only by negotiators totally dependent on American trade. Japanese army and navy representatives in Washington, however, concluded that there was now no further hope of reaching an agreement, and communicated that view to their Tokyo headquarters even before Nomura informed the Foreign Ministry. The urgency lay with the Japanese armed services, particularly the Imperial Navy, whose stocks of oil set a date—approximately six months in the future—after which offensive action would have been impractical. The Imperial Army, for its part, watched the German advance toward Moscow, assumed it would succeed, and feared it might be late for division of the spoils of European colonialism.

In a final Imperial Conference that was convened on November 2, Privy Council president Hara summed the matter up as follows: "It is impossible, from the standpoint of our present political situation and of our self-preservation, to accept all of the American demands. On the other hand we cannot let the present situation continue. If we miss the present opportunity to go to war, we will have to submit to American dictation. Therefore, I recognize that it is inevitable that we must decide to start a war against the United States. I will put my trust in what I have been told, namely that things will go well in the early part of the war; and that although we will experience increasing difficulties as the war progresses, there is some prospect of success."[11] Japan would negotiate for peace, but simultaneously prepare for war.

Japan's decision for war was made with forebodings of possible destruction, but was justified on grounds that acquiescence to the American requirements for trade would undo the efforts of generations who had pursued the dreams of national greatness. Japan now entered the last stage. The negotiations in Washington, though at this point clearly hopeless, were to continue to mask the fleet that put out from the Kurils to attack Pearl Harbor. There was discussion of a formal declaration of war. It was essential to retain the advantages of surprise, but also important to seem to play by the rules of nations. In 1905 much of the Western world, and particularly the British press, had applauded the Japanese surprise strike on the Russian Pacific Fleet at Port Arthur as a master stroke in courage and execution. In 1941 the reaction was sharply different.

A long, fourteen-point summary of the reasons for breaking off negotiations was prepared for transmittal to Admiral Nomura. He was to deliver it to Secretary of State Hull before the bombs fell, but not sufficiently so to lose the element of surprise. At the very last, even that minimal notice was lacking, and for a ludicrous reason. In preparation for war, the Japanese embassy had followed orders to dismantle all its code machines but one. By the time the last, longest, and most important paragraph came in, the only one on hand to type a clear copy was a young naval officer whose typing skills were poor. As he struggled with copy after copy in the effort to get a clean copy for his superiors, the appointed time for the emergency appointment that had been requested with Secretary Hull went by. Nomura phoned to apologize for a slight delay, and by the time he arrived the bombs had fallen at Pearl Harbor.

Much has been written in Japan deploring the failure to get the message to Hull on time, but it should be noted that the note in question merely broke off relations and implied, but did not specify, that Japan would now resort to war. In fact a formal declaration of war had been prepared, but was never sent, out of fear of breaking security. If it had been presented on time, Japan's act would have been within the strictures of international law, but there is no reason to think that the American response would have been very different.[12]

The imperial rescript officially declaring war was issued later that same day, and Professor Hiraizumi Kiyoshi had the honor of assisting in its preparation. The document described in lofty tones the factors that had made this decision a reluctant necessity to establish peace in greater East Asia. Unlike the rescripts the Meiji emperor had issued in 1894 and 1904 for the wars against the Ch'ing and the Russians, it did not exhort Japan's forces to abide by the code of international law. Japan, one could suggest, was no longer a "learner" in international society and was confident of its own rules and rhetoric, however inflated. Soon a commentary on the rescript was issued from the pen of the journalist Tokutomi Soho. The former Meiji reformer who had summoned Japanese youth to a new vision of modernization a half century earlier now spoke in hushed tones about the majesty of Japan's mission. In 1934 the government had ruled that the Chinese characters for Japan should be read as "Nippon" rather than "Nihon," to give the word more force and dignity.

Tokotomi's commentary was issued in English and carried this out. The imperial regalia of "Nippon," he said, represented sincerity (the mirror), love (the *magatama*, curved jewels), and intelligence (the sword). The Japanese way of life was ineffably superior to that of the West, based on individualism, and that of China, based on familism. Other Asian races looked on the Europeans and Americans as somehow superior, but it was now up to Nippon to show how wrong they were. "In other words, before we can expel the Anglo-Saxons and make them remove their traces from East Asia, we must annihilate them." This done, Japan would distribute the resources of East Asia more justly and lead in the creation of the Co-Prosperity Sphere.[13]

4. The Japanese People and the War

The tremendous victories Japan won in the first six months of fighting brought a sense of exhilaration and euphoria to most Japanese. The press gave only good news, and there was a great deal of it. Newspapers had special first-page corner space reserved for imperial rescripts that commented on the fall of country after country to the imperial forces, usually ending with the phrase "We are deeply gratified." It is understandable that ordinary people should have felt reassured, but it is worth noting that the euphoria extended to the well-informed and experienced. Prince Konoe's biographer describes a celebration at the imperial palace after the announcement of the success of the initial attack. Konoe found the senior statesmen—including Admiral Okada, fortuitous survivor of the February 26 rebellion—well in their cups and boisterous. Konoe had a deeper presentiment of what lay ahead; "how vulgar they are!" was his reaction.

Most intellectuals and men of letters rejoiced as well, and their response is of great interest. Takemura Kōtarō, a longtime rebel and free-form poet who had lived for years in Paris, returned to his roots with passionate intensity. In 1908 he had written that he had "first freed [his] soul in Paris," but in 1941 the news of war in Hawaii and the Pacific sealed his commitment: "I trembled as I heard the Imperial Proclamation. My thoughts distilled. Yesterday became long ago / And long ago became the now. / Our Emperor endangered! / That single statement / Fixed my course." The distinguished literary critic Itō Sei was no less moved, and wrote that on hearing the rescript, "I felt as if in one stroke I had become a new man, from the depths of my being."[14] No doubt silence would have been difficult. Many writers were accustomed to having the press seek them out and cite their comments as almost oracular, and found it difficult to abstain in the face of such extraordinary military success. The army, eager to utilize well-known men of letters, organized programs to send them off to distant battlefields. Reward was a greater danger than repression. What seems to stand out in the climate of exhilaration is a deep substratum consciousness of victimization and handicapping; Japan had been dragged into a world dominated by the Anglo-Saxon powers against its will, and it had found the cards stacked unfairly. The press and official commentary had worked to create that feeling for a decade and more, but without that substratum conviction they would not have been able to succeed. It must of course also be kept in mind that in 1941 Japan had already experienced a full decade of war and disruption. The idea that a resolution of the state of shortages, rallies, and torchlight processions was finally at hand must have contributed to the curious sense of relief and exhilaration so many felt.

Before long the initial exultation was replaced by foreboding and alarm, but many, probably most, writers remained faithful to the national cause. Some of Japan's most distinguished writers, to be sure, could afford to remain silent. Tanizaki Jun'ichirō (1886–1965), perhaps Japan's most distinguished man of letters, chose the war years to begin serial publication of *Sesame yuki*, a leisurely, nostalgic, and elegaic account of family life in prewar Japan. It was extremely well received, but after two installments had been printed in *Chūō Kōron* the editors were warned that the work would not contribute to the war spirit that was the need of the day. The editors, fearful of falling victim to the control the government could exercise by denying them supplies of paper, discontinued the serialization.[15] No less distinguished was Nagai Kafū (1879–1959), a man who lamented the disappearance of the old city and society.[16] Kafū refused to join the common front and preferred to rage in his diary against what he saw as the stupidities of an increasingly militarized state. Tanizaki and Nagai were distinguished senior figures, but the young leftist Takami Jun, who agreed to visit the Burma front, noted in his diary a dreary performance by a loud drunkard in an Imperial Army uniform and suggested that it would be as well if Japan were not to win.

Literary men might be accustomed to keeping diaries and expect the authorities to tolerate them, but for ordinary citizens it was a hazardous enterprise. Kiyosawa Kiyoshi (1890–1945) was a freelance writer on international affairs and historian of Japanese-American relations who began his wartime diary on the first anniversary of the Pearl Harbor attack.[17] He notes that his friends expressed surprise at his temerity. What he wanted, he writes, was a daily record, bolstered by newspaper clippings, for a history he planned to write when the guns had stilled. One suspects that he wrote this to clear himself in anticipation of possible police seizure and interrogation. It is striking to find that the shortage of materials and food was already severe when Kiyosawa began his diary. A visit to Viscount Makino Shinken finds the old gentleman unable to obtain an adequate supply of bread for the two meals he allows himself each day. The authorities trumpet the need for sacrifice, and bring the message home by felling magnificent old pines along the Tōkaidō route the daimyo used. (In the Kyushu castle town of Saga a magnificent old camphor tree along the castle moat was spared when old women formed a human chain around its base.)

Kiyosawa is dismayed by the crudity of authority and society. Japanese are bombarded with calls to remember their "spiritual" superiority over the enemy, and yet an ugly baggy outfit, the *monpe*, is required of all women and most men. Failure to appear properly dressed brings charges of malingering and indifference to "spiritual mobilization." Ordinary folk, given responsibility as block leaders under the IRAA structure, turn into petty tyrants and take particular pleasure in cowing their social superiors—a phenomenon one has witnessed in the People's Republic of China more recently. Kiyosawa reserves some of his most bitter remarks for Tokutomi Sohō, who, as grand old man of Japanese nationalism, is untiring in his calls for greater effort. Tokutomi, he suspects, had as much to do with the coming of the war as anyone. As the emergency mounts, the *Mainichi* and *Asahi* each add special columnists, who turn out to be Tōyama Mitsuru, longtime leader of ultra-rightist causes, and Tokutomi Sohō, to raise the level of martial fervor. Tokutomi's first article advocates death for downed B-29 airmen on the grounds that they contravene all rules of war by barbaric attacks on civilian targets.

Kiyosawa, no less than Nagai Kafū, is appalled by what he sees as the stupidity of the armed forces. He notes that conscripts are routinely brutalized by sadistic drill masters, in one case so severely as to be permanently disfigured. No less alarming, in his eyes, is the collapse of public morality. As shortages mount thievery becomes rampant; textiles become scarce, and cloth so rare that seat covers are ripped off of the seats of public transit vehicles. He and his friends are apprehensive about the resentment they see around them; they feel certain that defeat will be followed by social revolution, and wonder whether they will fare any better in the society that is to come. And yet, when the fire raids destroy Japan's cities, Kiyosawa is astonished by the quiet, dogged fortitude with which people accept their fate.

Kiyosawa's friends and confidants were the moderates; they included publishers and writers for major monthlies and economists like Ishibashi Tanzan (1884–1973), in postwar days an economic and political leader. Educated in America and once a reporter for West Coast Japanese newspapers, Kiyosawa had personal experience of injustice and discrimination, and knew only too well the futility of propaganda drives mobilizing hate. He died some months before the surrender and did not live to write his history, but the record he compiled is probably more valuable than his book would have been.

Kiyosawa's account gives some idea of how bleak the war years must have been for people who did not have his friends, his resources of land to farm, and his perspective. Throughout Japanese society the reach of the state and of minatory institutions grew ever longer. "Patriotic" *(hōkoku)* associations were formed to merge organizations and specialties of many kinds, from labor unions to writers—the last-named headed, once again, by Tokutomi. Protestant Christian denominations, separated from their overseas contacts, were merged into a single United Church of Christ in Japan. Pressure, but not repression, brought this about; the Episcopalians refused to come aboard, and the Roman Catholics were more difficult still to manage. The willingness of Protestant leaders to cooperate led to tumultuous disruptions and criticism in Japan two decades later.

Governmental monitoring of dissidence increased. The Special Higher Police *(tokkō ka),* established under the provisions of the Peace Preservation Law, had branches in all police precincts and were under the control of the Home Ministry, while prosecution was left to the Justice Ministry, which maintained special Thought Prosecutors. Particular care was given to monitoring religious sects, Koreans, and of course suspected leftists and pacifists. Japan also introduced German-inspired monitoring of Jews, although the possible targets were relatively few and the restrictions were not implemented very rigorously. Indeed, Jews in flight from Nazi terror often found supportive refuge in Japanese-occupied Harbin, Shanghai, and other cities. In addition to Christian suspects the police monitored and ultimately banned a number of Japanese "new" religions and sects, including the Nichiren Buddhist sect *Sōka gakkai.*

Another reason that repression advanced during the war years was that the power and influence of the military police *(kempeitai)* grew steadily, as they broadened their mandate from military personnel to anyone or anything that might seem to interfere with the war effort. This force of approximately 7,500 men became feared for its ruthless tactics and narrow construction of the national interest. Toward the end of the war, when Konoe, Yoshida Shigeru, and other members of the elite were discussing ways out of Japan's deepening disaster, it was the *kenpei* they had particularly to guard against.

During the war political life was to a large degree carried on under the auspices of the Imperial Rule Assistance Association. Political parties were dissolved in 1940, and after that date an IRAA committee endorsed candidates after vetting them for patriotism and spirit. Konoe had won approval for postponing an election scheduled for 1941, but Tōjō, who saw an election as useful for mass mobilization, went ahead with it a year later. The government used money and a captive press to influence the election of approved candidates. The now venerable Ozaki Yukio was reelected despite the fact that he was not among those approved. Ozaki was temporarily arrested during the campaign for a speech in which he was considered to have slurred the emperor; Ozaki had referred to a movement from "rags to riches," and back again, in three generations, with reference to the way Japan was apparently squandering the gains it had made under emperors Meiji and Taishō. But despite his difficulties with superpatriots, Ozaki was returned to office as usual. He did not find himself in congenial company, however, for in the 1942 elections "recommended" candidates gained two-thirds of the vote and 381 of the 466 seats.

The Tōjō government was intent on maintaining the forms of parliamentary procedure. The emperor opened Diet sessions with the panoply of earlier times. Despite this, the pattern of representative government became a facade for the military authorities. Budgets were submitted and passed, and occasional interpolations were addressed to Tōjō and other cabinet members, but it was clear that power lay elsewhere.[18]

There were also constructive aspects of life in Japan during the war. One, required by the shortage of male workers, was the increasing importance and confidence of women. The need for mobilization and unity led government officials to encourage and consolidate women's organizations as well, and major women leaders were eager to get more government help. The women's struggle for civil rights had, it will be recalled, been soundly defeated in 1931, and the increasing militarization of life thereafter held out little hope for a reverse on that front. Wartime shortages, however, also required frugality and domestic management, and to that effect the cooperation of women was essential. Prominent leaders in women's efforts in turn saw the opportunity offered by the situation. In 1931 the Greater Japan Federation of Women's Associations represented the first step in the rationalization and unification that the war years would bring to other sectors of society. With the China War of 1937 calls for more effective mobilization led to the Women's Patriotic Association, as women played their part in urging conformity with the drab *monpe* that replaced the kimono and Western dress. The same exhortations to greater effort and national unity characterized the women's press, and reflected a close cooperation with government bureaucrats.[19]

It has become customary in Japan to refer to the war years as a "dark valley" of unrelieved misery and pain.[20] It is understandable that in retrospect the despair of the final months should be reflected in this assessment, but one should also keep in mind the enthusiasm and euphoria that greeted the victories with which the war began. Japanese press and radio reported only victories, and although those victories gradually became closer to the home islands it was probably not until the great fire raids laid waste to Japan's cities in the spring of 1945 that serious doubts about the outcome of the war became common.

5. The Road to Hiroshima and Nagasaki

The story of the military and naval campaigns of the Pacific War has been told so well and so frequently[21] that it would be superfluous to treat it in detail here. Nevertheless its lessons and its memory have played so large a part in the history of Japan in the half century since the war that it is useful to make mention of its more contentious points.

The first relates to the surprise attack on Pearl Harbor. Admiral Yamamoto Isoroku, who commanded the Combined Fleet, was a man of experience and ability. He had studied at Harvard and served in Washington, and he had a healthy respect for American capabilities. He was also convinced that, if the standoff with America continued, the Japanese navy would be compelled to find sources for fuel in Southeast Asia. In 1940 President Roosevelt had moved the Pacific Fleet from San Diego to Pearl Harbor as a deterrent to Japanese action, and in Yamamoto's view this made it imperative that any plans for Southeast Asia be timed with action against the Pacific Fleet, lest it be able to cut the supply lines the Japanese would need. Yamamoto had an uphill fight persuading his associates of the feasibility of the air strike; the Imperial Navy admirals were dubious, and thought the idea far-fetched and dangerous. It required his threat to resign to bring them around. War games, map exercises, and preparations filled the summer months of 1941. Tactical planning was led by Genda Minoru, whose name will appear again. The task force that sailed from the Kurils in order to use the stormy and less used northern route was under the command of Admiral Nagumo Chūichi, a cautious member of the "fleet admiral" school who was not persuaded of the feasibility of the operation. The task force's progress was conducted under radio silence. Washington negotiations had been continued, and the Sunday morning attack caught United States forces so completely by surprise that the strike's success was even greater than expected. Subsequently there was criticism of Nagumo for withdrawing his forces rather than making another strike against the many targets that remained, but because the American fleet's carriers were at sea and their location was unknown caution carried the day.[22]

Disabling the American fleet gave Japanese invasion forces freedom of action for the assaults on the Philippines, Malaya, and Singapore that followed. Defenses were nowhere adequate to stem the Japanese attack, which was delivered with a force that won the reluctant admiration of even Winston Churchill, whose memoirs admitted that "the violence, fury, skill and might of Japan far exceeded anything we had been led to expect." With the exception of the resistance of American forces in the Philippines who stubbornly held on to Bataan and Corregidor, the pace of victory exceeded even Japanese projections; the invasion of Java was moved up a month earlier than the schedule that had been set. Within a few months of the opening of hostilities Japan seemed to have achieved its goals. Pacific islands became unsinkable aircraft carriers, oil stocks and facilities had been seized, Japanese troops were welcomed by colonial peoples in many parts of Southeast Asia, and the Co-Prosperity Sphere seemed to be on its way to realization. Southeast Asian army headquarters folded Intelligence into Operations, apparently assuming that the problem was in hand. The United States, in any case, had chosen to give priority to war in Europe, where interests and danger were greater.

Although Japan's strategic borders to the south and west seemed secure, the Pacific east, where the United States retained Hawaii, was harder to patrol. The Doolittle raid of April 1942, in which bombers took off from an American carrier a scant 600 miles from Japan, did slight material damage but had important psychological consequences. Yamamoto decided it would be necessary to add Midway atoll to the defense perimeter, and marshaled all his strength for a gigantic contest that took place in early June of 1942.

This time the Japanese came off second best, with the loss of four irreplaceable carriers. It became clear that the Pacific War would be waged on the Pacific, and by carriers rather than battleships. Consequently the loss of the ships on "battleship row" in Pearl Harbor loomed less serious. When replaced or rebuilt, they served as batteries to shell enemy bases prior to landings, but the carriers carried the burden. American industrial mobilization produced prodigious amounts of planes, ships, and weapons, while Japan's capabilities were far more limited. Submarines and flanking movements cut off Japanese bases in the South Pacific, and it was only briefly possible to exploit the riches of the territory that had been won. American technology and science were superior; radar, and the Japanese code that had been broken prior to the Pearl Harbor attack, gave American commanders critical advantages in planning operations and repulsing counterattacks.

Technology and matériel may have sealed the ultimate verdict, but the months ahead required grinding determination and immense hardship in battles that produced some of the highest battle casualty rates in United States history. Ultimately, however, the Japanese inability to maintain supply lines to distant outposts combined with the "island-hopping" strategy that isolated Japanese strongholds to turn the course of war against Japan. The American counterdrive was slowed by the necessity to tool and build for war, and by the decision to give priority to the European theater of operations, but once force came to bear the discrepancy of industrial capability led to dramatic advances against which Japan's long-vaunted "spirit" was helpless. Knowledgeable Japanese had seen this coming; Kiyosawa's wartime diary begins with news of German setbacks (which were reported, though Japanese setbacks were not) that the uneasy diarist realizes doom the hopes of the Axis partners. Japan's army leaders had gambled on a German victory and depletion of American enthusiasm in the face of a hostile Europe and Pacific setbacks, but instead the fury aroused by Pearl Harbor guaranteed a spirited response. Matsuoka came to lament the German tie as his greatest error.

Japan itself was hampered by service rivalries that were never overcome. Army and navy failed to coordinate plans or designs for plane production, and duplicated efforts continued despite the critical shortage of resources. What was true of industrial might was also true in technology. American superiority in radar, bombsights, aircraft, and ultimately the atomic bomb were far beyond the expectations of Japan's military leaders. On both sides submarine warfare was important; initially the Japanese had the advantage in ships and torpedoes, but soon American submarines were destroying merchant shipping at a rate that Japan could not replace. Japan entered the war with approximately ten million tons of steel bottom shipping, of which less than a half-million tons remained at the end. The resources of Southeast Asia that were supposed to fuel Japan's war efforts remained, unused, at their point of origin. Food supplies in Japan became ever more critical, and toward the end of the war most of what shipping remained was devoted to shipments of food to the home front. Other sectors of the Co-Prosperity Sphere, where civilian needs were given a far lower priority, fared even worse.

For postwar Japanese these issues have been blunted by focus on the use of fire and destruction against unarmed civilian targets through the use of American air power, culminating in the horror of the Hiroshima and Nagasaki bombings. Actions against civilians as an element of strategy had never taken place on the scale of the fire bombings of Tokyo or Dresden. Secretary of State Cordell Hull had denounced such tactics during the Spanish Civil War, declaring that "no theory of war can justify such conduct," but it proved only preliminary to far greater tolls of civilian dead in World War II. When American bombers began using bases prepared for General Chennault's Fourteenth Air Force in China the Japanese army struck against them with overwhelming force, but after the fall of Tinian Island in the Marshalls bases were speedily built beyond the range of Japanese response. The B-29 had been prepared as a precision bomber, but proved unsuitable to that task; instead American air force tactics concentrated on firebombs that rained down on Japan's highly flammable cities. In the spring of 1945 hundreds of planes combined to drop thousands upon thousands of firebombs on Japan's major cities. On March 9 and 10 fire storms in Tokyo claimed 120,000 lives and 23,000 homes; four days later Osaka was in flames, and in short order every major city except Kyoto was put to the torch.

While the bombers were bringing the reality of defeat home to Japanese civilians, army, navy and marine forces were moving up the Pacific road to Tokyo Bay. In the summer months of 1944 naval encounters cost Japan many of its warships and hundreds of naval air force planes, and American army and marine units invaded Saipan and followed it with seizure of Tinian. The Japanese high command had no set battle plans for this succession of disasters, and friction between the Imperial Navy and Army intensified. More significant was the fall of the Tōjō cabinet. Tōjō had staked his reputation on assurances that Saipan was invulnerable to attack, and the island's fall resulted in quiet maneuvering that unseated the prime minister on July 18, despite his best efforts to retain his post.

It was clear that things were going badly. Imperial Conferences and meetings of the Conference of Field Marshals and Fleet Admirals agreed on the importance of protecting the air space in what was now the inner perimeter of Japan's defense circle; further, they agreed on the importance of cooperation between the army and navy, and they vaguely held out hope for a "decisive battle" *(kessen)*. As the fighting neared Japan, the military argued, problems of coordination and supply would be simpler, and then discipline and spirit would take such a toll on American lives that Japan would be in a better position to think about ending the war. Meanwhile civilians began to drill with bamboo lances. There was stoic acceptance of hardship and danger, but little visible defeatism.

Tōjō was replaced by General Koiso Kuniaki. Koiso had won fame as an army planner, and subsequently served as governor general of Korea. His cabinet was strengthened by the return as navy minister and deputy prime minister of Admiral Yonai Mitsumasa, who had determined that Japan should marshal whatever strength it could to prevent the fall of the main bastions on the island chain to Tokyo. Next came the battle of the Philippines, which began with General MacArthur's landings on Luzon in October. The naval battle of Leyte Gulf, which followed, was the largest sea battle in history. Japanese tactics were daring and almost succeeded in intercepting the invading force, but ultimately they failed. At the end of the engagement the Imperial Navy, which had lost its carriers, planes, and best pilots, all of which were irreplaceable, was no longer an effective fighting force. The Japanese defense of Leyte was complicated by divided councils: the Tokyo high command wanted a frontal, "decisive" battle, while General Yamashita Tomoyuki, the "Tiger of Malaya," newly in command only days before the invasion, thought it wiser to plan for a long defensive battle. Worse, 80 percent of the shipping destined for the Philippines had been sunk en route by American air power and submarines. Although the outcome was never in doubt, the battle for the Philippines raged for months, and the Manila harbor was available to American shipping only in March. By then Yamashita's battered forces had retreated to the mountains. As Manila fell, the conduct of poorly trained and disciplined Japanese troops provided one more instance of mindless destruction and wanton rage. In mountain areas, fighting continued until the Japanese surrender, and Japanese casualties ultimately came to number 317,000.

One might have thought this would satisfy Imperial Headquarters' desire for a "decisive battle," but more was to follow. As the fighting came closer to Japan resistance became ever more desperate. In the struggle for the barren volcanic island of Iwo Jima, which extended from mid-February to March 1945, Japanese and American casualties in killed and wounded were close to 50,000, very nearly equally divided except that few Japanese survived. Possession of that island, only 650 miles from Tokyo, provided bases from which to support the bombardment of the home islands that now began in earnest.

In April 1945 American forces invaded Okinawa. In the struggle that followed, American casualties numbered 49,000, the highest during the Pacific War, and the casualty rate was the highest ever experienced in American military history. Japanese losses were higher still, with 107,000 dead, approximately 25,000 sealed in caves, and 11,000 taken prisoner. Imperial Headquarters was of little help to the Okinawa defense; one of the three divisions stationed there was moved to Taiwan to offset an expected invasion there, and air defense was shifted to the home islands late in the battle to conserve strength for the "decisive battle" that would now take place there. The tremendous toll of lives on Okinawa—almost one-quarter of the civilian population was killed—provided sobering indications of what lay ahead for Japanese and Americans in the anticipated invasion of the home islands.[23] As it was, the indifference of the Japanese military to Okinawans' defense and safety was seen by Okinawans as evidence of their marginality to Japan, and left wounds that fester a half century later.

By April of 1945 Italy had surrendered, German defeat was sure, and the American offensive was within reach of the Japanese home islands. General Koiso resigned as prime minister and proposed that Imperial Headquarters be put in charge. This was not acceptable to anyone, including the military, and instead retired admiral Suzuki Kantrō, the president of the Privy Council,

8. The Pacific War: Japanese advances and Allied counterattacks, with dates.

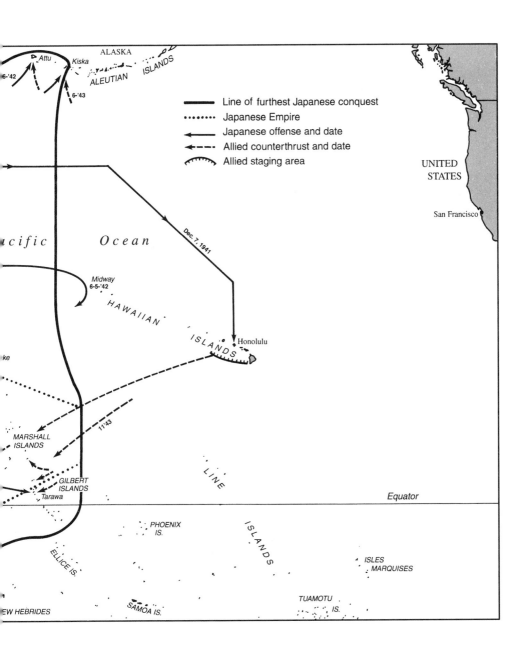

ALASKA

Attu Kiska ALEUTIAN ISLANDS

6-'42

6-'43

Line of furthest Japanese conquest
Japanese Empire
Japanese offense and date
Allied counterthrust and date
Allied staging area

UNITED
STATES

San Francisco

cific Ocean

Dec. 7, 1941

Midway
6-5-'42

HAWAIIAN

ISLANDS

Honolulu

ke

MARSHALL
ISLANDS

11-'43

GILBERT
ISLANDS

Tarawa

LINE

Equator

PHOENIX
IS.

ISLANDS

ISLES
MARQUISES

ELLICE IS.

EW HEBRIDES

SAMOA IS.

TUAMOTU
IS.

received the imperial command. Suzuki, who had narrowly escaped assassins in the February 1936 revolt, protested his inadequacy; he was old (78), and he was very deaf, but in vain. In retrospect it is clear that it was his assignment to end the war (although this was never put so baldly), but he was a master of cultivated obscurity and assured the Supreme Command that the war would go on while instructing his foreign minister, Tōgō Shigenori, to make every use of the resources of diplomacy. As the summer months came on Japan seemed frozen in inaction, its cities in ruin, its population nearing malnutrition, its factories and shipyards without materials, and daily life disoriented in every possible respect. The arrogance of military spokesmen and the intrusive surveillance by police and block leaders began to be replaced by a state of shock and shared misery. Kiyosawa Kiyoshi, attending a lunch with business leaders in April, noted in his diary that one man present regretted the news of President Roosevelt's death, for he had hoped Roosevelt would be in charge of a defeated Japan.

It was probably to be expected that Japanese army and navy leaders would grasp for ways to utilize the nation's "spirit," on which they so prided themselves, to overcome material disadvantages. The suicide mission seemed to offer such an instrument. Named for the "Divine Wind" (kamikaze), a term that had been applied to the great storms that sank the armada of Mongol ships that attacked Japan in the thirteenth century (and had been invoked, without success, against Perry in 1854), these suicide squads enlisted the courage and fatalism of young men who saw their country being destroyed and hoped to serve family and country by their fiery deaths. These young pilots were demonized as fanatics indifferent to loss of life, their own or the enemy's, by the American soldiers who were their target, and it came as some surprise to many that when collections of the kamikaze pilots' last letters, usually to their mothers, were published a few decades later they showed serious and sensitive young men, often well educated, who wrote affectionate letters expressing gratitude for the love they had received. As the fortunes of war turned against Japan a pathology of death made volunteering for such assignments less bizarre; death was everywhere, and the suicide flight offered the opportunity to combine it with possible service to home, country, and emperor. Many of the young pilots were or would have been members of the elite. Students were not conscripted until late in the war, and many had personal experience of the culture of the Special Higher Schools that were discussed earlier. Many survived because the war ended before their final call to attack was issued, and not a few lived on to leading careers in diplomacy and education.

On both sides the opportunity to know the enemy, stripped of his demon mask, brought changes in attitude. Donald Keene, later a distinguished authority on Japanese culture who was then a young interpreter questioning Japanese prisoners in Hawaii, writes of his discovery of the humanity of the men he encountered. "At first," he writes, "I would ask them the prescribed military questions, but soon I would shift to subjects completely unrelated to the war. For the first time, under these extraordinary conditions, I made friends with Japanese who shared my interests . . . But although I was impressed by their knowledge and intelligence, it baffled me that they remained convinced of the sacred nature of Japan's mission and the rest of the wartime ideology."[24] For the vast majority of servicemen, of course, opportunities for contact, indeed for reflection, were few and far between. But until late in the war very few Japanese prisoners were taken; they preferred to follow their commanders in final death charges. Japanese civilians on Saipan and again on Okinawa were urged, and sometimes forced, by Japanese officers to immolate themselves in caves or by leaps from rocky cliffs along the shore. Soldiers who found themselves in POW stockades, often taken when unconscious or desperately wounded, thought their lives were no less over; they had turned traitor to their country and would never be able to return.

The view of surrender as dishonorable combined with racism to shorten, and often to end, the lives of men who fell into Japanese hands. Forced labor by prisoners had been used in Meiji period mines, forced labor of Taiwanese and especially Koreans became frequent as war neared, and forced labor became the lot of Allied soldiers who entered Japanese captivity. The Pacific War was fought with ferocity. On both sides, as John Dower has pointed out,[25] there was race hatred as the enemy was painted in subhuman terms. Accounts that gradually filtered into the Allied world of Japanese treatment of prisoners, occupied lands, and women blackened Japan's image further. Japanese had shown their contempt for enemy prisoners in the China War, and as accounts of the treatment of American prisoners of war taken in the Philippines filtered out anger roused by the "sneak attack" at Pearl Harbor was compounded. Gavan Daws's study of Japan's treatment of 140,000 Allied prisoners taken during the Pacific War, almost all of them during its opening months, provides gripping details of the way Japan failed to honor the commitments it had signed, though not ratified, in Geneva for the treatment of prisoners of war.[26] The death rate for all nationalities was 27 percent and for Americans 34 percent, and it is Daws's opinion that if the war had continued another winter very few or none would have survived. Prisoners were systematically mistreated, denied medical treatment, and subjected to slave labor in Southeast Asia and later in Japan after being transported under inhuman conditions. Prisoners were compensated poorly in agreements worked out at the time of the San Francisco Treaty of Peace—British POWs received £78, and internees

£47—and long-smoldering anger flares, as on the occasion of a visit to England by Emperor Akihito in 1998, when organized protests demanded £14,000 per person. Even that sum, unlikely as it is, would probably not suffice to still the resentment that has continued to stir survivors in England and Holland. Oddly, American POWs, though they were not compensated any better, have been less vocal. At that, however, Chinese prisoners fared even worse, and figures for nonmilitary workers (rōmusha) rounded up in Southeast Asia cannot even be estimated. At most points of danger Koreans, who had been dragooned into a "Patriotic Work Force," were also to be found.

To these terrible tales has been added most recently the story of ianpu, quaintly rendered as "comfort women," who were rounded up to work in Japanese army brothels. The Imperial Army, more openly than other armed forces, had always provided and regulated brothels, in order to lessen disorder and decrease the incidence of venereal disease. Recruitment was normally through brothel contractors, and impoverished areas of Kyushu provided the largest number of women. Regulations specified that forcible recruitment was forbidden. As the army's numbers and fronts expanded, however, the usual sources of supply became inadequate and recruitment, initially of professional prostitutes but gradually of others who fell victim to lies or force, increased in amount. Death and shame served to seal the lips of victims until the 1990s. The moving complaints of long-silent Korean, Chinese, and even Dutch women became an international problem for Japan in the 1990s, and government moves to set up a (outwardly nongovernmental) fund for restitution and compensation showed that the complainants had justice on their side.

The final months of the war are among the most controversial. Deepset hatred and determination for revenge on the Allied and particularly the American side confronted the determination of the Japanese military to force one final bloodbath from which they might emerge with honor and some leverage on surrender negotiations. The Soviet Union, so long the object of suspicion and fear, now seemed to offer the last possibility for breaking out of the circle of fire that surrounded Japan. In July 1945, the Tokyo government indicated its wish to dispatch a mission to Moscow headed by Prince Konoe Fumimaro. Konoe had one last hope that high-level discussions could win Russian mediation with the Allies. He had realized the futility of further resistance and rethought the course of the last decade. In February, even before the invasion of Okinawa, he had addressed a rather bizarre memorandum to Emperor Hirohito, one he had discussed with the diplomat Yoshida Shigeru. In this he confessed to a new realization that the entire disaster of war had been the work of "Control faction" military leaders, who had ousted the Imperial Way faction and blunted its plans for a strike to the north. He now saw, he wrote, that their real purpose was Communist revolution in Japan, and that they had maneuvered to bring their country to the point of such a turnover. Japan, in other words, had been undone, and not by the military radicals who brought it to the brink of war with the Soviet Union, but by the calculating bureaucrats who won control of army policy after the February 1936 revolt; and they had structured matters to prepare the way for a Communist takeover. The upshot of the matter was that the emperor should lose no opportunity to bring the war to an end.

The emperor, however, was noncommittal and made no response to this strange document. The *kenpei* military police, suspecting some high-level defeatism, had put Konoe under surveillance and Yoshida in jail. In the months that followed the crisis had worsened, and Konoe now saw a mission to Moscow as his final contribution. Matsumoto Shigeharu later wrote that the Konoe he now knew was a quite different man from the suave aristocrat of earlier days. Grim in his determination and without thought of self or safety, he was prepared to come as supplicant to the Soviets he had feared.

But he was too late. The Russians could not receive the mission because Stalin, in a meeting with Roosevelt and Churchill at Yalta in February, had agreed to enter the war against Japan after the fall of Germany. After Japan requested a go-ahead for Konoe's trip the Russians asked for more details, and desultory talks conducted by Soviet ambassador Jacob Malik in Tokyo used up time. President Harry S Truman was informed about the Japanese request at Potsdam, where he had gone in late July to meet with Stalin and Churchill, but there he also received word of the successful test of an atom bomb. He rather hoped to forestall the Russian entry, since it would no longer be necessary. The bombs fell on Hiroshima and Nagasaki on August 6 and 9. One day before the second, the Soviet Union joined in the war against Japan, pouring across the border of Manchukuo—where, incidentally, they took Konoe's eldest son captive.[27]

Between the projected Konoe mission and the Soviet entry into the war momentous events had taken place. Late in July, when Truman, Stalin, and Churchill met in the old Prussian palace at Potsdam, they began to work out details for a postwar world. Truman came with one last ultimatum for Japan that was issued on July 26, in the name of the United States, China, and Great Britain, calling on Japan to surrender. It would receive firm, but also fair, treatment: Japan should decide "whether she will continue to be controlled by those self-willed militaristic advisers whose unintelligent calculations have brought the Empire of Japan to the threshold of annihilation, or whether she will follow the path of reason." The document went on to specify the removal of influence of the militarists, and that until evidence of this was clear, points in Japan would be occupied; Japan further would be limited to the home islands and "such minor islands as we determine," military forces would be disarmed and permitted to return to productive lives, Japan would be permitted to retain such industries as would "sustain her economy and permit the exaction of reparations in kind." "We do not intend" the Declaration went on, "that the Japanese shall be enslaved as a race or destroyed as a nation, but stern justice shall be meted out to all war criminals, including those who have visited cruelties upon our prisoners. The Japanese Government shall remove all obstacles to the revival and strengthening of democratic tendencies among the Japanese people. Freedom of speech, of religion, and of thought, as well as respect for the fundamental human rights, shall be established." The occupying forces would be withdrawn as soon as these goals were achieved.

The trouble with this was that it made no mention of the imperial institution, and to a generation of military men who had brought about the sacralization of *kokutai*, which centered on the imperial line, and whose own sense of identity as imperial servants was tied up with this, the omission of any reference to the throne was ominous. Former ambassador to Japan Joseph Grew, who had been under secretary of state, sensed this and urged inclusion of a provision that would speak to the retention of the imperial line, but his advice was ignored. In the American administration's mind the question of the emperor was still open; wartime rancor ruled out compromise, and nothing was to be allowed to defeat the terms of "unconditional surrender" that President Roosevelt had adopted from his reading of Civil War history. (Even so, some Japanese have argued that the Byrnes note, mentioned below, and the Potsdam language that the "following are our terms. We will not deviate from them" make it obvious that the surrender was not, after all, "unconditional.")

When the Declaration was received in Tokyo it was clear that the Japanese government was not ready to accept its terms. Prime Minister Suzuki turned aside a press question with the reply that the government's attitude toward the Declaration was one of *mokusatsu*, a somewhat ambiguous term usually translated literally as "kill with silence": that is, Japan would ignore it. Certainly that is the way it was interpreted in Washington. Preparations were now advanced for the use of the atom bomb, whose feasibility had been established by the Alamogordo test that was reported to President Truman at Potsdam. On August 6 (Japanese time) the atomic age began with the dropping of the first bomb on Hiroshima, and President Truman's announcement promised a "rain of death never equalled in history" if Japan did not surrender.

More hammer blows followed. Foreign Minister V. M. Molotov summoned the Japanese ambassador to the Soviet Union; instead of a reply to the proposed Konoe mission, he was presented with a declaration of war. As Secretary of State James Byrnes later phrased it, "It is doubtful whether ever before in history a government delivered a message indicating willingness to surrender and simultaneously was handed a declaration of war." The Soviet Union had accepted the American suggestion that its obligations under the United Nations Charter justified its failure to abide by its nonaggression pact with Japan, and later, in the International Tribunal that met in Tokyo, charged Japan with waging aggressive war at Nomonhan.

In Tokyo councils the hopeless argument continued: War Minister General Anami Korechika, who was under great pressure from his subordinates, continued to argue for a final battle unless the emperor's position was guaranteed. American planning for an invasion of Kyushu, scheduled for November 1, continued. Civilians had been removed from the southern half of Okinawa, and the Naha-Shuri area, so recently the scene of battle, was being converted into an immense base. American aircraft scoured the home islands for targets not yet burned, and the rain of death continued. On August 9 the second atomic bomb was dropped on Nagasaki.

Urgency mounted in the Tokyo bunker where the government leaders met. On August 10, a statement was issued indicating willingness to abide by the provisions of the Potsdam Declaration, but "with the understanding that that the said declaration does not comprise any demand which prejudices the prerogatives of His Majesty as a Sovereign Ruler." To this Secretary of State Byrnes returned a masterly obfuscation to the effect that "the Emperor and the Japanese Government" would be "subject to the Supreme Commander of the Allied Powers" and that "the ultimate form of government of Japan" would be established by "the freely expressed will of the Japanese people."

Once again the Tokyo council was deadlocked, as military leaders refused their assent. Optimists argued that a "subject emperor" was still an emperor, and that there need be no fear of how the Japanese people would express their will. Finally Prime Minister Suzuki asked Emperor Hirohito to decide the question himself. Hirohito then made the most important statement of his reign, saying that he agreed with the statement and that he agreed with those who spoke for peace. "Anami," he reassured his army minister and former aide-de-camp, "it's going to be all right."

That view was built into the rescript the emperor recorded for broadcast to his people on August 15. In this fascinating document that was phrased in terms of compassion and personal sacrifice he explained that "the enemy has begun to employ a new and most cruel bomb, the power of which to do damage is indeed incalculable, taking the toll of many innocent lives. Should

We continue to fight, not only would it result in an ultimate collapse and obliteration of the Japanese nation, but also it would lead to the total extinction of human civilization." As a result, he went on, choosing his words from the Buddhist *Sutra of 42 Sections,* "We have resolved to pave the way for a grand peace for all the generations to come by enduring the unendurable and suffering what is insufferable." The document went on to express sorrow for the dead and wounded, and it apologized to the faithful Asian allies who had joined in the struggle for the liberation of East Asia. Nevertheless, the rescript expressed an optimistic view of the future by assuring the Japanese people that, as the official translation phrased it, Japan had "been able to safeguard and maintain the structure of the Imperial State." The Japanese original made clear that the *kokutai* had been preserved.[28] The official translation of the Imperial Rescript of August 14, 1945, reads:

> To Our Good and Loyal Subjects:
>
> After pondering deeply the general trends of the world and the actual conditions obtaining in Our Empire today, We have decided to effect a settlement of the present situation by resorting to an extraordinary measure.
>
> We have ordered Our Government to communicate to the Governments of the United States, Great Britain, China and the Soviet Union that Our Empire accepts the provisions of their Joint [Potsdam] Declaration.
>
> To strive for the common prosperity and happiness of all nations as well as the security and well-being of Our subjects is the solemn obligation which has been handed down by Our Imperial Ancestors, and which We lay close to heart. Indeed, We declared war on America and Britain out of Our sincere desire to secure Japan's self-preservation and the stabilization of East Asia, it being far from Our thought either to infringe upon the sovereignty of other nations or to embark upon territorial aggrandizement. But now the war has lasted for nearly four years. Despite the best that has been done by everyone—the gallant fighting of military and naval forces, the diligence and assiduity of Our servants of the State and the devoted service of Our one hundred million people, the war situation has developed not necessarily to Japan's advantage, while the general trends of the world have all turned against her interest. Moreover, the enemy has begun to employ a new and most cruel bomb, the power of which to do damage is indeed incalculable, taking the toll of many innocent lives. Should We continue to fight, it would result not only in an ultimate collapse and obliteration of the Japanese nation, but also it would lead to the total extinction of human civilization. Such being the case, how are We

to save the millions of Our subjects, or to atone ourselves before the hallowed spirits of Our Imperial Ancestors? This is the reason why We have ordered the acceptance of the provisions of the Joint Declaration of the Powers.

We cannot but express the sense of deepest regret to our Allied nations of East Asia, who have consistently cooperated with the Empire towards the emancipation of East Asia. The thought of those officers and men as well as others who have fallen in the fields of battle, those who died at their posts of duty, or those who met with untimely death and all their bereaved families, pains Our heart night and day. The welfare of the wounded and the war-sufferers, and of those who have lost their homes and livelihood, are the objects of Our profound solicitude. The hardships and suffering to which Our nation is to be subjected hereafter will be certainly great. We are keenly aware of the inmost feelings of all ye, Our subjects. However, it is according to the dictate of time and fate that We have resolved to pave the way for a grand peace for all the generations to come by enduring the unendurable and suffering what is insufferable.

Having been able to safeguard and maintain the structure [*kokutai*] of the Imperial State, We are always with ye, Our good and loyal subjects, relying upon your sincerity and integrity. Beware most strictly of any outbursts of emotion which may engender or any fractional contention and strife which may create confusion, lead ye astray and cause ye to lose the confidence of the world. Let the entire nation continue as one family from generation to generation, ever firm in its faith in the imperishableness of this divine land, and mindful of its heavy burden of responsibilities, and the long road before it. Unite your total strength to be devoted to the construction for the future. Cultivate the ways of rectitude; foster nobility of spirit; and work with resolution so as ye may enhance the innate glory of the Imperial State and keep pace with the progress of the world.[29]

The emperor made no further mention of this matter until 1971, when he denied that his intervention had been in any sense unconstitutional. "The decision was taken on the responsibility of Prime Minister Suzuki," he said; "that was my interpretation." Nevertheless the fact remains that nothing short of a "divine decision," as nationalists phrased it, would have sufficed to bring the military to lay down their arms and give up their power.

Even so, not all military officers were ready to submit. The night before the recording of the rescript was to be broadcast a rebellion broke out. Staff and company grade officers led their men in groups to take over radio transmission facilities, murdered a general in the Imperial Guard to secure access to the palace, and rummaged through the chamber in which palace officials had hidden the recording. General Anami, who was aware of the plot but neither supported nor suppressed it, tendered his resignation in a traditional self-immolation on the veranda of his residence, where he expired in a prolonged and excruciatingly painful death.

Both services, the Imperial Army and Imperial Navy, prepared for possible Allied action against Hirohito and Crown Prince Akihito by assembling well-funded teams of zealots whose mission was to provide protective custody for a young Prince Kitashirakawa, whose descent from the Emperor Meiji was clear, in remote mountain areas. The navy's team was led by Genda Minoru, the planner of Pearl Harbor, who enlisted trusted associates in a setting of Wagnerian bathos. By the time their rather maladroit preparations were advanced it was clear that the emperor was probably not in danger, and the operations seem in retrospect ludicrous. It is also significant that even in these extreme moments the services could not work together, but also indicative of the state of crisis that they tried.[30]

6. The Pacific War in the History of the Twentieth Century

These cataclysmic events have spawned a rich harvest of controversy that centers around the beginning and the end of the war. It was not long after its conclusion that critics of President Roosevelt took aim at the manner in which the negotiations in Washington were carried out. The administration, it has been charged, was desperate to find some way of getting public support for intervention in the war in Europe, and once the Axis Pact was signed in 1940 it hardened its attitude toward Japan. Secretary of War Henry S. Stimson's diary of November 25, 1941, summarizing President Roosevelt to the effect that "the question was how we should maneuver them [the Japanese] into the position of firing the first shot without allowing too much danger ourselves," has been seized on by writers who feel that the Pacific Fleet at Pearl Harbor was there as a decoy to lure Japan to combat. Some go so far as to argue from the clumsy use that was made of intercepts that preceded the final message, in which Japan broke off negotiations, that Washington deliberately failed to inform its Hawaiian commanders of approaching danger.[31]

This charge, however, overlooks the consistent neglect of Japanese capabilities and equally consistent exaggeration of Allied preparedness in the Pacific. Prime Minister Churchill certainly did not send two of Great Britain's finest warships, the *Repulse* and the *Prince of Wales*, to Singapore without adequate air cover in a blithe expectation of losing them; rather, the Japanese were expected to be impressed and to be deterred from a move to the south. Similarly, President Roosevelt had assurances from his military advisers that Pearl Harbor and Hawaii were virtually impregnable to attack. Japanese military technology was also underrated. In the early stages of the war the Zero fighter was far more nimble than its foes, and the low-level torpedo bomb that did such damage to battleship row had been developed by Genda Minoru only months before and came as a brutal surprise.

The charge can easily be sustained that Japan was not taken seriously in intent or capability. In Tokyo the distinguished scholar of American constitutional law Takagi Yasaka was one of many who took the Konoe statements about a "new order" seriously and lamented the United States' inability or unwillingness to understand that the Roosevelt administration's hard line was courting danger. "The danger of war is by far the greatest," Takagi wrote Ambassador Joseph Grew, "not when Japan thinks that she can wage safely a war of aggression, as some people argue, but when she feels, rightly or wrongly, that she is driven into a corner and, therefore, desperately strikes back, defying consequences."[32]

In Washington the State Department's Stanley Hornbeck, on the other hand, predicted that Japan was bluffing. On July 23, 1941, he sent Undersecretary of State Sumner Welles a memorandum assuring him that "under existing circumstances it is altogether improbable that Japan would deliberately take action in response to any action which the United States is likely to take in the Pacific which action if taken by Japan would mean war between that country and this country." And on November 27, 1941, with Admiral Nagumo's fleet already at sea, he had the temerity to compose a memorandum which began, "In the opinion of the undersigned, the Japanese government does not desire or intend or expect to have forthwith armed conflict with the United States." He went on to offer odds, five to one that war would not come by December 15, three to one against war by January 15, and even money against war by March 1; "the undersigned," he concluded, "does not believe that this country is now on the immediate verge of 'war' in the Pacific."[33] Takagi proved the better prophet. Hornbeck's was a false confidence in which the military participated. In response to a report that no radio sounds had been received from the main Japanese fleet just before Pearl Harbor, Admiral Husband Kimmel asked, as an unlikely possibility, "Do you mean to say the Japanese fleet could be rounding Koko Head?"

More second guessing surrounds the administration's decision to discourage the talks that Konoe wanted so badly on the eve of war. It is argued that Konoe could have brought the emperor to bear on the military to accept a decision it might not have liked. Counter-to-fact arguments of what might have been are necessarily inconclusive, but it can be argued that Konoe's ability to utilize the emperor, if it existed, could also have been employed without discussions in Alaska; Konoe himself was expected to offer China a guarantee of withdrawal of Japanese troops when he came to power a second time in 1940, but those offers disappeared mysteriously and Matsumoto Shigeharu assumes that the Imperial Army intervened. The disgrace of Chamberlain's tragic performance at Munich was fresh in mind, and talks hinting of resolution of differences spoke of appeasement to Churchill and betrayal to Chiang Kai-shek. Nevertheless it is surely true that any and all attempts to ward off the carnage that followed should have been made, and that no statesman should leave a stone unturned in the pursuit of peace.

Once war did come the doctrines of earlier military history proved no more dependable than those of diplomacy, for air power changed the face of war. The Pacific, where capital ships had shown their worth as Admiral Tōgō sank the Russian Baltic fleet in 1905, now witnessed the end of a cycle that had begun with H.M.S. *Dreadnought* in 1908. At Pearl Harbor, where Americans never saw the Japanese fleet, and at Midway, where neither fleet saw the other, air power carried the day. Japan came to learn the lesson it had first taught at Pearl Harbor and in Malaya, where the British *Repulse* and *Prince of Wales* went down, when its own and even larger *Musashi* and *Yamato* were lost to American planes. On land as well, the vast distances between fortified outposts, instead of constituting handicaps, proved vulnerable to the imaginative island-hopping tactics used by United States forces in their progress from Guadalcanal to Okinawa.

Nothing more distinguished the Pacific War than the manner of its ending. The example of atomic weapons changed far more than Japanese policies. The experience transformed forever world strategic thinking and held up the picture of an Armageddon that has profound psychological consequences for people everywhere. Here the controversy swirls around the necessity and justification for the use of the bomb on Hiroshima and Nagasaki. As the realization of its awesome consequences began to sink in, those concerned, including Secretary Stimson, took refuge in the civilian and military casualties that were averted by its use. It is clear that it forced the argument in that humid Tokyo bunker, and provided the bridge over which the emperor could cross as compassionate Buddha to save his people.

The argument, however, centers on whether or not Japan would have surrendered by the fall of 1945 without its use. We have seen that intelligent commentators like the businessman Kiyosawa Kiyoshi writing in his diary knew, four months and hundreds of thousands of deaths before the end of the war, that American occupation was certain. The economic planner and later foreign minister Ōkita Saburō tells of a visit a professor at Tokyo Imperial

University, also in April 1945, in which he accepts the certainty of defeat philo-sophically. The two discuss a story (from Bagehot) of a warrior who starved himself to buy a coat of armor, only to find that he was too weak to fight in it. This was just what happened to Japan, they agreed. Japan would probably have to give up its arms, but this could be a blessing in disguise: it would achieve more of its aims in business suits than it had in uniforms.[34]

Intelligent people were ready to surrender. But most of them would proba-bly not have gone to war in the first place. Would the military have surren-dered sooner—or only slightly later, certainly before the landings scheduled for November—if the Potsdam Declaration had included a guarantee for the imperial line? The question cannot be answered, but as with the Konoe mis-sion in 1941, one can wish that the attempt had been made. It is irrelevant that Japan would have used the bomb if it had been at its disposal. It is poor comfort to balance noncombatant lives sacrificed against lives hypothetically saved by use of the bomb. Yet it is also true that, had Japan's military leaders succeeded in forcing a final "decisive battle," it would certainly have been more difficult to disengage the contending forces, and, given the indifference to civilian lives the Japanese command showed on Okinawa, one can only guess at the carnage that would have come in Kyushu. It is also interesting, if ironic, that much of the criticism of Presidents Roosevelt and Truman has come from what might be called the "liberal-left" persuasion, groups that were most vigilant against the appeasement of imperial Japan and military fascism.

There is, however, another aspect of the Pacific War on which there can be no disagreement: the war marked the end of colonial imperialism in Asia. The decline of European power and influence had begun in the years after World War I, but the Pacific War continued what was already under way. The humiliation and contempt that Japanese occupying forces visited on the colonial masters in Southeast Asia made it impossible to reassert the superior-ity they had long asserted for themselves. In Indonesia and Burma indepen-dence movements began to take shape with Japanese encouragement. It was not long before Japanese imperialism itself proved no less welcome, and fre-quently less humane, than the imperialisms it had displaced; the greater was the determination to be rid of all such outside control on the part of peoples once subject. Added to the expulsion of Japan from Korea and Taiwan, this marked a turning point in world history. Many postwar Japanese have fre-quently found comfort in this and cited it as a benefit for Asia. In this sense the war against the West can find defenders, while that against China cannot. Yet Japanese intervention was no less decisive in providing turning points in China, in a sense creating, and then destroying, the Kuomintang regime of

Chiang Kai-shek, while the peasant nationalism on which Mao Tse-tung rode to power was no less the product of Japanese destruction of the old society.

7. Dismantling the Meiji State

The Occupation forces required by the Potsdam Declaration began to arrive after the formal instrument of surrender was signed on board the U.S. battleship *Missouri* on September 2. The choice of General Douglas MacArthur as Supreme Commander of the Allied Powers (SCAP)—and simultaneously as commander of all American forces in the Far East, a designation scarcely less important—seems never to have been in doubt, although Admiral Chester Nimitz, under whose command so many of the Pacific battles had been won, might have had equal claim on the role. MacArthur had a larger reputation, longer administrative experience, and the confidence of Republican party leaders whose support was important in a Democratic administration. He was also a person of eloquence, bordering at times on grandiloquence, and fired by an idealistic vision of a future world of peace. He set his stamp on the Occupation in many ways. In 1950 Edwin Reischauer wrote that his name would "stand as one of the great names in Japanese history, surpassed by few in Japan's long annals and unrivaled by any since the stirring days of the Meiji period."[35] Those heroic estimates are well behind us today; it is striking to find how few current Japanese reference works give MacArthur more than cursory attention, but no one can deny that his was a fortunate match of man and task.

General Headquarters, GHQ, comprised several thousand military and civilian administrators divided into sections which included Government, Civil Information and Education, and Economic and Scientific. The highest slots were held by MacArthur loyalists, many of whom had followed his star since President Roosevelt had sent him to the Philippines as military adviser in the 1930s. Others were recruited in a wide search for talent and experience; a specialist in labor organizations,[36] a German judge who would recognize the roots of modern Japanese jurisprudence,[37] economists and bankers. In addition to the Potsdam terms MacArthur was directed by an Initial Post-Surrender Policy document drawn up by a State, War, and Navy departments committee, but the guidelines were general and not specific. American attention was still centered on Europe, and Japan came in a poor second. A Far Eastern Commission made up of the eleven Pacific War allies met in the former Japanese embassy in Washington to make and review policy, and an Allied Council with American, British Commonwealth, Soviet, and Chinese representatives met in Tokyo, theoretically to oversee implementation, but largely in vain. MacArthur would seldom brook interference, and his staff occasionally rushed measures in anticipation of directives from the commission. In addition to SCAP the army of occupation, initially the Eighth Army, spread throughout the country; gradually its functions were reduced to regional Military Government teams. There was some participation by British Commonwealth units, and the Soviet Union expressed interest in occupying Hokkaido, but was repulsed. Japan was spared the divided zones and councils of Germany. Chinese participation was minimal as the country was soon in civil war between Nationalist and Communist contenders for power.

The Japanese government remained in being. Its leaders had not gone to a fiery death or futile flight like those of Germany. The Potsdam Declaration spoke of its requirements for "the Japanese government." The Occupation was intensive, but ultimately indirect, with Japanese authorities responding to SCAP/GHQ directives.

The first order of the day was the elimination of militarism and other forces inimical to the establishment of democratic government in Japan. The Occupation proceeded in short order to strike some of the principal institutions of the Meiji state.

The military establishment was the first to fall. Army and navy equipment was seized and destroyed, and Japan's servicemen were demobilized, at home and as soon as ships could bring them from distant fronts. The Russians, however, held on to the large number of prisoners they took and used them in labor camps in the Soviet Far East for many years. Shame and remorse replaced the pride the returnees had felt as the "Emperor's soldiers." A defeated and hungry country did little to welcome them home. Many complained of avoidance and neglect. In the days of shortage and a breakdown of public services, demobilized men could expect little from their fellow citizens, and nothing from their government, which was forbidden to pay pensions. For some years threadbare mendicants with army caps pleaded for coppers from passengers on crowded trains who, more often than not, averted their eyes.

The dismantling of the military command and institutional structure proved effective and usually popular. At times, however, SCAP zealots went to absurd lengths in their war against Japanese militarism; publications were censored for warlike themes and classic kabuki dramas monitored for reference to the heroes of Japan's past. Swords were called in for registration by local Military Government units, and in the process not a few Japanese lost family heirlooms. Military schools and academies that had worked to create a separate caste disappeared into the larger structure of mass education. The Japanese military, which had so recently been able to dictate the makeup and policies of most levels of government, now ceased to exist, and in its place SCAP, through the agencies it set up, had the capability to influence all levels of Japanese government. It is impossible to overestimate the importance of the absence of the military for contemporary Japan. The Meiji leaders had seen to it that the armed services, under direct imperial command, would be beyond the reach of the heads of civil society.

The imperial institution was the pivotal point of the Meiji state, the center of its ideology and the fulcrum of state power. SCAP policies profited from that aura by utilizing the imperial institution during the days of surrender and compliance, and then gradually deflated and modernized the institution. Emperor Hirohito had presided over Japan's descent into aggressive war. His presence had legitimated council decisions of the greatest import. Service chiefs reported directly to him, and minutes of meetings found him occasionally questioning policy or procedure. He had to have been informed of the Pearl Harbor plan, although his chiefs had assured him of the prior delivery of the note breaking off negotiations. His rescripts had signaled his satisfaction with each of the early victories. On the other hand he had also been instrumental in bringing about the surrender, and his cooperation was important in securing that of his people, and certainly of the military. As we have seen, both the army and the navy had prepared contingency plans in the event action was taken against the emperor. During the war Allied government statements had been careful to avoid references to Hirohito personally; instead they had concentrated on Tōjō, but despite this the emperor had inevitably become a target of the hatred and rancor against Japan that welled up during the war. There was widespread support for including him as one of those on trial for war guilt.

In September 1945 a nervous, ill-at-ease monarch's ancient automobile picked its way through the potholes of his capital to the American embassy residence to pay a first courtesy call on General MacArthur. There was no American interpreter present, but MacArthur later wrote that Hirohito offered to take full responsibility for the actions of his ministers, thus showing himself, as the general wrote, "the first gentleman of Japan." However that talk may have gone, this encounter helped build Hirohito's position with the supreme commander. Through the fall of 1945, however, there was widespread discussion of putting the emperor on trial for war responsibility and perhaps abolishing the imperial institution altogether. Had this been done it is likely that, in the climate of the times, Hirohito would have been found guilty. Japanese newspaper polls, however, showed strong support for the retention of the monarchy, but there were also many who doubted the possibility of combining the imperial institution with democratic government. Washington queried

MacArthur to get his opinion on the matter, and on January 25, 1946, he weighed in with a strongly worded cable. Arrest of the emperor, he warned, would have enormous consequences throughout Japanese society; it would threaten if not doom the goals of the Occupation. "Civilized practices," he said, "would largely cease, and a condition of underground chaos and guerilla warfare in mountainous and outlying regions would result." The emperor, consequently, was essential to the achievement of the aims of the Occupation; if he were removed the occupying command would require an additional million men to keep order. The emperor, unaware of this, prepared comments for possible use in his defense that became available only in 1990.

To retain the emperor, however, it was essential to separate him from the ideology of State Shinto, for that had gradually become the central justification for Japan's wars and expansion. The Meiji government had from the first incorporated, and in a sense created, Shinto, and utilized its tales of the divine origin of the ruling house as the core of its ritual addressed to ancestors "of ages past." As the Japanese empire grew the affirmation of a divine mission for the Japanese race was emphasized more strongly. Shinto was imposed on colonial lands in Taiwan and Korea, and public funds were utilized to build and maintain new shrines there. Shinto priests were attached to army units as chaplains, and the cult of war dead, enshrined at the Yasukuni Jinja in Tokyo, took on ever greater proportions as their number grew. At the end of World War II they numbered 2,453,199, of which the vast majority, 2,123,651, were killed in the Pacific War, with an additional 188,196 enshrined as a result of the China War.[38]

It was thus inevitable that SCAP would make this an early target for reform. A directive of December 15, 1945, had as its subject the "Abolition of Government Sponsorship, Support, Preparation, Control, and Dissemination of State Shinto."[39] The state agencies that had been set up to protect the tie with Shinto were now abolished. A pivotal change came in Emperor Hirohito's New Year's message to his people, which ended with his deprecatory statement that his ties with his people "do not depend upon mere legends and myths. They are not predicated on the false conception that the emperor is divine and that the Japanese people are superior to other races and fated to rule the world." This renunciation of divinity, for that is what it was, had been worked out in negotiation between SCAP officials and the Imperial Household. Japanese negotiators succeeded in blunting its language to some extent, but the document remains important. For a generation that had been schooled in the imperial ideology it came as a devastating confession and even betrayal. Instead of mythology the emperor's statement pointed to the early Meiji Charter Oath of his grandfather, and held that up as precedent and guidepost for the remainder of his reign. The Charter Oath, it will be remembered, had been issued to reassure the feudal elite of justice and fairness and only later served as a beacon of the new. In similar fashion, its invocation now reassured the Occupation officials about the emperor's possible role.

The Meiji Constitution was the centerpiece of the institutional structure of Imperial Japan. Worked out by the *genrō* founding fathers with their German advisers, it had been presented to the nation as the spontaneous gift of a sovereign who retained his unique prerogatives. It was clearly in need of change for the new Japan. In October 1945 Prince Konoe requested a meeting with General MacArthur, in which he pleaded for gradualism in institutional reform. It was essential, he thought, to retain some of traditional features for a time to prevent the rapid rise of communism. MacArthur reminded him that the Imperial Diet and government existed solely at the pleasure of the Allied Powers. He did not doubt that there were many "technical" problems standing in the way of a new election law they had been talking about, but he went on to urge Konoe that, while he was a scion of the "feudal" forces, he was also young and cosmopolitan. If he would rally liberal leaders around him, and "lay before the public a proposal for constitutional revisions, I think the Diet would go along." The next day the Higashi-Kuni cabinet resigned rather than accept SCAP's Civil Rights Directive and a peremptory order to dismiss several thousand officials. Konoe, however, thought he had been delegated to lead in this,[40] and worked with friends and specialists in law to make some changes. Japanese and Western newspapermen soon began to publish articles critical of Konoe and his prewar role, and denounced him. He had, after all, been prime minister when the China War broke out, he had signed the pact with Germany and Italy, and he had authorized the move into French Indochina. As the criticism grew SCAP retreated and denied that Konoe had been given any authorization at all. Konoe's drafts were laid aside. Next, the Diet appointed a committee headed by Matsumoto Jōji, a conservative jurist, to propose changes. When this committee's proposed draft was presented to SCAP and made public, the Japanese press was quick to denounce it as face-saving and without substance. SCAP's Government Section ruled that the draft did not go far enough in reforming the shortcomings of the old constitution.

The next step was to show the Japanese what a new constitution should be, and out of this came the new, 1947 Constitution. General Courtney Whitney, head of the Government Section, convened a small team and impressed on them the fact that they were now a "constitutional convention." The group worked with a limited number of reference works and very little knowledge of Japanese procedures, but they were fired by their challenge, and produced a draft document in little more than a week. When complete it was presented to the prime minister as a model of what SCAP had in mind, but he correctly concluded that it was more than that. The Far Eastern Commission, to which the draft was submitted, suggested two changes, and in the course of Diet review more modification became possible. Conservative leaders were distressed by the fact that the draft differed so radically from the Meiji Constitution, but in Diet debate they were assured that the *kokutai* had been preserved. In 1946 both chambers in the Diet approved the document, and it became law the next year. Under its terms sovereignty was firmly vested in the people; the emperor, stripped of his political prerogatives, was described as the "symbol" of the unity of the people. The capstone of demilitarization was to be found in Article 9, in which the Japanese, "aspiring sincerely to an international peace based on justice and order," "forever renounce war as a sovereign right of the nation and the threat or use of force as means of settling international disputes . . . land, sea, and air forces, as well as other war potential, will never be maintained. The right of belligerency of the state will not be recognized."

It is one of the marvels of twentieth-century history that this document, with its echoes of the Gettysburg Address and Kellogg-Briand Pact, has stood for more than a half century and is indeed already one of the world's oldest constitutions. Internal and international politics combined to make it grow in popularity as a unique "Peace Constitution." And yet its wording is still under the shadow of the Pacific War; Japan protests its "sincerity," and the goal is that Japan should never again be a threat to peace. The Meiji Constitution had an early draft in German, the 1947 document in English. SCAP insisted its translation be in colloquial Japanese to prevent obfuscation by classical rhetoric; initially this offended many Japanese, but that argument is heard less frequently today. The document's content and implementation have stood for a half century, and it has proved, by interpretation and implementation, to permit the flexibility necessary for governing. We will return to these issues later.

With the change in the emperor's status came the abolition of the institutional structure the Meiji leaders had created to protect his otherness. The Privy Council and hereditary nobility found no place in the new constitution, and in voting to approve the new constitution the peers voted themselves out of existence. The lord privy seal who had headed the cabinet-level Imperial Household Ministry went by the board as well. Matters affecting the court were reduced to a subcabinet-level Imperial Household Agency.[41] Itō Hirobumi and his fellow *genrō* had considered the peerage a necessary buffer for the monarchy, but once abolished it disappeared almost without a ripple.

Japan, it seems, was as ready for the egalitarian measures of the Occupation years as it had been for the more hierarchical structure of Meiji when it was installed. In each case, social and economic change had moved beyond the previous—Tokugawa and then Meiji—institutions.

The Occupation was directed to remove from public office, national and local, all supporters of the military state. This was a tall order, for most Japanese had supported that state, whether voluntarily or involuntarily, and SCAP found it necessary to establish blanket categories. As the armed forces were demobilized their officers found themselves temporarily banned from public office. All right-wing organizations were ordered dissolved, and a purge program removed all their members from public office and participation in public affairs. In all, the program affected approximately 200,000 individuals. Those "purged" were listed by blanket categories; armed service officers, men involved in any aspect of Japan's colonies (like the South Manchurian Railroad and the Bank of Taiwan), and "all civilian officials of the civil service rank of *chokunin,* or above, or who occupy positions normally held by persons of such rank." Such blanket categories inevitably entailed individual instances of injustice, and rivalry and cliquism also came into play in the denunciation of individuals who escaped the initial listing, but it was deemed essential to move against those who had helped lead in militarist Japan. The enforced sidelining of so many executive administrators also opened opportunities to many otherwise locked out.

The problem of assigning responsibility for the decisions that led to the disaster of the Pacific War was more complex. In Europe the Nuremberg trials had found a clear conspiracy among top Nazis for aggression and genocide, and the attack on Poland and the horrors of Auschwitz cried out for satisfaction. The International Military Tribunal for the Far East that convened in the headquarters of the Imperial Army in Tokyo had the German trial as its model. In Europe, the atrocities of the Nazi death camps were central, and in Tokyo, the horror of Nanking received major attention; General Matsui Iwane, the commander there, was among those hanged. Sadly, little or no mention was made of the work in germ warfare in Manchuria conducted with great cruelty by Unit 731 under the command of General Ishii Shirō, who was spared prosecution in exchange for the transfer of the results of his "experiments" to United States hands. One additional precedent for the Tokyo trials had been set by a Manila army tribunal that sentenced General Yamashita Tomoyuki to the gallows for atrocities that had been committed in Manila, despite the contention of his defense that the units in question had been beyond his control. In addition, it should be added that the trials of "Class B" and "Class C" war criminals, who were charged with responsibility for or participation in specific wrongs, were held in the countries where they had been stationed. In all 1,068 men were executed. In addition, the Soviets may have executed as many as 3,000 Japanese as war criminals following summary proceedings, though details were not made public.[42]

The Tokyo trials have not received the approval accorded those in Germany. The prosecution charged defendants with carrying out a single, consistent plan of aggression that began in 1931, but neither the documentary basis nor the nature of Japanese politics, in which the prosecutors were neophytes, supported this. More awkward, the prosecution was under directions to avoid any mention of Emperor Hirohito, in whose name the Japanese had stormed through Asia. The Soviet Union, which had entered the war in violation of the Neutrality Pact Matsuoka had worked out, sat in judgment on Japanese leaders who honored it. It is not surprising that the proceedings are sometimes dismissed as "victors' justice."[43] The International Tribunal dealt only with "Class A" war criminals, those who were charged with conspiracy to wage aggressive war, and its deliberations lasted from 1946 to 1948. Among those whose names have figured prominently in this narrative, Prime Ministers Tōjō, Hirota, and General Itagaki Seishirō and also two other officers who had made their mark in the Kwantung Army were among the seven sentenced to be hung.[44] All defendants were found guilty; sixteen were sentenced to life imprisonment, one to twenty, and one to seven years. Imprisonment of Lord Privy Seal Kido Kōichi, grandson of the Meiji leader, brought the enterprise dangerously close to the throne. Konoe Fumimaro committed suicide rather than submit to the indignity of interrogation; Matsuoka Yōsuke died during the trial and former prime minister Koiso Kunaki while in confinement in 1950. Araki Sadao emerged from a long confinement as a self-styled Buddhist sage, and Ōkawa Shūmei, released for insanity, continued to find publishers for his writings until his death in 1957.

Many others were listed as "Class A" suspects but never brought to trial. Among them were prominent right-wing leaders who amassed great wealth and influence in postwar Japan like Kodama Yoshio and Sasegawa Ryōichi. Kishi Nobusuke, a Manchukuo bureaucrat and cabinet minister under Tōjō, emerged as prime minister in 1957. Thus it cannot be said that the trials succeeded in their purpose of demonstrating that aggression brought punishment. Most Japanese assumed that those charged would be found guilty, and in any case the desperate search for shelter and food amid the desolation of postsurrender Japan left little room for compassion on or concern for those who had ruled the land so recently.

During the long trauma of the Pacific War Japan had become increasingly isolated from the outside world. Communications suffered with shipping, and exchange diminished with encirclement. In one sense the appearance of United States forces brought an end to this isolation and provided Japan with its first close contact with outsiders—ultimately many hundreds of thousands of them. In addition visiting experts who were free with advice began to appear. Consequently it is not entirely inappropriate to call the period, as many have, a "second opening."

But the contrasts outweigh the similarities. The first opening was in response to perceived danger and it was carried out under indigenous leadership. At every point the first concern of the Japanese was with the retention of their national sovereignty. The "second," however, came as a response to the loss of that sovereignty, and the final authority was foreign in origin. Satisfaction of requirements imposed from outside was the condition for the resumption of sovereignty. The scorn Meiji people expressed for the shortcomings of their leaders was more than matched by the derogation of Japan's wartime establishment during the early Occupation years. Occupation propaganda and education administrators made every effort to ensure that Japanese would feel shame and, if not contrition, at least embarrassment for what their country had been and done. Of all the scapegoats, none provided a more inviting target of abuse than the military; like the samurai a century earlier, they had been found inferior and unable to protect their country. It did not prove difficult for millions of Japanese to look away while their recent leaders were being punished.

In another sense the "second opening" was accompanied by an isolation greater than any that had been known under the *sakoku* (closed country) years. No Japanese could go abroad. Japanese diplomats, from ambassadors to consuls, were called home from every corner of the globe. Some three million Japanese in Korea, China, and Southeast Asia returned home to already crowded islands in which food and shelter were hard to find, particularly in the burned-out wasteland of the metropolitan areas. Japanese servicemen so recently scattered throughout East and Southeast Asia searched for purpose and employment. As Occupation officials took early steps to restore a trickle of foreign trade in American ships, some of the world's most experienced traders from Mitsui and Mitsubishi sat on the sidelines. For many the isolation was broken only by the Far Eastern Network, American armed forces radio. The New Order that was to have led to a Greater East Asian Co-Prosperity Sphere had instead led to a desperately poor Japan cut off from Asia.

19

Between 1946 and 1953 Yoshida Shigeru (1878–1967) organized five cabinets, more than any other political leader in modern Japan. With the exception of a period in 1947–48, he occupied the post of prime minister during a time of wrenching political and social change. While in power he was frequently reviled as a bumbling relic of the past and quite unable to understand current trends, and his retirement was welcomed by political commentators. Subsequently it became clear that his ideas and his successors, the "Yoshida students," had put their stamp on a half century of postwar Japan; by the time of his death he was already being hailed as the grand old man of postsurrender Japan.

During his years in power Yoshida seemed a crusty and stubborn man totally lacking in the arts of public relations that modern politics require. He never quite belonged to the political establishment, and for many years his status was that of an adopted son. He was born the son of a Tosa leader of the Freedom and People's Rights Movement, Takeuchi Tsuna. Adopted by a wealthy merchant family, he soon developed a taste for the life he now inherited and rode his horse through Meiji Tokyo to attend classes at Tokyo Imperial University. Upon graduation he stood for the Foreign Ministry examinations and emerged one of a cohort of five. Marriage to a daughter of Makino Nobuaki (Shinken, 1861–1949) brought second-hand status in the inner circles of Japan's elite. Makino, son of the Meiji leader Ōkubo Toshimichi, had accompanied the Iwakura mission in early 1871, remained to study in Philadelphia, and returned to Japan after his father's assassination to take up a distinguished career in education (minister of education under Saionji), diplomacy (several ambassadorial posts, delegate to the Paris Peace Conference, and foreign minister under Yamamoto), and the palace (minister of the imperial household and, after 1925, lord privy seal).

Yoshida's record in diplomacy was uneven; he seems to have done a poor job of making arrangements for Saionji and Makino at the Paris Peace Conference. He served in a number of posts in China and attended Prime Minister General Tanaka's Far East Conference in 1927; his own preferences for Japanese China policy centered around support for conservative, pro-Japanese warlords who were swept away by the Nationalist revolution. The post that most affected Yoshida's outlook on world affairs was that of ambassador to the Court of St. James, a role in which he made some rather maladroit efforts to secure English understanding of Japan's early advances in the 1930s. Hirota Kōki wanted Yoshida as his minister of foreign affairs after the rebellion in 1936, but he was overruled by men who objected to Yoshida's relationship to Count Makino.

During the last year of the war Yoshida had cooperated with Konoe's efforts to bring the fighting to an end, a position that won him temporary confinement by investigators for the military police. Clearly this increased his acceptability for office in the postsurrender days. He emerged as minister of foreign affairs in the postsurrender cabinet of Prince Higashikuni Naruhiko, a prince of the blood who had been called out of obscurity to serve as prime minister in order to utilize the prestige of the imperial house to secure approval of the surrender; Yoshida retained that post under the successor cabinet of Shidehara Kijūrō.

Years later Yoshida described how he was summoned from Ōiso, some thirty miles west of Tokyo, early in the Occupation to take up his post. As his driver was maneuvering between the potholes on the way to Tokyo the car was suddenly halted by several American soldiers. Yoshida and his driver feared the worst, but were relieved to have the soldiers explain politely that they had lost their way and wondered whether they could have a lift. Once seated in the car, they pressed chewing gum, chocolate, and cigarettes on the startled Japanese. Later Yoshida wrote that "the incident surprised and pleased us, feelings that were probably shared by the majority of Japanese on their initial contact with the men of the Occupation forces." It must have suggested that the Occupation would be well-meaning; in effect, that it could be managed. Indeed, it would soon work to his advantage. Later, when he was appointed prime minister, Yoshida is said to have opened his first cabinet meeting by pointing out that there was such a thing as losing a war but winning the peace. One can take that as the unstated goal of his statecraft.

It was not an easy task. It involved work with the General Headquarters of the Supreme Commander, Allied Powers (SCAP), where reformers in the

Government Section headed by General Courtney Whitney saw it as their mission and opportunity to rid Japan of the incubus of its militarist past and remove all vestiges of "feudalism." The presence of this power provided tempting opportunities for Japanese to inform on and complain about their government and leaders, directly or through American reporters who were eager for a story and quick to relay anything negative about presurrender Japan. SCAP itself was dubious about the capacity of members of Japan's senior generation to lead in new paths, and looked for evidence of popular support and political vitality. Yoshida met this problem by dealing as much as possible directly with Generals MacArthur and Whitney and did his best to keep himself inaccessible to lesser figures. He seemed in the process to command more authority than he had in actuality; gradually, as the intensity of SCAP supervision weakened, appearance became reality.

In the spring of 1946 SCAP ordered general elections, the first in which women were accorded the vote. The reborn Jiyūtō (Liberal) party, which laid claim to the lineage and tradition of Itagaki Taisuke's call for representative government in 1874, emerged victorious. Its leader was the veteran Seiyūkai parliamentarian Hatoyama Ichirō. Hatoyama, unfortunately, had a mixed record in prewar years and one that the press insistently called attention to, and in May he was honored by a special SCAP directive ordering that he be purged from holding public office. As chief cabinet secretary under General Tanaka he bore partial responsibility for the violation of civil rights involved in the revision of the Peace Preservation Law and in the great police roundups of 1928, and as minister of education from 1931 to 1934 he had authorized the dismissal of suspected leftists and engineered the dismissal of Kyoto University professor Takigawa Yukitoki.

With Hatoyama unavailable, the Liberal Party turned to Yoshida as replacement. His Tosa origins, his association with prewar moderates, and his efforts to end the war all promised an acceptable candidacy.

Up to this point, in other words, Yoshida's emergence was marked by accident and good luck. Tosa combined with Satsuma in the Makino connection; diplomacy combined with rustication during the years of extremism; and his eligibility was enhanced by having been targeted by the military in the closing days of the war. Very little of the above would prepare one for the emergence of a crafty manager who guided Japan through reconstruction to the San Francisco Treaty of Peace under which Japan regained its sovereignty in 1952.

Yoshida's story is necessarily interwoven with the story of the MacArthur Occupation. Each contributed to the other's success. The impact of the surrender and Occupation was decisive in restructuring the pattern of Japanese social, political, and economic life. With the advantage of hindsight that a half century now provides, however, it is appropriate to speak of these affairs from the Japanese rather than from the American viewpoint, so that the MacArthur years become the Yoshida years.

1. The Social Context of Postsurrender Japan

Nevertheless, the Yoshida years were also the MacArthur years. Defeated Japan was a society in a process of rapid change. The austerity of wartime effort continued with even more critical shortages of food, fuel, and shelter for urban Japanese, though for those who could manage it, a new hedonism and self-indulgence began to give indications of what lay ahead. Amid urban ruins and in underground tunnels leading to train and subway stations tiny bars opened to serve commuters. American servicemen gradually had a range of entertainment from giant beer halls to greasy nightclubs. Capital and material resources were strained and scarce, but efforts were prodigious. Anxious to please the occupiers and also protect Japanese women, authorities recruited female entertainers only to have American headquarters forbid entry to servicemen; it was some time before fraternization with "indigenous personnel," as American authorities termed all Japanese, became common. Despite initial misgivings on both sides, hostility soon gave way to curiosity, tolerance, and usually friendship. Urban black markets, so long provisioned from country farms, awoke to new possibilities of canned goods, tobacco, and packaged foods frequently siphoned from the shelves of United States army service centers and post exchanges.

SCAP was by no means a single entity. Its Government Section, headed by General Whitney, was staffed by enthusiastic reformers, many of New Deal or even leftist persuasion, who saw themselves as liberators and felt it their mission to make Japan over in the American image. The G-2, or Intelligence Section, headed by General Charles A. Willoughby, was as much concerned with stability as with reform, and was particularly intent on monitoring the Communists and leftists who were released from confinement in the early months by order of SCAP. SCAP overall was intent on disbanding the Japanese military, but G-2 was not slow to compile files of former officers in case new struggles lay ahead. The Economic and Scientific Section, charged with management of the economy, was concerned with production and industrial peace as well as with reform of the monopolistic structure of big business under zaibatsu leadership. Its section chiefs, in their eagerness to get things moving once more, resisted decentralization they saw as inefficient and counterproductive. Yet the section also included a Labor Division, which worked with Japanese reform bureaucrats to implement a Trade Union Law that gave workers the right to bargain collectively and to strike a mere three months after the start of the Occupation. The Labor Relations Adjustment and Labor Standards laws followed a few months later.[1] Civil Information and Education was concerned with ideology, reproaching Japan for its militarist past, and emphasized the importance of the new democracy. There was no sector of Japanese life that failed to attract the attention of one or another section of MacArthur's headquarters. In all, SCAP came to number, with dependents, some 35,000 individuals. Like the military forces, who gradually numbered about 80,000 men, housing and provisions were born by the Japanese government. Initially American aid in foodstuffs was provided to prevent famine in the postsurrender days, but as matters stabilized, the costs of occupation came to constitute almost one-third of the Japanese government budget. Those costs were not negotiable.

General MacArthur ruled over this often contentious scene. His word was final, but he was too wise an administrator to try to micro-manage his section chiefs. Canny Japanese like Yoshida could sense the tensions in this structure and did their best to turn it to their advantage. Yoshida later wrote in his memoirs that the military men in SCAP, as opposed to the civilians, were reasonable and approachable. The military men, from MacArthur on down, were realists, while the idealists were more troublesome. Yoshida himself, as first minister, did his best to restrict his contacts to meetings with the Supreme Commander. Each man had a somewhat cautious and watchful attitude toward the other, but each realized the other's importance to his own success.[2]

At no time did SCAP try to invalidate or delegitimize the Japanese government. At the outset SCAP instructions were addressed to the "Imperial Japanese Government" despite the fact that its empire was no longer in being. The Japanese government, for its part, coped with this awkward division of authority by establishing a Liaison Office for dealing with the Occupation authorities. For those who served in it some command of English and of American and Anglo-Saxon values and mores was essential, and in a context in which there was no diplomacy it was natural for the Liaison Office to become staffed by former Foreign Ministry officials. On assuming the post of prime minister Yoshida initially set up shop in the Foreign Ministry. It is tempting to cite as precedent the office of *buke denso* through which the imperial court communicated with the bakufu in Tokugawa times, but while the Edo period court was essentially powerless the postsurrender "Imperial Japanese Government" continued to hold the administrative reins to a modernized and complex society.

SCAP directives altered Japanese practice in many respects. The first of these was the enfranchisement of women. The 1947 Constitution specified equality of sexes, and the formulations of the Civil Code put an end to the (samurai-style) pattern of family or house control (*ie*) that the Meiji government had enacted. A special division of SCAP, headed by a woman, took the liberation of Japanese women as its task.

Still others concerned themselves with the democratization of education. In the first months of the Occupation school officials strove to demilitarize their textbooks, often by crude and hasty measures like blacking out pictures of war ships and tanks, but soon a national education council was considering broader measures of institutional reform and curriculum. The Special Higher Schools of imperial Japan became undergraduate colleges in a new system modeled on that of the United States. Prefectural universities would play the role of American state universities, undergraduate education would begin with broad training in the liberal arts, and the elitism of the imperial universities would give way to more egalitarian organization.

All this required far greater resources than were available, and for many years the new structure was more hope than reality. The new institutions sometimes found themselves housed in former army barracks, and disparities of staff, libraries, and resources between these schools and older and more prestigious universities (like Tokyo, which now became the University of Tokyo), when added to traditional paths of elitist preference in entry into the bureaucracy, served to emphasize the distance between them rather than to lessen it. In education, as in many other areas, conservatives, eager to please new masters, often followed instructions blindly rather than arguing the merits of aspects of what was undergoing change. An American Education Mission that came to Japan advocated sweeping changes in approach and urged substitution of the "heroes of peace" for those of war.[3] Gradually, as travel abroad became possible for Japanese educators, first-hand acquaintance with the diversity of American education, public and private, served to enrich the debate in Japan upon their return. No sector of Japanese society responded more enthusiastically to the challenge of building a new Japan than that of education. It was not long before new textbooks and journals were berating the excesses of the prewar state with such vigor that conservative officials in the Ministry of Education began to take alarm. The debate this engendered has yet to run its course.

The abandonment of the sacred aura that surrounded the throne had repercussions throughout educational and political life. With the emperor's disavowal of divinity of January 1, 1946, and SCAP directives forbidding state support for Shinto, the structure of ideology established in the Meiji years lost its core. The surrender cabinet had called on the nation to prostrate itself in penitence for having failed the sovereign, but newspaper readers were soon treated to a famous photograph showing MacArthur in an open-necked shirt towering over a nervous emperor in formal dress. Yet the occupation felt its need of imperial support, and before long SCAP officials suggested that Hirohito, awkward in manner and fedora in hand, begin to make public appearances designed to encourage his people in difficult days—and incidentally shore up his own image. These trips were at first ridiculed by foreign reporters, but before long became so popular that SCAP officials who had initially suggested them became fearful that they would threaten the Supreme Commander's aura and began to criticize them as wasteful. The emperor himself, however, gradually learned how to interact with ordinary Japanese and gamely asked standardized questions.

MacArthur himself, it should be noted, never made the slightest attempt to ingratiate himself with the Japanese public. He maintained a stern and duty-oriented exterior and an inflexible routine. New Year's Day produced hortatory messages to the Japanese people that functioned somewhat like imperial rescripts in presurrender days. Daily his limousine swept from the American embassy residence to his offices in the Dai Ichi Insurance Building across the moat from the imperial palace. He traveled to Korea for the inauguration of Syngman Rhee as first president of the Republic of Korea, and the arrival of an unusually distinguished guest (Chief of Staff Dwight D. Eisenhower) brought him to the airport, but for the rest he maintained his routine. American visitors were received at his office and sometimes entertained at dinner in the embassy residence, but the number of Japanese he encountered was minimal. To this day the Dai Ichi Insurance Company maintains the general's office suite—silent and empty rooms—as a reminder of those days.

It must also be remembered that MacArthur's autonomy was seldom challenged. In Washington the Far Eastern Commission, which represented all the Pacific War allies, could propose but not dispose, and in Tokyo the Allied Council for Japan, with British Commonwealth, Soviet Union, Nationalist China, and American membership, could observe, but not obstruct. SCAP, alert to possible Soviet objections, walled off Soviet representatives in Tokyo and preempted Soviet suggestions in Washington. United States concern was focused on the reconstruction of Western Europe, and occasional visits from exhausted Washington emissaries who struggled with jet-lag while listening to well-rehearsed briefings offered little challenge to SCAP priorities and procedures.

2. Reform and Reconstruction

The setting within which postwar politics were played out included points at which Japanese and Allied plans converged, others where SCAP proposals initially shocked, but ultimately served, Japanese interests, and still others at which Japanese obstruction combined with American opposition to bring SCAP proposals to a halt. The first is exemplified by the program of land reform, the second by the Constitution of 1947, and the third by the program of industrial deconcentration.

It has already been noted that in the interwar years a lively tenant movement struggled for better terms and rights of tenancy. The turn to militarism in the 1930s doomed administrative efforts for the reform of tenant rights, but years of wartime shortages produced conditions that had the effect of weakening landlord control of agriculture. Rents were brought to the offices of local cooperatives instead of being delivered into the landlords' hands. This brought with it a certain leveling of the share of the crop that tenants delivered. Tenant sons conscripted for military service often sent part of their pay home, and however modest, that too helped tenant economy and confidence. Toward the end of the war the breakdown of the rationing system in the face of poor crop yields caused by inadequately fertilized paddies forced almost all Japanese to scour the countryside for food, and a thriving black market provided further opportunities for tenant incomes. Although thinking about land reform may have changed, however, conditions of ownership had not. One-third of Japan's 6 million farm families owned 90 percent of the land; holdings were fragmented and pitifully small; tenants spent an inordinate amount of time walking from plot to plot.

Japanese bureaucrats of the Agriculture and Home ministries had long waited for the opportunity to address this issue. In December 1945 the Diet approved a modest version of land reform, but SCAP ruled it inadequate on grounds that it favored resident landlords and permitted holdings that were too large. American interest in the issue had developed relatively late; the Initial Post-Surrender program made no mention of land reform out of fear of seeming to encourage collectivization in a setting of social chaos, but before long officials in SCAP saw the program as essential to the suppression of militaristic agrarianism. What followed saw an unusual degree of cooperation from the Allied Council for Japan, where the British Commonwealth representatives, SCAP specialists, and Japanese reform bureaucrats proposed changes. Under proposals that were to became law in October 1946, the Japanese government purchased land at preinflation prices. Local commissions with tenant, landlord, and owner-farmer representation set prices and selected eligible buyers. Resident landlords were limited to holdings that averaged two and a half acres in Japan's most crowded and productive areas, but appropriate provisions were made for areas farther from metropolitan markets. Strict regulations guaranteed tenants written contracts. Rent was to be paid in cash so that tenants would profit from higher prices, and it was not to exceed one-quarter of the yield. The percentage of owner-cultivated paddy land increased from 55.7 in 1947 to 88.9 in 1949.[4]

This was a stupendous feat of social engineering, easily comparable to the allocation of land to farmers under the seventh-century reforms of the early imperial state, the agricultural programs worked out by progressive daimyo in the seventeenth century, and the grant of certificates of ownership by the early Meiji government. Unlike the earlier programs, however, its goals were those of equity, and not of control; like them, however, it created a solid rural base for postwar politics. Before very long, the Occupation considered the program its greatest social accomplishment. The Yoshida government initially expressed fears of extremism and injustice to landlord interests, but then came to realize that a stable countryside created an almost invulnerable electoral base. Rural revolutionary protest had been forestalled, and tenant protests came to an end. In the years that followed the countryside, increasingly affluent, came to provide a vast internal market for urban manufactures.

The cooperation of reformist bureaucrats, many from the old Social Bureau of the Home Ministry, was also important in helping liberal SCAP officials who were determined to establish the rights of labor to organize. Labor leadership was strengthened by the numbers of Socialists and Communists, imprisoned during much of the last decade, who were released as part of SCAP efforts to protect civil liberties, but even without this the pace of labor organization, a movement that had been stopped by the militarism of the 1930s, was due to return in a new and stronger form. The fire raids and resulting destruction of Japan's industrial plant combined with shortages of food and of urban housing to create a dynamic and almost explosive discontent. New legislation quickly endorsed worker desires, and by 1950 nearly 56 percent of industrial workers were organized into labor unions which enrolled more than 6 million workers. Sheldon Garon has shown that these developments were by no means the exclusive product of American labor reformers in SCAP, but owed much to the efforts of bureaucrats who had long sought reforms, albeit less sweeping.[5] The issue is not without its importance. In area after area the heroic narrative has it that reforms thundered down from the Olympus of the Dai Ichi Building, but it is clear that the implementation of complex social engineering required the full cooperation of Japanese officials.

The Constitution of 1947 might seem an exception to this theme of cooperation. We have already seen how it was rushed to completion by a small team in General Whitney's Government Section. For guidelines they had only a handwritten note, probably from General MacArthur, that has since been lost, specifying quite generally that the emperor was to rule by consent of the people, that war should be abolished and Japan should rely on "higher ideals which are now stirring the world," and that the "feudal system of Japan will cease." The peerage would be abolished, and budgetary affairs arranged "after the British system."[6]

What began as a "model" for Japanese emulation became a draft the Japanese were obliged to accept in principle; General Whitney later recounted with pride how his assurance to Yoshida that he was "enjoying your atomic sunshine" during an outdoor reception at which cabinet members were huddling some distance away helped convince Japanese conservatives to accept the trial draft.

The document that emerged was the product of ten days of work carried on in utmost secrecy by some twenty-five persons from the Government Section who were charged by General Whitney to be a "constitutional convention." None were constitutional lawyers. One, a recent Vassar graduate and the only woman involved, concentrated her efforts on the formulation and inclusion of a women's equal rights clause.[7] The reason for the Government Section's haste was the knowledge that arrangements were being finalized for Soviet representation in the Far Eastern Commission; it seemed important to forestall possible interference. The same argument was useful in negotiating with the Japanese.

By the end of February 1946 group members had cobbled together a document that met their needs. It opened with a ringing affirmation of human rights with echoes of the Gettysburg Address and, as we have noted, began with the definition of the emperor as the "symbol" of the unity of the nation who derived his powers from the sovereign people. The provision for women's rights was one of thirty-eight that were guaranteed and not "subject to law" as had been true of all rights in the Meiji Constitution. These rights extended to "minimum standards of wholesome and cultured living." The new House of Representatives was far more powerful than its prewar counterpart, and the prime minister, who had to be a member, was elected by its vote. Constituencies were flexible. Yoshida stood for election to the House of Representatives from his father's old base of Tosa for many years, making brief appearances during election campaigns.

The executive process was clearly defined for the first time in modern Japanese history. Other changes specified that prefectural governors and local officials should be elected rather than appointed. Article 9, the renunciation of war as a national policy or sovereign right, has already been discussed.

The constitution's origins were foreign, but so were many of the provisions incorporated in the Meiji Constitution. The 1947 Constitution's idealistic language set standards that Japan would not reach for many years, but the powerful autocrat set forth in the Meiji Constitution was equally unfamiliar to Japanese of that day. The Yoshida government accepted the document, albeit reluctantly, for it was made aware that the maintenance of the imperial throne might very well hinge on its decision. The emperor added his approval in meetings with his ministers. Japanese arguments brought changes, some of them important, in Diet discussions of the draft; what had been a unicameral Diet, for instance, became a bicameral institution, with a House of Councillors, elected from national as well as local constituencies, replacing the peers, who were disestablished. Other changes seemed minor, but became significant later. The definition of "Japanese people," *kokumin,* came in time to discriminate against Japan-born Koreans and Taiwanese. Yet the principal thrust of the document remained unchanged. Loose interpretation of Article 9 permitted the establishment of Self-Defense Forces, but invocation of its language stood in the way of full-bodied commitment to collective security. When cautious steps toward establishment of a peace-keeping force became necessary in the 1990s, the operation was hedged about with such severe restrictions on the use of force that Japanese diplomacy was hard put to defend its nature. Nevertheless the "Peace Constitution," as it came to be called, became so popular that even conservative Japanese have so far resisted arguments that the language of Article 9 should be modified to permit Japan a larger role in world affairs, while liberal sentiment has opposed revision out of fear of even a partial restitution of prewar controls.

The entire Meiji Civil Code with its samurai-patriarchal family structure required rewriting to bring it into conformity with the constitution's assertions of equality of individuals and sexes; marriage was now to be based on mutual consent. When the constitution came up for discussion in the Diet, members had to be reassured that its provisions, particularly those pertaining to the throne, did not represent a violation of *kokutai.*

One might have expected a short life for a document drawn up under such conditions. Conservatives grumbled that its language, colloquial instead of classical, was imprecise as well as inelegant. In places its language betrayed translation from the prior English. Its guaranty that "no censorship shall be maintained, nor shall the secrecy of any means of communication be violated" (Article 22) was in glaring contrast to the fact that SCAP agencies were vigilantly censoring communications for possible threats to the security of Occupation forces. The soaring idealism of Article 9's renunciation of war was soon at variance with the arms race between the United States and the Soviet Union, and not a few Americans deplored it as inappropriate to the times.

The constitution does not lack critics. It is asserted by some that it was designed by MacArthur to save Emperor Hirohito and utilized by Yoshida to keep Japan out of cold war politics.[8] Japan's ruling conservatives have frequently been unenthusiastic about its references to the emperor, while the opposition left has championed its provisions. Nevertheless the Peace Constitution became firmly rooted in popular political attitudes and even affection in Japan. Far from having a short life, it is now one of the world's oldest and most durable constitutions, standing virtually unchallenged a half century after its adoption by the Diet—which, at Occupation urging, adopted it as an amendment to the Meiji Constitution in order to give it the stamp of continuity and legitimacy. "Realists" who regarded Article 9's renunciation of war as utopian came to see the advantages of that provision in resisting United States desires for greater reciprocity in defense arrangements. One must regard the 1947 Constitution as an astonishing success; like the Meiji Constitution, it proved capable, under a certain latitude of interpretation and implementation, of embracing a surprising variety of governmental positions. One might cite it as one more example of Japanese pragmatism in converting necessity to opportunity.

In economic reform the picture was more complicated. American planners began with ideas for sweeping relocation of much of Japan's industrial plant to countries that had suffered from Japanese aggression. Early missions, among them one headed by the Truman friend and oil executive Edwin Pauley, proposed drastic reductions in steel capacity, elimination of all aircraft capacity, and sharp reductions of other strategic materials. Unsure which firms were to be targeted, Japanese management delayed plans for resumption of production. Meanwhile, as the Japanese economy idled it became more difficult to decide what industrial capacity to take as reparations and where to send it; the countries of Southeast Asia, still struggling for independence, lacked the industrial base, while China was falling into civil war. Before long Japanese reluctance to, in effect, deindustrialize was rousing the backing of United States planners who argued that Japan could not rely indefinitely on United States aid and that its economy needed to be reinvigorated. From the first, however, Occupation officials spoke of the zaibatsu conglomerates as Japan's great war potential, and in extended flourishes of rhetoric MacArthur himself responded to critics of SCAP's plans for industrial deconcentration by denouncing the great firms. Japan's system of "private property," he asserted, "permitted ten family groups comprising only fifty-six families to control directly or indirectly every phase of slavery of the remainder of the Japanese people, permitted higher standards of life only through sufferance, and in a search of further plunder abroad furnished the tools for the military to embark upon its ill-fated venture into world conquest."[9]

Reformers in the Economic and Scientific Section thus drew up plans for sweeping change. The first step, which involved the separation of the zaibatsu families from the network of enterprises each group controlled, was simple enough. Further steps of economic deconcentration were far more difficult and challenging. Early plans called for dismantling industrial groups into their constituent parts and breaking up as many as 1,200 firms. A Holding Company Liquidation Commission was charged with the custody and resale of their stock shares, which were to be made available to public sale, and laws controlling monopoly were to prevent reconstitution of the commercial empires.

Japanese government bureaus whose expertise was essential to this were markedly unenthusiastic, and in the dismal economic climate of postwar Japan purchasers of stocks were more likely to be profiteers than productive capitalists. To this was added sharp criticism from the United States. *Newsweek* magazine devoted an entire issue to a scathing assessment of the program, a criticism drawn up by a lawyer who had practiced in prewar Tokyo, charging that New Dealers and radicals in SCAP were riding roughshod over personal property rights. The matter served as a catalyst for the formation of a Council on Japan, headed by former ambassador Joseph E. Grew, to urge caution.[10] Most important of all was the intervention of the State Department in the person of the head of the Policy Planning Staff, George F. Kennan, who traveled to Tokyo in 1948. Kennan was at first given the polite brush-off MacArthur reserved for visitors from Washington, but he succeeded in penetrating SCAP defenses for serious talks about the role of Japan and to question the wisdom of programs that sought to eliminate, as he saw it, tried for untried forces. Indeed, he later reflected, the policies pursued by "General MacArthur's headquarters, on cursory examination, seemed to be such that if they had been devised for the specific purpose of rendering Japanese society vulnerable to Communist political pressure and paving the way for a Communist takeover, they could scarcely have been other than what they were."[11] Kennan's observations confirmed his fears. Japan was substantially defenseless; the more than 80,000 American troops were of limited combined vitality. Japan itself was totally disarmed. The Occupation weighed heavily on the Japanese economy and consumed one-third of the annual budget for the support of its 35,000 civilians and the troops. Three-quarters of a million Japanese with administrative experience were on the sidelines because of the purge. It seemed high time to change priorities from reform to reconstruction.

In his talks with MacArthur, whom he described as a formidable proconsul, Kennan found the general aware of these concerns, but also hesitant to change course for fear of incurring opposition. Kennan argued that the aims of the Potsdam Declaration, which were limited, had been achieved, and suggested that MacArthur could change course while terming the Occupation a success. This provided the bridge for MacArthur's retreat; he could affirm that the Occupation's policies had been successful and then relax the schedule for deconcentration he had earlier asserted was necessary to the struggle against Japan's "feudal forces."

Plans for the deconcentration of some 1,200 firms were reduced to include only 325, and in the end only 28 were broken up. The giant trading firms associated with the Mitsubishi and Mitsui conglomerates were among them, but more of the firms targeted were electric power companies than manufacturers. The zaibatsu pattern of concentration, however, did not reappear. A spate of antimonopoly measures created new opportunity for outside forces, and the enforced retirement of wartime economic leaders under the terms of purge programs created an interval of opportunity for imaginative entrepreneurs. Great postwar firms like Toyota, Honda, and Sony were not affiliated with the prewar conglomerates. When enterprises were reconstituted it was in the form of networks of firms centering around one of the great banks, and such groupings became known as keiretsu.[12]

These few paragraphs illustrate the way in which the interplay of Occupation goals and Japanese response affected the course of social and economic change. In land and labor reform the cooperation of Japanese bureaucrats brought permanent change to the economy. In constitutional revision the initial reluctance of Japanese conservatives gave way to the grudging, and then grateful, realization that the changes were ones they could live with and that they enabled them to survive Diet challenges from the opposition Socialists. At every point the elimination of the institutional power of the prewar military brought breathing space for the development of new forces. Where initial goals were impractical and alarmed Japanese, as in the program of deconcentration, those fears found support in American economic and governmental circles and combined to blunt, indeed reverse, the process of reform. As the "opposite course," as Japanese critics called it, turned to programs of reconstruction and production, SCAP New Dealers began to feel themselves isolated, and most returned to the United States. The GHQ that remained in Tokyo gradually became routinized, more inclined to congratulate itself on past achievements than to call for new crusades.

Any discussion of the social context of postsurrender Japan must make mention of the turbulent and sometimes chaotic climate in which the new liberation was received. There was enthusiasm among American staffers, who saw themselves as liberators and warmed to the welcome accorded them by relieved Japanese who had feared retribution and rancor. On the part of Japanese liberals and especially academics, now free to speak their mind in denunciation of the old order, there was also, after the initial danger of famine had passed, an extraordinary flowering of debate and discussion. New magazines and pamphlets discussed the new and better society that should be built, and discussion clubs, seminars, and lectures drew attention that was astonishing in view of the hardships of housing, food, and transportation. Radicals released from prison and, in the case of Nozaka Sanzō, returned from flight and exile in China were uniquely fitted to provide effervescence and leadership in this setting. They cheered the lifting of restrictions on their activity, cheered MacArthur in the streets, and swiftly seized leadership of the union movement. Management was for the most part silent, unsure of its fate or that of its holdings. Strikes and demonstrations designed to show the superfluity of lackluster industrial leadership, as when unions seized facilities to speed production, contributed to labor confidence. Some of the denunciation of the recent past represented flattery to please the conquerors, and some of the literal acceptance of the new order on the part of the left represented opportunism, but overall there was a genuine and heartening efflorescence of hope. Commuters struggling to keep their feet on crowded trains read serious monthlies on their way to work; most Japanese thought they were building a new society that would be more just than the old had been.

Although there has been much talk about the "reverse course" of Occupation policy, it was also clear, well before the Kennan mission, that SCAP, for all its determination to reform, was by no means prepared to allow Japanese leftists to set the pace for change. When a nationwide general strike was called for February 1, 1947, General MacArthur ruled it out "with the greatest reluctance," explaining that under the conditions that prevailed a stoppage of utilities and of transport would cripple and derail whatever economic activity there was. A strike, led by a small minority of the Japanese people, he announced, "might well plunge the masses into disaster." This pronouncement astonished and dismayed labor leaders, who saw it as betrayal, and reassured the conservative and middle classes. Japanese historians, quick to assign a periodization to events, usually cite this prohibition as the beginning of a "reverse course" in American Occupation policy, though they would probably do better to reserve that designation for the abandonment of plans for industrial deconcentration. A general strike in 1947 might well have led to social disorganization and disorder in the cities, but it is difficult to argue that it would have been in furtherance of the announced aims of democratization.

Political leadership in a time of such extraordinary change required a realistic acceptance of restraints imposed by the Occupation and maintenance of a certain degree of independence. Yoshida managed this. He did not toady to the American overlord, but he was too wise to resist publicly. He cannot have been impressed by the campaign that SCAP's Civil Information section waged to convince the Japanese of the moral depravity of their government's recent actions, and indeed later provided his calligraphy for a stele commemorating the executed leaders as "Seven Patriots." On the other hand he had had personal experience of the militarists' irrationality, wanted no part of that for the future Japan, and used this to delay steps toward rearmament that would have slowed economic growth.

He himself was convinced that the Japanese people, far from being warlike and aggressive, were peacefully inclined and that it was the period of militarism that was the aberration. Japan's true course, he argued, had been to align itself with Great Britain in the Meiji period, and in the future it should certainly ally with the United States. To do so was to return to the course that had worked so well in earlier days.

Yoshida, as has been noted, divided SCAP headquarters into groups of "idealists" and "realists" and made clear that his preference lay with the latter and not with the reformers of the Government Section. He tried, on the whole successfully, to limit his contacts with SCAP to the Supreme Commander himself. In SCAP headquarters the "idealists" of the Government Section had their doubts about the stocky, brusque, and stubborn man they had to work with, but when they tried to replace him with a rival they found themselves outmaneuvered. The substitute candidate, no more prepared to do American bidding than Yoshida, declined to stand for election, and resigned instead.

As American policy focused increasingly on reconstruction Yoshida had fewer doubts about it, although he retained strong objections to the purge. In the eyes of the Americans, meanwhile, the old-fashioned Anglophile seemed able to deliver support when it mattered most. As a result there was a certain symbiosis in the MacArthur-Yoshida relationship, one that leads Richard Finn to describe them as "winners in peace."[13]

3. Planning for Recovery

The Japanese economy was in dire straits after the surrender. Inflation, which had been reined in to a certain extent by wartime controls, surged. The wholesale price index in 1946 was 16 times, and five years later 240 times, what it had been in the period between 1934 and 1936. Social and economic chaos typical of defeated countries contributed to this. There was a sudden flood of currency from government bonds that were losing their value. There were dark rumors that the armed services had released large supplies of bank notes they had hoarded, and that individuals who had access to raw materials they had assembled for the military turned those into personal fortunes. Meanwhile urban dwellers, their housing destroyed or badly damaged, had desperate need for every kind of product denied them by the blockade of the country and the destruction of war. Shortage of chemical fertilizers made for poor crops; the seas were overfished and the hills overcut; mines lay idle without the slave labor that had kept them going during the years of war. The government levied new taxes, including one on wartime profits, regulated banks, and decreed limits on prices, but in the slackening of discipline that accompanied defeat these measures could only be palliatives.

What was needed was a return of productivity. This was slow in coming, even more so in Japan than in Europe, and the level of the gross national product (GNP), which had sunk to one-half of the 1934–1936 level, did not return to that figure until 1953.[14]

This setting provided the background for the emergence of economic planners, some of whom who had carried out, and in some cases been punished for, studies of Japan's potential for war. They now faced the challenge of developing plans to revive the economy, and out of their work came the beginnings of a national industrial policy. Prime Minister Yoshida himself was convinced that state-led planning was inappropriate for a capitalist society, but the emergency Japan faced in the early postsurrender years provided an opportunity for others who had thought about these matters for many years.

Arisawa Hiromi has already been mentioned. He was thoroughly schooled in Marxist economic theories, and his period of study in interwar Germany had familiarized him with the work of the "total war" theorists. On his return to Japan he had participated in a study of Japan's resources that convinced him of the futility of its war efforts.[15] When the study was repressed he worked inconspicuously with the scholars in Prince Konoe's Shōwa Research Association, ghostwriting pieces that appeared under others' names. He was caught up in the red-baiters' "professors' group" in 1941 and dismissed from his post at Tokyo Imperial University, but with the return of peace he emerged as a leading figure in what now became the University of Tokyo. Together with a labor economist (Nakayama Ichirō) and two theorists of economic growth (Shimomura Osamu and Ōkita Saburō, an engineer turned economist) Arisawa became a principal architect of Japan's economic recovery. Each of these men went on to careers of extraordinary distinction in later days; under the ministry of Miki Kiyoshi, Ōkita served as foreign minister, and Arisawa, Nakayama, and Shimomura all appeared on the imperial honors list as recipients of the Order of the Rising Sun, First Class, with Star and Ribbon, the highest honor the Japanese state can bestow. In further recognition of the importance of their role Arisawa, Nakayama and Shimomura were sometimes referred to as a new *gosanke*, as the three great Tokugawa cadet houses of Kii, Owari, and Mito had been called.[16]

Economic planning was essential in the context of postsurrender Japan. On the one hand the giant zaibatsu conglomerates, which had bent to conform with state leadership during the war years, were being broken up into their constituent parts and were unavailable for a leading role. Occupation authorities, on the other hand, were in a position to centralize more in the process of reforming the old order, and their approval or at least tolerance was necessary to any large-scale activity that might be planned. The bureaucracy, essential to the implementation of Occupation decrees, stood almost unchallenged at the center of public life. Control of foreign exchange, which was at a premium, and allocation of material resources combined to make it possible and indeed necessary to shape the direction of the economy and maximize the return that might be expected from investment of the labor, capital, and resources at hand.

The origins of the thoughtful planning that followed can be found in a study group that began to meet before the arrival of the Americans. When defeat was imminent the Greater East Asia Ministry, which had been designed to take over Asian matters previously handled by the Foreign Ministry, was dismantled. Some of its most able men were transferred to the ministry's Research Bureau for Postwar Problems. Its members trudged through the ruins of Tokyo to meet in the badly damaged headquarters building of the South Manchurian Railroad, a remarkably ugly structure at the heart of Tokyo's Toranomon intersection that was later taken over by SCAP for its own office needs.

In the closing days of the war, ministry after ministry ordered the destruction of its files, and the Tokyo sky was black with the smoke sent up by burning paper. "This was a very stupid thing to do," Ōkita Saburō, one of the principal organizers of the study group, later recalled; "the documents being burned in courtyards and other places included mobilization documents, production capacity surveys and many basic economic materials, many of which would help our work in planning the postwar economy. But at the time people were shocked at losing the war and afraid of the occupation forces, who were a completely unknown quantity." Ōkita made it his business to go from courtyard to courtyard to try to salvage what remained from the smoldering piles of documents, and secretly smuggled them home. "One day, when engaged on such work, I ran into Inaba Hidezō and discovered he had come on the same mission as myself. During that time Inaba systematically collected those documents which were not burnt and used them to start the Research Institute of the National Economy."[17] From such modest beginnings did planning for the postwar economy grow. In the desperate shortage of goods of those days lunch for meetings was made possible by a few donations of yen that enabled secretaries to scrounge for black market food. Despite all this, enthusiasm ran high; Japan had to begin again, and time was short. Gotō Yōnosuke later recalled that thanks to the splendid briefings the meetings became more and more successful; a Foreign Ministry history noted that the report issued by the group, which gradually mobilized nearly all of Japan's economic experts, "engaged in discussion with all the *elan* of the patriots *(shishi)* of the Meiji Restoration."

The group's report, which was completed in March 1946 and distributed in 10,000 copies, was a document that looked far beyond the rubble of the present to consider Japan's future place in the world economy. Ōkita provides a few sentences of its introduction that suggest how astute he and the others who drafted it were.

> In considering Japan's future basic economic policies, we must rise above our immediate environment and proceed from a broad global and developmental standpoint. First we must discern the course of the progress of human society, its present state and future trends, and second, understand the nature of the world environment in which Japan now stands and in which it will stand in the future. With such an appreciation of the general environment, we must analyze the traditional and uniquely Japanese features of society and economy, as well as the new conditions we face in the postwar period. On the basis of this synthesis of the universal and the particular, our true course should be set in a constructive and positive spirit.[18]

There is no defeatism in these lines. One is struck by the fact that these economists, with so little to work with, saw themselves as successors to the Meiji Restoration activists. Ōkita notes that Saeki Kiichi, a prominent postwar planner, read the report "on his return from Manchuria and later realized that he found in it the inspiration to think of the future direction of his life."

The first problem the planners faced was that of possible reparations. The Potsdam Declaration had assured the Japanese that Japan would be permitted "such industries as will sustain her economy," but the level at which it should be sustained depended very much on the target date selected and the policies followed. The Pauley Commission of November 1945 advocated a Draconian course that would substantially have returned Japanese to their rice paddies, but it was not long before the "international environment" on which the planners kept their eyes intervened to raise questions of United States economic support, the feasibility of moving industrial equipment to less advanced economies, and the looming threat of the cold war with its priorities for Japanese stability and cooperation. Once a return to the standards of the period of

1930–1934 was set as a reasonable goal, the planners could point to the contradictions in the Pauley proposals. They proceeded methodically with calculations of per capita commodity consumption in those years and adjusted the totals to make allowance for Japan's population rise, newly augmented by 6 million Japanese repatriated from abroad.

When Yoshida first became prime minister in May 1946 he invited the economic planners to lunch with him each week, and noted that he found their talk more interesting than that at cabinet meetings. It was at one of these sessions that Arisawa Hiromi argued the importance of setting priorities in economic recovery. The overall level of production was so low, he pointed out, that it was impossible to work on all fronts simultaneously. At the time industrial energy came from coal, and in the depleted and often dangerous coal mines, where during the war years so much labor had been forced from prisoners of war and Koreans, production was particularly low. It did not help that Yoshida, in a New Year's radio address in 1947, castigated the miners as "insubordinate," thereby helping to bring on the threatened general strike on February 1 that was forbidden by GHQ. Shortly afterward, during a brief interlude of government led by members of the Socialist Party, the economist Wada Hirō was named to head the Economic Stabilization Board, and the now famous Priority Production Program went into effect. Coal was needed for steel, and steel was needed to improve the mine shafts and rails, and that would make possible more coal. GHQ cooperated by permitting the import of a limited amount of crude oil to reinforce the energy base. Now came a series of studies and reports, some inspired by the publications of England's Labor government. Ōkita, Arisawa, Inaba, and other economists, using the Economic Stabilization Board as their base, accumulated more and more documentation for key sectors of the economy to target.

One should not exaggerate the speed or degree of success achieved in these early months; real wages rose little, and the newly turbulent labor movement raised fears for social instability among conservatives. Intensification of the cold war encouraged the criticism of SCAP reforms by American Japan hands that has been described. The program of economic deconcentration was cut back and brought to a close long before its original goals were reached, as Washington's concerns for Japan's stability and self-sufficiency rose. "It is clear," United States secretary of the army Kenneth Royall stated in 1948, "that Japan cannot support itself as a nation of shopkeepers and craftsmen and small artisans any more than it can exist as an agricultural nation." From then on American policy and Japanese hopes coincided more and more. In the process the Japanese left, in politics, universities, and labor, began to decry the fact that policy was oriented more toward production than consumption, and that a "reverse course" had changed the thrust of American policy. Many of the original reform leaders in GHQ, among them Colonel Charles Kades of the Government Section, who had headed Whitney's "constitutional convention," resigned their posts. The men who took their place were more likely to be sympathetic with reconstruction.

The change in Occupation attitudes toward Japan is difficult to quantify, but important to remember. By the late 1940s the former enemy had in many ways become the new protégé.[19] Officials of the GHQ Economic Section had established a revolving fund to get foreign trade moving once more. Examination of the message files at the MacArthur Library in Norfolk, Virginia, leads to the astonishing realization that SCAP was doubling as an international trading company; telegrams discuss the optimum mixture of cotton and synthetic in textiles with an eye to customs duty, and others direct the import of materials unavailable in Japan from many corners of the world. The dictates of early Occupation years had been replaced by joint consultation and cooperation. The Japanese planners, in other words, had a favorable environment in which to work.

But basic differences remained. Some Japanese leaders, like Ishibashi Tanzan, favored expansionist policies that seemed reckless to American authorities, and the ready accessibility of Japanese firms to investment loans from the newly established Reconstruction Finance Bank seemed to be speeding an inflation. To meet this the United States dispatched a mission headed by the Detroit banker Joseph M. Dodge, in 1949. Dodge had served in a similar capacity in Germany. He was a no-nonsense fiscal conservative, and his recommendations, which became known as the "Dodge line," were that the Japanese government develop a consolidated and balanced national budget, close down the Reconstruction Finance Bank, reduce government intervention in matters of subsidies and price controls, and establish an exchange rate of 360 yen to the dollar. The economic slowdown this produced made life difficult for the labor movement. The Dodge measures were politically unpalatable; they led to unemployment and social distress that was reflected in the Japan Communist Party gains in the elections of 1949, in which it scored a historic high of almost 10 percent of the Diet seats. There were those who compared the Dodge measures to the "Matsukata deflation" of the 1880s. At the same time, the new policies were designed to prepare a base from which Japan could attain self-sufficiency through increased foreign trade, and the new exchange rate was instituted in order to guarantee the competitiveness of Japanese products. This rate obtained throughout the years of growth and came to an end only in 1970, when the administration of President Richard M. Nixon ended the set rate and allowed the yen to seek its true value.

With consumption temporarily, at least, reined in by deflation, and export productivity bolstered by a favorable exchange rate, the setting in which economic planners worked was a favorable one. Even so there would have been very great hardship and instability in Japan if it had not been for the Korean War, which broke out in June of 1950. Japan quickly became the workshop of the United Nations campaign to defend the Republic of Korea, and an enormous infusion of foreign exchange helped to fund the Dodge reforms.

4. Politics and the Road to San Francisco

In postwar Japan the old political groupings which were thought of as liberal found themselves reclassified as conservatives. In the 1920s and 1930s there had been the beginning of a left-wing opposition, and the so-called proletarian parties with their labor and farm constituencies had begun to garner appreciable votes in general elections. Government suppression combined with national support for Japan's wars to reduce their appeal and remove them from the political scene. After Japan's surrender Occupation directives for civil liberty brought Socialist and Communist leaders back into the open, and a discredited government and economic hardship offered opportunities for rapid growth of a left-wing opposition. Because the land reform stabilized the countryside, what had been labor-farmer coalitions were now overwhelmingly labor- and urban-centered. In this new climate of opinion the prewar liberals and moderates became postwar conservatives.

During the seven years of the Occupation Japanese conservatives profited from the approval of GHQ and the general popularity of Occupation measures to build a comfortably dominating position. Neither of these elements was a consistent plus, however; initially SCAP measures seemed certain to destabilize the conservatives and to favor the special opposition, but that likelihood lessened as Washington directives focused on Japan's role within a larger international structure. The land reform also left conservatives with a secure base in an electorate that was still predominantly agrarian. The course of politics was nevertheless uncertain and reflected in frequent cabinet change (see chart).

It would be tedious to detail the reasons for each of these shifts. Higashikuni and Shidehara were appointed under the prewar system, at the recommendation of Privy Seal Kido Kōichi, who was shortly tried and imprisoned after the Tokyo tribunal rendered its verdict. After his first cabinet, Yoshida came in under the new constitution with its specification that the prime minister be elected by the Lower House of the Diet. Thereafter general elections determined the makeup of the Lower House and the leading party elected its head as prime minister, in contrast to prewar days when elections had as often been plebiscites staged by a new cabinet to strengthen its position. Nevertheless, although there was great hope for a new era of democratic rule and voter turnout was high, it would be wrong to conclude that the election process was particularly interesting or inspiring. Ultimate power seemed to lie with SCAP. Prewar politicians returned to run for election. The House of Councillors came to include nationally prominent figures and women, but the political process changed relatively little. The chief difference, perhaps, was the sudden disappearance of the Japanese military and the failure of nationalist rhetoric and symbols to win support. SCAP, indeed, forbade display of the Japanese flag for some time and it remained controversial until the end of the century, when Diet action firmly established it as the national symbol.

Yoshida, as we have seen, originally became prime minister as surrogate for Hatoyama Ichirō, who received a personal purge thunderbolt from GHQ; he retained his post after Hatoyama became eligible once more, but ultimately gave way to him shortly after Japan regained its sovereignty. Officials in SCAP were not enthusiastic about Yoshida, especially at the first; they only tolerated him initially and tried to maneuver him out of office later, but without success. It can be concluded that although all postsurrender Japanese governments had to retain the confidence of the United States, the direct influence of SCAP, dominant at first, waned as the seven years of Occupation went on.

For the first two years it was SCAP that drove Japanese politics. The new constitution, land reform, civil rights, and labor directives fulfilled and indeed rather exceeded the goals of prewar liberals like Ozaki Yukio. Japanese leftists, however, had hoped for more and assumed optimistically that SCAP was on

---

Cabinets during the Allied Occupation

(Prince) Higashikuni Naruhiko	Aug.–Oct. 1945
Shidehara Kijūrō	Oct. 1945–Apr. 1946
Yoshida Shigeru (1st cabinet)	May 1946–May 1947
Katayama Tetsu (Socialist)	May 1947–Mar. 1948
Ashida Hitoshi	Mar.–Oct. 1948
Yoshida Shigeru (2nd)	Oct. 1948–Feb. 1949
Yoshida Shigeru (3rd)	Feb. 1949–Oct. 1952
Yoshida Shigeru (4th)	Oct. 1952–May 1953
Yoshida Shigeru (5th)	May 1953–Dec. 1954

their side. Conservatives also feared as much. Political prisoners who were released under the civil rights directives were told that their release was made possible by the direct intervention of General MacArthur. Communist leaders who had kept their integrity and refused to recant emerged as popular heroes of urban workers, and quickly assumed an important place in the burgeoning labor movement. In "production control" protests management representatives were barred from factories while worker-organized committees took over. In 1946 close to a million unionized workers participated in 1,260 industrial disputes, many of them involving such tactics.

That labor had overplayed its hand and misread the Occupation's intent became clear when MacArthur banned the general strike announced by transportation workers for February 1, 1947. Subsequently the Japanese government was able to deny public servants (who included railroad workers, the largest single union) the right to strike. Thereafter "slowdowns" might try commuters' patience, but total cessation of transport was ruled out.

As the possibility of malnutrition and famine declined and the economy began to show signs of life again, demonstrations became fewer and the conservative cause revived. The land reform had created a solid agricultural base for conservative political power, and the pressing need for food guaranteed farmers a market for their product. Rural revolution had been forestalled, but that was less the case with urban workers. Industrial wages began a slow recovery, but it was not until the end of Occupation in 1952 that they returned, in real terms, to prewar levels.

In a sense all politics during the Occupation years were a prelude to the recovery of sovereignty, however, and the story of the road to the San Francisco Peace Conference shifts the setting beyond Japan. As early as 1947, Japan specialists in the Department of State had begun work on the outlines of a peace treaty that would bring the Occupation to an end. Their thinking, however, was still that of postsurrender days: Kuomintang China was expected to be the United States' principal ally in Asia, and the problem was to restrain Japan while granting it sovereignty. Japan should be monitored to keep it disarmed, they thought, but for the rest a gradual return to sovereignty could be worked out. General MacArthur seemed supportive of this; he was not without hope for the Republican nomination for president in 1948—until he suffered a crushing setback in the Wisconsin primary of that year—and was prepared to return to national acclaim as a hero of peace as well as war.

The rising intensity of the cold war put an end to these plans. It became clear that the Communist cause would prevail in China. Pentagon planners were dismayed by the prospect of losing forward bases in Japan, and State Department realists feared for the stability of East Asian politics if a totally disarmed Japan was left to fend for itself. It was in this context that George F. Kennan came to Tokyo for talks with General MacArthur to urge restraint in the still incomplete program of industrial deconcentration and that Secretary of the Army Royall warned of the impossibility of Japan's retreating from its development as an industrial nation. Henceforth American policy was linked to the revival of the Japanese economy and vigilant in its concern for Communist activities in Japan. This in turn was naturally congenial to Japanese conservatives. United States labor unions, strongly anti-Communist, sent delegations and financial support for what were presumed (wrongly, in some cases) to be conservative Japanese unions. All this helped the conservative cause in Japan. It also helped the cause of industry and economic planners for industrial growth. Production was seen as requisite for future independence, and production was, for the present, more important than consumption. With time, benefits would inevitably extend throughout society. Delay in gratification of commodity needs would mean increased benefits in the future.[20] This was also the thrust of economic changes introduced by the "Dodge line" with its emphases on deflation and rationalization.

As the 1940s drew to a close, SCAP became increasingly concerned with possible Communist infiltration of the left, and the outbreak of the Korean War in 1950 heightened that alarm. Within SCAP the balance of power shifted; the New Dealers were fewer and less influential, while General Willoughby's Intelligence (G-2) Section became more powerful. A "red purge" now targeted Communists and suspected Communists in government posts from education to politics, and laws that had been used against the right in the early Occupation years were directed against the left instead. Japanese conservatives understandably took heart at these developments, and Communist strength in the Diet, which had approached 10 percent after the 1949 elections, virtually disappeared together with the Japan Communist Party leaders, who once again went underground.

Thanks in good measure to these pressures from trends outside Japan, then, it seemed to many that SCAP concerns shifted from reform to recovery and from preoccupation with right-wing activities to concern for Communist subversion. SCAP authorities, to be sure, argued that foreign-inspired radicals should not be allowed to interfere with the country's new-found freedoms, but for the most part Japanese reactions to these shifts were predictable. Most Japanese felt unthreatened by world politics, secure in the presence of the American military, and convinced from recent experience that participation in international politics was totally unprofitable. Japan had tried and failed to take a leading role.[21] Japan was surrounded by satisfied powers who had defeated it, and in the event of emergency its security would be provided by the United States. The average citizen was concerned with improving the conditions of life, and some of the shifts of American policy seemed dangerously reminiscent of trends in earlier days they had so recently been warned against. Intellectuals and Socialist leaders deplored the changes and developed a lively fear that political reforms of democratization might also be in danger of reversal. It did not help that a number of conservatives began to talk about revisions in the constitution that would permit the return of some kind of military structure and redefinition of the position of the emperor. The net result was a curious shift in which the left, highly critical of United States policy, championed the Peace Constitution as its own, while the conservatives, beneficiaries of the new political order, put their trust in American support.

There are grounds for crediting the imperial house and Emperor Hirohito with a role in preparations for a treaty of peace. During the Occupation years Hirohito met with General MacArthur eleven times. No American interpreters were present, and the record of the conversations has never been released. Fragments of the talks did slip out, on one occasion from an interpreter who was promptly dismissed.

The nervous and apprehensive Hirohito who first called on MacArthur at the outset of the Occupation gained in confidence as it became clear that the imperial institution would be maintained, and he seems to have become an astute spokesman for the Japanese conservative establishment. From the few scraps of discussion that became known, one finds him expressing fear that Japanese labor, without the experience and responsibility that American labor has gained over the years, may adopt irresponsible positions—presumably toward wages and toward security. More to the point with regard to Japan's position, he expresses apprehension about an disarmed Japan in world politics, and seems only partly assuaged by MacArthur's grandiose assurance that he would defend Japan as if it were California. Most striking, the emperor suggests that the United States might want to retain custody of Okinawa after a peace treaty as a base for its military forces, while granting Japan's residual sovereignty over the island. This proposal (which was in fact followed) did not endear the emperor to the residents of Okinawa; it was the only prefecture never visited by Hirohito, although plans for such a visit were being prepared at the time of his death in 1989. Some suggest that these conversations provided a unique transmission belt for the exchange of information and concern at the very highest level, and one scholar goes so far as to describe them as a new and updated form of "double diplomacy," in which the emperor could outflank even Prime Minister Yoshida.[22]

In this manner plans for the return of sovereignty to Japan—on the condition that the United States retain bases in Japan and full control of Okinawa—

began to take form. The Korean War had moved from near-defeat to near-victory, only to have Chinese intervention reverse the tide once more. MacArthur was replaced by General Matthew B. Ridgway in the fall of 1951; the Occupation was becoming an anachronism, and Japan was growing restive. Washington planners insisted, however, that Japan make preparations for its own security. President Truman appointed John Foster Dulles as special ambassador to work out arrangements for a treaty of peace in order to secure Republican congressional support. MacArthur, on his way home from Tokyo after his recall for open disagreement on Korean War policy, and Dulles, bound for Japan, were able to confer by radio as their planes crossed the Pacific in opposite directions. Dulles's goal was a Japan allied with the United States and able to participate in its own defense, but Yoshida, unwilling to underwrite American needs and burden Japan's economy, maintained—outwardly and politically—a reluctance to bypass Article 9 of the constitution.

In the negotiations that followed Yoshida showed himself a somewhat devious but skillful protagonist. He resisted proposals for a formal military, and when he did agree that Japan would in due time establish forces for its own defense he did so in a letter that became public only decades later. Now and later he argued the political cost of antagonizing the Socialist opposition to rearmament, although there are indications that he encouraged that opposition to strengthen his hand.

What emerged was compromise. Japan established a Police Reserve to take over some of the security role formerly played by United States forces now engaged in Korea, and that body in time became the Self-Defense Forces. The United States retained its right to maintain bases in Japan and kept full administrative control over Okinawa. Preparations now began for a formal treaty, prepared in bilateral talks with other allies. Since the Soviet Union could be expected to oppose any arrangements that left American forces in Japan, it was necessary to avoid the risk of debate at the upcoming conference. The Soviet Union did in fact send representatives to San Francisco, but they were outmaneuvered by Secretary of State Dean Acheson, who ruled them out of order at every turn. All this was in decided contrast to traditional patterns of peacemaking at Paris or Vienna.

The San Francisco Conference convened in September 1951. Prime Minister Yoshida journeyed to San Francisco to sign the document that restored sovereignty to Japan. Under the terms of the treaty Japan recognized the independence of Korea and renounced all claims to Taiwan, the Pescadores, the Kurils, South Sakhalin, and the Pacific islands it had held in trust since World War I. The Soviet Union was not a signatory, however, and the Kuril issue remained moot, especially as Japan contended that the southernmost islands had never been administered as part of the Kuril (Chishima) chain. Disagreement over ownership of the southernmost islands has stood in the way of a peace treaty with the Soviet Union (and now Russia) into the twenty-first century, although an agreement ending the state of war between the two countries was signed in 1956. Okinawa also remained in limbo, under American rule, and it was not returned to Japan until 1972.

The treaty recognized Japan's right to enter into arrangements for collective security and noted the United Nations' recognition of an "inherent right of individual or collective self-defense." That right—in actuality an obligation—was promptly exercised by the execution of a Security Treaty with the United States. Under its terms American forces would remain in Japan until Japan could "assume responsibility for its own defense." Japan agreed not to grant similar rights to any third power without American approval, and meanwhile United States assistance in defensive armament, technology, and training would prepare for the day when Japan would be prepared to defend itself. Since Japanese public opinion was then, and would remain for some time, unalterably opposed to remilitarization, it seemed unlikely that that would be very soon. Japan was also obliged to follow the American lead on the issue of a divided China. Arguing that it was essential to Senate ratification of the treaty, Dulles extracted from a reluctant Yoshida the assurance that Japan would recognize the Republic of China on Taiwan, rather than the People's Republic at Beijing, as the legitimate government of China.

The Treaty of Peace thus left Japan with sovereignty restored, but with limited options for setting its own course in world politics. American insistence on the arrangements of security, given the fact that war still raged against Chinese and North Korean armies in Korea, was natural; Japanese conservatives, doubtful of the feasibility of Japan's unilateral renunciation of force, welcomed an agreement that provided Japan with a "nuclear umbrella." Intellectuals by and large were critical, and their ambivalence on Japan's being drawn into policies not of its own choosing was also understandable. The arrangement set the stage for decades of negotiation in which the Americans asked for a greater contribution to mutual security from Japan, and decades of controversy within Japan about the desirability and cost of the Security Treaty.

5. The San Francisco System

Japan had regained its sovereignty and now reentered the international order after a prolonged period of relative isolation, but it did so under very unusual circumstances. In Meiji times the price of full sovereignty after the abolition of the unequal treaties had been the admission of foreigners to unrestricted residence throughout Japan. A half century later the price proved to be virtually unrestricted use of Japanese territory by the United States. Nevertheless the gains, from the point of view of Yoshida's conservative government, were greater than the drawbacks. The scale and pace of Japanese rearmament remained a Japanese decision. While holding this to the minimum for many years, Japan placed first priority on economic recovery and growth, confident that its defense needs against any eventuality were being met at modest cost. Japan reopened to foreign trade, but on its own terms. A favorable exchange rate made its manufactures competitive, and the strong tie with the United States opened the world's largest market to Japan. American manufacturers, confident that they had a long lead, were generous and even careless in providing technology for Japan's new industries.

The San Francisco system did, to be sure, cut Japan off from mainland China, and it was some time before South Korea, Taiwan, and the newly independent states of Southeast Asia could become promising markets. After the Korean armistice was worked out in 1953 East Asia was, however, stable, and Japanese recovery worked to speed economic development throughout maritime East Asia. Moreover the resources and markets of Southeast Asia and Australia were now available and no longer bound to imperial preferences. United States policy continued to favor the integration of Japan into the world trading order, and United States backing helped Japan win membership in the several regional trading systems that were established. In a sense, with an open field for the import of raw materials and access to foreign markets, Japan seemed to have achieved its chief war aims in defeat.

There were of course Japanese who deplored the fact that the peace was partial, since it did not include the Soviet Union and mainland China, and who protested that the commitment to Taiwan would cut Japan off from the People's Republic.

Yoshida himself was confident that the future would take care of these problems, and that Japan had returned to its proper historic past by allying itself with the world's strongest power. The arrangement enabled Japan to concentrate on economic growth and work toward a resolution of Article 9 in the Peace Constitution by separating "self-defense" from "war potential." For decades after Yoshida left office these priorities were maintained by graduates of what columnists called the "Yoshida academy," followers who shared his objectives. As these policies began to succeed, Yoshida's popularity, which was not high when he retired from office, began to grow, and with it his confidence. In his memoirs he was caustic in his dismissal of the many intellectuals who deplored Japan's continued seeming subservience to the United

States, and contrasted these attitudes to the late Meiji period when the Anglo-Japanese Alliance was negotiated. At that time, he pointed out,

> Great Britain was at the height of its power and mistress of the seven seas, while Japan was an insignificant island nation in the Far East which had only just begun its rise from obscurity. The difference in international significance and power potential between the two countries was far greater than the differences which exist between Japan and the United States today. Yet the Anglo-Japanese Alliance was welcomed by Government and people alike and no one viewed that document as meaning that Japan was truckling to British imperialism or in danger of becoming a glorified British colony.
>
> When I recall this historical fact, and then recall the way in which our so-called "progressive" intellectuals speak of Japan as little better than an American colony and the "orphan of Asia" and so forth, it makes me wonder if these critics belong to the same race of people who only fifty years ago had acted with such determination and judgment, and without any trace of what can only be termed a colonial sense of inferiority.[23]

In retrospect it is hard to fault Yoshida's estimate of the San Francisco system. The United States presence stabilized East Asia; the People's Republic of China was engulfed in the giant paroxysms of the Mao era and offered few possibilities, and Japan's enforced separation stabilized Japanese politics. Japan relied on the United States for its security, rearmed slowly and warily, and, thanks to the American presence, gradually managed to regain the trust of trading partners in maritime East Asia. The American tie, providing access to resources, technology, and markets, enabled Japan to regain its feet, resume economic growth, and become the locomotive of growth throughout maritime East Asia.[24]

6. Intellectuals and the Yoshida Structure

Admiration for Yoshida was far from unanimous, and as already noted, at the time of his retirement he was often portrayed as a political bumbler totally out of touch with most Japanese. The partial peace and security arrangement produced deep rifts in Japanese opinion, and these reached crisis proportions at the time of the renewal of the Security Treaty in 1960. Opposition to *Ampo*, the shorthand term for the pact, stirred a student generation and its mentors. The intellectual divisions of the 1950s were as deep as the class conflicts of the postsurrender years, and it will not do to dismiss the "progressive intellectuals" as contemptuously as Yoshida did.

The amuletic terms of the postwar era were "peace," "democracy," and "culture." Japan had vowed to reorient itself as a "nation of culture," and in that task intellectuals, "men of culture" *(bunkajin)*, played the central role. Austere, often self-righteous, poorly rewarded and yet sought out by the press, they were, some have commented, new and self-conscious successors to samurai moralists of an earlier day.[25]

The manner of Japan's recovery in the 1950s created divisions that dominated life into the 1960s. By the time Yoshida wrote his memoirs the great paroxysm of 1960 had passed, but few would have expected it to subside so suddenly. The most vocal and respected intellectuals of the day were usually ambivalent about the peace and security treaties, but in longer retrospect theirs was an uneasiness that began with the shift in Occupation priorities in 1948.

Nothing better illustrates this than the manner of dissemination of information to a publisher who went on to organize the most influential group of late-Occupation leaders. The publishing house of Iwanami launched as its postwar flagship the monthly *Sekai* (The World), which soon became a hugely popular platform for progressive intellectuals. The Occupation, it will be recalled, maintained censorship of periodicals in order to monitor the revival of militarism. In September 1949, the *Sekai* editor made one of his obligatory visits to the censorship division of the Civil Information and Education Section to secure clearance for his next issue. Such trips may have been galling at times, but they could also provide access to documents from beyond the seas. On this occasion the editor was given the text of a recent UNESCO statement drawn up by social scientists entitled "Factors That Make for War," with the suggestion that he might want to publish it. When he did so a few months later, it served as inspiration for the formation of a Peace Problems Discussion Group (Heiwa Mondai Danwakai) that all but dominated discussion—and also symbolize confusion—in a Japan still more or less isolated from world currents. The organization's founders concluded, from the fact that one of the eight scholars who had drafted the UNESCO statement, a relatively obscure Hungarian savant, was from the Soviet bloc, that this was a quiet signal that Soviet authorities favored peaceful coexistence, and this encouraged them to work for unarmed neutrality. They argued that a treaty that committed Japan to cold war partisanship was worse than none, and that it would be in violation of the new constitution as well.[26]

The intellectuals who went on from this to set the terms of debate had a major role in public opinion. The press, almost unanimously critical of the conservative government, eagerly sought their views, and they, wretchedly paid and cut off from the new commercialism that was developing around them, had to live by their pens. But there was a more profound impulse stirring them, and that was the determination to atone for their silence during the years of militarism and war. During those years many intellectuals and writers had been co-opted by the state, while those who declined to do so had retreated into silence. We have noted that the absence of a public dialogue on the road Japan was following, when it was still possible, is one of the striking features of the 1930s. Intellectuals were determined not to make the same error a second time. Marxist analysis, its prestige raised by its proscription during the war, dominated social science writing. The conservative heroes of the past were silenced or banished. Professor Hiraizumi Kiyoshi, whose "imperial history" had been so influential, ended his career in a minor post. Some, who had been co-opted by the military, were the more vehement in their support for the new democracy and peace.

Generational differences strengthened this. In the early discussions of the Peace Problems Discussion Group intellectuals of many stripes participated, but it was not long before deep divisions between "old liberals" and "new progressives" surfaced. With the exit of the old right and the military, prewar liberalism became postwar conservatism. The prewar generation of liberals did not, in any case, reproduce itself. The Taishō generation suffered disproportionate losses as a result of the war, and it was poorly prepared to face the vehemence of the new progressives.

The left too was ideologically divided by degrees of tolerance of communism, but it was firmly united in its determination to be heard in its opposition to what it saw as Japan's new pro-American conservatism. In a sense it marked a new, antistate intelligentsia. For these people Yoshida's disapproval was a badge of distinction, and they returned his scorn with their own.

A final element involved was confessional: the new intellectuals were as one in deploring Japan's role in China. It might be possible to see the Pacific War as motivated by resistance to Western imperialism and thereby ultimately progressive, but the China War, against a peaceful neighbor, had been one of inexcusable aggression. This penitence had a corollary of respect and often admiration for the revolution in progress in China, and heightened disapproval of policies that threatened to cut Japan off from the mainland. Throughout the 1950s a romantic and wistful yearning characterized much commentary about China, and even when stories of the extremism of class warfare or Chinese moves into Tibet and against India broke through, major figures like the Sinologist Takeuchi Yoshimi thought it incumbent upon Japan to look away; Japan, in view of its own behavior, was in no position to criticize China.

The 1950s also brought a number of issues on which it could plausibly be argued that the new arrangements for security spelled an end to Japan's priorities of peace and democracy. After Yoshida gave way to his old rival Hatoyama Ichirō in 1953, conservatives began serious study of the constitution with an eye to its revision. The Police Reserve that had been established at American urging became the Self-Defense Forces, with land, sea, and air divisions. Genda Minoru, the architect of the attack on Pearl Harbor, reemerged to organize the new air component. In several well-publicized events American military bases brought on public debate, as when a Japanese national was killed while scavenging on an artillery range. The roar of American jet fighters over nearby schools and residences helped make the change to independence seem illusory.

Contention came to center around the United States–Japan Security Treaty that had been signed within hours of the signing of the Treaty of Peace. In its original form the treaty began with the recognition that Japan, which was disarmed, did not have the "effective means to exercise its inherent right of self-defense," and that this brought danger to Japan because "irresponsible militarism has not yet been driven from the world." Therefore Japan asked that a Security Treaty come into force simultaneously with the Treaty of Peace, "as a provisional arrangement for its defense," and asked that "the United States of America should maintain armed forces of its own in and about Japan so as to deter armed attack." The United States agreed but in the expectation, however, that Japan would itself increasingly assume responsibility for its own defense against direct and indirect aggression but "always avoiding any armament which could be an offensive threat or serve other than to promote peace and security in accordance with the purposes and principles of the United Nations Charter." Accordingly Japan would grant, and the United States accept, the right "to dispose United States land, air and sea forces in and about Japan." These forces could be used "to contribute to the maintenance of international peace and security in the Far East," and could, if the Japanese government so requested, be used "to put down large-scale internal riots and disturbances in Japan caused through instigation or intervention by an outside power or powers."

The treaty did not provide for reciprocity: the United States was free to use its forces for the purposes of Japan's internal security and to maintain security in the Far East without prior consultation, while Japan would continue to defray the costs of American protection. Opponents denounced it as a new form of unequal treaty. Actually it was unequal in another sense, since America promised to defend Japan, but Japan, with nothing to reciprocate, was not bound to defend the United States.

In 1957, after the death of Ishibashi Tanzan two months after becoming prime minister, government leadership passed to Kishi Nobusuke, once a member of the cabinet of General Tōjō and subsequently interrogated, though never indicted and tried, as a "Class A" war criminal. The Security Treaty would be up for renewal in 1960, and the Kishi cabinet proposed changes that would provide for more reciprocity and consultation.

Critical intellectuals were little mollified by those changes, however, and felt Kishi a poor candidate for peace or democracy. They distrusted him and dismissed the improvements in the pact as cosmetic, and called for its abolition instead of accepting its revised version.

The Kishi government was determined to gain Diet approval for the renewal of the Security Treaty in time for a planned visit to Japan by President Dwight D. Eisenhower in 1960. That visit, however, originally planned in the relaxation of cold war tensions that was associated with the Soviet government of Nikita Khrushchev and scheduled to include a visit to Moscow, changed in imagery as a result of the U-2 spy plane incident that instead heightened suspicion.

In the Japanese Diet the Socialist opposition, determined to block approval of the Security Treaty renewal, tried to block the entrance of the House of Representatives Speaker. The government, too, resorted to force by calling in police to clear the entrance to the chamber. In response to this, the opposition boycotted the proceedings, and the government rammed approval through the Diet in the dead of night with no opposition members present.

It now seemed clear to many Japanese that both peace and democracy were endangered. Tokyo was rocked by gigantic demonstrations protesting the Kishi government's actions. President Eisenhower's press secretary, who arrived to plan his visit, was prevented from making his way from the airport into Tokyo. The Eisenhower visit was canceled.[27] Kishi prevailed, but at high cost: he himself was attacked and gravely wounded by a right-wing assailant. Later, another right-wing fanatic murdered the Japan Socialist Party's leader, Asanuma Inejirō, on television while he was addressing a rally.

These events tarnished the image of representative democracy in Japan and caused many to fear for its future. It was not yet two decades since Japan had tasted the ashes of war and defeat, and the wreckage of lives and of cities could still be seen. While it would be an exaggeration to credit the turbulence of the demonstrations to the intellectuals' dismay alone, there can be no question that the protests were the product of a climate of opinion that had developed by their doubts and suspicions, fanned by the government's maladroit response to the Diet obstruction and diffused and championed by press organs that were virtually unanimous in their denunciation of the government's policy and tactics. Clearly the events of 1960 have to be seen in the context of fears of a revival of militarism and war, suppression of dissent, and return of right-wing terrorism.

Beginning with May Day demonstrations in 1952, at the dawn of Japan's renewed independence, Socialist-led labor unions had provided the manpower for protests that frequently rocked Japan's major cities, especially Tokyo, and labor's contribution to the Security Treaty protests was important. What justified treating these events in the context of intellectuals' anger and dismay, however, is that the preponderance of demonstrators came from campuses within the metropolitan area and that they were frequently led by their instructors. Battalions were arrayed by school banners, and the only fatality of the riots was that of a woman student. But it has to be added that there was also a festive, ludic, sense about the protests, which in some psychological sense related them to the festivals of an earlier, agrarian society.

In commenting on these events many intellectuals drew the conclusion that the demonstrations marked something new and important in the process of democratization in Japan, and argued that for almost the first time a force for real change was boiling up from below and not responding to urgings from above; a revolutionary consciousness, they thought, was beginning to emerge in a society that had previously accepted, rather than initiated, change.

One might suggest that the only previous instance of this consciousness had come in the days of the Freedom and People's Rights Movement of the 1880s. With the enactment of the Meiji Constitution that spirit had been co-opted and diverted to goals of national, imperial power. In the 1960s the surge of participatory enthusiasm was once again diverted, into goals of economic growth and personal consumption.

For suddenly, and remarkably, the fears that brought on the demonstration subsided. Talk of doubling the national income replaced fears of losing the new-found democracy and peace. International affairs regained some kind of equilibrium. Growth stabilized Japan, and a resurgent Japanese economy seemed to stabilize maritime East Asia. A new cabinet headed by Yoshida's outstanding "disciple" Ikeda Hayato (1899–1965) substituted a "low posture" pose for Kishi's autocratic tactics. Japan gradually rejoined international society, signing a round of treaties with Southeast Asian nations and, in 1965, the Republic of Korea; the Self-Defense Forces, far from becoming a threat, had some difficulty in recruiting, and the goals set for the economy—including doubling the GNP in ten years—were soon exceeded. Intellectuals and their students traveled more, read more, and translated more. The fevered atmosphere of the 1950s was gradually replaced by one that was more varied and even relaxed.

7. Postwar Culture

In Tokugawa Japan the sword and the brush had been parallel skills, and the *Buke shohatto,* the Code for the Military Houses, for two centuries instructed samurai to cultivate the arts of peace as well as those of war. In the nineteenth century the modern state put first emphasis on gathering the instruments of power, and *bun,* "culture," had to take second place to arms; the emperor, so long the arbiter of the courtly arts of poetry and painting, now appeared at military reviews in uniform. In postwar Japan what had been parallel became opposite: a nation relieved to find it had survived turned its back on the arts of war and embraced the more enthusiastically those of culture. Peace, democracy, and culture were the trinity of the new age, and by January of 1946 schoolchildren were striving to emulate the crown prince's New Year calligraphic instruction to "build a nation of culture" in their copybooks.

That goal, however amorphous and indistinct, was a welcome change from the now empty rhetoric of war and domination, and once the immediate problems of physical needs had been met, the Japanese threw themselves into the task with enthusiasm. Journals of opinion that had been forced to accept "voluntary liquidation" by the authorities' refusal to give them newsprint reappeared as if by magic, and venerable favorites were soon challenged by numerous new voices that struggled to be heard and read. Japanese later recalled the exhilaration and excitement of a time when there were openings to ideas put forth by new writers in new formats.

"There was something akin to a creative outburst in the post-war years, when, in the midst of destruction and hunger, magazines were founded or re-established in great numbers and book production was resumed, giving the 'post-war generation' a platform for their works."[28] The writers Kawabata Yasunari (1899–1972) and Tanizaki Jun'ichirō (1886–1965), whose quiet nostalgia for an earlier day had resulted in their being silenced during the war, returned to the forefront. (Their major works have had the attention of a group of gifted translators, and are mentioned here by the titles under which they have become known to Western readers.) Tanizaki's *Makioka Sisters,* whose publication had been suppressed during the war, appeared to universal praise and quickly achieved the status of a modern classic. So too with Kawabata's *Snow Country* (1948).[29] Both Tanizaki and Kawabata went on to explore problems of age and declining sexual powers in works that harked back to the sensualist school through which they had become known in prewar days.

Personal experience of war figured importantly in the work of Ōoka Shohei (1909–1989), whose autobiography provides the setting for his fiction.[30] Dazai Osamu's *The Setting Sun* (1947), written from the depths of postwar despair and moral degeneration, also won great popularity. Mishima Yukio (1925–1970) was a brilliant stylist who lost sight of the distinction between art and reality. He became disenchanted with the postwar ethos and sought to re-create the ultranationalist ideal in fiction and in life, organizing a small private army and idealizing the young officers of the 1936 revolution. In 1970, having finished a tetralogy he felt completed his work, he scripted a carefully staged but hopeless putsch at a Self-Defense Forces center before disemboweling himself with a *seppuku* he thought would rival that of General Nogi in 1912. The response was one of astonishment.[31]

There was also a flood of writings by women, not a few who serialized in the new periodicals founded for women's interests. Ariyoshi Sawako (1931–1984) and others wrote of the hardships the old patriarchal society imposed on women. Women writers were nothing new, as seen in the enormously popular Meiji figure Yosano Akiko (to say nothing of the author of the *Tale of Genji*), but the new literary cohort wrote self-consciously as, and often, for, women, aware that they were creating a new genre.

Mishima's espousal of old-style nationalism was decidedly at odds with the views of the younger generation of writers and their readers. Ōe Kanzaburō (b. 1935) sprang to fame in the 1950s as an active exponent of liberal and progressive causes facing his generation, and became known (as in *A Personal Matter*) for his depiction of an antihero whose frustration in society finds an outlet in aggressive sexuality. There was also a great deal of writing about the atomic bomb, although it could not be published for some years because of Occupation censorship. Ōe affiliated himself with this in his documentary *Hiroshima Notes* in 1965. The best known of this category is Ibuse Masuji's *Black Rain*, which has been the basis of several films. Still other writers, many of them women, engaged contemporary social problems like the mercury pollution at Minamata in Kyushu.

Japanese literature had been deeply influenced by Western literature and thought since the Meiji period, and that influence strengthened with the sensualist and modernist influence on writers like Tanizaki and Kawabata in prewar times. In postwar days, however, that influence in a sense became stronger once more, with frequent asides referring to Western thinkers and writers. What was new was the fact that, with the growth of interest in Japan, major works found quick and often successful outlets in translation. While still a fraction of the compulsive coverage of European and American writing available to Japanese readers in translation, this brought Japanese writers attention they had never received before. In 1968 Kawabata was awarded the Nobel Prize for literature, an honor previously extended to only one Asian writer (Tagore). It was known that Mishima longed (in vain) for that honor, but it came to his critic Ōe Kenzaburō in 1994. Japanese literature seemed to be becoming a part of world literature. Japanese attached great importance to these recognitions of Japanese talent, as indications that the "nation of culture" was in fact at hand. On a different level, the selection of Tokyo as the site for the 1964 Olympics brought immense satisfaction.

Another aspect of postwar Japanese culture was the remarkable flowering of new religions. Over 3,000 claim a total enrollment of between 30 and 40 million believers. Of these 15 are major forces, with millions of followers. Sōka Gakkai ("value-creating organization") alone claims 12 million adherents. It maintains a university and has spawned a political party. Several maintain international networks and accumulate immense wealth devoted to massive headquarter buildings (Reiyūkai) and impressive art museums (MOA, Miho).

New religions are not an exclusively postwar phenomenon. Three important cults, Tenrikyō, Kurozumikyō, and Konkokyō, developed in late Tokugawa decades, each the product of the founder's revelations after experiencing a severe illness.[32] They developed in prosperous agricultural areas of central and western Japan. Under state pressure they tended to accept Shinto mythology and formulations and gradually came to resemble Shinto sects, though their autonomy brought official displeasure and, in several cases, proscription. In the early twentieth century another group of new religions sprang up, including the powerful Reiyūkai and Sōka Gakkai.[33] This time the origins were Buddhist, though a third, Seichō no ie, was more syncretic and preached the unity of all religions.

After Japan's surrender, with State Shinto proscribed, a constitution that specified the freedom of religion, and institutional Buddhism disadvantaged by collaboration with the state and massive social change and disorientation, new religions, especially those that had been frowned on by the authorities, came into their own. Their doctrines, while varied, tend to coalesce around the search for harmony and emphasize the core values of Japanese rural civilization like loyalty and sincerity. As economic development resulted in the migration of millions of Japanese from the countryside to urban workplaces, the new religions came to provide a sense of stability and association for their believers. Belief in faith healing is also common. In general the new religions are nonpolitical and conservative; the major exception is the Sōka Gakkai's Kōmeitō (Clean Government Party), which was established in 1964. Though it professed to reject traditional politics, by century's end it was in a coalition government with the Liberal Democratic Party and represented in the cabinet.

The new religions have developed extensive proselytizing programs and organized their followers into associations that provide meaning and belonging in Japan's changing society. They appeal to a membership that is, by and large, cut off from the more usual sources of prestige and recognition in Japanese society. Followers tend to be found in small enterprises and shops rather than in large firms, and many are women; indeed, from the beginning many founders have been women. "The provision of such alternative prestige structures is unquestionably one of the main reasons for the appeal of the new religions to women, whose opportunities for advancement in secular society remain limited."[34] In postwar Japan the sudden flood of new religions thus came as a response, both traditional and yet in its dimensions unexpected, to new provisions of religious freedom and new needs for social integration. Unfortunately the welter of new trends and religions did not always make for social cohesion. In 1995 Japan—and the world—suddenly became aware of a cult that called itself Aum Shinrikyō, phrases from Hindu esoteric practice, organized around a half-blind guru named Asahara who was credited with mystic powers. What astonished the nation was the realization that Asahara's followers included intelligent young scientists and graduates who, disaffected by the requirements for success in Japan's increasingly technological society, blindly followed the instructions of their seer to manufacture poisonous sarin gas and use it to produce death on Tokyo's crowded subway system. The death of twelve victims and the illness of thousands more brought some to question the scrupulous respect police had shown for laws forbidding interference with organizations incorporated as religions.

It was in film that postwar Japanese culture reached its greatest heights. The Japanese film industry had long been popular, but until the wartime insistence on themes of patriotism, patience, and valor its standard production had been focused on samurai battles in a national approximation of Hollywood westerns.[35] After the surrender SCAP officials frowned on such themes as militaristic, but with the lifting of Occupation controls in 1952 there was a remarkable outpouring of distinguished films by masterly directors whose work placed Japan at the forefront of world film.

It is impossible here to do justice to the variety and quality of this work. Three directors—Mizoguchi Kenji, Ozu Yasujirō, and Kurosawa Akira—received international fame, but it is essential to point to the role of Kurosawa Akira (1920–1998). Kurosawa began as an artist, and throughout his life his careful sketches show his sense of the way composition could be used for dramatic effect. His first film, released in 1943, drew criticism for its failure to conform with the requirements of wartime mobilization—but it was immensely popular.

In Kurosawa's work there is a central theme of truth versus illusion. Whether set in the grim reality of postsurrender Tokyo or in Japan's past, his films begin with the illusion and then, later, go on to explore the reality. *Rashomon* (1950), placed in medieval Japan and Kurosawa's first film to win international acclaim, is the account of a rape and murder as seen by a bandit, the victim, her husband's ghost, and an observer, with no clear identification of which account is correct. Clearly, each is correct to the one who has lived with his or her illusion. Kurosawa's producer argued that the film could not succeed, but after it did he was so willing to claim credit for it that the director later wrote that he thought himself back in the film itself. *Rashomon* has added a word to the world's vocabulary as a symbol of ambiguity and self-deception. Here and later Kurosawa worked with the actor Mifune Toshirō, whose stern visage and skillful movement are indelibly linked with viewers' memories of the films.

Kurosawa received the applause of Hollywood directors, who made versions of his *Seven Samurai, Rashomon,* and *Yojimbo* and adapted many other of his ideas and devices. He drew his material from a wide variety of sources—Western literature from Gorky to Shakespeare, Japanese folk tales, and Hollywood westerns. He was most active during the great age of Japanese cinema, making seventeen films between 1948 and 1965. On his death he was hailed by the *New York Times,* which devoted a full-page obituary to him, as a man who "personified Japanese movies to most of the world and who grew into one of the handful of truly important directors that the cinema has produced."

In retrospect the record of the Yoshida years gives force to his comment in that early cabinet meeting about losing a war but winning the peace. But that peace, in contrast to the war, was won without the conquest of an enemy. Japan and the United States had fought a war, the one losing, the other winning, but in the peace each gained an ally in the other.

20

The San Francisco Treaty of Peace came into force on April 28, 1952. Days later, on May Day, a demonstration on the grounds of the imperial palace plaza became disorderly as rioters, defying tear gas, struggled with police. American newspaper readers, suddenly made aware of the deep fissures in Japanese society, were alarmed and wondered about Japan's future. Labor was restless, a strident left was deeply hostile to the Security Treaty with the United States, and conservatives seemed eager to seize the opportunity to change and perhaps reverse changes incorporated in the 1947 Constitution. The Korean War had provided considerable stimulus to Japan's economy, but productivity was still very low. Coal, laboriously brought out of poorly maintained mines with narrow and often dangerous seams, was still the only source of energy. Forests were overcut, coastal waters overfished, and land was underfertilized. International trade languished. Housing remained scarce, and cities were full of makeshift buildings. Schools were poorly maintained, damp and cold. In central Tokyo a few major construction efforts saw building frameworks surrounded by a latticework of bamboo staging; rubber-soled workers carrying heavy loads of building materials slowly made their way up ladders to planks that served as platforms. Modernity and mechanization lay far in the future.

Fifty years later gleaming modern structures rose about those concrete monuments in central Tokyo. Sleek trains speeding into and out of the city on split-second schedules brought tens of thousands of travelers. Throngs of commuters who traveled on immaculate subways came from all directions of the compass to join the quiet march to home or office. New schools dotted the land; higher education was attracting more and more young people to campuses that often boasted splendid new libraries and laboratories. Japanese were better dressed and better fed. In every corner of the world neon signs proclaimed the attractions of Japanese products. Throughout Japan streets were more crowded than ever; the automobile had come within the range of millions. The culture of consumption had transformed the land. Japan had become one of the Group of Seven, more recently Eight, Developed Countries, and it was beginning to find its stride in world affairs.

1. Politics and the 1955 System

After the resumption of political life in postsurrender Japan, veterans of prewar days returned to lead political parties. On the right were the veterans of the Seiyūkai and Minseitō, the Liberals and Progressives, descendants of political wars of Meiji times, and facing them were the reform parties of Taishō and Shōwa, the Labor-Farmer Party survivors who, now that there were no restrictions on terminology, called themselves the Socialist Party (Shakaitō). In the first general elections in the spring of 1946 both conservative parties competed at a disadvantage because so many of their Diet members had been removed by the purge, which cost the Progressives over 90 percent and the Liberals 45 percent of their seats. The same arrangement cost the Socialists and Communists nothing, for both groups could wear their difficulties under the wartime regime as a badge of honor. In those elections the Liberals won a modest plurality, and the first Yoshida cabinet was the result.

Electoral districts also changed. For the first postwar election a new system in which entire prefectures constituted a single electoral district was introduced; voters cast ballots for three candidates. In the 1947 elections the system returned to the medium-size district that had been in force since 1925; a voter now cast a single ballot, and the highest-ranking candidates were seated. In party terms this put a premium on election management, since a larger than necessary plurality would represent a waste of votes that could otherwise be allocated to another candidate of the same party. This system stood until the reforms of 1990, when the Diet enacted measures to create single-member electoral districts.

In the 1947 elections the Socialists showed surprising strength and received a plurality, resulting in seating the short-lived Katayama and interim Ashida cabinets. They would not taste executive authority again until the end of the "1955 system" at the end of the Shōwa era, and then only briefly. Two years later, in 1949, the Socialists lost many of these seats to the Japan Communist Party which, as a result of the economic downturn that resulted from the deflation of the "Dodge line," scored virtually 10 percent of the total number of seats in the House of Representatives.

In 1950, the anti-Communist measures that the Korean War brought served to checkmate and substantially end Communist political influence, and the blush of economic health that accompanied Japan's role as a workshop for the United Nations campaign in defense of the Republic of Korea further lessened the economic distress that had contributed to Communist strength. Nonetheless Japanese politics remained in flux. On the one hand the "old liberals," now that the far right and military were out of the picture, began to seem an uninspiring group of aging moderate conservatives. Wada Hirō, a policy planner who had begun with Yoshida Shigeru, shifted to the Socialists in the mistaken expectation that an impending American withdrawal from Japan would doom the conservative cause.[1] Together with Suzuki Mōsaburō, a self-made man who had risen from poverty, worked his way through Waseda University, entered the world of journalism, and been imprisoned during the war, Wada set the line for old Labor-Farmer Party veterans who emerged as

Cabinets after Yoshida

Hatoyama Ichirō (3 cabinets)	Dec. 1954–Mar. 1955; –Nov. 1955; –Dec. 1956
Ishibashi Tanzan	Dec. 1956–Feb. 1957
Kishi Nobusuke (2 cabinets)	Feb. 1957–June 1958; –July 1960
Ikeda Hayato (3 cabinets)	July–Dec. 1960; –Dec. 1963; –Nov. 1964
Satō Eisaku (3 cabinets)	Nov. 1964–Feb. 1967; –Jan. 1970; –July 1972
Tanaka Kakuei (2 cabinets)	July–Dec. 1972; –Dec. 1974
Miki Takeo	Dec. 1974–Dec. 1976
Fukuda Takeo	Dec. 1976–Dec. 1978
Ōhira Masayoshi (2 cabinets)	Dec. 1978–Nov. 1979; –July 1980
Suzuki Zenko	July 1980–Nov. 1982
Nakasone Yasuhiro (3 cabinets)	Nov. 1982–Dec. 1983; –July 1986; –Nov. 1987
Takeshita Noboru	Nov. 1987–June 1989
Uno Sōsuke	June–Aug. 1989
Kaifu Toshiki (2 cabinets)	Aug. 1989–Feb. 1990; –Nov. 1991
Miyazawa Kiichi	Nov. 1991–Aug. 1993
Hosokawa Morihiro	Aug. 1993–Apr. 1994
Hata Tsutomu	Apr.–June 1994
Murayama Tomiichi	June 1994–Jan. 1996
Hashimoto Ryūtarō (2 cabinets)	Jan.–Nov. 1996; –July 1998
Obuchi Keizō	July 1998–April 2000
Mori Yoshirō	April 2000–

the new left Socialists. Competing with them as standard-bearers for the labor movement were figures from the prewar right-wing socialists, Nishio Suehiro and Asanuma Inejirō, a canny politician who was to lose his life to an assassin in 1960. On the right, the end of the purge decrees returned figures like the former diplomat Shigemitsu Mamoru (who had been among the signers of the surrender papers aboard the *Missouri*), longtime bureaucrat Kishi Nobu-suke (who had been a member of the Tōjō cabinet and was listed, though not tried, as a Class A war criminal), and the respected economic journalist Ishibashi Tanzan. Most of them were aging and unwell, and none seemed very inspiring. This context needs to be kept in mind when thinking about the intellectuals' dismay at the course Japan seemed to be taking.

A period of just under a half century in which cabinets had an average life of less than one and a half years, and prime ministers averaged a little more than two years in office (see chart), does not suggest very successful political leadership. There were, to be sure, deaths (Ishibashi, Ikeda, Ōhira), a stroke (Obuchi), and personal and especially financial scandals (Tanaka, Takeshita, Uno) that speeded changes in office. The fall of Kishi, brought on by the great swell of popular indignation that resulted from his handling of the Security Treaty revision in 1950, was the only instance of clear popular intervention in the political process, and even that came after the conservative government had achieved its immediate purpose.

Throughout the period there was a decline of class antagonism. In the late 1940s and throughout the 1950s Japanese society was rent by sharp conflict. Prior to 1960 a militant opposition was able to recruit support from the bur-geoning labor movement that saw itself threatened by the modernization of industry and rationalization of production. Labor responded vigorously. The General Council of Japanese Trade Unions (Sōhyō) provided the backbone for Socialist political strength. Although wages had returned to prewar levels by the end of the Occupation, dissatisfaction ran high; the demonstrations against the Security Treaty in 1960 marked the high point of that instability. Thereafter, however, politics gradually became less ideological. Economic growth was accompanied by a gradual rise in standards of living, and after Japan followed the American lead in China policy in the early 1970s much of the rhetoric of the left lost its relevance. In the 1990s even that rhetoric was abandoned as Socialists allied with conservatives to form the Murayama cab-inet.

In 1955, sensing victory at hand, the two wings of the Socialist movement combined to form the Japan Socialist Party (JSP). That same year the conser-vative Liberal and Democratic parties merged as the Liberal Democratic Party (LDP) to counter the danger of Socialist hegemony. The LDP held political power for four decades. Throughout those years the Socialists stood by as opposition, and were co-opted in Diet committee arrangements, with the result that some referred to Japan's politics as dominated by "one and a half" parties rather than a two-party system. The political structure this created is often referred to as the "1955 system."[2]

The LDP was divided along the lines of the parties that had united. That factionalism, however, was soon carried to a much higher level as clusters of politicians grouped around party leaders who could help them raise money for elections and advance them to office by service in faction posts or the larger LDP bureaucracy.

From an early point, bureaucrats who shifted from government to party politics constituted important elements in the LDP. Between 1958 and 1976 men who had previously been high bureaucrats—section chief or above—accounted for more than 10 percent of the House of Representatives' membership. Almost all of them were affiliated with the LDP.[3]

The party was formed at a time when it was clear that Prime Minister Hatoyama did not have long to serve or, in fact, live. In 1956 he traveled to Moscow to sign an agreement ending the war (though without a peace treaty) with the Soviet Union, but he was old and frail. The top figures of the new party were only slightly more healthy. Ogata Taketora, a prominent journalist with cabinet experience who was expected to be the party's first prime minister, died of a sudden heart attack, and Ishibashi Tanzan, who took office instead, also died two months after taking office. That left Kishi Nobusuke, who served as the first secretary general of the new party. Kishi's maladroit handling of the 1960 revision of the Security Treaty has already been described. The parliamentary imbroglio that followed cost him his job and very nearly his life, and opened the way for Ikeda Hayato, the most successful graduate of the "Yoshida academy."

Ikeda began with proposals for replacing his predecessor's high-handed stance with a low profile and announced as his goal a program to double the national income in ten years.[4] The auguries were good for Ikeda. He was personally popular. His administration coincided with a new era of youth and vigor in the United States. At this time, the new Kennedy administration replaced Ambassador Douglas MacArthur, nephew of the general, with Edwin O. Reischauer, who went on to become an extremely popular representative of his country, speaking often of a partnership between the two nations. A series of joint Japanese-American cabinet meetings seemed to give meaning to this language.

The income-doubling drive proved successful beyond all expectations, and the evidence of improvement in economic standards encouraged Japanese to think better of their society and its future. In 1964 Japan hosted the Olympic Games, and this produced a surprising boost to national pride and confidence. The games made an additional contribution to the quality of urban life as the government undertook massive construction projects for highways and stadiums to prepare for the anticipated influx of foreign visitors. The distinguished architect Tange Kenzō's Olympic buildings provided an impressive blend of contemporary technique with traditional design, and their unobtrusively monumental quality attracted international attention. It was only now that the average Japanese citizen began to see some resulting benefit from the efforts that had gone into reconstruction and economic growth.

Ikeda's early death led to the succession of Satō Eisaku, another "graduate" of the Yoshida academy who continued the popular policies that Ikeda had introduced. Toward the end of his period in office, negotiations with the United States resulted in the reversion of Okinawa to Japanese control in 1972. American military bases, now subject to the same restrictions that applied to those on the four main islands, continued to dominate life on Okinawa, however, although the Tokyo government began programs of development to offset the fact that it was asking Okinawa to bear the principal burdens of security arrangements. Satō maintained the Yoshida position on minimal military expenditure and added specific guarantees that Japan would not export arms or produce or house atomic weapons, and was awarded the Nobel Peace Prize as a result.

By this time the pattern of factionalism had become so deeply rooted in the LDP that political commentators concentrated more on factional strength than they did on the party's dominance. A faction's size was in the area of fifty Diet members; their leader was able to dispense financial support that helped them at election time, while they in turn provided the personnel base from which the leader could engage in party and Diet maneuvers. During the tenure of strong and highly visible politicians like Ikeda and Satō, election of the party leader to the post of prime minister was a foregone conclusion. More often it was the result of intense all-night negotiation among faction leaders. The successful candidate formed his cabinet with due respect to the factions that had supported his candidacy, and one reason for the realignment so common in the many cabinet shifts shown in the chart was to enable the prime minister to alter or broaden that pattern of reward.

There was frequent talk of abolishing the factions, but little success in doing so. In the 1980s a party primary was instituted for the selection of party leaders and for a time LDP party membership, previously confined mostly to participants in the political process, increased, but without much result. The pattern of factions served to moderate change in government policy, but it did not rule it out. To the contrary, it sometimes served to provide a measure of pluralism without the sacrifice of party dominance. Leaders of small factions could combine to form a majority. The Miki cabinet, though short in duration, was organized as a response to the revelation of corruption under Tanaka. Nakasone's base within the party was relatively tenuous, but by skillful management of the possibilities available to him he emerged as a strong leader, visible on the international stage as a friend of President Ronald Reagan and able to promote a program for increased attention to national defense.

Diet members themselves required predictable help within their electoral districts and organized *kōenkai* support groups for the burdensome requirements of attention to funerals, weddings, and other responsibilities that devolved upon politicians expecting votes. They had access to little governmental support for staff and travel.[5] Since organizations of this sort were directed to personal rather than to party ties, an electoral base could be "inherited" by a representative's relative. Toward the end of the 1980s some 40 percent or more of members of the House of Representatives were second- or third-generation politicians.

The LDP's electoral base was strongest in rural Japan. Rapid industrialization brought with it very large migration from countryside to city, and the reallocation of Diet seats lagged far behind the facts of demographic distribution despite several court rulings that challenged the constitutionality of electoral results. Electoral "management" tactics of distributing votes to secure the election of LDP candidates in multimember constituencies also worked best in areas where older patterns of influence and loyalty persisted.

Because there had been little ideological difference between the Liberal and Democratic parties that joined to create the LDP, previous identification rapidly gave way to factional divisions. This was not the case with the Socialists, where differences between the two groups that had coalesced were deep and principled. The party's left wing maintained an unyielding stand on disarmament, insisting that the Self-Defense Forces were unconstitutional, and called for total neutrality in the confrontation between the United States and the Soviet Union. This persisted until the right broke away once more as the Democratic Socialists in 1960. The fervent and rigid Marxist analysis of the national and international situation that was offered by the left made it increasingly irrelevant to conditions prevailing in Japan, but the more moderate right also failed to gain a large following despite several much-heralded programs that were described as "new visions."

The local support groups organized by Diet representatives kept them reasonably close to the constituencies they represented, but this did not translate into widespread support for the LDP. On the contrary its electoral majorities declined throughout the decades of its ascendancy, and there were recurrent predictions of the coming necessity for a coalition government. This did not become reality until the end of the 1955 system until the 1990s; in that decade the Hosokawa and Hata cabinets included members of the Socialist Party. Prime Minister Murayama brought in LDP members, and at the century's end the Kōmeitō too joined in a coalition cabinet under Prime Minister Obuchi.

After 1990 the collapse of the Soviet Union and improvement in relations with Japan's East Asian neighbors rendered moot the rhetoric about cold war dangers and isolation from Asia that had been the stock in trade of left-wing politics. The Japan Communist Party, in the meantime, had reemerged from the secrecy to which it had resorted upon its banishment at the time of the outbreak of the Korean War. It was generously funded through the sale of its newspaper the Red Flag (Akahata), left-wing unions, and foreign subsidies. But it faced a difficult problem in avoiding identification with the Soviet Union. The Soviet Union had inherited the misgivings with which prewar Japanese had regarded Russia; its treatment of several hundred thousand Japanese prisoners in Siberia had been harsh and well publicized by those who survived, and its retention of the islands off the Hokkaido coast, which it claimed as part of the Kuril chain, stirred resentment that was exploited by right-wing organizations whose sound trucks and slogans resounded at commuter stations and wherever large crowds converged in metropolitan centers. Knowledge of the violence of China's Cultural Revolution, too, did not help the party in an increasingly prosperous and bourgeois Japan.

In addition the Japan Communist Party had its own skeletons to deal with. There had been instances in which ideological factionalism had led to the betrayal of comrades to the police in presurrender Japan, and there was suspicion of intelligence service involvement with the Soviet Union. Under such conditions, leaders like Nozaka Sanzō, a popular figure who served in the House of Councillors, did their best to distance themselves from talk of revolution and violence and explained that since Japan was a developed country, the kind of upheaval carried out in China would not be necessary. For these and other reasons the party never surpassed, nor did it even re-create, the high-water mark of 10 percent of the popular vote that it had won in the general elections of 1949.

A period of rule this long by a single party could be expected to produce instances of corruption in any country. Japan was no exception, and the scandals became more impressive as the level of affluence rose. The administration of Prime Minister Tanaka Kakuei was brought to an end in 1974 by public and press uproar at the revelation that he had accepted bribes from the Lockheed Corporation in return for interceding on its behalf in aircraft purchases. Tanaka had been hailed as one of a new breed of politicians. He came from a relatively modest background, did not carry the cachet of elite university study, and marshaled commanding strength within the LDP through generous and judicious distribution of government funds for pork-barrel construction projects. He authored, or was credited with, a book arguing the desirability of restructuring the Japanese islands to lessen concentration in the metropolitan areas and broaden regional development. The response from business groups and remote areas was enthusiastic and it seemed likely that Tanaka the "bulldozer," as he was called, would make the rough places plain as he already had transformed the accessibility of his native Niigata by sweeping expressways and high-speed railways. But his popularity was not proof against the indignation that followed the revelation of bribery, and by a foreign contractor at that. His hold, however, on what was now the largest faction in the LDP, remained secure even as the ponderous machinery of investigation and condemnation ground its way through the court system. At Tanaka's death in 1997 his attorneys had still managed to avoid his incarceration. The historian is inevitably reminded of the Siemens scandal of 1914, in which German shipyards had bribed key figures in the Imperial Navy to secure lucrative contracts. It is worth noting, too, that the Tanaka exposé followed hard on the Watergate incident in the United States, and that Japanese journalists took as their example the investigative journalism practiced on the other side of the Pacific.

In 1964 one of the most powerful of the new religions, the Sōka Gakkai, launched a Clean Government Party (Kōmeitō) as a counter to perceived corruption within the political system, but although the party survived and even gained a cabinet foothold after the LDP system collapsed, it never became a major force in Japanese politics. It became somewhat more removed from its original sponsors, but remained sectarian. In time, it too showed the effects of factionalism compounded by suspicion that it shared in the evils it professed to combat.

The LDP's long tenure in power during a period of steady economic growth led to easy exchanges between big business, the bureaucracy, and political parties, creating relationships that came to exceed the boundaries of public and especially press tolerance. The Tanaka Lockheed scandal had served to give notice, if any was needed, of corruption in high places, but in the 1980s revelations of "money politics" and brazen dishonesty were so numerous and jarring that LDP rule was finally shaken. The problem was in large matter systemic, and related to the high cost of elections. Support from businesses that organized giant testimonials, in return for which they were rewarded with preference in government contracts and insider information about bureaucratic changes and rules, tarnished the image of politicians involved, who were treated with withering scorn in the press. When a leading member of party councils with particularly strong connections to construction companies was discovered to have large numbers of gold bars in his apartment, the judicial system once again went into action. Newspaper readers now began to become accustomed to pictures of virtual armies of young agents of the public prosecutor's office carrying boxes of reports out of the offices of party officials, banks, and security houses in order to investigate the trail of money. Within a short period of time LDP dominance had given way to a brief period of coalition government.

LDP reformers began to form splinter parties with the hope of organizing a major opposition conservative group. Socialists, after years in the political wilderness, reconsidered their ideological objections to Japanese defense policies and alliance with the United States and joined with the splinter parties to topple the LDP cabinet of Prime Minister Miyazawa Kiichi, an able and durable leader who would appear again as finance minister in the Obuchi cabinet. It was Miyazawa's bad luck to take office just as discontent with politics reached a new high.

What emerged was a cabinet headed by a popular former governor of Kumamoto, Hosokawa Morihiro. He seemed briefly to represent the future and the past, for he was a descendant of the Kumamoto daimyo and also a nephew of Prince Konoe Fumimaro. He and his cabinet seized the momentum of their rise by announcing a program of decentralization, liberalization, and electoral reform. A new electoral bill returned to small, single-member constituencies and added proportional representation in the hope of building party strength.

The 1955 system had been ended, but not replaced. Hosokawa and Hata Tsutomu, his immediate successor, held office only briefly. In the general election that toppled Hata the new electoral reforms virtually ended Socialist hopes of taking power. Hata was followed by a coalition cabinet balancing the Socialist and LDP parties, and after its tenure, in 1996 power passed once more into the hands of an LDP prime minister, Hashimoto Ryūtarō. The reform impulse seemed temporarily stilled, and the realization grew that the abuses of "money politics" were systemic unless other provisions could be made for financing elections. This is, to be sure, a pressing problem in other democratic societies, including the United States. Nevertheless LDP leadership, albeit reestablished, was not to be as sure as it had been since 1955. Without a firm majority, it needed the support of other parties in the Diet.

In the 1990s politics to some degree took a back seat to economics as Japan went into a decade-long slowdown and recession. The end of the economic bubble brought additional revelations of unsavory politics, and it began to seem that a new element, organized crime, had been added to the equation of business, party, and bureaucracy. Even the Ministry of Finance proved vulnerable to charges of impropriety in tolerating irregularities in bank loans during the high tide of prosperity in the 1980s. The one incorruptible element in the institutional order seemed to be the judiciary; its processes were slow and it was understaffed, but it was also unchallenged by charges of impropriety.

These events nevertheless brought important changes to Japanese political ideology. The Socialists had lost more than Diet seats, for they had also turned their backs on the rigid opposition to the Self-Defense Forces and security ties with America that had characterized them since the 1952. More important, Japanese democratic institutions showed a resilience and strength that suggested they had taken deep root. Civil rights were scrupulously respected, and the courts were no longer subject to administrative guidance from the Ministry of Justice as they had been before the war. Postwar reforms had brought Japan a more independent judiciary.

The most striking contrast with the prewar Japanese government was surely the absence of a military establishment that could claim the authority of the throne. The Self-Defense Forces, under the control of the prime minister's office, lacked the secure power base the prewar armed services had known. A half century after their establishment, they no longer seemed a threat to the institutions of the new Japan.

The long tenure of the LDP was in good measure possible because of its ability to modify course and compensate aggrieved elements that suffered under the strains of rapid industrialization. Agriculture, small business, construction, and regional interests all had their day in securing access to special consideration. The LDP majorities were possible because Japanese of many sorts were voting for their self-interest.[6]

It would be pleasant to be able to report general enthusiasm for, and great and growing participation in, the operation of the postwar political institutions, but in this respect Japan has followed the path of other developed countries. Voter turnout has declined over the years. The long period of conservative domination had as an inevitable consequence a decline in expectations of change. Postwar Japan experienced a steady rise in standards of living, but there were few issues—other than "China," which was resolved in the 1970s with the recognition of the Beijing government—to arouse voters. Security, especially the nuclear umbrella provided by the American alliance, seemed secure and in any case in others' hands. The factional arrangement of the LDP worked against the emergence of a strong leader, and with the exception of a few figures like Ikeda, Ōhira, and the articulate Nakasone few figures of strength stood out. In the 1990s the administration of Hosokawa Morihiro was extraordinarily popular, but its tenure proved very brief. Indeed, his cabinet fell on the very issue that brought it to power when he refused to undergo the indignity of detailing his personal financial dealings. Ōhira, serving in the late 1970s at a time when the rush for industrialization had begun to run its course, was a thoughtful analyst of world trends who felt it urgent to plan for a day when the LDP would become more truly popular and when Japan, its economic development assured, could prepare for a new role, but his early death cut short that promise.

Another reason Japanese politics failed to catch the popular imagination was related to the power of the bureaucracy. In contrast to members of the House of Representatives, who have access to few of the staff services to which their American counterparts are accustomed, Japanese representatives have received minimal support, and yet they have required offices and staffs within their electoral districts in order to function properly. This has brought with it reliance on local support circles and, at the center, faction leaders with access to large-scale, national-level financing. It was probably the administration of Tanaka Kakuei in the early 1970s that brought "money politics" to a new height.

Budgets and bills, in contrast, tended to be prepared within the ministries by career bureaucrats. The need for central allocation and direction was great in the early postwar decades, and the result was a web of guidelines and administrative regulations within which enterprises and citizens had to maneuver. Over time this began to change, and the regular invocations of "deregulation" by press and leaders testifies to the difficulty of bringing this about. The scandals of the 1980s and 1990s, and the prolonged economic slowdown at the century's end, began to give promise of lasting change in these circumstances.

2. The Rise to Economic Superpower

Ōkita Saburō, as has been noted, recalled in his memoir a friend's saying in the darkest days that preceded the surrender that it might be possible for Japanese to achieve in business suits what they had failed to bring about in uniform. A few decades later those words seemed prophetic. It was not, however, that Japan had achieved the regional domination that its military leaders had fought for, but something much more extraordinary: a position as a world economic superpower, with an economy second only to that of the United States. The course of this has now become clear, but the cause and explanation are still subjects of intense controversy.

Chalmers Johnson's description of Japan as a "developmental state," in contrast to the "regulatory state" of more advanced economies and particularly the United States, has come to serve as one extreme in the polarity that has characterized the discussion.[7] Focusing on the Ministry of International Trade and Industry, Johnson discussed the way in which the state had utilized industrial policy in Japan's rise to international economic stature. Other authorities have criticized Johnson's rhetoric as overblown, pointing to ways in which MITI's plans had often been rejected by the private sector. In the aftermath of the "Asian crisis" at the end of the century some economists have rejected the entire idea of "economic miracle," arguing that the spectacular growth rates of earlier decades had represented a combination of inexpensive labor and foreign investment, and that the economies of Southeast Asia and South Korea were doomed to lag until a proper infrastructure of regulation and fiscal systems had been developed. Nevertheless, whatever the degree of applicability of the category of "developmental state" to the events of the 1990s, few can deny that Japan was precisely such a state during its rise to affluence. It is therefore the historian's task to find the continuities and discontinuities between this rise, and to try to discern ways in which industrial policy did or did not make a critical difference. For we begin with the facts of Japan's economic strength. Despite a decade of recession, at the end of the century the Japanese economy was second only to that of the United States. It constituted two-thirds of the entire Asian economy, including that of China.

Japan's economic rebirth was aided by a mixture of external and internal factors. It has already been noted that the Korean War, disastrous as it was for the Korean peninsula, was almost providentially fortunate for Japan in boosting the economy. Yet it also spurred a new round of inflation that soon threatened to limit, if not to negate, those advantages. The international situation thereafter continued to serve Japanese interests. The United States, eager to promote Japanese recovery and bond Japan's economy to that of the anti-Soviet bloc, sponsored Japanese membership in international trading bodies beginning with the Colombo Plan and going on to the OECD, and provided Japan with ready access to the American market. Technological and scientific changes also came to bear. In textiles the introduction and perfection of synthetic materials reduced the need for imported fibers. Japan now had full access to the raw materials of Asia—excluding China—which it had fought and failed to dominate. New patterns of transportation helped to lessen the disadvantages of which a resource-poor Japan had complained. Japan's industrial plants were in port cities. Near Tokyo, government assistance in a large-scale land fill made it possible for the Kawasaki Steel Company to construct a facility at the water's edge. Giant ore carriers and supertankers lowered the unit price of imported raw materials, making Japanese plants competitive against inland providers in other countries whose plants, in addition to being less modern, were supplied by rail or river barge. Japan was beginning again, but so was much of the industrialized world. Japan was not as far behind its competitors as it seemed, and by having to replace virtually all of its industrial plants, it was able to adopt fabrication methods of the greatest efficiency. At the Kawasaki steel plant on the Chiba coast ore was transformed into high-grade steel in one continuous, almost unbroken conveyer process. Soon Japan was a world leader in the construction of ships. The same yards that had launched the *Yamato*, the world's largest battleship, now constructed giant supertankers. A final advantage was the indulgent condescension of many Western and particularly American producers in electronics, machine tools, and motor vehicles; they little imagined that Japan could become a competitor, and in transferring technology to Japan welcomed the opportunity to recover some of their development costs. After complaints of unfair competition began to be heard, United States policy put first emphasis on the importance of security ties with Japan and resisted calls for retaliation. And finally Japan was at every point one jump ahead of its neighbors in Asia. China, the one country that might have served as a counter, was immersed in the throes of Maoist revolution, with drive and counterdrive all but eliminating the entrepreneurial flexibility and rationalization that lay ahead.

Internal conditions were, in retrospect, no less favorable to economic growth. The Socialist opposition demanded, and LDP governments agreed, that defense costs be kept to the minimum. A defense budget ceiling of 1 percent of the GNP, originally forced on uneasy conservatives by those who championed peace and democracy, gradually became a shibboleth of political discourse; that line was not crossed until the administration of Nakasone in the 1980s, and then only barely. This modesty in armament became a point of reassurance to Japan's Asian neighbors and the bedrock of the national economy; in retirement Yoshida Shigeru saw the "Yoshida doctrine" implemented by the products of his "academy," and emerged as the patriarch of postwar politics and policy. Conservative governments also made no effort to combat the country's "nuclear allergy" and yielded to popular demand for explicit restrictions on American introduction of atomic weaponry into bases maintained in Japan. The process involved a measure of deception on both sides, but the platform of refusing to make, harbor, or introduce atomic weapons was powerful when enunciated by the leader of the world's only country to have experienced atomic horror; as we have noted, its explicit formulation was a major factor in the award of the Nobel Peace Prize to Prime Minister Satō in 1974.

Institutional measures also came into play, and it is these that underline

Johnson's concept of the industrial policy of a developmental state. The most obvious of these involved direct government subsidies for selected industries and government and tax encouragement for reducing and eliminating non-competitive technology and equipment. The Ministry of Finance made important contributions through its ability to allocate capital and encourage loans through the Japan Development Bank, and the Ministry of International Trade and Industry mapped out programs to make Japan more competitive. Tactics took the form of bureaucratic counsel and "guidance" rather than explicit tactics of command, and they did not always succeed, with mixed results. A group of engineers evaded the establishment and formed a small company that became known around the world as Sony. Again, MITI's plans to rationalize the automobile industry by merging small producers with the giant firms ended in failure. But the emphasis on competitiveness through scale and willingness to tolerate delayed rewards for stockholders and especially workers made long-range planning possible.

Institutional arrangements favored the accumulation of capital by almost enforcing a high rate of savings and limiting consumption. Interest earned on savings accounts was not taxed, and interest paid was not deductible. Legislation improving health insurance was slow in coming, increasing the importance of private savings for future needs. Business taxes were moderate. The government did not oppose cartels, but encouraged industrial cooperation. A triangular pattern of mutual support developed among business leaders of the Japan Management Association (Keidanren), conservative politicians, and bureaucrats, and the latter often moved to business as consultants upon retirement from their ministries. One would expect such arrangements to be accompanied by protectionism. This pattern extended from agriculture, where rice was barred from import until the cabinet under Hosokawa in 1994, to consumer goods of every sort to give Japanese manufacturers an opportunity to develop economies of scale that would make them competitive, by which time the domestic market was securely under their control. Throughout Japan, measures protected small shopkeepers by ruling out large stores and by regulating and limiting stores' ability to stock competing merchandise. It is understandable that for decades non-Japanese importers found it difficult to penetrate the complexity of Japan's distribution system and administrative pattern. Even after formal tariff barriers were reduced and removed, invisible but effective nontariff barriers operated to slow imports. What it came down to was that the Japanese market was "open," but Japanese business society was not.

In the climate of consensus that developed, management did its full share to organize and control the market. Great concerns and banks held one another's securities and equities. Shareholders' interests were secondary to considerations of growth. Stockholders fared poorly, and an occasional protest was frequently stifled by hired toughs called *sokaiya* who were drawn from the fringes of society. The "state," one concludes, was important but not omnipotent; there was no sharp duality between state and nonstate, but a much more flexible pattern of largely consensual cooperation.

For many years the Japanese consumers bore the brunt of this. They paid high prices, had little recourse to other suppliers, and worked for modest wages. Consumers were the objects of ingenious and many-sided campaigns that emphasized the traditional virtues of work, patience, and saving.[8]

By the 1970s the United States led Japan's trading partners in demanding freer access to the Japanese market. Success was slow but continuous. With affluence within reach and trade surpluses in the process of constant growth, the Japanese government also turned to measures of social policy and benefits.

The process and sequence of this growth is conveniently summarized by Kōsai Yutaka.[9] The process of starting again which was addressed by the priority production campaign was essential to what followed, but it represented a temporary and emergency step rather than a long-range solution. This campaign was followed by work and planning between government ministries and organizations like the Economic Planning Agency and industrial leaders. The modernization and rationalization of the steel industry was a case in point. So too were steps to modernize the electrical power industry and chemical industry. Early plans were to include coal, but the narrow seams and mediocre quality of Japanese coal deposits led to conclusions that it wold be more efficient to substitute imported crude oil, which was becoming more plentiful as new fields came on stream in the Near East, and electricity as sources of power. Coal mine unions, needless to say, resisted this change but were unsuccessful. Modernization of the electric and thermal power industries brought about dramatic rises in the amount of power available. Hydroelectric and carbide plants in turn allowed for an increase in the production of vinyl and other synthetics, while the development of the chemical industry produced the fertilizers that boosted agricultural production.

Because the pattern of interrelationship that characterizes advanced economies was squeezed into a relatively short period in Japan, it soon drew the attention of the outside world and came to serve as a model for other countries of maritime Asia. Nothing better illustrates the speed with which rags were turned to riches than the automobile industry. American manufacturers had established outposts in Japan in the 1930s, but military leaders with an eye to national security and self-sufficiency saw to their departure. What remained was a highly inefficient industry that was able to produce mostly trucks for the military. In 1950 Toyota Company executives were in the United States, bound for Detroit in hopes of a bailout, when they learned of the Korean War and returned to Tokyo. The war provided opportunities for resuscitation of the company and industry, but despite that serious thought was given to abandoning the effort to build a domestic industry. Then came a slow increase in production, a fair amount of which went to the ugly and uncomfortable taxis that raced through empty streets with scant regard for rules or safety. As late as 1955 even Toyota, the industry leader, set for itself a puny goal of 3,000 vehicles a month. But then quality improved and production grew, stimulated in part by a fierce competition with Nissan. Smaller makers— Honda, Mazda, Mitsubishi, Isuzu, Subaru—and the industry as a whole successfully resisted MITI's attempt to rationalize and merge. By the 1960s Japanese makers, particularly Toyota, were ready to enter the American market. Their timing was good; Near Eastern instability was threatening the supply of gasoline, which made fuel-efficient Japanese cars more attractive. And in the competition the smaller and economical imports from Japan soon proved their worth.[10]

In turn the automobile industry generated satellite industries for the manufacture of parts, stimulated the need for steel, tires, glass, and electronics, provided off-season employment and income for farm workers who returned to their villages in the spring, and became as central to Japanese industrialization as Detroit had long been for the United States.

For several decades there was a steadily increasing tide of technology introduced—and often improved—in Japan. The U.S. dollar value of items imported, taken by half-decade and beginning in 1949–1955, rose from $69 million to $3.2 billion in the early 1970s, with a tenfold increase in items. In many cases these began as joint ventures with foreign, especially American, firms, and gradually became entirely Japanese as economic power and bureaucratic muscle came to bear.

The result was a surge of exports and a dramatic change in the makeup of those exports. During the 1970s Japan's traditional exports of textiles were matched, and then far exceeded, by the products of heavy industry, of which automobiles were an important part. Television sets and other electronic products grew similarly. Light industries like textiles, Japan's major export for so long, now declined in importance and gradually concentrated on serving the growing home market. Publicists exulted in this growth, and, with thoughts of the urban flowering of Tokugawa times, characterized it as a "new Genroku," or reached back to the dawn of Japanese history to vaunt it as the greatest boom "since [the legendary first emperor] Jimmu." Domestic investment in new and ever larger and more modern plants suggested that Japan was becoming the world's workshop.

Industrial and government leaders, however, continued to warn of Japan's disadvantages in raw materials, in particular its dependence on imported (crude oil) energy, to counter complaints about foreign access to the Japanese market. They feared rising imports as inflationary and evidence of an "overheating" economy, pointing to a basic vulnerability. To some degree their protestations seemed borne out by the early 1980s when the period of high growth came to an end. In 1971 President Nixon moved to end the fixed exchange rates that, at 360 yen to $1, had created so favorable a setting for Japanese exports. The flexible and "floating" exchange rates proved that the yen had indeed been grossly undervalued as it rose to 300, and subsequently peaked at 87 yen to the dollar. Japan was becoming less a protégé of United States policy, and in fact the Nixon administration temporarily prohibited export of soybeans under ancient World War I era legislation banning trade with "enemy nations." Worse was to come as Near Eastern instability brought about the first oil crisis, which increased (in dollars) the price of oil fourfold. The oil crisis created a sense of national emergency. Government and industry leaders orchestrated a skillful campaign for the conservation of energy. The lights of the metropolis were suddenly dimmed. Police checked implementation of restrictions on heating and air conditioning in office buildings. Radio, television, and the press reminded housewives of the importance of saving energy. Planning and moralizing combined to limit the damage of the oil shock, and by the time a second round of shortages struck at the height of the Iranian revolution in 1978, Japan, though no less dependent on oil imports than it had been before, was better prepared to deal with it than many of its industrial competitors. Meanwhile the export of fuel-efficient vehicles flourished.

As Japan's export surpluses grew, pressure came from many countries, but especially from the United States, for trade liberalization and better access to the Japanese market. Japanese government negotiators moved slowly and grudgingly, raising the possibility of a domestic backlash as a deterrent, while their Washington counterparts warned of the possibility of protectionist legislation in the United States Congress in response to job loss. In fact, however, the security tie with Japan was so vital to Washington strategists that successive administrations were able to head off advocates of protectionism. Frequently the Japanese government, even more anxious to head off such legislation, committed itself to voluntary export restrictions (VERs) under which industrial export quotas were allocated to exporters. One might consider this an updated version of the "gentleman's agreement" earlier in the century by which the Japanese government had sought to ease frictions caused by immigration earlier in the century. It was an interim and unsatisfactory system, however, for it had the effect of strengthening the governmental role despite regular American requests for reducing it.

As Japanese exports increased, there was widespread admiration for their management systems that seemed to result in products of high quality with a minimum of labor disputes. "Permanent employment" that secured jobs and eased fears of technological innovation, a seniority system of pay that guaranteed equity, and "quality control circles" that institutionalized worker participation in shop-floor decisions seemed the harbingers of a more humane and rewarding system. Management, not subject to quarterly bottom-line judgments on profits, was able to plan for a longer future, and that future seemed one of indefinite expansion and growth. It was particularly the employment and management systems that attracted attention. Japanese and American publicists credited a good deal of this to the role of an American management consultant, W. Edwards Deming, who visited Japan at the end of the Occupation and returned periodically thereafter. Deming, credited with formative influence on the postwar Japanese economy through his emphasis on quality control, was depicted as the prophet of the new industrial order, and journalists in the United States lamented that it was Japanese management, rather than American, that had heeded his advice. Japanese journalists also lauded him as a great teacher from abroad. It is probable that Deming's emergence as imported icon needs to be placed in a context that includes Ernest Fenollosa and other Meiji instructors, Chinese painters at Nagasaki who were hailed as great teachers, and Buddhist evangelists like Ganjin much earlier. More sober evaluations serve to condition these assessments.[11] Lifetime employment and seniority pay were recent and not traditional Japanese patterns. They were furthermore restricted to approximately one-quarter of the labor force. Nor did Deming's management philosophy spring full-blown from the ashes of World War II, for Japanese managers had followed Western and particularly American management philosophy, including "Taylorism," since prewar days. As with Fenollosa, it was rather the fortuitous appearance of a foreign voice that could be credited with inspiring trends that benefited Japan and pleased the outside world; this resulted in the elevation of Deming to near-mythological status.

The economies of South Korea, Taiwan, Hong Kong, and Singapore seemed to be taking Japan as their model, and in the 1980s interest in a "Japanese miracle" was followed by talk of an "Asian miracle." Japanese banks and enterprises made massive investments in Southeast Asia and—less so— in China, and some grumbled that the Co-Prosperity Sphere was being realized after all. Speculative expansion fueled the Tokyo stock market to an unprecedented height. Banks, awash with capital, competed for borrowers uncritically and poured their resources into other lending institutions that were even less discriminating. Real estate prices became astronomical and minute plots were said to bring prices wildly out of range at any comparative level. Japanese firms purchased signature properties in the United States and Europe, and individual buyers drove the market for Impressionist paintings at auctions throughout the West. Japan, so long a debtor nation, became the largest creditor nation in the world; Japanese purchases of United States Treasury notes subsidized the budget deficits of the 1980s, and now it was the United States that was the world's largest debtor nation. It seemed to some that the Japanese had developed a new variety of capitalism. Deferred gratification, long-range planning with bureaucratic encouragement, and harmonious relations between labor and management in the furtherance of the "house" or enterprise had brought Japan prosperity with remarkably equitable income distribution. All this stood in contrast to the ruthlessly competitive forces unleashed by an American-style free market.

And then, in the last decade of the century, the "bubble," that classic symbol of arrogance, conceit, and overconfidence in seventeenth-century Dutch genre paintings, burst. In the early months of the last decade of the century the Tokyo stock market index fell from 33,000 to 13,000. Economic growth declined sharply, then became flat and even negative, and Japan entered a decade of deep recession, the most serious since the war. The economic institutions and tactics that had seemed so strong proved remarkably resistant to altered circumstances; it turned out that it was easier to encourage growth from a modest level than it was to sustain growth in a mature economy. Early steps in liberalization sometimes led to massive errors in judgment; stories of materialism, greed, and corruption greeted newspaper readers day after day. Observers who had sought the elements involved in Japanese success now wondered why the new situation was recognized so late, and why corrective steps were so slow in coming.

One can say that the bubble burst of its own momentum and that valuations of real estate and equities had reached prices that were wildly out of touch with profits and reality. As the speculative fever rose, bad money had followed good; organized crime vaulted beyond its usual sphere of protection rackets to join the real estate and securities frenzy, and careless lending practices led to multiple liens on many commercial properties which now became targets for squatters and furtive, fictive corporations.

Rash misjudgment in economic decisions brought with it equally rash and brazen corruption in politics. A series of highly publicized scandals revealed ties between LDP leaders, construction interests, and campaign funding that helped unseat the LDP and led to the establishment of the Hosokawa cabinet.

Next came the Asian economic crisis. In many countries of Southeast Asia the flood of foreign investment capital had come before regulatory rules of transparency had been established, creating personal and familial political empires that proved fragile.

These events struck giant Japanese banks that had become some of the world's largest financial institutions. The collapse of the real estate market left a plethora of nonperforming loans, and the Asian crisis intensified the banks' misfortunes. Soon they were scrambling to meet regulatory requirements for liquid assets, and efforts to include in such reports the (now depreciated) equities of client firms whose equities they held raised fears about the larger financial system. The government allowed several banks, among them the Long-Term Credit Bank, to fall, and tightened its requirements for reports. Toward the end of the decade a massive infusion of public money began to stabilize the banks. Analysts noted that the crisis was more extended, more expensive, and its solution less thoroughgoing than the process whereby the United States government had dealt with American savings and loans institutions a few years earlier.

During all this businessmen found themselves unable to borrow money and the economy slowly ground to a halt. Government measures reduced the interest rate to the world's lowest—0.25 percent—but that made it the more necessary to borrow and less rewarding to save and lend. Outsiders had seen Japanese recovery as leading that of Asia, but Japan, so recently the locomotive of Asian growth, seemed instead the caboose. Now the institutions on which so much had been predicated, particularly permanent employment and seniority pay, stood in the way of the restructuring and rationalization that the United States economy experienced in the 1980s. These brief paragraphs can only begin to suggest the complexity of the interrelationships at work, but they may suffice to explain the toll the decade of the 1990s took on the shibboleths of the 1980s: wise bureaucrats, cautious leaders, far-sighted planners, and familial consensus.

At century's end the Japanese government responded with impressive efforts to stimulate economic activity through public spending on infrastructure. Few streams remained unbridged, few shores lacked bulwarks, and the countryside changed as contractors searched for highways to repave. The return of free-spending habits nevertheless remained out of reach; instead consumers saved for an uncertain future. Japan's savings rate, always high, passed 20 percent, while America's, where confidence grew, entered the negative column.

A final and perhaps serious factor was that Japanese costs had outrun productivity gains. The years of the 1970s and 1980s left the country with price and salary levels that made Japan less competitive than it had been. Major Japanese exporters were moving production facilities to other shores. Within Japan a web of institutions and regulations that favored agriculture and small shops combined with a distribution system to keep prices the world's highest. Salaries were high, but prices even higher. This, at a time when the flow of the postwar generation into retirement was about to put maximum pressure on savings and pension provisions, promised more problems for the new century.

Remarkably, however, economic distress also brought with it relaxation of long-standing curbs on foreign investment. When a major Japanese brokerage house entered bankruptcy it was taken over by a New York firm. When the giant automobile maker Nissan found itself unable to borrow money in Japan it turned to the French government and Renault for a solution. The Ford Motor Company gained control of Mazda, Daimler-Chrysler negotiated with Mitsubishi Motors. New York financial institutions sent squadrons of executives to buy up real estate at bargain rates.

A thoroughgoing solution, if one was to be found, thus required more transparency, greater freedom from administrative guidance, and a more sensitive response to international trends and examples. Such globalization, however, would bring in train further rationalization, reduction of productive capacity, and a threat to the web—or womb—of security and safety that the postwar Japanese economy had made for itself. The social and political consequences of this were unclear; the Japanese establishment was not prepared to surrender unconditionally to the "rational choice" posed so confidently by overseas consultants.

These matters, even when presented in so cursory a discussion, are of considerable comparative and theoretical interest. The first concerns the significance of Japan's economic transformation from postwar orphan to economic superpower a few decades later. Writers who have discussed Japan's economic growth have made much of its industrial policy, sometimes going so far as to see in contemporary Japan a new sort of capitalism with severe challenges for classical economists who abhorred state intervention or control.[12] Some Japanese social scientists have placed this in larger theoretical context to class Japan's society as a "house" or "family" operated on post-Western and probably superior principles.[13] For over a decade, in addition, alarmists and prophets of many stripes held Japan up as a model or threat for other countries.[14] Paul Krugman, on the other hand, speaks for economists in dismissing Asian "miracles" and compares the analysts' enthusiasm to the respect that was accorded Soviet planning in the 1950s.[15] It is to be noted that Krugman differentiates between Japan and its neighbors. Their growth, he argues, was for the most part dependent on larger inputs, particularly of labor, while Japan increased individual productivity. The issue is not resolved, although Japan's extended recession in the 1990s has lessened the fears of those who viewed its growth with alarm. The argument continues to be refined and sharpened.[16]

3. Social Change

Japan has undergone immense social change since the end of the American Occupation. There is a large body of literature treating aspects of that change, and it may seem rash to deal with it within these confines. To some observers Japan seems almost an entirely different country; others emphasize the underlying continuities. Here it will be suggested that the changes, great as they have been, have come within a pattern in part universal, experienced in all developed and industrial societies, but also marked by distinctive features that stamp the result as quintessentially Japanese. The historian George Sansom once wrote that the Japanese, despite the appearance of "borrowing," had never surrendered their inner cultural citadel. The distinguished Chinese philosopher Hu Shih, meanwhile, wrote that Japan's changes, while far more rapid than those in China, were nevertheless superficial and that China's ultimate appropriation of Western culture would prove more enduring. Each comment suggests an underlying "Japaneseness" that resists transformation. One suspects that this is true with every long-established culture, especially one so long isolated and parochial as Japan's. Nevertheless it is clear that Japan has changed profoundly since 1952 in ways that inevitably have to affect its internal politics and external relations.

POPULATION

For the first three decades of the twentieth century Japanese leaders asserted that its growing population required outlets, and used that argument to justify expansion. By the year 2000, however, the Japanese islands supported twice the population they did in the 1930s and at a far higher standard of living. The greater Tokyo metropolitan area alone contained some 35 million people, more than the entire Japanese population in the early years of the Meiji period.

Japan's population swelled once again after World War II. In addition to several million servicemen recalled from distant fields of battle, tens of thousands of civilians were repatriated from all parts of Asia. The desperate shortage of housing was made worse by this population flow, and an already densely populated land had somehow to absorb the newcomers and returnees. As in every postwar society, birth rates rose. The Japanese government, which had discouraged birth control before the surrender, now reversed its policies and relaxed its prohibition of abortion by permitting exceptions for medical, eugenic, economic, or ethical reasons, though it continued to limit access to birth control pills until the late 1990s. With industrialization and the population flow to the cities birth rates began to level, and then fall.[17] Japan thus followed the pattern of other industrialized societies.

The postwar population bulge was thus slowed and finally stopped by a combination of social and economic factors. Mention should also be made of campaigns urging families to limit their size to two children, "one princess, one boy" *(ichi hime ichi Tarō)*. In time, as the population growth slowed, stopped, and then reversed, government leaders occasionally expressed alarm and seemed to advocate less career and more children for young women, but to little effect. Nor was Japan affected by flows of immigration that reinforced the work force; instead its population leveled off at approximately 125 million, making it number eight in the world.

The result of all this was a population differently structured from those of other industrialized societies, with a steady increase in the proportion of elderly Japanese, while the cohort of those younger was significantly smaller. Women married later and had fewer children. In addition Japanese were healthier and lived longer; indeed, the country achieved the world's highest longevity rates. The work force that was contributing to Japan's national health insurance and social security through its taxes and payroll deductions, while cost was rising steadily. The Ministry of Health and Welfare estimated that by the year 2020 one-fourth of all Japanese would be over the age of sixty-five. More specifically, the proportion of the population aged sixty-five or older, which numbered 12 percent in 1990, was 16.6 percent in 2000, and was projected to be 20.3 percent in 2010 and 24.5 percent in 2020, making Japan the "grayest" of the advanced economies. Japan thus faces problems in domestic social policy and international competitiveness in years to come.

During the half century that followed the war, Japan experienced urbanization that moved tens of millions from country to city. At the time of the San Francisco Treaty of Peace some 44 percent of the Japanese population was engaged in agriculture. By 1970 that percentage had fallen to 17, and by the end of the century it was closer to 4. Even among those who remained in the villages, agriculture was often a part-time occupation, its income supplemented by off-season employment in the factories of nearby cities.

In the face of such population density, land, of course, was more precious than ever. For many years income tax lists showed land developers prosperous out of all proportion. The nature of agriculture also changed. Rice continued to be the principal staple, but truck gardening for the urban market grew in importance. In the absence of bulk, quality and labor-intensive specialty took an ever more important part. Apples, grapes, and strawberries, protected from weather and insects by individual bags, were produced in growing amounts for metropolitan restaurants and as seasonal gifts at the exorbitant prices required to support the labor-intensive manner of production.

To supplement the ever smaller share of food produced domestically, Japan imported from abroad, principally the United States, and soon ranked as America's largest overseas market for agricultural goods. Rice, however, remained protected by legislation until a shortage in the 1990s forced the government to make at least a temporary change. Government measures to support agriculture predictably produced sharp criticism from abroad. United States producers of citrus and apples, to say nothing of rice, pressured their government to demand relaxation of Japanese import restrictions. Tokyo government leaders moved reluctantly and grudgingly, in part from a natural desire to avoid complete dependence on outside food, and more because of the strength of the Japanese farm lobby. At times they were caught in their own devices, as when the Ikeda government encouraged lemon growing on marginal dry land only to face pressure from overseas exporters who promised better fruit at lower prices. There were genuine concerns for the competitive ability of Japanese agriculture in an open market. These are reflected in the title of a massive volume, *Can Japanese Agriculture Survive?*[18]

In most parts of Japan the farm village changed radically. With government encouragement and subsidization there was a degree of rationalization of holdings in order to encourage more efficient tillage and higher individual productivity. This quickly led to a proliferation of ingenious farm machines, which, though small in comparison to what was used in Western countries, mechanized many tasks like rice planting, tilling, and reaping. The traditional villagewide tillage practices, beginning with seedbeds held in common and rice planting on a cooperative basis, celebrated in the "paddy planting" *(ta-ue)* chants, would never be the same again. But the government's plans for cooperative holding of machinery soon proved at odds with desires for autonomy and independence as even smaller machines were purchased by individual farm families. The result was a countryside overcapitalized in machinery just as it had formerly been overcapitalized in labor. Money needed to finance purchases and payments for the new machinery could be borrowed from the local agricultural cooperative, but the strains of repayment made off-season employment in factories, often in distant locales, a necessity. The country became dotted with small supplier firms whose reliance on such labor enabled the giant export-oriented firms to keep their costs low. There was little talk of permanent employment or seniority pay for these workers, although their contribution to Japan's international competitiveness was important.[19]

Farm village patterns changed. A large number of workers considered "agricultural" were only part-time; machinery, wives, and weekend work kept things going. Where the commuting distance made it possible, farm wives joined the flow of commuters to small factory-supplier firms. In this context, as William Kelly has shown, the mother-in-law, once the tyrannical despot who persecuted her son's wife as she entered the family, could become herself exploited, charged with the care and management of the children as well as farm tasks.[20] In other and more remote areas, where small-scale industrialization impinged less directly on rural life and emerging middle-class patterns of outside employment expectations were less common, the drudgery of rural life led to a large-scale exodus from the countryside. Farmers who stuck it out found themselves hard-pressed to find wives. One of the more remarkable consequences of this was a search abroad, especially in the Philippines, for young women willing to be recruited for marriage, life, and work in Japan. This practice never occurred, to be sure, on a very large scale, but was interesting for the way in which "internationalization" would affect patterns in that part of Japanese society most resistant to outside influences.

Another influence for change in rural Japan followed from the efforts of conservative governments to reward voter loyalties, increase economic effectiveness, and improve administrative rationalization. The Kumamoto village of Suye Mura, made famous to Western readers by John Embree's pioneering prewar study, gradually proved, in follow-up studies by a Japanese anthropologist, to lose its flavor and interest as it became a minor stop for a rural bus.[21] Motor roads came with motor vehicles. The local rail lines, many dating back to Meiji times, were becoming antiquated and their equipment expensive to maintain. Buses took their place. Administrative rationalization changed jurisdictions and boundaries. New marketing centers developed. Commerce, in turn, led to easier travel, and as metropolitan Japan became more pervasive, a nostalgia for what was being lost brought journalism, television, and tourism to areas that were once remote. Beginning in the 1960s the growth of high-speed rail travel, the much touted "bullet trains," brought more and more of Japan within reach of metropolitan travelers. Moving on new, standard-gauge rails and avoiding (expensive) population centers for lines and stations, the *shinkansen*, as the new train was known, opened up new areas of Japan. Prime Minister Tanaka's concern for his origins and backers in Niigata led to the opening of a service through the Japan Alps to the Japan Sea coast. The 1998 Winter Olympics at Nagano greatly benefited from this twentieth-century equivalent of the log-rolling that attended the expansion of the narrow-gauge local lines in the days of Prime Minister Hara in the first decade of the twentieth century.

CONSEQUENCES OF INDUSTRIAL GROWTH

Industrial growth drew the tens of millions added to Japan's population to the cities. In relative terms Japanese urbanization, as Gilbert Rozman has shown, was always high, but in the second half of the twentieth century this proportion grew sharply.[22] This was particularly evident in the two major metropolitan centers. In the countryside around them localities that had still been rural in the 1950s became completely developed, and as mass transportation improved, workers could come from ever farther settlements to work in the metropolis. Some had expressed the hope that better and faster transportation would result in a diffusion of what had been concentrated at the center, and that the development of new residential and industrial areas would reduce the pressures on major cities. Prime Minister Tanaka Kakuei published a book proposing full development of the Japanese archipelago, and used this as one argument for expansion of the network of high-speed rail lines. These goals were implemented to some extent; Kyushu became a center for high-technology industries, and small-scale and supplier industries developed all along the Pacific coast of the old Tōkaidō route. Nissan abandoned its principal factory near Tokyo for a new site in Kyushu. But in a more basic sense the new communications promoted even greater centralization than before. More and more firms felt the need for headquarters in the Tokyo area. "Salary men" commuters could come from ever greater distances. Academics found it easier to accept teaching responsibility at what had been regional institutions without changing their place of residence near the libraries and resources of the metropolitan area. At century's end there continued to be talk of moving or at least scattering government agencies and ministries to outer areas, and Gifu was proposed as a center for the new government. But no one expected this to happen, or lessen the importance of Tokyo or of Osaka in the development of national affairs and the economy. Indeed, the evidence that greater centralization was to some extent paralyzing local and regional administration often produced nostalgia for the regional autonomy of earlier days.

Drab worker flats proliferated on the outskirts of major cities, and the single-family homes of earlier suburbs became increasingly prized and expensive. Commuter rail stations were surrounded by acres of bicycles during the day. Those who could manage it added automobiles, but with the shortage of parking space and the extraordinarily expensive toll charges for bridges and expressways their utility for average workers was largely limited to weekend use. To qualify Japanese for the exacting requirements set by the government driving-lesson campuses sprang up, their small-scale evocation of reality in tortuous roads, narrow intersections, and turns making them modern equivalents to the suggestions of nature in Japanese gardens of earlier days. In fact the automobile frequently replaced the garden, for regulations requiring that vehicle owners provide off-street parking led to the sacrifice of garden walls and entrance porticos. Registration regulations added an early and thorough mechanical inspection of vehicles that often seemed to favor replacement over partial reconstruction.

In preparation for the 1964 Olympics, Tokyo authorities undertook the construction of an impressive network of thruways and overpasses that improved access to the downtown area. As these developed, old neighborhoods were sacrificed to construction or darkened by overpasses, and it became increasingly rare to find clusters of old-style, small-scale, family merchant shops near the center of major metropolitan areas.

Urban congestion made it more attractive and important to travel to other parts of Japan where this was less of a problem. The sense of something romantic and disappearing in the old Japan led the National Railways to sponsor travel under the slogan "Discover Japan." Government radio and television, the Nihon Hōsō Kyōkai (NHK), balanced this with feature coverage of provincial customs, festivals, and life. The historic capital of Kyoto, which was spared the wartime bombing, was naturally most visited, but distant mountain temples and holy places that had known only the quiet tread of straw-shod pilgrims' feet had to add parking lots for the tourist buses that charged up the mountain roads. Japanese who could manage it had long been formidable travelers, but in the postwar years virtually everyone could afford some travel. Lower- and middle-school children made "study tours" to Kyoto and other historic sites. Their elders scoured Japan for places of interest and relaxation and then turned to overseas journeys, beginning with Hawaii. By the late 1970s Japanese travelers overseas numbered 4 million, and within twenty years this number had climbed to 10 million.

Within the city limits life varied from the quiet dignity of upper-class dwellings to the squalid and crowded hostels of part-time workers in Tokyo and in Osaka, but in a material sense almost all Japanese were better off than they had been. There was, in fact, a remarkable uniformity about the urban society that had emerged. One aspect could be traced to the optimism that accompanied the years of unbroken economic growth. Conditions had improved and most people expected them to improve still more. Regulations and protections operated to keep prices and services high, but as salaries rose most Japanese accepted this as a form of social justice for the tiny shops and elderly clerks of neighborhood clusters. Government regulations ruling out "large stores" unless they had the concurrence of neighborhood consensus (in practice, bureaucratic approval) cemented the monopoly of small-scale shops and also, it should be noted, the ability of suppliers to enforce their own controls about competing lines and especially imports. As economic friction with Washington rose, each of these features would be the object of criticism and calls for structural change, and each such proposal had electoral and hence political consequences. A consumer movement was long in getting under way, and in its absence the interests of elements of the status quo naturally had priority. By the late 1990s the prolonged economic downturn and rising unemployment brought some cracks in the pattern, but although successive cabinets routinely called for administrative reform, this seldom led to action.

Poll after poll confirmed the fact that the great majority of Japanese saw themselves as members of the middle class. For seniors the recent experience of defeat and destitution brought this home; for others it was the fact and expectation of prosperity. During the first four of the five postwar decades these expectations were borne out; the media popularized slogans that indicated satisfaction with the diffusion of relatively inexpensive appliances like the electric rice cooker that lessened the drudgery of the traditional kitchen. By the 1970s tastes had turned to more expensive levels of consumption, encapsulated in the "three C's" of car, color television, and room cooler. In the 1980s salaries continued to improve, jobs were plentiful, and a large-scale market developed among young women for imported designer bags and styles. For those who could manage it, foreign travel provided access to such goods at their source. Goals of personal consumption had replaced, seemingly forever, the goals of national power.

Industrial growth of this order also brought with it environmental degradation of every sort. The Japanese had prior experience of pollution, to be sure; the agricultural wasteland produced by effluent from the copper mines at Ashio has been discussed earlier. What was new about Japan's environmental problems in postwar years was that they affected many more Japanese and bore most heavily on urban dwellers. By the early 1970s pollution from cars, trucks, and buses was so pervasive and deadly that morning radio news announcements posted emission readings for the most congested intersections. There were reports of schoolchildren collapsing on the playground, and of bizarre patterns in which particular elevations like the second floor might be more dangerous than the floors below or above. City rivers and canals were becoming oily and refuse-laden with pockets of stagnant water, and familiar landscapes disappeared from view in the smog. Government officials responded rapidly and on the whole effectively to the dismay shown by urban and suburban dwellers. The LDP, aware that public outrage would soon threaten its dominance, at last began to show interest in environmental issues, particularly from the standpoint of public health. A 1967 law still spoke of legislation that would "harmonize" the considerations of environment and economic growth, but by 1970 pollution became the principal concern of what became known as the "Pollution Diet."

Legislation was now toughened, and the following year an Environmental Agency was established within the prime minister's office to ensure implementation of the laws, oversee planning, and establish standards for water. Significantly, it also included an Atomic Energy Bureau to work for public safety in the drive to overcome public hostility to the development of atomic power plants. A decade of effort brought significant gains in air pollution, and by the mid-1980s Mt. Fuji was once again visible on the horizon for Tokyo residents. By then Japan was providing overseas aid for programs to fight pollution in Mexico City.

The movement for reform drew particular strength from a growing national revulsion over the case of Minamata, a disaster that attracted international attention. Minamata, in Kumamoto Prefecture in Kyushu, was the boyhood home of the journalist Tokutomi Sohō, whose call to young men to industrialize Japan and make it a "floating wharf" in the Pacific, its skies black from the smoke of factory chimneys, struck responsive chords in mid-Meiji ebullience. At Minamata a carbide plant allowed its mercury-laden effluent to run into the bay in disregard of warnings. The mercury entered the food chain as local fishermen worked in the bay, and resulted in the "Minamata disease." Dreadful symptoms of every description afflicted hundreds of villagers before the matter became clear. Through years of contest, corporate indifference and government disregard created a scandal that made Minamata a byword for the dangers of unchecked industrial pollution.

A final feature of urban life in twentieth-century Japan was its remarkable—by world standards—quality of public order and personal safety. The Japanese police seemed to have been transformed from the often harsh and minatory bullies who prided themselves on being the "Emperor's Police," into reasonable, helpful figures who showed solicitude for little children and drunks and directed anyone looking for an address in the maze of lanes and streets from giant neighborhood maps posted in ubiquitous police boxes. To some the polite presence remained more intrusive than desirable, and measures of preventive detention concerned many, but it was clear that the Japanese police system made for public safety and order that were the envy of observers from other countries.[23] Japan scored well in worldwide surveys of protection for individual civil rights. Police, in fact, were so careful about crossing the line of constitutional rights that on at least one occasion this operated to the advantage of Aum Shinrikyō, the sinister cult that had, as was described earlier, taken advantage of its status as a religious organization to plan large-scale terrorism in the Tokyo subways in 1995. Cultists had infiltrated the police and Self-Defense Forces. Police were not, to be sure, caught completely off guard, for they were assembling a file and were prepared with antidotes to the poison gas. Nevertheless it seems probable that their meticulous observance of constitutional protections for groups certified as "religious" worked to favor the cultists. In prewar Japan the police would have infiltrated the cultists instead of the other way around, and in this case their conduct stood in remarkable and admirable contrast to the intrusive vigilance of prewar days.

LABOR

Japan's economic growth in the years after 1955 was made smoother by the course of its labor relations. The immediate post-Occupation years, as we have noted, were ones of intense social and class friction. Industrial rationalization and productivity-oriented measures seemed threatened by the way the labor movement had developed, and they were not carried out without sharp conflict. The great strike of Miike coal miners provided an object lesson in the sort of disruption government and business leaders wanted to avoid. In the Nissan Motor Company, management plans to replace a plant that was fast becoming obsolete threatened worker jobs, and resulted in another bitter strike in 1953. Remarkably, no comparable disputes roiled the waters in the years that followed.

The postwar labor movement, it will be remembered, reproduced much of the factionalism of prewar times. A social-democratic right wing, a Socialist left wing, and a Communist-dominated group vied for power and influence. The radicals' goals were in part political; the planners of the February 1947 general strike that was banned by General MacArthur had hoped to unseat the Yoshida cabinet and share in whatever power arrangements might result. As the controls exerted in late Occupation years during the Korean War came to an end under an independent Japan, the labor scene in the 1950s seemed to many observers fraught with dangers of political instability.

It is useful to see the incorporation of labor into an overall organizational promotion of productivity, as a sort of "social contract."[24] When MITI established a Japan Productivity Center it included, in addition to bureaucratic and management leaders, labor leaders as well as academic experts. This should be understood as the product of bureaucratic concern in the administrative state, and it was part of a campaign to checkmate the radical left in the labor movement.

Management, in turn, gradually came to accept labor participation in its own councils. To have this make sense, though, it was important that a common goal of enterprise prosperity through productivity be accepted, and the union movement that resulted featured an organization by enterprise rather than by craft. In this pattern the largest unions, because they represented the largest national enterprises, were government workers, rail employees, and schoolteachers. As government servants, however, they did not have the right to strike, and in consequence they were limited to devices like rail slowdowns that did little to endear them to exasperated commuters. Salary raises, however, were worked out on a national scale by semiannual campaigns that established a bonus that became a regular part of worker expectations. And, coming as it did in one relatively large amount, the bonus in turn contributed to savings, and thereby to economic growth.

Management further solicited worker participation by the organization in major firms of quality control circles in which workers competed with proposals for improving the way things were done. It was this stress on quality, attributed fortuitously to the advice of a sage American management specialist, that caught the attention of observers overseas.

After the recession of the 1990s, however, there were indications that change was in the offing. Lifetime employment, even though limited to the industrial elite, was beginning to make enterprises slow and sluggish to change. A population in which the overwhelming majority considered themselves middle class did not offer a fertile field for labor struggle, but the loosening of corporate bonds—by choice for some, and by discharge for others— might change matters once again. In the decade of the 1990s unemployment rose to nearly 5 percent, and no one could be certain of its consequences. In addition there were signs that a generation that had experienced only prosperity was disenchanted with the prospect of lifetime employment in a single organization. Government regulations were beginning to be questioned in a mood for deregulation that, although it proceeded with tortuous slowness, was clearly moving in the direction of a more flexible labor market. The press carried tales of firms in which the labor force, including office "salary men," was downsized by a variety of tactics. There was less talk about "Learning from Japan," the theme that had been so common in the third quarter of the century. Nevertheless, characteristics of enterprise loyalty and productivity for international competitiveness seemed certain to continue to serve Japan well.

WOMEN

Throughout Japan's past, major crossroads in social history have found institutions that were obsolete brought up to date in dramatic feats of social engineering. This was true of the early Meiji period, and the postsurrender years saw a comparable shift in the institutional structure of the social order. Across-the-board change did more than bring institutions up to date, but often out-ran actuality. In the Meiji countryside feudal relationships could long outlive the progressive proclamations of the new government, and in postsurrender Japan sweeping announcements of change from SCAP, embodied in legislative reform, often described goals better than they did actualities.

This was particularly the case with women's rights. The 1947 Constitution contained provisions more advanced than those of the United States, where the political struggle for equal rights had required many decades of effort. The immediate gains for women in the postwar setting were immense. The recasting of the Meiji Civil Code that accompanied the constitution's provis-ions for equality dismantled the despotic samurai house system that the Meiji government had decreed for all Japanese. Suffrage, free choice in marriage, equal opportunity in education, and new opportunities in the work force changed the future for younger women and girls. As in other countries, war-time employment had also left some with expectations for a more equal future.

The rush to the cities and the burgeoning industrial growth of the 1960s of course required the contributions of female as well as male workers. It was to be expected that the obstacles to effective implementation of the new rights would be many. One was the modest expectation of many women in tradi-tional families who were programmed to put "house" *(ie)* and family values first. Another was the paternalistic attitudes of labor bureaucrats and indus-trial leaders who, by claiming to protect women from many kinds of work, kept them as male preserves. Most serious and lasting was the assumption of many industrialists that, while women might enter the labor force, they would do so chiefly before their years of child bearing. It was possible that they might return in their middle years, but would once again be restricted to lower levels of work and reward. The employment ceiling for women in major firms was more opaque than it was glass. In the last decades of the century a number of court cases saw women claim the rights they had been promised; out of this came remedial legislation that was hailed as pioneering, but most efforts lacked enforcement provisions and the struggle was far from won.[25] The de-pression of the 1990s brought a sharp end to industrial growth, and in that climate opportunities were unlikely to improve. As elsewhere, the last hired were the first released.

In other respects the position of women changed dramatically. Prosperity and employment produced urban streets thronged with fashionably dressed and confident young women. As suburbs grew in density and distance from the metropolitan center they produced a world run by women because men were at work in the city. Some recalled the Tokugawa days when samurai wives became the center of family and communal life while men were off on distant ceremonial duty in Edo to accompany their lords. Toward the end of the twentieth century Japanese men declined in status while women rose. Key decisions of residence, schooling, and consumption lay with the wife. "Managing" a household with an absentee husband and father became the subject of women's magazines that grew in number. Even at higher executive levels, the press occasionally reported instances of speedy and unanticipated divorce after the breadwinner returned home with his final lump sum severance payment. Women were important investors in the brokers' offices that opened in department stores. Their recreation, in classmate groups dating from elementary school, was visible in restaurants, domestic travel, and foreign tourism.

To many it seemed that Japan's slow progress in harnessing the ability of women in key positions was an important factor in its political and economic difficulties. A higher proportion of women in managerial positions must in time break up the old boys' network that works to unite the "iron triangle" of bureaucracy, business, and politics that has proved so difficult to reform through deregulation and administrative revision. This in turn would require a higher proportion of women admitted to key training grounds like the Law Faculty of Tokyo University, from which so much of the bureaucratic center in ministries like those of finance and foreign affairs is drawn. The present percentage of women in elite schools, some have suggested, needs to be increased by a factor of four or five to right this balance. The skill and integrity with which individual women in selected posts have worked—Ogata Sadako as the United Nations High Commissioner for Refugees is one example— indicates what can lie ahead for future growth. In the meantime politics continues to be a largely male world, even more so than in other developed countries, despite the constitution's promises of equal treatment.

4. The Examined Life

As Japan entered the road to full development, education became more important than it had ever been. Higher education grew rapidly. Former Special Higher Schools became prefectural universities, community or two-year colleges mushroomed, and in the cities private institutions grew to mammoth proportions. The proportion of high school graduates that continued on to higher education rose steadily. The growth of the student body outran the supply of adequate facilities for many years, but with the economic growth of the 1970s and 1980s new buildings and entire campuses began to relieve such pressures. It is true that from Meiji times on educational opportunities had beckoned able and ambitious youth, but the growth of higher education in the last quarter of the twentieth century marked a new stage in Japanese development and modernization. Entrance into the labor force at a proper level became the focus of domestic and family concern. Education provided that path.

As commuter "salary men" were absent from suburban homes for long hours each day, the job of readying children for the schooling that would determine their life path devolved upon wives and mothers. The "education mama," as they were termed, bore the responsibility of seeing to it that her children, especially sons, secured entrance into prestigious schools that would provide launching pads for further success. Examinations and preparation for examinations became the focus of early life and continued through entrance into college and university. Employers, not to be outdone, selected their cohort of privileged "permanent employment" workers through examination, as did the bureaucracy. Private universities, facing enormous numbers of applicants, employed entrance examinations that were, for reasons of efficiency and speed, increasingly factual and multiple choice. Proposals for a national educational testing service that could replace this multiplication of effort were frequent, but even when adopted and applied the examinations were usually supplemented by those set by institutions themselves.

Lower school education in consequence became oriented more and more toward the examinations that would follow. Instruction and application produced some of the developed world's most impressive test scores in mathematics and science, but the social sciences and humanities were too often set courses and chronological recitals of facts. For the accumulation of such facts an auxiliary industry of cram schools known as *juku* flourished throughout the land. Bonds of family weakened under the pressures of urbanization and commuting, and Japanese increasingly looked to the severity of school standards to supply the discipline that was no longer provided in the home. In prewar days the model pattern of organization and expression had been that of the military with its ranks and divisions, but postwar Japan came to rival this with its terminology of education. Even popular religions like the Sōka Gakkai frequently offered believers and catechists academic rank as steps toward advancement in belief and in the organization.

This new structure was not without its frustrations. City high schools, as Thomas Rohlen has shown, varied in quality and student makeup to constitute a multitrack system, and by high school years students' futures were often predictable.[26] Industries also differentiated between workers who entered with and without higher educational background, and listed and reported the groups separately. In higher education there was a distinction to be made between the private universities that financed themselves by tuition and entrance examination fees and the great national universities that were able to restrict student numbers and applicants. Consequently failure to enter a prestigious institution often resulted in one or more years spent preparing for another try at the examinations; during this period they were frequently referred to as *rōnin*, the term once reserved for masterless samurai.

Public lower school education became the battleground of politics and ideology. The contestants were the Teachers' Union (Nikkyōso), whose leadership ranged from liberal to left, and Education Ministry officials, who drew on public alarm over schools' lack of discipline to force their own agenda of character and patriotism on a generation that seemed in danger of losing both. Education Ministry approval of textbooks, secured in the 1960s, was followed by the rejection of several popular texts that had roundly denounced prewar and wartime policies and atrocities. These restrictions in turn were challenged in legal action by Professor Ienaga Saburō, whose text had been rejected. A long-running court case extended over decades and ended ambiguously with the judicial verdict that the ministry had the right to check textbooks before certifying them, but in this case had overreacted. Each side saw the other in darkest tones; liberals and leftists feared restoration of prewar indoctrination and whitewashing of wartime wrongs, while education bureaucrats and right-wing critics argued the dangers of producing a generation that would feel revulsion for its forebears. Right-wing ideologues were only too happy to enter this struggle, and made every effort to harass Teachers' Union activities and meetings. They did this by creating such disturbances through the use of sound trucks and threats of violence that communities thought twice before permitting the use of their facilities for Nikkyōso conventions.

In the great struggle against the Security Treaty in 1960 the armies that marched on the prime minister's residence and the Diet were overwhelmingly composed of students. They brought down the Kishi government but not the LDP and its policies. In the rapid economic growth that followed politics took a back seat for most Japanese, but student radicalism turned upon itself as conflicting ideologies and shades of radicalism made dormitories into battlegrounds in which the violence far exceeded that of the "storms" of prewar Special Higher Schools. The early 1970s marked a high point of violence with the revelation of startlingly brutal conflicts among student extremists. Some Japanese radicals went on to participate in international terrorism in Israel and Korea, but thereafter extremism gradually subsided.

The radicalism of the generational divide in education in the 1960s extended to other sectors of Japanese society. In the preparation of exhibits for the 1964 Olympics in Tokyo, the Japanese Christian community was torn by bitter recrimination between young radicals and their seniors who had, they charged, collaborated with wartime government policy. Few had opposed the war publicly, and most had accepted government directives to merge the denominational bodies into a United Church of Christ. Seminaries and even churches found themselves embroiled in disputes no less bitter than those that characterized education.

Within a decade, however, the prosperity and growth the economy produced increased attention to material comfort and rewards. More and more consumer concerns like the "three C's" became the focus of attention, and in the drive to obtain these products workaday values gradually came to replace ideology. As textbooks gradually became less "controversial" and said less about the war, many Japanese were astonished to find that they now drew criticism from abroad. Many felt it was easier to forget the past, and somehow kinder to the families and survivors of an era that had passed. Left-wing militancy declined, but right-wing militancy did not. One issue on which left and right could unite was the sense of Japan's victimization in the atomic holocaust of 1945.

It is not surprising that many young people reacted against the structured rigidity of Japan's examination life. As prosperity spread some found it possible to pursue their education abroad, particularly in the United States, where many private institutions were searching for students able to pay their higher tuitions. Of the thousands of Japanese students who went abroad, some were to be found even at unpromising community colleges, beneficiaries of their family's ability to free them from the rigors of the Japanese system. Many thousands more swarmed to the registers of new and less selective private institutions throughout Japan.

Some young people delayed their revolt until their higher education had been completed. So deviant a cult as Aum Shinrikyō, with its grim plans for mass terrorism that have been discussed above, was able to attract the loyalties and abilities of competent young graduates, some from major universities. Commentators focused on these events to relate them to a valueless generation of young Japanese with links to a more general, postnuclear philosophy of Armageddon. Japanese, not unlike people in other countries, sometimes spoke of their puzzlement with the younger generation, which they referred to as the "new species," *shin jinrui*. In the materialist drive for commodities, old bonds and loyalties seemed weaker. School officials wrestled with problems of violence in middle schools, sometimes directed against teachers, but most frequently against newcomers and outsiders. In the decade of the 1990s, marked as it was by a prolonged economic downturn, constant press coverage of scandals that rocked the banks, security houses, and even the Ministry of

Finance seemed to indicate that aberrations of traditional values were not exclusive to the younger generation.

An additional indication of changing times was the prominence of underworld forces in the last years of the twentieth century. The *yakuza* had roots in Tokugawa society, when samurai authorities permitted limited autonomy to these organizations in return for outward submission to government control and order. In prewar Japan, they developed close ties with right-wing nationalist and political organizations, and frequently benefited from the favor of the military, who found their jingoistic chauvinism useful in cowing critics. The disorder of postsurrender Japan offered new opportunities for protection rackets and the intimidation of otherwise law-abiding commercial interests. On the whole, however, underworld violence was directed against competitors, and the larger populace was unaware of, or indifferent to, such activities. Enterprises found it useful and sometimes politic to employ underworld-related toughs to police annual meetings in order to intimidate forces of dissent. *Yakuza* were structured and visible, with signs announcing the headquarters of regional gangs posted sedately in office buildings.

The immense prosperity of the new order with its startling profits brought *yakuza* new opportunities for respectability and wealth. Threats of violence found banks and security houses willing to make special arrangements in loans and rigged profits, and the feverish escalation of prices during the bubble years of the 1980s found land speculation on credit particularly profitable. In the downturn of the next decade, revelation of gang–business interrelationships brought this state of affairs into the open. By this point *yakuza* protection systems existed for virtually all restaurants, bars, and other places of pleasure, and the line between the licit and illicit, previously distinct, became blurred.

But commentators who lamented this as a sea change in Japanese social values were nevertheless exaggerating. What had changed was the new visibility of such activities, brought to the surface by a curious media and more confident gangsters. The vast majority of young people continued to conform to the demands of school and examination. As jobs became harder to find in the straightened circumstances of the late 1990s, the likelihood of hedonistic and ideological revolt became less common.

As Japan entered the new millennium a confluence of social and economic forces brought signs of profound change in the expansion of higher education that had so recently seemed irreversible. Years of a low birth rate, in which Japan barely sustained its population, and persistent recession threatened the future of many of the private colleges that had been established. Shrinking enrollment caused by demographic shifts was made worse by economic instability that made families think again about the costs of higher education for sons and especially daughters. The attrition was not likely to be limited to recently founded junior and two-year colleges. In 2000 the Ministry of Education, noting that enrollments in even long-popular faculties at national universities were declining sharply, announced a policy of privatization in which faculties would be required to have enough students to justify their continued existence. The postwar pattern of initial liberal education followed by specialization was also being rejected as expensive and outmoded. There was thus danger that higher education would become more specialized and employment oriented; the examined life for students was, some thought, going to be replaced by an examined life for institutions.

5. Japan in World Affairs

Japan's recovery of sovereignty in 1952 was not total, for the San Francisco Treaty of Peace was linked to acceptance of American leadership in the struggle with the Soviet Union. The treaty itself was signed by some but not all of Japan's wartime enemies, and it was left for the Ministry of Foreign Affairs to work out understandings with the new nations of Southeast Asia one by one. In each case the United States stood by to coordinate and help. The treaty was also partial in that it left unresolved the issue of both Okinawa, which remained under United States rule until 1972, and the four northern islands of Habomai, Shikotan, Kunashiri, and Etorofu, which the Soviet Union had occupied in the closing days of the war. By the treaty Japan renounced "title and claim to Sakhalin and the islands adjacent to it over which Japan acquired sovereignty as a consequence of the Treaty of Portsmouth of September 5, 1905," but that did not apply to the Kurils, which had been in Japanese hands since the Treaty of St. Petersburg in 1875. Prime Minister Hatoyama journeyed to Moscow in 1954 to work out an agreement to end the state of war with the Soviet Union. A formal treaty of peace, however, proved impossible to arrange because of the USSR's retention of four islands close to Hokkaido which it claimed as part of the Kuril island chain. Japan then and thereafter insisted that they were properly Japanese territory, and the "Northern Territories" issue, vigorously exploited by the Japanese right wing, remained a stumbling block to closer relations. A treaty of peace with the Republic of Korea was worked out only in the mid-1960s. Relations with China were also dependent on the approval of the United States. Secretary of State John Foster Dulles had tied Senate approval of the San Francisco treaty to Japan's recognition of the Republic of China on Taiwan rather than the People's Republic of China in Beijing as the legitimate government of China. Throughout the two decades that followed, Japanese intellectuals and commercial interests made numerous efforts to work out relations with the Chinese mainland and attempted to separate politics from economics, but it was not until the United States adopted the Shanghai Communiqué worked out by President Nixon and Premier Chou En-lai in 1972 that the Tokyo government felt it possible to follow suit. Prime Minister Tanaka Kakuei journeyed to Beijing to inaugurate formal relations with the People's Republic, while Japan's Taiwan representation was modified to nonstate, ostensibly nongovernmental form. For two decades Japanese policy was thus tied securely to Washington's requirements. Prime ministers or their surrogates routinely traveled to Washington for White House and Pentagon meetings before taking office, and Washington had reason to expect compliance and support from Japan on major issues of international relations.

For Japan the tie with the United States had great advantages. To a large degree it removed foreign policy issues from the realm of public debate by making it possible to shift responsibility to the United States. In the absence of the opportunity to take a stronger position in international affairs Japan's became a reactive posture, responding to but rarely initiating moves. During a period when any Japanese initiative would have been greeted with distrust and suspicion by other countries in Asia, this cautious stand had its advantages.

With United States sponsorship, Japan gradually gained membership in international organizations like the Colombo Plan, the OECD, and especially the United Nations, which brought it formal equality in world affairs. And then, as the Japanese recovery of the 1960s and 1970s took hold, it became clear that the "San Francisco system" had immense and favorable consequences for all of Asia. For Japan it meant low defense costs, American sponsorship in international trade, and ready access to American technology and the American market. In the three decades after 1951 more than 40,000 contracts for technological transfer cost Japanese purchasers $17 billion, less than the annual American expenditure for a single year during that period. This transfer provided the basis for virtually all of Japan's modern industries. American sellers were glad to recover part of the cost of development, and found it difficult to imagine that they would be faced with Japanese competition in the near future. By the 1980s Japan was no longer dependent on imported technology. Many United States commentators were prepared to lament the effects of technological transfer to Japan, but others, with a longer view, preferred to regard it as a triumph of statecraft comparable to the rebuilding of Europe through the Marshall Plan.

By then Japan had been stabilized, and through it the entire Pacific area. These policies first contained, and then co-opted, the People's Republic of

China, which in effect became part of the San Francisco system after 1972. The American presence operated to reassure the victims of Japanese aggression and gradually made the Japanese presence acceptable once more throughout the Pacific area. Japan rapidly became the world's largest trading power, and led in imports of resources of every description. One analyst speculated that Japan had grown the equivalent of the total GNP of France in the decade after 1985, or the equivalent of that of the Republic of Korea each year. By the 1980s Japanese manufacturers were spending more on new plants and technological research than their American counterparts, even though the American economy was still 40 percent larger.

More important, Japan began to serve as a locomotive of growth in the Pacific. In the 1990s it became clear that much of this growth had been marred by corruption and favoritism, but by then it had played a major role in developing societies that had lagged behind. Japan now had access to resources and markets it had long sought in the area, and its exports and technology began to change the face of Pacific Asia. The commentator Kaname Akamatsu described Japan as the point, or leader, in a formation of flying geese. The Republic of Korea, Taiwan, Hong Kong, Singapore, and the ASEAN nations seemed for a time destined for instant development, and talk of an "Asian miracle" and of South Korea, Hong Kong, Singapore, and Taiwan as the four "little tigers" expressed the optimism of the 1980s. One wing of geese became several as regional patterns developed. Taiwanese investment in the Philippines exceeded that of the United States, Hong Kong funneled investment money from Taiwan and other countries into the People's Republic, and very large sums of Japanese investment capital flowed into Thailand and Indonesia.

Japanese began to think of themselves as economic leaders of Asia. Bookstores reflected what many called the "Asianization" of Japan, and Fukuzawa Yukichi's call to his countrymen to "part with Asia" and embrace Europe seemed at last to be obsolete. In the early days of the San Francisco system, the Eurasian mainland had seemed stable and secure in contrast to the disorder of the Pacific periphery, but by the 1980s the reverse was the case. The power of this example was not lost on leaders of the People's Republic of China and related to their program of "four modernizations" inaugurated in the 1970s. Then, with the China "problem" solved, the single most divisive issue in Japanese politics and diplomacy had apparently been resolved. Adherence to the coalition of nations led by the United States no longer threatened to separate Japan from its neighbors.

It must be kept in mind that Japan was more the beneficiary than it was the initiator of policies that combined to favor it. The economic benefits of the Korean War have already been mentioned. The importance of Japanese bases to American prosecution of the war in Vietnam was also critical; Japan benefited once more, though less than before, and its economic gains were to some degree canceled out by the stimulus the war provided for political and particularly student protest. Soviet obduracy on the question of the Northern Territories was useful to a conservative government defending its close ties with the United States. Astonishment at the violence of the so-called Cultural Revolution in China counteracted sentimental pleas for a closer association with the People's Republic, and in 1989 the massacres at Tiananmen further served to consolidate the Japanese public's satisfaction with the course their leaders had been obliged to choose. Partly in its own defense, one suspects, the People's Republic chose this period to resurrect the atrocities committed by Japanese in Nanking, and graphic reminders of those outrages served to rally national cohesion among overseas Chinese as well.

To be sure, Japan's path within the Western alliance was not without its problems. The first item concerned trade and the burgeoning trade deficit incurred by the United States. Japan, although its agricultural purchases were important to American farmers, sold far more than it bought, and as Japanese automobiles gained market share in America at the same time that American factories fell idle, press and politics combined to see Japan as a menace once again. American critics charged that Japanese manufacturers profited unfairly from and infringed on patents and technology acquired through joint agreements, and contrasted the ease of penetrating the American market with the labyrinth of regulation and approvals that awaited them in Japan. Even after those barriers began to give way in response to increasing exasperation, the mutual cooperation of Japanese firms allied in the *keiretsu* system constituted additional obstacles of informal, nontariff barriers. Japan became the United States' most important trading partner after Canada, and Japan became America's largest market for agricultural goods, but at every turn—from citrus to apples to rice—it seemed that obstacles to free exchange remained in place. Japanese, for their part, pointed out that American manufacturers were slow to study the Japanese market and adjust manufactures to its needs, and contrasted this with the meticulous research carried on by Japan's great trading companies. Nevertheless on both sides progress, while slow, was steady. The prosperity of the 1980s brought a rapid growth of Japanese purchases of American manufactured goods as well as agricultural products and specialty goods, only to have the collapse of the bubble reverse this process once more. Thereafter circumstances seemed to operate in Japan's favor yet again. A prolonged period of economic expansion in the United States reduced sensitivity to issues of trade, while the rapid rise of American trade deficits with China lessened Japan's visibility.

A second area of contention concerned Japan's contribution to collective security under terms of the Security Treaty with the United States. American forces in Japan, which numbered 37,000 at the century's end, were virtually all stationed on Okinawa. They had only recently begun the practice of joint exercises with Self-Defense Forces units, and in a 1997 understanding Japan agreed to cooperate in the event of war, but only by agreeing to evacuate civilians from war zones. Over the half century of the treaty's existence the United States, in response to frequent congressional and editorial comment that Japan's was a "free ride" at American expense, had urged Japan to assume more of the costs of the U.S. bases, and did so with general success. In 1999 Japan's contribution was $4 billion, an impressive sum, particularly when compared with South Korea's $290 million or Germany's $60 million contributed for bases within their borders. This sum went to salaries, services, and especially land rent and constituted a major element in the economic balance sheet of Okinawa, helping to ease the islanders' discontent over the disproportionate share of the burden they carried. American negotiators, at least until the end of the cold war, also worked for greater Japanese spending on defense, but did not shake the Tokyo government's determination to hold that expenditure to approximately 1 percent of Japan's gross domestic product. Nevertheless, as the overall dimensions of that product grew the 1 percent also grew, and by the year 2000 the Japanese defense budget may have been second in the world after the American.

With economic recession in Japan in the 1990s even that expenditure became contentious. Leading politicians deplored the high cost of "host country" support of American forces, and in the 1999 elections for governor of Tokyo the successful candidate, Ishihara Shintarō, campaigned for the removal of Yokota, the largest remaining American air base on the home islands. Public opinion polls showed that 70 percent of Japanese supported the alliance, though 67 percent thought there should not be so many American troops in Japan.

In major issues of foreign affairs Japan held to the line set by the United States, but occasional American complaints of insufficient support constituted a third problem area. Japan's overwhelming reliance on Near Eastern oil led it to take a cautious stand on Israel in order to avoid offense to Arab states. By the 1980s imports of Near Eastern crude were rising so rapidly that commentators speculated on the possibility of an unbroken line of tankers navigating the seas between the Persian Gulf and Tokyo Bay. The oil shock of the 1970s, as has been mentioned, was particularly acute for Japan. When the Gulf War broke out following Iraq's seizure of Kuwait in 1989, Japan cited its constitutional restrictions to avoid sending even noncombatant help. On the other hand its financial contribution to the United Nations military campaign was so large that Japan virtually financed that effort, only to receive criticism of its "checkbook diplomacy" from its allies.

It now became urgent to devise some way of participating in allied efforts, and the unarmed "Peace-Keeping Operation" that was established during the brief cabinet headed by Prime Minister Miyazawa—related to, but distinct

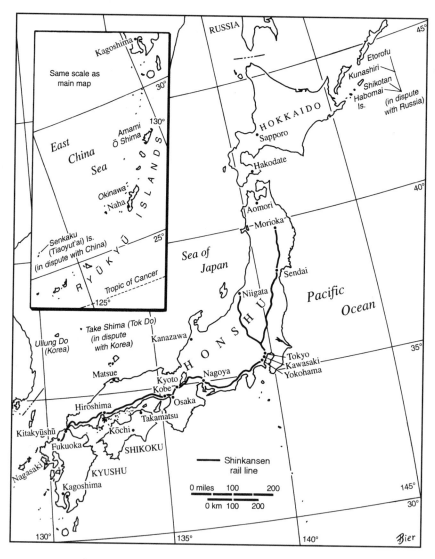

9. Postimperial Japan in 2000, showing "bullet train" (shinkansen) lines.

from, the Self-Defense Forces—soon made important contributions in Cambodia and other areas.

Japan's reluctance to violate or amend Article 9 of the 1947 Constitution also stood in the way of a more prominent role in the United Nations, whose charter Japan was pledged to uphold by the San Francisco Treaty of Peace. Collective security of the sort required in Korea or the Persian Gulf required more explicit participation than Japan felt itself free to offer, and as long as that was the case Japan's desire for a permanent seat in the Security Council, something that would restore the prestige it had known (and discarded) in the League of Nations, seemed likely to be denied. Even without such status, however, Japanese representatives had given distinguished service in Cambodia and in specialized agencies, notably the office of the High Commissioner for Refugees.

In a more basic sense, however, Japan was one of the Great Powers despite its failure to win a permanent seat in the United Nations Security Council, for its membership in the ranks of the Group of Seven Developed Nations had come several decades before the end of the century, and successive prime ministers beginning with Nakasone were photographed more nearly at the center of the group of leaders. In 1885 Fukuzawa Yukichi wrote, in a New Year's Day editorial, urging that Japan join the leading Western powers. He pictured a Treasure Ship with the Seven Gods of Fortune as passengers, but instead of Daikokuten and the others his gods were Britain, France, Russia, Germany, Austria, Italy and the United States. He expressed the wistful hope that on some future New Year's Day Japan would be on board with the others, an eighth god of wealth. A century later he had his way; Japan, instead of requiring an additional berth, was one of the original seven. By 2000 four such summit meetings had been convened in Japan, the last of them at Nago, in Okinawa. This would have astonished Fukuzawa even more.

6. Japan at Millennium's End

For many elderly Japanese the death of Emperor Hirohito in 1989 at the age of eighty-seven marked the end of an era. The sovereign, who would be posthumously known by his era as Emperor Shōwa, was the longest-lived emperor in Japan's history, and his reign of sixty-two years was far longer than that of his grandfather, Emperor Meiji. He had far outlived the other leaders of World War II. Born in the Meiji period, he was tutored and schooled by General Nogi, whose ritual suicide upon Meiji's death closed the age of samurai. He grew to manhood as an exemplar of Taishō liberalism, a symbol of its hope and failings. As crown prince his journey to England and Europe in

1921, the first venture abroad by a crown prince or emperor, found him astonished and delighted by the apparent freedom and popularity of the British
ruling family. On his return to Japan the stern formal caste that had enveloped
the imperial family since the Meiji Restoration once again closed around him.
He was reprimanded for the apparent insouciance of a party with his recent
schoolmates and friends. His father's mental illness brought him to the fore
as regent, and the disaster of the Tokyo earthquake forced postponement of
his marriage and accession ceremonies. Once united with his ancestral shades
in the mysteries of the Shinto accession ceremony in 1928, he soon encountered the effects of military insubordination in the Kwantung Army's murder
of Chang Tso-lin. When he had expressed his displeasure with the prime minister for his failure to follow up a promise to investigate that outrage, Tanaka
resigned and soon died in near disgrace.

Now his senior advisers expressed alarm; the emperor might be thought
to exceed his constitutional role, and in so doing he could subject himself
and them to displeasure and even danger. The young emperor resolved, he
later recalled, to maintain a low posture and limit himself to the formal requirements of his role.

In the 1930s those duties also led to his assumption of the role of generalissimo, mounted—albeit awkwardly at first—on his white charger, reviewing
endless lines of marching men, honoring the Kwantung Army commander
after the seizure of Mukden, and even installing him as his aide-de-camp in
the very heart of the palace.

The violence and terrorism of the army revolt of February 1936 broke his
resolve to remain inactive. "They are killing my ministers!" he fumed, and
he helped force his military chiefs to suppress the mutiny and execute its
leaders, over the anguished pleas of General Honjō, his aide-de-camp.

The year following Hirohito began to preside over councils of war, first
against China and then against the Western democracies, unable or unwilling
to deflect the disastrous course Japan pursued in its determination to bend
China to its will and strike at those whose resources would make possible a
regional command. Frustrated by the factional feuding and ideological postur-
ing of those who professed to worship him, he was comfortable with Konoe
Fumimaro and respected Tōjō Hideki, the men who presided over the initia-
tion of the China and Pacific wars. His sense of duty and reserve made him
a silent presence at every major council in those fevered years, no doubt gratified by the early victories he greeted with congratulatory rescripts to his soldiers and sailors, then sharing the sense of fatalism with which they waited
for a final "decisive battle," not recognizing that battle when it came on Okinawa, and bowing to the certainty of atomic annihilation at the last.

The early successes of the Pacific War found the emperor greeting each advance with a rescript expressing deep satisfaction in the valor and dash of the imperial forces. When success was followed by distress and danger Hirohito chose to remain at his palace command post, sharing—in form, at least—in the deprivations of his subjects and watching from the bunkers of the Fukuage garden in the palace compound the collapse of the realm he had inherited. But when the Suzuki cabinet, unable to resolve the issue in the face of army demands for one more battle, turned to ask Hirohito to decide, he chose surrender, optimistic that the *kokutai* would somehow be preserved. Not to do so, his recorded statement told a people that had never heard his voice, would lead to the total extinction of human civilization as well as violate the solemn obligation handed down by the Imperial Ancestors to strive for the happiness of all nations as well as the well-being of his subjects.

Soldiers on distant islands, young pilots in *kamikaze* Zeros, and sailors on every ship had gone into battle in the emperor's name, and frequently to their death with his name on their lips, but on the Allied side hatred had focused more on Tōjō than on Hirohito, from fear of stiffening resistance and feelings that he might be instrumental in future plans. Despite this, reprieve and retention for the Son of Heaven were far from certain, and if United States—including MacArthur's—strength had not been brought to bear, Hirohito would almost surely have been in the dock at the Tokyo trials that convened in 1946. His absence, as we have noted, was awkward for prosecutors and defendants alike, and his retention and resurrection, though as the "symbol" of the unity of the people, eased immediate transitions while complicating the longer retrospect.

Events bore out Hirohito's optimism that the national polity would be preserved. The Americans, convinced of his importance to secure compliance and ward off radicalism, managed to spare him the indignity of the Tokyo tribunal. He was advised to renounce his claims to divinity—claims he had never made and was uncomfortable with—and he was prevailed upon to support the efforts to make him a "People's Emperor." SCAP officials encouraged him to leave the palace to meet his people, and he himself began to find the promises of the Charter Oath of 1868 a way of reconciling his new stance with his grandfather's early image.

Then, as economic growth began to change the face of Japanese society, the emperor changed once more. He now became the model of the family man in a new era of privatism and prosperity. Cautious sparring in carefully structured press conferences began to show a grandfatherly, kindly gentleman, rather elegant in his simplicity and reticence. He ventured to visit Europe once again, and then, with more success, the United States. Everywhere he went people waited to see what he would say about the recent past, but learned little from formulations that expressed regret rather than remorse. Hirohito had become the ultimate survivor. When he lay at death's door throngs of Japanese gathered outside the palace gates, and even former American president Jimmy Carter appeared at the Double Bridge to add his name to those who wished him well.[27]

It is interesting to note that Hirohito's long rule had only one previous counterpart, in that of the Emperor Go-Mizuno-o (1596–1680) at the very beginning of the Tokugawa era. Go-Mizuno-o dutifully issued the Code for the Nobility *(Kuge shohatto)* at the shogun's behest, but when he became irritated by shogunal interference he abdicated in favor of his daughter (the second shogun's granddaughter), though he continued to be a force in Kyoto for another half century. Hirohito may have considered abdication after the Tokyo tribunal had rendered its decision, but instead presided over the court for the half century that followed. Both sovereigns were subject to military pressure, the one to abdicate, and the other to MacArthur's determination that he remain on the throne. Earlier emperors, shrouded in the mystery of divinity, lived in obscurity, and the aura that surrounded them was a form of folk religion. In contrast Hirohito's final illness was chronicled by the media in excruciating detail, with daily blood counts and transfusions carefully recorded. Even Emperor Meiji's final illness, we are told, found doctors hampered by taboos that made it difficult for them to diagnose and treat him, but Hirohito lingered, almost forbidden to die. When the end did come the ceremonies were part private, a faithful re-creation of Shinto mysteries culled from centuries past, and part public, as world leaders led by President George Bush sat quietly on uncomfortable chairs in a chilling rain under a large tent, before coming forward to bow slightly in respect. After this the catafalque, borne silently by young men from a village near Kyoto traditionally assigned this task, was transferred to a vehicle that then moved slowly through the crowded streets bound for the tomb in Hachioji. Few lives have known more change or more contrast; grandson of the first modernizer and the last divine ruler, Hirohito somehow symbolized the ambiguities of Japan's twentieth century.

Hirohito was succeeded by his son, Akihito, whose era was proclaimed to be Heisei, a couplet with an essential reference to peace. The new emperor began his reign with a pledge to support the 1947 Constitution. He had had foreign tutors in his youth, and his marriage to a commoner was hailed as significant for the new democracy. It was even more so with his son, the new crown prince, who had studied at Oxford and whose bride had a degree from Harvard. An awkward term, "internationalization," *kokusaika,* was briefly the slogan of the day. Colleges and universities competed for Ministry of Education approval for new schools of international studies, and the ruling family, far more "international" in its orientation than would have been thought possible a century before, exemplified this enthusiasm. But adherence to the constitution meant that decisions would be made on the far side of the moat that surrounds the palace, and in any case the kind of charisma that Hirohito, for all his reticence, had exerted was unattainable for his successors. They will never have been revered as demigods, nor remembered as symbols of the restoration of a devastated country.

The last decade of the millennium was also the first of the new reign, and it quickly found the Japanese polity in uncharted seas. The disintegration of the Soviet Union brought a new world order, or more properly disorder, in which long-smoldering nationalism and racism in Eastern Europe, the Near East, and Africa led to crises and joint action for collective security in which Japan played little part. The Soviet collapse made it certain that United States priorities, which had placed security so far above commerce, would change in time.

The dramatic growth of the Chinese economy and the attraction that it seemed to offer to Americans led to talk of a "strategic partnership" that made even doubters in Japan think better of the security arrangement with the United States. Abroad, the image of a Japan in recession contrasted with a China showing new vitality. That China, furthermore, was flexing its muscles at Japan's expense, often to the cheers of overseas Chinese and students. As the Chinese state gained confidence—or perhaps because it lacked confidence—it frequently selected Japan as its target. Claims to the Senkaku (Tiao-yu-tai) Islands off Taiwan and vigorous exploitation of the Nanking outrages of 1937 roiled those waters frequently. Japanese reluctance to offer more than "regret" helped keep the issue of the China War alive. In such a climate Japanese trade and investment consequently moved farther south, to the ASEAN countries of Southeast Asia. This was not the world a generation of Japanese had come to expect.

There were also continuities. In the separation of Taiwan from the mainland that began with its acquisition by Japan in 1895 there lay seeds of further problems, as Beijing grew more truculent and Taiwanese voters elected governments less willing to talk of reunion on terms set by Beijing. The possibility of an attempt to subdue Taiwan by force disturbed policymakers in both Washington and Tokyo. Korea remained divided and isolated; a hostile North Korea was provocative in occasional forays into Japanese waters, and it alarmed Japanese by testing missiles that overflew Japan to land in the North Pacific.

Fortunately, however, relations with the Republic of Korea improved dramatically in the late 1990s. Democratically elected governments replaced the military dictatorships that had ruled the southern half of the peninsula since the 1950s. Greater confidence and prosperity were reflected in moderation of animus against Japan, and Japan and the Republic of Korea joined with the United States in efforts to deal with North Korea on issues of power and atomic development. A visit to Japan by Korean president Kim Dae Jung in 1999 left far warmer feelings than had prevailed since the Pacific War, and raised hopes of healing the many rifts between the two democracies. Efforts went forward for talks between North and South Korea, but they had made little headway by 2000. Japan and its Washington ally had vital stakes in this, for a renewed outbreak of war on the peninsula would involve United States forces on Okinawa and, inevitably, Japan.

In many postwar years such uncertainties would immediately have been reflected in Japanese politics, but in 2000 this did not seem to be the case. There was greater confidence, and more unity, in Tokyo. The long sway of the Liberal Democratic Party ended when a Diet vote of no confidence toppled the Miyazawa government in 1993, and for a brief moment a "reform" administration under Hosokawa Morihiro, wildly popular in Japan and welcomed overseas, held out the hope of a new politics. Before the Hosokawa cabinet fell, as it soon did, an electoral system in place since the 1920s had been reshaped and the import of rice, long banned, became possible.

Then came the full consequences of the bubble economy that had burst; revelation of scandals, dishonesty, clumsy delay in taking remedial steps, bankruptcies, threats to job security, and rising unemployment all combined to shake faith in the wisdom and integrity of Japan's long-respected bureaucrats. Japanese investors beat a hasty retreat from the signature properties in the United States whose purchase had alarmed Americans. Additional problems related to Japan's success in treating public health and improving the environment. The Japanese population was living longer and also aging rapidly, and the system of health insurance and social security support was coming under heavy strain. A generation of Japanese was moving toward retirement, and their pension funds, given the puny interest rate that would prevail for a decade, offered little guaranty for the future. Economic recovery became ever more urgent, at home and abroad.

Clearly there was no lack of problems facing Japan as it entered the new millennium. It is reasonable to suppose that the San Francisco system that prevailed for half a century is due for change. Japan is fated to become once again an active participant in world affairs. Its Security Treaty with the United States holds good, but in the absence of the former Soviet threat its priority must decline. Yet this is not to suggest a new military role, for Japan's abhorrence of war seems deep and firm. Nevertheless American hegemony will lessen, and some new balance of the United States, Russia, China, Japan, and one or both Koreas must emerge.

Japan's society has shown enormous resilience and strength in the past millennium. A thousand years ago the court society of Lady Murasaki's *Tale of Genji* was giving way to that of warriors whose rule was fastened on the country for eight hundred years. The Meiji revolution disarmed those samurai and armed the state instead. The new Meiji empire flourished briefly, but in defeat that state was itself disarmed. Reconstruction brought enormous economic influence and power, but that structure too was not immune to cyclical decline. Yet no student of the Japanese past could doubt that a nation so gifted, resourceful, and courageous was destined to play a major role in the millennium now begun.

FURTHER READING

NOTES

CREDITS

INDEX

Until the end of World War II serious study of the history of Japan was seldom undertaken in the Western world, and the few hardy pioneers who did so received little or no institutional support. The Pacific War, as the Japanese term it, changed that; governments and military authorities sponsored programs in Japanese language study, and after the war was over a number of products of such programs set about to develop Japanese history as a field of study and establish it as an academic discipline and regular field in schools of historical study. It requires little space to say what was available in English at the outset. The three volumes of *History of Japan* by James Murdoch, published in London by Kegan Paul, Trench Trubner and Co. in 1925, took the story through the Tokugawa period but concentrated its attention on "the Century of Early Foreign Intercourse (1542–1651)," its middle and best volume. This emphasis on Western contact foreshadows a great deal of writing by Westerners, and if accepted uncritically could lead to a distorted view, as though the arrivals of St. Francis Xavier, Commodore Perry, and General MacArthur constituted in each case the appearance of a deus ex machina, with supporting roles for Will Adams, Townsend Harris, and W. Edwards Deming—on which everything would hinge. Murdoch taught Latin and Greek in Japan, and had among his students Natsume Sōseki, who had difficulty in distinguishing between his Scotch brogue and Greek; he presented old-fashioned political history with old-fashioned judgments rendered pontifically and provided, as George Sansom later wrote, a view of Japan "as seen through spectacles made in Aberdeen about 1880." What gave the work its value was the collaboration of Isoh Yamagata, whose diligence in scouring historical records Murdoch announced as his own.

Very different in quality was George B. Sansom's classic *Japan: A Short Cultural History*, published in London by the Cresset Press in 1932. Sansom, an English diplomat, was commercial attaché. Fluent in Japanese, he tapped Japanese secondary scholarship as well as providing his own insights into art and culture, a field of which Murdoch was totally ignorant, and produced a work of enduring value. It was a time, he once wrote me, when diplomats were not harassed by the close observation made possible by modern communications; he was seldom expected to appear at his office before noon, and indeed wrote much of the manuscript while floating in a sampan on Lake Chūzenji above Nikko. The unhurried elegance of his prose reflects those times.

He too ended with the Tokugawa period, but said relatively little about the "foreign intercourse" that was Murdoch's emphasis. In postwar years he was to teach at Columbia University and made good this lacuna in *The Western World and Japan* (New York: Knopf, 1951), a thoughtful study of the Westernization of the Meiji period, and, after his retirement, a three-volume *History of Japan* (Stanford: Stanford University Press, 1958–1963), which he reined in at the end of the Tokugawa period.

Postwar scholars had two other monuments against which to measure what they built. Ruth Benedict's *The Chrysanthemum and the Sword: Patterns of Japanese Culture* (Boston: Houghton Mifflin, 1946) was the product of a study of Japanese national character undertaken in the United States' Office of War Information to see whether Japan was likely to surrender or whether its leaders would force their countrymen into a final suicidal stand against superior American firepower. Benedict was an anthropologist and a student of Native Americans of the Southwest. She knew no Japanese—though some of her assistants did—but she did know how to look for patterns of culture that would provide clues to future action. Unable to consult contemporary Japanese, however, she studied Japanese Americans, pioneers of a flow that had been stopped in the early-twentieth-century restrictions on immigration, and inevitably called forth an old-fashioned, nineteenth-century ideal type. Much of postwar American social science, and not a little Japanese scholarship, would test and deepen the analysis of Benedict's pioneering work.

One more, and quite different, work was E. Herbert Norman's *Japan's Emergence as a Modern State* (New York: Institute of Pacific Relations, 1940), the work of a young Canadian diplomat born in Japan of missionary parents. The book's subtitle, *Political and Economic Problems of the Meiji Period,* indicated that his focus was on the problems or flaws in Japan's modern transformation that brought on Japanese militarism and expansionism. His work drew heavily on the secondary scholarship of Japanese Marxists who sought the "contradictions" in Japan's structure during the early 1930s, and his skillful summary and pointed argument set the standard against which most postwar scholarship would measure itself.

In the half century since then the scene has changed beyond recognition. Sansom and Norman remain important figures, but the scene is far richer and its products much more diverse. To begin with, Japanese scholarship, which Western specialists ignore at their peril, has been liberated from the cocoon of emperor-centered piety and Ministry of Education–imposed orthodoxy to pursue theory and facts wherever they may lead. In the first postwar decades that scholarship was produced in an intellectual climate that was overwhelmingly Marxist; most prewar writing was condemned as pusillanimous and political history replaced by "scientific" materialism that sought the roots of superstructures described by conventional history. Gradually that focus broadened and changed. Greater affluence brought freedom from the urgency to publish and permitted time for reflection and research, the socialist ideal waned with the travails of socialism overseas, and Japanese society and institutions, however imperfect, proved once more to have redeeming characteristics.

Now the way was open for the production of magnificent reference works of quality and scope. Some had their origins in prewar projects, but economic disasters of war and defeat left some incomplete, while political conformity, as in an eleven-volume biographical dictionary in which all dates were calculated from the mythical accession to rule of the emperor Jimmu in 660 B.C., seriously compromised their utility. Today historians are blessed with a *Dictionary of National History (Kokushi jiten),* 15 massive volumes (Tokyo: Yoshikawa, 1973–1998), a model work enlisting the talents of hundreds of scholars, whose entries add references, complete with fine maps and charts. In the 1960s a "history boom" saw Japanese publishers produce multivolume national histories by leading academic historians who proved wonderfully skilled at readable and popular expositions of the state of their field. Chūō Kōron, to name only one of three houses, enlisted the services of major scholars to issue a twenty-eight-volume *History of Japan* that sold in such large numbers that a paperback series followed the cloth. One step farther came with a series of academic monographs; the great house of Iwanamai, which has been mentioned in these pages, produced three series of "Lectures on Japanese History" *(Iwanami Kōza Nihon rekishi)* that reflect every shift and facet of historical convention.

English-language readers have also benefited from this age of compilation. Kodansha Publishers issued a nine-volume *Encyclopedia of Japan* in 1983 that was reduced in length to two packed volumes ten years later, in which most Western, and many Japanese, authorities contributed often extensive essays on virtually any topic the reader might want to investigate. Different in organization, but equally compelling in quality, is the *Cambridge Encyclopedia of Japan* (Cambridge: Cambridge University Press, 1993), whose editors (Richard Bowring and Peter Kornicki) have assembled highly respected peers to provide chronological treatment under the headings of Geography, History, Literature, Religion, Society, and the like.

Also valuable are three stout volumes published by Kodansha for the International Society for Cultural Information, *Biographical Dictionary of Japanese History* (Sei'ichi Iwao, ed., and Burton Watson, trans., 1978), *Biographical Dictionary of Japanese Literature* (Sen'ichi Hisamatsu, ed., 1976), and *Biographical Dictionary of Japanese Art* (Yutaka Tazawa, ed., 1981). Yet another sweeping survey is provided in the *Cultural Atlas of Japan* (Oxford: Phaidon, 1988), a lavishly illustrated book in which Martin Collcutt, Isao Kumakura, and Marius Jansen offer surveys of early, Tokugawa, and modern Japanese history and culture. Readers who want to examine particular aspects of Japan's early modern and modern history may not find their needs fully satisfied by these works, but they will be ill-advised indeed if they neglect to consult and sample them.

Most recently, a fresh survey of writings on Japanese history—by periods—that goes on to discuss developments in writings on history, art, religion, anthropology, law, and politics, each essay from the pen of a major figure, can be found in Helen Hardacre, ed., *The Postwar Development of Japanese Studies in the United States* (Leiden, Boston, and Cologne: Brill, 1998).

For translations of primary sources one begins with an irreplaceable work edited by Ryusaku Tsunoda, Wm. Theodore de Bary, and Donald Keene, *Sources of Japanese Tradition* (New York: Columbia University Press, 1958). This work, from which liberal use has been made in selections and quotations for this book, provides a rich sampling of excerpts from basic sources relating to thought, religion, and cultural history generally. At this writing it is in process of revision and augmentation for a two-volume edition. There is now an impressive library of translations from Japanese literature, for a generation of specialists have made it their first concern to introduce and annotate works of quality and importance.

Two major research and publishing projects that required the collaborative efforts of a large number of scholars next require mention. The first is the product of the Conference on Modern Japan, an organization created within the Association for Asian Studies, attempting to bring together social science and comparative viewpoints for the consideration of Japan's modern transformation. The products of this enterprise defined to a large extent the field of Japanese studies, and although their emphasis on modernization fell out of favor in the 1970s and 1980s the volumes remain important for concerns of intellectual history, political and economic development, and cultural and social change. Published by Princeton University Press, the titles in the series Studies in the Modernization of Japan are *Changing*

Japanese Attitudes toward Modernization (Marius B. Jansen, ed., 1965), *The State and Economic Enterprise in Japan* (William W. Lockwood, ed., 1965), *Aspects of Social Change in Modern Japan* (R. P. Dore, ed., 1967), *Political Development in Modern Japan* (Robert E. Ward, ed., 1968), *Tradition and Modernization in Japanese Culture* (Donald H. Shively, ed., 1971), and *Dilemmas of Growth in Prewar Japan* (James W. Morley, ed., 1971).

The second of these collaborative enterprises spanned two decades and enlisted senior scholars in Japan and in the West to provide the most complete and authoritative survey of Japanese history ever undertaken in the West. The *Cambridge History of Japan,* 6 vols. (Cambridge: Cambridge University Press, 1988–1999), effectively places the study of Japanese history on a new level, and readers of this volume will have noted my reliance on its monographic chapters at many points. In chronological order of coverage its volumes treat *Ancient Japan* (Delmer M. Brown, ed., 1993), *Heian Japan* (Donald H. Shively, ed., 1999), *Medieval Japan* (Kozo Yamamura, ed., 1990), *Early Modern Japan* (John W. Hall, ed., 1991), *The Nineteenth Century* (Marius B. Jansen, ed., 1989), and *The Twentieth Century* (Peter Duus, ed., 1988). The editors of the *Cambridge History,* which will hereafter be referred to as *CHJ,* felt it necessary to leave cultural history, especially that of art and literature, to other works, and instead concentrated their attention on political, institutional, economic, international, and social developments in Japanese history, but in those areas they have compiled a record whose scope and quality is not likely to be surpassed.

If to these works one adds the quality of periodical coverage provided by the *Journal of Japanese Studies* (Seattle, University of Washington, 1974–present, hereafter *JJS*), *Monumenta Nipponica* (Tokyo, Sophia University, hereafter *MN*), the *Journal of Asian Studies* (Ann Arbor, Mich., Association for Asian Studies, hereafter *JAS*), and *Transactions of the Asiatic Society of Japan* (hereafter *TASJ*), one can follow the transformation of the field of Japanese history from its cloistered beginning as Japanology, a branch of Oriental Studies, to a robust present in which it is represented in every major institution of learning.

Sengoku Unifiers and Tokugawa Establishment

Conrad Totman, *Early Modern Japan* (Berkeley: University of California Press, 1993), provides a work of erudition and scope that contributes to the understanding of every aspect of Tokugawa times. Asao Naohiro, "The Sixteenth Century Unification," in *CHJ,* vol. 4, lays out the terrain. The age of the unifiers is treated with color and care by the essays brought together in *Japan before Tokugawa,* ed. John Whitney Hall, Nagahara Keiji, and Kozo Yamamura (Princeton: Princeton University Press, 1981), and *Warlords, Artists, and Commoners,* ed. George Elison and Bradwell L. Smith (Honolulu: University Press of Hawaii, 1981). Nobunaga has not yet been given close study in the West, but Hideyoshi has fared better. George Elison (who later writes under the name Jurges Elisonas) is the author of a splendid essay, "Hideyoshi the Bountiful Provider" in the volume just mentioned, and Mary Elizabeth Berry's *Hideyoshi* (Cambridge, Mass.: Harvard University Press, 1982) provides a highly readable and richly documented account of that extraordinary man's life. Adriana Boscaro gives a first-hand look in *101 Letters of Hideyoshi: The Private Correspondence of Toyotomi Hideyoshi* (Tokyo: Sophia University, 1975). Alternately boastful, greedy, generous, and lethal (as when he tells young Hideyori to have four men who have displeased him tied up and promises that "when I arrive I shall beat them to death; don't let them free"—hardly Lord Chesterton's tone with his son!), they provide an extraordinary feel for an exciting and violent age. Sengoku Japan, as seen by intrepid European travelers and missionaries, provides the background for the fascinating excerpts of contemporary correspondence assembled by Michael Cooper, S.J., in *They Came to Japan: An Anthology of European Reports on Japan, 1543–1640* (Berkeley: University of California Press, 1965).

The Tokugawa political order is discussed by Conrad Totman in *Politics in the Tokugawa Bakufu, 1600–1843* (Cambridge, Mass.: Harvard University Press, 1967), who provides a convenient periodization of changes as personal rule gave way to the bureaucratic. It has not gone without criticism, implicitly in Harold Bolitho's *Treasures among Men: The Fudai Daimyo in Tokugawa Japan* (New Haven: Yale University Press, 1974) and in review exchanges between the two. For many years the standard work on the Tokugawa system was that of Matsudaira Tarō, *Edo jidai seido no kenkyū* (Studies in the institutions of the Edo period) (Tokyo: Buke Seido Kenkyukai, 1919), but it has been overtaken by the exhaustive research with which Fujino Tamotsu, in *Bakuhan taisei shi no kenkyū* (Studies in the bakuhan system), rev. ed. (Tokyo: Yoshikawa Kobunkan, 1975) and other works, catalogued and analyzed changes in tenure made by successive shoguns. The charts used above have their ultimate origin in Professor Fujino's pages.

The han represented the limits of political activity and consciousness for most samurai, however, and provides the best point of departure for the way national developments impinged on localities. Kanai Madoka's *Hansei* (The *han* system) (Tokyo: Shibundo, 1962) lays out the structure with great clarity, and Harold Bolitho, in Chapter 6, "The *han*," in *CHJ*, vol. 4, and in *Treasures among Men*, provides engrossing detail. The classic study of the interrelationships between national and regional trends, however, remains John W. Hall's *Government and Local Power in Japan, 500 to 1700: A Study Based on Bizen Province* (Princeton: Princeton University Press, 1966). Early in his career Hall stumbled upon the records of Bizen (Okayama) Province, one of the few such repositories to survive natural and man-made disasters, and his fascination with their richness and bureaucratic routine never left him. He returned to them for several chapters in *Studies in the Institutional History of Early Modern Japan*, a collection of essays which he edited with Marius Jansen which was published by Princeton University Press in 1968.

Hall's study of the national through the local was one of a number of such efforts, albeit his was the most ambitious. Study of the institutions of Satsuma produced translations and commentary by Torao Haraguchi, Robert K. Sakai, Mitsugu Sakihara, Kazuko Yamada, and Masato Matsui in *The Status System and Social Organization of Satsuma* (Tokyo: University of Tokyo Press, 1975), in which Sakai's long introduction provided splendid detail on that domain. Philip C. Brown, in *Central Authority and Local Autonomy in the Formation of Early Modern Japan: The Case of Kaga Domain* (Stanford: Stanford University Press, 1993) extended this to the Japan Sea domain of Kanazawa, a locality already chronicled by James L. McClain in *Kanazawa: A Seventeenth-Century Japanese Castle Town* (New Haven: Yale University Press, 1982). Background chapters of several studies that approach the Meiji Restoration through the examination of regional dynamics, notably Albert M. Craig, *Chōshū in the Meiji Restoration* (Cambridge, Mass.: Harvard University Press, 1961), Marius B. Jansen, *Sakamoto Ryōma and the Meiji Restoration* (Princeton: Princeton University Press, 1961) for the domain of Tosa, and James C. Baxter, *The Meiji Unification through the Lens of Ishikawa Prefecture* (Cambridge, Mass.: Harvard University Press, 1994), for Kanazawa, help fill out the story. Charles L. Yates's *Saigō Takamori: The Man behind the Myth* (London: Kegan Paul, 1996) begins with its subject's Satsuma setting, though with much less detail than was true of the Princeton University dissertation from which it is drawn. Most recently Luke S. Roberts, in *Mercantilism in a Japanese Domain: The Merchant Origins of Economic Nationalism in 18th-Century Tosa* (Cambridge: Cambridge University Press, 1998), has provided an authoritative and challenging thesis based on the domain of Tosa.

The International Setting

The arrival of the Portuguese at Tanegashima in the 1540s and the century of European activity that came to an end with the edicts of the 1640s has drawn the attention of many historians; it was an era when Westerners and Western products affected Japanese political developments, and Western sources provide unusual access to sixteenth-century Japan. Dictionaries compiled by missionaries have value for the study of the spoken vernacular of that day, as do the products of the Jesuit mission press in Nagasaki. James Murdoch began his *History* with the middle volume on the century of foreign intercourse, and while he was quite unsympathetic to the Catholic cause he made extensive use of its sources. Much better coverage, however, is provided by C. R. Boxer in *The Christian Century in Japan, 1549–1650* (Berkeley: University of California Press, 1951), a book soundly based and richly flavored by first-hand accounts. The selection of Western, largely Iberian, reports on Japan arranged by topic of Michael Cooper, S.J., *They Came to Japan: An Anthology of European Reports on Japan, 1543–1640* is a rich resource, as is the same author's *Rodrigues the Interpreter: An Early Jesuit in Japan and China* (New York: Weatherhill, 1974), a work of intellectual and artistic elegance. In *Deus Destroyed: The Image of Christianity in Early Modern Japan* (Cambridge, Mass.: Harvard University Press, 1973), George Elison provides a splendidly documented account of the rise and extirpation of Christianity before proceeding to the translation of four pamphlets issued to refute missionary teachings, the first of which is by Fabian Fucan, an apostate Japanese Jesuit, and provides Elison's title. The same author (now Jurgis Elisonas) examines the political effects of the mission movement in "Christianity and the Daimyo," chapter 7 of *CHJ*, vol. 4.

The participation of the English East India Company in early Tokugawa days is given magisterial coverage in Derek Massarella's *A World Elsewhere: Europe's Encounter with Japan in the Sixteenth and Seventeenth Centuries* (New Haven: Yale University Press, 1990). The *Diary of Richard Cocks*, the EIC's principal agent in Japan from 1615 to 1622, was published in two volumes in Tokyo in 1899 and provides a first-hand account.

Ronald Toby's *State and Diplomacy in Early Modern Japan: Asia in the Development of the Tokugawa Bakufu* (Princeton: Princeton University Press, 1984) marked an important advance in interpreting the foreign relations of the early bakufu. He earlier signaled this in "Reopening the Question of *sakoku*: Diplomacy in the Legitimation of the Tokugawa Bakufu," *JJS* (1977). Tokugawa relations with Korea have been illumined by the work of Tashiro Kazui of Keio University, "Foreign Relations during the Edo Period: *Sakoku* Reexamined" (*JJS*, 1982), and numerous works in Japanese, of which the central work is *Kinsei Ni-Chō tsūkō bōekishi no kenkyū* (Studies in trade and contact between Japan and Korea in the early modern period) (Tokyo: Sobunsha, 1981). Korean missions to Japan have been studied by Yi Won-sik, *Chōsen tsūshinshi no kenkyū* (Kyoto: Shibunkaku Shuppan, 1997).

The study of Tokugawa relations with China have been the life work of Ōba Osamu, whose works follow the import of books (*Edo jidai ni okeru Tōsen mochiwatarisho no kenkyū;* Kyoto: Kansai Daigaku Shuppanbu, 1967), cultural contacts (*Edo jidai ni okeru Chūgoku bunka juyō no kenkyū;* Kyoto: Dohosha, 1984), and a delightfully anecdotal *Edo jidai no Ni-Chū hiwa* (Secret tales of Edo period Sino-Japanese relations) (Tokyo: Toho Shoten, 1980). I have drawn frequently on his work in *China in the Tokugawa World* (Cambridge, Mass.: Harvard University Press, 1992).

The Nagasaki system of trade receives impressive documentation in Robert Leroy Innes, "The Door Ajar: Japan's Foreign Trade in the Seventeenth Century" (Ph.D. dissertation, University of Michigan, 1980). The system has been the focus of numerous works by scholars in Japan, of which I have found Nakamura Tadashi, *Kinsei Nagasaki bōekishi no kenkyū* (Studies in Nagasaki trade in the early modern era) (Tokyo: Yoshikawa Kobunkan, 1988), particularly helpful. The Dutch contact is treated by Grant Goodman, *Japan: The Dutch Experience* (London: Athlone, 1986) and C. R. Boxer, *Jan Compagnie in Japan: 1600–1860* (The Hague: Nijhoff, 1950), whose focus is, however, more on the Dutch influence than on the Dutch role. Mention should be made of a magnificent bilingual volume of illustrations of life at the Dutch station issued by the city of Nagasaki, *Deshima: Its Pictorial Heritage* (Tokyo: Chūō Kōron, 1987). In 2000 the Japan-Netherlands Institute issued identical volumes in Dutch, Japanese, and English edited by Leonard Blussé, W. Remmelink, and Ivo Smits, *Bridging the Divide: 400 Years, the Netherlands–Japan* (Tokyo: Hotei Pub.; Ede: Teleac/not). Kanai Madoka, *Taigai kōshōshi no kenkyū* (Studies in foreign relations) (Yokohama: Yurindo, 1988), provides an abundance of data on Deshima missions to Edo.

The daily reports kept by the Deshima chief factor and files in the Hague archives constitute a resource so vast that it has discouraged investigation by most scholars. In recent years, however, L. Blussé and W. G. J. Remmelink of Leiden University, working with the cooperation of the Japan-Netherlands Institute, have made available the marginal summaries that scribes provided to ease access to the archives, and these offer fascinating details of and insights into life at Deshima and on the journey to Edo (during which a parallel diary was kept by the second-in-command). To date there is one hardcover volume, *Deshima Diaries: Marginalia, 1700–1740,* ed. Paul van der Velde and Rudolf Bachofner (Tokyo: Japan-Netherlands Institute, 1992), and a series entitled *The Deshima Dagregisters: Their Original Tables of Contents* in ten volumes beginning in 1680 and currently extending through vol. X, for the years *1780–1800* and edited by Cynthia Vallé and L. Blussé, which appeared in 1997. Mention must also be made of an engaging account of a Japanese woman stranded in Java by the shogunal decrees, L. Blussé's *Strange Company: Chinese Settlers, Mestizo Women, and the Dutch in VOC Batavia* (Dordrecht: Foris Publications, 1986).

The classic account of life in Deshima and the chief factor's trips to Edo remains *The History of Japan* by Engelbert Kaempfer in the English translation by J. C. Scheuchzer, first published in 1728 and republished in 1906 in three volumes in Scotland. The famous last chapter, "An Inquiry, whether it be conducive for the good of the Japanese Empire, to keep it shut up, as it now is, and not to suffer its inhabitants to have any commerce with foreign nations, either at home or abroad," marked, as I mention in the text, the opening shot in the debate over *sakoku* (closed country) policy that has never quite ended. Kaempfer, surprisingly, thought it was for the best that things remain as they were, and he was also not greatly troubled by the persecution of Christians. Some explanation of this emerges in an interesting set of essays edited by Beatrice M. Bodart-Bailey and Derek Massarella, *The Furthest Goal: Engelbert Kaempfer's Encounter with Tokugawa Japan* (London: Curzon, 1955), in which we learn that Kaempfer's native Lemgo in Westphalia burned a record thirty-eight people as witches, one a clergyman uncle who had inveighed against the practice from his pulpit. Contributions trace the history of the manuscript, identify (through VOC archives) the young Japanese who was Kaempfer's informant, and Kaempfer's description of the Kyoto emperor. Beatrice Bodart-Bailey, author of several studies relating to Kaempfer, has made a modern and full translation: *Kaempfer's Japan: Tokugawa Culture Observed,* ed., trans., and annot. Beatrice M. Bodart-Bailey (Honolulu: University of Hawai'i Press, 1999).

Status

A good place to begin is *Daily Life in Traditional Japan* by C. J. Dunn (London: B. T. Batsford, 1969), an engaging and attractively produced little book that discusses and presents illustrations depicting each of the four traditional status groups. David Howell's forthcoming *Geographics of Japanese Identity: Polity, Status, and Civilization in the Nineteenth Century* is an important contribution; in this and other works its author includes discussion of Ainu identity, an issue not always treated. John W. Hall's essay in the opening (1974) issue of *JJS*, "Rule by Status in Tokugawa Japan," was an early reflection of the concern of Japanese scholarship with *mibunsei*. The outpouring of studies and discussion in Japan in recent years is suggested by the invaluable volume edited by Asao Naohiro, *Mibun to kakushiki* (Status and rank), vol. 7 in *Nihon no kinsei* (Japan's early modern) (Tokyo: Chūō Kōron, 1992), a collection of illuminating essays on aspects of the status system. The Japanese court is best treated in Herschel Webb's *The Imperial Institution in the Tokugawa Period* (New York: Columbia University Press, 1968). Samurai ranks and divisions differed from domain to domain, and are invariably discussed in the prefectural and domain-centered studies listed above. For soundly based and discerning studies of the countryside and village life nothing surpasses, or indeed comes up to, Thomas C. Smith's *The Agrarian Origins of Modern Japan* (Stanford: Stanford University Press, 1959), supplemented by later essays on the seventeenth-century village and land tax reprinted in Hall and Jansen, *Studies in the Institutional History of Early Modern Japan,* and also in Smith's *Native Sources for Industrialization in Japan, 1750–1920* (Berkeley: University of California Press, 1988), a collection of ten articles, all of them important. Village demographics are treated in the same author's *Nagahara: Family Framing and Population in a Japanese Village, 1717–1830* (Stanford: Stanford University Press, 1977). Demographics (usually based on the temple registers compiled to monitor Christianity) have been the special province of a group of economists led by Hayami Akira, long of Keio University, and while their work is reflected in every discussion of population and economic growth no single translation has yet emerged. The significance of population study for the consideration of larger problems of economic history can be seen in the excellent work by Susan B. Hanley and Kozo Yamamura, *Economic and Demographic Change in Preindustrial Japan, 1600–1868* (Princeton: Princeton University Press, 1977). Urban developments will receive fuller attention below, but the study of Gary P. Leupp, *Servants, Shophands, and Laborers in the Cities of Tokugawa Japan* (Princeton: Princeton University Press, 1992), marks a great advance in this area.

Urbanization and Communications

Gilbert Rozman, *Urban Networks in Ch'ing China and Tokugawa Japan* (Princeton: Princeton University Press, 1973), provides a great deal of information about Edo in the course of his comparison of that city with Peking. John W. Hall, "The Castle Town and Japan's Urban Modernization," in Hall and Jansen, *Studies in the Institutional History of Early Modern Japan*, marked an important contribution, as did Rozman's "Castle Towns in Transition," in Rozman and Jansen, eds., *Japan in Transition: From Tokugawa to Meiji* (Princeton: Princeton University Press, 1986). *Edo and Paris: Urban Life and the State in the Early Modern Era*, a conference volume edited by James L. McClain, John M. Merriman, and Ugawa Kaoru (Ithaca, N.Y.: Cornell University Press, 1994), has a rich supply of essays on Edo governance and social organization. Henry D. Smith II, whose essay on comparing Edo publishing with that of Paris is in that volume, is also the author of "Edo and London: Comparative Conceptions of the City" in Albert M. Craig, ed., *Japan: A Comparative View* (Princeton: Princeton University Press, 1979). Jinnai Hidenobu, *Tokyo: A Spatial Anthropology*, trans. Kimiko Nishimura (Berkeley: University of California Press, 1995), provides a fascinating "reading" of the modern city from its early modern perspective. As one would expect, the literature on Edo and castle towns in Japanese is enormous. Some feeling for its richness can be gained from Yoshida Nobuyuki, ed., *Toshi no jidai* (The era of cities), which is the seventh volume in the magisterial enterprise under the direction of Asao Naohiro, *Nihon no kinsei* (Japan's early modern).

The study of Tokugawa communications has been enriched by the work of Constantine Nomikos Vaporis, *Breaking Barriers: Travel and the State in Early Modern Japan* (Cambridge, Mass.: Harvard University Press, 1994). Vaporis is also the author of several studies that center on communication between Tosa and Edo and has in preparation a study of the system of alternate attendance. The early work of Toshio G. Tsukahira, *Feudal Control in Tokugawa Japan: The Sankin-kōtai System* (Cambridge, Mass.: Harvard University Press, 1966), remains the standard study. I have profited from, and quoted extensively, the account of the Dutch representative Dirk de Graeff van Polsbroek, *Journaal 1857–1870: Belevenissen van een Nederlands diplomaat om het negentiende eeuwse Japan* (Assen/Maastricht: Vangorcum, 1987), whose journey from Nagasaki to Edo followed by a century and a half the famous account provided by Kaempfer in volume 3 of his *History*.

Education and Literacy

Since its appearance in 1965 R. P. Dore's *Education in Tokugawa Japan* (Berkeley: University of California Press) has been the standard work and one against which others can be measured. Richard Rubinger's *Private Academies of Tokugawa Japan* (Princeton: Princeton University Press, 1982) adds important material on the many sorts of *shijuku* that existed throughout the land. A useful discussion of commoner schools that makes clear that they were less "parish" or "temple" centered than one would suppose can be found in Brian W. Platt, "School, Community and State in Nineteenth Century Japan" (Ph.D. dissertation, University of Illinois, 1998). Some interesting comparisons with educational developments in England are provided in Lawrence Stone and Marius B. Jansen, "Education and Modernization in Japan and England," *Comparative Studies in Society and History*, 9, 2 (January

1967). For the development of publishing one should consult Henry D. Smith II's comparison with developments in Paris in McClain, Merriman, and Ugawa ed., *Edo and Paris,* and Donald H. Shively's discussion of popular culture in *CHJ,* vol. 4. Peter Kornicki, *The Book in Japan: A Cultural History from the Beginnings to the Nineteenth Century* (Leiden: Brill, 1998), traces the development of the book.

Intellectual Concerns

The selections and commentary in Tsunoda, de Bary, and Keene, *Sources of Japanese Tradition,* furnish an admirable guide to Tokugawa thought, with particular strength on Confucianism and *kokugaku.* W. J. Boot, *The Adoption and Adaptation of Neo-Confucianism in Japan: The Role of Fujiwara Seika and Hayashi Razan* (Leiden, 1992), shows that Hayashi Razan was far less important than that individual would have had his readers believe. Early Tokugawa thought and ideology, with particular focus on Yamazaki Ansai, is treated in Herman Oom's *Tokugawa Ideology: Early Constructs, 1570–1680* (Princeton: Princeton University Press, 1985). Tetsuo Najita's "History and Nature in Eighteenth Century Thought" in *CHJ,* vol. 4, is a good place to begin consideration of this voluminous literature. The same author's *Visions of Virtue in Tokugawa Japan* (Chicago: University of Chicago Press, 1987) and *Japanese Thought in the Tokugawa Period,* ed. with Irwin Schiner (Chicago: University of Chicago Press, 1978), and other works too numerous to list here add important dimensions.

Among individual Tokugawa scholars Ogyū Sorai has probably attracted the most attention, for reasons that are apparent from his treatment in the text. A seminal study is that of Maruyama Masao, *Nihon seiji shisōshi kenkyū* (1952), translated by Mikiso Hane as *Studies in the Intellectual History of Tokugawa Japan* (Princeton: Princeton University Press, 1974). Sorai's life is discussed by Olof Lidin in *The Life of Ogyū Sorai, a Tokugawa Confucian Philosopher,* Scandinavian Institute of Asian Studies Monograph Series (Lund: Studentlitt., 1973). Translations of several works are available, but J. R. McEwan's *The Political Writings of Ogyū Sorai* (Cambridge: Cambridge University Press, 1962), with long excerpts from proposals Sorai offered to Yoshimune, is most useful for the social scientist.

Arai Hakuseki is studied by Kate Wildman Nakai in *Shogunal Politics: Arai Hakuseki and the Premises of Tokugawa Rule* (Cambridge, Mass.: Harvard University Press, 1988), and two major works have been translated by Joyce Ackroyd: *Told Round a Brushwood Fire: The Autobiography of Arai Hakuseki* (Princeton: Princeton University Press, 1979) and *Lessons from History: Arai Hakuseki's* Tokushi Yoron (St. Lucia: University of Queensland Press, 1982). Other discussions and translations of individual scholars include Joseph John Spae's *Itō Jinsai: A Philosopher, Educator, and Sinologist of the Tokugawa Period* (Peking: Catholic University of Peking, 1948), Yoshikawa Kōjirō's invaluable *Jinsai, Sorai, Norinaga: Three Classical Philologists of Tokugawa Japan* (Tokyo: Tōhō Gakkai, 1983), and Mary Evelyn Tucker, *Moral and Spiritual Cultivation in Japanese Confucianism: The Life and Thought of Kaibara Ekken (1630–1714).* It will be seen that the literature is vast. An additional title that should be mentioned indicates more of its promise: Peter Nosco, ed., *Confucianism and Tokugawa Culture* (Princeton: Princeton University Press, 1984). The relationship between China-oriented Confucian scholars and their sense of nationality is also an important area of study. I have discussed aspects of this in *China in the Tokugawa World* (Cambridge, Mass.:

Harvard University Press, 1992), and in intellectual history the terrain has been mapped by Kate Wildman Nakai, "The Naturalization of Confucianism in Tokugawa Japan: The Problem of Sinocentrism," in *Harvard Journal of Asiatic Studies,* 40 (June 1980). A focus on intellectuals can, however, lead to the conclusion that Edo Japan was more "Confucian" than it was in fact. These cautions are well shown in Martin Collcutt's "The Legacy of Confucianism in Japan," in Gilbert Rozman, ed., *The East Asian Region: Confucian Heritage and Its Modern Adaptation* (Princeton: Princeton University Press, 1991).

The Mito School, a synthesis of Confucian and nativist concerns, receives treatment in two studies of the nineteenth-century scholar Aizawa Seishisai, J. Victor Koschmann, *The Mito Ideology* (Berkeley: University of California Press, 1987), and Bob T. Wakabayashi, *Anti-Foreignism and Western Learning in Early Modern Japan: The* New Theses *of 1825* (Cambridge, Mass.: Harvard University Press, 1986).

Kokugaku and early Shinto are more of a problem because of their amorphous nature. One of the few accessible studies of the great nativist scholars is that of Shigeru Matsumoto, *Motoori Norinaga* (Cambridge, Mass.: Harvard University Press, 1970). Harry Harootunian, in *Things Seen and Unseen: Discourse and Ideology in Tokugawa Nativism* (Chicago: University of Chicago Press, 1988), and, more accessibly, in "Late Tokugawa Culture and Thought," in vol. 5 of *CHJ*, relates *kokugaku* to many aspects of commoner culture and belief. Kuroda Toshio, "Shinto in the History of Japanese Religion," *JJS*, 7, 1 (1981), provides a splendid survey of the problem, and the early sections of Helen Hardacre's *Shinto and the State, 1866–1988* (Princeton: Princeton University Press, 1989) add further detail. The network of circuit preachers, *oshi*, who supported popular religions and above all the Ise shrine, is discussed by Takano Toshihiko in "Ido suru mibun: shinshoku to hyakushō no aida" (The itinerant status: between priest and farmer) in Asao, *Nihon no kinsei* (Japan's early modern), vol. 7, *Mibun to kakushiki*. Pilgrimages are the subject of an article by Winston Davis, "Pilgrimage and World Renewal: A Study of Religion and Social Values in Japan," republished in his *Japanese Religion and Society: Paradigms of Structure and Change* (Albany: State University of New York, 1992).

For Dutch studies the pertinent references in "The International Setting," above, apply, especially Goodman's *Japan: The Dutch Experience*. I have surveyed some problems of interpretation in "Rangaku and Westernization," *Modern Asian Studies,* 18, 4 (October 1984) and in *Japan and Its World: Two Centuries of Change* (Princeton: Princeton University Press, 1980). Donald Keene's *The Japanese Discovery of Europe* (Stanford: Stanford University Press, 1969) is an engaging discussion of the "Dutch" scholar Honda Toshiaki. One discussion of the impact on art is that of Timon Screech, *The Western Scientific Gaze and Popular Imagery in Later Edo Japan* (Cambridge: Cambridge University Press, 1996). Tadashi Yoshida, "The *rangaku* of Shizuki Tadao" (Ph.D. dissertation, Princeton University, 1974), gives an insight into the difficulties translators faced. Shizuki, it may be remembered, was also the translator whose rendering of Kaempfer's "closed country" as *sakoku* left its mark on future histories.

Crisis and Response

The "consensus" view of Japanese society has problems dealing with the clear evidence of conflict. A good place to begin is Tetsuo Najita and Victor Koschmann, eds., *Conflict in*

Modern Japanese History: The Neglected Tradition (Princeton: Princeton University Press, 1982). For many years the only source in English on peasant protests was Hugh Borton, "Peasant Uprisings in Japan of the Tokugawa Period," *TASJ*, 2nd ser., 16 (May 1938), a study based principally on the work of Kokushō Iwao. In postwar years, especially in the 1970s and 1980s, there has been an outpouring of studies, and much of this literature on Tokugawa peasant protests is surveyed by Conrad Totman in "Tokugawa Peasants: Win, Lose, or Draw?", *MN* 41, 4 (1986): 457–476. James W. White, *Ikki: Social Conflict and Political Protest in Early Modern Japan* (Ithaca, N.Y.: Cornell University Press, 1995) structures the field in impressive detail, classifying and analyzing the statistics compiled by Aoki Kōji and other Japanese scholars. Anne Walthall has added to her *Social Protest and Popular Culture in Eighteenth-Century Japan* (Tucson: University of Arizona Press, 1986) a splendid anthology of peasant narratives in *Peasant Uprisings in Japan: A Critical Anthology of Peasant Histories* (Chicago: University of Chicago Press, 1991). Stephen Vlastos, *Peasant Protests and Uprisings in Tokugawa Japan* (Berkeley: University of California Press, 1986), gives a skillful account and analysis of discontent in a sericulture region, and Herbert Bix, *Peasant Protest in Japan, 1590–1884* (New Haven: Yale University Press, 1986) maintains a consistent interpretation throughout a longer period of time. William W. Kelley, *Deference and Defiance in Nineteenth-Century Japan* (Princeton: Princeton University Press, 1985) gives a splendid account of the campaign samurai and commoners in Shōnai waged to thwart bakufu plans to transfer their daimyo in the early nineteenth century. Selçuk Esenbel, *Even the Gods Rebel: The Peasants of Takaino and the 1871 Nakano Uprising in Japan* (Ann Arbor, Mich.: Association for Asian Studies, 1998) provides a fascinating study at the turn of the Tokugawa-Meiji change that tells a great deal about both the early modern and the modern state. And, while the literature in Japanese is too vast to attempt to summarize, mention should be made of an engaging study by Yokoyama Toshio, *Hyakushō ikki no gimin denshō* (Peasant rebellion traditions of righteous martyrs) (Tokyo: Kyoikusha, 1977), that arranges, analyzes, and discusses such narratives.

The Opening

The literature surrounding issues raised by Japan's encounter with the nineteenth-century West is so extensive that I can mention only the items I find most useful. On the American side the official account is contained in Francis Hawks, *Narrative of the Expedition of an American Squadron to the China Seas and Japan,* 2 vols., pub. by order of the government of the United States (Washington, D.C., 1856). Samuel Eliot Morison's *"Old Bruin": Commodore Matthew Calbraith Perry* (Boston: Little, Brown, 1967) gives a good account in his treatment of Perry's biography, and Perry's own account has been edited by Roger Pineau in *The Japan Expedition of 1852–1854: The Personal Journal of Commodore Matthew C. Perry* (Washington, D.C.: Smithsonian Institution, 1968). Peter Booth Wiley, in *Yankees in the Land of the Gods: Commodore Perry and the Opening of Japan* (New York: Viking, 1990), has worked with Japanese historians to round out the story. The matter of the white flags that Perry used as device to intimidate the Japanese is the subject of a recent study by Miwa Kimitada, *Kakusareta Perii no "shirohata"* (Perry's hidden "white flags") (Tokyo: Sophia University Press, 1999). It has long been noted that General MacArthur took many of his leads from reading about Perry, though he of course had no need for white flags.

Townsend Harris's role, and difficulties, were if anything greater. *The Complete Journal of Townsend Harris,* ed. Mario Cosenza (Rutland and Tokyo: Tuttle, 1959), is an essential account, but, since Harris was a difficult man, it is wise to add the account of his Dutch interpreter Henry Heusken, *Japan Journal, 1855–1861* (New Brunswick, N.J.: Rutgers University Press, 1964), and Oliver Statler's *Shimoda Story* (New York: Random House, 1969).

The Russian role has its classical treatment in George Alexander Lensen, *The Russian Push toward Japan: Russo-Japanese Relations, 1697–1875* (Princeton: Princeton University Press, 1959), and *Russia's Japan Expedition of 1852–1855* (Gainesville: University of Florida Press, 1955). John J. Stephan's *The Kuril Islands: Russo-Japanese Frontier in the Pacific* (Oxford: Clarendon, 1974) focuses on the dispute over the Northern Islands, but gives an excellent summary of early relations.

The northern approach is complicated by the very unusual pattern of Japanese control and expansion in Hokkaido. David Howell discusses this in *Capitalism from Within: Economy, Society and the State in a Japanese Fishery* (Berkeley: University of California Press, 1995). Brett L. Walker, *Marsumae Domain and the Conquest of Ainu Lands: Ecology and Commerce in Tokugawa Expansion* (Berkeley: University of California Press, 1999), is based on a 1997 University of Oregon dissertation.

The British role is the subject of W. G. Beasley's standard *Great Britain and the Opening of Japan* (London: Luzac, 1951), while the Dutch role is covered in the richly documented account by J. A. van der Chijs, *Neerlands Streven tot Openstelling van Japan* (Amsterdam: Frederik Muller, 1867).

But of course it is the Japanese side of the story that is the most interesting and important. W. G. Beasley's treatment in *CHJ*, vol. 5, provides a skillful summary, and it is especially his *Select Documents on Japanese Foreign Policy, 1853–1868* (Oxford: Oxford University Press, 1955) that is the standard source. A rich assortment of contemporary memorials and memoranda is introduced by an extensive discussion of issues and problems in a work that will not need to be done again.

The Meiji Restoration

Because the Restoration is the central event in Japan's modern history an enormous amount of writing has been devoted to it, and it is not possible to do more than sketch the contours of the field. Volume 5 of *CHJ, The Nineteenth Century,* is a good place to begin, with particular attention to the contributions by Bolitho, Harootunian, Beasley, Hirakawa, and Jansen. W. G. Beasley's *The Meiji Restoration* (Stanford University Press, 1972) is the standard survey. Problems of interpretation are the focus of George M. Wilson, *Patriots and Redeemers in Japan: Motives in the Meiji Restoration* (Chicago: University of Chicago Press, 1992). An extremely important book is that of Conrad Totman, *The Fall of the Tokugawa Bakufu, 1862–1868* (Honolulu: University of Hawaii Press, 1980). While other accounts tend to center on the future winners in Kyoto and Chōshū, Totman's focus is on problems, actions, and actors of the Edo bakufu; his discussion of sources is also invaluable. H. D. Harootunian, *Toward Restoration* (University of California Press, 1970), provides a challenging and lively account of Restoration era men whose thought impelled their contemporaries to action.

The first serious study of this in English was that of E. Herbert Norman, *Japan's Emergence as a Modern State*, which relied on Japanese Marxist scholarship of the 1930s and provided a vivid and compelling account centered on social change in Chōshū. Albert M. Craig, *Chōshū in the Meiji Restoration* (Cambridge, Mass.: Harvard University Press, 1961), questioned the factual basis for Norman's evaluation of "lower samurai," but Thomas M. Huber, in *The Revolutionary Origins of Modern Japan* (University of Chicago Press, 1981), centered his attention on Yoshida Shōin and his disciples to emphasize the elements of social revolution. Satsuma politics have been less chronicled, probably because they lacked colorful turnovers. Robert K. Sakai's "Shimazu Nariakira and the Emergence of National Leadership in Satsuma," in Albert Craig and Donald Shively, eds., *Personality in Japanese History* (Berkeley: University of California Press, 1970) and Charles L. Yates's *Saigō Takamori: The Man behind the Myth* indicate the riches of the terrain. I have taken the Tosa setting as background for my study *Sakamoto Ryōma and the Meiji Restoration* (Princeton University Press, 1961). Saga still lacks a study in a Western language, though Franklyn Odo's dissertation on the institutional structure of the Saga domain (Princeton University, 1975) provides a good structural study of that domain. While there has been an understandable preoccupation with domains that "moved" the Restoration, it is no less important to ask why other large and powerful domains did not take part, and James G. Baxter's *The Meiji Unification through the Lens of Ishikawa Prefecture* does just that for Kaga, the largest non-Tokugawa domain of them all.

As Westerners and Japanese came to know more about each other the impact of the opening and of travel became steadily larger. Haga Tōru's *Taikun no shisetsu: Bakumatsu Nihonjin no seiyō taiken* (The shogun's missions: the experience of late Tokugawa Japanese in the West) (Tokyo, 1968) provides a compelling account in remarkably brief compass. The famous *Autobiography of Fukuzawa Yukichi* is probably the best individual account by a Japanese traveler. In larger context, however, the most remarkable experience of the West was that gained by the Iwakura embassy, which included almost half of the top leadership of early Meiji Japan, and visited the United States and Europe in 1871–1873. The embassy's scribe was Kume Kunitake, and his account, a five volume *Tokumei zenken taishi Bei-Ō kairan jikki* (A true account of the observations of the ambassadors plenipotentiary of America and Europe), first published in 1878, is the subject of Marlene J. Mayo's "The Western Education of Kume Kunitake," *MN*, 38, 1 (1973). Since then interest in the embassy and in Kume's account has grown steadily. Tanaka Akira and Takada Seiji have edited a splendid volume, [*Bei-Ō kairan jikki*] *no gakusaiteki kenkyū* (International studies of the *Bei-Ō Kairan jikki*) (Sapporo: Hokkaido University Library, 1993), and we have adapted map 5, showing the route taken by the ambassadors, from this work. Plans for publication in English translation of the entire Kume account are far advanced.

Among Western observers of mid-nineteenth-century Japan the account by Sir Ernest Satow, *A Diplomat in Japan* (Philadelphia: Lippincott, 1921), is by far the richest, written by a man who was himself a participant in the years in which he served as Harry Parkes's interpreter. And nongovernmental Westerners played their role, as can be seen in the revealing F. G. Notehelfer, ed., *Japan through American Eyes* (Princeton University Press, 1992), the journal of Francis Hall, an American freelance journalist and settler at Yokohama from 1859 to 1866.

Meiji Japan

It is well to begin at the end. Carol Gluck's *Japan's Modern Myths: Ideology in the Late Meiji Period* (Princeton University Press, 1985) gives a richly documented and carefully argued account of the construction of twentieth-century ideology.

The turn to Meiji is treated from a number of angles in Marius B. Jansen and Gilbert N. Rozman, ed., *Japan in Transition from Tokugawa to Meiji* (Princeton: Princeton University Press, 1986). The political process that ended with unification is the subject of Michio Umegaki's *After the Restoration: The Beginning of Japan's Modern State* (New York: New York University Press, 1988). The first decade is also treated through the study of its leaders, notably the three-volume *Diary of Kido Takayoshi*, translated by Sidney D. Brown and Akiko Hirota, and published by the University of Tokyo Press between 1983 and 1986. Masakazu Iwata, *Ōkubo Toshimichi: The Bismarck of Japan* (Berkeley: University of California Press, 1964), and Charles L. Yates's *Saigō Takamori: The Man behind the Myth*, cited earlier, complete biographical coverage of the three principal leaders of the first decade. The creation of the army is the subject of Roger F. Hackett's *Yamagata Aritomo in the Rise of Modern Japan, 1838–1922* (Cambridge, Mass.: Harvard University Press, 1971). A splendidly documented discussion of the evolution of the Imperial Precepts to Soldiers and Sailors is now at hand in Umetani Noboru, *Gunjin chokuron seiritsushi: Tennōsei kokkakan no seiritsu* (Tokyo: Seishi shuppan, 2000). Yoshitake Oka, in *Five Political Leaders of Modern Japan*, trans. Andrew Fraser and Patricia Murray (Tokyo: University of Tokyo Press, 1986), gives brief sketches of the lives and personalities of Itō, Ōkubo, Hara, Inukai, and Saionji.

The "civilization and enlightenment" (*bunmei kaika*) movement cannot be treated without study of the life of Fukuzawa Yukichi. His autobiography, translated by Eiichi Kiyooka, is available in several editions, and his *Outline of a Theory of Civilization*, trans. David A. Dilworth and G. Cameron Hurst (Tokyo: Sophia University Press, 1973), can be supplemented by translations of other works, notably *An Encouragement of Learning*, trans. David A. Dilworth and Umeyo Hirano (Tokyo: Sophia University, 1969). Carmen Blacker's *The Japanese Enlightenment: A Study of the Writings of Fukuzawa Yukichi* (Cambridge: Cambridge University Press, 1964), and Albert M. Craig, "Fukuzawa Yukichi: The Philosophical Foundations of Meiji Nationalism," in Robert E. Ward, ed., *Political Development in Modern Japan* (Princeton: Princeton University Press, 1968), are essential studies of this thinker, and Albert Craig has in preparation a longer study. The "Meiji Six Society" of which Fukuzawa was the center can be followed in the translation by William R. Braisted, *Meiroku Zasshi: Journal of the Japanese Enlightenment* (Cambridge, Mass.: Harvard University Press, 1976). Mori Arinori, who was an important member of this group, is the subject of Ivan Parker Hall, *Mori Arinori* (Cambridge, Mass.: Harvard University Press, 1973), and Nishi Amane, another stalwart who went on to be a Meiji bureaucrat, is studied in Thomas R. H. Havens, *Nishi Amane and Modern Japanese Thought* (Princeton: Princeton University Press, 1970).

The problem of reconciling scientific history with the requirements of the state ideology was first brought home to me by Haga Tōru's discussion of Kume Kunitake in "Meiji shoki ichi chishikijin no seiyō taiken" (An early Meiji intellectual's experience of the West) in a set of essays published to honor Professor Shimada Keinji in 1961; more detail has been provided by Margaret Mehl, "Scholarship and Ideology in Conflict: The Kume Affair, 1892," in *Monumenta Nipponica*, 48, 3 (Winter 1993). The larger issue received compelling treatment in John S. Brownlee, *Japanese Historians and the National Myths, 1600–1945: The Age of the Gods and Emperor Jimmu* (Vancouver: University of British Columbia Press, 1997). The linkage between Ogyū Sorai scholarship and the iconoclastic stance taken by Shigeno Yasutsugu toward national myths is discussed by Tao De-min, "The Influence of Sorai in Meiji Japan: Shigeno Yasutsugu as an Advocate of 'Practical Sinology,'" in *Nihon Kangaku shisōshi ronkō* (Essays on the history of Japanese Sinology) (Suita City: Kansai Daigaku Shuppanbu, 1999), a volume of essays in Chinese, Japanese, and (in this case) English.

Foreign advisers and Japanese overseas study are the subject of H. J. Jones, *Live Machines: Hired Foreigners and Meiji Japan* (Vancouver: University of British Columbia Press, 1980) and Ardath W. Burks, ed., *The Modernizers: Overseas Students, Foreign Employees, and Meiji Japan* (Boulder, Colo.: Westview, 1985). A study that focuses on the importance of foreign experience or training is Bernard S. Silberman, *Ministers of Modernization: Elite Mobility in the Meiji Restoration, 1868–1873* (Tucson: University of Arizona Press, 1964). The path to success, immortalized in the slogan *risshin shusse* (be a success!), is well treated in Earl H. Kinmonth, *The Self-Made Man in Meiji Japanese Thought: From Samurai to Salary Man* (Berkeley: University of California Press, 1981).

Religion first received structured treatment in Kishimoto Hideo ed., *Japanese Religion in the Meiji Era*, trans. John Howes (Tokyo: Ōbunsha, 1956). James Edward Ketelaar, *Of Heretics and Martyrs in Meiji Japan: Buddhism and Its Persecution* (Princeton: Princeton University Press, 1990). The modern Protestant Christian movement can be followed at Kumamoto, one of its points of entry, in F. G. Notehelfer, *American Samurai: Captain L. L. Janes and Japan,* and Irwin Scheiner's thoughtful *Christian Converts and Social Protest in Meiji Japan* (University of California Press, 1970). The only book-length treatment of the Sapporo disciples of Dr. Clark is John Howes, ed., *Nitobe Inazō: Japan's Bridge across the Pacific* (Boulder, Colo.: Westview, 1995).

Tokutomi Sohō, one of the graduates of Janes's Kumamoto academy, is the subject of John D. Pierson, *Tokutomi Sohō (1863–1957): A Journalist for Modern Japan* (Princeton: Princeton University Press, 1980), and his most important Meiji book, *The Future Japan,* has been translated by Vinh Sinh (Edmonton: University of Alberta Press, 1989), who is also the author of *Tokutomi Sohō (1863–1957): The Later Career* (Toronto: University of Toronto/York University Centre on Modern East Asia, 1986). Tokutomi also figures frequently in the important study by Kenneth B. Pyle, *The New Generation in Meiji Japan: Problems of Cultural Identity, 1885–1895* (Stanford: Stanford University Press, 1969).

Meiji politics were one of the first areas of inquiry, and W. W. McLaren's old *A Political History of Japan during the Meiji Era, 1867–1912* (London: Allen and Unwin, 1916) is still useful, though less so than the long-standard work by Robert A. Scalapino, *Democracy and the Party Movement in Prewar Japan: The Failure of the First Attempt* (Berkeley: University of California Press, 1953). Nobutaka Ike, *Beginnings of Political Democracy in Japan* (Baltimore: Johns Hopkins, 1960), is particularly useful for its consideration of Ueki Emori and Nakae Chōmin, two Jiyūtō theorists. One can also examine the participation of nonsamurai in the 1880s, notably in Irokawa Daikichi's *The Culture of the Meiji Period,* ed. M. B. Jansen (Princeton: Princeton University Press, 1985), and Roger W. Bowen, *Rebellion and Democracy in Meiji Japan: A Study of Commoners in the Popular Rights Movement* (Berkeley: University of California Press, 1980).

It is, however, simplistic to see the Meiji Constitution as something "wrung from the hands of a reluctant oligarchy," although its founders did indeed take great care to make sure that things would not get away from them. George M. Beckmann's *The Making of the Meiji Constitution* (Lawrence: University of Kansas, 1957) is particularly useful for its attention to the initial drafts proposed by government leaders, and Joseph Pittau, S.J., *Political Thought in Early Meiji Japan, 1868–1889* (Cambridge, Mass.: Harvard University Press, 1967) gives a careful account of the drafting of that document. Johannes Siems, S.J., *Hermann Roesler and the Making of the Meiji Constitution* (Tokyo: Sophia University, 1966), adds that important adviser's commentaries. R. H. P. Mason *Japan's First General Election, 1890* (Cambridge: Cambridge University Press, 1969) adds wonderful detail on how things actually worked. The inauguration and experience of government under the new charter is illumined by George Akita in *Foundations of Constitutional Government in Modern Japan, 1868–1900* (Cambridge, Mass.: Harvard University Press, 1967), and the decade after 1900 is treated in Tetsuo Najita, *Hara Kei in the Politics of Compromise, 1905–1915* (Cambridge, Mass.: Harvard University Press, 1967), who provides an illuminating picture of how things worked in the "mature" constitutional government of late Meiji years. The role and power of the Imperial Household Ministry are the subject of David A. Titus, *Palace and Politics in Prewar Japan* (Columbia University Press, 1974).

The economic changes of the Meiji period are limned by Kazushi Ohkawa and Henry Rosovsky in "A Century of Japanese Economic Growth," in Lockwood, *The State and Economic Enterprise in Japan,* and at greater length in the same two authors' *Japanese Economic Growth: Trend Acceleration in the Twentieth Century* (Stanford: Stanford University Press, 1973). Lockwood's *The Economic Development of Japan: Growth and Structural Change, 1868–1939* (Princeton: Princeton University Press, 1955), however, stands as the study that opened the field of Japanese economic history, and remains important. Thomas C. Smith's *Political Change and Industrial Development in Japan: Government Enterprise, 1868–1880* (Stanford: Stanford University Press, 1955) is essential for the question of zaibatsu origins, and William D. Wray's *Mitsubishi and the N.Y.K. Line, 1870–1894* (Cambridge, Mass.: Harvard University Press, 1984) details the birth of the modern shipping giant. Johannes Hirschmeier, S.V.D., *The Origins of Entrepreneurship in Meiji Japan* (Cambridge, Mass.: Harvard University Press, 1964) is full of interest for its studies of individual businessmen. Byron K. Marshall, *Capitalism and Nationalism in Prewar Japan: The Ideology of the Business Elite, 1868–1941* (Stanford: Stanford University Press, 1967), helps one to understand the way profit and patriotism could be combined.

The modern agricultural system is the subject of Thomas C. Smith's classic *The Agrarian Origins of Modern Japan* (Stanford: Stanford University Press, 1959), a book that, with the same author's collection of essays in *Native Sources of Japanese Industrialization, 1750–1920* (Berkeley: University of California Press, 1988), is must reading for any student of modern Japanese history. Richard J. Smethurst, in *Agricultural Development and Tenancy Disputes in Japan, 1870–1940* (Princeton: Princeton University Press, 1986), discerns better living standards in the Meiji transition of peasants into farmers, though his critics reproach him with selecting a relatively favored area for examination. The tenancy situation and movement have been treated by Ann Waswo, *Japanese Landlords: The Decline of a Rural Elite* (Berkeley: University of California Press, 1977), who takes the story into the 1930s.

Diplomacy and War

It is easy, but wrong, to overlook the formal diplomatic history approach of Sterling Tatsuji Takeuchi, *War and Diplomacy in the Japanese Empire* (New York: Doubleday, 1935), who gives concise and soundly documented accounts of matters from the revision of the unequal treaties to the Manchurian crisis, with careful exposition of the mechanisms provided by the Meiji constitutional order. Meiji foreign relations begin with the squabble over policy toward Korea, and that story, through its annexation in 1910, is treated in F. Hilary Conroy, *The Japanese Seizure of Korea, 1868–1910* (Philadelphia: University of Pennsylvania Press, 1960). More recently Peter Duus, *The Abacus and the Sword: The Japanese Penetration of Korea, 1895–1910* (Berkeley: University of California Press, 1995) provides more richly documented economic as well as political details, and becomes the best study of the annexation. Neither work, however, makes use of Korean sources. The Sino-Japanese War of 1894–95 is the subject of Morinosuke Kajima, *The Diplomacy of Japan, 1894–1922,* vol. 1: *Sino-Japanese War and Triple Intervention* (Tokyo: Kajima Institute of International Peace, 1976); Foreign Minister Mutsu Munemitsu's account of his stewardship, *Kenkenroku: A Diplomatic Record of the Sino-Japanese War, 1894–95,* trans. Gordon Mark Berger (Tokyo: Japan Foundation, 1982), is an essential supplement. The war is put in its social history context by Stewart Lone, *Japan's First Modern War: Army and Society in the Conflict with China, 1894–95* (London: St. Martin's Press, 1994).

Ian Nish has put his stamp on the Russo-Japanese War. His *Origins of the Russo-Japanese War* (London: Longman, 1985) is the place to begin. His study of the alliance with Great Britain, *The Anglo-Japanese Alliance: A Study of Two Island Empires, 1894–1907* (London: Athlone Press, 1966), lays the groundwork. Vol. 2 of the Kajima Institute's *Diplomacy of Japan, Anglo-Japanese Alliance and Russo-Japanese War* (Tokyo: Kajima Institute of International Peace, 1978), contains useful documentation, though one is wise to move beyond it for interpretation. Shumpei Okamoto's *The Japanese Oligarchy and the Russo-Japanese War* (New York: Columbia University Press, 1970) is unique for its coverage of the decision process and the Hibiya riots.

Social Conditions, Radicalism, and Protest

E. Patricia Tsurumi, *Factory Girls: Women in the Thread Mills of Meiji Japan* (Princeton: Princeton University Press, 1990), is a balanced and careful study, but there is so far a dearth of books that concentrate on conditions in Japan's cities and factories. There are, however, some collections and works that try to counter the "consensus" model of Japan's as a cooperative, if not completely "familial," society. Tetsuo Najita and J. Victor Koschmann, eds., *Conflict in Japan: The Neglected Tradition* (Princeton: Princeton University Press, 1982) from a historical perspective, and Ellis S. Krauss, Thomas P. Rohlen, and Patricia G. Steinhoff, eds., *Conflict in Japan* (Honolulu: University of Hawaii Press, 1984), from a sociological and anthropological perspective, address this need. Mikiso Hane, *Peasants, Rebels, and Outcasts: The Underside of Modern Japan* (New York: Pantheon, 1982), and *Reflections on the Way to the Gallows: Rebel Women in Prewar Japan* (Berkeley: University of California Press, 1988), comes close to positing a "two Japan," or upper side and underside, alternative to "consensus." Tanaka Shōzō, who devoted his life to a fight against the Ashio copper mine pollution (also treated, as noted, by F. G. Notehelfer in a symposium in *JJS*, 1, 2, 1975), is the subject of Kenneth Strong, *Ox against the Storm: A Biography of Tanaka Shōzō, Japan's Conservationist Pioneer (1841–1913)* (Vancouver: University of British Columbia Press, 1977). The anarchist movement and the High Treason Trial are the subject of F. G. Notehelfer, *Kōtoku Shūsui: Portrait of a Japanese Radical* (Cambridge: Cambridge University Press, 1971). There are a number of studies of the Japan Communist Party, among them Rodger Swearingen and Paul Langer, *Red Flag in Japan* (Cambridge, Mass.: Harvard University Press, 1952) and George M. Beckmann and Okubo Genji, *The Japanese Communist Party, 1922–1945* (Stanford University Press, 1969). Hyman Kublin's *Asian Revolutionary: The Life of Sen Katayama* (Princeton: Princeton University Press, 1964), treats a communist who ended his days in Moscow.

The 1920s

The Taishō era has received surprisingly little attention, as historians have focused on the more tumultuous events that followed. A welcome step in making good this lack is a volume edited by Sharon A. Minichiello, *Japan's Competing Modernities: Issues in Culture and Democracy, 1900–1930* (Honolulu: University of Hawaii Press, 1998). Thomas Rimer, ed., *Culture and Identity: Japanese Intellectuals during the Interwar Years* (Princeton: Princeton University Press, 1990) provides compelling pen portraits of aspects of Taishō culture.

The politics of the interwar years are the subject of Peter Duus, *Party Rivalry and Political Change in Taishō Japan* (Cambridge, Mass.: Harvard University Press, 1968). *Japan in Crisis: Essays on Taishō Democracy*, ed. Bernard S. Silberman and H. D. Harootunian (Princeton: Princeton University Press, 1974), has a fine set of essays dealing with the ambiguities of the interwar period. A particularly challenging interpretation is that of Andrew Gordon, *Imperial Democracy in Prewar Japan* (Berkeley: University of California Press, 1991). There are interesting studies of political figures. The short life of Ōsugi Sakae is treated by Thomas A. Stanley in *Ōsugi Sakae: Anarchist in Taishō Japan* (Cambridge, Mass.: Harvard University Press, 1982), and Byron K. Marshall has translated *The Autobiography of Ōsugi Sakae* (Berkeley: University of California Press, 1992). Sharon M. Minichiello's *Retreat from Reform: Patterns of Political Behavior in Interwar Japan* (Honolulu: University of Hawaii Press, 1984) takes up the case of Nagai Ryūtarō (1881–1944).

Intellectual and cultural life of the period receives increasing attention. Tatsuo Arima, *The Failure of Freedom: A Portrait of Modern Japanese Intellectuals* (Cambridge, Mass.: Harvard University Press, 1969), discusses a fascinating group of writers. The Special Higher School ethos is the subject of Donald Roden's splendid *Schooldays in Imperial Japan: A Study in the Culture of a Student Elite* (Berkeley: University of California Press, 1980). Henry DeWitt Smith II, *Japan's First Student Radicals* (Cambridge, Mass.: Harvard University Press, 1972), published during the stormy days of postwar student radicalism, takes the Special Higher School students on to Tokyo Imperial University and Yoshino Sakuzō's Shinjinkai (New Man Society). The government's concern with university radicalism is treated in Byron K. Marshall's *Academic Freedom and the Japanese Imperial University, 1868–1939* (Berkeley: University of California Press, 1992). An extremely useful dimension of cultural life is to be found in Gregory J. Kasza, *The State and the Mass Media in Japan, 1918–1945* (Berkeley: University of California Press, 1988). Popular culture of the era is also beginning to receive its due, as in Jennifer Robertson, *Takarazuka: Sexual Politics and Popular Culture in Modern Japan* (Berkeley: University of California Press, 1988), and Gennifer Weisenfeld, "Maruyama, MAVO, and Modernity: Constructions of the Modern in Taishō Japan Avant-garde Art" (Ph.D. dissertation, Princeton University, 1987).

Interwar political relations with China have drawn much attention, but the dimensions of cultural relations are only now coming into focus. There is a large Japanese literature, and the studies of student exchanges by Sanetō Keishū are discussed in my *Japan and China from War to Peace, 1894–1972* (Chicago: Rand McNally, 1975). Joshua Fogel has made this area his own. Mention should be made of *The Literature of Travel in the Japanese Rediscovery of China, 1862–1945* (Stanford: Stanford University Press, 1996), *Nakae Ushikichi in China* (Cambridge, Mass.: Harvard University Press, 1989), and *Life along the South Manchurian Railway: The Memoirs of Itō Takeo* (Armonk, N.Y.: Sharpe, 1988).

In Japanese foreign policy the work of Akira Iriye takes first place. His *After Imperialism: The Search for a New Order in the Far East, 1921–1931* (Cambridge, Mass.: Harvard University Press, 1965) took up the Soviet, Japanese, and Chinese responses to the Washington Conference order, and three books examined aspects of Japanese-American relations: *Across the Pacific: An Inner History of American-East Asian Relations* (New York: Harcourt Brace, 1967), *Pacific Estrangement: Japanese and American Expansion, 1897–1911* (Cambridge, Mass.: Harvard University Press, 1972), and *Power and Culture: The Japanese-American War, 1941–1945* (Cambridge, Mass.: Harvard University Press, 1981). The same author's *The Origins of the Second World War in Asia and the Pacific* (New York: Longman, 1987), gives a skillful and soundly based summary. Ernest R. May and James C. Thomson, Jr., have edited a set of essays that follow the full course of the exchange in *American–East Asian Relations: A Survey* (Cambridge, Mass.: Harvard University Press, 1972), which give some idea of the complexity of the field and the immense quantity of material available.

The field of Japanese colonialism has expanded manyfold thanks to the contents of three conference volumes: *The Japanese Colonial Empire, 1895–1945*, ed. Ramon H. Myers and Mark R. Peattie; *The Japanese Informal Empire in China, 1895–1937*, ed. Peter Duus, Ramon H. Myers, and Mark R. Peattie; and *The Japanese Wartime Empire, 1931–1945*, ed. Peter Duus, Ramon H. Myers and Mark R. Peattie, all from Princeton University Press, 1984, 1989, and 1996. To these must be added Louise Young, *Japan's Total Empire: Manchuria and the Culture of Wartime Imperialism* (Berkeley: University of California Press, 1998).

The 1930s

As one enters the 1930s the amount of reading available increases dramatically, and it is possible to offer only a few guideposts. The last holdover of the old Meiji elite was Saionji Kinmochi, who is the subject of Lesley Connors, *The Emperor's Adviser: Saionji Kinmochi and Pre-war Japanese Politics* (London: Croom Helm, 1987). His secretary, Harada Kumao, kept a careful diary during the 1930s that has been the source for much political coverage. The first volume has been translated by Thomas Francis Mayer-Oakes as *Fragile Victory: Prince Saionji and the 1930 London Treaty Issue* (New York: Weatherhill, 1968), a handsome volume that gets surprisingly little attention. Oka Yoshitake's biography of Konoe, translated by Shumpei Okamoto and Patricia Murray as *Konoe Fumimaro: A Political Biography*

(Tokyo: University of Tokyo Press, 1983), leaves many questions about that enigmatic aristocrat. Gordon Berger, *Parties out of Power in Japan, 1931–1941* (Princeton: Princeton University Press, 1977) is essential for its coverage of the parties during the 1930s and the development of the Imperial Rule Assistance Association. Ben-Ami Shillony, *Politics and Culture in Wartime Japan* (Oxford: Clarendon, 1981), follows politics to the surrender.

The factional struggles in the Imperial Army lie behind each of the "incidents," and are well treated in James B. Crowley, "Japanese Army Factionalism in the Early 1930s," *JAS*, 21, 3 (May 1962). The classic treatment of the February 1936 revolt is that of Ben-Ami Shillony, *Revolt in Japan: The Young Officers and the February 26, 1936 Incident* (Princeton: Princeton University Press, 1973). There are many accounts of right-wing organizations and terrorism. A highly readable one is by Richard Storry, *The Double Patriots: A Study of Japanese Nationalism* (London: Chatto and Windus, 1957). More structured and carefully documented is the Marxist account by O. Tanin and E. Yohan, *Militarism and Fascism in Japan* (New York: International Publishers, 1934), two scholars who fell victim to Stalin's purges. Civilian nationalists were no less important. George M. Wilson, *Radical Nationalist in Japan: Kita Ikki, 1883–1937* (Cambridge, Mass.: Harvard University Press, 1969), treats a man involved in (and executed for) the 1936 revolt, and Thomas R. H. Havens, *Farm and Nation in Modern Japan: Agrarian Nationalism, 1870–1940* (Princeton: Princeton University Press, 1974), studies Gondo Seikyō and Tachibana Kōzaburō, two men whose writings and ideas had explosive consequences.

From the Manchurian Incident to the Surrender

The literature here is vast, but also repetitious, so these notes remain brief. Sadako N. Ogata, *Defiance in Manchuria: The Making of Japanese Foreign Policy, 1931–32* (University of California, 1964), an early work by a scholar who has gone on to become a distinguished United Nations official, remains probably the best account. Ian Nish, *Japan's Struggle with Internationalism: Japan, China, and the League of Nations, 1931–3* (London: Kegan Paul, 1993) provides a carefully argued account of the response to the Lytton Commission. The matter looked quite different to defense specialists, and James B. Crowley, *Japan's Quest for Autonomy: National Security and Foreign Policy, 1930–1938* (Princeton: Princeton University Press, 1966), remains one of the best accounts of matters as Japanese military leaders saw them.

Robert J. C. Butow's *Tojo and the Coming of the War* (Princeton: Princeton University Press, 1961) bridges the career of an army bureaucrat with the Washington negotiations and war decisions, with explicit normative judgments. The same author's *The John Doe Associates: Backdoor Diplomacy for Peace, 1941* (Stanford: Stanford University Press, 1974) details for the first time the strange and ultimately unhelpful efforts of well-meaning meddlers to help the Washington negotiations along. They failed, unfortunately, and Roberta Wohlstetter, *Pearl Harbor: Warning and Decision* (Stanford: Stanford University Press, 1962) is a brilliant account that helps explain the many things that went wrong on Hawaii in December 1941. Dorothy Borg and Shumpei Okamoto have edited a splendid set of papers that take up in tandem the setting in comparable bureaus, agencies, and ministries in Japan and the United States in *Pearl Harbor as History: Japanese-American Relations, 1931–1941* (New York: Columbia University Press, 1973). And for a close study of the immediate prelude to and unfolding of that fateful day, with particular attention to the Japanese planning and execution, Gordon W. Prange, *At Dawn We Slept: The Untold Story of Pearl Harbor* (New York: McGraw-Hill, 1981) remains a classic account.

Japan's path to war can best be studied in the selected translations by many specialists from the massive Japanese set *Taiheiyō senso e no michi*, published in five volumes, all from Columbia University Press, and edited by James William Morley. In sequence of the material covered they are *Deterrent Diplomacy: Japan, Germany, and the U.S.S.R., 1935–1940* (1976), *Japan Erupts: The London Naval Conference and the Manchurian Incident, 1928–1932* (1984), *The China Quagmire: Japan's Expansion on the Asian Continent, 1933–1941* (1983), *The Fateful Choice: Japan's Advance into Southeast Asia, 1939–1941* (1980), and *The Final Confrontation: Japan's Negotiations with the United States* (1984). Finally, Nobutaka Ike's translation of the minutes of the key conferences that were held in connection with the decision for war with the United States, *Japan's Decision for War: Records of the 1941 Policy Conferences* (Stanford: Stanford University Press, 1967), is a priceless resource.

Life in Japan during the war is discussed by the French reporter Robert Guillain, who was there, in *Le Peuple japonaise et la guerre* (Paris: Julliard, 1947), a book hard to find and seldom cited. Thomas R. H. Havens, *Valley of Darkness: The Japanese People and World War Two* (New York: Norton, 1978), has used it and many other Japanese sources, and the diary of Kiyosawa Kiyoshi, *Diary of Darkness: The Wartime Diary of Kiyosawa Kiyoshi* (Princeton: Princeton University Press, 1999) gives a gripping and depressing account of years that seem well named. There are two invaluable collections of memories of the war. Frank Gibney, ed., and Beth Cary, trans., provide some of the thousands of letters that were sent to the editor of the *Asahi Shinbun* in 1986 and 1987 telling about war experiences, some in military and others in civilian life, in *Senso: The Japanese Remember the Pacific War* (Armonk, N.Y.: Sharpe, 1995). Somewhat similar is a splendid collection of memories dredged out in interviews by Haruko Taya Cook and Theodore F. Cook, *Japan at War: An Oral History* (New York: New Press, 1992). These materials give the reader entry into the minds of survivors of the war; the memories from victims and victimizers, shamed and shameless, explain why so many Japanese found it best to try to forget and move on.

The shattering events that ended the war—atomic bombs, huge casualty lists, imperial conferences and the emperor's decision, abortive revolt and ultimate acquiescence—have produced more titles than can be suggested here. The work of Robert J. C. Butow, *Japan's Decision to Surrender* (Stanford: Stanford University Press, 1954), remains the standard account. There is a highly readable account by the Pacific War Research Society, *Japan's Longest Day* (Tokyo: Kodansha International, 1968) in which the emperor emerges as hero. The discovery of a "monologue" Hirohito prepared for possible use in the event he was questioned by the International Military Tribunal, however, permits other readings, some of them suggested by Herbert P. Bix, "The Showa Emperor's 'Monologue' and the Problem of War Responsibility," *JJS* 18, 2 (Summer 1992), and especially Bix, "Hiroshima in History and Memory: Japan's Delayed Surrender—a Reinterpretation," *Diplomatic History*, 19, 2 (Spring 1966): 197–235. The "Monologue" is also utilized by Bob T. Wakabayashi, "Emperor Hirohito on Localized Aggression in China," *Sino-Japanese Studies*, 4, 1 (October 1991): 4–27. An overall biography of Hirohito is the work of Stephen S. Large, *Emperor Hirohito and Shōwa Japan* (London: Routledge, 1992).

The Yoshida and MacArthur Years

There is of course an abundance of material dealing with the Allied Occupation of Japan. Notes to the text identify some of the sources available on early steps taken for the demolition of the old order. Particular interest attaches to the Tokyo Tribunal for the Far East, Japan's equivalent of the Nuremberg tribunal. Richard H. Minear has written a particularly sharp attack on its procedures in *Victor's Justice: The Tokyo War Crimes Trial* (Princeton: Princeton University Press, 1971). It is interesting to note, however, that there has been relatively little critical writing about the trial in Japan, perhaps because progressive historians want no part of the prewar establishment and its policy, although there has been at least one major film effort at revisionism. An interesting study by Kazuko Tsurumi, *Social Change and the Individual: Japan before and after Defeat in World War II* (Princeton: Princeton University Press, 1970), concludes that the tribunal and other trials brought little change.

The official history prepared by General Courtney Whitney's Government Section, *Political Reorientation of Japan: September 1945 to September 1948*, issued by the Government Printing Office in two massive volumes in 1948, contains an uncritical summary and, in its larger volume, an essential collection of documents. There are of course memoirs by MacArthur himself and his aides, Whitney among them. A good guide through this forest is the lucid account by Richard B. Finn, *Winners in Peace: MacArthur, Yoshida, and Postwar Japan* (Berkeley: University of California Press, 1992). The Yoshida side of the story is contained in *The Yoshida Memoirs* (Boston: Houghton Mifflin, 1962), a translation in Churchillian prose by his son from a slightly longer and often more acerbic original. John W. Dower's *Empire and Aftermath: Yoshida Shigeru and the Japanese Experience, 1878–1954* (Cambridge, Mass.: Harvard University Press, 1979), consistently critical of Yoshida and the overall Occupation turn away from reform, is carefully based on the right sources.

But the story of the Occupation goes far beyond MacArthur's staff in SCAP and Yoshida's mobilization of former diplomats and politicians, and it has now received highly praised treatment in John W. Dower's *Embracing Defeat: Japan in the Wake of World War II* (New York: Norton, 1999), an impressive survey I wish we had had earlier. Dower is concerned with ordinary people in extraordinary days of defeat and determination. He views retention of the throne as foreshadowing the turn from reform to reconstruction, and captures the mood of postwar years with skill.

When one knows how the story came out, more or less, it is particularly interesting to see how it looked to those who wrote before they could have known. *Japan's Economy in War and Reconstruction* by Jerome B. Cohen (Minneapolis: University of Minnesota Press, Institute of Pacific Relations, 1949), with a foreword by George B. Sansom, regrets abandonment of early and more draconian plans but has wonderful detail on Japan's wartime fumbling. Eleanor M. Hadley, who was involved in the implementation of the Occupation, describes the abandonment of plans for economic deconcentration in *Anti-Trust in Japan* (Princeton: Princeton University Press, 1970). Edwin O. Reischauer's *The United States and Japan* (Cambridge, Mass.: Harvard University Press, 1950) was probably the more authoritative and balanced account in its successive revisions for twenty years. The land reform received classic treatment in R. P. Dore, *Land Reform in Japan* (Oxford: Oxford University Press, 1959). Labor reforms, implemented by SCAP and recounted by Theodore Cohen in

Remaking Japan: The American Occupation as New Deal (New York: Free Press, 1987), edited by Herbert Passin, conveys some of the zest reformist SCAP officials took in their work; that the final product was to an important extent an outcome prepared by Japanese officials, however, is clear from Sheldon Garon's scholarly *The State and Labor in Japan* (Berkeley: University of California Press, 1987).

Probably the single most important contribution to postwar Japan is a splendid set of essays edited by Andrew Gordon, *Postwar Japan as History* (Berkeley: University of California Press, 1993), a set of sixteen essays that range over many aspects of Japanese society. The death of Emperor Hirohito in 1989 brought many evaluations of an era and life that had spanned the twentieth century, and Carol Gluck edited a set of essays by Japanese and American commentators that appeared as a special issue of *Daedalus* (American Academy of Arts and Sciences, Summer 1990), entitled *Showa: The Japan of Hirohito,* that was subsequently published separately.

It was inevitable that Japan's economic resurgence should bring with it a flood of studies and commentaries on its significance for other industrializing and industrialized societies. Management and labor arrangements brought studies that began with James Abegglen's *The Japanese Factory: Aspects of Its Social Organization* (Glencoe, Ill.: Free Press, 1958), which viewed the permanent employment system as a residue of traditional Japanese social practices. Further research, notably R. P. Dore's *British Factory—Japanese Factory: The Origins of National Diversity in Industrial Relations* (London: Allen & Unwin, 1973), showed this was in no sense a product of tradition or continuity, and soon Garon's *State and Labor* and especially Andrew Gordon's magisterial *The Evolution of Labor Relations in Japan: Heavy Industry, 1853–1955* (Cambridge, Mass.: Council on East Asian Studies, Harvard University, 1985), showed that the system, while it resonated with Japanese perceptions of social justice and mutuality, came into existence during the labor shortages immediately prior to World War II.

Next scholars began to ask about the relations between the state and private enterprise in Japan. William W. Lockwood, ed., *The State and Economic Enterprise in Japan* (Princeton: Princeton University Press, 1965), one of the Modernization series volumes, strove for a balanced assessment in these matters, but as Japan's economy grew and seemed to threaten the predominance of the United States positions became stronger and the perception of "Japanese capitalism" as structurally different was heard more often. A major contribution to this discussion was Chalmers Johnson's *MITI and the Japanese Miracle: The Growth of Industrial Policy, 1925–1975* (Stanford University Press, 1982), which distinguished between the "regulatory state" of the United States and other industrial democracies and the "developmental state" best exemplified by Japan but mirrored by other latecomers whose governments worked actively to discipline, direct, fund, and ultimately promote heavy and export industries. Other scholars have refined this by emphasizing the function of the market and internal politics. Bai Gao, *Economic Ideology and Japanese Industrial Policy* (Cambridge: Cambridge University Press, 1997), Daniel I. Okimoto, *Between MITI and the Market* (Stanford: Stanford University Press, 1988), and Kent Calder, *Crisis and Compensation* (Princeton: Princeton University Press, 1988) make important contributions. All in all, one can conclude, Japanese economics history, a field in which William W. Lockwood's *The Economic Development of Japan: Growth and Structural Change* stood almost alone when it was published by Princeton University Press in 1955, has experienced a growth as robust as that of Japan itself.

For years the issues seemed so pressing that journalists and other pundits took up the cry, notably Karel van Wolferen, *The Enigma of Japanese Power: People and Politics in a Stateless Nation* (New York: Knopf, 1989); the "enigma" lay in the author's inability to identify a central, "state" spider in the web of Japanese interrelationships. Many others, for example Patrick Smith, *Japan: A Reinterpretation* (New York: Vintage, 1997) leaped aboard this vehicle, determined to denounce as somehow subversive figures like Edwin Reischauer who had argued the long-range convergence of Japan and the West. Meanwhile a group of scholars organized by Murakami Yasusuke and Hugh T. Patrick rethought the paradigms of the "modernization" school of the 1960s in a series of conferences that produced three fine volumes on the *Political Economy of Japan* published by Stanford University Press: *The Domestic Transformation*, edited by Kozo Yamamura and Yasukichi Yasuba (1987), *The Changing International Context*, edited by Takeshi Inoguchi and Daniel I. Okimoto (1988), and *Cultural and Social Dynamics*, edited by Shumpei Kumon and Henry Rosovsky, (1992).

The 1990s, during which the Japanese economy experienced its first postwar and longest slump, were remarkably free of this controversy. Japan no longer seemed as remarkable to its neighbors or as threatening to its competitors. Nevertheless it would be as great a mistake to dismiss the dormant giant of the 1990s as it was to accept the demonic interpretations of the 1980s.

NOTES

Excerpts from *Sources of Japanese Tradition* (1958), comp. Ryusaku Tsunoda, Wm. Theodore de Bary, and Donald Keene, and *Society and Education in Japan* (Columbia Teachers College, 1965), trans. Herbert Passin, are republished with permission of Columbia University Press, 562 W. 113th St., New York, N.Y. 10025. Reproduced by permission of the publisher via Copyright Clearance Center, Inc.

1. Sekigahara

1. George Elison, "Introduction," in George Elison and Baldwell L. Smith, eds., *Warlords, Artists, and Commoners: Japan in the Sixteenth Century* (Honolulu: University Press of Hawaii, 1981), pp. 1ff.

2. Jurgis Elisonas, "The Inseparable Trinity: Japan's Relations with China and Korea," in *Cambridge History of Japan* [hereafter *CHJ*], vol. 4: *Early Modern Japan*, ed. John Whitney Hall (Cambridge: Cambridge University Press, 1991), p. 255.

3. Jurgis Elisonas, "Christianity and the Daimyo," in *CHJ*, 4:303.

4. *Teppō-ki*, in Ryusaku Tsunoda, Wm. Theodore de Bary, and Donald Keene, comps., *Sources of Japanese Tradition* (New York: Columbia University Press, 1958), pp. 319–320.

5. Asao Naohiro with Marius B. Jansen, "Shogun and Tennō," in John Whitney Hall, Nagahara Keiji, and Kozo Yamamura, eds., *Japan before Tokugawa: Political Consolidation and Economic Growth, 1500–1650* (Princeton: Princeton University Press, 1981), p. 249.

6. Nagahara Keiji with Kozo Yamamura, "The Sengoku Daimyo and the Kandaka System," in Hall, Nagahara, and Yamamura, *Japan before Tokugawa*, p. 50.

7. One finds these claims repeated in the nineteenth century as the moral standing of samurai rule weakened. In the province of Tosa, on the island of Shikoku, a league of village leaders secretly distributed criticism of samurai rule that argued "we were once commissioned directly by the Imperial Court . . . should we not say that village heads, the head of the commoners, are superior to the retainers who are the hands or feet of the nobles?" Marius B. Jansen, "Tosa during the Last Century of Tokugawa Rule," in John Whitney Hall and Marius B. Jansen, eds., *Studies in the Institutional History of Early Modern Japan* (Princeton: Princeton University Press, 1968), p. 341.

8. Asao with Jansen, "Shogun and Tennō," pp. 252–253.

9. George Sansom, *A History of Japan, 1334–1640* (Stanford: Stanford University Press, 1981), p. 310.

10. Tsunoda, de Bary, and Keene, *Sources of Japanese Tradition,* pp. 315–316.

11. Fujiki Hisashi with George Elison, "The Political Posture of Oda Nobunaga," in Hall, Nagahara, and Yamamura, *Japan before Tokugawa,* pp. 155–173.

12. Asao with Jansen, "Shogun and Tennō," p. 255.

13. Michael Cooper, S.J., *They Came to Japan: An Anthology of European Reports on Japan, 1543–1640* (Berkeley: University of California Press, 1965), pp. 93–95.

14. Ibid., pp. 134–135.

15. James Murdoch, *A History of Japan,* vol. 2 (London: Kegan, Trench, Trubner, 1925), p. 386.

16. Mary Elizabeth Berry, *Hideyoshi* (Cambridge, Mass.: Harvard University Press, 1982), is the best biography. See also John Whitney Hall, "Hideyoshi's Domestic Policies," and Elison, "Hideyoshi, the Bountiful Minister," both in Hall, Nagahara, and Yamamura, *Japan before Tokugawa.*

17. Quoted from a contemporary translation in Berry, *Hideyoshi,* p. 219.

18. Yoshio Kuno, *Japanese Expansion on the Asiatic Continent* (Berkeley: University of California Press, 1937), 1:311–312.

19. John W. Hall, *Government and Local Power in Japan, 500 to 1700: A Study Based on Bizen Province* (Princeton: Princeton University Press, 1966), p. 288.

20. Tsunoda, de Bary, and Keene, *Sources of Japanese Tradition,* p. 330.

21. Marius B. Jansen, "Tosa in the Sixteenth Century," in Hall and Jansen, *Studies in the Institutional History,* and Hall, "Hideyoshi's Domestic Policies."

22. Philip C. Brown, *Central Authority and Local Autonomy in the Formation of Modern Japan: The Case of Kaga Domain* (Stanford: Stanford University Press, 1993), pp. 76–84.

23. Berry, *Hideyoshi,* p. 105.

24. Quoted in C. R. Boxer, *The Christian Century in Japan, 1549–1650* (Berkeley: University of California Press, 1951), pp. 54–55.

2. The Tokugawa State

1. Lee Butler, "Tokugawa Ieyasu's Regulations for the Court: A Reappraisal," *Harvard Journal of Asiatic Studies,* 54, 2 (1994): 451–509, provides the best study of this document.

2. Hall, *Government and Local Power in Japan,* pp. 6–7.

3. Thomas C. Smith, "The Japanese Village in the Seventeenth Century," in Hall and Jansen, *Studies in Institutional History,* pp. 263–282.

4. Albert M. Craig, *Chōshū in the Meiji Restoration* (Cambridge, Mass.: Harvard University Press, 1961), p. 22.

5. William Coaldrake, *Architecture and Authority in Japan* (London: Routledge, 1996).

6. Bob T. Wakabayashi, "In Name Only: Imperial Sovereignty in Early Modern Japan," *Journal of Japanese Studies,* 17, 1 (1991): 41.

7. John W. Hall, "The *bakuhan* System," in *CHJ,* 4:152.

8. Kären Wigen, *The Making of a Japanese Periphery* (Berkeley: University of California Press, 1995).

9. Quoted in George M. Wilson, "Hashimoto Sanai in the Political Crisis of 1858," in Albert M. Craig and Donald H. Shively, eds., *Personality in Japanese History* (Berkeley: University of California Press, 1970), p. 260.

10. Conrad Totman, *Politics in the Tokugawa Bakufu, 1600–1843* (Cambridge, Mass.: Harvard University Press, 1967), pp. 213ff.

11. Donald H. Shively, "Tokugawa Tsunayoshi, the Genroku Shogun," in Craig and Shively, *Personality in Japanese History*, pp. 85–126.

12. Beatrice Bodart-Bailey, "The Laws of Compassion," *Monumenta Nipponica*, 40, 2 (Summer 1985): 163–189.

13. Hall, "The *bakuhan* System," in *CHJ*, 4:166–167, and Totman, *Politics in the Tokugawa Bakufu*, pp. 270–277.

14. Thomas C. Smith, " 'Merit' as Ideology in the Tokugawa Period," in R. P. Dore, ed., *Aspects of Social Change in Modern Japan* (Princeton: Princeton University Press, 1967), pp. 75–76.

15. Robert K. Sakai et al., eds., *The Status System and Social Organization of Satsuma* (Tokyo: University of Tokyo Press, 1975).

16. Bonnie Abiko, "Watanabe Kazan, His Life and Times" (Ph.D. dissertation, Princeton University, 1982).

17. Marius B. Jansen, "Tosa in the Sixteenth Century: The 100 Article Code of Chōsokabe Motochika," in Hall and Jansen, *Studies in Institutional History*, pp. 89–114.

18. Jansen, "Tosa in the Seventeenth Century: The Establishment of Yamauchi Rule," in Hall and Jansen, *Studies in Institutional History*, pp. 115–139, and Luke S. Roberts, *Mercantilism in a Japanese Domain* (Cambridge: Cambridge University Press, 1998), chap. 2, "The Geography and Politics of Seventeenth Century Tosa."

19. Philip C. Brown, *Central Authority and Local Autonomy in the Formation of Early Modern Japan: The Case of Kaga Domain* (Stanford: Stanford University Press, 1993), pp. 24ff.

20. Ronald DiCenzo, "Daimyo Domain and Retainer Band in the Seventeenth Century" (Ph.D. dissertation, Princeton University, 1978).

21. Hall, "The *bakuhan* System," in *CHJ*, 4:159.

22. Harold Bolitho, "The *han*," in *CHJ*, 4:194.

23. Hall, *Government and Local Power in Japan*, pp. 414–418.

24. Harold Bolitho, *Treasures among Men: The Fudai Daimyo in Tokugawa Japan* (New Haven: Yale University Press, 1974), p. 35, and William Kelley, *Deference and Defiance in Nineteenth-Century Japan* (Princeton: Princeton University Press, 1985), pp. 78ff., take up the event as social history.

25. Yoon Byung-nam, "Domain and Bakufu in Tokugawa Japan: The Copper Trade and Development of Akita Domain Mines" (Ph.D. dissertation, Princeton University, 1994).

26. Hiraide Kojirō, "kataiuchi" (vendetta), in *Kokushi daijiten*, vol. 3 (Tokyo, 1983), pp. 350–352.

27. Constantine N. Vaporis, "Post Station and Assisting Villages: Labor and Peasant Contention," *Monumenta Nipponica*, 41 (1986): 377–414.

28. Mary Elizabeth Berry, "Public Policy and Private Attachment: The Goals and Conduct of Power in Early Modern Japan," *Journal of Japanese Studies*, 12, 2 (1986).

29. James W. White, "State Growth and Popular Protest in Tokugawa Japan," *Journal of Japanese Studies*, 14, 1 (1988).

30. A leading voice in this is Watanabe Hiroshi, whose *Higashi Ajiya no Ōken to shisō*

(Tokyo: Tokyo Daigaku Shuppankai, 1997) is introduced by Luke Roberts's translation of its introduction in *Sino-Japanese Studies*, 10, 2 (April 1998). Some recent histories use the term *bakufu* only beginning in the mid-ninetenth century, and Asao Naohiro, who was cited earlier, avoids the entire "*bakuhan* state" terminology as problematic and prefers simply "Tokugawa political structure."

3. Foreign Relations

1. Olof G. Lidin, *The Life of Ogyū Sorai, a Tokugawa Confucian Philosopher*, Scandinavian Institute of Asian Studies Monograph Series (Lund: Studentlitt., 1973), p. 120.

2. *Japanese Family Storehouse*, trans. G. W. Sargent (Cambridge: Cambridge University Press, 1959), pp. 85–86.

3. Leonard Blussé, *Strange Company* (Dordrecht: Foris Publications, 1986), pp. 99, 103.

4. George Elison, *Deus Destroyed: The Image of Christianity in Early Modern Japan* (Cambridge, Mass.: Harvard University Press, 1973), p. 116.

5. Tashiro Kazui, "Foreign Relations during the Edo Period: *Sakoku* Reexamined," *Journal of Japanese Studies*, 8, 2 (Summer 1982), and her magisterial *Kinsei Ni-Chō tsūkō-bōekishi no kenkyū* (Tokyo: Sobunsha, 1981).

6. Ronald P. Toby, *State and Diplomacy in Early Modern Japan: Asia in the Development of the Tokugawa Bakufu* (Princeton: Princeton University Press, 1984), provides the definitive statement of this position.

7. Arai Hakuseki's autobiography, Joyce Ackroyd, trans., *Told Round a Brushwood Fire* (Princeton: Princeton University Press, 1979), p. 62.

8. Dan F. Henderson, "Chinese Legal Studies in Early Eighteenth Century Japan: Scholars and Sources," *Journal of Asian Studies*, 30 (November 1970): 21–50.

9. Sin Yu-han, *Haeyurok* (Seoul: Chongumsa), trans. Byungnam Yoon, unpublished paper, 1976.

10. *Deshima Diaries: Marginalia, 1700–1740*, ed. Paul van der Velde and Rudolf Bachofner (Tokyo: Japan-Netherlands Institute, 1992), p. 148.

11. On whom see Michael Cooper, S.J., *Rodrigues the Interpreter: An Early Jesuit in Japan and China* (New York: Weatherhill, 1974).

12. Kamigaito Kenichi, *Sakoku no hikaku bummei ron* (Tokyo: Kodansha, 1994), pp. 42ff.

13. Derek Massarella, *A World Elsewhere: Europe's Encounter with Japan in the Sixteenth and Seventeenth Centuries* (New Haven: Yale University Press, 1990), a work solidly based on EIC records.

14. See Ivan I. Morris, *The Nobility of Failure: Tragic Heroes in the History of Japan* (New York: Holt, Rinehart and Winston, 1975), pp. 143–179, for an account of the rebellion and Amakusa Shirō as one of many tragic figures who have gained posthumous fame as righteous martyrs in Japan.

15. *Dai Nihon Shiryō*, 34, sect. 12.

16. Sakai et al., *The Status System and Social Organization of Satsuma*, p. 45.

17. Elison, *Deus Destroyed*, takes his title from one such pamphlet, of which he provides a translation.

18. Reinier H. Hesselink, "The Prisoners from Nambu: The *Beskens* Affair in Historical and Historiographical Perspective" (Ph.D. dissertation, University of Hawaii, 1992), a

striking account of an affair in which Dutch prisoners were used to denounce imprisoned priests.

19. Endō Shūsaku's novel *Chinboku*, translated as *Silence*, is built around the fate of two priests who reached Japan in an effort to reconvert an apostate priest and instead fell into the inquisitor's hands.

20. Grant K. Goodman, *Japan: The Dutch Experience* (London: Athlone Press, 1986), and Kanai Madoka, *Tai gaikōshōshi no kenkyū: kaikokuki no tōzai bunka kōryū* (Yokohama: Yurindo, 1988), provide an abundance of detail.

21. Robert LeRoy Innes, "The Door Ajar: Japan's Foreign Trade in the Seventeenth Century" (Ph.D. dissertation, University of Michigan, 1980), the fullest account of the Nagasaki trade.

22. Engelbert Kaempfer, *History*, trans. J. Scheuchzer (Glasgow: James MacLehose, 1906), 3:167–168. For Kaempfer and the history of his manuscript, see Beatrice M. Bodart-Bailey and Derek Massarella, eds., *The Furthest Goal: Engelbert Kaempfer's Encounter with Tokugawa Japan* (London: Curzon Press, Japan Library, 1995).

23. Kaempfer, *History*, 3:334. Kaempfer argued that Japan was fortunate in having a ruler who wisely shut it off from unnecessary goods and temptations. "Happy and flourishing," he concluded, "is the condition of [Tsunayoshi's] subjects under his reign."

24. Toby, *State and Diplomacy*, provides the classic account.

25. Ibid., p. 126.

26. Ōba Osamu, *Edo jidai no Ni-Chū hiwa* (Tokyo: Toho Shoten, 1980), and *Edo jidai ni okeru Chūgoku bunka juyō no kenkyū* (Kyoto: Dōhōsha, 1984).

27. Ironically, though, it was Kaempfer, and Thunberg, Titsingh, and von Siebold after him, who managed, despite the restrictions under which they lived, to scrape together the information on life in Edo Japan that still serves to educate us. The Chinese guests, with much better opportunities, did nothing of the sort. What would we not give for Ingen's account of the conversations, seminars, and banquets with his Japanese hosts!

28. Wai-ming Benjamin Ng, *The I Ching in Tokugawa Thought and Culture* (Honolulu: Association for Asian Studies and University of Hawaii Press, 2000), pp. 66–67.

29. Letter from Ogyū Sorai to the abbot Yüeh-feng (Japan's Eppō, 1635–1734), who arrived in Nagasaki in 1655 and was invited to lecture before the shogun Tsunayoshi in 1708. Sorai was in touch with him for the remainder of his life. Lidin, *The Life of Ogyū Sorai*, pp. 116–117.

30. William S. Atwell, "Ming China and the Emerging World Economy, c. 1470–1650," chap. 8 in Denis Twitchett and Frederick W. Mote, eds., *Cambridge History of China*, vol. 8: *The Ming Dynasty* (Cambridge: Cambridge University Press, 1998), pp. 376–416.

31. Marius B. Jansen, *China in the Tokugawa World* (Cambridge, Mass.: Harvard University Press, 1992), p. 68, and De-min Tao, "Traditional Chinese Social Ethics in Japan, 1721–1943," *Gest Library Journal*, 4, 2 (Winter 1991): 68–84.

32. In 1710, for example, the Dutch Deshima Diary noted that "seventeen Japanese were sentenced. Eight of them were crucified, nine were decapitated. All on charges of smuggling." And a few days later, "The rampant smuggling by the Chinese during the past hundred years has drained Japan of silver and gold. Added to the fact that

for over sixty years there has been no new prospecting for precious metals, it explains why there is a scarcity of these metals." *Deshima Diaries*, pp. 128–129. Also Fred G. Notehelfer, "Smuggling in the Kyōhō Period," *Princeton Papers on Japan* (1972).

33. Quoted in Marius B. Jansen, "New Materials for the Intellectual History of Nineteenth Century Japan," *Harvard Journal of Asiatic Studies*, 20, 2–3 (1957): 597, quoting from *Ihi nyūkō roku* (Tokyo, 1931).

34. Leonard Bussé, "Japanese Historiography and European Sources," in P. C. Emmer and H. L. Wesseling, eds., *Reappraisals in Overseas History* (Leiden: Leiden University Press, 1979).

4. Status Groups

1. Kōsaka Masaaki, ed., *Japanese Thought in the Meiji Period*, trans. David Abosch (Tokyo: Pan-Pacific Press, 1958), p. 203.

2. John W. Hall, "Rule by Status in Tokugawa Japan," *Journal of Japanese Studies*, 1, 1 (Autumn 1974).

3. Lafcadio Hearn, *Japan: An Attempt at Interpretation* (New York: Macmillan, 1907), pp. 386–387.

4. Herschel Webb, *The Imperial Institution in the Tokugawa Period* (New York: Columbia University Press, 1968), the best study.

5. Asao Naohiro, ed., *Mibun to kakushiki*, vol. 7 of *Nihon no kinsei* (Tokyo: Chūō Kōron, 1992), pp. 193ff.

6. Bob T. Wakabayashi, "In Name Only: Imperial Sovereignty in Early Modern Japan," *Journal of Japanese Studies*, 17, 1 (Winter 1991): 48.

7. Ibid., p. 49. One offspring of such a marriage succeeded to the throne (the Empress Meishō) and one to the shogunate (Tokugawa Ieharu).

8. Adapted from F. G. Notehelfer, "Ebina Danjō: A Christian Samurai of the Meiji Period," *Papers on Japan* (Harvard University, 1963), 2:6.

9. Tamamoto Tsunetomo, *The Hagakure: A Code to the Way of the Samurai*, trans. Takao Mukoh (Tokyo: Hokuseido, 1980), p. 35. See also Yukio Mishima, *The Way of the Samurai*, trans. Kathryn Sparling (Putnam, N.Y.: Pegasus, 1977), pp. 110–112.

10. Quoted from Tsunoda, de Bary, and Keene, *Sources of Japanese Tradition*, p. 399.

11. Asao, *Mibun to kakushiki*, pp. 14ff., for the principal Chinese and Japanese texts.

12. Donald H. Shively, "Popular Culture," in *CHJ*, 4:708.

13. Recent scholarship refines this somewhat. Takagi Shunsaku argues that the edicts were initially the products of wartime emergency, and concerned less with samurai than with their servants and designed to prevent desertion, but no one doubts that the separate "class" as such dates from that period. Cf. Asao, *Mibun to kakushiki*, p. 45.

14. W. G. Beasley, "Feudal Revenue in Japan at the Time of the Meiji Restoration," *Journal of Asian Studies*, 19 (1960): 235–275.

15. E. Herbert Norman, *Japan's Emergence as a Modern State* (1940; New York: Institute of Pacific Relations, 1946), p. 81.

16. Carmen Blacker, "*Kūhanjō*, by Fukuzawa Yukichi," *Monumenta Nipponica*, 13 (1953): 304–329.

17. John W. Hall, "The Ikeda House and Its Retainers," in Hall and Jansen, *Studies in Institutional History*, p. 87.

18. Kate Wildman Nakai, *Women of the Mito Domain* (Tokyo: University of Tokyo Press, 1992), p. xiii, for Yūkoku's humble origins.

19. Kozo Yamamura, *A Study of Samurai Income and Entrepreneurship* (Cambridge, Mass.: Harvard University Press, 1974).

20. Luke Roberts, trans., "'From a Parrot's Cage'—The Diary of a Samurai," unpublished diary of Asahi Monzaemon (1674–1718).

21. *Musui's Story: The Autobiography of a Tokugawa Samurai*, trans. Teruko Craig (Tucson: University of Arizona Press, 1988). For more detail on the context of the diary, see *Journal of Japanese Studies*, 16, 2 (1990).

22. Gary P. Leupp, *Servants, Shophands, and Laborers in the Cities of Tokugawa Japan* (Princeton: Princeton University Press, 1992), p. 32.

23. Donald H. Shively, "Sumptuary Regulation and Status in Early Tokugawa Japan," *Harvard Journal of Asiatic Studies*, 25, 4–5 (1965): 152.

24. Nakai, *Women of the Mito Domain*, p. 54.

25. Brown, *Central Authority and Local Autonomy*, presents a (Kaga-based) challenge to the acceptance of sweeping claims made for the effect of Hideyoshi's measures.

26. Adapted from Dan Fenno Henderson, *Village "Contracts" in Tokugawa Japan* (Seattle: University of Washington Press, 1975), p. 188.

27. This is argued persuasively by Luke Roberts in *Mercantilism in a Japanese Domain*.

28. Smith, "The Japanese Village in the Seventeenth Century," p. 265.

29. See Harumi Befu, "Village Autonomy and Articulation with the State," in Hall and Jansen, *Studies in Institutional History*, pp. 301–316, and Befu, "Duty, Reward, Sanction, and Power: Four-cornered Office of the Tokugawa Village Headman" in B. S. Silberman and H. Harootunian, eds., *Modern Japanese Leadership* (Tucson: University of Arizona Press, 1966), pp. 25–50.

30. Thomas C. Smith's *The Agrarian Origins of Modern Japan* (Stanford: Stanford University Press, 1959) is the classic work.

31. Kodama Kōta, *Kinsei nōmin seikatsu shi* (Tokyo: Yoshikawa Kobunkan, 1957), pp. 215ff.

32. Jansen, "Tosa in the Seventeenth Century," p. 120. But if things became sufficiently difficult emigration would take place. See the discussion of movement from Tosa to Satsuma in Roberts, *Mercantilism in a Japanese Domain*, pp. 68ff.

33. George Sansom, *A History of Japan, 1615–1867* (Stanford: Stanford University Press, 1963), p. 99.

34. Shively, "Sumptuary Legislation," pp. 154–155.

35. Smith, *Agrarian Origins*, p. 280.

36. Thomas C. Smith, "The Land Tax during the Tokugawa Period," in Hall and Jansen, *Studies in Institutional History*, pp. 283–300.

37. Hayami Akira, *Keizai shakai no seiritsu 17–18 seiki* (Tokyo: Iwanami, 1988).

38. Naitō Jirō, *Kinsei Nihon keizaishi ron* (Tokyo: Yachiyo, 1981), pp. 57ff.

39. Kumakura Isao, *Kan'ei bunka no kenkyū* (Tokyo: Yoshikawa Kobunkan, 1988), and Kumakura, "From the Outlandish to the Refined: Art and Power at the Outset of the Edo Period," *Asian Cultural Studies*, 17 (March 1989): 59–68.

40. Attractively presented in Yoshikazu Hayashi with the unfortunate title *Seventeenth-century Japan: A Time of Mystery and Isolation—120 Paintings by Yusetsu Kaiho* (Tokyo, 1991). Another, roughly contemporaneous collection of artisan professions, *Jinrin kinmōzu*, depicts four hundred occupations.

41. Sasamoto Shōji in Asao, *Nihon no kinsei*, 4:90ff.

42. It is worth noting that Hideyoshi's turn against the Christian missionaries in 1587 included the wording, "the sale of Japanese to China, South Barbary, and Korea is outrageous. In Japan trade in human beings is prohibited." Elison, *Deus Destroyed*, p. 118.

43. Leupp, *Servants, Shophands, and Laborers*, p. 41.

44. David Howell, *Geographics of Japanese Identity: Polity, Status, and Civilization in the Nineteenth Century* (forthcoming, University of California Press).

45. Edwin McClellan, *Woman in the Crested Kimono: The Life of Shibue Io and Her Family Drawn from Mori Ōgai's "Shibue Chūsai"* (New Haven: Yale University Press, 1985), a literary work with rich materials for social history.

46. Bitō Masahide, in Japan Foundation *Newsletter*, 1981, a useful summary of a large body of work.

5. Urbanization and Communications

1. Toshio G. Tsukahira, *Feudal Control in Tokugawa Japan: The Sankin Kōtai System* (Cambridge, Mass.: Harvard University Press, 1966), and Bolitho, "The han," in *CHJ*, 4:198ff.

2. Constantine Vaporis, "To Edo and Back: Alternate Attendance and Japanese Culture in the Early Modern Period," *Journal of Japanese Studies*, 23, 1 (Winter 1997): 30.

3. F. G. Notehelfer, ed., *Japan through American Eyes: The Journal of Francis Hall, Kanagawa and Yokohama, 1859–1866* (Princeton: Princeton University Press, 1992), pp. 133, 382.

4. Kaempfer, *History of Japan*, 2:336.

5. *Journaal van Dirk de Graeff van Polsbroek* (Maastricht, 1978), pp. 33, 34.

6. DiCenzo, "Daimyo Domain and Retainer Band," p. 44.

7. The authoritative study is that of Constantine Novikos Vaporis, *Breaking Barriers: Travel and the State in Early Modern Japan* (Cambridge, Mass.: Harvard University Press, 1994).

8. One might compare this with the cumbersome distribution system of contemporary Japan, maintained to protect the uneconomic and the weak.

9. William Wray, "Shipping: From Sail to Steam," in Marius B. Jansen and Gilbert Rozman, eds., *Japan in Transition: From Tokugawa to Meiji* (Princeton: Princeton University Press, 1986), pp. 250–254, provides a convenient summary.

10. Van Polsbroek, *Journaal*, p. 34.

11. Vaporis, "To Edo and Back," provides a richly documented discussion of Tosa samurai travels and purchases on such trips. See also the same author's discussion in *Kōtsūshi kenkyū* (1995).

12. Tsukahira, *Feudal Control*, p. 68.

13. Roberts, *Mercantilism in a Japanese Domain*, persuasively points out that arguments

for such policies frequently, as in Tosa, had their origins in merchant opinion and proposals.

14. As in Yokkaichi, "fourth-day market," in memory of market days on the fourth, fourteenth, and twenty-fourth day of the month.

15. Jinnai Hidenobu, *Tokyo: A Spatial Anthropology,* trans. Kimiko Nishimura (Berkeley: University of California Press, 1995); see also the same author's "The Spatial Structure of Edo" in Chie Nakane and Shinzaburo Ōishi, eds., *Tokugawa Japan: The Social and Economic Antecedents of Modern Japan* (Tokyo: University of Tokyo Press, 1990).

16. Jinnai, *Tokyo,* p. 40.

17. Coaldrake, *Architecture and Authority in Japan,* and William H. Coaldrake, "Building a New Establishment," in James L. McClain, John M. Merriman, and Ugawa Kaoru, eds., *Edo and Paris: Urban Life and the State in the Early Modern Era* (Ithaca, N.Y.: Cornell University Press, 1994). The only gate that has survived in place is the "Red Gate" of the University of Tokyo, designed to be a "guardian gate" for the shogun Ienari's daughter when she entered the daimyo (Maeda) family as a bride.

18. One might extend this comparison to modern Tokyo, whose central space, like that of New York, is given over to a world of green which, unlike Central Park, is off limits.

19. Miyazaki Katsumi, "Edo no tochi—daimyo, bakushin no tochi mondai," in Yoshida Nobuyuki, ed., *Toshi no jidai,* vol. 9 in *Nihon no kinsei* (Tokyo: Chūō Kōron, 1992), provides illuminating details and figures for warrior holdings in Edo. See also, for spatial allocation, Gilbert Rozman, *Urban Networks in Ch'ing China and Tokugawa Japan* (Princeton: Princeton University Press, 1973).

20. Constantine Vaporis, "Edo to Tosa—Edo hantei no ichi kōsatsu," *Tosa shidan* (Kochi, 1995).

21. Notehelfer, *Japan through American Eyes,* p. 592.

22. McClellan, *Woman in the Crested Kimono,* pp. 28–29.

23. Jinnai, *Tokyo,* p. 39.

24. On the history and role of the Sensōji temple at Asakusa, see Nam-il Hur, *Prayer and Play in Tokugawa Japan: Asakusa's Sensōji and Edo Society* (Cambridge, Mass.: Harvard University Press, 2000).

25. James L. McClain, "Edobashi: Power, Space and Popular Culture in Edo," in McClain, Merriman, and Ugawa, *Edo and Paris,* pp. 105ff.

26. Quoted by McClain, in ibid., pp. 105ff.

27. William W. Kelley, "Incendiary Action: Fires and Fire Fighting in the Shogun's Capital and the People's City," in McClain, Merriman, and Ugawa, *Edo and Paris,* pp. 310–331.

28. Hatano Jun, "Edo's Water Supply," in McClain, Merriman, and Ugawa, *Edo and Paris,* pp. 234–250.

29. Ōoka (1677–1751) was city magistrate for twenty years and then commissioner of shrines and temples for another twenty-five. He served as a judge at the shogunal court (Hyōjōsho) throughout the entire period and attained a legendary fame for Solomonic wisdom.

30. Thus Dan Fenno Henderson, *Conciliation and Japanese Law* (Seattle: University of Washington Press, 1965), pp. 142–162, gives the transcript of hearings in a breach of

contract complaint, brought by men living in different jurisdictions, in which the judge tries to force a private settlement by threatening to punish both parties if they fail to work things out.

31. Katō Takashi, "Governing Edo," in McClain, Merriman, and Ugawa, *Edo and Paris,* pp. 57ff.

32. Misbehavior on the part of persons lower in status was treated quite differently. For a thoughtful discussion of the interrelationships between status society and punishment, see Daniel V. Botsman, "Crime, Punishment, and the Making of Modern Japan, 1790–1895" (Ph.D. dissertation, Princeton University, 1999).

33. Katsu, *Musui's Story,* pp. 101, 155, 68. Mori Ōgai finds a doctor's family resorting to the same measure in an effort to curb behavior by a son who is disgracing the family. "Chūsai, in utter despair, had a room of incarceration built upstairs, with bars on the windows and doorway, so that his son could be thrown into it." McClellan, *Woman in the Crested Kimono,* p. 46.

34. *The Autobiography of Fukuzawa Yukichi,* trans. Eiichi Kiyooka (Tokyo: Hokuseido, 1948), pp. 252–253.

6. The Development of a Mass Culture

1. Shively, "Popular Culture," in *CHJ,* 4:716.

2. Yoshiaki Shimizu, *Japan: The Shaping of Daimyo Culture, 1185–1868* (Washington, D.C.: National Gallery of Art, 1988), and Shimizu, "Workshop Management of the Early Kano Painters *circa* A.D. 1590–1600," *Archives of Asian Art,* 34 (1981).

3. Quoted from Robert Treat Paine and Alexander Soper, *The Art and Architecture of Japan* (London: Penguin, 1955), pp. 273–274.

4. Henry D. Smith II, "The Book," in McClain, Merriman, and Ugawa, *Edo and Paris,* p. 333.

5. Smith, in ibid., gives an admirably succinct discussion of the process.

6. See the discussion by Ekkehard May, *Die Kommerzialisierung der japanishen Literature in späten Edo—Zeit 1750–1868* (Wiesbaden: Harrassowitz, 1985).

7. Shively, "Popular Culture," pp. 718–720.

8. Mary Elizabeth Berry, *The Culture of Civil War in Kyoto* (Berkeley: University of California Press, 1994), p. 186.

9. Paine and Soper, *Art and Architecture,* pp. 268–269.

10. Berry, *The Culture of Civil War in Kyoto,* p. 210.

11. The many works of the Osaka historian Miyamoto Mataji explore the intricacies of this system.

12. Nishizi Yasushi, in Yoshida Nobuyuki, ed., *Toshi no jidai,* vol. 9 in Asao, *Nihon no kinsei,* pp. 173ff. It is ironic that present-day Japan, in the interests of equity within its distribution system, limits store size through its "Big Store Law" (*Daiten Hō*).

13. The code, or *kahō,* is translated in full in Sansom, *History of Japan, 1615–1867,* 2:251–253.

14. Translated with commentary by E. S. Crawcour in *Transactions of the Asiatic Society of Japan,* 3d ser., 8 (1961).

15. Mitsui history is discussed in an authorized volume, John G. Roberts, *Mitsui: Three*

Centuries of Japanese Business (New York: Weatherhill, 1973), and authoritatively in *Mitsui jigyō shi* (Tokyo: Mitsui Library, 1980), 3 vols., and by Hayashi Reiko in *Shōnin no katsudō*, vol. 5 of Asao, ed., *Nihon no kinsei*.

16. J. Mark Ramseyer, "Thrift and Diligence: House Codes of Tokugawa Merchant Families," in *Monumenta Nipponica*, 34, 2 (1979): 219–230.

17. Nishizaka Yasushi in Yoshida, *Tōshi no jidai*, pp. 203–206.

18. Donald Keene, *World within Walls: Japanese Literature of the Pre-Modern Era, 1600–1867* (New York: Holt, Rinehart and Winston, 1976), p. 93.

19. Yoshikawa Kōjirō, *Jinsai, Sorai, Norinaga: Three Classical Philologists of Mid-Tokugawa Japan* (Tokyo: Tōhō Gakkai, 1983), p. 268.

20. Shively, "Popular Culture," pp. 728ff., and Keene, *World within Walls,* pp. 156ff.

21. Keene, *World within Walls,* p. 156.

22. Howard Hibbett, *The Floating World in Japanese Fiction* (New York: Oxford University Press, 1959), p. 63.

23. See Shively, "Popular Culture," pp. 742ff.

24. See Liza Crihfield, "Geisha," in *Encyclopedia of Japan* (Tokyo: Kodansha International, 1988), 3:14–15, and Liza Dalby, *Geisha* (New York: Vintage Books, 1985).

25. Donald H. Shively, *The Love Suicide at Amijima: A Study of a Japanese Domestic Tragedy by Chikamatsu Monzaemon* (Cambridge, Mass.: Harvard University Press, 1953), pp. 26–27.

26. See the discussion by Donald H. Shively in ibid.

27. The play is translated by Donald Keene in *Major Plays of Chikamatsu* (New York: Columbia University Press, 1961), pp. 39–56.

28. Translated by Donald Keene: *Chūshingura: The Treasury of Loyal Retainers* (New York: Columbia University Press, 1971).

7. Education, Thought, and Religion

1. Tetsuo Najita, *Visions of Virtue in Tokugawa Japan: The Kaitokudō Merchant Academy of Osaka* (Chicago: University of Chicago Press, 1987), and Tao De-min, *Kaitokudō Shushigaku no Kenkyū* (Osaka: Osaka University Press, 1994).

2. R. P. Dore, *Education in Tokugawa Japan* (Berkeley: University of California Press, 1965), pp. 76ff.; the standard work.

3. Richard Rubinger, *Private Academies of Tokugawa Japan* (Princeton: Princeton University Press, 1982).

4. See, for example, the picture of Seizan Sensei in the Meiji novel by Tokutomi Roka, *Omoide no ki,* translated by Kenneth Strong as *Footprints in the Snow* (Tokyo: Tuttle, 1971), pp. 8off.

5. John W. Hall, "The Confucian Teacher in Tokugawa Japan," in David S. Nivison and Arthur E. Wright, eds., *Confucianism in Action* (Stanford: Stanford University Press, 1959), and Kate Wildman Nakai, "The Naturalization of Confucianism in Tokugawa Japan: The Problem of Sino-Centrism," *Harvard Journal of Asiatic Studies,* 40, 1 (June 1980).

6. Arai is among the most studied and translated of the scholars. In addition to Kate Wildman Nakai's splendid study *Shogunal Politics: Arai Hakuseki and the Premises of*

Tokugawa Rule (Cambridge, Mass.: Harvard University Press, 1988), there are two translations by Joyce Ackroyd: *Told Round a Brushwood Fire: The Autobiography of Arai Hakuseki* (Princeton: Princeton University Press, 1979) and *Lessons from History: Arai Hakuseki's Tokushi Yoron* (St. Lucia: University of Queensland Press, 1982).

7. Hall, "The Confucian Teacher," and John W. Hall, "Ikeda Mitsumasa and the Bizen Flood of 1654," in Craig and Shively, *Personality in Japanese History*, pp. 57ff.

8. *Told Round a Brushwood Fire*, trans. Ackroyd, pp. 202–203.

9. Ansai is most accessible in the study by Herman Ooms, *Tokugawa Ideology: Early Constructs, 1570–1680* (Princeton: Princeton University Press, 1985).

10. Tsunoda, de Bary, and Keene, *Sources of Japanese Tradition*, pp. 369–370.

11. See Mary Evelyn Tucker, *Moral and Spiritual Cultivation in Japanese Neo-Confucianism: The Life and Thought of Kaibara Ekken (1630–1714)* (Albany: State University of New York Press, 1989).

12. Kaibara Ekken, "The Greater Learning for Women," trans. Basil Hall Chamberlain; first published in *Journal of the Royal Asiatic Society of Great Britain* (X, pt. 3, July 1878), and republished by him in *Things Japanese* (Tokyo, 1905), pp. 502–508.

13. Masao Maruyama, *Studies in the Intellectual History of Tokugawa Japan*, trans. Mikiso Hane (Princeton: Princeton University Press, 1974); Yoshikawa, *Jinsai, Sorai, Norinaga*; Lidin, *The Life of Ogyū Sorai*, and Olof G. Lidin, trans., *Ogyū Sorai's "Distinguishing the Way": An Annotated English Translation of the Bendo* (Tokyo: Sophia University, 1970); J. R. McEwan, *The Political Writings of Ogyū Sorai* (Cambridge: Cambridge University Press, 1962); and Samuel Hideo Yamashita, *Master Sorai's Responsals: An Annotated Translation of "Sorai sensei tōmonshō"* (Honolulu: University of Hawaii Press, 1994).

14. Tetsuo Najita, "History and Nature in Eighteenth-Century Tokugawa Thought," in *CHJ*, 4:599.

15. From the fine exposition of Sumie Jones, "Language in Crisis: Ogyū Sorai's Philological Thought and Hiraga Gennai's Creative Practice," in Earl Miner, ed., *Principles of Classical Japanese Literature* (Princeton: Princeton University Press, 1985), p. 221.

16. W. J. Boot, *The Adoption and Adaptation of Neo-Confucianism in Japan: The Role of Fujiwara Seika and Hayashi Razan* (Leiden, 1992), p. 244.

17. Bob Tadashi Wakabayashi, *Japanese Loyalism Reconstrued: Yamagata Daini's Ryūshi shinron of 1759* (Honolulu: University of Hawaii Press, 1995), p. 105, and Martin Collcutt, "The Legacy of Confucianism in Japan," in Gilbert Rozman, ed., *The East Asian Region: Confucian Heritage and Its Modern Adaptation* (Princeton: Princeton University Press, 1991).

18. Robert L. Backus, "The Kansei Prohibition of Heterodoxy and Its Effects on Education," and "The Motivation of Confucian Orthodoxy in Tokugawa Japan," in *Harvard Journal of Asiatic Studies*, 39, 1, and 39, 2 (June and December 1979): 55–106 and 275–358.

19. Some have related the statecraft of the Meiji Restoration leaders, who constructed a new institutional order, to Sorai's praise of inventive system builders. See Robert Bellah, "Baigan and Sorai," in Tetsuo Najita and Irwin Scheiner, eds., *Japanese Thought in the Tokugawa Period* (Chicago: University of Chicago Press, 1978), p. 148.

20. Nakai, "The Naturalization of Confucianism," pp. 157ff.

21. Tsunoda, de Bary, Keene, *Sources of Japanese Tradition,* pp. 389–400.

22. Bob Tadashi Wakabayashi, *Anti-Foreignism and Western Learning in Early-Modern Japan: The New Theses of 1825* (Cambridge, Mass.: Harvard University Press, 1986), p. 149.

23. Nakai, "The Naturalization of Confucianism," p. 173.

24. Quoted in Tsunoda, de Bary, and Keene, *Sources of Japanese Tradition,* pp. 538–540.

25. Ibid., pp. 512–514.

26. Heinrich Dumoulinn, "Kamo Mabuchi: Kokuikō," *Monumenta Nipponica,* 2, 1 (1939): 165–192. Pledges of this sort were not uncommon, for most private academy heads demanded full loyalty from their charges. This was true also of the authority structure of the *iemoto* ("house head") system in applied arts like flowers, tea, and incense. Nevertheless its application here to instruction in historical poetics indicates something of the instructor's intensity.

27. Shigeru Matsumoto, *Motoori Norinaga, 1730–1801* (Cambridge, Mass.: Harvard University Press, 1970), an important character study from the perspective of Eriksonian psychology.

28. Harry D. Harootunian, "The Functions of China in Tokugawa Thought," in Akira Iriye, ed., *The Chinese and the Japanese: Essays in Political and Cultural Interactions* (Princeton: Princeton University Press, 1980), pp. 9–36.

29. Tsunoda, de Bary, and Keene, *Sources of Japanese Tradition,* pp. 544–548.

30. Donald Keene, *The Japanese Discovery of Europe* (Stanford: Stanford University Press, 1969), chap. 7, "Hirata Atsutane and Western Learning," p. 170.

31. Thomas C. Smith, "Ōkura Nagatsune and the Technologists," in Craig and Shively, *Personality in Japanese History,* p. 129.

32. Harry Harootunian, "Late Tokugawa Culture and Thought," in *Cambridge History of Japan,* vol. 5: *The Nineteenth Century,* ed. Marius B. Jansen (Cambridge: Cambridge University Press, 1989), pp. 198–215.

33. These doctors are the subject of a forthcoming study by Professor Harm Beuker of Leiden University.

34. Yoshida Tadashi, "The *rangaku* of Shizuki Tadao: The Introduction of Western Science in Tokugawa Japan" (Ph.D. dissertation, Princeton University, 1974).

35. Adapted from Keene, *The Japanese Discovery of Europe,* p. 22, as used in Marius B. Jansen, *Japan and Its World: Two Centuries of Change* (Princeton: Princeton University Press, 1980), pp. 32–33.

36. Jansen, *Japan and Its World,* pp. 38–39.

37. All Sugita texts quoted can be found in Haga Tōru, ed., *Sugita Genpaku, Hiraga Gennai, Shiba Kōkan,* vol. 22 of *Nihon meicho* (Tokyo: Chūō Kōron, 1971).

38. Paul B. Watt, "Jiun Sonja (1718–1804): A Response to Confucianism within the Context of Buddhist Reform," in Peter Nosco, ed., *Confucianism and Tokugawa Culture* (Princeton: Princeton University Press, 1984), pp. 188ff.

39. Kuroda Toshio, "Shinto in the History of Japanese Religion," *Journal of Japanese Studies,* 7, 1 (1981): "The word Shinto by itself probably means popular beliefs in general" (p. 5), and Helen Hardacre, *Shinto and the State, 1868–1988* (Princeton: Princeton University Press, 1989), pp. 15ff.

40. Helen Hardacre, "Conflict between Shugendō and the New Religions of Bakumatsu Japan," *Japanese Journal of Religious Studies,* 21, 2–3 (1994), and Carmen Blacker, *The Catalpa Bow: A Study of Shamanistic Practices in Japan* (London: Allen & Unwin, 1975).

41. Hardacre, "Shugendō," p. 147.

42. For a sample of the fare that held them spellbound, see "A Sermon Given by Hosoi Heishū on 14 December 1783" in Michiko Y. Aoki and Margaret B. Dardess, "The Popularization of Samurai Values," *Monumenta Nipponica,* 30, 4 (Winter 1976): 401–413.

43. Janine Sawada, *Confucian Values and Popular Zen: Sekimon Shingaku in Eighteenth-Century Japan* (Honolulu: University of Hawaii Press, 1993), p. 45; see also the older study by Robert Bellah, *Tokugawa Religion: The Values of Pre-Industrial Japan* (Glenco, Ill.: Free Press, 1957).

8. Change, Protest, and Reform

1. Conrad Totman, "Tokugawa Peasants: Win, Lose, or Draw?" *Monumenta Nipponica,* 41, 4 (1986): 468.

2. Susan B. Hanley and Kozo Yamamura, *Economic and Demographic Change in Pre-industrial Japan, 1600–1868* (Princeton: Princeton University Press, 1977).

3. Ann Bowman Jannetta, *Epidemics and Mortality in Early Modern Japan* (Princeton: Princeton University Press, 1987), discusses outbreaks of smallpox, measles, and dysentery. Japan was fortunately spared an outbreak of plague, probably thanks to its relative isolation. Note also the work in progress of William S. Atwell tracing the effect of volcanic eruptions on climate change, crop failure, and political unrest in Japan and China simultaneously.

4. Hayami Akira, *Kinsei nōson no rekishi jinkōgakuteki kenkyū* (Tokyo: Tōyō keizai shinpō, 1973), and other works.

5. Laurel Cornell, "Infanticide in Early Modern Japan? Demography, Culture, and Population," *Journal of Asian Studies,* 55, 1 (February 1996): 22–50.

6. Thomas C. Smith, *Nakahara: Family Farming and Population in a Japanese Village, 1717–1830* (Stanford: Stanford University Press, 1977).

7. Thomas C. Smith, "The Land Tax in the Tokugawa Period," *Journal of Asian Studies* 18, 1 (November 1958), and reprinted in Hall and Jansen, *Studies in the Institutional History,* pp. 283–299, and in Smith, *Native Sources of Japanese Industrialization, 1750–1920* (Berkeley: University of California Press, 1988).

8. Matsudaira Sadanobu, *Kokuhonron,* quoted in David Lu, ed., *Sources of Japanese History* (New York: McGraw-Hill, 1974), 2:6–7.

9. Haruko Iwasaki, "Writing in Circles: Cultural Networks of Edo Gesaku Literature, 1760–1790" (Ph.D. dissertation, Harvard University, 1991), pp. 318, 148–151.

10. Kozo Yamamura, *A Study of Samurai Income and Entrepreneurship* (Cambridge, Mass.: Harvard University Press, 1974), p. 133.

11. Lu, *Sources of Japanese History,* 2:4.

12. Yamamura, *Samurai Income,* pp. 47–48.

13. Kelley, *Deference and Defiance in Nineteenth-Century Japan,* chap. 3, and Bolitho, *Treasures among Men,* p. 35.

14. James W. White, *Ikki: Social Conflict and Political Protest in Early Modern Japan* (Ithaca, N.Y.: Cornell University Press, 1995), is now the standard study.

15. Studies of "peasant rebellions" in Japan flourished during the 1970s and 1980s, both in Japan and abroad, partly, some have suggested, in response to the "Cultural" (more accurately, counter-cultural) Revolution in China, and more generally in rejection of the consensus model of Japanese society. This literature is reviewed and appraised in Conrad Totman, "Tokugawa Peasants: Win, Lose, or Draw?" pp. 457–476. See also Tetsuo Najita and J. Victor Koschmann, eds., *Conflict in Modern Japanese History: The Neglected Tradition* (Princeton: Princeton University Press, 1982).

16. See, in this connection, Irwin Scheiner, "Benevolent Lords and Honorable Peasants: Rebellion and Peasant Consciousness in Tokugawa Japan" in Tetsuo Najita and Irwin Scheiner, eds., *Japanese Thought in the Tokugawa Period* (Chicago: University of Chicago Press, 1978).

17. The subject of Anne Walthall, *Peasant Uprisings in Japan: A Critical Anthology of Peasant Histories* (Chicago: University of Chicago Press, 1991).

18. The martyr tradition in rebellions is explored by Yokoyama Toshio, *Hyakushō ikki to gimin denshō* (Tokyo: Kyōikusha, 1977). Reference to this splendid little book is one of many debts I owe Hayami Akira. Similar themes of "restless spirits" *(onryō)* in Japanese culture generally and Nō drama in particular are the subject of several studies by Umehara Takeshi.

19. Jansen, "Tosa in the Seventeenth Century," p. 120. Luke Roberts uncovers a case in which the flight of Tosa residents from overpopulated areas to Satsum led to an emigration agreement worked out by Edo representatives of the two domains, but agrees that arrangements for extradition would have been more common. Roberts, *Mercantilism in a Japanese Domain,* p. 68, with documentation.

20. Marius B. Jansen, "Tosa during the Last Century of Tokugawa Rule," in *Studies in Institutional History,* p. 335, following Hirao Michio, *Tosa nōmin ikki shikō* (Kōchi: Shimin toshokan, 1953), pp. 32–61.

21. Herbert Bix, "Leader of Peasant Rebellions: Miura Meisuke," in Murakami Hyoei and Thomas Harper, eds., *Great Historical Figures of Japan* (Tokyo: Japan Culture Institute, 1978), pp. 243–260. See also Bix, *Peasant Protest in Japan, 1590–1884* (New Haven: Yale University Press, 1986).

22. White, *Ikki,* p. 125.

23. The opposite, in other words, of the arrangement of signatures on the Declaration of Independence, in which John Hancock allegedly led off by inscribing his name so large that the king would be able to read it without his spectacles.

24. David L. Howell, *Capitalism from Within: Economy, Society, and the State in a Japanese Fishery* (Berkeley: University of California Press, 1994).

25. Tsuji Tatsuya, "Politics in the Eighteenth Century," in *CHJ,* 4:445ff.

26. Luke Roberts, "The Petition Box in Eighteenth-Century Tosa," *Journal of Japanese Studies,* 20, 2 (1994): 423–458.

27. A revealing instance of this principle is an 1808 litigation, mentioned earlier, studied and translated by Dan Fenno Henderson. The litigants, after making their way into a lower court with some difficulty, were repeatedly ordered to settle things themselves on penalty of punishment for both parties. Henderson, *Conciliation and Japanese Law* (Seattle: University of Washington Press, 1965), 1:135ff.

28. Tsuji, "Politics in the Eighteenth Century," in *CHJ*, 4:456.

29. Najita, *Visions of Virtue*, pp. 148ff.

30. This is the persuasive argument of Luke Roberts in *Mercantilism in a Japanese Domain*, who contends that domain merchants espoused this form of protectionism earlier than domain administrators.

31. Byung-nam Yoon, "The Akita Copper Trade" (Ph.D. dissertation, Princeton University, 1994).

32. John W. Hall, *Tanuma Okitsugu (1719–1788): Forerunner of Modern Japan* (Cambridge, Mass.: Harvard University Press, 1955), the standard source.

33. Ibid., pp. 119ff.

34. Sadanobu is the subject of Herman Ooms, *Charismatic Bureaucrat: A Political Biography of Matsudaira Sadanobu* (Chicago: University of Chicago Press, 1975).

35. Keene, *The Japanese Discovery of Europe*, p. 75.

36. I have discussed these trends at greater length in Chapter 1, "Japan in the Early Nineteenth Century," *CHJ*, 5:71–87.

37. Gilbert Rozman, "Edo's Importance in Changing Tokugawa Society," *Journal of Japanese Studies*, 1, 1 (1974): 94.

38. Katsuhisa Moriya, "Urban Networks and Information Networks," in Nakane and Ōishi, *Tokugawa Japan*, pp. 97–123.

39. Buyo Inshi, *Seji kemmonroku* (Tokyo: Misuzu shobō, 1969).

40. Harold Bolitho, "The Tempō Crisis," in *CHJ*, 5:117.

41. Ivan Morris, *The Nobility of Failure* (New York: Holt, Rinehart and Winston, 1975), p. 197, offers a highly readable account of the rebellion. For an analysis of Ōshio's thought, see Tetsuo Najita, "Ōshio Heihachirō, 1793–1838," in Craig and Shively, *Personality in Japanese History*, pp. 155–179.

42. Lu, *Sources of Japanese History*, 2:8.

43. *Keisei hisaku* (A secret plan of government), translated in Keene, *The Japanese Discovery of Europe*, p. 191.

44. Charles L. Yates, *Saigō Takamori* (London and New York: Kegan Paul, 1995), p. 19, and, in greater detail, "Restoration and Rebellion in Satsuma: The Life of Saigō Takamori" (Ph.D. dissertation, Princeton University, 1987), pp. 57–75. See also Nishikawa Shunsaku, *Edo jidai no poriteikaru-ekonomii* (Tokyo: Nihon Hyōronsha, 1974), pp. 161–182.

45. Craig, *Chōshū in the Meiji Restoration*, chap. 2, "Chōshū and the Tempō Reform," and Nishikawa Shunsaku, "Grain Consumption: The Case of Chōshū," in Jansen and Rozman, *Japan in Transition*, pp. 421–446.

46. See Ooms, *Charismatic Bureaucrat*, pp. 85–86.

47. Bolitho, "The Tempō Crisis," p. 156.

48. Ibid., p. 151.

49. Tōyama Shigeki, *Meiji Ishin* (Tokyo: Iwanami, 1950), perhaps the classical statement of this view.

9. The Opening to the World

1. Howell, *Capitalism from Within,* provides the first careful description of this enterprise.

2. Yoshikazu Nakamura, "The Satsuma Dialect in St. Petersburg, or the Adventures of Gonza the Castaway," *Japan Foundation Newsletter* (Tokyo), 26, 3, November 1998, pp. 1–3. This story, discovered by a scholar researching Bogdanov, has so delighted Kagoshima residents that a street has been named for Gonza.

3. John J. Stephan, *The Kuril Islands: Russo-Japanese Frontiers in the Pacific* (Oxford: Oxford University Press, 1974), p. 55.

4. W. G. Beasley, "The Foreign Threat and the Opening of the Ports," in *CHJ,* 5:265–266.

5. Haga Tōru, ed., *Nihon no meicho: Sugita Genpaku, Hiraga Gennai, Shiba Kōkan* (Tokyo, 1971), pp. 269–295, for text.

6. See the fine summary by Takakura Shin'ichirō in *Kokushi Daijiten,* vol. 2 (Tokyo, 1980), pp. 271–273.

7. Honda's "Secret Plan of Government" (*Keisei hissaku*) is discussed and translated in part by Donald Keene in *The Japanese Discovery of Europe.*

8. In the same period the English East India Company was becoming an arm of government, a change that was completed in 1834.

9. Kanai Madoka, *Nichi-Ran kōshōshi no kenkyū* (Kyoto: Shibunkaku Shuupan, 1986), gives the details of ships and captains.

10. Jansen, "New Materials for the Intellectual History of Nineteenth Century Japan," p. 575.

11. Translation by Bob T. Wakabayashi, *Anti-Foreignism and Western Learning in Early-Modern Japan,* p. 60.

12. Wakabayashi, *Anti-Foreignism and Western Learning in Early-Modern Japan,* p. 103.

13. The work and influence of Philipp Franz von Siebold are the subject of a massive biographical study by Kure Shōzō, *Shiiboruto sensei* (Tokyo, 1926) and a journal, *Shiiboruto kenkyū,* issued for several years beginning in 1982 by the Von Siebold Society of Hōsei University in Tokyo. His *Nippon: Archiv zur Beschreibung von Japan* (Leiden, 1832) was the basis for a popular work entitled *Manners and Customs of the Japanese* that was published in London and New York in 1852 and taken to Japan as textbook by Commodore Perry the next year.

14. Abiko, "Watanabe Kazan: The Man and His Times."

15. Satō Shōsuke, *Yōgakushi no kenkyū* (Tokyo: Chūō Kōron, 1980). Haruko Iwakasi first called this to my attention.

16. Wakabayashi, *Anti-Foreignism and Western Learning in Early-Modern Japan,* p. 149, translates the entire work.

17. From Aizawa's "New Theses," as translated by Wakabayashi in ibid., p. 169.

18. I have discussed this at greater length in *China in the Tokugawa World,* pp. 74–75.

19. Tsunoda, de Bary, and Keene, *Sources of Japanese Tradition,* p. 613.

20. Bob T. Wakabayashi, "Opium, Expulsion, Sovereignty: China's Lessons for Bakumatsu Japan," *Monumenta Nipponica,* 47, 1 (Spring 1992): 5.

21. Robert van Gulik, "*Kakkaron:* A Japanese Echo of the Opium War," *Monumenta Serica* (1939): 516–540.

22. C. R. Boxer, *Jan Compagnie in Japan 1600–1850* (The Hague: Nijhoff, 1950), app. V, p. 186.

23. J. A. van der Chijs, *Neërlands Streven tot Openstelling van Japan voor den Wereldhandel* (Amsterdam, 1867), pp. 47–52, for full text. The Lao Tzu reference was lost on bakufu scholars, who promised to research the matter.

24. For many years scholars credited Mizuno with a desire for opening Japan to trade and related his resignation to his failure, but Mitani Hiroshi finds little basis for this. "Kaikoku zen'ya," in *Nihon gaikō no kiki ishiki* (Tokyo: Kindai Nihon kenkyūkai, 1985), pp. 7ff.

25. W. G. Beasley, *Great Britain and the Opening of Japan, 1834–1858* (London: Luzac, 1951), p. 93.

26. For the flags, Miwa Kimitada, "Perri 'daiyon no shokan,'" in *Kokusai seiji*, no. 102 (Tokyo: Kokusai seiji gakkai, February 1993), pp. 1–21; a discussion expanded and enriched in the same author's *Kakurareta Peri no "shirohata"* (Tokyo: Sophia University Press, 1999). Peter Booth Wiley, *Yankees in the Land of the Gods: Commodore Perry and the Opening of Japan* (New York: Viking, 1990), gives the fullest account of the mission. Perry's own account appeared in 1856 as F. J. Hawks, ed., *Narrative of an Expedition of an American Squadron to the China Seas and Japan*, 2 vols. (Washington, D.C.: "Published by Order of the Congress," 1856). Perry's personal account, *The Japan Expedition of 1852–1854: The Personal Journal of Commodore Matthew C. Perry*, ed. Roger Pineau, appeared in 1968 from the Smithsonian Institution in Washington, D.C.

27. See, on this point, W. G. Beasley, "Japanese Castaways and British Interpreters," *Monumenta Nipponica*, 46, 1 (Spring 1991), who notes that the English too decided that negotiations in Dutch went better than those in Chinese.

28. A contemporary painting shows those hulls as brown, but the more ominous black had long served to distinguish ships from beyond the borders from the "white" ships from China. Printmakers emphasized their blackness, and the term has become standard in Japan.

29. In his diary S. Wells Williams, whose help was necessary for a Chinese version of the treaty, deplored Perry's hauteur. "I do not at all like the way in which this nation is spoken of by the commodore and most of his officers, calling them savages, liars, a pack of fools, poor devils; cursing them and then denying practically all of it by supposing them worth making a treaty with. Truly, what sort of instruments does God work with!" Wiley, *Yankees in the Land of the Gods*, p. 398.

30. From W. G. Beasley, *Select Documents on Japanese Foreign Policy, 1853–1868* (Oxford: Oxford University Press, 1955), pp. 102–107.

31. From ibid., pp. 117–119.

32. Conrad Totman, "Political Reconciliation in the Tokugawa Bakufu: Abe Masahiro and Tokugawa Nariaki, 1844–1852," in Craig and Shively, *Personality in Japanese History*, pp. 180–208, and, a less favorable view, Harold Bolitho, "Abe Masahiro and the New Japan," in Jeffrey P. Mass and William B. Hauser, eds., *The Bakufu in Japanese History* (Stanford: Stanford University Press, 1985), pp. 173–188.

33. Harris can be followed in his *Complete Journal*, ed. Mario Cosenza (Rutland and Tokyo: C. E. Tuttle, 1959); see also the account by his Dutch-speaking interpreter

Henry C. J. Heusken, *Japan Journal 1855–1861* (New Brunswick, N.J.: Rutgers University Press, 1964), and Oliver Statler's more critical, carefully researched, and highly readable *Shimoda Story* (New York: Random House, 1969).

34. Text of Nariaki's letter in Beasley, *Select Documents on Japanese Foreign Policy,* pp. 168–169.

35. Letter in *Ishin shi,* 6 vols. (Tokyo: Meiji shoin, 1941), 2:442–443. See also the discussion of one such daimyo agent in George M. Wilson, "The Bakumatsu Intellectual in Action: Hashimoto Sanai in the Political Crisis of 1858," in Craig and Shively, *Personality in Japanese History,* pp. 234–263.

36. The classic work by G. B. Sansom, *The Western World and Japan* (New York: Knopf, 1950), pp. 248–274, "Forerunners of the Restoration Movement," and especially H. D. Harootunian, *Toward Restoration: The Growth of Political Consciousness in Tokugawa Japan* (Berkeley: University of California Press, 1970), provide appealing detail (Sansom) and incisive analysis (Harootunian) of the men considered here.

37. Text in Beasley, *Select Documents on Japanese Foreign Policy,* pp. 102–107, a work that has as preface a masterly discussion of competing views about Japan's opening. Fujita is also discussed in Richard T. Chang, *From Prejudice to Tolerance: A Study of the Japanese Image of the West, 1826–1864* (Tokyo: Sophia University, 1970), pp. 21–97.

38. From Sakuma Shōzan, "Reflections on My Errors," in Tsunoda, de Bary, and Keene, *Sources of Japanese Tradition,* pp. 608f.

39. A formula also worked out by Chinese reformers like Chang Chih-tung, but only at the end of the century.

40. Adapted from Chang, *From Prejudice to Tolerance,* p. 124. Miyamoto Chū, *Sakuma Shōzan* (Tokyo, 1940), provides Sakuma's major writings as well as full biographical coverage.

41. Quoted in Thomas M. Huber, *The Revolutionary Origins of Modern Japan* (Stanford: Stanford University Press, 1981), p. 13, who provides good biographical detail.

42. Sukehiro Hirakawa, "Japan's Turn to the West," in *CHJ,* 5:451.

43. From Tsunoda, de Bary, and Keene, *Sources of Japanese Tradition,* pp. 618–622, and (the last), *CHJ,* 5:452.

10. The Tokugawa Fall

1. Text in *Ishin shi,* 2:731–739.

2. Marius B. Jansen, *Sakamoto Ryōma and the Meiji Restoration* (Princeton: Princeton University Press, 1961), pp. 108–109.

3. In addition to Richardson, the party consisted of a Mr. Marshall and Mrs. Boradaile; Marshall received a chest wound, and the lady sustained a head wound from a blow partially deflected by her pith helmet. A Dutch diplomat wrote that "Marshall later told me that it was entirely Richardson's fault. They could have let the procession pass, but Richardson paid no attention to Marshall, who called 'For God's sake let's not have a row! Turn back!' Richardson, a great braggart, cut right through the escort and was cut down immediately." *Journal van Jonkheer Dirk de Graeff van Polsbroek* (Assen: Van Gorcum, 1987), p. 60.

4. Harold Bolitho, "Aizu, 1853–1868," *Proceedings* of the British Association for Japanese Studies, 2 (1977): 8ff.

5. Shimazaki Tōson's epic account of the Restoration, *Yoake mae* (translated by William Naff as *Before the Dawn;* University of Hawaii Press, 1987), details these events as experienced by his father, a station *(honjin)* master on the central mountain highway.

6. The best account is to be found in Conrad Totman, *The Collapse of the Tokugawa Bakufu, 1862–1868* (Honolulu: University Press of Hawaii, 1980), pp. 108–122.

7. Jansen, *Sakamoto Ryōma and the Meiji Restoration,* p. 300.

8. From ibid., pp. 295–296.

9. Lu, *Sources of Japanese History,* 2:29.

10. Sugitami Akira draws a pointed contrast between Saga and bakufu officials in their reaction to the miniature railroad Perry presented the bakufu at Shimoda in 1854. Edo representatives, quite innocent of the engine which provided its power, sat on the roof of the little passenger cars and whooped with pleasure as the engine carried them along; Saga men, by contrast, selected for their training, headed straight for the engine room of the Dutch steamer they boarded, asked the right questions, and set out to build their own as soon as possible. "Kaikoku zengo ni okeru Nichi-Ran kankei" in Marius B. Jansen, ed., *Kyūshū to Nihon no rekishi,* Monograph Series no. 1 (Singapore: National University of Singapore, 1991), pp. 113–139.

11. W. G. Beasley, "The Foreign Threat and the Opening of the Ports," in *CHJ,* 5:301.

12. Rutherford Alcock, minister to Japan, to Lord Russell, November 19, 1864. Quoted in ibid., 5:297.

13. Shinya Sugiyama, "Thomas B. Glover: A British Merchant in Japan, 1861–70," *Business History,* 26, 2 (July 1984): 115–138.

14. *Japan through American Eyes: The Journal of Francis Hall, Kanagawa and Yokohama, 1859–1866,* ed. Notehelfer.

15. Jansen, "New Materials for the Intellectual History of Nineteenth Century Japan," p. 579.

16. I have discussed the missions abroad in *Japan and Its World,* pp. 45ff. The diaries of members of the first mission are discussed in Masao Miyoshi, *As We Saw Them: The First Japanese Embassy to the United States (1860)* (Berkeley: University of California Press, 1979).

17. Carmen Blacker, *The Japanese Enlightenment: A Study of the Writings of Fukuzawa Yukichi* (Cambridge: Cambridge University Press, 1964), p. 8.

18. *The Autobiography of Fukuzawa Yukichi,* trans. Eiichi Kiyooka (Tokyo: Hokuseido, 1948), pp. 143–144.

19. Jansen, "Tosa during the Last Century of Tokugawa Rule," p. 341. This intermediate role is also clear in Anne Walthall, "Caught in the Middle: *Gunchū Sōdai* in the Restoration Era," *Asian Cultural Studies,* 18 (February 1992): 164ff.

20. See *Before the Dawn,* trans. Naff; see also Naff, "Shimazaki Toson's *Before the Dawn:* Historical Fiction as History and as Literature" in James White, Michio Umegaki and Thomas Havens, eds., *The Ambivalence of Nationalism: Modern Japan between East and West* (Lanham, Md.: University Press of America, 1990), pp. 79–114.

21. M. William Steele, "Goemon's New World View: Popular Representations of the Opening of Japan," *Asian Cultural Studies*, 17 (March 1989): 79.

22. This is most sharply seen in comparing Conrad Totman's *Collapse of the Tokugawa Bakufu, 1862–1868*, with the Chōshū-centered account by Albert Craig, *Chōshū in the Meiji Restoration*, or Marius Jansen's *Sakamoto Ryōma and the Meiji Restoration*.

23. Jansen, *Sakamoto Ryōma and the Meiji Restoration*, pp. 108–109; for Takechi, p. 133.

24. Reinier Hesselink, "The Assassination of Henry Heusken," *Monumenta Nipponica*, 49, 3 (Autumn 1994): 351.

25. Conrad Totman, "From *Sakoku* to *Kaikoku:* The Transformation of Foreign-Policy Attitudes, 1853–1868" *Monumenta Nipponica*, 36, 1 (1980), and Totman, *The Collapse of the Tokugawa Bakufu, 1862–1868*.

26. Bob T. Wakabayashi, "Rival Statesmen on a Loose Rein," in White, Umegaki, and Havens, *The Ambivalence of Nationalism*, p. 33.

27. Sensaku Nakagawa, *Kutani Ware*, trans. John Bester (New York: Kodansha, 1979), pp. 104–143. I owe this reference to Louise Cort.

28. Bolitho, "Aizu, 1853–1868."

29. Takie Sugiyama Lebra, *Above the Clouds: Status Culture of Modern Japanese Nobility* (Berkeley: University of California Press, 1993), p. 92.

30. Sir Ernest Satow, *A Diplomat in Japan* (Philadelphia: Lippincott, 1921), p. 184.

11. The Meiji Revolution

1. See, on this point, the discussion by Thomas C. Smith, "Japan's Aristocratic Revolution," reprinted in his *Native Sources of Japanese Industrialization, 1750–1820* (Berkeley: University of California Press, 1988).

2. Tsunoda, de Bary, and Keene, *Sources of Japanese Tradition*, p. 644.

3. Slightly variant translations of the three drafts can be found in Lu, *Sources of Japanese History*, 2:35–36. I follow the analysis of Inoue Kiyoshi, *Meiji ishin*, Nihon no rekishi, no. 20 (Tokyo: Chūō Kōron, 1966), pp. 84–90.

4. For Kido, Jansen, *Japan and Its World*, p. 63, following Kume Kunitake memoirs; for the emperor's rescript renouncing his divinity, Government Section, Supreme Commander for the Allied Powers, *Political Reorientation of Japan*, vol. II, appendices (Washington, D.C.: U.S. Government Printing Office, 1949), p. 470.

5. James Edward Ketelaar, *Of Heretics and Martyrs in Meiji Japan: Buddhism and Its Persecution* (Princeton: Princeton University Press, 1990), pp. 88–89. See also John Breen, "The Imperial Oath of 1868: Ritual, Politics, and Power in the Restoration," *Monumenta Nipponica*, 51, 4 (Winter 1996): 407–429.

6. Inoue, *Meiji ishin*, pp. 77ff., provides a deft summary of the tensions involved.

7. Albert M. Craig, "The Central Government," in Jansen and Rozman, *Japan in Transition*, p. 45.

8. *The Diary of Kido Takayoshi*, trans. Sidney Devere Brown and Akiko Hirota (Tokyo: University of Tokyo Press, 1983), 1:71 (entry of August 6, 1868).

9. Craig, "The Central Government," p. 48.

10. Ibid., p. 47.

11. *The Autobiography of Fukuzawa Yukichi*, p. 212.

12. Lu, *Sources of Japanese History*, 2:38.

13. Michio Umegaki, *After the Restoration: The Beginning of Japan's Modern State* (New York: New York University Press, 1988), p. 124.

14. *The Diary of Kido Takayoshi*, 1:186 (entry of February 28, 1869).

15. From the petition submitted by the daimyo of Satsuma, Choshū, Tosa, and Hizen in March 1869; Kan'ichi Asakawa, *The Documents of Iriki* (Tokyo, reprint 1955), pp. 377–378.

16. Translation modified from Umegaki, *After the Restoration*, p. 61.

17. On whom see Edward R. Beauchamp, *An American Teacher in Early Meiji Japan* (Honolulu: University Press of Hawaii, 1976).

18. F. G. Notehelfer, *American Samurai: Captain L. L. Janes and Japan* (Princeton: Princeton University Press, 1985). Janes, and a number of other Americans including Griffis, were recruited from Nagasaki by the Dutch-American missionary-educator Guido Verbeck through his contacts with the Dutch Reformed Seminary at Rutgers, New Brunswick, New Jersey.

19. Umegaki, *After the Restoration*, p. 63.

20. Craig, "Central Government," p. 55.

21. Ibid., p. 54.

22. Quoted in Beasley, "Meiji Political Institutions," in *CHJ*, 5:634.

23. W. E. Griffis, *The Mikado's Empire* (New York, 1876), pp. 526, 534, 536. Griffis left Japan in 1874, but his book went through twelve editions by 1912, and it was probably the most-read work on Japan for a half century in the United States.

24. The site was to become the impact center of the second atomic bomb of August 9, 1945.

25. Martin Collcutt, "Buddhism: The Threat of Eradication," in Jansen and Rozman, *Japan in Transition*, pp. 144–153.

26. Griffis, *The Mikado's Empire*, pp. 336–337.

27. Collcutt, "Buddhism: The Threat of Eradication," p. 159; Ketelaar, *Of Heretics and Martyrs in Meiji Japan*.

28. Fukuda Gyōkai, quoted in *Japanese Religion in the Meiji Era*, ed. Kishimoto Hideo and trans. John F. Howes (Tokyo: Obunsha, 1956), p. 111.

29. Helen Hardacre, *Shintō and the State, 1868–1988* (Princeton: Princeton University Press, 1989), pp. 28–29, provides a succinct summary of a very complex process.

30. Barbara Rose, *Tsuda Umeko and Women's Education in Japan* (New Haven: Yale University Press, 1992), and Akiko Kuno, *Unexpected Destinations: The Poignant Story of Japan's First Vassar Graduate* (New York: Kodansha, 1993), follow the careers of two of these, the one a pioneer educator and founder of Tsuda College, the other the wife of General Ōyama Iwao.

31. Marlene Mayo, "The Western Education of Kume Kunitake," *Monumenta Nipponica*, 27, no. 1 (1973): 3–67; Tanaka Akira, *"Bei-Ō kairan jikki" no gakusaiteki kenkyū* (Sapporo, 1993); and Kume's five-volume account, *Bei-Ō kairan jikki*, first published in 1875 and again in edited form by Professor Tanaka in the 1970s. At this writing the entire journal is being prepared for publication in English.

32. Irokawa Daikichi, *The Culture of the Meiji Period* (translation of Irokawa, *Meiji no bunka*), ed. Marius B. Jansen (Princeton: Princeton University Press, 1985), pp. 55ff., discusses Kido's observations.

33. *The Diary of Kido Takayoshi*, 2:187.
34. Fukuzawa Yukichi, *An Encouragement of Learning*, trans. David A. Dilworth and Umeyo Hirano (Tokyo: Sophia University, 1969), p. 15. Fukuzawa later built this into a longer *Outline of a Theory of Civilization*, trans. David A. Dilworth and G. Cameron Hurst (Tokyo: Sophia University, 1973).
35. Quoted in Mayo, "The Western Education of Kume Kunitake," p. 48.
36. Quoted in Tsunoda, de Bary, and Keene, *Sources of Japanese Tradition*, pp. 650–651.
37. Quoted in Eugene Soviak, "On the Nature of Western Progress: The Journal of the Iwakuea Embassy" in Donald Shively, ed., *Tradition and Modernization in Japanese Culture* (Princeton: Princeton University Press, 1971), p. 31.
38. James F. Conte, "Overseas Study in the Meiji Period: Japanese Students in America, 1867–1902" (Ph.D. dissertation, Princeton University, 1977). Also Ishizuki Minoru, *Kindai Nihon no kaigai ryūgakushi* (Kyoto: Mineruba shobō, 1972).
39. *The Diary of Kido Takayoshi*, 1:167–168.
40. *Ibid.*, 1:191 (entry for March 12, 1869).
41. Inoue, *Meiji ishin*, pp. 314–340; the most thoughtful treatment of Saigō in this struggle is that of Charles L. Yates, *Saigō Takamori: The Man behind the Myth* (London: Kegan Paul, 1994), pp. 130–155, who argues that Saigō may have expected to work out a peaceful compromise like those he masterminded in the bakufu's first expedition against Chōshū and the surrender of Edo with Katsu Kaishū.
42. The Fifteenth National Bank, established in 1877, was capitalized at 17,820,000 yen, almost eight times the next largest, and its 484 investors were all *kazoku*.
43. Stephen Vlastos, "Opposition Movements in Early Meiji," in *CHJ*, 5:367–382.
44. See the striking case detailed by Selçuk Esenbel in *Even the Gods Rebel: The Peasants of Takaino and the 1871 Nakano Uprising in Japan* (Ann Arbor, Mich.: Association for Asian Studies, 1998).
45. A convenient summary can be found in Kozo Yamamura, "The Meiji Land Tax Reform and Its Effects," in Jansen and Rozmen, *Japan in Transition*, pp. 382–397.
46. Neil Waters finds this to be the case in Kawasaki; *Japan's Local Pragmatists* (Cambridge, Mass.: Harvard University Press, 1983); James C. Baxter, *The Meiji Unification through the Lens of Ishikawa Prefecture* (Cambridge, Mass.: Harvard University Press, 1994), pp. 100–108, though in basic agreement, notes that changes that followed the abolition of the Kaga domain included a conscious effort to bypass old village leaders that took effect gradually.
47. *Meiji kenpakusho shūsei*, 6 vols. (Tokyo, 1986–).

12. Building the Meiji State

1. Roger F. Hackett, "Political Modernization and the Meiji *Genrō*," in Robert E. Ward, ed., *Political Development in Modern Japan* (Princeton: Princeton University Press, 1968), and Lesley Connors, *The Emperor's Adviser: Saionji Kinmochi and Pre-war Japanese politics* (London: Croom Helm, 1987).
2. *Samurai and Silk*, by his granddaughter Haru Matsukata Reischauer (Cambridge, Mass.: Harvard University Press, 1986), gives a warm and understandably favorable account of Matsukata's career.

3. Sydney Crawcour, "Economic Change in the Nineteenth Century," in *CHJ*, 5:606.

4. Adapted from translation from *Itō Hirobumi den* (Tokyo, 1940), 1:622–623, by D. W. Anthony and G. H. Healey, "The Iwakura Embassy in Sheffield," *Research Papers in East Asian Studies*, no. 2 (University of Sheffield, December 1994): 14.

5. Crawcour, "Economic Change," p. 614, quoting Thomas C. Smith, *Political Change and Industrial Development in Japan: Government Enterprise, 1868–1880* (Stanford: Stanford University Press, 1955), pp. 96–97.

6. Ann Waswo, *Japanese Landlords: The Decline of a Rural Elite* (Berkeley: University of California Press, 1977).

7. Richard J. Smethurst, *Agricultural Development and Tenancy Disputes in Japan, 1870–1940* (Princeton: Princeton University Press, 1986), grants the hardship of the Matsukata decade, but emphasizes instead land reclamation and entrepreneurial vitality as elements in the growth of owner-tenant categories. The Smethurst study, based on a relatively favored area, has drawn sharp criticism from scholars he takes to task, a controversy that can be located and followed in his own response in the *Journal of Japanese Studies*, 15, 2 (Summer 1989): 417–437.

8. Smith, *Political Change and Industrial Development in Japan*.

9. Kazushi Okawa and Henry Rosovsky, "A Century of Japanese Economic Growth," in W. W. Lockwood, ed., *The State and Economic Enterprise in Japan* (Princeton: Princeton University Press, 1965), pp. 47–92.

10. Adapted from W. W. McLaren, *Japanese Government Documents* (Transactions of the Asiatic Society of Japan), 42, May 1914, pp. 426–433, who translated the entire document. Nobutaka Ike, *The Beginnings of Political Democracy in Japan* (Baltimore: Johns Hopkins Press, 1950), remains the standard account of the birth of the party movement.

11. Itagaki's bearded, John Brown–like visage appeared on the basic 100-yen note that served as the center of the post–World War II currency until inflation changed the unit to a metal coin.

12. George M. Beckmann, *The Making of the Meiji Constitution: The Oligarchs and the Constitutional Development of Japan, 1868–1891* (Lawrence: University of Kansas, 1957), provides in appendices the views of Kido, Ōkubo, Yamagata, Itō, and Iwakura in addition to Ōkuma's, which proposed elections by the end of 1882.

13. From the translation in ibid., p. 149.

14. Ozaki Yukio, *Nihon kenseishi o kataru*, in vol. 11 of *Ozaki Gakudō zenshū* (Tokyo: Kōronsha, 1956). An English translation by Fujiko Hara is forthcoming from Princeton University Press.

15. Irokawa, *The Culture of the Meiji Period* (translation of Irokawa, *Meiji no bunka*), ed. Marius B. Jansen, p. 45.

16. Irokawa, *The Culture of the Meiji Period*. For another such spiritual pilgrimage, see *My Thirty-three Years' Dream: The Autobiography of Miyazaki Torazō*, trans. Etō Shinkichi and Marius B. Jansen (Princeton: Princeton University Press, 1982), which shows a comparable hegira of another intense young man who found purpose in life by serving Sun Yat-sen in order to save Asia from Western imperialism.

17. Ivan Parker Hall, *Mori Arinori* (Cambridge, Mass.: Harvard University Press, 1973), p. 292.

18. Lafcadio Hearn, *Japan: An Attempt at Interpretation* (New York: 1907), appendix, p. 531; letter to Kaneko Kentarō, who had relayed a query from Itō Hirobumi, dated August 26, 1892.

19. See W. G. Beasley, "Meiji Political Institutions," in *CHJ*, 5:651–665; Johannes Siemes, S.J., *Hermann Roesler and the Making of the Meiji State* (Tokyo: Sophia University Press, 1966); and Joseph Pittau, S.J., *Political Thought in Early Meiji Japan, 1868–1889* (Cambridge, Mass.: Harvard University Press, 1967).

20. Pittau, *Political Thought*, pp. 177–178.

21. Ibid.

22. Theodore F. Cook, "Soldiers in Meiji Society and State: Japan Joins the World," in Banno Junji, ed., *Nihon kin-gendai shi* (Tokyo, 1993).

23. David C. Evans and Mark R. Peattie, *Kaigun: Strategy, Tactics, and Technology in the Imperial Japanese Navy, 1887–1941* (Annapolis: Naval Institute Press, 1997), now the standard authority.

24. Text in Tsunoda, de Bary, and Keene, *Sources of Japanese Tradition*, pp. 705–707. World War II would show, unfortunately, that these values were not always "easy to practice."

25. Ōsawa Hiroaki, "Emperor versus Army Leaders: The 'Complications' Incident of 1886," in *Acta Asiatica*, 59 (Tokyo, 1990): 10.

26. Roger Hackett, *Yamagata Aritomo in the Rise of Modern Japan* (Cambridge, Mass.: Harvard University Press, 1971), p. 111.

27. The structure and problems of the police system are discussed by D. Eleanor Westney in *Imitation and Innovation: The Transfer of Western Organizational Patterns to Meiji Japan* (Cambridge, Mass.: Harvard University Press, 1987), pp. 35–99.

28. Hall, *Mori Arinori*, provides a full account.

29. Adapted from text translated in Herbert Passin, *Society and Education in Japan* (New York: Columbia Teachers College, 1965), pp. 210–211.

30. See the summary by Richard Rubinger, "Education: From One Room to One System," in Jansen and Rozman, *Japan in Transition*, pp. 195–230.

31. Ibid., pp. 212–213.

32. Cook, "Soldiers in Meiji Society and State," p. 14.

33. The subject of Brian Wesley Platt, "School, Community, and State in Nineteenth Century Japan" (Ph.D. dissertation, University of Illinois, 1998).

34. Donald H. Shively, "Motoda Eifu: Confucian Lecturer to the Meiji Emperor," in David S. Nivison and Arthur F. Wright, eds., *Confucianism in Action* (Stanford: Stanford University Press, 1959), pp. 302–334.

35. From translation in Passin, *Society and Education in Japan*, p. 227.

36. Cook, "Soldiers in Meiji Society and State," pp. 26–27.

37. Donald H. Shively, "Nishimura Shigeki: A Confucian View of Modernization," in Marius B. Jansen, ed., *Changing Japanese Attitudes toward Modernization* (Princeton: Princeton University Press, 1965), pp. 193–241.

38. Hall, *Mori Arinori*.

39. Masamichi Inoki, "The Civil Bureaucracy: Japan," in Robert A. Ward and Dankwart K. Rustow, eds., *Political Modernization in Japan and Turkey* (Princeton: Princeton University Press, 1964), pp. 296–297. See also Byron K. Marshall's chapter "The Aca-

demic Elite," in his *Academic Freedom and the Japanese Imperial University, 1868–1939* (Berkeley: University of California Press, 1992), pp. 21–52.

40. For a study of student culture in these institutions, see Donald T. Roden, *Schooldays in Imperial Japan: A Study in the Culture of a Student Elite* (Berkeley: University of California Press, 1980).

41. Quotations from Hall, *Mori Arinori,* pp. 426, 430, 424.

42. Shively, "Motoda Eifu," p. 330.

43. Tsunoda, de Bary, and Keene, *Sources of Japanese Tradition,* pp. 646–647.

44. Hirakawa Sukehiro, "Japan's Turn to the West," in *CHJ,* 5:497.

45. See Carol Gluck, *Japan's Modern Myths: Ideology in the Late Meiji Period* (Princeton: Princeton University Press, 1985), for a brilliant study of the context and content of the new imperial ideology.

13. Imperial Japan

1. R. H. P. Mason, *Japan's First General Election, 1890* (London: Cambridge University Press, 1969), provides much of the information below.

2. Ibid., p. 208.

3. Adapted from quotation in ibid., p. 189.

4. The provision was in fact not so different from that in the United States Congress, which can enact the previous year's allocations by a "Continuing Resolution" when agreement on a new budget is not forthcoming.

5. The discussion that follows owes a great deal to Andrew Fraser, "The House of Peers (1890–1905): Structure, Groups, and Role," and "Land Tax Increase: The Debates of December 1898," in Andrew Fraser, R. H. P. Mason, and Philip Mitchell, eds., *Japan's Early Parliaments, 1890–1905* (London: Routledge, 1995), and to George Akita, *Foundations of Constitutional Government in Japan, 1868–1900* (Cambridge, Mass.: Harvard University Press, 1967).

6. Fraser, "Land Tax Increase."

7. Though now part of a newly defined Japan, Okinawa and the rest of Ryukyu were not yet given full equality. Reform and voting rights would come more slowly than they did elsewhere, the islands were sacrificed as buffers for the defense of the main Japanese islands in World War II, they were left under American control long after the occupation of Japan came to an end, and they were required to bear the burden of American military bases after reversion to Japan in 1972.

8. Akira Iriye, "Japan's Drive to Great-Power Status," in *CHJ,* 5:747ff., provides an admirable overview of domestic politics and overseas expansion.

9. Chin Young Choe, *The Rule of the Taewon'gun, 1864–1873* (Cambridge, Mass.: Harvard University Press, 1972).

10. These machinations have been treated by Hilary Conroy, *The Japanese Seizure of Korea, 1868–1910* (Philadelphia: University of Pennsylvania Press, 1960), and more recently by Peter Duus, *The Abacus and the Sword: The Japanese Penetration of Korea, 1895–1910* (Berkeley: University of California Press, 1995), which now becomes the standard work.

11. Sugimura Fukashi in 1894, quoted in Duus, *Abacus and Sword,* p. 60.

12. Akira Iriye, "Japan's Drive," in *CHJ*, 5:758.

13. See Alan Takeo Moriyama, *Imingaisha: Japanese Emigration Companies and Hawaii* (Honolulu: University of Hawaii Press, 1985).

14. Actually even the *Times* thought this unreasonable, and argued that "it is idle to pretend that the institutions of Japan are not sufficiently civilized to afford adequate security for the rights and interests of British subjects." Quoted in Tatsuji Takeuchi, *War and Diplomacy in the Japanese Empire* (Garden City, N.Y.: Doubleday, 1935), p. 95.

15. On whom, see Marius B. Jansen, "Ōi Kentarō (1843–1922): Radicalism and Chauvinism," *Far Eastern Quarterly*, 6, no. 3 (May 1952).

16. See Marius B. Jansen, "Mutsu Munemitsu," in Craig and Shively, *Personality in Japanese History* (Berkeley: University of California Press, 1970), pp. 309–334.

17. The standard study of this interesting movement, which combined social protest with syncretic religion, is Benjamin B. Weems, *Reform, Rebellion, and the Heavenly Way* (Tucson: University of Arizona Press, 1964).

18. Mutsu's account of the diplomacy of the Sino-Japanese War, *Kenkenroku*, has been translated by Gordon Berger (Tokyo: Japan Foundation, 1982). Quotation taken from *Hakushaku Mutsu Munemitsu ikō* (Tokyo: Iwanami Shoten, 1929), p. 322.

19. I have discussed these events at some length in *Japan and China from War to Peace, 1894–1972* (Chicago: Rand McNally, 1975), and "Mutsu Munemitsu."

20. See, in this connection, Donald Keene, "The Sino-Japanese War of 1894–95 and Its Cultural Effect on Japan," in Shively, *Tradition and Modernization in Japanese Culture*.

21. Stuart Lone, *Japan's First Modern War: Army and Society in the Conflict with China, 1894–95* (London: St. Martin's Press, 1994).

22. Duus, *Abacus and Sword*, p. 81.

23. I have discussed his travels in China in "Konoe Atsumaro," in Akira Iriye, ed., *The Chinese and the Japanese: Essays in Political and Cultural Interactions* (Princeton: Princeton University Press, 1980), pp. 107–123.

24. A prime example is Miyazaki Tōten (Torazō), whose autobiography, *My Thirty-three Years' Dream*, is available in translation by Etō Shinkichi and Marius B. Jansen (Princeton: Princeton University Press, 1982).

25. Akira Iriye, "Japan's Drive," in *CHJ*, 5:774, notes that its reverberations were enormous, in that it forced France closer to Britain while maintaining its Russian ties, and thus contributing to the conflagration of 1914.

26. The extensive literature is surveyed and summarized in Ian Nish, *The Anglo-Japanese Alliance: The Diplomacy of Two Island Empires, 1894–1907* (London: Athlone Press, 1966), and Nish, *The Origins of the Russo-Japanese War* (London: Longman, 1985).

27. Marius B. Jansen, *The Japanese and Sun Yat-sen* (Cambridge, Mass.: Harvard University Press, 1954), and Jansen, "Japan and the Chinese Revolution of 1911," in John K. Fairbank and Kwang-ching Liu, eds., *Late Ch'ing*, vol. 11 of *Cambridge History of China* (Cambridge: Cambridge University Press, 1980).

28. Duus, *Abacus and Sword*, pp. 181–187.

29. Ibid., p. 189.

30. Quoted in Jansen, *Japan and China from War to Peace*, pp. 124–125.

31. Quoted in Duus, *Abacus and Sword*, p. 190.

32. Akira Iriye, *Pacific Estrangement: Japanese and American Expansion, 1897–1911* (Chicago: Imprint Publications, 1994, reprint of the 1972 Harvard University Press edition), p. 101.

33. Andrew Gordon, *Labor and Imperial Democracy in Prewar Japan* (Berkeley: University of California Press, 1991), p. 33. The fullest analysis of the event is that of Shumpei Okamoto, *The Japanese Oligarchy and the Russo-Japanese War* (New York: Columbia University Press, 1970), pp. 167–223, and Okamoto, "The Emperor and the Crowd: The Historical Significance of the Hibiya Riot" in Najita and Koschmann, *Conflict in Modern Japanese History*. Portsmouth negotiations are described in John Albert White, *The Diplomacy of the Russo-Japanese War* (Princeton University Press, 1964).

34. Akita, *Foundations of Constitutional Government*, p. 142.

35. Ozaki Yukio recalled later that "as the leader of a political party Hoshi held a stick in his right hand and money in his left. If money did not work he used the stick. He conquered one after another, and within a short period he became a powerful figure. Not surprisingly, he needed money . . . To be sure, his objective was not money itself but power." Ozaki, *Nihon kenseishi o kataru.*

36. Yoshida's examination standing is taken from Inoki Masamichi, *Hyōden: Yoshida Shigeru* (Tokyo: Yomiuri Shinbunsha, 1978), pp. 66–68. A full account of the diplomatic/consular (and other) examinations can be found in Robert M. Spaulding, Jr., *Imperial Japan's Higher Civil Service Examinations* (Princeton: Princeton University Press, 1967), pp. 100ff.

37. Nagatsuka Takashi, *The Soil*, trans. Ann Waswo as *A Portrait of Rural Life in Meiji Japan* (London: Routledge, 1989).

38. Susan Hanley, "The Material Culture: Stability in Transition," in Jansen and Rozman, *Japan in Transition*, p. 468.

14. Meiji Culture

1. Mention should be made of Donald Keene, *Dawn to the West*, 2 vols. (New York: Holt, Rinehart, and Winston, 1984); Christine Guth, *Art, Tea, and Industry: Matsuda Takashi and the Mitsui Circle* (Princeton: Princeton University Press, 1993); Kishimoto Hideo, ed., *Japanese Religion in the Meiji Era* (Tokyo: Ōbunsha, 1956); Dallas Finn, *Meiji Revisited: The Sites of Victorian Japan* (New York: Weatherhill, 1995); and Ellen P. Conant, *Nihonga: Transcending the Past: Japanese-Style Painting, 1868–1958* (St. Louis: St. Louis Art Museum, 1995).

2. Irokawa, *The Culture of the Meiji Period*, p. 51.

3. Quoted by Isamu Fukuchi, "*Kokoro* and the Spirit of Meiji," *Monumenta Nipponica*, 48, 4 (1993): 469.

4. Breen, "The Imperial Oath of April 1868."

5. Irokawa Daikichi, "The Impact on Popular Culture," in Nagai Michio and Miguel Urrutia, eds., *Meiji Ishin: Restoration and Revolution* (Tokyo: United Nations University, 1985), pp. 120–133.

6. Hazel Jones, *Live Machines: Hired Foreigners and Meiji Japan* (Vancouver: University

of British Columbia Press, 1980), analyzes the number and contributions of the foreign experts.

7. Ōta Yūzō, *Eigo to Nihonjin* (Tokyo: Kōdansha), 1995, characterizes those who dominated this era as "Gods of English."

8. Carmen Blacker, *The Japanese Enlightenment: A Study of the Writings of Fukuzawa Yukichi* (Cambridge: Cambridge University Press, 1964). Translations exist of *An Encouragement of Learning,* trans. David Dilworth and Umeyo Hirano (Tokyo: Sophia University, 1969) and *An Outline of a Theory of Civilization,* trans. David A. Dilworth and Cameron Hurst (Tokyo: Sophia University, 1973).

9. There is a complete translation by William R. Braisted, *Meiroku Zasshi: Journal of the Japanese Enlightenment* (Cambridge, Mass.: Harvard University Press, 1976).

10. See Earl H. Kinmonth, *The Self-Made Man in Meiji Japanese Thought: From Samurai to Salary Man* (Berkeley: University of California Press, 1981).

11. F. G. Notehelfer, *American Samurai: Captain L. L. Janes and Japan* (Princeton: Princeton University Press, 1985), p. 205; for the oath, pp. 196–197.

12. John F. Howes, "Japanese Christians and American Missionaries," in Jansen, *Changing Japanese Attitudes toward Modernization,* p. 339.

13. Masatake Oshima, "Memories of Dr. Clark," *Japan Christian Intelligencer,* 2, 2 (April 5, 1926), the only eye-witness account. I owe this reference to Atsushi Fukushima.

14. On whom see John F. Howes, ed., *Nitobe Inazō: Japan's Bridge across the Pacific* (Boulder, Colo.: Westview Press, 1995).

15. Naganawa Mitsuo, "The Japanese Orthodox Church in the Meiji Era," in J. Thomas Rimer, ed., *A Hidden Fire: Russian and Japanese Cultural Encounters, 1868–1926* (Stanford: Stanford University Press and Woodrow Wilson Center Press, 1995), pp. 158–169. There is a recent biography by Nakamura Kennosuke, *Senkyōshi Nikorai to Meiji Nihon* (Tokyo: Iwanami, 1996).

16. Quoted in Masaharu Anesaki, *History of Japnese Religion* (London: Kegan Paul, Trench, Trubner, 1930), p. 342.

17. James Edward Ketelaar, *Of Heretics and Martyrs in Meiji Japan,* p. 206.

18. See the collected petitions in Irokawa Daikichi and Gabe Masato, eds., *Meiji kempaku shusei* (Tokyo: Chikuma shobō, 1980).

19. See Hirakawa Sukehiro, "Japan's Turn to the West," in *CHJ,* 5:477ff.

20. Sansom, *The Western World and Japan,* p. 414.

21. Translated by Kenneth Strong as *Footprints in the Snow: A Novel of Meiji Japan* (Tokyo: Tuttle, 1970).

22. *My Thirty-three Years' Dream: The Autobiography of Miyazaki Tōten,* trans. Ēto and Jansen, pp. 12–13.

23. Tokutomi Sohō, *The Future Japan,* trans. Vinh Sinh (Edmonton: University of Alberta Press, 1989), p. 126. Tokutomi's life can be followed in John Pierson, *Tokutomi Sohō, 1863–1957* (Princeton: Princeton University Press, 1980), and Vinh Sinh, *Tokutomi Sohō (1863–1957): The Later Career* (Toronto: University of Toronto/York University Joint Centre on Modern East Asia, 1986).

24. These issues are taken up by Kenneth B. Pyle in *The New Generation in Meiji Japan: Problems of Cultural Identity, 1885–1895* (Stanford: Stanford University Press, 1969), and Pyle, "Meiji Conservatism," in *CHJ,* 5: 674–720.

25. On whom, see Thomas R. H. Havens, *Nishi Amane and Modern Japanese Thought* (Princeton: Princeton University Press, 1970).

26. J. Scott Miller, "Japanese Shorthand and *Sokkibon*," *Monumenta Nipponica*, 49, 4 (Winter 1994): 471–487.

27. Translated by Marleigh Grayer Ryan, in *Japan's First Modern Novel: Ukigumo of Futabatei Shimei* (New York: Columbia University Press, 1967).

28. Quoted by Ury Eppstein, "Musical Instruction in Meiji Education: A Study of Adaptation and Assimilation," *Monumenta Nipponica*, 40, 1 (Spring 1985): 32.

29. See William Malm, "The Modern Music of Meiji Japan," in Shively, *Tradition and Modernization in Japanese Culture.*

30. Quoted in Eppstein, "Musical Instruction," p. 12.

31. The recent work of Dallas Finn, *Meiji Revisited: The Sites of Victorian Japan* (New York: Weatherhill, 1995), provides an authoritative illustrated guide and commentary.

32. I owe this point to William Coaldrake.

33. These reflections owe much to a forthcoming study of Fenollosa by Ellen Conant.

34. See Conant, *Nihonga: Transcending the Past,* and Michiyo Morioka and Paul Berry, eds., *The Transformation of Japanese Painting Traditions:* Nihonga *from the Griffith and Patricia Way Collection* (Seattle, Wash.: Seattle Art Museum, 1999).

35. Shūji Takashina, J. Thomas Rimer, and Gerald Bolas, eds., *Paris in Japan: The Japanese Encounter with European Painting* (Tokyo: Japan Foundation; St. Louis: Washington University, 1987).

36. The magisterial survey by Donald Keene, *Dawn to the West,* and the distinguished translations of major authors by Keene, Edward Seidensticker, Howard S. Hibbett, and Edwin McClellan deserve mention, though they are too numerous to itemize.

37. Edwin McClellan, *Two Japanese Novelists: Sōseki and Tōson* (Chicago: University of Chicago, 1969), p. 5.

38. Hearn (1850–1904), a freelance writer, came to Japan in 1890 and after teaching English in Matsue and Kumamoto, was appointed lecturer on English literature at the Imperial University. He was enthralled by traditional Japan, married the daughter of a former samurai, and was adopted as Koizumi Yakumo, thereby becoming a Japanese citizen. (As such his salary was sharply reduced to put him on the Japanese pay scale.) He became famous for a stream of books derived from Japanese folklore. His last work, *Japan: An Attempt at Interpretation* (New York: Macmillan, 1904), has been drawn on earlier. See also Sukehiro Hirakawa, ed., *Rediscovering Lafcadio Hearn: Japanese Legends, Life, and Culture* (Kent: Global Books, 1997).

39. *Kokoro: A Novel by Natsume Sōseki* (Chicago: Henry Regnery, 1957), p. 245. See Isamu Fukui, "*Kokoro* and the Spirit of Meiji," *Monumenta Nipponica*, 48, 4 (1993), for a discussion of alternate explanations of that "spirit" by Japanese critics.

40. Richard Bowring, *Mori Ōgai and the Modernization of Japanese Culture* (Cambridge: Cambridge University Press, 1979), p. 19.

41. Many translated by David Dilworth and J. Thomas Rimer in *The Incident at Sakai and Other Stories* and *Saiki kōi and Other Stories* (both Honolulu: University Press of Hawaii, 1977).

42. Translation by William E. Naff (Honolulu: University of Hawaii Press, 1987).

43. See, for the larger question, the splendid study by Carol Gluck, *Japan's Modern Myths.*

44. See, for example, Kate Wildman Nakai, "Tokugawa Confucian Historiography: The Hayashi, Early Mito School, and Arai Hakuseki," in Nosco, *Confucianism and Tokugawa Culture,* pp. 62–91.

45. Tao De-min, "The Influence of Sorai in Meiji Japan: Shigeno Yasutsugu as an Advocate of 'Practical Sinology,' " in Tao, *Nihon kangaku shisōshi ronkō* (Osaka: Kansai University, 2000), pp. 69–81.

46. Quoted in Numata Jirō, "Shigeno Yasutsugu and the Modern Tokyo Tradition of Writing," in W. G. Beasley and E. G. Pulleyblank, eds., *Historians of China and Japan* (London: Oxford University Press, 1961), p. 277.

47. John S. Brownlee, *Japanese Historians and the National Myths, 1600–1945: The Age of the Gods and Emperor Jimmu* (Vancouver: University of British Columbia Press, 1997), p. 86.

48. Japan and the United States adopted the German system of graduate instruction through seminars in the same era, and developed historical research as an academic profession in the same decade. The American Historical Association was founded in 1885, the Japanese Shigakkai in 1889, with Shigeno as president.

49. Margaret Mehl, "Scholarship and Ideology in Conflict: The Kume Affair, 1892," *Monumenta Nipponica,* 48, 3 (Winter 1993): 342. See also the longer discussion in Brownlee, *Japanese Historians.*

50. Brownlee, *Japanese Historians,* p. 96.

51. The larger problem of censorship of literature is treated by Jay Rubin in *Injurious to Public Morals: Writers and the Meiji State* (Seattle: University of Washington Press, 1984).

52. Brownlee, *Japanese Historians,* p. 109.

53. *The Works of Inazo Nitobe,* 5 vols. (Tokyo: University of Tokyo, 1972), 1:138–141.

54. See the chart and discussion of riots in Andrew Gordon, *Labor and Imperial Democracy in Prewar Japan* (Berkeley: University of California, 1991), pp. 26ff.

55. See Richard J. Smethurst, *A Social Basis for Prewar Japanese Militarism: The Army and the Rural Community* (Berkeley: University of California Press, 1973), the standard work.

56. From the introduction by Ann Waswo, trans., *The Soil by Nagatsuka Takashi: A Portrait of Rural life in Meiji Japan* (London: Routledge, 1989), p. xv.

57. Irokawa, *The Culture of the Meiji Period,* p. 219.

58. Quoted in ibid., p. 241. Irokawa is also author of a recent biography, *Kitamura Tōkoku* (Tokyo: Tokyo Daigaku Shuppankai, 1994).

59. Eiji Yoshikawa, *Fragments of a Past: A Memoir,* trans. Edwin McClellan (Tokyo: Kodansha, 1992), pp. 112, 186.

60. Quoted in F. G. Notehelfer, *Kōtoku Shūsui: Portrait of a Japanese Radical* (Cambridge: Cambridge University Press, 1971), p. 203. Nitobe Inazō, then head of the First Higher School, was held responsible fort Tokutomi's talk, and the Ministry of Education requested his resignation, which he submitted without protest. Howes, *Nitobe Inazō,* p. 148. The prison diary of Kano Sugako, Kōtoku's common-law wife and the only woman hanged, is translated by Mikiso Hane in *Reflections on the Way to the Gallows: Rebel Women in Prewar Japan* (Berkeley: University of California Press, 1988).

61. Brownlee, *Japanese Historians*. The controversy is also discussed in H. Paul Varley, *Imperial Restoration in Medieval Japan* (New York: Columbia University Press, 1971).

15. Japan between the Wars

1. See the discussion by Taichirō Mitani in "The Establishment of Party Cabinets, 1898–1932," in *CHJ*, 6.

2. His career can be followed in Leslie Connors, *The Emperor's Adviser: Saionji Kinmochi and Pre-war Japanese Politics* (London: Croom Helm, 1987).

3. Tetsuo Najita, *Hara Kei in the Politics of Compromise, 1905–1915* (Cambridge, Mass.: Harvard University Press, 1967), provides the best coverage of these tactics.

4. Ozaki autobiography, *Nihon kenseishi o kataru*, chap. 9.

5. Richard H. Mitchell, *Censorship in Imperial Japan* (Princeton: Princeton University Press, 1983), pp. 132ff., provides the standard treatment of censorship. For censorship of literature the basic work is that by Rubin, *Injurious to Public Morals*.

6. Byron K. Marshall, trans., *The Autobiography of Ōsugi Sakae* (Berkeley: University of California Press, 1992), pp. 132–133.

7. Harry Emerson Wildes, *Social Currents in Japan: With Special Reference to the Press* (Chicago: University of Chicago Press, 1927), p. 108. I am grateful to Soowon Kim for identification of the unfortunate Mr. Min.

8. Mitchell, *Censorship in Imperial Japan*, pp. 196–197. See also Richard H. Mitchell, *Thought Control in Prewar Japan* (Ithaca, N.Y.: Cornell University Press, 1976).

9. Ben-Ami Shillony, "The Meiji Restoration: Japan's Attempt to Inherit China," in Ian Neary, ed., *War, Revolution, and Japan* (Kent: Sandgate, Folkestone, 1993), pp. 20–32.

10. These events are discussed in greater detail in Jansen, *The Japanese and Sun Yat-sen*, and Etō and Jansen, trans., *My Thirty-three Years' Dream*.

11. Ikuhiko Hata, "Continental Expansion, 1905–1941," in *CHJ*, 6:271–277.

12. The standard study is that by James W. Morley, *The Japanese Thrust into Siberia, 1918* (New York: Columbia University Press, 1957).

13. Frank P. Baldwin, "The March First Movement: Korean Challenge, Japanese Response" (Ph.D. dissertation, Columbia University, 1969), and Baldwin, "Participatory Anti-Imperialism: The 1919 Independence Movement," *Journal of Korean Studies*, 1 (1979): 123–162.

14. See Joshua A. Fogel, *The Literature of Travel in the Japanese Rediscovery of China* (Stanford: Stanford University Press, 1996), and Carter J. Eckert, *Offspring of Empire: the Koch'ang Kims and the Cultural Origins of Korean Capitalism, 1876–1945* (Seattle: University of Washington Press, 1991).

15. Ian Nish, *Japan's Struggle with Internationalism: Japan, China, and the League of Nations, 1931–33* (London: Kegan Paul, 1993), p. 10.

16. Joshua Fogel, *Politics and Sinology: The Case of Naitō Konan (1860–1934)* (Cambridge, Mass.: Harvard University Press, 1984), and Yue-him Tam, "In Search of the Oriental Past: The Life and Thought of Naitō Konan (1860–1934)" (Ph.D. dissertation, Princeton University, 1975).

17. The authoritative work is Arthur Waldron, *From War to Nationalism: China's Turning Point, 1924–1925* (Cambridge: Cambridge University Press, 1995).

18. Akira Iriye, *After Imperialism: The Search for a New Order in the Far East, 1921–1931* (Cambridge, Mass.: Harvard University Press, 1965). For Chang Tso-lin, see Gavan McCormack, *Chang Tso-lin in Northeast China, 1911–1928: China, Japan, and the Manchurian Idea* (Stanford: Stanford University Press, 1977).

19. Quoted from translation by Herbert Bix, "The Showa Emperor's 'Monologue' and the Problem of War Responsibility," *Journal of Japanese Studies*, 18, 2 (Summer 1992): 339, and also discussed in Marius B. Jansen, "The Pacific War and the Twentieth Century," published in Japanese as "Nijū seiki ni okeru Taiheiyō sensō no imi," in Hosoya Chihiro, Homma Nagayo, Iriye Akira, and Hatano Sumiyo, *Taiheiyō sensō* (Tokyo: University of Tokyo Press, 1993), p. 599.

20. On whom, see George Akita, "The Other Itō: A Political Failure," in Craig and Shively, *Personality in Japanese History*, pp. 335–372.

21. Sterling Tatsuji Takeuchi, *War and Diplomacy in the Japanese Empire* (New York: Doubleday, 1935), pp. 262–274, provides a full account.

22. On the slow pace at which daily life changed, see Susan B. Hanley, "The Material Culture: Stability in Transition," in Jansen and Rozman, *Japan in Transition from Tokugawa to Meiji*, pp. 447–469.

23. The most cogent discussion of these issues is that of E. Sydney Crawcour, "Industrialization and Technological Change, 1885–1920," in *CHJ*, 6:420. The Crawcour, Nakamura, and Taira essays referred to below have also been reprinted in Kozo Yamamura, ed., *The Economic Emergence of Modern Japan* (Cambridge: Cambridge University Press, 1997), chaps. 1, 2, 3, 6.

24. See Mikiso Hane in *Peasants, Rebels, and Outcasts: The Underside of Modern Japan* (New York: Pantheon Books, 1982), pp. 172ff., and E. Patricia Tsurumi, *Factory Girls: Women in the Thread Mills of Meiji Japan* (Princeton: Princeton University Press, 1990).

25. Followed more closely in Marius B. Jansen, "Yawata, Hanyehping, and the 21 Demands," *Pacific Historical Review*, 23, 1 (1954): 31–48.

26. Peter Duus, "Zaikabō: Japanese Cotton Mills in China, 1895–1937," in Peter Duus, Ramon H. Myers, and Mark R. Peattie, eds., *The Japanese Informal Empire in China, 1895–1937* (Princeton: Princeton University Press, 1989), pp. 65–100.

27. Crawcour, "Industrialization and Technological Change," p. 443.

28. There is a magisterial summary by Takafusa Nakamura, "Depression, Recovery, and War, 1920–1945," in *CHJ*, 6:451–493, and a pointed discussion by Hugh Patrick, "The Economic Muddle of the 1920's" in James W. Morley, ed., *Dilemmas of Growth in Prewar Japan* (Princeton: Princeton University Press, 1971), pp. 211–266.

29. From his statement reprinted in Tsunoda, de Bary, and Keene, *Sources of Japanese Tradition*, pp. 767–769.

30. And commemorated on its sixtieth anniversary in 1989 with a sumptuous volume detailing its elegance from the Corinthian columns that circle the building to (imported) marble mantels to washroom fixtures. *Mitsui honkan* (Mitsui Real Estate Development Co, Inc., 1989). Prestige still lay with the import.

31. Thomas Schalow, "The Role of the Financial Panic of 1927 and Failure of the 15th Bank in the Economic Decline of the Japanese Aristocracy" (Ph.D. dissertation, Princeton University, 1989), p. 160.

32. Nakamura, "Depression, Recovery, and War," p. 459.
33. Ibid., p. 466.

16. Taishō Culture and Society

1. The standard source for these schools and the environment they created is the work of Donald Roden, *Schooldays in Imperial Japan* (Berkeley: University of California Press, 1980).
2. Ibid., p. 137.
3. *Bushido,* in *The Works of Inazo Nitobe* (Tokyo: University of Tokyo Press, 1972), 1: 131–132.
4. This was also true in military schools, though flagrant conduct was punished, as was the case with the future anarchist Ōsugi Sakae. See Byron Marshall, trans., *The Autobiography of Ōsugi Sakae* (Berkeley: University of California Press, 1992), p. 77.
5. The army cadet schools did the same; "they made me stand at attention in the middle of a large group while they took turns punching me . . . I could not raise a hand to protect myself—to do so would be insubordination against an upperclassman. As I was struck I remained still, mainly careful to keep my feet. I feared being kicked if I fell." *Ōsugi,* trans. Marshall, pp. 71–72.
6. Roden, *Schooldays,* p. 210.
7. These cases are the subject of Byron K. Marshall's *Academic Freedom and the Japanese Imperial University, 1868–1939* (Berkeley: University of California Press, 1992).
8. William J. Cummings, *Education and Equality in Japan* (Princeton: Princeton University Press, 1980), pp. 26–29. These figures are conservative, for other sources add universities and graduates.
9. Henry DeWitt Smith II, *Japan's First Student Radicals* (Cambridge, Mass.: Harvard University Press, 1972), pp. 7–8.
10. Minobe is the subject of Frank O. Miller, *Minobe Tatsukichi: Interpreter of Constitutionalism in Japan* (Berkeley: University of California Press, 1965).
11. Peter Duus, "Yoshino Sakuzō: The Christian as Social Critic," *Journal of Japanese Studies,* 4, 2 (Summer 1978): 301–320.
12. References are to "Minpon shugi ron," translated with some excisions in Tsunoda, de Bary and Keene, *Sources of Japanese Tradition,* pp. 724–746. See also Peter Duus and Irwin Scheiner, "Socialism, Liberalism, and Marxism" in *CHJ,* 6:673–681.
13. See, on this point, Tetsuo Najita, "Some Reflections on Idealism in the Political Thought of Yoshino Sakuzō" in Bernard Silberman and Harry D. Harootunian, eds., *Japan in Crisis: Essays on Taishō Democracy* (Princeton: Princeton University Press, 1974), pp. 29–66.
14. Smith, *Japan's First Student Radicals,* pp. 52ff.
15. The career of Abe (1865–1949) illustrates many of the themes discussed here. When a student at Dōshisha, he was baptized by Niijima Jō. He later traveled to America to study theology and socialism. He played a leading role in the early (and abortive) socialist organizations. As Japanese radicalism turned left he became a leader of the "right wing" socialist movement.
16. For details, see F. G. Notehelfer, "Japan's First Pollution Incident," *Journal of Japa-*

nese Studies, 1, 2 (Spring 1975): 351–383. The struggle was led by a political maverick who died in 1913; see Kenneth Strong, *Ox against the Storm: A Biography of Tanaka Shōzō, Japan's Conservationist Pioneer* (Vancouver: University of British Columbia Press, 1977).

17. Yamakawa's wife Kikue is the author of the *Women of the Mito Domain: Recollections of Samurai Family Life*, to which reference was made in Chapter 4.

18. Haruko Taya Cook and Theodore F. Cook, *Japan at War: An Oral History* (New York: New Press, 1992), p. 51.

19. I find persuasive Donald Roden's discussion of this in "Taishō Culture and the Problem of Gender," in J. Thomas Rimer, ed., *Culture and Identity: Japanese Intellectuals during the Interwar Years* (Princeton: Princeton University Press, 1990), p. 39.

20. See Earl H. Kinmonth in *The Self-Made Man in Meiji Japanese Thought* (Berkeley: University of California Press, 1981), chap. 6, "Anguished Youth."

21. Quotations are from Roden, *Schooldays*, pp. 212–215. For details, see Stephen W. Kohn, "Abe Jirō and *The Diary of Santarō*" and J. Thomas Rimer, "Kurata Hyakuzō and *The Origins of Love and Understanding*," in Rimer, *Culture and Identity*, pp. 7–36.

22. Valdo H. Viglielmo, "Nishida Kitarō: The Early Years," in Shively, *Tradition and Modernization in Japanese Culture*, pp. 507–562.

23. Isaiah Berlin, "Kant as an Unfamiliar Source of Nationalism," in Berlin, *The Sense of Reality: Studies in Ideas and Their History* (New York: Farrar, Straus and Giroux, 1997), pp. 232–248.

24. Gennifer Weisenfeld, "Murayama, MAVO, and Modernity: Constructions of the Modern in Taishō Japan Avant-garde Art" (Ph.D. dissertation, Princeton University, 1997), and Miriam Silverberg, "Constructing the Japanese Ethnography of Modernity," *Journal of Asian Studies*, 51, 1 (February 1992): 30–54.

25. See the excellent discussion by Peter Duus and Irwin Scheiner, "Socialism, Liberalism, and Marxism, 1901–1931," in *CHJ*, 6:654–710.

26. Ronald A. Morse, *Yanagita Kunio and the Folklore Movement: The Search for Japan's National Character and Distinctive Culture* (New York: Garland, 1990). Yanagita's best-known work, "Legends of Tōno," appeared in translation by Ronald Morse (Tokyo: Japan Foundation, 1975). See also Yanagita's thoughtful *About Our Ancestors: The Japanese Family System*, trans. Fanny Hagin Mayer and Ishiwara Yasuyo (Tokyo: Japan Society for the Promotion of Science—Ministry of Education, 1970).

27. See Leslie Pincus, *Authenticating Culture in Imperial Japan: Kuki Shūzō and the Rise of National Aesthetics* (Berkeley: University of California Press, 1996).

28. Kathleen and Barbara Molony, *One Woman Who Dared: Ichikawa Fusae and the Japanese Women's Suffrage Movement* (Stanford: Stanford University Press, 1995).

29. Shizue Ishimoto, *Facing Two Ways: The Story of My Life* (New York: Farrar and Rinehart, 1935), and Dorothy Robins-Mowry, *The Hidden Sun: Women of Modern Japan* (Boulder, Co.: Westview Press, 1983). For the Einstein tour, Marius B. Jansen, "Einstein in Japan," *Princeton Library Chronicle*, 50, 3 (Winter 1989): 145–154.

30. See particularly Andrew Gordon, *Labor and Imperial Democracy in Prewar Japan* (Berkeley: University of California Press, 1991); Gordon, *The Evolution of Labor Relations in Japan: Heavy Industry, 1853–1955* (Cambridge, Mass.: Harvard University Press, 1985); Sheldon Garon, *The State and Labor in Modern Japan* (Berkeley: Univer-

sity of California Press, 1987); and Koji Taira, "Economic Development, Labor Markets, and Industrial Relations in Japan, 1905–1955," in *CHJ*, 6:606–653.

31. Thomas O. Wilkinson, *The Urbanization of Japanese Labor, 1860–1955* (Amherst: University of Massachusetts Press, 1965).

32. See Tsurumi, *Factory Girls*, and Mikiso Hane, *Peasants, Outcasts, and Rebels: The Underside of Modern Japan* (New York: Pantheon, 1982), pp. 172–204.

33. Gordon, *Evolution of Labor Relations*.

34. Yoshikawa Eiji, *Fragments of a Past: A Memoir*, trans. Edwin McClellan (Tokyo: Kodansha International, 1992), pp. 204–205. Yokohama Dock is one of the enterprises studied in Gordon, *Evolution of Labor Relations*.

35. Thomas C. Smith, "The Right to Benevolence: Dignity and Japanese Workers, 1890–1920," in Smith, *Native Sources of Japanese Industrialization, 1750–1920* (Berkeley: University of California Press, 1988), p. 242. Here one remembers the contemporary Japanese worker with coat and tie carrying his lunch in a briefcase.

36. Quoted in Smith, *Native Sources*, p. 268.

37. See Gordon, *Labor and Imperial Democracy*, pp. 17–18, for the overtones of this term at the time. More recently, however, its thrust is to exclude outsiders and narrow the sense of ethnicity.

38. See Gordon's biographical sketches of the victims of the Kameido Incident, as it is known, in *Labor and Imperial Democracy*, pp. 345–348.

39. The standard coverage is that of Garon, *The State and Labor in Modern Japan*.

40. See Kenneth Pyle, "Advantages of Followership: German Economics and Japanese Bureaucrats, 1890–1925," *Journal of Japanese Studies*, 1 (August 1974): 127–164, and Garon, *The State and Labor in Modern Japan*, pp. 25–26.

41. R. P. Dore, *Land Reform in Japan* (Oxford: Oxford University Press, 1959), p. 33.

42. Ann Waswo, *Japanese Landlords: The Decline of a Rural Elite* (Berkeley: University of California Press, 1977), and Waswo, "The Transformation of Rural Society, 1900–1950," in *CHJ*, 6:541–605.

43. Dore, *Land Reform in Japan*, pp. 69ff.

44. Waswo, "The Transformation of Rural Society," p. 586.

45. As doctor, medical school chief, bureaucrat, colonial administrator in Taiwan, head of the South Manchurian Railroad, cabinet member holding the posts of foreign affairs, communications, and home ministry, mayor of Tokyo, and architect of Japan's recognition of the new Soviet state, Gotō's career provides a vivid history of modern Japan. For a recent biography, see Kitaoka Shin'ichi, *Gotō Shinpei: Gaikō to vuishion* (Tokyo: Chūō Kōron, 1988).

46. Figures from Gregory J. Kasza, *The State and the Mass Media in Japan, 1918–1945* (Berkeley: University of California Press, 1988), p. 28.

47. Edward Seidensticker, *Tokyo Rising: The City since the Great Earthquake* (Cambridge, Mass.: Harvard University Press, 1991), p. 30. Together with Seidensticker's *Low City, High City* (Cambridge, Mass.: Harvard University Press, 1991), *Tokyo Rising* provides engaging and thoughtful descriptions of Edo and Tokyo life, richly documented by extracts from major Japanese authors.

48. See Jennifer Robertson, *Takarazuka: Sexual Politics and Popular Culture in Modern Japan* (Berkeley: University of California Press, 1998).

49. Thomas R. H. Havens, *Architects of Affluence: The Tsutsumi Family and the Seibu-Saison Enterprises in Twentieth-Century Japan* (Cambridge, Mass.: Harvard University Press, 1994), p. 5.

50. Weisenfeld, "Murayama, MAVO, and Modernity."

51. Shunsuke Tsurumi, "Edo Period in Contemporary Popular Culture" in William Beasley, ed., *Edo Culture and Its Modern Legacy*, a special issue of *Modern Asian Studies*, 18, 4 (October 1984): 748ff.

52. Miriam Silverberg, "Constructing the Japanese Ethnography of Modernity," *Journal of Asian Studies*, 51, 1 (February 1992): 31.

17. The China War

1. Jansen, *China in the Tokugawa World*, p. 90.

2. Ramon H. Myers, "Japanese Imperialism in Manchuria: The South Manchuria Railway Company, 1906–1933," in Duus, Myers, and Peattie, *The Japanese Informal Empire in China, 1895–1937*, pp. 101–132. See also John Young, *The Research Activities of the South Manchurian Railway Company, 1907–1945: A History and Bibliography* (New York: Columbia University, East Asian Institute, 1966).

3. Alvin D. Coox, "The Kwantung Army Dimension," in Duus, Myers, and Peattie, *The Japanese Informal Empire in China, 1895–1937*, pp. 395–428, and, in greater detail, Coox, *Nomonhan: Japan against Russia, 1939* (Stanford University Press, 1985), 1:1–16.

4. The standard work on Ishiwara is Mark R. Peattie, *Ishiwara Kanji and Japan's Confrontation with the West* (Princeton: Princeton University Press, 1975); the details of the preparation for and carrying out of the Incident can be followed in Sadako N. Ogata, *Defiance in Manchuria: The Making of Japanese Foreign Policy, 1931–1932* (Berkeley: University of California Press, 1964), and Hiroharu Seki, "The Manchurian Incident," trans. Marius B. Jansen, in James W. Morley, ed., *Japan Erupts: The London Conference and the Manchurian Incident* (New York: Columbia University Press, 1984), pp. 123–240.

5. Hata Ikuhiko, *Hirohito Tennō itsutsu no ketsudan* (Tokyo: Kōdansha, 1984), p. 1. Honjō went on to become the emperor's aide-de-camp; his memoirs have been translated by Mikiso Hane as *Emperor Hirohito and His Chief Aide-de-Camp: The Honjō Diary, 1933–1936* (Tokyo: University of Tokyo Press, 1982).

6. The Lytton Commission and its impact on Japan receive careful study in Nish, *Japan's Struggle with Internationalism*.

7. This section owes much to Louise Young, "Imagined Empire: The Cultural Construction of Manchukuo" in Peter Duus, Ramon H. Myers, and Mark R. Peattie, eds., *The Japanese Wartime Empire, 1933–1945* (Princeton: Princeton University Press, 1996), pp. 71–96, and especially her important *Japan's Total Empire: Manchuria and the Culture of Wartime Imperialism* (Berkeley: University of California Press, 1997), p. 456.

8. Joshua Fogel, *Life along the South Manchurian Railway: The Memoirs of Itō Takeo* (Armonk, N.Y.: M. E. Sharpe, 1988), discusses this phenomenon and translates Itō's memoir.

9. These tactics were considered possible models for Vietnam a quarter century later.

See Chang-sik Lee, "Counterinsurgency in Manchuria: The Japanese Experience, 1931–1940," memorandum RM-5012-ARPA, RAND Corporation, 1967, p. 352.

10. This trade is the subject of a forthcoming study by Bob T. Wakabayashi of York University, Toronto.

11. Young, *Total Empire*, p. 411.

12. Figures from Roger F. Hackett "The Military," in Ward and Rustow, *Political Modernization in Japan and Turkey*, p. 346.

13. See the discussion in Connors, *The Emperor's Adviser*, pp. 126ff.

14. See Masaru Ikei, "Ugaki Kazushige's View of China and His China Policy, 1915–1930," in Iriye, *The Chinese and the Japanese*, pp. 199–219.

15. These tangled politics receive authoritative treatment in Kitaoka Shin'ichi, *Nihon rikugun to tairiku seisaku, 1906–1918* (Tokyo: Tokyo University Press, 1978), and Kitaoka, "China Experts in the Army," in Duus, Myers, and Peattie, *The Japanese Informal Empire in China, 1895–1937*, pp. 330–368. Note also Kitaoka's deft summary in "The Army as a Bureaucracy: Japanese Militarism Revisited," *Journal of Military History*, 57 (October 1993): 67–86.

16. "Designs on North China, 1933–1937" by Shimada Toshihiko, translation and commentary by James B. Crowley, in James William Morley, ed., *The China Quagmire: Japanese Expansion on the Asian Continent, 1933–1941* (New York: Columbia University Press, 1983).

17. James B. Crowley, *Japan's Quest for Autonomy: National Security and Foreign Policy, 1930–1938* (Princeton: Princeton University Press, 1966), p. 195.

18. The standard study of the rebellion is that of Ben-Ami Shillony, *Revolt in Japan: The Young Officers and the February 26, 1936 Incident* (Princeton: Princeton University Press, 1973). The Ugaki quotation is from p. 203, Hata, *Hirohito Tennō itsutsu no ketsudan*.

19. The second volume of Mishima Yukio's final tetrology, *Honba*, translated by Michael Gallagher as *Runaway Horses* (New York: Knopf, 1973), attempts a sympathetic recreation of the romantic and murderous nationalism of the 1930s.

20. The documents included the makeup of the proposed cabinet to be led by General Mazaki and numerous other details. *Asahi Shinbum*, February 15, 1988.

21. See Robert J. C. Butow, *Tōjō and the Coming of the War* (Princeton: Princeton University Press, 1964).

22. One of the author's first assignments in 1945 was to act as interpreter so a U.S. Army doctor could question Ugaki, who was living in an Izu Peninsula hot spring village, to see whether his health would permit a flight to Manila, where General Yamashita Tomoyuki had asked for him as a witness in the trial that preceded his execution. The doctor decided against the flight; Ugaki, for his part, told the author that Yamashita's rank was so far below his own that he scarcely knew him. When Ugaki stood for the House of Councillors under the new constitution in 1953 he received the largest vote of any candidate in Japan.

23. Araki was sentenced to prison by the International Tribunal that met in Tokyo, after which he steeped himself in Buddhist philosophy, was released for illness, and then was pardoned; he died in 1966.

24. Translated by Owen Guntlett, with introduction by Robert King Hall, as *Kokutai no*

Hongi: Cardinal Principles of the National Entity of Japan (Cambridge: Harvard University Press, 1949).

25. For a thoughtful treatment of this current, see Tetsuo Najita and H. D. Harootunian, "Japanese Revolt against the West: Political and Cultural Criticism in the Twentieth Century," in *CHJ*, 6:711–734.

26. R. P. Dore, "Tenancy and Aggression," chap. 5 in Dore, *Land Reform in Japan*; and Dore and Tsutomu Ōuchi, "Rural Origins of Japanese Fascism," in Morley, *Dilemmas of Growth in Prewar Japan*, pp. 181–209.

27. The standard study of Kita is that of George M. Wilson, *Radical Nationalist in Japan: Kita Ikki, 1883–1937* (Cambridge, Mass.: Harvard University Press, 1969).

28. To this day Japanese universities have separate departments of Japanese, Asian, and Western history.

29. Irokawa Daikichi, *Aru Shōwa shi: jibunshi no kokoromi* (Tokyo: Chūō Kōron, 1975), p. 92.

30. Takafusa Nakamura, "Depression, Recovery, and War," in *CHJ*, 6:451–493, and reprinted in Kozo Yamamura, ed., *The Economic Development of Modern Japan* (Cambridge: Cambridge University Press, 1997), pp. 116–158.

31. Haruko Taya Cook and Theodore F. Cook, *Japan at War: An Oral History* (New York: New Press, 1992), p. 49.

32. Bai Gao, *Economic Ideology and Japanese Industrial Policy: Developmentalism from 1931 to 1965* (Cambridge: Cambridge University Press, 1997).

33. Yasukichi Yasuba, "Did Japan Ever Suffer from a Shortage of Natural Resources before World War II?" *Journal of Economic History*, 56, 3 (September 1996).

34. The extensive literature on *tenkō* is capped by a multivolume compilation edited by Tsurumi Shunsuke, for the Society for the Scientific History of Thought (Shisō no kagakkai), from which he has drawn in *An Intellectual History of Wartime Japan, 1931–1945* (London: Routledge and Kegan Paul, 1986), workbook material pp. 10–11. See also George M. Beckmann and Okubo Genji, *The Japanese Communist Party, 1922–1945* (Stanford: Stanford University Press, 1969).

35. Germaine A. Hoston, "Marxists and Japanese Expansionists: Takahashi Kamekichi and the Theory of 'Petty Imperialism,'" *Journal of Japanese Studies*, 10, 1 (Winter 1984), and, for the Marxist debates on Japan's historical stage, Hoston, *Marxism and the Crisis of Development in Prewar Japan* (Princeton: Princeton University Press, 1986).

36. See, for this and other cases, Byron K. Marshall, *Academic Freedom in the Imperial Japanese University, 1868–1939* (Berkeley: University of California Press, 1992).

37. The organization's scope and importance are discussed by James Crowley, "Intellectuals as Visionaries of the New Asian Order," in Morley, *Dilemmas of Growth in Prewar Japan*. See also Miles Fletcher, "Intellectuals and Fascism in Early Shōwa Japan," *Journal of Asian Studies*, 29, 9 (November 1979).

38. Bai Gao, "Arisawa Hiromichi and His Theory for a Managed Economy," *Journal of Japanese Studies*, 20, 1 (Winter 1994): 115–153, and Gao, *Economic Ideology and Japanese Industrial Policy: Developmentalism from 1931 to 1965* (Cambridge: Cambridge University Press, 1997).

39. The literature here is vast. I have discussed the incident in *Japan and China from War to Peace, 1894–1972*, pp. 425–426.

40. The most accessible study is that by Yoshitake Oka, *Konoe Fumimaro: A Political Biography* (Tokyo: University of Tokyo Press, 1983), a translation by Shumpei Okamoto and Patricia Murray of the 1972 original.

41. Morley, *The China Quagmire.*

42. Daqing Yang, "A Sino-Japanese Controversy: The Nanking Atrocity in History," *Sino-Japanese Studies*, 3, 1 (November 1990), and Yang, *The Rape of Nanjing in History and Public Memory: A Critical Anthology* (forthcoming, Westview Press). For the most reasonable of many Japanese studies, see Hata Ikuhiko, *Nankin jiken* (Tokyo: Chūō Kōron, 1986).

18. The Pacific War

1. A more detailed discussion of nomenclature draws on a extensive and still unpublished essay by Bob T. Wakabayashi of York University. The translation of the Japan's Road to the Pacific War series was published under the editorship of James William Morley by Columbia University Press as *Japan Erupts: The London Conference and the Manchurian Incident, 1928–1932* (1984), *Deterrent Diplomacy: Japan, Germany, and the USSR, 1935–1940* (1976), *The China Quagmire: Japan's Expansion on the Asian Continent, 1933–1941* (1983), and *The Fateful Choice: Japan's Advance in Southeast Asia, 1939–1941* (1980).

2. Chronicled in a splendid two-volume study by Alvin D. Coox, *Nomonhan: Japan against Russia, 1939.*

3. Some writers, among them Irokawa Daikichi, however, argue that Hirohito's actions then constituted an assertion of direct rule that made him directly responsible for everything that followed.

4. Gordon M. Berger, *Parties out of Power in Japan, 1931–1941* (Princeton: Princeton University Press, 1977), provides the standard coverage of this period.

5. See the account of those days by Matsumoto Shigeharu, *Konoe jidai*, 2 vols. (Tokyo: Chūō Kōron, 1986), 2:28ff.

6. Akira Iriye, *The Origins of the Second World War in Asia and the Pacific* (London and New York: Longman, 1987), p. 107.

7. This curious chapter in diplomacy has been unraveled by Robert J. C. Butow, who entitles his study by the code name that was used for Father Walsh and his associates. *The John Doe Associates: Backdoor Diplomacy for Peace, 1941* (Stanford: Stanford University Press, 1974). See also his earlier *Tojo and the Coming of the War* (Princeton: Princeton University Press, 1961), pp. 129ff.

8. See Chalmers Johnson, *An Instance of Treason: Ozaki Hotsumi and the Sorge Spy Ring* (Stanford: Stanford University Press, 1964, and expanded ed., 1990).

9. Nobutaka Ike, ed. and trans., *Japan's Decision for War: Records of the 1941 Policy Conferences* (Stanford: Stanford University Press, 1967), gives the documents and transcripts of the discussions. Quote from p. 79.

10. James B. Crowley, "Japan's Military Foreign Policies," in James William Morley, ed., *Japan's Foreign Policy, 1868–1941* (New York: Columbia University Press, 1974), p. 98.

11. I have discussed this in *Japan and China from War to Peace, 1894–1972*, pp. 397–409.

12. For the note that was never sent, see Robert J. C. Butow, "Marching off to War on

the Wrong Foot: The Final Note that Tokyo Did *Not* Send to Washington," *Pacific Historical Review,* 62, 1 (February 1994): 67–79.

13. Excerpts from Tokutomi's commentary can be found in Tsunoda, de Bary, and Keene, *Sources of Japanese Tradition,* pp. 798–801.

14. For Takemura, Irokawa, *The Culture of the Meiji Period,* p. 11; for Itō and other writers, Donald Keene, "Japanese Writers and the Greater East Asian War," in Keene, *Landscapes and Portraits: Appreciations of Japanese Culture* (Tokyo and Palo Alto: Kodansha International, 1971), pp. 300–321.

15. Translated by Edward Seidensticker as *The Makioka Sisters* (New York: Knopf, 1957).

16. See Edward Seidensticker, *Kafū the Scribbler: The Life and Writings of Nagai Kafū, 1879–1959* (Stanford: Stanford University Press, 1965).

17. Translated by Eugene Soviak and Kamiyama Tamie as *Diary of Darkness: The Wartime Diary of Kiyosawa Kiyoshi* (Princeton: Princeton University Press, 1998).

18. Ben-Ami Shillony, *Politics and Culture in Wartime Japan* (Oxford: Clarendon Press, 1981), surveys these and other trends.

19. Treated in depth with discernment by Sheldon Garon in *Molding Japanese Minds: The State in Everyday Life* (Princeton: Princeton University Press, 1997).

20. See Thomas R. H. Havens, *Valley of Darkness: The Japanese People and World War II* (New York: Norton, 1978), and the dispassionate account by a French correspondent, Robert Guillain, *Le Peuple Japonais et la Guerre* (Paris: René Julliard, 1947).

21. Admirably summarized by Alvin D. Coox in chapter 7, "The Pacific War," in *CHJ,* 6: 315–382.

22. Gordon W. Prange, *At Dawn We Slept: The Untold Story of Pearl Harbor* (New York: McGraw Hill, 1981) gives the fullest account.

23. See the eyewitness and critical account by Colonel Hiromichi Yahara, a high staff officer, *The Battle for Okinawa* (New York: Wiley, 1995), translated by Roger Pinneau and Masatoshi Uehara with an introduction by Frank Gibney. Gibney was Yahara's interrogator. For the civilian side, see the gripping account by Masahide Ōta, *The Battle of Okinawa: Typhoon of Steel and Bombs* (Tokyo: Kume Publishers, 1984). Mr. Ōta became governor of Okinawa in the 1990s.

24. Donald Keene, *Meeting with Japan* (Tokyo: Gakuseisha, 1979), p. 45.

25. John W. Dower, *War without Mercy: Race and Power in the Pacific War* (New York: Pantheon, 1986).

26. Gavan Daws, *Prisoners of the Japanese: POWs of World War II in the Pacific* (New York: William Morrow, 1994).

27. Konoe Fumitaka was tried and found guilty of "aiding the international bourgeoisie" and died at Ivanovo outside Moscow in 1956.

28. The classic account of the surrender decision remains that of Robert J. C. Butow, *Japan's Decision to Surrender* (Stanford: Stanford University Press, 1954). See also the gripping account compiled by the Pacific War Research Society, *Japan's Longest Day* (Tokyo: Kōdansha, 1968).

29. As given in Butow, *Japan's Decision to Surrender,* p. 248.

30. These attempts are detailed in Hata, *Hirohito Tennō itsutsu no ketsudan.* Genda, who died in 1989, became a leading figure in Japan's postwar air defense, for which he received the Legion of Merit, the highest United States honor awarded to foreigners.

31. Robert J. C. Butow, the most careful student of these negotiations, scouts revisionist views in "How Roosevelt Attacked Japan at Pearl Harbor: Myth Masquerading as History," *Prologue*, 28, 3 (Fall 1996): 209–221.

32. Takagi letter of October 7, 1941, in *Toward International Understanding*, vol. 5 of *Takagi Yasaka chosakushū* (Tokyo: Tokyo University Press, 1971), pp. 100–101.

33. James C. Thomson, Jr., "The Role of the Department of State," in Dorothy Borg and Shumpei Okamoto, eds., *Pearl Harbor as History: Japanese-American Relations, 1931–41* (New York: Columbia University Press, 1973), p. 103.

34. Ōkita Saburō, *Japan's Challenging Years: Reflections on My Lifetime* (Canberra: Australian National University, 1983).

35. Edwin O. Reischauer, *The United States and Japan* (Cambridge, Mass.: Harvard University Press, 1950), p. 224.

36. For whose account, Theodore E. Cohen, *Remaking Japan: The American Occupation as New Deal* (New York: Free Press, 1987).

37. Alfred D. Oppler, *Legal Reform in Occupied Japan: A Participant Looks Back* (Princeton: Princeton University Press, 1976).

38. Helen Hardacre, *Shintō and the State* (Princeton: Princeton University Press, 1989), p. 25.

39. Text in Government Section, Supreme Commander for the Allied Powers, *Political Reorientation of Japan*, 2 vols. (Washington, D.C.: Government Printing Office, 1949), 2:467.

40. This may not have been entirely his fault. According to one account MacArthur's interpreter rendered Konoe's explanation (about changing election laws) that there were problems about the "organization of government" *(seifu no soshiki)* as "the constitution of the government," at which MacArthur fired back that in that case the constitution would have be be revised to incorporate "the essential elements of liberalism" (in this case women's suffrage), and that Konoe ought to be in a position to do something about that. See Dale M. Hellegers, "The Konoe Affair," in L. H. Redford, ed., *The Occupation of Japan: Impact of Legal Reform* (Norfolk, Va.: MacArthur Memorial, 1977), p. 168.

41. David Anson Titus, *Palace and Politics in Prewar Japan* (New York: Columbia University Press, 1974), is the standard study of the reach of palace power and politics in Japan.

42. Kazuko Tsurumim, *Social Change and the Individual: Japan before and after Defeat in World War II* (Princeton: Princeton University Press, 1970), pp. 139ff., discusses the testaments left by those executed. For Soviets, John W. Dower, *Embracing Defeat: Japan in the Wake of World War II* (New York: W. W. Norton/New Press, 1999), p. 449.

43. See Richard H. Minear, *Victors' Justice: The Tokyo War Crimes Trial* (Princeton: Princeton University Press, 1971). It may be added that the United States had suggested that the Soviet Union justify its violation of its treaty obligations to Japan by citing the United Nations as higher authority, advice that was gratefully followed. To be sure, a half-decade earlier many Japanese leaders had advocated that Japan sack the Neutrality Pact and attack to the north.

44. The executions took place in Sugamo Prison. It has since been demolished, and the developers have named the high rise built on the site Sunshine City.

19. The Yoshida Years

1. For the participants' view, see Theodore Cohen, *Remaking Japan: The American Occupation as New Deal*, ed. Herbert Passin (New York: Free Press, 1987); for the process, see Sheldon Garon, *The State and Labor in Modern Japan* (Berkeley: University of California Press, 1987).

2. The relationship is well described by Richard B. Finn in *Winners in Peace: MacArthur, Yoshida, and Postwar Japan* (Berkeley: University of California Press, 1992).

3. See the *Report of the United States Education Mission to Japan* (Washington: Government Printing Office, 1946), submitted by a delegation of twenty-seven educators in March 1946.

4. The standard work is Dore, *Land Reform in Japan*.

5. Garon, *The State and Labor in Modern Japan*. For the SCAP side, see Cohen, *Remaking Japan*.

6. MacArthur had initially said that constitutional revision was beyond his authority, but responded to a memorandum from General Whitney arguing that he did indeed have that authority. See Robert E. Ward, "The Origins of the Present Japanese Constitution," *American Political Science Review*, 50, 4 (December 1956), and more recently Finn, *Winners in Peace*, pp. 89–106. Most recently, Theodore McNelly summarizes decades of research and publishing in *The Origins of Japan's Democratic Constitution* (Lanham, Md.: University Press of America, 2000).

7. Beate Gordon, *The Only Woman in the Room* (New York: Kodansha, 1997).

8. See Tetsuya Kataoka, *The Price of a Constitution: The Origin of Japan's Postwar Politics* (New York: Taylor & Francis, 1991).

9. Douglas MacArthur, "Reply to Criticism of Economic Policy," February 1948, in SCAP, *Political Reorientation of Japan*, 2:762.

10. Best described in Howard B. Schonberger, *Aftermath of War: Americans and the Remaking of Japan, 1945–1952* (Kent: Kent State University Press, 1989).

11. George F. Kennan, *Memoirs, 1925–1950* (New York: Little, Brown and Co., 1967), p. 376.

12. The standard work, by a SCAP participant in the process, is that of Eleanor M. Hadley, *Antitrust in Japan* (Princeton: Princeton University Press, 1970).

13. Finn, *Winners in Peace*. Mention must also be made of the critical biography by John W. Dower, *Empire and Aftermath: Yoshida Shigeru and the Japanese Empire, 1878–1954* (Cambridge, Mass.: Harvard University Press, 1979), and Yoshida Shigeru's own account, translated as *The Yoshida Memoir: The Story of Japan in Crisis* (Boston: Houghton Mifflin, 1962).

14. Yutaka Kōsai, "The Postwar Japanese Economy, 1945–1970," in *CHJ*, 6:494–537.

15. Gao, "Arisawa Hiromi and His Theory for a Managed Economy."

16. Gao, *Economic Ideology and Japanese Industrial Policy*, p. 20.

17. Saburō Ōkita, *Japan's Challenging Years: Reflections on My Lifetime* (Canberra: Australian National University, 1983), pp. 32–33.

18. Ibid., p. 34.

19. This shift, with heavy emphasis on the role of the cold war and Pentagon priorities, is the subject of Michael Schaller, *The American Occupation of Japan: The Origins of the Cold War in Asia* (New York: Oxford University Press, 1985).

20. These cursory comments receive careful treatment in Andrew Gordon, ed., *Postwar Japan as History* (Berkeley: University of California Press, 1993).

21. John K. Emmerson, a diplomat assigned an office in the Mitsui Bank Building, describes moving in as a Mitsui executive was taking his leave: "Before turning to go out the door, he hesitated, pointing to a map on the wall of Japan's Co-Prosperity Sphere in Eastern Asia. 'There it is,' he said smiling, 'We tried. See what you can do with it.'" *The Japanese Thread: A Life in the U.S. Foreign Service* (New York: Holt, Rinehart, and Winston, 1978), p. 256.

22. Hata, *Hirohito Tennō itsutsu no ketsudan,* and Toyoshita Haruhiko, "Japanese Peace Negotiations and 'Double Diplomacy,'" paper presented at "Social Change and International Affairs," Paris, December 1994.

23. Yoshida, *The Yoshida Memoirs,* p. 4.

24. For a discussion of what the author calls a "Yoshida doctrine," see Kenneth B. Pyle, *The Japanese Question: Power and Purpose in a New Era* (Washington, D.C.: American Enterprise Institute, 1992).

25. See Herbert Passin, "Modernization and the Japanese Intellectual: Some Comparative Observations" in Jansen, *Changing Japanese Attitudes toward Modernization,* pp. 425–446.

26. Masaru Tanimoto, "Unwanted Peace: Japanese Intellectuals in American Occupied Japan, 1948–52" (Ph.D. dissertation, Johns Hopkins University, 1988).

27. The standard account of these events is George R. Packard, *Protest in Tokyo: The Security Treaty Crisis of 1960* (Princeton: Princeton University Press, 1966).

28. Irmela Hijiya-Kirchnereit in Richard Bowring and Peter Kornicke, eds., *Cambridge Encyclopedia of Japan* (Cambridge: Cambridge University Press, 1993), p. 145.

29. Both works translated by Edward G. Seidensticker: *Makioka Sisters* (New York: Knopf, 1957) and *Snow Country* (New York: Knopf, 1956).

30. Ōoka Shōhei, *Taken Captive: A Japanese POW's Story,* trans. Wayne P. Lammers (New York: John Wiley, 1996).

31. For a study of this strange man, John Nathan, *Mishima: A Biography* (Boston: Little, Brown and Co., 1974).

32. On Tenrikyō, see Henry van Staelen, *The Religion of Divine Wisdom: Japan's Most Powerful Religious Movement* (Kyoto: Veritas Shoin, 1957); on Kurozumikyō, see Helen Hardacre, *Kurozumikyō and the New Religions of Japan* (Princeton: Princeton University Press, 1986).

33. On Reiyūkai, see Helen Hardacre, *Lay Buddhism in Contemporary Japan: Reiyūkai yōdan* (Princeton: Princeton University Press, 1984). On Sōka Gakkai, see James W. White, *The Soka Gakkai and Mass Society* (Stanford: Stanford University Press, 1970), and Noah S. Brannen, *Soka Gakkai: Japan's Militant Buddhists* (Richmond, Va.: John Knox, 1968).

34. Helen Hardacre, in Bowring and Kornicke, *Cambridge Encyclopedia of Japan,* p. 177.

35. For a full account, Joseph L. Anderson and Donald Richie, *The Japanese Film,* expanded edition (Princeton: Princeton University Press, 1982).

20. Japan since Independence

1. Wada (1903–1967) played an important role in postwar politics. Elected to the House of Councillors, he was appointed minister of agriculture by Yoshida in his first cabinet and it fell to him to implement the land reform program. He also took steps to counter the critical food shortage. Wada then shifted his affiliation to the Japan Socialist Party after the emergence of the Katayama cabinet, in which he headed the Economic Stabilization Board, and subsequently affiliated with the party's left wing.

2. The system has been studied by numerous political scientists and their studies are too numerous to list. Mention need only be made of Masumi Junnosuke's authoritative *Gendai seiji*, 2 vols. (Tokyo: Tokyo Daigaku Shuppankai, 1985), translated by Lonny E. Carlile as *Contemporary Politics in Japan* (Berkeley: University of California Press, 1995).

3. For charts and a wealth of detail, see Masumi, *Contemporary Politics*, pp. 205ff.

4. For excerpts from the plan, T. J. Pempel, *Party Politics in Japan: Creative Conservatism* (Philadelphia: Temple University Press, 1982), pp. 78ff.

5. See the engrossing study of a local politician provided by Gerald L. Curtis, *Election Campaigning Japanese Style* (New York: Columbia University Press, 1972).

6. See, on this point, Kent Calder, *Crisis and Compensation: Public Policy and Political Stability in Japan, 1949–1980* (Princeton: Princeton University Press, 1988).

7. Chalmers Johnson, *MITI and the Japanese Miracle* (Stanford: Stanford University Press, 1982).

8. The subject of Garon, *Molding Japanese Minds.*

9. Yutaka Kōsai, "The Postwar Japanese Economy, 1945–1975," in *CHJ*, 6:518ff.

10. The best history is by Michael A. Cusumano, *The Japanese Automobile Industry, Technology, and Management: Nissan and Toyota* (Cambridge, Mass.: Harvard University Press, 1985).

11. William N. Tsutsui, "W. Edwards Deming and the Origins of Quality Control in Japan," *Journal of Japanese Studies* (Summer 1996): 295–326, and Tsutsui, *Manufacturing Ideology: Scientific Management in Twentieth-Century Japan* (Princeton: Princeton University Press, 1998).

12. Johnson, *MITI and the Japanese Miracle,* is central here. See also David Williams, *Japan and the Emergence of Open Political Science* (London: Routledge, 1996).

13. Yasusuke Murakami, *An Anticlassical Political and Economic Analysis: A Vision for the Next Century,* trans. Kozo Yamamura (Stanford: Stanford University Press, 1996).

14. See Ezra Vogel, *Japan as Number One: Lessons for America* (Cambridge, Mass.: Harvard University Press, 1979), for a highly favorable view, and Karl van Wolferen, *The Enigma of Japanese Power: People and Politics in a Stateless Nation* (London: Macmillan, 1989), for a sharply contrasting view by an author who seems to discern a conspiracy directed by dark-suited graduates of Tokyo University.

15. Paul Krugman, "The Myth of Asia's Miracle," *Foreign Affairs* (November/December 1994), and elsewhere. For a more extended comparative study of Japan and Russia, see Cyril E. Black, Marius B. Jansen, Herbert S Levine, Marion J. Levy Jr., Henry Rosovsky, Gilbert Rozman, Henry D. Smith II, and F. Fredrick Starr, *The Modernization of Japan and Russia* (New York: Free Press, 1975).

16. See Bai Gao, *Economic Ideology and Japanese Industrial Policy,* who relates "private" organization to "public" policy formation, and Kent Calder, *Strategic Capitalism: Private Business and Public Purpose in Japanese Industrial Finance* (Princeton: Princeton University Press, 1993), who tries to find a middle ground; Daniel I. Okimoto, *Between MITI and the Market: Japanese Industrial Policy for High Technology* (Stanford: Stanford University Press, 1988); and finally three volumes edited respectively by Kozo Yamamura and Yasukichi Yasuba, Takashi Inoguchi and Daniel Okimoto, and Shumpei Kumon and Henry Rosovsky, *The Political Economy of Japan: The Domestic Transformation* (I), *The Changing International Context* (II), and *Cultural and Social Dynamics* (III) (Stanford: Stanford University Press, 1989, 1990, and 1992).

17. There was—and is—a special poignancy about the provision that Buddhist temples and cemeteries make for aborted fetuses, the *mizuko,* discussed by William LaFleur in *Liquid Life: Abortion and Buddhism in Japan* (Princeton: Princeton University Press, 1992). Oddly, there was relatively little debate about the origins of life that was waged so vigorously in the United States, but a great deal about the end of life in connection with organ transplants.

18. Takekazu Ogura, *Can Japanese Agriculture Survive?* (Tokyo: Agricultural Policy Research Center, 1980).

19. For a first-hand description by a reporter posing as a part-time farmer-hand, see Satoshi Kamata, *Japan in the Passing Lane: An Inside Account of Life in a Japanese Auto Factory* (New York: Pantheon, 1982).

20. William W. Kelly, "Rationalization and Nostalgia: Cultural Dynamics of New Middle-Class Japan." *American Ethnologist,* 13, 4 (November 1986).

21. John F. Embree, *Suye Mura: A Japanese Village* (Chicago: University of Chicago Press, 1939); Ushijima Morimitsu, *Henbo suru Suemura* (Kyoto: Mineruva Shobō, 1971), and *Suemura, 1935–1985* (Tokyo: Nihon Keizai Hyōronsha, 1988).

22. Rozman, *Urban Networks in Ch'ing China and Tokugawa Japan.*

23. See David M. Bayley, *Forces of Order: Police Behavior in Japan and the United States* (Berkeley: University of California Press, 1976).

24. Sheldon Garon and Mike Mochizuki, "Negotiating Social Contracts," in Gordon, *Postwar Japan as History,* pp. 144–186. Similar consideration was shown, as Garon and Mochizuki write, for small and medium-sized business through an agency established for that purpose.

25. See the optimistic view of Sumiko Iwao, *The Japanese Woman: Traditional Image and Changing Reality* (New York: Free Press, 1993).

26. Thomas Rohlen, *Japan's High Schools* (Berkeley: University of California Press, 1983).

27. The ambiguities of those final days are captured in Norma Field, *In the Realm of a Dying Emperor* (New York: Pantheon Books, 1991), and Thomas Crump, *The Death of an Emperor: Japan at the Crossroads* (New York: Oxford University Press, 1991).

CREDITS

1. Sekigahara screen, Osaka Municipal Art Museum.
2. Nagashino screen, Naruse Collection. Reprinted in *Nihon no kinsei,* vol. 4 (Tokyo: Chūō Kōron, 1992), pl. 1.
3. *Genshoku Nihon no bijutsu,* vol. 10, *Shiro to Shoin* (Tokyo: Shogakukan, 1968), pp. 12–13.
4. Author's collection.
5. Nagasaki Deshima Historical Association, *Deshima: Its Pictorial Heritage* (Tokyo: Chūō Kōron, 1987), pl. 10.
6. Photograph in author's collection.
7. Woodcut from Masahiro Murai, *Tanki Yōryaku* (A single horseman: Summary on how to wear armor), 2d ed. (1837). The Metropolitan Museum of Art, The Bashford Dean Memorial Collection.
8. *Nōgyō zensho;* Princeton University, Gest Oriental Library and East Asian Collections.
9. Hikone screen, Hikone Castle Art Museum.
10. Neil Skene Smith, "Materials on Japanese Social and Economic History: Tokugawa Japan," Asiatic Society of Japan, *Transactions,* 2nd ser., 14 (June 1937, Tokyo): 84. (Hereafter *TASJ.*)
11. Engelbert Kaempfer, *History of Japan,* trans. J. Scheuchzer (Glasgow: James Mac-Lehose, 1906), 3:368.
12. Yamauchi archives, Kōchi.
13. *Jōkamachi ezu shū: Kantō* (Tokyo: Shōwa reibunsha, 1981), n.p.
14. *TASJ* 1937, p. 52.
15. Author's collection.
16. *Edo meisho zu byōbu* (Tokyo: Mainichi shinbunsha, 1972), "Hakkoku issō."
17. *TASJ* 1937, p. 155.
18. *TASJ* 1937, p. 127.
19. Photograph in author's collection.
20. Reprinted in *Nihon no kinsei,* vol. 17 (Tokyo: Chūō Kōron, 1994), pl. 7.
21. Lithograph, U.S. Naval Academy Museum, Annapolis.
22. *Journaal van Dirk de Graeff van Polsbroek,* ed. Herman J. Moeshart (Maastricht, 1987).
23. Meiji Jingu Gaien, Seitoku Kinen Kaigakan, Tokyo.
24. Author's collection.
25. Meiji Jingu Gaien, Seitoku Kinen Kaigakan, Tokyo.
26. Photograph taken in San Francisco and reproduced, inter alia, in Kodama Kōta, ed., *Zusetsu Nihon bunka shi taikei* (Tokyo: Shogakukan, 1956).

27. Biographies as follows: *Kōshaku Matsukata Masayoshi den* (1935); *Itō Hirobumi den* (1940); *Kōshaku Yamagata Aritomo den* (1933); Ivan Parker Hall, *Mori Arinori* (Cambridge, Mass.: Harvard University Press, 1973), frontispiece; and for Itagaki, Marius B. Jansen, *Sakamoto Ryōma and the Meiji Restoration* (Princeton: Princeton University Press, 1961), n.p.

28. Ienaga Saburō, ed., *Nihon no rekishi*, vol. 6 (Tokyo: Harp shuppan, 1977), p. 21.

29. *Nihon no rekishi*, suppl. vol. 4 (Tokyo: Chūō Kōron, 1967), pp. 144–145.

30. Collection of H. Kwan Lau, New York.

31. *Ōkuma Kō hachijū-gonen shi*, vol. 2 (Tokyo, 1926).

32. Author's collection.

33. Author's collection.

34. Meiji Jingu Gaien, Seitoku Kinen Kaigakan, Tokyo.

35. Author's collection.

36. 1999 currency.

37. Jennifer Robertson, *Takarazuka: Sexual Politics and Popular Culture in Modern Japan* (Berkeley: University of California Press; ©1998 The Regents of the University of California).

38. Griffith and Patricia Way Collection. Photograph by Eduardo Calderón, courtesy Seattle Art Museum.

39. Author's collection.

40. Takahara Tomiyasu, ed., *Ichiokunin no Shōwa shi*, vol. 1, *Manshū jihen zengo* (Tokyo: Mainichi, 1974), p. 220.

41. Takahara Tomiyasu, ed., *Ichiokunin no Shōwa shi*, vol. 2, *Ni niroku jiken to Ni-Chū sensō* (Tokyo: Mainichi, 1975), p. 8.

42. Iwase Junzō, ed., *Gōka shashin shiriizu*, vol. 3, *Natsukashi no Shōwa jidai* (Tokyo: Besuto seraazu K.K., 1972), p. 149.

43. Takahara Tomiyasu, ed., *Ichiokunin no Shōwa shi*, vol. 4, *Kūgeki-haisen-hikiage* (Tokyo: Mainichi, 1975), p. 128.

44. Top and bottom right: *Asahi Graph*, special issue devoted to the emperor's trip to Europe, October 25, 1971.

45. Takahara Tomiyasu, ed., *Ichiokunin no Shōwa shi*, vol. 6, *Dokuritsu, jiritsu e no kunō* (Tokyo: Mainichi, 1976), pp. 8–9.

46. Author's photograph, taken at Yoshida's Ōiso villa in 1961.

47. Takahara Tomiyasu, *Ichiokunin no Shōwa shi*, vol. 7, *Kōdo seichō no kiseki* (Tokyo: Mainichi, 1976), p. 220.